PRO FOOTBALL REGISTER

1996 EDITION

Editors/Pro Football Register
MARK BONAVITA
SEAN STEWART

PUBLISHING CO.

Efrem Zimbalist III, President and Chief Executive Officer, Times Mirror Magazines; **Nicholas H. Niles,** President and Chief Executive Officer; **Francis X. Farrell,** Senior Vice President, Publisher; **John D. Rawlings,** Senior Vice President, Editorial Director; **John Kastberg,** Vice President, General Manager; **Kathy Kinkeade,** Vice President, Operations; **Mike Nahrstedt,** Managing Editor; **Kyle Veltrop,** Associate Editor; **Craig Carter,** Statistical Editor; **Mark Bonavita and Sean Stewart,** Assistant Editors; **Fred Barnes,** Director of Graphics; **Terry Shea,** Database Analyst; **Marilyn Kasal,** Production Manager; **Michael Behrens and Anita Cechowski,** Macintosh Production Artists.

A Times Mirror
Company

CONTENTS

EXPLANATION OF ABBREVIATIONS

LEAGUES: AFL: American Football League. **Ar.FL., Arena Football:** Arena Football League. **CFL:** Canadian Football League. **CoFL:** Continental Football League. **NFL:** National Football League. **USFL:** United States Football League. **WFL:** World Football League. **W.L.:** World League. **WLAF:** World League of American Football.

TEAMS: Birm.: Birmingham. **Jack.:** Jacksonville. **L.A. Raiders:** Los Angeles Raiders. **L.A. Rams:** Los Angeles Rams. **New Eng.:** New England. **N.Y. Giants:** New York Giants. **N.Y. Jets:** New York Jets. **N.Y./N.J.:** New York/New Jersey. **San Ant.:** San Antonio. **San Fran.:** San Francisco. **Sask.:** Saskatchewan. **StL.:** St. Louis.

STATISTICS: Att.: Attempts. **Avg.:** Average. **Blk.:** Blocked punts. **Cmp.:** Completions. **FGA:** Field goals attempted. **FGM:** Field goals made. **50+:** Field goals of 50 yards or longer. **F., Fum.:** Fumbles. **G:** Games. **In. 20:** Punts inside 20-yard line. **Int.:** Interceptions. **Lg.:** Longest made field goal. **L:** Lost. **Net avg.:** Net punting average. **No.:** Number. **Rat.:** Passer rating. **Pct.:** Percentage. **Pts.:** Points scored. **T:** Tied. **TD:** Touchdowns. **2-pt.:** Two-point conversions. **W:** Won. **XPA:** Extra points attempted. **XPM:** Extra points made. **Yds.:** Yards.

EXPLANATION OF AWARDS

AWARDS: Butkus Award: Nation's top college linebacker. **Davey O'Brien Award:** Nation's top college quarterback. **Doak Walker Award:** Nation's top college junior or senior running back. **Fred Biletnikoff Award:** Nation's top college wide receiver. **Harlon Hill Trophy:** Nation's top college Division II player. **Heisman Trophy:** Nation's top college player. **Jim Thorpe Award:** Nation's top college defensive back. **Lombardi Award:** Nation's top college lineman. **Lou Groza Award:** Nation's top college kicker. **Maxwell Award:** Nation's top college player. **Outland Trophy:** Nation's top college interior lineman. **Walter Payton Award:** Nation's top college Division I-AA player.

ON THE COVER: Quarterback Brett Favre led the Green Bay Packers to the NFC championship game and was named the NFL's MVP after leading the league with 4,413 passing yards and 38 TD tosses. (Photo by Otto Grevle/Allsport)

Spine photo of Troy Aikman by The Sporting News.

ISBN: 0-89204-554-X (perfect-bound)
     0-89204-556-6 (comb-bound)

10 9 8 7 6 5 4 3 2 1

VETERAN PLAYERS

Please note for statistical comparisons: In 1982, only nine of 16 games were played due to the cancellation of games because of a player's strike. In 1987, only 15 of 16 games were played due to the cancellation of games in the third week because of a players' strike. Most NFL players also missed games scheduled in the fourth, fifth and sixth weeks.

Sacks became an official NFL statistic in 1982.

Two-point conversions became an official NFL statistic in 1994.

*Indicates league leader.

†Indicates tied for league lead.

ABRAHAM, CLIFTON　　　　　CB　　　　　BUCCANEERS

PERSONAL: Born December 9, 1971, in Dallas. ... 5-9/184.
HIGH SCHOOL: David W. Carter (Dallas).
COLLEGE: Florida State.
TRANSACTIONS/CAREER NOTES: Selected by Tampa Bay Buccaneers in fifth round (143rd pick overall) of 1995 NFL draft. ... Signed by Buccaneers (May 3, 1995).
PLAYING EXPERIENCE: Tampa Bay NFL, 1995. ... Games: 1995 (6).
HONORS: Named defensive back on THE SPORTING NEWS college All-America first team (1994).

ABRAMS, BOBBY　　　　　LB　　　　　PATRIOTS

PERSONAL: Born April 12, 1967, in Detroit. ... 6-4/242.
HIGH SCHOOL: Henry Ford (Detroit).
COLLEGE: Michigan.
TRANSACTIONS/CAREER NOTES: Signed as non-drafted free agent by New York Giants (April 26, 1990). ... Granted free agency (February 1, 1992). ... Re-signed by Giants (1992). ... Claimed on waivers by Dallas Cowboys (September 1, 1992). ... Released by Cowboys (October 6, 1992). ... Signed by Cleveland Browns (October 8, 1992). ... Released by Browns (November 7, 1992). ... Signed by Giants (November 9, 1992). ... Released by Giants (November 21, 1992). ... Signed by Cowboys (April 26, 1993). ... Released by Cowboys (August 30, 1993). ... Re-signed by Cowboys (August 31, 1993). ... Released by Cowboys (November 26, 1993). ... Signed by Minnesota Vikings (December 7, 1993). ... Granted unconditional free agency (February 17, 1995). ... Signed by New England Patriots (March 1, 1995).
PLAYING EXPERIENCE: New York Giants NFL, 1990 and 1991; Dallas (4)-Cleveland (3)-New York Giants (1) NFL, 1992; Dallas (5)-Minnesota (4) NFL, 1993; Minnesota NFL, 1994; New England NFL, 1995. ... Games: 1990 (16), 1991 (16), 1992 (8), 1993 (9), 1994 (16), 1995 (9). Total: 74.
CHAMPIONSHIP GAME EXPERIENCE: Played in NFC championship game (1990 season). ... Member of Super Bowl championship team (1990 season).

ADAMS, SAM　　　　　DT　　　　　SEAHAWKS

PERSONAL: Born June 13, 1973, in Houston. ... 6-3/297. ... Full name: Sam Aaron Adams. ... Son of Sam Adams Sr., guard, New England Patriots (1972-80) and New Orleans Saints (1981).
HIGH SCHOOL: Cypress Creek (Houston).
COLLEGE: Texas A&M.
TRANSACTIONS/CAREER NOTES: Selected after junior season by Seattle Seahawks in first round (eighth pick overall) of 1994 NFL draft. ... Signed by Seahawks (July 30, 1994).
HONORS: Named defensive lineman on THE SPORTING NEWS college All-America first team (1993).

Year　Team	G	SACKS
1994—Seattle NFL	12	4.0
1995—Seattle NFL	16	3.5
Pro totals (2 years)	28	7.5

ADAMS, SCOTT　　　　　OT　　　　　BUCCANEERS

PERSONAL: Born September 28, 1966, in Lake City, Fla. ... 6-5/305.
HIGH SCHOOL: Columbia (Lake City, Fla.).
COLLEGE: Georgia (degree in marketing).
TRANSACTIONS/CAREER NOTES: Signed as non-drafted free agent by Dallas Cowboys (April 25, 1989). ... Released by Cowboys (September 5, 1989). ... Signed by Atlanta Falcons (1990). ... Released by Falcons (February 1990). ... Signed by WLAF (January 2, 1991). ... Selected by Barcelona Dragons in third round (16th offensive lineman) of 1991 WLAF positional draft. ... Signed by Minnesota Vikings (June 22, 1991). ... Released by Vikings (August 26, 1991). ... Re-signed by Vikings to practice squad (August 27, 1991). ... Activated (December 20, 1991). ... On inactive list for one game (1991). ... Released by Vikings (August 31, 1992). ... Re-signed by Vikings to practice squad (September 1, 1992). ... Activated (September 8, 1992). ... Granted free agency (February 17, 1994). ... Re-signed by Vikings (July 12, 1994). ... Released by Vikings (August 22, 1994). ... Signed by New Orleans Saints (September 28, 1994). ... Granted free agency (February 17, 1995). ... Signed by Chicago Bears (March 21, 1995). ... Granted unconditional free agency (February 16, 1996). ... Signed by Tampa Bay Buccaneers (March 23, 1996).
PLAYING EXPERIENCE: Barcelona W.L., 1991; Minnesota NFL, 1992 and 1993; New Orleans NFL, 1994; Chicago NFL, 1995. ... Games: 1991 (10), 1992 (15), 1993 (15), 1994 (11), 1995 (4). Total W.L.: 10. Total NFL: 45. Total Pro: 55.
PRO STATISTICS: NFL: 1992—Returned one kickoff for no yards and fumbled once. 1994—Recovered one fumble.

ADAMS, THEO　　　　　G

PERSONAL: Born April 24, 1966, in San Francisco. ... 6-5/300.
HIGH SCHOOL: McKinley (Honolulu).

COLLEGE: Hawaii.
TRANSACTIONS/CAREER NOTES: Signed as non-drafted free agent by Los Angeles Rams (March 30, 1990). ... Released by Rams (August 29, 1990). ... Signed by WLAF (January 3, 1991). ... Selected by London Monarchs in second round (11th offensive lineman) of 1991 WLAF positional draft. ... Signed by Rams (July 17, 1991). ... Released by Rams (August 19, 1991). ... Signed by Seattle Seahawks to practice squad (September 11, 1991). ... Assigned by Seahawks to Monarchs in 1992 World League enhancement allocation program (February 20, 1992). ... Released by Seahawks (September 26, 1992). ... Re-signed by Seahawks to practice squad (September 30, 1992). ... Activated (October 24, 1992). ... Released by Seahawks (August 30, 1993). ... Signed by Tampa Bay Buccaneers (September 7, 1993). ... Released by Buccaneers (August 21, 1994). ... Signed by Philadelphia Eagles (August 25, 1994). ... Released by Eagles (August 29, 1994). ... Signed by San Francisco 49ers (February 15, 1995). ... Released by 49ers (August 27, 1995). ... Signed by Eagles (September 2, 1995). ... Released by Eagles (October 3, 1995). ... Selected by Frankfurt Galaxy in 1996 World League draft (February 22, 1996).
PLAYING EXPERIENCE: London W.L., 1991 and 1992; Seattle NFL, 1992; Tampa Bay NFL, 1993; Philadelphia NFL, 1995. ... Games: 1991 (10), 1992 W.L. (10), 1992 NFL (10), 1993 (7). Total W.L.: 20. Total NFL: 17. Total Pro: 37.

ADAMS, VASHONE — S — RAVENS

PERSONAL: Born September 12, 1973, in Aurora, Colo. ... 5-10/196. ... Full name: Vashone LaRey Adams. ... Name pronounced vash-ON.
HIGH SCHOOL: Overland (Kan.) Christian.
JUNIOR COLLEGE: Butte Junior College (Calif.).
COLLEGE: Fort Hays State (Kan.), then Eastern Michigan.
TRANSACTIONS/CAREER NOTES: Signed as non-drafted free agent by Cleveland Browns (May 2, 1995). ... Released by Browns (August 21, 1995). ... Re-signed by Browns to practice squad (August 30, 1995). ... Activated (November 4, 1995). ... Browns franchise moved to Baltimore and renamed Ravens for 1996 season (March 11, 1996).
PLAYING EXPERIENCE: Cleveland NFL, 1995. ... Games: 1995 (8).

AGEE, MEL — DL

PERSONAL: Born November 22, 1968, in Chicago. ... 6-5/298.
HIGH SCHOOL: George Washington (Chicago).
COLLEGE: Illinois.
TRANSACTIONS/CAREER NOTES: Selected by Indianapolis Colts in sixth round (152nd pick overall) of 1991 NFL draft. ... Signed by Colts (July 11, 1991). ... Released by Colts (September 11, 1992). ... Signed by Atlanta Falcons (December 23, 1992). ... Active for one game with Falcons (1992); did not play. ... Granted unconditional free agency (February 17, 1994). ... Re-signed by Falcons (April 8, 1994). ... Granted free agency (February 17, 1995). ... Re-signed by Falcons (May 8, 1995). ... Granted unconditional free agency (February 16, 1996).

Year Team	G	SACKS
1991—Indianapolis NFL	16	0.0
1992—Indianapolis NFL	1	0.0
—Atlanta NFL	Did not play.	
1993—Atlanta NFL	11	2.5
1994—Atlanta NFL	16	0.0
1995—Atlanta NFL	10	0.0
Pro totals (5 years)	54	2.5

AGNEW, RAY — DT — GIANTS

PERSONAL: Born December 9, 1967, in Winston-Salem, N.C. ... 6-3/285. ... Full name: Raymond Mitchell Agnew.
HIGH SCHOOL: Carver (Winston-Salem, N.C.).
COLLEGE: North Carolina State.
TRANSACTIONS/CAREER NOTES: Selected by New England Patriots in first round (10th pick overall) of 1990 NFL draft. ... Signed by Patriots (July 19, 1990). ... On injured reserve with knee injury (December 29, 1990-remainder of season). ... Granted unconditional free agency (February 17, 1995). ... Signed by New York Giants (March 10, 1995).
PRO STATISTICS: 1990—Recovered one fumble. 1992—Recovered one fumble. 1995—Recovered one fumble.

Year Team	G	SACKS
1990—New England NFL	12	2.5
1991—New England NFL	13	2.0
1992—New England NFL	14	1.0
1993—New England NFL	16	1.5
1994—New England NFL	11	0.5
1995—New York Giants NFL	16	1.0
Pro totals (6 years)	82	8.5

AGUIAR, LOUIE — P — CHIEFS

PERSONAL: Born June 30, 1966, in Livermore, Calif. ... 6-2/219. ... Name pronounced AG-ee-ar.
HIGH SCHOOL: Granada (Livermore, Calif.).
COLLEGE: Utah State.
TRANSACTIONS/CAREER NOTES: Signed as non-drafted free agent by Buffalo Bills (May 8, 1989). ... Released by Bills (August 14, 1989). ... Re-signed by Bills (March 27, 1990). ... Released by Bills (August 7, 1990). ... Signed by WLAF (January 8, 1991). ... Selected by Barcelona Dragons in first round (first punter) of 1991 WLAF positional draft. ... Signed by New York Jets (June 14, 1991). ... Granted free agency (February 17, 1994). ... Signed by Kansas City Chiefs (April 1994).
PRO STATISTICS: NFL: 1991—Rushed once for 18 yards and recovered one fumble. 1993—Rushed three times for minus 27 yards, attempted two passes without a completion and an interception, fumbled twice and recovered one fumble for minus 10 yards.

			PUNTING					KICKING					
Year Team	G	No.	Yds.	Avg.	Net avg.	In. 20	Blk.	XPM	XPA	FGM	FGA	Lg.	50+	Pts.
1991—Barcelona W.L.	10	49	2029	41.4	33.8	15	1	0	0	0	0	...	0-0	0
—New York Jets NFL	16	64	2521	39.4	34.6	14	0	0	0	1	2	23	0-0	3

Year Team	G	No.	Yds.	PUNTING Avg.	Net avg.	In. 20	Blk.	XPM	XPA	KICKING FGM	FGA	Lg.	50+	Pts.
1992—New York Jets NFL	16	73	2993	41.0	37.6	21	0	0	0	0	0	...	0-0	0
1993—New York Jets NFL	16	73	2806	38.4	34.8	21	0	0	0	0	0	...	0-0	0
1994—Kansas City NFL	16	85	3582	42.1	34.5	15	0	0	0	0	0	...	0-0	0
1995—Kansas City NFL	16	91	3990	43.8	36.5	29	0	0	0	0	0	...	0-0	0
W.L. totals (1 year)	10	49	2029	41.4	33.8	15	1	0	0	0	0	...	0-0	0
NFL totals (5 years)	80	386	15892	41.2	35.5	100	0	0	0	1	2	23	0-0	3
Pro totals (6 years)	90	435	17921	41.2	35.4	115	1	0	0	1	2	23	0-0	3

AHANOTU, CHIDI — DE/DT — BUCCANEERS

PERSONAL: Born October 11, 1970, in Modesto, Calif. ... 6-2/283. ... Full name: Chidi Obioma Ahanotu. ... Name pronounced chee-dee a-ha-nah-too.
HIGH SCHOOL: Berkeley (Calif.).
COLLEGE: California (degree in physical education).
TRANSACTIONS/CAREER NOTES: Selected by Tampa Bay Buccaneers in sixth round (145th pick overall) of 1993 NFL draft. ... Signed by Buccaneers (July 9, 1993). ... Granted free agency (February 16, 1996). ... Re-signed by Buccaneers (February 20, 1996).

Year Team	G	SACKS
1993—Tampa Bay NFL	16	1.5
1994—Tampa Bay NFL	16	1.0
1995—Tampa Bay NFL	16	3.0
Pro totals (3 years)	48	5.5

AIKMAN, TROY — QB — COWBOYS

PERSONAL: Born November 21, 1966, in West Covina, Calif. ... 6-4/228. ... Full name: Troy Kenneth Aikman.
HIGH SCHOOL: Henryetta (Okla.).
COLLEGE: Oklahoma, then UCLA.
TRANSACTIONS/CAREER NOTES: Selected by Dallas Cowboys in first round (first pick overall) of 1989 NFL draft. ... Signed by Cowboys (April 20, 1989). ... On injured reserve with shoulder injury (December 28, 1990-remainder of season).
CHAMPIONSHIP GAME EXPERIENCE: Played in NFC championship game (1992-1995 seasons). ... Member of Super Bowl championship team (1992, 1993 and 1995 seasons).
HONORS: Named quarterback on The Sporting News college All-America second team (1987). ... Davey O'Brien Award winner (1988). ... Named quarterback on The Sporting News college All-America first team (1988). ... Played in Pro Bowl (1991, 1992 and 1994 seasons). ... Named Most Valuable Player of Super Bowl XXVII (1992 season). ... Named quarterback on The Sporting News NFL All-Pro team (1993). ... Named to play in Pro Bowl (1993 season); replaced by Bobby Hebert due to injury. ... Named to play in Pro Bowl (1995 season); replaced by Warren Moon due to injury.
POSTSEASON RECORDS: Holds Super Bowl career record for highest percentage of passes completed (minimum 40 attempts)—70.0. ... Holds NFL postseason career records for highest percentage of passes completed (minimum 150 attempts)—68.3; highest average gain (minimum 150 attempts)—8.64; and longest pass completion (to Alvin Harper)—94 yards (January 8, 1995, vs. Green Bay).
PRO STATISTICS: 1989—Caught one pass for minus 13 yards, fumbled six times and recovered three fumbles. 1990—Fumbled five times and recovered one fumble. 1991—Caught one pass for minus six yards and fumbled four times. 1992—Fumbled four times and recovered one fumble. 1993—Fumbled seven times and recovered three fumbles for minus three yards. 1994—Fumbled twice and recovered two fumbles. 1995—Fumbled five times and recovered two fumbles for minus 15 yards.
STATISTICAL PLATEAUS: 300-yard passing games: 1989 (1), 1990 (1), 1991 (1), 1993 (1), 1994 (1), 1995 (2). Total: 7.
MISCELLANEOUS: Regular-season record as starting NFL quarterback: 60-38 (.612).

Year Team	G	PASSING Att.	Cmp.	Pct.	Yds.	TD	Int.	Avg.	Rat.	RUSHING Att.	Yds.	Avg.	TD	TOTALS TD	2pt.	Pts.
1989—Dallas NFL	11	293	155	52.9	1749	9	18	5.97	55.7	38	302	8.0	0	0	...	0
1990—Dallas NFL	15	399	226	56.6	2579	11	18	6.46	66.6	40	172	4.3	1	1	...	6
1991—Dallas NFL	12	363	237	65.3	2754	11	10	7.59	86.7	16	5	.3	1	1	...	6
1992—Dallas NFL	16	473	302	63.9	3445	23	14	7.28	89.5	37	105	2.8	1	1	...	6
1993—Dallas NFL	14	392	271	*69.1	3100	15	6	7.91	99.0	32	125	3.9	0	0	...	0
1994—Dallas NFL	14	361	233	64.5	2676	13	12	7.41	84.9	30	62	2.1	1	1	0	6
1995—Dallas NFL	16	432	280	64.8	3304	16	7	7.65	93.6	21	32	1.5	1	1	0	6
Pro totals (7 years)	98	2713	1704	62.8	19607	98	85	7.23	83.5	214	803	3.8	5	5	0	30

ALBERTS, TREV — LB — COLTS

PERSONAL: Born August 8, 1970, in Cedar Falls, Iowa. ... 6-4/245.
HIGH SCHOOL: Northern University (Cedar Falls, Iowa).
COLLEGE: Nebraska.
TRANSACTIONS/CAREER NOTES: Selected by Indianapolis Colts in first round (fifth pick overall) of 1994 NFL draft. ... Signed by Colts (July 25, 1994).
CHAMPIONSHIP GAME EXPERIENCE: Played in AFC championship game (1995 season).
HONORS: Butkus Award winner (1993). ... Named linebacker on The Sporting News college All-America first team (1993).

Year Team	G	SACKS
1994—Indianapolis NFL	5	2.0
1995—Indianapolis NFL	15	2.0
Pro totals (2 years)	20	4.0

ALBRIGHT, ETHAN — OL — DOLPHINS

PERSONAL: Born May 1, 1971, in Greensboro, N.C. ... 6-5/283. ... Full name: Lawrence Ethan Albright.

HIGH SCHOOL: Grimsley (Greensboro, N.C.).
COLLEGE: North Carolina.
TRANSACTIONS/CAREER NOTES: Signed as non-drafted free agent by Miami Dolphins (April 28, 1994). ... Released by Dolphins (August 22, 1994). ... Re-signed by Dolphins to practice squad (August 29, 1994). ... Released by Dolphins (September 14, 1994). ... Re-signed by Dolphins to practice squad (September 28, 1994). ... Released by Dolphins (November 2, 1994). ... Re-signed by Dolphins (February 16, 1995). ... On injured reserve with knee injury (November 15, 1995-remainder of season).
PLAYING EXPERIENCE: Miami NFL, 1995. ... Games: 1995 (10).

ALDRIDGE, ALLEN — LB — BRONCOS

PERSONAL: Born May 30, 1972, in Houston. ... 6-1/245. ... Full name: Allen Ray Aldridge. ... Son of Allen Aldridge, defensive end, Houston Oilers and Cleveland Browns (1971, 1972 and 1974).
HIGH SCHOOL: Willowridge (Sugar Land, Texas).
JUNIOR COLLEGE: Tyler (Texas) Junior College.
COLLEGE: Houston.
TRANSACTIONS/CAREER NOTES: Selected by Denver Broncos in second round (51st pick overall) of 1994 NFL draft. ... Signed by Broncos (July 12, 1994).
PLAYING EXPERIENCE: Denver NFL, 1994 and 1995. ... Games: 1994 (16), 1995 (16). Total: 32.
PRO STATISTICS: 1995—Credited with 11/2 sack s and recovered one fumble.

ALDRIDGE, MELVIN — S

PERSONAL: Born July 22, 1970, in Pittsburg, Texas. ... 6-2/195. ... Full name: Melvin Keith Aldridge.
HIGH SCHOOL: Pittsburg (Texas).
COLLEGE: Murray State.
TRANSACTIONS/CAREER NOTES: Signed as non-drafted free agent by Houston Oilers (May 5, 1993). ... Released by Oilers (August 30, 1993). ... Re-signed by Oilers to practice squad (August 31, 1993). ... Activated (January 1, 1994). ... Released by Oilers (August 22, 1994). ... Selected by Amsterdam Admirals in 36th round (214th pick overall) of 1995 World League Draft. ... Signed by Arizona Cardinals (August 2, 1995). ... Released by Cardinals (September 11, 1995).
PLAYING EXPERIENCE: Houston NFL, 1993; Arizona NFL, 1995. ... Games: 1993 (1), 1995 (2). Total: 3.

ALEX, KEITH — G — VIKINGS

PERSONAL: Born June 9, 1969, in Kountze, Texas. ... 6-4/307. ... Full name: Hiram Keith Alex.
HIGH SCHOOL: Beaumont (Texas) Central.
COLLEGE: Texas A&M.
TRANSACTIONS/CAREER NOTES: Selected by Atlanta Falcons in ninth round (243rd pick overall) of 1992 NFL draft. ... Signed by Falcons (1992). ... Released by Falcons (August 29, 1992). ... Re-signed by Falcons to practice squad (September 2, 1992). ... Released by Falcons (September 12, 1992). ... Re-signed by Falcons (February 26, 1993). ... Released by Falcons (August 29, 1994). ... Signed by Minnesota Vikings (December 30, 1994); inactive for 1994 playoffs.
PLAYING EXPERIENCE: Atlanta NFL, 1993; Minnesota NFL, 1995. ... Games: 1993 (14), 1995 (1). Total: 15.

ALEXANDER, BRENT — DB — CARDINALS

PERSONAL: Born July 10, 1970, in Gallatin, Tenn. ... 5-10/184.
HIGH SCHOOL: Gallatin (Tenn.).
COLLEGE: Tennessee State.
TRANSACTIONS/CAREER NOTES: Signed as non-drafted free agent by Arizona Cardinals (April 28, 1994).
PRO STATISTICS: 1995—Credited with ½ sack and recovered one fumble.

Year Team	G	No.	Yds.	Avg.	TD
		INTERCEPTIONS			
1994—Arizona NFL	16	0	0	...	0
1995—Arizona NFL	16	2	14	7.0	0
Pro totals (2 years)	32	2	14	7.0	0

ALEXANDER, DAVID — C — JETS

PERSONAL: Born July 28, 1964, in Silver Spring, Md. ... 6-3/275.
HIGH SCHOOL: Broken Arrow (Okla.).
COLLEGE: Tulsa.
TRANSACTIONS/CAREER NOTES: Selected by Philadelphia Eagles in fifth round (121st pick overall) of 1987 NFL draft. ... Signed by Eagles (August 5, 1987). ... Released by Eagles (June 26, 1995). ... Signed by New York Jets (August 4, 1995). ... On injured reserve with knee injury (August 21, 1995-entire season).
PLAYING EXPERIENCE: Philadelphia NFL, 1987-1994. ... Games: 1987 (12), 1988 (16), 1989 (16), 1990 (16), 1991 (16), 1992 (16), 1993 (16), 1994 (16). Total: 124.
PRO STATISTICS: 1988—Recovered one fumble. 1989—Fumbled once and recovered one fumble for minus four yards. 1991—Recovered two fumbles for four yards. 1994—Caught two passes for one yard and recovered one fumble.

ALEXANDER, DERRICK — DE — VIKINGS

PERSONAL: Born November 3, 1973, in Jacksonville. ... 6-4/276.

HIGH SCHOOL: Raines (Jacksonville).
COLLEGE: Florida State.
TRANSACTIONS/CAREER NOTES: Selected after junior season by Minnesota Vikings in first round (11th pick overall) of 1995 NFL draft. ... Signed by Vikings (August 16, 1995).
HONORS: Named defensive lineman on THE SPORTING NEWS college All-America second team (1994).
PRO STATISTICS: 1995—Recovered one fumble.

Year Team	G	SACKS
1995—Minnesota NFL	15	2.0

ALEXANDER, DERRICK   WR   RAVENS

PERSONAL: Born November 6, 1971, in Detroit. ... 6-2/195. ... Full name: Derrick Scott Alexander.
HIGH SCHOOL: Benedictine (Detroit).
COLLEGE: Michigan.
TRANSACTIONS/CAREER NOTES: Selected by Cleveland Browns in first round (29th pick overall) of 1994 NFL draft. ... Signed by Browns (August 3, 1994). ... Browns franchise moved to Baltimore and renamed Ravens for 1996 season (March 11, 1996).
PRO STATISTICS: 1995—Fumbled three times and recovered one fumble.
STATISTICAL PLATEAUS: 100-yard receiving games: 1994 (3).

		RUSHING				RECEIVING				PUNT RETURNS				KICKOFF RETURNS				TOTALS		
Year Team	G	Att.	Yds.	Avg.	TD	No.	Yds.	Avg.	TD	No.	Yds.	Avg.	TD	No.	Yds.	Avg.	TD	TD	2pt.	Pts.
1994—Cleveland NFL	14	4	38	9.5	0	48	828	17.3	2	0	0	...	0	0	0	...	0	2	1	14
1995—Cleveland NFL	14	1	29	29.0	0	15	216	14.4	0	9	122	13.6	†1	21	419	20.0	0	1	0	6
Pro totals (2 years)	28	5	67	13.4	0	63	1044	16.6	2	9	122	13.6	1	21	419	20.0	0	3	1	20

ALEXANDER, ELIJAH   LB

PERSONAL: Born August 8, 1970, in Fort Worth, Texas. ... 6-2/230. ... Full name: Elijah Alfred Alexander III.
HIGH SCHOOL: Dunbar Senior (Fort Worth, Texas).
COLLEGE: Kansas State.
TRANSACTIONS/CAREER NOTES: Selected by Tampa Bay Buccaneers in 10th round (254th pick overall) of 1992 NFL draft. ... Signed by Buccaneers (June 3, 1992). ... Released by Buccaneers (August 31, 1992). ... Re-signed by Buccaneers (September 1, 1992). ... Released by Buccaneers (October 16, 1992). ... Re-signed by Buccaneers to practice squad (October 22, 1992). ... Activated (November 10, 1992). ... Claimed on waivers by Denver Broncos (August 31, 1993). ... On injured reserve with shoulder injury (November 22, 1995-remainder of season). ... Granted unconditional free agency (February 16, 1996).
PRO STATISTICS: 1994—Recovered one fumble for nine yards.

		INTERCEPTIONS				SACKS
Year Team	G	No.	Yds.	Avg.	TD	No.
1992—Tampa Bay NFL	12	0	0	...	0	0.0
1993—Denver NFL	16	0	0	...	0	0.0
1994—Denver NFL	16	1	2	2.0	0	1.0
1995—Denver NFL	9	2	5	2.5	0	0.5
Pro totals (4 years)	53	3	7	2.3	0	1.5

ALIPATE, TUINEAU   LB   VIKINGS

PERSONAL: Born August 21, 1967, in Union City, Calif. ... 6-2/239. ... Name pronounced TOO-know al-a-PA-tay.
HIGH SCHOOL: Logan (Union City, Calif.).
COLLEGE: Washington State.
TRANSACTIONS/CAREER NOTES: Signed as non-drafted free agent by Los Angeles Raiders (April 1993). ... Released by Raiders (July 27, 1993). ... Signed by New York Jets (August 1993). ... Released by Jets (August 27, 1993). ... Re-signed by Jets for 1994season. ... Released by Jets (August 29, 1994). ... Re-signed by Jets to practice squad (August 31, 1994). ... Activated (September 17, 1994). ... Released by Jets (September 20, 1994). ... Re-signed by Jets (October 7, 1994). ... Released by Jets (October 20, 1994). ... Re-signed by Jets to practice squad (October 20, 1994). ... Activated (November 5, 1994). ... Released by Jets (November 8, 1994). ... Re-signed by Jets (November 1994).... Released by Jets (December 16, 1994). ... Re-signed by Jets to practice squad (December 16, 1994). ... Released by Jets (December 1994).... Signed by Green Bay Packers to practice squad (January 5, 1995). ... Released by Packers (June 12, 1995). ... Signed by Minnesota Vikings (July 5, 1995).
PLAYING EXPERIENCE: New York Jets NFL, 1994; Minnesota NFL, 1995. ... Games: 1994 (8); 1995 (16). Total: 24.
PRO STATISTICS: 1994—Recovered one fumble.

ALLEN, DEREK   C   GIANTS

PERSONAL: Born January 30, 1971, in Geneseo, Ill. ... 6-4/290.
HIGH SCHOOL: Darnell (Geneseo, Ill.), then Naval Preparatory Academy (Newport, R.I.).
COLLEGE: Illinois.
TRANSACTIONS/CAREER NOTES: Signed as non-drafted free agent by New York Giants (April 29, 1995).
PLAYING EXPERIENCE: New York Giants NFL, 1995. ... Games: 1995 (1).

ALLEN, ERIC   CB   SAINTS

PERSONAL: Born November 22, 1965, in San Diego. ... 5-10/180. ... Full name: Eric Andre Allen.
HIGH SCHOOL: Point Loma (San Diego).
COLLEGE: Arizona State (degree in broadcasting, 1988).
TRANSACTIONS/CAREER NOTES: Selected by Philadelphia Eagles in second round (30th pick overall) of 1988 NFL draft. ... Signed by Eagles

(July 19, 1988). ... Granted free agency (February 1, 1992). ... Re-signed by Eagles (September 2, 1992). ... Granted roster exemption (September 2-4, 1992). ... Designated by Eagles as transition player (February 25, 1993). ... Tendered offer sheet by New Orleans Saints (March 20, 1995). ... Eagles declined to match offer (March 27, 1995).

HONORS: Played in Pro Bowl (1989 and 1991-1995 seasons).

RECORDS: Shares NFL single-season record for most touchdowns by interception—4 (1993). ... Shares NFL single-game record for most touchdowns by interception—2 (December 26, 1993, vs. New Orleans).

PRO STATISTICS: 1989—Fumbled once for seven yards. 1990—Returned one kickoff for two yards and recovered one fumble. 1991—Recovered one fumble. 1992—Recovered two fumbles. 1993—Credited with two sacks. 1994—Recovered one fumble for 30 yards.

MISCELLANEOUS: Shares Philadelphia Eagles all-time record for most interceptions (34).

		INTERCEPTIONS			
Year Team	G	No.	Yds.	Avg.	TD
1988—Philadelphia NFL	16	5	76	15.2	0
1989—Philadelphia NFL	15	8	38	4.8	0
1990—Philadelphia NFL	16	3	37	12.3	1
1991—Philadelphia NFL	16	5	20	4.0	0
1992—Philadelphia NFL	16	4	49	12.3	0
1993—Philadelphia NFL	16	6	*201	33.5	*4
1994—Philadelphia NFL	16	3	61	20.3	0
1995—New Orleans NFL	16	2	28	14.0	0
Pro totals (8 years)	127	36	510	14.2	5

ALLEN, LARRY — G — COWBOYS

PERSONAL: Born November 27, 1971, in Los Angeles. ... 6-3/325. ... Full name: Larry Christopher Allen.

HIGH SCHOOL: Vintage (Napa, Calif.).

JUNIOR COLLEGE: Butte Junior College (Calif.).

COLLEGE: Sonoma State (Calif.).

TRANSACTIONS/CAREER NOTES: Selected by Dallas Cowboys in second round (46th pick overall) of 1994 NFL draft. ... Signed by Cowboys (July 16, 1994).

PLAYING EXPERIENCE: Dallas NFL, 1994 and 1995. ... Games: 1994 (16); 1995 (16). Total: 32.

CHAMPIONSHIP GAME EXPERIENCE: Played in NFC championship game (1994 and 1995 seasons). ... Member of Super Bowl championship team (1995 season).

HONORS: Named guard on THE SPORTING NEWS NFL All-Pro team (1995). ... Played in Pro Bowl (1995 season).

PRO STATISTICS: 1995—Recovered one fumble.

ALLEN, MARCUS — RB — CHIEFS

PERSONAL: Born March 26, 1960, in San Diego. ... 6-2/210. ... Brother of Damon Allen, quarterback, Ottawa Rough Riders, Edmonton Eskimos and Hamilton Tiger-Cats of CFL (1985-1995).

HIGH SCHOOL: Lincoln (San Diego).

COLLEGE: Southern California.

TRANSACTIONS/CAREER NOTES: Selected by Los Angeles Raiders in first round (10th pick overall) of 1982 NFL draft. ... On reserve/did not report list (July 26-August 30, 1989). ... On injured reserve with knee injury (October 13-November 29, 1989). ... Moved to developmental squad (November 30, 1989). ... Activated (December 2, 1989). ... Granted free agency (February 1, 1990). ... Re-signed by Raiders (July 27, 1990). ... Granted free agency (February 1, 1991). ... Re-signed by Raiders (July 13, 1991). ... On injured reserve (September 4-October 30, 1991). ... Granted free agency (February 1, 1992). ... Re-signed by Raiders (August 12, 1992). ... Granted unconditional free agency (March 1, 1993). ... Signed by Kansas City Chiefs (June 9, 1993). ... Granted unconditional free agency (February 16, 1996). ... Re-signed by Chiefs (April 24, 1996).

CHAMPIONSHIP GAME EXPERIENCE: Played in AFC championship game (1983, 1990 and 1993 seasons). ... Member of Super Bowl championship team (1983 season).

HONORS: Heisman Trophy winner (1981). ... Maxwell Award winner (1981). ... Named College Football Player of the Year by THE SPORTING NEWS (1981). ... Named running back on THE SPORTING NEWS college All-America first team (1981). ... Named NFL Rookie of the Year by THE SPORTING NEWS (1982). ... Played in Pro Bowl (1982, 1984, 1985, 1987 and 1993 seasons). ... Named Most Valuable Player of Super Bowl XVIII (1983 season). ... Named NFL Player of the Year by THE SPORTING NEWS (1985). ... Named running back on THE SPORTING NEWS NFL All-Pro team (1985). ... Named to play in Pro Bowl (1986 season); replaced by Sammy Winder due to injury.

RECORDS: Holds NFL record for most consecutive games with 100 or more yards rushing—11 (October 28, 1985-September 14, 1986).

POSTSEASON RECORDS: Holds Super Bowl career records for highest average gain (minimum 20 attempts)—9.5; longest touchdown run—74 yards; and longest run from scrimmage—74 yards (January 22, 1984, vs. Washington). ... Shares Super Bowl single-game record for most rushing touchdowns—2 (January 22, 1984, vs. Washington).

PRO STATISTICS: 1982—Attempted four passes with one completion for 47 yards and recovered two fumbles. 1983—Attempted seven passes with four completions for 111 yards and three touchdowns and recovered two fumbles (including one in end zone for a touchdown). 1984—Attempted four passes with one completion for 38 yards and recovered three fumbles. 1985—Attempted two passes with one completion for 16 yards and recovered one fumble. 1986—Recovered one fumble. 1987—Attempted two passes with one completion for 23 yards. 1988—Attempted two passes with one completion for 21 yards. 1990—Attempted one pass without a completion and recovered one fumble. 1991—Attempted two passes with one completion for 11 yards and a touchdown. 1993—Recovered one fumble. 1995—Recovered one fumble.

STATISTICAL PLATEAUS: 100-yard rushing games: 1982 (2), 1983 (1), 1984 (3), 1985 (11), 1986 (2), 1987 (1), 1988 (1), 1994 (1), 1995 (2). Total: 24. ... 100-yard receiving games: 1983 (1), 1984 (1), 1986 (1). Total: 3.

MISCELLANEOUS: Active NFL and AFC leader for career rushing yards (10,908). ... Active AFC leader for most touchdowns (125). ... Holds Raiders franchise all-time record for most yards rushing (8,545) and most touchdowns (98).

		RUSHING				RECEIVING				TOTALS			
Year Team	G	Att.	Yds.	Avg.	TD	No.	Yds.	Avg.	TD	TD	2pt.	Pts.	Fum.
1982—Los Angeles Raiders NFL	9	160	697	4.4	*11	38	401	10.6	3	*14	...	*84	5
1983—Los Angeles Raiders NFL	15	266	1014	3.8	9	68	590	8.7	2	12	...	72	*14
1984—Los Angeles Raiders NFL	16	275	1168	4.3	13	64	758	11.8	5	†18	...	108	8
1985—Los Angeles Raiders NFL	16	380	*1759	4.6	11	67	555	8.3	3	14	...	84	3
1986—Los Angeles Raiders NFL	13	208	759	3.7	5	46	453	9.9	2	7	...	42	7
1987—Los Angeles Raiders NFL	12	200	754	3.8	5	51	410	8.0	0	5	...	30	3
1988—Los Angeles Raiders NFL	15	223	831	3.7	7	34	303	8.9	1	8	...	48	5

Year Team	G	RUSHING				RECEIVING				TOTALS			
		Att.	Yds.	Avg.	TD	No.	Yds.	Avg.	TD	TD	2pt.	Pts.	Fum.
1989—Los Angeles Raiders NFL	8	69	293	4.3	2	20	191	9.6	0	2	...	12	2
1990—Los Angeles Raiders NFL	16	179	682	3.8	12	15	189	12.6	1	13	...	78	1
1991—Los Angeles Raiders NFL	8	63	287	4.6	2	15	131	8.7	0	2	...	12	1
1992—Los Angeles Raiders NFL	16	67	301	4.5	2	28	277	9.9	1	3	...	18	1
1993—Kansas City NFL	16	206	764	3.7	*12	34	238	7.0	3	15	...	90	4
1994—Kansas City NFL	13	189	709	3.8	7	42	349	8.3	0	7	1	44	3
1995—Kansas City NFL	16	207	890	4.3	5	27	210	7.8	0	5	0	30	2
Pro totals (14 years)	189	2692	10908	4.1	103	549	5055	9.2	21	125	1	752	59

A

ALLEN, TERRY   RB   REDSKINS

PERSONAL: Born February 21, 1968, in Commerce, Ga. ... 5-10/208. ... Full name: Terry Thomas Allen Jr.
HIGH SCHOOL: Banks County (Homer, Ga.).
COLLEGE: Clemson.
TRANSACTIONS/CAREER NOTES: Selected after junior season by Minnesota Vikings in ninth round (241st pick overall) of 1990 NFL draft. ... Signed by Vikings (July 2, 1990). ... On injured reserve with knee injury (August 28, 1990-entire season). ... On injured reserve with knee injury (August 23, 1993-entire season). ... Released by Vikings (May 8, 1995). ... Signed by Washington Redskins (June 15, 1995). ... Granted free agency (February 16, 1996).
PRO STATISTICS: 1991—Returned one kickoff for 14 yards and recovered one fumble. 1992—Recovered two fumbles. 1994—Recovered two fumbles for four yards. 1995—Recovered one fumble.
STATISTICAL PLATEAUS: 100-yard rushing games: 1991 (1), 1992 (3), 1994 (3), 1995 (4). Total: 11. ... 100-yard receiving games: 1992 (1).

Year Team	G	RUSHING				RECEIVING				TOTALS			
		Att.	Yds.	Avg.	TD	No.	Yds.	Avg.	TD	TD	2pt.	Pts.	Fum.
1990—Minnesota NFL					Did not play—injured.								
1991—Minnesota NFL	15	120	563	4.7	2	6	49	8.2	1	3	...	18	4
1992—Minnesota NFL	16	266	1201	4.5	13	49	478	9.8	2	15	...	90	9
1993—Minnesota NFL					Did not play—injured.								
1994—Minnesota NFL	16	255	1031	4.0	8	17	148	8.7	0	8	1	50	3
1995—Washington NFL	16	338	1309	3.9	10	31	232	7.5	1	11	0	66	6
Pro totals (4 years)	63	979	4104	4.2	33	103	907	8.8	4	37	1	224	22

ALT, JOHN   OT   CHIEFS

PERSONAL: Born May 30, 1962, in Stuttgart, West Germany. ... 6-8/307. ... Full name: John Michael Alt.
HIGH SCHOOL: Columbia Heights (Minn.).
COLLEGE: Iowa (degree in business, 1984).
TRANSACTIONS/CAREER NOTES: Selected by Oklahoma Outlaws in third round (46th pick overall) of 1984 USFL draft. ... Selected by Kansas City Chiefs in first round (21st pick overall) of 1984 NFL draft. ... Signed by Chiefs (July 18, 1984). ... On injured reserve with back injury (December 6, 1985-remainder of season). ... On reserve/physically unable to perform list with back injury (August 18-November 8, 1986). ... On injured reserve with knee injury (December 9, 1987-remainder of season). ... Granted free agency (February 1, 1991). ... Re-signed by Chiefs (August 11, 1991). ... Designated by Chiefs as transition player (February 15, 1994).
PLAYING EXPERIENCE: Kansas City NFL, 1984-1995. ... Games: 1984 (15), 1985 (13), 1986 (7), 1987 (9), 1988 (14), 1989 (16), 1990 (16), 1991 (16), 1992 (16), 1993 (16), 1994 (13), 1995 (16). Total: 167.
CHAMPIONSHIP GAME EXPERIENCE: Played in AFC championship game (1993 season).
HONORS: Named offensive tackle on THE SPORTING NEWS NFL All-Pro team (1990). ... Played in Pro Bowl (1992 and 1993 seasons).

AMBROSE, ASHLEY   DB   BENGALS

PERSONAL: Born September 17, 1970, in New Orleans. ... 5-10/182. ... Full name: Ashley Avery Ambrose.
HIGH SCHOOL: Fortier (New Orleans).
COLLEGE: Mississippi Valley State.
TRANSACTIONS/CAREER NOTES: Selected by Indianapolis Colts in second round (29th pick overall) of 1992 NFL draft. ... Signed by Colts (August 11, 1992). ... On injured reserve with leg injury (September 14-October 29, 1992); on practice squad (October 21-29, 1992). ... Granted free agency (February 17, 1995). ... Re-signed by Colts (April 29, 1995). ... Granted unconditional free agency (February 16, 1996). ... Signed by Cincinnati Bengals (February 26, 1996).
CHAMPIONSHIP GAME EXPERIENCE: Played in AFC championship game (1995 season).
PRO STATISTICS: 1994—Recovered one fumble.

Year Team	G	INTERCEPTIONS				KICKOFF RETURNS				TOTALS			
		No.	Yds.	Avg.	TD	No.	Yds.	Avg.	TD	TD	2pt.	Pts.	Fum.
1992—Indianapolis NFL	10	0	0	...	0	8	126	15.8	0	0	...	0	0
1993—Indianapolis NFL	14	0	0	...	0	0	0	...	0	0	...	0	0
1994—Indianapolis NFL	16	2	50	25.0	0	0	0	...	0	0	0	0	0
1995—Indianapolis NFL	16	3	12	4.0	0	0	0	...	0	0	0	0	0
Pro totals (4 years)	56	5	62	12.4	0	8	126	15.8	0	0	0	0	0

ANDERS, KIMBLE   FB

PERSONAL: Born September 10, 1966, in Galveston, Texas. ... 5-11/230. ... Full name: Kimble Lynard Anders.
HIGH SCHOOL: Ball (Galveston, Texas).
COLLEGE: Houston.
TRANSACTIONS/CAREER NOTES: Signed as non-drafted free agent by Pittsburgh Steelers (April 25, 1990). ... Released by Steelers (September 3, 1990). ... Signed by Kansas City Chiefs (March 13, 1991). ... On injured reserve with hand injury (September 15, 1991-remainder of season). ... On injured reserve with knee injury (September 12-October 17, 1992); on practice squad (October 7-17, 1992). ... Granted

unconditional free agency (February 16, 1996).
CHAMPIONSHIP GAME EXPERIENCE: Played in AFC championship game (1993 season).
HONORS: Played in Pro Bowl (1995 season).
PRO STATISTICS: 1994—Recovered two fumbles.

Year Team	G	RUSHING				RECEIVING				KICKOFF RETURNS				TOTALS			
		Att.	Yds.	Avg.	TD	No.	Yds.	Avg.	TD	No.	Yds.	Avg.	TD	TD	2pt.	Pts.	Fum.
1991—Kansas City NFL	2	0	0	...	0	2	30	15.0	0	0	0	...	0	0	...	0	0
1992—Kansas City NFL	11	1	1	1.0	0	5	65	13.0	0	1	20	20.0	0	0	...	0	1
1993—Kansas City NFL	16	75	291	3.9	0	40	326	8.2	1	1	47	47.0	0	1	...	6	1
1994—Kansas City NFL	16	62	231	3.7	2	67	525	7.8	1	2	36	18.0	0	3	0	18	1
1995—Kansas City NFL	16	58	398	6.9	2	55	349	6.4	1	0	0	...	0	3	0	18	1
Pro totals (5 years)	61	196	921	4.7	4	169	1295	7.7	3	4	103	25.8	0	7	0	42	4

ANDERSEN, MORTEN — K — FALCONS

PERSONAL: Born August 19, 1960, in Struer, Denmark. ... 6-2/221.
HIGH SCHOOL: Ben Davis (Indianapolis).
COLLEGE: Michigan State.
TRANSACTIONS/CAREER NOTES: Selected by New Orleans Saints in fourth round (86th pick overall) of 1982 NFL draft. ... On injured reserve with sprained ankle (September 15-November 20, 1982). ... Designated by Saints as transition player (February 25, 1993). ... Released by Saints (July 19, 1995). ... Signed by Atlanta Falcons (July 21, 1995).
HONORS: Named place-kicker on THE SPORTING NEWS college All-America first team (1981). ... Named kicker on THE SPORTING NEWS NFL All-Pro team (1985-1987 and 1995). ... Played in Pro Bowl (1985-1988, 1990, 1992 and 1995 seasons).
RECORDS: Holds NFL career record for most field goals of 50 or more yards—30. ... Holds NFL record for most consecutive games scoring—190 (December 11, 1983-December 24, 1995). ... Holds NFL single-season record for most field goals of 50 or more yards—8 (1995). ... Holds NFL single-game record for most field goals of 50 or more yards—3 (December 11, 1983, at Philadelphia).

Year Team	G	KICKING						
		XPM	XPA	FGM	FGA	Lg.	50+	Pts.
1982—New Orleans NFL	8	6	6	2	5	45	0-1	12
1983—New Orleans NFL	16	37	38	18	24	52	3-4	91
1984—New Orleans NFL	16	34	34	20	27	53	2-3	94
1985—New Orleans NFL	16	27	29	31	35	55	3-4	120
1986—New Orleans NFL	16	30	30	26	30	53	2-5	108
1987—New Orleans NFL	12	37	37	*28	*36	52	2-6	121
1988—New Orleans NFL	16	32	33	26	36	51	1-4	110
1989—New Orleans NFL	16	44	45	20	29	49	0-4	104
1990—New Orleans NFL	16	29	29	21	27	52	3-4	92
1991—New Orleans NFL	16	38	38	25	32	60	2-4	113
1992—New Orleans NFL	16	33	34	29	34	52	3-3	†120
1993—New Orleans NFL	16	33	33	28	35	56	1-5	117
1994—New Orleans NFL	16	32	32	28	*39	48	0-6	116
1995—Atlanta NFL	16	29	30	31	37	59	8-9	122
Pro totals (14 years)	212	441	448	333	426	60	30-62	1440

ANDERSON, DARREN — CB — CHIEFS

PERSONAL: Born January 11, 1969, in Cincinnati. ... 5-10/187. ... Full name: Darren Hunter Anderson.
HIGH SCHOOL: Walnut Hills (Cincinnati).
COLLEGE: Toledo.
TRANSACTIONS/CAREER NOTES: Selected by New England Patriots in fourth round (93rd pick overall) of 1992 NFL draft. ... Signed by Patriots (July 21, 1992). ... Released by Patriots (September 3, 1992). ... Re-signed by Patriots to practice squad (September 9, 1992). ... Activated (September 26, 1992). ... Released by Patriots (October 2, 1992). ... Re-signed by Patriots to practice squad (October 6, 1992). ... Released by Patriots (October 28, 1992). ... Signed by Tampa Bay Buccaneers to practice squad (October 31, 1992). ... Activated (December 26, 1992). ... Traded by Buccaneers to Kansas City Chiefs for seventh-round pick (DE Jeffrey Rodgers) in 1995 draft (August 23, 1994). ... Granted free agency (February 16, 1996).
PLAYING EXPERIENCE: New England (1)-Tampa Bay (1) NFL, 1992; Tampa Bay NFL, 1993; Kansas City NFL, 1994 and 1995. ... Games: 1992 (2), 1993 (14), 1994 (15), 1995 (16). Total: 47.
PRO STATISTICS: 1993—Intercepted one pass for six yards. 1994—Recovered one fumble.

ANDERSON, EDDIE — S — RAIDERS

PERSONAL: Born July 22, 1963, in Warner Robins, Ga. ... 6-1/210. ... Full name: Eddie Lee Anderson Jr.
HIGH SCHOOL: Warner Robins (Ga.).
COLLEGE: Fort Valley (Ga.) State.
TRANSACTIONS/CAREER NOTES: Selected by Seattle Seahawks in sixth round (153rd pick overall) of 1986 NFL draft. ... Signed by Seahawks (July 16, 1986). ... On injured reserve with back injury (September 11-November 21, 1986). ... Released by Seahawks (September 1, 1987). ... Signed as replacement player by Los Angeles Raiders (September 24, 1987). ... Granted free agency (February 1, 1991). ... Re-signed by Raiders (July 12, 1991). ... Raiders franchise moved to Oakland (July 21, 1995).
CHAMPIONSHIP GAME EXPERIENCE: Played in AFC championship game (1990 season).
PRO STATISTICS: 1987—Recovered one fumble. 1990—Recovered one fumble. 1991—Recovered one fumble. 1993—Recovered one fumble. 1994—Recovered one fumble. 1995—Recovered two fumbles.

Year Team	G	INTERCEPTIONS				SACKS
		No.	Yds.	Avg.	TD	No.
1986—Seattle NFL	5	0	0	...	0	0.0
1987—Los Angeles Raiders NFL	13	1	58	58.0	0	0.0
1988—Los Angeles Raiders NFL	16	2	-6	-3.0	0	0.0

Year Team	G	INTERCEPTIONS				SACKS
		No.	Yds.	Avg.	TD	No.
1989—Los Angeles Raiders NFL	15	5	*233	46.6	*2	0.0
1990—Los Angeles Raiders NFL	16	3	49	16.3	0	0.0
1991—Los Angeles Raiders NFL	16	2	14	7.0	0	0.0
1992—Los Angeles Raiders NFL	16	3	131	43.7	1	1.0
1993—Los Angeles Raiders NFL	16	2	52	26.0	0	1.0
1994—Los Angeles Raiders NFL	14	0	0	...	0	2.0
1995—Oakland NFL	14	1	0	0.0	0	0.0
Pro totals (10 years)	141	19	531	28.0	3	4.0

ANDERSON, FLIPPER   WR   COLTS

PERSONAL: Born March 7, 1965, in Philadelphia. ... 6-0/176. ... Full name: Willie Lee Anderson Jr.
HIGH SCHOOL: Paulsboro (N.J.).
COLLEGE: UCLA.
TRANSACTIONS/CAREER NOTES: Selected by Los Angeles Rams in second round (46th pick overall) of 1988 NFL draft. ... Signed by Rams (July 17, 1988). ... Granted unconditional free agency (February 17, 1995). ... Signed by Indianapolis Colts (March 7, 1995). ... On injured reserve with knee injury (September 14, 1995-remainder of season).
CHAMPIONSHIP GAME EXPERIENCE: Played in NFC championship game (1989 season).
RECORDS: Holds NFL single-game record for most yards receiving—336 (November 26, 1989, OT, at New Orleans).
PRO STATISTICS: 1989—Rushed once for minus one yard. 1990—Rushed once for 13 yards and recovered one fumble. 1991—Recovered one fumble. 1992—Returned one kickoff for nine yards. 1993—Recovered one fumble. 1994—Rushed once for 11 yards and recovered one fumble for seven yards.
STATISTICAL PLATEAUS: 100-yard receiving games: 1989 (2), 1990 (4), 1991 (1), 1994 (2). Total: 9.

Year Team	G	RECEIVING				TOTALS			
		No.	Yds.	Avg.	TD	TD	2pt.	Pts.	Fum.
1988—Los Angeles Rams NFL	16	11	319	29.0	0	0	...	0	0
1989—Los Angeles Rams NFL	16	44	1146	*26.1	5	5	...	30	0
1990—Los Angeles Rams NFL	16	51	1097	*21.5	4	4	...	24	0
1991—Los Angeles Rams NFL	12	32	530	16.6	1	1	...	6	2
1992—Los Angeles Rams NFL	15	38	657	17.3	7	7	...	42	1
1993—Los Angeles Rams NFL	15	37	552	14.9	4	4	...	24	0
1994—Los Angeles Rams NFL	16	46	945	20.5	5	5	0	30	0
1995—Indianapolis NFL	2	8	111	13.9	2	2	0	12	0
Pro totals (8 years)	108	267	5357	20.1	28	28	0	168	3

ANDERSON, GARY   K   EAGLES

PERSONAL: Born July 16, 1959, in Parys, Orange Free State, South Africa. ... 5-11/179. ... Full name: Gary Allan Anderson. ... Son of Rev. Douglas Anderson, former professional soccer player in England.
HIGH SCHOOL: Brettonwood (Durban, South Africa).
COLLEGE: Syracuse (degree in management and accounting, 1982).
TRANSACTIONS/CAREER NOTES: Selected by Buffalo Bills in seventh round (171st pick overall) of 1982 NFL draft. ... Claimed on waivers by Pittsburgh Steelers (September 7, 1982). ... Designated by Steelers as transition player (February 15, 1994). ... On reserve/did not report list (August 23-25, 1994). ... Free agency status changed by Steelers from transition to unconditional (February 17, 1995). ... Signed by Philadelphia Eagles (July 23, 1995).
CHAMPIONSHIP GAME EXPERIENCE: Played in AFC championship game (1984 and 1994 seasons).
HONORS: Played in Pro Bowl (1983, 1985 and 1993 seasons).
PRO STATISTICS: 1994—Rushed once for three yards.

Year Team	G	KICKING						
		XPM	XPA	FGM	FGA	Lg.	50+	Pts.
1982—Pittsburgh NFL	9	22	22	10	12	48	0-1	52
1983—Pittsburgh NFL	16	38	39	27	31	49	0-0	119
1984—Pittsburgh NFL	16	45	45	24	32	55	2-3	117
1985—Pittsburgh NFL	16	40	40	*33	*42	52	1-4	139
1986—Pittsburgh NFL	16	32	32	21	32	45	0-3	95
1987—Pittsburgh NFL	12	21	21	22	27	52	2-2	87
1988—Pittsburgh NFL	16	34	35	28	36	52	1-2	118
1989—Pittsburgh NFL	16	28	28	21	30	49	0-0	91
1990—Pittsburgh NFL	16	32	32	20	25	48	0-2	92
1991—Pittsburgh NFL	16	31	31	23	33	54	1-6	100
1992—Pittsburgh NFL	16	29	31	28	36	49	0-2	113
1993—Pittsburgh NFL	16	32	32	28	30	46	0-0	116
1994—Pittsburgh NFL	16	32	32	24	29	50	1-2	104
1995—Philadelphia NFL	16	32	33	22	30	43	0-3	98
Pro totals (14 years)	213	448	453	331	425	55	8-30	1441

ANDERSON, JAMAL   RB   FALCONS

PERSONAL: Born March 6, 1972, in Woodland Hills, Calif. ... 5-10/240. ... Full name: Jamal Sharif Anderson.
HIGH SCHOOL: El Camino Real (Monterey Park, Calif.).
COLLEGE: Utah.
TRANSACTIONS/CAREER NOTES: Selected by Atlanta Falcons in seventh round (201st pick overall) of 1994 NFL draft. ... Signed by Falcons (June 21, 1994).
PRO STATISTICS: 1995—Caught four passes for 42 yards.

Year Team	G	RUSHING				KICKOFF RETURNS				TOTALS			
		Att.	Yds.	Avg.	TD	No.	Yds.	Avg.	TD	TD	2pt.	Pts.	Fum.
1994—Atlanta NFL	3	2	-1	-0.5	0	1	11	11.0	0	0	0	0	0
1995—Atlanta NFL	16	39	161	4.1	1	24	541	22.5	0	1	0	6	0
Pro totals (2 years)	19	41	160	3.9	1	25	552	22.1	0	1	0	6	0

ANDERSON, RICHIE   RB   JETS

PERSONAL: Born September 13, 1971, in Sandy Spring, Md. ... 6-2/225. ... Full name: Richard Darnoll Anderson.
HIGH SCHOOL: Sherwood (Sandy Spring, Md.).
COLLEGE: Penn State.
TRANSACTIONS/CAREER NOTES: Selected after junior season by New York Jets in sixth round (144th pick overall) of 1993 NFL draft. ... Signed by Jets (June 10, 1993). ... On injured reserve with ankle injury (December 31, 1993-remainder of season). ... On injured reserve with ankle injury (November 30, 1995-remainder of season).
PRO STATISTICS: 1993—Recovered one fumble. 1994—Recovered one fumble. 1995—Attempted one pass without a completion.

Year Team	G	RUSHING				RECEIVING				KICKOFF RETURNS				TOTALS			
		Att.	Yds.	Avg.	TD	No.	Yds.	Avg.	TD	No.	Yds.	Avg.	TD	TD	2pt.	Pts.	Fum.
1993—New York Jets NFL	7	0	0	...	0	0	0	...	0	4	66	16.5	0	0	...	0	1
1994—New York Jets NFL	13	43	207	4.8	1	25	212	8.5	1	3	43	14.3	0	2	0	12	1
1995—New York Jets NFL	10	5	17	3.4	0	5	26	5.2	0	0	0	...	0	0	0	0	2
Pro totals (3 years)	30	48	224	4.7	1	30	238	7.9	1	7	109	15.6	0	2	0	12	4

ANDERSON, STEVIE   WR   CARDINALS

PERSONAL: Born May 12, 1970, in Monroe, La. ... 6-5/215. ... Brother of Anthony Anderson, safety, San Diego Chargers (1987).
HIGH SCHOOL: Jonesboro (La.)-Hodge.
COLLEGE: Grambling State.
TRANSACTIONS/CAREER NOTES: Selected by Phoenix Cardinals in eighth round (215th pick overall) of 1993 NFL draft. ... Signed by Cardinals (July 20, 1993). ... Released by Cardinals (August 23, 1993). ... Re-signed by Cardinals to practice squad (August 30, 1993). ... Signed by New York Jets off Cardinals practice squad (September 1, 1993). ... Activated (December 31, 1993). ... Claimed on waivers by Arizona Cardinals (August 22, 1995).
PRO STATISTICS: 1995—Returned one kickoff for 17 yards.

Year Team	G	RECEIVING				TOTALS			
		No.	Yds.	Avg.	TD	TD	2pt.	Pts.	Fum.
1994—New York Jets NFL	10	9	90	10.0	0	0	0	0	0
1995—Arizona NFL	5	3	34	11.3	1	1	2	10	0
Pro totals (2 years)	15	12	124	10.3	1	1	2	10	0

ARBUCKLE, CHARLES   TE

PERSONAL: Born September 13, 1968, in Beaumont, Texas. ... 6-3/248. ... Full name: Charles Edward Arbuckle.
HIGH SCHOOL: Willowridge (Sugar Land, Texas).
COLLEGE: UCLA.
TRANSACTIONS/CAREER NOTES: Selected by New Orleans Saints in fifth round (125th pick overall) of 1990 NFL draft. ... Signed by Saints (July 21, 1990). ... On injured reserve with knee injury (September 4, 1990-entire season). ... Granted unconditional free agency (February 1, 1991). ... Signed by Cleveland Browns (March 25, 1991). ... Released by Browns (August 18, 1991). ... Signed by San Diego Chargers to practice squad (November 13, 1991). ... Released by Chargers (November 19, 1991). ... Signed by Indianapolis Colts (February 20, 1992). ... Granted free agency (February 17, 1994). ... Re-signed by Colts (May 6, 1994). ... Claimed on waivers by Green Bay Packers (July 28, 1994). ... Released by Packers (August 17, 1994). ... Signed by Colts (November 1, 1994). ... Released by Colts (September 21, 1995).
STATISTICAL PLATEAUS: 100-yard receiving games: 1992 (1). Total: 1.

Year Team	G	RECEIVING				TOTALS			
		No.	Yds.	Avg.	TD	TD	2pt.	Pts.	Fum.
1990—New Orleans NFL				Did not play—injured.					
1991—San Diego NFL				Did not play.					
1992—Indianapolis NFL	16	13	152	11.7	1	1	...	6	0
1993—Indianapolis NFL	16	15	90	6.0	0	0	...	0	1
1994—Indianapolis NFL	7	1	7	7.0	0	0	0	0	0
1995—Indianapolis NFL	3	4	33	8.3	0	0	0	0	0
Pro totals (4 years)	42	33	282	8.6	1	1	0	6	1

ARCHAMBEAU, LESTER   DE   FALCONS

PERSONAL: Born June 27, 1967, in Montville, N.J. ... 6-5/275. ... Full name: Lester Milward Archambeau.
HIGH SCHOOL: Montville (N.J.).
COLLEGE: Stanford (degree in industrial engineering).
TRANSACTIONS/CAREER NOTES: Selected by Green Bay Packers in seventh round (186th pick overall) of 1990 NFL draft. ... Signed by Packers (July 22, 1990). ... On injured reserve with back injury (October 6, 1990-remainder of season). ... Granted free agency (February 1, 1992). ... Re-signed by Packers (August 12, 1992). ... Traded by Packers to Atlanta Falcons for WR James Milling (June 3, 1993). ... Granted unconditional free agency (February 17, 1994). ... Re-signed by Falcons (March 7, 1994).
PRO STATISTICS: 1995—Recovered one fumble.

Year Team	G	SACKS
1990—Green Bay NFL	4	0.0
1991—Green Bay NFL	16	4.5
1992—Green Bay NFL	16	1.0
1993—Atlanta NFL	15	0.0

Year	Team	G	SACKS
1994—Atlanta NFL		16	2.0
1995—Atlanta NFL		16	3.0
Pro totals (6 years)		83	10.5

ARMOUR, JUSTIN   WR   BILLS

PERSONAL: Born January 1, 1973, in Colorado Springs, Colo. ... 6-4/209. ... Full name: Justin Hugh Armour.
HIGH SCHOOL: Manitou Springs (Colo.).
COLLEGE: Stanford.
TRANSACTIONS/CAREER NOTES: Selected by Buffalo Bills in fourth round (113th pick overall) of 1995 NFL draft. ... Signed by Bills (June 27, 1995).
PRO STATISTICS: 1995—Rushed four times for minus five yards, attempted one pass without a completion and recovered two fumbles.

			RECEIVING				TOTALS			
Year	Team	G	No.	Yds.	Avg.	TD	TD	2pt.	Pts.	Fum.
1995—Buffalo NFL		15	26	300	11.5	3	3	0	18	1

ARMSTEAD, JESSIE   LB   GIANTS

PERSONAL: Born October 26, 1970, in Dallas. ... 6-1/232.
HIGH SCHOOL: David W. Carter (Dallas).
COLLEGE: Miami, Fla. (degree in criminal justice, 1992).
TRANSACTIONS/CAREER NOTES: Selected by New York Giants in eighth round (207th pick overall) of 1993 NFL draft. ... Signed by Giants (July 19, 1993).
PRO STATISTICS: 1995—Recovered one fumble.

			INTERCEPTIONS				SACKS
Year	Team	G	No.	Yds.	Avg.	TD	No.
1993—New York Giants NFL		16	1	0	0.0	0	0.0
1994—New York Giants NFL		16	1	0	0.0	0	3.0
1995—New York Giants NFL		16	1	58	58.0	1	0.5
Pro totals (3 years)		48	3	58	19.3	1	3.5

ARMSTRONG, ANTONIO   DE/LB   DOLPHINS

PERSONAL: Born October 15, 1973, in Houston ... 6-1/234. ... Full name: Antonio Donnell Armstrong. ... Formerly known as Antonio Shorter.
HIGH SCHOOL: Kashmere (Houston).
COLLEGE: Texas A&M.
TRANSACTIONS/CAREER NOTES: Selected by San Francisco 49ers in sixth round (201st pick overall) of 1995 NFL draft. ... Signed by 49ers (July 17, 1995). ... Released by 49ers (August 27, 1995). ... Re-signed by 49ers to practice squad (August 29, 1995). ... Released by 49ers (October 16, 1995). ... Signed by Miami Dolphins to practice squad (October 18, 1995). ... Activated (October 25, 1995).
PLAYING EXPERIENCE: Miami NFL, 1995. ... Games: 1995 (4).

ARMSTRONG, BRUCE   OT   PATRIOTS

PERSONAL: Born September 7, 1965, in Miami. ... 6-4/295. ... Full name: Bruce Charles Armstrong.
HIGH SCHOOL: Central (Miami).
COLLEGE: Louisville.
TRANSACTIONS/CAREER NOTES: Selected by New England Patriots in first round (23rd pick overall) of 1987 NFL draft. ... Signed by Patriots (July 23, 1987). ... On injured reserve with knee injury (November 2, 1992-remainder of season). ... On active/physically unable to perform list (July 16-July 27, 1993).
PLAYING EXPERIENCE: New England NFL, 1987-1995. ... Games: 1987 (12), 1988 (16), 1989 (16), 1990 (16), 1991 (16), 1992 (8), 1993 (16), 1994 (16), 1995 (16). Total: 132.
HONORS: Named offensive tackle on THE SPORTING NEWS NFL All-Pro team (1988). ... Played in Pro Bowl (1990, 1991, 1994 and 1995 seasons).
PRO STATISTICS: 1990—Recovered two fumbles for four yards. 1992—Recovered one fumble. 1993—Recovered one fumble for one yard. 1995—Recovered one fumble.

ARMSTRONG, TRACE   DE   DOLPHINS

PERSONAL: Born October 5, 1965, in Bethesda, Md. ... 6-4/260. ... Full name: Raymond Lester Armstrong.
HIGH SCHOOL: John Carroll (Birmingham, Ala.).
COLLEGE: Arizona State, then Florida (degree in psychology, 1989).
TRANSACTIONS/CAREER NOTES: Selected by Chicago Bears in first round (12th pick overall) of 1989 NFL draft. ... Signed by Bears (August 18, 1989). ... On injured reserve with knee injury (September 24-November 3, 1991). ... Granted free agency (March 1, 1993). ... Re-signed by Bears (March 14, 1993). ... Traded by Bears to Miami Dolphins for second-round (P Todd Sauerbrun) and third-round picks (OG Evan Pilgrim) in 1995 draft (April 4, 1995).
HONORS: Named defensive lineman on THE SPORTING NEWS college All-America first team (1988).
PRO STATISTICS: 1989—Recovered one fumble. 1990—Recovered two fumbles. 1992—Recovered one fumble. 1993—Recovered three fumbles for three yards. 1995—Recovered one fumble.

Year	Team	G	SACKS
1989—Chicago NFL		15	5.0
1990—Chicago NFL		16	10.0

Year Team	G	SACKS
1991—Chicago NFL	12	1.5
1992—Chicago NFL	14	6.5
1993—Chicago NFL	16	11.5
1994—Chicago NFL	15	7.5
1995—Miami NFL	15	4.5
Pro totals (7 years)	103	46.5

ARMSTRONG, TYJI   TE   BUCCANEERS

PERSONAL: Born October 3, 1970, in Inkster, Mich. ... 6-4/277. ... Full name: Tyji Donrapheal Armstrong. ... Name pronounced TY-JAY.
HIGH SCHOOL: Robichaud (Dearborn, Mich.).
JUNIOR COLLEGE: Iowa Central Community College.
COLLEGE: Mississippi.
TRANSACTIONS/CAREER NOTES: Selected by Tampa Bay Buccaneers in third round (79th pick overall) of 1992 NFL draft. ... Signed by Buccaneers (July 27, 1992). ... Granted free agency (February 17, 1995). ... Re-signed by Buccaneers (May 19, 1995).
PRO STATISTICS: 1993—Rushed twice for five yards. 1994—Rushed once for minus one yard, returned one kickoff for six yards and recovered one fumble. 1995—Returned one kickoff for six yards and recovered one fumble.

Year Team	G	RECEIVING No.	Yds.	Avg.	TD	TOTALS TD	2pt.	Pts.	Fum.
1992—Tampa Bay NFL	15	7	138	19.7	1	1	...	6	0
1993—Tampa Bay NFL	12	9	86	9.6	1	1	...	6	0
1994—Tampa Bay NFL	16	22	265	12.1	1	1	0	6	2
1995—Tampa Bay NFL	16	7	68	9.7	0	0	0	0	1
Pro totals (4 years)	59	45	557	12.4	3	3	0	18	3

ARTHUR, MIKE   C   PACKERS

PERSONAL: Born May 7, 1968, in Minneapolis. ... 6-3/280. ... Full name: Michael Scott Arthur.
HIGH SCHOOL: Spring Woods (Houston).
COLLEGE: Texas A&M.
TRANSACTIONS/CAREER NOTES: Selected by Cincinnati Bengals in fifth round (130th pick overall) of 1991 NFL draft. ... Signed by Bengals (1991). ... Claimed on waivers by New England Patriots (September 1, 1993). ... Granted free agency (February 17, 1994). ... Re-signed by Patriots (March 25, 1994). ... Traded by Patriots to Green Bay Packers for TE Jeff Wilner and WR Bill Schroeder (August 11, 1995).
PLAYING EXPERIENCE: Cincinnati NFL, 1991 and 1992; New England NFL, 1993 and 1994; Green Bay NFL, 1995. ... Games: 1991 (7), 1992 (16), 1993 (13), 1994 (12), 1995 (11). Total: 59.
CHAMPIONSHIP GAME EXPERIENCE: Played in NFC championship game (1995 season).
PRO STATISTICS: 1991—Recovered one fumble. 1992—Fumbled four times for minus 33 yards. 1993—Recovered one fumble. 1994—Fumbled once and recovered one fumble for minus two yards. 1995—Returned one kickoff for 10 yards.

ARVIE, HERMAN   OT   RAVENS

PERSONAL: Born October 12, 1970, in Opelousas, La. ... 6-4/305. ... Full name: Herman Joseph Arvie.
HIGH SCHOOL: Opelousas (La.).
COLLEGE: Grambling State.
TRANSACTIONS/CAREER NOTES: Selected by Cleveland Browns in fifth round (124th pick overall) of 1993 NFL draft. ... Signed by Browns (July 14, 1993). ... Browns franchise moved to Baltimore and renamed Ravens for 1996 season (March 11, 1996).
PLAYING EXPERIENCE: Cleveland NFL, 1993-1995. ... Games: 1993 (16), 1994 (16), 1995 (16). Total: 48.

ASHER, JAMIE   TE   REDSKINS

PERSONAL: Born October 31, 1972, in Indianapolis. ... 6-3/243.
HIGH SCHOOL: Warren Central (Indianapolis).
COLLEGE: Louisville.
TRANSACTIONS/CAREER NOTES: Selected by Washington Redskins in fifth round (137th pick overall) of 1995 NFL draft. ... Signed by Redskins (June 1, 1995).
PRO STATISTICS: Returned one kickoff for 13 yards.

Year Team	G	RECEIVING No.	Yds.	Avg.	TD	TOTALS TD	2pt.	Pts.	Fum.
1995—Washington	7	14	172	12.3	0	0	0	0	0

ASHMORE, DARRYL   OT   RAMS

PERSONAL: Born November 1, 1969, in Peoria, Ill. ... 6-7/310. ... Full name: Darryl Allan Ashmore.
HIGH SCHOOL: Peoria (Ill.) Central.
COLLEGE: Northwestern (degree in business).
TRANSACTIONS/CAREER NOTES: Selected by Los Angeles Rams in seventh round (171st pick overall) of 1992 NFL draft. ... Signed by Rams (July 13, 1992). ... On injured reserve with knee injury (September 3-October 7, 1992). ... On practice squad (October 7, 1992-remainder of season). ... Granted free agency (February 17, 1995). ... Rams franchise moved to St. Louis (April 12, 1995). ... Re-signed by Rams (July 20, 1995).
PLAYING EXPERIENCE: Los Angeles Rams NFL, 1993 and 1994; St. Louis NFL, 1995. ... Games: 1993 (9), 1994 (11), 1995 (16). Total: 36.

ASKA, JOE   RB   RAIDERS

PERSONAL: Born July 14, 1972, in St. Croix, Virgin Islands ... 5-11/230.
HIGH SCHOOL: Putnam City (Okla.).
JUNIOR COLLEGE: Cisco (Texas) Junior College, then Coffeyville (Kan.) Junior College.
COLLEGE: Central Oklahoma.
TRANSACTIONS/CAREER NOTES: Selected by Los Angeles Raiders in third round (86th pick overall) of 1995 NFL draft. ... Signed by Raiders (June 1, 1995). ... Raiders franchise moved to Oakland (July 21, 1995).
PLAYING EXPERIENCE: Oakland NFL, 1995. ... Games: 1995 (1).

ATKINS, GENE   S   DOLPHINS

PERSONAL: Born November 22, 1964, in Tallahassee, Fla. ... 5-11/201. ... Full name: Gene Reynard Atkins.
HIGH SCHOOL: James S. Rickards (Tallahassee, Fla.).
COLLEGE: Florida A&M.
TRANSACTIONS/CAREER NOTES: Selected by New Orleans Saints in seventh round (179th pick overall) of 1987 NFL draft. ... Signed by Saints (July 25, 1987). ... On injured reserve with eye injury (September 7-October 1, 1987). ... Crossed picket line during players strike (October 1, 1987). ... Granted free agency (February 1, 1990). ... Re-signed by Saints (July 15, 1990). ... Granted free agency (February 1, 1992). ... Re-signed by Saints (August 22, 1992). ... Granted unconditional free agency (February 17, 1994). ... Signed by Miami Dolphins (February 19, 1994).
PRO STATISTICS: 1987—Recovered one fumble. 1988—Recovered two fumbles. 1989—Recovered two fumbles. 1990—Recovered three fumbles. 1991—Recovered two fumbles. 1992—Recovered one fumble for nine yards. 1993—Recovered two fumbles for four yards. 1995—Recovered one fumble for one yard.

		INTERCEPTIONS			SACKS	KICKOFF RETURNS				TOTALS			
Year Team	G	No.	Yds.	Avg.	TD	No.	No.	Yds.	Avg.	TD	TD 2pt.	Pts.	Fum.
1987—New Orleans NFL	13	3	12	4.0	0	0.0	0	0	...	0	0 ...	0	0
1988—New Orleans NFL	16	4	42	10.5	0	0.0	20	424	21.2	0	0 ...	0	1
1989—New Orleans NFL	14	1	-2	-2.0	0	0.0	12	245	20.4	0	0 ...	0	1
1990—New Orleans NFL	16	2	15	7.5	0	3.0	19	471	24.8	0	0 ...	0	1
1991—New Orleans NFL	16	5	*198	39.6	0	3.0	20	368	18.4	0	0 ...	0	0
1992—New Orleans NFL	16	3	0	0.0	0	0.0	0	0	...	0	0 ...	0	0
1993—New Orleans NFL	16	3	59	19.7	0	1.0	0	0	...	0	0 ...	0	0
1994—Miami NFL	15	3	24	8.0	0	1.0	0	0	...	0	0 0	0	0
1995—Miami NFL	16	1	0	0.0	0	0.0	0	0	...	0	0 0	0	0
Pro totals (9 years)	138	25	348	13.9	0	8.0	71	1508	21.2	0	0 0	0	3

ATKINS, JAMES   G   SEAHAWKS

PERSONAL: Born January 28, 1970, in Amite, La. ... 6-6/303.
HIGH SCHOOL: Woodland (Amite, La.).
COLLEGE: Southwestern Louisiana.
TRANSACTIONS/CAREER NOTES: Signed as non-drafted free agent by Houston Oilers (May 26, 1993). ... Released by Oilers (August 31, 1993). ... Signed by Seattle Seahawks to practice squad (October 11, 1993). ... Granted free agency (January 10, 1994). ... Re-signed by Seahawks for 1994 season.
PLAYING EXPERIENCE: Seattle NFL, 1994 and 1995. ... Games: 1994 (4), 1995 (16). Total: 20.
PRO STATISTICS: 1995—Recovered one fumble.

ATWATER, STEVE   S   BRONCOS

PERSONAL: Born October 28, 1966, in Chicago. ... 6-3/217. ... Full name: Stephen Dennis Atwater. ... Cousin of Mark Ingram, wide receiver, New York Giants, Miami Dolphins and Green Bay Packers (1987-1995).
HIGH SCHOOL: Lutheran North (St. Louis).
COLLEGE: Arkansas (degree in business administration, 1989).
TRANSACTIONS/CAREER NOTES: Selected by Denver Broncos in first round (20th pick overall) of 1989 NFL draft. ... Signed by Broncos (August 1, 1989). ... Designated by Broncos as transition player (February 25, 1993). ... Designated by Broncos as franchise player (February 15, 1995).
CHAMPIONSHIP GAME EXPERIENCE: Played in AFC championship game (1989 and 1991 seasons). ... Played in Super Bowl XXIV (1989 season).
HONORS: Named defensive back on The Sporting News college All-America second team (1988). ... Played in Pro Bowl (1990-1995 seasons). ... Named free safety on The Sporting News NFL All-Pro team (1992).
PRO STATISTICS: 1989—Recovered one fumble for 29 yards. 1990—Returned one kickoff for no yards. 1991—Recovered one fumble. 1992—Recovered two fumbles for one yard. 1994—Recovered two fumbles for 17 yards.

		INTERCEPTIONS				SACKS
Year Team	G	No.	Yds.	Avg.	TD	No.
1989—Denver NFL	16	3	34	11.3	0	0.0
1990—Denver NFL	15	2	32	16.0	0	1.0
1991—Denver NFL	16	5	104	20.8	0	1.0
1992—Denver NFL	15	2	22	11.0	0	1.0
1993—Denver NFL	16	2	81	40.5	0	1.0
1994—Denver NFL	14	1	24	24.0	0	0.0
1995—Denver NFL	16	3	54	18.0	0	0.0
Pro totals (7 years)	108	18	351	19.5	0	4.0

AUZENNE, TROY — OT — COLTS

PERSONAL: Born June 26, 1969, in El Monte, Calif. ... 6-7/305. ... Full name: Troy Anthony Auzenne. ... Name pronounced aw-ZEEN.
HIGH SCHOOL: Bishop Amat (La Puente, Calif.).
COLLEGE: California.
TRANSACTIONS/CAREER NOTES: Selected by Chicago Bears in second round (49th pick overall) of 1992 NFL draft. ... Signed by Bears (July 23, 1992). ... Granted unconditional free agency (February 16, 1996). ... Signed by Indianapolis Colts (February 29, 1996).
PLAYING EXPERIENCE: Chicago NFL, 1992-1995. ... Games: 1992 (16), 1993 (11), 1994 (11), 1995 (11). Total: 49.
PRO STATISTICS: 1992—Recovered one fumble.

AVERY, STEVE — RB — STEELERS

PERSONAL: Born August 18, 1966, in Milwaukee. ... 6-2/229. ... Full name: Steven George Avery.
HIGH SCHOOL: Brookfield (Wis.) Central.
COLLEGE: Northern Michigan (bachelor of science degree in management).
TRANSACTIONS/CAREER NOTES: Signed as non-drafted free agent by Houston Oilers (May 1989). ... Released by Oilers (September 1989). ... Signed by Kansas City Chiefs to developmental squad (September 26, 1989). ... Released by Chiefs (November 1, 1989). ... Signed by Green Bay Packers for 1990. ... Released by Packers (August 27, 1990). ... Re-signed by Packers to practice squad (October 23, 1990). ... Released by Packers (November 23, 1990). ... Re-signed by Packers to practice squad (December 6, 1990). ... Released by Packers (December 11, 1990). ... Signed by WLAF (January 8, 1991). ... Selected by Birmingham Fire in third round (29th running back) of 1991 WLAF positional draft. ... Signed by Pittsburgh Steelers to practice squad (December 3, 1991). ... Signed by Steelers to practice squad (December 17, 1991). ... Granted unconditional free agency (February 1-April 1, 1992). ... Re-signed by Packers (1992). ... Assigned by Packers to Fire in 1992 World League enhancement allocation program (February 20, 1992). ... Released by Packers (August 31, 1992). ... Signed by Steelers (March 10, 1993). ... Released by Steelers (August 23, 1993). ... Re-signed by Steelers (January 1, 1994).
CHAMPIONSHIP GAME EXPERIENCE: Played in AFC championship game (1994 season). ... Member of Steelers for AFC championship game (1995 season); inactive.
PRO STATISTICS: W.L.: 1992—Attempted one pass with one completion for minus three yards.

		RUSHING				RECEIVING				TOTALS			
Year Team	G	Att.	Yds.	Avg.	TD	No.	Yds.	Avg.	TD	TD	2pt.	Pts.	Fum.
1989—Houston NFL	1	0	0	...	0	0	0	...	0	0	...	0	0
1990—							Did not play.						
1991—Birmingham W.L.	10	25	102	4.1	1	17	197	11.6	2	3		18	1
—Green Bay NFL	1	0	0	...	0	0	0	...	0	0	...	0	0
1992—Birmingham W.L.	10	24	80	3.3	0	15	167	11.1	1	1		6	1
1993—							Did not play.						
1994—Pittsburgh NFL	14	2	4	2.0	0	1	2	2.0	0	0	0	0	0
1995—Pittsburgh NFL	11	1	3	3.0	0	11	82	7.5	1	1	0	6	0
W.L. totals (2 years)	20	49	182	3.7	1	32	364	11.4	3	4	0	24	2
NFL totals (4 years)	27	3	7	2.3	0	12	84	7.0	1	1	0	6	0
Pro totals (6 years)	47	52	189	3.6	1	44	448	10.2	4	5	0	30	2

BAHR, MATT — K — PATRIOTS

PERSONAL: Born July 6, 1956, in Philadelphia. ... 5-10/175. ... Full name: Matthew David Bahr. ... Brother of Chris Bahr, kicker, Cincinnati Bengals, Oakland/Los Angeles Raiders and San Diego Chargers (1976-1989).
HIGH SCHOOL: Neshaminy Langhorne (Langhorne, Pa.).
COLLEGE: Penn State (degree in electrical engineering, 1979).
TRANSACTIONS/CAREER NOTES: Selected by Pittsburgh Steelers in sixth round (165th pick overall) of 1979 NFL draft. ... Released by Steelers (August 31, 1981). ... Signed by San Francisco 49ers (September 8, 1981). ... Traded by 49ers to Cleveland Browns for ninth-round pick (traded to Chicago) in 1983 draft (October 6, 1981). ... On injured reserve with knee injury (November 26, 1986-remainder of season). ... On physically unable to perform list with knee injury (September 1-December 11, 1987). ... Released by Browns (September 3, 1990). ... Signed by New York Giants (September 28, 1990). ... Granted unconditional free agency (February 1-April 1, 1991). ... Re-signed by Giants for 1991 season. ... Granted unconditional free agency (February 1-April 1, 1992). ... Re-signed by Giants for 1992 season. ... On inactive list (November 21-December 6, 1992). ... On injured reserve with knee injury (December 6, 1992-remainder of season). ... Granted unconditional free agency (March 1, 1993). ... Re-signed by Giants (July 1, 1993). ... Released by Giants (August 30, 1993). ... Signed by Philadelphia Eagles (September 9, 1993). ... Claimed on waivers by New England Patriots (December 14, 1993). ... Granted unconditional free agency (February 17, 1995). ... Re-signed by Patriots (March 24, 1995).
CHAMPIONSHIP GAME EXPERIENCE: Played in AFC championship game (1979, 1987 and 1989 seasons). ... Played in NFC championship game (1990 season). ... Member of Super Bowl championship team (1979 and 1990 seasons).
POSTSEASON RECORDS: Shares NFL postseason single-game record for most field goals—5; and most field goals attempted—6 (January 20, 1991, at San Francisco).
PRO STATISTICS: 1988—Rushed once for minus eight yards. 1995—Punted once for 29 yards.
MISCELLANEOUS: Played with Colorado Caribous and Tulsa Roughnecks of North American Soccer League (1978; 26 games, 3 assists).

		KICKING						
Year Team	G	XPM	XPA	FGM	FGA	Lg.	50+	Pts.
1979—Pittsburgh NFL	16	*50	52	18	30	47	0-1	104
1980—Pittsburgh NFL	16	39	42	19	28	48	0-1	96
1981—San Francisco NFL	4	12	12	2	6	47	0-0	18
—Cleveland NFL	11	22	22	13	20	39	0-1	61
1982—Cleveland NFL	9	17	17	7	15	46	0-0	38
1983—Cleveland NFL	16	38	40	21	24	47	0-1	101
1984—Cleveland NFL	16	25	25	24	32	50	1-1	97
1985—Cleveland NFL	16	35	35	14	18	45	0-1	77
1986—Cleveland NFL	12	30	30	20	26	52	1-3	90
1987—Cleveland NFL	3	9	10	4	5	31	0-0	21
1988—Cleveland NFL	16	32	33	24	29	47	0-0	104
1989—Cleveland NFL	16	40	40	16	24	50	1-2	88

A
B

Year Team	G	XPM	XPA	FGM	FGA	Lg.	50+	Pts.
1990—New York Giants NFL	13	29	30	17	23	49	0-2	80
1991—New York Giants NFL	13	24	25	22	29	54	1-3	90
1992—New York Giants NFL	12	29	29	16	21	47	0-2	77
1993—Philadelphia NFL	11	18	19	8	13	48	0-0	42
—New England NFL	3	10	10	5	5	37	0-0	25
1994—New England NFL	16	36	36	27	34	48	0-0	117
1995—New England NFL	16	27	27	23	33	55	2-5	96
Pro totals (17 years)	235	522	534	300	415	55	6-23	1422

BAILEY, AARON　　　　　WR　　　　　COLTS

PERSONAL: Born October 24, 1971, in Ann Arbor, Mich. ... 5-10/184.
HIGH SCHOOL: Pioneer (Ann Arbor, Mich.).
COLLEGE: Louisville.
TRANSACTIONS/CAREER NOTES: Signed as non-drafted free agent by Indianapolis Colts (May 5, 1994).
CHAMPIONSHIP GAME EXPERIENCE: Played in AFC championship game (1995 season).
PRO STATISTICS: 1995—Rushed once for 34 yards and recovered one fumble.

		RECEIVING				KICKOFF RETURNS				TOTALS			
Year Team	G	No.	Yds.	Avg.	TD	No.	Yds.	Avg.	TD	TD	2pt.	Pts.	Fum.
1994—Indianapolis NFL	13	2	30	15.0	0	0	0	...	0	0	0	0	0
1995—Indianapolis NFL	15	21	379	18.1	3	21	495	23.6	1	4	0	24	0
Pro totals (2 years)	28	23	409	17.8	3	21	495	23.6	1	4	0	24	0

BAILEY, CARLTON　　　　　LB　　　　　PANTHERS

PERSONAL: Born December 15, 1964, in Baltimore. ... 6-3/242. ... Full name: Carlton Wilson Bailey.
HIGH SCHOOL: Woodlawn (Baltimore).
COLLEGE: North Carolina (degree in sociology, 1988).
TRANSACTIONS/CAREER NOTES: Selected by Buffalo Bills in ninth round (235th pick overall) of 1988 NFL draft. ... Signed by Bills (July 15, 1988). ... On injured reserve with knee injury (August 30-November 14, 1988). ... Granted unconditional free agency (March 1, 1993). ... Signed by New York Giants (March 22, 1993). ... Released by Giants (April 5, 1995). ... Signed by Carolina Panthers (May 2, 1995).
CHAMPIONSHIP GAME EXPERIENCE: Played in AFC championship game (1988 and 1990-1992 seasons). ... Played in Super Bowl XXV (1990 season), Super Bowl XXVI (1991 season) and Super Bowl XXVII (1992 season).
PRO STATISTICS: 1989—Intercepted one pass for 16 yards. 1990—Recovered one fumble. 1991—Recovered one fumble. 1993—Recovered one fumble and fumbled once. 1994—Recovered one fumble for two yards.

Year Team	G	SACKS
1988—Buffalo NFL	6	0.0
1989—Buffalo NFL	16	0.0
1990—Buffalo NFL	16	2.0
1991—Buffalo NFL	16	0.0
1992—Buffalo NFL	16	1.0
1993—New York Giants NFL	16	1.5
1994—New York Giants NFL	16	0.0
1995—Carolina NFL	16	3.0
Pro totals (8 years)	118	7.5

BAILEY, JOHNNY　　　　　RB/KR

PERSONAL: Born March 17, 1967, in Houston. ... 5-8/180. ... Full name: Johnny Lee Bailey.
HIGH SCHOOL: Jack Yates (Houston).
COLLEGE: Texas A&I.
TRANSACTIONS/CAREER NOTES: Selected by Chicago Bears in ninth round (228th pick overall) of 1990 NFL draft. ... Signed by Bears (July 24, 1990). ... Granted unconditional free agency (February 1, 1992). ... Signed by Phoenix Cardinals (March 11, 1992). ... Granted unconditional free agency (February 17, 1994). ... Signed by Los Angeles Rams (July 22, 1994). ... Granted unconditional free agency (February 17, 1995). ... Re-signed by Rams (April 4, 1995). ... Rams franchise moved to St. Louis (April 12, 1995). ... Granted unconditional free agency (February 16, 1996).
HONORS: Harlon Hill Trophy winner (1987-89). ... Played in Pro Bowl (1992 season).
PRO STATISTICS: 1990—Attempted one pass with one completion for 22 yards, fumbled eight times and recovered four fumbles. 1991—Fumbled four times and recovered two fumbles. 1992—Fumbled twice and recovered two fumbles. 1993—Fumbled four times. 1994—Fumbled twice. 1995—Fumbled once and recovered one fumble.
STATISTICAL PLATEAUS: 100-yard receiving games: 1994 (1).

		RUSHING				RECEIVING				PUNT RETURNS				KICKOFF RETURNS				TOTALS		
Year Team	G	Att.	Yds.	Avg.	TD	No.	Yds.	Avg.	TD	No.	Yds.	Avg.	TD	No.	Yds.	Avg.	TD	TD	2pt.	Pts.
1990—Chicago NFL	16	26	86	3.3	0	0	0	...	0	36	399	11.1	†1	23	363	15.8	0	1	...	6
1991—Chicago NFL	14	15	43	2.9	1	0	0	...	0	36	281	7.8	0	16	311	19.4	0	1	...	6
1992—Phoenix NFL	12	52	233	4.5	1	33	331	10.0	1	20	263	*13.2	0	28	690	24.6	0	2	...	12
1993—Phoenix NFL	13	49	253	5.2	1	32	243	7.6	0	35	282	8.1	1	31	699	22.6	0	2	...	12
1994—L.A. Rams NFL	14	11	35	3.2	1	58	516	8.9	0	19	153	8.1	0	12	260	21.7	0	1	0	6
1995—St. Louis NFL	12	36	182	5.1	2	38	265	7.0	0	2	42	21.0	0	5	97	19.4	0	2	1	14
Pro totals (6 years)	81	189	832	4.4	6	161	1355	8.4	1	148	1420	9.6	2	115	2420	21.1	0	9	1	56

BAILEY, ROBERT　　　　　CB　　　　　DOLPHINS

PERSONAL: Born September 3, 1968, in Miami. ... 5-9/174. ... Full name: Robert Martin Bailey.

HIGH SCHOOL: Miami Southridge Senior.
COLLEGE: Miami (Fla.).
TRANSACTIONS/CAREER NOTES: Selected by Los Angeles Rams in fourth round (107th pick overall) of 1991 NFL draft. ... Signed by Rams (July 17, 1991). ... On injured reserve with broken hand (August 27-October 11, 1991). ... On injured reserve with finger injury (November 19, 1991-remainder of season). ... On injured reserve with knee injury (December 11, 1993-remainder of season). ... Granted free agency (February 17, 1994). ... Re-signed by Rams (June 10, 1994). ... Released by Rams (August 22, 1995). ... Signed by Washington Redskins (September 11, 1995). ... Released by Redskins (October 17, 1995). ... Signed by Dallas Cowboys (October 19, 1995). ... Granted unconditional free agency (February 16, 1996). ... Signed by Miami Dolphins (March 7, 1996).
CHAMPIONSHIP GAME EXPERIENCE: Played in NFC championship game (1995 season). ... Member of Super Bowl championship team (1995 season).
RECORDS: Holds NFL record for longest punt return—103 yards, touchdown (October 23, 1994, at New Orleans).
PRO STATISTICS: 1994—Returned one punt for 103 yards and a touchdown and recovered one fumble.

		INTERCEPTIONS			
Year Team	G	No.	Yds.	Avg.	TD
1991—Los Angeles Rams NFL	6	0	0	...	0
1992—Los Angeles Rams NFL	16	3	61	20.3	1
1993—Los Angeles Rams NFL	9	2	41	20.5	0
1994—Los Angeles Rams NFL	16	0	0	...	0
1995—Washington NFL	4	0	0	...	0
—Dallas NFL	9	0	0	...	0
Pro totals (5 years)	60	5	102	20.4	1

BAILEY, THOMAS — WR — BENGALS

PERSONAL: Born December 6, 1971, in Dallas. ... 6-0/196.
HIGH SCHOOL: Enterprise (Ala.).
COLLEGE: Auburn.
TRANSACTIONS/CAREER NOTES: Signed as non-drafted free agent by Cincinnati Bengals (April 26, 1995). ... Released by Bengals (August 27, 1995). ... Re-signed by Bengals to practice squad (August 28, 1995). ... Activated (October 31, 1995).
PLAYING EXPERIENCE: Cincinnati NFL, 1995. ... Games: 1995 (1).

BAILEY, VICTOR — WR — CHIEFS

PERSONAL: Born July 3, 1970, in Fort Worth, Texas. ... 6-2/203.
HIGH SCHOOL: Dunbar Senior (Fort Worth, Texas).
COLLEGE: Texas-El Paso, then Missouri.
TRANSACTIONS/CAREER NOTES: Selected by Philadelphia Eagles in second round (50th pick overall) of 1993 NFL draft. ... Signed by Eagles (July 17, 1993). ... Traded by Eagles with fourth-round pick (traded to New England) in 1995 draft to Kansas City Chiefs for second-round pick (DB Bobby Taylor) in 1995 draft (April 22, 1995). ... Granted free agency (February 16, 1996).

		RECEIVING				TOTALS			
Year Team	G	No.	Yds.	Avg.	TD	TD	2pt.	Pts.	Fum.
1993—Philadelphia NFL	16	41	545	13.3	1	1	...	6	0
1994—Philadelphia NFL	16	20	311	15.6	1	1	0	6	0
Pro totals (2 years)	32	61	856	14.0	2	2	0	12	0

BAKER, JON — K — 49ERS

PERSONAL: Born August 13, 1972, in ... 6-1/170.
HIGH SCHOOL: Foothill (Bakersfield, Calif.).
JUNIOR COLLEGE: Bakersfield (Calif.) Community College.
COLLEGE: Arizona State.
TRANSACTIONS/CAREER NOTES: Signed as non-drafted free agent by Dallas Cowboys (April 27, 1995). ... Released by Cowboys (September 19, 1995). ... Signed by San Francisco 49ers (May 16, 1996).
PLAYING EXPERIENCE: Dallas NFL, 1995. ... Games: 1995 (3),

BAKER, MYRON — LB — BEARS

PERSONAL: Born January 6, 1971, in Haughton, La. ... 6-1/232. ... Full name: Myron Tobias Baker.
HIGH SCHOOL: Haughton (La.).
COLLEGE: Louisiana Tech.
TRANSACTIONS/CAREER NOTES: Selected by Chicago Bears in fourth round (100th pick overall) of 1993 NFL draft. ... Signed by Bears (July 15, 1993). ... Granted free agency (February 16, 1996). ... Re-signed by Bears (April 18, 1996).
PLAYING EXPERIENCE: Chicago NFL, 1993-1995. ... Games: 1993 (16), 1994 (16), 1995 (16). Total: 48.
PRO STATISTICS: 1993—Returned blocked punt for five yards and a touchdown and recovered two fumbles for eight yards and a touchdown.

BALDWIN, RANDY — RB/KR — PACKERS

PERSONAL: Born August 19, 1967, in Griffin, Ga. ... 5-10/216. ... Full name: Randy Chadwick Baldwin.
HIGH SCHOOL: Griffin (Ga.).
JUNIOR COLLEGE: Holmes Junior College (Miss.).
COLLEGE: Mississippi.

TRANSACTIONS/CAREER NOTES: Selected after junior season by Minnesota Vikings in fourth round (92nd pick overall) of 1991 NFL draft. ... Signed by Vikings (July 18, 1991). ... Released by Vikings (September 28, 1991). ... Re-signed by Vikings to practice squad (October 1, 1991). ... Signed by Cleveland Browns off Vikings practice squad (November 13, 1991). ... On inactive list for four games with Browns (1991). ... Granted free agency (February 17, 1994). ... Re-signed by Browns (July 20, 1994). ... Granted unconditional free agency (February 17, 1995). ... Signed by Carolina Panthers (February 27, 1995). ... Released by Panthers (November 7, 1995). ... Signed by San Francisco 49ers (December 13, 1995). ... Claimed on waivers by Green Bay Packers (January 12, 1996).

PRO STATISTICS: 1993—Recovered one fumble. 1994—Recovered one fumble.

			RUSHING			RECEIVING				KICKOFF RETURNS				TOTALS		
Year Team	G	Att.	Yds.	Avg.	TD	No.	Yds.	Avg.	TD	No.	Yds.	Avg.	TD	TD 2pt.	Pts. Fum.
1991—Minnesota NFL	4	0	0	...	0	0	0	...	0	1	14	14.0	0	0 ...	0
1992—Cleveland NFL	15	10	31	3.1	0	2	30	15.0	0	30	675	22.5	0	0 ...	0 1
1993—Cleveland NFL	14	18	61	3.4	0	1	5	5.0	1	24	444	18.5	0	1 ...	6 2
1994—Cleveland NFL	16	23	78	3.4	0	3	15	5.0	0	28	753	26.9	1	1 0	6 1
1995—Carolina NFL	7	23	61	2.7	0	0	0	...	0	14	316	22.6	0	0 0	0 1
Pro totals (5 years)	56	74	231	3.1	0	6	50	8.3	1	97	2202	22.7	1	2 0	12 5

BALL, ERIC   RB

PERSONAL: Born July 1, 1966, in Cleveland. ... 6-2/220. ... Full name: Eric Clinton Ball.
HIGH SCHOOL: Ypsilanti (Mich.).
COLLEGE: UCLA.
TRANSACTIONS/CAREER NOTES: Selected by Cincinnati Bengals in second round (35th pick overall) of 1989 NFL draft. ... Signed by Bengals (July 21, 1989). ... On injured reserve with ankle injury (October 21, 1991-remainder of season). ... Granted unconditional free agency (February 17, 1994). ... Re-signed by Bengals (May 19, 1994). ... Selected by Carolina Panthers from Bengals in NFL expansion draft (February 15, 1995). ... Released by Panthers (May 23, 1995). ... Signed by Oakland Raiders (July 1994). ... Granted unconditional free agency (February 16, 1996).
PRO STATISTICS: 1992—Recovered two fumbles for minus six yards. 1994—Recovered one fumble.

			RUSHING			RECEIVING				KICKOFF RETURNS				TOTALS		
Year Team	G	Att.	Yds.	Avg.	TD	No.	Yds.	Avg.	TD	No.	Yds.	Avg.	TD	TD 2pt.	Pts. Fum.
1989—Cincinnati NFL	15	98	391	4.0	3	6	44	7.3	0	1	19	19.0	0	3 ...	18 3
1990—Cincinnati NFL	13	22	72	3.3	1	2	46	23.0	1	16	366	22.9	0	2 ...	12 1
1991—Cincinnati NFL	6	10	21	2.1	1	3	17	5.7	0	13	262	20.2	0	1 ...	6 1
1992—Cincinnati NFL	16	16	55	3.4	2	6	66	11.0	2	20	411	20.6	0	4 ...	24 1
1993—Cincinnati NFL	15	8	37	4.6	1	4	39	9.8	0	23	501	21.8	0	1 ...	6 0
1994—Cincinnati NFL	16	2	0	0.0	0	1	4	4.0	0	42	915	21.8	0	0 0	0 1
1995—Oakland NFL	16	2	10	5.0	0	0	0	...	0	0	0	...	0	0 0	0 0
Pro totals (7 years)	97	158	586	3.7	8	22	216	9.8	3	115	2474	21.5	0	11 0	66 7

BALL, JERRY   DT   RAIDERS

PERSONAL: Born December 15, 1964, in Beaumont, Texas. ... 6-1/315. ... Full name: Jerry Lee Ball. ... Related to Mel Farr Sr., running back, Detroit Lions (1967-1973); cousin of Mel Farr Jr., running back, Los Angeles Rams and Sacramento Surge of World League (1989 and 1991); and cousin of Mike Farr, wide receiver, Detroit Lions (1990-1992).
HIGH SCHOOL: Westbrook (Texas).
COLLEGE: Southern Methodist.
TRANSACTIONS/CAREER NOTES: Selected by Detroit Lions in third round (63rd pick overall) of 1987 NFL draft. ... Signed by Lions (July 6, 1987). ... On injured reserve with knee injury (December 12, 1991-remainder of season). ... On injured reserve with ankle injury (December 13, 1992-remainder of season). ... Traded by Lions to Cleveland Browns for third-round pick (LB Antonio London) in 1993 draft (April 23, 1993). ... Granted unconditional free agency (February 17, 1994). ... Signed by Los Angeles Raiders (June 21, 1994). ... Raiders franchise moved to Oakland (July 21, 1995).
HONORS: Played in Pro Bowl (1989 and 1990 seasons). ... Named to play in Pro Bowl (1991 season); replaced by Henry Thomas due to injury.
PRO STATISTICS: 1987—Returned two kickoffs for 23 yards. 1989—Recovered three fumbles. 1991—Credited with a safety. 1992—Recovered three fumbles for 21 yards and a touchdown. 1994—Recovered one fumble. 1995—Recovered one fumble.

Year Team	G	SACKS
1987—Detroit NFL	12	1.0
1988—Detroit NFL	16	2.0
1989—Detroit NFL	16	9.0
1990—Detroit NFL	15	2.0
1991—Detroit NFL	13	2.0
1992—Detroit NFL	12	2.5
1993—Cleveland NFL	16	3.0
1994—Los Angeles Raiders NFL	16	3.0
1995—Oakland NFL	15	3.0
Pro totals (9 years)	131	27.5

BALLARD, HOWARD   OT   SEAHAWKS

PERSONAL: Born November 3, 1963, in Ashland, Ala. ... 6-6/325. ... Full name: Howard Louis Ballard.
HIGH SCHOOL: Clay County (Ashland, Ala.).
COLLEGE: Alabama A&M.
TRANSACTIONS/CAREER NOTES: Selected by Buffalo Bills in 11th round (283rd pick overall) of 1987 NFL draft (elected to return to college for final year of eligibility). ... Signed by Bills (March 30, 1988). ... Granted unconditional free agency (February 17, 1994). ... Signed by Seattle Seahawks (February 28, 1994).
PLAYING EXPERIENCE: Buffalo NFL, 1988-1993; Seattle NFL, 1994 and 1995. ... Games: 1988 (16), 1989 (16), 1990 (16), 1991 (16), 1992 (16), 1993 (16), 1994 (16), 1995 (16). Total: 128.

CHAMPIONSHIP GAME EXPERIENCE: Played in AFC championship game (1988 and 1990-1993 seasons). ... Played in Super Bowl XXV (1990 season), Super Bowl XXVI (1991 season), Super Bowl XXVII (1992 season) and Super Bowl XXVIII (1993 season).
HONORS: Played in Pro Bowl (1992 and 1993 seasons).

BANDISON, ROMEO — DT — REDSKINS

PERSONAL: Born February 12, 1971, in The Hague, Netherlands ... 6-5/290.
HIGH SCHOOL: Mill Valley (Calif.)-Tamalpais.
COLLEGE: Oregon.
TRANSACTIONS/CAREER NOTES: Selected by Cleveland Browns in third round (75th pick overall) of 1994 NFL draft. ... On inactive list for 16 games (1994). ... Released by Browns (September 26, 1995). ... Signed by Washington Redskins (October 3, 1995).
PLAYING EXPERIENCE: Washington NFL, 1995. ... Games: 1995 (4).

B

BANKS, CARL — LB

PERSONAL: Born August 29, 1962, in Flint, Mich. ... 6-4/235.
HIGH SCHOOL: Beecher (Flint, Mich.).
COLLEGE: Michigan State.
TRANSACTIONS/CAREER NOTES: Selected by Michigan Panthers in 1984 USFL territorial draft. ... Selected by New York Giants in first round (third pick overall) of 1984 NFL draft. ... Signed by Giants (July 12, 1984). ... On injured reserve with knee injury (October 12-November 9, 1985). ... Granted free agency (February 1, 1988). ... Re-signed by Giants (August 29, 1988). ... Granted roster exemption (August 29-September 5, 1988). ... On injured reserve with dislocated wrist (October 17-December 1, 1990). ... Granted free agency (February 1, 1992). ... Re-signed by Giants (August 25, 1992). ... Granted roster exemption (August 25-September 5, 1992). ... Designated by Giants as transition player (February 25, 1993). ... Free agency status changed by Giants from transitional to unconditional (June 10, 1993). ... Signed by Washington Redskins (June 14, 1993). ... Released by Redskins (March 8, 1994). ... Signed by Cleveland Browns (June 2, 1994). ... Granted unconditional free agency (February 17, 1995). ... Re-signed by Browns (April 13, 1995). ... Released by Browns (February 1996).
CHAMPIONSHIP GAME EXPERIENCE: Played in NFC championship game (1986 and 1990 seasons). ... Member of Super Bowl championship team (1986 and 1990 seasons).
HONORS: Named linebacker on THE SPORTING NEWS college All-America first team (1983). ... Played in Pro Bowl (1987 season). ... Named outside linebacker on THE SPORTING NEWS NFL All-Pro team (1987).
PRO STATISTICS: 1984—Recovered one fumble. 1985—Recovered one fumble. 1986—Recovered two fumbles for five yards. 1989—Caught one pass for 22 yards and a touchdown and recovered one fumble. 1990—Recovered one fumble.

| | | INTERCEPTIONS | | | | SACKS |
Year Team	G	No.	Yds.	Avg.	TD	No.
1984—New York Giants NFL	16	0	0	...	0	3.0
1985—New York Giants NFL	12	0	0	...	0	3.0
1986—New York Giants NFL	16	0	0	...	0	6.5
1987—New York Giants NFL	12	1	0	0.0	0	9.0
1988—New York Giants NFL	14	1	15	15.0	1	1.5
1989—New York Giants NFL	16	1	6	6.0	0	4.0
1990—New York Giants NFL	9	0	0	...	0	1.0
1991—New York Giants NFL	16	0	0	...	0	4.0
1992—New York Giants NFL	15	0	0	...	0	4.0
1993—Washington NFL	15	0	0	...	0	1.0
1994—Cleveland NFL	16	0	0	...	0	1.5
1995—Cleveland NFL	16	0	0	...	0	1.0
Pro totals (12 years)	173	3	21	7.0	1	39.5

BANKSTON, MICHAEL — DL — CARDINALS

PERSONAL: Born March 12, 1970, in East Bernard, Texas. ... 6-3/280.
HIGH SCHOOL: East Bernard (Texas).
COLLEGE: Sam Houston State.
TRANSACTIONS/CAREER NOTES: Selected by Phoenix Cardinals in fourth round (100th pick overall) of 1992 NFL draft. ... Signed by Cardinals (July 20, 1992). ... Cardinals franchise renamed Arizona Cardinals for 1994 season.
PRO STATISTICS: 1993—Recovered five fumbles for 16 yards. 1994—Recovered one fumble for two yards. 1995—Intercepted one pass for 28 yards and fumbled once.

Year Team	G	SACKS
1992—Phoenix NFL	16	2.0
1993—Phoenix NFL	16	3.0
1994—Arizona NFL	16	7.0
1995—Arizona NFL	16	2.0
Pro totals (4 years)	64	14.0

BANTA, BRADFORD — TE — COLTS

PERSONAL: Born December 14, 1970, in Baton Rouge, La. ... 6-6/257. ... Full name: Dennis Bradford Banta.
HIGH SCHOOL: University (Baton Rouge, La.).
COLLEGE: Southern California.
TRANSACTIONS/CAREER NOTES: Selected by Indianapolis Colts in fourth round (106th pick overall) of 1994 NFL draft. ... Signed by Colts (July 22, 1994).
PLAYING EXPERIENCE: Indianapolis NFL, 1994 and 1995. ... Games: 1994 (16), 1995 (16). Total: 32.
CHAMPIONSHIP GAME EXPERIENCE: Played in AFC championship game (1995 season).
PRO STATISTICS: 1995—Caught one pass for six yards.

BARBER, KURT — LB

PERSONAL: Born January 5, 1969, in Paducah, Ky. ... 6-4/249.
HIGH SCHOOL: Paducah (Ky.) Tilghman.
COLLEGE: Southern California (degree in communications).
TRANSACTIONS/CAREER NOTES: Selected by New York Jets in second round (42nd pick overall) of 1992 NFL draft. ... Signed by Jets (July 14, 1992). ... Granted unconditional free agency (February 16, 1996).

Year Team	G	SACKS
1992—New York Jets NFL	16	0.5
1993—New York Jets NFL	13	0.0
1994—New York Jets NFL	15	1.0
1995—New York Jets NFL	6	2.0
Pro totals (4 years)	50	3.5

BARBER, MICHAEL — LB — SEAHAWKS

PERSONAL: Born November 9, 1971, in Edgemore, S.C. ... 6-1/252.
HIGH SCHOOL: Lewisville (Richburg, S.C.).
COLLEGE: Auburn.
TRANSACTIONS/CAREER NOTES: Signed as non-drafted free agent by Seattle Seahawks (April 26, 1995).
PLAYING EXPERIENCE: Seattle NFL, 1995. ... Games: 1995 (2).

BARKER, BRYAN — P — JAGUARS

PERSONAL: Born June 28, 1964, in Jacksonville Beach, Fla. ... 6-2/189. ... Full name: Bryan Christopher Barker.
HIGH SCHOOL: Miramonte (Orinda, Calif.).
COLLEGE: Santa Clara (degree in economics).
TRANSACTIONS/CAREER NOTES: Signed as non-drafted free agent by Denver Broncos (May 1988). ... Released by Broncos (July 19, 1988). ... Signed by Seattle Seahawks (1989). ... Released by Seahawks (August 30, 1989). ... Signed by Kansas City Chiefs (May 1, 1990). ... Released by Chiefs (August 28, 1990). ... Re-signed by Chiefs (September 26, 1990). ... Granted unconditional free agency (February 1-April 1, 1991). ... Re-signed by Chiefs for 1991 season. ... Granted unconditional free agency (February 1-April 1, 1992). ... Re-signed by Chiefs for 1992 season. ... Released by Chiefs (1994). ... Signed by Minnesota Vikings (May 18, 1994). ... Released by Vikings (August 30, 1994). ... Signed by Philadelphia Eagles (October 11, 1994). ... Granted unconditional free agency (February 17, 1995). ... Signed by Jacksonville Jaguars (March 7, 1995).
CHAMPIONSHIP GAME EXPERIENCE: Played in AFC championship game (1993 season).

				PUNTING			
Year Team	G	No.	Yds.	Avg.	Net avg.	In. 20	Blk.
1990—Kansas City NFL	13	64	2479	38.7	33.4	16	0
1991—Kansas City NFL	16	57	2303	40.4	35.0	14	0
1992—Kansas City NFL	15	75	3245	43.3	35.3	16	1
1993—Kansas City NFL	16	76	3240	42.6	35.4	19	1
1994—Philadelphia NFL	11	66	2696	40.8	36.3	20	0
1995—Jacksonville NFL	16	82	3591	43.8	*38.6	19	0
Pro totals (6 years)	87	420	17554	41.8	35.8	104	2

BARKER, ROY — DE — 49ERS

PERSONAL: Born February 14, 1969, in New York. ... 6-5/290.
HIGH SCHOOL: Central Islip (N.Y.).
COLLEGE: North Carolina (degree in speech communications).
TRANSACTIONS/CAREER NOTES: Selected by Minnesota Vikings in fourth round (98th pick overall) of 1992 NFL draft. ... Signed by Vikings (July 16, 1992). ... On injured reserve with knee injury (September 1-30, 1992). ... Granted unconditional free agency (February 16, 1996). ... Signed by San Francisco 49ers (February 28, 1996).
PRO STATISTICS: 1993—Recovered one fumble. 1994—Recovered one fumble. 1995—Intercepted one pass for minus two yards.

Year Team	G	SACKS
1992—Minnesota NFL	8	0.0
1993—Minnesota NFL	16	6.0
1994—Minnesota NFL	16	3.5
1995—Minnesota NFL	16	3.0
Pro totals (4 years)	56	12.5

BARNES, JOHNNIE — WR — STEELERS

PERSONAL: Born July 21, 1968, in Suffolk, Va. ... 6-1/185. ... Full name: Johnnie Darnell Barnes.
HIGH SCHOOL: John F. Kennedy (Suffolk, Va.).
COLLEGE: Hampton (Va.).
TRANSACTIONS/CAREER NOTES: Selected by San Diego Chargers in ninth round (231st pick overall) of 1992 NFL draft. ... Signed by Chargers (July 16, 1992). ... Released by Chargers (August 31, 1992). ... Re-signed by Chargers to practice squad (September 1, 1992). ... Activated (September 25, 1992). ... On injured reserve with shoulder injury (October 30, 1992-remainder of season). ... Granted unconditional free agency (February 17, 1995). ... Signed by Pittsburgh Steelers (March 30, 1995). ... On injured reserve with knee injury (November 3, 1995-remainder of season).
PLAYING EXPERIENCE: San Diego NFL, 1992-1994; Pittsburgh NFL, 1995. ... Games: 1992 (1), 1993 (14), 1994 (11), 1995 (3). Total: 29.
CHAMPIONSHIP GAME EXPERIENCE: Member of Chargers for AFC championship game and Super Bowl XXIX (1994 season); inactive.
PRO STATISTICS: 1993—Caught 10 passes for 137 yards. 1994—Caught one pass for six yards. 1995—Caught three passes for 48 yards.

B

BARNES, REGGIE   LB   PACKERS

PERSONAL: Born October 23, 1969, in Arlington, Texas. ... 6-1/237. ... Full name: Reginald Keith Barnes.
HIGH SCHOOL: South Grand Prairie (Texas).
COLLEGE: Oklahoma (degree in organizational communications, 1993).
TRANSACTIONS/CAREER NOTES: Signed as non-drafted free agent by Pittsburgh Steelers (May 2, 1993). ... Released by Steelers (August 28, 1994). ... Signed by Dallas Cowboys (February 13, 1995). ... Released by Cowboys (October 19, 1995). ... Signed by Green Bay Packers (January 3, 1996).
PLAYING EXPERIENCE: Pittsburgh NFL, 1993; Dallas NFL, 1995. ... Games: 1993 (16), 1995 (7). Total: 23.
PRO STATISTICS: 1995—Recovered one fumble.

BARNES, TOMUR   CB   OILERS

B

PERSONAL: Born September 8, 1970, in McNair, Texas. ... 5-10/188.
HIGH SCHOOL: Ross Sterling (Baytown, Texas).
COLLEGE: North Texas.
TRANSACTIONS/CAREER NOTES: Signed as non-drafted free agent by San Francisco 49ers (May 7, 1993). ... Released by 49ers (July 16, 1993). ... Re-signed by 49ers (August 12, 1993). ... Released by 49ers (August 24, 1993). ... Re-signed by 49ers to practice squad (September 22, 1993). ... Released by 49ers (November 8, 1993). ... Re-signed by 49ers to practice squad (December 1, 1993). ... Released by 49ers (December 15, 1993). ... Re-signed by 49ers (May 4, 1994). ... Released by 49ers (August 23, 1994). ... Signed by Houston Oilers to practice squad (August 30, 1994). ... Activated (December 23, 1994).
PRO STATISTICS: 1995—Returned one kickoff for minus four yards and recovered one fumble.

		INTERCEPTIONS			
Year Team	G	No.	Yds.	Avg.	TD
1994—Houston NFL	1	0	0	...	0
1995—Houston NFL	15	2	6	3.0	0
Pro totals (2 years)	16	2	6	3.0	0

BARNETT, FRED   WR   DOLPHINS

PERSONAL: Born June 17, 1966, in Shelby, Miss. ... 6-0/199. ... Full name: Fred Lee Barnett Jr. ... Nephew of John Barnett, running back, Los Angeles Express of USFL (1983); and cousin of Tim Barnett, wide receiver, Kansas City Chiefs (1991-1993) and Scottish Claymores of World League (1995).
HIGH SCHOOL: Rosedale (Miss.).
COLLEGE: Arkansas State.
TRANSACTIONS/CAREER NOTES: Selected by Philadelphia Eagles in third round (77th pick overall) of 1990 NFL draft. ... Signed by Eagles (August 13, 1990). ... Granted free agency (March 1, 1993). ... Re-signed by Eagles (August 21, 1993). ... On injured reserve with knee injury (October 4, 1993-remainder of season). ... Granted unconditional free agency (February 16, 1996). ... Signed by Miami Dolphins (March 11, 1996).
HONORS: Played in Pro Bowl (1992 season).
PRO STATISTICS: 1991—Recovered one fumble. 1995—Recovered one fumble.
STATISTICAL PLATEAUS: 100-yard receiving games: 1990 (3), 1991 (3), 1992 (3), 1994 (3), 1995 (1). Total: 13.

		RUSHING				RECEIVING				KICKOFF RETURNS				TOTALS			
Year Team	G	Att.	Yds.	Avg.	TD	No.	Yds.	Avg.	TD	No.	Yds.	Avg.	TD	TD	2pt.	Pts.	Fum.
1990—Philadelphia NFL	16	2	13	6.5	0	36	721	20.0	8	4	65	16.3	0	8	...	48	0
1991—Philadelphia NFL	15	1	0	0.0	0	62	948	15.3	4	0	0	...	0	4	...	24	2
1992—Philadelphia NFL	16	1	-15	-15.0	0	67	1083	16.2	6	0	0	...	0	6	...	36	1
1993—Philadelphia NFL	4	0	0	...	0	17	170	10.0	0	0	0	...	0	0	...	0	1
1994—Philadelphia NFL	16	0	0	...	0	78	1127	14.5	5	0	0	...	0	5	0	30	1
1995—Philadelphia NFL	14	0	0	...	0	48	585	12.2	5	0	0	...	0	5	1	32	0
Pro totals (6 years)	81	4	-2	-0.5	0	308	4634	15.1	28	4	65	16.3	0	28	1	170	5

BARNETT, HARLON   S   VIKINGS

PERSONAL: Born January 2, 1967, in Cincinnati. ... 5-11/203.
HIGH SCHOOL: Princeton (Cincinnati).
COLLEGE: Michigan State.
TRANSACTIONS/CAREER NOTES: Selected by Cleveland Browns in fourth round (101st pick overall) of 1990 NFL draft. ... Signed by Browns (July 22, 1990). ... On injured reserve with back injury (September 8-November 24, 1990). ... Granted unconditional free agency (February 1-April 1, 1992). ... Re-signed by Browns for 1992 season. ... Granted free agency (March 1, 1993). ... Re-signed by Browns (July 24, 1993). ... Claimed on waivers by New England Patriots (August 31, 1993). ... Granted unconditional free agency (February 17, 1995). ... Signed by Minnesota Vikings (February 27, 1995).
HONORS: Named defensive back on THE SPORTING NEWS college All-America first team (1989).
PRO STATISTICS: 1990—Returned one kickoff for 15 yards. 1991—Credited with a sack. 1994—Recovered two fumbles for seven yards.

		INTERCEPTIONS			
Year Team	G	No.	Yds.	Avg.	TD
1990—Cleveland NFL	6	0	0	...	0
1991—Cleveland NFL	16	0	0	...	0
1992—Cleveland NFL	16	0	0	...	0
1993—New England NFL	14	1	40	40.0	0
1994—New England NFL	16	3	51	17.0	0
1995—Minnesota NFL	15	0	0	...	0
Pro totals (6 years)	83	4	91	22.8	0

BARNETT, OLIVER   DE   49ERS

PERSONAL: Born April 9, 1966, in Louisville, Ky. ... 6-3/285. ... Full name: Oliver Wesley Barnett.
HIGH SCHOOL: Jeffersontown (Ky.).
COLLEGE: Kentucky, then Georgia State (did not play football; degree in social work).
TRANSACTIONS/CAREER NOTES: Selected by Atlanta Falcons in third round (55th pick overall) of 1990 NFL draft. ... Signed by Falcons (July 27, 1990). ... Granted free agency (March 1, 1993). ... Signed by Buffalo Bills (April 13, 1993); Falcons received third-round pick (P Harold Alexander) in 1993 draft as compensation. ... Granted unconditional free agency (February 17, 1995). ... Signed by San Francisco 49ers (March 10, 1995).
CHAMPIONSHIP GAME EXPERIENCE: Played in AFC championship game (1993 season). ... Played in Super Bowl XXVIII (1993 season).
PRO STATISTICS: 1991—Recovered one fumble for 75 yards and a touchdown. 1992—Returned one kickoff for 13 yards.

Year Team	G	SACKS
1990—Atlanta NFL	15	0.0
1991—Atlanta NFL	15	1.0
1992—Atlanta NFL	16	0.0
1993—Buffalo NFL	16	2.0
1994—Buffalo NFL	16	1.0
1995—San Francisco NFL	7	1.0
Pro totals (6 years)	85	5.0

B

BARNETT, TROY   DE   PATRIOTS

PERSONAL: Born May 24, 1971, in Jacksonville. ... 6-5/293. ... Full name: Troy Anthony Barnett.
HIGH SCHOOL: Southwest (Jacksonville).
COLLEGE: North Carolina.
TRANSACTIONS/CAREER NOTES: Signed as non-drafted free agent by New England Patriots (April 25, 1994).
PRO STATISTICS: 1995—Recovered one fumble.

Year Team	G	SACKS
1994—New England NFL	14	1.0
1995—New England NFL	16	2.0
Pro totals (2 years)	30	3.0

BARNHARDT, TOMMY   P   BUCCANEERS

PERSONAL: Born June 11, 1963, in Salisbury, N.C. ... 6-2/207. ... Full name: Tommy Ray Barnhardt.
HIGH SCHOOL: South Rowan (China Grove, N.C.).
COLLEGE: East Carolina, then North Carolina (degree in industrial relations, 1986).
TRANSACTIONS/CAREER NOTES: Selected by Baltimore Stars in 1986 USFL territorial draft. ... Selected by Tampa Bay Buccaneers in ninth round (223rd pick overall) of 1986 NFL draft. ... Signed by Buccaneers (July 16, 1986). ... Released by Buccaneers (August 25, 1986). ... Re-signed by Buccaneers (February 6, 1987). ... Released by Buccaneers (August 5, 1987). ... Signed as replacement player by New Orleans Saints (September 23, 1987). ... Released by Saints (November 3, 1987). ... Signed by Chicago Bears (December 16, 1987). ... Released by Bears (August 24, 1988). ... Signed by Washington Redskins (September 9, 1988). ... On injured reserve with pulled quadricep (October 11, 1988-remainder of season). ... Granted unconditional free agency (February 1-April 1, 1989). ... Re-signed by Redskins (May 11, 1989). ... Released by Redskins (June 27, 1989). ... Signed by Detroit Lions (July 20, 1989). ... Released by Lions (August 30, 1989). ... Signed by Saints (October 11, 1989). ... Granted unconditional free agency (February 1-April 1, 1992). ... Re-signed by Saints for 1992 season. ... Granted unconditional free agency (March 1, 1993). ... Re-signed by Saints (July 15, 1993). ... Granted unconditional free agency (February 17, 1995). ... Signed by Carolina Panthers (March 2, 1995). ... Released by Panthers (May 7, 1996). ... Signed by Buccaneers (May 13, 1996).
PRO STATISTICS: 1987—Had 35.2-yard net-punting average and rushed once for minus 13 yards. 1991—Rushed once for no yards. 1992—Rushed four times for minus two yards and fumbled twice for minus 16 yards. 1993—Attempted one pass with one completion for seven yards and rushed once for 18 yards. 1994—Rushed once for 21 yards and attempted one pass without a completion.

Year Team	G	No.	Yds.	Avg.	Net avg.	In. 20	Blk.
1987—New Orleans NFL	3	11	483	43.9	...	4	0
—Chicago NFL	2	6	236	39.3	...	2	0
1988—Washington NFL	4	15	628	41.9	34.3	1	0
1989—New Orleans NFL	11	55	2179	39.6	35.0	17	0
1990—New Orleans NFL	16	70	2990	42.7	36.2	20	1
1991—New Orleans NFL	16	86	*3743	43.5	35.3	20	1
1992—New Orleans NFL	16	67	2947	44.0	37.7	19	0
1993—New Orleans NFL	16	77	3356	43.6	37.5	26	0
1994—New Orleans NFL	16	67	2920	43.6	33.5	14	0
1995—Carolina NFL	16	95	3906	41.1	35.2	27	0
Pro totals (9 years)	116	549	23388	42.6	35.7	150	2

(Header: PUNTING)

BARR, DAVE   QB

PERSONAL: Born May 9, 1972, in Oakland. ... 6-3/210.
HIGH SCHOOL: Concord (Calif.).
COLLEGE: California.
TRANSACTIONS/CAREER NOTES: Selected by Philadelphia Eagles in fourth round (119th pick overall) of 1995 NFL draft. ... Signed by Eagles (July 19, 1995). ... Claimed on waivers by St. Louis Rams (August 30, 1995). ... Released by Rams (April 27, 1996).

Year Team	G	PASSING Att.	Cmp.	Pct.	Yds.	TD	Int.	Avg.	Rat.	RUSHING Att.	Yds.	Avg.	TD	TOTALS TD	2pt.	Pts.
1995—St. Louis NFL	2	9	5	55.6	42	0	0	4.67	67.8	1	5	5.0	0	0	0	0

BARRIE, SEBASTIAN   DE   EAGLES

PERSONAL: Born May 26, 1970, in Dallas. ... 6-2/280.
HIGH SCHOOL: Lincoln (Dallas).
COLLEGE: Prairie View A&M, then Liberty (Va.).
TRANSACTIONS/CAREER NOTES: Signed as non-drafted free agent by Green Bay Packers (May 7, 1992). ... Released by Packers (August 31, 1992). ... Re-signed by Packers to practice squad (September 2, 1992). ... Activated (October 23, 1992). ... On injured reserve with knee injury (November 12, 1992-remainder of season). ... Released by Packers (August 30, 1993). ... Signed by San Francisco 49ers (June 10, 1994). ... Released by 49ers (July 28, 1994). ... Signed by Arizona Cardinals (August 3, 1994). ... Released by Cardinals (August 27, 1995). ... Signed by San Diego Chargers (October 18, 1995). ... Released by Chargers (December 5, 1995). ... Re-signed by Chargers (December 6, 1995). ... Granted unconditional free agency (February 16, 1996). ... Signed by Philadelphia Eagles (April 18, 1996).
PLAYING EXPERIENCE: Green Bay NFL, 1992; Arizona NFL, 1994; San Diego NFL, 1995. ... Games: 1992 (3), 1994 (10), 1995 (7). Total: 20.

BARROW, MICHEAL   LB   OILERS

PERSONAL: Born April 19, 1970, in Homestead, Fla. ... 6-1/236. ... Full name: Micheal Calvin Barrow.
HIGH SCHOOL: Homestead (Fla.) Senior.
COLLEGE: Miami, Fla. (degree in accounting, 1992).
TRANSACTIONS/CAREER NOTES: Selected by Houston Oilers in second round (47th pick overall) of 1993 NFL draft. ... Signed by Oilers (July 30, 1993). ... Granted free agency (February 16, 1996).
HONORS: Named linebacker on THE SPORTING NEWS college All-America first team (1992).
PRO STATISTICS: 1995—Recovered one fumble.

Year Team	G	SACKS
1993—Houston NFL	16	1.0
1994—Houston NFL	16	2.5
1995—Houston NFL	13	3.0
Pro totals (3 years)	**45**	**6.5**

BARTON, HARRIS   OT   49ERS

PERSONAL: Born April 19, 1964, in Atlanta. ... 6-4/286. ... Full name: Harris Scott Barton.
HIGH SCHOOL: Dunwoody (Ga.).
COLLEGE: North Carolina (bachelor of science degree, 1987).
TRANSACTIONS/CAREER NOTES: Selected by San Francisco 49ers in first round (22nd pick overall) of 1987 NFL draft. ... Signed by 49ers (July 22, 1987). ... Granted free agency (February 1, 1990). ... Re-signed by 49ers (July 30, 1990).
PLAYING EXPERIENCE: San Francisco NFL, 1987-1995. ... Games: 1987 (12), 1988 (16), 1989 (16), 1990 (16), 1991 (16), 1992 (13), 1993 (15), 1994 (9), 1995 (12). Total: 125.
CHAMPIONSHIP GAME EXPERIENCE: Played in NFC championship game (1988-1990 and 1992-1994 seasons). ... Member of Super Bowl championship team (1988, 1989 and 1994 seasons).
HONORS: Named offensive tackle on THE SPORTING NEWS college All-America second team (1986). ... Named offensive tackle on THE SPORTING NEWS NFL All-Pro team (1993). ... Played in Pro Bowl (1993 season).
PRO STATISTICS: 1987—Recovered one fumble. 1991—Recovered one fumble.

BARTRUM, MICHAEL   TE   PACKERS

PERSONAL: Born June 23, 1970, in Gallipolis, Ohio. ... 6-4/243. ... Full name: Michael Weldon Bartrum.
HIGH SCHOOL: Meigs (Pomeroy, Ohio).
COLLEGE: Marshall (degree in education).
TRANSACTIONS/CAREER NOTES: Signed as non-drafted free agent by Kansas City Chiefs (May 5, 1993). ... Released by Chiefs (August 30, 1993). ... Re-signed by Chiefs to practice squad (August 31, 1993). ... Activated (October 27, 1993). ... Released by Chiefs (August 23, 1994). ... Signed by Green Bay Packers (January 20, 1995). ... On injured reserve with broken arm (October 11, 1995-remainder of season).
PLAYING EXPERIENCE: Kansas City NFL, 1993; Green Bay NFL, 1995. ... Games: 1993 (3), 1995 (4). Total: 7.
CHAMPIONSHIP GAME EXPERIENCE: Member of Chiefs for AFC championship game (1993 season); inactive.

BASS, ROBERT   LB   PACKERS

PERSONAL: Born November 10, 1970, in Brooklyn, N.Y. ... 6-1/239.
HIGH SCHOOL: Samuel J. Tilden (Brooklyn, N.Y.).
JUNIOR COLLEGE: Nassau Community College (N.Y.).
COLLEGE: Miami, Fla. (degree in criminal justice).
TRANSACTIONS/CAREER NOTES: Signed as non-drafted free agent by Chicago Bears (April 28, 1994). ... On injured reserve with knee injury (August 23, 1994-entire season). ... Released by Bears (August 22, 1995). ... Re-signed by Bears (September 12, 1995). ... Released by Bears (September 27, 1995). ... Signed by Green Bay Packers to practice squad (October 30, 1995). ... Activated (January 4, 1996).
PLAYING EXPERIENCE: Chicago NFL, 1995. ... Games: 1995 (2).
CHAMPIONSHIP GAME EXPERIENCE: Member of Packers for NFC championship game (1995 season); inactive.

BATES, BILL   S   COWBOYS

PERSONAL: Born June 6, 1961, in Knoxville, Tenn. ... 6-1/210. ... Full name: William Frederick Bates.
HIGH SCHOOL: Farragut (Knoxville, Tenn.).
COLLEGE: Tennessee.

TRANSACTIONS/CAREER NOTES: Selected by New Jersey Generals in 1983 USFL territorial draft. ... Signed as non-drafted free agent by Dallas Cowboys (April 28, 1983). ... On injured reserve with hip injury (September 3-28, 1984). ... Granted unconditional free agency (February 1-April 1, 1991). ... Re-signed by Cowboys for 1991 season. ... Granted unconditional free agency (February 1-April 1, 1992). ... Re-signed by Cowboys for 1992 season. ... On injured reserve with knee injury (October 14, 1992-remainder of season). ... Granted unconditional free agency (March 1, 1993). ... Re-signed by Cowboys (June 15, 1993). ... Released by Cowboys (August 30, 1993). ... Re-signed by Cowboys (August 31, 1993). ... Granted unconditional free agency (February 17, 1994). ... Re-signed by Cowboys (July 14, 1994). ... Granted unconditional free agency (February 16, 1996). ... Re-signed by Cowboys (March 29, 1996).
CHAMPIONSHIP GAME EXPERIENCE: Played in NFC championship game (1993-1995 seasons). ... Member of Super Bowl championship team (1992, 1993 and 1995 seasons).
HONORS: Played in Pro Bowl (1984 season).
PRO STATISTICS: 1983—Recovered two fumbles. 1984—Recovered one fumble. 1988—Recovered one fumble. 1989—Rushed once for no yards. 1990—Rushed once for four yards. 1991—Recovered two fumbles. 1993—Recovered one fumble.

Year Team	G	INTERCEPTIONS No.	Yds.	Avg.	TD	SACKS No.	PUNT RETURNS No.	Yds.	Avg.	TD	TOTALS TD	2pt.	Pts.	Fum.
1983—Dallas NFL	16	1	29	29.0	0	4.0	0	0	...	0	0	...	0	1
1984—Dallas NFL	12	1	3	3.0	0	5.0	0	0	...	0	0	...	0	0
1985—Dallas NFL	16	4	15	3.8	0	1.0	22	152	6.9	0	0	...	0	0
1986—Dallas NFL	15	0	0	...	0	2.5	0	0	...	0	0	...	0	0
1987—Dallas NFL	12	3	28	9.3	0	3.0	0	0	...	0	0	...	0	0
1988—Dallas NFL	16	1	0	0.0	0	0.5	0	0	...	0	0	...	0	0
1989—Dallas NFL	16	1	18	18.0	0	0.0	0	0	...	0	0	...	0	0
1990—Dallas NFL	16	1	4	4.0	0	0.0	0	0	...	0	0	...	0	0
1991—Dallas NFL	16	0	0	...	0	0.0	0	0	...	0	0	...	0	0
1992—Dallas NFL	5	0	0	...	0	0.0	0	0	...	0	0	...	0	0
1993—Dallas NFL	16	2	25	12.5	0	0.0	0	0	...	0	0	...	0	0
1994—Dallas NFL	15	0	0	...	0	1.0	0	0	...	0	0	0	0	0
1995—Dallas NFL	16	0	0	...	0	0.0	0	0	...	0	0	0	0	0
Pro totals (13 years)	187	14	122	8.7	0	17.0	22	152	6.9	0	0	0	0	1

BATES, MARIO — RB — SAINTS

PERSONAL: Born January 16, 1973, in Tucson, Ariz. ... 6-1/217. ... Brother of Michael Bates, wide receiver/kick returner, Carolina Panthers.
HIGH SCHOOL: Amphitheater (Tucson, Ariz.).
COLLEGE: Arizona State.
TRANSACTIONS/CAREER NOTES: Selected after junior season by New Orleans Saints in second round (44th pick overall) of 1994 NFL draft. ... Signed by Saints (July 6, 1994).
PRO STATISTICS: 1994—Recovered one fumble. 1995—Recovered one fumble.
STATISTICAL PLATEAUS: 100-yard rushing games: 1994 (1), 1995 (3). Total: 4.

Year Team	G	RUSHING Att.	Yds.	Avg.	TD	RECEIVING No.	Yds.	Avg.	TD	KICKOFF RETURNS No.	Yds.	Avg.	TD	TOTALS TD	2pt.	Pts.	Fum.
1994—New Orleans NFL	11	151	579	3.8	6	8	62	7.8	0	1	20	20.0	0	6	0	36	3
1995—New Orleans NFL	16	244	951	3.9	7	18	114	6.3	0	0	0	...	0	7	0	42	2
Pro totals (2 years)	27	395	1530	3.9	13	26	176	6.8	0	1	20	20.0	0	13	0	78	5

BATES, MICHAEL — WR/KR — PANTHERS

PERSONAL: Born December 19, 1969, in Tucson, Ariz. ... 5-10/189. ... Brother of Mario Bates, running back, New Orleans Saints.
HIGH SCHOOL: Amphitheater (Tucson, Ariz.).
COLLEGE: Arizona.
TRANSACTIONS/CAREER NOTES: Selected after sophomore season by Seattle Seahawks in sixth round (151st pick overall) of 1992 NFL draft. ... Missed 1992 season due to contract dispute. ... Signed by Seahawks (March 7, 1993). ... Released by Seahawks (August 27, 1995). ... Claimed on waivers by Carolina Panthers (August 28, 1995). ... Traded by Panthers to Cleveland Browns for LB Travis Hill (August 29, 1995). ... Granted unconditional free agency (February 16, 1996). ... Signed by Panthers (March 11, 1996).
PRO STATISTICS: 1993—Recovered two fumbles for three yards.
MISCELLANEOUS: Won bronze medal in 200-meter dash in 1992 Summer Olympics.

Year Team	G	RUSHING Att.	Yds.	Avg.	TD	RECEIVING No.	Yds.	Avg.	TD	KICKOFF RETURNS No.	Yds.	Avg.	TD	TOTALS TD	2pt.	Pts.	Fum.
1992—Seattle NFL								Did not play.									
1993—Seattle NFL	16	2	12	6.0	0	1	6	6.0	0	30	603	20.1	0	0	...	0	1
1994—Seattle NFL	15	2	-4	-2.0	0	5	112	22.4	1	26	508	19.5	0	1	0	6	3
1995—Cleveland NFL	13	0	0	...	0	0	0	...	0	9	176	19.6	0	0	0	0	0
Pro totals (3 years)	44	4	8	2.0	0	6	118	19.7	1	65	1287	19.8	0	1	0	6	4

BATES, PATRICK — S — FALCONS

PERSONAL: Born November 27, 1970, in Galveston, Texas. ... 6-3/215. ... Full name: Patrick James Bates.
HIGH SCHOOL: Ball (Galveston, Texas).
COLLEGE: Texas A&M.
TRANSACTIONS/CAREER NOTES: Selected after junior season by Los Angeles Raiders in first round (12th pick overall) of 1993 NFL draft. ... Signed by Raiders (1993). ... Raiders franchise moved to Oakland (July 21, 1995). ... Inactive for 16 games (1995 season). ... Traded by Raiders to Atlanta Falcons for second-round pick (traded to Houston) in 1996 draft (April 18, 1996).
PLAYING EXPERIENCE: Los Angeles Raiders NFL, 1993 and 1994. ... Games: 1993 (13), 1994 (16). Total: 29.
HONORS: Named defensive back on THE SPORTING NEWS college All-America first team (1992).
PRO STATISTICS: 1993—Intercepted one pass for no yards. 1994—Recovered two fumbles.

BATISTE, MICHAEL   G   COWBOYS

PERSONAL: Born December 24, 1970, in Beaumont, Texas. ... 6-3/305.
HIGH SCHOOL: Westbrook (Texas).
COLLEGE: Tulane.
TRANSACTIONS/CAREER NOTES: Signed as non-drafted free agent by Dallas Cowboys (April 28, 1994). ... Released by Cowboys (August 23, 1994). ... Re-signed by Cowboys (April 10, 1995).
PLAYING EXPERIENCE: Dallas NFL. 1995. ... Games: 1995 (2).
CHAMPIONSHIP GAME EXPERIENCE: Member of Cowboys for NFC championship game (1995 season); inactive.

BAXTER, BRAD   RB   JETS

PERSONAL: Born May 5, 1967, in Dothan, Ala. ... 6-1/235. ... Full name: Herman Bradley Baxter.
HIGH SCHOOL: Slocomb (Ala.).
COLLEGE: Alabama State.
TRANSACTIONS/CAREER NOTES: Selected by Minnesota Vikings in 11th round (303rd pick overall) of 1989 NFL draft. ... Signed by Vikings (July 26, 1989). ... Released by Vikings (August 30, 1989). ... Signed by New York Jets to developmental squad (October 5, 1989). ... Activated (December 20, 1989). ... Granted free agency (March 1, 1993). ... Re-signed by Jets (May 5, 1993). ... Granted unconditional free agency (February 17, 1995). ... Re-signed by Jets (February 24, 1995).
PRO STATISTICS: 1990—Recovered one fumble. 1991—Recovered one fumble. 1992—Recovered one fumble. 1993—Recovered two fumbles.
STATISTICAL PLATEAUS: 100-yard rushing games: 1992 (1).

		RUSHING				RECEIVING				TOTALS			
Year Team	G	Att.	Yds.	Avg.	TD	No.	Yds.	Avg.	TD	TD	2pt.	Pts.	Fum.
1989—New York Jets NFL	1	0	0	...	0	0	0	...	0	0	...	0	0
1990—New York Jets NFL	16	124	539	4.4	6	8	73	9.1	0	6	...	36	4
1991—New York Jets NFL	16	184	666	3.6	11	12	124	10.3	0	11	...	66	6
1992—New York Jets NFL	15	152	698	4.6	6	4	32	8.0	0	6	...	36	3
1993—New York Jets NFL	16	174	559	3.2	7	20	158	7.9	0	7	...	42	3
1994—New York Jets NFL	15	60	170	2.8	4	10	40	4.0	0	4	0	24	0
1995—New York Jets NFL	15	85	296	3.5	1	26	160	6.2	0	1	0	6	0
Pro totals (7 years)	94	779	2928	3.8	35	80	587	7.3	0	35	0	210	16

BAXTER, FRED   TE   JETS

PERSONAL: Born June 14, 1971, in Brundidge, Ala. ... 6-3/260. ... Full name: Frederick Denard Baxter.
HIGH SCHOOL: Pike County (Brundidge, Ala.).
COLLEGE: Auburn.
TRANSACTIONS/CAREER NOTES: Selected by New York Jets in fifth round (115th pick overall) of 1993 NFL draft. ... Signed by Jets (July 13, 1993).
PRO STATISTICS: 1994—Returned one kickoff for 20 yards and recovered one fumble. 1995—Returned six kickoffs for 36 yards and recovered two fumbles for eight yards.

		RECEIVING				TOTALS			
Year Team	G	No.	Yds.	Avg.	TD	TD	2pt.	Pts.	Fum.
1993—New York Jets NFL	7	3	48	16.0	1	1	...	6	0
1994—New York Jets NFL	11	3	11	3.7	1	1	0	6	0
1995—New York Jets NFL	15	18	222	12.3	1	1	0	6	1
Pro totals (3 years)	33	24	281	11.7	3	3	0	18	1

BAYLESS, MARTIN   S

PERSONAL: Born October 11, 1962, in Dayton, Ohio. ... 6-2/219. ... Full name: Martin Ashley Bayless. ... Name pronounced BAY-liss.
HIGH SCHOOL: Belmont (Dayton, Ohio).
COLLEGE: Bowling Green State (degree in architectural design).
TRANSACTIONS/CAREER NOTES: Selected by Memphis Showboats in first round (20th pick overall) of 1984 USFL draft. ... Selected by St. Louis Cardinals in fourth round (101st pick overall) of 1984 NFL draft. ... Signed by Cardinals (July 20, 1984). ... Claimed on waivers by Buffalo Bills (September 20, 1984). ... On injured reserve with pinched nerve in neck (December 6, 1985-remainder of season). ... Traded by Bills to San Diego Chargers for CB Wayne Davis (August 26, 1987). ... Released by Chargers (August 26, 1991). ... Re-signed by Chargers (August 27, 1991). ... Granted unconditional free agency (February 1, 1992). ... Signed by Kansas City Chiefs (April 1, 1992). ... Released by Chiefs (August 31, 1993). ... Re-signed by Chiefs (September 1, 1993). ... Granted unconditional free agency (February 17, 1994). ... Signed by Washington Redskins (July 22, 1994). ... Granted unconditional free agency (February 17, 1995). ... Signed by Chiefs (September 27, 1995). ... Granted unconditional free agency (February 16, 1996).
CHAMPIONSHIP GAME EXPERIENCE: Played in AFC championship game (1993 season).
PRO STATISTICS: 1985—Recovered one fumble. 1989—Recovered one fumble. 1990—Recovered one fumble. 1991—Recovered one fumble. 1994—Recovered one fumble for 60 yards and a touchdown. 1995—Recovered one fumble.

		INTERCEPTIONS				SACKS
Year Team	G	No.	Yds.	Avg.	TD	No.
1984—St. Louis NFL	3	0	0	...	0	0.0
—Buffalo NFL	13	0	0	...	0	0.0
1985—Buffalo NFL	12	2	10	5.0	0	0.0
1986—Buffalo NFL	16	1	0	0.0	0	1.0
1987—San Diego NFL	12	0	0	...	0	2.5
1988—San Diego NFL	15	0	0	...	0	1.0
1989—San Diego NFL	16	1	0	0.0	0	1.0

Year Team	G	INTERCEPTIONS				SACKS
		No.	Yds.	Avg.	TD	No.
1990—San Diego NFL	14	1	0	0.0	0	3.0
1991—San Diego NFL	16	1	0	0.0	0	0.0
1992—Kansas City NFL	16	1	0	0.0	0	0.0
1993—Kansas City NFL	16	2	14	7.0	0	1.0
1994—Washington NFL	16	3	38	12.7	0	0.0
1995—Kansas City NFL	11	0	0	...	0	1.0
Pro totals (12 years)	176	12	62	5.2	0	10.5

BEAMON, WILLIE   CB   GIANTS

PERSONAL: Born June 14, 1970, in Belle Glade, Fla. ... 5-11/184.
HIGH SCHOOL: Suncoast (Riviera Beach, Fla.).
COLLEGE: Northern Iowa.
TRANSACTIONS/CAREER NOTES: Signed as non-drafted free agent by New York Giants (May 1, 1993). ... Granted free agency (February 16, 1996).
PLAYING EXPERIENCE: New York Giants NFL, 1993-1995. ... Games: 1993 (13), 1994 (15), 1995 (16). Total: 44.
PRO STATISTICS: 1993—Intercepted one pass for no yards. 1994—Credited with one sack and recovered two fumbles.

B

BEAVERS, AUBREY   LB   DOLPHINS

PERSONAL: Born August 30, 1971, in Houston. ... 6-3/231. ... Full name: Aubrey Tod Beavers.
HIGH SCHOOL: Jack Yates (Houston).
COLLEGE: Oklahoma.
TRANSACTIONS/CAREER NOTES: Selected by Miami Dolphins in second round (54th pick overall) of 1994 NFL draft. ... Signed by Dolphins (July 19, 1994).

Year Team	G	INTERCEPTIONS			
		No.	Yds.	Avg.	TD
1994—Miami NFL	16	2	0	0.0	0
1995—Miami NFL	16	1	8	8.0	0
Pro totals (2 years)	32	3	8	2.7	0

BECKLES, IAN   G   BUCCANEERS

PERSONAL: Born July 20, 1967, in Montreal. ... 6-1/304. ... Full name: Ian Harold Beckles.
HIGH SCHOOL: Lindsay Place (Montreal).
JUNIOR COLLEGE: Wadorf Junior College (Iowa).
COLLEGE: Indiana (degree in general studies).
TRANSACTIONS/CAREER NOTES: Selected by Tampa Bay Buccaneers in fifth round (114th pick overall) of 1990 NFL draft. ... Signed by Buccaneers (July 19, 1990). ... Granted free agency (February 1, 1992). ... Re-signed by Buccaneers (July 17, 1992). ... On injured reserve with knee injury (September 1-October 16, 1992). ... On injured reserve with knee injury (December 22, 1993-remainder of season). ... Granted unconditional free agency (February 17, 1994). ... Re-signed by Buccaneers (March 29, 1994).
PLAYING EXPERIENCE: Tampa Bay NFL, 1990-1995. ... Games: 1990 (16), 1991 (16), 1992 (11), 1993 (14), 1994 (16), 1995 (15). Total: 88.
PRO STATISTICS: 1993—Recovered one fumble. 1994—Recovered two fumbles. 1995—Recovered two fumbles.

BEEBE, DON   WR   PACKERS

PERSONAL: Born December 18, 1964, in Aurora, Ill. ... 5-11/183. ... Full name: Don Lee Beebe. ... Name pronounced BEE-BEE.
HIGH SCHOOL: Kaneland (Maple Park, Ill.).
COLLEGE: Western Illinois, then Aurora, Ill. (did not play football), then Chadron (Neb.) State College.
TRANSACTIONS/CAREER NOTES: Selected by Buffalo Bills in third round (82nd pick overall) of 1989 NFL draft. ... Signed by Bills (May 8, 1989). ... On injured reserve with broken leg (December 29, 1990-remainder of season). ... On injured reserve with broken collarbone (November 23, 1991-January 5, 1992). ... Granted free agency (February 1, 1992). ... Re-signed by Bills (1992). ... On injured reserve with pulled hamstring (September 19-October 26, 1992). ... Granted unconditional free agency (February 17, 1995). ... Signed by Carolina Panthers (April 25, 1995). ... Released by Panthers (February 14, 1996). ... Signed by Green Bay Packers (April 1, 1996).
CHAMPIONSHIP GAME EXPERIENCE: Played in AFC championship game (1991-1993 seasons). ... Played in Super Bowl XXVI (1991 season), Super Bowl XXVII (1992 season) and Super Bowl XXVIII (1993 season).
PRO STATISTICS: 1993—Recovered one fumble.
STATISTICAL PLATEAUS: 100-yard receiving games: 1991 (1), 1992 (4), 1993 (1), 1994 (1). Total: 7.

Year Team	G	RUSHING				RECEIVING				KICKOFF RETURNS				TOTALS			
		Att.	Yds.	Avg.	TD	No.	Yds.	Avg.	TD	No.	Yds.	Avg.	TD	TD	2pt.	Pts.	Fum.
1989—Buffalo NFL	14	0	0	...	0	17	317	18.7	2	16	353	22.1	0	2	...	12	1
1990—Buffalo NFL	12	1	23	23.0	0	11	221	20.1	1	6	119	19.8	0	1	...	6	0
1991—Buffalo NFL	11	0	0	...	0	32	414	12.9	6	7	121	17.3	0	6	...	36	3
1992—Buffalo NFL	12	1	-6	-6.0	0	33	554	16.8	2	0	0	...	0	2	...	12	1
1993—Buffalo NFL	14	0	0	...	0	31	504	16.3	3	10	160	16.0	0	3	...	18	1
1994—Buffalo NFL	13	2	11	5.5	0	40	527	13.2	4	12	230	19.2	0	4	0	24	3
1995—Carolina NFL	14	0	0	...	0	14	152	10.9	1	9	215	23.9	0	1	0	6	0
Pro totals (7 years)	90	4	28	7.0	0	178	2689	15.1	19	60	1198	20.0	0	19	0	114	9

BEER, THOMAS   LB   LIONS

PERSONAL: Born March 27, 1969, in Bay Port, Mich. ... 6-1/237.

HIGH SCHOOL: Elkton-Pigeon-Bay Port (Bay Port, Mich.).
COLLEGE: Saginaw Valley State (Mich.), then Wayne State (Neb.).
TRANSACTIONS/CAREER NOTES: Selected by Detroit Lions in seventh round (215th pick overall) of 1994 NFL draft. ... Signed by Lions (July 13, 1994).
PLAYING EXPERIENCE: Detroit NFL, 1994 and 1995. ... Games: 1994 (9), 1995 (16). Total: 25.

BELIN, CHUCK G RAMS

PERSONAL: Born October 27, 1970, in Milwaukee. ... 6-2/305. ... Full name: Charles Edward Belin. ... Name pronounced BELL-in.
HIGH SCHOOL: Vincent (Milwaukee).
COLLEGE: Wisconsin.
TRANSACTIONS/CAREER NOTES: Selected by Los Angeles Rams in fifth round (157th pick overall) of 1993 NFL draft. ... Signed by Rams (1993). ... Released by Rams (August 30, 1993). ... Re-signed by Rams to practice squad (August 31, 1993). ... Activated (November 2, 1993). ... Rams franchise moved to St. Louis (April 12, 1995). ... Granted free agency (February 16, 1996).
PLAYING EXPERIENCE: Los Angeles Rams NFL, 1994; St. Louis NFL, 1995. ... Games: 1994 (14), 1995 (6). Total: 20.
PRO STATISTICS: 1994—Recovered one fumble.

BELL, COLEMAN TE REDSKINS

PERSONAL: Born April 22, 1970, in Tampa. ... 6-2/243.
HIGH SCHOOL: Thomas Jefferson (Tampa).
COLLEGE: Miami (Fla.).
TRANSACTIONS/CAREER NOTES: Signed as non-drafted free agent by Miami Dolphins (April 29, 1993). ... Released by Dolphins (August 23, 1993). ... Signed by Dallas Cowboys to practice squad (August 31, 1993). ... Granted free agency after 1993 season. ... Re-signed by Cowboys (April 28, 1993). ... Released by Cowboys (November 21, 1994). ... Signed by Washington Redskins (December 20, 1994).

		RECEIVING				TOTALS			
Year Team	G	No.	Yds.	Avg.	TD	TD	2pt.	Pts.	Fum.
1995—Washington NFL	11	14	166	11.9	1	1	0	6	1

BELL, MYRON S STEELERS

PERSONAL: Born September 15, 1971, in Toledo, Ohio. ... 5-11/203.
HIGH SCHOOL: Macomber-Whitney (Toledo, Ohio).
COLLEGE: Michigan State.
TRANSACTIONS/CAREER NOTES: Selected by Pittsburgh Steelers in fifth round (140th pick overall) of 1994 NFL draft. ... Signed by Steelers (July 18, 1994).
CHAMPIONSHIP GAME EXPERIENCE: Played in AFC championship game (1994 and 1995 seasons). ... Played in Super Bowl XXX (1995 season).
PRO STATISTICS: 1995—Recovered one fumble.

		INTERCEPTIONS			
Year Team	G	No.	Yds.	Avg.	TD
1994—Pittsburgh NFL	15	0	0	...	0
1995—Pittsburgh NFL	16	2	4	2.0	0
Pro totals (2 years)	31	2	4	2.0	0

BELL, WILLIAM RB REDSKINS

PERSONAL: Born July 22, 1971, in Miami. ... 5-11/212.
HIGH SCHOOL: Edison (Miami).
COLLEGE: Georgia Tech.
TRANSACTIONS/CAREER NOTES: Signed as non-drafted free agent by Washington Redskins (April 28, 1994). ... Released by Redskins (August 29, 1994). ... Re-signed by Redskins to practice squad (August 31, 1994). ... Activated (September 7, 1994).
PRO STATISTICS: 1995—Rushed four times for 13 yards.

		KICKOFF RETURNS				TOTALS			
Year Team	G	No.	Yds.	Avg.	TD	TD	2pt.	Pts.	Fum.
1994—Washington NFL	7	2	43	21.5	0	0	0	0	0
1995—Washington NFL	16	8	121	15.1	0	0	0	0	0
Pro totals (2 years)	23	10	164	16.4	0	0	0	0	0

BELLAMY, JAY S SEAHAWKS

PERSONAL: Born July 8, 1972, in Perth Amboy, N.J. ... 5-11/198. ... Full name: John Lee Bellamy.
HIGH SCHOOL: Matawan (N.J.).
COLLEGE: Rutgers.
TRANSACTIONS/CAREER NOTES: Signed as non-drafted free agent by Seattle Seahawks (April 27, 1994). ... On injured reserve with shoulder injury (November 11, 1994-remainder of season).
PLAYING EXPERIENCE: Seattle NFL, 1994 and 1995. ... Games: 1994 (3), 1995 (14). Total: 17.

BELSER, JASON DB COLTS

PERSONAL: Born May 28, 1970, in Kansas City, Mo. ... 5-9/185. ... Son of Caeser Belser, defensive back, Kansas City Chiefs (1968-1971)

and linebacker, San Francisco 49ers (1974).
HIGH SCHOOL: Raytown (Mo.) South.
COLLEGE: Oklahoma.
TRANSACTIONS/CAREER NOTES: Selected by Indianapolis Colts in eighth round (197th pick overall) of 1992 NFL draft. ... Signed by Colts (July 22, 1992). ... Granted free agency (February 17, 1995). ... Tendered offer sheet by Carolina Panthers (April 17, 1995). ... Offer matched by Colts (April 19, 1995).
CHAMPIONSHIP GAME EXPERIENCE: Played in AFC championship game (1995 season).
PRO STATISTICS: 1992—Fumbled once and recovered two fumbles. 1993—Recovered three fumbles. 1995—Returned one kickoff for 15 yards and recovered two fumbles.

		INTERCEPTIONS			
Year Team	G	No.	Yds.	Avg.	TD
1992—Indianapolis NFL	16	3	27	9.0	0
1993—Indianapolis NFL	16	1	14	14.0	0
1994—Indianapolis NFL	13	1	31	31.0	0
1995—Indianapolis NFL	16	1	0	0.0	0
Pro totals (4 years)	61	6	72	12.0	0

BENFATTI, LOU   DT   JETS

PERSONAL: Born March 9, 1971, in Green Pond, N.J. ... 6-4/278. ... Full name: Lewis Vincent Benfatti.
HIGH SCHOOL: Morris Knolls (Denville, N.J.).
COLLEGE: Penn State.
TRANSACTIONS/CAREER NOTES: Selected by New York Jets in third round (94th pick overall) of 1994 NFL draft. ... Signed by Jets (July 21, 1994).
PLAYING EXPERIENCE: New York Jets NFL, 1994 and 1995. ... Games: 1994 (7), 1995 (12). Total: 19.
HONORS: Named defensive lineman on THE SPORTING NEWS college All-America second team (1992 and 1993).
PRO STATISTICS: 1995—Returned one kickoff for 25 yards.

BENNETT, CORNELIUS   LB   FALCONS

PERSONAL: Born August 25, 1966, in Birmingham, Ala. ... 6-2/238. ... Full name: Cornelius O'landa Bennett.
HIGH SCHOOL: Ensley (Birmingham, Ala.).
COLLEGE: Alabama.
TRANSACTIONS/CAREER NOTES: Selected by Indianapolis Colts in first round (second pick overall) of 1987 NFL draft. ... Placed on reserve/unsigned list (August 31-October 30, 1987). ... Rights traded by Colts to Buffalo Bills in exchange for Bills trading first-round pick (RB Gaston Green) in 1988 draft, first-round (RB Cleveland Gary) and second-round (CB Darryl Henley) picks in 1989 draft and RB Greg Bell to Los Angeles Rams (October 31, 1987); Rams also traded RB Eric Dickerson to Colts for first-round (WR Aaron Cox) and second-round (LB Fred Strickland) picks in 1988 draft, second-round pick (LB Frank Stams) in 1989 draft and RB Owen Gill. ... Signed by Bills (October 31, 1987). ... Granted roster exemption (October 31-November 7, 1987). ... Granted free agency (February 1, 1992). ... Re-signed by Bills (August 31, 1992). ... Designated by Bills as franchise player (February 15, 1995). ... Granted unconditional free agency (February 16, 1996). ... Signed by Atlanta Falcons (March 1, 1996).
CHAMPIONSHIP GAME EXPERIENCE: Played in AFC championship game (1988 and 1990-1993 seasons). ... Played in Super Bowl XXV (1990 season), Super Bowl XXVI (1991 season), Super Bowl XXVII (1992 season) and Super Bowl XXVIII (1993 season).
HONORS: Named linebacker on THE SPORTING NEWS college All-America first team (1984-1986). ... Lombardi Award winner (1986). ... Named outside linebacker on THE SPORTING NEWS All-pro team (1988). ... Played in Pro Bowl (1988 and 1990-1993 seasons).
PRO STATISTICS: 1988—Recovered three fumbles. 1989—Recovered two fumbles for five yards. 1990—Returned blocked field-goal attempt 80 yards for a touchdown and recovered two fumbles. 1991—Recovered two fumbles for nine yards and a touchdown. 1992—Recovered three fumbles. 1993—Recovered two fumbles for 40 yards and fumbled once. 1994—Recovered three fumbles for 14 yards. 1995—Recovered two fumbles.

		INTERCEPTIONS				SACKS
Year Team	G	No.	Yds.	Avg.	TD	No.
1987—Buffalo NFL	8	0	0	...	0	8.5
1988—Buffalo NFL	16	2	30	15.0	0	9.5
1989—Buffalo NFL	12	2	5	2.5	0	5.5
1990—Buffalo NFL	16	0	0	...	0	4.0
1991—Buffalo NFL	16	0	0	...	0	9.0
1992—Buffalo NFL	15	0	0	...	0	4.0
1993—Buffalo NFL	16	1	5	5.0	0	5.0
1994—Buffalo NFL	16	0	0	...	0	5.0
1995—Buffalo NFL	14	1	69	69.0	1	2.0
Pro totals (9 years)	129	6	109	18.2	1	52.5

BENNETT, DARREN   P   CHARGERS

PERSONAL: Born January 9, 1965, in Sydney, Australia. ... 6-5/235. ... Full name: Darren Leslie Bennett.
HIGH SCHOOL: Applecross (Western Australia).
COLLEGE: None.
TRANSACTIONS/CAREER NOTES: Played Australian Rules Football (1987-1993). ... Signed as free agent by San Diego Chargers (April 14, 1994). ... Released by Chargers (August 28, 1994). ... Re-signed by Chargers to practice squad (August 29, 1994). ... Granted free agency after 1994 season. ... Re-signed by Chargers (February 18, 1995). ... Assigned by Chargers to Amersterdam Admirals in 1995 World League enhancement allocation program (February 20, 1995).
HONORS: Named punter on THE SPORTING NEWS NFL All-Pro team (1995). ... Played in Pro Bowl (1995 season).

		PUNTING					
Year Team	G	No.	Yds.	Avg.	Net avg.	In. 20	Blk.
1995—Amsterdam W.L.	...	60	2296	38.3	35.1	24	1

Year Team	G	No.	Yds.	PUNTING Avg.	Net avg.	In. 20	Blk.
—San Diego NFL	16	72	3221	44.7	36.6	28	0
W.L. totals (1 year)	...	60	2296	38.3	35.1	24	1
NFL totals (1 year)	16	72	3221	44.7	36.6	28	0
Pro totals (1 year)	...	132	5517	41.8	35.9	52	1

BENNETT, DONNELL — FB — CHIEFS

PERSONAL: Born September 14, 1972, in Fort Lauderdale. ... 6-0/241.
HIGH SCHOOL: Cardinal Gibbons (Fort Lauderdale).
COLLEGE: Miami (Fla.).
TRANSACTIONS/CAREER NOTES: Selected after junior season by Kansas City Chiefs in second round (58th pick overall) of 1994 NFL draft. ... Signed by Chiefs (May 6, 1994). ... On injured reserve with knee injury (December 20, 1994-remainder of season). ... On physically unable to perform list with knee injury (August 22, 1995-October 31, 1995).
PRO STATISTICS: 1994—Recovered one fumble.

		RUSHING				RECEIVING				KICKOFF RETURNS				TOTALS			
Year Team	G	Att.	Yds.	Avg.	TD	No.	Yds.	Avg.	TD	No.	Yds.	Avg.	TD	TD	2pt.	Pts.	Fum.
1994—Kansas City NFL	15	46	178	3.9	2	7	53	7.6	0	1	12	12.0	0	2	0	12	2
1995—Kansas City NFL	3	7	11	1.6	0	1	12	12.0	0	0	0	...	0	0	0	0	0
Pro totals (2 years)	18	53	189	3.6	2	8	65	8.1	0	1	12	12.0	0	2	0	12	2

BENNETT, EDGAR — FB — PACKERS

PERSONAL: Born February 15, 1969, in Jacksonville. ... 6-0/217.
HIGH SCHOOL: Robert E. Lee Senior (Jacksonville).
COLLEGE: Florida State.
TRANSACTIONS/CAREER NOTES: Selected by Green Bay Packers in fourth round (103rd pick overall) of 1992 NFL draft. ... Signed by Packers (July 22, 1992). ... Granted free agency (February 17, 1995). ... Re-signed by Packers (May 5, 1995).
CHAMPIONSHIP GAME EXPERIENCE: Played in NFC championship game (1995 season).
PRO STATISTICS: 1993—Recovered one fumble. 1994—Recovered one fumble. 1995—Recovered one fumble.
STATISTICAL PLATEAUS: 100-yard rushing games: 1992 (1), 1994 (3), 1995 (1). Total: 5. ... 100-yard receiving games: 1994 (1).

		RUSHING				RECEIVING				KICKOFF RETURNS				TOTALS			
Year Team	G	Att.	Yds.	Avg.	TD	No.	Yds.	Avg.	TD	No.	Yds.	Avg.	TD	TD	2pt.	Pts.	Fum.
1992—Green Bay NFL	16	61	214	3.5	0	13	93	7.2	0	5	104	20.8	0	0	...	0	2
1993—Green Bay NFL	16	159	550	3.5	9	59	457	7.8	1	0	0	...	0	10	0	60	0
1994—Green Bay NFL	16	178	623	3.5	5	78	546	7.0	4	0	0	...	0	9	0	54	1
1995—Green Bay NFL	16	316	1067	3.4	3	61	648	10.6	4	0	0	...	0	7	0	42	2
Pro totals (4 years)	64	714	2454	3.4	17	211	1744	8.3	9	5	104	20.8	0	26	0	156	5

BENNETT, TONY — LB — COLTS

PERSONAL: Born July 1, 1967, in Alligator, Miss. ... 6-2/242. ... Full name: Tony Lydell Bennett.
HIGH SCHOOL: Coahoma County (Clarksdale, Miss.).
COLLEGE: Mississippi (degree in physical education and recreation).
TRANSACTIONS/CAREER NOTES: Selected by Green Bay Packers in first round (18th pick overall) of 1990 NFL draft. ... Signed by Packers (July 22, 1990). ... Granted free agency (March 1, 1993). ... Re-signed by Packers (October 27, 1993). ... Activated (October 30, 1993). ... Granted unconditional free agency (February 17, 1994). ... Signed by Indianapolis Colts (March 26, 1994).
CHAMPIONSHIP GAME EXPERIENCE: Played in AFC championship game (1995 season).
HONORS: Named defensive end on THE SPORTING NEWS college All-America second team (1989).
PRO STATISTICS: 1990—Recovered one fumble. 1992—Recovered three fumbles for 18 yards and a touchdown. 1994—Recovered one fumble for 75 yards and a touchdown. 1995—Credited with a safety, recovered one fumble for 32 yards and a touchdown.

Year Team	G	SACKS
1990—Green Bay NFL	14	3.0
1991—Green Bay NFL	16	13.0
1992—Green Bay NFL	16	13.5
1993—Green Bay NFL	10	6.5
1994—Indianapolis NFL	16	9.0
1995—Indianapolis NFL	16	10.5
Pro totals (6 years)	88	55.5

BENSON, DARREN — DT — COWBOYS

PERSONAL: Born August 25, 1974, in Memphis. ... 6-7/305.
HIGH SCHOOL: Craigmont (Memphis).
JUNIOR COLLEGE: Trinity Valley Community College (Texas).
COLLEGE: None.
TRANSACTIONS/CAREER NOTES: Selected by Dallas Cowboys in third round of 1995 NFL supplemental draft. ... Signed by Cowboys (July 21, 1995).
PLAYING EXPERIENCE: Dallas NFL, 1995. ... Games: 1995 (6).
CHAMPIONSHIP GAME EXPERIENCE: Played in NFC championship game (1995 season). ... Member of Super Bowl championship team (1995 season).

BERCICH, PETER   LB   VIKINGS

PERSONAL: Born December 23, 1971, in Joliet, Ill. ... 6-1/237. ... Full name: Peter James Bercich.
HIGH SCHOOL: Providence Catholic (New Lenox, Ill.).
COLLEGE: Notre Dame.
TRANSACTIONS/CAREER NOTES: Selected by Minnesota Vikings in seventh round (211th pick overall) of 1994 NFL draft. ... Signed by Vikings (July 11, 1994). ... Released by Vikings (August 28, 1994). ... Re-signed by Vikings to practice squad (August 29, 1994). ... Granted free agency after 1994 season. ... Re-signed by Vikings (March 27, 1995).
PLAYING EXPERIENCE: Minnesota NFL, 1995. ... Games: 1995 (9).

BERGER, MITCH   P   VIKINGS

PERSONAL: Born June 24, 1972, in Kamloops, British Columbia. ... 6-2/231.
HIGH SCHOOL: North Delta (Vancouver).
JUNIOR COLLEGE: Tyler (Texas) Junior College.
COLLEGE: Colorado.
TRANSACTIONS/CAREER NOTES: Selected by Philadelphia Eagles in sixth round (193rd pick overall) of 1994 NFL draft. ... Signed by Eagles (July 11, 1994). ... Released by Eagles (October 10, 1994). ... Signed by Cincinnati Bengals to practice squad (October 13, 1994). ... Released by Bengals (November 30, 1994). ... Signed by Chicago Bears (March 7, 1995). ... Released by Bears (May 4, 1995). ... Signed by Indianapolis Colts (May 16, 1995). ... Claimed on waivers by Green Bay Packers (August 24, 1995). ... Released by Packers (August 27, 1995). ... Signed by Bears (November 7, 1995). ... Released by Bears (November 13, 1995). ... Signed by Minnesota Vikings (April 17, 1996).

				PUNTING			
Year Team	G	No.	Yds.	Avg.	Net avg.	In. 20	Blk.
1994—Philadelphia NFL	5	25	951	38.0	31.3	8	0
1995—				Did not play.			

BERNSTINE, ROD   RB

PERSONAL: Born February 8, 1965, in Fairfield, Calif. ... 6-3/238. ... Full name: Rod Earl Bernstine.
HIGH SCHOOL: Bryan (Texas).
COLLEGE: Texas A&M.
TRANSACTIONS/CAREER NOTES: Selected by San Diego Chargers in first round (24th pick overall) of 1987 NFL draft. ... Signed by Chargers (August 11, 1987). ... On injured reserve with hamstring injury (September 8-October 24, 1987). ... On injured reserve with knee injury (December 9, 1988-remainder of season). ... On injured reserve with knee injury (November 25, 1989-remainder of season). ... On injured reserve with hamstring injury (November 21-December 22, 1990). ... Granted free agency (February 1, 1991). ... Re-signed by Chargers (May 16, 1991). ... On injured reserve with back injury (October 26-November 23, 1991). ... Granted free agency (February 1, 1992). ... Re-signed by Chargers (July 27, 1992). ... On injured reserve with shoulder injury (October 22-December 9, 1992). ... On practice squad (December 9-11, 1992). ... Granted unconditional free agency (March 1, 1993). ... Signed by Denver Broncos (March 13, 1993). ... On injured reserve with shoulder injury (December 28, 1993-remainder of season). ... Granted unconditional free agency (February 17, 1994). ... Re-signed by Broncos (1994). ... On injured reserve with knee injury (October 7, 1994-remainder of season). ... Released by Broncos (September 27, 1995).
HONORS: Named tight end on THE SPORTING NEWS college All-America second team (1986).
PRO STATISTICS: 1987—Returned one kickoff for 13 yards and recovered one fumble. 1991—Attempted one pass with one completion for 11 yards and a touchdown and returned one kickoff for seven yards. 1993—Recovered one fumble. 1995—Recovered one fumble.
STATISTICAL PLATEAUS: 100-yard rushing games: 1990 (1), 1991 (3), 1992 (1), 1993 (2). Total: 7.

		RUSHING				RECEIVING				TOTALS			
Year Team	G	Att.	Yds.	Avg.	TD	No.	Yds.	Avg.	TD	TD	2pt.	Pts.	Fum.
1987—San Diego NFL	10	1	9	9.0	0	10	76	7.6	1	1	...	6	0
1988—San Diego NFL	14	2	7	3.5	0	29	340	11.7	0	0	...	0	0
1989—San Diego NFL	5	15	137	9.1	1	21	222	10.6	1	2	...	12	0
1990—San Diego NFL	12	124	589	4.8	4	8	40	5.0	0	4	...	24	1
1991—San Diego NFL	13	159	766	4.8	8	11	124	11.3	0	8	...	48	1
1992—San Diego NFL	9	106	499	4.7	4	12	86	7.2	0	4	...	24	2
1993—Denver NFL	15	223	816	3.7	4	44	372	8.5	0	4	...	24	3
1994—Denver NFL	3	17	91	5.4	0	9	70	7.8	0	0	0	0	0
1995—Denver NFL	3	23	76	3.3	1	5	54	10.8	0	1	0	6	0
Pro totals (9 years)	84	670	2990	4.5	22	149	1384	9.3	2	24	0	144	7

BERTI, TONY   OT   CHARGERS

PERSONAL: Born June 21, 1972, in Rock Springs, Wyo. ... 6-5/287. ... Full name: Charles Anton Berti Jr.
HIGH SCHOOL: Skyview (Thornton, Colo.).
COLLEGE: Colorado.
TRANSACTIONS/CAREER NOTES: Selected by San Diego Chargers in sixth round (200th pick overall) of 1995 NFL draft. ... Signed by Chargers (July 12, 1995).
PLAYING EXPERIENCE: San Diego NFL, 1995. ... Games: (1).

BETTIS, JEROME   RB   STEELERS

PERSONAL: Born February 16, 1972, in Detroit. ... 5-11/243. ... Full name: Jerome Abram Bettis.
HIGH SCHOOL: Mackenzie (Detroit).
COLLEGE: Notre Dame.
TRANSACTIONS/CAREER NOTES: Selected after junior season by Los Angeles Rams in first round (10th pick overall) of 1993 NFL draft. ... Signed by Rams (July 22, 1993). ... Rams franchise moved to St. Louis (April 12, 1995). ... Traded by Rams with third-round pick (LB Steven

B

Conley) in 1996 draft to Pittsburgh Steelers for second-round pick (TE Ernie Conwell) in 1996 draft and fourth-round pick in 1997 draft (April 20, 1996).
HONORS: Named NFL Rookie of the Year by THE SPORTING NEWS (1993). ... Played in Pro Bowl (1993 and 1994 seasons).
PRO STATISTICS: 1994—Recovered three fumbles. 1995—Recovered two fumbles.
STATISTICAL PLATEAUS: 100-yard rushing games: 1993 (7), 1994 (4). Total: 11.

		RUSHING				RECEIVING				TOTALS			
Year Team	G	Att.	Yds.	Avg.	TD	No.	Yds.	Avg.	TD	TD	2pt.	Pts.	Fum.
1993—Los Angeles Rams NFL	16	294	1429	4.9	7	26	244	9.4	0	7	...	42	4
1994—Los Angeles Rams NFL	16	319	1025	3.2	3	31	293	9.5	1	4	2	28	5
1995—St. Louis NFL	15	183	637	3.5	3	18	106	5.9	0	3	0	18	4
Pro totals (3 years)	47	796	3091	3.9	13	75	643	8.6	1	14	2	88	13

BEUERLEIN, STEVE — QB — PANTHERS

PERSONAL: Born March 7, 1965, in Hollywood, Calif. ... 6-3/210. ... Full name: Stephen Taylor Beuerlein. ... Name pronounced BURR-line.
HIGH SCHOOL: Servite (Anaheim, Calif.).
COLLEGE: Notre Dame (degree in American studies, 1987).
TRANSACTIONS/CAREER NOTES: Selected by Los Angeles Raiders in fourth round (110th pick overall) of 1987 NFL draft. ... Signed by Raiders (July 24, 1987). ... On injured reserve with elbow and shoulder injuries (September 7, 1987-entire season). ... Granted free agency (February 1, 1990). ... Re-signed by Raiders (September 3, 1990). ... Granted roster exemption (September 3-16, 1990). ... On inactive list for all 16 games (1990). ... Granted free agency (February 1, 1991). ... Re-signed by Raiders (July 8, 1991). ... Traded by Raiders to Dallas Cowboys for fourth-round pick in 1992 draft (August 25, 1991). ... Granted unconditional free agency (March 1, 1993). ... Signed by Phoenix Cardinals (April 21, 1993). ... Cardinals franchise renamed Arizona Cardinals for 1994 season. ... Selected by Jacksonville Jaguars from Cardinals in NFL expansion draft (February 15, 1995). ... Granted free agency (February 16, 1996). ... Signed by Carolina Panthers (April 2, 1996).
CHAMPIONSHIP GAME EXPERIENCE: Member of Raiders for AFC championship game (1990 season); inactive. ... Played in NFC championship game (1992 season). ... Member of Super Bowl championship team (1992 season).
PRO STATISTICS: 1988—Caught one pass for 21 yards, fumbled six times and recovered two fumbles for minus one yard. 1989—Fumbled six times and recovered three fumbles for minus eight yards. 1993—Fumbled eight times and recovered two fumbles. 1994—Fumbled eight times and recovered three fumbles for minus 13 yards. 1995—Fumbled three times.
STATISTICAL PLATEAUS: 300-yard passing games: 1988 (1), 1993 (2). Total: 3.
MISCELLANEOUS: Regular-season record as starting NFL quarterback: 22-24 (.478).

		PASSING								RUSHING				TOTALS		
Year Team	G	Att.	Cmp.	Pct.	Yds.	TD	Int.	Avg.	Rat.	Att.	Yds.	Avg.	TD	TD	2pt.	Pts.
1987—Los Angeles Raiders NFL					Did not play—injured.											
1988—Los Angeles Raiders NFL	10	238	105	44.1	1643	8	7	6.90	66.6	30	35	1.2	0	0	...	0
1989—Los Angeles Raiders NFL	10	217	108	49.8	1677	13	9	7.73	78.4	16	39	2.4	0	0	...	0
1990—Los Angeles Raiders NFL					Did not play.											
1991—Dallas NFL	8	137	68	49.6	909	5	2	6.64	77.2	7	-14	-2.0	0	0	...	0
1992—Dallas NFL	16	18	12	66.7	152	0	1	8.45	69.7	4	-7	-1.8	0	0	...	0
1993—Phoenix NFL	16	418	258	61.7	3164	18	17	7.57	82.5	22	45	2.1	0	0	...	0
1994—Arizona NFL	9	255	130	51.0	1545	5	9	6.06	61.6	22	39	1.8	1	1	0	6
1995—Jacksonville NFL	7	142	71	50.0	952	4	7	6.71	60.5	5	32	6.4	0	0	0	0
Pro totals (7 years)	76	1425	752	52.8	10042	53	52	7.05	72.6	106	169	1.6	1	1	0	6

BIASUCCI, DEAN — K

PERSONAL: Born July 25, 1962, in Niagara Falls, N.Y. ... 6-0/190.
HIGH SCHOOL: Miramar (Fla.).
COLLEGE: Western Carolina.
TRANSACTIONS/CAREER NOTES: Signed as non-drafted free agent by Atlanta Falcons (May 16, 1984). ... Released by Falcons (August 14, 1984). ... Signed by Indianapolis Colts (September 8, 1984). ... Released by Colts (August 27, 1985). ... Re-signed by Colts (April 22, 1986). ... Granted free agency (February 1, 1990). ... Re-signed by Colts (July 27, 1990). ... Granted unconditional free agency (March 1, 1993). ... Re-signed by Colts (July 18, 1993). ... Granted unconditional free agency (February 17, 1995). ... Signed by Pittsburgh Steelers (July 6, 1995). ... Released by Steelers (August 28, 1995). ... Signed by St. Louis Rams (November 1, 1995). ... Granted unconditional free agency (February 16, 1996).
HONORS: Played in Pro Bowl (1987 season). ... Named kicker on THE SPORTING NEWS NFL All-Pro team (1988).
PRO STATISTICS: 1988—Recovered one fumble.

		KICKING						
Year Team	G	XPM	XPA	FGM	FGA	Lg.	50+	Pts.
1984—Indianapolis NFL	15	13	14	3	5	50	1-3	22
1985—				Did not play.				
1986—Indianapolis NFL	16	26	27	13	25	52	2-8	65
1987—Indianapolis NFL	12	24	24	24	27	50	1-2	96
1988—Indianapolis NFL	16	39	40	25	32	52	6-8	114
1989—Indianapolis NFL	16	31	32	21	27	55	1-4	94
1990—Indianapolis NFL	16	32	33	17	24	55	2-5	83
1991—Indianapolis NFL	16	14	14	15	26	54	1-3	59
1992—Indianapolis NFL	16	24	24	16	29	52	1-3	72
1993—Indianapolis NFL	16	15	16	26	31	53	1-2	93
1994—Indianapolis NFL	16	37	37	16	24	50	2-2	85
1995—St. Louis NFL	8	13	14	9	12	51	1-3	40
Pro totals (11 years)	163	268	275	185	262	55	19-43	823

BICKETT, DUANE — LB — PANTHERS

PERSONAL: Born December 1, 1962, in Los Angeles. ... 6-5/245. ... Full name: Duane Clair Bickett. ... Name pronounced BIK-ett.

HIGH SCHOOL: Glendale (Calif.).
COLLEGE: Southern California (degree in accounting, 1986).
TRANSACTIONS/CAREER NOTES: Selected by Los Angeles Express in 1985 USFL territorial draft. ... Selected by Indianapolis Colts in first round (fifth pick overall) of 1985 NFL draft. ... Signed by Colts (August 7, 1985). ... Designated by Colts as franchise player (February 25, 1993). ... Released by Colts (February 17, 1994). ... Signed by Seattle Seahawks (June 29, 1994). ... On injured reserve with back injury (December 20, 1994-remainder of season). ... Granted unconditional free agency (February 16, 1996). ... Signed by Carolina Panthers (April 25, 1996).
HONORS: Named linebacker on THE SPORTING NEWS college All-America first team (1984). ... Played in Pro Bowl (1987 season).
PRO STATISTICS: 1985—Recovered two fumbles. 1986—Recovered one fumble. 1987—Fumbled once and recovered two fumbles for 32 yards. 1988—Recovered one fumble. 1989—Recovered three fumbles for two yards. 1990—Recovered two fumbles. 1992—Recovered two fumbles. 1993—Recovered one fumble.

| | | INTERCEPTIONS | | | | SACKS |
Year Team	G	No.	Yds.	Avg.	TD	No.
1985—Indianapolis NFL	16	1	0	0.0	0	6.0
1986—Indianapolis NFL	16	2	10	5.0	0	5.0
1987—Indianapolis NFL	12	0	0	...	0	8.0
1988—Indianapolis NFL	16	3	7	2.3	0	3.5
1989—Indianapolis NFL	16	1	6	6.0	0	8.0
1990—Indianapolis NFL	15	1	9	9.0	0	4.5
1991—Indianapolis NFL	16	0	0	...	0	5.0
1992—Indianapolis NFL	15	1	14	14.0	0	6.5
1993—Indianapolis NFL	15	0	0	...	0	3.5
1994—Seattle NFL	7	0	0	...	0	0.0
1995—Seattle NFL	13	0	0	...	0	1.0
Pro totals (11 years)	157	9	46	5.1	0	51.0

BIEKERT, GREG　　　　LB　　　　RAIDERS

PERSONAL: Born March 14, 1969, in Iowa City, Iowa. ... 6-2/240.
HIGH SCHOOL: Longmont (Colo.).
COLLEGE: Colorado (degree in marketing, 1992).
TRANSACTIONS/CAREER NOTES: Selected by Los Angeles Raiders in seventh round (181st pick overall) of 1993 NFL draft. ... Signed by Raiders (July 13, 1993). ... Raiders franchise moved to Oakland (July 21, 1995).

| | | INTERCEPTIONS | | | | SACKS |
Year Team	G	No.	Yds.	Avg.	TD	No.
1993—Los Angeles Raiders NFL	16	0	0	...	0	0.0
1994—Los Angeles Raiders NFL	16	1	11	11.0	0	1.5
1995—Oakland NFL	16	0	0	...	0	1.0
Pro totals (3 years)	48	1	11	11.0	0	2.5

BIENIEMY, ERIC　　　　RB　　　　BENGALS

PERSONAL: Born August 15, 1969, in New Orleans. ... 5-7/198.
HIGH SCHOOL: Bishop Amat (La Puente, Calif.).
COLLEGE: Colorado.
TRANSACTIONS/CAREER NOTES: Selected by San Diego Chargers in second round (39th pick overall) of 1991 NFL draft. ... Signed by Chargers (July 19, 1991). ... Granted free agency (February 17, 1994). ... Re-signed by Chargers (June 6, 1994). ... Granted unconditional free agency (February 17, 1995). ... Signed by Cincinnati Bengals (March 27, 1995).
CHAMPIONSHIP GAME EXPERIENCE: Played in AFC championship game (1994 season). ... Played in Super Bowl XXIX (1994 season).
HONORS: Named running back on THE SPORTING NEWS college All-America first team (1990).
PRO STATISTICS: 1992—Fumbled four times and recovered one fumble. 1993—Fumbled once. 1994—Fumbled once and recovered one fumble. 1995—Attempted two passes without a completion, fumbled once and recovered one fumble.

| | | RUSHING | | | | RECEIVING | | | | PUNT RETURNS | | | | KICKOFF RETURNS | | | | TOTALS | | |
Year Team	G	Att.	Yds.	Avg.	TD	No.	Yds.	Avg.	TD	No.	Yds.	Avg.	TD	No.	Yds.	Avg.	TD	TD	2pt.	Pts.
1991—San Diego NFL	15	3	17	5.7	0	0	0	...	0	0	0	...	0	0	0	...	0	0	...	0
1992—San Diego NFL	15	74	264	3.6	3	5	49	9.8	0	30	229	7.6	0	15	257	17.1	0	3	...	18
1993—San Diego NFL	16	33	135	4.1	1	1	0	0.0	0	0	0	...	0	7	110	15.7	0	1	...	6
1994—San Diego NFL	16	73	295	4.0	0	5	48	9.6	0	0	0	...	0	0	0	...	0	0	0	0
1995—Cincinnati NFL	16	98	381	3.9	3	43	424	9.9	0	7	47	6.7	0	8	168	21.0	0	3	0	18
Pro totals (5 years)	78	281	1092	3.9	7	54	521	9.7	0	37	276	7.5	0	30	535	17.8	0	7	0	42

BINN, DAVE　　　　C　　　　CHARGERS

PERSONAL: Born February 6, 1972, in San Mateo, Calif. ... 6-3/240. ... Full name: David Aaron Binn.
HIGH SCHOOL: San Mateo (Calif.).
COLLEGE: California.
TRANSACTIONS/CAREER NOTES: Signed as non-drafted free agent by San Diego Chargers (April 28, 1994).
PLAYING EXPERIENCE: San Diego NFL, 1994 and 1995. ... Games: 1994 (16), 1995 (16). Total: 32.
CHAMPIONSHIP GAME EXPERIENCE: Played in AFC championship game (1994 season). ... Played in Super Bowl XXIX (1994 season).

BIRDEN, J.J.　　　　WR　　　　FALCONS

PERSONAL: Born June 16, 1965, in Portland, Ore. ... 5-9/170.
HIGH SCHOOL: Lakeridge (Lake Oswego, Ore.).

COLLEGE: Oregon (degree in leisure studies and services).

TRANSACTIONS/CAREER NOTES: Selected by Cleveland Browns in eighth round (216th pick overall) of 1988 NFL draft. ... On physically unable to perform list with knee injury (August 23, 1988-entire season). ... Released by Browns (September 5, 1989). ... Signed by Dallas Cowboys to developmental squad (November 1, 1989). ... Released by Cowboys (January 5, 1990). ... Signed by Kansas City Chiefs (April 3, 1990). ... Released by Chiefs (September 3, 1990). ... Re-signed by Chiefs to practice squad (October 1, 1990). ... Activated (October 10, 1990). ... Granted unconditional free agency (February 1-April 1, 1991). ... Re-signed by Chiefs (1991). ... Granted free agency (March 1, 1993). ... Re-signed by Chiefs for 1993 season. ... Granted unconditional free agency (February 17, 1995). ... Signed by Atlanta Falcons (March 6, 1995).

CHAMPIONSHIP GAME EXPERIENCE: Played in AFC championship game (1993 season).

PRO STATISTICS: 1990—Returned one kickoff for 14 yards. 1992—Recovered one fumble. 1994—Recovered one fumble. 1995—Recovered one fumble.

STATISTICAL PLATEAUS: 100-yard receiving games: 1991 (1), 1994 (2). Total: 3.

			RECEIVING				PUNT RETURNS				TOTALS		
Year Team	G	No.	Yds.	Avg.	TD	No.	Yds.	Avg.	TD	TD	2pt.	Pts.	Fum.
1988—Cleveland NFL						Did not play.							
1989—						Did not play.							
1990—Kansas City NFL	11	15	352	23.5	3	10	72	7.2	0	3	...	18	1
1991—Kansas City NFL	15	27	465	17.2	2	0	0	...	0	2	...	12	1
1992—Kansas City NFL	16	42	644	15.3	3	0	0	...	0	3	...	18	3
1993—Kansas City NFL	16	51	721	14.1	2	5	43	8.6	0	2	...	12	1
1994—Kansas City NFL	13	48	637	13.3	4	0	0	...	0	4	1	26	1
1995—Atlanta NFL	10	31	303	9.8	1	0	0	...	0	1	0	6	0
Pro totals (6 years)	81	214	3122	14.6	15	15	115	7.7	0	15	1	92	7

BISHOP, BLAINE　　　　　S　　　　　OILERS

PERSONAL: Born July 24, 1970, in Indianapolis. ... 5-9/197. ... Full name: Blaine Elwood Bishop.

HIGH SCHOOL: Cathedral (Indianapolis).

COLLEGE: Saint Joseph's (Ind.) College, then Ball State (degree in insurance, 1993).

TRANSACTIONS/CAREER NOTES: Selected by Houston Oilers in eighth round (214th pick overall) of 1993 NFL draft. ... Signed by Oilers (July 16, 1993). ... Granted free agency (February 16, 1996).

HONORS: Played in Pro Bowl (1995 season).

PRO STATISTICS: 1993—Fumbled once and recovered one fumble. 1994—Returned two kickoffs for 18 yards and recovered one fumble. 1995—Recovered four fumbles for six yards.

		INTERCEPTIONS				SACKS
Year Team	G	No.	Yds.	Avg.	TD	No.
1993—Houston NFL	16	1	1	1.0	0	1.0
1994—Houston NFL	16	1	21	21.0	0	1.5
1995—Houston NFL	16	1	62	62.0	1	1.5
Pro totals (3 years)	48	3	84	28.0	1	4.0

BISHOP, GREG　　　　　OT　　　　　GIANTS

PERSONAL: Born May 2, 1971, in Stockton, Calif. ... 6-5/300. ... Full name: Gregory Lawrence Bishop.

HIGH SCHOOL: Lodi (Calif.).

COLLEGE: Pacific.

TRANSACTIONS/CAREER NOTES: Selected by New York Giants in fourth round (93rd pick overall) of 1993 NFL draft. ... Signed by Giants (July 19, 1993).

PLAYING EXPERIENCE: New York Giants NFL, 1993-1995. ... Games: 1993 (8), 1994 (16), 1995 (16). Total: 40.

PRO STATISTICS: 1994—Recovered two fumbles. 1995—Recovered one fumble.

BISHOP, HAROLD　　　　　TE　　　　　RAVENS

PERSONAL: Born April 8, 1970, in Tuscaloosa, Ala. ... 6-4/250. ... Full name: Harold Lucius Bishop.

HIGH SCHOOL: Central (Tuscaloosa, Ala.).

COLLEGE: Louisiana State.

TRANSACTIONS/CAREER NOTES: Selected by Tampa Bay Buccaneers in third round (69th pick overall) of 1994 NFL draft. ... Signed by Buccaneers (July 19, 1994). ... Traded by Buccaneers to Cleveland Browns for second-round pick (FB Mike Alstott) in 1996 draft (May 19, 1995). ... Browns franchise moved to Baltimore and renamed Ravens for 1996 season (March 11, 1996).

		RECEIVING				TOTALS			
Year Team	G	No.	Yds.	Avg.	TD	TD	2pt.	Pts.	Fum.
1994—Tampa Bay NFL	6	0	0	...	0	0	0	0	0
1995—Cleveland NFL	13	16	135	8.4	0	0	0	0	0
Pro totals (2 years)	19	16	135	8.4	0	0	0	0	0

BJORNSON, ERIC　　　　　TE　　　　　COWBOYS

PERSONAL: Born December 15, 1971, in San Francisco. ... 6-4/215.

HIGH SCHOOL: Bishop O'Dowd (Oakland).

COLLEGE: Washington.

TRANSACTIONS/CAREER NOTES: Selected by Dallas Cowboys in fourth round (110th pick overall) of 1995 NFL draft. ... Signed by Cowboys (July 18, 1995).

CHAMPIONSHIP GAME EXPERIENCE: Played in NFC championship game (1995 season). ... Member of Super Bowl championship team (1995 season).

Year Team		G	No.	Yds.	Avg.	TD	TD	2pt.	Pts.	Fum.
			RECEIVING				**TOTALS**			
1995—Dallas NFL		14	7	53	7.6	0	0	0	0	0

BLACKMON, ROBERT   S   SEAHAWKS

PERSONAL: Born May 12, 1967, in Bay City, Texas. ... 6-0/208. ... Full name: Robert James Blackmon.
HIGH SCHOOL: Van Vleck (Texas).
COLLEGE: Baylor (degree in therapy recreation).
TRANSACTIONS/CAREER NOTES: Selected by Seattle Seahawks in second round (34th pick overall) of 1990 NFL draft. ... Signed by Seahawks (July 29, 1990). ... Granted free agency (March 1, 1993). ... Tendered offer sheet by Philadelphia Eagles (April 21, 1993). ... Offer matched by Seahawks (April 23, 1993). ... Designated by Seahawks as franchise player (February 16, 1996).
PRO STATISTICS: 1990—Recovered one fumble. 1991—Recovered one fumble. 1992—Recovered one fumble for nine yards. 1993—Recovered one fumble for five yards and a touchdown. 1993—Recovered one fumble for five yards. 1994—Recovered three fumbles for 18 yards.

B

			INTERCEPTIONS				**SACKS**
Year Team		G	No.	Yds.	Avg.	TD	No.
1990—Seattle NFL		15	0	0	...	0	0.0
1991—Seattle NFL		16	3	59	19.7	0	1.0
1992—Seattle NFL		15	1	69	69.0	0	3.5
1993—Seattle NFL		16	2	0	0.0	0	0.0
1994—Seattle NFL		15	1	24	24.0	0	0.0
1995—Seattle NFL		13	5	46	9.2	0	1.0
Pro totals (6 years)		90	12	198	16.5	0	5.5

BLACKSHEAR, JEFF   G   RAVENS

PERSONAL: Born March 29, 1969, in Fort Pierce, Fla. ... 6-6/323.
HIGH SCHOOL: Fort Pierce (Fla.) Westwood.
JUNIOR COLLEGE: Northeast Mississippi Junior College.
COLLEGE: Northeast Louisiana.
TRANSACTIONS/CAREER NOTES: Selected by Seattle Seahawks in eighth round (197th pick overall) of 1993 NFL draft. ... Signed by Seahawks (July 15, 1993). ... Traded by Seahawks to Cleveland Browns for fourth-round pick in 1997 draft (March 12, 1996). ... Browns franchise moved to Baltimore and renamed Ravens for 1996 season (March 11, 1996).
PLAYING EXPERIENCE: Seattle NFL, 1993 and 1994; Cleveland NFL, 1995. ... Games: 1993 (15), 1994 (16), 1995 (16). Total: 47.

BLADES, BENNIE   S   LIONS

PERSONAL: Born September 3, 1966, in Fort Lauderdale. ... 6-1/221. ... Full name: Horatio Benedict Blades. ... Brother of Brian Blades, wide receiver, Seattle Seahawks.
HIGH SCHOOL: Piper (Sunrise, Fla.).
COLLEGE: Miami (Fla.).
TRANSACTIONS/CAREER NOTES: Selected by Detroit Lions in first round (third pick overall) of 1988 NFL draft. ... Signed by Lions (July 14, 1988). ... Granted free agency (February 1, 1992). ... Re-signed by Lions (August 26, 1992). ... Granted roster exemption (August 26-September 4, 1992). ... Designated by Lions as transition player (February 25, 1993). ... On injured reserve (January 7, 1994-remainder of 1993 playoffs).
CHAMPIONSHIP GAME EXPERIENCE: Played in NFC championship game (1991 season).
HONORS: Named defensive back on The Sporting News college All-America first team (1986 and 1987). ... Jim Thorpe Award co-winner (1987). ... Played in Pro Bowl (1991 season).
PRO STATISTICS: 1988—Recovered four fumbles for 22 yards. 1989—Recovered one fumble. 1990—Recovered one fumble. 1991—Recovered three fumbles for 21 yards. 1992—Returned blocked punt seven yards for a touchdown. 1994—Recovered two fumbles. 1995—Credited with a safety.

			INTERCEPTIONS				**SACKS**
Year Team		G	No.	Yds.	Avg.	TD	No.
1988—Detroit NFL		15	2	12	6.0	0	1.0
1989—Detroit NFL		16	0	0	...	0	0.0
1990—Detroit NFL		12	2	25	12.5	0	1.0
1991—Detroit NFL		16	1	14	14.0	0	0.0
1992—Detroit NFL		16	3	56	18.7	0	0.0
1993—Detroit NFL		4	0	0	...	0	0.0
1994—Detroit NFL		16	1	0	0.0	0	1.0
1995—Detroit NFL		16	1	0	0.0	0	1.0
Pro totals (8 years)		111	10	107	10.7	0	4.0

BLADES, BRIAN   WR   SEAHAWKS

PERSONAL: Born July 24, 1965, in Fort Lauderdale. ... 5-11/188. ... Full name: Brian Keith Blades. ... Brother of Bennie Blades, safety, Detroit Lions.
HIGH SCHOOL: Piper (Sunrise, Fla.).
COLLEGE: Miami (Fla.).
TRANSACTIONS/CAREER NOTES: Selected by Seattle Seahawks in second round (49th pick overall) of 1988 NFL draft. ... Signed by Seahawks (May 19, 1988). ... Granted free agency (February 1, 1992). ... Re-signed by Seahawks (September 2, 1992). ... Granted roster exemption (September 2-5, 1992). ... On injured reserve with broken clavicle (September 8-November 25, 1992); on practice squad (November 18-25, 1992). ... Designated by Seahawks as transition player (February 25, 1993). ... Free agency status changed from transitional to unconditional (February 17, 1994). ... Re-signed by Seahawks (May 17, 1994). ... Granted unconditional free agency (February 16,

1996). ... Re-signed by Seahawks (April 10, 1996).
HONORS: Played in Pro Bowl (1989 season).
PRO STATISTICS: 1988—Recovered one fumble. 1989—Recovered one fumble. 1994—Recovered two fumbles.
STATISTICAL PLATEAUS: 100-yard receiving games: 1988 (2), 1989 (5), 1991 (3), 1992 (1), 1993 (2), 1994 (1), 1995 (3). Total: 17.

		RUSHING				RECEIVING				TOTALS			
Year Team	G	Att.	Yds.	Avg.	TD	No.	Yds.	Avg.	TD	TD	2pt.	Pts.	Fum.
1988—Seattle NFL	16	5	24	4.8	0	40	682	17.1	8	8	...	48	1
1989—Seattle NFL	16	1	3	3.0	0	77	1063	13.8	5	5	...	30	3
1990—Seattle NFL	16	3	19	6.3	0	49	525	10.7	3	3	...	18	0
1991—Seattle NFL	16	2	17	8.5	0	70	1003	14.3	2	2	...	12	1
1992—Seattle NFL	6	1	5	5.0	0	19	256	13.5	1	1	...	6	1
1993—Seattle NFL	16	5	52	10.4	0	80	945	11.8	3	3	...	18	
11994—Seattle NFL	16	2	32	16.0	0	81	1086	13.4	4	4	1	26	1
1995—Seattle NFL	16	2	4	2.0	0	77	1001	13.0	4	4	0	24	0
Pro totals (8 years)	118	21	156	7.4	0	493	6561	13.3	30	30	1	182	8

BLAKE, JEFF   QB   BENGALS

PERSONAL: Born December 4, 1970, in Daytona Beach, Fla. ... 6-0/202. ... Son of Emory Blake, running back, Toronto Argonauts of CFL (1974).
HIGH SCHOOL: Seminole (Sanford, Fla.).
COLLEGE: East Carolina.
TRANSACTIONS/CAREER NOTES: Selected by New York Jets in sixth round (166th pick overall) of 1992 NFL draft. ... Signed by Jets (July 14, 1992). ... Claimed on waivers by Cincinnati Bengals (August 29, 1994). ... Granted free agency (February 17, 1995). ... Re-signed by Bengals (May 8, 1995).
HONORS: Played in Pro Bowl (1995 season).
PRO STATISTICS: 1992—Fumbled once. 1994—Fumbled six times. 1995—Fumbled 10 times for minus seven yards.
STATISTICAL PLATEAUS: 300-yard passing games: 1994 (2), 1995 (1). Total: 3.
MISCELLANEOUS: Regular-season record as starting NFL quarterback: 10-15 (.400).

		PASSING								RUSHING				TOTALS		
Year Team	G	Att.	Cmp.	Pct.	Yds.	TD	Int.	Avg.	Rat.	Att.	Yds.	Avg.	TD	TD	2pt.	Pts.
1992—New York Jets NFL	3	9	4	44.4	40	0	1	4.45	18.1	2	-2	-1.0	0	0	...	0
1993—New York Jets NFL								Did not play.								
1994—Cincinnati NFL	10	306	156	51.0	2154	14	9	7.04	76.9	37	204	5.5	1	1	1	8
1995—Cincinnati NFL	16	567	326	57.5	3822	28	17	6.74	82.1	53	309	5.8	2	2	1	14
Pro totals (3 years)	29	882	486	55.1	6016	42	27	6.82	79.5	92	511	5.6	3	3	2	22

BLANCHARD, CARY   K   COLTS

PERSONAL: Born November 5, 1968, in Fort Worth, Texas. ... 6-1/225.
HIGH SCHOOL: L.D. Bell (Hurst, Texas).
COLLEGE: Oklahoma State.
TRANSACTIONS/CAREER NOTES: Signed as non-drafted free agent by Dallas Cowboys (April 25, 1991). ... Released by Cowboys (August 4, 1991). ... Signed by Sacramento Surge of World League (1992). ... Signed by New Orleans Saints (July 7, 1992). ... Released by Saints (August 31, 1992). ... Re-signed by Saints to practice squad (September 7, 1992). ... Activated (September 14, 1992). ... Active for one game with Saints (1992); did not play. ... Claimed on waivers by New York Jets (September 29, 1992). ... Released by Jets (June 24, 1994). ... Signed by Minnesota Vikings (July 12, 1994). ... Released by Vikings (August 28, 1994). ... Signed by New Orleans Saints (April 18, 1995). ... Released by Saints (August 27, 1995). ... Signed by Indianapolis Colts (October 3, 1995).
CHAMPIONSHIP GAME EXPERIENCE: Played in AFC championship game (1995 season).

		KICKING						
Year Team	G	XPM	XPA	FGM	FGA	Lg.	50+	Pts.
1991—					Did not play.			
1992—Sacramento W.L.	4	17	17	5	8	42	0-0	32
—New York Jets NFL	11	17	17	16	22	47	0-1	65
1993—New York Jets NFL	16	31	31	17	26	45	0-2	82
1994—					Did not play.			
1995—Indianapolis NFL	12	25	25	19	24	50	1-1	82
W.L. totals (1 year)	4	17	17	5	8	42	0-0	32
NFL totals (3 years)	39	73	73	52	72	50	1-4	229
Pro totals (4 years)	43	90	90	57	80	50	1-4	261

BLEDSOE, DREW   QB   PATRIOTS

PERSONAL: Born February 14, 1972, in Ellensburg, Wash. ... 6-5/233.
HIGH SCHOOL: Walla Walla (Wash.).
COLLEGE: Washington State.
TRANSACTIONS/CAREER NOTES: Selected after junior season by New England Patriots in first round (first pick overall) of 1993 NFL draft. ... Signed by Patriots (July 6, 1993).
HONORS: Played in Pro Bowl (1994 season).
RECORDS: Holds NFL single-season record for most passes attempted—691 (1994). ... Holds NFL single-game records for most passes completed—45; most passes attempted—70; and most passes attempted without an interception—70 (November 13, 1994, vs. Minnesota).
PRO STATISTICS: 1993—Fumbled eight times and recovered five fumbles for minus 23 yards. 1994—Fumbled nine times and recovered three fumbles for minus five yards. 1995—Caught one pass for minus nine yards, fumbled 11 times and recovered one fumble for minus eight yards.
STATISTICAL PLATEAUS: 300-yard passing games: 1993 (1), 1994 (6), 1995 (2). Total: 9.

MISCELLANEOUS: Regular-season record as starting NFL quarterback: 21-22 (.488).

			PASSING								RUSHING				TOTALS		
Year Team	G	Att.	Cmp.	Pct.	Yds.	TD	Int.	Avg.	Rat.	Att.	Yds.	Avg.	TD	TD	2pt.	Pts.
1993—New England NFL...............	13	429	214	49.9	2494	15	15	5.81	65.0	32	82	2.6	0	0	...	0
1994—New England NFL...............	16	*691	*400	57.9	*4555	25	*27	6.59	73.6	44	40	0.9	0	0	0	0
1995—New England NFL...............	15	*636	323	50.8	3507	13	16	5.52	63.7	20	28	1.4	0	0	0	0
Pro totals (3 years)...................	44	1756	937	53.4	10556	53	58	6.01	67.9	96	150	1.6	0	0	0	0

BOATSWAIN, HARRY — OT — JETS

PERSONAL: Born June 26, 1969, in Brooklyn, N.Y. ... 6-4/295. ... Full name: Harry Kwane Boatswain.
HIGH SCHOOL: James Madison (Brooklyn, N.Y.).
COLLEGE: New Haven, Conn. (degree in business administration and marketing, 1991).
TRANSACTIONS/CAREER NOTES: Selected by San Francisco 49ers in fifth round (137th pick overall) of 1991 NFL draft. ... Signed by 49ers (July 11, 1991). ... On injured reserve with back and knee injuries (August 27, 1991-entire season). ... Granted unconditional free agency (February 1-April 1, 1992). ... Re-signed by 49ers for 1992 season. ... Selected by Carolina Panthers from 49ers in NFL expansion draft (February 15, 1995). ... Released by Panthers (August 16, 1995). ... Signed by Philadelphia Eagles (September 12, 1995). ... Granted unconditional free agency (February 16, 1996). ... Signed by New York Jets (May 13, 1996).
PLAYING EXPERIENCE: San Francisco NFL, 1992-1994; Philadelphia NFL, 1995. ... Games: 1992 (16), 1993 (16), 1994 (13), 1995 (13). Total: 58.
CHAMPIONSHIP GAME EXPERIENCE: Played in NFC championship game (1992-1994 seasons). ... Member of Super Bowl championship team (1994 season).
PRO STATISTICS: 1995—Recovered one fumble.

BOCK, JOHN — C — JETS

PERSONAL: Born February 11, 1971, in Crystal Lake, Ill. ... 6-3/285. ... Full name: John Matthew Bock. ... Nephew of Wayne Bock, tackle, Chicago Cardinals (1957).
HIGH SCHOOL: Crystal Lake (Ill.).
COLLEGE: Louisville, then Indiana State.
TRANSACTIONS/CAREER NOTES: Signed as non-drafted free agent by Buffalo Bills (May 7, 1994). ... Released by Bills (August 22, 1994). ... Selected by Amsterdam Admirals in 1995 World League draft. ... Signed by New York Jets (June 22, 1995).
PLAYING EXPERIENCE: New York Jets NFL, 1995. ... Games: 1995 (10).
PRO STATISTICS: 1995—Fumbled once for minus one yard.

BONHAM, SHANE — DL — LIONS

PERSONAL: Born October 18, 1970, in Fairbanks, Alaska. ... 6-2/275. ... Full name: Steven Shane Bonham.
HIGH SCHOOL: Lathrop (Fairbanks, Alaska).
COLLEGE: Air Force, then Tennessee.
TRANSACTIONS/CAREER NOTES: Selected by Detroit Lions in third round (93rd pick overall) of 1994 NFL draft. ... Signed by Lions (July 21, 1994).
PLAYING EXPERIENCE: Detroit NFL, 1994 and 1995. ... Games: 1994 (15), 1995, (16). Total: 31.
PRO STATISTICS: 1995—Credited with one sack.

BONIOL, CHRIS — K — COWBOYS

PERSONAL: Born December 9, 1971, in Alexandria, La. ... 5-11/159.
HIGH SCHOOL: Alexandria (La.).
COLLEGE: Louisiana Tech.
TRANSACTIONS/CAREER NOTES: Signed as non-drafted free agent by Dallas Cowboys (April 28, 1994).
CHAMPIONSHIP GAME EXPERIENCE: Played in NFC championship game (1994 and 1995 season). ... Member of Super Bowl championship team (1995 season).
PRO STATISTICS: 1995—Punted twice for 77 yards.

		KICKING						
Year Team	G	XPM	XPA	FGM	FGA	Lg.	50+	Pts.
1994—Dallas NFL................................	16	48	48	22	29	47	0-1	114
1995—Dallas NFL................................	16	46	†48	27	28	45	0-0	127
Pro totals (2 years)	32	94	96	49	57	47	0-1	241

BONO, STEVE — QB — CHIEFS

PERSONAL: Born May 11, 1962, in Norristown, Pa. ... 6-4/215. ... Full name: Steven Christopher Bono.
HIGH SCHOOL: Norristown (Pa.).
COLLEGE: UCLA.
TRANSACTIONS/CAREER NOTES: Selected by Memphis Showboats in 1985 USFL territorial draft. ... Selected by Minnesota Vikings in sixth round (142nd pick overall) of 1985 NFL draft. ... Signed by Vikings (July 10, 1985). ... Released by Vikings (October 4, 1986). ... Re-signed by Vikings (November 19, 1986). ... Released by Vikings (December 9, 1986). ... Signed by Pittsburgh Steelers (March 25, 1987). ... Released by Steelers (September 7, 1987). ... Re-signed as replacement player by Steelers (September 24, 1987). ... Released by Steelers (April 13, 1989). ... Signed by San Francisco 49ers (June 13, 1989). ... Active for seven games with 49ers (1990); did not play. ... Granted free agency (February 1, 1991). ... Re-signed by 49ers (1991). ... Granted unconditional free agency (March 1, 1993). ... Re-signed by 49ers (April 7, 1993). ... Released by 49ers (April 29, 1994). ... Re-signed by 49ers and traded to Kansas City Chiefs for conditional draft pick (May 2, 1994).
CHAMPIONSHIP GAME EXPERIENCE: Member of 49ers for NFC championship game (1989 and 1990 seasons); inactive. ... Member of Super

Bowl championship team (1989 season). ... Played in NFC championship game (1992 and 1993 seasons).
HONORS: Played in Pro Bowl (1995 season).
PRO STATISTICS: 1987—Caught one pass for two yards, fumbled five times and recovered three fumbles. 1991—Fumbled seven times for minus eight yards. 1992—Fumbled twice and recovered one fumble for minus three yards. 1995—Fumbled 10 times and recovered one fumble for minus five yards.
STATISTICAL PLATEAUS: 300-yard passing games: 1991 (2), 1994 (2). Total: 4.
MISCELLANEOUS: Regular-season record as starting NFL quarterback: 20-7 (.741).

				PASSING							RUSHING				TOTALS		
Year Team	G	Att.	Cmp.	Pct.	Yds.	TD	Int.	Avg.	Rat.	Att.	Yds.	Avg.	TD	TD	2pt.	Pts.
1985—Minnesota NFL	1	10	1	10.0	5	0	0	.50	39.6	0	0	...	0	0	...	0
1986—Minnesota NFL	1	1	1	100.0	3	0	0	3.00	79.2	0	0	...	0	0	...	0
1987—Pittsburgh NFL	3	74	34	46.0	438	5	2	5.92	76.3	8	27	3.4	1	1	...	6
1988—Pittsburgh NFL	2	35	10	28.6	110	1	2	3.14	25.9	0	0	...	0	0	...	0
1989—San Francisco NFL	1	5	4	80.0	62	1	0	12.40	157.9	0	0	...	0	0	...	0
1990—San Francisco NFL							Did not play.									
1991—San Francisco NFL	9	237	141	59.5	1617	11	4	6.82	88.5	17	46	2.7	0	0	...	0
1992—San Francisco NFL	16	56	36	64.3	463	2	2	8.27	87.1	15	23	1.5	0	0	...	0
1993—San Francisco NFL	8	61	39	63.9	416	0	1	6.82	76.9	12	14	1.2	1	1	...	6
1994—Kansas City NFL	7	117	66	56.4	796	4	4	6.80	74.6	4	-1	-03	0	0	0	0
1995—Kansas City NFL	16	520	293	56.4	3121	21	10	6.00	79.5	28	113	4.0	5	5	0	30
Pro totals (10 years)	64	1116	625	56.0	7031	45	25	6.30	79.1	84	222	2.7	7	7	0	42

BOOKER, VAUGHN   DE   CHIEFS

PERSONAL: Born February 24, 1968, in Cincinnati. ... 6-5/293. ... Full name: Vaughn Jamel Booker.
HIGH SCHOOL: Taft (Cincinnati).
COLLEGE: Cincinnati.
TRANSACTIONS/CAREER NOTES: Signed as non-drafted free agent by Winnipeg Blue Bombers of CFL (June 1992). ... Granted free agency after 1994 season. ... Signed as free agent by Kansas City Chiefs (May 2, 1994).
PRO STATISTICS: CFL: 1992—Recovered four fumbles and returned one kickoff for three yards. NFL: 1994—Recovered two fumbles for six yards and returned two kickoffs for 10 yards. 1995—Recovered one fumble for 14 yards and a touchdown.
MISCELLANEOUS: Served in U.S. Army (1988-90).

Year Team	G	SACKS
1992—Winnipeg CFL	15	2.0
1993—Winnipeg CFL	9	4.0
1994—Kansas City NFL	13	0.0
1995—Kansas City NFL	16	1.5
CFL totals (2 years)	24	6.0
NFL totals (2 years)	29	1.5
Pro totals (4 years)	53	7.5

BOOTH, ISSAC   DB   RAVENS

PERSONAL: Born May 23, 1971, in Indianapolis. ... 6-3/190. ... Full name: Issac Ramoun Booth.
HIGH SCHOOL: Perry Meridan (Indianapolis).
COLLEGE: California.
TRANSACTIONS/CAREER NOTES: Selected by Cleveland Browns in fifth round (141st pick overall) of 1994 NFL draft. ... Signed by Browns (1994). ... On injured reserve with knee injury (December 8, 1995). ... Browns franchise moved to Baltimore and renamed Ravens for 1996 season (March 11, 1996).

		INTERCEPTIONS			
Year Team	G	No.	Yds.	Avg.	TD
1994—Cleveland NFL	16	1	4	4.0	0
1995—Cleveland NFL	8	1	11	11.0	0
Pro totals (2 years)	24	2	15	7.5	0

BOOTY, JOHN   S   BUCCANEERS

PERSONAL: Born October 9, 1965, in Deberry, Texas. ... 6-0/185. ... Full name: John Fitzgerald Booty.
HIGH SCHOOL: Carthage (Texas
JUNIOR COLLEGE: Cisco (Texas) Junior College.
COLLEGE: Texas Christian (degree in speech communications, 1988).
TRANSACTIONS/CAREER NOTES: Selected by New York Jets in 10th round (257th pick overall) of 1988 NFL draft. ... Signed by Jets (June 7, 1988). ... On injured reserve with neck injury (September 5-October 17, 1989). ... Granted free agency (February 1, 1990). ... Re-signed by Jets (July 17, 1990). ... On injured reserve with knee injury (December 1-28, 1990). ... Granted unconditional free agency (February 1, 1991). ... Signed by Philadelphia Eagles (April 1, 1991). ... Granted unconditional free agency (March 1, 1993). ... Signed by Phoenix Cardinals (March 17, 1993). ... Released by Cardinals (June 2, 1994). ... Signed by New York Giants (July 18, 1994). ... Granted unconditional free agency (February 17, 1995). ... Signed by Tampa Bay Buccaneers (June 1, 1995). ... On injured reserve with hamstring injury (November 29, 1995-remainder of season).
PRO STATISTICS: 1988—Recovered two fumbles. 1991—Recovered one fumble. 1992—Returned one kickoff for 11 yards and recovered one fumble. 1994—Recovered two fumbles for five yards. 1995—Caught one pass for 48 yards.

		INTERCEPTIONS				SACKS
Year Team	G	No.	Yds.	Avg.	TD	No.
1988—New York Jets NFL	16	3	0	0.0	0	0.0
1989—New York Jets NFL	9	1	13	13.0	0	0.0

| Year Team | G | INTERCEPTIONS | | | | SACKS |
		No.	Yds.	Avg.	TD	No.
1990—New York Jets NFL	13	0	0	...	0	0.0
1991—Philadelphia NFL	13	1	24	24.0	0	1.0
1992—Philadelphia NFL	16	3	22	7.3	0	0.0
1993—Phoenix NFL	12	2	24	12.0	0	3.0
1994—New York Giants NFL	16	3	95	31.7	0	0.0
1995—Tampa Bay NFL	7	1	21	21.0	0	0.0
Pro totals (8 years)	102	14	199	14.2	0	4.0

BORGELLA, JOCELYN   CB   LIONS

PERSONAL: Born August 26, 1971, in Nassau, Bahamas. ... 5-10/180. ... Full name: Jocelyn Kenza Borgella.
HIGH SCHOOL: Edison (Miami).
COLLEGE: Cincinnati.
TRANSACTIONS/CAREER NOTES: Selected by Detroit Lions in sixth round (183rd pick overall) of 1994 NFL draft. ... Signed by Lions (June 8, 1994). ... Assigned by Lions to Scottish Claymores in 1995 World League enhancement allocation program (February 20, 1995).

| Year Team | G | INTERCEPTIONS | | | |
		No.	Yds.	Avg.	TD
1994—Detroit NFL	4	0	0	...	0
1995—Scottish W.L.	...	3	45	15.0	0
Pro totals (2 years)	...	3	45	15.0	0

BORGOGNONE, DIRK   K

PERSONAL: Born January 9, 1968, in Elko, Nev. ... 6-2/221. ... Full name: Dirk Ronald Borgognone. ... Name pronounced borg-a-NO-nee.
HIGH SCHOOL: Reno (Nev.).
JUNIOR COLLEGE: Truckee Meadows (Nev.).
COLLEGE: Tennessee, then Pacific.
TRANSACTIONS/CAREER NOTES: Signed as non-drafted free agent by Minnesota Vikings (August 11, 1990). ... Released by Vikings (August 17, 1990). ... Signed by Atlanta Falcons (1991). ... Released by Falcons (1991). ... Signed by Cleveland Browns (1992). ... Released by Browns (August 11, 1992). ... Signed by Indianapolis Colts (April 30, 1993). ... Released by Colts (August 23, 1993). ... Signed by Miami Dolphins (April 29, 1994). ... Released by Dolphins (August 24, 1994). ... Signed by Green Bay Packers (January 20, 1995). ... Released by Packers (August 24, 1995). ... Re-signed by Packers to practice squad (September 6, 1995). ... Activated (September 13, 1995). ... Released by Packers (September 26, 1995).
PLAYING EXPERIENCE: Green Bay NFL, 1995. ... Games: 1995 (2).

BOSELLI, TONY   OT   JAGUARS

PERSONAL: Born April 17, 1972, in Boulder, Colo. ... 6-7/323. ... Full name: Don Anthony Boselli Jr.
HIGH SCHOOL: Fairview (Boulder, Colo.).
COLLEGE: Southern California.
TRANSACTIONS/CAREER NOTES: Selected by Jacksonville Jaguars in first round (second pick overall) of 1995 NFL draft. ... Signed by Jaguars (June 1, 1995).
PLAYING EXPERIENCE: Jacksonville NFL, 1995. ... Games: 1995 (13).
HONORS: Named offensive lineman on THE SPORTING NEWS college All-America first team (1994).

BOTKIN, KIRK   TE   SAINTS

PERSONAL: Born March 19, 1971, in Baytown, Texas. ... 6-3/245.
HIGH SCHOOL: Robert E. Lee (Baytown, Texas).
COLLEGE: Arkansas.
TRANSACTIONS/CAREER NOTES: Signed as non-drafted free agent by New England Patriots (April 25, 1994). ... Released by Patriots (August 24, 1994). ... Signed by New Orleans Saints to practice squad (September 28, 1994). ... Activated (December 9, 1994).
PLAYING EXPERIENCE: New Orleans NFL, 1994 and 1995. ... Games: 1994 (3), 1995 (16). Total: 19.
PRO STATISTICS: 1995—Caught one pass for eight yards.

BOUIE, TONY   S   BUCCANEERS

PERSONAL: Born August 7, 1972, in New Orleans. ... 5-10/187. ... Full name: Tony Vanderson Bouie. ... BOO-ee
HIGH SCHOOL: Holy Cross (New Orleans).
COLLEGE: Arizona.
TRANSACTIONS/CAREER NOTES: Signed as non-drafted free agent by Tampa Bay Buccaneers (April 26, 1995). ... Released by Buccaneers (August 21, 1995). ... Re-signed by Buccaneers to practice squad (October 4, 1995). ... Activated (October 17, 1995).
PLAYING EXPERIENCE: Tampa Bay NFL, 1995. ... Games: 1995 (9).
HONORS: Named defensive back on THE SPORTING NEWS college All-America second team (1994).
PRO STATISTICS: 1995—Intercepted one pass for 19 yards

BOUTTE, MARC   DT   REDSKINS

PERSONAL: Born July 25, 1969, in Lake Charles, La. ... 6-4/311. ... Full name: Marc Anthony Boutte. ... Name pronounced BOO-TAY.

HIGH SCHOOL: Lake Charles (La.)-Boston.
COLLEGE: Louisiana State.
TRANSACTIONS/CAREER NOTES: Selected by Los Angeles Rams in third round (57th pick overall) of 1992 NFL draft. ... Signed by Rams (July 13, 1992). ... Claimed on waivers by Washington Redskins (August 29, 1994). ... Granted free agency (February 17, 1995). ... Re-signed by Redskins (April 21, 1995). ... Granted unconditional free agency (February 16, 1996). ... Re-signed by Redskins (February 18, 1996).
PRO STATISTICS: 1993—Recovered one fumble. 1995—Recovered one fumble.

Year Team	G	SACKS
1992—Los Angeles Rams NFL	16	1.0
1993—Los Angeles Rams NFL	16	1.0
1994—Washington NFL	9	0.0
1995—Washington NFL	16	2.0
Pro totals (4 years)	57	4.0

BOUWENS, SHAWN — G — JAGUARS

PERSONAL: Born May 25, 1968, in Lincoln, Neb. ... 6-5/293. ... Name pronounced BOW-ens.
HIGH SCHOOL: Lincoln (Neb.) Northeast.
COLLEGE: Nebraska Wesleyan.
TRANSACTIONS/CAREER NOTES: Selected by New England Patriots in ninth round (226th pick overall) of 1990 NFL draft. ... Signed by Patriots (July 18, 1990). ... Released by Patriots (September 3, 1990). ... Signed by Cleveland Browns to practice squad (October 3, 1990). ... Granted free agency after 1990 season. ... Signed by Detroit Lions (February 27, 1991). ... Granted unconditional free agency (February 17, 1995). ... Signed by Jacksonville Jaguars (February 28, 1995).
PLAYING EXPERIENCE: Detroit NFL, 1991-1994; Jacksonville NFL, 1995. ... Games: 1991 (16), 1992 (16), 1993 (15), 1994 (16), 1995 (10). Total: 73.
CHAMPIONSHIP GAME EXPERIENCE: Played in NFC championship game (1991 season).
PRO STATISTICS: 1992—Recovered one fumble. 1994—Recovered three fumbles and fumbled once.

BOWDEN, JOE — LB — OILERS

PERSONAL: Born February 25, 1970, in Dallas. ... 5-11/230. ... Full name: Joseph Tarrod Bowden.
HIGH SCHOOL: North Mesquite (Mesquite, Texas).
COLLEGE: Oklahoma.
TRANSACTIONS/CAREER NOTES: Selected by Houston Oilers in fifth round (133rd pick overall) of 1992 NFL draft. ... Signed by Oilers (July 16, 1992). ... Granted free agency (February 17, 1995). ... Re-signed by Oilers (June 6, 1995). ... Granted unconditional free agency (February 16, 1996). ... Re-signed by Oilers (February 22, 1996).
PLAYING EXPERIENCE: Houston NFL, 1992-1995. ... Games: 1992 (14), 1993 (16), 1994 (14), 1995 (16). Total: 60.
PRO STATISTICS: 1993—Credited with a sack and recovered one fumble. 1995—Credited with one sack, returned one kickoff for six yards and recovered one fumble.

BOWENS, TIM — DT — DOLPHINS

PERSONAL: Born February 7, 1973, in Okolona, Miss. ... 6-4/310.
HIGH SCHOOL: Okolona (Miss.).
JUNIOR COLLEGE: Itawamba Junior College (Miss.).
COLLEGE: Mississippi.
TRANSACTIONS/CAREER NOTES: Selected after junior season by Miami Dolphins in first round (20th pick overall) of 1994 NFL draft. ... Signed by Dolphins (June 2, 1994).
PRO STATISTICS: 1994—Recovered one fumble. 1995—Recovered two fumbles.

Year Team	G	SACKS
1994—Miami NFL	16	3.0
1995—Miami NFL	16	2.0
Pro totals (2 years)	32	5.0

BOWNES, FABIEN — WR — BEARS

PERSONAL: Born February 29, 1972, in Aurora, Ill. ... 5-11/180. ... Name pronounced BOW-ens.
HIGH SCHOOL: Waubonsie Valley (Aurora, Ill.).
COLLEGE: Western Illinois.
TRANSACTIONS/CAREER NOTES: Signed as non-drafted free agent by Chicago Bears (April 27, 1995). ... Released by Bears (August 27, 1995). ... Re-signed by Bears to practice squad (August 29, 1995). ... Activated (December 14, 1995).
PLAYING EXPERIENCE: Chicago NFL, 1995. ... Games: 1995 (1).

BOYD, STEPHEN — LB — LIONS

PERSONAL: Born August 22, 1972, in Valley Stream, N.Y. ... 6-0/247. ... Full name: Stephen Gerard Boyd.
HIGH SCHOOL: Valley Stream (N.Y.).
COLLEGE: Boston College.
TRANSACTIONS/CAREER NOTES: Selected by Detroit Lions in fifth round (141st pick overall) of 1995 NFL draft. ... Signed by Lions (July 19, 1995).
HONORS: Named linebacker on THE SPORTING NEWS college All-America first team (1994).
PLAYING EXPERIENCE: Detroit NFL, 1995. ... Games: 1995 (16).

BOYER, BRANT   LB   JAGUARS

PERSONAL: Born June 27, 1971, in Ogden, Utah. ... 6-1/235.
HIGH SCHOOL: North Summit (Coalville, Utah).
JUNIOR COLLEGE: Snow College (Utah).
COLLEGE: Arizona.
TRANSACTIONS/CAREER NOTES: Selected by Miami Dolphins in sixth round (177th pick overall) of 1994 NFL draft. ... Signed by Dolphins (July 11, 1994). ... Released by Dolphins (September 21, 1994). ... Re-signed by Dolphins to practice squad (September 22, 1994). ... Activated (October 5, 1994). ... Selected by Jacksonville Jaguars from Dolphins in NFL expansion draft (February 15, 1995). ... Released by Jaguars (August 27, 1995). ... Re-signed by Jaguars (December 13, 1995).
PLAYING EXPERIENCE: Miami NFL, 1994; Jacksonville NFL, 1995. ... Games: 1994 (14), 1995 (2). Total: 16.

BOYKIN, DERAL   S   EAGLES   B

PERSONAL: Born September 2, 1970, in Kent, Ohio. ... 5-11/198. ... Full name: Deral Lamont Boykin. ... Nephew of Greg Boykin, running back, New Orleans Saints and San Francisco 49ers (1977 and 1978).
HIGH SCHOOL: Roosevelt (Kent, Ohio).
COLLEGE: Louisville.
TRANSACTIONS/CAREER NOTES: Selected by Los Angeles Rams in sixth round (149th pick overall) of 1993 NFL draft. ... Signed by Rams for 1993 season. ... Released by Rams (August 28, 1994). ... Signed by Washington Redskins (August 29, 1994). ... Released by Redskins (November 28, 1994). ... Signed by Jacksonville Jaguars (December 27, 1994). ... Released by Jaguars (August 27, 1995). ... Re-signed by Jaguars (September 28, 1995). ... Released by Jaguars (November 17, 1995). ... Signed by Philadelphia Eagles (March 19, 1996).
PLAYING EXPERIENCE: Los Angeles Rams NFL, 1993; Washington NFL, 1994; Jacksonville NFL, 1995. ... Games: 1993 (16), 1994 (12), 1995 (5). Total: 33.
PRO STATISTICS: 1993—Returned 13 kickoffs for 216 yards, fumbled once and recovered two fumbles for six yards and a touchdown.

BRADFORD, RONNIE   CB   BRONCOS

PERSONAL: Born October 1, 1970, in Minot, N.D. ... 5-10/188.
HIGH SCHOOL: Adams City (Commerce City, Colo.).
COLLEGE: Colorado.
TRANSACTIONS/CAREER NOTES: Selected by Miami Dolphins in fourth round (105th pick overall) of 1993 NFL draft. ... Signed by Dolphins (July 14, 1993). ... Released by Dolphins (August 24, 1993). ... Signed by Denver Broncos to practice squad (September 1, 1993). ... Activated (October 12, 1993). ... On injured reserve with knee injury (September 28, 1995-remainder of season).
PLAYING EXPERIENCE: Denver NFL, 1993-1995. ... Games: 1993 (10), 1994 (12), 1995 (4). Total: 26.
PRO STATISTICS: 1993—Intercepted one pass for no yards, returned one punt for no yards and fumbled once. 1994—Credited with one sack and recovered two fumbles.

BRADY, DONNY   DB   RAVENS

PERSONAL: Born November 24, 1973, in North Bellmore, N.Y. ... 6-2/195.
HIGH SCHOOL: Mepham (Bellmore, N.Y.).
JUNIOR COLLEGE: Nassau Community College (N.Y.).
COLLEGE: Wisconsin.
TRANSACTIONS/CAREER NOTES: Signed as non-drafted free agent by Cleveland Browns (May 2, 1995). ... Released by Browns (August 21, 1995). ... Re-signed by Browns to practice squad (December 13, 1995). ... Activated (December 16, 1995). ... Browns franchise moved to Baltimore and renamed Ravens for 1996 season (March 11, 1996).
PLAYING EXPERIENCE: Cleveland NFL, 1995. ... Games: 1995 (2).

BRADY, ED   LB

PERSONAL: Born June 17, 1962, in Morris, Ill. ... 6-2/238. ... Full name: Ed John Brady.
HIGH SCHOOL: Morris (Ill.).
COLLEGE: Illinois.
TRANSACTIONS/CAREER NOTES: Selected by Chicago Blitz in 1984 USFL territorial draft. ... Selected by Los Angeles Rams in eighth round (215th pick overall) of 1984 NFL draft. ... Signed by Rams (July 14, 1984). ... Released by Rams (August 27, 1984). ... Re-signed by Rams (August 28, 1984). ... Claimed on waivers by Cincinnati Bengals (September 2, 1986). ... Granted unconditional free agency (February 1-April 1, 1991). ... Re-signed by Bengals for 1991 season. ... Granted unconditional free agency (February 1, 1992). ... Signed by Tampa Bay Buccaneers (March 6, 1992). ... Granted unconditional free agency (February 17, 1995). ... Re-signed by Buccaneers (February 21, 1995). ... Granted unconditional free agency (February 16, 1996).
PLAYING EXPERIENCE: Los Angeles Rams NFL, 1984 and 1985; Cincinnati NFL, 1986-1991; Tampa Bay NFL, 1992-1995. ... Games: 1984 (16), 1985 (16), 1986 (16), 1987 (12), 1988 (16), 1989 (16), 1990 (16), 1991 (16), 1992 (16), 1993 (16), 1994 (16), 1995 (16). Total: 188.
CHAMPIONSHIP GAME EXPERIENCE: Played in NFC championship game (1985 season). ... Played in AFC championship game (1988 season). ... Played in Super Bowl XXIII (1988 season).
PRO STATISTICS: 1985—Recovered one fumble. 1986—Fumbled once for minus seven yards. 1987—Recovered one fumble. 1990—Recovered one fumble. 1992—Recovered one fumble. 1994—Recovered one fumble. 1995—Fumbled once for minus 18 yards.

BRADY, JEFF   LB   VIKINGS

PERSONAL: Born November 9, 1968, in Cincinnati. ... 6-1/238. ... Full name: Jeffrey Thomas Brady.
HIGH SCHOOL: Newport (Ky.) Central Catholic.
COLLEGE: Kentucky (degree in telecommunications, 1990).

TRANSACTIONS/CAREER NOTES: Selected by Pittsburgh Steelers in 12th round (323rd pick overall) of 1991 NFL draft. ... Signed by Steelers (July 10, 1991). ... Granted unconditional free agency (February 1, 1992). ... Signed by Green Bay Packers (March 30, 1992). ... On injured reserve with knee injury (September 26-November 21, 1992). ... Claimed on waivers by Los Angeles Rams (August 31, 1993). ... Released by Rams (October 20, 1993). ... Signed by San Diego Chargers (October 25, 1993). ... Granted free agency (February 17, 1994). ... Signed by Tampa Bay Buccaneers (May 4, 1994). ... Granted unconditional free agency (February 17, 1995). ... Signed by Minnesota Vikings (April 13, 1995). ... Granted unconditional free agency (February 16, 1996). ... Re-signed by Vikings (February 28, 1996).
PLAYING EXPERIENCE: Pittsburgh NFL, 1991; Green Bay NFL, 1992; Los Angeles Rams (6)-San Diego (3) NFL, 1993; Tampa Bay NFL, 1994; Minnesota NFL, 1995. ... Games: 1991 (16), 1992 (8), 1993 (9), 1994 (16), 1995 (16). Total: 65.
PRO STATISTICS: 1993—Recovered one fumble. 1995—Credited with three sacks, intercepted two passes for seven yards and recovered two fumbles.

B

BRADY, KYLE — TE — JETS

PERSONAL: Born January 14, 1972, in New Cumberland, Pa. ... 6-6/260. ... Full name: Kyle James Brady.
HIGH SCHOOL: Cedar Cliff (Camp Hill, Pa.).
COLLEGE: Penn State.
TRANSACTIONS/CAREER NOTES: Selected by New York Jets in first round (ninth pick overall) of 1995 NFL draft. ... Signed by Jets (July 17, 1995).
HONORS: Named tight end on THE SPORTING NEWS college All-America second team (1994).

Year Team	G	RECEIVING				KICKOFF RETURNS				TOTALS			
		No.	Yds.	Avg.	TD	No.	Yds.	Avg.	TD	TD	2pt.	Pts.	Fum.
1995—New York Jets NFL	15	26	252	9.7	2	2	25	12.5	0	2	0	12	0

BRAHAM, RICH — C/G — BENGALS

PERSONAL: Born November 6, 1970, in Morgantown, W.Va. ... 6-4/290. ... Name pronounced bray-HAM.
HIGH SCHOOL: University (Morgantown, W.Va.).
COLLEGE: West Virginia.
TRANSACTIONS/CAREER NOTES: Selected by Arizona Cardinals in third round (76th pick overall) of 1994 NFL draft. ... Signed by Cardinals (July 30, 1994). ... Claimed on waivers by Cincinnati Bengals (November 18, 1994). ... On injured reserve with ankle injury (August 29, 1995-entire season).
PLAYING EXPERIENCE: Cincinnati NFL, 1994. ... Games: 1994 (3).
HONORS: Named offensive lineman on THE SPORTING NEWS college All-America second team (1993).

BRANDON, DAVID — LB — FALCONS

PERSONAL: Born February 9, 1965, in Memphis. ... 6-4/240. ... Full name: David Sherrod Brandon.
HIGH SCHOOL: Mitchell (Memphis).
COLLEGE: Memphis State.
TRANSACTIONS/CAREER NOTES: Selected by Buffalo Bills in third round (60th pick overall) of 1987 NFL draft. ... Signed by Bills (July 25, 1987). ... Traded by Bills with fourth-round pick (OL Stacy Searels) in 1988 draft to San Diego Chargers for WR Trumaine Johnson and seventh-round pick (NT Jeff Wright) in 1988 draft (August 31, 1987). ... On injured reserve with knee injury (July 23, 1990-entire season). ... Granted unconditional free agency (February 1, 1991). ... Signed by Cleveland Browns (April 1, 1991). ... Granted free agency (February 1, 1992). ... Re-signed by Browns (July 19, 1992). ... Granted unconditional free agency (March 1, 1993). ... Re-signed by Browns (April 20, 1993). ... Released by Browns (October 26, 1993). ... Signed by Seattle Seahawks (November 10, 1993). ... Granted unconditional free agency (February 17, 1994). ... Re-signed by Seahawks (April 6, 1994). ... Released by Seahawks (August 27, 1995). ... Signed by San Diego Chargers (August 28, 1995). ... Granted unconditional free agency (February 16, 1996). ... Signed by Atlanta Falcons (May 3, 1996).
PRO STATISTICS: 1987—Recovered blocked punt in end zone for a touchdown. 1992—Recovered three fumbles for 32 yards and a touchdown.

Year Team	G	INTERCEPTIONS				SACKS
		No.	Yds.	Avg.	TD	No.
1987—San Diego NFL	8	0	0	...	0	0.0
1988—San Diego NFL	8	0	0	...	0	0.0
1989—San Diego NFL	13	0	0	...	0	0.0
1990—San Diego NFL			Did not play—injured.			
1991—Cleveland NFL	16	2	70	35.0	1	3.0
1992—Cleveland NFL	16	2	123	61.5	1	1.0
1993—Cleveland NFL	6	0	0	...	0	0.0
—Seattle NFL	7	0	0	...	0	0.0
1994—Seattle NFL	13	0	0	...	0	0.0
1995—San Diego NFL	16	0	0	...	0	1.0
Pro totals (8 years)	103	4	193	48.3	2	5.0

BRANDON, MIKE — DE — 49ERS

PERSONAL: Born July 30, 1968, in Perry, Fla. ... 6-4/290. ... Full name: Michael Breon Brandon.
HIGH SCHOOL: Taylor County (Perry, Fla.).
COLLEGE: Florida.
TRANSACTIONS/CAREER NOTES: Signed as non-drafted free agent by Indianapolis Colts (July 17, 1992). ... Released by Colts (August 31, 1992). ... Re-signed by Colts to practice squad (September 2, 1992). ... Released by Colts (October 8, 1992). ... Signed by Miami Dolphins (October 12, 1992). ... Released by Dolphins (December 2, 1992). ... Signed by New Orleans Saints to practice squad (December 9, 1992). ... Granted free agency after 1992 season. ... Signed by Colts (February 8, 1993). ... Released by Colts (April 26, 1994). ... Re-signed by Colts (July 11, 1994). ... Claimed on waivers by Arizona Cardinals (July 17, 1994). ... Released by Cardinals (September 7, 1994). ... Selected by Scottish Claymores in seventh round (41st pick overall) of 1995 World League Draft. ... Signed by San Francisco 49ers (July 28, 1995).

PLAYING EXPERIENCE: Indianapolis NFL, 1993; Arizona NFL, 1994; San Francisco NFL, 1995. ... Games: 1993 (15), 1994 (1), 1995 (11). Total: 27.

BRATZKE, CHAD   DE   GIANTS

PERSONAL: Born September 15, 1971, in Brandon, Fla. ... 6-4/273. ... Full name: Chad Allen Bratzke.
HIGH SCHOOL: Blooming Dale Senior (Valcro, Fla.).
COLLEGE: Eastern Kentucky.
TRANSACTIONS/CAREER NOTES: Selected by New York Giants in fifth round (155th pick overall) of 1994 NFL draft. ... Signed by Giants (July 17, 1994).
PLAYING EXPERIENCE: New York Giants NFL, 1994 and 1995. ... Games: 1994 (2), 1995 (6). Total: 8.

BRAXTON, TYRONE   CB

PERSONAL: Born December 17, 1964, in Madison, Wis. ... 5-11/185. ... Full name: Tyrone Scott Braxton. ... Related to Jim Braxton, fullback, Buffalo Bills and Miami Dolphins (1971-1978).
HIGH SCHOOL: James Madison Memorial (Madison, Wis.).
COLLEGE: North Dakota State.
TRANSACTIONS/CAREER NOTES: Selected by Denver Broncos in 12th round (334th pick overall) of 1987 NFL draft. ... Signed by Broncos (July 18, 1987). ... On injured reserve with shoulder injury (September 1-December 18, 1987). ... On injured reserve with knee injury (September 25, 1990-remainder of season). ... Granted unconditional free agency (February 17, 1994). ... Signed by Miami Dolphins (May 13, 1994). ... Released by Dolphins (April 20, 1995). ... Signed by Broncos (May 5, 1995). ... Granted unconditional free agency (February 16, 1996).
CHAMPIONSHIP GAME EXPERIENCE: Played in AFC championship game (1987, 1989 and 1991 seasons). ... Played in Super Bowl XXII (1987 season) and Super Bowl XXIV (1989 season).
PRO STATISTICS: 1988—Recovered one fumble. 1989—Recovered two fumbles for 35 yards. 1991—Fumbled once and recovered one fumble. 1993—Recovered two fumbles for six yards. 1994—Returned one kickoff for 34 yards.

| | | INTERCEPTIONS | | | | SACKS |
Year Team	G	No.	Yds.	Avg.	TD	No.
1987—Denver NFL	2	0	0	...	0	0.0
1988—Denver NFL	16	2	6	3.0	0	1.0
1989—Denver NFL	16	6	103	17.2	1	0.0
1990—Denver NFL	3	1	10	10.0	0	0.0
1991—Denver NFL	16	4	55	13.8	1	1.0
1992—Denver NFL	16	2	54	27.0	0	0.0
1993—Denver NFL	16	3	37	12.3	0	0.0
1994—Miami NFL	16	2	3	1.5	0	0.0
1995—Denver NFL	16	2	36	18.0	0	0.0
Pro totals (9 years)	117	22	304	13.8	2	2.0

BREWER, DEWELL   RB/KR   PANTHERS

PERSONAL: Born May 22, 1970, in Lawton, Okla. ... 5-8/201.
HIGH SCHOOL: Lawton (Okla.).
COLLEGE: Oklahoma.
TRANSACTIONS/CAREER NOTES: Signed as non-drafted free agent by Chicago Bears (April 29, 1993). ... Released by Bears (August 24, 1993). ... Signed by Indianapolis Colts (July 19, 1994). ... Selected by Carolina Panthers from Colts in NFL expansion draft (February 15, 1995). ... On injured reserve with knee injury (August 27, 1995-entire season).
PRO STATISTICS: 1994—Recovered one fumble.

| | | PUNT RETURNS | | | | KICKOFF RETURNS | | | | TOTALS | | | |
Year Team	G	No.	Yds.	Avg.	TD	No.	Yds.	Avg.	TD	TD	2pt.	Pts.	Fum.
1993—						Did not play.							
1994—Indianapolis NFL	16	*42	339	8.1	1	18	358	19.9	0	1	0	6	3
1995—Carolina NFL						Did not play—injured.							

BRICE, ALUNDIS   CB   COWBOYS

PERSONAL: Born May 1, 1970, in Brookhaven, Miss. ... 5-10/178.
HIGH SCHOOL: Brookhaven (Miss.).
COLLEGE: Mississippi.
TRANSACTIONS/CAREER NOTES: Selected by Dallas Cowboys in fourth round (129th pick overall) of 1995 NFL draft. ... Signed by Cowboys (July 19, 1995).
CHAMPIONSHIP GAME EXPERIENCE: Played in NFC championship game (1995 season). ... Member of Super Bowl championship team (1995 season).

| | | INTERCEPTIONS | | | |
Year Team	G	No.	Yds.	Avg.	TD
1995—Dallas NFL	10	1	2	2.0	0

BRIEN, DOUG   K   SAINTS

PERSONAL: Born November 24, 1970, in Bloomfield, N.J. ... 6-0/180. ... Full name: Douglas Robert Zachariah Brien.
HIGH SCHOOL: De La Salle Catholic (Concord, Calif.).

COLLEGE: California.
TRANSACTIONS/CAREER NOTES: Selected by San Francisco 49ers in third round (85th pick overall) of 1994 NFL draft. ... Signed by 49ers (July 27, 1994). ... Released by 49ers (October 16, 1995). ... Signed by New Orleans Saints (October 31, 1995).
CHAMPIONSHIP GAME EXPERIENCE: Played in NFC championship game (1994 season). ... Member of Super Bowl championship team (1994 season).
POSTSEASON RECORDS: Shares Super Bowl single-game record for most extra points—7 (January 29, 1995, vs. San Diego).

| | | | KICKING | | | | | |
Year Team	G	XPM	XPA	FGM	FGA	Lg.	50+	Pts.
1994—San Francisco NFL	16	*60	*62	15	20	48	0-1	105
1995—San Francisco NFL	6	19	19	7	12	51	1-1	40
—New Orleans NFL	8	16	16	12	17	47	0-1	52
Pro totals (2 years)	30	95	97	34	49	51	1-3	197

BRIGGS, GREG   S

PERSONAL: Born October 1, 1968, in Meadville, Miss. ... 6-3/212.
HIGH SCHOOL: Franklin (Meadville, Miss.).
JUNIOR COLLEGE: Copiah-Lincoln Junior College (Miss.).
COLLEGE: Arkansas-Pine Bluff, then Texas Southern.
TRANSACTIONS/CAREER NOTES: Selected by Dallas Cowboys in fifth round (120th pick overall) of 1992 NFL draft. ... Signed by Cowboys (June 10, 1992). ... On physically unable to perform list with right hip injury (August 25, 1992-entire season). ... Released by Cowboys (August 23, 1993). ... Signed by Cleveland Browns to practice squad (December 15, 1993). ... Granted free agency after 1993 season. ... Re-signed by Browns (March 18, 1994). ... Released by Browns (July 21, 1994). ... Signed by Frankfurt Galaxy of World League (1995). ... Signed by Cowboys (August 14, 1995). ... Released by Cowboys (August 27, 1995). ... Re-signed by Cowboys (September 20, 1995). ... Granted unconditional free agency (February 16, 1996).
PLAYING EXPERIENCE: Dallas NFL, 1995. ... Games: 1995 (11).
CHAMPIONSHIP GAME EXPERIENCE: Played in NFC championship game (1995 season). ... Member of Super Bowl championship team (1995 season).

BRILZ, DARRICK   C   BENGALS

PERSONAL: Born February 14, 1964, in Richmond, Calif. ... 6-3/287. ... Full name: Darrick Joseph Brilz.
HIGH SCHOOL: Pinole (Calif.) Valley.
COLLEGE: Oregon State.
TRANSACTIONS/CAREER NOTES: Signed as non-drafted free agent by Washington Redskins (May 1, 1987). ... Released by Redskins (August 31, 1987). ... Re-signed as replacement player by Redskins (September 23, 1987). ... On injured reserve with pinched nerve in neck (December 12, 1987-remainder of season). ... Claimed on waivers by San Diego Chargers (August 30, 1988). ... Released by Chargers (August 1, 1989). ... Signed by Seattle Seahawks (August 16, 1989). ... Released by Seahawks (September 5, 1989). ... Re-signed by Seahawks (September 21, 1989). ... Granted unconditional free agency (February 17, 1994). ... Signed by Cincinnati Bengals (March 28, 1994).
PLAYING EXPERIENCE: Washington NFL, 1987; San Diego NFL, 1988; Seattle NFL, 1989-1993; Cincinnati NFL, 1994 and 1995. ... Games: 1987 (7), 1988 (14), 1989 (14), 1990 (16), 1991 (16), 1992 (16), 1993 (16), 1994 (15), 1995 (16). Total: 130.
PRO STATISTICS: 1991—Recovered one fumble. 1994—Recovered one fumble.

BRIM, MIKE   CB

PERSONAL: Born January 23, 1966, in Danville, Va. ... 6-0/192. ... Full name: Michael Anthony Brim.
HIGH SCHOOL: George Washington (Danville, Va.).
COLLEGE: Virginia Union (degree in history, 1988).
TRANSACTIONS/CAREER NOTES: Selected by Phoenix Cardinals in fourth round (95th pick overall) of 1988 NFL draft. ... Signed by Cardinals (July 10, 1988). ... On injured reserve with cracked ribs (August 29-November 25, 1988). ... Released by Cardinals (September 5, 1989). ... Signed by Detroit Lions (September 20, 1989). ... Released by Lions (October 25, 1989). ... Signed by Minnesota Vikings (November 8, 1989). ... Granted free agency (February 1, 1990). ... Re-signed by Vikings (July 30, 1990). ... Granted unconditional free agency (February 1, 1991). ... Signed by New York Jets (March 11, 1991). ... Granted unconditional free agency (March 1, 1993). ... Signed by Cincinnati Bengals (May 19, 1993). ... On injured reserve with back injury (December 11, 1995-remainder of season). ... Released by Bengals (April 18, 1996).
PRO STATISTICS: 1991—Credited with a sack and recovered one fumble. 1993—Recovered two fumbles. 1994—Recovered one fumble.

| | | INTERCEPTIONS | | | |
Year Team	G	No.	Yds.	Avg.	TD
1988—Phoenix NFL	4	0	0	...	0
1989—Detroit NFL	2	0	0	...	0
—Minnesota NFL	7	0	0	...	0
1990—Minnesota NFL	16	2	11	5.5	0
1991—New York Jets NFL	16	4	52	13.0	0
1992—New York Jets NFL	16	6	139	23.2	1
1993—Cincinnati NFL	16	3	74	24.7	1
1994—Cincinnati NFL	16	2	72	36.0	0
1995—Cincinnati NFL	1	0	0	...	0
Pro totals (8 years)	94	17	348	20.5	2

BRISBY, VINCENT   WR   PATRIOTS

PERSONAL: Born January 25, 1971, in Lake Charles, La. ... 6-2/188. ... Full name: Vincent Cole Brisby.
HIGH SCHOOL: Washington-Marion Magnet (Lake Charles, La.).

COLLEGE: Northeast Louisiana.
TRANSACTIONS/CAREER NOTES: Selected by New England Patriots in second round (56th pick overall) of 1993 NFL draft. ... Signed by Patriots (July 30, 1993). ... Granted free agency (February 16, 1996).
PRO STATISTICS: 1993—Recovered one fumble.
STATISTICAL PLATEAUS: 100-yard receiving games: 1994 (2), 1995 (3). Total: 5.

		RECEIVING				TOTALS			
Year Team	G	No.	Yds.	Avg.	TD	TD	2pt.	Pts.	Fum.
1993—New England NFL	16	45	626	13.9	2	2	...	12	1
1994—New England NFL	14	58	904	15.6	5	5	0	30	1
1995—New England NFL	16	66	974	14.8	3	3	0	18	0
Pro totals (3 years)	46	169	2504	14.8	10	10	0	60	2

BRISTER, BUBBY — QB — B

PERSONAL: Born August 15, 1962, in Alexandria, La. ... 6-3/207. ... Full name: Walter Andrew Brister III.
HIGH SCHOOL: Neville (Monroe, La.).
COLLEGE: Tulane, then Northeast Louisiana.
TRANSACTIONS/CAREER NOTES: Selected by Pittsburgh Steelers in third round (67th pick overall) of 1986 NFL draft. ... Selected by New Jersey Generals in 11th round (80th pick overall) of 1986 USFL draft. ... Signed by Steelers (July 25, 1986). ... Granted free agency (February 1, 1992). ... Re-signed by Steelers (June 16, 1992). ... Released by Steelers (June 4, 1993). ... Signed by Philadelphia Eagles (July 19, 1993). ... Granted unconditional free agency (February 17, 1994). ... Re-signed by Eagles (April 6, 1994). ... Granted unconditional free agency (February 17, 1995). ... Signed by New York Jets (March 17, 1995). ... Released by Jets (February 29, 1996).
PRO STATISTICS: 1986—Fumbled once. 1988—Recovered two fumbles. 1989—Caught one pass for minus 10 yards, fumbled eight times and recovered one fumble. 1990—Fumbled nine times. 1991—Fumbled four times and recovered two fumbles. 1992—Fumbled twice and recovered two fumbles for minus two yards. 1993—Fumbled three times. 1995—Caught one pass for two yards, fumbled four times and recovered three fumbles for minus nine yards.
STATISTICAL PLATEAUS: 300-yard passing games: 1988 (2), 1993 (1), 1994 (1). Total: 4.
MISCELLANEOUS: Regular-season record as starting NFL quarterback: 33-39 (.458).

		PASSING								RUSHING				TOTALS		
Year Team	G	Att.	Cmp.	Pct.	Yds.	TD	Int.	Avg.	Rat.	Att.	Yds.	Avg.	TD	TD	2pt.	Pts.
1986—Pittsburgh NFL	2	60	21	35.0	291	0	2	4.85	37.6	6	10	1.7	1	1	...	6
1987—Pittsburgh NFL	2	12	4	33.3	20	0	3	1.67	2.8	0	0	...	0	0	...	0
1988—Pittsburgh NFL	13	370	175	47.3	2634	11	14	7.12	65.3	45	209	4.6	6	6	...	36
1989—Pittsburgh NFL	14	342	187	54.7	2365	9	10	6.92	73.1	27	25	.9	0	0	...	0
1990—Pittsburgh NFL	16	387	223	57.6	2725	20	14	7.04	81.6	25	64	2.6	0	0	...	0
1991—Pittsburgh NFL	8	190	103	54.2	1350	9	9	7.11	72.9	11	17	1.6	0	0	...	0
1992—Pittsburgh NFL	6	116	63	54.3	719	2	5	6.20	61.0	10	16	1.6	0	0	...	0
1993—Philadelphia NFL	10	309	181	58.6	1905	14	5	6.17	84.9	20	39	2.0	0	0	...	0
1994—Philadelphia NFL	7	76	51	67.1	507	2	1	6.67	89.1	1	7	7.0	0	0	0	0
1995—New York Jets NFL	9	170	93	54.7	726	4	8	4.27	53.7	16	18	1.1	0	0	0	0
Pro totals (10 years)	87	2032	1101	54.2	13242	71	71	6.52	71.5	161	405	2.5	7	7	0	42

BROCK, MATT — DT — JETS

PERSONAL: Born January 14, 1966, in Ogden, Utah. ... 6-5/290. ... Full name: Matthew Lee Brock. ... Son of Clyde Brock, defensive tackle, Dallas Cowboys and San Francisco 49ers (1962 and 1963).
HIGH SCHOOL: University City (San Diego).
COLLEGE: Oregon.
TRANSACTIONS/CAREER NOTES: Selected by Green Bay Packers in third round (58th pick overall) of 1989 NFL draft. ... Signed by Packers (July 24, 1989). ... On injured reserve with broken bone in hand (November 14, 1989-remainder of season). ... Granted free agency (February 1, 1991). ... Re-signed by Packers (July 30, 1991). ... Granted free agency (March 1, 1993). ... Re-signed by Packers (August 9, 1993). ... Granted unconditional free agency (February 17, 1994). ... Re-signed by Packers (August 24, 1994). ... Granted unconditional free agency (February 17, 1995). ... Signed by New York Jets (April 4, 1995).
PRO STATISTICS: 1992—Recovered two fumbles for 34 yards. 1993—Intercepted one pass for no yards. 1993—Recovered one fumble. 1995—Intercepted one pass for nine yards, recovered two fumbles for three yards and one touchdown.

Year Team	G	SACKS
1989—Green Bay NFL	7	0.0
1990—Green Bay NFL	16	4.0
1991—Green Bay NFL	16	2.5
1992—Green Bay NFL	16	4.0
1993—Green Bay NFL	16	2.0
1994—Green Bay NFL	5	0.0
1995—New York Jets NFL	16	5.0
Pro totals (7 years)	92	17.5

BROCK, STAN — OT — CHARGERS

PERSONAL: Born June 8, 1958, in Portland, Ore. ... 6-6/295. ... Full name: Stanley James Brock. ... Brother of Pete Brock, center, New England Patriots (1976-1987); and brother of Willie Brock, center, Detroit Lions (1978).
HIGH SCHOOL: Jesuit (Beaverton, Ore.).
COLLEGE: Colorado.
TRANSACTIONS/CAREER NOTES: Selected by New Orleans Saints in first round (12th pick overall) of 1980 NFL draft. ... On injured reserve with knee injury (December 5, 1984-remainder of season). ... On injured reserve with knee injury (October 22, 1988-remainder of season). ... Granted free agency (February 1, 1990). ... Re-signed by Saints (August 12, 1990). ... Granted unconditional free agency (February 1-April 1, 1992). ... Re-signed by Saints for 1992 season. ... Granted unconditional free agency (March 1, 1993). ... Signed by San Diego Chargers (May 18, 1993). ... Released by Chargers (August 30, 1993). ... Re-signed by Chargers (August 31, 1993). ... Granted unconditional free

agency (February 17, 1994). ... Re-signed by Chargers (April 7, 1994). ... Released by Chargers (February 16, 1995). ... Re-signed by Chargers (July 18, 1995).
PLAYING EXPERIENCE: New Orleans NFL, 1980-1992; San Diego NFL, 1993-1995. ... Games: 1980 (16), 1981 (16), 1982 (9), 1983 (16), 1984 (14), 1985 (16), 1986 (16), 1987 (12), 1988 (7), 1989 (16), 1990 (16), 1991 (16), 1992 (16), 1993 (16), 1994 (16), 1995 (16). Total: 234.
CHAMPIONSHIP GAME EXPERIENCE: Played in AFC championship game (1994 season). ... Played in Super Bowl XXIX (1994 season).
HONORS: Named offensive tackle on THE SPORTING NEWS college All-America first team (1979).
PRO STATISTICS: 1980—Recovered one fumble. 1981—Returned two kickoffs for 18 yards and recovered two fumbles. 1983—Returned one kickoff for 15 yards and recovered one fumble. 1985—Recovered one fumble. 1987—Returned one kickoff for 11 yards. 1989—Recovered one fumble. 1990—Recovered one fumble.

BROCKERMEYER, BLAKE   OT   PANTHERS

PERSONAL: Born April 11, 1973, in Fort Worth, Texas. ... 6-4/300.
HIGH SCHOOL: Arlington Heights (Texas).
COLLEGE: Texas.
TRANSACTIONS/CAREER NOTES: Selected after junior season by Carolina Panthers in first round (29th pick overall) of 1995 NFL draft. ... Signed by Panthers (July 14, 1995).
PLAYING EXPERIENCE: Carolina NFL, 1995. ... Games: 1995 (16).
HONORS: Named offensive lineman on THE SPORTING NEWS college All-America first team (1994).

BRONSON, BEN   WR   LIONS

PERSONAL: Born September 9, 1972, in Jasper, Texas. ... 5-9/159.
HIGH SCHOOL: Jasper (Texas).
JUNIOR COLLEGE: Tyler (Texas) Junior College.
COLLEGE: Baylor.
TRANSACTIONS/CAREER NOTES: Signed as non-drafted free agent by Indianapolis Colts (April 27, 1995). ... Released by Colts (November 10, 1995). ... Signed by Detroit Lions to practice squad (November 29, 1995).
PLAYING EXPERIENCE: Indianapolis NFL, 1995. ... Games: 1995 (9).
PRO STATISTICS: 1995—Returned one kickoff for 31 yards, returned 13 punts for 79 yards and fumbled twice.

BROOKS, BARRETT   OT   EAGLES

PERSONAL: Born May 5, 1972, in St. Louis. ... 6-4/309.
HIGH SCHOOL: McCluer North (Florissant, Mo.).
COLLEGE: Kansas State.
TRANSACTIONS/CAREER NOTES: Selected by Philadelphia Eagles in second round (58th pick overall) of 1995 NFL draft. ... Signed by Eagles (July 19, 1995).
PLAYING EXPERIENCE: Philadelphia NFL, 1995. ... Games: 1995 (16).

BROOKS, BILL   WR   REDSKINS

PERSONAL: Born April 6, 1964, in Boston. ... 6-0/188.
HIGH SCHOOL: North (Framingham, Mass.).
COLLEGE: Boston University (degree in business administration, 1986).
TRANSACTIONS/CAREER NOTES: Selected by Indianapolis Colts in fourth round (86th pick overall) of 1986 NFL draft. ... Signed by Colts (June 23, 1986). ... Granted unconditional free agency (March 1, 1993). ... Signed by Buffalo Bills (March 31, 1993). ... Released by Bills (April 25, 1995). ... Re-signed by Bills (June 12, 1995). ... Granted unconditional free agency (February 16, 1996). ... Signed by Washington Redskins (May 10, 1996).
CHAMPIONSHIP GAME EXPERIENCE: Played in AFC championship game (1993 season). ... Played in Super Bowl XXVIII (1993 season).
PRO STATISTICS: 1986—Returned eight kickoffs for 143 yards and recovered one fumble. 1988—Recovered two fumbles. 1991—Recovered one fumble. 1992—Recovered one fumble.
STATISTICAL PLATEAUS: 100-yard receiving games: 1986 (2), 1987 (1), 1988 (2), 1989 (3), 1991 (1), 1995 (3). Total: 12.

		RUSHING				RECEIVING				PUNT RETURNS				TOTALS			
Year Team	G	Att.	Yds.	Avg.	TD	No.	Yds.	Avg.	TD	No.	Yds.	Avg.	TD	TD	2pt.	Pts.	Fum.
1986—Indianapolis NFL	16	4	5	1.3	0	65	1131	17.4	8	18	141	7.8	0	8	...	48	2
1987—Indianapolis NFL	12	2	-2	-1.0	0	51	722	14.2	3	22	136	6.2	0	3	...	18	3
1988—Indianapolis NFL	16	5	62	12.4	0	54	867	16.1	3	3	15	5.0	0	3	...	18	1
1989—Indianapolis NFL	16	2	-3	-1.5	0	63	919	14.6	4	0	0	...	0	4	...	24	1
1990—Indianapolis NFL	16	0	0	...	0	62	823	13.3	5	0	0	...	0	5	...	30	0
1991—Indianapolis NFL	16	0	0	...	0	72	888	12.3	4	0	0	...	0	4	...	24	0
1992—Indianapolis NFL	14	2	14	7.0	0	44	468	10.6	1	0	0	...	0	1	...	6	0
1993—Buffalo NFL	16	3	30	10.0	0	60	714	11.9	5	1	3	3.0	0	5	...	30	0
1994—Buffalo NFL	16	0	0	...	0	42	482	11.5	2	0	0	...	0	2	0	12	1
1995—Buffalo NFL	15	3	7	2.3	0	53	763	14.4	11	6	35	5.8	0	11	0	66	0
Pro totals (10 years)	153	21	113	5.4	0	566	7777	13.8	46	50	330	6.6	0	46	0	276	8

BROOKS, BUCKY   CB   PACKERS

PERSONAL: Born January 22, 1971, in Raleigh, N.C. ... 6-0/185. ... Full name: William Eldridge Brooks Jr.
HIGH SCHOOL: Millbrook (Raleigh, N.C.).
COLLEGE: North Carolina.

TRANSACTIONS/CAREER NOTES: Selected by Buffalo Bills in second round (48th pick overall) of 1994 NFL draft. ... Signed by Bills (July 15, 1994). ... On injured reserve (November 17, 1994-remainder of season). ... Released by Bills (August 22, 1995). ... Signed by Green Bay Packers (December 12, 1995). ... Inactive for two games (1995).
CHAMPIONSHIP GAME EXPERIENCE: Member of Packers for NFC championship game (1995 season); inactive.
PRO STATISTICS: 1994—Recovered one fumble.

			KICKOFF RETURNS				TOTALS			
Year Team	G	No.	Yds.	Avg.	TD	TD	2pt.	Pts.	Fum.
1994—Buffalo NFL	3	9	162	18.0	0	0	0	0	1
1995—Green Bay NFL						Did not play.			

BROOKS, CARLOS   CB   CARDINALS

PERSONAL: Born May 8, 1971, in Hamilton, Ohio. ... 6-0/200.
HIGH SCHOOL: Middletown (Ohio).
COLLEGE: Bowling Green.
TRANSACTIONS/CAREER NOTES: Played with Arizona Rattlers of Arena Football League (1994). ... Signed by Arizona Cardinals (May 1995). ... Released by Cardinals (August 27, 1995). ... Re-signed by Cardinals to practice squad (August 30, 1995). ... Activated (October 31, 1995).
PLAYING EXPERIENCE: Arizona NFL, 1995. ... Games: 1995 (7).

BROOKS, DERRICK   LB   BUCCANEERS

PERSONAL: Born April 18, 1973, in Pensacola, Fla. ... 6-0/225.
HIGH SCHOOL: Washington (Pensacola, Fla.).
COLLEGE: Florida State (degree in communications, 1994).
TRANSACTIONS/CAREER NOTES: Selected by Tampa Bay Buccaneers in first round (28th pick overall) of 1995 NFL draft. ... Signed by Buccaneers (May 3, 1995).
HONORS: Named linebacker on The Sporting News college All-America first team (1993 and 1994).

Year Team	G	SACKS
1995—Tampa Bay NFL	16	1.0

BROOKS, MICHAEL   LB   LIONS

PERSONAL: Born March 2, 1964, in Ruston, La. ... 6-1/236.
HIGH SCHOOL: Ruston (La.).
COLLEGE: Louisiana State.
TRANSACTIONS/CAREER NOTES: Selected by Denver Broncos in third round (86th pick overall) of 1987 NFL draft. ... Signed by Broncos (July 24, 1987). ... Granted free agency (February 1, 1990). ... Re-signed by Broncos (July 29, 1990). ... Granted free agency (February 1, 1991). ... Re-signed by Broncos (July 12, 1991). ... Designated by Broncos as transition player (February 25, 1993). ... Free agency status changed by Broncos from transitional to unconditional (May 28, 1993). ... Signed by New York Giants (June 7, 1993). ... Granted unconditional free agency (February 16, 1996). ... Signed by Detroit Lions (March 7, 1996).
CHAMPIONSHIP GAME EXPERIENCE: Played in AFC championship game (1987, 1989 and 1991 seasons). ... Played In Super Bowl XXII (1987 season) and Super Bowl XXIV (1989 season).
HONORS: Named linebacker on The Sporting News college All-America second team (1984 and 1985). ... Played in Pro Bowl (1992 season).
PRO STATISTICS: 1987—Recovered one fumble. 1989—Credited with a safety and recovered two fumbles. 1992—Recovered two fumbles for 55 yards and a touchdown. 1993—Recovered one fumble. 1994—Recovered three fumbles.

		INTERCEPTIONS				SACKS
Year Team	G	No.	Yds.	Avg.	TD	No.
1987—Denver NFL	12	0	0	...	0	1.0
1988—Denver NFL	16	0	0	...	0	0.0
1989—Denver NFL	16	0	0	...	0	1.0
1990—Denver NFL	16	0	0	...	0	2.0
1991—Denver NFL	14	2	7	3.5	0	0.0
1992—Denver NFL	15	1	17	17.0	0	0.0
1993—New York Giants NFL	13	0	0	...	0	1.0
1994—New York Giants NFL	16	1	10	10.0	0	1.0
1995—New York Giants NFL	16	0	0	...	0	1.0
Pro totals (9 years)	134	4	34	8.5	0	7.0

BROOKS, REGGIE   RB   REDSKINS

PERSONAL: Born January 19, 1971, in Tulsa, Okla. ... 5-8/211. ... Full name: Reginald Arthur Brooks. ... Brother of Tony Brooks, running back, Philadelphia Eagles (1992) and London Monarchs of World League (1995); and nephew of Tony Peters, safety, Washington Redskins (1979-1985).
HIGH SCHOOL: Booker T. Washington (Tulsa, Okla.).
COLLEGE: Notre Dame.
TRANSACTIONS/CAREER NOTES: Selected by Washington Redskins in second round (45th pick overall) of 1993 NFL draft. ... Signed by Redskins (1993). ... Granted free agency (February 16, 1996).
HONORS: Named running back on The Sporting News college All-America second team (1992).
PRO STATISTICS: 1993—Returned one kickoff for 12 yards and recovered one fumble.
STATISTICAL PLATEAUS: 100-yard rushing games: 1993 (4).

		RUSHING				RECEIVING				TOTALS			
Year Team	G	Att.	Yds.	Avg.	TD	No.	Yds.	Avg.	TD	TD	2pt.	Pts.	Fum.
1993—Washington NFL	16	223	1063	4.8	3	21	186	8.9	0	3	...	18	4

Year Team	G	RUSHING				RECEIVING				TOTALS			
		Att.	Yds.	Avg.	TD	No.	Yds.	Avg.	TD	TD	2pt.	Pts.	Fum.
1994—Washington NFL	13	100	297	3.0	2	13	68	5.2	0	2	0	12	3
1995—Washington NFL	1	2	-2	-1.0	0	0	0	...	0	0	0	0	0
Pro totals (3 years)	30	325	1358	4.2	5	34	254	7.5	0	5	0	30	7

BROOKS, ROBERT — WR/KR — PACKERS

PERSONAL: Born June 23, 1970, in Greenwood, S.C. ... 6-0/180. ... Full name: Robert Darren Brooks.
HIGH SCHOOL: Greenwood (S.C.).
COLLEGE: South Carolina (bachelor of science degree in retailing).
TRANSACTIONS/CAREER NOTES: Selected by Green Bay Packers in third round (62nd pick overall) of 1992 NFL draft. ... Signed by Packers (July 22, 1992). ... Granted free agency (February 17, 1995). ... Re-signed by Packers (June 1, 1995).
CHAMPIONSHIP GAME EXPERIENCE: Played in NFC championship game (1995 season).
RECORDS: Shares NFL record for longest pass reception (from Brett Favre)—99 yards, touchdown (September 11, 1995, at Chicago).
PRO STATISTICS: 1993—Fumbled once and recovered one fumble. 1994—Fumbled four times and recovered one fumble.
STATISTICAL PLATEAUS: 100-yard receiving games: 1994 (1), 1995 (9). Total: 10.

Year Team	G	RUSHING				RECEIVING				PUNT RETURNS				KICKOFF RETURNS				TOTALS		
		Att.	Yds.	Avg.	TD	No.	Yds.	Avg.	TD	No.	Yds.	Avg.	TD	No.	Yds.	Avg.	TD	TD	2pt.	Pts.
1992—Green Bay NFL	16	2	14	7.0	0	12	126	10.5	1	11	102	9.3	0	18	338	18.8	0	1	...	6
1993—Green Bay NFL	14	3	17	5.7	0	20	180	9.0	0	16	135	8.4	0	23	611	*26.6	†1	1	...	6
1994—Green Bay NFL	16	1	0	0.0	0	58	648	11.2	4	40	352	8.8	1	9	260	28.9	1	6	0	36
1995—Green Bay NFL	16	4	21	5.3	0	102	1497	14.7	13	0	0	...	0	1	28	28.0	0	13	0	78
Pro totals (4 years)	62	10	52	5.2	0	192	2451	12.8	18	67	589	8.8	1	51	1237	24.3	2	21	0	126

BROSTEK, BERN — C — RAMS

PERSONAL: Born September 11, 1966, in Honolulu. ... 6-3/300. ... Name pronounced BRAH-stek.
HIGH SCHOOL: Iolani (Honolulu).
COLLEGE: Washington.
TRANSACTIONS/CAREER NOTES: Selected by Los Angeles Rams in first round (23rd pick overall) of 1990 NFL draft. ... Signed by Rams (July 29, 1990). ... Rams franchise moved to St. Louis (April 12, 1995).
PLAYING EXPERIENCE: Los Angeles Rams NFL, 1990-1994; St. Louis NFL, 1995. ... Games: 1990 (16), 1991 (14), 1992 (16), 1993 (16), 1994 (10), 1995 (16). Total: 88.
HONORS: Named center on THE SPORTING NEWS college All-America first team (1989).
PRO STATISTICS: 1992—Recovered one fumble. 1993—Fumbled once.

BROUGHTON, WILLIE — DT — SAINTS

PERSONAL: Born September 9, 1964, in Fort Pierce, Fla. ... 6-5/285. ... Full name: Willie Lee Broughton. ... Brother of Dock Luckie, nose tackle, Winnipeg Blue Bombers of CFL (1981).
HIGH SCHOOL: Central (Fort Pierce, Fla.).
COLLEGE: Miami (Fla.).
TRANSACTIONS/CAREER NOTES: Selected by Orlando Renegades in 1985 USFL territorial draft. ... Selected by Indianapolis Colts in fourth round (88th pick overall) of 1985 NFL draft. ... Signed by Colts (August 9, 1985). ... On injured reserve with knee injury (August 5, 1987-entire season). ... Crossed picket line during players strike (September 29, 1987). ... Released by Colts (August 24, 1988). ... Signed by Dallas Cowboys (July 18, 1989). ... On injured reserve with back injury (October 8, 1990-remainder of season). ... Granted unconditional free agency (February 1-April 1, 1991). ... Re-signed by Cowboys for 1991 season. ... Released by Cowboys (August 20, 1991). ... Signed by Los Angeles Raiders (March 1992). ... Released by Raiders (August 30, 1993). ... Re-signed by Raiders (August 31, 1993). ... Released by Raiders after 1993 season. ... Signed by Miami Dolphins (November 23, 1994). ... Released by Dolphins (December 31, 1994). ... Signed by Raiders for 1995 season. ... Traded by Raiders to New Orleans Saints for seventh-round pick (DE Sedric Clark) in 1996 draft (August 27, 1995).
PRO STATISTICS: 1986—Recovered one fumble.

Year Team	G	SACKS
1985—Indianapolis NFL	15	1.0
1986—Indianapolis NFL	15	1.0
1987—Indianapolis NFL	Did not play.	
1988—	Did not play.	
1989—Dallas NFL	16	3.0
1990—Dallas NFL	4	0.0
1991—Dallas NFL	Did not play.	
1992—Los Angeles Raiders NFL	16	1.0
1993—Los Angeles Raiders NFL	15	1.0
1994—Miami	Did not play.	
1995—New Orleans NFL	16	2.0
Pro totals (7 years)	97	9.0

BROUSSARD, STEVE — RB — SEAHAWKS

PERSONAL: Born February 22, 1967, in Los Angeles. ... 5-7/201. ... Name pronounced BREW-sard.
HIGH SCHOOL: Manual Arts (Los Angeles).
COLLEGE: Washington State.
TRANSACTIONS/CAREER NOTES: Selected by Atlanta Falcons in first round (20th pick overall) of 1990 NFL draft. ... Signed by Falcons (July 12, 1990). ... Released by Falcons (February 17, 1994). ... Signed by Cincinnati Bengals (April 8, 1994). ... On injured reserve with concussion (December 21, 1994-remainder of season). ... Released by Bengals (May 3, 1995). ... Signed by Seattle Seahawks (June 13, 1995).
HONORS: Named running back on THE SPORTING NEWS college All-America second team (1988).
PRO STATISTICS: 1992—Recovered one fumble for minus two yards. 1994—Attempted one pass without a completion and recovered one fumble. 1995—Recovered one fumble.

B

STATISTICAL PLATEAUS: 100-yard rushing games: 1991 (2), 1993 (1). Total: 3.

Year Team	G	RUSHING				RECEIVING				KICKOFF RETURNS				TOTALS			
		Att.	Yds.	Avg.	TD	No.	Yds.	Avg.	TD	No.	Yds.	Avg.	TD	TD	2pt.	Pts.	Fum.
1990—Atlanta NFL	13	126	454	3.6	4	24	160	6.7	0	3	45	15.0	0	4	...	24	6
1991—Atlanta NFL	14	99	449	4.5	4	12	120	10.0	1	0	0	...	0	5	...	30	1
1992—Atlanta NFL	15	84	363	4.3	1	11	96	8.7	1	0	0	...	0	2	...	12	3
1993—Atlanta NFL	8	39	206	5.3	1	1	4	4.0	0	0	0	...	0	1	...	6	0
1994—Cincinnati NFL	13	94	403	4.3	2	34	218	6.4	0	7	115	16.4	0	2	1	14	5
1995—Seattle NFL	15	46	222	4.8	1	10	94	9.4	0	43	1064	24.7	0	1	0	6	4
Pro totals (6 years)	78	488	2097	4.3	13	92	692	7.5	2	53	1224	23.1	0	15	1	92	19

BROWN, ANTHONY · OT/G · BENGALS

PERSONAL: Born November 6, 1972, in Okinawa, Japan. ... 6-5/310.
HIGH SCHOOL: American (Wurzburg, Germany).
COLLEGE: Utah.
TRANSACTIONS/CAREER NOTES: Signed as non-drafted free agent by Cincinnati Bengals (April 26, 1995).
PLAYING EXPERIENCE: Cincinnati NFL, 1995. ... Games: 1995 (7).

B

BROWN, CHAD · DE · CARDINALS

PERSONAL: Born July 9, 1971, in Thomasville, Ga. ... 6-7/265. ... Full name: Chadrick Chico Brown.
HIGH SCHOOL: Thomasville (Ga.).
COLLEGE: Mississippi.
TRANSACTIONS/CAREER NOTES: Selected by Phoenix Cardinals in eighth round (199th pick overall) of 1993 NFL draft. ... Signed by Cardinals (July 15, 1993). ... Cardinals franchise renamed Arizona Cardinals for 1994 season. ... Released by Cardinals (November 29, 1995). ... Granted free agency (February 16, 1996). ... Re-signed by Cardinals (March 22, 1996).
PLAYING EXPERIENCE: Phoenix NFL, 1993; Arizona NFL, 1994 and 1995. ... Games: 1993 (5), 1994 (8), 1995 (5). Total: 18.
PRO STATISTICS: 1995—Credited with ½ sack.

BROWN, CHAD · LB · STEELERS

PERSONAL: Born July 12, 1970, in Pasadena, Calif. ... 6-2/240. ... Full name: Chadwick Everett Brown.
HIGH SCHOOL: John Muir (Pasadena, Calif.).
COLLEGE: Colorado (degree in marketing, 1992).
TRANSACTIONS/CAREER NOTES: Selected by Pittsburgh Steelers in second round (44th pick overall) of 1993 NFL draft. ... Signed by Steelers (July 26, 1993).
CHAMPIONSHIP GAME EXPERIENCE: Played in AFC championship game (1994 and 1995 seasons). ... Played in Super Bowl XXX (1995 season).

Year Team	G	INTERCEPTIONS				SACKS
		No.	Yds.	Avg.	TD	No.
1993—Pittsburgh NFL	16	0	0	...	0	3.0
1994—Pittsburgh NFL	16	1	9	9.0	0	8.5
1995—Pittsburgh NFL	10	0	0	...	0	5.5
Pro totals (3 years)	42	1	9	9.0	0	17.0

BROWN, CORWIN · S · PATRIOTS

PERSONAL: Born April 25, 1970, in Chicago. ... 6-1/200. ... Full name: Corwin Alan Brown.
HIGH SCHOOL: Percy L. Julian (Chicago).
COLLEGE: Michigan.
TRANSACTIONS/CAREER NOTES: Selected by New England Patriots in fourth round (110th pick overall) of 1993 NFL draft. ... Signed by Patriots (July 16, 1993). ... Granted free agency (February 16, 1996). ... Re-signed by Patriots (February 27, 1996).
PLAYING EXPERIENCE: New England NFL, 1993-1995. ... Games: 1993 (15), 1994 (16), 1995 (16). Total: 47.
PRO STATISTICS: 1993—Recovered one fumble. 1995—Recovered one fumble.

BROWN, DAVE · QB · GIANTS

PERSONAL: Born February 25, 1970, in Summit, N.J. ... 6-5/223. ... Full name: David Michael Brown.
HIGH SCHOOL: Westfield (N.J.).
COLLEGE: Duke.
TRANSACTIONS/CAREER NOTES: Selected by New York Giants in first round of 1992 NFL supplemental draft. ... Signed by Giants (August 12, 1992). ... On injured reserve with thumb injury (December 18, 1992-remainder of season). ... Granted unconditional free agency (February 16, 1996). ... Re-signed by Giants (May 3, 1996).
PRO STATISTICS: 1994—Punted twice for 57 yards, fumbled 11 times and recovered four fumbles for minus 15 yards. 1995—Punted once for 15 yards, fumbled 10 times and recovered two fumbles for minus eight yards.
MISCELLANEOUS: Regular-season record as starting NFL quarterback: 14-17 (.452).

Year Team	G	PASSING								RUSHING				TOTALS		
		Att.	Cmp.	Pct.	Yds.	TD	Int.	Avg.	Rat.	Att.	Yds.	Avg.	TD	TD	2pt.	Pts.
1992—New York Giants NFL	2	7	4	57.1	21	0	0	3.00	62.2	2	-1	-0.5	0	0	...	0
1993—New York Giants NFL	1	0	0	...	0	0	0	...	...	3	-4	-1.3	0	0	...	0
1994—New York Giants NFL	15	350	201	57.4	2536	12	16	7.25	72.5	60	196	3.3	2	2	0	12

Year Team	G	PASSING Att	Cmp	Pct	Yds	TD	Int	Avg	Rat	RUSHING Att	Yds	Avg	TD	TOTALS TD	2pt	Pts
1995—New York Giants NFL	16	456	254	55.7	2814	11	10	6.17	73.1	45	228	5.1	4	4	0	24
Pro totals (4 years)	34	813	455	56.0	5371	23	26	6.61	72.8	110	419	3.8	6	6	0	36

BROWN, DENNIS — DE

PERSONAL: Born November 6, 1967, in Los Angeles. ... 6-4/290. ... Full name: Dennis Trammel Brown.
HIGH SCHOOL: Long Beach (Calif.) Jordan.
COLLEGE: Washington.
TRANSACTIONS/CAREER NOTES: Selected by San Francisco 49ers in second round (47th pick overall) of 1990 NFL draft. ... Signed by 49ers (July 27, 1990). ... Granted free agency (March 1, 1993). ... Re-signed by 49ers (May 10, 1993). ... Released by 49ers (April 2, 1996).
CHAMPIONSHIP GAME EXPERIENCE: Played in NFC championship game (1990 and 1992-1994 seasons). ... Member of Super Bowl championship team (1994 season).
PRO STATISTICS: 1995—Recovered two fumbles.

Year Team	G	INTERCEPTIONS No.	Yds.	Avg.	TD	SACKS No.
1990—San Francisco NFL	15	0	0	...	0	6.0
1991—San Francisco NFL	16	0	0	...	0	3.0
1992—San Francisco NFL	16	1	0	0.0	0	3.5
1993—San Francisco NFL	16	0	0	...	0	5.5
1994—San Francisco NFL	16	1	0	0.0	0	3.0
1995—San Francisco NFL	16	0	0	...	0	1.5
Pro totals (6 years)	95	2	0	0.0	0	22.5

BROWN, DEREK — RB — SAINTS

PERSONAL: Born April 15, 1971, in Banning, Calif. ... 5-9/205. ... Full name: Derek Darnell Brown.
HIGH SCHOOL: Servite (Anaheim, Calif.).
COLLEGE: Nebraska.
TRANSACTIONS/CAREER NOTES: Selected after junior season by New Orleans Saints in fourth round (109th pick overall) of 1993 NFL draft. ... Signed by Saints (June 2, 1993). ... Granted free agency (February 16, 1996).
PRO STATISTICS: 1994—Recovered two fumbles.
STATISTICAL PLATEAUS: 100-yard rushing games: 1993 (1).

Year Team	G	RUSHING Att	Yds.	Avg.	TD	RECEIVING No.	Yds.	Avg.	TD	KICKOFF RETURNS No.	Yds.	Avg.	TD	TOTALS TD	2pt.	Pts.	Fum.
1993—New Orleans NFL	13	180	705	3.9	2	21	170	8.1	1	3	58	19.3	0	3	...	18	1
1994—New Orleans NFL	16	146	489	3.4	3	44	428	9.7	1	1	3	3.0	0	4	0	24	4
1995—New Orleans NFL	16	49	159	3.2	1	35	266	7.6	1	0	0	...	0	2	0	12	0
Pro totals (3 years)	45	375	1353	3.6	6	100	864	8.7	3	4	61	15.3	0	9	0	54	5

BROWN, DEREK — TE — JAGUARS

PERSONAL: Born March 31, 1970, in Fairfax, Va. ... 6-6/262. ... Full name: Derek Vernon Brown.
HIGH SCHOOL: Merritt Island (Fla.).
COLLEGE: Notre Dame.
TRANSACTIONS/CAREER NOTES: Selected by New York Giants in first round (14th pick overall) of 1992 NFL draft. ... Signed by Giants (July 29, 1992). ... Selected by Jacksonville Jaguars from Giants in NFL expansion draft (February 15, 1995). ... On injured reserve with rib injury (October 10, 1995-remainder of season).
PRO STATISTICS: 1994—Returned one kickoff for one yard and recovered one fumble.

Year Team	G	RECEIVING No.	Yds.	Avg.	TD	TOTALS TD	2pt.	Pts.	Fum.
1992—New York Giants NFL	16	4	31	7.8	0	0	...	0	0
1993—New York Giants NFL	16	7	56	8.0	0	0	...	0	0
1994—New York Giants NFL	13	0	0	...	0	0	0	0	0
1995—Jacksonville NFL				Did not play—injured.					
Pro totals (3 years)	45	11	87	7.9	0	0	0	0	0

BROWN, GARY — OT/G — PACKERS

PERSONAL: Born June 25, 1971, in Amityville, N.Y. ... 6-4/315. ... Full name: Gary Lee Brown.
HIGH SCHOOL: Brentwood (N.Y.).
COLLEGE: Georgia Tech.
TRANSACTIONS/CAREER NOTES: Selected by Pittsburgh Steelers in fifth round (148th pick overall) of 1994 NFL draft. ... Signed by Steelers (June 6, 1994). ... Claimed on waivers by Green Bay Packers (August 30, 1994).
PLAYING EXPERIENCE: Green Bay NFL, 1994 and 1995. ... Games: 1994 (1), 1995 (16). Total: 17.
CHAMPIONSHIP GAME EXPERIENCE: Played in NFC championship game (1995 season).

BROWN, GARY — RB

PERSONAL: Born July 1, 1969, in Williamsport, Pa. ... 5-11/233. ... Full name: Gary Leroy Brown.
HIGH SCHOOL: Williamsport (Pa.) Area.
COLLEGE: Penn State.

TRANSACTIONS/CAREER NOTES: Selected by Houston Oilers in eighth round (214th pick overall) of 1991 NFL draft. ... Signed by Oilers (July 15, 1991). ... Granted free agency (February 17, 1994). ... Re-signed by Oilers (July 15, 1994). ... Released by Oilers (April 19, 1996).
PRO STATISTICS: 1992—Recovered one fumble. 1993—Recovered two fumbles for four yards. 1995—Recovered one fumble.
STATISTICAL PLATEAUS: 100-yard rushing games: 1993 (5), 1995 (1). Total: 6.

Year Team	G	RUSHING				RECEIVING				KICKOFF RETURNS				TOTALS			
		Att.	Yds.	Avg.	TD	No.	Yds.	Avg.	TD	No.	Yds.	Avg.	TD	TD	2pt.	Pts.	Fum.
1991—Houston NFL	11	8	85	10.6	1	2	1	.5	0	3	30	10.0	0	1	...	6	0
1992—Houston NFL	16	19	87	4.6	1	1	5	5.0	0	1	15	15.0	0	1	...	6	
01993—Houston NFL	16	195	1002	5.1	6	21	240	11.4	2	2	29	14.5	0	8	...	48	4
1994—Houston NFL	12	169	648	3.8	4	18	194	10.8	1	0	0	...	0	5	0	30	6
1995—Houston NFL	9	86	293	3.4	0	6	16	2.7	0	0	0	...	0	0	0	0	2
Pro totals (5 years)	64	477	2115	4.4	12	48	456	9.5	3	6	74	12.3	0	15	0	90	12

BROWN, GILBERT — DT — PACKERS

B

PERSONAL: Born February 22, 1971, in Farmington, Mich. ... 6-2/325. ... Full name: Gilbert Jesse Brown.
HIGH SCHOOL: Mackenzie (Detroit).
COLLEGE: Kansas.
TRANSACTIONS/CAREER NOTES: Selected by Minnesota Vikings in third round (79th pick overall) of 1993 NFL draft. ... Signed by Vikings (July 16, 1993). ... Claimed on waivers by Green Bay Packers (August 31, 1993). ... On injured reserve with knee injury (December 6, 1994-remainder of season).
CHAMPIONSHIP GAME EXPERIENCE: Played in NFC championship game (1995 season).

Year Team	G	SACKS
1993—Green Bay NFL	2	0.0
1994—Green Bay NFL	13	3.0
1995—Green Bay NFL	13	0.0
Pro totals (3 years)	28	3.0

BROWN, JAMES — OT — DOLPHINS

PERSONAL: Born January 3, 1970, in Philadelphia. ... 6-6/329. ... Full name: James Lamont Brown.
HIGH SCHOOL: Mastbaum Area Vo-Tech (Philadelphia).
COLLEGE: Virginia State.
TRANSACTIONS/CAREER NOTES: Selected by Dallas Cowboys in third round (82nd pick overall) of 1992 NFL draft. ... Signed by Cowboys (July 15, 1992). ... Released by Cowboys (August 17, 1992). ... Signed by Indianapolis Colts (August 19, 1992). ... Released by Colts (August 31, 1992). ... Signed by New York Jets to practice squad (September 2, 1992). ... Granted free agency after 1992 season. ... Re-signed by Jets (1993). ... Traded by Jets to Miami Dolphins for fifth-round pick in 1997 draft (March 4, 1996).
PLAYING EXPERIENCE: New York Jets NFL, 1993-1995. ... Games: 1993 (14), 1994 (16), 1995 (14). Total: 44.
PRO STATISTICS: 1994—Recovered one fumble.

BROWN, JAMIE — OT — BRONCOS

PERSONAL: Born April 24, 1972, in Miami. ... 6-8/320.
HIGH SCHOOL: Miami Killian.
COLLEGE: Florida A&M.
TRANSACTIONS/CAREER NOTES: Selected by Denver Broncos in fourth round (121st pick overall) of 1995 NFL draft. ... Signed by Broncos (May 25, 1995). ... On injured reserve with foot injury (November 29, 1995-remainder of season).
PLAYING EXPERIENCE: Denver NFL, 1995. ... Games: 1995 (6).

BROWN, J.B. — CB — DOLPHINS

PERSONAL: Born January 5, 1967, in Washington, D.C. ... 6-0/191. ... Full name: James Harold Brown.
HIGH SCHOOL: DeMatha Catholic (Hyattsville, Md.).
COLLEGE: Maryland.
TRANSACTIONS/CAREER NOTES: Selected by Miami Dolphins in 12th round (315th pick overall) of 1989 NFL draft. ... Signed by Dolphins (July 16, 1989). ... Granted free agency (February 1, 1991). ... Re-signed by Dolphins (August 29, 1991). ... Activated (September 7, 1991). ... Granted free agency (March 1, 1993). ... Re-signed by Dolphins (July 21, 1993).
CHAMPIONSHIP GAME EXPERIENCE: Played in AFC championship game (1992 season).
PRO STATISTICS: 1990—Credited with one sack. 1992—Recovered one fumble. 1993—Fumbled once. 1995—Fumbled once and recovered two fumbles.

Year Team	G	INTERCEPTIONS			
		No.	Yds.	Avg.	TD
1989—Miami NFL	16	0	0	...	0
1990—Miami NFL	16	0	0	...	0
1991—Miami NFL	15	1	0	0.0	0
1992—Miami NFL	16	4	119	29.8	1
1993—Miami NFL	16	5	43	8.6	0
1994—Miami NFL	16	3	82	27.3	0
1995—Miami NFL	13	2	20	10.0	0
Pro totals (7 years)	108	15	264	17.6	1

BROWN, KEN — LB — BRONCOS

PERSONAL: Born May 5, 1971, in Wiesbaden, Germany. ... 6-1/235. ... Full name: Kenneth Anderson Brown.

HIGH SCHOOL: Monacan (Richmond, Va.), then Fork Union (Va.) Military Academy.
COLLEGE: Virginia Tech.
TRANSACTIONS/CAREER NOTES: Selected by Denver Broncos in fourth round (124th pick overall) of 1995 NFL draft. ... Signed by Broncos for 1995 season.
PLAYING EXPERIENCE: Denver NFL, 1995. ... Games: 1995 (2).

BROWN, LANCE — DB — CARDINALS

PERSONAL: Born February 2, 1972, in Jacksonville. ... 6-0/200.
HIGH SCHOOL: Terry Parker (Jacksonville).
COLLEGE: Indiana.
TRANSACTIONS/CAREER NOTES: Selected by Pittsburgh Steelers in fifth round (161st pick overall) of 1995 NFL draft. ... Signed by Steelers (July 18, 1995). ... Claimed on waivers by Arizona Cardinals (September 25, 1995).
PLAYING EXPERIENCE: Arizona NFL, 1995. ... Games: 1995 (11).
PRO STATISTICS: 1995—Recovered one fumble.

BROWN, LARRY — CB — RAIDERS

PERSONAL: Born November 30, 1969, in Miami. ... 5-11/186.
HIGH SCHOOL: Los Angeles (Calif.).
JUNIOR COLLEGE: Southwestern College (Calif.).
COLLEGE: Texas Christian (degree in criminal justice).
TRANSACTIONS/CAREER NOTES: Selected by Dallas Cowboys in 12th round (320th pick overall) of 1991 NFL draft. ... Granted unconditional free agency (February 16, 1996). ... Signed by Oakland Raiders (February 20, 1996).
CHAMPIONSHIP GAME EXPERIENCE: Played in NFC championship game (1992-1995 seasons). ... Member of Super Bowl championship team (1992, 1993 and 1995 seasons).
HONORS: Named Most Valuable Player of Super Bowl XXX (1995 season).
POSTSEASON RECORDS: Holds Super Bowl career and single-game records for most interception return yards—77 (January 28, 1996). ... Shares Super Bowl career record for most interceptions—3.
PRO STATISTICS: 1991—Recovered one fumble. 1992—Recovered one fumble.

| | | | INTERCEPTIONS | | | |
Year Team	G	No.	Yds.	Avg.	TD
1991—Dallas NFL	16	2	31	15.5	0
1992—Dallas NFL	16	1	30	30.0	0
1993—Dallas NFL	16	0	0	...	0
1994—Dallas NFL	15	4	21	5.3	0
1995—Dallas NFL	16	6	124	20.7	†2
Pro totals (5 years)	79	13	206	15.9	2

BROWN, LOMAS — OT — CARDINALS

PERSONAL: Born March 30, 1963, in Miami. ... 6-4/275. ... Cousin of Joe Taylor, defensive back, Chicago Bears (1967-1974); cousin of Guy McIntyre, guard, San Francisco 49ers and Green Bay Packers (1984-1994); and cousin of Eric Curry, defensive end, Tampa Bay Buccaneers.
HIGH SCHOOL: Miami Springs Senior.
COLLEGE: Florida.
TRANSACTIONS/CAREER NOTES: Selected by Orlando Renegades in second round (18th pick overall) of 1985 USFL draft. ... Selected by Detroit Lions in first round (sixth pick overall) of 1985 NFL draft. ... Signed by Lions (August 9, 1985). ... Designated by Lions as franchise player (February 25, 1993). ... Granted roster exemption (September 1-3, 1993). ... Designated by Lions as franchise player (February 15, 1995). ... Re-signed by Lions (September 7, 1995). ... Granted unconditional free agency (February 16, 1996). ... Signed by Arizona Cardinals (February 28, 1996).
PLAYING EXPERIENCE: Detroit NFL, 1985-1995. ... Games: 1985 (16), 1986 (16), 1987 (11), 1988 (16), 1989 (16), 1990 (16), 1991 (15), 1992 (16), 1993 (11), 1994 (16), 1995 (15). Total: 164.
CHAMPIONSHIP GAME EXPERIENCE: Played in NFC championship game (1991 season).
HONORS: Named tackle on THE SPORTING NEWS college All-America first team (1984). ... Played in Pro Bowl (1990-1995 seasons). ... Named offensive tackle on THE SPORTING NEWS NFL All-Pro team (1992).
PRO STATISTICS: 1989—Rushed once for three yards and recovered one fumble. 1991—Recovered one fumble.

BROWN, MONTY — LB — PATRIOTS

PERSONAL: Born April 13, 1970, in Bridgeport, Mich. ... 6-0/233.
HIGH SCHOOL: Bridgeport (Mich.).
COLLEGE: Ferris State (Mich.).
TRANSACTIONS/CAREER NOTES: Signed as non-drafted free agent by Buffalo Bills (May 10, 1993). ... On physically unable to perform list (July 16, 1993). ... Activated (July 23, 1993). ... On injured reserve with quad injury (November 30, 1994-remainder of season). ... Granted free agency (February 16, 1996). ... Tendered offer sheet by New England Patriots (April 16, 1996). ... Bills declined to match offer (April 17, 1996).
PLAYING EXPERIENCE: Buffalo NFL, 1993-1995. ... Games: 1993 (13), 1994 (3), 1995 (16). Total: 32.
CHAMPIONSHIP GAME EXPERIENCE: Played in AFC championship game (1993 season). ... Played in Super Bowl XXVIII (1993 season).

BROWN, ORLANDO — OT — RAVENS

PERSONAL: Born December 12, 1970, in Washington, D.C. ... 6-7/340. ... Full name: Orlando Claude Brown.
HIGH SCHOOL: Howard D. Woodson (Washington, D.C.).

COLLEGE: Central State (Ohio), then South Carolina State.
TRANSACTIONS/CAREER NOTES: Signed as non-drafted free agent by Cleveland Browns (May 13, 1993). ... On injured reserve with shoulder injury (August 30, 1993-entire season). ... Browns franchise moved to Baltimore and renamed Ravens for 1996 season (March 11, 1996).
PLAYING EXPERIENCE: Cleveland NFL, 1994 and 1995. ... Games: 1994 (14), 1995 (16). Total: 30.
PRO STATISTICS: 1995—Recovered one fumble.

BROWN, RAY   OT   49ERS

PERSONAL: Born December 12, 1962, in West Memphis, Ark. ... 6-5/315. ... Full name: Leonard Ray Brown Jr.
HIGH SCHOOL: Marion (Ark.).
COLLEGE: Memphis State, then Arizona State, then Arkansas State.
TRANSACTIONS/CAREER NOTES: Selected by St. Louis Cardinals in eighth round (201st pick overall) of 1986 NFL draft. ... Signed by Cardinals (July 14, 1986). ... On injured reserve with knee injury (October 17-November 21, 1986). ... Released by Cardinals (September 7, 1987). ... Re-signed by Cardinals as replacement player (September 25, 1987). ... On injured reserve with finger injury (November 12-December 12, 1987). ... Cardinals franchise moved to Phoenix (March 15, 1988). ... Granted unconditional free agency (February 1, 1989). ... Signed by Washington Redskins (March 10, 1989). ... On injured reserve with knee injury (September 5-November 4, 1989). ... On injured reserve with knee injury (September 4, 1990-January 4, 1991). ... Granted unconditional free agency (February 1-April 1, 1991). ... Re-signed by Redskins for 1991 season. ... On injured reserve with elbow injury (August 27, 1991-entire season). ... Granted unconditional free agency (February 16, 1996). ... Signed by San Francisco 49ers (February 25, 1996).
PLAYING EXPERIENCE: St. Louis NFL, 1986 and 1987; Phoenix NFL, 1988; Washington NFL, 1989, 1992-1995. ... Games: 1986 (11), 1987 (7), 1988 (15), 1989 (7), 1992 (16), 1993 (16), 1994 (16), 1995 (16). Total: 104.

BROWN, RICHARD   LB

PERSONAL: Born September 21, 1965, in Western Samoa. ... 6-3/240. ... Full name: Richard Solomon Brown.
HIGH SCHOOL: Westminster (Calif.).
COLLEGE: San Diego State.
TRANSACTIONS/CAREER NOTES: Signed as non-drafted free agent by Los Angeles Rams (May 14, 1987). ... On injured reserve with hamstring injury (August 31-November 3, 1987). ... Released by Rams (August 30, 1988). ... Re-signed by Rams (March 10, 1989). ... Released by Rams (September 4, 1989). ... Re-signed by Rams (September 5, 1989). ... Released by Rams (December 15, 1989). ... Signed by San Diego Chargers (May 18, 1990). ... On injured reserve with hamstring injury (November 21, 1990-remainder of season). ... Granted unconditional free agency (February 1, 1991). ... Signed by Cleveland Browns (March 29, 1991). ... On injured reserve with knee injury (November 17, 1992-remainder of season). ... Granted unconditional free agency (March 1, 1993). ... Re-signed by Browns (1993). ... On injured reserve with knee injury (September 2, 1993-entire season). ... Released by Browns (August 16, 1994). ... Signed by Minnesota Vikings (December 5, 1994). ... Granted unconditional free agency (February 17, 1995). ... Re-signed by Vikings (March 9, 1995). ... Granted unconditional free agency (February 16, 1996).
PLAYING EXPERIENCE: Los Angeles Rams NFL, 1987 and 1989; San Diego NFL, 1990; Cleveland NFL, 1991 and 1992; Minnesota NFL, 1994 and 1995. ... Games: 1987 (8), 1989 (13), 1990 (11), 1991 (16), 1992 (10), 1994 (3), 1995 (16). Total: 77.
PRO STATISTICS: 1989—Recovered two fumbles. 1990—Recovered one fumble. 1991—Intercepted one pass for 19 yards, credited with one sack and recovered one fumble. 1992—Credited with one sack. 1994—Recovered one fumble.

BROWN, RUBEN   OT   BILLS

PERSONAL: Born February 13, 1972, in Lynchburg, Va. ... 6-3/304. ... Full name: Ruben Pernell Brown.
HIGH SCHOOL: E.C. Glass (Lynchburg, Va.).
COLLEGE: Pittsburgh.
TRANSACTIONS/CAREER NOTES: Selected by Buffalo Bills in first round (14th pick overall) of 1995 NFL draft. ... Signed by Bills (June 20, 1995).
PLAYING EXPERIENCE: Buffalo NFL, 1995. ... Games: 1995 (16).
HONORS: Named offensive lineman on THE SPORTING NEWS college All-America second team (1994).

BROWN, TIM   WR   RAIDERS

PERSONAL: Born July 22, 1966, in Dallas. ... 6-0/195. ... Full name: Timothy Donell Brown.
HIGH SCHOOL: Woodrow Wilson (Dallas).
COLLEGE: Notre Dame (degree in sociology).
TRANSACTIONS/CAREER NOTES: Selected by Los Angeles Raiders in first round (sixth pick overall) of 1988 NFL draft. ... Signed by Raiders (July 14, 1988). ... On injured reserve with knee injury (September 12, 1989-remainder of season). ... Granted free agency (February 1, 1992). ... Re-signed by Raiders (August 13, 1992). ... Designated by Raiders as transition player (February 25, 1993). ... Tendered offer sheet by Denver Broncos (March 11, 1994). ... Offer matched by Raiders (March 16, 1994). ... Raiders franchise moved to Oakland (July 21, 1995).
CHAMPIONSHIP GAME EXPERIENCE: Played in AFC championship game (1990 season).
HONORS: Named wide receiver on THE SPORTING NEWS college All-America first team (1986 and 1987). ... Heisman Trophy winner (1987). ... Named College Football Player of the Year by THE SPORTING NEWS (1987). ... Named kick returner on THE SPORTING NEWS NFL All-Pro team (1988). ... Played in Pro Bowl (1988, 1991, 1993-1995 seasons).
RECORDS: Holds NFL rookie-season record for most combined yards gained—2,317 (1988).
PRO STATISTICS: 1988—Fumbled five times and recovered one fumbled for seven yards. 1989—Fumbled once. 1990—Fumbled three times. 1991—Fumbled once. 1992—Fumbled six times and recovered one fumble. 1993—Fumbled once. 1994—Fumbled three times. 1995—Recovered one fumble for three yards.
STATISTICAL PLATEAUS: 100-yard receiving games: 1988 (1), 1991 (1), 1992 (1), 1993 (4), 1994 (4), 1995 (6). Total: 17.

		RUSHING				RECEIVING				PUNT RETURNS				KICKOFF RETURNS				TOTALS		
Year	Team	G	Att.	Yds.	Avg.	TD	No.	Yds.	Avg.	TD	No.	Yds.	Avg.	TD	No.	Yds.	Avg.	TD	TD	2pt.	Pts.
1988—L.A. Raiders NFL		16	14	50	3.6	1	43	725	16.9	5	49	444	9.1	0	*41	*1098	*26.8	†1	7	...	42
1989—L.A. Raiders NFL		1	0	0	...	0	1	8	8.0	0	4	43	10.8	0	3	63	21.0	0	0	...	0
1990—LA Raiders NFL		16	0	0	...	0	18	265	14.7	3	34	295	8.7	0	0	0	...	0	3	...	18
1991—LA Raiders NFL		16	5	16	3.2	0	36	554	15.4	5	29	330	11.4	1	1	29	29.0	0	6	...	36
1992—LA Raiders NFL		15	3	-4	-1.3	0	49	693	14.1	7	37	383	10.4	0	2	14	7.0	0	7	...	42

Year Team	G	RUSHING				RECEIVING				PUNT RETURNS				KICKOFF RETURNS				TOTALS		
		Att.	Yds.	Avg.	TD	No.	Yds.	Avg.	TD	No.	Yds.	Avg.	TD	No.	Yds.	Avg.	TD	TD	2pt.	Pts.
1993—LA Raiders NFL	16	2	7	3.5	0	80	1180	14.8	7	40	465	11.6	1	0	0	...	0	8	...	48
1994—LA Raiders NFL	16	0	0	...	0	89	1309	14.7	9	40	*487	12.2	0	0	0	...	0	9	0	54
1995—Oakland NFL	16	0	0	...	0	89	1342	15.1	10	36	364	10.1	0	0	0	...	0	10	0	60
Pro totals (8 years)	112	24	69	2.9	1	405	6076	15.0	46	269	2811	10.5	2	47	1204	25.6	1	50	0	300

BROWN, TONY — CB

PERSONAL: Born May 15, 1970, in Bangkok, Thailand. ... 5-9/183. ... Full name: Anthony Lamar Brown.
HIGH SCHOOL: John F. Kennedy (Granada Hills, Calif.).
COLLEGE: Fresno State.
TRANSACTIONS/CAREER NOTES: Selected by Houston Oilers in fifth round (135th pick overall) of 1992 NFL draft. ... Signed by Oilers (July 16, 1992). ... Released by Oilers (August 28, 1994). ... Signed by Seattle Seahawks (September 20, 1994). ... Granted free agency (February 17, 1995). ... Re-signed by Seahawks (April 25, 1995). ... Granted unconditional free agency (February 16, 1996).
PLAYING EXPERIENCE: Houston NFL, 1992 and 1993; Seattle NFL, 1994 and 1995. ... Games: 1992 (12), 1993 (16), 1994 (13), 1995 (16). Total: 57.

BROWN, TROY — WR/KR — PATRIOTS

PERSONAL: Born July 2, 1971, in Blackville, S.C. ... 5-9/190. ... Full name: Troy Fitzgerald Brown.
HIGH SCHOOL: Blackville (S.C.)-Hilda.
COLLEGE: Lees-McRae College (N.C.), then Marshall.
TRANSACTIONS/CAREER NOTES: Selected by New England Patriots in eighth round (198th pick overall) of 1993 NFL draft. ... Signed by Patriots (July 16, 1993). ... On injured reserve with quadriceps injury (December 31, 1993-remainder of season). ... Released by Patriots (August 28, 1994). ... Re-signed by Patriots (October 19, 1994).
PRO STATISTICS: 1993—Recovered one fumble. 1994—Recovered two fumbles. 1995—Recovered one fumble for 75 yards and a touchdown.

Year Team	G	RECEIVING				PUNT RETURNS				KICKOFF RETURNS				TOTALS			
		No.	Yds.	Avg.	TD	No.	Yds.	Avg.	TD	No.	Yds.	Avg.	TD	TD	2pt.	Pts.	Fum.
1993—New England NFL	12	2	22	11.0	0	25	224	9.0	0	15	243	16.2	0	0	...	0	2
1994—New England NFL	9	0	0	...	0	24	202	8.4	0	1	14	14.0	0	0	0	0	2
1995—New England NFL	16	14	159	11.4	0	0	0	...	0	31	672	21.7	0	1	0	6	1
Pro totals (3 years)	37	16	181	11.3	0	49	426	8.7	0	47	929	19.8	0	1	0	6	5

BROWN, TYRONE — WR — FALCONS

PERSONAL: Born January 3, 1973, in Cincinnati. ... 5-11/164.
HIGH SCHOOL: Withrow (Cincinnati).
COLLEGE: Toledo.
TRANSACTIONS/CAREER NOTES: Signed as non-drafted free agent by Atlanta Falcons (April 24, 1995).

Year Team	G	RECEIVING				TOTALS			
		No.	Yds.	Avg.	TD	TD	2pt.	Pts.	Fum.
1995—Atlanta NFL	6	17	198	11.6	0	0	0	0	1

BROWN, VINCENT — LB

PERSONAL: Born January 9, 1965, in Atlanta. ... 6-2/245. ... Full name: Vincent Bernard Brown.
HIGH SCHOOL: Walter F. George (Atlanta).
COLLEGE: Mississippi Valley State (degree in criminal justice, 1988).
TRANSACTIONS/CAREER NOTES: Selected by New England Patriots in second round (43rd pick overall) of 1988 NFL draft. ... Signed by Patriots (July 20, 1988). ... Granted free agency (February 1, 1992). ... Re-signed by Patriots (June 10, 1992). ... On injured reserve with knee injury (December 24, 1992-remainder of season). ... Designated by Patriots as transition player (February 25, 1993). ... Released by Patriots (March 26, 1996).
PRO STATISTICS: 1989—Recovered two fumbles. 1991—Recovered one fumble. 1992—Recovered two fumbles for 25 yards and a touchdown. 1994—Recovered one fumble for five yards. 1995—Recovered one fumble.

Year Team	G	INTERCEPTIONS				SACKS
		No.	Yds.	Avg.	TD	No.
1988—New England NFL	16	0	0	...	0	0.0
1989—New England NFL	14	1	-1	-1.0	0	4.0
1990—New England NFL	16	0	0	...	0	2.5
1991—New England NFL	16	0	0	...	0	3.0
1992—New England NFL	13	1	49	49.0	1	0.5
1993—New England NFL	16	1	24	24.0	0	1.0
1994—New England NFL	16	3	22	7.3	0	1.5
1995—New England NFL	16	4	1	0.3	0	4.0
Pro totals (8 years)	123	10	95	9.5	1	16.5

BROWNLOW, DARRICK — LB — REDSKINS

PERSONAL: Born December 28, 1968, in Indianapolis. ... 6-0/243. ... Full name: Darrick Dewayne Brownlow.
HIGH SCHOOL: Cathedral (Indianapolis).
COLLEGE: Illinois (degree in speech communications).

TRANSACTIONS/CAREER NOTES: Selected by Dallas Cowboys in fifth round (132nd pick overall) of 1991 NFL draft. ... Granted unconditional free agency (February 1, 1992). ... Signed by Buffalo Bills (March 11, 1992). ... Released by Bills (August 31, 1992). ... Signed by Tampa Bay Buccaneers (September 1, 1992). ... Released by Buccaneers (August 31, 1993). ... Re-signed by Buccaneers (September 11, 1993). ... Granted free agency (February 17, 1994). ... Signed by Cowboys (July 18, 1994). ... Granted unconditional free agency (February 17, 1995). ... Signed by Washington Redskins (March 16, 1995).

PLAYING EXPERIENCE: Dallas NFL, 1991 and 1994; Tampa Bay NFL, 1992 and 1993; Washington NFL, 1995. ... Games: 1991 (16), 1992 (16), 1993 (15), 1994 (16), 1995 (16). Total: 79.

CHAMPIONSHIP GAME EXPERIENCE: Played in NFC championship game (1994 season).

HONORS: Named linebacker on THE SPORTING NEWS college All-America second team (1990).

PRO STATISTICS: 1991—Returned one punt for no yards.

BRUCE, AUNDRAY — DE — RAIDERS

PERSONAL: Born April 30, 1966, in Montgomery, Ala. ... 6-5/260. ... Uncle of Ricky Shaw, linebacker, New York Giants and Philadelphia Eagles (1988-1990).

HIGH SCHOOL: George Washington Carver (Montgomery, Ala.).

COLLEGE: Auburn.

TRANSACTIONS/CAREER NOTES: Signed by Atlanta Falcons (April 6, 1988). ... Selected officially by Falcons in first round (first pick overall) of 1988 NFL draft. ... Granted unconditional free agency (February 1, 1992). ... Signed by Los Angeles Raiders (February 14, 1992). ... Granted unconditional free agency (February 17, 1995). ... Re-signed by Oakland Raiders (September 6, 1995). ... Raiders franchise moved to Oakland (July 21, 1995).

HONORS: Named linebacker on THE SPORTING NEWS college All-America first team (1987).

PRO STATISTICS: 1989—Returned one kickoff for 15 yards. 1991—Caught one pass for 11 yards. 1993—Recovered one fumble.

| | | INTERCEPTIONS | | | | SACKS |
Year Team	G	No.	Yds.	Avg.	TD	No.
1988—Atlanta NFL	16	2	10	5.0	0	6.0
1989—Atlanta NFL	16	1	0	0.0	0	6.0
1990—Atlanta NFL	16	0	0	...	0	4.0
1991—Atlanta NFL	14	0	0	...	0	0.0
1992—Los Angeles Raiders NFL	16	0	0	...	0	3.5
1993—Los Angeles Raiders NFL	16	0	0	...	0	2.0
1994—Los Angeles Raiders NFL	16	0	0	...	0	0.0
1995—Oakland NFL	14	1	1	1.0	1	5.5
Pro totals (8 years)	124	4	11	2.8	1	27.0

BRUCE, ISAAC — WR — RAMS

PERSONAL: Born November 10, 1972, in Fort Lauderdale. ... 6-0/180. ... Full name: Isaac Isidore Bruce.

HIGH SCHOOL: Dillard (Fort Lauderdale).

COLLEGE: Memphis State.

TRANSACTIONS/CAREER NOTES: Selected by Los Angeles Rams in second round (33rd pick overall) of 1994 NFL draft. ... Signed by Rams (July 13, 1994). ... On injured reserve with sprained right knee (December 9, 1994-remainder of season). ... Rams franchise moved to St. Louis (April 12, 1995).

PRO STATISTICS: 1995—Ran 52 yards with lateral from punt return and recovered one fumble.

STATISTICAL PLATEAUS: 100-yard receiving games: 1995 (9).

| | | RUSHING | | | | RECEIVING | | | | TOTALS | | | |
Year Team	G	Att.	Yds.	Avg.	TD	No.	Yds.	Avg.	TD	TD	2pt.	Pts.	Fum.
1994—Los Angeles Rams NFL	12	1	2	2.0	0	21	272	13.0	3	3	0	18	0
1995—St. Louis NFL	16	3	17	5.7	0	119	1781	15.0	13	13	1	80	2
Pro totals (2 years)	28	4	19	4.8	0	140	2053	14.7	16	16	1	98	2

BRUENER, MARK — TE — STEELERS

PERSONAL: Born September 16, 1972, in Olympia, Wash. ... 6-4/254. ... Name pronounced BREW-ner.

HIGH SCHOOL: Aberdeen (Wash.).

COLLEGE: Washington.

TRANSACTIONS/CAREER NOTES: Selected by Pittsburgh Steelers in first round (27th pick overall) of 1995 NFL draft. ... Signed by Steelers (July 25, 1995).

CHAMPIONSHIP GAME EXPERIENCE: Played in AFC championship game (1995 season). ... Played in Super Bowl XXX (1995 season).

PRO STATISTICS: 1995—Returned two kickoffs for 19 yards.

| | | RECEIVING | | | | TOTALS | | | |
Year Team	G	No.	Yds.	Avg.	TD	TD	2pt.	Pts.	Fum.
1992—Pittsburgh NFL	16	26	238	9.2	3	3	0	18	0

BRUMFIELD, SCOTT — G — BENGALS

PERSONAL: Born August 19, 1970, in Salt Lake City. ... 6-8/320.

HIGH SCHOOL: Spanish Fork (Utah).

JUNIOR COLLEGE: Dixie College (Utah).

COLLEGE: Brigham Young.

TRANSACTIONS/CAREER NOTES: Signed as non-drafted free agent by Cincinnati Bengals (April 28, 1993). ... Released by Bengals (August 29, 1994). ... Re-signed by Bengals (November 7, 1994). ... Granted free agency (February 16, 1996). ... Re-signed by Bengals (April 26, 1996).

PLAYING EXPERIENCE: Cincinnati NFL, 1993-1995. ... Games: 1993 (16), 1994 (2), 1995 (14). Total: 32.

BRUNELL, MARK — QB — JAGUARS

PERSONAL: Born September 17, 1970, in Los Angeles. ... 6-0/217. ... Full name: Mark Allen Brunell.
HIGH SCHOOL: St. Joseph (Santa Maria, Calif.).
COLLEGE: Washington (degree in history).
TRANSACTIONS/CAREER NOTES: Selected by Green Bay Packers in fifth round (118th pick overall) of 1993 NFL draft. ... Signed by Packers (July 1, 1993). ... Traded by Packers to Jacksonville Jaguars for third-round (FB William Henderson) and fifth-round (RB Travis Jervey) picks in 1995 draft (April 21, 1995).
PRO STATISTICS: 1994—Fumbled once. 1995—Fumbled five times and recovered three fumbles.
STATISTICAL PLATEAUS: 300-yard passing games: 1995 (2).
MISCELLANEOUS: Regular-season record as NFL starting quarterback: 3-7 (.300). ... Holds Carolina Panthers all-time records for most yards passing (2,168) and most touchdown passes (14).

				PASSING							RUSHING				TOTALS		
Year Team	G	Att.	Cmp.	Pct.	Yds.	TD	Int.	Avg.	Rat.	Att.	Yds.	Avg.	TD	TD	2pt.	Pts.
1993—Green Bay NFL								Did not play.								
1994—Green Bay NFL	2	27	12	44.4	95	0	0	3.52	53.8	6	7	1.2	1	1	0	6
1995—Jacksonville NFL	13	346	201	58.1	2168	15	7	6.27	82.6	67	480	7.2	4	4	0	24
Pro totals (2 years)	15	373	213	57.1	2263	15	7	6.07	80.5	73	487	6.7	5	5	0	30

BRYANT, JUNIOR — DE — 49ERS

PERSONAL: Born January 16, 1971, in Omaha, Neb. ... 6-4/275.
HIGH SCHOOL: Creighton Prep (Omaha, Neb.).
COLLEGE: Notre Dame.
TRANSACTIONS/CAREER NOTES: Signed as non-drafted free agent by San Francisco 49ers (May 3, 1993). ... Released by 49ers (August 30, 1993). ... Re-signed by 49ers to practice squad (August 31, 1993). ... Released by 49ers (August 27, 1994). ... Re-signed by 49ers to practice squad (August 31, 1994). ... Granted free agency after 1994 season. ... Re-signed by 49ers (March 29, 1994).
PLAYING EXPERIENCE: San Francisco NFL, 1995. ... Games: 1995 (16).
PRO STATISTICS: 1995—Credited with one sack.

BUCHANAN, RAY — DB — COLTS

PERSONAL: Born September 29, 1971, in Chicago. ... 5-9/189. ... Full name: Raymond Louis Buchanan.
HIGH SCHOOL: East Proviso (Ill.).
COLLEGE: Louisville.
TRANSACTIONS/CAREER NOTES: Selected by Indianapolis Colts in third round (65th pick overall) of 1993 NFL draft. ... Signed by Colts (July 26, 1993).
CHAMPIONSHIP GAME EXPERIENCE: Played in AFC championship game (1995 season).
PRO STATISTICS: 1994—Credited with one sack and recovered one fumble. 1995—Credited with one sack, returned one kickoff for 22 yards and recovered two fumbles.

		INTERCEPTIONS				PUNT RETURNS				TOTALS			
Year Team	G	No.	Yds.	Avg.	TD	No.	Yds.	Avg.	TD	TD	2pt.	Pts.	Fum.
1993—Indianapolis NFL	16	4	45	11.3	0	0	0	...	0	0		0	0
1994—Indianapolis NFL	16	8	221	27.6	†3	0	0	...	0	3		18	0
1995—Indianapolis NFL	16	2	60	30.0	0	16	113	7.1	0	0	0	0	1
Pro totals (3 years)	48	14	326	23.3	3	16	113	7.1	0	3	0	18	1

BUCK, MIKE — QB — DOLPHINS

PERSONAL: Born April 22, 1967, in Long Island, N.Y. ... 6-3/227. ... Full name: Mike Eric Buck.
HIGH SCHOOL: Sayville (N.Y.).
COLLEGE: Maine (degree in physical education).
TRANSACTIONS/CAREER NOTES: Selected by New Orleans Saints in sixth round (156th pick overall) of 1990 NFL draft. ... Signed by Saints (July 16, 1990). ... Active for eight games (1990); did not play. ... Granted free agency (February 1, 1992). ... Re-signed by Saints (July 21, 1992). ... Granted free agency (March 1, 1993). ... Re-signed by Saints (April 23, 1993). ... Released by Saints (June 1, 1994). ... Signed by Arizona Cardinals (January 24, 1995). ... Granted unconditional free agency (February 16, 1996). ... Signed by Miami Dolphins (April 11, 1996).
PRO STATISTICS: 1995—Fumbled once and recovered one fumble.
MISCELLANEOUS: Regular-season record as starting NFL quarterback: 0-1 (.000).

				PASSING							RUSHING				TOTALS		
Year Team	G	Att.	Cmp.	Pct.	Yds.	TD	Int.	Avg.	Rat.	Att.	Yds.	Avg.	TD	TD	2pt.	Pts.
1990—New Orleans NFL								Did not play.								
1991—New Orleans NFL	2	2	1	50.0	61	0	1	30.50	56.3	0	0	...	0	0	...	0
1992—New Orleans NFL	2	4	2	50.0	10	0	0	2.50	56.3	3	-4	-1.3	0	0	...	0
1993—New Orleans NFL	4	54	32	59.3	448	4	3	8.30	87.6	1	0	0.0	0	0	...	0
1994—								Did not play.								
1995—Arizona NFL	4	32	20	62.5	271	1	0	8.47	99.9	1	0	0.0	0	0	...	0
Pro totals (4 years)	12	92	55	59.8	790	5	4	8.59	87.7	5	-4	-0.8	0	0	0	0

BUCK, VINCE — CB — SAINTS

PERSONAL: Born January 12, 1968, in Owensboro, Ky. ... 6-0/198. ... Full name: Vincent Lamont Buck.
HIGH SCHOOL: Owensboro (Ky.).
COLLEGE: Central State (Ohio).

TRANSACTIONS/CAREER NOTES: Selected by New Orleans Saints in second round (44th pick overall) of 1990 NFL draft. ... Signed by Saints (May 7, 1990). ... On injured reserve with neck injury (December 6, 1991-remainder of season). ... On injured reserve with knee injury (September 8-October 26, 1992). ... Granted unconditional free agency (February 17, 1994). ... Re-signed by Saints (February 17, 1994). ... On injured reserve with leg injury (December 7, 1995-remainder of season).
PRO STATISTICS: 1990—Returned three kickoffs for 38 yards and recovered two fumbles. 1991—Recovered three fumbles. 1993—Recovered two fumbles for six yards. 1994—Recovered one fumble. 1995—Fumbled once and recovered four fumbles for 10 yards.

		INTERCEPTIONS			SACKS	PUNT RETURNS				TOTALS			
Year Team	G	No.	Yds.	Avg.	TD	No.	No.	Yds.	Avg.	TD	TD	2pt.	Pts.	Fum.
1990—New Orleans NFL	16	0	0	...	0	0.0	37	305	8.2	0	0	...	0	2
1991—New Orleans NFL	13	5	12	2.4	0	0.0	31	260	8.4	0	0	...	0	0
1992—New Orleans NFL	10	2	51	25.5	1	0.5	2	4	2.0	0	1	...	6	0
1993—New Orleans NFL	16	2	28	14.0	0	3.0	0	0	...	0	0	...	0	0
1994—New Orleans NFL	16	1	0	0.0	0	1.0	0	0	...	0	0	0	0	0
1995—New Orleans NFL	13	0	0	...	0	0.0	0	0	...	0	0	0	0	1
Pro totals (6 years)	84	10	91	9.1	1	4.5	70	569	8.1	0	1	0	6	3

BUCKLEY, CURTIS　　　　　S　　　　　49ERS

PERSONAL: Born September 25, 1970, in Oakdale, Calif. ... 6-1/191. ... Full name: Curtis Ladonn Buckley.
HIGH SCHOOL: Silsbee (Texas).
JUNIOR COLLEGE: Kilgore (Texas) College.
COLLEGE: East Texas State.
TRANSACTIONS/CAREER NOTES: Signed as non-drafted free agent by Tampa Bay Buccaneers (May 3, 1993). ... Released by Buccaneers (August 30, 1993). ... Re-signed by Buccaneers (August 31, 1993). ... Released by Buccaneers (September 7, 1993). ... Re-signed by Buccaneers (September 9, 1993). ... Activated (November 5, 1993). ... Released by Buccaneers (August 30, 1994). ... Re-signed by Buccaneers (September 7, 1994). ... Released by Buccaneers (September 17, 1994). ... Re-signed by Buccaneers (September 30, 1994). ... Granted free agency (February 16, 1996). ... Tendered offer sheet by San Francisco 49ers (February 21, 1996). ... Buccaneers declined to match offer (February 28, 1996).
PRO STATISTICS: 1994—Recovered two fumbles.

		KICKOFF RETURNS				TOTALS			
Year Team	G	No.	Yds.	Avg.	TD	TD	2pt.	Pts.	Fum.
1993—Tampa Bay NFL	10	0	0	...	0	0	...	0	0
1994—Tampa Bay NFL	13	8	177	22.1	0	0	0	0	1
1995—Tampa Bay NFL	15	2	29	14.5	0	0	0	0	0
Pro totals (3 years)	38	10	206	20.6	0	0	0	0	1

BUCKLEY, MARCUS　　　　　LB　　　　　GIANTS

PERSONAL: Born February 3, 1971, in Fort Worth, Texas. ... 6-3/240. ... Full name: Marcus Wayne Buckley.
HIGH SCHOOL: Eastern Hills (Fort Worth, Texas).
COLLEGE: Texas A&M.
TRANSACTIONS/CAREER NOTES: Selected by New York Giants in third round (66th pick overall) of 1993 NFL draft. ... Signed by Giants (July 23, 1993). ... Granted free agency (February 16, 1996). ... Re-signed by Giants (April 15, 1996).
PLAYING EXPERIENCE: New York Giants NFL, 1993-1995. ... Games: 1993 (16), 1994 (16), 1995 (16). Total: 48.
HONORS: Named linebacker on THE SPORTING NEWS college All-America first team (1992).
PRO STATISTICS: 1993—Recovered one fumble. 1995—Recovered one fumble.

BUCKLEY, TERRELL　　　　　CB　　　　　DOLPHINS

PERSONAL: Born June 7, 1971, in Pascagoula, Miss. ... 5-9/176. ... Full name: Douglas Terrell Buckley.
HIGH SCHOOL: Pascagoula (Miss.).
COLLEGE: Florida State.
TRANSACTIONS/CAREER NOTES: Selected after junior season by Green Bay Packers in first round (fifth pick overall) of 1992 NFL draft. ... Signed by Packers (September 11, 1992). ... Granted roster exemption for one game (September 1992). ... Traded by Packers to Miami Dolphins for past considerations (April 3, 1995).
HONORS: Named defensive back on THE SPORTING NEWS college All-America second team (1990). ... Jim Thorpe Award winner (1991). ... Named defensive back on THE SPORTING NEWS college All-America first team (1991).
PRO STATISTICS: 1992—Recovered four fumbles. 1994—Recovered one fumble. 1995—Returned one kickoff for 16 yards.

		INTERCEPTIONS			PUNT RETURNS				TOTALS			
Year Team	G	No.	Yds.	Avg.	TD	No.	Yds.	Avg.	TD	TD	2pt.	Pts.	Fum.
1992—Green Bay NFL	14	3	33	11.0	1	21	211	10.1	1	2	...	12	7
1993—Green Bay NFL	16	2	31	15.5	0	11	76	6.9	0	0	...	0	1
1994—Green Bay NFL	16	5	38	7.6	0	0	0	...	0	0	0	0	0
1995—Miami NFL	16	1	0	0.0	0	0	0	...	0	0	0	0	0
Pro totals (4 years)	62	11	102	9.3	1	32	287	9.0	1	2	0	12	8

BUCKNER, BRENTSON　　　　　DE　　　　　STEELERS

PERSONAL: Born September 30, 1971, in Columbus, Ga. ... 6-2/305. ... Full name: Brentson Andre Buckner.
HIGH SCHOOL: Carver (Columbus, Ga.).
COLLEGE: Clemson.
TRANSACTIONS/CAREER NOTES: Selected by Pittsburgh Steelers in second round (50th pick overall) of 1994 NFL draft. ... Signed by Steelers (July 23, 1994).
CHAMPIONSHIP GAME EXPERIENCE: Played in AFC championship game (1994 and 1995 seasons). ... Played in Super Bowl XXX (1995 season).

PRO STATISTICS: 1994—Recovered one fumble. 1995—Recovered one fumble for 46 yards and a touchdown.

Year Team	G	SACKS
1994—Pittsburgh NFL	13	2.0
1995—Pittsburgh NFL	16	3.0
Pro totals (2 years)	29	5.0

BURGER, TODD   G   BEARS

PERSONAL: Born March 20, 1970, in Clark, N.J. ... 6-3/301.
HIGH SCHOOL: A.L. Johnson Regional (Clark, N.J.).
COLLEGE: Penn State.
TRANSACTIONS/CAREER NOTES: Signed as non-drafted free agent by Chicago Bears (April 29, 1993). ... Released by Bears (August 30, 1993). ... Re-signed by Bears to practice squad (August 31, 1993). ... Activated (December 12, 1993).
PLAYING EXPERIENCE: Chicago NFL, 1994 and 1995. ... Games: 1994 (4), 1995 (16). Total: 20.

BURKE, JOHN   TE   PATRIOTS

PERSONAL: Born September 7, 1971, in Elizabeth, N.J. ... 6-3/255. ... Full name: John Richard Burke.
HIGH SCHOOL: Holmdel (N.J.).
COLLEGE: Virginia Tech.
TRANSACTIONS/CAREER NOTES: Selected by New England Patriots in fourth round (121st pick overall) of 1994 NFL draft. ... Signed by Patriots (May 25, 1994).
PRO STATISTICS: 1995—Recovered one fumble.

Year Team	G	RECEIVING No.	Yds.	Avg.	TD	KICKOFF RETURNS No.	Yds.	Avg.	TD	TOTALS TD	2pt.	Pts.	Fum.
1994—New England NFL	16	9	86	9.6	0	3	11	3.7	0	0	0	0	0
1995—New England NFL	16	15	136	9.1	0	1	7	7.0	0	0	0	0	0
Pro totals (2 years)	32	24	222	9.3	0	4	18	4.5	0	0	0	0	0

BURNETT, ROB   DE   RAVENS

PERSONAL: Born August 27, 1967, in Livingston, N.J. ... 6-4/280. ... Full name: Robert Barry Burnett.
HIGH SCHOOL: Newfield (Selden, N.Y.).
COLLEGE: Syracuse.
TRANSACTIONS/CAREER NOTES: Selected by Cleveland Browns in fifth round (129th pick overall) of 1990 NFL draft. ... Signed by Browns (July 22, 1990). ... Granted free agency (March 1, 1993). ... Re-signed by Browns (June 11, 1993). ... Browns franchise moved to Baltimore and renamed Ravens for 1996 season (March 11, 1996).
HONORS: Played in Pro Bowl (1994 season).
PRO STATISTICS: 1991—Recovered one fumble for nine yards. 1992—Recovered two fumbles. 1993—Recovered two fumbles. 1994—Recovered one fumble. 1995—Recovered one fumble.

Year Team	G	SACKS
1990—Cleveland NFL	16	2.0
1991—Cleveland NFL	13	3.0
1992—Cleveland NFL	16	9.0
1993—Cleveland NFL	16	9.0
1994—Cleveland NFL	16	10.0
1995—Cleveland NFL	16	7.5
Pro totals (6 years)	93	40.5

BURNS, JASON   RB   BENGALS

PERSONAL: Born November 27, 1972, in Chicago. ... 5-7/196.
HIGH SCHOOL: Julian (Chicago).
COLLEGE: Wisconsin.
TRANSACTIONS/CAREER NOTES: Signed as non-drafted free agent by Cincinnati Bengals (April 26, 1995).
PLAYING EXPERIENCE: Cincinnati NFL, 1995. ... Games: 1995 (1).
PRO STATISTICS: 1995—Rushed once for one yard.

BURNS, KEITH   LB   BRONCOS

PERSONAL: Born May 16, 1972, in Greelyville, S.C. ... 6-2/245. ... Full name: Keith Bernard Burns.
HIGH SCHOOL: T. C. Williams (Alexandria, Va.).
JUNIOR COLLEGE: Navarro College (Texas).
COLLEGE: Oklahoma State.
TRANSACTIONS/CAREER NOTES: Selected by Denver Broncos in seventh round (210th pick overall) of 1994 NFL draft. ... Signed by Broncos (July 12, 1994).
PLAYING EXPERIENCE: Denver NFL, 1994 and 1995. ... Games: 1994 (11), 1995 (16). Total: 27.
PRO STATISTICS: 1995—Credited with 1½ sack, returned one kickoff for five yards and recovered two fumbles.

BURRIS, JEFF   CB/PR   BILLS

PERSONAL: Born June 7, 1972, in York, S.C. ... 6-0/204. ... Full name: Jeffrey Lamar Burris.

HIGH SCHOOL: Northwestern (Rockhill, S.C.).
COLLEGE: Notre Dame.
TRANSACTIONS/CAREER NOTES: Selected by Buffalo Bills in first round (27th pick overall) of 1994 NFL draft. ... Signed by Bills (July 18, 1994). ... On injured reserve (November 20, 1995-remainder of season).
HONORS: Named defensive back on THE SPORTING NEWS college All-America second team (1993).
PRO STATISTICS: 1994—Recovered one fumble.

Year Team	G	INTERCEPTIONS				PUNT RETURNS				TOTALS			
		No.	Yds.	Avg.	TD	No.	Yds.	Avg.	TD	TD	2pt.	Pts.	Fum.
1994—Buffalo NFL	16	2	24	12.0	0	32	332	10.4	0	0	0	0	2
1995—Buffalo NFL	9	1	19	19.0	0	20	229	11.5	0	0	0	0	0
Pro totals (2 years)	25	3	43	14.3	0	52	561	10.8	0	0	0	0	2

BURROUGH, JOHN   DL   FALCONS

PERSONAL: Born May 17, 1972, in Laramie, Wyo. ... 6-5/265.
HIGH SCHOOL: Pinedale (Wyo.).
COLLEGE: Wyoming.
TRANSACTIONS/CAREER NOTES: Selected by Atlanta Falcons in seventh round (245th pick overall) of 1995 NFL draft. ... Signed by Falcons (June 30, 1995).
PLAYING EXPERIENCE: Atlanta NFL, 1995. ... Games: 1995 (16).

BURTON, JAMES   CB   BEARS

PERSONAL: Born April 22, 1971, in Torrance, Calif. ... 5-9/181.
HIGH SCHOOL: Long Beach (Calif.) Polytechnic.
COLLEGE: Fresno State.
TRANSACTIONS/CAREER NOTES: Selected by Kansas City Chiefs in fifth round (151st pick overall) of 1994 NFL draft. ... Signed by Chiefs (July 20, 1994). ... Released by Chiefs (August 29, 1994). ... Signed by Chicago Bears (August 31, 1994). ... On injured reserve with shoulder injury (November 22, 1995-remainder of season).
PLAYING EXPERIENCE: Chicago NFL, 1994 and 1995. ... Games: 1994 (13), 1995 (11). Total: 24.

BUSH, DEVIN   S   FALCONS

PERSONAL: Born July 3, 1973, in Miami. ... 5-11/208.
HIGH SCHOOL: Hialeah Miami Lakes.
COLLEGE: Florida State.
TRANSACTIONS/CAREER NOTES: Selected after junior season by Atlanta Falcons in first round (26th pick overall) of 1995 NFL draft. ... Signed by Falcons (August 8, 1995).
PRO STATISTICS: 1995—Recovered one fumble.

Year Team	G	INTERCEPTIONS			
		No.	Yds.	Avg.	TD
1995—Atlanta NFL	11	1	0	0.0	0

BUSH, LEWIS   LB   CHARGERS

PERSONAL: Born December 2, 1969, in Atlanta. ... 6-2/245. ... Full name: Lewis Fitzgerald Bush.
HIGH SCHOOL: Washington (Tacoma, Wash.).
COLLEGE: Washington State.
TRANSACTIONS/CAREER NOTES: Selected by San Diego Chargers in fourth round (99th pick overall) of 1993 NFL draft. ... Signed by Chargers (July 9, 1993). ... Granted free agency (February 16, 1996).
PLAYING EXPERIENCE: San Diego NFL, 1993-1995. ... Games: 1993 (16), 1994 (16), 1995 (16). Total: 48.
CHAMPIONSHIP GAME EXPERIENCE: Played in AFC championship game (1994 season). ... Played in Super Bowl XXIX (1994 season).
PRO STATISTICS: 1994—Recovered one fumble. 1995—Intercepted one pass and recovered two fumbles.

BUSSEY, BARNEY   S

PERSONAL: Born May 20, 1962, in Lincolnton, Ga. ... 6-0/215.
HIGH SCHOOL: Lincoln County (Lincolnton, Ga.).
COLLEGE: South Carolina State.
TRANSACTIONS/CAREER NOTES: Selected by Memphis Showboats in first round (fourth pick overall) of 1984 USFL draft. ... Selected by Cincinnati Bengals in fifth round (119th pick overall) of 1984 NFL draft. ... Signed by Showboats (May 8, 1984). ... Granted roster exemption (May 8-15, 1984). ... On developmental squad for one game (March 16-24, 1985). ... Granted free agency when USFL suspended operations (August 7, 1986). ... Signed by Bengals (August 12, 1986). ... Granted free agency (February 1, 1991). ... Re-signed by Bengals (July 12, 1991). ... On injured reserve with thumb injury (August 27-October 4, 1991). ... Granted unconditional free agency (March 1, 1993). ... Signed by Tampa Bay Buccaneers (April 23, 1993). ... Released by Buccaneers (August 30, 1993). ... Re-signed by Buccaneers (August 31, 1993). ... Granted unconditional free agency (February 17, 1995). ... Re-signed by Buccaneers (February 21, 1995). ... On injured reserve with neck injury (November 15, 1995-remainder of season). ... Announced retirement (April 25, 1996).
CHAMPIONSHIP GAME EXPERIENCE: Played in AFC championship game (1988 season). ... Played in Super Bowl XXIII (1988 season).
HONORS: Named strong safety on THE SPORTING NEWS USFL All-Star team (1985).
PRO STATISTICS: USFL: 1984—Recovered one fumble. 1985—Recovered one fumble for 12 yards. NFL: 1988—Recovered one fumble. 1989—Recovered blocked punt in end zone for a touchdown. 1990—Recovered one fumble for 70 yards and a touchdown. 1991—Recovered one fumble. 1993—Recovered one fumble. 1994—Recovered one fumble. 1995—Recovered one fumble.

Year Team	G	INTERCEPTIONS				SACKS	KICKOFF RETURNS				TOTALS			
		No.	Yds.	Avg.	TD	No.	No.	Yds.	Avg.	TD	TD	2pt.	Pts.	Fum.
1984—Memphis USFL	6	0	0	...	0	0.0	0	0	...	0	0	0	0	0
1985—Memphis USFL	17	3	11	3.7	0	1.0	0	0	...	0	0	0	0	0
1986—Cincinnati NFL	16	1	19	19.0	0	1.0	0	0	...	0	0	...	0	0
1987—Cincinnati NFL	12	1	0	0.0	0	2.0	21	406	19.3	0	0	...	0	1
1988—Cincinnati NFL	16	0	0	...	0	4.0	7	83	11.9	0	0	...	0	1
1989—Cincinnati NFL	16	1	0	0.0	0	2.5	0	0	...	0	1	...	6	0
1990—Cincinnati NFL	16	4	37	9.3	0	2.0	0	0	...	0	1	...	6	0
1991—Cincinnati NFL	12	2	18	9.0	0	0.0	0	0	...	0	0	...	0	0
1992—Cincinnati NFL	16	1	3	3.0	0	0.0	1	18	18.0	0	0	...	0	0
1993—Tampa Bay NFL	16	0	0	...	0	0.0	0	0	...	0	0	...	0	0
1994—Tampa Bay NFL	16	0	0	...	0	1.5	0	0	...	0	0	...	0	0
1995—Tampa Bay NFL	8	0	0	...	0	0.0	0	0	...	0	0	0	0	0
USFL totals (2 years)	23	3	11	3.7	0	1.0	0	0	...	0	0	0	0	0
NFL totals (10 years)	144	10	77	7.7	0	13.0	29	507	17.5	0	2	0	12	2
Pro totals (12 years)	167	13	88	6.8	0	14.0	29	507	17.5	0	2	0	12	2

BUTCHER, PAUL — LB

PERSONAL: Born November 8, 1963, in Detroit. ... 6-0/240. ... Full name: Paul Martin Butcher.
HIGH SCHOOL: St. Alphonsus (Dearborn, Mich.).
COLLEGE: Wayne State, Mich. (degree in mechanical engineering, 1986).
TRANSACTIONS/CAREER NOTES: Signed as non-drafted free agent by Detroit Lions (July 23, 1986). ... Released by Lions (August 18, 1986). ... Re-signed by Lions (October 3, 1986). ... Granted unconditional free agency (February 1, 1989). ... Signed by Philadelphia Eagles (March 27, 1989). ... Released by Eagles (August 30, 1989). ... Signed by Los Angeles Rams (January 4, 1990). ... On injured reserve with groin injury (January 10, 1990-remainder of 1989 season playoffs). ... Granted unconditional free agency (February 1-April 1, 1991). ... Re-signed by Rams (May 6, 1991). ... Granted unconditional free agency (February 1-April 1, 1992). ... Re-signed by Rams for 1992 season. ... On injured reserve with foot injury (September 22-October 7, 1992). ... Released by Rams (October 7, 1992). ... Signed by Indianapolis Colts (April 30, 1993). ... Released by Colts (August 30, 1993). ... Re-signed by Colts (August 31, 1993). ... Granted unconditional free agency (February 17, 1994). ... Re-signed by Colts (June 17, 1994). ... Selected by Carolina Panthers from Colts in NFL expansion draft (February 15, 1995). ... Granted unconditional free agency (February 16, 1996).
PLAYING EXPERIENCE: Detroit NFL, 1986-1988; Los Angeles Rams NFL, 1990-1992; Indianapolis NFL, 1993 and 1994; Carolina NFL, 1995. ... Games: 1986 (12), 1987 (12), 1988 (16), 1990 (16), 1991 (16), 1992 (1), 1993 (16), 1994 (13), 1995 (16). Total: 118.
PRO STATISTICS: 1991—Recovered one fumble. 1993—Returned two kickoffs for two yards. 1995—Returned one kickoff for five yards.

BUTLER, KEVIN — K — BEARS

PERSONAL: Born July 24, 1962, in Savannah, Ga. ... 6-1/205. ... Full name: Kevin Gregory Butler.
HIGH SCHOOL: Redan (Stone Mountain, Ga.).
COLLEGE: Georgia.
TRANSACTIONS/CAREER NOTES: Selected by Jacksonville Bulls in 1985 USFL territorial draft. ... Selected by Chicago Bears in fourth round (105th pick overall) of 1985 NFL draft. ... Signed by Bears (July 23, 1985). ... Granted free agency (February 1, 1991). ... Re-signed by Bears (August 6, 1991). ... Granted unconditional free agency (February 17, 1994). ... Re-signed by Bears (June 4, 1994).
CHAMPIONSHIP GAME EXPERIENCE: Played in NFC championship game (1985 and 1988 seasons). ... Member of Super Bowl championship team (1985 season).
HONORS: Named kicker on THE SPORTING NEWS college All-America second team (1984).
RECORDS: Holds NFL rookie-season record for most points—144 (1985).

Year Team	G	KICKING							
		XPM	XPA	FGM	FGA	Lg.	50+	Pts.	
1985—Chicago NFL	16	51	51	31	37	46	0-2	*144	
1986—Chicago NFL	16	36	37	28	*41	52	1-6	120	
1987—Chicago NFL	12	28	30	19	28	52	2-6	85	
1988—Chicago NFL	16	37	38	15	19	45	0-0	82	
1989—Chicago NFL	16	43	45	15	19	46	0-1	88	
1990—Chicago NFL	16	36	37	26	37	52	4-7	114	
1991—Chicago NFL	16	32	34	19	29	50	1-3	89	
1992—Chicago NFL	16	34	34	19	26	50	1-3	91	
1993—Chicago NFL	16	21	22	27	36	55	5-8	102	
1994—Chicago NFL	15	24	24	21	29	52	2-4	87	
1995—Chicago NFL	16	45	45	23	31	47	0-2	114	
Pro totals (11 years)	171	387	397	243	332	55	16-42	1116	

BUTLER, LeROY — S — PACKERS

PERSONAL: Born July 19, 1968, in Jacksonville. ... 6-0/200.
HIGH SCHOOL: Robert E. Lee Senior (Jacksonville).
COLLEGE: Florida State.
TRANSACTIONS/CAREER NOTES: Selected by Green Bay Packers in second round (48th pick overall) of 1990 NFL draft. ... Signed by Packers (July 25, 1990). ... On suspended list (December 9, 1992). ... Designated by Packers as transition player (February 15, 1994).
CHAMPIONSHIP GAME EXPERIENCE: Played in NFC championship game (1995 season).
HONORS: Named strong safety on THE SPORTING NEWS NFL All-Pro team (1993). ... Played in Pro Bowl (1993 season).
PRO STATISTICS: 1991—Recovered one fumble. 1992—Recovered one fumble for 17 yards. 1993—Credited with one sack and ran 25 yards with lateral from fumble recovery for a touchdown. 1994—Credited with one sack. 1995—Credited with one sack.

Year Team	G	INTERCEPTIONS			
		No.	Yds.	Avg.	TD
1990—Green Bay NFL	16	3	42	14.0	0

Year Team	G	INTERCEPTIONS			
		No.	Yds.	Avg.	TD
1991—Green Bay NFL	16	3	6	2.0	0
1992—Green Bay NFL	15	1	0	0.0	0
1993—Green Bay NFL	16	6	131	21.8	0
1994—Green Bay NFL	13	3	68	22.7	0
1995—Green Bay NFL	16	5	105	21.0	0
Pro totals (6 years)	92	21	352	16.8	0

BUTTS, MARION   RB

PERSONAL: Born August 1, 1966, in Sylvester, Ga. ... 6-1/248. ... Full name: Marion Stevenson Butts Jr.
HIGH SCHOOL: Worth Academy (Sylvester, Ga.).
COLLEGE: Northeastern Oklahoma A&M, then Florida State.
TRANSACTIONS/CAREER NOTES: Selected after junior season by San Diego Chargers in seventh round (183rd pick overall) of 1989 NFL draft. ... Signed by Chargers (July 21, 1989). ... On reserve/left squad list (July 18-August 31, 1991). ... Traded by Chargers with third-round pick (NT Ervin Collier) in 1994 NFL draft to New England Patriots for third-round (WR Andre Coleman) and fifth-round (TE Aaron Laing) picks in 1994 NFL draft (April 25, 1994). ... Granted unconditional free agency (February 17, 1995). ... Signed by San Francisco 49ers (August 7, 1995). ... Released by 49ers (August 27, 1995). ... Signed by Houston Oilers (September 28, 1995). ... Granted unconditional free agency (February 16, 1996).
HONORS: Named to play in Pro Bowl (1990 season); replaced by James Brooks due to injury. ... Played in Pro Bowl (1991 season).
PRO STATISTICS: 1989—Recovered one fumble. 1990—Recovered one fumble. 1991—Returned one kickoff for no yards. 1992—Recovered one fumble. 1994—Recovered one fumble. 1995—Returned two kickoffs for 14 yards.
STATISTICAL PLATEAUS: 100-yard rushing games: 1989 (1), 1990 (5), 1992 (2). Total: 8.

Year Team	G	RUSHING				RECEIVING				TOTALS			
		Att.	Yds.	Avg.	TD	No.	Yds.	Avg.	TD	TD	2pt.	Pts.	Fum.
1989—San Diego NFL	15	170	683	4.0	9	7	21	3.0	0	9	...	54	2
1990—San Diego NFL	14	265	1225	4.6	8	16	117	7.3	0	8	...	48	0
1991—San Diego NFL	16	193	834	4.3	6	10	91	9.1	1	7	...	42	3
1992—San Diego NFL	15	218	809	3.7	4	9	73	8.1	0	4	...	24	4
1993—San Diego NFL	16	185	746	4.0	4	15	105	7.0	0	4	...	24	0
1994—New England NFL	16	243	703	2.9	8	9	54	6.0	0	8	0	48	1
1995—Houston NFL	12	71	185	2.6	4	2	10	5.0	0	4	0	24	0
Pro totals (7 years)	104	1345	5185	3.9	43	68	471	6.9	1	44	0	264	10

BYARS, KEITH   FB   DOLPHINS

PERSONAL: Born October 14, 1963, in Dayton, Ohio. ... 6-1/255.
HIGH SCHOOL: Nettie Lee Roth (Dayton, Ohio).
COLLEGE: Ohio State.
TRANSACTIONS/CAREER NOTES: Selected by New Jersey Generals in 1986 USFL territorial draft. ... Selected by Philadelphia Eagles in first round (10th pick overall) of 1986 NFL draft. ... Signed by Eagles (July 25, 1986). ... Granted free agency (February 1, 1990). ... Re-signed by Eagles (August 10, 1990). ... Granted unconditional free agency (March 1, 1993). ... Signed by Miami Dolphins (July 15, 1993). ... On injured reserve with knee injury (November 9, 1994-remainder of season). ... Released by Dolphins (February 15, 1996). ... Re-signed by Dolphins (March 21, 1996).
HONORS: Named running back on THE SPORTING NEWS college All-America first team (1984). ... Played in Pro Bowl (1993 season).
PRO STATISTICS: 1986—Attempted two passes with one completion for 55 yards and a touchdown, returned two kickoffs for 47 yards and recovered two fumbles. 1987—Recovered two fumbles. 1988—Attempted two passes without a completion, returned two kickoffs for 20 yards and recovered two fumbles for 14 yards. 1989—Recovered four fumbles for six yards and returned one kickoff for 27 yards. 1990—Attempted four passes with four completions for 53 yards and four touchdowns and recovered one fumble. 1991—Attempted two passes without a completion and with one interception. 1992—Attempted one pass without a completion and recovered one fumble. 1993—Attempted two passes with one completion for 11 yards and a touchdown.
STATISTICAL PLATEAUS: 100-yard rushing games: 1986 (1), 1987 (1). Total: 2. ... 100-yard receiving games: 1989 (2), 1990 (2), 1991 (1). Total: 5.

Year Team	G	RUSHING				RECEIVING				TOTALS			
		Att.	Yds.	Avg.	TD	No.	Yds.	Avg.	TD	TD	2pt.	Pts.	Fum.
1986—Philadelphia NFL	16	177	577	3.3	1	11	44	4.0	0	1	...	6	3
1987—Philadelphia NFL	10	116	426	3.7	3	21	177	8.4	1	4	...	24	3
1988—Philadelphia NFL	16	152	517	3.4	6	72	705	9.8	4	10	...	60	5
1989—Philadelphia NFL	16	133	452	3.4	5	68	721	10.6	0	5	...	30	4
1990—Philadelphia NFL	16	37	141	3.8	0	81	819	10.1	3	3	...	18	4
1991—Philadelphia NFL	16	94	383	4.1	1	62	564	9.1	3	4	...	24	5
1992—Philadelphia NFL	15	41	176	4.3	1	56	502	9.0	2	3	...	18	1
1993—Miami NFL	16	64	269	4.2	3	61	613	10.1	3	6	...	36	3
1994—Miami NFL	9	19	64	3.4	2	49	418	8.5	5	7	0	42	0
1995—Miami NFL	16	15	44	2.9	1	51	362	7.1	2	3	0	18	0
Pro totals (10 years)	146	848	3049	3.6	23	532	4925	9.3	23	46	0	276	28

BYNER, EARNEST   RB

PERSONAL: Born September 15, 1962, in Milledgeville, Ga. ... 5-10/215. ... Full name: Earnest Alexander Byner.
HIGH SCHOOL: Baldwin (Milledgeville, Ga.).
COLLEGE: East Carolina.
TRANSACTIONS/CAREER NOTES: Selected by Cleveland Browns in 10th round (280th pick overall) of 1984 NFL draft. ... On injured reserve with ankle injury (October 21, 1986-January 10, 1987). ... Granted free agency (February 1, 1989). ... Re-signed by Browns and traded to Washington Redskins for RB Mike Oliphant (April 23, 1989). ... Granted unconditional free agency (February 17, 1994). ... Signed by Browns

B

(May 5, 1994). ... Browns franchise moved to Baltimore and renamed Ravens for 1996 season (March 11, 1996). ... Granted-unconditional free agency (February 16, 1996).

CHAMPIONSHIP GAME EXPERIENCE: Played in AFC championship game (1986 and 1987 seasons). ... Played in NFC championship game (1991 season). ... Member of Super Bowl championship team (1991 season).

HONORS: Played in Pro Bowl (1990 and 1991 seasons).

PRO STATISTICS: 1984—Recovered two fumbles for 55 yards and a touchdown. 1985—Recovered four fumbles. 1987—Recovered one fumble. 1988—Recovered two fumbles. 1989—Attempted one pass without a completion and recovered two fumbles. 1990—Attempted two passes with one completion for 31 yards and a touchdown and recovered one fumble. 1991—Attempted four passes with one completion for 18 yards and a touchdown and recovered one fumble. 1992—Attempted three passes with one completion for 41 yards and a touchdown. 1993—Recovered one fumble. 1995—Recovered one fumble.

STATISTICAL PLATEAUS: 100-yard rushing games: 1984 (1), 1985 (2), 1989 (1), 1990 (5), 1991 (4), 1992 (2), 1995 (1). Total: 16.

			RUSHING				RECEIVING				KICKOFF RETURNS				TOTALS		
Year Team	G	Att.	Yds.	Avg.	TD	No.	Yds.	Avg.	TD	No.	Yds.	Avg.	TD	TD	2pt.	Pts.	Fum.
1984—Cleveland NFL	16	72	426	5.9	2	11	118	10.7	0	22	415	18.9	0	3	...	18	3
1985—Cleveland NFL	16	244	1002	4.1	8	45	460	10.2	2	0	0	...	0	10	...	60	5
1986—Cleveland NFL	7	94	277	3.0	2	37	328	8.9	2	0	0	...	0	4	...	24	1
1987—Cleveland NFL	12	105	432	4.1	8	52	552	10.6	2	1	2	2.0	0	10	...	60	5
1988—Cleveland NFL	16	157	576	3.7	3	59	576	9.8	2	0	0	...	0	5	...	30	5
1989—Washington NFL	16	134	580	4.3	7	54	458	8.5	2	0	0	...	0	9	...	54	2
1990—Washington NFL	16	*297	1219	4.1	6	31	279	9.0	1	0	0	...	0	7	...	42	2
1991—Washington NFL	16	274	1048	3.8	5	34	308	9.1	0	0	0	...	0	5	...	30	3
1992—Washington NFL	16	262	998	3.8	6	39	338	8.7	1	0	0	...	0	7	...	42	1
1993—Washington NFL	16	23	105	4.6	1	27	194	7.2	0	0	0	...	0	1	...	6	0
1994—Cleveland NFL	16	75	219	2.9	2	11	102	9.3	0	0	0	...	0	2	0	12	0
1995—Cleveland NFL	16	115	432	3.8	2	61	494	8.1	2	5	98	19.6	0	4	0	24	1
Pro totals (12 years)	179	1852	7314	4.0	52	461	4207	9.1	14	28	515	18.4	0	67	0	402	28

BY'NOT'E, BUTLER — CB — PANTHERS

PERSONAL: Born September 29, 1972, in St. Louis. ... 5-9/190. ... Name pronounced by-NO-tay.
HIGH SCHOOL: Vashon (St. Louis).
COLLEGE: Ohio State.
TRANSACTIONS/CAREER NOTES: Selected by Denver Broncos in seventh round (212th pick overall) of 1994 NFL draft. ... Signed by Broncos (July 8, 1994). ... Released by Broncos (August 22, 1995). ... Claimed on waivers by Carolina Panthers (April 24, 1995).

		KICKOFF RETURNS				TOTALS		
Year Team	G	No.	Yds.	Avg.	TD	TD	2pt.	Pts.	Fum.
1994—Denver NFL	9	24	545	22.7	0	0	0	0	0
1995—Carolina NFL	7	18	335	18.6	0	0	0	0	0
Pro totals (2 years)	16	42	880	21.0	0	0	0	0	0

BYRD, ISRAEL — CB — SAINTS

PERSONAL: Born February 1, 1971, in St. Louis. ... 5-11/184.
HIGH SCHOOL: Parkway Central (St. Louis).
JUNIOR COLLEGE: Allan Hancock Junior College (Calif.).
COLLEGE: Utah State.
TRANSACTIONS/CAREER NOTES: Signed as non-drafted free agent by New Orleans Saints (May 7, 1993). ... Released by Saints (August 24, 1993). ... Re-signed by Saints to practice squad (September 8, 1993). ... Activated (December 29, 1993); did not play. ... Released by Saints (August 28, 1994). ... Re-signed by Saints to practice squad (August 30, 1994). ... Activated (October 21, 1994). ... Released by Saints (November 23, 1994). ... Re-signed by Saints to practice squad (November 25, 1994). ... Activated (December 22, 1994). ... Assigned by Saints to Scottish Claymores in 1996 World League enhancement allocation program (February 19, 1996).
PLAYING EXPERIENCE: New Orleans NFL, 1994 and 1995. ... Games: 1994 (3), 1995 (4). Total: 7.

CADE, EDDIE — S — PATRIOTS

PERSONAL: Born August 4, 1973, in Casa Grande, Ariz. ... 6-1/206. ... Full name: Eddie Ray Cade.
HIGH SCHOOL: Santa Cruz Valley Union (Eloy, Ariz.).
COLLEGE: Arizona State.
TRANSACTIONS/CAREER NOTES: Signed as non-drafted free agent by New England Patriots (April 24, 1995).
PLAYING EXPERIENCE: Miami NFL, 1995. ... Games: 1995 (10).

CADREZ, GLENN — LB — BRONCOS

PERSONAL: Born January 2, 1970, in El Centro, Calif. ... 6-3/245. ... Name pronounced kuh-DREZ.
HIGH SCHOOL: El Centro (Calif.) Central Union.
JUNIOR COLLEGE: Chaffey College (Calif.).
COLLEGE: Houston.
TRANSACTIONS/CAREER NOTES: Selected by New York Jets in sixth round (154th pick overall) of 1992 NFL draft. ... Signed by Jets (July 13, 1992). ... Released by Jets (September 19, 1995). ... Signed by Denver Broncos (September 27, 1995).
PLAYING EXPERIENCE: New York Jets NFL, 1992-1994; New York Jets (1)-Denver (10) NFL, 1995. ... Games: 1992 (16), 1993 (16), 1994 (16), 1995 (11). Total: 59.
PRO STATISTICS: 1992—Recovered one fumble. 1994—Returned one kickoff for 10 yards and recovered one fumble. 1995—Credited with two sacks and recovered one fumble.

CAIN, JOE LB BEARS

PERSONAL: Born June 11, 1965, in Los Angeles. ... 6-1/239. ... Full name: Joseph Harrison Cain Jr.
HIGH SCHOOL: Compton (Calif.).
COLLEGE: Stanford, then Oregon Tech.
TRANSACTIONS/CAREER NOTES: Selected by Minnesota Vikings in eighth round (210th pick overall) of 1988 NFL draft. ... Signed by Vikings (July 24, 1988). ... Released by Vikings (August 30, 1988). ... Signed by Seattle Seahawks (March 31, 1989). ... Released by Seahawks (September 5, 1989). ... Re-signed by Seahawks to developmental squad (September 6, 1989). ... Activated (October 13, 1989). ... Granted unconditional free agency (February 1-April 1, 1992). ... Re-signed by Seahawks (July 23, 1992). ... Granted free agency (March 1, 1993). ... Tendered offer sheet by Chicago Bears (March 10, 1993). ... Seahawks declined to match offer (March 15, 1993); Seahawks received eighth-round pick (DE Antonio Edwards) in 1993 draft as compensation. ... Granted unconditional free agency (February 17, 1995). ... Re-signed by Bears (February 27, 1995).
PRO STATISTICS: 1992—Recovered one fumble. 1994—Recovered one fumble.

			INTERCEPTIONS		
Year Team	G	No.	Yds.	Avg.	TD
1989—Seattle NFL	9	0	0	...	0
1990—Seattle NFL	16	0	0	...	0
1991—Seattle NFL	16	1	5	5.0	0
1992—Seattle NFL	16	2	3	1.5	0
1993—Chicago NFL	15	0	0	...	0
1994—Chicago NFL	16	0	0	...	0
1995—Chicago NFL	16	0	0	...	0
Pro totals (7 years)	104	3	8	2.7	0

CALDWELL, MIKE WR 49ERS

PERSONAL: Born March 28, 1971, in Cleveland. ... 6-2/200.
HIGH SCHOOL: San Ramon (Calif.).
COLLEGE: California.
TRANSACTIONS/CAREER NOTES: Signed as non-drafted free agent by New Orleans Saints (April 28, 1994). ... Released by Saints (August 22, 1994). ... Signed by San Francisco 49ers to practice squad (September 14, 1994). ... Activated from practice squad (September 8, 1995). ... Released by 49ers (October 31, 1995). ... Re-signed by 49ers to practice squad (November 1, 1995). ... On injured reserve with ankle injury (November 14, 1995-remainder of season).
PLAYING EXPERIENCE: San Francisco NFL, 1995. ... Games: 1995 (2).
PRO STATISTICS: 1995—Returned two kickoffs for 40 yards.

CALDWELL, MIKE LB RAVENS

PERSONAL: Born August 31, 1971, in Oak Ridge, Tenn. ... 6-2/235. ... Full name: Mike Isiah Caldwell.
HIGH SCHOOL: Oak Ridge (Tenn.).
COLLEGE: Middle Tennessee State.
TRANSACTIONS/CAREER NOTES: Selected by Cleveland Browns in third round (83rd pick overall) of 1993 NFL draft. ... Signed by Browns (July 14, 1993). ... Granted free agency (February 16, 1996). ... Browns franchise moved to Baltimore and renamed Ravens for 1996 season (March 11, 1996).
PRO STATISTICS: 1993—Recovered one fumble. 1994—Returned one punt for two yards.

			INTERCEPTIONS		
Year Team	G	No.	Yds.	Avg.	TD
1993—Cleveland NFL	15	0	0	...	0
1994—Cleveland NFL	16	1	0	0.0	0
1995—Cleveland NFL	16	2	24	12.0	1
Pro totals (3 years)	47	3	24	8.0	1

CALLOWAY, CHRIS WR GIANTS

PERSONAL: Born March 29, 1968, in Chicago. ... 5-10/191. ... Full name: Christopher Fitzpatrick Calloway.
HIGH SCHOOL: Mount Carmel (Chicago).
COLLEGE: Michigan (degree in communications and film, 1990).
TRANSACTIONS/CAREER NOTES: Selected by Pittsburgh Steelers in fourth round (97th pick overall) of 1990 NFL draft. ... Signed by Steelers (July 18, 1990). ... On injured reserve with knee injury (November 25, 1991-remainder of season). ... Granted unconditional free agency (February 1, 1992). ... Signed by New York Giants (April 1, 1992). ... Granted unconditional free agency (February 17, 1994). ... Re-signed by Giants (July 18, 1994). ... Granted unconditional free agency (February 16, 1996). ... Re-signed by Giants (April 2, 1996).
PRO STATISTICS: 1991—Recovered one fumble. 1993—Recovered one fumble.
STATISTICAL PLATEAUS: 100-yard receiving games: 1995 (1).

		RUSHING				RECEIVING				KICKOFF RETURNS				TOTALS			
Year Team	G	Att.	Yds.	Avg.	TD	No.	Yds.	Avg.	TD	No.	Yds.	Avg.	TD	TD	2pt.	Pts.	Fum.
1990—Pittsburgh NFL	16	0	0	...	0	10	124	12.4	1	0	0	...	0	1	...	6	0
1991—Pittsburgh NFL	12	0	0	...	0	15	254	16.9	1	0	0	...	0	1	...	6	0
1992—New York Giants NFL	16	0	0	...	0	27	335	12.4	1	2	29	14.5	0	1	...	6	0
1993—New York Giants NFL	16	0	0	...	0	35	513	14.7	3	6	89	14.8	0	3	...	18	0
1994—New York Giants NFL	16	8	77	9.6	0	43	666	15.5	2	0	0	...	0	2	0	12	1
1995—New York Giants NFL	16	2	-9	-4.5	0	56	796	14.2	3	0	0	...	0	3	0	18	0
Pro totals (6 years)	92	10	68	6.8	0	186	2688	14.5	11	8	118	14.8	0	11	0	66	1

C

CAMARILLO, RICH — P

PERSONAL: Born November 29, 1959, in Whittier, Calif. ... 5-11/202. ... Full name: Richard Jon Camarillo.
HIGH SCHOOL: El Rancho (Pico Rivera, Calif.).
JUNIOR COLLEGE: Cerritos College (Calif.).
COLLEGE: Washington.
TRANSACTIONS/CAREER NOTES: Signed as non-drafted free agent by New England Patriots (May 11, 1981). ... Released by Patriots (August 24, 1981). ... Re-signed by Patriots (October 20, 1981). ... On injured reserve with knee injury (August 28-November 3, 1984). ... Released by Patriots (August 30, 1988). ... Signed by Los Angeles Rams (August 31, 1988). ... Released by Rams (November 2, 1988). ... Signed by Phoenix Cardinals (April 7, 1989). ... Granted free agency (February 1, 1990). ... Re-signed by Cardinals (August 1, 1990). ... Granted free agency (February 1, 1992). ... Re-signed by Cardinals (July 19, 1992). ... Granted unconditional free agency (February 17, 1994). ... Signed by Houston Oilers (April 29, 1994). ... Granted unconditional free agency (February 16, 1996).
CHAMPIONSHIP GAME EXPERIENCE: Played in AFC championship game (1985 season). ... Played in Super Bowl XX (1985 season).
HONORS: Named punter on THE SPORTING NEWS NFL All-Pro team (1983). ... Played in Pro Bowl (1983, 1989 and 1991-1993 seasons).
POSTSEASON RECORDS: Holds NFL postseason career record for highest average (minimum 25 punts)—44.5.
PRO STATISTICS: 1981—Fumbled once and recovered one fumble. 1987—Rushed once for no yards. 1989—Attempted one pass with one completion for no yards. 1990—Rushed once for minus 11 yards and fumbled once. 1991—Attempted one pass without a completion and recovered one fumble. 1992—Missed one extra-point attempt. 1993—Rushed once for no yards and recovered one fumble. 1994—Attempted one pass without a completion, fumbled once and recovered one fumble. 1995—Attempted one pass without a completion, fumbled once and recovered one fumble.

| | | | | PUNTING | | | |
Year Team	G	No.	Yds.	Avg.	Net avg.	In. 20	Blk.
1981—New England NFL	9	47	1959	41.7	33.4	12	0
1982—New England NFL	9	49	2140	43.7	37.7	10	0
1983—New England NFL	16	81	3615	44.6	*37.1	25	0
1984—New England NFL	7	48	2020	42.1	34.7	12	0
1985—New England NFL	16	92	*3953	43.0	33.6	16	0
1986—New England NFL	16	89	3746	42.1	33.1	16	*3
1987—New England NFL	12	62	2489	40.1	31.7	14	1
1988—Los Angeles Rams NFL	9	40	1579	39.5	34.8	11	0
1989—Phoenix NFL	15	76	3298	*43.4	37.5	21	0
1990—Phoenix NFL	16	67	2865	42.8	37.4	16	0
1991—Phoenix NFL	16	76	3445	45.3	*38.9	19	1
1992—Phoenix NFL	15	54	2317	42.9	*39.6	23	0
1993—Phoenix NFL	16	73	3189	43.7	37.8	23	0
1994—Houston NFL	16	96	*4115	42.9	36.4	35	0
1995—Houston NFL	16	77	3165	41.1	34.8	26	1
Pro totals (15 years)	204	1027	43895	42.8	35.9	279	6

CAMPBELL, JESSE — S — GIANTS

PERSONAL: Born April 11, 1969, in Washington, N.C. ... 6-1/215.
HIGH SCHOOL: West Craven (Vanceboro, N.C.).
COLLEGE: North Carolina State.
TRANSACTIONS/CAREER NOTES: Selected after junior season by Philadelphia Eagles in second round (48th pick overall) of 1991 NFL draft. ... Signed by Eagles (July 17, 1991). ... On injured reserve with knee injury (August 27-October 23, 1991). ... On practice squad (October 23, 1991-remainder of season). ... Released by Eagles (September 4, 1992). ... Signed by New York Giants (September 7, 1992). ... Released by Giants (September 21, 1992). ... Signed by Giants to practice squad (September 23, 1992). ... Activated (October 21, 1992). ... Granted free agency (February 17, 1994). ... Re-signed by Giants (July 17, 1994). ... Granted unconditional free agency (February 17, 1995). ... Re-signed by Giants (February 24, 1995).
HONORS: Named defensive back on THE SPORTING NEWS college All-America first team (1990).
PRO STATISTICS: 1992—Recovered one fumble. 1994—Recovered two fumbles for three yards.

| | | INTERCEPTIONS | | | |
Year Team	G	No.	Yds.	Avg.	TD
1992—New York Giants NFL	11	0	0	...	0
1993—New York Giants NFL	16	1	0	0.0	0
1994—New York Giants NFL	14	2	3	1.5	0
1995—New York Giants NFL	16	0	0	...	0
Pro totals (4 years)	57	3	3	1.0	0

CAMPBELL, MATTHEW — TE — PANTHERS

PERSONAL: Born July 14, 1972, in North Augusta, S.C. ... 6-4/270.
HIGH SCHOOL: North Augusta (S.C.).
COLLEGE: South Carolina.
TRANSACTIONS/CAREER NOTES: Signed as non-drafted free agent by New Orleans Saints (April 28, 1994). ... Released by Saints (August 23, 1994). ... Re-signed by Saints to practice squad (August 30, 1994). ... Released by Saints (September 20, 1994). ... Signed by Carolina Panthers (December 15, 1994).
PLAYING EXPERIENCE: Carolina NFL, 1995. ... Games: 1995 (10).
PRO STATISTICS: 1995—Caught three passes for 32 yards and fumbled once.

CARNEY, JOHN — K — CHARGERS

PERSONAL: Born April 20, 1964, in Hartford, Conn. ... 5-11/170. ... Full name: John Michael Carney.
HIGH SCHOOL: Cardinal Newman (West Palm Beach, Fla.).

C

COLLEGE: Notre Dame (degree in marketing, 1987).

TRANSACTIONS/CAREER NOTES: Signed as non-drafted free agent by Cincinnati Bengals (May 1, 1987). ... Released by Bengals (August 10, 1987). ... Signed as replacement player by Tampa Bay Buccaneers (September 24, 1987). ... Released by Buccaneers (October 14, 1987). ... Re-signed by Buccaneers (April 5, 1988). ... Released by Buccaneers (August 23, 1988). ... Re-signed by Buccaneers (November 22, 1988). ... Granted unconditional free agency (February 1-April 1, 1989). ... Re-signed by Buccaneers (April 13, 1989). ... Released by Buccaneers (September 5, 1989). ... Re-signed by Buccaneers (December 13, 1989). ... Granted unconditional free agency (February 1, 1990). ... Signed by San Diego Chargers (April 1, 1990). ... Released by Chargers (August 28, 1990). ... Signed by Los Angeles Rams (September 21, 1990). ... Released by Rams (September 26, 1990). ... Signed by Chargers (October 3, 1990). ... Granted free agency (February 1, 1992). ... Re-signed by Chargers (July 27, 1992). ... Granted free agency (March 1, 1993). ... Re-signed by Chargers (June 9, 1993). ... Granted unconditional free agency (February 17, 1994). ... Re-signed by Chargers (April 6, 1994).

CHAMPIONSHIP GAME EXPERIENCE: Played in AFC championship game (1994 season). ... Played in Super Bowl XXIX (1994 season).

HONORS: Named kicker on THE SPORTING NEWS NFL All-Pro team (1994). ... Played in Pro Bowl (1994 season).

PRO STATISTICS: 1993—Punted four times for 155 yards (38.8-yard average).

						KICKING			
Year Team	G	XPM	XPA	FGM	FGA	Lg.	50+	Pts.
1988—Tampa Bay NFL	4	6	6	2	5	29	0-0	12
1989—Tampa Bay NFL	1	0	0	0	0	...	0-0	0
1990—San Diego NFL	12	27	28	19	21	43	0-1	84
—Los Angeles Rams NFL	1	0	0	0	0	...	0-0	0
1991—San Diego NFL	16	31	31	19	29	54	2-4	88
1992—San Diego NFL	16	35	35	26	32	50	1-3	113
1993—San Diego NFL	16	31	33	31	40	51	2-3	124
1994—San Diego NFL	16	33	33	*34	38	50	2-2	*135
1995—San Diego NFL	16	32	33	21	26	45	0-2	95
Pro totals (8 years)	98	195	199	152	191	54	7-15	651

CAROLAN, BRETT　　　　　TE　　　　　49ERS

PERSONAL: Born March 16, 1971, in San Rafael, Calif. ... 6-3/241. ... Son of Reg Carolan, tight end, San Diego Chargers and Kansas City Chiefs (1962-1968).

HIGH SCHOOL: San Marin (Novato, Calif.).

COLLEGE: Washington State.

TRANSACTIONS/CAREER NOTES: Signed as non-drafted free agent by San Francisco 49ers (May 4, 1994).

CHAMPIONSHIP GAME EXPERIENCE: Member of 49ers for NFC championship game (1994 season); inactive. ... Member of Super Bowl championship team (1994 season).

		RECEIVING				TOTALS			
Year Team	G	No.	Yds.	Avg.	TD	TD	2pt.	Pts.	Fum.
1994—San Francisco NFL	4	2	10	5.0	0	0	0	0	0
1995—San Francisco NFL	14	1	3	3.0	0	0	0	0	0
Pro totals (2 years)	18	3	13	4.3	0	0	0	0	0

CARPENTER, ROB　　　　　WR

PERSONAL: Born August 1, 1968, in Amityville, N.Y. ... 6-2/190.

HIGH SCHOOL: Amityville (N.Y.) Memorial.

COLLEGE: Notre Dame, then Syracuse.

TRANSACTIONS/CAREER NOTES: Selected after junior season by Cincinnati Bengals in fourth round (109th pick overall) of 1991 NFL draft. ... Claimed on waivers by New England Patriots (August 27, 1991). ... On injured reserve with hamstring injury (November 7-December 4, 1991). ... Granted unconditional free agency (February 1, 1992). ... Signed by New York Jets (March 15, 1992). ... Granted free agency (February 17, 1994). ... Re-signed by Jets (May 3, 1994). ... Released by Jets (September 20, 1994). ... Signed by Philadelphia Eagles (July 21, 1995). ... Granted unconditional free agency (February 16, 1996).

PRO STATISTICS: 1992—Attempted one pass without a completion and rushed once for two yards. 1995—Recovered one fumble.

STATISTICAL PLATEAUS: 100-yard receiving games: 1992 (1).

		RECEIVING				PUNT RETURNS				TOTALS			
Year Team	G	No.	Yds.	Avg.	TD	No.	Yds.	Avg.	TD	TD	2pt.	Pts.	Fum.
1991—New England NFL	8	3	45	15.0	0	0	0	...	0	0	...	0	0
1992—New York Jets NFL	16	13	161	12.4	1	28	208	7.4	0	1	...	6	3
1993—New York Jets NFL	16	6	83	13.8	0	0	0	...	0	0	...	0	0
1994—New York Jets NFL	3	0	0	...	0	0	0	...	0	0	0	0	0
1995—Philadelphia NFL	16	29	318	11.0	0	12	79	6.6	0	0	0	0	2
Pro totals (5 years)	59	51	607	11.9	1	40	287	7.2	0	1	0	6	5

CARPENTER, RON　　　　　S　　　　　JETS

PERSONAL: Born January 20, 1970, in Cincinnati. ... 6-1/189.

HIGH SCHOOL: Princeton (Cincinnati).

COLLEGE: Miami of Ohio.

TRANSACTIONS/CAREER NOTES: Signed as non-drafted free agent by Minnesota Vikings (May 1, 1993). ... Claimed on waivers by Cincinnati Bengals (November 3, 1993). ... Released by Bengals (July 29, 1994). ... Signed by Minnesota Vikings (August 2, 1994). ... Released by Vikings (August 22, 1994). ... Selected by Amsterdam Admirals in fifth round (27th pick overall) of 1995 World League Draft. ... Signed by New York Jets (June 28, 1995).

		INTERCEPTIONS				KICKOFF RETURNS				TOTALS			
Year Team	G	No.	Yds.	Avg.	TD	No.	Yds.	Avg.	TD	TD	2pt.	Pts.	Fum.
1993—Cincinnati NFL	6	0	0	...	0	0	0	...	0	0	...	0	0
—Minnesota NFL	7	0	0	...	0	0	0	...	0	0	...	0	0

Year Team	G	INTERCEPTIONS				KICKOFF RETURNS				TOTALS			
		No.	Yds.	Avg.	TD	No.	Yds.	Avg.	TD	TD	2pt.	Pts.	Fum.
1994—									Did not play.				
1995—Amsterdam W.L.	...	7	93	13.3	1	7	219	31.3	0	1	0	6	...
—New York Jets NFL	13	0	0	...	0	20	553	27.7	0	0	0	0	3
W.L. totals (1 year)	...	7	93	13.3	1	7	219	31.3	0	1	0	6	...
NFL totals (2 years)	26	0	0	...	0	20	553	27.7	0	0	0	0	3
Pro totals (2 years)	...	7	93	13.3	1	27	772	28.6	0	1	0	6	

CARRIER, MARK   S   BEARS

PERSONAL: Born April 28, 1968, in Lake Charles, La. ... 6-1/190. ... Full name: Mark Anthony Carrier. ... Related to Mark Carrier, wide receiver, Tampa Bay Buccaneers, Cleveland Browns and Carolina Panthers (1987-1995).
HIGH SCHOOL: Polytechnic (Long Beach, Calif.).
COLLEGE: Southern California (degree in communications).
TRANSACTIONS/CAREER NOTES: Selected after junior season by Chicago Bears in first round (sixth pick overall) of 1990 NFL draft. ... Signed by Bears (April 22, 1990). ... Designated by Bears as transition player (February 25, 1993).
HONORS: Named defensive back on THE SPORTING NEWS college All-America second team (1988). ... Jim Thorpe Award winner (1989). ... Named defensive back on THE SPORTING NEWS college All-America first team (1989). ... Played in Pro Bowl (1990, 1991 and 1993 seasons). ... Named free safety on THE SPORTING NEWS NFL All-Pro team (1991).
PRO STATISTICS: 1990—Recovered two fumbles for 16 yards. 1991—Recovered one fumble for two yards. 1992—Recovered two fumbles. 1995—Recovered one fumble.

Year Team	G	INTERCEPTIONS			
		No.	Yds.	Avg.	TD
1990—Chicago NFL	16	*10	39	3.9	0
1991—Chicago NFL	16	2	54	27.0	0
1992—Chicago NFL	16	0	0	...	0
1993—Chicago NFL	16	4	94	23.5	1
1994—Chicago NFL	16	2	10	5.0	0
1995—Chicago NFL	16	0	0	...	0
Pro totals (6 years)	96	18	197	11.0	1

CARRIER, MARK   WR

PERSONAL: Born October 28, 1965, in Lafayette, La. ... 6-0/185. ... Full name: John Mark Carrier. ... Related to Mark Carrier, safety, Chicago Bears.
HIGH SCHOOL: Church Point (La.).
COLLEGE: Nicholls State (La.).
TRANSACTIONS/CAREER NOTES: Selected by Tampa Bay Buccaneers in third round (57th pick overall) of 1987 NFL draft. ... Signed by Buccaneers (July 18, 1987). ... Granted free agency (February 1, 1990). ... Re-signed by Buccaneers (August 13, 1990). ... Granted unconditional free agency (March 1, 1993). ... Signed by Cleveland Browns (April 7, 1993). ... Selected by Carolina Panthers from Browns in NFL expansion draft (February 15, 1995). ... Granted unconditional free agency (February 16, 1996).
HONORS: Played in Pro Bowl (1989 season).
PRO STATISTICS: 1987—Returned one kickoff for no yards. 1991—Recovered one fumble. 1993—Rushed four times for 26 yards and a touchdown. 1994—Rushed once for 14 yards and a touchdown and recovered one fumble. 1995—Rushed three times for minus four yards and recovered one fumble.
STATISTICAL PLATEAUS: 100-yard receiving games: 1987 (1), 1988 (1), 1989 (8), 1990 (1), 1991 (1), 1992 (1), 1993 (2), 1995 (3). Total: 18.
MISCELLANEOUS: Holds Tampa Bay Buccaneers all-time record for most yards receiving (5,018). ... Holds Carolina Panthers all-time record for most yards receiving (1,002).

Year Team	G	RECEIVING				PUNT RETURNS				TOTALS			
		No.	Yds.	Avg.	TD	No.	Yds.	Avg.	TD	TD	2pt.	Pts.	Fum.
1987—Tampa Bay NFL	10	26	423	16.3	3	0	0	...	0	3	...	18	0
1988—Tampa Bay NFL	16	57	970	17.0	5	0	0	...	0	5	...	30	2
1989—Tampa Bay NFL	16	86	1422	16.5	9	0	0	...	0	9	...	54	1
1990—Tampa Bay NFL	16	49	813	16.6	4	0	0	...	0	4	...	24	0
1991—Tampa Bay NFL	16	47	698	14.9	2	0	0	...	0	2	...	12	2
1992—Tampa Bay NFL	14	56	692	12.4	4	0	0	...	0	4	...	24	1
1993—Cleveland NFL	16	43	746	17.4	3	6	92	15.3	1	5	...	30	0
1994—Cleveland NFL	16	29	452	15.6	5	9	112	12.4	0	6	0	36	1
1995—Carolina NFL	16	66	1002	15.2	3	6	25	4.2	0	3	0	18	0
Pro totals (9 years)	136	459	7218	15.7	38	21	229	10.9	1	41	0	246	7

CARRINGTON, DARREN   S   RAIDERS

PERSONAL: Born October 10, 1966, in Bronx, N.Y. ... 6-2/200. ... Full name: Darren Russell Carrington.
HIGH SCHOOL: James Monroe (Bronx, N.Y.).
COLLEGE: Northern Arizona.
TRANSACTIONS/CAREER NOTES: Selected by Denver Broncos in fifth round (134th pick overall) of 1989 NFL draft. ... Signed by Broncos (July 19, 1989). ... Released by Broncos (September 8, 1990). ... Signed by Detroit Lions (September 21, 1990). ... Granted unconditional free agency (February 1, 1991). ... Signed by San Diego Chargers (March 29, 1991). ... Released by Chargers (August 26, 1991). ... Re-signed by Chargers (August 27, 1991). ... Granted free agency (March 1, 1993). ... Tendered offer sheet by Tampa Bay Buccaneers (April 13, 1993). ... Offer matched by Chargers (April 19, 1993). ... Selected by Jacksonville Jaguars from Chargers in NFL expansion draft (February 15, 1995). ... On injured reserve with groin injury (October 17, 1995-remainder of season). ... Granted unconditional free agency (February 16, 1996). ... Signed by Oakland Raiders (April 20, 1996).
CHAMPIONSHIP GAME EXPERIENCE: Played in AFC championship game (1989 and 1994 seasons). ... Played in Super Bowl XXIV (1989 season) and Super Bowl XXIX (1994 season).
PRO STATISTICS: 1989—Returned one punt for no yards. 1990—Recovered one fumble. 1991—Ran 24 yards with lateral from kickoff

return. 1993—Credited with a sack and recovered one fumble. 1994—Recovered two fumbles. 1995—Recovered one fumble.

			INTERCEPTIONS				KICKOFF RETURNS				TOTALS			
Year Team	G	No.	Yds.	Avg.	TD	No.	Yds.	Avg.	TD	TD	2pt.	Pts.	Fum.
1989—Denver NFL	16	1	2	2.0	0	6	152	25.3	0	0	...	0	1
1990—Detroit NFL	12	0	0	...	0	0	0	...	0	0	...	0	0
1991—San Diego NFL	16	3	30	10.0	0	0	24	...	0	0	...	0	0
1992—San Diego NFL	16	6	152	25.3	1	0	0	...	0	1	...	6	0
1993—San Diego NFL	16	7	104	14.9	0	0	0	...	0	0	...	0	1
1994—San Diego NFL	16	3	51	17.0	0	0	0	...	0	0	0	0	0
1995—Jacksonville NFL	6	1	17	17.0	0	0	0	...	0	0	0	0	0
Pro totals (7 years)	98	21	356	17.0	1	6	176	29.3	0	1	0	6	2

CARSWELL, DWAYNE TE BRONCOS

PERSONAL: Born January 18, 1972, in Jacksonville, Fla.. ... 6-3/261.
HIGH SCHOOL: University Christian (Jacksonville, Fla.).
COLLEGE: Liberty (Va.).
TRANSACTIONS/CAREER NOTES: Signed as non-drafted free agent by Denver Broncos (May 2, 1994). ... Released by Broncos (August 26, 1994). ... Re-signed by Broncos to practice squad (August 30, 1994). ... Activated (November 25, 1994).
PLAYING EXPERIENCE: Denver NFL, 1994 and 1995. ... Games: 1994 (4), 1995 (9). Total: 13.
PRO STATISTICS: 1994—Returned one kickoff for no yards and recovered one fumble. 1995—Caught three passes for 37 yards.

CARTER, ANTHONY WR

C

PERSONAL: Born September 17, 1960, in Riviera Beach, Fla. ... 5-11/168. ... Cousin of Leonard Coleman, defensive back, Memphis Showboats of USFL, Indianapolis Colts and San Diego Chargers (1985-1989).
HIGH SCHOOL: Sun Coast (Riviera Beach, Fla.).
COLLEGE: Michigan.
TRANSACTIONS/CAREER NOTES: Selected by Michigan Panthers in 1983 USFL territorial draft. ... Signed by Panthers (February 26, 1983). ... Selected by Miami Dolphins in 12th round (334th pick overall) of 1983 NFL draft. ... On injured reserve with broken arm (April 5, 1984-remainder of season). ... Protected in merger of Panthers and Oakland Invaders (December 6, 1984). ... On developmental squad for one game with Invaders (June 24-30, 1985). ... NFL rights traded by Dolphins to Minnesota Vikings for LB Robin Sendlein and second-round pick (traded to Tampa Bay) in 1986 draft (August 15, 1985). ... Released by Invaders (August 23, 1985). ... Signed by Vikings (August 25, 1985). ... Granted roster exemption (August 25-29, 1985). ... On injured reserve with knee injury (September 5-October 4, 1986). ... Granted free agency (February 1, 1990). ... Re-signed by Vikings (July 30, 1990). ... Granted unconditional free agency (February 17, 1994). ... Signed by Detroit Lions (June 9, 1994). ... Granted unconditional free agency (February 17, 1995). ... Re-signed by Lions (June 22, 1995). ... Announced retirement (October 5, 1995).
CHAMPIONSHIP GAME EXPERIENCE: Played in USFL championship game (1983 and 1985 seasons). ... Played in NFC championship game (1987 season).
HONORS: Named wide receiver on THE SPORTING NEWS college All-America first team (1981 and 1982). ... Named punt returner on THE SPORTING NEWS USFL All-Star team (1983). ... Named wide receiver on THE SPORTING NEWS USFL All-Star team (1985). ... Played in Pro Bowl (1987 and 1988 seasons).
POSTSEASON RECORDS: Holds NFL postseason career records for most yards by punt return—259; longest punt return—84 yards (January 3, 1988, at New Orleans); and highest average (minimum 10 punt returns)—15.2. ... Shares NFL postseason career record for most touchdowns by punt return—1 (January 3, 1988, at New Orleans). ... Holds NFL postseason single-game records for most yards receiving—227 (January 9, 1988, at San Francisco); and most yards by punt return—143 (January 3, 1988, at New Orleans).
PRO STATISTICS: USFL: 1983—Recovered three fumbles. 1984—Recovered one fumble. 1985—Attempted one pass without a completion and recovered one fumble in end zone for a touchdown. NFL: 1985—Recovered one fumble. 1988—Returned one kickoff for no yards and recovered one fumble. 1989—Returned one kickoff for 19 yards and recovered one fumble. 1992—Attempted one pass without a completion. 1995—Returned two kickoffs for 46 yards.
STATISTICAL PLATEAUS: USFL: 100-yard receiving games: 1983 (5), 1984 (3), 1985 (3). Total: 11. ... NFL: 100-yard receiving games: 1985 (5), 1986 (1), 1987 (3), 1988 (3), 1989 (3), 1990 (3), 1992 (1), 1993 (3). Total: 22.
MISCELLANEOUS: Holds Minnesota Vikings all-time record for most yards receiving (7,636).

		RUSHING				RECEIVING				PUNT RETURNS				TOTALS			
Year Team	G	Att.	Yds.	Avg.	TD	No.	Yds.	Avg.	TD	No.	Yds.	Avg.	TD	TD	2pt.	Pts.	Fum.
1983—Michigan USFL	18	3	1	0.3	0	60	1181	19.7	9	40	387	9.7	*1	10	0	60	6
1984—Michigan USFL	6	0	0	...	0	30	538	17.9	4	5	21	4.2	0	4	0	24	2
1985—Oakland USFL	17	0	0	...	0	70	1323	18.9	14	0	0	...	0	15	0	90	0
—Minnesota NFL	16	0	0	...	0	43	821	19.1	8	9	117	13.0	0	8	...	48	1
1986—Minnesota NFL	12	1	12	12.0	0	38	686	18.1	7	0	0	...	0	7	...	42	1
1987—Minnesota NFL	12	0	0	...	0	38	922	*24.3	7	3	40	13.3	0	7	...	42	0
1988—Minnesota NFL	16	4	41	10.3	0	72	1225	17.0	6	1	3	3.0	0	6	...	36	1
1989—Minnesota NFL	16	3	18	6.0	0	65	1066	16.4	4	1	2	2.0	0	4	...	24	0
1990—Minnesota NFL	15	3	16	5.3	0	70	1008	14.4	8	0	0	...	0	8	...	48	2
1991—Minnesota NFL	15	13	117	9.0	1	51	553	10.8	5	0	0	...	0	6	...	36	0
1992—Minnesota NFL	16	16	66	4.1	0	41	580	14.2	2	0	0	...	0	3	...	18	1
1993—Minnesota NFL	15	7	19	2.7	0	60	775	12.9	5	0	0	...	0	5	...	30	1
1994—Detroit NFL	4	0	0	...	0	8	97	12.1	3	0	0	...	0	3	0	18	0
1995—Detroit NFL	3	0	0	...	0	0	0	...	0	1	3	3.0	0	0	0	0	0
USFL totals (3 years)	41	3	1	0.3	0	160	3042	19.0	27	45	408	9.1	1	29	0	174	8
NFL totals (11 years)	140	47	289	6.2	2	486	7733	15.9	55	15	165	11.0	0	57	0	342	7
Pro totals (14 years)	181	50	290	5.8	2	646	10775	16.7	82	60	573	9.6	1	86	0	516	15

CARTER, BERNARD LB JAGUARS

PERSONAL: Born August 22, 1971, in Tallahassee, Fla. ... 6-3/238. ... Full name: Edward Bernard Carter. ... Brother of Kevin Carter, defensive end, St. Louis Rams.

HIGH SCHOOL: Lincoln (Tallahassee, Fla.).
COLLEGE: East Carolina (degree in industrial technology).
TRANSACTIONS/CAREER NOTES: Selected by Tampa Bay Buccaneers in sixth round (165th pick overall) of 1994 NFL draft. ... Signed by Buccaneers (May 20, 1994). ... Claimed on waivers by Green Bay Packers (August 24, 1994). ... Released by Packers (August 28, 1994). ... Re-signed by Packers to practice squad (August 30, 1994). ... Activated (January 6, 1995). ... Released by Packers (August 27, 1995). ... Signed by Jacksonville Jaguars to practice squad (October 10, 1995). ... Released by Jaguars (October 17, 1995). ... Re-signed by Jaguars to practice squad (October 18, 1995). ... Activated (November 21, 1995). ... Assigned by Jaguars to Frankfurt Galaxy in 1996 World League enhancement allocation program (February 19, 1996).
PLAYING EXPERIENCE: Jacksonville NFL, 1995. ... Games: 1995 (5). Total: 5.

CARTER, CRIS — WR — VIKINGS

PERSONAL: Born November 25, 1965, in Middletown, Ohio. ... 6-3/206. ... Brother of Butch Carter, guard/forward with four NBA teams (1980-81 through 1985-86).
HIGH SCHOOL: Middletown (Ohio).
COLLEGE: Ohio State.
TRANSACTIONS/CAREER NOTES: Selected by Philadelphia Eagles in fourth round of 1987 NFL supplemental draft (September 4, 1987). ... Signed by Eagles (September 17, 1987). ... Granted roster exemption (September 17-October 26, 1987). ... Claimed on waivers by Minnesota Vikings (September 4, 1990). ... Granted free agency (February 1, 1991). ... Re-signed by Vikings (July 9, 1991). ... Granted free agency (February 1, 1992). ... Re-signed by Vikings (July 26, 1992). ... On injured reserve with collarbone injury (December 4-30, 1992).
HONORS: Played in Pro Bowl (1993-1995 seasons). ... Named wide receiver on THE SPORTING NEWS NFL All-Pro team (1994).
PRO STATISTICS: 1987—Attempted one pass without a completion. 1988—Recovered one fumble in end zone for a touchdown. 1989—Recovered one fumble. 1993—Recovered one fumble.
STATISTICAL PLATEAUS: 100-yard receiving games: 1988 (1), 1989 (1), 1990 (2), 1991 (4), 1992 (1), 1993 (3), 1994 (5), 1995 (5). Total: 22.

Year Team	G	RUSHING				RECEIVING				KICKOFF RETURNS				TOTALS			
		Att.	Yds.	Avg.	TD	No.	Yds.	Avg.	TD	No.	Yds.	Avg.	TD	TD	2pt.	Pts.	Fum.
1987—Philadelphia NFL	9	0	0	...	0	5	84	16.8	2	12	241	20.1	0	2	...	12	0
1988—Philadelphia NFL	16	1	1	1.0	0	39	761	19.5	6	0	0	...	0	7	...	42	0
1989—Philadelphia NFL	16	2	16	8.0	0	45	605	13.4	11	0	0	...	0	11	...	66	1
1990—Minnesota NFL	16	2	6	3.0	0	27	413	15.3	3	0	0	...	0	3	...	18	0
1991—Minnesota NFL	16	0	0	...	0	72	962	13.4	5	0	0	...	0	5	...	30	1
1992—Minnesota NFL	12	5	15	3.0	0	53	681	12.9	6	0	0	...	0	6	...	36	1
1993—Minnesota NFL	16	0	0	...	0	86	1071	12.5	9	0	0	...	0	9	...	54	0
1994—Minnesota NFL	16	0	0	...	0	*122	1256	10.3	7	0	0	...	0	7	2	46	4
1995—Minnesota NFL	16	1	0	0.0	0	122	1371	11.2	†17	0	0	...	0	17	0	102	0
Pro totals (9 years)	133	11	38	3.5	0	571	7204	12.6	66	12	241	20.1	0	67	2	406	7

CARTER, DALE — CB/PR — CHIEFS

PERSONAL: Born November 28, 1969, in Covington, Ga. ... 6-1/188. ... Full name: Dale Lavelle Carter. ... Brother of Jake Reed, wide receiver, Minnesota Vikings.
HIGH SCHOOL: Newton County (Covington, Ga.).
JUNIOR COLLEGE: Ellsworth (Iowa) Community College.
COLLEGE: Tennessee.
TRANSACTIONS/CAREER NOTES: Selected by Kansas City Chiefs in first round (20th pick overall) of 1992 NFL draft. ... Signed by Chiefs (June 2, 1992). ... Designated by Chiefs as transition player (February 25, 1993). ... On injured reserve with broken arm (January 7, 1994-remainder of 1993 playoffs).
HONORS: Named kick returner on THE SPORTING NEWS college All-America first team (1990). ... Named defensive back on THE SPORTING NEWS college All-America first team (1991). ... Played in Pro Bowl (1994 and 1995 seasons).
PRO STATISTICS: 1992—Recovered two fumbles. 1993—Rushed once for two yards and recovered two fumbles. 1994—Recovered one fumble. 1995—Recovered two fumbles.

Year Team	G	INTERCEPTIONS				PUNT RETURNS				KICKOFF RETURNS				TOTALS			
		No.	Yds.	Avg.	TD	No.	Yds.	Avg.	TD	No.	Yds.	Avg.	TD	TD	2pt.	Pts.	Fum.
1992—Kansas City NFL	16	7	65	9.3	1	38	398	10.5	†2	11	190	17.3	0	3	...	18	7
1993—Kansas City NFL	15	1	0	0.0	0	27	247	9.2	0	0	0	...	0	0	...	0	4
1994—Kansas City NFL	16	2	24	12.0	0	16	124	7.8	0	0	0	...	0	0	0	0	1
1995—Kansas City NFL	16	4	45	11.3	0	0	0	...	0	0	0	...	0	0	0	0	0
Pro totals (4 years)	63	14	134	9.6	1	81	769	9.5	2	11	190	17.3	0	3	0	18	12

CARTER, DEXTER — RB/KR — 49ERS

PERSONAL: Born September 15, 1967, in Baxley, Ga. ... 5-9/175. ... Full name: Dexter Anthony Carter.
HIGH SCHOOL: Appling County (Baxley, Ga.).
COLLEGE: Florida State (degree in child development).
TRANSACTIONS/CAREER NOTES: Selected by San Francisco 49ers in first round (25th pick overall) of 1990 NFL draft. ... Signed by 49ers (July 26, 1990). ... On injured reserve with shoulder injury (September 1-November 21, 1992); on practice squad (October 7-November 21, 1992). ... On injured reserve with knee injury (December 10, 1992-remainder of season). ... Granted unconditional free agency (February 17, 1994). ... Re-signed by 49ers (May 4, 1994). ... Granted unconditional free agency (February 17, 1995). ... Signed by New York Jets (March 1, 1995). ... Claimed on waivers by 49ers (November 8, 1995).
CHAMPIONSHIP GAME EXPERIENCE: Played in NFC championship game (1990, 1993 and 1994 seasons). ... Member of Super Bowl championship team (1994 season).
PRO STATISTICS: 1990—Fumbled eight times and recovered two fumbles. 1991—Fumbled five times and recovered one fumble. 1993—Fumbled five times and recovered one fumble. 1994—Fumbled twice and recovered two fumbles. 1995—Fumbled eight times and recovered four fumbles.

STATISTICAL PLATEAUS: 100-yard rushing games: 1990 (1).

Year Team	G	RUSHING Att.	Yds.	Avg.	TD	RECEIVING No.	Yds.	Avg.	TD	PUNT RETURNS No.	Yds.	Avg.	TD	KICKOFF RETURNS No.	Yds.	Avg.	TD	TOTALS TD	2pt.	Pts.
1990—San Francisco NFL	16	114	460	4.0	1	25	217	8.7	0	0	0	...	0	41	783	19.1	0	1	...	6
1991—San Francisco NFL	16	85	379	4.5	2	23	253	11.0	1	0	0	...	0	37	839	22.7	†1	4	...	24
1992—San Francisco NFL	3	4	9	2.3	0	1	43	43.0	1	0	0	...	0	2	55	27.5	0	1	...	6
1993—San Francisco NFL	16	10	72	7.2	1	3	40	13.3	0	34	411	12.1	1	25	494	19.8	0	2	...	12
1994—San Francisco NFL	16	8	34	4.3	0	7	99	14.1	0	38	321	8.5	0	48	1105	23.0	1	1	0	6
1995—New York Jets NFL.....	10	0	0	...	0	1	0	0.0	0	21	145	6.9	0	33	705	21.4	0	0	0	0
—San Francisco NFL.....	7	7	22	3.1	0	1	4	4.0	0	9	164	18.2	†1	23	522	22.7	0	1	0	6
Pro totals (6 years)	84	228	976	4.3	4	61	656	10.8	2	102	1041	10.2	2	209	4503	21.6	2	10	0	60

CARTER, KEVIN   DE   RAMS

PERSONAL: Born September 21, 1973, in Tallahassee, Fla. ... 6-5/274. ... Full name: Kevin Louis Carter. ... Brother of Bernard Carter, linebacker, Jacksonville Jaguars.
HIGH SCHOOL: Lincoln (Tallahassee, Fla.).
COLLEGE: Florida.
TRANSACTIONS/CAREER NOTES: Selected by St. Louis Rams in first round (sixth pick overall) of 1995 NFL draft. ... Signed by Rams (July 17, 1995).
HONORS: Named defensive lineman on THE SPORTING NEWS college All-America first team (1994).
PRO STATISTICS: 1995—Recovered one fumble.

Year Team	G	SACKS
1995—St. Louis NFL...	16	6.0

CARTER, KI-JANA   RB   BENGALS

PERSONAL: Born September 12, 1973, in Westerville, Ohio. ... 5-10/227. ... Full name: Kenneth Leonard Carter. ... Name pronounced ki-JOHN-ah.
HIGH SCHOOL: Westerville (Ohio) South.
COLLEGE: Penn State.
TRANSACTIONS/CAREER NOTES: Selected after junior season by Cincinnati Bengals in first round (first pick overall) of 1995 NFL draft. ... Signed by Bengals (July 19, 1995). ... On injured reserve with knee injury (August 22, 1995- entire season).
HONORS: Named running back on THE SPORTING NEWS college All-America first team (1994).

CARTER, MARTY   S   BEARS

PERSONAL: Born December 17, 1969, in LaGrange, Ga. ... 6-1/209. ... Full name: Marty LaVincent Carter.
HIGH SCHOOL: LaGrange (Ga.).
COLLEGE: Middle Tennessee State.
TRANSACTIONS/CAREER NOTES: Selected by Tampa Bay Buccaneers in eighth round (207th pick overall) of 1991 NFL draft. ... Signed by Buccaneers (July 19, 1991). ... Granted unconditional free agency (February 17, 1995). ... Signed by Chicago Bears (March 3, 1995).
PRO STATISTICS: 1993—Recovered two fumbles. 1994—Caught one pass for 21 yards and returned one kickoff for no yards. 1995—Recovered one fumble.

Year Team	G	INTERCEPTIONS No.	Yds.	Avg.	TD	SACKS No.
1991—Tampa Bay NFL..	14	1	5	5.0	0	0.0
1992—Tampa Bay NFL..	16	3	1	0.3	0	2.0
1993—Tampa Bay NFL..	16	1	0	0.0	0	0.0
1994—Tampa Bay NFL..	16	0	0	...	0	1.0
1995—Chicago NFL..	16	2	20	10.0	0	0.0
Pro totals (5 years)..	78	7	26	3.7	0	3.0

CARTER, PAT   TE   CARDINALS

PERSONAL: Born August 1, 1966, in Sarasota, Fla. ... 6-4/258. ... Full name: Wendell Patrick Carter.
HIGH SCHOOL: Riverview (Sarasota, Fla.).
COLLEGE: Florida State.
TRANSACTIONS/CAREER NOTES: Selected by Detroit Lions in second round (32nd pick overall) of 1988 NFL draft. ... Signed by Lions (June 13, 1988). ... Traded by Lions to Los Angeles Rams for fourth-round pick (LB Rob Hinckley) in 1990 draft (August 18, 1989). ... Granted free agency (February 1, 1992). ... Re-signed by Rams (July 21, 1992). ... Granted unconditional free agency (February 17, 1994). ... Signed by Houston Oilers (March 30, 1994). ... Released by Oilers (August 27, 1995). ... Signed by St. Louis Rams (August 29, 1995). ... Granted unconditional free agency (February 16, 1996). ... Signed by Arizona Cardinals (April 22, 1996).
CHAMPIONSHIP GAME EXPERIENCE: Played in NFC championship game (1989 season).
HONORS: Named tight end on THE SPORTING NEWS college All-America first team (1987).
PRO STATISTICS: 1991—Returned one kickoff for 18 yards.

Year Team	G	RECEIVING No.	Yds.	Avg.	TD	TOTALS TD	2pt.	Pts.	Fum.
1988—Detroit NFL	15	13	145	11.2	0	0	...	0	0
1989—Los Angeles Rams NFL	16	0	0	...	0	0	...	0	0
1990—Los Angeles Rams NFL	16	8	58	7.3	0	0	...	0	0
1991—Los Angeles Rams NFL	16	8	69	8.6	2	2	...	12	1
1992—Los Angeles Rams NFL	16	20	232	11.6	3	3	...	18	0
1993—Los Angeles Rams NFL	11	14	166	11.9	1	1	...	6	0

C

Year Team	G	No.	Yds.	Avg.	TD	TD	2pt.	Pts.	Fum.
1994—Houston NFL	16	11	74	6.7	1	1	0	6	0
1995—St. Louis NFL	16	0	0	...	0	0	0	0	0
Pro totals (8 years)	122	74	744	10.1	7	7	0	42	1

The header above the last four columns reads RECEIVING (No., Yds., Avg., TD) and TOTALS (TD, 2pt., Pts., Fum.).

CARTER, PERRY   CB   CHIEFS

PERSONAL: Born August 15, 1971, in McComb, Miss. ... 5-11/206. ... Full name: Perry Lynn Carter.
HIGH SCHOOL: McComb (Miss.).
COLLEGE: Southern Mississippi.
TRANSACTIONS/CAREER NOTES: Selected by Arizona Cardinals in fourth round (107th pick overall) of 1994 NFL draft. ... Released by Cardinals (August 27, 1994). ... Re-signed by Cardinals to practice squad (August 30, 1994). ... Released by Cardinals (September 5, 1994). ... Signed by Washington Redskins to practice squad (September 13, 1994). ... Released by Redskins (September 20, 1994). ... Signed by Kansas City Chiefs to practice squad (December 15, 1994). ... Granted free agency after 1994 season. ... Re-signed by Chiefs (February 28, 1995). ... Released by Chiefs (August 22, 1995). ... Re-signed by Chiefs to practice squad (August 29, 1995). ... Activated (December 10, 1995).
PLAYING EXPERIENCE: Kansas City NFL, 1995. ... Games: 1995 (2).

CARTER, TOM   CB   REDSKINS

PERSONAL: Born September 5, 1972, in St. Petersburg, Fla. ... 6-0/181.
HIGH SCHOOL: Lakewood Senior (St. Petersburg, Fla.).
COLLEGE: Notre Dame.
TRANSACTIONS/CAREER NOTES: Selected after junior season by Washington Redskins in first round (17th pick overall) of 1993 NFL draft. ... Signed by Redskins for 1993 season. ... Designated by Redskins as transition player (February 15, 1994).

			INTERCEPTIONS		
Year Team	G	No.	Yds.	Avg.	TD
1993—Washington NFL	14	6	54	9.0	0
1994—Washington NFL	16	3	58	19.3	0
1995—Washington NFL	16	4	116	29.0	1
Pro totals (3 years)	46	13	228	17.5	1

CARTER, TONY   FB   BEARS

PERSONAL: Born August 23, 1972, in Columbus, Ohio. ... 5-11/232.
HIGH SCHOOL: South (Columbus, Ohio).
COLLEGE: Minnesota.
TRANSACTIONS/CAREER NOTES: Signed as non-drafted free agent by Chicago Bears (April 28, 1994).

		RECEIVING				KICKOFF RETURNS				TOTALS			
Year Team	G	No.	Yds.	Avg.	TD	No.	Yds.	Avg.	TD	TD	2pt.	Pts.	Fum.
1994—Chicago NFL	14	1	24	24.0	0	6	99	16.5	0	0	0	0	0
1995—Chicago NFL	16	40	329	8.2	1	3	24	8.0	0	1	0	6	1
Pro totals (2 years)	30	41	353	8.6	1	9	123	13.7	0	1	0	6	1

CARVER, SHANTE   DE   COWBOYS

PERSONAL: Born February 12, 1971, in Stockton, Calif. ... 6-5/242.
HIGH SCHOOL: Lincoln (Stockton, Calif.).
COLLEGE: Arizona State.
TRANSACTIONS/CAREER NOTES: Selected by Dallas Cowboys in first round (23rd pick overall) of 1994 NFL draft. ... Signed by Cowboys (July 16, 1994).
CHAMPIONSHIP GAME EXPERIENCE: Member of Cowboys for NFC championship game (1994 season); inactive. ... Played in NFC championship game (1995 season). ... Member of Super Bowl championship team (1995 season).
HONORS: Named defensive lineman on THE SPORTING NEWS college All-America first team (1993).
PRO STATISTICS: 1995—Recovered one fumble.

Year Team	G	SACKS
1994—Dallas NFL	10	0.0
1995—Dallas NFL	16	2.5
Pro totals (2 years)	26	2.5

CASCADDEN, CHAD   LB   JETS

PERSONAL: Born May 14, 1972, in Chippewa Falls, Wis. ... 6-1/225.
HIGH SCHOOL: Chippewa Falls (Wis.).
COLLEGE: Wisconsin.
TRANSACTIONS/CAREER NOTES: Signed as non-drafted free agent by New York Jets (April 28, 1995). ... Released by Jets (August 27, 1995). ... Re-signed by Jets to practice squad (August 29, 1995). ... Activated (September 19, 1995).
PLAYING EXPERIENCE: New York Jets NFL, 1995. ... Games: 1995 (12).

CASE, SCOTT   S

PERSONAL: Born May 17, 1962, in Waynoka, Okla. ... 6-1/188. ... Full name: Jeffrey Scott Case.

HIGH SCHOOL: Alva (Okla.) and Memorial (Edmond, Okla.).
COLLEGE: Northeastern Oklahoma A&M, then Oklahoma.
TRANSACTIONS/CAREER NOTES: Selected by Oklahoma Outlaws in 1984 USFL territorial draft. ... Selected by Atlanta Falcons in second round (32nd pick overall) of 1984 NFL draft. ... Signed by Falcons (July 20, 1984). ... Granted free agency (February 1, 1988). ... Re-signed by Falcons (August 29, 1988). ... On injured reserve with foot injury (December 23, 1989-remainder of season). ... Granted unconditional free agency (February 17, 1994). ... Re-signed by Falcons (July 21, 1994). ... Granted unconditional free agency (February 17, 1995). ... Signed by Dallas Cowboys (August 24, 1995). ... Granted unconditional free agency (February 16, 1996).
CHAMPIONSHIP GAME EXPERIENCE: Played in NFC championship game (1995 season). ... Member of Super Bowl championship team (1995 season).
HONORS: Played in Pro Bowl (1988 season).
PRO STATISTICS: 1985—Credited with a safety and recovered one fumble for 13 yards. 1990—Returned one kickoff for 13 yards and recovered two fumbles. 1991—Recovered two fumbles for two yards. 1992—Recovered two fumbles.

			INTERCEPTIONS				SACKS
Year Team	G	No.	Yds.	Avg.	TD		No.
1984—Atlanta NFL	16	0	0	...	0		0.0
1985—Atlanta NFL	14	4	78	19.5	0		1.0
1986—Atlanta NFL	16	4	41	10.3	0		0.0
1987—Atlanta NFL	11	1	12	12.0	0		0.0
1988—Atlanta NFL	16	*10	47	4.7	0		1.0
1989—Atlanta NFL	14	2	13	6.5	0		1.0
1990—Atlanta NFL	16	3	38	12.7	1		3.0
1991—Atlanta NFL	16	2	23	11.5	0		0.0
1992—Atlanta NFL	12	2	0	0.0	0		0.0
1993—Atlanta NFL	16	0	0	...	0		1.5
1994—Atlanta NFL	15	2	12	6.0	0		0.0
1995—Dallas NFL	16	0	0	...	0		0.0
Pro totals (12 years)	178	30	264	8.8	1		7.5

CASE, STONEY — QB — CARDINALS

PERSONAL: Born July 7, 1972, in Odessa, Texas. ... 6-2/206. ... Full name: Stoney Jarrod Case.
HIGH SCHOOL: Permian (Odessa, Texas).
COLLEGE: New Mexico.
TRANSACTIONS/CAREER NOTES: Selected by Arizona Cardinals in third round (80th pick overall) of 1995 NFL draft. ... Signed by Cardinals for 1995 season.

		PASSING							RUSHING				TOTALS		
Year Team	G	Att.	Cmp.	Pct.	Yds.	TD	Int.	Avg.	Rat.	Att.	Yds.	Avg.	TD	TD	2pt.	Pts.
1995—Arizona NFL	2	2	1	50.0	19	0	1	9.50	43.8	1	4	4.0	0	0	0	0

CASH, KEITH — TE — CHIEFS

PERSONAL: Born August 7, 1969, in San Antonio. ... 6-4/242. ... Full name: Keith Lovell Cash. ... Twin brother of Kerry Cash, tight end, Oakland Raiders.
HIGH SCHOOL: Holmes (San Antonio).
COLLEGE: Texas.
TRANSACTIONS/CAREER NOTES: Selected by Washington Redskins in seventh round (188th pick overall) of 1991 NFL draft. ... Released by Redskins (August 20, 1991). ... Signed by Pittsburgh Steelers to practice squad (September 3, 1991). ... Activated (November 23, 1991). ... Granted unconditional free agency (February 1, 1992). ... Signed by Kansas City Chiefs (April 1, 1992).
CHAMPIONSHIP GAME EXPERIENCE: Played in AFC championship game (1993 season).
PRO STATISTICS: 1991—Returned one punt for six yards. 1992—Returned one kickoff for 36 yards and recovered one fumble. 1993—Rushed once for no yards and recovered two fumbles. 1995—Recovered one fumble.
STATISTICAL PLATEAUS: 100-yard receiving games: 1995 (1).

		RECEIVING				TOTALS			
Year Team	G	No.	Yds.	Avg.	TD	TD	2pt.	Pts.	Fum.
1991—Pittsburgh NFL	5	7	90	12.9	1	1	...	6	0
1992—Kansas City NFL	15	12	113	9.4	2	2	...	12	0
1993—Kansas City NFL	15	24	242	10.1	4	4	...	24	1
1994—Kansas City NFL	6	19	192	10.1	2	2	0	12	0
1995—Kansas City NFL	14	42	419	10.0	1	1	0	6	0
Pro totals (5 years)	55	104	1056	10.2	10	10	0	60	1

CASH, KERRY — TE — RAIDERS

PERSONAL: Born August 7, 1969, in San Antonio. ... 6-4/245. ... Full name: Kerry Lenard Cash. ... Twin brother of Keith Cash, tight end, Kansas City Chiefs.
HIGH SCHOOL: Holmes (San Antonio).
COLLEGE: Texas.
TRANSACTIONS/CAREER NOTES: Selected by Indianapolis Colts in fifth round (125th pick overall) of 1991 NFL draft. ... Signed by Colts (July 14, 1991). ... On injured reserve with leg injury (September 24, 1991-remainder of season). ... Granted free agency (February 17, 1994). ... Re-signed by Colts (August 12, 1994). ... Granted unconditional free agency (February 17, 1995). ... Signed by Los Angeles Raiders (March 20, 1995). ... Raiders franchise moved to Oakland (July 21, 1995).
PRO STATISTICS: 1992—Recovered two fumbles. 1993—Returned one kickoff for 11 yards and recovered one fumble. 1994—Recovered one fumble. 1995—Fumbled two times and recovered two fumbles for three yards.
STATISTICAL PLATEAUS: 100-yard receiving games: 1992 (1).

Year—Team	G	No.	Yds.	Avg.	TD	TD	2pt.	Pts.	Fum.
		RECEIVING				**TOTALS**			
1991—Indianapolis NFL	4	1	18	18.0	0	0	...	0	0
1992—Indianapolis NFL	16	43	521	12.1	3	3	...	18	0
1993—Indianapolis NFL	16	43	402	9.4	3	3	...	18	2
1994—Indianapolis NFL	16	16	190	11.9	1	1	0	6	1
1995—Oakland NFL	16	25	254	10.2	2	2	0	12	2
Pro totals (5 years)	68	128	1385	10.8	9	9	0	54	5

CASILLAS, TONY   DT

PERSONAL: Born October 26, 1963, in Tulsa, Okla. ... 6-3/278. ... Full name: Tony Steven Casillas.
HIGH SCHOOL: East Central (Tulsa, Okla.).
COLLEGE: Oklahoma (degree in communications, 1986).
TRANSACTIONS/CAREER NOTES: Selected by Atlanta Falcons in first round (second pick overall) of 1986 NFL draft. ... Selected by Arizona Outlaws in first round (second pick overall) of 1986 USFL draft. ... Signed by Falcons (July 20, 1986). ... Granted roster exemption (September 13-24, 1990). ... On reserve/suspended list (October 23-November 5, 1990). ... On injured reserve with fractured elbow (December 27, 1990-remainder of season). ... Traded by Falcons to Dallas Cowboys for second-round (DE Chuck Smith) and eighth-round (TE Reggie Dwight) picks in 1992 draft (July 22, 1991). ... Granted unconditional free agency (February 17, 1994). ... Signed by Kansas City Chiefs (April 5, 1994). ... Released by Chiefs (August 4, 1994). ... Signed by New York Jets (September 19, 1994). ... Granted unconditional free agency (February 17, 1995). ... Re-signed by Jets (March 7, 1995). ... Released by Jets (March 1, 1996).
CHAMPIONSHIP GAME EXPERIENCE: Played in NFC championship game (1992 and 1993 seasons). ... Member of Super Bowl championship team (1992 and 1993 seasons).
HONORS: Named defensive lineman on THE SPORTING NEWS college All-America first team (1984 and 1985). ... Lombardi Award winner (1985).
PRO STATISTICS: 1986—Recovered one fumble. 1987—Recovered one fumble. 1988—Recovered one fumble. 1989—Recovered three fumbles. 1991—Recovered one fumble. 1992—Recovered one fumble for three yards. 1993—Recovered one fumble.

Year—Team	G	SACKS
1986—Atlanta NFL	16	1.0
1987—Atlanta NFL	9	2.0
1988—Atlanta NFL	16	2.0
1989—Atlanta NFL	16	2.0
1990—Atlanta NFL	9	1.0
1991—Dallas NFL	16	2.5
1992—Dallas NFL	15	3.0
1993—Dallas NFL	15	2.0
1994—New York Jets NFL	12	1.5
1995—New York Jets NFL	11	3.0
Pro totals (10 years)	135	20.0

CASTLE, ERIC   S   CHARGERS

PERSONAL: Born March 15, 1970, in Longview, Wash. ... 6-3/212. ... Full name: Eric Dean Castle.
HIGH SCHOOL: Lebanon (Ore.) Union.
COLLEGE: Oregon.
TRANSACTIONS/CAREER NOTES: Selected by San Diego Chargers in sixth round (161st pick overall) of 1993 NFL draft. ... Signed by Chargers (June 10, 1993). ... Released by Chargers (August 30, 1993). ... Re-signed by Chargers (August 31, 1993). ... Granted free agency (February 16, 1996). ... Re-signed by Chargers (May 8, 1996).
PLAYING EXPERIENCE: San Diego NFL, 1993-1995. ... Games: 1993 (5), 1994 (16), 1995 (16). Total: 37.
CHAMPIONSHIP GAME EXPERIENCE: Played in AFC championship game (1994 season). ... Played in Super Bowl XXIX (1994 season).

CATANHO, ALCIDES   LB   PATRIOTS

PERSONAL: Born January 20, 1972, in Elizabeth, N.J. ... 6-3/216.
HIGH SCHOOL: Elizabeth (N.J.).
COLLEGE: Rutgers.
TRANSACTIONS/CAREER NOTES: Signed as non-drafted free agent by New England Patriots (April 24, 1995). ... Released by Patriots (August 19, 1995). ... Signed by Washington Redskins to practice squad (August 28, 1995). ... Signed by Patriots off Redskins practice squad (September 13, 1995).
PLAYING EXPERIENCE: New England NFL, 1995. ... Games: 1995 (12).
PRO STATISTICS: 1995—Recovered one fumble.

CEASER, CURTIS   WR   JETS

PERSONAL: Born August 11, 1972, in Lincoln, Neb. ... 6-2/190.
HIGH SCHOOL: Westbrook (Beaumont, Texas).
COLLEGE: Grambling State.
TRANSACTIONS/CAREER NOTES: Selected by New York Jets in seventh round (217th pick overall) of 1995 NFL draft. ... Signed by Jets (May 15, 1995). ... Released by Jets (August 27, 1995). ... Re-signed by Jets (August 29, 1995). ... Released by Jets (October 10, 1995). ... Re-signed by Jets to practice squad (October 12, 1995).
PLAYING EXPERIENCE: New York Jets NFL, 1995. ... Games: 1995 (4).

CECIL, CHUCK   S

PERSONAL: Born November 8, 1964, in Red Bluff, Calif. ... 6-0/185. ... Full name: Charles Douglas Cecil.

HIGH SCHOOL: Helix (La Mesa, Calif.).
COLLEGE: Arizona.
TRANSACTIONS/CAREER NOTES: Selected by Green Bay Packers in fourth round (89th pick overall) of 1988 NFL draft. ... Signed by Packers (July 17, 1988). ... On injured reserve with hamstring injury (September 15-October 12, 1990). ... On injured reserve with strained knee (December 20, 1990-remainder of season). ... Granted free agency (February 1, 1991). ... Re-signed by Packers (July 31, 1991). ... Granted unconditional free agency (March 1, 1993). ... Signed by Phoenix Cardinals (April 8, 1993). ... Released by Cardinals (June 2, 1994). ... Re-signed by Cardinals (June 6, 1994). ... Released by Cardinals (August 15, 1994). ... Signed by Cleveland Browns (May 11, 1995). ... Released by Browns (August 22, 1995). ... Signed by Houston Oilers (August 31, 1995). ... Granted unconditional free agency (February 16, 1996).
HONORS: Named defensive back on THE SPORTING NEWS college All-America second team (1986 and 1987). ... Played in Pro Bowl (1992 season).
PRO STATISTICS: 1988—Recovered one fumble. 1992—Returned one punt for no yards and fumbled once.

			INTERCEPTIONS		
Year Team	G	No.	Yds.	Avg.	TD
1988—Green Bay NFL	16	4	56	14.0	0
1989—Green Bay NFL	9	1	16	16.0	0
1990—Green Bay NFL	9	1	0	0.0	0
1991—Green Bay NFL	16	3	76	25.3	0
1992—Green Bay NFL	16	4	52	13.0	0
1993—Phoenix NFL	15	0	0	...	0
1994—			Did not play.		
1995—Houston NFL	14	3	35	11.7	1
Pro totals (7 years)	95	16	235	14.7	1

CENTERS, LARRY   RB   CARDINALS

PERSONAL: Born June 1, 1968, in Tatum, Texas. ... 5-11/215.
HIGH SCHOOL: Tatum (Texas).
COLLEGE: Stephen F. Austin State.
TRANSACTIONS/CAREER NOTES: Selected by Phoenix Cardinals in fifth round (115th pick overall) of 1990 NFL draft. ... Signed by Cardinals (July 23, 1990). ... On injured reserve with broken foot (September 11-October 30, 1991). ... Granted free agency (February 1, 1992). ... Re-signed by Cardinals (July 23, 1992). ... Granted unconditional free agency (February 17, 1994). ... Re-signed by Cardinals (March 15, 1994). ... Cardinals franchise renamed Arizona Cardinals for 1994 season.
HONORS: Played in Pro Bowl (1995 season).
PRO STATISTICS: 1991—Returned five punts for 30 yards and recovered two fumbles. 1993—Recovered two fumbles. 1994—Recovered two fumbles for 27 yards. 1995—Had only pass attempt intercepted and recovered one fumble.
STATISTICAL PLATEAUS: 100-yard receiving games: 1995 (2).

		RUSHING				RECEIVING				KICKOFF RETURNS				TOTALS			
Year Team	G	Att.	Yds.	Avg.	TD	No.	Yds.	Avg.	TD	No.	Yds.	Avg.	TD	TD	2pt.	Pts.	Fum.
1990—Phoenix NFL	6	0	0	...	0	0	0	...	0	16	272	17.0	0	0	...	0	1
1991—Phoenix NFL	9	14	44	3.1	0	19	176	9.3	0	16	330	20.6	0	0	...	0	4
1992—Phoenix NFL	16	37	139	3.8	0	50	417	8.3	2	0	0	...	0	2	...	12	1
1993—Phoenix NFL	16	25	152	6.1	0	66	603	9.1	3	0	0	...	0	3	...	18	1
1994—Arizona NFL	16	115	336	2.9	5	77	647	8.4	2	0	0	...	0	7	0	42	2
1995—Arizona NFL	16	78	254	3.3	2	101	962	9.5	2	1	15	15.0	0	4	0	24	2
Pro totals (6 years)	79	269	925	3.4	7	313	2805	9.0	9	33	617	18.7	0	16	0	96	11

CHALENSKI, MIKE   DL   JETS

PERSONAL: Born January 28, 1970, in Elizabeth, N.J. ... 6-5/285.
HIGH SCHOOL: David Brearley Regional (Kenilworth, N.J.).
COLLEGE: Pittsburgh, then UCLA.
TRANSACTIONS/CAREER NOTES: Signed as non-drafted free agent by Philadelphia Eagles (April 30, 1993). ... On injured reserve with knee injury (August 23, 1994-entire season). ... Granted unconditional free agency (February 16, 1996). ... Signed by New York Jets (April 18, 1996).
PLAYING EXPERIENCE: Philadelphia NFL, 1993 and 1995. ... Games: 1993 (15), 1995 (9). Total: 24.

CHAMBERLAIN, BYRON   WR   BRONCOS

PERSONAL: Born October 17, 1971, in Honolulu. ... 6-1/225.
HIGH SCHOOL: Eastern Hills (Ft. Worth, Texas).
COLLEGE: Missouri, then Wayne (Neb.) State.
TRANSACTIONS/CAREER NOTES: Selected by Denver Broncos in seventh round (222nd pick overall) of 1995 NFL draft. ... Signed by Broncos (August 27, 1995). ... Released by Broncos (August 27, 1995). ... Re-signed by Broncos to practice squad (August 28, 1995). ... Activated (November 24, 1995). ... Assigned by Broncos to Rhein Fire in 1996 World League enhancement allocation program (February 19, 1996).
PLAYING EXPERIENCE: Denver NFL, 1995. ... Games: 1995 (5).
PRO STATISTICS: 1995—Caught one pass for 11 yards.

CHANDLER, CHRIS   QB   OILERS

PERSONAL: Born October 12, 1965, in Everett, Wash. ... 6-4/225. ... Full name: Christopher Mark Chandler. ... Brother of Greg Chandler, catcher, San Francisco Giants organization (1978); and son-in-law of John Brodie, quarterback, San Francisco 49ers (1957-1973).
HIGH SCHOOL: Everett (Wash.).
COLLEGE: Washington (degree in economics, 1988).
TRANSACTIONS/CAREER NOTES: Selected by Indianapolis Colts in third round (76th pick overall) of 1988 NFL draft. ... Signed by Colts (July 23, 1988). ... On injured reserve with knee injury (October 3, 1989-remainder of season). ... Traded by Colts to Tampa Bay Buccaneers for first round pick (DL Steve Emtman) in 1992 draft (August 7, 1990). ... Claimed on waivers by Phoenix Cardinals (November 6, 1991). ... Granted unconditional free agency (February 17, 1994). ... Signed by Los Angeles Rams (May 6, 1994). ... Granted unconditional free agency

(February 17, 1995). ... Signed by Houston Oilers (March 10, 1995).
PRO STATISTICS: 1988—Fumbled eight times and recovered five fumbles for minus six yards. 1990—Fumbled five times and recovered one fumble for minus two yards. 1991—Fumbled six times and recovered two fumbles for minus seven yards. 1992—Fumbled nine times and recovered two fumbles for minus 11 yards. 1993—Fumbled twice. 1994—Fumbled three times. 1995—Fumbled 12 times and recovered five fumbles for minus nine yards.
STATISTICAL PLATEAUS: 300-yard passing games: 1992 (1), 1995 (1). Total: 2.
MISCELLANEOUS: Regular-season record as starting NFL quarterback: 22-36 (.379).

			PASSING								RUSHING				TOTALS		
Year Team	G	Att.	Cmp.	Pct.	Yds.	TD	Int.	Avg.	Rat.	Att.	Yds.	Avg.	TD	TD	2pt.	Pts.
1988—Indianapolis NFL	15	233	129	55.4	1619	8	12	6.95	67.2	46	139	3.0	3	3	...	18
1989—Indianapolis NFL	3	80	39	48.8	537	2	3	6.71	63.4	7	57	8.1	1	1	...	6
1990—Tampa Bay NFL	7	83	42	50.6	464	1	6	5.59	41.4	13	71	5.5	1	1	...	6
1991—Tampa Bay NFL	6	104	53	51.0	557	4	8	5.36	47.6	18	79	4.4	0	0	...	0
—Phoenix NFL	3	50	25	50.0	289	1	2	5.78	57.8	8	32	4.0	0	0	...	0
1992—Phoenix NFL	15	413	245	59.3	2832	15	15	6.86	77.1	36	149	4.1	1	1	...	6
1993—Phoenix NFL	4	103	52	50.5	471	3	2	4.57	64.8	3	2	.7	0	0	...	0
1994—Los Angeles Rams NFL	12	176	108	61.4	1352	7	2	7.68	93.8	18	61	3.4	1	1	0	6
1995—Houston NFL	13	356	225	63.2	2460	17	10	6.91	87.8	28	58	2.1	2	2	1	14
Pro totals (8 years)	78	1598	918	57.5	10581	58	60	6.62	74.0	177	648	3.7	9	9	1	56

CHILDRESS, RAY — DT

C

PERSONAL: Born October 20, 1962, in Memphis. ... 6-6/272. ... Full name: Raymond Clay Childress Jr.
HIGH SCHOOL: J.J. Pearce (Richardson, Texas).
COLLEGE: Texas A&M.
TRANSACTIONS/CAREER NOTES: Selected by Houston Gamblers in 1985 USFL territorial draft. ... Selected by Houston Oilers in first round (third pick overall) of 1985 NFL draft. ... Signed by Oilers (August 24, 1985). ... Granted roster exemption (August 24-30, 1985). ... Crossed picket line during players strike (October 14, 1987). ... Granted free agency (February 1, 1989). ... Tendered offer sheet by Chicago Bears (March 30, 1989). ... Offer matched by Oilers (April 3, 1989). ... On injured reserve with shoulder injury (November 30, 1995-remainder of season). ... Released by Oilers (February 15, 1996).
HONORS: Named defensive lineman on THE SPORTING NEWS college All-America first team (1984). ... Played in Pro Bowl (1988, 1990, 1992 and 1993 seasons). ... Named to play in Pro Bowl (1991 season); replaced by Cortez Kennedy due to injury. ... Named defensive tackle on THE SPORTING NEWS NFL All-Pro team (1990).
RECORDS: Shares NFL single-game record for most opponents' fumbles recovered—3 (October 30, 1988, vs. Washington).
PRO STATISTICS: 1985—Recovered one fumble. 1986—Recovered one fumble. 1987—Recovered one fumble for one yard. 1988—Recovered seven fumbles. 1989—Recovered one fumble. 1990—Credited with a safety and recovered one fumble. 1991—Recovered one fumble. 1992—Recovered two fumbles for eight yards and a touchdown. 1993—Recovered three fumbles (including one in end zone for a touchdown). 1995—Recovered one fumble.

Year Team	G	SACKS
1985—Houston NFL	16	3.5
1986—Houston NFL	16	5.0
1987—Houston NFL	13	6.0
1988—Houston NFL	16	8.5
1989—Houston NFL	14	8.5
1990—Houston NFL	16	8.0
1991—Houston NFL	15	7.0
1992—Houston NFL	16	13.0
1993—Houston NFL	16	9.0
1994—Houston NFL	16	6.0
1995—Houston NFL	6	1.0
Pro totals (11 years)	160	75.5

CHILDS, RON — LB — SAINTS

PERSONAL: Born September 18, 1971, in Kennewick, Wash. ... 5-11/212. ... Full name: Ron Lee Childs.
HIGH SCHOOL: Kamiakin (Kennewick, Wash.).
COLLEGE: Washington State.
TRANSACTIONS/CAREER NOTES: Signed as non-drafted free agent by Kansas City Chiefs (May 1, 1995). ... Claimed on waivers by New Orleans Saints (August 28, 1995).
PLAYING EXPERIENCE: New Orleans NFL, 1995. ... Games: 1995 (9).

CHMURA, MARK — TE — PACKERS

PERSONAL: Born February 22, 1969, in Deerfield, Mass. ... 6-5/250. ... Full name: Mark William Chmura.
HIGH SCHOOL: Frontier Regional (South Deerfield, Mass.).
COLLEGE: Boston College.
TRANSACTIONS/CAREER NOTES: Selected by Green Bay Packers in sixth round (157th pick overall) of 1992 NFL draft. ... Signed by Packers (July 22, 1992). ... On injured reserve with back injury (August 24, 1992-entire season).
CHAMPIONSHIP GAME EXPERIENCE: Played in NFC championship game (1995 season).
HONORS: Named tight end on THE SPORTING NEWS college All-America second team (1991). ... Played in Pro Bowl (1995 season).
PRO STATISTICS: 1993—Returned one kickoff for no yards and recovered one fumble.
STATISTICAL PLATEAUS: 100-yard receiving games: 1995 (2).

		RECEIVING				TOTALS			
Year Team	G	No.	Yds.	Avg.	TD	TD	2pt.	Pts.	Fum.
1992—Green Bay NFL				Did not play—injured.					
1993—Green Bay NFL	14	2	13	6.5	0	0	...	0	1

Year Team	G	No.	Yds.	Avg.	TD	TD	2pt.	Pts.	Fum.
			RECEIVING				**TOTALS**		
1994—Green Bay NFL	14	14	165	11.8	0	0	0	0	0
1995—Green Bay NFL	16	54	679	12.6	7	7	1	44	0
Pro totals (3 years)	44	70	857	12.3	7	7	1	44	1

CHREBET, WAYNE — WR — JETS

PERSONAL: Born August 14, 1973, in Garfield, N.J. ... 5-10/180. ... Name pronounced kra-BET.
HIGH SCHOOL: Garfield (N.J.).
COLLEGE: Hofstra.
TRANSACTIONS/CAREER NOTES: Signed as non-drafted free agent by New York Jets (April 25, 1995).
PRO STATISTICS: 1995—Rushed once for one yard.

Year Team	G	No.	Yds.	Avg.	TD	TD	2pt.	Pts.	Fum.
			RECEIVING				**TOTALS**		
1995—New York Jets NFL	16	66	726	11.0	4	4	0	24	1

CHRISTIAN, BOB — RB — PANTHERS

PERSONAL: Born November 14, 1968, in St. Louis. ... 5-10/230. ... Full name: Robert Douglas Christian.
HIGH SCHOOL: McCluer North (Florissant, Mo.).
COLLEGE: Northwestern.
TRANSACTIONS/CAREER NOTES: Selected by Atlanta Falcons in 12th round (310th pick overall) of 1991 NFL draft. ... Signed by Falcons (July 18, 1991). ... Released by Falcons (August 20, 1991). ... Selected by London Monarchs in 16th round (175th pick overall) of 1992 World League draft. ... Signed by San Diego Chargers (July 10, 1992). ... Released by Chargers (August 25, 1992). ... Signed by Chicago Bears to practice squad (September 8, 1992). ... Activated (December 18, 1992). ... On injured reserve with knee injury (December 2, 1994-remainder of season). ... Selected by Carolina Panthers from Bears in NFL expansion draft (February 15, 1995). ... Granted free agency (February 16, 1996).
PRO STATISTICS: 1995—Recovered one fumble.

Year Team	G	Att.	Yds.	Avg.	TD	No.	Yds.	Avg.	TD	TD	2pt.	Pts.	Fum.
			RUSHING				**RECEIVING**				**TOTALS**		
1992—Chicago NFL	2	0	0	...	0	0	0	...	0	0	...	0	0
1993—Chicago NFL	14	8	19	2.4	0	16	160	10.0	0	0	0	0	0
1994—Chicago NFL	12	7	29	4.1	0	2	30	15.0	0	0	0	0	0
1995—Carolina NFL	14	41	158	3.9	0	29	255	8.8	1	1	1	8	1
Pro totals (4 years)	42	56	206	3.7	0	47	445	9.5	1	1	1	8	1

CHRISTIE, STEVE — K — BILLS

PERSONAL: Born November 13, 1967, in Oakville, Ontario. ... 6-0/185. ... Full name: Geoffrey Stephen Christie.
HIGH SCHOOL: Oakville (Ont.) Trafalgar.
COLLEGE: William & Mary.
TRANSACTIONS/CAREER NOTES: Signed as non-drafted free agent by Tampa Bay Buccaneers (May 8, 1990). ... Granted unconditional free agency (February 1, 1992). ... Signed by Buffalo Bills (February 5, 1992).
CHAMPIONSHIP GAME EXPERIENCE: Played in AFC championship game (1992 and 1993 seasons). ... Played in Super Bowl XXVII (1992 season) and Super Bowl XXVIII (1993 season).
POSTSEASON RECORDS: Holds Super Bowl single-game record for longest field goal—54 yards (January 30, 1994, vs. Dallas). ... Shares NFL postseason single-game record for most field goals—5; and most field goals attempted—6 (January 17 1993, at Miami).
PRO STATISTICS: 1994—Recovered one fumble.

Year Team	G	XPM	XPA	FGM	FGA	Lg.	50+	Pts.
				KICKING				
1990—Tampa Bay NFL	16	27	27	23	27	54	2-2	96
1991—Tampa Bay NFL	16	22	22	15	20	49	0-0	67
1992—Buffalo NFL	16	43	44	24	30	54	3-5	115
1993—Buffalo NFL	16	36	37	23	32	59	1-6	105
1994—Buffalo NFL	16	38	38	24	28	52	2-2	110
1995—Buffalo NFL	16	33	35	31	40	51	2-5	126
Pro totals (6 years)	96	199	203	140	177	59	10-20	619

CHRISTOPHERSON, RYAN — FB — JAGUARS

PERSONAL: Born July 26, 1972, in Sioux Falls, S.D. ... 5-11/237.
HIGH SCHOOL: Cactus (Glendale, Ariz.).
COLLEGE: Wyoming.
TRANSACTIONS/CAREER NOTES: Selected by Jacksonville Jaguars in fifth round (169th pick overall) of 1995 NFL draft. ... Signed by Jaguars (June 1, 1995).
PRO STATISTICS: 1995—Caught one pass for minus one yard.

Year Team	G	Att.	Yds.	Avg.	TD	TD	2pt.	Pts.	Fum.
			RUSHING				**TOTALS**		
1995—Jacksonville NFL	16	16	16	1.0	1	1	0	6	1

CHRISTY, JEFF — C — VIKINGS

PERSONAL: Born February 3, 1969, in Natrona Heights, Pa. ... 6-3/284. ... Full name: Jeffrey Alan Christy. ... Brother of Greg Christy, tackle,

Buffalo Bills (1985).
HIGH SCHOOL: Freeport (Pa.) Area.
COLLEGE: Pittsburgh.
TRANSACTIONS/CAREER NOTES: Selected by Phoenix Cardinals in fourth round (91st pick overall) of 1992 NFL draft. ... Signed by Cardinals (July 21, 1992). ... Released by Cardinals (August 31, 1992). ... Signed by Minnesota Vikings (March 16, 1993).
PLAYING EXPERIENCE: Minnesota NFL, 1993-1995. ... Games: 1993 (9), 1994 (16), 1995 (16). Total: 41.

CHUNG, EUGENE — G/OT — 49ERS

PERSONAL: Born June 14, 1969, in Prince George's County, Md. ... 6-5/311. ... Full name: Yon Eugene Chung.
HIGH SCHOOL: Oakton (Vienna, Va.).
COLLEGE: Virginia Tech (degree in hotel, restaurant and institutional management).
TRANSACTIONS/CAREER NOTES: Selected by New England Patriots in first round (13th pick overall) of 1992 NFL draft. ... Signed by Patriots (July 29, 1992). ... Selected by Jacksonville Jaguars from Patriots in NFL expansion draft (February 15, 1995). ... Granted unconditional free agency (February 16, 1996). ... Signed by San Francisco 49ers (March 20, 1996).
PLAYING EXPERIENCE: New England NFL, 1992-1994; Jacksonville NFL, 1995. ... Games: 1992 (15), 1993 (16), 1994 (3), 1995 (11). Total: 45.

C

CLARK, GARY — WR

PERSONAL: Born May 1, 1962, in Radford, Va. ... 5-9/175.
HIGH SCHOOL: Pulaski County (Dublin, Va.).
COLLEGE: James Madison.
TRANSACTIONS/CAREER NOTES: Selected by Jacksonville Bulls in first round (sixth pick overall) of 1984 USFL draft. ... Signed by Bulls (January 16, 1984). ... On developmental squad (May 9-16, 1984). ... On developmental squad for two games (June 4-12, 1984). ... Selected by Washington Redskins in second round (55th pick overall) of 1984 NFL supplemental draft. ... On developmental squad for one game with Bulls (March 17-20, 1985). ... Released by Bulls (May 1, 1985). ... Signed by Redskins (May 13, 1985). ... Granted unconditional free agency (March 1, 1993). ... Signed by Phoenix Cardinals (March 22, 1993). ... Cardinals franchise renamed Arizona Cardinals for 1994 season. ... Granted unconditional free agency (February 17, 1995). ... Signed by Miami Dolphins (April 30, 1995). ... Released by Dolphins (February 5, 1996).
CHAMPIONSHIP GAME EXPERIENCE: Played in NFC championship game (1986, 1987 and 1991 seasons). ... Member of Super Bowl championship team (1987 and 1991 seasons).
HONORS: Played in Pro Bowl (1986, 1987, 1990 and 1991 seasons).
PRO STATISTICS: USFL: 1984—Fumbled five times and recovered four fumbles. 1985—Fumbled once and recovered one fumble. NFL: 1986—Fumbled once and recovered one fumble. 1987—Fumbled three times. 1988—Fumbled twice. 1989—Fumbled once. 1992—Fumbled once. 1993—Fumbled once.
STATISTICAL PLATEAUS: USFL: 100-yard receiving games: 1984 (2). ... NFL: 100-yard receiving games: 1985 (3), 1986 (5), 1987 (5), 1989 (5), 1990 (4), 1991 (3), 1992 (1), 1993 (3), 1994 (2). Total: 31.
MISCELLANEOUS: Active AFC leader for career receiving yards (10,856).

Year Team	G	RUSHING				RECEIVING				PUNT RETURNS				KICKOFF RETURNS				TOTALS		
		Att.	Yds.	Avg.	TD	No.	Yds.	Avg.	TD	No.	Yds.	Avg.	TD	No.	Yds.	Avg.	TD	TD	2pt.	Pts.
1984—Jacksonville USFL	16	2	9	4.5	0	56	760	13.6	2	20	84	4.2	0	19	341	18.0	0	2	0	12
1985—Jacksonville USFL	9	0	0	...	0	10	61	6.1	1	7	44	6.3	0	3	56	18.7	0	1	0	6
—Washington NFL	16	0	0	...	0	72	926	12.9	5	0	0	...	0	0	0	...	0	5	...	30
1986—Washington NFL	15	2	10	5.0	0	74	1265	17.1	7	1	14	14.0	0	0	0	...	0	7	...	42
1987—Washington NFL	12	1	0	0.0	0	56	1066	19.0	7	0	0	...	0	0	0	...	0	7	...	42
1988—Washington NFL	16	2	6	3.0	0	59	892	15.1	7	8	48	6.0	0	0	0	...	0	7	...	42
1989—Washington NFL	15	2	19	9.5	0	79	1229	15.6	9	0	0	...	0	0	0	...	0	9	...	54
1990—Washington NFL	16	1	1	1.0	0	75	1112	14.8	8	0	0	...	0	0	0	...	0	8	...	48
1991—Washington NFL	16	1	0	0.0	0	70	1340	19.1	10	0	0	...	0	0	0	...	0	10	...	60
1992—Washington NFL	16	2	18	9.0	0	64	912	14.3	5	0	0	...	0	0	0	...	0	5	...	30
1993—Phoenix NFL	14	0	0	...	0	63	818	13.0	4	0	0	...	0	0	0	...	0	4	...	24
1994—Arizona NFL	15	0	0	...	0	50	771	15.4	1	0	0	...	0	0	0	...	0	1	0	6
1995—Miami NFL	16	0	0	...	0	37	525	14.2	2	0	0	...	0	0	0	...	0	2	0	12
USFL totals (2 years)	25	2	9	4.5	0	66	821	12.4	3	27	128	4.8	0	22	397	18.1	0	3	0	18
NFL totals (11 years)	167	11	54	4.9	0	699	10856	15.5	65	9	62	6.9	0	0	0	...	0	65	0	390
Pro totals (13 years)	192	13	63	4.9	0	765	11677	15.3	68	36	190	5.3	0	22	397	18.1	0	68	0	408

CLARK, REGGIE — LB — JAGUARS

PERSONAL: Born October 17, 1967, in Charlotte. ... 6-3/245.
HIGH SCHOOL: Providence Day (Charlotte).
COLLEGE: North Carolina.
TRANSACTIONS/CAREER NOTES: Signed as non-drafted free agent by New England Patriots (April 27, 1991). ... Released by Patriots (August 26, 1991). ... Signed by Patriots to practice squad (August 28, 1991). ... Granted free agency after 1991 season. ... Re-signed by Patriots (February 1, 1992). ... Assigned by Patriots to Montreal Machine in 1992 World League enhancement allocation program (February 20, 1992). ... Released by Patriots (August 31, 1992). ... Re-signed by Patriots to practice squad (September 2, 1992). ... Released by Patriots (September 9, 1992). ... Signed by San Diego Chargers to practice squad (September 30, 1992). ... Granted free agency after 1992 season. ... Re-signed by Chargers (February 8, 1993). ... Released by Chargers (August 24, 1993). ... Signed by Pittsburgh Steelers (July 28, 1994). ... Released by Steelers (October 21, 1994). ... Signed by Jacksonville Jaguars (January 10, 1995). ... On injured reserve with knee injury (October 10, 1995-remainder of season).
PLAYING EXPERIENCE: Montreal W.L., 1992; Pittsburgh NFL, 1994; Jacksonville NFL, 1995. ... Games: 1992 (10), 1994 (5), 1995 (5). Total W.L.: 10. Total NFL: 10. Total Pro: 20.
PRO STATISTICS: W.L.: 1992—Credited with one sack and recovered one fumble. NFL: 1994—Recovered one fumble. 1995—Recovered one fumble.

CLARK, VINNIE   CB   JAGUARS

PERSONAL: Born January 22, 1969, in Cincinnati. ... 6-0/204. ... Full name: Vincent Eugene Clark.
HIGH SCHOOL: Cincinnati Academy of Physical Education.
COLLEGE: Ohio State.
TRANSACTIONS/CAREER NOTES: Selected by Green Bay Packers in first round (19th pick overall) of 1991 NFL draft. ... Signed by Packers (July 16, 1991). ... Traded by Packers to Atlanta Falcons for fourth-round pick in 1993 draft (April 1, 1993). ... Claimed on waivers by New Orleans Saints (November 23, 1994). ... Granted unconditional free agency (February 17, 1995). ... Signed by Jacksonville Jaguars (March 3, 1995).
PRO STATISTICS: 1992—Returned one punt for no yards. 1993—Returned one punt for no yards and recovered one fumble for 46 yards and a touchdown.

			INTERCEPTIONS		
Year Team	G	No.	Yds.	Avg.	TD
1991—Green Bay NFL	16	2	42	21.0	0
1992—Green Bay NFL	16	2	70	35.0	0
1993—Atlanta NFL	15	2	59	29.5	0
1994—Atlanta NFL	11	4	119	29.8	0
—New Orleans NFL	5	1	30	30.0	0
1995—Jacksonville NFL	16	1	0	0.0	0
Pro totals (5 years)	79	12	320	26.7	0

CLARK, WILLIE   CB   CHARGERS

PERSONAL: Born January 6, 1972, in New Haven, Conn. ... 5-10/186. ... Full name: Willie Calvin Clark.
HIGH SCHOOL: Wheatland (Calif.).
COLLEGE: Notre Dame.
TRANSACTIONS/CAREER NOTES: Selected by San Diego Chargers in third round (82nd pick overall) of 1994 NFL draft. ... Signed by Chargers (July 12, 1994).
PLAYING EXPERIENCE: San Diego NFL, 1994 and 1995. ... Games: 1994 (6), 1995 (16). Total: 22.
CHAMPIONSHIP GAME EXPERIENCE: Played in AFC championship game (1994 season). ... Played in Super Bowl XXIX (1994 season).
PRO STATISTICS: 1995—Intercepted two passes for 14 yards and recovered one fumble.

CLARKS, CONRAD   DB   COLTS

PERSONAL: Born April 21, 1969, in Franklin, La. ... 5-10/200.
HIGH SCHOOL: Franklin (La.).
JUNIOR COLLEGE: Pearl River Community College (Miss.).
COLLEGE: Northeast Louisiana.
TRANSACTIONS/CAREER NOTES: Signed as non-drafted free agent by Indianapolis Colts (April 27, 1995).
PLAYING EXPERIENCE: Indianapolis NFL, 1995. ... Games: 1995 (6).
CHAMPIONSHIP GAME EXPERIENCE: Played in AFC championship game (1995 season).

CLAVELLE, SHANNON   DE   PACKERS

PERSONAL: Born December 12, 1973, in Lafayette, La. ... 6-2/287.
HIGH SCHOOL: O. Perry Walker (New Orleans).
COLLEGE: Colorado.
TRANSACTIONS/CAREER NOTES: Selected after junior season by Buffalo Bills in sixth round (185th pick overall) of 1995 NFL draft. ... Signed by Bills (June 27, 1995). ... Released by Bills (August 27, 1995). ... Signed by Green Bay Packers to practice squad (September 18, 1995). ... Activated (October 25, 1995).
PLAYING EXPERIENCE: Green Bay NFL, 1995. ... Games: 1995 (1).
CHAMPIONSHIP GAME EXPERIENCE: Member of Packers for NFC championship game (1995 season); inactive.

CLAY, WILLIE   S   PATRIOTS

PERSONAL: Born September 5, 1970, in Pittsburgh. ... 5-9/184. ... Full name: Willie James Clay.
HIGH SCHOOL: Linsly (Wheeling, W.Va.).
COLLEGE: Georgia Tech.
TRANSACTIONS/CAREER NOTES: Selected by Detroit Lions in eighth round (221st pick overall) of 1992 NFL draft. ... Signed by Lions (July 25, 1992). ... Released by Lions (September 4, 1992). ... Re-signed by Lions to practice squad (September 8, 1992). ... Activated (November 20, 1992). ... Granted free agency (February 17, 1995). ... Re-signed by Lions (May 16, 1995). ... Granted unconditional free agency (February 16, 1996). ... Signed by New England Patriots (March 13, 1996).
HONORS: Named defensive back on THE SPORTING NEWS college All-America second team (1991).
PRO STATISTICS: 1993—Credited with one sack, returned two kickoffs for 34 yards and recovered two fumbles for 54 yards and two touchdowns.

			INTERCEPTIONS		
Year Team	G	No.	Yds.	Avg.	TD
1992—Detroit NFL	6	0	0	...	0
1993—Detroit NFL	16	0	0	...	0
1994—Detroit NFL	16	3	54	18.0	1
1995—Detroit NFL	16	8	*173	21.6	0
Pro totals (4 years)	54	11	227	20.7	1

CLIFTON, KYLE　　　　　　LB　　　　　　JETS

PERSONAL: Born August 23, 1962, in Onley, Texas. ... 6-4/236.
HIGH SCHOOL: Bridgeport (Texas).
COLLEGE: Texas Christian (degree in business management).
TRANSACTIONS/CAREER NOTES: Selected by Birmingham Stallions in first round (12th pick overall) of 1984 USFL draft. ... Selected by New York Jets in third round (64th pick overall) of 1984 NFL draft. ... Signed by Jets (July 12, 1984). ... Granted unconditional free agency (February 16, 1996). ... Re-signed by Jets (April 22, 1996).
PRO STATISTICS: 1984—Recovered one fumble. 1986—Recovered one fumble. 1985—Recovered two fumbles. 1988—Recovered two fumbles for six yards. 1989—Recovered one fumble. 1990—Recovered one fumble. 1992—Recovered four fumbles. 1993—Recovered two fumbles. 1994—Returned one kickoff for 13 yards and recovered one fumble.

			INTERCEPTIONS			SACKS
Year Team	G	No.	Yds.	Avg.	TD	No.
1984—New York Jets NFL	16	1	0	0.0	0	0.0
1985—New York Jets NFL	16	3	10	3.3	0	0.0
1986—New York Jets NFL	16	2	8	4.0	0	0.0
1987—New York Jets NFL	12	0	0	...	0	0.0
1988—New York Jets NFL	16	0	0	...	0	0.0
1989—New York Jets NFL	16	0	0	...	0	2.0
1990—New York Jets NFL	16	3	49	16.3	0	0.5
1991—New York Jets NFL	16	1	3	3.0	0	1.0
1992—New York Jets NFL	16	1	1	1.0	0	1.0
1993—New York Jets NFL	16	1	3	3.0	0	1.0
1994—New York Jets NFL	16	0	0	...	0	0.0
1995—New York Jets NFL	16	0	0	...	0	0.0
Pro totals (12 years)	188	12	74	6.2	0	5.5

CLINE, TONY　　　　　　TE　　　　　　BILLS

PERSONAL: Born November 24, 1971, in Davis, Calif. ... 6-4/247. ... Full name: Anthony Francis Cline. ... Son of Tony Cline, defensive lineman, Oakland Raiders and San Francisco 49ers (1970-1976).
HIGH SCHOOL: Davis (Calif.).
COLLEGE: Stanford.
TRANSACTIONS/CAREER NOTES: Selected by Buffalo Bills in fourth round (131st pick overall) of 1995 NFL draft. ... Signed by Bills (July 10, 1995).
PLAYING EXPERIENCE: Buffalo NFL, 1995. ... Games: 1995 (16).
PRO STATISTICS: 1995—Caught eight passes for 64 yards and returned one kickoff for 11 yards.

COATES, BEN　　　　　　TE　　　　　　PATRIOTS

PERSONAL: Born August 16, 1969, in Greenwood, S.C. ... 6-5/245. ... Full name: Ben Terrence Coates.
HIGH SCHOOL: Greenwood (S.C.).
COLLEGE: Livingstone College, N.C. (degree in sports management).
TRANSACTIONS/CAREER NOTES: Selected after junior season by New England Patriots in fifth round (124th pick overall) of 1991 NFL draft. ... Signed by Patriots (April 25, 1991). ... Granted free agency (February 17, 1994). ... Re-signed by Patriots (April 2, 1994).
HONORS: Named tight end on THE SPORTING NEWS NFL All-Pro team (1994 and 1995). ... Played in Pro Bowl (1994 and 1995 seasons).
RECORDS: Holds NFL single-season record for most receptions by tight end—96 (1994).
PRO STATISTICS: 1991—Rushed once for minus six yards and returned one kickoff for six yards. 1992—Rushed once for two yards. 1994—Rushed once for no yards and recovered two fumbles.
STATISTICAL PLATEAUS: 100-yard receiving games: 1993 (1), 1994 (5), 1995 (1). Total: 7.

		RECEIVING				TOTALS			
Year Team	G	No.	Yds.	Avg.	TD	TD	2pt.	Pts.	Fum.
1991—New England NFL	16	10	95	9.5	1	1	...	6	0
1992—New England NFL	16	20	171	8.6	3	3	...	18	1
1993—New England NFL	16	53	659	12.4	8	8	...	48	0
1994—New England NFL	16	96	1174	12.2	7	7	0	42	2
1995—New England NFL	16	84	915	10.9	6	6	0	36	4
Pro totals (5 years)	80	263	3014	11.5	25	25	0	150	7

COBB, REGGIE　　　　　　RB　　　　　　JETS

PERSONAL: Born July 7, 1968, in Knoxville, Tenn. ... 6-0/215. ... Full name: Reginald John Cobb.
HIGH SCHOOL: Central (Knoxville, Tenn.).
COLLEGE: Tennessee.
TRANSACTIONS/CAREER NOTES: Selected after junior season by Tampa Bay Buccaneers in second round (30th pick overall) of 1990 NFL draft. ... Signed by Buccaneers (August 6, 1990). ... Granted free agency (February 1, 1992). ... Re-signed by Buccaneers (July 23, 1992). ... Designated by Buccaneers as transition player (February 25, 1993). ... Free agency status changed by Buccaneers from transition to unconditional (February 17, 1994). ... Signed by Green Bay Packers (April 22, 1994). ... Selected by Jacksonville Jaguars from Packers in NFL expansion draft (February 15, 1995). ... Released by Jaguars (September 6, 1995). ... Signed by New York Jets (May 13, 1996).
PRO STATISTICS: 1990—Recovered six fumbles. 1992—Recovered one fumble. 1993—Recovered one fumble.
STATISTICAL PLATEAUS: 100-yard rushing games: 1991 (2), 1992 (4), 1993 (1). Total: 7.

		RUSHING				RECEIVING				KICKOFF RETURNS				TOTALS			
Year Team	G	Att.	Yds.	Avg.	TD	No.	Yds.	Avg.	TD	No.	Yds.	Avg.	TD	TD	2pt.	Pts.	Fum.
1990—Tampa Bay NFL	16	151	480	3.2	2	39	299	7.7	0	11	223	20.3	0	2	...	12	8

Year Team	G	RUSHING Att.	Yds.	Avg.	TD	RECEIVING No.	Yds.	Avg.	TD	KICKOFF RETURNS No.	Yds.	Avg.	TD	TOTALS TD	2pt.	Pts.	Fum.
1991—Tampa Bay NFL	16	196	752	3.8	7	15	111	7.4	0	2	15	7.5	0	7	...	42	3
1992—Tampa Bay NFL	16	310	1171	3.8	9	21	156	7.4	0	0	0	...	0	9	...	54	3
1993—Tampa Bay NFL	12	221	658	3.0	3	9	61	6.8	1	0	0	...	0	4	...	24	5
1994—Green Bay NFL	16	153	579	3.8	3	35	299	8.5	1	0	0	...	0	4	0	24	1
1995—Jacksonville NFL	1	9	18	2.0	0	0	0	...	0	0	0	...	0	0	0	0	1
Pro totals (6 years)	77	1040	3658	3.5	24	119	926	7.8	2	13	238	18.3	0	26	0	156	21

COCOZZO, JOE　　　　　　G　　　　　　CHARGERS

PERSONAL: Born August 7, 1970, in Mechanicville, N.Y. ... 6-4/300. ... Full name: Joseph Ramond Cocozzo. ... Name pronounced cuh-COE-zoe.
HIGH SCHOOL: Mechanicville (N.Y.).
COLLEGE: Michigan (degree in communications, 1993).
TRANSACTIONS/CAREER NOTES: Selected by San Diego Chargers in third round (64th pick overall) of 1993 NFL draft. ... Signed by Chargers (July 14, 1993). ... Granted free agency (February 16, 1996).
PLAYING EXPERIENCE: San Diego NFL, 1993-1995. ... Games: 1993 (16), 1994 (13), 1995 (16). Total: 45.
CHAMPIONSHIP GAME EXPERIENCE: Played in AFC championship game (1994 season). ... Played in Super Bowl XXIX (1994 season).
HONORS: Named guard on THE SPORTING NEWS college All-America second team (1992).

COFER, MIKE　　　　　　K

PERSONAL: Born February 19, 1964, in Columbia, S.C. ... 6-1/195. ... Full name: James Michael Cofer.
HIGH SCHOOL: Country Day (Charlotte).
COLLEGE: North Carolina State (degree in business management and political science).
TRANSACTIONS/CAREER NOTES: Signed as non-drafted free agent by Cleveland Browns (May 5, 1987). ... Released by Browns (September 1, 1987). ... Signed as replacement player by New Orleans Saints (September 24, 1987). ... Released by Saints (October 16, 1987). ... Signed by San Francisco 49ers (April 5, 1988). ... Granted free agency (February 1, 1990). ... Re-signed by 49ers (May 8, 1990). ... Granted unconditional free agency (February 1-April 1, 1992). ... Re-signed by 49ers for 1992 season. ... Granted unconditional free agency (March 1, 1993). ... Re-signed by 49ers (July 19, 1993). ... Released by 49ers (August 30, 1993). ... Re-signed by 49ers (August 31, 1993). ... Granted unconditional free agency (February 17, 1994). ... Signed by Indianapolis Colts (April 7, 1995). ... Released by Colts (October 2, 1995).
CHAMPIONSHIP GAME EXPERIENCE: Played in NFC championship game (1988-1990, 1992 and 1993 seasons). ... Member of Super Bowl championship team (1988 and 1989 seasons).
POSTSEASON RECORDS: Holds Super Bowl career record for most extra points—9. ... Shares Super Bowl single-game record for most extra points—7 (January 28, 1990, vs. Denver).

				KICKING				
Year Team	G	XPM	XPA	FGM	FGA	Lg.	50+	Pts.
1987—New Orleans NFL	2	5	7	1	1	27	0-0	8
1988—San Francisco NFL	16	40	41	27	*38	52	1-5	121
1989—San Francisco NFL	16	49	†51	29	36	47	0-1	*136
1990—San Francisco NFL	16	39	39	24	36	56	2-6	111
1991—San Francisco NFL	16	49	50	14	28	50	2-3	91
1992—San Francisco NFL	16	*53	*54	18	27	46	0-1	107
1993—San Francisco NFL	16	*59	*61	16	26	46	0-3	107
1994—				Did not play.				
1995—Indianapolis NFL	4	9	9	4	9	52	1-1	21
Pro totals (8 years)	102	303	312	133	201	56	6-20	702

COLEMAN, ANDRE　　　　　　WR/KR　　　　　　CHARGERS

PERSONAL: Born January 18, 1971, in Hermitage, Pa. ... 5-9/165. ... Full name: Andre Clintonian Coleman.
HIGH SCHOOL: Hickory (Hermitage, Pa.).
COLLEGE: Kansas State.
TRANSACTIONS/CAREER NOTES: Selected by San Diego Chargers in third round (70th pick overall) of 1994 NFL draft. ... Signed by Chargers (July 12, 1994).
CHAMPIONSHIP GAME EXPERIENCE: Played in AFC championship game (1994 season). ... Played in Super Bowl XXIX (1994 season).
POSTSEASON RECORDS: Shares Super Bowl career records for most touchdowns by kickoff return—1; and longest kickoff return—98 yards (January 29, 1995, vs. San Francisco). ... Holds Super Bowl single-game records for most kickoff returns—8; and most yards by kickoff return—242 (January 29, 1995, vs. San Francisco). ... Holds NFL postseason single-game record for most yards yards by kickoff return—242 (January 29, 1995, vs. San Francisco). ... Shares NFL postseason career record for most touchdowns by kickoff return—1; and longest kickoff return—98 yards (January 29, 1995, vs. San Francisco). ... Shares NFL postseason single-game record for most kickoff returns—8 (January 29, 1995, vs. San Francisco).
PRO STATISTICS: 1994—Recovered one fumble. 1995—Caught four passes for 78 yards and recovered three fumbles.

		PUNT RETURNS				KICKOFF RETURNS				TOTALS			
Year Team	G	No.	Yds.	Avg.	TD	No.	Yds.	Avg.	TD	TD	2pt.	Pts.	Fum.
1994—San Diego NFL	13	0	0	...	0	49	1293	26.4	2	2	0	12	3
1995—San Diego NFL	15	28	326	11.6	†1	62	1411	22.8	†2	3	0	18	10
Pro totals (2 years)	28	28	326	11.7	1	111	2704	24.4	4	5	0	30	13

COLEMAN, BEN　　　　　　G/OT　　　　　　JAGUARS

PERSONAL: Born May 18, 1971, in South Hill, Va. ... 6-6/315. ... Full name: Benjamin Leon Coleman.
HIGH SCHOOL: Park View Senior (South Hill, Va.).
COLLEGE: Wake Forest.

C

TRANSACTIONS/CAREER NOTES: Selected by Phoenix Cardinals in second round (32nd pick overall) of 1993 NFL draft. ... Signed by Cardinals (July 6, 1993). ... Cardinals franchise renamed Arizona Cardinals for 1994 season. ... Claimed on waivers by Jacksonville Jaguars (September 27, 1995). ... Granted free agency (February 16, 1996). ... Re-signed by Jaguars (June 6, 1996).
PLAYING EXPERIENCE: Phoenix NFL, 1993; Arizona NFL, 1994; Arizona (3)-Jacksonville (10) NFL, 1995. ... Games: 1993 (12), 1994 (15), 1995 (13). Total: 40.
PRO STATISTICS: 1995—Recovered one fumble.

COLEMAN, LINCOLN RB FALCONS

PERSONAL: Born August 12, 1969, in Dallas. ... 6-1/239. ... Full name: Lincoln Cales Coleman. ... Cousin of Billy Sims, running back, Detroit Lions (1980-1984); and cousin of Everson Walls, cornerback, Dallas Cowboys, New York Giants and Cleveland Browns (1981-1993).
HIGH SCHOOL: Bryan Adams (Dallas).
COLLEGE: Notre Dame, then Baylor.
TRANSACTIONS/CAREER NOTES: Signed as non-drafted free agent after junior season by Dallas Cowboys (August 12, 1993). ... Released by Cowboys (August 30, 1993). ... Re-signed by Cowboys to practice squad (August 31, 1993). ... Activated (November 17, 1993). ... Released by Cowboys (September 6, 1994). ... Re-signed by Cowboys (September 10, 1994). ... Released by Cowboys (July 17, 1995). ... Signed by Atlanta Falcons (July 22, 1995). ... Released by Falcons (August 27, 1995). ... Re-signed by Falcons (February 1, 1996).
CHAMPIONSHIP GAME EXPERIENCE: Member of Cowboys for NFC championship game (1993 and 1994 seasons); did not play. ... Member of Super Bowl championship team (1993 season).

Year Team	G	RUSHING				RECEIVING				TOTALS			
		Att.	Yds.	Avg.	TD	No.	Yds.	Avg.	TD	TD	2pt.	Pts.	Fum.
1993—Dallas NFL	7	34	132	3.9	2	4	24	6.0	0	2	...	12	1
1994—Dallas NFL	11	64	180	2.8	1	8	46	5.8	0	1	0	6	2
1995—						Did not play.							
Pro totals (2 years)	18	98	312	3.2	3	12	70	5.8	0	3	0	18	3

COLEMAN, MARCO DE CHARGERS

PERSONAL: Born December 18, 1969, in Dayton, Ohio. ... 6-3/297. ... Full name: Marco Darnell Coleman.
HIGH SCHOOL: Patterson Co-op (Dayton, Ohio).
COLLEGE: Georgia Tech.
TRANSACTIONS/CAREER NOTES: Selected after junior season by Miami Dolphins in first round (12th pick overall) of 1992 NFL draft. ... Signed by Dolphins (August 1, 1992). ... Designated by Dolphins as transition player (February 25, 1993). ... Tendered offer sheet by San Diego Chargers (February 28, 1996). ... Dolphins declined to match offer (March 7, 1996).
CHAMPIONSHIP GAME EXPERIENCE: Played in AFC championship game (1992 season).
HONORS: Named linebacker on THE SPORTING NEWS college All-America second team (1991).

Year Team	G	SACKS
1992—Miami NFL	16	6.0
1993—Miami NFL	15	5.5
1994—Miami NFL	16	6.0
1995—Miami NFL	16	6.5
Pro totals (4 years)	63	24.0

COLLINS, ANDRE LB BENGALS

PERSONAL: Born May 4, 1968, in Riverside, N.J. ... 6-1/231. ... Full name: Andre Pierre Collins.
HIGH SCHOOL: Cinnaminson (N.J.).
COLLEGE: Penn State (degree in health planning and administration, 1991).
TRANSACTIONS/CAREER NOTES: Selected by Washington Redskins in second round (46th pick overall) of 1990 NFL draft. ... Signed by Redskins (July 22, 1990). ... Granted free agency (March 1, 1993). ... Re-signed by Redskins for 1993 season. ... Released by Redskins (April 11, 1995). ... Signed by Cincinnati Bengals (May 7, 1995). ... Granted free agency (February 16, 1996).
CHAMPIONSHIP GAME EXPERIENCE: Played in NFC championship game (1991 season). ... Member of Super Bowl championship team (1991 season).
HONORS: Named inside linebacker on THE SPORTING NEWS college All-America second team (1989).
PRO STATISTICS: 1991—Fumbled once. 1992—Recovered one fumble for 40 yards. 1994—Returned one kickoff for no yards and recovered one fumble for 16 yards. 1995—Returned one kickoff for minus three yards.

Year Team	G	INTERCEPTIONS				SACKS
		No.	Yds.	Avg.	TD	No.
1990—Washington NFL	16	0	0	...	0	6.0
1991—Washington NFL	16	2	33	16.5	1	3.0
1992—Washington NFL	14	1	59	59.0	0	2.0
1993—Washington NFL	13	1	5	5.0	0	6.0
1994—Washington NFL	16	4	150	37.5	2	1.5
1995—Cincinnati NFL	16	2	3	1.5	0	4.0
Pro totals (6 years)	91	10	250	25.0	3	22.5

COLLINS, GERALD LB BENGALS

PERSONAL: Born February 13, 1971, in St. Louis. ... 6-2/250.
HIGH SCHOOL: Roosevelt (St. Louis).
COLLEGE: Vanderbilt.
TRANSACTIONS/CAREER NOTES: Signed as non-drafted free agent by Cincinnati Bengals (April 26, 1995). ... On injured reserve with ankle injury (September 25, 1995-remainder of season).
PLAYING EXPERIENCE: Cincinnati NFL, 1995. ... Games: 1995 (3).

COLLINS, KERRY   QB   PANTHERS

PERSONAL: Born December 30, 1972, in West Lawn, Pa. ... 6-5/240. ... Full name: Kerry Michael Collins.
HIGH SCHOOL: Wilson-West Lawn (Pa.).
COLLEGE: Penn State.
TRANSACTIONS/CAREER NOTES: Selected by Carolina Panthers in first round (fifth pick overall) of 1995 NFL draft. ... Signed by Panthers (July 17, 1995).
HONORS: Maxwell Award winner (1994). ... Davey O'Brien Award winner (1994). ... Named quarterback on THE SPORTING NEWS college All-America first team (1994).
PRO STATISTICS: 1995—Fumbled 13 times and recovered four fumbles for minus 15 yards.
STATISTICAL PLATEAUS: 300-yard passing games: 1995 (2).
MISCELLANEOUS: Selected by Detroit Tigers organization in 26th round of free-agent draft (June 4, 1990); did not sign. ... Selected by Toronto Blue Jays organization in 58th round of free-agent draft (June 4, 1994); did not sign. ... Regular-season record as starting NFL quarterback: 7-6 (.538). ... Holds Carolina Panthers all-time records for most yards passing (2,717) and most touchdown passes (14).

			PASSING							RUSHING			TOTALS		
Year Team	G	Att.	Cmp.	Pct.	Yds.	TD	Int.	Avg.	Rat.	Att.	Yds.	Avg.	TD	TD	2pt.	Pts.
1995—Carolina NFL	15	433	214	49.4	2717	14	19	6.28	61.9	42	74	1.8	3	3	0	18

COLLINS, MARK   S/CB   CHIEFS

C

PERSONAL: Born January 16, 1964, in San Bernardino, Calif. ... 5-10/196. ... Full name: Mark Anthony Collins.
HIGH SCHOOL: Pacific (San Bernardino, Calif.).
COLLEGE: Cal State Fullerton.
TRANSACTIONS/CAREER NOTES: Selected by New York Giants in second round (44th pick overall) of 1986 NFL draft. ... Signed by Giants (July 30, 1986). ... On injured reserve with back injury (December 23, 1987-remainder of season). ... On injured reserve with pulled groin (December 3, 1988-remainder of season). ... On injured reserve with sprained ankle (September 19-October 19, 1990). ... Granted free agency (February 1, 1992). ... Re-signed by Giants (August 7, 1992). ... On injured reserve with rib injury (December 24, 1992-remainder of season). ... Granted unconditional free agency (February 17, 1994). ...Signed by Kansas City Chiefs (April 26, 1994).
CHAMPIONSHIP GAME EXPERIENCE: Played in NFC championship game (1986 and 1990 seasons). ... Member of Super Bowl championship team (1986 and 1990 seasons).
HONORS: Named defensive back on THE SPORTING NEWS college All-America first team (1985).
PRO STATISTICS: 1986—Returned three punts for 11 yards and recovered three fumbles for five yards. 1988—Credited with one safety. 1989—Recovered two fumbles for eight yards. 1991—Recovered two fumbles. 1994—Recovered two fumbles. 1995—Recovered one fumble for 34 yards and a touchdown.

		INTERCEPTIONS				SACKS	KICKOFF RETURNS				TOTALS			
Year Team	G	No.	Yds.	Avg.	TD	No.	No.	Yds.	Avg.	TD	TD	2pt.	Pts.	Fum.
1986—New York Giants NFL	15	1	0	0.0	0	0.0	11	204	18.6	0	0	...	0	2
1987—New York Giants NFL	11	2	28	14.0	0	1.5	0	0	...	0	0	...	0	0
1988—New York Giants NFL	11	1	13	13.0	0	0.0	4	67	16.8	0	0	...	2	0
1989—New York Giants NFL	16	2	12	6.0	0	1.0	1	0	0.0	0	0	...	0	0
1990—New York Giants NFL	13	2	0	0.0	0	0.0	0	0	...	0	0	...	0	0
1991—New York Giants NFL	16	4	77	19.3	0	0.0	0	0	...	0	0	...	0	0
1992—New York Giants NFL	14	1	0	0.0	0	0.0	0	0	...	0	0	...	0	0
1993—New York Giants NFL	16	4	77	19.3	1	1.0	0	0	...	0	1	...	6	0
1994—Kansas City NFL	14	2	83	41.5	1	2.0	0	0	...	0	1	0	6	0
1995—Kansas City NFL	16	1	8	8.0	0	0.0	0	0	...	0	1	0	6	1
Pro totals (10 years)	142	20	298	14.9	2	5.5	16	271	16.9	0	3	0	20	3

COLLINS, TODD   QB   BILLS

PERSONAL: Born November 5, 1971, in Walpole, Mass. ... 6-4/224.
HIGH SCHOOL: Walpole (Mass.).
COLLEGE: Michigan.
TRANSACTIONS/CAREER NOTES: Selected by Buffalo Bills in second round (45th pick overall) of 1995 NFL draft. ... Signed by Bills (July 10, 1995).
MISCELLANEOUS: Regular-season record as starting NFL quarterback: 0-1 (.000).

			PASSING							RUSHING			TOTALS		
Year Team	G	Att.	Cmp.	Pct.	Yds.	TD	Int.	Avg.	Rat.	Att.	Yds.	Avg.	TD	TD	2pt.	Pts.
1995—Buffalo NFL	7	29	14	48.3	112	0	1	3.86	44.0	9	23	2.6	0	0	0	0

COLLINS, TODD   LB   PATRIOTS

PERSONAL: Born May 27, 1970, in New Market, Tenn. ... 6-2/242. ... Full name: Todd Franklin Collins.
HIGH SCHOOL: Jefferson County (Dandridge, Tenn.).
COLLEGE: Georgia (did not play football), then Tennessee (did not play football), then Carson-Newman College (Tenn.).
TRANSACTIONS/CAREER NOTES: Selected after junior season by New England Patriots in third round (64th pick overall) of 1992 NFL draft. ... Signed by Patriots (July 23, 1992). ... On injured reserve with neck injury (October 16-November 13, 1992); on practice squad (November 11-13, 1992). ... On injured reserve with knee injury (November 15, 1994-remainder of season). ... Granted free agency (February 17, 1995). ... Re-signed by Patriots (April 20, 1995). ... Placed on reserved/retired list (July 21, 1995-April 16, 1996).
PLAYING EXPERIENCE: New England NFL, 1992-1994. ... Games: 1992 (10), 1993 (16), 1994 (7). Total: 33.
PRO STATISTICS: 1992—Recovered two fumbles. 1993—Credited with one sack, intercepted one pass for eight yards and recovered one fumble for two yards.

COLLONS, FERRIC — DE — PATRIOTS

PERSONAL: Born December 4, 1969, in Scott Air Force Base (Belleville, Ill.). ... 6-6/285. ... Full name: Ferric Jason Collons.
HIGH SCHOOL: Jesuit (Carmichael, Calif.).
COLLEGE: California.
TRANSACTIONS/CAREER NOTES: Signed as non-drafted free agent by Los Angeles Raiders (April 1992). ... Released by Raiders (August 31, 1992). ... Re-signed by Raiders to practice squad (September 2, 1992). ... Granted free agency after 1992 season. ... Re-signed by Raiders (February 1993). ... Inactive for all 16 games (1993). ... Released by Raiders (August 23, 1994). ... Signed by Jacksonville Jaguars (December 15, 1994). ... Released by Jaguars (May 1, 1995). ... Signed by Green Bay Packers (May 22, 1995). ... Traded by Packers to New England Patriots for past considerations (August 27, 1995).
PLAYING EXPERIENCE: New England NFL, 1995. ... Games: 1995 (16).
PRO STATISTICS: 1995—Credited with four sacks.

COLON, HARRY — S — JAGUARS

PERSONAL: Born February 14, 1969, in Kansas City, Kan. ... 6-0/203.
HIGH SCHOOL: Washington (Kansas City, Kan.).
COLLEGE: Missouri.
TRANSACTIONS/CAREER NOTES: Selected by New England Patriots in eighth round (196th pick overall) of 1991 NFL draft. ... Signed by Patriots (July 12, 1991). ... Granted unconditional free agency (February 1, 1992). ... Signed by Detroit Lions (March 30, 1992). ... Granted free agency (February 15, 1994). ... Re-signed by Lions (July 20, 1994). ... Selected by Jacksonville Jaguars from Lions in NFL expansion draft (February 15, 1995).
PRO STATISTICS: 1991—Recovered two fumbles for minus eight yards. 1992—Recovered two fumbles. 1993—Credited with a sack.
MISCELLANEOUS: Holds Jacksonville Jaguars all-time record for most interceptions (3).

| | | | INTERCEPTIONS | | |
Year Team	G	No.	Yds.	Avg.	TD
1991—New England NFL	16	0	0	...	0
1992—Detroit NFL	16	0	0	...	0
1993—Detroit NFL	15	2	28	14.0	0
1994—Detroit NFL	16	1	3	3.0	0
1995—Jacksonville NFL	16	3	46	15.3	0
Pro totals (5 years)	79	6	77	12.8	0

COMPTON, MIKE — C/G — LIONS

PERSONAL: Born September 18, 1970, in Richlands, Va. ... 6-6/297. ... Full name: Michael Eugene Compton.
HIGH SCHOOL: Richlands (Va.).
COLLEGE: West Virginia.
TRANSACTIONS/CAREER NOTES: Selected by Detroit Lions in third round (68th pick overall) of 1993 NFL draft. ... Signed by Lions (June 4, 1993).
PLAYING EXPERIENCE: Detroit NFL, 1993-1995. ... Games: 1993 (8), 1994 (2), 1995 (16). Total: 26.
HONORS: Named center on THE SPORTING NEWS college All-America first team (1992).

CONKLIN, CARY — QB

PERSONAL: Born February 29, 1968, in Yakima, Wash. ... 6-4/215.
HIGH SCHOOL: Eisenhower (Yakima, Wash.).
COLLEGE: Washington.
TRANSACTIONS/CAREER NOTES: Selected by Washington Redskins in fourth round (86th pick overall) of 1990 NFL draft. ... On injured reserve (entire 1990 season). ... On injured reserve with knee injury (entire 1991 season). ... Granted free agency (February 1, 1992). ... Re-signed by Redskins for 1992 season. ... Granted unconditional free agency (February 17, 1994). ... Signed by Philadelphia Eagles (March 22, 1995). ... Released by Eagles (May 3, 1995). ... Signed by San Francisco 49ers (June 14, 1995). ... Granted unconditional free agency (February 16, 1996).
MISCELLANEOUS: Selected by Cleveland Indians organization in 47th round of free-agent baseball draft (June 5, 1989); did not sign. ... Regular-season record as starting NFL quarterback: 0-2 (.000).

| | | PASSING | | | | | | | | RUSHING | | | | TOTALS | | |
Year Team	G	Att.	Cmp.	Pct.	Yds.	TD	Int.	Avg.	Rat.	Att.	Yds.	Avg.	TD	TD	2pt.	Pts.
1990—Washington NFL							Did not play—injured.									
1991—Washington NFL							Did not play—injured.									
1992—Washington NFL	1	2	2	100.0	16	1	0	8.00	139.6	3	-4	-1.3	0	0	...	0
1993—Washington NFL	4	87	46	52.9	496	4	3	5.70	70.9	2	-2	-1.0	0	0	...	0
1994—							Did not play.									
1995—San Francisco NFL	2	12	4	33.3	48	0	0	4.00	46.5	0	0	...	0	0	0	0
Pro totals (3 years)	7	101	52	51.5	560	5	3	5.55	72.2	5	-6	-1.2	0	0	0	0

CONLAN, SHANE — LB

PERSONAL: Born March 4, 1964, in Frewsburg, N.Y. ... 6-3/235. ... Full name: Shane Patrick Conlan.
HIGH SCHOOL: Central (Frewsburg, N.Y.).
COLLEGE: Penn State (degree in administration of justice, 1987).
TRANSACTIONS/CAREER NOTES: Selected by Buffalo Bills in first round (eighth pick overall) of 1987 NFL draft. ... Signed by Bills (August 9, 1987). ... On injured reserve with knee injury (September 21-November 3, 1989). ... Granted unconditional free agency (March 1, 1993). ... Signed by Los Angeles Rams (April 11, 1993). ... Rams franchise moved to St. Louis (April 12, 1995). ... On injured reserve with left knee injury (December 20, 1995-remainder of season). ... Granted unconditional free agency (February 16, 1996).

CHAMPIONSHIP GAME EXPERIENCE: Played in AFC championship game (1988 and 1990-1992 seasons). ... Played in Super Bowl XXV (1990 season), Super Bowl XXVI (1991 season) and Super Bowl XXVII (1992 season).
HONORS: Named linebacker on THE SPORTING NEWS college All-America second team (1986). ... Named inside linebacker on THE SPORTING NEWS NFL All-Pro team (1988). ... Member of Pro Bowl squad (1988 season); did not play. ... Played in Pro Bowl (1989 and 1990 seasons).
PRO STATISTICS: 1988—Recovered one fumble. 1991—Recovered two fumbles. 1995—Recovered two fumbles.

| | | | INTERCEPTIONS | | | SACKS |
Year Team	G	No.	Yds.	Avg.	TD	No.
1987—Buffalo NFL	12	0	0	...	0	0.5
1988—Buffalo NFL	13	1	0	0.0	0	1.5
1989—Buffalo NFL	10	1	0	0.0	0	1.0
1990—Buffalo NFL	16	0	0	...	0	1.0
1991—Buffalo NFL	16	0	0	...	0	0.0
1992—Buffalo NFL	13	1	7	7.0	0	2.0
1993—Los Angeles Rams NFL	12	1	28	28.0	0	0.0
1994—Los Angeles Rams NFL	15	0	0	...	0	1.0
1995—St. Louis NFL	13	1	1	1.0	0	0.0
Pro totals (9 years)	120	5	36	7.2	0	7.0

CONNER, DARION   LB   PANTHERS

PERSONAL: Born September 28, 1967, in Macon, Ga. ... 6-2/250.
HIGH SCHOOL: Noxubee County (Macon, Ga.).
COLLEGE: Jackson State.
TRANSACTIONS/CAREER NOTES: Selected by Atlanta Falcons in second round (27th pick overall) of 1990 NFL draft. ... Signed by Falcons (July 12, 1990). ... Granted free agency (March 1, 1993). ... Re-signed by Falcons (August 13, 1993). ... Granted unconditional free agency (February 17, 1994). ... Signed by New Orleans Saints (July 18, 1994). ... Granted unconditional free agency (February 17, 1995). ... Signed by Carolina Panthers (April 6, 1995). ... Granted free agency (February 16, 1996).
PRO STATISTICS: 1991—Fumbled once and recovered one fumble for five yards. 1994—Intercepted one pass for 58 yards and recovered one fumble.

Team Year	G	SACKS
1990—Atlanta NFL	16	2.0
1991—Atlanta NFL	15	3.5
1992—Atlanta NFL	16	7.0
1993—Atlanta NFL	14	1.5
1994—New Orleans NFL	16	10.5
1995—Carolina NFL	16	7.0
Pro totals (6 years)	93	31.5

CONOVER, SCOTT   OT   LIONS

PERSONAL: Born September 27, 1968, in Neptune, N.J. ... 6-4/285. ... Full name: Kelsey Scott Conover.
HIGH SCHOOL: Freehold (N.J.) Boro.
COLLEGE: Purdue.
TRANSACTIONS/CAREER NOTES: Selected by Detroit Lions in fifth round (118th pick overall) of 1991 NFL draft. ... Signed by Lions (July 10, 1991). ... Granted unconditional free agency (February 17, 1995). ... Re-signed by Lions (April 3, 1995).
PLAYING EXPERIENCE: Detroit NFL, 1991-1995. ... Games: 1991 (16), 1992 (15), 1993 (1), 1994 (11), 1995 (14). Total: 57.
CHAMPIONSHIP GAME EXPERIENCE: Played in NFC championship game (1991 season).
PRO STATISTICS: 1994—Caught one pass for one yard and a touchdown.

CONWAY, CURTIS   WR/KR   BEARS

PERSONAL: Born March 13, 1971, in Los Angeles. ... 6-0/193. ... Full name: Curtis LaMont Conway.
HIGH SCHOOL: Hawthorne (Calif.).
JUNIOR COLLEGE: El Camino Junior College (Calif.).
COLLEGE: Southern California.
TRANSACTIONS/CAREER NOTES: Selected after junior season by Chicago Bears in first round (seventh pick overall) of 1993 NFL draft. ... Signed by Bears (May 24, 1993). ... Granted free agency (February 16, 1996). ... Re-signed by Bears (March 4, 1996).
HONORS: Named kick returner on THE SPORTING NEWS college All-America second team (1992).
PRO STATISTICS: 1993—Fumbled once. 1994—Attempted one pass with one completion for 23 yards and a touchdown, fumbled twice and recovered one fumble. 1995—Attempted one pass without a completion.
STATISTICAL PLATEAUS: 100-yard receiving games: 1994 (1), 1995 (3). Total: 4.

| | | RUSHING | | | | RECEIVING | | | | PUNT RETURNS | | | | KICKOFF RETURNS | | | | TOTALS | | |
Year Team	G	Att.	Yds.	Avg.	TD	No.	Yds.	Avg.	TD	No.	Yds.	Avg.	TD	No.	Yds.	Avg.	TD	TD	2pt.	Pts.
1993—Chicago NFL	16	5	44	8.8	0	19	231	12.2	2	0	0	...	0	21	450	21.4	0	2	...	12
1994—Chicago NFL	13	6	31	5.2	0	39	546	14.0	2	8	63	7.9	0	10	228	22.8	0	2	1	14
1995—Chicago NFL	16	5	77	15.4	0	62	1037	16.7	12	0	0	...	0	0	0	...	0	12	0	72
Pro totals (3 years)	45	16	152	9.5	0	120	1814	15.1	16	8	63	7.9	0	31	678	21.9	0	16	1	98

COOK, ANTHONY   DL   OILERS

PERSONAL: Born May 30, 1972, in Bennettsville, S.C. ... 6-3/293.
HIGH SCHOOL: Marlboro County (Bennettsville, S.C.).
COLLEGE: South Carolina State.
TRANSACTIONS/CAREER NOTES: Selected by Houston Oilers in second round (35th pick overall) of 1995 NFL draft. ... Signed by Oilers (July 20, 1995).

Year Team	G	SACKS
1995—Houston NFL	10	4.5

COOK, MARV   TE   RAMS

PERSONAL: Born February 24, 1966, in Iowa City, Iowa. ... 6-4/234. ... Full name: Marvin Eugene Cook.
HIGH SCHOOL: West Branch (Iowa).
COLLEGE: Iowa.
TRANSACTIONS/CAREER NOTES: Selected by New England Patriots in third round (63rd pick overall) of 1989 NFL draft. ... Signed by Patriots (August 1, 1989). ... Released by Patriots (April 21, 1994). ... Signed by Chicago Bears (May 6, 1994). ... Released by Bears (February 17, 1995). ... Signed by St. Louis Rams (May 31, 1995). ... Granted free agency (February 16, 1996).
HONORS: Named tight end on The Sporting News NFL All-Pro team (1991). ...Played in Pro Bowl (1991 and 1992 seasons).
PRO STATISTICS: 1991—Recovered two fumbles. 1992—Recovered one fumble for minus 26 yards. 1993—Returned one kickoff for eight yards. 1994—Recovered one fumble.

		RECEIVING				TOTALS			
Year Team	G	No.	Yds.	Avg.	TD	TD	2pt.	Pts.	Fum.
1989—New England NFL	16	3	13	4.3	0	0	...	0	0
1990—New England NFL	16	51	455	8.9	5	5	...	30	2
1991—New England NFL	16	82	808	9.9	3	3	...	18	2
1992—New England NFL	16	52	413	7.9	2	2	...	12	3
1993—New England NFL	16	22	154	7.0	1	1	...	6	1
1994—Chicago NFL	16	21	212	10.1	1	1	0	6	0
1995—St. Louis NFL	16	26	135	5.2	1	1	0	6	1
Pro totals (7 years)	112	257	2190	8.5	13	13	0	78	9

COOK, TOI   CB   BRONCOS

PERSONAL: Born December 3, 1964, in Chicago. ... 5-11/188. ... Full name: Toi Fitzgerald Cook. ... Name pronounced TOY.
HIGH SCHOOL: Montclair (Calif.).
COLLEGE: Stanford.
TRANSACTIONS/CAREER NOTES: Selected by New Orleans Saints in eighth round (207th pick overall) of 1987 NFL draft. ... Signed by Saints (July 24, 1987). ... Granted free agency (February 1, 1990). ... Re-signed by Saints (August 13, 1990). ... On injured reserve with forearm injury (December 9, 1991-remainder of season). ... Granted free agency (February 1, 1992). ... Re-signed by Saints (August 24, 1992). ... Granted roster exemption (August 24-September 5, 1992). ... Granted unconditional free agency (February 17, 1994). ... Signed by San Francisco 49ers (August 22, 1994). ... Re-signed by 49ers (August 19, 1995). ... On injured reserve with shoulder injury (September 27, 1995-remainder of season). ... Granted unconditional free agency (February 16, 1996). ... Signed by Denver Broncos (April 12, 1996).
CHAMPIONSHIP GAME EXPERIENCE: Played in NFC championship game (1994 season). ... Member of Super Bowl championship team (1994 season).
PRO STATISTICS: 1987—Returned one punt for three yards. 1989—Caught one pass for eight yards and fumbled once. 1993—Recovered three fumbles.
MISCELLANEOUS: Selected by Minnesota Twins organization in 38th round of free-agent baseball draft (June 2, 1987); did not sign.

		INTERCEPTIONS				SACKS
Year Team	G	No.	Yds.	Avg.	TD	No.
1987—New Orleans NFL	7	0	0	...	0	0.0
1988—New Orleans NFL	16	1	0	0.0	0	0.0
1989—New Orleans NFL	16	3	81	27.0	1	1.0
1990—New Orleans NFL	16	2	55	27.5	0	1.0
1991—New Orleans NFL	14	3	54	18.0	0	0.0
1992—New Orleans NFL	16	6	90	15.0	1	1.0
1993—New Orleans NFL	16	1	0	0.0	0	1.0
1994—San Francisco NFL	16	1	18	18.0	0	0.0
1995—San Francisco NFL	2	0	0	...	0	0.0
Pro totals (9 years)	119	17	298	17.5	2	4.0

COONS, ROBERT   TE   BILLS

PERSONAL: Born September 18, 1969, in Brea, Calif. ... 6-5/249. ... Full name: Robert Allen Coons.
HIGH SCHOOL: El Dorado (Calif.).
JUNIOR COLLEGE: Fullerton (Calif.) Junior College.
COLLEGE: Pittsburgh.
TRANSACTIONS/CAREER NOTES: Signed as non-drafted free agent by Miami Dolphins (April 29, 1993). ... Released by Dolphins (August 30, 1993). ... Re-signed by Dolphins to practice squad (August 31, 1993). ... Released by Dolphins (November 10, 1993). ... Re-signed by Dolphins to practice squad (November 18, 1993). ... Granted free agency after 1993 season. ... Re-signed by Dolphins (April 15, 1994). ... On injured reserve (August 29-November 23, 1994). ... Released by Dolphins (November 23, 1994). ... Signed by Buffalo Bills (April 19, 1995).
PLAYING EXPERIENCE: Buffalo NFL, 1995. ... Games: 1995 (4). .

COOPER, ADRIAN   TE   49ERS

PERSONAL: Born April 27, 1968, in Denver. ... 6-5/255.
HIGH SCHOOL: South (Denver).
COLLEGE: Oklahoma (bachelor of arts degree in communication, 1991).
TRANSACTIONS/CAREER NOTES: Selected by Pittsburgh Steelers in fourth round (103rd pick overall) of 1991 NFL draft. ... Signed by Steelers (July 16, 1991). ... Traded by Steelers to Minnesota Vikings for third-round (LB Jason Gildon) and sixth-round (LB Eric Ravotti) picks

in 1994 NFL draft (March 18, 1994). ... On injured reserve with shoulder injury (December 5, 1994-remainder of season). ... Granted unconditional free agency (February 16, 1996). ... Signed by San Francisco 49ers (April 2, 1996).
PRO STATISTICS: 1992—Returned one kickoff for eight yards. 1993—Returned one kickoff for two yards. 1994—Recovered one fumble. 1995—Recovered one fumble for one yard.
STATISTICAL PLATEAUS: 100-yard receiving games: 1994 (1).

		RECEIVING				TOTALS			
Year Team	G	No.	Yds.	Avg.	TD	TD	2pt.	Pts.	Fum.
1991—Pittsburgh NFL	16	11	147	13.4	2	0	...	0	0
1992—Pittsburgh NFL	16	16	197	12.3	3	3	...	18	1
1993—Pittsburgh NFL	14	9	112	12.4	0	0	...	0	1
1994—Minnesota NFL	12	32	363	11.3	0	0	0	0	2
1995—Minnesota NFL	13	18	207	11.5	0	0	0	0	0
Pro totals (5 years)	71	86	1026	11.9	5	3	0	18	4

COOPER, RICHARD　　　　　OT　　　　　EAGLES

PERSONAL: Born November 1, 1964, in Memphis. ... 6-5/290. ... Full name: Richard Warren Cooper.
HIGH SCHOOL: Melrose (Memphis).
COLLEGE: Tennessee.
TRANSACTIONS/CAREER NOTES: Signed as non-drafted free agent by Seattle Seahawks (May 1988). ... Released by Seahawks (August 1, 1988). ... Signed by New Orleans Saints (February 2, 1989). ... Released by Saints (September 5, 1989). ... Re-signed by Saints to developmental squad (September 6, 1989). ... Released by Saints (December 29, 1989). ... Re-signed by Saints (February 2, 1990). ... Granted free agency (March 1, 1993). ... Re-signed by Saints (April 19, 1993). ... On injured reserve with elbow injury (December 22, 1994-remainder of season). ... Granted unconditional free agency (February 16, 1996). ... Signed by Philadelphia Eagles (February 29, 1996).
PLAYING EXPERIENCE: New Orleans NFL, 1990-1995. ... Games: 1990 (2), 1991 (15), 1992 (16), 1993 (16), 1994 (14), 1995 (14). Total: 77.
PRO STATISTICS: 1991—Recovered one fumble. 1992—Recovered one fumble. 1993—Recovered one fumble. 1995—Recovered one fumble.

C

COPELAND, HORACE　　　　　WR　　　　　BUCCANEERS

PERSONAL: Born January 2, 1971, in Orlando. ... 6-3/222. ... Full name: Horace Nathaniel Copeland.
HIGH SCHOOL: Maynard Evans (Orlando).
COLLEGE: Miami, Fla. (degree in criminal justice, 1992).
TRANSACTIONS/CAREER NOTES: Selected by Tampa Bay Buccaneers in fourth round (104th pick overall) of 1993 NFL draft. ... Signed by Buccaneers (June 22, 1993).
PRO STATISTICS: 1993—Rushed three times for 34 yards.
STATISTICAL PLATEAUS: 100-yard receiving games: 1993 (2), 1995 (2). Total: 4.

		RECEIVING				TOTALS			
Year Team	G	No.	Yds.	Avg.	TD	TD	2pt.	Pts.	Fum.
1993—Tampa Bay NFL	14	30	633	21.1	4	4	...	24	0
1994—Tampa Bay NFL	16	17	308	18.1	0	0	1	2	0
1995—Tampa Bay NFL	15	35	605	17.3	2	2	0	12	0
Pro totals (3 years)	45	82	1546	18.9	6	6	1	38	0

COPELAND, JOHN　　　　　DE　　　　　BENGALS

PERSONAL: Born September 20, 1970, in Lanett, Ala. ... 6-3/286.
HIGH SCHOOL: Valley (Ala.).
JUNIOR COLLEGE: Hinds Community College (Miss.).
COLLEGE: Alabama.
TRANSACTIONS/CAREER NOTES: Selected by Cincinnati Bengals in first round (fifth pick overall) of 1993 NFL draft. ... Signed by Bengals (August 13, 1993).
HONORS: Named defensive lineman on THE SPORTING NEWS college All-America first team (1992).

Year Team	G	SACKS
1993—Cincinnati NFL	14	3.0
1994—Cincinnati NFL	12	1.0
1995—Cincinnati NFL	16	9.0
Pro totals (3 years)	42	13.0

COPELAND, RUSSELL　　　　　WR/KR　　　　　BILLS

PERSONAL: Born November 4, 1971, in Tupelo, Miss. ... 6-0/200.
HIGH SCHOOL: Tupelo (Miss.).
COLLEGE: Memphis State.
TRANSACTIONS/CAREER NOTES: Selected after junior season by Buffalo Bills in fourth round (111th pick overall) of 1993 NFL draft. ... Signed by Bills (July 12, 1993). ... Granted free agency (February 16, 1996). ... Re-signed by Bills (June 5, 1996).
CHAMPIONSHIP GAME EXPERIENCE: Played in AFC championship game (1993 season). ... Played in Super Bowl XXVIII (1993 season).
PRO STATISTICS: 1994—Rushed once for minus seven yards. 1995—Rushed once for minus one yard and recovered one fumble.
STATISTICAL PLATEAUS: 100-yard receiving games: 1995 (1). .

		RECEIVING				PUNT RETURNS				KICKOFF RETURNS				TOTALS			
Year Team	G	No.	Yds.	Avg.	TD	No.	Yds.	Avg.	TD	No.	Yds.	Avg.	TD	TD	2pt.	Pts.	Fum.
1993—Buffalo NFL	16	13	242	18.6	0	31	274	8.8	1	24	436	18.2	0	1	...	6	1
1994—Buffalo NFL	15	21	255	12.1	1	1	11	11.0	0	12	232	19.3	0	1	0	6	0

Year Team	G	RECEIVING				PUNT RETURNS				KICKOFF RETURNS				TOTALS			
		No.	Yds.	Avg.	TD	No.	Yds.	Avg.	TD	No.	Yds.	Avg.	TD	TD	2pt.	Pts.	Fum.
1995—Buffalo NFL	16	42	646	15.4	1	2	8	4.0	0	0	0	...	0	1	0	6	1
Pro totals (3 years)	47	76	1143	15.0	2	34	293	8.6	1	36	668	18.6	0	3	0	18	2

CORNISH, FRANK — C/G

PERSONAL: Born September 24, 1967, in Chicago. ... 6-4/287. ... Full name: Frank Edgar Cornish. ... Son of Frank Cornish, defensive tackle, Chicago Bears, Miami Dolphins and Buffalo Bills (1966-1972).
HIGH SCHOOL: Mt. Carmel (Ill.).
COLLEGE: UCLA.
TRANSACTIONS/CAREER NOTES: Selected by San Diego Chargers in sixth round (143rd pick overall) of 1990 NFL draft. ... Signed by Chargers (July 19, 1990). ... Granted unconditional free agency (February 1, 1992). ... Signed by Dallas Cowboys (April 1, 1992). ... Granted unconditional free agency (February 17, 1994). ... Signed by Minnesota Vikings (July 12, 1994). ... Released by Vikings (November 11, 1994). ... Signed by Cowboys (November 21, 1994). ... Granted unconditional free agency (February 17, 1995). ... Signed by Jacksonville Jaguars (August 6, 1995). ... Released by Jaguars (September 18, 1995). ... Signed by Philadelphia Eagles (November 21, 1995). ... Granted unconditional free agency (February 16, 1996).
PLAYING EXPERIENCE: San Diego NFL, 1990 and 1991; Dallas NFL, 1992 and 1993; Minnesota NFL, 1994; Jacksonville (3)-Philadelphia (2) NFL. ... Games: 1990 (16), 1991 (16), 1992 (11), 1993 (14); 1994 (7), 1995 (5). Total: 69.
CHAMPIONSHIP GAME EXPERIENCE: Played in NFC championship game (1992-1994 seasons). ... Member of Super Bowl championship team (1992 and 1993 seasons).
HONORS: Named center on THE SPORTING NEWS college All-America second team (1988).

C

CORYATT, QUENTIN — LB — COLTS

PERSONAL: Born August 1, 1970, in St. Croix, Virgin Islands. ... 6-3/246. ... Full name: Quentin John Coryatt.
HIGH SCHOOL: Robert E. Lee (Baytown, Texas).
COLLEGE: Texas A&M.
TRANSACTIONS/CAREER NOTES: Selected by Indianapolis Colts in first round (second pick overall) of 1992 NFL draft. ... Signed by Colts (April 24, 1992). ... On injured reserve with displaced wrist bone (October 27, 1992-remainder of season). ... Designated by Colts as transition player (February 25, 1993). ... Tendered offer sheet by Jacksonville Jaguars (February 21, 1996). ... Offer matched by Colts (February 28, 1996).
CHAMPIONSHIP GAME EXPERIENCE: Played in AFC championship game (1995 season).
PRO STATISTICS: 1992—Recovered one fumble. 1994—Recovered one fumble for 78 yards and a touchdown. 1995—Intercepted one pass for six yards and recovered three fumbles.

Year Team	G	SACKS
1992—Indianapolis NFL	7	2.0
1993—Indianapolis NFL	16	1.0
1994—Indianapolis NFL	16	1.0
1995—Indianapolis NFL	16	2.5
Pro totals (4 years)	55	6.5

COTA, CHAD — S — PANTHERS

PERSONAL: Born August 13, 1971, in Ashland, Ore. ... 6-1/188. ... Full name: Chad Garrett Cota.
HIGH SCHOOL: Ashland (Ore.).
COLLEGE: Oregon.
TRANSACTIONS/CAREER NOTES: Selected by Carolina Panthers in seventh round (209th pick overall) of 1995 NFL draft. ... Signed by Panthers (July 14, 1995).
PLAYING EXPERIENCE: Carolina NFL, 1995. ... Games: 1995 (16).
PRO STATISTICS: 1995—Recovered one fumble.

COTHRAN, JEFF — FB — BENGALS

PERSONAL: Born June 28, 1971, in Middletown, Ohio. ... 6-1/249.
HIGH SCHOOL: Middletown (Ohio).
COLLEGE: Ohio State.
TRANSACTIONS/CAREER NOTES: Selected by Cincinnati Bengals in third round (66th pick overall) of 1994 NFL draft. ... Signed by Bengals (July 19, 1994).

Year Team	G	RUSHING				RECEIVING				TOTALS			
		Att.	Yds.	Avg.	TD	No.	Yds.	Avg.	TD	TD	2pt.	Pts.	Fum.
1994—Cincinnati NFL	14	26	85	3.3	0	4	24	6.0	1	1	0	6	0
1995—Cincinnati NFL	14	16	62	3.9	0	8	44	5.5	0	0	0	0	1
Pro totals (2 years)	28	42	147	3.5	0	12	68	5.7	1	1	0	6	1

COVINGTON, DAMIEN — LB — BILLS

PERSONAL: Born December 4, 1972, in Berlin, N.J. ... 5-11/236.
HIGH SCHOOL: Overbrook (Berlin, N.J.).
COLLEGE: North Carolina State.
TRANSACTIONS/CAREER NOTES: Selected by Buffalo Bills in third round (96th pick overall) of 1995 NFL draft. ... Signed by Bills (July 5, 1995).
PLAYING EXPERIENCE: Buffalo NFL, 1995. ... Games: 1995 (13).

COVINGTON, TONY   S   SEAHAWKS

PERSONAL: Born December 26, 1967, in Winston-Salem, N.C. ... 5-11/196. ... Full name: Anthony Lavonne Covington.
HIGH SCHOOL: Parkland (Winston-Salem, N.C.).
COLLEGE: Virginia (degree in rhetoric and communication studies).
TRANSACTIONS/CAREER NOTES: Selected by Tampa Bay Buccaneers in fourth round (93rd pick overall) of 1991 NFL draft. ... Signed by Buccaneers (July 15, 1991). ... On injured reserve with knee injury (September 8, 1992-remainder of season). ... On injured reserve with back injury (September 2, 1993-entire season). ... Granted unconditional free agency (February 17, 1995). ... Signed by Seattle Seahawks (April 12, 1995).
PRO STATISTICS: 1991—Credited with one sack and recovered one fumble.

		INTERCEPTIONS			
Year Team	G	No.	Yds.	Avg.	TD
1991—Tampa Bay NFL	16	3	21	7.0	0
1992—Tampa Bay NFL	1	0	0	...	0
1993—Tampa Bay NFL			Did not play—injured.		
1994—Tampa Bay NFL	14	1	38	38.0	0
1995—Seattle NFL	11	0	0	...	0
Pro totals (4 years)	42	4	59	14.8	0

COX, BRYAN   LB   BEARS

C

PERSONAL: Born February 17, 1968, in St. Louis. ... 6-4/248. ... Full name: Bryan Keith Cox.
HIGH SCHOOL: East St. Louis (Ill.) Senior.
COLLEGE: Western Illinois (bachelor of science degree in mass communications).
TRANSACTIONS/CAREER NOTES: Selected by Miami Dolphins in fifth round (113th pick overall) of 1991 NFL draft. ... Signed by Dolphins (July 11, 1991). ... On injured reserve with sprained ankle (October 5-November 2, 1991). ... Granted unconditional free agency (February 16, 1996). ... Signed by Chicago Bears (February 21, 1996).
CHAMPIONSHIP GAME EXPERIENCE: Played in AFC championship game (1992 season).
HONORS: Played in Pro Bowl (1992, 1994 and 1995 seasons).
PRO STATISTICS: 1992—Recovered one fumble. 1993—Recovered four fumbles for one yard. 1995—Recovered one fumble.

		INTERCEPTIONS				SACKS
Year Team	G	No.	Yds.	Avg.	TD	No.
1991—Miami NFL	13	0	0	...	0	2.0
1992—Miami NFL	16	1	0	0.0	0	14.0
1993—Miami NFL	16	1	26	26.0	0	5.0
1994—Miami NFL	16	0	0	...	0	3.0
1995—Miami NFL	16	1	12	12.0	0	7.5
Pro totals (5 years)	77	3	38	12.7	0	31.5

COX, RON   LB   PACKERS

PERSONAL: Born February 27, 1968, in Fresno, Calif. ... 6-2/235.
HIGH SCHOOL: Washington Union (Fresno, Calif.).
COLLEGE: Fresno State.
TRANSACTIONS/CAREER NOTES: Selected after junior season by Chicago Bears in second round (33rd pick overall) of 1990 NFL draft. ... Signed by Bears (July 25, 1990). ... On injured reserve with knee injury (September 25-October 31, 1991). ... On injured reserve with knee injury (November 27, 1991-remainder of season). ... Granted unconditional free agency (February 17, 1994). ... Re-signed by Bears (May 16, 1994). ... Granted free agency (February 16, 1996). ... Tendered offer sheet by Green Bay Packers (March 29, 1996). ... Bears declined to match offer (April 4, 1996).
HONORS: Named outside linebacker on THE SPORTING NEWS college All-America second team (1989).
PRO STATISTICS: 1992—Recovered one fumble. 1993—Recovered one fumble. 1995—Intercepted one pass for one yard.

Year Team	G	SACKS
1990—Chicago NFL	13	3.0
1991—Chicago NFL	6	1.0
1992—Chicago NFL	16	1.0
1993—Chicago NFL	16	2.0
1994—Chicago NFL	15	0.0
1995—Chicago NFL	16	0.0
Pro totals (6 years)	82	7.0

CRAVER, AARON   RB   BRONCOS

PERSONAL: Born December 18, 1968, in Los Angeles. ... 6-0/220. ... Full name: Aaron LeRenze Craver.
HIGH SCHOOL: Compton (Calif.).
JUNIOR COLLEGE: El Camino College (Calif.).
COLLEGE: Fresno State.
TRANSACTIONS/CAREER NOTES: Selected by Miami Dolphins in third round (60th pick overall) of 1991 NFL draft. ... Signed by Dolphins (July 23, 1991). ... On injured reserve with pulled hamstring (October 21, 1992-December 12, 1992). ... On practice squad (December 12, 1992-January 9, 1993). ... On injured reserve with knee injury (August 23, 1993-entire season). ... Granted free agency (February 17, 1994). ... Re-signed by Dolphins (May 31, 1994). ... Released by Dolphins (August 28, 1994). ... Re-signed by Dolphins (September 26, 1994). ... Released by Dolphins (October 4, 1994). ... Re-signed by Dolphins (November 9, 1994). ... Granted unconditional free agency (February 17, 1995). ... Signed by Denver Broncos (March 9, 1995).
CHAMPIONSHIP GAME EXPERIENCE: Played in AFC championship game (1992 season).

PRO STATISTICS: 1991—Recovered two fumbles. 1994—Recovered one fumble. 1995—Recovered one fumble.
STATISTICAL PLATEAUS: 100-yard rushing games: 1995 (1).

			RUSHING				RECEIVING				KICKOFF RETURNS				TOTALS			
Year Team	G	Att.	Yds.	Avg.	TD	No.	Yds.	Avg.	TD	No.	Yds.	Avg.	TD	TD	2pt.	Pts.	Fum.
1991—Miami NFL	14	20	58	2.9	1	8	67	8.4	0	32	615	19.2	0	1	...	6	2
1992—Miami NFL	6	3	9	3.0	0	0	0	...	0	8	174	21.8	0	0	...	0	0
1993—Miami NFL								Did not play—injured.									
1994—Miami NFL	8	6	43	7.2	0	24	237	9.9	0	0	0	...	0	0	1	2	1
1995—Denver NFL	16	73	333	4.6	5	43	369	8.6	1	7	50	7.1	0	6	0	36	1
Pro totals (4 years)	44	102	443	4.4	6	75	673	9.0	1	47	839	17.9	0	7	1	44	4

CRAWFORD, KEITH   CB   PACKERS

PERSONAL: Born November 21, 1970, in Palestine, Texas. ... 6-2/198.
HIGH SCHOOL: Westwood (Palestine, Texas).
COLLEGE: Howard Payne (Texas).
TRANSACTIONS/CAREER NOTES: Signed as non-drafted free agent by New York Giants (May 1, 1993). ... Released by Giants (October 7, 1993). ... Re-signed by Giants to practice squad (October 8, 1993). ... Activated (October 20, 1993). ... Released by Giants (August 22, 1994). ... Signed by Green Bay Packers (October 28, 1994). ... Released by Packers (November 22, 1994). ... Re-signed by Packers (December 27, 1994).
PLAYING EXPERIENCE: Green Bay NFL, 1993 and 1995. ... Games: 1993 (7), 1995 (13). Total: 20.
CHAMPIONSHIP GAME EXPERIENCE: Played in NFC championship game (1995 season).
PRO STATISTICS: 1993—Caught one pass for six yards.

CREWS, TERRY   LB   REDSKINS

PERSONAL: Born July 30, 1968, in Flint, Mich. ... 6-2/245.
HIGH SCHOOL: Academy (Flint, Mich.).
COLLEGE: Western Michigan.
TRANSACTIONS/CAREER NOTES: Selected by Los Angeles Rams in 11th round (281st pick overall) of 1991 NFL draft. ... Signed by Rams (June 27, 1991). ... Released by Rams (August 26, 1991). ... Signed by Rams to practice squad (August 28, 1991). ... Activated (September 11, 1991). ... Released by Rams (September 27, 1991). ... Re-signed by Rams to practice squad (October 1, 1991). ... Activated (October 18, 1991). ... Released by Rams (October 25, 1991). ... Re-signed by Rams to practice squad (October 30, 1991). ... Activated (November 29, 1991). ... Released by Rams (December 20, 1991). ... Re-signed by Rams for 1992 season. ... Released by Rams (August 24, 1992). ... Signed by Green Bay Packers (February 8, 1993). ... Released by Packers (August 29, 1993). ... Signed by San Diego Chargers (September 1, 1993). ... Released by Chargers (September 19, 1993). ... Re-signed by Chargers (September 22, 1993). ... Granted free agency (February 17, 1994). ... Re-signed by Chargers (April 20, 1994). ... Released by Chargers (August 29, 1994). ... Selected by Rhein Fire in 10th round (60th pick overall) of 1995 World League Draft. ... Signed by Washington Redskins (June 22, 1995). ... Granted free agency (February 16, 1996). ... Re-signed by Redskins (April 16, 1996).
PLAYING EXPERIENCE: Los Angeles Rams NFL, 1991; San Diego NFL, 1993; Washington NFL, 1995. ... Games: 1991 (6), 1993 (10), 1995 (16). Total: 32.
MISCELLANEOUS: Played with Rhein Fire of World League in 1995 and was credited with five sacks.

CRISWELL, JEFF   OT   CHIEFS

PERSONAL: Born March 7, 1964, in Grinnell, Iowa. ... 6-7/294.
HIGH SCHOOL: Lynnville-Sully (Sully, Iowa).
COLLEGE: Graceland College (Iowa). (degree in physical education, health and secondary education).
TRANSACTIONS/CAREER NOTES: Signed as free-agent replacement player by Indianapolis Colts (September 26, 1987). ... Released by Colts (October 19, 1987). ... Signed by New York Jets (May 3, 1988). ... On injured reserve with foot injury (December 24, 1992-remainder of season). ... Granted unconditional free agency (February 17, 1995). ... Signed by Kansas City Chiefs (March 9, 1995).
PLAYING EXPERIENCE: Indianapolis NFL, 1987; New York Jets NFL, 1988-1994; Kansas City NFL, 1995. ... Games: 1987 (3), 1988 (15), 1989 (16), 1990 (16), 1991 (16), 1992 (14), 1993 (16), 1994 (15), 1995 (15). Total: 126.
PRO STATISTICS: 1989—Recovered one fumble. 1990—Recovered one fumble. 1994—Recovered one fumble.

CRITTENDEN, RAY   WR/KR   PANTHERS

PERSONAL: Born March 1, 1970, in Washington, D.C. ... 6-1/188.
HIGH SCHOOL: Annandale (Va.).
COLLEGE: Virginia Tech.
TRANSACTIONS/CAREER NOTES: Signed as non-drafted free agent by New England Patriots (May 20, 1993). ... Released by Patriots (August 22, 1995). ... Claimed on waivers by Carolina Panthers (August 24, 1995); released after failing physical. ...Signed by Panthers for 1996 season.
PRO STATISTICS: 1993—Rushed once for minus three yards. 1994—Recovered one fumble.

		RECEIVING				PUNT RETURNS				KICKOFF RETURNS				TOTALS			
Year Team	G	No.	Yds.	Avg.	TD	No.	Yds.	Avg.	TD	No.	Yds.	Avg.	TD	TD	2pt.	Pts.	Fum.
1993—New England NFL	16	16	293	18.3	1	2	37	18.5	0	23	478	20.8	0	1	...	6	0
1994—New England NFL	16	28	379	13.5	3	19	155	8.2	0	24	460	19.2	0	3	0	18	1
1995—								Did not play.									
Pro totals (2 years)	32	44	672	15.3	4	21	192	9.2	0	47	938	20.0	0	4	0	24	1

CROCKETT, RAY   CB   BRONCOS

PERSONAL: Born January 5, 1967, in Dallas. ... 5-10/185. ... Full name: Donald Ray Crockett.
HIGH SCHOOL: Duncanville (Texas).
COLLEGE: Baylor.
TRANSACTIONS/CAREER NOTES: Selected by Detroit Lions in fourth round (86th pick overall) of 1989 NFL draft. ... Signed by Lions (July 18, 1989). ... Granted unconditional free agency (February 17, 1994). ... Signed by Denver Broncos (March 9, 1994).
CHAMPIONSHIP GAME EXPERIENCE: Played in NFC championship game (1991 season).
PRO STATISTICS: 1989—Returned one kickoff for eight yards and recovered one fumble. 1990—Recovered two fumbles for 22 yards and a touchdown. 1992—Recovered one fumble for 15 yards. 1993—Recovered one fumble. 1994—Recovered two fumbles for 43 yards. 1995—Ran four yards with lateral from punt return and recovered one fumble for 50 yards and a touchdown.

		INTERCEPTIONS				SACKS
Year Team	G	No.	Yds.	Avg.	TD	No.
1989—Detroit NFL	16	1	5	5.0	0	0.0
1990—Detroit NFL	16	3	17	5.7	0	1.0
1991—Detroit NFL	16	6	141	23.5	1	1.0
1992—Detroit NFL	15	4	50	12.5	0	1.0
1993—Detroit NFL	16	2	31	15.5	0	1.0
1994—Denver NFL	14	2	6	3.0	0	0.0
1995—Denver NFL	16	0	0	...	0	3.0
Pro totals (7 years)	109	18	250	13.9	1	7.0

CROCKETT, ZACK   FB   COLTS   C

PERSONAL: Born December 2, 1972, in Pompano Beach, Fla. ... 6-2/241.
HIGH SCHOOL: Ely (Pompano Beach, Fla.).
JUNIOR COLLEGE: Hinds Community College (Miss.).
COLLEGE: Florida State.
TRANSACTIONS/CAREER NOTES: Selected by Indianapolis Colts in third round (79th pick overall) of 1995 NFL draft. ... Signed by Colts (July 21, 1995).
CHAMPIONSHIP GAME EXPERIENCE: Played in AFC championship game (1995 season).

		RUSHING				receiving				TOTALS			
Year Team	G	Att.	Yds.	Avg.	TD	No.	Yds.	Avg.	TD	TD	2pt.	Pts.	Fum.
1995—Indianapolis NFL	16	1	0	0.0	0	2	35	17.5	0	0	0	0	0

CROEL, MIKE   LB

PERSONAL: Born June 6, 1969, in Detroit. ... 6-3/235. ... Name pronounced KROLL.
HIGH SCHOOL: Lincoln-Sudbury (Mass.) Regional.
COLLEGE: Nebraska.
TRANSACTIONS/CAREER NOTES: Selected by Denver Broncos in first round (fourth pick overall) of 1991 NFL draft. ... Signed by Broncos (August 9, 1991). ... Released by Broncos (March 7, 1995). ... Signed by New York Giants (April 5, 1995). ... Granted unconditional free agency (February 16, 1996).
CHAMPIONSHIP GAME EXPERIENCE: Played in AFC championship game (1991 season).
HONORS: Named linebacker on THE SPORTING NEWS college All-America second team (1990). ... Named NFL Rookie of the Year by THE SPORTING NEWS (1991).
PRO STATISTICS: 1992—Recovered one fumble. 1993—Intercepted one pass for 22 yards and a touchdown and recovered two fumbles.

Year Team	G	SACKS
1991—Denver NFL	13	10.0
1992—Denver NFL	16	5.0
1993—Denver NFL	16	5.0
1994—Denver NFL	13	0.0
1995—New York Giants NFL	16	1.0
Pro totals (5 years)	74	21.0

CROOM, COREY   RB/KR   PATRIOTS

PERSONAL: Born May 22, 1971, in Sandusky, Ohio. ... 5-11/208. ... Full name: Corey Vincent Croom.
HIGH SCHOOL: Sandusky (Ohio).
COLLEGE: Ball State.
TRANSACTIONS/CAREER NOTES: Signed as non-drafted free agent by New England Patriots (April 30, 1993). ... Released by Patriots (August 30, 1993). ... Re-signed by Patriots to practice squad (August 31, 1993). ... Activated (September 19, 1993).

		RUSHING				RECEIVING				KICKOFF RETURNS				TOTALS			
Year Team	G	Att.	Yds.	Avg.	TD	No.	Yds.	Avg.	TD	No.	Yds.	Avg.	TD	TD	2pt.	Pts.	Fum.
1993—New England NFL	14	60	198	3.3	1	8	92	11.5	0	0	0	...	0	1	...	6	1
1994—New England NFL	16	0	0	...	0	0	0	...	0	10	172	17.2	0	0	...	0	1
1995—New England NFL	13	13	54	4.2	0	1	8	8.0	0	0	0	...	0	0	0	0	0
Pro totals (3 years)	43	73	252	3.5	1	9	100	11.1	0	10	172	17.2	0	1	0	6	2

CROSS, HOWARD   TE   GIANTS

PERSONAL: Born August 8, 1967, in Huntsville, Ala. ... 6-5/265.

HIGH SCHOOL: New Hope (Ala.).
COLLEGE: Alabama.
TRANSACTIONS/CAREER NOTES: Selected by New York Giants in sixth round (158th pick overall) of 1989 NFL draft. ... Signed by Giants (July 24, 1989). ... Granted free agency (February 1, 1991). ... Re-signed by Giants (July 24, 1991). ... Granted free agency (March 1, 1993). ... Re-signed by Giants (July 16, 1993). ... Designated by Giants as transition player (February 15, 1994).
CHAMPIONSHIP GAME EXPERIENCE: Played in NFC championship game (1990 season). ... Member of Super Bowl championship team (1990 season).
PRO STATISTICS: 1992—Recovered one fumble. 1993—Recovered one fumble. 1994—Recovered one fumble.

		RECEIVING				KICKOFF RETURNS				TOTALS		
Year Team	G	No.	Yds.	Avg.	TD	No.	Yds.	Avg.	TD	TD	2pt.	Pts.	Fum.
1989—New York Giants NFL	16	6	107	17.8	1	0	0	...	0	1	...	6	1
1990—New York Giants NFL	16	8	106	13.3	0	1	10	10.0	0	0	...	0	0
1991—New York Giants NFL	16	20	283	14.2	2	1	11	11.0	0	2	...	12	1
1992—New York Giants NFL	16	27	357	13.2	2	0	0	...	0	2	...	12	2
1993—New York Giants NFL	16	21	272	13.0	5	2	15	7.5	0	5	...	30	0
1994—New York Giants NFL	16	31	364	11.7	4	0	0	...	0	4	0	24	0
1995—New York Giants NFL	15	18	197	10.9	0	0	0	...	0	0	0	0	0
Pro totals (7 years)	111	131	1686	12.9	14	4	36	9.0	0	14	0	84	4

CROSS, JEFF   DE   DOLPHINS

PERSONAL: Born March 25, 1966, in Riverside, Calif. ... 6-4/280. ... Full name: Jeffrey Allen Cross.
HIGH SCHOOL: Blythe (Calif.)-Palo Verde Valley.
JUNIOR COLLEGE: Riverside (Calif.) Community College.
COLLEGE: Missouri.
TRANSACTIONS/CAREER NOTES: Selected by Miami Dolphins in ninth round (239th pick overall) of 1988 NFL draft. ... Signed by Dolphins (July 11, 1988). ... Granted free agency (February 1, 1992). ... Re-signed by Dolphins (July 20, 1992).
CHAMPIONSHIP GAME EXPERIENCE: Played in AFC championship game (1992 season).
HONORS: Played in Pro Bowl (1990 season).
PRO STATISTICS: 1990—Recovered two fumbles. 1993—Recovered two fumbles. 1994—Intercepted one pass for no yards and recovered one fumble. 1995—Fumbled once and recovered two fumbles for 11 yards.

Year Team	G	SACKS
1988—Miami NFL	16	0.0
1989—Miami NFL	16	10.0
1990—Miami NFL	16	11.5
1991—Miami NFL	16	7.0
1992—Miami NFL	16	5.0
1993—Miami NFL	16	10.5
1994—Miami NFL	13	9.5
1995—Miami NFL	16	6.0
Pro totals (8 years)	125	59.5

CRUMPLER, CARLESTER   TE   SEAHAWKS

PERSONAL: Born September 5, 1971, in Greenville, N.C. ... 6-6/260.
HIGH SCHOOL: Greenville (N.C.).
COLLEGE: East Carolina.
TRANSACTIONS/CAREER NOTES: Selected by Seattle Seahawks in seventh round (202nd pick overall) of 1994 NFL draft. ... Signed by Seahawks (July 6, 1994).
HONORS: Named tight end on The Sporting News college All-America second team (1993).

		RECEIVING				TOTALS			
Year Team	G	No.	Yds.	Avg.	TD	TD	2pt.	Pts.	Fum.
1994—Seattle NFL	9	2	19	9.5	0	0	0	0	0
1995—Seattle NFL	16	23	254	11.0	1	1	0	6	1
Pro totals (2 years)	25	25	273	10.9	1	1	0	6	1

CULPEPPER, BRAD   DT   BUCCANEERS

PERSONAL: Born May 8, 1969, in Tallahassee, Fla. ... 6-1/270. ... Full name: John Broward Culpepper.
HIGH SCHOOL: Leon (Tallahassee, Fla.).
COLLEGE: Florida (degree in history).
TRANSACTIONS/CAREER NOTES: Selected by Minnesota Vikings in 10th round (264th pick overall) of 1992 NFL draft. ... Signed by Vikings (July 20, 1992). ... On injured reserve with toe injury (November 23, 1992-remainder of season). ... Claimed on waivers by Tampa Bay Buccaneers (August 30, 1994).
HONORS: Named defensive lineman on The Sporting News college All-America first team (1991).
PRO STATISTICS: 1994—Returned two kickoffs for 30 yards and recovered one fumble. 1995—Recovered one fumble for 10 yards.

Year Team	G	SACKS
1992—Minnesota NFL	11	0.0
1993—Minnesota NFL	15	0.0
1994—Tampa Bay NFL	16	4.0
1995—Tampa Bay NFL	16	4.0
Pro totals (4 years)	58	8.0

IN MEMORIAM — RODNEY CULVER

PERSONAL: Born December 23, 1969, in Detroit. ... Died May 11, 1996. ... 5-9/224. ... Full name: Rodney Dwayne Culver. ... Played running back.
HIGH SCHOOL: Saint Martin De Porres (Detroit).
COLLEGE: Notre Dame.
TRANSACTIONS/CAREER NOTES: Selected by Indianapolis Colts in fourth round (85th pick overall) of 1992 NFL draft. ... Signed by Colts (July 19, 1992). ... Granted free agency (February 17, 1994). ... Re-signed by Colts (August 12, 1994). ... Claimed on waivers by San Diego Chargers (August 29, 1994). ... Granted free agency (February 17, 1995). ... Re-signed by Chargers (April 25, 1995).
CHAMPIONSHIP GAME EXPERIENCE: Member of Chargers for AFC championship game (1994 season); did not play. ... Played in Super Bowl XXIX (1994 season).
PRO STATISTICS: 1992—Recovered one fumble. 1993—Returned three kickoffs for 51 yards and recovered two fumbles for 56 yards and a touchdown.

		RUSHING				RECEIVING				TOTALS		
Year Team	G	Att.	Yds.	Avg.	TD	No.	Yds.	Avg.	TD	TD	2pt.	Pts. Fum.
1992—Indianapolis NFL	16	121	321	2.7	7	26	210	8.1	2	9	...	54	2
1993—Indianapolis NFL	16	65	150	2.3	3	11	112	10.2	1	5	...	30	3
1994—San Diego NFL	3	8	63	7.9	0	0	0	...	0	0	...	0	0
1995—San Diego NFL	8	47	155	3.3	3	5	21	4.2	0	3	0	18	0
Pro totals (4 years)	43	241	689	2.9	13	42	343	8.2	3	17	0	102	5

CUNNINGHAM, ED   C   BEARS   C

PERSONAL: Born August 17, 1969, in Washington, D.C. ... 6-3/285.
HIGH SCHOOL: Mount Vernon (Alexandria, Va.).
COLLEGE: Washington.
TRANSACTIONS/CAREER NOTES: Selected by Phoenix Cardinals in third round (61st pick overall) of 1992 NFL draft. ... Signed by Cardinals (July 23, 1992). ... Cardinals franchise renamed Arizona Cardinals for 1994 season. ... Granted free agency (February 17, 1995). ... Re-signed by Cardinals (July 17, 1995). ... Granted unconditional free agency (February 16, 1996). ... Signed by Chicago Bears (February 29, 1996).
PLAYING EXPERIENCE: Phoenix NFL, 1992 and 1993; Arizona NFL, 1994 and 1995. ... Games: 1992 (10); 1993 (15), 1994 (16), 1995 (9). Total: 50.
PRO STATISTICS: 1995—Fumbled once for minus 25 yards.

CUNNINGHAM, RANDALL   QB

PERSONAL: Born March 27, 1963, in Santa Barbara, Calif. ... 6-4/205. ... Brother of Sam Cunningham, running back, New England Patriots (1973-1979 and 1981).
HIGH SCHOOL: Santa Barbara (Calif.).
COLLEGE: UNLV.
TRANSACTIONS/CAREER NOTES: Selected by Arizona Outlaws in 1985 USFL territorial draft.... Selected by Philadelphia Eagles in second round (37th pick overall) of 1985 NFL draft. ... Signed by Eagles (July 22, 1985). ... On injured reserve with knee injury (September 3, 1991-remainder of season).... Granted unconditional free agency (February 16, 1996).
HONORS: Named punter on The Sporting News college All-America first team (1984). ... Played in Pro Bowl (1988-1990 seasons). ... Named Outstanding Player of Pro Bowl (1988 season).
RECORDS: Holds NFL single-season record for most times sacked—72 (1986). ... Shares NFL single-game records for most own fumbles recovered—4 (November 30, 1986, OT, at Los Angeles Raiders); and most own and opponents' fumbles recovered—4 (November 30, 1986, OT, at Los Angeles Raiders).
PRO STATISTICS: 1985—Fumbled three times. 1986—Punted twice for 54 yards and fumbled seven times and recovered four fumbles. 1987—Caught one pass for minus three yards, led league with 12 fumbles and recovered six fumbles for minus seven yards. 1988—Punted 3 three times for 167 yards and led league with 12 fumbles and recovered six fumbles. 1989—Punted six times for 319 yards and fumbled 17 times and recovered four fumbles for minus six yards. 1990—Fumbled nine times and recovered three fumbles for minus four yards. 1992—Led league with 13 fumbles and recovered three fumbles. 1993—Fumbled three times. 1994—Punted once for 80 yards and fumbled 10 times and recovered two fumbles for minus 15 yards. 1995—Fumbled three times and recovered one fumble for minus five yards.
STATISTICAL PLATEAUS: 300-yard passing games: 1987 (1), 1988 (2), 1989 (3), 1992 (1), 1993 (1), 1994 (4). Total: 12. ... 100-yard rushing games: 1986 (1), 1990 (1), 1992 (1). Total: 3.
MISCELLANEOUS: Regular-season record as starting NFL quarterback: 63-43-1 (.593).

		PASSING								RUSHING				TOTALS		
Year Team	G	Att.	Cmp.	Pct.	Yds.	TD	Int.	Avg.	Rat.	Att.	Yds.	Avg.	TD	TD	2pt.	Pts.
1985—Philadelphia NFL	6	81	34	42.0	548	1	8	6.77	29.8	29	205	7.1	0	0	...	0
1986—Philadelphia NFL	15	209	111	53.1	1391	8	7	6.66	72.9	66	540	8.2	5	5	...	30
1987—Philadelphia NFL	12	406	223	54.9	2786	23	12	6.86	83.0	76	505	6.6	3	3	...	18
1988—Philadelphia NFL	16	560	301	53.8	3808	24	16	6.80	77.6	93	624	6.7	6	6	...	36
1989—Philadelphia NFL	16	532	290	54.5	3400	21	15	6.39	75.5	104	621	*6.0	4	4	...	24
1990—Philadelphia NFL	16	465	271	58.3	3466	30	13	7.45	91.6	118	942	*8.0	5	5	...	30
1991—Philadelphia NFL	1	4	1	25.0	19	0	0	4.75	46.9	0	0	...	0	0	...	0
1992—Philadelphia NFL	15	384	233	60.7	2775	19	11	7.23	87.3	87	549	6.3	5	5	...	30
1993—Philadelphia NFL	4	110	76	69.1	850	5	5	7.73	88.1	18	110	6.1	1	1	...	6
1994—Philadelphia NFL	14	490	265	54.1	3229	16	13	6.59	74.4	65	288	4.4	3	3	0	18
1995—Philadelphia NFL	7	121	69	57.0	605	3	5	5.00	61.5	21	98	4.7	0	0	0	0
Pro totals (11 years)	122	3362	1874	55.8	22877	150	105	6.81	78.7	677	4482	6.6	32	32	0	192

CUNNINGHAM, RICK   OT

PERSONAL: Born January 4, 1967, in Los Angeles. ... 6-6/307. ... Full name: Patrick Dante Ross Cunningham.
HIGH SCHOOL: Beverly Hills (Calif.).

JUNIOR COLLEGE: Sacramento City College.
COLLEGE: Texas A&M.
TRANSACTIONS/CAREER NOTES: Selected by Indianapolis Colts in fourth round (106th pick overall) of 1990 NFL draft. ... Signed by Colts (July 17, 1990). ... Released by Colts (August 26, 1991). ... Selected by Orlando Thunder in third round (28th pick overall) of 1992 World League draft. ... Signed by Phoenix Cardinals (June 16, 1992). ... On injured reserve with forearm injury (December 4, 1992-remainder of season). ... Cardinals franchise renamed Arizona Cardinals for 1994 season. ... Granted unconditional free agency (February 17, 1995). ... Signed by Minnesota Vikings (April 3, 1995). ... Granted unconditional free agency (February 16, 1996).
PLAYING EXPERIENCE: Indianapolis NFL, 1990; Orlando W.L., 1992; Phoenix NFL, 1992 and 1993; Arizona NFL, 1994; Minnesota NFL, 1995. ... Games: 1990 (2), 1992 W.L. (10), 1992 NFL (8), 1993 (16), 1994 (11), 1995 (11). Total NFL: 48. Total Pro: 58.
HONORS: Named offensive tackle on All-World League team (1992).
PRO STATISTICS: W.L.: 1992—Recovered one fumble. NFL: 1993—Recovered one fumble. 1995—Recovered one fumble.

CURRY, ERIC   DE   BUCCANEERS

PERSONAL: Born February 3, 1970, in Thomasville, Ga. ... 6-5/270. ... Full name: Eric Felece Curry. ... Cousin of William Andrews, running back, Atlanta Falcons (1979-1983 and 1986); cousin of Lomas Brown, tackle, Arizona Cardinals; and cousin of Guy McIntyre, guard, San Francisco 49ers and Green Bay Packers (1984-1994).
HIGH SCHOOL: Thomasville (Ga.).
COLLEGE: Alabama (degree in criminal justice, 1992).
TRANSACTIONS/CAREER NOTES: Selected by Tampa Bay Buccaneers in first round (sixth pick overall) of 1993 NFL draft. ... Signed by Buccaneers (August 16, 1993). ... Designated by Buccaneers as transition player (February 15, 1994).
HONORS: Named defensive lineman on THE SPORTING NEWS college All-America first team (1992).
PRO STATISTICS: 1993—Recovered one fumble. 1995—Recovered one fumble.

Year Team	G	SACKS
1993—Tampa Bay NFL	10	5.0
1994—Tampa Bay NFL	15	3.0
1995—Tampa Bay NFL	16	2.0
Pro totals (3 years)	41	10.0

DAFNEY, BERNARD .   OL   STEELERS

PERSONAL: Born November 1, 1968, in Los Angeles. ... 6-5/329. ... Full name: Bernard Eugene Dafney.
HIGH SCHOOL: John C. Fremont (Los Angeles).
JUNIOR COLLEGE: Los Angeles Southwest Community College.
COLLEGE: Tennessee.
TRANSACTIONS/CAREER NOTES: Selected by Houston Oilers in ninth round (247th pick overall) of 1992 NFL draft. ... Signed by Oilers (July 9, 1992). ... Released by Oilers (August 31, 1992). ... Signed by Minnesota Vikings to practice squad (September 9, 1992). ... Activated (October 29, 1992). ... On injured reserve (August 25, 1995). ... Released by Vikings (August 31, 1995). ... Signed by Arizona Cardinals (September 15, 1995). ... Granted unconditional free agency (February 16, 1996). ... Signed by Pittsburgh Steelers (April 11, 1996).
PLAYING EXPERIENCE: Minnesota NFL, 1992-1994; Arizona NFL, 1995. ... Games: 1992 (2), 1993 (16), 1994 (16), 1995 (11). Total: 45.
PRO STATISTICS: 1994—Recovered one fumble.

DAHL, BOB   G   REDSKINS

PERSONAL: Born November 5, 1968, in Chicago. ... 6-5/310. ... Full name: Robert Allen Dahl.
HIGH SCHOOL: Chagrin Falls (Ohio).
COLLEGE: Notre Dame.
TRANSACTIONS/CAREER NOTES: Selected by Cincinnati Bengals in third round (72nd pick overall) of 1991 NFL draft. ... Signed by Bengals (July 15, 1991). ... Released by Bengals (August 26, 1991). ... Signed by Bengals to practice squad (August 28, 1991). ... Released by Bengals (November 12, 1991). ... Signed by Cleveland Browns (March 3, 1992). ... Released by Browns (September 11, 1992). ... Re-signed by Browns to practice squad (September 16, 1992). ... Activated (October 31, 1992). ... Released by Browns after 1995 season. ... Signed by Washington Redskins (March 4, 1996).
PLAYING EXPERIENCE: Cleveland NFL, 1992-1995. ... Games: 1992 (9), 1993 (16), 1994 (15), 1995 (16). Total: 56.
PRO STATISTICS: 1993—Recovered one fumble.

DALMAN, CHRIS   G/C   49ERS

PERSONAL: Born March 15, 1970, in Salinas, Calif. ... 6-3/285. ... Full name: Chris William Dalman.
HIGH SCHOOL: Palma (Salinas, Calif.).
COLLEGE: Stanford (degree in political science, 1992).
TRANSACTIONS/CAREER NOTES: Selected by San Francisco 49ers in sixth round (166th pick overall) of 1993 NFL draft. ... Signed by 49ers (June 24, 1993).
PLAYING EXPERIENCE: San Francisco NFL, 1993-1995. ... Games: 1993 (15), 1994 (16), 1995 (15). Total: 46.
CHAMPIONSHIP GAME EXPERIENCE: Played in NFC championship game (1993 and 1994 seasons). ... Member of Super Bowl championship team (1994 season).
PRO STATISTICS: 1993—Recovered one fumble. 1994—Fumbled once. 1995—Caught one pass for minus one yard, returned three kickoffs for 29 yards and recovered one fumble.

DALUISO, BRAD   K   GIANTS

PERSONAL: Born December 31, 1967, in San Diego. ... 6-2/210. ... Full name: Bradley William Daluiso. ... Name pronounced DOLL-uh-WEE-so.
HIGH SCHOOL: Valhalla (El Cajon, Calif.).
JUNIOR COLLEGE: Grossmont (Calif.) College.

COLLEGE: San Diego State, then UCLA.

TRANSACTIONS/CAREER NOTES: Signed as non-drafted free agent by Green Bay Packers (May 2, 1991). ... Traded by Packers to Atlanta Falcons for an undisclosed pick in 1992 draft (August 26, 1991). ... Claimed on waivers by Buffalo Bills (September 10, 1991). ... Granted unconditional free agency (February 1, 1992). ... Signed by Dallas Cowboys (February 18, 1992). ... Claimed on waivers by Denver Broncos (September 1, 1992). ... Released by Broncos (August 23, 1993). ... Signed by New York Giants (September 1, 1993). ... Granted free agency (February 17, 1994). ... Re-signed by Giants (June 21, 1994). ... Granted unconditional free agency (February 17, 1995). ... Re-signed by Giants (February 22, 1995).

CHAMPIONSHIP GAME EXPERIENCE: Played in AFC championship game (1991 season). ... Played in Super Bowl XXVI (1991 season).

PRO STATISTICS: 1992—Punted 10 times for 467 yards.

Year Team	G	XPM	XPA	FGM	FGA	Lg.	50+	Pts.
					KICKING			
1991—Atlanta NFL	2	2	2	2	3	23	0-0	8
—Buffalo NFL	14	0	0	0	0	0	0-0	0
1992—Denver NFL	16	0	0	0	1	0	0-1	0
1993—New York Giants NFL	15	0	0	1	3	54	1-3	3
1994—New York Giants NFL	16	5	5	11	11	52	1-1	38
1995—New York Giants NFL	16	28	28	20	28	51	2-2	88
Pro totals (5 years)	79	35	35	34	46	54	4-7	137

DANIEL, EUGENE　　　　DB　　　　COLTS

PERSONAL: Born May 4, 1961, in Baton Rouge, La. ... 5-11/180.

HIGH SCHOOL: Robert E. Lee (Baton Rouge, La.).

COLLEGE: Louisiana State (degree in marketing, 1984).

TRANSACTIONS/CAREER NOTES: Selected by New Orleans Breakers in 1984 USFL territorial draft. ... Selected by Indianapolis Colts in eighth round (205th pick overall) of 1984 NFL draft. ... Signed by Colts (June 21, 1984). ... Granted free agency (February 1, 1991). ... Re-signed by Colts (July 25, 1991). ... Granted unconditional free agency (February 17, 1994). ... Re-signed by Colts (March 9, 1994).

CHAMPIONSHIP GAME EXPERIENCE: Played in AFC championship game (1995 season).

PRO STATISTICS: 1985—Returned one punt for six yards, fumbled once and recovered three fumbles for 25 yards. 1986—Returned blocked punt 13 yards for a touchdown and recovered one fumble. 1989—Recovered one fumble for five yards. 1990—Returned one punt for no yards. 1992—Credited with two sacks.

Year Team	G	No.	Yds.	Avg.	TD
		INTERCEPTIONS			
1984—Indianapolis NFL	15	6	25	4.2	0
1985—Indianapolis NFL	16	8	53	6.6	0
1986—Indianapolis NFl	15	3	11	3.7	0
1987—Indianapolis NFL	12	2	34	17.0	0
1988—Indianapolis NFL	16	2	44	22.0	1
1989—Indianapolis NFL	15	1	34	34.0	0
1990—Indianapolis NFL	15	0	0	...	0
1991—Indianapolis NFL	16	3	22	7.3	0
1992—Indianapolis NFL	14	1	0	0.0	0
1993—Indianapolis NFL	16	1	17	17.0	0
1994—Indianapolis NFL	16	2	6	3.0	0
1995—Indianapolis NFL	16	3	142	47.3	1
Pro totals (12 years)	182	32	388	12.1	2

DARBY, MATT　　　　S　　　　CARDINALS

PERSONAL: Born November 19, 1968, in Virginia Beach, Va. ... 6-1/200. ... Full name: Matthew Lamont Darby.

HIGH SCHOOL: Green Run (Virginia Beach, Va.).

COLLEGE: UCLA.

TRANSACTIONS/CAREER NOTES: Selected by Buffalo Bills in fifth round (139th pick overall) of 1992 NFL draft. ... Signed by Bills (July 22, 1992). ... Released by Bills (February 16, 1996). ... Signed by Arizona Cardinals (April 9, 1996).

CHAMPIONSHIP GAME EXPERIENCE: Played in AFC championship game (1992 and 1993 seasons). ... Played in Super Bowl XXVII (1992 season) and Super Bowl XXVIII (1993 season).

HONORS: Named defensive back on THE SPORTING NEWS college All-America second team (1991).

PRO STATISTICS: 1992—Recovered one fumble. 1993—Recovered one fumble.

Year Team	G	No.	Yds.	Avg.	TD
		INTERCEPTIONS			
1992—Buffalo NFL	16	0	0	...	0
1993—Buffalo NFL	16	2	32	16.0	0
1994—Buffalo NFL	16	4	20	5.0	0
1995—Buffalo NFL	7	2	37	18.5	0
Pro totals (4 years)	55	8	89	11.1	0

DAR DAR, KIRBY　　　　WR　　　　DOLPHINS

PERSONAL: Born March 27, 1972, in Morgan City, La. ... 5-9/183. ... Full name: Kirby David Dar Dar.

HIGH SCHOOL: Thomas Jefferson (Tampa).

COLLEGE: Syracuse.

TRANSACTIONS/CAREER NOTES: Signed as non-drafted free agent by Miami Dolphins (April 27, 1995). ... Released by Dolphins (August 22, 1995). ... Re-signed by Dolphins to practice squad (August 30, 1995). ... Activated (December 23, 1995).

PLAYING EXPERIENCE: Miami NFL, 1995. ... Games: 1995 (1).

PRO STATISTICS: 1995—Returned one kickoff for 22 yards.

DAVEY, DON — DE/DT — JAGUARS

PERSONAL: Born April 8, 1968, in Scottsville, N.Y. ... 6-4/275. ... Full name: Donald Vincent Davey.
HIGH SCHOOL: Lincoln (Manitowoc, Wis.).
COLLEGE: Wisconsin (bachelor's and master's degree in mechanical engineering).
TRANSACTIONS/CAREER NOTES: Selected by Green Bay Packers in third round (67th pick overall) of 1991 NFL draft. ... Signed by Packers (June 14, 1991). ... Released by Packers (September 16, 1992). ... Re-signed by Packers (November 12, 1992). ... Granted free agency (February 17, 1994). ... Re-signed by Packers (April 11, 1994). ... Granted unconditional free agency (February 17, 1995). ... Signed by Jacksonville Jaguars (February 28, 1995).
PLAYING EXPERIENCE: Green Bay NFL, 1991-1994; Jacksonville NFL, 1995. ... Games: 1991 (16), 1992 (9), 1993 (9), 1994 (16), 1995 (16). Total: 66.
PRO STATISTICS: 1991—Returned one kickoff for eight yards. 1992—Returned one kickoff for eight yards. 1994—Credited with 1½ sacks and returned one kickoff for six yards. 1995—Credited with three sacks.

DAVIDSON, KENNY — DE

PERSONAL: Born August 17, 1967, in Shreveport, La. ... 6-5/288. ... Full name: Kenneth Darrell Davidson.
HIGH SCHOOL: Huntington (Shreveport, La.).
COLLEGE: Louisiana State (degree in business administration, 1991).
TRANSACTIONS/CAREER NOTES: Selected by Pittsburgh Steelers in second round (43rd pick overall) of 1990 NFL draft. ... Signed by Steelers (July 19, 1990). ... Granted free agency (March 1, 1993). ... Re-signed by Steelers (July 22, 1993). ... Granted unconditional free agency (February 17, 1994). ... Signed by Houston Oilers (May 25, 1994). ... Granted unconditional free agency (February 16, 1996).
PRO STATISTICS: 1993—Intercepted one pass for six yards and recovered one fumble for 18 yards and a touchdown. 1995—Intercepted one pass for three yards and recovered one fumble.

Year Team	G	SACKS
1990—Pittsburgh NFL	14	3.5
1991—Pittsburgh NFL	13	0.0
1992—Pittsburgh NFL	16	2.0
1993—Pittsburgh NFL	16	2.5
1994—Houston NFL	16	6.0
1995—Houston NFL	15	2.0
Pro totals (6 years)	90	16.0

DAVIS, ANTHONY — LB — CHIEFS

PERSONAL: Born March 7, 1969, in Pasco, Wash. ... 6-0/231.
HIGH SCHOOL: Pasco (Wash.).
JUNIOR COLLEGE: Spokane Falls Community College (Wash.).
COLLEGE: Utah.
TRANSACTIONS/CAREER NOTES: Selected by Houston Oilers in 11th round (301st pick overall) of 1992 NFL draft. ... Released by Oilers (August 24, 1992). ... Re-signed by Oilers to practice squad (September 2, 1992). ... Released by Oilers (October 6, 1992). ... Signed by Seattle Seahawks to practice squad (December 9, 1992). ... Granted free agency after 1992 season. ... Re-signed by Seahawks (February 24, 1993). ... Released by Seahawks (August 30, 1993). ... Re-signed by Seahawks to practice squad (September 1, 1993). ... Activated (October 11, 1993). ... Released by Seahawks (August 22, 1994). ... Signed by Kansas City Chiefs (November 24, 1994).
PLAYING EXPERIENCE: Seattle NFL, 1993; Kansas City NFL, 1994 and 1995. ... Games: 1993 (10), 1994 (5), 1995 (16). Total: 31.
PRO STATISTICS: 1995—Credited with two sacks and intercepted one pass for 11 yards.

DAVIS, ANTONE — OT — FALCONS

PERSONAL: Born February 28, 1967, in Sweetwater, Tenn. ... 6-4/325. ... Full name: Antone Eugene Davis.
HIGH SCHOOL: Peach County (Fort Valley, Ga.).
COLLEGE: Tennessee (degree in city planning).
TRANSACTIONS/CAREER NOTES: Selected by Philadelphia Eagles in first round (ninth pick overall) of 1991 NFL draft. ... Signed by Eagles (August 5, 1991). ... Granted unconditional free agency (February 16, 1996). ... Signed by Atlanta Falcons (May 13, 1996).
PLAYING EXPERIENCE: Philadelphia NFL, 1991-1995. ... Games: 1991 (16), 1992 (15), 1993 (16), 1994 (16), 1995 (15). Total: 78.
HONORS: Named offensive tackle on THE SPORTING NEWS college All-America first team (1990).

DAVIS, BILLY — WR — COWBOYS

PERSONAL: Born July 6, 1972, in El Paso, Texas. ... 6-1/199. ... Full name: William Augusta Davis III.
HIGH SCHOOL: Irvin (El Paso, Texas).
COLLEGE: Pittsburgh.
TRANSACTIONS/CAREER NOTES: Signed as non-drafted free agent by Dallas Cowboys (April 27, 1995).
PLAYING EXPERIENCE: Dallas NFL, 1995. ... Games: 1995 (16).
CHAMPIONSHIP GAME EXPERIENCE: Played in NFC championship game (1995 season). ... Member of Super Bowl championship team (1995 season).

DAVIS, DEXTER — CB — RAMS

PERSONAL: Born March 20, 1970, in Brooklyn, N.Y. ... 5-10/185. ... Full name: Dexter Wendell Davis.
HIGH SCHOOL: Sumter (S.C.).
COLLEGE: Clemson.

TRANSACTIONS/CAREER NOTES: Selected after junior season by Phoenix Cardinals in fourth round (89th pick overall) of 1991 NFL draft. ... Signed by Cardinals (July 18, 1991). ... On injured reserve with finger injury (October 15-November 21, 1991). ... Released by Cardinals (October 19, 1993). ... Signed by Los Angeles Rams (November 24, 1993). ... Granted free agency (February 17, 1994). ... Re-signed by Rams (June 6, 1994). ... Granted free agency (February 17, 1995). ... Rams franchise moved to St. Louis (April 12, 1995). ... Re-signed by Rams (June 16, 1995).

PRO STATISTICS: 1991—Recovered two fumbles. 1994—Recovered one fumble. 1995—Credited with one sack and recovered one fumble for seven yards.

		INTERCEPTIONS			
Year Team	G	No.	Yds.	Avg.	TD
1991—Phoenix NFL	11	0	0	...	0
1992—Phoenix NFL	16	2	27	13.5	0
1993—Phoenix NFL	6	0	0	...	0
—Los Angeles Rams NFL	6	0	0	...	0
1994—Los Angeles Rams NFL	4	0	0	...	0
1995—St. Louis NFL	16	0	0	...	0
Pro totals (5 years)	59	2	27	13.5	0

DAVIS, ERIC CB PANTHERS

PERSONAL: Born January 26, 1968, in Anniston, Ala. ... 5-11/186. ... Full name: Eric Wayne Davis.
HIGH SCHOOL: Anniston (Ala.).
COLLEGE: Jacksonville (Ala.) State.
TRANSACTIONS/CAREER NOTES: Selected by San Francisco 49ers in second round (53rd pick overall) of 1990 NFL draft. ... Signed by 49ers (July 28, 1990). ... On injured reserve with shoulder injury (September 11, 1991-remainder of season). ... Granted free agency (March 1, 1993). ... Re-signed by 49ers (July 20, 1993). ... Granted unconditional free agency (February 16, 1996). ... Signed by Carolina Panthers (February 19, 1996).
CHAMPIONSHIP GAME EXPERIENCE: Played in NFC championship game (1990 and 1992-1994 seasons). ... Member of Super Bowl championship team (1994 season).
HONORS: Played in Pro Bowl (1995 season).
POSTSEASON RECORDS: Shares NFL postseason career record for most consecutive games with one or more interception—3.
PRO STATISTICS: 1990—Recovered one fumble for 34 yards. 1992—Recovered two fumbles. 1993—Recovered one fumble for 47 yards and a touchdown. 1994—Recovered two fumbles. 1995—Credited with one sack.

		INTERCEPTIONS				PUNT RETURNS				TOTALS			
Year Team	G	No.	Yds.	Avg.	TD	No.	Yds.	Avg.	TD	TD	2pt.	Pts.	Fum.
1990—San Francisco NFL	16	1	13	13.0	0	5	38	7.6	0	0	...	0	0
1991—San Francisco NFL	2	0	0	...	0	0	0	...	0	0	...	0	0
1992—San Francisco NFL	16	3	52	17.3	0	0	0	...	0	0	...	0	0
1993—San Francisco NFL	16	4	45	11.3	1	0	0	...	0	2	...	12	0
1994—San Francisco NFL	16	1	8	8.0	0	0	0	...	0	0	0	0	1
1995—San Francisco NFL	15	3	84	28.0	1	0	0	...	0	1	0	6	0
Pro totals (6 years)	81	12	202	16.8	2	5	38	7.6	0	3	0	18	1

DAVIS, GREG K CARDINALS

PERSONAL: Born October 29, 1965, in Rome, Ga. ... 6-0/205. ... Full name: Gregory Brian Davis.
HIGH SCHOOL: Lakeside (Atlanta).
COLLEGE: The Citadel (degree in physical education, 1987).
TRANSACTIONS/CAREER NOTES: Selected by Tampa Bay Buccaneers in ninth round (246th pick overall) of 1987 NFL draft. ... Signed by Buccaneers (July 18, 1987). ... Released by Buccaneers (September 7, 1987). ... Signed as replacement player by Atlanta Falcons (September 24, 1987). ... Claimed on waivers by Buccaneers (October 20, 1987). ... Released by Buccaneers (November 2, 1987). ... Signed by Falcons (December 24, 1987). ... Granted unconditional free agency (February 1, 1989). ... Signed by New England Patriots (March 9, 1989). ... Released by Patriots (November 8, 1989). ... Signed by Falcons (November 15, 1989). ... Granted unconditional free agency (February 1, 1991). ... Signed by Phoenix Cardinals (February 21, 1991). ... Granted unconditional free agency (March 1, 1993). ... Re-signed by Cardinals (July 15, 1993). ... Cardinals franchise renamed Arizona Cardinals for 1994 season.

		PUNTING					KICKING						
Year Team	G	No.	Yds.	Avg.	Net avg.	In. 20	Blk.	XPM	XPA	FGM	FGA	Lg.	50+	Pts.
1987—Atlanta NFL	3	6	191	31.8	27.5	0	0	6	6	3	4	42	0-0	15
1988—Atlanta NFL	16	0	0	...	...	0	0	25	27	19	30	52	1-4	82
1989—New England NFL	9	0	0	...	...	0	0	13	16	16	23	52	2-2	61
—Atlanta NFL	6	0	0	...	...	0	0	12	12	7	11	47	0-0	33
1990—Atlanta NFL	16	0	0	...	...	0	0	40	40	22	33	53	2-5	106
1991—Phoenix NFL	16	0	0	...	...	0	0	19	19	21	30	52	3-7	82
1992—Phoenix NFL	16	4	167	41.8	36.8	0	0	28	28	13	26	49	0-3	67
1993—Phoenix NFL	16	0	0	...	...	0	0	37	37	21	28	55	4-5	100
1994—Arizona NFL	14	0	0	...	...	0	0	17	17	20	26	51	1-4	77
1995—Arizona NFL	16	0	0	...	...	0	0	19	19	30	39	55	1-6	109
Pro totals (10 years)	128	10	358	35.8	31.2	0	0	216	221	172	250	55	14-36	732

DAVIS, ISAAC G CHARGERS

PERSONAL: Born April 8, 1972, in Malvern, Ark. ... 6-3/320. ... Full name: John Isaac Davis. ... Cousin of Keith Traylor, defensive tackle, Kansas City Chiefs.
HIGH SCHOOL: Malvern (Ark.).
COLLEGE: Arkansas.
TRANSACTIONS/CAREER NOTES: Selected by San Diego Chargers in second round (43rd pick overall) of 1994 NFL draft. ... Signed by Chargers (July 13, 1994).

PLAYING EXPERIENCE: San Diego NFL, 1994 and 1995. ... Games: 1994 (13), 1995 (16). Total: 29.
CHAMPIONSHIP GAME EXPERIENCE: Played in AFC championship game (1994 season). ... Played in Super Bowl XXIX (1994 season).

DAVIS, MICHAEL   CB   RAVENS

PERSONAL: Born January 14, 1972, in Springfield, Ohio. ... 6-0/195. ... Full name: Michael Allen Davis.
HIGH SCHOOL: North (Springfield, Ohio).
COLLEGE: Cincinnati.
TRANSACTIONS/CAREER NOTES: Selected by Houston Oilers in fourth round (119th pick overall) of 1994 NFL draft. ... Signed by Oilers (June 6, 1995). ... Selected by Jacksonville Jaguars from Oilers in NFL expansion draft (February 15, 1995). ... Released by Jaguars (August 19, 1995). ... Claimed on waivers by Cleveland Browns (August 22, 1995). ... Browns franchise moved to Baltimore and renamed Ravens for 1996 season (March 11, 1996).
PLAYING EXPERIENCE: Houston NFL, 1994; Cleveland NFL, 1995. ... Games: 1994 (16), 1995 (3). Total: 19.

DAVIS, PASCHALL   LB   RAMS

PERSONAL: Born July 5, 1969, in Bryan, Texas. ... 6-2/225. ... Full name: Paschall Tederall Davis.
HIGH SCHOOL: Hearne (Texas).
JUNIOR COLLEGE: Trinity Valley Community College (Texas).
COLLEGE: Texas A&I.
TRANSACTIONS/CAREER NOTES: Signed as non-drafted free agent by Denver Broncos (April 30, 1992). ... Released by Broncos (August 18, 1992). ... Signed by Sacramento Gold Miners of CFL (March 1993). ... Released by Sacramento (1994). ... Signed by Shreveport Pirates of CFL (1994). ... Granted free agency (February 15, 1995). ... Signed by St. Louis Rams (June 6, 1995). ... Released by Rams (August 29, 1995). ... Re-signed by Rams to practice squad (October 16, 1995). ... Released by Rams (November 14, 1995). ... Re-signed by Rams (November 22, 1995). ... Released by Rams (December 5, 1995). ... Re-signed by Rams to practice squad (December 6, 1995). ... Activated (December 22, 1995).
PLAYING EXPERIENCE: Sacramento CFL, 1993; Shreveport CFL, 1994; St. Louis Rams NFL, 1995. ... Games: 1993 (18), 1994 (18), 1995 (3). Total CFL: 36. Total NFL: 3. Total Pro: 39.
PRO STATISTICS: CFL: 1993—Intercepted two passes for 46 yards and one touchdown, returned one kickoff for 13 yards and recovered one fumble.

DAVIS, REUBEN   DT   CHARGERS

PERSONAL: Born May 7, 1965, in Greensboro, N.C. ... 6-5/320. ... Full name: Reuben Cordell Davis.
HIGH SCHOOL: Grimsley (Greensboro, N.C.).
COLLEGE: North Carolina (degree in journalism and mass communications, 1988).
TRANSACTIONS/CAREER NOTES: Selected by Tampa Bay Buccaneers in ninth round (225th pick overall) of 1988 NFL draft. ... Signed by Buccaneers (July 6, 1988). ... Granted free agency (February 1, 1990). ... Re-signed by Buccaneers (July 22, 1990). ... On injured reserve with knee injury (December 3, 1991-remainder of season). ... Granted free agency (February 1, 1992). ... Re-signed by Buccaneers (August 20, 1992). ... Granted roster exemption (August 20-28, 1992). ... Traded by Buccaneers to Phoenix Cardinals for third-round pick (traded to San Diego) in 1993 draft (October 12, 1992). ... Granted unconditional free agency (February 17, 1994). ... Signed by San Diego Chargers (March 18, 1994).
CHAMPIONSHIP GAME EXPERIENCE: Played in AFC championship game (1994 season). ... Played in Super Bowl XXIX (1994 season).
POSTSEASON RECORDS: Shares NFL postseason single-game record for most safeties—1 (January 8, 1995, vs. Miami).
PRO STATISTICS: 1989—Intercepted one pass for 13 yards and recovered two fumbles. 1990—Recovered one fumble. 1993—Recovered one fumble. 1994—Recovered one fumble.

Year Team	G	SACKS
1988—Tampa Bay NFL	16	3.0
1989—Tampa Bay NFL	16	3.0
1990—Tampa Bay NFL	16	1.0
1991—Tampa Bay NFL	12	3.5
1992—Tampa Bay NFL	5	0.0
—Phoenix NFL	11	2.0
1993—Phoenix NFL	16	1.0
1994—San Diego NFL	16	0.5
1995—San Diego NFL	16	3.5
Pro totals (8 years)	124	17.5

DAVIS, RONALD   CB   FALCONS

PERSONAL: Born February 24, 1972, in Bartlett, Tenn. ... 5-10/190. ... Full name: Ronald Rozelle Davis.
HIGH SCHOOL: Bartlett (Tenn.).
COLLEGE: Tennessee.
TRANSACTIONS/CAREER NOTES: Selected by Atlanta Falcons in second round (41st pick overall) of 1995 NFL draft. ... Signed by Falcons (July 25, 1995).
PLAYING EXPERIENCE: Atlanta NFL, 1995. ... Games: 1995 (12).
PRO STATISTICS: 1995—Recovered one fumble.

DAVIS, SCOTT   G   GIANTS

PERSONAL: Born January 29, 1970, in Glenwood, Iowa. ... 6-3/292.
HIGH SCHOOL: Glenwood (Iowa).
COLLEGE: Iowa.

TRANSACTIONS/CAREER NOTES: Selected by New York Giants in sixth round (150th pick overall) of 1993 NFL draft. ... Signed by Giants (July 19, 1993). ... On injured reserve with knee injury (August 22, 1995-entire season).
PLAYING EXPERIENCE: New York Giants NFL, 1993 and 1994. ... Games: 1993 (4), 1994 (15). Total: 19.

DAVIS, TERRELL   RB   BRONCOS

PERSONAL: Born October 28, 1972, in San Diego. ... 5-11/200.
HIGH SCHOOL: Abraham Lincoln Prep (San Diego).
COLLEGE: Long Beach State, then Georgia.
TRANSACTIONS/CAREER NOTES: Selected by Denver Broncos in sixth round (196th pick overall) of 1995 NFL draft.
PRO STATISTICS: 1995—Recovered one fumble.
STATISTICAL PLATEAUS: 100-yard rushing games: 1995 (3).

		RUSHING				RECEIVING				TOTALS		
Year Team	G	Att.	Yds.	Avg.	TD	No.	Yds.	Avg.	TD	TD 2pt.	Pts.	Fum.
1995—Denver NFL.................................	14	237	1117	4.7	7	49	367	7.5	1	8 0	48	5

DAVIS, TRAVIS   S   JAGUARS

PERSONAL: Born January 10, 1973, in Harbor City, Calif. ... 6-0/200.
HIGH SCHOOL: Banning (Wilmington, Calif.).
COLLEGE: Notre Dame.
TRANSACTIONS/CAREER NOTES: Selected by New Orleans Saints in seventh round (242nd pick overall) of 1995 NFL draft. ... Signed by Saints (July 14, 1995). ... Released by Saints (September 5, 1995). ... Re-signed by Saints to practice squad (September 6, 1995). ... Signed by Jacksonville Jaguars off Saints practice squad (October 17, 1995).
PLAYING EXPERIENCE: Jacksonville NFL, 1995. ... Games: 1995 (9).
PRO STATISTICS: Recovered one fumble.

DAVIS, TYREE   WR   BENGALS

PERSONAL: Born September 28, 1970, in Altheimer, Ark. ... 5-9/175. ... Brother of Willie Davis, wide receiver, Houston Oilers.
HIGH SCHOOL: Altheimer (Ark.).
COLLEGE: Central Arkansas.
TRANSACTIONS/CAREER NOTES: Selected by Tampa Bay Buccaneers in seventh round (176th pick overall) of 1993 NFL draft. ... Signed by Buccaneers (June 22, 1993). ... Released by Buccaneers (August 24, 1993). ... Re-signed by Buccaneers to practice squad (August 31, 1993). ... Granted free agency (January 10, 1994). ... Re-signed by Buccaneers (March 29, 1994). ... Released by Buccaneers (August 28, 1994). ... Re-signed by Buccaneers to practice squad (August 30, 1994). ... Activated (December 16, 1994). ... Assigned by Buccaneers to Barcelona Dragons in 1995 World League enhancement allocation program (February 20, 1995). ... Released by Buccaneers (October 17, 1995). ... Signed by Cincinnati Bengals (February 22, 1996).

		RECEIVING				PUNT RETURNS				KICKOFF RETURNS				TOTALS		
Year Team	G	No.	Yds.	Avg.	TD	No.	Yds.	Avg.	TD	No.	Yds.	Avg.	TD	TD 2pt.	Pts.	Fum.
1995—Barcelona W.L.	...	56	855	15.3	6	18	143	7.9	0	13	286	22.0	0	6 0	36	...
—Tampa Bay NFL	1	0	0	...	0	0	0	...	0	0	0	...	0	0 0	0	0
W.L. totals (1 year)	...	56	855	15.3	6	18	143	8.0	0	13	286	22.0	0	6 0	36	...
NFL totals (1 year).....................	1	0	0	...	0	0	0	...	0	0	0	...	0	0 0	0	0
Pro totals (1 year)......................	...	56	855	15.3	6	18	143	8.0	0	13	286	22.0	0	6 0	36	...

DAVIS, TYRONE   WR   JETS

PERSONAL: Born June 30, 1972, in Halifax, Va. ... 6-4/229.
HIGH SCHOOL: Halifax (Va.), then Fork Union (Va.) Military Academy.
COLLEGE: Virginia.
TRANSACTIONS/CAREER NOTES: Selected by New York Jets in fourth round (107th pick overall) of 1995 NFL draft. ... Signed by Jets (June 14, 1995). ... Released by Jets (September 13, 1995). ... Re-signed by Jets to practice squad (September 15, 1995). ... Activated (December 11, 1995).
PLAYING EXPERIENCE: New York Jets NFL, 1995. ... Games: 1995 (4).
PRO STATISTICS: 1995—Caught one pass for nine yards.

DAVIS, WILLIE   WR   OILERS

PERSONAL: Born October 10, 1967, in Little Rock, Ark. ... 6-0/181. ... Full name: Willie Clark Davis. ... Brother of Tyree Davis, wide receiver, Cincinnati Bengals.
HIGH SCHOOL: Altheimer (Ark.).
COLLEGE: Central Arkansas.
TRANSACTIONS/CAREER NOTES: Signed as non-drafted free agent by Kansas City Chiefs (May 2, 1990). ... Released by Chiefs (September 3, 1990). ... Signed by Chiefs to practice squad (1990). ... Granted free agency after 1990 season. ... Re-signed by Chiefs (February 2, 1991). ... Released by Chiefs (August 26, 1991). ... Signed by Chiefs to practice squad (August 28, 1991). ... Activated (November 23, 1991). ... Moved to practice squad (November 26, 1991). ... Granted free agency after 1991 season. ... Re-signed by Chiefs (February 20, 1992). ... Assigned by Chiefs to Orlando Thunder in 1992 World League enhancement allocation program (February 20, 1992). ... Granted unconditional free agency (February 16, 1996). ... Signed by Houston Oilers (March 7, 1996).
CHAMPIONSHIP GAME EXPERIENCE: Played in AFC championship game (1993 season).
PRO STATISTICS: W.L.: 1992—Recovered one fumble and rushed once for 12 yards. NFL: 1992—Rushed once for minus 11 yards.

D

STATISTICAL PLATEAUS: 100-yard receiving games: 1992 (3), 1993 (2), 1994 (2), 1995 (1). Total: 8.

Year Team	G	RECEIVING				TOTALS			
		No.	Yds.	Avg.	TD	TD	2pt.	Pts.	Fum.
1991—Kansas City NFL	1	0	0	...	0	0	...	0	0
1992—Orlando W.L.	6	20	242	12.1	1	1		6	0
—Kansas City NFL	16	36	756	*21.0	3	3	...	18	0
1993—Kansas City NFL	16	52	909	17.5	7	7		42	0
1994—Kansas City NFL	14	51	822	16.1	5	5	1	32	1
1995—Kansas City NFL	16	33	527	16.0	5	5	0	30	0
W.L. totals (1 year)	6	20	242	12.1	1	1	0	6	0
NFL totals (5 years)	63	172	3014	17.5	20	20	1	122	1
Pro totals (5 years)	69	192	3256	17.0	21	21	1	128	1

DAWKINS, SEAN — WR — COLTS

PERSONAL: Born February 3, 1971, in Red Bank, N.J. ... 6-4/211. ... Full name: Sean Russell Dawkins.
HIGH SCHOOL: Homestead (Cupertino, Calif.).
COLLEGE: California.
TRANSACTIONS/CAREER NOTES: Selected after junior season by Indianapolis Colts in first round (16th pick overall) of 1993 NFL draft. ... Signed by Colts (August 4, 1993).
CHAMPIONSHIP GAME EXPERIENCE: Played in AFC championship game (1995 season).
HONORS: Named wide receiver on THE SPORTING NEWS college All-America first team (1992).
STATISTICAL PLATEAUS: 100-yard receiving games: 1993 (1), 1994 (1), 1995 (2). Total: 4.

Year Team	G	RECEIVING				TOTALS			
		No.	Yds.	Avg.	TD	TD	2pt.	Pts.	Fum.
1993—Indianapolis NFL	16	26	430	16.5	1	1	...	6	0
1994—Indianapolis NFL	16	51	742	14.6	5	5	0	30	1
1995—Indianapolis NFL	16	52	784	15.1	3	3	0	18	1
Pro totals (3 years)	48	129	1956	15.2	9	9	0	54	2

DAWSEY, LAWRENCE — WR

PERSONAL: Born November 16, 1967, in Dothan, Ala. ... 6-0/192.
HIGH SCHOOL: Northview (Dothan, Ala.).
COLLEGE: Florida State.
TRANSACTIONS/CAREER NOTES: Selected by Tampa Bay Buccaneers in third round (66th pick overall) of 1991 NFL draft. ... Signed by Buccaneers (July 17, 1991). ... On injured reserve with knee injury (October 5, 1993-remainder of season). ... On physically unable to perform list (August 28-October 21, 1994). ... Released by Buccaneers (May 13, 1996).
HONORS: Named wide receiver on THE SPORTING NEWS college All-America second team (1990).
PRO STATISTICS: 1991—Rushed once for nine yards and a touchdown. 1992—Recovered one fumble.
STATISTICAL PLATEAUS: 100-yard receiving games: 1991 (1), 1992 (1), 1993 (1), 1994 (1). Total: 4.

Year Team	G	RECEIVING				TOTALS			
		No.	Yds.	Avg.	TD	TD	2pt.	Pts.	Fum.
1991—Tampa Bay NFL	16	55	818	14.9	3	4	...	24	0
1992—Tampa Bay NFL	15	60	776	12.9	1	1	...	6	1
1993—Tampa Bay NFL	4	15	203	13.5	0	0	...	0	0
1994—Tampa Bay NFL	10	46	673	14.6	1	1	0	6	0
1995—Tampa Bay NFL	12	30	372	12.4	0	0	0	0	0
Pro totals (5 years)	57	206	2842	13.8	5	6	0	36	1

DAWSON, DERMONTTI — C — STEELERS

PERSONAL: Born June 17, 1965, in Lexington, Ky. ... 6-2/288. ... Full name: Dermontti Farra Dawson. ... Cousin of Marc Logan, running back, Washington Redskins; and cousin of George Adams, running back, New York Giants and New England Patriots (1985-1991).
HIGH SCHOOL: Bryan Station (Lexington, Ky.).
COLLEGE: Kentucky (degree in education, 1988).
TRANSACTIONS/CAREER NOTES: Selected by Pittsburgh Steelers in second round (44th pick overall) of 1988 NFL draft. ... Signed by Steelers (August 1, 1988). ... On injured reserve with knee injury (September 26-November 26, 1988). ... Designated by Steelers as transition player (February 25, 1993).
PLAYING EXPERIENCE: Pittsburgh NFL, 1988-1995. ... Games: 1988 (8), 1989 (16), 1990 (16), 1991 (16), 1992 (16), 1993 (16), 1994 (16), 1995 (16). Total: 120.
CHAMPIONSHIP GAME EXPERIENCE: Played in AFC championship game (1994 and 1995 seasons). ... Played in Super Bowl XXX (1995 season).
HONORS: Played in Pro Bowl (1992-1995 seasons). ... Named center on THE SPORTING NEWS NFL All-Pro team (1994 and 1995).
PRO STATISTICS: 1991—Fumbled twice and recovered one fumble for two yards. 1993—Fumbled once.

DAWSON, LAKE — WR — CHIEFS

PERSONAL: Born January 2, 1972, in Boston. ... 6-1/207.
HIGH SCHOOL: Federal Way (Wash.).
COLLEGE: Notre Dame (degree in telecommunications).
TRANSACTIONS/CAREER NOTES: Selected by Kansas City Chiefs in third round (92nd pick overall) of 1994 NFL draft. ... Signed by Chiefs (May 5, 1994).

STATISTICAL PLATEAUS: 100-yard receiving games: 1994 (1).

		RUSHING				RECEIVING				TOTALS			
Year Team	G	Att.	Yds.	Avg.	TD	No.	Yds.	Avg.	TD	TD	2pt.	Pts.	Fum.
1994—Kansas City NFL	12	3	24	8.0	0	37	537	14.5	2	2	0	12	1
1995—Kansas City NFL	16	1	-9	-9.0	0	40	513	12.8	5	5	0	30	0
Pro totals (2 years)	28	4	15	3.8	0	77	1050	13.6	7	7	0	42	1

DEESE, DERRICK   G   49ERS

PERSONAL: Born May 17, 1970, in Culver City, Calif. ... 6-3/270.
HIGH SCHOOL: Culver City (Calif.).
JUNIOR COLLEGE: El Camino Junior College (Calif.).
COLLEGE: Southern California.
TRANSACTIONS/CAREER NOTES: Signed as non-drafted free agent by San Francisco 49ers (May 8, 1992). ... On injured reserve with elbow injury (August 4, 1992-entire season). ... On inactive list for six games with 49ers (1993). ... On injured reserve with broken wrist (October 23, 1993-remainder of season). ... Granted free agency (February 17, 1995). ... Tendered offer sheet by St. Louis Rams (April 20, 1995). ... Offer matched by 49ers (April 21, 1995). ... Granted unconditional free agency (February 16, 1996). ... Re-signed by 49ers (June 4, 1996).
PLAYING EXPERIENCE: San Francisco NFL, 1994 and 1995. ... Games: 1994 (16), 1995 (2). Total: 18.
CHAMPIONSHIP GAME EXPERIENCE: Played in NFC championship game (1994 season). ... Member of Super Bowl championship team (1994 season).

DeGRAFFENREID, ALLEN   WR   PACKERS

PERSONAL: Born May 1, 1970, in Cincinnati. ... 6-2/210.
HIGH SCHOOL: Princeton (Cincinnati).
COLLEGE: Ohio State.
TRANSACTIONS/CAREER NOTES: Signed as non-drafted free agent by Cincinnati Bengals (April 27, 1993). ... Released by Bengals (August 30, 1993). ... Re-signed by Bengals (November 27, 1993). ... Released by Bengals (December 15, 1993). ... Signed by Kansas City Chiefs to practice squad (December 17, 1993). ... Granted free agency after 1993 season. ... Re-signed by Chiefs (May 18, 1994). ... Released by Chiefs (August 23, 1994). ... Re-signed by Chiefs to practice squad (August 31, 1994). ... Released by Chiefs (October 12, 1994). ... Re-signed by Chiefs to practice squad (October 19, 1994). ... Assigned by Chiefs to Scottish Claymores in 1995 World League enhancement allocation program (February 20, 1995). ... Released by Chiefs (August 22, 1995). ... Signed by Green Bay Packers (January 4, 1996).
PRO STATISTICS: W.L.: 1995— Attempted three field goals (missed all three) and kicked one extra-point try (in one attempt).

		RECEIVING				PUNT RETURNS				KICKOFF RETURNS				TOTALS			
Year Team	G	No.	Yds.	Avg.	TD	No.	Yds.	Avg.	TD	No.	Yds.	Avg.	TD	TD	2pt	Pts.	Fum.
1993—								Did not play.									
1994—Cincinnati	2	0	0	...	0	0	0	...	0	0	0	...	0	0	0	0	0
1995—Scottish W.L.	...	44	624	14.2	4	8	70	8.8	0	21	490	23.3	0	4	0	24	...
Pro totals (2 years)	...	44	624	14.2	4	8	70	8.8	0	21	490	23.3	0	4	0	24	...

DEL GRECO, AL   K   OILERS

PERSONAL: Born March 2, 1962, in Providence, R.I. ... 5-10/200. ... Full name: Albert Louis Del Greco Jr.
HIGH SCHOOL: Coral Gables (Fla.).
COLLEGE: Auburn.
TRANSACTIONS/CAREER NOTES: Signed as non-drafted free agent by Miami Dolphins (May 17, 1984). ... Released by Dolphins (August 27, 1984). ... Signed by Green Bay Packers (October 17, 1984). ... Released by Packers (November 25, 1987). ... Signed by St. Louis Cardinals (December 8, 1987). ... Cardinals franchise moved to Phoenix (March 15, 1988). ... Granted unconditional free agency (February 1-April 1, 1991). ... Re-signed by Cardinals (July 1, 1991). ... Released by Cardinals (August 19, 1991). ... Signed by Houston Oilers (November 5, 1991). ... Granted unconditional free agency (February 1-April 1, 1992). ... Re-signed by Oilers for 1992 season. ... Granted unconditional free agency (February 17, 1995). ... Re-signed by Oilers (June 2, 1995).
PRO STATISTICS: 1988—Rushed once for eight yards. 1990—Recovered one fumble. 1995—Punted once for 15 yards.

		KICKING							
Year Team	G	XPM	XPA	FGM	FGA	Lg.	50+	Pts.	
1984—Green Bay NFL	9	34	34	9	12	45	0-1	61	
1985—Green Bay NFL	16	38	40	19	26	46	0-1	95	
1986—Green Bay NFL	16	29	29	17	27	50	2-4	80	
1987—Green Bay NFL	5	11	11	5	10	47	0-0	26	
—St. Louis NFL	3	8	9	4	5	37	0-0	20	
1988—Phoenix NFL	16	42	44	12	21	51	1-2	78	
1989—Phoenix NFL	16	28	29	18	26	50	1-2	82	
1990—Phoenix NFL	16	31	31	17	27	50	2-6	82	
1991—Houston NFL	7	16	16	10	13	52	1-1	46	
1992—Houston NFL	16	41	41	21	27	54	1-1	104	
1993—Houston NFL	16	39	40	29	34	52	4-7	126	
1994—Houston NFL	16	18	18	16	20	50	1-3	66	
1995—Houston NFL	16	33	33	27	31	53	3-5	114	
Pro totals (12 years)	168	368	375	204	279	54	16-33	980	

DELLENBACH, JEFF   C   PATRIOTS

PERSONAL: Born February 14, 1963, in Wausau, Wis. ... 6-6/300. ... Full name: Jeffrey Alan Dellenbach. ... Name pronounced del-en-BOK.
HIGH SCHOOL: East (Wausau, Wis.).
COLLEGE: Wisconsin.

TRANSACTIONS/CAREER NOTES: Selected by Jacksonville Bulls in 1985 USFL territorial draft. ... Selected by Miami Dolphins in fourth round (111th pick overall) of 1985 NFL draft. ... Signed by Dolphins (July 15, 1985). ... Granted free agency (February 1, 1990). ... Re-signed by Dolphins (August 30, 1990). ... Granted roster exemption (August 30-September 8, 1990). ... Granted free agency (February 1, 1992). ... Re-signed by Dolphins (May 4, 1992). ... Granted unconditional free agency (February 17, 1995). ... Signed by New England Patriots (March 6, 1995).
PLAYING EXPERIENCE: Miami NFL, 1985-1994; New England NFL, 1995. ... Games: 1985 (11), 1986 (13), 1987 (11), 1988 (16), 1989 (16), 1990 (15), 1991 (15), 1992 (16), 1993 (16), 1994 (16), 1995 (15). Total: 160.
CHAMPIONSHIP GAME EXPERIENCE: Played in AFC championship game (1985 and 1992 seasons).
PRO STATISTICS: 1987—Fumbled once for minus 13 yards. 1988—Fumbled once for minus nine yards. 1991—Returned one kickoff for no yards. 1992—Recovered one fumble. 1993—Fumbled once and recovered one fumble for minus six yards. 1994—Fumbled once.

DeLONG, GREG   TE   VIKINGS

PERSONAL: Born April 3, 1973, in Orefield, Pa. ... 6-4/245.
HIGH SCHOOL: Parkland Senior (Orefield, Pa.).
COLLEGE: North Carolina.
TRANSACTIONS/CAREER NOTES: Signed as non-drafted free agent by Cleveland Browns (May 2, 1995). ... Released by Browns (August 21, 1995). ... Signed by Minnesota Vikings to practice squad (August 28, 1995). ... Activated (November 15, 1995).
PLAYING EXPERIENCE: Minnesota NFL, 1995. ... Games: 1995 (2)
PRO STATISTICS: 1995—Caught six passes for 38 yards.

DEL RIO, JACK   LB   DOLPHINS

PERSONAL: Born April 4, 1963, in Castro Valley, Calif. ... 6-4/246.
HIGH SCHOOL: Hayward (Calif.).
COLLEGE: Southern California.
TRANSACTIONS/CAREER NOTES: Selected by Los Angeles Express in 1985 USFL territorial draft. ... Selected by New Orleans Saints in third round (68th pick overall) of 1985 NFL draft. ... Signed by Saints (July 31, 1985). ... Traded by Saints to Kansas City Chiefs for fifth-round pick (TE Greg Scales) in 1988 draft (August 17, 1987). ... On injured reserve with knee injury (December 13, 1988-remainder of season). ... Claimed on waivers by Dallas Cowboys (August 31, 1989). ... Granted free agency (February 1, 1991). ... Re-signed by Cowboys (July 25, 1991). ... Granted unconditional free agency (February 1, 1992). ... Signed by Minnesota Vikings (March 3, 1992). ... Released by Vikings (February 13, 1996). ...Signed by Miami Dolphins (June 2, 1996).
HONORS: Played in Pro Bowl (1994 season).
PRO STATISTICS: 1985—Recovered five fumbles for 22 yards and one touchdown. 1986—Rushed once for 16 yards. 1988—Recovered one fumble. 1989—Returned two fumbles for 57 yards and one touchdown. 1991—Recovered one fumble. 1992—Recovered two fumbles. 1993—Returned one kickoff for four yards. 1994—Recovered two fumbles. 1995—Recovered one fumble.
MISCELLANEOUS: Selected by Toronto Blue Jays organization in 22nd round of free-agent baseball draft (June 8, 1981); did not sign.

		INTERCEPTIONS				SACKS
Year Team	G	No.	Yds.	Avg.	TD	No.
1985—New Orleans NFL	16	2	13	6.5	0	0.0
1986—New Orleans NFL	16	0	0	...	0	0.0
1987—Kansas City NFL	10	0	0	...	0	3.0
1988—Kansas City NFL	15	1	0	0.0	0	1.0
1989—Dallas NFL	14	0	0	...	0	0.0
1990—Dallas NFL	16	0	0	...	0	1.5
1991—Dallas NFL	16	0	0	...	0	0.0
1992—Minnesota NFL	16	2	92	46.0	1	2.0
1993—Minnesota NFL	16	4	3	.8	0	0.5
1994—Minnesota NFL	16	3	5	1.7	0	2.0
1995—Minnesota NFL	9	1	15	15.0	0	3.0
Pro totals (11 years)	160	13	128	9.9	1	13.0

DeMARCO, BRIAN   G   JAGUARS

PERSONAL: Born April 9, 1972, in Berea, Ohio. ... 6-7/321.
HIGH SCHOOL: Admiral King (Lorain, Ohio).
COLLEGE: Michigan State.
TRANSACTIONS/CAREER NOTES: Selected by Jacksonville Jaguars in second round (40th pick overall) of 1995 NFL draft. ... Signed by Jaguars (June 1, 1995).
PLAYING EXPERIENCE: Jacksonville NFL, 1995. ... Games: 1995 (16).

DeOSSIE, STEVE   LB   PATRIOTS

PERSONAL: Born November 22, 1962, in Tacoma, Wash. ... 6-2/248. ... Full name: Steven Leonard DeOssie.
HIGH SCHOOL: Don Bosco Technical (Boston).
COLLEGE: Boston College (degree in communications, 1984).
TRANSACTIONS/CAREER NOTES: Selected by New Jersey Generals in first round (14th pick overall) of 1984 USFL draft. ... Selected by Dallas Cowboys in fourth round (110th pick overall) of 1984 NFL draft. ... Signed by Cowboys (May 3, 1984). ... Traded by Cowboys to New York Giants for sixth-round pick (traded to San Diego) in 1990 draft (June 2, 1989). ... On injured reserve with broken toe (September 27-November 15, 1989). ... On developmental squad (November 16-18, 1989). ... On injured reserve with ankle injury (December 6, 1992-remainder of season). ... Granted unconditional free agency (March 1, 1993). ... Re-signed by Giants (July 9, 1993). ... Released by Giants (August 31, 1993). ... Re-signed by Giants (September 1, 1993). ... Released by Giants (November 10, 1993). ... Signed by New York Jets (November 16, 1993). ... Granted unconditional free agency (February 17, 1994). ... Signed by New England Patriots (March 25, 1994). ... Granted unconditional free agency (February 16, 1996). ... Re-signed by Patriots (February 21, 1996).
PLAYING EXPERIENCE: Dallas NFL, 1984-1988; New York Giants NFL, 1989-1992; New York Giants (8)-New York Jets (7) NFL, 1993; New

England NFL, 1994 and 1995. ... Games: 1984 (16), 1985 (16), 1986 (16), 1987 (11), 1988 (16), 1989 (9), 1990 (16), 1991 (16), 1992 (12), 1993 (15), 1994 (16), 1995 (16). Total: 175.
CHAMPIONSHIP GAME EXPERIENCE: Played in NFC championship game (1990 season). ... Member of Super Bowl championship team (1990 season).
PRO STATISTICS: 1989—Intercepted one pass for 10 yards. 1990—Recovered one fumble. 1994—Returned one kickoff for 14 yards.

DeRAMUS, LEE — WR — SAINTS

PERSONAL: Born August 24, 1972, in Sicklerville, N.J. ... 6-0/191.
HIGH SCHOOL: Edgewood Regional (Atco, N.J.).
COLLEGE: Wisconsin.
TRANSACTIONS/CAREER NOTES: Selected after junior season by New Orleans Saints in sixth round (184th pick overall) of 1995 NFL draft. ... Signed by Saints (July 14, 1995). ... On reserve/non-football injury list with leg injury (August 22, 1995). ... Activated (October 30, 1995).
PLAYING EXPERIENCE: New Orleans NFl, 1995. ... Games: 1995 (8).
PRO STATISTICS: 1995—Caught six passes for 76 yards.

DENNIS, MARK — OT — PANTHERS

PERSONAL: Born April 15, 1965, in Junction City, Kan. ... 6-6/296. ... Full name: Mark Francis Dennis.
HIGH SCHOOL: Washington (Ill.).
COLLEGE: Illinois.
TRANSACTIONS/CAREER NOTES: Selected by Miami Dolphins in eighth round (212th pick overall) of 1987 NFL draft. ... Signed by Dolphins (July 23, 1987). ... On injured reserve with knee injury (November 28, 1988-remainder of season). ... On reserve/physically unable to perform list with knee injury (August 29-November 4, 1989). ... Granted unconditional free agency (February 1-April 1, 1990). ... Re-signed by Dolphins (July 31, 1990). ... Granted free agency (February 1, 1991). ... Re-signed by Dolphins (1991). ... Granted unconditional free agency (February 17, 1994). ... Re-signed by Dolphins (May 31, 1994). ... Released by Dolphins (August 28, 1994). ... Signed by Cincinnati Bengals (September 20, 1994). ... Released by Bengals (November 18, 1994). ... Signed by Carolina Panthers (June 12, 1995). ... Granted unconditional free agency (February 16, 1996). ... Re-signed by Panthers (March 28, 1996).
PLAYING EXPERIENCE: Miami NFL, 1987-1993; Cincinnati NFL, 1994; Carolina NFL, 1995. ... Games: 1987 (5), 1988 (13), 1989 (8), 1990 (16), 1991 (16), 1992 (16), 1993 (16), 1994 (7), 1995 (12). Total: 109.
CHAMPIONSHIP GAME EXPERIENCE: Played in AFC championship game (1992 season).
PRO STATISTICS: 1991—Recovered one fumble. 1993—Recovered one fumble. 1995—Caught one pass for three yards.

D

DENT, RICHARD — DE

PERSONAL: Born December 13, 1960, in Atlanta. ... 6-5/265. ... Full name: Richard Lamar Dent. ... Cousin of Vince Marrow, tight end, Buffalo Bills (1994).
HIGH SCHOOL: Murphy (Atlanta).
COLLEGE: Tennessee State.
TRANSACTIONS/CAREER NOTES: Selected by Philadelphia Stars in eighth round (89th pick overall) of 1983 USFL draft. ... Selected by Chicago Bears in eighth round (203rd pick overall) of 1983 NFL draft. ... Signed by Bears (May 12, 1983). ... On non-football injury list for substance abuse (September 8, 1988). ... Activated (September 9, 1988). ... On injured reserve with fractured fibula (November 29, 1988-remainder of season). ... Released by Bears (April 27, 1994). ... Signed by San Francisco 49ers (June 9, 1994). ... Released by 49ers (February 14, 1995). ... Signed by Bears (September 18, 1995). ... Released by Bears (October 24, 1995).
CHAMPIONSHIP GAME EXPERIENCE: Played in NFC championship game (1984 and 1985 seasons). ... Member of Super Bowl championship team (1985 and 1994 seasons). ... Member of 49ers for NFC championship game (1994 season); inactive.
HONORS: Played in Pro Bowl (1984, 1985, 1990 and 1993 seasons). ... Named Most Valuable Player of Super Bowl XX (1985 season).
POSTSEASON RECORDS: Shares NFL postseason single-game record for most sacks—3½ (January 5, 1986, vs. New York Giants).
PRO STATISTICS: 1984—Recovered one fumble. 1985—Recovered two fumbles. 1987—Recovered two fumbles for 11 yards. 1988—Recovered one fumble. 1989—Recovered two fumbles. 1990—Recovered three fumbles for 45 yards and one touchdown. 1991—Recovered one fumble. 1992—Recovered one fumble.
MISCELLANEOUS: Holds Chicago Bears all-time record for most sacks (124.5)

| | | INTERCEPTIONS | | | | SACKS |
Year Team	G	No.	Yds.	Avg.	TD	No.
1983—Chicago NFL	16	0	0	...	0	3.0
1984—Chicago NFL	16	0	0	...	0	17.5
1985—Chicago NFL	16	2	10	5.0	1	*17.0
1986—Chicago NFL	15	0	0	...	0	11.5
1987—Chicago NFL	12	0	0	...	0	12.5
1988—Chicago NFL	13	0	0	...	0	10.5
1989—Chicago NFL	15	1	30	30.0	0	9.0
1990—Chicago NFL	16	3	21	7.0	0	12.0
1991—Chicago NFL	16	1	4	4.0	0	10.5
1992—Chicago NFL	16	0	0	...	0	8.5
1993—Chicago NFL	16	1	24	24.0	0	12.5
1994—San Francisco NFL	2	0	0	...	0	2.0
1995—Chicago NFL	3	0	0	...	0	0.0
Pro totals (13 years)	172	8	89	11.1	1	126.5

DETMER, TY — QB — EAGLES

PERSONAL: Born October 30, 1967, in San Marcos, Texas. ... 6-0/194. ... Full name: Ty Hubert Detmer.
HIGH SCHOOL: Southwest (San Antonio).
COLLEGE: Brigham Young (degree in recreation administration).
TRANSACTIONS/CAREER NOTES: Selected by Green Bay Packers in ninth round (230th pick overall) of 1992 NFL draft. ... Signed by Packers

(July 22, 1992). ... Active for two games (1992); did not play. ... Activefor five games (1994); did not play. ... On injured reserve with thumb injury (November 8, 1995-remainder of season). ... Granted unconditional free agency (February 16, 1996). ... Signed by Philadelphia Eagles (February 29, 1996).

HONORS: Heisman Trophy winner (1990). ... Maxwell Award winner (1990). ... Davey O'Brien Award winner (1990 and 1991). ... Named quarterback on THE SPORTING NEWS college All-America first team (1990 and 1991).

PRO STATISTICS: 1995—Fumbled once and recovered one fumble.

Year—Team	G	Att.	Cmp.	Pct.	Yds.	TD	Int.	Avg.	Rat.	Att.	Yds.	Avg.	TD	TD	2pt.	Pts.
					PASSING						**RUSHING**				**TOTALS**	
1992—Green Bay NFL							Did not play.									
1993—Green Bay NFL	3	5	3	60.0	26	0	0	5.20	73.8	1	-2	-2.0	0	0	...	0
1994—Green Bay NFL							Did not play.									
1995—Green Bay NFL	4	16	8	50.0	81	1	1	5.06	59.6	3	3	1.0	0	0	0	0
Pro totals (2 years)	7	21	11	52.4	107	1	1	5.10	63.0	4	1	0.3	0	0	0	0

DEVLIN, MIKE — OL — CARDINALS

PERSONAL: Born November 16, 1969, in Marlton, N.J. ... 6-2/300. ... Cousin of Joe Devlin, offensive tackle/offensive guard, Buffalo Bills (1976-1982 and 1984-1989).

HIGH SCHOOL: Cherokee (Marlton, N.J.).

COLLEGE: Iowa.

TRANSACTIONS/CAREER NOTES: Selected by Buffalo Bills in fifth round (136th pick overall) of 1993 NFL draft. ... Signed by Bills (July 12, 1993). ... Granted unconditional free agency (February 16, 1996). ... Signed by Arizona Cardinals (March 8, 1996).

PLAYING EXPERIENCE: Buffalo NFL, 1993-1995. ... Games: 1993 (12), 1994 (16), 1995 (16). Total: 44.

CHAMPIONSHIP GAME EXPERIENCE: Played in AFC championship game (1993 season). ... Played in Super Bowl XXVIII (1993 season).

DeVRIES, JED — OL — RAVENS

PERSONAL: Born January 6, 1971, in Ogden, Utah. ... 6-6/300.

HIGH SCHOOL: Weber (Ogden, Utah).

COLLEGE: Utah State.

TRANSACTIONS/CAREER NOTES: Signed as non-drafted free agent by Seattle Seahawks (April 28, 1994). ... Released by Seahawks (August 22, 1994). ... Signed by Cleveland Browns to practice squad (August 30, 1994). ... Activated (December 30, 1994); did not play. ... Browns franchise moved to Baltimore and renamed Ravens for 1996 season (March 11, 1996).

PLAYING EXPERIENCE: Cleveland NFL, 1995. ... Games: 1995 (2).

DICKERSON, BRYAN — RB — JAGUARS

PERSONAL: Born March 22, 1971, in Louisville, Ky. ... 6-1/245.

HIGH SCHOOL: Desales High School for Boys (Louisville, Ky.).

COLLEGE: Eastern Kentucky.

TRANSACTIONS/CAREER NOTES: Signed as non-drafted free agent by Cincinnati Bengals (April 26, 1995). ... Released by Bengals (August 22, 1995). ... Re-signed by Bengals to practice squad (August 28, 1995). ... Signed by Jacksonville Jaguars off Bengals practice squad (December 6, 1995).

DILFER, TRENT — QB — BUCCANEERS

PERSONAL: Born March 13, 1972, in Santa Cruz, Calif. ... 6-4/235. ... Full name: Trent Farris Dilfer.

HIGH SCHOOL: Aptos (Calif.).

COLLEGE: Fresno State.

TRANSACTIONS/CAREER NOTES: Selected after junior season by Tampa Bay Buccaneers in first round (sixth pick overall) of 1994 NFL draft. ... Signed by Buccaneers (August 3, 1994).

PRO STATISTICS: 1994—Fumbled twice. 1995—Fumbled 13 times and recovered one fumble for minus nine yards.

STATISTICAL PLATEAUS: 300-yard passing games: 1995 (1).

MISCELLANEOUS: Regular-season record as starting NFL quarterback: 7-11 (.389).

Year—Team	G	Att.	Cmp.	Pct.	Yds.	TD	Int.	Avg.	Rat.	Att.	Yds.	Avg.	TD	TD	2pt.	Pts.
					PASSING						**RUSHING**				**TOTALS**	
1994—Tampa Bay NFL	5	82	38	46.3	433	1	6	5.28	36.3	2	27	13.5	0	0	0	0
1995—Tampa Bay NFL	16	415	224	54.0	2774	4	18	6.69	60.1	23	115	5.0	2	2	0	12
Pro totals (2 years)	21	497	262	52.7	3207	5	24	6.45	56.1	25	142	5.7	2	2	0	12

DILGER, KEN — TE — COLTS

PERSONAL: Born February 2, 1971, in Mariah Hill, Ind. ... 6-5/256.

HIGH SCHOOL: Heritage Hills (Lincoln City, Ind.).

COLLEGE: Illinois.

TRANSACTIONS/CAREER NOTES: Selected by Indianapolis Colts in second round (48th pick overall) of 1995 NFL draft. ... Signed by Colts (July 15, 1995).

CHAMPIONSHIP GAME EXPERIENCE: Played in AFC championship game (1995 season).

STATISTICAL PLATEAUS: 100-yard receiving games: 1995 (1).

Year—Team	G	No.	Yds.	Avg.	TD	TD	2pt.	Pts.	Fum.
		RECEIVING					**TOTALS**		
1995—Indianapolis NFL	16	42	635	15.1	4	4	0	24	0

DILL, SCOTT   OT/G   BUCCANEERS

PERSONAL: Born April 5, 1966, in Birmingham, Ala. ... 6-5/295. ... Full name: Gerald Scott Dill.
HIGH SCHOOL: W.A. Berry (Birmingham, Ala.).
COLLEGE: Memphis State.
TRANSACTIONS/CAREER NOTES: Selected by Phoenix Cardinals in ninth round (233rd pick overall) of 1988 NFL draft. ... Signed by Cardinals (July 13, 1988). ... Granted unconditional free agency (February 1, 1990). ... Signed by Tampa Bay Buccaneers (March 16, 1990). ... On injured reserve with back injury (October 19, 1990-remainder of season). ... Granted unconditional free agency (February 1-April 1, 1991). ... Re-signed by Buccaneers for 1991 season. ... Granted free agency (February 1, 1992). ... Re-signed by Buccaneers (July 23, 1992). ... On injured reserve with foot injury (September 1-November 13, 1992). ... Granted unconditional free agency (February 17, 1995). ... Re-signed by Buccaneers (February 17, 1995).
PLAYING EXPERIENCE: Phoenix NFL, 1988 and 1989; Tampa Bay NFL, 1990-1995. ... Games: 1988 (13), 1989 (16), 1990 (3), 1991 (8), 1992 (4), 1993 (16), 1994 (16), 1995 (12). Total: 88.
PRO STATISTICS: 1989—Recovered one fumble. 1993—Recovered one fumble.

DILLARD, STACEY   DT   GIANTS

PERSONAL: Born September 17, 1968, in Clarksville, Texas. ... 6-5/290. ... Full name: Stacey Bertrand Dillard.
HIGH SCHOOL: Clarksville (Texas).
COLLEGE: Oklahoma.
TRANSACTIONS/CAREER NOTES: Selected by New York Giants in sixth round (153rd pick overall) of 1992 NFL draft. ... Signed by Giants (July 21, 1992). ... Released by Giants (August 31, 1992). ... Re-signed by Giants to practice squad (September 2, 1992). ... Activated (September 21, 1992). ... Granted free agency (February 17, 1995). ... Re-signed by Giants (July 23, 1995). ... Granted unconditional free agency (February 16, 1996). ... Re-signed by Giants (April 26, 1996).

Year Team	G	SACKS
1992—New York Giants NFL	12	0.0
1993—New York Giants NFL	16	3.0
1994—New York Giants NFL	16	1.5
1995—New York Giants NFL	15	1.0
Pro totals (4 years)	**59**	**5.5**

DIMRY, CHARLES   CB   BUCCANEERS   D

PERSONAL: Born January 31, 1966, in San Diego. ... 6-0/176. ... Full name: Charles Louis Dimry III.
HIGH SCHOOL: Oceanside (Calif.).
COLLEGE: UNLV.
TRANSACTIONS/CAREER NOTES: Selected by Atlanta Falcons in fifth round (110th pick overall) of 1988 NFL draft. ... Signed by Falcons (July 16, 1988). ... Granted unconditional free agency (February 1, 1991). ... Signed by Denver Broncos (March 28, 1991). ... Granted unconditional free agency (February 17, 1994). ... Signed by Tampa Bay Buccaneers (May 23, 1994).
CHAMPIONSHIP GAME EXPERIENCE: Played in AFC championship game (1991 season).
PRO STATISTICS: 1989—Credited with one sack. 1991—Recovered one fumble. 1992—Returned one punt for four yards. 1994—Recovered one fumble. 1995—Recovered two fumbles.

		INTERCEPTIONS			
Year Team	G	No.	Yds.	Avg.	TD
1988—Atlanta NFL	16	0	0	...	0
1989—Atlanta NFL	16	2	72	36.0	0
1990—Atlanta NFL	16	3	16	5.3	0
1991—Denver NFL	16	3	35	11.7	1
1992—Denver NFL	16	1	2	2.0	0
1993—Denver NFL	12	1	0	0.0	0
1994—Tampa Bay NFL	16	1	0	0.0	0
1995—Tampa Bay NFL	16	1	0	0.0	0
Pro totals (8 years)	**124**	**12**	**125**	**10.4**	**1**

DINGLE, NATE   LB   CHIEFS

PERSONAL: Born July 23, 1971, in Wells, Maine. ... 6-2/242.
HIGH SCHOOL: Wells (Maine).
COLLEGE: Cincinnati.
TRANSACTIONS/CAREER NOTES: Signed as non-drafted free agent by Washington Redskins (April 28, 1994). ... Released by Redskins (August 15, 1994). ... Signed by San Diego Chargers (June 29, 1995). ... Released by Chargers (August 28, 1995). ... Signed by Philadelphia Eagles to practice squad (September 8, 1995). ... Activated (September 17, 1995); did not play. ... Released by Eagles (October 31, 1995). ... Re-signed by Eagles to practice squad (November 1, 1995). ... Activated (December 1, 1995); did not play. ... Released by Eagles (December 22, 1995). ... Re-signed by Eagles to practice squad (December 22, 1995). ... Signed by Kansas City Chiefs (April 1996).
PLAYING EXPERIENCE: Kansas City NFL, 1995. ... Games: 1995 (6).

DISHMAN, CRIS   CB   OILERS

PERSONAL: Born August 13, 1965, in Louisville, Ky. ... 6-0/188. ... Full name: Cris Edward Dishman.
HIGH SCHOOL: DeSales (Louisville, Ky.).
COLLEGE: Purdue.
TRANSACTIONS/CAREER NOTES: Selected by Houston Oilers in fifth round (125th pick overall) of 1988 NFL draft. ... Signed by Oilers (July 15, 1988). ... Granted free agency (February 1, 1991). ... Re-signed by Oilers (August 18, 1991). ... Granted free agency (February 1, 1992). ... Re-signed by Oilers (September 10, 1992). ... Designated by Oilers as transition player (February 15, 1994). ... Free agency status changed

by Oilers from transitional to franchise player (February 16, 1996).
HONORS: Played in Pro Bowl (1991 season).
PRO STATISTICS: 1988—Returned blocked punt 10 yards for a touchdown and recovered one fumble. 1989—Returned blocked punt seven yards for a touchdown and recovered one fumble. 1991—Recovered three fumbles for 19 yards and one touchdown. 1993—Recovered two fumbles for 69 yards and a touchdown. 1994—Returned one punt for no yards and recovered one fumble for 29 yards. 1995—Recovered two fumbles for 15 yards.

		INTERCEPTIONS			
Year Team	G	No.	Yds.	Avg.	TD
1988—Houston NFL	15	0	0	...	0
1989—Houston NFL	16	4	31	7.8	0
1990—Houston NFL	16	4	50	12.5	0
1991—Houston NFL	15	6	61	10.2	0
1992—Houston NFL	15	3	34	11.3	0
1993—Houston NFL	16	6	74	12.3	0
1994—Houston NFL	16	4	74	18.5	1
1995—Houston NFL	15	3	17	5.7	0
Pro totals (8 years)	124	30	341	11.4	1

DIXON, CAL   C/G

PERSONAL: Born October 11, 1969, in Fort Lauderdale. ... 6-4/302. ... Full name: Calvert Ray Dixon III.
HIGH SCHOOL: Merritt Island (Fla.).
COLLEGE: Florida (degree in exercise and sports science).
TRANSACTIONS/CAREER NOTES: Selected by New York Jets in fifth round (127th pick overall) of 1992 NFL draft. ... Signed by Jets (July 14, 1992). ... Granted unconditional free agency (February 16, 1996).
PLAYING EXPERIENCE: New York Jets NFL, 1992-1995. ... Games: 1992 (11), 1993 (16), 1994 (15), 1995 (13). Total: 55.
HONORS: Named center on THE SPORTING NEWS college All-America second team (1991).
PRO STATISTICS: 1992—Returned one kickoff for six yards. 1995—Recovered one fumble.

DIXON, DAVID   G/OT   VIKINGS

PERSONAL: Born January 5, 1969, in Auckland, New Zealand. ... 6-5/359.
JUNIOR COLLEGE: Ricks Junior College (Idaho).
COLLEGE: Arizona State.
TRANSACTIONS/CAREER NOTES: Signed as non-drafted free agent by Minnesota Vikings to practice squad (October 20, 1992). ... Granted free agency after 1992 season. ... Re-signed by Vikings (February 23, 1993). ... Released by Vikings (August 23, 1993). ... Signed by Dallas Cowboys to practice squad (September 8, 1993). ... Granted free agency after 1993 season. ... Signed by Vikings (July 12, 1994).
PLAYING EXPERIENCE: Minnesota NFL, 1994 and 1995. ... Games: 1994 (1), 1995 (15). Total: 16.

DIXON, ERNEST   LB   SAINTS

PERSONAL: Born October 17, 1971, in Fort Mill, S.C. ... 6-1/240.
HIGH SCHOOL: Fort Mill (S.C.).
COLLEGE: South Carolina.
TRANSACTIONS/CAREER NOTES: Signed as non-drafted free agent by New Orleans Saints (April 28, 1994).
PLAYING EXPERIENCE: New Orleans NFL, 1994 and 1995. ... Games: 1994 (1), 1995 (16). Total: 17.
PRO STATISTICS: 1995—Fumbled once.

		INTERCEPTIONS				SACKS
Year Team	G	No.	Yds.	Avg.	TD	No.
1994—New Orleans NFL	15	0	0	...	0	0.0
1995—New Orleans NFL	16	2	17	8.5	0	4.0
Pro totals (2 years)	31	2	17	8.5	0	4.0

DIXON, GERALD   LB   BENGALS

PERSONAL: Born June 20, 1969, in Charlotte. ... 6-3/250. ... Full name: Gerald Scott Dixon.
HIGH SCHOOL: Rock Hill (S.C.).
COLLEGE: South Carolina.
TRANSACTIONS/CAREER NOTES: Selected by Cleveland Browns in third round (78th pick overall) of 1992 NFL draft. ... Signed by Browns (July 15, 1992). ... On injured reserve with ankle injury (September 2, 1992-remainder of season). ... Granted free agency (February 17, 1995). ... Re-signed by Browns for 1995 season. ... Granted unconditional free agency (February 16, 1996). ... Signed by Cincinnati Bengals (March 14, 1996).
PRO STATISTICS: 1995—Intercepted two passes for 48 yards and a touchdown, returned one kickoff for 10 yards and recovered one fumble.

Year Team	G	SACKS
1992—Cleveland NFL	Did not play.	
1993—Cleveland NFL	11	0.0
1994—Cleveland NFL	16	1.0
1995—Cleveland NFL	16	0.0
Pro totals (3 years)	43	1.0

DIXON, RANDY   G

PERSONAL: Born March 12, 1965, in Clewiston, Fla. ... 6-3/305. ... Full name: Randall Charles Dixon. ... Related to Titus Dixon, wide receiv-

er, New York Jets, Indianapolis Colts and Detroit Lions (1989).
HIGH SCHOOL: Clewiston (Fla.).
COLLEGE: Pittsburgh.
TRANSACTIONS/CAREER NOTES: Selected by Indianapolis Colts in fourth round (85th pick overall) of 1987 NFL draft. ... Signed by Colts (July 24, 1987). ... Granted free agency (February 1, 1990). ... Re-signed by Colts (September 12, 1990). ... Activated (September 14, 1990). ... On injured reserve with calf injury (October 3-November 1, 1991). ... Granted free agency (February 17, 1995). ... Re-signed by Colts (September 23, 1995). ... Granted unconditional free agency (February 16, 1996).
PLAYING EXPERIENCE: Indianapolis NFL, 1987-1995. ... Games: 1987 (3), 1988 (16), 1989 (16), 1990 (15), 1991 (12), 1992 (15), 1993 (15), 1994 (14), 1995 (12). Total: 118.
CHAMPIONSHIP GAME EXPERIENCE: Played in AFC championship game (1995 season).
HONORS: Named offensive tackle on THE SPORTING NEWS college All-America first team (1986).
PRO STATISTICS: 1989—Recovered one fumble in end zone for a touchdown. 1991—Recovered one fumble.

DIXON, RONNIE　　　　DL　　　　EAGLES

PERSONAL: Born May 10, 1971, in Clinton, N.C. ... 6-3/292. ... Full name: Ronnie Christopher Dixon.
HIGH SCHOOL: Clinton (N.C.).
COLLEGE: Cincinnati.
TRANSACTIONS/CAREER NOTES: Selected by New Orleans Saints in sixth round (165th pick overall) of 1993 NFL draft. ... Signed by Saints (July 2, 1993). ... Released by Saints (August 30, 1993). ... Re-signed by Saints (August 31, 1993). ... Released by Saints (August 22, 1994). ... Selected by Frankfurt Galaxy in 17th round (98th pick overall) of 1995 World League Draft. ... Signed by Cleveland Browns for 1995 season. ... Traded by Browns to Philadelphia Eagles for seventh-round pick (QB Jon Stark) in 1996 draft (August 21, 1995).
PLAYING EXPERIENCE: New Orleans NFL, 1993; Philadelphia NFL, 1995. ... Games: 1993 (2), 1995 (16). Total: 18.

DODGE, DEDRICK　　　　S　　　　49ERS

PERSONAL: Born June 14, 1967, in Neptune, N.J. ... 6-2/184. ... Full name: Dedrick Allen Dodge. ... Name pronounced DEAD-rik.
HIGH SCHOOL: East Brunswick (N.J.) and Mulberry (Fla.).
COLLEGE: Florida State (degree in criminology).
TRANSACTIONS/CAREER NOTES: Signed as non-drafted free agent by Seattle Seahawks (May 1, 1990). ... Released by Seahawks (August 29, 1990). ... Signed by WLAF (January 31, 1991). ... Selected by London Monarchs in fourth round (40th defensive back) of 1991 WLAF positional draft. ... Signed by Seahawks (August 13, 1991). ... Released by Seahawks (August 26, 1991). ... Signed by Seahawks to practice squad (August 28, 1991). ... Activated (October 5, 1991). ... Assigned by Seahawks to Monarchs in 1992 World League enhancement allocation program (February 20, 1992). ... On injured reserve with knee injury (December 19, 1992-remainder of season). ... Granted free agency (March 1, 1993). ... Re-signed by Seahawks (July 2, 1993). ... Released by Seahawks (August 30, 1993). ... Signed by San Francisco 49ers (June 1, 1994). ... Granted unconditional free agency (February 17, 1995). ... Re-signed by 49ers (April 13, 1995).
CHAMPIONSHIP GAME EXPERIENCE: Played in NFC championship game (1994 season). ... Member of Super Bowl championship team (1994 season).
HONORS: Named strong safety on All-World League team (1992).
PRO STATISTICS: W.L.: 1991—Recovered one fumble. NFL: 1992—Credited with one sack.

		INTERCEPTIONS			
Year　Team	G	No.	Yds.	Avg.	TD
1991—London W.L.	10	6	202	33.7	*2
—Seattle NFL	11	0	0	...	0
1992—London W.L.	10	3	35	11.7	0
—Seattle NFL	14	1	13	13.0	0
1993—			Did not play.		
1994—San Francisco NFL	15	0	0	...	0
1995—San Francisco NFL	16	1	13	13.0	0
W.L. totals (2 years)	20	9	237	26.3	2
NFL totals (4 years)	56	2	26	13.0	0
Pro totals (4 years)	76	11	263	23.9	2

DOLEMAN, CHRIS　　　　DE　　　　49ERS

PERSONAL: Born October 16, 1961, in Indianapolis. ... 6-5/275. ... Full name: Christopher John Doleman.
HIGH SCHOOL: Valley Forge Military Academy (Wayne, Pa.), then William Penn (York, Pa.).
COLLEGE: Pittsburgh.
TRANSACTIONS/CAREER NOTES: Selected by Baltimore Stars in 1985 USFL territorial draft. ... Selected by Minnesota Vikings in first round (fourth pick overall) of 1985 NFL draft. ... Signed by Vikings (August 8, 1985). ... Granted free agency (February 1, 1991). ... Re-signed by Vikings (July 25, 1991). ... Traded by Vikings with second-round pick (WR Bert Emanuel) in 1994 draft to Atlanta Falcons for second-round pick (RB/WR/KR David Palmer) in 1994 draft and first-round pick (DE Derrick Alexander) in 1995 draft (April 24, 1994). ... Granted unconditional free agency (February 16, 1996). ... Signed by San Francisco 49ers (March 14, 1996).
CHAMPIONSHIP GAME EXPERIENCE: Played in NFC championship game (1987 season).
HONORS: Played in Pro Bowl (1987-1990, 1992, 1993 and 1995 seasons). ... Named defensive end on THE SPORTING NEWS NFL All-Pro team (1989 and 1992).
PRO STATISTICS: 1985—Recovered three fumbles. 1989—Recovered five fumbles for seven yards. 1990—Credited with a safety. 1991—Recovered two fumbles for seven yards. 1992—Credited with a safety and recovered three fumbles. 1993—Recovered one fumble. 1995—Recovered two fumbles.

		INTERCEPTIONS				SACKS
Year　Team	G	No.	Yds.	Avg.	TD	No.
1985—Minnesota NFL	16	1	5	5.0	0	0.5
1986—Minnesota NFL	16	1	59	59.0	1	3.0
1987—Minnesota NFL	12	0	0	...	0	11.0
1988—Minnesota NFL	16	0	0	...	0	8.0

| Year Team | G | INTERCEPTIONS | | | | SACKS |
		No.	Yds.	Avg.	TD	No.
1989—Minnesota NFL	16	0	0	...	0	*21.0
1990—Minnesota NFL	16	1	30	30.0	0	11.0
1991—Minnesota NFL	16	0	0	...	0	7.0
1992—Minnesota NFL	16	1	27	27.0	1	14.5
1993—Minnesota NFL	16	1	-3	-3.0	0	12.5
1994—Atlanta NFL	14	1	2	2.0	0	7.0
1995—Atlanta NFL	16	0	0	...	0	9.0
Pro totals (11 years)	170	6	120	20.0	2	104.5

DOMBROWSKI, JIM G/OT SAINTS

PERSONAL: Born October 19, 1963, in Williamsville, N.Y. ... 6-5/300. ... Full name: James Matthew Dombrowski. ... Name pronounced dum-BROW-skee.
HIGH SCHOOL: South (Williamsville, N.Y.).
COLLEGE: Virginia (degree in biology, 1986).
TRANSACTIONS/CAREER NOTES: Selected by Orlando Renegades in 1986 USFL territorial draft. ... Selected by New Orleans Saints in first round (sixth pick overall) of 1986 NFL draft. ... Signed by Saints (August 1, 1986). ... On injured reserve with broken foot (September 22, 1986-remainder of season). ... Granted free agency (February 1, 1990). ... Re-signed by Saints (July 17, 1990). ... Designated by Saints as transition player (February 25, 1993).
PLAYING EXPERIENCE: New Orleans NFL, 1986-1995. ... Games: 1986 (3), 1987 (10), 1988 (16), 1989 (16), 1990 (16), 1991 (16), 1992 (16), 1993 (16), 1994 (16), 1995 (16). Total: 141.
HONORS: Named offensive tackle on THE SPORTING NEWS college All-America second team (1984). ... Named offensive tackle on THE SPORTING NEWS college All-America first team (1985).
PRO STATISTICS: 1988—Recovered one fumble. 1989—Recovered one fumble. 1992—Recovered one fumble.

DONALDSON, RAY C COWBOYS

PERSONAL: Born May 18, 1958, in Rome, Ga. ... 6-3/300. ... Full name: Raymond Canute Donaldson. ... Step-brother of John Tutt, minor league outfielder, Baltimore Orioles and San Diego Padres organizations (1981-1986) and Aguas of Mexican league (1983); and cousin of Robert Lavette, running back, Dallas Cowboys and Philadelphia Eagles (1985-1987).
HIGH SCHOOL: East (Rome, Ga.).
COLLEGE: Georgia.
TRANSACTIONS/CAREER NOTES: Selected by Baltimore Colts in second round (32nd pick overall) of 1980 NFL draft. ... Colts franchise moved to Indianapolis (March 31, 1984). ... On injured reserve with leg injury (September 17, 1991-remainder of season). ... Released by Colts (February 18, 1993). ... Signed by Seattle Seahawks (April 20, 1993). ... Granted unconditional free agency (February 17, 1995). ... Signed by Dallas Cowboys (March 20, 1995). ... On injured reserve with broken ankle (November 28, 1995-remainder of season).
PLAYING EXPERIENCE: Baltimore NFL, 1980-1983; Indianapolis NFL, 1984-1992; Seattle NFL, 1993 and 1994; Dallas NFL, 1995. ... Games: 1980 (16), 1981 (16), 1982 (9), 1983 (16), 1984 (16), 1985 (16), 1986 (16), 1987 (12), 1988 (16), 1989 (16), 1990 (16), 1991 (3), 1992 (16), 1993 (16), 1994 (16), 1995 (12). Total: 228.
HONORS: Played in Pro Bowl (1986-1989 seasons). ... Named to play in Pro Bowl (1995 season); replaced by Bart Oates due to injury.
PRO STATISTICS: 1981—Recovered one fumble. 1982—Recovered one fumble. 1983—Fumbled once. 1985—Recovered one fumble. 1986—Fumbled twice for minus four yards. 1988—Caught one pass for minus three yards. 1989—Fumbled once and recovered one fumble for minus 22 yards. 1991—Recovered one fumble. 1992—Fumbled once for minus 17 yards. 1993—Fumbled once. 1994—Fumbled twice.

DONNALLEY, KEVIN OT/G OILERS

PERSONAL: Born June 10, 1968, in St. Louis. ... 6-5/305. ... Full name: Kevin Thomas Donnalley. ... Brother of Rick Donnalley, center, Pittsburgh Steelers, Washington Redskins and Kansas City Chiefs (1982-1987).
HIGH SCHOOL: Athens Drive Senior (Raleigh, N.C.).
COLLEGE: Davidson, then North Carolina (degree in economics).
TRANSACTIONS/CAREER NOTES: Selected by Houston Oilers in third round (79th pick overall) of 1991 NFL draft. ... Signed by Oilers (July 10, 1991). ... Granted free agency (February 17, 1994). ... Tendered offer sheet by Los Angeles Rams (March 17, 1994). ... Offer matched by Oilers (March 23, 1994).
PLAYING EXPERIENCE: Houston NFL, 1991-1995. ... Games: 1991 (16), 1992 (16), 1993 (16), 1994 (13), 1995 (16). Total: 77.
PRO STATISTICS: 1995—Recovered one fumble.

DORN, TORIN CB RAMS

PERSONAL: Born February 29, 1968, in Greenwood, S.C. ... 6-0/190.
HIGH SCHOOL: Southfield (Mich.) Senior.
COLLEGE: North Carolina.
TRANSACTIONS/CAREER NOTES: Selected by Los Angeles Raiders in fourth round (95th pick overall) of 1990 NFL draft. ... Signed by Raiders (June 9, 1990). ... Granted free agency (February 1, 1992). ... Re-signed by Raiders for 1992 season. ... Granted free agency (March 1, 1993). ... Re-signed by Raiders for 1993 season. ... On injured reserve with hamstring injury (August 29-September 16, 1994). ... Released by Raiders (September 16, 1994). ... Signed by Los Angeles Rams (March 22, 1995). ... Rams franchise moved to St. Louis (April 12, 1995).
PLAYING EXPERIENCE: Los Angeles Raiders NFL, 1990-1993; St. Louis NFL, 1995. ... Games: 1990 (16), 1991 (16), 1992 (15), 1993 (15), 1995 (12). Total: 74.
CHAMPIONSHIP GAME EXPERIENCE: Played in AFC championship game (1990 season).
PRO STATISTICS: 1991—Credited with one safety and recovered one fumble. 1992—Intercepted one pass for seven yards. 1995—Intercepted one pass for 24 yards and a touchdown, recovered one fumble for 26 yards and a touchdown.

DORSETT, MATTHEW   CB   PACKERS

PERSONAL: Born August 23, 1973, in New Orleans. ... 5-11/187. ... Full name: Matthew Herbert Dorsett.
HIGH SCHOOL: Eleanor McMain (New Orleans).
COLLEGE: Southern.
TRANSACTIONS/CAREER NOTES: Signed as non-drafted free agent by Green Bay Packers (April 27, 1995).
PLAYING EXPERIENCE: Green Bay NFL, 1995. ... Games: 1995 (10).
CHAMPIONSHIP GAME EXPERIENCE: Member of Packers for NFC championship game (1995 season); inactive.

DOTSON, DeWAYNE   FB   DOLPHINS

PERSONAL: Born June 10, 1971, in Hendersonville, Tenn. ... 6-1/256. ... Full name: Jack Dewayne Dotson.
HIGH SCHOOL: Hendersonville (Tenn.).
COLLEGE: Tennessee, then Mississippi.
TRANSACTIONS/CAREER NOTES: Selected by Dallas Cowboys in fourth round (131st pick overall) of 1994 NFL draft. ... Signed by Cowboys (July 15, 1994). ... Released by Cowboys (August 27, 1994). ... Signed by Miami Dolphins to practice squad (September 7, 1994). ... Released by Dolphins (September 28, 1994). ... Re-signed by Dolphins to practice squad (October 5, 1994). ... Activated (December 31, 1994).
PLAYING EXPERIENCE: Miami NFL, 1995. ... Games: 1995 (15).
PRO STATISTICS: 1995—Recovered one fumble.

DOTSON, EARL   OT   PACKERS

PERSONAL: Born December 17, 1970, in Beaumont, Texas. ... 6-3/310. ... Full name: Earl Christopher Dotson.
HIGH SCHOOL: West Brook (Beaumont, Texas).
JUNIOR COLLEGE: Tyler (Texas) Junior College.
COLLEGE: Texas A&I.
TRANSACTIONS/CAREER NOTES: Selected by Green Bay Packers in third round (81st pick overall) of 1993 NFL draft. ... Signed by Packers (June 14, 1993).
PLAYING EXPERIENCE: Green Bay NFL, 1993-1995. ... Games: 1993 (13), 1994 (4), 1995 (16). Total: 33.
CHAMPIONSHIP GAME EXPERIENCE: Played in NFC championship game (1995 season).

DOTSON, SANTANA   DT   PACKERS

PERSONAL: Born December 19, 1969, in New Orleans. ... 6-5/275. ... Son of Alphonse Dotson, defensive tackle, Kansas City Chiefs, Miami Dolphins and Oakland Raiders (1965, 1966 and 1968-1970).
HIGH SCHOOL: Jack Yates (Houston).
COLLEGE: Baylor.
TRANSACTIONS/CAREER NOTES: Selected by Tampa Bay Buccaneers in fifth round (132nd pick overall) of 1992 NFL draft. ... Signed by Buccaneers (July 7, 1992). ... Granted free agency (February 17, 1995). ... Re-signed by Buccaneers (June 14, 1995). ... Granted unconditional free agency (February 16, 1996). ... Signed by Green Bay Packers (March 7, 1996).
HONORS: Named defensive lineman on THE SPORTING NEWS college All-America first team (1991). ... Named NFL Rookie of the Year by THE SPORTING NEWS (1992).
PRO STATISTICS: 1992—Recovered two fumbles for 42 yards and a touchdown. 1995—Recovered two fumbles.

Year Team	G	SACKS
1992—Tampa Bay NFL	16	10.0
1993—Tampa Bay NFL	16	5.0
1994—Tampa Bay NFL	16	3.0
1995—Tampa Bay NFL	16	5.0
Pro totals (4 years)	64	23.0

DOUGLAS, HUGH   DE   JETS

PERSONAL: Born August 23, 1971, in Mansfield, Ohio. ... 6-2/265.
HIGH SCHOOL: Mansfield (Ohio).
COLLEGE: Central State (Ohio).
TRANSACTIONS/CAREER NOTES: Selected after junior season by New York Jets in first round (16th pick overall) of 1995 NFL draft. ... Signed by Jets (June 8, 1995).
PRO STATISTICS: 1995—Recovered two fumbles.

Year Team	G	SACKS
1995—New York Jets NFL	15	10.0

DOUGLAS, OMAR   WR   GIANTS

PERSONAL: Born June 3, 1972, in New Orleans. ... 5-10/182.
HIGH SCHOOL: Isidore Newman (New Orleans).
COLLEGE: Minnesota.
TRANSACTIONS/CAREER NOTES: Signed as non-drafted free agent by New York Giants (April 29, 1994).
PLAYING EXPERIENCE: New York Giants NFL, 1994 and 1995. ... Games: 1994 (6), 1995 (8). Total: 14.
PRO STATISTICS: 1995—Caught two passes for 15 yards, returned one kickoff for 13 yards, fumbled once and recovered two fumbles for 41 yards and a touchdown.

DOUGLASS, MAURICE   S   GIANTS

PERSONAL: Born February 12, 1964, in Muncie, Ind. ... 5-11/210. ... Full name: Maurice Gerrard Douglass.
HIGH SCHOOL: Madison (Trotwood, Ohio).
JUNIOR COLLEGE: Coffeyville (Kan.) Community College.
COLLEGE: Kentucky.
TRANSACTIONS/CAREER NOTES: Selected by Chicago Bears in eighth round (221st pick overall) of 1986 NFL draft. ... Signed by Bears (June 22, 1986). ... Released by Bears (September 1, 1986). ... Re-signed by Bears (November 28, 1986). ... On reserve/non-football injury list for steroid use (August 29-September 25, 1989). ... Reinstated and granted roster exemption (September 26-October 2, 1989). ... On injured reserve with neck injury (December 14, 1989-remainder of season). ... On injured reserve with ankle injury (October 23-November 24, 1990). ... Granted unconditional free agency (February 1-April 1, 1991). ... Re-signed by Bears for 1991 season. ... Granted unconditional free agency (February 1-April 1, 1992). ... Re-signed by Bears for 1992 season. ... Released by Bears (August 31, 1992). ... Re-signed by Bears (September 2, 1992). ... Granted unconditional free agency (March 1, 1993). ... Re-signed by Bears (May 20, 1993). ... Granted unconditional free agency (February 17, 1995). ... Signed by New York Giants (April 18, 1995). ... On injured reserve with broken leg (November 8, 1995-remainder of season).
CHAMPIONSHIP GAME EXPERIENCE: Played in NFC championship game (1988 season).
PRO STATISTICS: 1987—Recovered one fumble. 1988—Fumbled once and recovered three fumbles. 1989—Recovered one fumble. 1990—Recovered one fumble. 1991—Recovered two fumbles. 1994—Credited with 1½ sacks and recovered one fumble. 1995—Credited with one sack and recovered two fumbles for five yards.

		INTERCEPTIONS			
Year Team	G	No.	Yds.	Avg.	TD
1986—Chicago NFL	4	0	0	...	0
1987—Chicago NFL	12	2	0	0.0	0
1988—Chicago NFL	15	1	35	35.0	0
1989—Chicago NFL	10	1	0	0.0	0
1990—Chicago NFL	11	0	0	...	0
1991—Chicago NFL	16	0	0	...	0
1992—Chicago NFL	16	0	0	...	0
1993—Chicago NFL	16	0	0	...	0
1994—Chicago NFL	16	1	18	18.0	0
1995—New York Giants NFL	8	0	0	...	0
Pro totals (10 years)	124	5	53	10.6	0

DOWDELL, MARCUS   WR/KR   CARDINALS

PERSONAL: Born May 22, 1970, in Birmingham, Ala. ... 5-10/179.
HIGH SCHOOL: Banks (Birmingham, Ala.).
COLLEGE: Tennessee State.
TRANSACTIONS/CAREER NOTES: Selected by New Orleans Saints in 10th round (276th pick overall) of 1992 NFL draft. ... Signed by Saints (July 21, 1992). ... Released by Saints (August 31, 1992). ... Signed by Saints to practice squad (September 2, 1992). ... Activated (October 10, 1992). ... Released by Saints (November 10, 1992). ... Re-signed by Saints to practice squad (November 12, 1992). ... Granted free agency after 1992 season. ... Re-signed by Saints (March 8, 1993). ... Released by Saints (August 30, 1993). ... Re-signed by Saints (August 31, 1993). ... Released by Saints (August 23, 1994). ... Signed by Winnipeg Blue Bombers of CFL (1995). ... Signed by Arizona Cardinals (August 7, 1995). ... Released by Cardinals after 1995 season . ... Re-signed by Cardinals (April 25, 1996).
PRO STATISTICS: 1992—Recovered three fumbles. 1995—Fumbled once and recovered one fumble.

		RECEIVING				PUNT RETURNS				TOTALS			
Year Team	G	No.	Yds.	Avg.	TD	No.	Yds.	Avg.	TD	TD	2pt.	Pts.	Fum.
1992—New Orleans NFL	4	1	6	6.0	0	12	37	3.1	0	0	...	0	4
1993—New Orleans NFL	9	6	46	7.7	1	0	0	...	0	1	...	6	1
1994—					Did not play.								
1995—Arizona NFL	13	10	96	9.6	0	1	0	0.0	0	0	0	0	1
Pro totals (3 years)	26	17	148	8.7	1	13	37	2.9	0	1	0	6	6

DOWNS, GARY   RB   BRONCOS

PERSONAL: Born June 28, 1971, in Columbus, Ga. ... 6-0/212. ... Full name: Gary McLinton Downs.
HIGH SCHOOL: William H. Spencer (Columbus, Ga.).
COLLEGE: North Carolina State.
TRANSACTIONS/CAREER NOTES: Selected by New York Giants in third round (95th pick overall) of 1994 NFL draft. ... Signed by Giants (July 19, 1994). ... Released by Giants (August 27, 1995). ... Signed by Denver Broncos (August 28, 1995).

		RUSHING				RECEIVING				TOTALS			
Year Team	G	Att.	Yds.	Avg.	TD	No.	Yds.	Avg.	TD	TD	2pt.	Pts.	Fum.
1994—New York Giants NFL	14	15	51	3.4	0	2	15	7.5	0	0	0	0	1
1995—Denver NFL	2	0	0	...	0	0	0	...	0	0	0	0	0
Pro totals (2 years)	16	15	51	3.4	0	2	15	7.5	0	0	0	0	1

DRAKE, JERRY   DL   CARDINALS

PERSONAL: Born July 9, 1969, in Kingston, N.Y. ... 6-4/292.
HIGH SCHOOL: Kingston (N.Y.).
JUNIOR COLLEGE: Ulster Community College (N.Y.).
COLLEGE: Hastings (Neb.) College.
TRANSACTIONS/CAREER NOTES: Signed as non-drafted free agent by Arizona Cardinals (May 2, 1995). ... Released by Cardinals (August

21, 1995). ... Re-signed by Cardinals to practice squad (August 30, 1995). ... Activated (November 24, 1995).
PLAYING EXPERIENCE: Arizona NFL, 1995. ... Games: 1995 (2).

DRAKE, TROY　　　　　OT　　　　　EAGLES

PERSONAL: Born May 15, 1972, in Rockford, Ill. ... 6-6/289.
HIGH SCHOOL: Byron (Ill.).
COLLEGE: Indiana.
TRANSACTIONS/CAREER NOTES: Signed as non-drafted free agent by Philadelphia Eagles (April 26, 1995). ... Released by Eagles (October 23, 1995). ... Re-signed by Eagles to practice squad (October 25, 1995). ... Activated (November 12, 1995). ... Released by Eagles (November 14, 1995). ... Re-signed by Eagles to practice squad (November 15, 1995).
PLAYING EXPERIENCE: Philadelphia NFL, 1995. ... Games: 1995 (1).

DRAKEFORD, TYRONNE　　　　　CB　　　　　49ERS

PERSONAL: Born June 21, 1971, in Camden, S.C. ... 5-9/185. ... Full name: Tyronne James Drakeford.
HIGH SCHOOL: Camden (S.C.) County.
COLLEGE: Virginia Tech.
TRANSACTIONS/CAREER NOTES: Selected by San Francisco 49ers in second round (62nd pick overall) of 1994 NFL draft. ... Signed by 49ers (July 20, 1994).
CHAMPIONSHIP GAME EXPERIENCE: Played in NFC championship game (1994 season). ... Member of Super Bowl championship team (1994 season).
PRO STATISTICS: 1995—Credited with one sack, fumbled once and recovered one fumble for 12 yards.

		INTERCEPTIONS			
Year Team	G	No.	Yds.	Avg.	TD
1994—San Francisco NFL	13	1	6	6.0	0
1995—San Francisco NFL	16	5	54	10.8	0
Pro totals (2 years)	29	6	60	10.0	0

DRAYTON, TROY　　　　　TE　　　　　RAMS

PERSONAL: Born June 29, 1970, in Harrisburg, Pa. ... 6-3/255. ... Full name: Troy Anthony Drayton.
HIGH SCHOOL: Highspire (Steelton, Pa.).
COLLEGE: Penn State.
TRANSACTIONS/CAREER NOTES: Selected by Los Angeles Rams in second round (39th pick overall) of 1993 NFL draft. ... Signed by Rams (July 20, 1993). ... Rams franchise moved to St. Louis (April 12, 1995). ... Granted free agency (February 16, 1996).
PRO STATISTICS: 1993—Rushed once for seven yards and returned one kickoff for minus 15 yards. 1994—Rushed once for four yards.
STATISTICAL PLATEAUS: 100-yard receiving games: 1995 (1).

		RECEIVING				TOTALS			
Year Team	G	No.	Yds.	Avg.	TD	TD	2pt.	Pts.	Fum.
1993—Los Angeles Rams NFL	16	27	319	11.8	4	4	...	24	1
1994—Los Angeles Rams NFL	16	32	276	8.6	6	6	0	36	0
1995—St. Louis NFL	16	47	458	9.7	4	4	0	24	2
Pro totals (3 years)	48	106	1053	9.9	14	14	0	84	3

DRONETT, SHANE　　　　　DE　　　　　FALCONS

PERSONAL: Born January 12, 1971, in Orange, Texas. ... 6-6/275.
HIGH SCHOOL: Bridge City (Texas).
COLLEGE: Texas.
TRANSACTIONS/CAREER NOTES: Selected after junior season by Denver Broncos in second round (54th pick overall) of 1992 NFL draft. ... Signed by Broncos (July 15, 1992). ... Granted free agency (February 17, 1995). ... Re-signed by Broncos (May 12, 1995). ... Granted unconditional free agency (February 16, 1996). ... Signed by Atlanta Falcons (April 9, 1996).
PRO STATISTICS: 1992—Recovered two fumbles for minus five yards.

		INTERCEPTIONS				SACKS
Year Team	G	No.	Yds.	Avg.	TD	No.
1992—Denver NFL	16	0	0	...	0	6.5
1993—Denver NFL	16	2	13	6.5	0	7.0
1994—Denver NFL	16	0	0	...	0	6.0
1995—Denver NFL	13	0	0	...	0	2.0
Pro totals (4 years)	61	2	13	6.5	0	21.5

DuBOSE, DEMETRIUS　　　　　LB　　　　　BUCCANEERS

PERSONAL: Born March 23, 1971, in Seattle. ... 6-1/235. ... Full name: Adolphus Demetrius DuBose.
HIGH SCHOOL: O'Dea (Seattle).
COLLEGE: Notre Dame (degree in government, 1992).
TRANSACTIONS/CAREER NOTES: Selected by Tampa Bay Buccaneers in second round (34th pick overall) of 1993 NFL draft. ... Signed by Buccaneers (July 20, 1993). ... Granted free agency (February 16, 1996).
PLAYING EXPERIENCE: Tampa Bay NFL, 1993-1995. ... Games: 1993 (15), 1994 (16), 1995 (15). Total: 46.

DUFF, JAMAL   DE   GIANTS

PERSONAL: Born March 11, 1972, in Columbus, Ohio. ... 6-7/271. ... Full name: Jamal Edwin Duff. ... Brother of John Duff, tight end, Dallas Cowboys, Los Angeles Raiders and Jacksonville Jaguars (1989-1995).
HIGH SCHOOL: Foothill (Tustin, Calif.).
COLLEGE: San Diego State.
TRANSACTIONS/CAREER NOTES: Selected by New York Giants in sixth round (204th pick overall) of 1995 NFL draft.... Signed by Giants (July 23, 1995).

Year Team	G	SACKS
1995—New York Giants NFL	15	4.0

DUFFY, ROGER   G/C   JETS

PERSONAL: Born July 16, 1967, in Pittsburgh. ... 6-3/311. ... Full name: Roger Thomas Duffy.
HIGH SCHOOL: Canton (Ohio) Central Catholic.
COLLEGE: Penn State (degree in communications, 1990).
TRANSACTIONS/CAREER NOTES: Selected by New York Jets in eighth round (196th pick overall) of 1990 NFL draft. ... Signed by Jets (July 18, 1990). ... Granted free agency (February 1, 1992). ... Re-signed by Jets (May 15, 1992). ... Granted unconditional free agency (February 17, 1994). ... Re-signed by Jets (March 2, 1994). ... Granted unconditional free agency (February 16, 1996). ... Re-signed by Jets (April 1, 1996).
PLAYING EXPERIENCE: New York Jets NFL, 1990-1995. ... Games: 1990 (16), 1991 (12), 1992 (16), 1993 (16), 1994 (16), 1995 (16). Total: 92.
PRO STATISTICS: 1991—Returned one kickoff for eight yards. 1992—Returned one kickoff for seven yards and recovered one fumble. 1993—Recovered one fumble. 1995—Recovered two fumbles.

DUKES, JAMIE   C   JAGUARS

PERSONAL: Born June 14, 1964, in Schenectady, N.Y. ... 6-1/285. ... Full name: Jamie Donnell Dukes.
HIGH SCHOOL: Evans (Orlando).
COLLEGE: Florida State.
TRANSACTIONS/CAREER NOTES: Selected by Tampa Bay Bandits in 1986 USFL territorial draft. ... Signed as non-drafted free agent by Atlanta Falcons (May 4, 1986). ... On injured reserve with toe injury (November 23, 1988-remainder of season). ... Granted free agency (February 1, 1990). ... Re-signed by Falcons (July 17, 1990). ... Granted free agency (February 1, 1992). ... Re-signed by Falcons (1992). ... Released by Falcons (May 3, 1994). ... Signed by Green Bay Packers (July 6, 1994). ... Granted unconditional free agency (February 17, 1995). ... Signed by Arizona Cardinals (May 24, 1995). ... On injured reserve with knee injury (December 6, 1995-remainder of season). ... Granted unconditional free agency (February 16, 1996). ... Signed by Jacksonville Jaguars (April 20, 1996).
PLAYING EXPERIENCE: Atlanta NFL, 1986-1993; Green Bay NFL, 1994; Arizona NFL, 1995. ... Games: 1986 (14), 1987 (4), 1988 (12), 1989 (16), 1990 (16), 1991 (16), 1992 (16), 1993 (16), 1994 (6), 1995 (8). Total: 124.
PRO STATISTICS: 1986—Recovered one fumble. 1988—Returned one kickoff for 13 yards. 1990—Fumbled once and recovered one fumble for minus six yards. 1991—Recovered one fumble. 1992—Recovered two fumbles. 1993—Recovered one fumble.

DUMAS, MIKE   S

PERSONAL: Born March 18, 1969, in Grand Rapids, Mich. ... 5-11/181. ... Full name: Michael Dion Dumas.
HIGH SCHOOL: Lowell (Mich.).
COLLEGE: Indiana.
TRANSACTIONS/CAREER NOTES: Selected by Houston Oilers in second round (28th pick overall) of 1991 NFL draft. ... Signed by Oilers (August 12, 1991). ... On injured reserve with Achilles tendon injury (August 23, 1993-entire season). ... Granted free agency (February 17, 1994). ... Re-signed by Oilers (June 1994). ... Released by Oilers (July 14, 1994). ... Signed by Buffalo Bills (July 25, 1994). ... Granted unconditional free agency (February 17, 1995). ... Signed by Jacksonville Jaguars (April 24, 1995). ... Released by Jaguars (April 24, 1996).
HONORS: Named defensive back on THE SPORTING NEWS college All-America second team (1990).
PRO STATISTICS: 1991—Recovered three fumbles for 19 yards and a touchdown. 1992—Recovered one fumble. 1994—Recovered two fumbles for 40 yards. 1995—Recovered two fumbles.

Year Team	G	INTERCEPTIONS No.	Yds.	Avg.	TD
1991—Houston NFL	13	1	19	19.0	0
1992—Houston NFL	16	1	0	0.0	0
1993—Houston NFL			Did not play—injured.			
1994—Buffalo NFL	14	0	0	...	0
1995—Jacksonville NFL	14	1	0	0.0	0
Pro totals (4 years)	57	3	19	6.3	0

DUNBAR, KARL   DE   CARDINALS

PERSONAL: Born May 18, 1967, in Opelousas, La. ... 6-4/275.
HIGH SCHOOL: Plaisance (Opelousas, La.).
COLLEGE: Louisiana State (degree in criminal justice).
TRANSACTIONS/CAREER NOTES: Selected by Pittsburgh Steelers in eighth round (209th pick overall) of 1990 NFL draft. ... Signed by Steelers (1990). ... On physically unable to perform list (August 28-November 6, 1990). ... On injured reserve with foot injury (November 17, 1990-remainder of season). ... Released by Steelers (August 19, 1991). ... Selected by Orlando Thunder in second round (18th pick overall) of 1992 World League draft. ... Signed by New Orleans Saints (June 26, 1992). ... Released by Saints (August 31, 1992). ... Re-signed by Saints to practice squad (September 2, 1992). ... Released by Saints (August 30, 1993). ... Re-signed by Saints (August 31, 1993). ... Released by Saints (August 22, 1994). ... Signed by Arizona Cardinals (August 27, 1994). ... Released by Cardinals (November 9, 1994). ...

Re-signed by Cardinals (February 16, 1995). ... Assigned by Cardinals to Rhein Fire in 1995 World League enhancement allocation program (February 20, 1995). ... Granted unconditional free agency (February 16, 1996). ... Re-signed by Cardinals (April 9, 1996).

Year Team	G	SACKS
1990—Pittsburgh NFL	Did not play.	
1991—	Did not play.	
1992—Orlando W.L.	10	5.5
1993—New Orleans NFL	13	0.0
1994—Arizona NFL	4	0.0
1995—Arizona NFL	4	0.0
W.L. totals (1 year)	10	5.5
NFL totals (3 years)	21	0.0
Pro totals (4 years)	31	5.5

DUNBAR, VAUGHN   RB

PERSONAL: Born September 4, 1968, in Fort Wayne, Ind. ... 5-10/204. ... Full name: Vaughn Allen Dunbar.
HIGH SCHOOL: R. Nelson Snider (Fort Wayne, Ind.).
COLLEGE: Northeastern Oklahoma A&M, then Indiana.
TRANSACTIONS/CAREER NOTES: Selected by New Orleans Saints in first round (21st pick overall) of 1992 NFL draft. ... Signed by Saints (July 15, 1992). ... On injured reserve with knee injury (August 24, 1993-entire season). ... Granted free agency (February 17, 1995). ... Re-signed by Saints (July 20, 1995). ... Claimed on waivers by Jacksonville Jaguars (September 6, 1995). ... Granted unconditional free agency (February 16, 1996).
HONORS: Named running back on The Sporting News college All-America first team (1991).

		RUSHING				RECEIVING				KICKOFF RETURNS				TOTALS			
YearTeam	G	Att.	Yds.	Avg.	TD	No.	Yds.	Avg.	TD	No.	Yds.	Avg.	TD	TD	2pt.	Pts.	Fum.
1992—New Orleans NFL	16	154	565	3.7	3	9	62	6.9	0	10	187	18.7	0	3	...	18	3
1993—New Orleans NFL								Did not play—injured.									
1994—New Orleans NFL	8	3	9	3.0	0	0	0	...	0	1	28	28.0	0	0	0	0	0
1995—New Orleans NFL	1	0	0	...	0	0	0	...	0	0	0	...	0	0	0	0	0
—Jacksonville NFL	14	110	361	3.3	2	2	11	5.5	0	2	32	16.0	0	2	0	12	0
Pro totals (3 years)	39	267	935	3.5	5	11	73	6.6	0	13	247	19.0	0	5	0	30	3

DUNN, DAVID   WR/KR   BENGALS

PERSONAL: Born June 10, 1972, in San Diego. ... 6-3/210.
HIGH SCHOOL: Morse (San Diego).
JUNIOR COLLEGE: Bakersfield (Calif.) College.
COLLEGE: Fresno State.
TRANSACTIONS/CAREER NOTES: Selected by Cincinnati Bengals in fifth round (139th pick overall) of 1995 NFL draft. ... Signed by Bengals (July 31, 1995).
PLAYING EXPERIENCE: Cincinnati NFL, 1995. ... Games: 1995 (16).
HONORS: Named kick returner on The Sporting News college All-America second team (1994).
PRO STATISTICS: 1995—Rushed once for minus 13 yards and fumbled twice.

DYE, ERNEST   G   CARDINALS

PERSONAL: Born July 15, 1971, in Greenwood, S.C. ... 6-6/325. ... Full name: Ernest Thaddius Dye.
HIGH SCHOOL: Greenwood (S.C.).
JUNIOR COLLEGE: Itawamba Junior College (Miss.).
COLLEGE: South Carolina.
TRANSACTIONS/CAREER NOTES: Selected by Phoenix Cardinals in first round (18th pick overall) of 1993 NFL draft. ... Signed by Cardinals (July 23, 1993). ... Cardinals franchise renamed Arizona Cardinals for 1994 season.
PLAYING EXPERIENCE: Phoenix NFL, 1993; Arizona NFL, 1994 and 1995. ... Games: 1993 (7), 1994 (16), 1995 (6). Total: 29.
PRO STATISTICS: 1994—Recovered one fumble.

DYSON, MATT   LB   RAIDERS

PERSONAL: Born August 1, 1972, in La Plata, Md. ... 6-4/275.
HIGH SCHOOL: La Plata (Md.).
COLLEGE: Michigan.
TRANSACTIONS/CAREER NOTES: Selected by Los Angeles Raiders in fifth round (138th pick overall) of 1995 NFL draft. ... Signed by Raiders (July 21, 1995). ... Raiders franchise moved to Oakland (July 21, 1995).
PLAYING EXPERIENCE: Oakland NFL, 1995. ... Games: 1995 (4).

EARLY, QUINN   WR   BILLS

PERSONAL: Born April 13, 1965, in West Hempstead, N.Y. ... 6-0/190. ... Full name: Quinn Remar Early.
HIGH SCHOOL: Great Neck (N.Y.).
COLLEGE: Iowa (degree in art, 1988).
TRANSACTIONS/CAREER NOTES: Selected by San Diego Chargers in third round (60th pick overall) of 1988 NFL draft. ... Signed by Chargers (July 11, 1988). ... On injured reserve with knee injury (October 21-December 13, 1989). ... On developmental squad (December 14-15, 1989). ... Activated (December 16, 1989). ... Granted unconditional free agency (February 1, 1991). ... Signed by New Orleans Saints (April 1, 1991). ... Granted unconditional free agency (February 16, 1996). ... Signed by Buffalo Bills (March 6, 1996).

D

E

STATISTICAL PLATEAUS: 100-yard receiving games: 1991 (1), 1994 (1), 1995 (2). Total: 4.

		RUSHING				RECEIVING				KICKOFF RETURNS				TOTALS			
Year Team	G	Att.	Yds.	Avg.	TD	No.	Yds.	Avg.	TD	No.	Yds.	Avg.	TD	TD	2pt.	Pts.	Fum.
1988—San Diego NFL	16	7	63	9.0	0	29	375	12.9	4	0	0	...	0	4	...	24	1
1989—San Diego NFL	6	1	19	19.0	0	11	126	11.5	0	0	0	...	0	0	...	0	0
1990—San Diego NFL	14	0	0	...	0	15	238	15.9	1	0	0	...	0	1	...	6	0
1991—New Orleans NFL	15	3	13	4.3	0	32	541	16.9	2	9	168	18.7	0	2	...	12	2
1992—New Orleans NFL	16	3	-1	-.3	0	30	566	18.9	5	0	0	...	0	5	...	30	0
1993—New Orleans NFL	16	2	32	16.0	0	45	670	14.9	6	0	0	...	0	6	...	36	1
1994—New Orleans NFL	16	2	10	5.0	0	82	894	10.9	4	0	0	...	0	4	0	24	0
1995—New Orleans NFL	16	2	-3	-1.5	0	81	1087	13.4	8	0	0	...	0	8	0	48	0
Pro totals (8 years)	115	20	133	6.7	0	325	4497	13.8	30	9	168	18.7	0	30	0	180	5

EATMAN, IRV   OT   OILERS

PERSONAL: Born January 1, 1961, in Birmingham, Ala. ... 6-7/305. ... Full name: Irvin Humphrey Eatman.
HIGH SCHOOL: Meadowdale (Dayton, Ohio).
COLLEGE: UCLA.
TRANSACTIONS/CAREER NOTES: Selected by Philadelphia Stars in first round (eighth pick overall) of 1983 USFL draft. ... Signed by Stars (February 8, 1983). ... Selected by Kansas City Chiefs in eighth round (204th pick overall) of 1983 NFL draft. ... Stars franchise moved to Baltimore (November 1, 1984). ... Granted free agency when USFL suspended operations (August 7, 1986). ... Signed by Chiefs (August 10, 1986). ... Granted free agency (February 1, 1990). ... Re-signed by Chiefs (August 15, 1990). ... Traded by Chiefs to New York Jets for DL Ron Stallworth (February 1, 1991). ... On injured reserve with ankle injury (November 29, 1992-remainder of season). ... Granted unconditional free agency (March 1, 1993). ... Signed by Los Angeles Rams (March 6, 1993). ... Released by Rams (April 27, 1994). ... Signed by Atlanta Falcons (June 2, 1994). ... Released by Falcons (March 9, 1995). ... Signed by Houston Oilers (June 6, 1995).
PLAYING EXPERIENCE: Philadelphia USFL, 1983 and 1984; Baltimore USFL, 1985; Kansas City NFL, 1986-1990; New York Jets NFL, 1991 and 1992, Los Angeles Rams NFL, 1993; Atlanta NFL, 1994; Houston NFL, 1995. ... Games: 1983 (18), 1984 (18), 1985 (18), 1986 (16), 1987 (12), 1988 (16), 1989 (13), 1990 (12), 1991 (16), 1992 (12), 1993 (16), 1994 (4), 1995 (16). Total USFL: 54. Total NFL: 133. Total Pro: 187.
CHAMPIONSHIP GAME EXPERIENCE: Played in USFL championship game (1983-1985 seasons).
HONORS: Named offensive tackle on THE SPORTING NEWS USFL All-Star team (1983 and 1984).
PRO STATISTICS: 1989—Recovered one fumble. 1991—Recovered one fumble. 1993—Recovered one fumble. 1995—Recovered one fumble.

EDMONDS, BOBBY JOE   RB/KR

PERSONAL: Born September 26, 1964, in Nashville. ... 5-11/186. ... Full name: Bobby Joe Edmonds Jr. ... Son of Bobby Joe Edmonds Sr., forward, Indiana Pacers of American Basketball Association (1967-68 and 1969-70).
HIGH SCHOOL: Lutheran North (St. Louis).
COLLEGE: Arkansas.
TRANSACTIONS/CAREER NOTES: Selected by Memphis Showboats in 1986 USFL territorial draft. ... Selected by Seattle Seahawks in fifth round (126th pick overall) of 1986 NFL draft. ... Signed by Seahawks (July 19, 1986). ... Granted unconditional free agency (February 1, 1989). ... Signed by Detroit Lions (March 16, 1989). ... Released by Lions (September 5, 1989). ... Signed by Los Angeles Raiders (September 19, 1989). ... On injured reserve with ankle injury (November 1-December 12, 1989). ... Moved to developmental squad (December 12, 1989). ... Granted unconditional free agency (February 1, 1990). ... Signed by Seahawks (April 1, 1990). ... Released by Seahawks (August 23, 1990). ... Signed by Tampa Bay Buccaneers (March 23, 1995). ... Released by Buccaneers (April 23, 1996).
HONORS: Named punt returner on THE SPORTING NEWS NFL All-Pro team (1986). ... Played in Pro Bowl (1986 season).
PRO STATISTICS: 1986—Rushed once for minus 11 yards and recovered one fumble. 1987—Recovered one fumble. 1988—Recovered one fumble. 1995—Recovered one fumble.
MISCELLANEOUS: Selected by St. Louis Cardinals baseball organization in 12th round of free-agent draft (June 7, 1982); did not sign. ... Selected by Cardinals organization in secondary phase of free-agent draft (June 6, 1983); did not sign.

		PUNT RETURNS				KICKOFF RETURNS				TOTALS			
Year Team	G	No.	Yds.	Avg.	TD	No.	Yds.	Avg.	TD	TD	2pt.	Pts.	Fum.
1986—Seattle NFL	15	34	419	*12.3	1	34	764	22.5	0	1	...	6	4
1987—Seattle NFL	11	20	251	12.6	0	27	564	20.9	0	0	...	0	1
1988—Seattle NFL	16	35	340	9.7	0	40	900	22.5	0	0	...	0	2
1989—Los Angeles Raiders NFL	7	16	168	10.5	0	14	271	19.4	0	0	...	0	0
1990—						Did not play.							
1991—						Did not play.							
1992—						Did not play.							
1993—						Did not play.							
1994—						Did not play.							
1995—Tampa Bay NFL	16	29	293	10.1	0	58	1147	19.8	0	0	0	0	1
Pro totals (5 years)	65	134	1471	11.0	1	173	3646	21.1	0	1	0	6	8

EDWARDS, ANTHONY   WR   CARDINALS

PERSONAL: Born May 26, 1966, in Casa Grande, Ariz. ... 5-10/190.
HIGH SCHOOL: Union (Casa Grande, Ariz.).
COLLEGE: New Mexico Highlands.
TRANSACTIONS/CAREER NOTES: Signed as non-drafted free agent by Philadelphia Eagles (July 7, 1989). ... Released by Eagles (September 5, 1989). ... Re-signed by Eagles to developmental squad (September 6, 1989). ... Activated (October 20, 1989). ... On injured reserve with knee injury (September 4-October 1, 1990). ... On practice squad (October 1-30, 1990). ... Released by Eagles (October 30, 1990). ... Re-signed by Eagles (October 31, 1990). ... Released by Eagles (December 12, 1990). ... Signed by Phoenix Cardinals (May 1991). ... Released by Cardinals (August 26, 1991). ... Re-signed by Cardinals (September 18, 1991). ... Granted unconditional free agency (February 1-April 1, 1992). ... Re-signed by Cardinals for 1992 season. ... Granted unconditional free agency (February 17, 1994). ... Re-signed by Cardinals (April 14, 1994). ... Cardinals franchise renamed Arizona Cardinals for 1994 season. ... On injured reserve with knee injury (August 12, 1994-entire season).

E

PRO STATISTICS: 1989—Recovered one fumble. 1995—Recovered one fumble.
STATISTICAL PLATEAUS: 100-yard receiving games: 1993 (1).

		RECEIVING				PUNT RETURNS				KICKOFF RETURNS				TOTALS			
Year Team	G	No.	Yds.	Avg.	TD	No.	Yds.	Avg.	TD	No.	Yds.	Avg.	TD	TD	2pt.	Pts.	Fum.
1989—Philadelphia NFL	9	2	74	37.0	0	7	64	9.1	0	3	23	7.7	0	0	...	0	2
1990—Philadelphia NFL	5	0	0	...	0	8	60	7.5	0	3	36	12.0	0	0	...	0	2
1991—Phoenix NFL	13	0	0	...	0	1	7	7.0	0	13	261	20.1	0	0	...	0	0
1992—Phoenix NFL	16	14	147	10.5	1	0	0	...	0	8	143	17.9	0	1	...	6	0
1993—Phoenix NFL	16	13	326	25.1	1	3	12	4.0	0	3	51	17.0	0	1	...	6	0
1994—Arizona NFL								Did not play—injured.									
1995—Arizona NFL	15	29	417	14.4	2	18	131	7.3	0	3	50	16.7	0	2	0	12	0
Pro totals (6 years)	74	58	964	16.6	4	37	274	7.4	0	33	564	17.1	0	4	0	24	4

EDWARDS, ANTONIO   DE   SEAHAWKS

PERSONAL: Born March 10, 1970, in Moultrie, Ga. ... 6-3/271.
HIGH SCHOOL: Colquitt County (Moultrie, Ga.).
COLLEGE: Valdosta (Ga.) State.
TRANSACTIONS/CAREER NOTES: Selected by Seattle Seahawks in eighth round (204th pick overall) of 1993 NFL draft. ... Signed by Seahawks (July 14, 1993).
PRO STATISTICS: 1993—Credited with one safety. 1995—Recovered one fumble for 83 yards and a touchdown.

Year Team	G	SACKS
1993—Seattle NFL	9	3.0
1994—Seattle NFL	15	2.5
1995—Seattle NFL	13	5.5
Pro totals (3 years)	37	11.0

EDWARDS, BRAD   S   FALCONS

PERSONAL: Born March 22, 1966, in Lumberton, N.C. ... 6-2/207. ... Full name: Bradford Wayne Edwards. ... Son of Wayne Edwards, infielder, Baltimore Orioles organization (1962-1965).
HIGH SCHOOL: Douglas Byrd (Fayetteville, N.C.).
COLLEGE: South Carolina (degree in business management, 1988).
TRANSACTIONS/CAREER NOTES: Selected by Minnesota Vikings in second round (54th pick overall) of 1988 NFL draft. ... Signed by Vikings (July 20, 1988). ... On injured reserve with neck injury (September 14-November 4, 1989). ... Granted unconditional free agency (February 1, 1990). ... Signed by Washington Redskins (March 7, 1990). ... Granted unconditional free agency (March 1, 1993). ... Re-signed by Redskins (March 1, 1993). ... Released by Redskins (July 18, 1994). ... Signed by Atlanta Falcons (November 25, 1994). ... Granted unconditional free agency (February 17, 1995). ... Re-signed by Falcons (April 5, 1995). ... Granted unconditional free agency (February 16, 1996). ... Re-signed by Falcons (February 20, 1996).
CHAMPIONSHIP GAME EXPERIENCE: Played in NFC championship game (1991 season). ... Member of Super Bowl championship team (1991 season).
PRO STATISTICS: 1993—Recovered one fumble.

		INTERCEPTIONS			
Year Team	G	No.	Yds.	Avg.	TD
1988—Minnesota NFL	16	2	47	23.5	1
1989—Minnesota NFL	9	1	18	18.0	0
1990—Washington NFL	16	2	33	16.5	0
1991—Washington NFL	16	4	52	13.0	0
1992—Washington NFL	16	6	157	26.2	1
1993—Washington NFL	16	1	17	17.0	0
1994—Atlanta NFL	4	0	0	...	0
1995—Atlanta NFL	13	0	0	...	0
Pro totals (8 years)	106	16	324	20.3	2

EDWARDS, DIXON   LB   VIKINGS

PERSONAL: Born March 25, 1968, in Cincinnati. ... 6-1/225. ... Full name: Dixon Voldean Edwards III.
HIGH SCHOOL: Aiken (Cincinnati).
COLLEGE: Michigan State.
TRANSACTIONS/CAREER NOTES: Selected by Dallas Cowboys in second round (37th pick overall) of 1991 NFL draft. ... Signed by Cowboys (April 22, 1991). ... On injured reserve with hamstring injury (August 27-September 25, 1991). ... Granted unconditional free agency (February 16, 1996). ... Signed by Minnesota Vikings (February 26, 1996).
CHAMPIONSHIP GAME EXPERIENCE: Played in NFC championship game (1992-1995 seasons). ... Member of Super Bowl championship team (1992, 1993 and 1995 seasons).
PRO STATISTICS: 1991—Intercepted one pass for 36 yards and a touchdown. 1992—Returned one kickoff for no yards. 1993—Recovered one fumble. 1994—Recovered one fumble for 21 yards.

Year Team	G	SACKS
1991—Dallas NFL	11	0.0
1992—Dallas NFL	16	0.0
1993—Dallas NFL	16	1.5
1994—Dallas NFL	16	1.0
1995—Dallas NFL	15	0.0
Pro totals (5 years)	74	2.5

E

EILERS, PAT   S

PERSONAL: Born September 3, 1966, in St. Paul, Minn. ... 5-11/197. ... Full name: Patrick Christopher Eilers.
HIGH SCHOOL: St. Thomas Academy (St. Paul, Minn.).
COLLEGE: Notre Dame (degrees in mechanical engineering and biology).
TRANSACTIONS/CAREER NOTES: Signed as non-drafted free agent by Minnesota Vikings (April 27, 1990). ... Released by Vikings (September 3, 1990). ... Re-signed by Vikings to practice squad (October 1, 1990). ... Activated (November 9, 1990). ... Granted unconditional free agency (February 1-April 1, 1991). ... Re-signed by Vikings (April 9, 1991). ... Granted unconditional free agency (February 1, 1992). ... Signed by Phoenix Cardinals (April 1, 1992). ... Released by Cardinals (September 1, 1992). ... Signed by Washington Redskins (December 16, 1992). ... Released by Redskins (December 25, 1992). ... Re-signed by Redskins (May 3, 1993). ... On injured reserve with knee injury (December 1, 1993-remainder of season). ... Granted unconditional free agency (February 17, 1995). ... Signed by Chicago Bears (April 22, 1995). ... Released by Bears (September 27, 1995). ... Re-signed by Bears (November 22, 1995). ... Granted unconditional free agency (February 16, 1996).
PLAYING EXPERIENCE: Minnesota NFL, 1990 and 1991; Washington NFL, 1992-1994; Chicago NFL, 1995. ... Games: 1990 (8), 1991 (16), 1992 (1), 1993 (11), 1994 (16), 1995 (9). Total: 61.
PRO STATISTICS: 1990—Recovered one fumble. 1991—Returned five kickoffs for 99 yards and recovered two fumbles. 1993—Recovered three fumbles. 1995—Recovered one fumble.

ELAM, JASON   K   BRONCOS

PERSONAL: Born March 8, 1970, in Fort Walton Beach, Fla. ... 5-11/192.
HIGH SCHOOL: Brookwood (Snellville, Ga.).
COLLEGE: Hawaii.
TRANSACTIONS/CAREER NOTES: Selected by Denver Broncos in third round (70th pick overall) of 1993 NFL draft. ... Signed by Broncos (July 12, 1993).
HONORS: Named kicker on THE SPORTING NEWS college All-America second team (1989 and 1991). ... Played in Pro Bowl (1995 season).
PRO STATISTICS: 1995—Punted once for 17 yards.

Year Team	G	XPM	XPA	FGM	FGA	Lg.	50+	Pts.
					KICKING			
1993—Denver NFL	16	41	42	26	35	54	4-6	119
1994—Denver NFL	16	29	29	30	37	54	1-3	119
1995—Denver NFL	16	39	39	31	38	56	5-7	132
Pro totals (3 years)	48	109	110	87	110	56	10-16	370

ELEWONIBI, MO   OT

PERSONAL: Born December 16, 1965, in Lagos, Nigeria. ... 6-4/286. ... Full name: Mohammed Thomas David Elewonibi. ... Name pronounced EL-eh-wa-NEE-bee.
HIGH SCHOOL: Mount Douglas Secondary (Victoria, B.C.).
JUNIOR COLLEGE: Snow College (Utah).
COLLEGE: Brigham Young.
TRANSACTIONS/CAREER NOTES: Selected by Washington Redskins in third round (76th pick overall) of 1990 NFL draft. ... On injured reserve with shoulder injury (September 4, 1990-entire season). ... On injured reserve with knee injury (August 27, 1991-entire season). ... On injured reserve with shoulder injury (September 1-October 8, 1992). ... On injured reserve with sprained knee (November 11, 1992-remainder of season). ... Granted free agency (March 1, 1993). ... Re-signed by Redskins for 1993 season. ... Released by Redskins (August 1, 1994). ... Signed by Buffalo Bills (August 3, 1994). ... Released by Bills (August 23, 1994). ... Selected by Barcelona Dragons in seventh round (42nd pick overall) of 1995 World League Draft. ... Signed by Philadelphia Eagles (November 14, 1995). ... Granted unconditional free agency (February 16, 1996).
PLAYING EXPERIENCE: Washington NFL, 1992 and 1993; Philadelphia NFL, 1995. ... Games: 1992 (5), 1993 (15), 1995 (6). Total: 26.
HONORS: Outland Trophy winner (1989). ... Named guard on THE SPORTING NEWS college All-America second team (1989).
PRO STATISTICS: 1993—Recovered two fumbles for 10 yards. 1995—Recovered one fumble.
MISCELLANEOUS: Selected by Vancouver in 1985 North American Soccer League draft.

ELIAS, KEITH   RB   GIANTS

PERSONAL: Born February 3, 1972, in Lacey Township, N.J. ... 5-9/203.
HIGH SCHOOL: Lacey Township (N.J.).
COLLEGE: Princeton.
TRANSACTIONS/CAREER NOTES: Signed as non-drafted free agent by New York Giants (April 29, 1994).
PRO STATISTICS: 1995—Caught nine passes for 69 yards.

Year Team	G	Att.	Yds.	Avg.	TD	TD	2pt.	Pts.	Fum.
		RUSHING				TOTALS			
1994—New York Giants NFL	2	2	4	2.0	0	0	0	0	0
1995—New York Giants NFL	15	10	44	4.4	0	0	0	0	0
Pro totals (2 years)	17	12	48	4.0	0	0	0	0	0

ELLARD, HENRY   WR   REDSKINS

PERSONAL: Born July 21, 1961, in Fresno, Calif. ... 5-11/185. ... Full name: Henry Austin Ellard. ... Name pronounced EL-lard.
HIGH SCHOOL: Hoover (Fresno, Calif.).
COLLEGE: Fresno State.
TRANSACTIONS/CAREER NOTES: Selected by Oakland Invaders in 1983 USFL territorial draft. ... Selected by Los Angeles Rams in second

round (32nd pick overall) of 1983 NFL draft. ... Signed by Rams (July 22, 1983). ... Granted free agency (February 1, 1986). ... Re-signed by Rams (October 22, 1986). ... Granted roster exemption (October 22-25, 1986). ... Granted unconditional free agency (February 17, 1994). ... Signed by Washington Redskins (April 13, 1994). ... Granted unconditional free agency (February 16, 1996). ... Re-signed by Redskins (February 18, 1996).

CHAMPIONSHIP GAME EXPERIENCE: Played in NFC championship game (1985 and 1989 seasons).

HONORS: Named punt returner on THE SPORTING NEWS NFL All-Pro team (1984 and 1985). ... Played in Pro Bowl (1984, 1988 and 1989 seasons). ... Named wide receiver on THE SPORTING NEWS NFL All-Pro team (1988).

PRO STATISTICS: 1983—Fumbled twice and recovered two fumbles. 1984—Fumbled four times and recovered two fumbles. 1985—Fumbled three times and recovered five fumbles. 1986—Fumbled three times and recovered one fumble. 1987—Fumbled three times and recovered one fumble. 1988—Fumbled three times. 1990—Fumbled four times. 1991—Fumbled once and recovered one fumble. 1994—Fumbled once. 1995—Fumbled once.

STATISTICAL PLATEAUS: 100-yard receiving games: 1985 (2), 1986 (2), 1987 (1), 1988 (5), 1989 (5), 1990 (6), 1991 (1), 1993 (3), 1994 (5), 1995 (3). Total: 33.

MISCELLANEOUS: Holds Rams franchise all-time record for most yards receiving (9,761).

		RUSHING				RECEIVING				PUNT RETURNS				KICKOFF RETURNS				TOTALS		
Year Team	G	Att.	Yds.	Avg.	TD	No.	Yds.	Avg.	TD	No.	Yds.	Avg.	TD	No.	Yds.	Avg.	TD	TD	2pt.	Pts.
1983—Los Angeles Rams NFL..	12	3	7	2.3	0	16	268	16.8	0	16	217	*13.6	†1	15	314	20.9	0	1	...	6
1984—Los Angeles Rams NFL..	16	3	-5	-1.7	0	34	622	18.3	6	30	403	13.4	*2	2	24	12.0	0	8	...	48
1985—Los Angeles Rams NFL..	16	3	8	2.7	0	54	811	15.0	5	37	501	13.5	1	0	0	...	0	6	...	36
1986—Los Angeles Rams NFL..	9	1	-15	-15.0	0	34	447	13.2	4	14	127	9.1	0	1	18	18.0	0	4	...	24
1987—Los Angeles Rams NFL..	12	1	4	4.0	0	51	799	15.7	3	15	107	7.1	0	1	8	8.0	0	3	...	18
1988—Los Angeles Rams NFL..	16	1	7	7.0	0	86	*1414	16.4	10	17	119	7.0	0	0	0	...	0	10	...	60
1989—Los Angeles Rams NFL..	14	2	10	5.0	0	70	1382	19.7	8	2	20	10.0	0	0	0	...	0	8	...	48
1990—Los Angeles Rams NFL..	15	2	21	10.5	0	76	1294	17.0	4	2	15	7.5	0	0	0	...	0	4	...	24
1991—Los Angeles Rams NFL..	16	0	0	...	0	64	1052	16.4	3	0	0	...	0	0	0	...	0	3	...	18
1992—Los Angeles Rams NFL..	16	0	0	...	0	47	727	15.5	3	0	0	...	0	0	0	...	0	3	...	18
1993—Los Angeles Rams NFL..	16	2	18	9.0	0	61	945	15.5	2	2	18	9.0	0	0	0	...	0	2	...	12
1994—Washington NFL	16	1	-5	-5.0	0	74	1397	18.9	6	0	0	...	0	0	0	...	0	6	0	36
1995—Washington NFL	15	0	0	...	0	56	1005	18.0	5	0	0	...	0	0	0	...	0	5	0	30
Pro totals (13 years)	189	19	50	2.6	0	723	12163	16.8	59	135	1527	11.3	4	19	364	19.2	0	63	0	378

ELLIOTT, JUMBO — OT — JETS

PERSONAL: Born April 1, 1965, in Lake Ronkonkoma, N.Y. ... 6-7/308. ... Full name: John Elliott.

HIGH SCHOOL: Sachem (Lake Ronkonkoma, N.Y.).

COLLEGE: Michigan (received undergraduate degree, 1988).

TRANSACTIONS/CAREER NOTES: Selected by New York Giants in second round (36th pick overall) of 1988 NFL draft. ... Signed by Giants (July 18, 1988). ... Granted free agency (February 1, 1991). ... Re-signed by Giants (August 22, 1991). ... Designated by Giants as franchise player (February 25, 1993). ... On injured reserve (January 7, 1994-remainder of 1993 playoffs). ... Granted unconditional free agency (February 16, 1996). ... Signed by New York Jets (February 24, 1996).

PLAYING EXPERIENCE: New York Giants NFL, 1988-1995. ... Games: 1988 (16), 1989 (13), 1990 (8), 1991 (16), 1992 (16), 1993 (11), 1994 (16), 1995 (16). Total: 112.

CHAMPIONSHIP GAME EXPERIENCE: Played in NFC championship game (1990 season). ... Member of Super Bowl championship team (1990 season).

HONORS: Played in Pro Bowl (1993 season).

PRO STATISTICS: 1988—Recovered one fumble.

ELLIOTT, LIN — K

PERSONAL: Born November 11, 1968, in Euless, Texas. ... 6-0/182. ... Full name: Lindley Franklin Elliott Jr.

HIGH SCHOOL: Waco (Texas).

COLLEGE: Texas Tech.

TRANSACTIONS/CAREER NOTES: Signed as non-drafted free agent by Dallas Cowboys (April 29, 1992). ... Released by Cowboys (September 14, 1993). ... Signed by Atlanta Falcons (October 13, 1993). ... Released by Falcons (October 15, 1993). ... Signed by Kansas City Chiefs (April 6, 1994). ... Granted unconditional free agency (February 16, 1996).

CHAMPIONSHIP GAME EXPERIENCE: Played in NFC championship game (1992 season). ... Member of Super Bowl championship team (1992 season).

POSTSEASON RECORDS: Shares Super Bowl single-game record for most extra points—7 (January 31, 1993, vs. Buffalo).

PRO STATISTICS: 1994—Recovered one fumble.

		KICKING						
Year Team	G	XPM	XPA	FGM	FGA	Lg.	50+	Pts.
1992—Dallas NFL.....................................	16	47	48	24	35	53	3-4	119
1993—Dallas NFL.....................................	2	2	3	2	4	43	0-0	8
1994—Kansas City NFL.............................	16	30	30	25	30	49	0-0	105
1995—Kansas City NFL.............................	16	34	37	24	30	49	0-0	106
Pro totals (4 years)	50	113	118	75	99	53	3-4	338

ELLIOTT, MATT — C/G — PANTHERS

PERSONAL: Born October 1, 1968, in Carmel, Ind. ... 6-3/295.

HIGH SCHOOL: Carmel (Ind.).

COLLEGE: Michigan.

TRANSACTIONS/CAREER NOTES: Selected by Washington Redskins in 12th round (336th pick overall) of 1992 NFL draft. ... Signed by

E

Redskins for 1992 season. ... On injured reserve (August 20, 1993-entire season). ... Released by Redskins (August 23, 1994). ... Signed by Carolina Panthers (January 10, 1995). ... Granted free agency (February 16, 1996).
PLAYING EXPERIENCE: Washington NFL, 1992; Carolina NFL, 1995. ... Games: 1992 (16), 1995 (15). Total: 31.

ELLISON, JERRY　　　　　RB　　　　　BUCCANEERS

PERSONAL: Born December 20, 1971, in Augusta, Ga. ... 5-10/198.
HIGH SCHOOL: Glenn Hills (Augusta, Ga.).
COLLEGE: UT-Chattanooga.
TRANSACTIONS/CAREER NOTES: Signed as non-drafted free agent by Tampa Bay Buccaneers (May 5, 1994). ... Released by Buccaneers (August 23, 1994). ... Re-signed by Buccaneers to practice squad (September 7, 1994). ... Released by Buccaneers (September 12, 1994). ... Re-signed by Buccaneers to practice squad (September 27, 1994). ... Granted free agency after 1994 season. ... Re-signed by Buccaneers (January 24, 1995).
PRO STATISTICS: 1995—Recovered one fumble.

| | | RUSHING | | | | RECEIVING | | | | TOTALS | | |
Year Team	G	Att.	Yds.	Avg.	TD	No.	Yds.	Avg.	TD	TD	2pt.	Pts.	Fum.
1995—Tampa Bay NFL	16	26	218	8.4	5	7	44	6.3	0	5	0	30	0

ELLISON, 'OMAR　　　　　WR　　　　　CHARGERS

PERSONAL: Born October 8, 1971, in Griffin, Ga. ... 6-0/200.
HIGH SCHOOL: Griffin (Ga.).
COLLEGE: Florida State.
TRANSACTIONS/CAREER NOTES: Selected by San Diego Chargers in fifth round (162nd pick overall) of 1995 NFL draft. ... Signed by Chargers (July 17, 1995).
PLAYING EXPERIENCE: San Diego NFL, 1995. ... Games: 1995 (2).
PRO STATISTICS: 1995—Caught one pass for six yards.

ELLISS, LUTHER　　　　　DE　　　　　LIONS

PERSONAL: Born March 22, 1973, in Mancos, Colo. ... 6-5/291.
HIGH SCHOOL: Mancos (Colo.).
COLLEGE: Utah.
TRANSACTIONS/CAREER NOTES: Selected by Detroit Lions in first round (20th pick overall) of 1995 NFL draft. ... Signed by Lions (July 19, 1995).
PLAYING EXPERIENCE: Detroit NFL, 1995. ... Games: 1995 (16).
HONORS: Named defensive lineman on THE SPORTING NEWS college All-America first team (1994).

E

EL-MASHTOUB, HICHAM　　　　　C/G　　　　　OILERS

PERSONAL: Born May 11, 1972, in Lebanon. ... 6-2/288. ... Name pronounced EE-shum el-mash-toob.
HIGH SCHOOL: Polyvalente Georges-Vanier (Montreal).
COLLEGE: Arizona.
TRANSACTIONS/CAREER NOTES: Selected by Edmonton Eskimos in first round (fifth pick overall) of 1995 CFL draft. ... Selected by Houston Oilers in sixth round (174th pick overall) of 1995 NFL draft. ... Signed with Oilers (July 20, 1995).
PLAYING EXPERIENCE: Houston NFL, 1995. ... Games: 1995 (2).

ELWAY, JOHN　　　　　QB　　　　　BRONCOS

PERSONAL: Born June 28, 1960, in Port Angeles, Wash. ... 6-3/215. ... Full name: John Albert Elway. ... Son of Jack Elway, scout, Denver Broncos.
HIGH SCHOOL: Granada Hills (Calif.).
COLLEGE: Stanford (degree in economics, 1983).
TRANSACTIONS/CAREER NOTES: Selected by Oakland Invaders in 1983 USFL territorial draft. ... Selected by Baltimore Colts in first round (first pick overall) of 1983 NFL draft. ... Rights traded by Colts to Denver Broncos for QB Mark Herrmann, rights to OL Chris Hinton and first-round pick (OG Ron Solt) in 1984 draft (May 2, 1983). ... Signed by Broncos (May 2, 1983).
CHAMPIONSHIP GAME EXPERIENCE: Played in AFC championship game (1986, 1987, 1989 and 1991 seasons). ... Played in Super Bowl XXI (1986 season), Super Bowl XXII (1987 season) and Super Bowl XXIV (1989 season).
HONORS: Named quarterback on THE SPORTING NEWS college All-America first team (1980 and 1982). ... Played in Pro Bowl (1986, 1987, 1993 and 1994 seasons). ... Named quarterback on THE SPORTING NEWS NFL All-Pro team (1987). ... Named to play in Pro Bowl (1989 season); replaced by Dave Krieg due to injury. ... Named to play in Pro Bowl as replacement for Dan Marino (1991); replaced by Ken O'Brien due to injury.
POSTSEASON RECORDS: Shares Super Bowl career record for most fumbles recovered—2.
PRO STATISTICS: 1983—Fumbled six times and recovered three fumbles. 1984—Fumbled 14 times and recovered five fumbles for minus 10 yards. 1985—Fumbled seven times and recovered two fumbles for minus 35 yards. 1986—Caught one pass for 23 yards and a touchdown, fumbled eight times and recovered one fumble for minus 13 yards. 1987—Punted once for 31 yards and fumbled twice. 1988—Punted three times for 117 yards, fumbled seven times and recovered five fumbles for minus nine yards. 1989—Punted once for 34 yards, fumbled nine times and recovered two fumbles for minus four yards. 1990—Punted once for 37 yards, fumbled eight times and recovered one fumble for minus three yards. 1991—Caught one pass for 24 yards, punted once for 34 yards, led league with 12 fumbles and recovered two fumbles. 1992—Fumbled 12 times and recovered one fumble. 1993—Fumbled eight times and recovered five fumbles for minus five yards. 1994—Fumbled 11 times and recovered two fumbles for minus five yards. 1995—Fumbled nine times and recovered one fumble for minus seven yards.
STATISTICAL PLATEAUS: 300-yard passing games: 1983 (1), 1984 (1), 1985 (3), 1986 (2), 1987 (4), 1988 (1), 1989 (1), 1990 (2), 1991 (1),

1992 (1), 1993 (3), 1994 (4), 1995 (5). Total: 29.

MISCELLANEOUS: Regular-season record as starting NFL quarterback: 113-74-1 (.604). ... Holds Denver Broncos all-time records for most yards passing (41,706) and most touchdown passes (225).

					PASSING						RUSHING				TOTALS		
Year	Team	G	Att.	Cmp.	Pct.	Yds.	TD	Int.	Avg.	Rat.	Att.	Yds.	Avg.	TD	TD	2pt.	Pts.
1983—Denver NFL		11	259	123	47.5	1663	7	14	6.42	54.9	28	146	5.2	1	1	...	6
1984—Denver NFL		15	380	214	56.3	2598	18	15	6.84	76.8	56	237	4.2	1	1	...	6.
1985—Denver NFL		16	*605	327	54.1	3891	22	23	6.43	70.2	51	253	5.0	0	0	...	0
1986—Denver NFL		16	504	280	55.6	3485	19	13	6.92	79.0	52	257	4.9	1	2	...	12
1987—Denver NFL		12	410	224	54.6	3198	19	12	7.80	83.4	66	304	4.6	4	4	...	24
1988—Denver NFL		15	496	274	55.2	3309	17	19	6.67	71.4	54	234	4.3	1	1	...	6
1989—Denver NFL		15	416	223	53.6	3051	18	18	7.34	73.7	48	244	5.1	3	3	...	18
1990—Denver NFL		16	502	294	58.6	3526	15	14	7.02	78.5	50	258	5.2	3	3	...	18
1991—Denver NFL		16	451	242	53.7	3253	13	12	7.21	75.4	55	255	4.6	6	6	...	36
1992—Denver NFL		12	316	174	55.1	2242	10	17	7.10	65.7	34	94	2.8	2	2	...	12
1993—Denver NFL		16	*551	*348	63.2	*4030	25	10	7.31	92.8	44	153	3.5	0	0	...	0
1994—Denver NFL		14	494	307	62.2	3490	16	10	7.07	85.7	58	235	4.1	4	4	0	24
1995—Denver NFL		16	542	316	58.3	3970	26	14	7.33	86.4	41	176	4.3	1	1	1	8
Pro totals (13 years)		190	5926	3346	56.5	41706	225	191	7.04	77.7	637	2846	4.5	27	28	1	170

RECORD AS BASEBALL PLAYER

TRANSACTIONS/CAREER NOTES: Threw right, batted left. ... Selected by Kansas City Royals organization in 18th round of free-agent draft (June 5, 1979); did not sign. ... Selected by New York Yankees organization in second round of free-agent draft (June 8, 1981). ... On temporary inactive list (August 2-September 13, 1982). ... On suspended list (April 8-18, 1983). ... Placed on restricted list (April 18, 1983).

							BATTING								FIELDING		
Year	Team (League)	Pos.	G	AB	R	H	2B	3B	HR	RBI	Avg.	BB	SO	SB	PO	A	E	Avg.
1982—Oneonta (NYP)	OF	42	151	26	48	6	2	4	25	.318	28	25	13	69	8	0	1.000

EMANUEL, BERT   WR   FALCONS

PERSONAL: Born October 27, 1970, in Kansas City, Mo. ... 5-10/175. ... Full name: Bert Tyrone Emanuel.
HIGH SCHOOL: Langham Creek (Houston).
COLLEGE: Rice.
TRANSACTIONS/CAREER NOTES: Selected by Atlanta Falcons in second round (45th pick overall) of 1994 NFL draft. ... Signed by Falcons (July 11, 1994).
PRO STATISTICS: 1994—Rushed twice for four yards and had only pass attempt intercepted. 1995—Rushed once for no yards.
STATISTICAL PLATEAUS: 100-yard receiving games: 1994 (1), 1995 (4). Total: 5.
MISCELLANEOUS: Selected by Toronto Blue Jays organization in 75th round of free-agent baseball draft (June 5, 1989); did not sign. ... Selected by Pittsburgh Pirates organization in 49th round of free-agent baseball draft (June 1, 1992); did not sign.

		RUSHING				RECEIVING				TOTALS			
Year	Team	G	Att.	Yds.	Avg.	TD	No.	Yds.	Avg.	TD	TD	2pt.	Pts.	Fum.
1994—Atlanta NFL	16	2	4	2.0	0	46	649	14.1	4	4	0	24	0
1995—Atlanta NFL	16	1	0	0.0	0	74	1039	14.0	5	5	0	30	2
Pro totals (2 years)	32	3	4	1.3	0	120	1688	14.1	9	9	0	54	2

EMTMAN, STEVE   DE   DOLPHINS

PERSONAL: Born April 16, 1970, in Spokane, Wash. ... 6-4/284. ... Full name: Steven Charles Emtman.
HIGH SCHOOL: Cheney (Wash.).
COLLEGE: Washington.
TRANSACTIONS/CAREER NOTES: Selected after junior season by Indianapolis Colts in first round (first pick overall) of 1992 NFL draft. ... Signed by Colts (April 25, 1992). ... On injured reserve with knee injury (November 11, 1992-remainder of season). ... Designated by Colts as transition player (February 25, 1993). ... On injured reserve with knee injury (October 12, 1993-remainder of season). ... Released by Colts (July 15, 1995). ... Signed by Miami Dolphins (July 27, 1995).
HONORS: Named defensive lineman on THE SPORTING NEWS college All-America second team (1990). ... Lombardi Award winner (1991). ... Outland Trophy winner (1991). ... Named defensive lineman on THE SPORTING NEWS college All-America first team (1991).
PRO STATISTICS: 1992—Intercepted one pass for 90 yards and a touchdown. 1994—Recovered one fumble. 1995—Recovered one fumble.

Year	Team	G	SACKS
1992—Indianapolis NFL	9	3.0
1993—Indianapolis NFL	5	1.0
1994—Indianapolis NFL	4	1.0
1995—Miami NFL	16	1.0
Pro totals (4 years)	34	6.0

ENGEL, GREG   C   CHARGERS

PERSONAL: Born January 18, 1971, in Davenport, Iowa. ... 6-3/285. ... Full name: Gregory Allen Engel.
HIGH SCHOOL: Bloomington (Ill.).
COLLEGE: Illinois.
TRANSACTIONS/CAREER NOTES: Signed as non-drafted free agent by San Diego Chargers (April 28, 1994). ... On inactive list for 16 games (1994).
PLAYING EXPERIENCE: San Diego NFL, 1995. ... Games: 1995 (10).

ENGLAND, ERIC   DE   CARDINALS

PERSONAL: Born March 25, 1971, in Fort Wayne, Ind. ... 6-2/283. ... Full name: Eric Jevon England.

HIGH SCHOOL: Willowridge (Sugar Land, Texas).
COLLEGE: Texas A&M.
TRANSACTIONS/CAREER NOTES: Selected by Arizona Cardinals in third round (89th pick overall) of 1994 NFL draft. ... Signed by Cardinals (July 30, 1994).
PLAYING EXPERIENCE: Arizona NFL, 1994 and 1995. ... Games: 1994 (11), 1995 (15). Total: 26.
PRO STATISTICS: 1995—Recovered two fumbles.

EPPS, TORY　　　　　　　　　DT　　　　　　　　　SAINTS

PERSONAL: Born May 28, 1967, in Uniontown, Pa. ... 6-1/280.
HIGH SCHOOL: Uniontown (Pa.) Area.
COLLEGE: Memphis State.
TRANSACTIONS/CAREER NOTES: Selected by Atlanta Falcons in eighth round (195th pick overall) of 1990 NFL draft. ... Signed by Falcons (July 27, 1990). ... Granted free agency (February 1, 1992). ... Re-signed by Falcons (July 27, 1992). ... Released by Falcons (October 15, 1993). ... Claimed on waivers by San Diego Chargers (October 19, 1993). ... Released by Chargers (October 29, 1993). ... Signed by Chicago Bears (November 9, 1993). ... Granted unconditional free agency (February 17, 1995). ... Signed by New Orleans Saints (April 27, 1995).
PRO STATISTICS: 1991—Recovered one fumble. 1992—Recovered one fumble.

Year　Team	G	SACKS
1990—Atlanta NFL	16	3.0
1991—Atlanta NFL	16	1.5
1992—Atlanta NFL	16	0.0
1993—Atlanta NFL	2	0.0
—Chicago NFL	3	0.0
1994—Chicago NFL	5	1.0
1995—New Orleans NFL	12	0.0
Pro totals (6 years)	70	5.5

ERICKSON, CRAIG　　　　　　　QB　　　　　　　　　COLTS

PERSONAL: Born May 17, 1969, in Boynton Beach, Fla. ... 6-2/205. ... Full name: Craig Neil Erickson.
HIGH SCHOOL: Cardinal Newman (West Palm Beach, Fla.).
COLLEGE: Miami, Fla. (degree in business).
TRANSACTIONS/CAREER NOTES: Selected by Philadelphia Eagles in fifth round (131st pick overall) of 1991 NFL draft; did not sign. ... Selected by Tampa Bay Buccaneers in fourth round (86th pick overall) of 1992 NFL draft. ... Signed by Buccaneers (July 10, 1992). ... Granted free agency (February 17, 1995). ... Re-signed by Buccaneers (April 26, 1995). ... Traded by Buccaneers to Indianapolis Colts for first-round pick (DT Marcus Jones) and conditional fourth-round picks in 1996 draft (April 26, 1995).
CHAMPIONSHIP GAME EXPERIENCE: Member of Colts for AFC championship game (1995 season); did not play.
PRO STATISTICS: 1993—Fumbled nine times and recovered six fumbles for minus two yards. 1994—Fumbled six times and recovered one fumble for minus one yard. 1995—Fumbled twice for minus four yards.
STATISTICAL PLATEAUS: 300-yard passing games: 1993 (1), 1994 (1). Total: 2.
MISCELLANEOUS: Graduate assistant football coach, University of Georgia (1991). ... Regular-season record as starting NFL quarterback: 13-19 (.406).

Year　Team	G		PASSING								RUSHING				TOTALS	
		Att.	Cmp.	Pct.	Yds.	TD	Int.	Avg.	Rat.	Att.	Yds.	Avg.	TD	TD	2pt.	Pts.
1992—Tampa Bay NFL	6	26	15	57.7	121	0	0	4.65	69.6	1	-1	-1.0	0	0	...	0
1993—Tampa Bay NFL	16	457	233	51.0	3054	18	21	6.68	66.4	26	96	3.7	0	0	...	0
1994—Tampa Bay NFL	15	399	225	56.4	2919	16	10	7.32	82.5	26	68	2.6	1	1	0	6
1995—Indianapolis NFL	6	83	50	60.2	586	3	4	7.06	73.7	9	14	1.6	0	0	0	0
Pro totals (4 years)	43	965	523	54.2	6680	37	35	6.92	73.8	62	177	2.9	1	1	0	6

ERVINS, RICKY　　　　　　　　RB

PERSONAL: Born December 7, 1968, in Fort Wayne, Ind. ... 5-7/195.
HIGH SCHOOL: John Muir (Pasadena, Calif.).
COLLEGE: Southern California.
TRANSACTIONS/CAREER NOTES: Selected by Washington Redskins in third round (76th pick overall) of 1991 NFL draft. ... Signed by Redskins for 1991 season. ... Granted free agency (February 17, 1994). ... Re-signed by Redskins (June 14, 1994). ... Granted unconditional free agency (February 17, 1995). ... Signed by San Francisco 49ers (July 15, 1995). ... Granted unconditional free agency (February 16, 1996).
CHAMPIONSHIP GAME EXPERIENCE: Played in NFC championship game (1991 season). ... Member of Super Bowl championship team (1991 season).
PRO STATISTICS: 1991—Recovered one fumble. 1992—Recovered one fumble.
STATISTICAL PLATEAUS: 100-yard rushing games: 1991 (1).

Year　Team	G		RUSHING				RECEIVING				KICKOFF RETURNS				TOTALS	
		Att.	Yds.	Avg.	TD	No.	Yds.	Avg.	TD	No.	Yds.	Avg.	TD	TD	2pt.	Pts.	Fum.
1991—Washington NFL	15	145	680	4.7	3	16	181	11.3	1	11	232	21.1	0	4	...	24	1
1992—Washington NFL	16	151	495	3.3	2	32	252	7.9	0	0	0	...	0	2	...	12	1
1993—Washington NFL	15	50	201	4.0	0	16	123	7.7	0	2	29	14.5	0	0	...	0	2
1994—Washington NFL	16	185	650	3.5	3	51	293	5.8	1	1	17	17.0	0	4	0	24	1
1995—San Francisco NFL	14	23	88	3.8	0	2	21	10.5	0	5	32	6.4	0	0	0	0	0
Pro totals (5 years)	76	554	2114	3.8	8	117	870	7.4	2	19	310	16.3	0	10	0	60	5

ESIASON, BOOMER　　　　　　QB　　　　　　　CARDINALS

PERSONAL: Born April 17, 1961, in West Islip, N.Y. ... 6-5/224. ... Full name: Norman Julius Esiason.

HIGH SCHOOL: East Islip (Islip Terrace, N.Y.).

COLLEGE: Maryland.

TRANSACTIONS/CAREER NOTES: Selected by Washington Federals in 1984 USFL territorial draft. ... Selected by Cincinnati Bengals in second round (38th pick overall) of 1984 NFL draft. ... Signed by Bengals (June 19, 1984). ... Traded by Bengals to New York Jets for third-round pick (DT Ty Parten) in 1993 draft (March 17, 1993). ... Granted unconditional free agency (February 16, 1996). ... Signed by Arizona Cardinals (April 8, 1996).

CHAMPIONSHIP GAME EXPERIENCE: Played in AFC championship game (1988 season). ... Played in Super Bowl XXIII (1988 season).

HONORS: Named quarterback on THE SPORTING NEWS college All-America second team (1983). ... Played in Pro Bowl (1986 and 1993 seasons). ... Named NFL Player of the Year by THE SPORTING NEWS (1988). ... Named quarterback on THE SPORTING NEWS NFL All-Pro team (1988). ... Named to play in Pro Bowl (1988 season); replaced by Jim Kelly due to injury. ... Named to play in Pro Bowl (1989 season); replaced by John Elway due to injury.

PRO STATISTICS: 1984—Fumbled four times and recovered two fumbles for minus two yards. 1985—Fumbled nine times and recovered four fumbles for minus five yards. 1986—Punted once for 31 yards, fumbled 12 times and recovered five fumbles for minus 10 yards. 1987—Punted twice for 68 yards, fumbled 10 times and recovered four fumbles for minus eight yards. 1988—Punted once for 21 yards, fumbled five times and recovered four fumbles. 1989—Fumbled eight times and recovered two fumbles for minus four yards. 1990—Fumbled 11 times and recovered two fumbles for minus 23 yards. 1991—Fumbled 10 times and recovered three fumbles for minus five yards. 1992—Fumbled 12 times. 1993—Caught one pass for minus eight yards, fumbled 13 times and recovered five fumbles for minus 10 yards. 1994—Fumbled 11 times and recovered three fumbles for minus 11 yards. 1995—Fumbled 12 times and recovered four fumbles for minus 27 yards.

STATISTICAL PLATEAUS: 300-yard passing games: 1985 (4), 1986 (3), 1987 (5), 1988 (3), 1989 (4), 1990 (1), 1991 (2), 1993 (2), 1994 (1), 1995 (1). Total: 26.

MISCELLANEOUS: Regular-season record as starting NFL quarterback: 73-86 (.459).

		PASSING								RUSHING				TOTALS		
Year Team	G	Att.	Cmp.	Pct.	Yds.	TD	Int.	Avg.	Rat.	Att.	Yds.	Avg.	TD	TD	2pt.	Pts.
1984—Cincinnati NFL	10	102	51	50.0	530	3	3	5.20	62.9	19	63	3.3	2	2	...	12
1985—Cincinnati NFL	15	431	251	58.2	3443	27	12	7.99	93.2	33	79	2.4	1	1	...	6
1986—Cincinnati NFL	16	469	273	58.2	3959	24	17	*8.44	87.7	44	146	3.3	1	1	...	6
1987—Cincinnati NFL	12	440	240	54.6	3321	16	19	7.55	73.1	52	241	4.6	0	0	...	0
1988—Cincinnati NFL	16	388	223	57.5	3572	28	14	*9.21	*97.4	43	248	5.8	1	1	...	6
1989—Cincinnati NFL	16	455	258	56.7	3525	28	11	7.75	92.1	47	278	5.9	0	0	...	0
1990—Cincinnati NFL	16	402	224	55.7	3031	24	*22	7.54	77.0	49	157	3.2	0	0	...	0
1991—Cincinnati NFL	14	413	233	56.4	2883	13	16	6.98	72.5	24	66	2.8	0	0	...	0
1992—Cincinnati NFL	12	278	144	51.8	1407	11	15	5.06	57.0	21	66	3.1	0	0	...	0
1993—New York Jets NFL	16	473	288	60.9	3421	16	11	7.23	84.5	45	118	2.6	1	1	...	6
1994—New York Jets NFL	15	440	255	58.0	2782	17	13	6.32	77.3	28	59	2.1	0	0	...	0
1995—New York Jets NFL	12	389	221	56.8	2275	16	15	5.85	71.4	19	14	.7	0	0	...	0
Pro totals (12 years)	170	4680	2661	56.9	34149	223	168	7.30	80.8	424	1535	3.6	6	6	0	36

EVANS, CHUCK — FB — VIKINGS

PERSONAL: Born April 16, 1967, in Augusta, Ga. ... 6-1/240.

HIGH SCHOOL: Glenn Hills (Augusta, Ga.).

COLLEGE: Clark Atlanta (Ga.).

TRANSACTIONS/CAREER NOTES: Selected by Minnesota Vikings in 11th round (295th pick overall) of 1992 NFL draft. ... Signed by Vikings (June 10, 1992). ... Released by Vikings (August 31, 1992). ... Re-signed by Vikings (February 10, 1993). ... On injured reserve with wrist injury (October 11, 1993-remainder of season). ... Granted free agency (February 16, 1996).

		RUSHING				RECEIVING				KICKOFF RETURNS				TOTALS			
Year Team	G	Att.	Yds.	Avg.	TD	No.	Yds.	Avg.	TD	No.	Yds.	Avg.	TD	TD	2pt.	Pts.	Fum.
1992—							Did not play.										
1993—Minnesota NFL	3	14	32	2.3	0	4	39	9.8	0	1	11	11.0	0	0	...	0	0
1994—Minnesota NFL	14	6	20	3.3	0	1	2	2.0	0	1	4	4.0	0	0	0	0	0
1995—Minnesota NFL	16	19	59	3.1	1	18	119	6.6	1	0	0	...	0	2	0	12	0
Pro totals (3 years)	33	39	111	2.9	1	23	160	7.0	1	2	15	7.5	0	2	0	12	0

EVANS, DONALD — DE/DT

PERSONAL: Born March 14, 1964, in Raleigh, N.C. ... 6-2/282. ... Full name: Donald Lee Evans.

HIGH SCHOOL: Athens Drive Senior (Raleigh, N.C.).

COLLEGE: Winston-Salem State (N.C.).

TRANSACTIONS/CAREER NOTES: Selected by Los Angeles Rams in second round (47th pick overall) of 1987 NFL draft. ... Signed by Rams (August 1, 1987). ... On injured reserve with strained abdomen (September 7-December 8, 1987). ... Released by Rams (August 30, 1988). ... Signed by Philadelphia Eagles (September 8, 1988). ... On injured reserve with fractured jaw (October 13, 1988-remainder of season). ... Released by Eagles (September 5, 1989). ... Signed by Pittsburgh Steelers (April 24, 1990). ... Granted unconditional free agency (February 17, 1994). ... Signed by New York Jets (March 14, 1994). ... On injured reserve with ankle injury (November 1, 1995-remainder of season). ... Released by Jets (March 26, 1996).

PRO STATISTICS: 1987—Rushed three times for 10 yards. 1990—Recovered three fumbles for 59 yards. 1991—Recovered one fumble. 1992—Recovered two fumbles. 1994—Recovered one fumble. 1995—Recovered one fumble.

Year Team	G	SACKS
1987—Los Angeles Rams NFL	1	0.0
1988—Philadelphia NFL	5	0.0
1989—	Did not play.	
1990—Pittsburgh NFL	16	3.0
1991—Pittsburgh NFL	16	2.0
1992—Pittsburgh NFL	16	3.0
1993—Pittsburgh NFL	16	6.5
1994—New York Jets NFL	16	0.5
1995—New York Jets NFL	4	2.0
Pro totals (8 years)	90	17.0

EVANS, DOUG   CB   PACKERS

PERSONAL: Born May 13, 1970, in Shreveport, La. ... 6-0/190. ... Full name: Douglas Edwards Evans. ... Brother of Bobby Evans, safety, Winnipeg Blue Bombers of CFL (1990-1994).
HIGH SCHOOL: Haynesville (La.).
COLLEGE: Louisiana Tech (degree in finance).
TRANSACTIONS/CAREER NOTES: Selected by Green Bay Packers in sixth round (141st pick overall) of 1993 NFL draft. ... Signed by Packers (July 9, 1993).
CHAMPIONSHIP GAME EXPERIENCE: Played in NFC championship game (1995 season).
PRO STATISTICS: 1993—Recovered two fumbles. 1994—Credited with one sack and recovered one fumble for three yards. 1995—Credited with one sack, returned one punt for no yards and fumbled once.

		INTERCEPTIONS			
Year Team	G	No.	Yds.	Avg.	TD
1993—Green Bay NFL	16	1	0	0.0	0
1994—Green Bay NFL	16	1	0	0.0	0
1995—Green Bay NFL	16	2	24	12.0	0
Pro totals (3 years)	48	4	24	6.0	0

EVANS, GREG   S   BILLS

PERSONAL: Born June 28, 1971, in Daingerfield, Texas. ... 6-1/208.
HIGH SCHOOL: Daingerfield (Texas).
COLLEGE: Texas Christian (degree in criminal justice).
TRANSACTIONS/CAREER NOTES: Signed as non-drafted free agent by Buffalo Bills (May 19, 1994). ... Released by Bills (August 22, 1994). ... Re-signed by Bills to practice squad (August 26, 1994). ... Activated (December 24, 1994); did not play.
PLAYING EXPERIENCE: Buffalo NFL, 1995. ... Games: 1995 (16).
PRO STATISTICS: 1995—Intercepted one pass for 18 yards and recovered one fumble for three yards.

EVANS, JERRY   TE   BRONCOS

PERSONAL: Born September 28, 1968, in Lorain, Ohio. ... 6-4/250. ... Full name: Gerald Kristin Evans.
HIGH SCHOOL: Admiral King (Lorain, Ohio).
COLLEGE: Toledo.
TRANSACTIONS/CAREER NOTES: Selected by Phoenix Cardinals in eighth round (204th pick overall) of 1991 NFL draft. ... Signed by Cardinals (July 13, 1991). ... Released by Cardinals (August 26, 1991). ... Re-signed by Cardinals to practice squad (August 27, 1991). ... Released by Cardinals (September 23, 1991). ... Signed by Green Bay Packers to practice squad (November 15, 1991). ... Released by Packers (December 10, 1991). ... Re-signed by Packers to practice squad (December 19, 1991). ... Assigned by Packers to Barcelona Dragons in 1992 World League allocation enhancement program (February 20, 1992). ... Released by Dragons (April 1, 1992). ... Released by Packers (August 31, 1992). ... Signed by Denver Broncos (April 13, 1993). ... On injured reserve with knee injury (December 5, 1995-remainder of season). ... Granted free agency (February 16, 1996).
PRO STATISTICS: 1994—Returned one kickoff for six yards.

		RECEIVING				TOTALS			
Year Team	G	No.	Yds.	Avg.	TD	TD	2pt.	Pts.	Fum.
1991—					Did not play.				
1992—Barcelona W.L.	2	3	34	11.3	0	0		0	0
1993—Denver NFL	14	0	0	...	0	0	...	0	0
1994—Denver NFL	16	13	127	9.8	2	2	0	12	0
1995—Denver NFL	13	12	124	10.3	1	1	0	6	1
W.L. totals (1 year)	2	3	34	11.3	0	0	0	0	0
NFL totals (3 years)	43	25	251	10.1	3	3	0	18	1
Pro totals (4 years)	45	28	285	10.2	3	3	0	18	1

EVANS, JOSH   DL   OILERS

PERSONAL: Born September 6, 1972, in Langdale, Ala. ... 6-0/280. ... Full name: Mijoshki Antwon Evans.
HIGH SCHOOL: Lanett (Ala.).
COLLEGE: Alabama-Birmingham.
TRANSACTIONS/CAREER NOTES: Signed as non-drafted free agent by Dallas Cowboys (April 27, 1995). ... Released by Cowboys (August 22, 1995). ... Signed by Houston Oilers to practice squad (September 1, 1995). ... Activated (November 10, 1995).
PLAYING EXPERIENCE: Houston NFL, 1995. ... Games: 1995 (7).

EVANS, VINCE   QB

PERSONAL: Born June 14, 1955, in Greensboro, N.C. ... 6-2/215. ... Full name: Vincent Tobias Evans.
HIGH SCHOOL: Benjamin L. Smith (Greensboro, N.C.).
JUNIOR COLLEGE: Los Angeles City College.
COLLEGE: Southern California.
TRANSACTIONS/CAREER NOTES: Selected by Chicago Bears in sixth round (140th pick overall) of 1977 NFL draft. ... On injured reserve with staph infection (October 12, 1979-remainder of season). ... USFL rights traded by Los Angeles Express to Washington Federals for rights to CB Johnny Lynn (November 11, 1983). ... Signed by Chicago Blitz of USFL (November 14, 1983), for contract to take effect after being granted free agency (February 1, 1984). ... USFL rights traded by Federals to Blitz for LB Ben Apuna and rights to WR Waddell Smith (December 27, 1983). ... Blitz franchise disbanded (November 20, 1984). ... Traded by Blitz with LB Kelvin Atkins, LB Jay Wilson and LB Ed Thomas to Denver Gold for past considerations (December 6, 1984). ... Contract rights returned to Blitz (August 2, 1985). ... Granted free agency when

USFL suspended operations (August 7, 1986). ... Signed as replacement player by Los Angeles Raiders (September 24, 1987). ... Released by Raiders (October 10, 1988). ... Re-signed by Raiders (November 30, 1988). ... Active for six games with Raiders (1988); did not play. ... Released by Raiders (September 3, 1990). ... Re-signed by Raiders (September 4, 1990). ... Granted unconditional free agency (February 1-April 1, 1991). ... Re-signed by Raiders for 1991 season. ... Released by Raiders (August 26, 1991). ... Re-signed by Raiders (August 27, 1991). ... Granted unconditional free agency (February 1-April 1, 1992). ... Re-signed by Raiders for 1992 season. ... Released by Raiders (August 31, 1992). ... Re-signed by Raiders (September 2, 1992). ... Released by Raiders (September 4, 1992). ... Re-signed by Raiders (October 1, 1992). ... Released by Raiders (October 13, 1992). ... Re-signed by Raiders (October 21, 1992). ... Granted unconditional free agency (March 1, 1993). ... Re-signed by Raiders for 1993 season. ... Raiders franchise moved to Oakland (July 21, 1995). ... Granted unconditional free agency (February 16, 1996).
CHAMPIONSHIP GAME EXPERIENCE: Played in AFC championship game (1990 season).
PRO STATISTICS: NFL: 1977—Returned 13 kickoffs for 253 yards (19.5-yard avg.), fumbled three times and recovered two fumbles. 1979—Fumbled once. 1980—Fumbled four times. 1981—Fumbled 13 times and recovered two fumbles for minus 10 yards. 1982—Fumbled once. 1983—Fumbled four times. 1989—Fumbled once. 1992—Fumbled once. 1993—Fumbled four times. 1994—Recovered one fumble. 1995—Fumbled five times for minus four yards. USFL: 1984—Fumbled six times and recovered two fumbles. 1985—Fumbled three times.
STATISTICAL PLATEAUS: NFL: 300-yard passing games: 1980 (1), 1981 (1), 1983 (1), 1995 (1). Total: 4. ... USFL: 300-yard passing games: 1984 (1), 1985 (1). Total: 2.
MISCELLANEOUS: Regular-season record as starting NFL quarterback: 14-25 (.359).

				PASSING						RUSHING				TOTALS		
Year Team	G	Att.	Cmp.	Pct.	Yds.	TD	Int.	Avg.	Rat.	Att.	Yds.	Avg.	TD	TD	2pt.	Pts.
1977—Chicago NFL	13	0	0	...	0	0	0	...	...	1	0	0.0	0	0	...	0
1978—Chicago NFL	3	3	1	33.3	38	0	1	12.67	42.4	6	23	3.8	0	0	...	0
1979—Chicago NFL	4	63	32	50.8	508	4	5	8.06	66.1	12	72	6.0	1	1	...	6
1980—Chicago NFL	13	278	148	53.2	2039	11	16	7.34	66.2	60	306	5.1	8	8	...	48
1981—Chicago NFL	16	436	195	44.7	2354	11	20	5.40	51.1	43	218	5.1	3	3	...	18
1982—Chicago NFL	4	28	12	42.9	125	0	4	4.47	16.8	2	0	0.0	0	0	...	0
1983—Chicago NFL	9	145	76	52.4	1108	5	7	7.64	69.0	22	142	6.5	1	1	...	6
1984—Chicago USFL	15	411	200	48.7	2624	14	22	6.39	58.3	30	144	4.8	6	6	0	36
1985—Denver USFL	14	325	157	48.3	2259	12	16	6.95	63.1	43	283	6.6	7	7	0	42
1986—							Did not play.									
1987—Los Angeles Raiders NFL	3	83	39	47.0	630	5	4	7.59	72.9	11	144	13.1	1	1	...	6
1988—Los Angeles Raiders NFL							Did not play.									
1989—Los Angeles Raiders NFL	1	2	2	100.0	50	0	0	25.00	118.8	1	16	16.0	0	0	...	0
1990—Los Angeles Raiders NFL	5	1	1	100.0	36	0	0	36.00	118.8	1	-2	-2.0	0	0	...	0
1991—Los Angeles Raiders NFL	4	14	6	42.9	127	1	2	9.07	59.8	8	20	2.5	0	0	...	0
1992—Los Angeles Raiders NFL	5	53	29	54.7	372	4	3	7.02	78.5	11	79	7.2	0	0	...	0
1993—Los Angeles Raiders NFL	8	76	45	59.2	640	3	4	8.42	77.7	14	51	3.6	0	0	...	0
1994—Los Angeles Raiders NFL	9	33	18	54.6	222	2	0	6.73	95.8	6	24	4.0	0	0	...	0
1995—Oakland NFL	9	175	100	57.1	1236	6	8	7.06	71.5	14	36	2.6	0	0	...	0
USFL totals (2 years)	29	736	357	485	4883	26	38	6.64	60.4	73	427	5.9	13	13	0	78
NFL totals (15 years)	106	1390	704	507	9485	52	74	6.82	63.0	212	1129	5.3	14	14	0	84
Pro totals (17 years)	135	2126	1061	49.9	14368	78	112	6.76	62.1	285	1556	5.5	27	27	0	162

EVERETT, JIM   QB   SAINTS

E

PERSONAL: Born January 3, 1963, in Emporia, Kan. ... 6-5/212. ... Full name: James Samuel Everett III.
HIGH SCHOOL: Eldorado (Albuquerque, N.M.).
COLLEGE: Purdue (degree in finance, 1986).
TRANSACTIONS/CAREER NOTES: Selected by Houston Oilers in first round (third pick overall) of 1986 NFL draft. ... Selected by Memphis Showboats in first round (fourth pick overall) of 1986 USFL draft. ... NFL rights traded by Oilers to Los Angeles Rams for G Kent Hill, DE William Fuller, first-round (WR Haywood Jeffires) and fifth-round (RB Spencer Tillman) picks in 1987 draft and first-round pick (traded to Rams) in 1988 draft (September 18, 1986). ... Signed by Rams (September 25, 1986). ... Granted roster exemption (September 25-30, 1986). ... Crossed picket line during players strike (October 14, 1987). ... Designated by Rams as transition player (February 25, 1993). ... Traded by Rams to New Orleans Saints for seventh-round pick (CB Herman O'Berry) in 1995 draft (March 18, 1994).
CHAMPIONSHIP GAME EXPERIENCE: Played in NFC championship game (1989 season).
HONORS: Named to play in Pro Bowl (1989 season); replaced by Randall Cunningham due to injury. ... Played in Pro Bowl (1990 season).
PRO STATISTICS: 1986—Fumbled twice. 1987—Fumbled twice and recovered one fumble. 1988—Fumbled seven times. 1989—Fumbled four times and recovered four fumbles for minus one yard. 1990—Fumbled four times. 1991—Led league with 12 fumbles and recovered one fumble for minus four yards. 1992—Fumbled five times. 1993—Fumbled seven times and recovered one fumble for minus one yard. 1994—Fumbled three times. 1995—Fumbled six times for minus six yards.
STATISTICAL PLATEAUS: 300-yard passing games: 1987 (1), 1988 (5), 1989 (4), 1990 (4), 1991 (4), 1992 (1), 1993 (1), 1994 (2), 1995 (2). Total: 24.
MISCELLANEOUS: Regular-season record as starting NFL quarterback: 60-77 (.438). ... Holds Rams franchise all-time record for most yards passing (23,758).

				PASSING						RUSHING				TOTALS		
Year Team	G	Att.	Cmp.	Pct.	Yds.	TD	Int.	Avg.	Rat.	Att.	Yds.	Avg.	TD	TD	2pt.	Pts.
1986—Los Angeles Rams NFL	6	147	73	49.7	1018	8	8	6.93	67.8	16	46	2.9	1	1	...	6
1987—Los Angeles Rams NFL	11	302	162	53.6	2064	10	13	6.84	68.4	18	83	4.6	1	1	...	6
1988—Los Angeles Rams NFL	16	517	308	59.6	3964	*31	18	7.67	89.2	34	104	3.1	0	0	...	0
1989—Los Angeles Rams NFL	16	518	304	58.7	4310	*29	17	8.32	90.6	25	31	1.2	1	1	...	6
1990—Los Angeles Rams NFL	16	554	307	55.4	3989	23	17	7.20	79.3	20	31	1.6	1	1	...	6
1991—Los Angeles Rams NFL	16	490	277	56.5	3438	11	20	7.02	68.9	27	44	1.6	0	0	...	0
1992—Los Angeles Rams NFL	16	475	281	59.2	3323	22	18	7.00	80.2	32	133	4.2	0	0	...	0
1993—Los Angeles Rams NFL	10	274	135	49.3	1652	8	12	6.03	59.7	19	38	2.0	0	0	...	0
1994—New Orleans NFL	16	540	346	64.1	3855	22	18	7.14	84.9	15	35	2.3	0	0	...	0
1995—New Orleans NFL	16	567	345	60.9	3970	26	14	7.00	87.0	24	42	1.8	0	0	...	0
Pro totals (10 years)	139	4384	2538	57.9	31583	190	155	7.21	80.1	230	587	2.6	4	4	0	24

EVERETT, THOMAS   S

PERSONAL: Born November 21, 1964, in Daingerfield, Texas. ... 5-9/190. ... Full name: Thomas Gregory Everett. ... Brother of Eric Everett,

cornerback with four NFL teams (1988-1992).
HIGH SCHOOL: Daingerfield (Texas).
COLLEGE: Baylor (degree in physical education).
TRANSACTIONS/CAREER NOTES: Selected by Pittsburgh Steelers in fourth round (94th pick overall) of 1987 NFL draft. ... Signed by Steelers (July 26, 1987). ... Granted free agency (February 1, 1992). ... Traded by Steelers to Dallas Cowboys for fifth-round pick (LB Marc Woodard) in 1993 draft (September 19, 1992). ... Signed by Cowboys (September 19, 1992). ... Activated (October 3, 1992). ... Traded by Cowboys to Tampa Bay Buccaneers for fourth-round pick (WR Willie Jackson) in 1994 draft (April 5, 1994). ... Released by Buccaneers (March 21, 1996).
CHAMPIONSHIP GAME EXPERIENCE: Played in NFC championship game (1992 and 1993 seasons). ... Member of Super Bowl championship team (1992 and 1993 seasons).
HONORS: Named defensive back on THE SPORTING NEWS college All-America second team (1985). ... Jim Thorpe Award winner (1986). ... Named defensive back on THE SPORTING NEWS college All-America first team (1986). ... Named to play in Pro Bowl (1993 season); replaced by LeRoy Butler due to injury.
PRO STATISTICS: 1987—Returned four punts for 22 yards, fumbled once and recovered two fumbles for seven yards. 1988—Recovered two fumbles for 38 yards. 1989—Fumbled once and recovered one fumble for 21 yards. 1991—Recovered two fumbles for 18 yards. 1992—Recovered two fumbles for 15 yards. 1994—Returned two punts for two yards and recovered one fumble. 1995—Credited with one sack and recovered one fumble.

			INTERCEPTIONS		
Year Team	G	No.	Yds.	Avg.	TD
1987—Pittsburgh NFL	12	3	22	7.3	0
1988—Pittsburgh NFL	14	3	31	10.3	0
1989—Pittsburgh NFL	16	3	68	22.7	0
1990—Pittsburgh NFL	15	3	2	0.7	0
1991—Pittsburgh NFL	16	4	53	13.3	0
1992—Dallas NFL	11	2	28	14.0	0
1993—Dallas NFL	16	2	25	12.5	0
1994—Tampa Bay NFL	15	1	26	26.0	0
1995—Tampa Bay NFL	13	0	0	...	0
Pro totals (9 years)	128	21	255	12.2	0

EVERITT, STEVE   C   RAVENS

PERSONAL: Born August 21, 1970, in Miami. ... 6-5/290. ... Full name: Steven Michael Everitt.
HIGH SCHOOL: Southridge (Miami).
COLLEGE: Michigan (degree in fine arts, 1993).
TRANSACTIONS/CAREER NOTES: Selected by Cleveland Browns in first round (14th pick overall) of 1993 NFL draft. ... Signed by Browns (July 15, 1993). ... Designated by Browns as transition player (February 15, 1994). ... Browns franchise moved to Baltimore and renamed Ravens for 1996 season (March 11, 1996).
PLAYING EXPERIENCE: Cleveland NFL, 1993-1995. ... Games: 1993 (16), 1994 (15), 1995 (15). Total: 46.
HONORS: Named center on THE SPORTING NEWS college All-America second team (1992).
PRO STATISTICS: 1993—Recovered two fumbles. 1995—Recovered one fumble.

FANN, CHAD   TE   CARDINALS

PERSONAL: Born June 7, 1970, in Jacksonville. ... 6-3/250. ... Full name: Chad Fitzgerald Fann.
HIGH SCHOOL: Ribault (Jacksonville).
COLLEGE: Mississippi, then Florida A&M.
TRANSACTIONS/CAREER NOTES: Signed as non-drafted free agent by Phoenix Cardinals (April 28, 1993). ... Released by Cardinals (August 23, 1993). ... Re-signed by Cardinals to practice squad (October 24, 1993). ... Activated (November 4, 1993). ... Cardinals franchise renamed Arizona Cardinals for 1994 season. ... Granted free agency (February 16, 1996).

		RECEIVING				TOTALS			
Year Team	G	No.	Yds.	Avg.	TD	TD	2pt.	Pts.	Fum.
1993—Phoenix NFL	1	0	0	...	0	0	...	0	0
1994—Arizona NFL	16	12	96	8.0	0	0	0	0	1
1995—Arizona NFL	16	5	41	8.2	0	0	0	0	1
Pro totals (3 years)	33	17	137	8.1	0	0	0	0	2

FARR, D'MARCO   DT   RAMS

PERSONAL: Born June 9, 1971, in San Pablo, Calif. ... 6-1/270. ... Cousin of Mel Farr Sr., running back, Detroit Lions (1967-1973); cousin of Mel Farr Jr., running back, Los Angeles Rams and Sacramento Surge of World League (1989 and 1991); and cousin of Mike Farr, wide receiver, Detroit Lions (1990-1992).
HIGH SCHOOL: John F. Kennedy (Richmond, Calif.).
COLLEGE: Washington.
TRANSACTIONS/CAREER NOTES: Signed as non-drafted free agent by Los Angeles Rams (May 4, 1994). ... On injured reserve with dislocated left elbow (December 7, 1994-remainder of season). ... Rams franchise moved to St. Louis (April 12, 1995).
PRO STATISTICS: 1994—Returned one kickoff for 16 yards. 1995—Intercepted one pass for five yards.

Year Team	G	No.
1994—Los Angeles Rams NFL	10	1.0
1995—St. Louis NFL	16	11.5
Pro totals (2 years)	26	12.5

FARYNIARZ, BRETT   LB

PERSONAL: Born July 23, 1965, in Carmichael, Calif. ... 6-3/230. ... Full name: Brett Allen Faryniarz. ... Name pronounced FAIR-in-nezz.

E

F

HIGH SCHOOL: Cordova Senior (Rancho Cordova, Calif.).

COLLEGE: San Diego State.

TRANSACTIONS/CAREER NOTES: Signed as non-drafted free agent by Los Angeles Rams (June 17, 1988). ... Granted free agency (February 1, 1990). ... Re-signed by Rams (July 27, 1990). ... Granted free agency (February 1, 1991). ... Re-signed by Rams (July 17, 1991). ... Granted unconditional free agency (February 1, 1992). ... Signed by Atlanta Falcons (March 31, 1992). ... Released by Falcons prior to 1992 season. ... Signed by San Francisco 49ers (April 30, 1993). ... Released by 49ers (August 30, 1993). ... Re-signed by 49ers (September 1, 1993). ... Released by 49ers (September 21, 1993). ... Signed by Houston Oilers (July 7, 1994). ... Granted unconditional free agency (February 17, 1995). ... Signed by Carolina Panthers (July 15, 1995). ... Granted unconditional free agency (February 16, 1996).

CHAMPIONSHIP GAME EXPERIENCE: Played in NFC championship game (1989 season).

PRO STATISTICS: 1989—Recovered two fumbles. 1991—Recovered one fumble.

Year Team	G	No.
1988—Los Angeles Rams NFL	15	1.0
1989—Los Angeles Rams NFL	16	3.0
1990—Los Angeles Rams NFL	16	2.0
1991—Los Angeles Rams NFL	12	0.0
1992—	Did not play.	
1993—San Francisco NFL	2	0.0
1994—Houston NFL	16	0.0
1995—Carolina NFL	15	0.0
Pro totals (7 years)	92	6.0

FAULK, MARSHALL   RB   COLTS

PERSONAL: Born February 26, 1973, in New Orleans. ... 5-10/205. ... Full name: Marshall William Faulk.

HIGH SCHOOL: George Washington Carver (New Orleans).

COLLEGE: San Diego State.

TRANSACTIONS/CAREER NOTES: Selected after junior season by Indianapolis Colts in first round (second pick overall) of 1994 NFL draft. ... Signed by Colts (July 24, 1994).

CHAMPIONSHIP GAME EXPERIENCE: Member of Colts for AFC championship game (1995 season); inactive.

HONORS: Named running back on THE SPORTING NEWS college All-America first team (1991-1993). ... Named NFL Rookie of the Year by THE SPORTING NEWS (1994). ... Played in Pro Bowl (1994 and 1995 seasons). ... Named Outstanding Player of Pro Bowl (1994 season).

PRO STATISTICS: 1994—Recovered one fumble. 1995—Recovered one fumble.

STATISTICAL PLATEAUS: 100-yard rushing games: 1994 (4), 1995 (1). Total: 5. ... 100-yard receiving games: 1994 (1).

		RUSHING				RECEIVING				TOTALS			
Year Team	G	Att.	Yds.	Avg.	TD	No.	Yds.	Avg.	TD	TD	2pt.	Pts.	Fum.
1994—Indianapolis NFL	16	314	1282	4.1	11	52	522	10.0	1	12	0	72	5
1995—Indianapolis NFL	16	289	1078	3.7	11	56	475	8.5	3	14	0	84	8
Pro totals (2 years)	32	603	2360	3.9	22	108	997	9.2	4	26	0	156	13

FAULKERSON, MIKE   FB   BEARS

PERSONAL: Born September 9, 1970, in Kingsport, Tenn. ... 6-0/237. ... Full name: Michael Wayne Faulkerson.

HIGH SCHOOL: Dobyns-Bennett (Kingsport, Tenn.).

COLLEGE: North Carolina.

TRANSACTIONS/CAREER NOTES: Played in Arena Football League with Albany Firebirds (1995). ... Signed as free agent by Chicago Bears (July 17, 1995). ... Released by Bears (August 27, 1995). ... Re-signed by Bears to practice squad (August 29, 1995). ... Activated (September 22, 1995). ... Released by Bears (September 25, 1995). ... Re-signed by Bears to practice squad (September 27, 1995). ... Activated (November 29, 1995).

PLAYING EXPERIENCE: Chicago NFL, 1995. ... Games: 1995 (5).

PRO STATISTICS: 1995—Caught two passes for 22 yards.

FAUMUI, TA'ASE   DL   STEELERS

PERSONAL: Born March 19, 1971, in Western Samoa. ... 6-3/278. ... Name pronounced tah-ah-SAY fah-oo-MOO-ee.

HIGH SCHOOL: Farrington (Honolulu).

COLLEGE: Hawaii.

TRANSACTIONS/CAREER NOTES: Selected by Pittsburgh Steelers in fourth round (122nd pick overall) of 1994 NFL draft. ... Signed by Steelers (July 13, 1994).

PLAYING EXPERIENCE: Pittsburgh NFL, 1994 and 1995. ... Games: 1994 (5), 1995 (3). Total: 8.

CHAMPIONSHIP GAME EXPERIENCE: Member of Steelers for AFC championship game (1994 season); did not play. ... Member of Steelers for AFC championship game and Super Bowl XXX (1995 season); inactive.

FAURIA, CHRISTIAN   TE   SEAHAWKS

PERSONAL: Born September 22, 1971, in Harbor City, Calif. ... 6-4/245. ... Name pronounced FOUR-ee-a.

HIGH SCHOOL: Crespi Carmelite (Encino, Calif.).

COLLEGE: Colorado.

TRANSACTIONS/CAREER NOTES: Selected by Seattle Seahawks in second round (39th pick overall) of 1995 NFL draft. ... Signed by Seahawks (July 17, 1995).

		RECEIVING				TOTALS			
Year Team	G	No.	Yds.	Avg.	TD	TD	2pt.	Pts.	Fum.
1995—Seattle NFL	14	17	181	10.7	1	1	0	6	0

F

FAVRE, BRETT   QB   PACKERS

PERSONAL: Born October 10, 1969, in Pass Christian, Miss. ... 6-2/220. ... Full name: Brett Lorenzo Favre. ... Name pronounced FAHRV.
HIGH SCHOOL: Hancock North Central (Pass Christian, Miss.).
COLLEGE: Southern Mississippi.
TRANSACTIONS/CAREER NOTES: Selected by Atlanta Falcons in second round (33rd pick overall) of 1991 NFL draft. ... Signed by Falcons (July 18, 1991). ... Traded by Falcons to Green Bay Packers for first-round pick (OT Bob Whitfield) in 1992 draft (February 11, 1992). ... Granted free agency (February 17, 1994). ... Re-signed by Packers (July 14, 1994).
CHAMPIONSHIP GAME EXPERIENCE: Played in NFC championship game (1995 season).
HONORS: Played in Pro Bowl (1992, 1993 and 1995 seasons). ... Named NFL Player of the Year by THE SPORTING NEWS (1995). ... Named quarterback on THE SPORTING NEWS NFL All-Pro team (1995).
RECORDS: Shares NFL record for longest pass completion (to Robert Brooks)—99 yards, touchdown (September 11, 1995, at Chicago).
PRO STATISTICS: 1992—Caught one pass for minus seven yards, fumbled 12 times and recovered three fumbles for minus 12 yards. 1993—Fumbled 12 times and recovered two fumbles for minus one yard. 1994—Fumbled seven times and recovered one fumble for minus two yards. 1995—Fumbled eight times.
STATISTICAL PLATEAUS: 300-yard passing games: 1993 (1), 1994 (4), 1995 (7). Total: 12.
MISCELLANEOUS: Regular-season record as starting NFL quarterback: 37-24 (.607).

Year—Team	G	PASSING Att.	Cmp.	Pct.	Yds.	TD	Int.	Avg.	Rat.	RUSHING Att.	Yds.	Avg.	TD	TOTALS TD	2pt.	Pts.
1991—Atlanta NFL	2	5	0	0.0	0	0	2	.00	0.0	0	0	...	0	0	...	0
1992—Green Bay NFL	15	471	302	64.1	3227	18	13	6.85	85.3	47	198	4.2	1	1	...	6
1993—Green Bay NFL	16	522	318	60.9	3303	19	*24	6.33	72.2	58	216	3.7	1	1	...	6
1994—Green Bay NFL	16	582	363	62.4	3882	33	14	6.67	90.7	42	202	4.8	2	2	0	12
1995—Green Bay NFL	16	570	359	63.0	*4413	*38	13	7.74	99.5	39	181	4.6	3	3	0	18
Pro totals (5 years)	65	2150	1342	62.4	14825	108	66	6.90	86.8	186	797	4.3	7	7	0	42

FEAGLES, JEFF   P   CARDINALS

PERSONAL: Born March 7, 1966, in Scottsdale, Ariz. ... 6-1/205. ... Full name: Jeffrey Allan Feagles.
HIGH SCHOOL: Gerard Catholic (Phoenix).
JUNIOR COLLEGE: Scottsdale (Ariz.) Community College.
COLLEGE: Miami, Fla. (degree in business administration, 1988).
TRANSACTIONS/CAREER NOTES: Signed as non-drafted free agent by New England Patriots (May 1, 1988). ... Claimed on waivers by Philadelphia Eagles (June 5, 1990). ... Granted unconditional free agency (February 1-April 1, 1992). ... Re-signed by Eagles for 1992 season. ... Granted unconditional free agency (February 17, 1994). ... Signed by Phoenix Cardinals (March 2, 1994). ... Cardinals franchise renamed Arizona Cardinals for 1994 season.
HONORS: Played in Pro Bowl (1995 season).
PRO STATISTICS: 1988—Rushed once for no yards and recovered one fumble. 1989—Attempted two passes without a completion, fumbled once and recovered one fumble. 1990—Attempted one pass without a completion and rushed twice for three yards. 1991—Rushed three times for minus one yard, fumbled once and recovered one fumble. 1993—Rushed twice for six yards and recovered one fumble. 1994—Rushed twice for eight yards. 1995—Rushed twice for four yards and fumbled once for minus 22 yards.

Year—Team	G	PUNTING No.	Yds.	Avg.	Net avg.	In. 20	Blk.
1988—New England NFL	16	91	3482	38.3	34.1	24	0
1989—New England NFL	16	63	2392	38.0	31.3	13	1
1990—Philadelphia NFL	16	72	3026	42.0	35.5	20	2
1991—Philadelphia NFL	16	*87	3640	41.8	34.0	29	1
1992—Philadelphia NFL	16	82	3459	42.2	36.9	26	0
1993—Philadelphia NFL	16	83	3323	40.0	35.3	31	0
1994—Arizona NFL	16	*98	3997	40.8	36.0	33	0
1995—Arizona NFL	16	72	3150	43.8	38.2	20	0
Pro totals (8 years)	128	648	26469	40.9	35.2	196	4

FENNER, DERRICK   RB   RAIDERS

PERSONAL: Born April 6, 1967, in Washington, D.C. ... 6-3/230. ... Full name: Derrick Steven Fenner.
HIGH SCHOOL: Oxon Hill (Md.).
COLLEGE: North Carolina, then Gardner-Webb College, N.C. (did not play football).
TRANSACTIONS/CAREER NOTES: Selected after sophomore season by Seattle Seahawks in 10th round (268th pick overall) of 1989 NFL draft. ... Signed by Seahawks (July 22, 1989). ... Granted free agency (February 1, 1991). ... Re-signed by Seahawks (August 4, 1991). ... Granted unconditional free agency (February 1, 1992). ... Signed by Cincinnati Bengals (March 24, 1992). ... Granted free agency (March 1, 1993). ... Tendered offer sheet by New York Jets (April 17, 1993). ... Offer matched by Bengals (April 24, 1993). ... Granted unconditional free agency (February 17, 1995). ... Signed by Los Angeles Raiders (March 27, 1995). ... Raiders franchise moved to Oakland (July 21, 1995).
PRO STATISTICS: 1990—Recovered one fumble. 1992—Returned two kickoffs for 38 yards and recovered one fumble. 1993—Recovered two fumbles. 1994—Recovered one fumble. 1995—Recovered two fumbles.
STATISTICAL PLATEAUS: 100-yard rushing games: 1990 (2).

Year—Team	G	RUSHING Att.	Yds.	Avg.	TD	RECEIVING No.	Yds.	Avg.	TD	TOTALS TD	2pt.	Pts.	Fum.
1989—Seattle NFL	5	11	41	3.7	1	3	23	7.7	0	1	...	6	0
1990—Seattle NFL	16	215	859	4.0	†14	17	143	8.4	1	15	...	90	3
1991—Seattle NFL	11	91	267	2.9	4	11	72	6.6	0	4	...	24	2
1992—Cincinnati NFL	16	112	500	4.5	7	7	41	5.9	1	8	...	48	1
1993—Cincinnati NFL	15	121	482	4.0	1	48	427	8.9	0	1	...	6	1
1994—Cincinnati NFL	16	141	468	3.3	1	36	276	7.7	1	2	0	12	6
1995—Oakland NFL	16	39	110	2.8	0	35	252	7.2	3	3	0	18	2
Pro totals (7 years)	95	730	2727	3.7	28	157	1234	7.9	6	34	0	204	15

F

FIEDLER, JAY   QB   EAGLES

PERSONAL: Born December 29, 1971, in Oceanside, N.Y. ... 6-1/214.
HIGH SCHOOL: Oceanside (N.Y.).
COLLEGE: Dartmouth.
TRANSACTIONS/CAREER NOTES: Signed as non-drafted free agent by Philadelphia Eagles for 1994 season. ... Inactive for 16 games (1994). ... Inactive for 16 games (1995).

FIELDINGS, ANTHONY   LB

PERSONAL: Born July 7, 1971, in Eustis, Fla. ... 6-1/237.
HIGH SCHOOL: Eustis (Fla.).
COLLEGE: Morningside (Iowa).
TRANSACTIONS/CAREER NOTES: Signed as non-drafted free agent by Buffalo Bills (March 25, 1994). ... Released by Bills (August 22, 1994). ... Signed by Dallas Cowboys (July 31, 1995). ... Released by Cowboys (October 3, 1995).
PLAYING EXPERIENCE: Dallas NFL, 1995. ... Games: 1995 (4).

FIELDS, JEFF   DT   SAINTS

PERSONAL: Born July 3, 1967, in Jackson, Miss. ... 6-3/320.
HIGH SCHOOL: Jim Hill (Jackson, Miss.).
JUNIOR COLLEGE: Hinds Community College (Miss.).
COLLEGE: Arkansas State.
TRANSACTIONS/CAREER NOTES: Selected by Los Angeles Rams in ninth round (228th pick overall) of 1991 NFL draft. ... Signed by Rams (June 27, 1991). ... Released by Rams (August 20, 1991). ... Signed by Hamilton Tiger-Cats of CFL (October 1991). ... Granted free agency (February 1993). ... Signed by Seattle Seahawks (June 22, 1993). ... Released by Seahawks (August 23, 1993). ... Traded by Tiger-Cats with LB Glenn Young to Toronto Argonauts for QB Reggie Slack (September 1994)... Signed by Carolina Panthers (March 27, 1995). ... Released by Panthers (August 27, 1995). ... Re-signed by Panthers to practice squad (August 29, 1995). ... Released by Panthers (September 15, 1995). ... Signed by Washington Redskins to practice squad (September 20, 1995). ... Signed by Panthers to practice squad off Redskins practice squad (August 29, 1995). ... Activated (November 28, 1995). ... Released by Panthers (December 13, 1995). ... Signed by New Orleans Saints (February 26, 1996).
PRO EXPERIENCE: CFL: 1992—Intercepted one pass for 10 yards and a touchdown.

Year Team	G	SACKS
1991—Hamilton CFL	5	2.0
1992—Hamilton CFL	18	7.0
1993—Hamilton CFL	5	2.0
1994—Toronto CFL	9	2.0
1995—Carolina NFL	2	0.0
CFL totals (4 years)	37	13.0
NFL totals (1 year)	2	0.0
Pro totals (5 years)	39	13.0

FIELDS, MARK   LB   SAINTS

PERSONAL: Born November 9, 1972, in Los Angeles. ... 6-2/244. ... Full name: Mark Lee Fields.
HIGH SCHOOL: Washington (Cerritos, Calif.).
JUNIOR COLLEGE: Los Angeles Southwest College.
COLLEGE: Washington State.
TRANSACTIONS/CAREER NOTES: Selected by New Orleans Saints in first round (13th pick overall) of 1995 NFL draft. ... Signed by Saints (July 20, 1995).

Year Team	G	SACKS
1995—New Orleans NFL	16	1.0

FIGARO, CEDRIC   LB

PERSONAL: Born August 17, 1966, in Lafayette, La. ... 6-3/255. ... Full name: Cedric Noah Figaro.
HIGH SCHOOL: Lafayette (La.).
COLLEGE: Notre Dame.
TRANSACTIONS/CAREER NOTES: Selected by San Diego Chargers in sixth round (152nd pick overall) of 1988 NFL draft. ... Signed by Chargers (July 13, 1988). ... On injured reserve with back injury (August 29-November 12, 1988). ... Granted free agency (February 1, 1990). ... Re-signed by Chargers (August 1, 1990). ... Granted unconditional free agency (February 1, 1991). ... Signed by Indianapolis Colts (March 22, 1991). ... Released by Colts (August 26, 1991). ... Re-signed by Colts (September 11, 1991). ... Released by Colts (September 18, 1991). ... Signed by Cleveland Browns (September 25, 1991). ... Released by Browns (August 31, 1992). ... Re-signed by Browns (September 3, 1992). ... Released by Browns (September 9, 1992). ... Re-signed by Browns (September 11, 1992). ... Granted unconditional free agency (March 1, 1993). ... Rights relinquished by Browns (June 7, 1993). ... Signed by Atlanta Falcons (May 13, 1994). ... Released by Falcons (August 22, 1994). ... Selected by Amsterdam Admirals in fourth round (22nd pick overall) of 1995 World League Draft. ... Signed by St. Louis Rams (July 5, 1995). ... Granted unconditional free agency (February 16, 1996).
PRO STATISTICS: NFL: 1989—Returned one kickoff for 21 yards, returned one punt for no yards and recovered one fumble. 1991—Recovered one fumble. 1992—Recovered one fumble. 1995—Credited with one sack and recovered one fumble. W.L.: 1995—Credited with one sack.

		INTERCEPTIONS			
Year Team	G	No.	Yds.	Avg.	TD
1988—San Diego NFL	6	0	0	...	0
1989—San Diego NFL	16	1	2	2.0	0

Year Team	G	No.	INTERCEPTIONS Yds.	Avg.	TD
1990—San Diego NFL	16	0	0	...	0
1991—Indianapolis NFL	1	0	0	...	0
—Cleveland NFL	12	1	9	9.0	0
1992—Cleveland NFL	16	0	0	...	0
1993—		Did not play.			
1994—		Did not play.			
1995—Amsterdam W.L.	...	2	23	11.5	1
—St. Louis NFL	16	0	0	...	0
W.L. totals (1 year)	...	2	23	11.5	1
NFL totals (6 years)	83	2	11	5.5	0
Pro totals (6 years)	...	4	34	8.5	1

FIGURES, DEON   CB   STEELERS

PERSONAL: Born January 10, 1970, in Bellflower, Calif. ... 6-0/192. ... Full name: Deon Juniel Figures.
HIGH SCHOOL: Serra (Compton, Calif.).
COLLEGE: Colorado.
TRANSACTIONS/CAREER NOTES: Selected by Pittsburgh Steelers in first round (23rd pick overall) of 1993 NFL draft. ... Signed by Steelers (July 21, 1993).
CHAMPIONSHIP GAME EXPERIENCE: Played in AFC championship game (1994 and 1995 seasons). ... Played in Super Bowl XXX (1995 season).
HONORS: Jim Thorpe Award winner (1992). ... Named defensive back on THE SPORTING NEWS college All-America first team (1992).
PRO STATISTICS: 1993—Recovered two fumbles for six yards. 1994—Credited with one sack and recovered one fumble.

Year Team	G	No.	INTERCEPTIONS Yds.	Avg.	TD	No.	PUNT RETURNS Yds.	Avg.	TD	TD	2pt.	TOTALS Pts.	Fum.
1993—Pittsburgh NFL	15	1	78	78.0	0	5	15	3.0	0	0	...	0	2
1994—Pittsburgh NFL	16	0	0	...	0	0	0	...	0	0	0	0	0
1995—Pittsburgh NFL	14	0	0	...	0	0	0	...	0	0	0	0	0
Pro totals (3 years)	45	1	78	78.0	0	5	15	3.0	0	0	0	0	2

FINA, JOHN   OT   BILLS

PERSONAL: Born March 11, 1969, in Rochester, Minn. ... 6-4/285. ... Full name: John Joseph Fina. ... Name pronounced FEE-nuh.
HIGH SCHOOL: Salpointe Catholic (Tucson, Ariz.).
COLLEGE: Arizona.
TRANSACTIONS/CAREER NOTES: Selected by Buffalo Bills in first round (27th pick overall) of 1992 NFL draft. ... Signed by Bills (July 21, 1992). ... Designated by Bills as franchise player (February 16, 1996).
PLAYING EXPERIENCE: Buffalo NFL, 1992-1995. ... Games: 1992 (16), 1993 (16), 1994 (12), 1995 (16). Total: 60.
CHAMPIONSHIP GAME EXPERIENCE: Played in AFC championship game (1992 and 1993 seasons). ... Played in Super Bowl XXVII (1992 season) and Super Bowl XXVIII (1993 season).
PRO STATISTICS: 1992—Caught one pass for one yard and a touchdown. 1993—Rushed once for minus two yards.

FISK, JASON   DT   VIKINGS

PERSONAL: Born September 4, 1972, in Davis, Calif. ... 6-3/284.
HIGH SCHOOL: Davis (Calif.).
COLLEGE: Stanford.
TRANSACTIONS/CAREER NOTES: Selected by Minnesota Vikings in seventh round (243rd pick overall) of 1995 NFL draft. ... Signed by Vikings (July 24, 1995).
PLAYING EXPERIENCE: Minnesota NFL, 1995. ... Games: 1995 (8).

FLANIGAN, JIM   DT   BEARS

PERSONAL: Born August 27, 1971, in Green Bay. ... 6-2/280. ... Full name: James Michael Flanigan.
HIGH SCHOOL: Southern Door (Brussels, Wis.).
COLLEGE: Notre Dame.
TRANSACTIONS/CAREER NOTES: Selected by Chicago Bears in third round (74th pick overall) of 1994 NFL draft. ... Signed by Bears (July 14, 1994).
PRO STATISTICS: 1994—Returned two kickoffs for 26 yards. 1995—Rushed once for no yards, caught two passes for six yards and two touchdowns and recovered one fumble.

Year Team	G	SACKS
1994—Chicago NFL	14	0.0
1995—Chicago NFL	16	11.0
Pro totals (2 years)	30	11.0

FLEMING, CORY   WR

PERSONAL: Born March 19, 1971, in Nashville. ... 6-1/216. ... Full name: Cory Lamont Fleming.
HIGH SCHOOL: Stratford (Nashville).
COLLEGE: Tennessee.
TRANSACTIONS/CAREER NOTES: Selected by San Francisco 49ers in third round (87th pick overall) of 1994 NFL draft. ... Draft rights relin-

quished by 49ers (July 21, 1994). ... Signed by Dallas Cowboys (August 3, 1994). ... Released by Cowboys (February 6, 1996).
PLAYING EXPERIENCE: Dallas NFL, 1994 and 1995. ... Games: 1994 (2), 1995 (16). Total: 18.
CHAMPIONSHIP GAME EXPERIENCE: Member of Cowboys for NFC championship game (1994 season); inactive. ... Member of Super Bowl championship team (1995 season).
PRO STATISTICS: 1995—Caught six passes for 83 yards.

FLETCHER, SIMON   LB

PERSONAL: Born February 18, 1962, in Bay City, Texas. ... 6-5/240. ... Full name: Simon Raynard Fletcher. ... Related to Pat Franklin, fullback, Tampa Bay Buccaneers and Cincinnati Bengals (1986 and 1987).
HIGH SCHOOL: Bay City (Texas).
COLLEGE: Houston.
TRANSACTIONS/CAREER NOTES: Selected by Houston Gamblers in 1985 USFL territorial draft. ... Selected by Denver Broncos in second round (54th pick overall) of 1985 NFL draft. ... Signed by Broncos (July 16, 1985). ... Granted free agency (February 1, 1992). ... Re-signed by Broncos (July 27, 1992). ... Granted unconditional free agency (February 16, 1996).
CHAMPIONSHIP GAME EXPERIENCE: Played in AFC championship game (1986, 1987, 1989 and 1991 seasons). ... Played in Super Bowl XXI (1986 season), Super Bowl XXII (1987 season) and Super Bowl XXIV (1989 season).
PRO STATISTICS: 1986—Recovered two fumbles. 1987—Recovered one fumble. 1988—Intercepted one pass for four yards and recovered one fumble. 1989—Recovered one fumble. 1990—Credited with one safety and recovered one fumble. 1993—Recovered one fumble. 1994—Intercepted one pass for four yards and recovered two fumbles.
MISCELLANEOUS: Holds Denver Broncos all-time record for most sacks (97.5).

Year Team	G	SACKS
1985—Denver NFL	16	1.0
1986—Denver NFL	16	5.5
1987—Denver NFL	12	4.0
1988—Denver NFL	16	9.0
1989—Denver NFL	16	12.0
1990—Denver NFL	16	11.0
1991—Denver NFL	16	13.5
1992—Denver NFL	16	16.0
1993—Denver NFL	16	13.5
1994—Denver NFL	16	7.0
1995—Denver NFL	16	5.0
Pro totals (11 years)	**172**	**97.5**

FLETCHER, TERRELL   RB   CHARGERS

PERSONAL: Born September 14, 1973, in St. Louis. ... 5-8/196.
HIGH SCHOOL: Hazelwood East (St. Louis).
COLLEGE: Wisconsin.
TRANSACTIONS/CAREER NOTES: Selected by San Diego Chargers in second round (51st pick overall) of 1995 NFL draft. ... Signed by Chargers (July 12, 1995).
PRO STATISTICS: 1995—Fumbled twice and recovered two fumbles.

		RUSHING				RECEIVING				PUNT RETURNS				KICKOFF RETURNS				TOTALS		
Year Team	G	Att.	Yds.	Avg.	TD	No.	Yds.	Avg.	TD	No.	Yds.	Avg.	TD	No.	Yds.	Avg.	TD	TD	2pt.	Pts.
1995—San Diego NFL	16	26	140	5.4	1	3	26	8.7	0	3	12	4.0	0	4	65	16.3	0	1	0	6

FLORES, MIKE   DE

PERSONAL: Born December 1, 1966, in Youngstown, Ohio. ... 6-3/256.
HIGH SCHOOL: East (Youngstown, Ohio).
COLLEGE: Louisville (degree in art).
TRANSACTIONS/CAREER NOTES: Selected by Philadelphia Eagles in 11th round (300th pick overall) of 1991 NFL draft. ... Signed by Eagles (July 3, 1991). ... Released by Eagles (August 30, 1991). ... Re-signed by Eagles (September 3, 1991). ... Granted free agency (February 17, 1994). ... Re-signed by Eagles (July 24, 1994). ... Granted unconditional free agency (February 17, 1995). ... Signed by Cincinnati Bengals (April 12, 1995). ... Released by Bengals (August 27, 1995). ... Signed by Washington Redskins (August 29, 1995). ... Released by Redskins (November 7, 1995). ... Signed by San Francisco 49ers (November 22, 1995). ... Released by 49ers (December 5, 1995). ... Signed by Redskins (December 8, 1995). ... Granted unconditional free agency (February 16, 1996).
PRO STATISTICS: 1993—Credited with one safety and recovered one fumble. 1994—Recovered one fumble.

Year Team	G	Sacks
1991—Philadelphia NFL	4	0.0
1992—Philadelphia NFL	15	0.0
1993—Philadelphia NFL	16	3.0
1994—Philadelphia NFL	15	3.0
1995—Washington NFL	11	0.0
Pro totals (5 years)	**61**	**7.0**

FLOWERS, LETHON   CB   STEELERS

PERSONAL: Born January 14, 1973, in Columbia, S.C. ... 6-0/207. ... Name pronounced LEE-thon.
HIGH SCHOOL: Spring Valley (Columbia, S.C.).
COLLEGE: Georgia Tech.
TRANSACTIONS/CAREER NOTES: Selected by Pittsburgh Steelers in fifth round (151st pick overall) of 1995 NFL draft. ... Signed by Steelers (July 18, 1995).

FLOYD, ERIC　　　　　　　　　　G　　　　　　　　　　BRONCOS

PERSONAL: Born October 28, 1965, in Rome, Ga. ... 6-5/310. ... Full name: Eric Cunningham Floyd.
HIGH SCHOOL: West Rome (Rome, Ga.).
COLLEGE: Auburn.
TRANSACTIONS/CAREER NOTES: Signed as non-drafted free agent by San Diego Chargers (May 1988). ... Released by Chargers (August 25, 1988). ... Re-signed by Chargers (offseason, 1989). ... Released by Chargers (August 30, 1989). ... Signed by Chargers to developmental squad (September 7, 1989). ... Released by Chargers (December 7, 1989). ... Re-signed by Chargers (March 5, 1990). ... On injured reserve with back injury (October 12, 1991-remainder of season). ... Granted unconditional free agency (February 1, 1992). ... Signed by Philadelphia Eagles (April 1, 1992). ... On injured reserve with knee injury (September 20, 1993-remainder of season). ... Released by Eagles (August 27, 1994). ... Signed by Arizona Cardinals (July 6, 1995). ... Released by Cardinals (August 21, 1995). ... Re-signed by Cardinals (October 11, 1995). ... Released by Cardinals (November 21, 1995). ... Signed by Denver Broncos (November 29, 1995).
PLAYING EXPERIENCE: San Diego NFL, 1990 and 1991; Philadelphia NFL, 1992 and 1993; Arizona NFL, 1995. ... Games: 1990 (16), 1991 (2), 1992 (16), 1993 (3), 1995 (1). Total: 38.
PRO STATISTICS: 1993—Recovered one fumble for five yards.

FLOYD, WILLIAM　　　　　　　　FB　　　　　　　　　49ERS

PERSONAL: Born February 17, 1972, in St. Petersburg, Fla. ... 6-1/242. ... Full name: William Ali Floyd.
HIGH SCHOOL: Lakewood Senior (St. Petersburg, Fla.).
COLLEGE: Florida State.
TRANSACTIONS/CAREER NOTES: Selected after junior season by San Francisco 49ers in first round (28th pick overall) of 1994 NFL draft. ... Signed by 49ers (July 28, 1994). ... On injured reserve with knee injury (October 31, 1995-remainder of season).
CHAMPIONSHIP GAME EXPERIENCE: Played in NFC championship game (1994 season). ... Member of Super Bowl championship team (1994 season).
POSTSEASON RECORDS: Holds postseason single-game record for most touchdowns by rookie—3 (January 7, 1995, vs Chicago).

Year Team	G	RUSHING				RECEIVING				TOTALS			
		Att.	Yds.	Avg.	TD	No.	Yds.	Avg.	TD	TD	2pt.	Pts.	Fum.
1994—San Francisco NFL	16	87	305	3.5	6	19	145	7.6	0	6	0	36	0
1995—San Francisco NFL	8	64	237	3.7	2	47	348	7.4	1	3	0	18	1
Pro totals (2 years)	24	151	542	3.6	8	66	493	7.5	1	9	0	54	1

FOLEY, GLENN　　　　　　　　　QB　　　　　　　　　　JETS

PERSONAL: Born October 10, 1970, in Cherry Hill, N.J. ... 6-2/210. ... Full name: Glenn Edward Foley.
HIGH SCHOOL: Cherry Hill (N.J.) East.
COLLEGE: Boston College.
TRANSACTIONS/CAREER NOTES: Selected by New York Jets in seventh round (208th pick overall) of 1994 NFL draft. ... Signed by Jets (June 21, 1994). ... On injured reserve with shoulder injury (November 8, 1995-remainder of season).
PRO STATISTICS: 1995—Caught one pass for minus nine yards.

Year Team	G	PASSING								RUSHING				TOTALS		
		Att.	Cmp.	Pct.	Yds.	TD	Int.	Avg.	Rat.	Att.	Yds.	Avg.	TD	TD	2pt.	Pts.
1994—New York Jets NFL	1	8	5	62.5	45	0	1	5.63	38.0	0	0	...	0	0	0	0
1995—New York Jets NFL	1	29	16	55.2	128	0	1	4.41	52.1	1	9	9.00	0	0	0	0
Pro totals (2 years)	2	37	21	56.8	173	0	2	4.68	46.3	1	9	9.0	0	0	0	0

F

FOLSTON, JAMES　　　　　　　　DE　　　　　　　　RAIDERS

PERSONAL: Born August 14, 1971, in Cocoa, Fla. ... 6-3/235. ... Full name: James Edward Folston.
HIGH SCHOOL: Cocoa (Fla.).
COLLEGE: Northeast Louisiana.
TRANSACTIONS/CAREER NOTES: Selected by Los Angeles Raiders in second round (52nd pick overall) of 1994 NFL draft. ... Signed by Raiders (July 13, 1994). ... Raiders franchise moved to Oakland (July 21, 1995).
PLAYING EXPERIENCE: Los Angeles Raiders NFL, 1994; Oakland NFL, 1995. ... Games: 1994 (7), 1995 (14). Total: 21.

FONTENOT, ALBERT　　　　　　　DE　　　　　　　　　BEARS

PERSONAL: Born September 17, 1970, in Houston. ... 6-4/275. ... Full name: Albert Paul Fontenot. ... Name pronounced FAHN-tuh-no
HIGH SCHOOL: Jack Yates (Houston).
JUNIOR COLLEGE: Navarro (Texas) College.
COLLEGE: Baylor.
TRANSACTIONS/CAREER NOTES: Selected by Chicago Bears in fourth round (112th pick overall) of 1993 NFL draft. ... Signed by Bears (July 16, 1993). ... Granted free agency (February 16, 1996). ... Re-signed by Bears (April 18, 1996).
PRO STATISTICS: 1993—Returned one kickoff for eight yards. 1995—Credited with one safety and recovered one fumble.

Year Team	G	SACKS
1993—Chicago NFL	16	1.0
1994—Chicago NFL	16	4.0
1995—Chicago NFL	13	2.5
Pro totals (3 years)	45	7.5

FONTENOT, JERRY   C   BEARS

PERSONAL: Born November 21, 1966, in Lafayette, La. ... 6-3/285. ... Full name: Jerry Paul Fontenot. ... Name pronounced FAHN-tuh-no.
HIGH SCHOOL: Lafayette (La.).
COLLEGE: Texas A&M.
TRANSACTIONS/CAREER NOTES: Selected by Chicago Bears in third round (65th pick overall) of 1989 NFL draft. ... Signed by Bears (July 27, 1989). ... Granted free agency (March 1, 1993). ... Re-signed by Bears (June 16, 1993). ... Granted free agency (February 16, 1996).
PLAYING EXPERIENCE: Chicago NFL, 1989-1995. ... Games: 1989 (16), 1990 (16), 1991 (16), 1992 (16), 1993 (16), 1994 (16), 1995 (16). Total: 112.
PRO STATISTICS: 1989—Recovered one fumble. 1990—Fumbled once. 1992—Fumbled once for minus two yards. 1993—Recovered one fumble.

FOOTMAN, DAN   DE   RAVENS

PERSONAL: Born January 13, 1969, in Tampa. ... 6-5/290. ... Full name: Dan Ellis Footman.
HIGH SCHOOL: Hillsborough (Tampa).
COLLEGE: Florida State.
TRANSACTIONS/CAREER NOTES: Selected by Cleveland Browns in second round (42nd pick overall) of 1993 NFL draft. ... Signed by Browns (July 15, 1993). ... Granted free agency (February 16, 1996). ... Browns franchise moved to Baltimore and renamed Ravens for 1996 season (March 11, 1996). ... Signed by Ravens (April 3, 1996).
PRO STATISTICS: 1995—Recovered one fumble.

Year Team	G	SACKS
1993—Cleveland NFL	8	1.0
1994—Cleveland NFL	16	2.5
1995—Cleveland NFL	16	5.0
Pro totals (3 years)	**40**	**8.5**

FORD, COLE   K   RAIDERS

PERSONAL: Born December 31, 1972, in Tucson, Ariz. ... 6-2/195.
HIGH SCHOOL: Sabino (Tucson, Ariz.).
COLLEGE: Southern California.
TRANSACTIONS/CAREER NOTES: Selected by Pittsburgh Steelers in seventh round (247th pick overall) of 1995 NFL draft. ... Signed by Steelers (July 17, 1995). ... Released by Steelers (August 15, 1995). ... Signed by Oakland Raiders to practice squad (August 31, 1995). ... Activated (September 2, 1995). ... Released by Raiders (September 5, 1995). ... Re-signed by Raiders to practice squad (September 6, 1995). ...Activated (September 9, 1995).

| Year   Team | G | KICKING | | | | | | |
		XPM	XPA	FGM	FGA	Lg.	50+	Pts.
1995—Oakland NFL	5	17	18	8	9	46	0-1	41

FORD, HENRY   DE   OILERS

PERSONAL: Born October 30, 1971, in Fort Worth, Texas. ... 6-3/284.
HIGH SCHOOL: Trimble Technical (Fort Worth, Texas).
COLLEGE: Arkansas.
TRANSACTIONS/CAREER NOTES: Selected by Houston Oilers in first round (26th pick overall) of 1994 NFL draft.... Signed by Oilers (June 16, 1994).

Year Team	G	SACKS
1994—Houston NFL	11	0.0
1995—Houston NFL	16	4.5
Pro totals (2 years)	**27**	**4.5**

FORTIN, ROMAN   C   FALCONS

PERSONAL: Born February 26, 1967, in Columbus, Ohio. ... 6-5/295. ... Full name: Roman Brian Fortin.
HIGH SCHOOL: Ventura (Calif.).
COLLEGE: Oregon, then San Diego State.
TRANSACTIONS/CAREER NOTES: Selected by Detroit Lions in eighth round (203rd pick overall) of 1990 NFL draft. ... On injured reserve (September 5, 1990-entire season). ... Granted unconditional free agency (February 1, 1992). ... Signed by Atlanta Falcons (March 31, 1992). ... Granted unconditional free agency (February 17, 1994). ... Re-signed by Falcons (February 24, 1994). ... Granted unconditional free agency (February 16, 1996). ... Re-signed by Falcons (February 20, 1996).
PLAYING EXPERIENCE: Detroit NFL, 1991; Atlanta NFL, 1992-1995. ... Games: 1991 (16), 1992 (16), 1993 (16), 1994 (16), 1995 (16). Total: 80.
CHAMPIONSHIP GAME EXPERIENCE: Played in NFC championship game (1991 season).
PRO STATISTICS: 1991—Caught one pass for four yards. 1992—Returned one kickoff for five yards and recovered one fumble. 1995—Fumbled two times for minus six yards.

FOUNTAINE, JAMAL   DE   PANTHERS

PERSONAL: Born January 29, 1971, in San Francisco. ... 6-3/240.
HIGH SCHOOL: Abraham Lincoln (San Francisco).
COLLEGE: Washington.
TRANSACTIONS/CAREER NOTES: Signed as non-drafted free agent by San Francisco 49ers (May 4, 1994). ... Released by 49ers (August 23,

F

1994). ... Re-signed by 49ers to practice squad (August 31, 1994). ... Granted free agency after 1994 season. ... Re-signed by 49ers (March 2, 1995). ... Released by 49ers (November 14, 1995). ... Signed by Carolina Panthers (April 12, 1995).
PLAYING EXPERIENCE: San Francisco NFL, 1995. ... Games: 1995 (7).
PRO STATISTICS: 1995—Credited with one sack.

FOX, MIKE   DE   PANTHERS

PERSONAL: Born August 5, 1967, in Akron, Ohio. ... 6-8/296.
HIGH SCHOOL: Akron (Ohio) North.
COLLEGE: West Virginia.
TRANSACTIONS/CAREER NOTES: Selected by New York Giants in second round (51st pick overall) of 1990 NFL draft. ... Signed by Giants (July 31, 1990). ... Granted free agency (March 1, 1993). ... Re-signed by Giants (August 13, 1993). ... Granted unconditional free agency (February 17, 1995). ... Signed by Carolina Panthers (February 20, 1995).
CHAMPIONSHIP GAME EXPERIENCE: Played in NFC championship game (1990 season). ... Member of Super Bowl championship team (1990 season).
PRO STATISTICS: 1993—Recovered one fumble for two yards.

Year Team	G	SACKS
1990—New York Giants NFL	16	1.5
1991—New York Giants NFL	15	0.0
1992—New York Giants NFL	16	2.5
1993—New York Giants NFL	16	4.5
1994—New York Giants NFL	16	1.0
1995—Carolina NFL	16	4.5
Pro totals (6 years)	95	14.0

FOXX, DION   LB   REDSKINS

PERSONAL: Born June 11, 1971, in Richmond, Va. ... 6-3/250. ... Full name: Dion Lamont Foxx.
HIGH SCHOOL: Meadowbrook (Richmond, Va.).
COLLEGE: James Madison.
TRANSACTIONS/CAREER NOTES: Signed as non-drafted free agent by Miami Dolphins (April 28, 1994). ... Released by Dolphins (October 21, 1995). ... Signed by Washington Redskins (December 5, 1995).
PLAYING EXPERIENCE: Miami NFL, 1994; Miami (1)-Washington (2) NFL, 1995. ... Games: 1994 (16), 1995 (3). Total: 19.
PRO STATISTICS: 1995—Credited with ½ sack.

FRANCIS, JAMES   LB   BENGALS

PERSONAL: Born August 4, 1968, in Houston. ... 6-5/252. ... Brother of Ron Francis, cornerback, Dallas Cowboys (1987-1990).
HIGH SCHOOL: La Marque (Texas).
COLLEGE: Baylor.
TRANSACTIONS/CAREER NOTES: Selected by Cincinnati Bengals in first round (12th pick overall) of 1990 NFL draft. ... Signed by Bengals (July 19, 1990). ... On injured reserve with knee injury (December 26, 1992-remainder of season). ... Designated by Bengals as transition player (February 25, 1993). ... On injured reserve with broken leg (November 22, 1995-remainder of season).
HONORS: Named special-teams player on THE SPORTING NEWS college All-America first team (1989).
PRO STATISTICS: 1990—Credited with one safety. 1991—Recovered one fumble. 1992—Recovered two fumbles for three yards. 1993—Recovered one fumble.

Year Team	G	INTERCEPTIONS No.	Yds.	Avg.	TD	SACKS No.
1990—Cincinnati NFL	16	1	17	17.0	1	8.0
1991—Cincinnati NFL	16	1	0	0.0	0	3.0
1992—Cincinnati NFL	14	3	108	36.0	1	6.0
1993—Cincinnati NFL	14	2	12	6.0	0	2.0
1994—Cincinnati NFL	16	0	0	...	0	4.5
1995—Cincinnati NFL	11	0	0	...	0	3.0
Pro totals (6 years)	87	7	137	19.6	2	26.5

FRANK, DONALD   CB   VIKINGS

PERSONAL: Born October 24, 1965, in Edgecombe County, N.C. ... 6-0/192. ... Full name: Donald Lee Frank. ... Cousin of Kelvin Bryant, running back, Baltimore/Philadelphia Stars of USFL and Washington Redskins (1983-1990).
HIGH SCHOOL: Tarboro (N.C.).
COLLEGE: Winston-Salem (N.C.) State.
TRANSACTIONS/CAREER NOTES: Signed as non-drafted free agent by San Diego Chargers (April 26, 1990). ... Granted free agency (March 1, 1993). ... Re-signed by Chargers for 1993 season. ... Traded by Chargers to Cleveland Browns for sixth-round pick (QB Craig Whelihan) in 1995 draft (March 4, 1994). ... Released by Browns (August 25, 1994). ... Signed by Los Angeles Raiders (August 29, 1994). ... Granted unconditional free agency (February 17, 1995). ... Signed by Minnesota Vikings (April 14, 1995). ... Granted free agency (February 16, 1996).
PRO STATISTICS: 1994—Recovered one fumble for 30 yards.

Year Team	G	INTERCEPTIONS No.	Yds.	Avg.	TD	KICKOFF RETURNS No.	Yds.	Avg.	TD	TOTALS TD	2pt.	Pts.	Fum.
1990—San Diego NFL	16	2	8	4.0	0	8	172	21.5	0	0	...	0	0
1991—San Diego NFL	16	1	71	71.0	1	0	0	...	0	1	...	6	0
1992—San Diego NFL	16	4	37	9.3	0	0	0	...	0	0	...	0	0
1993—San Diego NFL	16	3	119	39.7	1	0	0	...	0	1	...	6	0
1994—Los Angeles Raiders NFL	16	1	8	8.0	0	0	0	...	0	0	0	0	0

F

Year Team	G	INTERCEPTIONS				KICKOFF RETURNS				TOTALS			
		No.	Yds.	Avg.	TD	No.	Yds.	Avg.	TD	TD	2pt.	Pts.	Fum.
1995—Minnesota NFL	12	3	72	24.0	0	0	0	...	0	0	0	0	0
Pro totals (6 years)	92	14	315	22.5	2	8	172	21.5	0	2	0	12	0

FRANKLIN, KEITH   LB   RAIDERS

PERSONAL: Born March 4, 1970, in Los Angeles. ... 6-2/230.
HIGH SCHOOL: Dorsey (Los Angeles).
JUNIOR COLLEGE: Glendale (Calif.) College.
COLLEGE: South Carolina.
TRANSACTIONS/CAREER NOTES: Signed as non-drafted free agent by Phoenix Cardinals (April 24, 1993). ... Released by Cardinals (August 23, 1993). ... Signed by Los Angeles Raiders (April 1994). ... Released by Raiders (August 22, 1994). ... Signed by St. Louis Rams (July 10, 1994). ... Released by Rams (August 22, 1994). ... Signed by Oakland Raiders (December 10, 1995).
PLAYING EXPERIENCE: Oakland NFL, 1995. ... Games: 1995 (2).

FRASE, PAUL   DE/DT   JAGUARS

PERSONAL: Born May 5, 1965, in Elmira, N.Y. ... 6-5/276. ... Full name: Paul Miles Frase. ... Name pronounced FRAZE.
HIGH SCHOOL: Spaulding (Rochester, N.H.).
COLLEGE: Syracuse (degree in psychology).
TRANSACTIONS/CAREER NOTES: Selected by New York Jets in sixth round (146th pick overall) of 1988 NFL draft. ... Signed by Jets (June 21, 1988). ... On reserve/non-football illness list with hyperthyroidism (August 27, 1990-entire season). ... Granted unconditional free agency (February 1-April 1, 1991). ... Re-signed by Jets for 1991 season. ... Granted free agency (February 1, 1992). ... Re-signed by Jets (July 13, 1992). ... Granted free agency (March 1, 1993). ... Re-signed by Jets (April 12, 1993). ... Granted unconditional free agency (February 17, 1994). ... Re-signed by Jets (April 6, 1994). ... Selected by Jacksonville Jaguars from Jets in NFL expansion draft (February 15, 1995).
PRO STATISTICS: 1991—Fumbled once. 1993—Recovered two fumbles. 1994—Recovered one fumble.

Year Team	G	SACKS
1988—New York Jets NFL	16	1.0
1989—New York Jets NFL	16	2.0
1990—New York Jets NFL	Did not play.	
1991—New York Jets NFL	16	0.0
1992—New York Jets NFL	16	5.0
1993—New York Jets NFL	16	1.0
1994—New York Jets NFL	16	1.0
1995—Jacksonville NFL	9	1.0
Pro totals (7 years)	105	11.0

FRAZIER, DERRICK   CB   COLTS

PERSONAL: Born April 29, 1970, in Sugar Land, Texas. ... 5-11/183.
HIGH SCHOOL: Clements (Sugar Land, Texas).
COLLEGE: Texas A&M.
TRANSACTIONS/CAREER NOTES: Selected by Philadelphia Eagles in third round (75th pick overall) of 1993 NFL draft. ... Signed by Eagles (July 14, 1993). ... On injured reserve with knee injury (entire 1993 season). ... Granted unconditional free agency (February 16, 1996). ... Signed by Indianapolis Colts (April 26, 1996).
PLAYING EXPERIENCE: Philadelphia NFL, 1994 and 1995. ... Games: 1994 (12), 1995 (7). Total: 19.
PRO STATISTICS: 1994—Recovered one fumble for three yards. 1995—Intercepted one pass for three yards.

FREDERICK, MIKE   DE   RAVENS

PERSONAL: Born August 6, 1972, in Abington, Pa. ... 6-5/280. ... Full name: Thomas Michael Frederick.
HIGH SCHOOL: Neshaminy (Langhorne, Pa.).
COLLEGE: Virginia (degree in management).
TRANSACTIONS/CAREER NOTES: Selected by Cleveland Browns in third round (94th pick overall) of 1995 NFL draft. ... Signed by Browns (July 14, 1995). ... Browns franchise moved to Baltimore and renamed Ravens for 1996 season (March 11, 1996).
PRO STATISTICS: 1995—Returned two kickoffs for 16 yards.

Year Team	G	SACKS
1995—Cleveland NFL	16	1.0

FREDRICKSON, ROB   LB   RAIDERS

PERSONAL: Born May 13, 1971, in Saint Joseph, Mich. ... 6-4/240.
HIGH SCHOOL: Saint Joseph (Mich.) Senior.
COLLEGE: Michigan State.
TRANSACTIONS/CAREER NOTES: Selected by Los Angeles Raiders in first round (22nd pick overall) of 1994 NFL draft. ... Signed by Raiders (July 19, 1994). ... Raiders franchise moved to Oakland (July 21, 1995).
PRO STATISTICS: 1995—Intercepted one pass for 14 yards and recovered four fumbles for 35 yards and one touchdown.

Year Team	G	SACKS
1994—Los Angeles Raiders NFL	16	3.0
1995—Oakland NFL	16	0.0
Pro totals (2 years)	32	3.0

F

FREEMAN, ANTONIO WR PACKERS

PERSONAL: Born May 27, 1972, in Baltimore. ... 6-0/187. ... Full name: Antonio Michael Freeman.
HIGH SCHOOL: Baltimore Polytechnic.
COLLEGE: Virginia Tech.
TRANSACTIONS/CAREER NOTES: Selected by Green Bay Packers in third round (90th pick overall) of 1995 NFL draft. ... Signed by Packers (June 22, 1995).
CHAMPIONSHIP GAME EXPERIENCE: Played in NFC championship game (1995 season).
POSTSEASON RECORDS: Shares NFL postseason record for most touchdowns by punt return—1 (December 31, 1995, vs. Atlanta).
PRO STATISTICS: 1995—Recovered four fumbles.

		RECEIVING				PUNT RETURNS				KICKOFF RETURNS				TOTALS			
Year Team	G	No.	Yds.	Avg.	TD	No.	Yds.	Avg.	TD	No.	Yds.	Avg.	TD	TD	2pt.	Pts.	Fum.
1995—Green Bay NFL	11	8	106	13.3	1	37	292	7.9	0	24	556	23.2	0	1	0	6	7

FREEMAN, RUSSELL OT RAIDERS

PERSONAL: Born September 2, 1969, in Homestead, Pa. ... 6-7/290. ... Full name: Russell Williams Freeman.
HIGH SCHOOL: Allderdice (Pittsburgh).
COLLEGE: Georgia Tech.
TRANSACTIONS/CAREER NOTES: Signed as non-drafted free agent by Denver Broncos (April 30, 1992). ... Granted free agency (February 17, 1995). ... Signed by Oakland Raiders (July 28, 1995).
PLAYING EXPERIENCE: Denver NFL, 1992-1994; Oakland NFL, 1995. ... Games: 1992 (16), 1993 (14), 1994 (13), 1995 (15). Total: 58.

FREROTTE, GUS QB REDSKINS

PERSONAL: Born July 31, 1971, in Kittanning, Pa. ... 6-2/221. ... Full name: Gustave Joseph Frerotte.
HIGH SCHOOL: Ford City (Pa.) Junior-Senior.
COLLEGE: Tulsa.
TRANSACTIONS/CAREER NOTES: Selected by Washington Redskins in seventh round (197th pick overall) of 1994 NFL draft. ... Signed by Redskins (July 19, 1994).
PRO STATISTICS: 1994—Fumbled four times and recovered two fumbles for minus four yards. 1995—Fumbled seven times and recovered four fumbles for minus 16 yards.
STATISTICAL PLATEAUS: 300-yard passing games: 1995 (1).
MISCELLANEOUS: Regular-season record as starting NFL quarterback: 3-12 (.200).

		PASSING								RUSHING				TOTALS		
Year Team	G	Att.	Cmp.	Pct.	Yds.	TD	Int.	Avg.	Rat.	Att.	Yds.	Avg.	TD	TD	2pt.	Pts.
1994—Washington NFL	4	100	46	46.0	600	5	5	6.00	61.3	4	1	0.3	0	0	0	0
1995—Washington NFL	16	396	199	50.3	2751	13	13	6.95	70.2	22	16	0.7	1	1	0	6
Pro totals (2 years)	20	496	245	49.4	3351	18	18	6.76	68.4	26	17	0.7	1	1	0	6

FRIESZ, JOHN QB SEAHAWKS

PERSONAL: Born May 19, 1967, in Missoula, Mont. ... 6-4/211. ... Full name: John Melvin Friesz. ... Name pronounced FREEZE.
HIGH SCHOOL: Coeur D'Alene (Idaho).
COLLEGE: Idaho.
TRANSACTIONS/CAREER NOTES: Selected by San Diego Chargers in sixth round (138th pick overall) of 1990 NFL draft. ... Signed by Chargers (July 20, 1990). ... On injured reserve with elbow injury (September 4-October 3, 1990). ... On practice squad (October 3-December 28, 1990). ... Granted free agency (February 1, 1992). ... Re-signed by Chargers (July 27, 1992). ... On injured reserve with knee injury (August 25, 1992-entire season). ... Granted unconditional free agency (February 17, 1994). ... Signed by Washington Redskins (April 18, 1994). ... Granted unconditional free agency (February 17, 1995). ... Signed by Seattle Seahawks (March 17, 1995).
HONORS: Walter Payton Award winner (1989).
PRO STATISTICS: 1991—Fumbled 10 times and recovered two fumbles for minus 21 yards. 1993—Fumbled twice and recovered one fumble for minus three yards. 1994—Fumbled twice and recovered one fumble. 1995—Fumbled twice and recovered one fumble for minus three yards.
STATISTICAL PLATEAUS: 300-yard passing games: 1991 (2), 1994 (1). Total: 3.
MISCELLANEOUS: Regular-season record as starting NFL quarterback: 8-22 (.267).

		PASSING								RUSHING				TOTALS		
Year Team	G	Att.	Cmp.	Pct.	Yds.	TD	Int.	Avg.	Rat.	Att.	Yds.	Avg.	TD	TD	2pt.	Pts.
1990—San Diego NFL	1	22	11	50.0	98	1	1	4.46	58.5	1	3	3.0	0	0	...	0
1991—San Diego NFL	16	487	262	53.8	2896	12	15	5.95	67.1	10	18	1.8	0	0	...	0
1992—San Diego NFL						Did not play—injured.										
1993—San Diego NFL	12	238	128	53.8	1402	6	4	5.89	72.8	10	3	0.3	0	0	...	0
1994—Washington NFL	16	180	105	58.3	1266	10	9	7.03	77.7	1	1	1.0	0	0	0	0
1995—Seattle NFL	6	120	64	53.3	795	6	3	6.63	80.4	11	0	0.0	0	0	0	0
Pro totals (5 years)	51	1047	570	54.5	6457	35	32	6.17	71.6	33	25	0.8	0	0	0	0

FRISCH, DAVID TE VIKINGS

PERSONAL: Born June 22, 1970, in Kirkwood, Mo. ... 6-7/260. ... Full name: David Joseph Frisch.
HIGH SCHOOL: Northwest (House Springs, Mo.).
JUNIOR COLLEGE: Iowa Central Community College.
COLLEGE: Missouri, then Colorado State.
TRANSACTIONS/CAREER NOTES: Signed as non-drafted free agent by Cincinnati Bengals (April 27, 1993). ... Released by Bengals (August 20, 1995). ... Signed by New England Patriots (October 25, 1995). ... Released by Patriots (December 19, 1995). ... Signed by Minnesota

Vikings (February 13, 1996).
PLAYING EXPERIENCE: Cincinnati NFL, 1993 and 1994; New England NFL, 1995. ... Games: 1993 (11), 1994 (16), 1995 (2). Total: 29.
PRO STATISTICS: 1993—Caught six passes for 43 yards. 1995—Returned one kickoff for eight yards.

FRYAR, IRVING   WR   EAGLES

PERSONAL: Born September 28, 1962, in Mount Holly, N.J. ... 6-0/200. ... Full name: Irving Dale Fryar.
HIGH SCHOOL: Rancocas Valley Regional (Mount Holly, N.J.).
COLLEGE: Nebraska.
TRANSACTIONS/CAREER NOTES: Selected by Chicago Blitz in first round (third pick overall) of 1984 USFL draft. ... Signed by New England Patriots (April 11, 1984). ... Selected officially by Patriots in first round (first pick overall) of 1984 NFL draft. ... Traded by Patriots to Miami Dolphins for second-round pick (OL Todd Rucci) in 1993 draft and third-round pick (C Joe Burch) in 1994 draft (April 1, 1993). ... Granted unconditional free agency (February 16, 1996). ... Signed by Philadelphia Eagles (March 19, 1996).
CHAMPIONSHIP GAME EXPERIENCE: Played in Super Bowl XX (1985 season).
HONORS: Named wide receiver on THE SPORTING NEWS college All-America first team (1983). ... Played in Pro Bowl (1985, 1993 and 1994 seasons).
PRO STATISTICS: 1984—Fumbled four times and recovered one fumble. 1985—Fumbled four times. 1986—Fumbled four times and recovered one fumble. 1987—Fumbled twice. 1988—Fumbled twice. 1989—Fumbled twice. 1990—Fumbled once and recovered one fumble. 1991—Attempted one pass without a completion and fumbled twice. 1994—Ran two yards with lateral from reception for a touchdown and recovered one fumble for seven yards.
STATISTICAL PLATEAUS: 100-yard receiving games: 1985 (1), 1986 (2), 1987 (1), 1988 (1), 1989 (1), 1990 (1), 1991 (3), 1992 (2), 1993 (2), 1994 (6), 1995 (2). Total: 22.

Year Team	G	RUSHING				RECEIVING				PUNT RETURNS				KICKOFF RETURNS				TOTALS		
		Att.	Yds.	Avg.	TD	No.	Yds.	Avg.	TD	No.	Yds.	Avg.	TD	No.	Yds.	Avg.	TD	TD	2pt.	Pts.
1984—New England NFL	14	2	-11	-5.5	0	11	164	14.9	1	36	347	9.6	0	5	95	19.0	0	1	...	6
1985—New England NFL	16	7	27	3.9	1	39	670	17.2	7	37	520	*14.1	*2	3	39	13.0	0	10	...	60
1986—New England NFL	14	4	80	20.0	0	43	737	17.1	6	35	366	10.5	1	10	192	19.2	0	7	...	42
1987—New England NFL	12	9	52	5.8	0	31	467	15.1	5	18	174	9.7	0	6	119	19.8	0	5	...	30
1988—New England NFL	15	6	12	2.0	0	33	490	14.9	5	38	398	10.5	0	1	3	3.0	0	5	...	30
1989—New England NFL	11	2	15	7.5	0	29	537	18.5	3	12	107	8.9	0	1	47	47.0	0	3	...	18
1990—New England NFL	16	0	0	...	0	54	856	15.9	4	28	133	4.8	0	0	0	...	0	4	...	24
1991—New England NFL	16	2	11	5.5	0	68	1014	14.9	3	2	10	5.0	0	0	0	...	0	3	...	18
1992—New England NFL	15	1	6	6.0	0	55	791	14.4	4	0	0	...	0	0	0	...	0	4	...	24
1993—Miami NFL	16	3	-4	-1.3	0	64	1010	15.8	5	0	0	...	0	1	10	10.0	0	5	...	30
1994—Miami NFL	16	0	0	...	0	73	1270	17.4	7	0	0	...	0	0	0	...	0	7	2	46
1995—Miami NFL	16	0	0	...	0	62	910	14.7	8	0	0	...	0	0	0	...	0	8	0	48
Pro totals (12 years)	177	36	188	5.2	1	562	8916	15.9	58	206	2055	10.0	3	27	505	18.7	0	62	2	376

FULLER, COREY   CB   VIKINGS

PERSONAL: Born May 11, 1971, in Tallahassee, Fla. ... 5-10/198.
HIGH SCHOOL: James S. Rickards (Tallahassee, Fla.).
COLLEGE: Florida State.
TRANSACTIONS/CAREER NOTES: Selected by MInnesota Vikings in second round (55th pick overall) of 1995 NFL draft. ... Signed by Vikings (July 24, 1995).
PRO STATISTICS: 1995—Credited with ½ sack and recovered one fumble for 12 yards and a touchdown.

		INTERCEPTIONS			
Year Team	G	No.	Yds.	Avg.	TD
1995—Minnesota NFL	16	1	0	0.0	0

FULLER, RANDY   CB   STEELERS

PERSONAL: Born June 2, 1970, in Columbus, Ga. ... 5-10/175. ... Full name: Randy Lamar Fuller.
HIGH SCHOOL: William H. Spencer (Columbus, Ga.).
COLLEGE: Tennessee State.
TRANSACTIONS/CAREER NOTES: Selected by Denver Broncos in fourth round (123rd pick overall) of 1994 NFL draft. ... Signed by Broncos (July 22, 1994). ... Released by Broncos (August 22, 1995). ... Signed by Pittsburgh Steelers (September 12, 1995).
PLAYING EXPERIENCE: Denver NFL, 1994; Pittsburgh NFL, 1995. ... Games: 1994 (10), 1995 (13). Total: 23.
CHAMPIONSHIP GAME EXPERIENCE: Played in AFC championship game (1995 season). ... Played in Super Bowl XXX (1995 season).

FULLER, WILLIAM   DE   EAGLES

PERSONAL: Born March 8, 1962, in Norfolk, Va. ... 6-3/280. ... Full name: William Henry Fuller Jr.
HIGH SCHOOL: Indian River (Chesapeake, Va.).
COLLEGE: North Carolina.
TRANSACTIONS/CAREER NOTES: Selected by Philadelphia Stars in 1984 USFL territorial draft. ... Signed by Stars (February 6, 1984). ... On injured reserve with fractured ankle (May 18-June 23, 1984). ... Selected by Los Angeles Rams in first round (21st pick overall) of 1984 NFL supplemental draft. ... Stars franchise moved to Baltimore (November 1, 1984). ... Granted free agency when USFL suspended operations (August 7, 1986). ... Signed by Rams (September 10, 1986). ... Traded by Rams with G Kent Hill, first-round (WR Haywood Jeffires) and fifth-round (RB Spencer Tillman) picks in 1987 draft and first-round pick (traded to Los Angeles Raiders) in 1988 draft to Houston Oilers for rights to QB Jim Everett (September 8, 1986). ... Granted roster exemption (September 18-22, 1986). ... Granted free agency (February 1, 1992). ... Re-signed by Oilers (September 11, 1992). ... Granted unconditional free agency (February 17, 1994). ... Signed by Philadelphia Eagles (March 31, 1994).
CHAMPIONSHIP GAME EXPERIENCE: Played in USFL championship game (1984 and 1985 seasons).
HONORS: Named defensive tackle on THE SPORTING NEWS college All-America first team (1983). ... Named defensive end on THE SPORTING NEWS USFL All-Star team (1985). ... Played in Pro Bowl (1991, 1994 and 1995 seasons).

F

PRO STATISTICS: USFL: 1984—Recovered one fumble. 1985—Intercepted one pass for 35 yards and recovered four fumbles for 17 yards. NFL: 1987—Returned one kickoff for no yards and recovered one fumble. 1988—Intercepted one pass for nine yards. 1990—Recovered one fumble. 1991—Recovered two fumbles for three yards. 1992—Recovered one fumble for 10 yards and a touchdown. 1994—Credited with one safety and recovered one fumble. 1995—Recovered one fumble.

Year Team	G	SACKS
1984—Philadelphia USFL	13	2.0
1985—Baltimore USFL	18	8.5
1986—Houston NFL	13	1.0
1987—Houston NFL	12	2.0
1988—Houston NFL	16	8.5
1989—Houston NFL	15	6.5
1990—Houston NFL	16	8.0
1991—Houston NFL	16	15.0
1992—Houston NFL	15	8.0
1993—Houston NFL	16	10.0
1994—Philadelphia NFL	16	9.5
1995—Philadelphia NFL	14	13.0
USFL totals (2 years)	31	10.5
NFL totals (10 years)	149	81.5
Pro totals (12 years)	180	92.0

FURRER, WILL — QB

PERSONAL: Born February 5, 1968, in Danville, Pa. ... 6-3/210. ... Full name: William Mason Furrer.
HIGH SCHOOL: Pullman (Wash.) and Fork Union (Va.) Military Academy.
COLLEGE: Virginia Tech.
TRANSACTIONS/CAREER NOTES: Selected by Chicago Bears in fourth round (107th pick overall) of 1992 NFL draft.... Signed by Bears (July 23, 1992).... Claimed on waivers by Phoenix Cardinals (August 31, 1993).... Cardinals franchise renamed Arizona Cardinals for 1994 season.... Released by Cardinals (August 22, 1994).... Signed by Denver Broncos (August 24, 1994).... Granted unconditional free agency (February 17, 1995).... Assigned by Broncos to Amsterdam Admirals in 1995 World League enhancement allocation program (February 20, 1995).... Signed by Houston Oilers (July 21, 1995).... Released by Oilers (February 15, 1996).
PRO STATISTICS: 1992—Fumbled once. 1995—Fumbled three times.
MISCELLANEOUS: Regular-season record as starting NFL quarterback: 0-1 (.000).

Year Team	G	PASSING Att.	Cmp.	Pct.	Yds.	TD	Int.	Avg.	Rat.	RUSHING Att.	Yds.	lAvg.	TD	TOTALS TD	2pt.	Pts.
1992—Chicago NFL	2	25	9	36.0	89	0	3	3.56	7.3	0	0	0	0	0	0	0
1993—							Did not play.									
1994—Denver NFL	0	0	0	...	0	0	0	...	...	0	0	0	0	0	0	0
1995—Amsterdam W.L.	...	85	51	60.0	542	4	2	6.38	84.5	14	32	2.3	1	1	0	6
—Houston NFL	7	99	48	48.5	483	2	7	4.88	40.1	8	20	2.5	0	0	0	0
W.L. totals (1 year)	...	85	51	600	542	4	2	6.38	84.5	14	32	2.3	1	1	0	6
NFL totals (3 years)	9	124	57	460	572	2	10	4.61	31.4	8	20	2.5	0	0	0	0
Pro totals (3 years)	...	209	108	51.7	1114	6	12	5.33	53.0	22	52	2.4	1	1	0	6

GAINES, WENDALL — DE — PACKERS

PERSONAL: Born January 17, 1972, in Vernon, Texas. ... 6-4/293. ... Related to Jason Gildon, linebacker, Pittsburgh Steelers.
HIGH SCHOOL: Frederick (Okla.).
JUNIOR COLLEGE: Rose State College (Okla.).
COLLEGE: Oklahoma State.
TRANSACTIONS/CAREER NOTES: Signed as non-drafted free agent by Arizona Cardinals to practice squad (September 12, 1994). ... Activated (November 9, 1994); did not play. ... Released by Cardinals (March 27, 1996). ... Signed by Green Bay Packers (May 15, 1996).
PLAYING EXPERIENCE: Arizona NFL, 1995. ... Games: 1995 (16).
PRO STATISTICS: 1995—Caught 14 passes for 117 yards and two touchdowns and recovered one fumble.
MISCELLANEOUS: Played tight end during the 1995 season.

GAINES, WILLIAM — DT — REDSKINS

PERSONAL: Born June 20, 1971, in Jackson, Miss. ... 6-5/303. ... Full name: William Albert Gaines.
HIGH SCHOOL: Lanier (Jackson, Miss.).
COLLEGE: Florida.
TRANSACTIONS/CAREER NOTES: Selected by Miami Dolphins in fifth round (147th pick overall) of 1994 NFL draft. ... Signed by Dolphins (July 11, 1994). ... Released by Dolphins (August 27, 1995). ... Claimed on waivers by Washington Redskins (August 28, 1995).

Year Team	G	SACKS
1994—Miami NFL	7	0.0
1995—Washington NFL	15	2.0
Pro totals (2 years)	22	2.0

GALBRAITH, SCOTT — TE

PERSONAL: Born January 7, 1967, in Sacramento. ... 6-2/255. ... Full name: Alan Scott Galbraith. ... Name pronounced GAL-breath.
HIGH SCHOOL: Highlands (North Highlands, Calif.).
COLLEGE: Southern California.
TRANSACTIONS/CAREER NOTES: Selected by Cleveland Browns in seventh round (178th pick overall) of 1990 NFL draft. ... Signed by Browns (July 17, 1990). ... Granted free agency (February 1, 1992). ... Re-signed by Browns (August 30, 1992). ... Activated (September 15,

F
G

1992). ... Granted free agency (March 1, 1993). ... Re-signed by Browns (July 24, 1993). ... Released by Browns (August 30, 1993). ... Signed by Dallas Cowboys (November 11, 1993). ... Granted unconditional free agency (February 17, 1995). ... Signed by Washington Redskins (May 16, 1995). ... Granted unconditional free agency (February 16, 1996).
CHAMPIONSHIP GAME EXPERIENCE: Played in NFC championship game (1993 and 1994 seasons). ... Member of Super Bowl championship team (1993 season).
PRO STATISTICS: 1990—Recovered one fumble. 1991—Recovered one fumble.

		RECEIVING				KICKOFF RETURNS				TOTALS			
Year Team	G	No.	Yds.	Avg.	TD	No.	Yds.	Avg.	TD	TD	2pt.	Pts.	Fum.
1990—Cleveland NFL	16	4	62	15.5	0	3	16	5.3	0	0	...	0	0
1991—Cleveland NFL	16	27	328	12.2	0	2	13	6.5	0	0	...	0	0
1992—Cleveland NFL	14	4	63	15.8	1	0	0	...	0	1	...	6	0
1993—Dallas NFL	7	1	1	1.0	1	0	0	...	0	1	...	6	0
1994—Dallas NFL	16	4	31	7.8	0	0	0	...	0	0	0	0	0
1995—Washington NFL	16	10	80	8.0	2	0	0	...	0	2	0	12	0
Pro totals (6 years)	85	50	565	11.3	4	5	29	5.8	0	4	0	24	0

GALBREATH, HARRY   G

PERSONAL: Born January 1, 1965, in Clarksville, Tenn. ... 6-1/285. ... Full name: Harry Curtis Galbreath.
HIGH SCHOOL: Clarksville (Tenn.).
COLLEGE: Tennessee (degree in human services).
TRANSACTIONS/CAREER NOTES: Selected by Miami Dolphins in eighth round (212th pick overall) of 1988 NFL draft. ... Signed by Dolphins (July 12, 1988). ... Granted free agency (February 1, 1991). ... Re-signed by Dolphins (August 26, 1991). ... Activated (September 1, 1991). ... Granted unconditional free agency (March 1, 1993). ... Signed by Green Bay Packers (March 23, 1993). ... Granted unconditional free agency (February 16, 1996).
PLAYING EXPERIENCE: Miami NFL, 1988-1992; Green Bay NFL, 1993-1995. ... Games: 1988 (16), 1989 (14), 1990 (16), 1991 (16), 1992 (16), 1993 (16), 1994 (16), 1995 (16). Total: 126.
CHAMPIONSHIP GAME EXPERIENCE: Played in AFC championship game (1992 season). ... Played in NFC championship game (1995 season).
HONORS: Named guard on THE SPORTING NEWS college All-America first team (1987).
PRO STATISTICS: 1989—Recovered one fumble.

GALLOWAY, JOEY   WR/KR   SEAHAWKS

PERSONAL: Born November 20, 1971, in Bellaire, Ohio. ... 5-11/188.
HIGH SCHOOL: Bellaire (Ohio).
COLLEGE: Ohio State.
TRANSACTIONS/CAREER NOTES: Selected by Seattle Seahawks in first round (eighth pick overall) of 1995 NFL draft. ... Signed by Seahawks (July 20, 1995).
PRO STATISTICS: 1995—Fumbled once.
STATISTICAL PLATEAUS: 100-yard receiving games: 1995 (3).

		RUSHING				RECEIVING				PUNT RETURNS				KICKOFF RETURNS				TOTALS		
Year Team	G	Att.	Yds.	Avg.	TD	No.	Yds.	Avg.	TD	No.	Yds.	Avg.	TD	No.	Yds.	Avg.	TD	TD	2pt.	Pts.
1995—Seattle NFL	16	11	154	14.0	1	67	1039	15.5	7	36	360	10.0	†1	2	30	15.0	0	9	0	54

GAMMON, KENDALL   C   STEELERS

PERSONAL: Born October 23, 1968, in Wichita, Kan. ... 6-4/288. ... Full name: Kendall Robert Gammon.
HIGH SCHOOL: Rose Hill (Kan.).
COLLEGE: Pittsburg (Kan.) State.
TRANSACTIONS/CAREER NOTES: Selected by Pittsburgh Steelers in 11th round (291st pick overall) of 1992 NFL draft. ... Signed by Steelers (July 14, 1992). ... Released by Steelers (August 30, 1993). ... Re-signed by Steelers (August 31, 1993). ... Granted unconditional free agency (February 17, 1995). ... Re-signed by Steelers (May 8, 1995).
PLAYING EXPERIENCE: Pittsburgh NFL, 1992-1995. ... Games: 1992 (16), 1993 (16), 1994 (16), 1995 (16). Total: 64.
CHAMPIONSHIP GAME EXPERIENCE: Played in AFC championship game (1994 and 1995 seasons). ... Played in Super Bowl XXX (1995 season).

GANDY, WAYNE   OT   RAMS

PERSONAL: Born February 10, 1971, in Haines City, Fla. ... 6-4/292. ... Full name: Wayne Lamar Gandy.
HIGH SCHOOL: Haines City (Fla.).
COLLEGE: Auburn.
TRANSACTIONS/CAREER NOTES: Selected by Los Angeles Rams in first round (15th pick overall) of 1994 NFL draft. ... Signed by Rams (July 23, 1994). ... Rams franchise moved to St. Louis (April 12, 1995).
PLAYING EXPERIENCE: Los Angeles Rams NFL, 1994 and 1995. ... Games: 1994 (16), 1995 (16). Total: 32.
HONORS: Named offensive lineman on THE SPORTING NEWS college All-America first team (1993).

G

GANNON, RICH   QB   CHIEFS

PERSONAL: Born December 20, 1965, in Philadelphia. ... 6-3/205. ... Full name: Richard Joseph Gannon.
HIGH SCHOOL: St. Joseph's Prep (Philadelphia).
COLLEGE: Delaware (degree in criminal justice, 1987).
TRANSACTIONS/CAREER NOTES: Selected by New England Patriots in fourth round (98th pick overall) of 1987 NFL draft. ... Rights traded by Patriots to Minnesota Vikings for fourth-round (WR Sammy Martin) and 11th-round (traded) picks in 1988 draft (May 6, 1987). ... Signed

by Vikings (July 30, 1987). ... Active for 13 games with Vikings (1989); did not play. ... Granted free agency (February 1, 1990). ... Re-signed by Vikings (July 30, 1990). ... Granted free agency (February 1, 1991). ... Re-signed by Vikings (July 25, 1991). ... Granted free agency (February 1, 1992). ... Re-signed by Vikings (August 8, 1992). ... Traded by Vikings to Washington Redskins for conditional draft pick (August 20, 1993). ... Granted unconditional free agency (February 17, 1994). ... Signed by Kansas City Chiefs (March 29, 1995). ... Released by Chiefs (February 15, 1996). ... Re-signed by Chiefs (April 3, 1996).

CHAMPIONSHIP GAME EXPERIENCE: Member of Vikings for NFC championship game (1987 season); did not play.
PRO STATISTICS: 1990—Recovered six fumbles for minus three yards. 1991—Caught one pass for no yards. 1993—Recovered one fumble.
STATISTICAL PLATEAUS: 300-yard passing games: 1991 (1), 1992 (1). Total: 2.
MISCELLANEOUS: Regular-season record as starting NFL quarterback: 20-19 (.513).

| | | | PASSING | | | | | | | | RUSHING | | | | TOTALS | | |
Year Team	G	Att.	Cmp.	Pct.	Yds.	TD	Int.	Avg.	Rat.	Att.	Yds.	Avg.	TD	TD	2pt.	Pts.
1987—Minnesota NFL	4	6	2	33.3	18	0	1	3.00	2.8	0	0	...	0	0	...	0
1988—Minnesota NFL	3	15	7	46.7	90	0	0	6.00	66.0	4	29	7.3	0	0	...	0
1989—Minnesota NFL							Did not play.									
1990—Minnesota NFL	14	349	182	52.2	2278	16	16	6.53	68.9	52	268	5.2	1	1	...	6
1991—Minnesota NFL	15	354	211	59.6	2166	12	6	6.12	81.5	43	236	5.5	2	2	...	12
1992—Minnesota NFL	12	279	159	57.0	1905	12	13	6.83	72.9	45	187	4.2	0	0	...	0
1993—Washington NFL	8	125	74	59.2	704	3	7	5.63	59.6	21	88	4.2	1	1	...	6
1994—							Did not play.									
1995—Kansas City NFL	2	11	7	63.6	57	0	0	5.18	76.7	8	25	3.1	1	0	0	0
Pro totals (7 years)	58	1139	642	56.4	7218	43	43	6.34	72.3	173	833	4.8	5	4	0	24

GANT, KENNETH　　　　　S　　　　　BUCCANEERS

PERSONAL: Born April 18, 1967, in Lakeland, Fla. ... 5-11/195. ... Full name: Kenneth Dwayne Gant.
HIGH SCHOOL: Kathleen (Lakeland, Fla.).
COLLEGE: Albany (Ga.) State.
TRANSACTIONS/CAREER NOTES: Selected by Dallas Cowboys in ninth round (221st pick overall) of 1990 NFL draft. ... Signed by Cowboys (July 18, 1990). ... On injured reserve with hamstring injury (September 6-October 1, 1990). ... Granted free agency (March 1, 1993). ... Re-signed by Cowboys (April 23, 1993). ... Granted unconditional free agency (February 17, 1995). ... Signed by Tampa Bay Buccaneers (March 24, 1995).
CHAMPIONSHIP GAME EXPERIENCE: Played in NFC championship game (1992-1994 seasons). ... Member of Super Bowl championship team (1992 and 1993 seasons).
PRO STATISTICS: 1991—Recovered one fumble. 1992—Recovered one fumble. 1995—Recovered one fumble for 13 yards.

| | | INTERCEPTIONS | | | | SACKS | KICKOFF RETURNS | | | | TOTALS | | | |
Year Team	G	No.	Yds.	Avg.	TD	No.	No.	Yds.	Avg.	TD	TD	2pt.	Pts.	Fum.
1990—Dallas NFL	12	1	26	26.0	0	0.0	0	0	...	0	0	...	0	0
1991—Dallas NFL	16	1	0	0.0	0	0.0	6	114	19.0	0	0	...	0	0
1992—Dallas NFL	16	3	19	6.3	0	3.0	0	0	...	0	0	...	0	0
1993—Dallas NFL	12	1	0	0.0	0	0.0	1	18	18.0	0	0	...	0	0
1994—Dallas NFL	16	1	0	0.0	0	0.0	0	0	...	0	0	0	0	0
1995—Tampa Bay NFL	16	0	0		0	0.0	0	0	...	0	0	0	0	0
Pro totals (6 years)	88	7	45	6.4	0	3.0	7	132	18.9	0	0	0	0	0

GARCIA, FRANK　　　　　C　　　　　PANTHERS

PERSONAL: Born January 28, 1972, in Phoenix. ... 6-1/295.
HIGH SCHOOL: Maryvale (Phoenix).
COLLEGE: Washington.
TRANSACTIONS/CAREER NOTES: Selected by Carolina Panthers in fourth round (132nd pick overall) of 1995 NFL draft. ... Signed by Panthers (July 14, 1995).
PLAYING EXPERIENCE: Carolina NFL, 1995. ... Games: 1995 (15).
PRO STATISTICS: 1995—Fumbled once and recovered one fumble for 10 yards.

GARDNER, CARWELL　　　　　FB

G

PERSONAL: Born November 27, 1966, in Louisville, Ky. ... 6-2/244. ... Full name: Carwell Ernest Gardner. ... Brother of Donnie Gardner, defensive lineman, San Antonio Riders of World League and Miami Dolphins (1991).
HIGH SCHOOL: Trinity High School for Boys (Louisville, Ky.).
COLLEGE: Kentucky, then Louisville.
TRANSACTIONS/CAREER NOTES: Selected by Buffalo Bills in second round (42nd pick overall) of 1990 NFL draft. ... Signed by Bills (July 28, 1990). ... On injured reserve with knee injury (September 4-November 3, 1990). ... Granted free agency (March 1, 1993). ... Re-signed by Bills (May 21, 1993). ... Granted unconditional free agency (February 17, 1995). ... Re-signed by Bills (April 21, 1995). ... Released by Bills (February 16, 1996).
CHAMPIONSHIP GAME EXPERIENCE: Played in AFC championship game (1990-1993 seasons). ... Played in Super Bowl XXV (1990 season), Super Bowl XXVI (1991 season), Super Bowl XXVII (1992 season) and Super Bowl XXVIII (1993 season).
PRO STATISTICS: 1991—Recovered three fumbles and returned one kickoff for 10 yards. 1992—Recovered two fumbles. 1994—Returned one kickoff for six yards. 1995—Recovered two fumbles.

| | | RUSHING | | | | RECEIVING | | | | TOTALS | | | |
Year Team	G	Att.	Yds.	Avg.	TD	No.	Yds.	Avg.	TD	TD	2pt.	Pts.	Fum.
1990—Buffalo NFL	7	15	41	2.7	0	0	0	...	0	0	...	0	0
1991—Buffalo NFL	16	42	146	3.5	4	3	20	6.7	0	4	...	24	4
1992—Buffalo NFL	16	40	166	4.2	2	7	67	9.6	0	2	...	12	0
1993—Buffalo NFL	13	20	56	2.8	0	4	50	12.5	1	1	...	6	1
1994—Buffalo NFL	16	41	135	3.3	4	11	89	8.1	0	4	0	24	1

Year Team		G	Att.	Yds.	Avg.	TD	No.	Yds.	Avg.	TD	TD	2pt.	Pts.	Fum.
	RUSHING						RECEIVING				TOTALS			
1995—Buffalo NFL		15	20	77	3.9	0	2	17	8.5	0	1	1	8	0
Pro totals (6 years)		83	178	621	3.5	10	27	243	9.0	1	12	1	74	6

GARDNER, MOE   NT   FALCONS

PERSONAL: Born August 10, 1968, in Indianapolis. ... 6-2/265.
HIGH SCHOOL: Cathedral (Indianapolis).
COLLEGE: Illinois (degree in sociology).
TRANSACTIONS/CAREER NOTES: Selected by Atlanta Falcons in fourth round (87th pick overall) of 1991 NFL draft. ... Signed by Falcons (July 20, 1991). ... Granted unconditional free agency (February 16, 1996). ... Re-signed by Falcons (May 13, 1996).
HONORS: Named nose tackle on THE SPORTING NEWS college All-America second team (1989). ... Named defensive lineman on THE SPORTING NEWS college All-America second team (1990).
PRO STATISTICS: 1994—Recovered one fumble.

Year Team	G	SACKS
1991—Atlanta NFL	16	3.0
1992—Atlanta NFL	16	4.5
1993—Atlanta NFL	16	2.0
1994—Atlanta NFL	16	0.0
1995—Atlanta NFL	16	0.5
Pro totals (5 years)	80	10.0

GARDOCKI, CHRIS   P   COLTS

PERSONAL: Born February 7, 1970, in Stone Mountain, Ga. ... 6-1/199. ... Full name: Christopher Allen Gardocki.
HIGH SCHOOL: Redan (Stone Mountain, Ga.).
COLLEGE: Clemson.
TRANSACTIONS/CAREER NOTES: Selected after junior season by Chicago Bears in third round (78th pick overall) of 1991 NFL draft. ... Signed by Bears (June 24, 1991). ... On injured reserve with groin injury (August 27-November 27, 1991). ... Granted unconditional free agency (February 17, 1995). ... Signed by Indianapolis Colts (February 24, 1995).
CHAMPIONSHIP GAME EXPERIENCE: Played in AFC championship game (1995 season).
HONORS: Named kicker on THE SPORTING NEWS college All-America second team (1990).
PRO STATISTICS: 1992—Attempted three passes with one completion for 43 yards and recovered one fumble. 1993—Attempted two passes without a completion, fumbled once and recovered one fumble. 1995—Attempted one pass without a completion.

Year Team	G	No.	Yds.	Avg.	Net avg.	In. 20	Blk.
				PUNTING			
1991—Chicago NFL	4	0	0	...	...	0	0
1992—Chicago NFL	16	79	3393	42.9	36.2	19	0
1993—Chicago NFL	16	80	3080	38.5	36.6	28	0
1994—Chicago NFL	16	76	2871	37.8	32.4	23	0
1995—Indianapolis NFL	16	63	2681	42.6	33.4	16	0
Pro totals (5 years)	68	298	12025	40.4	34.8	86	0

GARNER, CHARLIE   RB   EAGLES

PERSONAL: Born February 13, 1972, in Falls Church, Va. ... 5-9/187.
HIGH SCHOOL: J. E. B. Stuart (Falls Church, Va.).
COLLEGE: Tennessee.
TRANSACTIONS/CAREER NOTES: Selected by Philadelphia Eagles in second round (42nd pick overall) of 1994 NFL draft. ... Signed by Eagles (July 18, 1994).
STATISTICAL PLATEAUS: 100-yard rushing games: 1994 (2), 1995 (1). Total: 3.

Year Team	G	Att.	Yds.	Avg.	TD	No.	Yds.	Avg.	TD	No.	Yds.	Avg.	TD	TD	2pt.	Pts.	Fum.
		RUSHING				RECEIVING				KICKOFF RETURNS				TOTALS			
1994—Philadelphia NFL	10	109	399	3.7	3	8	74	9.3	0	0	0	...	0	3	0	18	3
1995—Philadelphia NFL	15	108	588	*5.4	6	10	61	6.1	0	29	590	20.3	0	6	0	36	2
Pro totals (2 years)	25	217	987	4.6	9	18	135	7.5	0	29	590	20.4	0	9	0	54	5

GARNETT, DAVE   LB   VIKINGS

G

PERSONAL: Born December 6, 1970, in Pittsburgh. ... 6-2/219. ... Full name: David Eugene Garnett.
HIGH SCHOOL: Naperville (Ill.) North.
COLLEGE: Stanford.
TRANSACTIONS/CAREER NOTES: Signed as non-drafted free agent by Minnesota Vikings (May 4, 1993). ... Selected by Carolina Panthers from Vikings in NFL expansion draft (February 15, 1995). ... Released by Panthers (May 22, 1995). ... Signed by Denver Broncos (May 31, 1995). ... Released by Broncos (August 22, 1995). ... Re-signed by Broncos (October 3, 1995). ... Released by Broncos (October 24, 1995). ... Signed by Minnesota Vikings (February 22, 1996).
PLAYING EXPERIENCE: Minnesota NFL, 1993 and 1994; Denver NFL, 1995. ... Games: 1993 (16), 1994 (9), 1995 (3). Total: 28.
PRO STATISTICS: 1994—Returned one kickoff for no yards and recovered two fumbles.

GARRETT, JASON   QB   COWBOYS

PERSONAL: Born March 28, 1966, in Abington, Pa. ... 6-2/195. ... Full name: Jason Calvin Garrett. ... Son of Jim Garrett, scout, Dallas Cowboys and brother of John Garrett, wide receiver, Cincinnati Bengals and San Antonio Riders of World League (1989 and 1991).

HIGH SCHOOL: University (Hunting Valley, Ohio).
COLLEGE: Princeton (degree in history).
TRANSACTIONS/CAREER NOTES: Signed as non-drafted free agent by New Orleans Saints (1989). ... Released by Saints (August 30, 1989). ... Re-signed by Saints to developmental squad (September 6, 1989). ... Released by Saints (December 29, 1989). ... Re-signed by Saints for 1990 season. ... Released by Saints (September 3, 1990). ... Signed by WLAF (January 3, 1991). ... Selected by San Antonio Riders in first round (seventh quarterback) of 1991 WLAF positional draft. ... Signed by Ottawa Rough Riders of CFL (1991). ... Released by San Antonio Riders (March 3, 1992). ... Signed by Dallas Cowboys (March 23, 1992). ... Released by Cowboys (August 31, 1992). ... Re-signed by Cowboys to practice squad (September 1, 1992). ... Granted unconditional free agency (February 16, 1996). ... Re-signed by Cowboys (April 3, 1996).
CHAMPIONSHIP GAME EXPERIENCE: Member of Cowboys for NFC championship game (1993-1995 seasons); inactive. ... Member of Super Bowl championship team (1993 and 1995 seasons).
PRO STATISTICS: W.L.: 1991—Fumbled twice. CFL: 1991—Fumbled once. NFL: 1993—Fumbled once. 1994—Recovered one fumble.
STATISTICAL PLATEAUS: 300-yard passing games: 1994 (1).
MISCELLANEOUS: Regular-season record as starting NFL quarterback: 2-0 (1.000).

Year Team	G	PASSING Att.	Cmp.	Pct.	Yds.	TD	Int.	Avg.	Rat.	RUSHING Att.	Yds.	Avg.	TD	TOTALS TD	2pt.	Pts.
1991—San Antonio W.L.	5	113	66	58.4	609	3	3	5.39	71.0	7	7	1.0	0	0	0	0
—Ottawa CFL	13	3	2	66.7	28	0	0	9.33	96.5	0	0	...	0	0	0	0
1992—Dallas NFL							Did not play.									
1993—Dallas NFL	5	19	9	47.4	61	0	0	3.21	54.9	8	-8	-1.0	0	0	...	0
1994—Dallas NFL	2	31	16	51.6	315	2	1	10.16	95.5	3	-2	-0.7	0	0	0	0
1995—Dallas NFL	1	5	4	80.0	46	1	0	9.20	144.6	1	-1	-1.0	0	0	0	0
W.L. totals (1 year)	5	113	66	584	609	3	3	5.39	71.0	7	7	1.0	0	0	0	0
CFL totals (1 year)	13	3	2	667	28	0	0	9.33	96.5	0	0		0	0	0	0
NFL totals (3 years)	8	55	29	527	422	3	1	7.67	88.6	12	-11	-0.9	0	0	0	0
Pro totals (4 years)	26	171	97	56.7	1059	6	4	6.19	77.1	19	-4	-0.2	0	0	0	0

GASH, SAM   FB   PATRIOTS

PERSONAL: Born March 7, 1969, in Hendersonville, N.C. ... 5-11/224. ... Full name: Samuel Lee Gash Jr. ... Cousin of Thane Gash, safety, Cleveland Browns and San Francisco 49ers (1988-1993).
HIGH SCHOOL: Hendersonville (N.C.).
COLLEGE: Penn State (degree in liberal arts).
TRANSACTIONS/CAREER NOTES: Selected by New England Patriots in eighth round (205th pick overall) of 1992 NFL draft. ... Signed by Patriots (June 10, 1992). ... Granted free agency (February 17, 1995). ... Re-signed by Patriots (May 5, 1995).
PRO STATISTICS: 1992—Recovered two fumbles. 1994—Returned one kickoff for nine yards and recovered one fumble.

Year Team	G	RUSHING Att.	Yds.	Avg.	TD	RECEIVING No.	Yds.	Avg.	TD	TOTALS TD	2pt.	Pts.	Fum.
1992—New England NFL	15	5	7	1.4	1	0	0	...	0	1	...	6	1
1993—New England NFL	15	48	149	3.1	1	14	93	6.6	0	1	...	6	1
1994—New England NFL	13	30	86	2.9	0	9	61	6.8	0	0	0	0	1
1995—New England NFL	15	8	24	3.0	0	26	242	9.3	1	1	0	6	0
Pro totals (4 years)	58	91	266	2.9	2	49	396	8.1	1	3	0	18	3

GAYLE, SHAUN   S   CHARGERS

PERSONAL: Born March 8, 1962, in Newport News, Va. ... 5-11/202. ... Full name: Shaun Lanard Gayle.
HIGH SCHOOL: Bethel (Hampton, Va.).
COLLEGE: Ohio State (degree in education, 1984).
TRANSACTIONS/CAREER NOTES: Selected by Michigan Panthers in 14th round (288th pick overall) of 1984 USFL draft. ... Selected by Chicago Bears in 10th round (271st pick overall) of 1984 NFL draft. ... Signed by Bears (June 21, 1984). ... On injured reserve with broken ankle (December 12, 1984-remainder of season). ... On injured reserve with ankle injury (September 8-November 6, 1987). ... On injured reserve with neck injury (October 14, 1988-remainder of season). ... On injured reserve with stress fracture in shins (August 27-September 25, 1991). ... On injured reserve with ankle injury (September 2-October, 1992). ... Granted unconditional free agency (February 17, 1994). ... Re-signed by Bears (May 31, 1994). ... Granted unconditional free agency (February 17, 1995). ... Signed by San Diego Chargers (March 28, 1995).
CHAMPIONSHIP GAME EXPERIENCE: Played in NFC championship game (1985 season). ... Member of Super Bowl championship team (1985 season).
HONORS: Played in Pro Bowl (1991 season).
POSTSEASON RECORDS: Shares NFL postseason career record for most touchdowns by punt return—1 (January 5, 1986, vs. New York Giants).
PRO STATISTICS: 1985—Recovered one fumble. 1986—Recovered one fumble. 1989—Recovered two fumbles for 11 yards. 1990—Credited with one sack and recovered three fumbles for two yards. 1992—Recovered three fumbles. 1993—Credited with one sack. 1994—Recovered one fumble for nine yards. 1995—Recovered one fumble in end zone for a touchdown.

Year Team	G	INTERCEPTIONS No.	Yds.	Avg.	TD
1984—Chicago NFL	15	1	-1	-1.0	0
1985—Chicago NFL	16	0	0	...	0
1986—Chicago NFL	16	1	13	13.0	0
1987—Chicago NFL	8	1	20	20.0	1
1988—Chicago NFL	4	1	0	0.0	0
1989—Chicago NFL	14	3	39	13.0	0
1990—Chicago NFL	16	2	5	2.5	0
1991—Chicago NFL	12	1	11	11.0	0
1992—Chicago NFL	11	2	39	19.5	0
1993—Chicago NFL	16	0	0	...	0
1994—Chicago NFL	16	2	33	16.5	0
1995—San Diego NFL	16	2	99	49.5	1
Pro totals (12 years)	160	16	258	16.1	2

G

GEATHERS, JUMPY — DT

PERSONAL: Born June 26, 1960, in Georgetown, S.C. ... 6-7/290. ... Full name: James Allen Geathers. ... Brother of Robert Geathers, defensive end, Boston Breakers of USFL (1983).
HIGH SCHOOL: Choppee (Georgetown, S.C.).
JUNIOR COLLEGE: Paducah (Ky.) Community College.
COLLEGE: Wichita State.
TRANSACTIONS/CAREER NOTES: Selected by Oklahoma Outlaws in 1984 USFL territorial draft. ... Selected by New Orleans Saints in second round (42nd pick overall) of 1984 NFL draft. ... Signed by Saints (May 30, 1984). ... On injured reserve with knee injury (September 1-December 26, 1987). ... On injured reserve with knee injury (December 21, 1989-remainder of season). ... Granted unconditional free agency (February 1, 1990). ... Signed by Washington Redskins (March 30, 1990). ... On physically unable to perform list with knee injury (August 28-November 3, 1990). ... Granted unconditional free agency (March 1, 1993). ... Signed by Atlanta Falcons (March 19, 1993). ... Released by Falcons (April 5, 1995). ... Re-signed by Falcons (June 6, 1995). ... Released by Falcons (February 16, 1996).
CHAMPIONSHIP GAME EXPERIENCE: Played in NFC championship game (1991 season). ... Member of Super Bowl championship team (1991 season).
PRO STATISTICS: 1986—Recovered one fumble. 1988—Recovered three fumbles. 1989—Recovered five fumbles.

Year—Team	G	SACKS
1984—New Orleans NFL	16	6.0
1985—New Orleans NFL	16	6.5
1986—New Orleans NFL	16	9.0
1987—New Orleans NFL	1	0.0
1988—New Orleans NFL	16	3.5
1989—New Orleans NFL	15	1.0
1990—Washington NFL	9	3.0
1991—Washington NFL	16	4.5
1992—Washington NFL	16	5.0
1993—Atlanta NFL	14	3.5
1994—Atlanta NFL	16	8.0
1995—Atlanta NFL	16	7.0
Pro totals (12 years)	**167**	**57.0**

GEDNEY, CHRIS — TE — BEARS

PERSONAL: Born August 9, 1970, in Liverpool, N.Y. ... 6-5/265. ... Full name: Christopher Joseph Gedney.
HIGH SCHOOL: Liverpool (N.Y.).
COLLEGE: Syracuse.
TRANSACTIONS/CAREER NOTES: Selected by Chicago Bears in third round (61st pick overall) of 1993 NFL draft. ... Signed by Bears (June 16, 1994). ... On injured reserve with broken right fibula (October 24, 1994-remainder of season). ... Granted free agency (February 16, 1996). ... Re-signed by Bears (March 29, 1996).
HONORS: Named tight end on THE SPORTING NEWS college All-America first team (1992).

		RECEIVING				TOTALS			
Year—Team	G	No.	Yds.	Avg.	TD	TD	2pt.	Pts.	Fum.
1993—Chicago NFL	7	10	98	9.8	0	0	...	0	1
1994—Chicago NFL	7	13	157	12.1	3	3	0	18	1
1995—Chicago NFL	14	5	52	10.4	0	0	0	0	0
Pro totals (3 years)	**28**	**28**	**307**	**11.0**	**3**	**3**	**0**	**18**	**2**

GELBAUGH, STAN — QB

PERSONAL: Born December 4, 1962, in Carlisle, Pa. ... 6-3/215. ... Full name: Stanley Morris Gelbaugh.
HIGH SCHOOL: Cumberland Valley (Mechanicsburg, Pa.).
COLLEGE: Maryland (degree in marketing, 1986).
TRANSACTIONS/CAREER NOTES: Selected by Baltimore Stars in 1986 USFL territorial draft. ... Selected by Dallas Cowboys in sixth round (150th pick overall) of 1986 NFL draft. ... Signed by Cowboys (July 5, 1986). ... Released by Cowboys (August 18, 1986). ... Signed by Saskatchewan Roughriders of CFL (August 27, 1986). ... Released by Roughriders (October 7, 1986). ... Signed by Buffalo Bills (November 18, 1986). ... Active for five games with Bills (1986); did not play. ... On injured reserve with elbow injury (September 8, 1987-entire season). ... Released by Bills (September 16, 1988). ... Re-signed by Bills (September 20, 1988). ... Active for three games (1988); did not play. ... Released by Bills (September 5, 1989). ... Re-signed by Bills (October 11, 1989). ... Released by Bills (October 24, 1989). ... Re-signed by Bills (October 25, 1989). ... Released by Bills (November 6, 1989). ... Signed by Cincinnati Bengals (March 5, 1990). ... Released by Bengals prior to 1990 season. ... Signed by WLAF for 1991. ... Selected by London Monarchs in first round of 1991 WLAF supplemental draft (February 28, 1991). ... Signed by Hamilton Tiger-Cats of CFL (July 29, 1991). ... Released by Tiger-Cats (August 1991). ... Signed by Kansas City Chiefs (August 12, 1991). ... Released by Chiefs (August 19, 1991). ... Signed by Phoenix Cardinals (September 18, 1991). ... Granted unconditional free agency (February 1, 1992). ... Signed by Seattle Seahawks (February 13, 1992). ... Assigned by Seahawks to Monarchs in 1992 World League enhancement allocation program (February 20, 1992). ... Granted free agency (March 1, 1993). ... Re-signed by Seahawks (July 14, 1993). ... Granted unconditional free agency (February 17, 1994). ... Re-signed by Seahawks (May 20, 1994). ... Granted unconditional free agency (February 16, 1996).
CHAMPIONSHIP GAME EXPERIENCE: Member of Bills for AFC championship game (1988 season); inactive.
HONORS: Named quarterback on All-World League team (1991).
PRO STATISTICS: CFL: 1986: Credited with a single and punted 45 times for 1,811 yards (40.2-yard avg.). NFL: 1991—Recovered one fumble. 1992—Recovered two fumbles for minus 11 yards. 1993—Fumbled once. W.L.: 1991—Fumbled twice and recovered one fumble. 1992—Fumbled 10 times and recovered five fumbles for 12 yards.
MISCELLANEOUS: Regular-season record as starting NFL quarterback: 0-11 (.000).

		PASSING								RUSHING				TOTALS		
Year—Team	G	Att.	Cmp.	Pct.	Yds.	TD	Int.	Avg.	Rat.	Att.	Yds.	Avg.	TD	TD	2pt.	Pts.
1986—Saskatchewan CFL	5	0	0	...	0	0	0	...		0	0	...	0	0	0	1
1987—Buffalo NFL					Did not play—injured.											
1988—Buffalo NFL					Did not play—injured.											

G

Year Team	G	PASSING								RUSHING				TOTALS		
		Att.	Cmp.	Pct.	Yds.	TD	Int.	Avg.	Rat.	Att.	Yds.	Avg.	TD	TD	2pt.	Pts.
1989—Buffalo NFL	1	0	0	...	0	0	0	...	...	1	-3	-3.0	0	0	...	0
1990—					Did not play.											
1991—London W.L.	10	303	*189	*62.4	*2655	*17	12	8.76	*92.8	9	66	7.3	0	0	0	0
—Phoenix NFL	6	118	61	51.7	674	3	10	5.71	42.1	9	23	2.6	0	0	0	0
1992—London W.L.	10	279	147	52.7	1966	11	*12	7.05	70.6	21	91	4.3	0	0	0	0
—Seattle NFL	10	255	121	47.5	1307	6	11	5.13	52.9	16	79	4.9	0	0	...	0
1993—Seattle NFL	1	5	3	60.0	39	0	1	7.80	45.0	1	-1	-1.0	0	0	...	0
1994—Seattle NFL	1	11	7	63.6	80	1	0	7.27	115.7	1	10	10.0	0	0	0	0
1995—Seattle NFL					Did not play.											
W.L. totals (2 years)	20	582	336	577	4621	28	24	7.94	82.1	30	157	5.2	0	0	0	0
CFL totals (1 year)	5	0	0	...	0	0	0	...	...	0	0	...	0	0	0	1
NFL totals (5 years)	19	389	192	494	2100	10	22	5.40	50.7	28	108	3.9	0	0	0	0
Pro totals (6 years)	44	971	528	54.4	6721	38	46	6.92	69.5	58	265	4.6	0	0	0	1

GEORGE, JEFF   QB   FALCONS

PERSONAL: Born December 8, 1967, in Indianapolis. ... 6-4/210. ... Full name: Jeffrey Scott George.

HIGH SCHOOL: Warren Central (Indianapolis).

COLLEGE: Purdue, then Illinois (degree in speech communications, 1991).

TRANSACTIONS/CAREER NOTES: Signed after junior season by Indianapolis Colts (April 20, 1990). ... Selected officially by Colts in first round (first pick overall) of 1990 NFL draft. ... On reserve/did not report list (July 23-August 6, 1990). ... Traded by Colts to Atlanta Falcons for first-round (LB Trev Alberts) and third-round (OT Jason Mathews) picks in 1994 draft and a first-round pick (WR Marvin Harrison) in 1996 draft (March 24, 1994). ... Designated by Falcons as transition player (February 16, 1996).

PRO STATISTICS: 1990—Fumbled four times and recovered two fumbles. 1991—Fumbled eight times and recovered two fumbles for minus four yards. 1992—Fumbled six times and recovered one fumble for minus two yards. 1993—Fumbled four times. 1994—Led league with 12 fumbles and recovered six fumbles for minus 12 yards. 1995—Fumbled six times and recovered two fumbles for minus 15 yards.

STATISTICAL PLATEAUS: 300-yard passing games: 1991 (2), 1992 (3), 1993 (2), 1994 (2), 1995 (3). Total: 12.

MISCELLANEOUS: Regular-season record as starting NFL quarterback: 30-51 (.370).

Year Team	G	PASSING								RUSHING				TOTALS		
		Att.	Cmp.	Pct.	Yds.	TD	Int.	Avg.	Rat.	Att.	Yds.	Avg.	TD	TD	2pt.	Pts.
1990—Indianapolis NFL	13	334	181	54.2	2152	16	13	6.44	73.8	11	2	0.2	1	1	...	6
1991—Indianapolis NFL	16	485	292	60.2	2910	10	12	6.00	73.8	16	36	2.3	0	0	...	0
1992—Indianapolis NFL	10	306	167	54.6	1963	7	15	6.42	61.5	14	26	1.9	1	1	...	6
1993—Indianapolis NFL	13	407	234	57.5	2526	8	6	6.21	76.3	13	39	3.0	0	0	...	0
1994—Atlanta NFL	16	524	322	61.5	3734	23	18	7.13	83.3	30	66	2.2	0	0	0	0
1995—Atlanta NFL	16	557	336	60.3	4143	24	11	7.44	89.5	27	17	0.6	0	0	0	0
Pro totals (6 years)	84	2613	1532	58.6	17428	88	75	6.67	78.0	111	186	1.7	2	2	0	12

GEORGE, RON   LB   FALCONS

PERSONAL: Born March 20, 1970, in Heidelberg, Germany. ... 6-2/225.

HIGH SCHOOL: Heidelberg (Germany) American.

COLLEGE: Air Force, then Stanford (degree in economics, 1992).

TRANSACTIONS/CAREER NOTES: Selected by Atlanta Falcons in fifth round (121st pick overall) of 1993 NFL draft. ... Signed by Falcons (June 4, 1993). ... Granted free agency (February 16, 1996).

PLAYING EXPERIENCE: Atlanta NFL, 1993-1995. ... Games: 1993 (12), 1994 (16), 1995 (16). Total: 44.

HONORS: Named linebacker on THE SPORTING NEWS college All-America second team (1992).

PRO STATISTICS: 1993—Credited with one sack. 1994—Recovered one fumble. 1995—Returned three kickoffs for 45 yards.

GERAK, JOHN   TE/G   VIKINGS

PERSONAL: Born January 6, 1970, in Youngstown, Ohio. ... 6-3/269. ... Full name: John Matthew Gerak.

HIGH SCHOOL: Struthers (Ohio).

COLLEGE: Penn State.

TRANSACTIONS/CAREER NOTES: Selected by Minnesota Vikings in third round (57th pick overall) of 1993 NFL draft. ... Signed by Vikings (July 17, 1993).

PLAYING EXPERIENCE: Minnesota NFL, 1993-1995. ... Games: 1993 (4), 1994 (13), 1995 (16). Total: 33.

PRO STATISTICS: 1995—Caught one pass for three yards and returned one kickoff for 19 yards.

GESEK, JOHN   G/C   REDSKINS

PERSONAL: Born February 18, 1963, in San Francisco. ... 6-5/282. ... Full name: John Christian Gesek Jr. ... Name pronounced GEE-sik.

HIGH SCHOOL: San Ramon Valley (Danville, Calif.) and Bellflower (Calif.).

JUNIOR COLLEGE: Diablo Valley College, Calif. (did not play football).

COLLEGE: Sacramento State.

TRANSACTIONS/CAREER NOTES: Selected by Los Angeles Raiders in 10th round (265th pick overall) of 1987 NFL draft. ... Signed by Raiders (July 11, 1987). ... On injured reserve with back injury (September 7-October 14, 1987). ... Crossed picket line during players strike (October 13, 1987). ... On injured reserve with knee injury (October 19-December 5, 1987). ... On injured reserve with knee injury (November 30, 1988-remainder of season). ... Traded by Raiders to Dallas Cowboys for fifth-round pick in 1991 draft (September 3, 1990). ... Granted free agency (February 1, 1991). ... Re-signed by Cowboys (July 24, 1991). ... Granted unconditional free agency (February 17, 1994). ... Signed by Washington Redskins (March 16, 1994).

PLAYING EXPERIENCE: Los Angeles Raiders NFL, 1987-1989; Dallas NFL, 1990-1993; Washington NFL, 1994 and 1995. ... Games: 1987 (3), 1988 (12), 1989 (16), 1990 (15), 1991 (16), 1992 (16), 1993 (14), 1994 (15), 1995 (16). Total: 123.

G

CHAMPIONSHIP GAME EXPERIENCE: Played in NFC championship game (1992 and 1993 seasons). ... Member of Super Bowl championship team (1992 and 1993 seasons).
PRO STATISTICS: 1988—Fumbled once. 1990—Recovered two fumbles. 1992—Caught one pass for four yards and fumbled once. 1994—Recovered one fumble.

GIBSON, DENNIS — LB

PERSONAL: Born February 8, 1964, in Des Moines, Iowa. ... 6-2/240. ... Full name: Dennis Michael Gibson.
HIGH SCHOOL: Ankeny (Iowa).
COLLEGE: Iowa State.
TRANSACTIONS/CAREER NOTES: Selected by Detroit Lions in eighth round (203rd pick overall) of 1987 NFL draft. ... Signed by Lions (July 25, 1987). ... On injured reserve with shoulder injury (September 18-November 6, 1989). ... On developmental squad (November 7-22, 1989). ... On injured reserve with arch injury (December 14, 1990-remainder of season). ... Granted free agency (February 1, 1992). ... Re-signed by Lions (August 26, 1992). ... Granted roster exemption (August 26-September 4, 1992). ... Granted unconditional free agency (February 17, 1994). ... Signed by San Diego Chargers (March 30, 1994). ... Granted unconditional free agency (February 16, 1996).
CHAMPIONSHIP GAME EXPERIENCE: Played in NFC championship game (1991 season). ... Played in AFC championship game (1994 season). ... Played in Super Bowl XXIX (1994 season).
PRO STATISTICS: 1988—Recovered one fumble. 1989—Recovered three fumbles for minus four yards. 1990—Recovered one fumble. 1993—Recovered one fumble for two yards.

			INTERCEPTIONS				SACKS
Year Team	G	No.	Yds.	Avg.	TD		No.
1987—Detroit NFL	12	1	5	5.0	0		1.0
1988—Detroit NFL	16	0	0	...	0		0.5
1989—Detroit NFL	6	1	10	10.0	0		0.0
1990—Detroit NFL	11	0	0	...	0		0.0
1991—Detroit NFL	16	0	0	...	0		0.0
1992—Detroit NFL	16	0	0	...	0		0.0
1993—Detroit NFL	15	1	0	0.0	0		1.0
1994—San Diego NFL	16	0	0	...	0		0.0
1995—San Diego NFL	13	0	0	...	0		0.0
Pro totals (9 years)	121	3	15	5.0	0		2.5

GIBSON, OLIVER — DT — STEELERS

PERSONAL: Born March 15, 1972, in Chicago. ... 6-2/283. ... Full name: Oliver Donnovan Gibson. ... Cousin of Godfrey Myles, linebacker, Dallas Cowboys.
HIGH SCHOOL: Romeoville (Ill.).
COLLEGE: Notre Dame (degree in economics, 1994).
TRANSACTIONS/CAREER NOTES: Selected by Pittsburgh Steelers in fourth round (120th pick overall) of 1995 NFL draft. ... Signed by Steelers (July 18, 1995).
PLAYING EXPERIENCE: Pittsburgh NFL, 1995. ... Games: 1995 (12).
CHAMPIONSHIP GAME EXPERIENCE: Member of Steelers for AFC championship game (1995 season); inactive.
PRO STATISTICS: 1995—Returned one kickoff for 10 yards.

GILBERT, GALE — QB

PERSONAL: Born December 20, 1961, in Red Bluff, Calif. ... 6-3/209. ... Full name: Gale Reed Gilbert.
HIGH SCHOOL: Red Bluff (Calif.).
COLLEGE: California (degree in physical education).
TRANSACTIONS/CAREER NOTES: Selected by Oakland Invaders in 1985 USFL territorial draft. ... Signed as non-drafted free agent by Seattle Seahawks (May 2, 1985). ... On injured reserve with knee injury (September 8, 1987-entire season). ... Granted free agency (February 1, 1988). ... Rights relinquished by Seahawks (June 8, 1988). ... Signed by Buffalo Bills (May 11, 1989). ... On injured reserve with ribs injury (September 14, 1989-remainder of season). ... Active for three games with Bills (1991); did not play. ... Active for three games with Bills (1992); did not play. ... Granted unconditional free agency (February 17, 1994). ... Signed by San Diego Chargers (April 29, 1994). ... Granted unconditional free agency (February 16, 1996).
CHAMPIONSHIP GAME EXPERIENCE: Member of Bills for AFC championship game and Super Bowl XXV (1990 season); did not play. ... Member of Bills for AFC championship game and Super Bowl XXVI (1991 season); inactive. ... Member of Bills for AFC championship game and Super Bowl XXVII (1992 season); inactive. ... Member of Bills for AFC championship game and Super Bowl XXVIII (1993 season); inactive. ... Played in AFC championship game (1994 season). ... Played in Super Bowl XXIX (1994 season).
PRO STATISTICS: 1985—Fumbled once and recovered one fumble for minus five yards. 1986—Fumbled once. 1995—Fumbled twice.
MISCELLANEOUS: Regular-season record as starting NFL quarterback: 0-4 (.000).

		PASSING								RUSHING				TOTALS		
Year Team	G	Att.	Cmp.	Pct.	Yds.	TD	Int.	Avg.	Rat.	Att.	Yds.	Avg.	TD	TD	2pt.	Pts.
1985—Seattle NFL	9	40	19	47.5	218	1	2	5.45	51.9	7	4	0.6	0	0	...	0
1986—Seattle NFL	16	76	42	55.3	485	3	3	6.38	71.4	3	8	2.7	0	0	...	0
1987—Seattle NFL							Did not play—injured.									
1988—							Did not play.									
1989—Buffalo NFL							Did not play—injured.									
1990—Buffalo NFL	1	15	8	53.3	106	2	2	7.07	76.0	0	0	...	0	0	...	0
1991—Buffalo NFL							Did not play.									
1992—Buffalo NFL							Did not play.									
1993—Buffalo NFL	1	0	0	...	0	0	0	...	...	0	0	...	0	0	...	0
1994—San Diego NFL	15	67	41	61.2	410	3	1	6.12	87.3	8	-3	-0.4	0	0	0	0
1995—San Diego NFL	16	61	36	59.0	325	0	4	5.33	46.1	6	11	1.8	0	0	0	0
Pro totals (6 years)	58	259	146	56.4	1544	9	12	5.96	66.2	24	20	0.8	0	0	0	0

G

GILBERT, SEAN · DT · REDSKINS

PERSONAL: Born April 10, 1970, in Aliquippa, Pa. ... 6-5/310.
HIGH SCHOOL: Aliquippa (Pa.).
COLLEGE: Pittsburgh.
TRANSACTIONS/CAREER NOTES: Selected after junior season by Los Angeles Rams in first round (third pick overall) of 1992 NFL draft. ... Signed by Rams (July 28, 1992). ... Designated by Rams as transition player (February 25, 1993). ... Rams franchise moved to St. Louis (April 12, 1995). ... Traded by Rams to Washington Redskins for first-round pick (RB Lawrence Phillips) in 1996 draft (April 8, 1996).
HONORS: Played in Pro Bowl (1993 season).
PRO STATISTICS: 1992—Recovered one fumble. 1994—Credited with a safety. 1995—Recovered one fumble.

Year Team	G	SACKS
1992—Los Angeles Rams NFL	16	5.0
1993—Los Angeles Rams NFL	16	10.5
1994—Los Angeles Rams NFL	14	3.0
1995—St. Louis NFL	14	5.5
Pro totals (4 years)	60	24.0

GILDON, JASON · LB · STEELERS

PERSONAL: Born July 31, 1972, in Altus, Okla. ... 6-3/245. ... Full name: Jason Larue Gildon. ... Related to Wendall Gaines, defensive end, Green Bay Packers.
HIGH SCHOOL: Altus (Okla.).
COLLEGE: Oklahoma State.
TRANSACTIONS/CAREER NOTES: Selected by Pittsburgh Steelers in third round (88th pick overall) of 1994 NFL draft. ... Signed by Steelers (July 15, 1994).
CHAMPIONSHIP GAME EXPERIENCE: Played in AFC championship game (1994 and 1995 seasons). ... Played in Super Bowl XXX (1995 season).
PRO STATISTICS: 1995—Recovered one fumble.

Year Team	G	SACKS
1994—Pittsburgh NFL	16	2.0
1995—Pittsburgh NFL	16	3.0
Pro totals (2 years)	32	5.0

GISLER, MIKE · G/C · PATRIOTS

PERSONAL: Born August 26, 1969, in Runge, Texas. ... 6-4/300.
HIGH SCHOOL: Runge (Texas).
COLLEGE: Houston.
TRANSACTIONS/CAREER NOTES: Selected by New Orleans Saints in 11th round (303rd pick overall) of 1992 NFL draft. ... Signed by Saints (July 15, 1992). ... Released by Saints (August 31, 1992). ... Re-signed by Saints to practice squad (September 2, 1992). ... Released by Saints (September 7, 1992). ... Signed by Houston Oilers to practice squad (September 9, 1992-remainder of season). ... Granted free agency after 1992 season. ... Signed by New England Patriots (March 3, 1993). ... Granted free agency (February 16, 1996).
PLAYING EXPERIENCE: New England NFL, 1993-1995. ... Games: 1993 (12), 1994 (15), 1995 (16). Total: 43.
PRO STATISTICS: 1995—Returned two kickoffs for 19 yards and fumbled once.

GIVINS, ERNEST · WR

PERSONAL: Born September 3, 1964, in St. Petersburg, Fla. ... 5-9/178. ... Full name: Ernest Pastell Givins Jr.
HIGH SCHOOL: Lakewood Senior (St. Petersburg, Fla.).
COLLEGE: Northeastern Oklahoma A&M, then Louisville.
TRANSACTIONS/CAREER NOTES: Selected by Houston Oilers in second round (34th pick overall) of 1986 NFL draft. ... Selected by Tampa Bay Bandits in first round (eighth pick overall) of 1986 USFL draft. ... Signed by Oilers (August 1, 1986). ... Designated by Oilers as transition player (February 25, 1993). ... Released by Oilers (May 15, 1995). ... Signed by Jacksonville Jaguars (June 2, 1995). ... Released by Jaguars (December 5, 1995).
HONORS: Played in Pro Bowl (1990 and 1992 seasons).
PRO STATISTICS: 1986—Attempted two passes without a completion. 1989—Recovered one fumble. 1992—Recovered one fumble. 1994—Returned one kickoff for 27 yards and recovered three fumbles.
STATISTICAL PLATEAUS: 100-yard receiving games: 1986 (4), 1987 (2), 1988 (4), 1989 (1), 1990 (1), 1991 (1), 1992 (2), 1993 (1). Total: 16.
MISCELLANEOUS: Holds Houston Oilers all-time record for most yards receiving (7,935).

Year Team	G	RUSHING				RECEIVING				PUNT RETURNS				TOTALS			
		Att.	Yds.	Avg.	TD	No.	Yds.	Avg.	TD	No.	Yds.	Avg.	TD	TD	2pt.	Pts.	Fum.
1986—Houston NFL	15	9	148	16.4	1	61	1062	17.4	3	8	80	10.0	0	4	...	24	0
1987—Houston NFL	12	1	-13	-13.0	0	53	933	17.6	6	0	0	...	0	6	...	36	2
1988—Houston NFL	16	4	26	6.5	0	60	976	16.3	5	0	0	...	0	5	...	30	1
1989—Houston NFL	15	0	0	...	0	55	794	14.4	3	0	0	...	0	3	...	18	0
1990—Houston NFL	16	3	65	21.7	0	72	979	13.6	9	0	0	...	0	9	...	54	1
1991—Houston NFL	16	4	30	7.5	0	70	996	14.2	5	11	107	9.7	0	5	...	30	3
1992—Houston NFL	16	7	75	10.7	0	67	787	11.8	10	0	0	...	0	10	...	60	3
1993—Houston NFL	16	6	19	3.2	0	68	887	13.0	4	0	0	...	0	4	...	24	2
1994—Houston NFL	16	1	-5	-5.0	0	36	521	14.5	1	37	210	5.7	1	2	...	12	3
1995—Jacksonville NFL	9	0	0	...	0	29	280	9.7	3	2	-7	-3.5	0	3	0	18	1
Pro totals (10 years)	147	35	345	9.9	1	571	8215	14.4	49	58	390	6.7	1	51	0	306	16

GLENN, AARON · CB/KR · JETS

PERSONAL: Born July 16, 1972, in Humble, Texas. ... 5-9/185. ... Full name: Aaron DeVon Glenn.

G

HIGH SCHOOL: Nimitz (Houston).
COLLEGE: Texas A&M.
TRANSACTIONS/CAREER NOTES: Selected by New York Jets in first round (12th pick overall) of 1994 NFL draft. ... Signed by Jets (July 21, 1994).
HONORS: Named defensive back on THE SPORTING NEWS college All-America first team (1993).
PRO STATISTICS: 1994—Recovered one fumble. 1995—Recovered one fumble for 20 yards.

		INTERCEPTIONS				KICKOFF RETURNS				TOTALS			
Year Team	G	No.	Yds.	Avg.	TD	No.	Yds.	Avg.	TD	TD	2pt.	Pts.	Fum.
1994—New York Jets NFL	15	0	0	...	0	27	582	21.6	0	0	0	0	2
1995—New York Jets NFL	16	1	17	17.0	0	1	12	12.0	0	0	0	0	0
Pro totals (2 years)	31	1	17	17.0	0	28	594	21.2	0	0	0	0	2

GLENN, VENCIE   S

PERSONAL: Born October 26, 1964, in Grambling, La. ... 6-0/205. ... Full name: Vencie Leonard Glenn.
HIGH SCHOOL: John F. Kennedy (Silver Spring, Md.).
COLLEGE: Indiana State.
TRANSACTIONS/CAREER NOTES: Selected by New England Patriots in second round (54th pick overall) of 1986 NFL draft. ... Signed by Patriots (July 29, 1986). ... Traded by Patriots to San Diego Chargers for fifth-round pick (OT Danny Villa) in 1987 draft and cash (September 29, 1986). ... Granted free agency (February 1, 1990). ... Re-signed by Chargers (August 7, 1990). ... Granted unconditional free agency (February 1, 1991). ... Signed by Los Angeles Raiders (March 1991). ... Traded by Raiders to New Orleans Saints for an undisclosed draft pick (August 13, 1991). ... Granted unconditional free agency (February 1, 1992). ... Signed by Minnesota Vikings (March 18, 1992). ... Granted unconditional free agency (February 17, 1994). ... Re-signed by Vikings (March 21, 1994). ... Traded by Vikings to New York Giants for sixth-round pick (LB John Solomon) in 1995 draft (April 23, 1995). ... Released by Giants (June 4, 1996).
RECORDS: Shares NFL record for longest interception return—103 yards, touchdown (November 29, 1987).
PRO STATISTICS: 1986—Recovered two fumbles for 32 yards. 1987—Recovered one fumble. 1988—Recovered two fumbles. 1989—Recovered one fumble for 81 yards and a touchdown. 1991—Returned one kickoff for 10 yards and recovered one fumble. 1995—Recovered two fumbles.

		INTERCEPTIONS				SACKS
Year Team	G	No.	Yds.	Avg.	TD	No.
1986—New England NFL	4	0	0		0	0.0
—San Diego NFL	12	2	31	15.5	0	0.0
1987—San Diego NFL	12	4	*166	41.5	1	0.5
1988—San Diego NFL	16	1	0	0.0	0	1.0
1989—San Diego NFL	16	4	52	13.0	0	1.0
1990—San Diego NFL	14	1	0	0.0	0	0.0
1991—New Orleans NFL	16	4	35	8.8	0	0.0
1992—Minnesota NFL	16	5	65	13.0	0	0.0
1993—Minnesota NFL	16	5	49	9.8	0	0.0
1994—Minnesota NFL	16	4	55	13.8	0	1.0
1995—New York Giants NFL	15	5	91	18.2	1	0.0
Pro totals (10 years)	153	35	544	15.6	2	3.5

GLOVER, ANDREW   TE   RAIDERS

PERSONAL: Born August 12, 1967, in New Orleans. ... 6-6/245. ... Full name: Andrew Lee Glover.
HIGH SCHOOL: East Ascension (Gonzales, La.).
COLLEGE: Grambling State (degree in criminal justice).
TRANSACTIONS/CAREER NOTES: Selected by Los Angeles Raiders in 10th round (274th pick overall) of 1991 NFL draft. ... Signed by Raiders (1991). ... On injured reserve with knee injury (December 27, 1993-remainder of season). ... Raiders franchise moved to Oakland (July 21, 1995). ... Granted unconditional free agency (February 16, 1996). ... Re-signed by Raiders (May 24, 1996).
PRO STATISTICS: 1992—Recovered one fumble.

		RECEIVING				TOTALS			
Year Team	G	No.	Yds.	Avg.	TD	TD	2pt.	Pts.	Fum.
1991—Los Angeles Raiders NFL	16	5	45	9.0	3	3	...	18	0
1992—Los Angeles Raiders NFL	16	15	178	11.9	1	1	...	6	1
1993—Los Angeles Raiders NFL	15	4	55	13.8	1	1	...	6	0
1994—Los Angeles Raiders NFL	16	33	371	11.2	2	2	0	12	0
1995—Oakland NFL	16	26	220	8.5	3	3	0	18	0
Pro totals (5 years)	79	83	869	10.5	10	10	0	60	1

GLOVER, KEVIN   C   LIONS

PERSONAL: Born June 17, 1963, in Washington, D.C. ... 6-2/282. ... Full name: Kevin Bernard Glover.
HIGH SCHOOL: Largo (Md.).
COLLEGE: Maryland.
TRANSACTIONS/CAREER NOTES: Selected by Tampa Bay Bandits in 1985 USFL territorial draft. ... Selected by Detroit Lions in second round (34th pick overall) of 1985 NFL draft. ... Signed by Lions (July 23, 1985). ... On injured reserve with knee injury (December 7, 1985-remainder of season). ... On injured reserve with knee injury (September 29-December 20, 1986). ... Granted free agency (February 1, 1992). ... Re-signed by Lions (August 25, 1992). ... Activated (August 26, 1992). ... On injured reserve with ankle injury (October 27, 1992-remainder of season). ... Designated by Lions as franchise player (February 16, 1996).
PLAYING EXPERIENCE: Detroit NFL, 1985-1995. ... Games: 1985 (10), 1986 (4), 1987 (12), 1988 (16), 1989 (16), 1990 (16), 1991 (16), 1992 (7), 1993 (16), 1994 (16), 1995 (16). Total: 145.
CHAMPIONSHIP GAME EXPERIENCE: Played in NFC championship game (1991 season).
HONORS: Named center on THE SPORTING NEWS college All-America first team (1984). ... Played in Pro Bowl (1995 season).
PRO STATISTICS: 1987—Returned one kickoff for 19 yards. 1988—Recovered two fumbles. 1990—Recovered one fumble. 1992—Recovered one fumble. 1995—Fumbled twice and recovered one fumble for minus 14 yards.

G

GOAD, TIM   NT

PERSONAL: Born February 28, 1966, in Claudville, Va. ... 6-3/280. ... Full name: Timothy Ray Goad. ... Name pronounced GODE.
HIGH SCHOOL: Patrick County (Stuart, Va.).
COLLEGE: North Carolina.
TRANSACTIONS/CAREER NOTES: Selected by New England Patriots in fourth round (87th pick overall) of 1988 NFL draft. ... Signed by Patriots (July 15, 1988). ... Granted free agency (February 1, 1991). ... Re-signed by Patriots (August 23, 1991). ... Activated (August 30, 1991). ... On injured reserve with right leg injury (December 7, 1994-remainder of season). ... Granted unconditional free agency (February 17, 1995). ... Signed by Cleveland Browns (April 17, 1995). ... Granted unconditional free agency (February 16, 1996).
PRO STATISTICS:1990—Recovered one fumble. 1992—Recovered one fumble for 19 yards and a touchdown. 1993—Recovered one fumble. 1994—Recovered one fumble for eight yards. 1995—Recovered two fumbles for 24 yards.

Year Team	G	SACKS
1988—New England NFL	16	2.0
1989—New England NFL	16	1.0
1990—New England NFL	16	2.5
1991—New England NFL	16	0.0
1992—New England NFL	16	2.5
1993—New England NFL	16	0.5
1994—New England NFL	13	3.0
1995—Cleveland NFL	16	0.0
Pro totals (8 years)	125	11.5

GOEAS, LEO   G/OT

PERSONAL: Born August 15, 1966, in Honolulu. ... 6-4/300. ... Full name: Leo Douglas Goeas. ... Name pronounced GO-az.
HIGH SCHOOL: Kamehameha (Honolulu).
COLLEGE: Hawaii.
TRANSACTIONS/CAREER NOTES: Selected by San Diego Chargers in third round (60th pick overall) of 1990 NFL draft. ... Signed by Chargers (July 19, 1990). ... Granted free agency (February 1, 1992). ... Re-signed by Chargers (July 24, 1992). ... Granted free agency (March 1, 1993). ... Re-signed by Chargers (April 15, 1993). ... Traded by Chargers to Los Angeles Rams for fourth-round pick in 1993 draft (April 15, 1993). ... Rams franchise moved to St. Louis (April 12, 1995). ... Granted unconditional free agency (February 16, 1996).
PLAYING EXPERIENCE: San Diego NFL, 1990-1992; Los Angeles Rams NFL, 1993 and 1994; St. Louis NFL, 1995. ... Games: 1990 (15), 1991 (9), 1992 (16), 1993 (16), 1994 (13), 1995 (15). Total: 84.
PRO STATISTICS: 1990—Recovered one fumble. 1992—Recovered one fumble. 1994—Recovered one fumble.

GOFF, ROBERT   DE/NT

PERSONAL: Born October 2, 1965, in Rochester, N.Y. ... 6-3/280. ... Full name: Robert Lamar Goff.
HIGH SCHOOL: Bayshore (Bradenton, Fla.).
JUNIOR COLLEGE: Butler County (Kan.) Community College.
COLLEGE: Auburn.
TRANSACTIONS/CAREER NOTES: Selected by Tampa Bay Buccaneers in fourth round (83rd pick overall) of 1988 NFL draft. ... Signed by Buccaneers (July 10, 1988). ... Traded by Buccaneers to New Orleans Saints for 10th-round pick (RB Hyland Hickson) in 1991 draft (September 3, 1990). ... Granted free agency (February 1, 1991). ... Re-signed by Saints (July 27, 1991). ... Granted unconditional free agency (March 1, 1993). ... Re-signed by Saints (April 13, 1993). ... Granted unconditional free agency (February 16, 1996).
RECORDS: Shares NFL single-season record for most touchdowns by fumble recovery—2 (1992); and most touchdowns by recovery of opponents' fumbles—2 (1992).
PRO STATISTICS: 1988—Recovered three fumbles. 1989—Recovered one fumble. 1990—Recovered one fumble for 13 yards. 1992—Recovered three fumbles for 47 yards and two touchdowns.

Year Team	G	SACKS
1988—Tampa Bay NFL	16	2.0
1989—Tampa Bay NFL	12	4.0
1990—New Orleans NFL	15	0.0
1991—New Orleans NFL	15	2.0
1992—New Orleans NFL	16	0.0
1993—New Orleans NFL	16	2.0
1994—New Orleans NFL	16	0.0
1995—New Orleans NFL	11	1.5
Pro totals (8 years)	117	11.5

GOGAN, KEVIN   G/OT   RAIDERS

PERSONAL: Born November 2, 1964, in San Francisco. ... 6-7/320. ... Full name: Kevin Patrick Gogan.
HIGH SCHOOL: Sacred Heart (San Francisco).
COLLEGE: Washington (degree in sociology, 1987).
TRANSACTIONS/CAREER NOTES: Selected by Dallas Cowboys in eighth round (206th pick overall) of 1987 NFL draft. ... Signed by Cowboys (July 18, 1987). ... On non-football injury list with substance abuse problem (August 5-31, 1988). ... Granted roster exemption (August 31-September 5, 1988). ... Granted unconditional free agency (February 17, 1994). ... Signed by Los Angeles Raiders (April 18, 1994). ... Raiders franchise moved to Oakland (July 21, 1995).
PLAYING EXPERIENCE: Dallas NFL, 1987-1993; Los Angeles Raiders NFL, 1994; Oakland NFL, 1995. ... Games: 1987 (11), 1988 (15), 1989 (13), 1990 (16), 1991 (16), 1992 (16), 1993 (16), 1994 (16), 1995 (16). Total: 135.
CHAMPIONSHIP GAME EXPERIENCE: Played in NFC championship game (1992 and 1993 seasons). ... Member of Super Bowl championship team (1992 and 1993 seasons).
HONORS: Played in Pro Bowl (1994 season).
PRO STATISTICS: 1987—Recovered one fumble. 1990—Recovered one fumble.

GOGANIOUS, KEITH LB

PERSONAL: Born December 7, 1968, in Virginia Beach, Va. ... 6-2/239. ... Full name: Keith Lorenzo Goganious. ... Name pronounced go-GAY-nus.
HIGH SCHOOL: Green Run (Virginia Beach, Va.).
COLLEGE: Penn State.
TRANSACTIONS/CAREER NOTES: Selected by Buffalo Bills in third round (83rd pick overall) of 1992 NFL draft. ... Signed by Bills (July 22, 1992). ... Selected by Jacksonville Jaguars from Bills in NFL expansion draft (February 15, 1995). ... Granted free agency (February 17, 1995). ... Signed by Jaguars (June 7, 1995). ... Granted unconditional free agency (February 16, 1996).
PLAYING EXPERIENCE: Buffalo NFL, 1992-1994; Jacksonville NFL, 1995. ... Games: 1992 (13), 1993 (16), 1994 (16), 1995 (16). Total: 61.
CHAMPIONSHIP GAME EXPERIENCE: Played in AFC championship game (1992 and 1993 seasons). ... Played in Super Bowl XXVII (1992 season) and Super Bowl XXVIII (1993 season).
PRO STATISTICS: 1993—Credited with a sack and recovered one fumble. 1995—Intercepted two passes for 11 yards.

GORDON, DARRIEN CB CHARGERS

PERSONAL: Born November 14, 1970, in Shawnee, Okla. ... 5-11/182. ... Full name: Darrien X. Jamal Gordon.
HIGH SCHOOL: Shawnee (Okla.).
COLLEGE: Stanford.
TRANSACTIONS/CAREER NOTES: Selected by San Diego Chargers in first round (22nd pick overall) of 1993 NFL draft. ... Signed by Chargers (July 16, 1993). ... Inactive for 16 games due to shoulder injury (1995 season).
CHAMPIONSHIP GAME EXPERIENCE: Played in AFC championship game (1994 season). ... Played in Super Bowl XXIX (1994 season).
PRO STATISTICS: 1993—Recovered two fumbles for minus two yards. 1994—Recovered three fumbles for 15 yards.

		INTERCEPTIONS				PUNT RETURNS				TOTALS			
Year Team	G	No.	Yds.	Avg.	TD	No.	Yds.	Avg.	TD	TD	2pt.	Pts.	Fum.
1993—San Diego NFL	16	1	3	3.0	0	31	395	12.7	0	0	...	0	4
1994—San Diego NFL	16	4	32	8.0	0	36	475	13.2	†2	2	0	12	2
1995—San Diego NFL							Did not play.						
Pro totals (2 years)	32	5	35	7.0	0	67	870	13.0	2	2	0	12	6

GORDON, DWAYNE LB CHARGERS

PERSONAL: Born November 2, 1969, in White Plains, N.Y. ... 6-1/240.
HIGH SCHOOL: Arlington North (Lagrangeville, N.Y.).
COLLEGE: New Hampshire.
TRANSACTIONS/CAREER NOTES: Selected by Miami Dolphins in eighth round (218th pick overall) of 1993 NFL draft. ... Released by Dolphins (July 12, 1993). ... Signed by Atlanta Falcons (July 19, 1993). ... Released by Falcons (August 27, 1995). ... Signed by San Diego Chargers (August 28, 1995). ... Granted free agency (February 16, 1996).
PLAYING EXPERIENCE: Atlanta NFL, 1993 and 1994; San Diego NFL, 1995. ... Games: 1993 (5), 1994 (16), 1995 (16). Total: 37.
PRO STATISTICS: 1993—Fumbled once. 1995—Credited with one sack and recovered one fumble.

GOSS, ANTONIO LB 49ERS

PERSONAL: Born August 11, 1966, in Randleman, N.C. ... 6-4/228. ... Full name: Antonio Derrell Goss.
HIGH SCHOOL: Randleman (N.C.).
COLLEGE: North Carolina.
TRANSACTIONS/CAREER NOTES: Selected by San Francisco 49ers in 12th round (319th pick overall) of 1989 NFL draft. ... Signed by 49ers (July 20, 1989). ... Released by 49ers (September 5, 1989). ... Re-signed by 49ers to developmental squad (September 7, 1989). ... Released by 49ers (September 3, 1990). ... Signed by San Diego Chargers (November 21, 1990). ... On inactive list for two games with Chargers (1990). ... Released by Chargers (December 5, 1990). ... Signed by 49ers (April 12, 1991). ... Released by 49ers (August 26, 1991). ... Re-signed by 49ers (September 11, 1991). ... Granted free agency (March 1, 1993). ... Re-signed by 49ers (July 19, 1993). ... Released by 49ers (August 30, 1993). ... Re-signed by 49ers (August 31, 1993). ... Released by 49ers (February 17, 1994). ... Re-signed by 49ers (June 1, 1994). ... Granted unconditional free agency (February 17, 1995). ... Re-signed by 49ers (May 6, 1995).
PLAYING EXPERIENCE: San Francisco NFL, 1989, 1991-1995. ... Games: 1989 (8), 1991 (14), 1992 (16), 1993 (14), 1994 (16), 1995 (16). Total: 84.
CHAMPIONSHIP GAME EXPERIENCE: Member of 49ers for NFC championship game and Super Bowl XXIV (1989 season); inactive. ... Played in NFC championship game (1992-1994 seasons). ... Member of Super Bowl championship team (1994 season).
PRO STATISTICS: 1989—Recovered one fumble.

GOSSETT, JEFF P RAIDERS

PERSONAL: Born January 25, 1957, in Charleston, Ill. ... 6-2/190. ... Full name: Jeffery Alan Gossett.
HIGH SCHOOL: Charleston (Ill.).
COLLEGE: Eastern Illinois (degree in physical education, 1982).
TRANSACTIONS/CAREER NOTES: Signed as non-drafted free agent by Dallas Cowboys (May 1980). ... Released by Cowboys (August 25, 1980). ... Signed by San Diego Chargers (April 6, 1981). ... Released by Chargers (August 31, 1981). ... Signed by Kansas City Chiefs (November 5, 1981). ... Released by Chiefs (December 14, 1982). ... Re-signed by Chiefs (December 21, 1982). ... Claimed on waivers by Cleveland Browns (August 30, 1983). ... Signed by Chicago Blitz of USFL (December 20, 1983), for contract to take effect after being granted free agency (February 1, 1984). ... USFL rights traded by Pittsburgh Maulers with K Efren Herrera to Blitz for rights to LB Bruce Huther (December 30, 1983). ... Blitz franchise disbanded (November 20, 1984). ... Signed as free agent by Portland Breakers (February 4, 1985). ... Signed by Browns (May 20, 1985). ... Released by Breakers (June 26, 1985). ... Crossed picket line during players strike (October 14, 1987). ... Released by Browns (November 17, 1987). ... Signed by Houston Oilers (December 3, 1987). ... Traded by Oilers to Los Angeles Raiders for past considerations (August 16, 1988). ... Granted unconditional free agency (February 1-April 1, 1991). ... Re-signed by Raiders

G

(July 13, 1991). ... Granted unconditional free agency (March 1, 1993). ... Re-signed by Raiders for 1993 season. ... Released by Raiders (August 30, 1993). ... Re-signed by Raiders (August 31, 1993). ... Granted unconditional free agency (February 17, 1995). ... Re-signed by Raiders (February 17, 1995). ... Raiders franchise moved to Oakland (July 21, 1995).

CHAMPIONSHIP GAME EXPERIENCE: Played in AFC championship game (1986 and 1990 seasons).

HONORS: Played in Pro Bowl (1991 season). ... Named punter on THE SPORTING NEWS NFL All-Pro team (1991).

PRO STATISTICS: NFL: 1982—Recovered one fumble. 1985—Attempted one pass without a completion. 1986—Attempted two passes with one completion for 30 yards and one interception. 1987—Had 31.6-yard net punting average. 1989—Attempted one pass without a completion. 1991—Attempted one pass with one completion for 34 yards. 1992—Rushed once for minus 12 yards and fumbled once. 1993—Rushed once for minus 10 yards. USFL: 1984—Rushed once for no yards. 1985—Attempted one pass with one interception, rushed once for minus four yards, fumbled once and recovered one fumble.

| | | | PUNTING | | | | | |
Year Team	G	No.	Yds.	Avg.	Net avg.	In. 20	Blk.
1981—Kansas City NFL	7	29	1141	39.3	32.9	4	0
1982—Kansas City NFL	8	33	1366	41.4	30.9	6	0
1983—Cleveland NFL	16	70	2854	40.8	34.1	17	0
1984—Chicago USFL	18	85	3608	42.4	35.5	18	0
1985—Portland USFL	18	74	3120	42.2	33.2	19	0
—Cleveland NFL	16	81	3261	40.3	34.5	18	0
1986—Cleveland NFL	16	83	3423	41.2	35.6	21	0
1987—Cleveland NFL	5	19	769	40.5	...	4	0
—Houston NFL	4	25	1010	40.4	...	0	1
1988—Los Angeles Raiders NFL	16	91	3804	41.8	35.7	27	0
1989—Los Angeles Raiders NFL	16	67	2711	40.5	33.9	12	0
1990—Los Angeles Raiders NFL	16	60	2315	38.6	33.6	19	2
1991—Los Angeles Raiders NFL	16	67	2961	44.2	38.5	26	0
1992—Los Angeles Raiders NFL	16	77	3255	42.3	36.5	17	0
1993—Los Angeles Raiders NFL	16	71	2971	41.8	35.1	19	0
1994—Los Angeles Raiders NFL	16	77	3377	43.9	35.2	19	0
1995—Oakland NFL	16	75	3089	41.2	34.7	22	1
USFL totals (2 years)	36	159	6728	42.3	34.4	37	0
NFL totals (14 years)	200	925	38307	41.4	34.8	231	4
Pro totals (16 years)	236	1084	45035	41.6	34.8	268	4

GOUVEIA, KURT   LB   CHARGERS

PERSONAL: Born September 14, 1964, in Honolulu. ... 6-1/240. ... Full name: Kurt Keola Gouveia. ... Name pronounced goo-VAY-uh.

HIGH SCHOOL: Waianae (Hawaii).

COLLEGE: Brigham Young.

TRANSACTIONS/CAREER NOTES: Selected by Washington Redskins in eighth round (213th pick overall) of 1986 NFL draft. ... Signed by Redskins (July 18, 1986). ... On injured reserve with knee injury (August 25, 1986-entire season). ... Granted unconditional free agency (March 1, 1993). ... Re-signed by Redskins for 1993 season. ... Granted free agency (February 17, 1995). ... Signed by Philadelphia Eagles (April 23, 1995). ... Granted unconditional free agency (February 1, 1996). ... Signed by San Diego Chargers (February 27, 1996).

CHAMPIONSHIP GAME EXPERIENCE: Played in NFC championship game (1987 and 1991 seasons). ... Member of Super Bowl championship team (1987 and 1991 seasons).

POSTSEASON RECORDS: Shares NFL postseason career record for most consecutive games with one or more interception—3.

PRO STATISTICS: 1990—Recovered one fumble for 39 yards and a touchdown. 1995—Recovered one fumble.

| | | INTERCEPTIONS | | | | SACKS | KICKOFF RETURNS | | | | TOTALS | | | |
Year Team	G	No.	Yds.	Avg.	TD	No.	No.	Yds.	Avg.	TD	TD	2pt.	Pts.	Fum.
1986—Washington NFL						Did not play—injured.								
1987—Washington NFL	11	0	0	...	0	0.0	0	0	...	0	0	...	0	0
1988—Washington NFL	16	0	0	...	0	0.0	0	0	...	0	0	...	0	0
1989—Washington NFL	15	1	1	1.0	0	0.0	1	0	0.0	0	0	...	0	0
1990—Washington NFL	16	0	0	...	0	1.0	2	23	11.5	0	1	...	6	0
1991—Washington NFL	14	1	22	22.0	0	0.0	3	12	4.0	0	0	...	0	0
1992—Washington NFL	16	3	43	14.3	0	1.0	1	7	7.0	0	0	...	0	0
1993—Washington NFL	16	1	59	59.0	1	1.5	0	0	...	0	1	...	6	0
1994—Washington NFL	14	1	7	7.0	0	0.0	0	0	...	0	0	0	0	0
1995—Philadelphia NFL	16	1	20	20.0	0	0.0	0	0	...	0	0	0	0	0
Pro totals (9 years)	134	8	152	19.0	1	3.5	7	42	6.0	0	2	0	12	0

GRAGG, SCOTT   OT   GIANTS

PERSONAL: Born February 28, 1972, in Altus, Okla. ... 6-8/325.

HIGH SCHOOL: Silverton (Ore.) Union.

COLLEGE: Montana.

TRANSACTIONS/CAREER NOTES: Selected by New York Giants in second round (54th pick overall) of 1995 NFL draft. ... Signed by Giants (July 23, 1995).

PLAYING EXPERIENCE: New York Giants NFL, 1995. ... Games: 1995 (13).

GRAHAM, DERRICK   G   SEAHAWKS

PERSONAL: Born March 18, 1967, in Groveland, Fla. ... 6-4/315. ... Full name: Dettrice Andrew Graham.

HIGH SCHOOL: Groveland (Fla.).

COLLEGE: Appalachian State (degree in criminal justice).

TRANSACTIONS/CAREER NOTES: Selected by Kansas City Chiefs in fifth round (124th pick overall) of 1990 NFL draft. ... Signed by Chiefs (July 28, 1990). ... On injured reserve with ankle injury (November 3, 1990-remainder of season). ... On injured reserve with knee injury (September 16, 1992-remainder of season). ... Granted unconditional free agency (February 17, 1995). ... Signed by Carolina Panthers

G

(February 21, 1995). ... Released by Panthers (February 14, 1996). ... Signed by Seattle Seahawks (February 29, 1996).
PLAYING EXPERIENCE: Kansas City NFL, 1990-1994; Carolina NFL, 1995. ... Games: 1990 (6), 1991 (16), 1992 (2), 1993 (11), 1994 (16), 1995 (11). Total: 62.
CHAMPIONSHIP GAME EXPERIENCE: Played in AFC championship game (1993 season).

GRAHAM, HASON — WR — PATRIOTS

PERSONAL: Born March 21, 1971, in Decatur, Ga. ... 5-10/176. ... Full name: Hason Aaron Graham.
HIGH SCHOOL: Southwest Dekalb (Decatur, Ga.).
JUNIOR COLLEGE: hinds Community College.
COLLEGE: Georgia.
TRANSACTIONS/CAREER NOTES: Signed as non-drafted free agent by New England Patriots (April 24, 1995).

		RECEIVING				TOTALS			
Year Team	G	No.	Yds.	Avg.	TD	TD	2pt.	Pts.	Fum.
1995—New England NFL	10	10	156	15.6	2	2	0	12	0

GRAHAM, JEFF — WR/PR — JETS

PERSONAL: Born February 14, 1969, in Dayton, Ohio. ... 6-2/200. ... Full name: Jeff Todd Graham.
HIGH SCHOOL: Alter (Kettering, Ohio).
COLLEGE: Ohio State.
TRANSACTIONS/CAREER NOTES: Selected by Pittsburgh Steelers in second round (46th pick overall) of 1991 NFL draft. ... Signed by Steelers (August 3, 1991). ... Traded by Steelers to Chicago Bears for fifth-round pick (DB Lethon Flowers) in 1995 draft (April 29, 1994). ... Granted unconditional free agency (February 16, 1996). ... Signed by New York Jets (March 14, 1996).
PRO STATISTICS: 1991—Returned three kickoffs for 48 yards. 1994—Recovered one fumble. 1995—Returned one kickoff for 12 yards.
STATISTICAL PLATEAUS: 100-yard receiving games: 1992 (2), 1993 (2), 1994 (2), 1995 (7). Total: 13.

		RECEIVING				PUNT RETURNS				TOTALS			
Year Team	G	No.	Yds.	Avg.	TD	No.	Yds.	Avg.	TD	TD	2pt.	Pts.	Fum.
1991—Pittsburgh NFL	13	2	21	10.5	0	8	46	5.8	0	0	...	0	0
1992—Pittsburgh NFL	14	49	711	14.5	1	0	0	...	0	1	...	6	0
1993—Pittsburgh NFL	15	38	579	15.2	0	0	0	...	0	0	...	0	0
1994—Chicago NFL	16	68	944	13.9	4	15	140	9.3	1	5	1	32	1
1995—Chicago NFL	16	82	1301	15.9	4	23	183	8.0	0	4	0	24	3
Pro totals (5 years)	74	239	3556	14.9	9	46	369	8.0	1	10	1	62	4

GRAHAM, KENT — QB — CARDINALS

PERSONAL: Born November 1, 1968, in Winfield, Ill. ... 6-5/242. ... Full name: Kent Douglas Graham.
HIGH SCHOOL: Wheaton (Ill.) North.
COLLEGE: Notre Dame, then Ohio State.
TRANSACTIONS/CAREER NOTES: Selected by New York Giants in eighth round (211th pick overall) of 1992 NFL draft. ... Signed by Giants (July 21, 1992). ... On injured reserve with elbow injury (September 18-October 14, 1992). ... Granted free agency (February 17, 1995). ... Re-signed by Giants (July 1995). ... Released by Giants (August 30, 1995). ... Signed by Detroit Lions (September 5, 1995). ... Granted unconditional free agency (February 16, 1996). ... Signed by Arizona Cardinals (March 7, 1996).
PRO STATISTICS: 1992—Fumbled once and recovered one fumble. 1994—Fumbled twice and recovered one fumble.
MISCELLANEOUS: Regular-season record as starting NFL quarterback: 0-4 (.000).

		PASSING							RUSHING				TOTALS		
Year Team	G	Att.	Cmp.	Pct.	Yds.	TD	Int.	Avg.	Rat.	Att.	Yds.	Avg.	TD	TD	2pt.	Pts.
1992—New York Giants NFL	6	97	42	43.3	470	1	4	4.85	44.6	6	36	6.0	0	0	...	0
1993—New York Giants NFL	9	22	8	36.4	79	0	0	3.59	47.3	2	-3	-1.5	0	0	...	0
1994—New York Giants NFL	13	53	24	45.3	295	3	2	5.57	66.2	2	11	5.5	0	0	0	0
1995—Detroit NFL	2	0	0	...	0	0	0	...	...	0	0	...	0	0	0	0
Pro totals (4 years)	30	172	74	43.0	844	4	6	4.91	51.6	10	44	4.4	0	0	0	0

GRAHAM, SCOTTIE — RB — VIKINGS

PERSONAL: Born March 28, 1969, in Long Beach, N.Y. ... 5-9/222. ... Full name: James Otis Graham.
HIGH SCHOOL: Long Beach (N.Y.).
COLLEGE: Ohio State (degree in recreation education).
TRANSACTIONS/CAREER NOTES: Selected by Pittsburgh Steelers in seventh round (188th pick overall) of 1992 NFL draft. ... Signed by Steelers (July 16, 1992). ... Released by Steelers (August 31, 1992). ... Re-signed by Steelers to practice squad (September 1, 1992). ... Signed by New York Jets off Steelers practice squad (December 15, 1992). ... Released by Jets (August 23, 1993). ... Signed by Minnesota Vikings to practice squad (September 29, 1993). ... Activated (November 9, 1993). ... Granted free agency (February 16, 1996).
PRO STATISTICS: 1993—Returned one kickoff for 16 yards.
STATISTICAL PLATEAUS: 100-yard rushing games: 1993 (2), 1995 (1). Total: 3.

		RUSHING				RECEIVING				TOTALS			
Year Team	G	Att.	Yds.	Avg.	TD	No.	Yds.	Avg.	TD	TD	2pt.	Pts.	Fum.
1992—New York Jets NFL	2	14	29	2.1	0	0	0	...	0	1	...	6	0
1993—Minnesota NFL	7	118	488	4.1	3	7	46	6.6	0	3	...	18	0
1994—Minnesota NFL	16	64	207	3.2	2	1	1	1.0	0	2	0	12	0
1995—Minnesota NFL	16	110	406	3.7	2	4	30	7.5	0	2	0	12	0
Pro totals (4 years)	41	306	1130	3.7	7	12	77	6.4	0	8	0	48	0

G

GRANT, RUPERT   RB   PATRIOTS

PERSONAL: Born November 5, 1973, in Washington, D.C. ... 6-1/233.
HIGH SCHOOL: Coolidge (Washington, D.C.).
COLLEGE: Howard.
TRANSACTIONS/CAREER NOTES: Signed as non-drafted free agent by New England Patriots (April 24, 1995). ... Released by Patriots (October 25, 1995). ... Re-signed by Patriots to practice squad (October 26, 1995). ... Activated (December 19, 1995).
PLAYING EXPERIENCE: New England NFL, 1995. ... Games: 1995 (7).
PRO STATISTICS: 1995—Caught one pass for four yards, returned one kickoff for seven yards and recovered one fumble.

GRANT, STEPHEN   LB   COLTS

PERSONAL: Born December 23, 1969, in Miami. ... 6-0/240.
HIGH SCHOOL: Miami Southridge Sr.
COLLEGE: West Virginia.
TRANSACTIONS/CAREER NOTES: Selected by Indianapolis Colts in 10th round (253rd pick overall) of 1992 NFL draft. ... Signed by Colts (July 17, 1992). ... Granted free agency (February 17, 1995). ... Re-signed by Colts (May 31, 1995).
PLAYING EXPERIENCE: Indianapolis NFL, 1992-1995. ... Games: 1992 (16), 1993 (16), 1994 (16), 1995 (15). Total: 63.
CHAMPIONSHIP GAME EXPERIENCE: Played in AFC championship game (1995 season).
PRO STATISTICS: 1994—Recovered one fumble for two yards. 1995—Credited with two sacks, intercepted one pass for nine yards and recovered three fumbles for two yards.

GRAY, CARLTON   CB   SEAHAWKS

PERSONAL: Born June 26, 1971, in Cincinnati. ... 6-0/200. ... Full name: Carlton Patrick Gray.
HIGH SCHOOL: Forest Park (Cincinnati).
COLLEGE: UCLA.
TRANSACTIONS/CAREER NOTES: Selected by Seattle Seahawks in second round (30th pick overall) of 1993 NFL draft. ... Signed by Seahawks (July 22, 1993). ... On injured reserve with forearm injury (November 23, 1994-remainder of season). ... Granted free agency (February 16, 1996).
HONORS: Named defensive back on THE SPORTING NEWS college All-America first team (1992).
PRO STATISTICS: 1993—Credited with one sack. 1995—Fumbled once.

		INTERCEPTIONS			
Year Team	G	No.	Yds.	Avg.	TD
1993—Seattle NFL	10	3	33	11.0	0
1994—Seattle NFL	11	2	0	0.0	0
1995—Seattle NFL	16	4	45	11.3	0
Pro totals (3 years)	37	9	78	8.7	0

GRAY, CECIL   OT

PERSONAL: Born February 16, 1968, in Harlem, N.Y. ... 6-4/305. ... Full name: Cecil Talik Gray.
HIGH SCHOOL: Norfolk (Va.) Catholic.
COLLEGE: North Carolina (degree in journalism, 1990).
TRANSACTIONS/CAREER NOTES: Selected by Philadelphia Eagles in ninth round (245th pick overall) of 1990 NFL draft. ... Signed by Eagles (August 1, 1990). ... On injured reserve with knee injury (September 11-October 23, 1991). ... Moved to practice squad (October 23, 1991). ... Granted free agency (February 1, 1992). ... Re-signed by Eagles (July 22, 1992). ... Released by Eagles (August 29, 1992). ... Signed by Green Bay Packers (October 27, 1992). ... Released by Packers (August 24, 1993). ... Signed by New Orleans Saints (August 31, 1993). ... Released by Saints (October 7, 1993). ... Signed by Indianapolis Colts (October 12, 1993). ... On injured reserve with foot injury (December 21, 1993-remainder of season). ... Released by Colts (July 26, 1994). ... Re-signed by Colts (July 27, 1994). ... Granted unconditional free agency (February 17, 1995). ... Signed by Los Angeles Raiders (May 8, 1995). ... Released by Raiders (August 21, 1995). ... Signed by Arizona Cardinals (October 17, 1995). ... Granted unconditional free agency (February 16, 1996).
PLAYING EXPERIENCE: Philadelphia NFL, 1990 and 1991; Green Bay NFL, 1992; Indianapolis NFL, 1993 and 1994; Arizona NFL, 1995. ... Games: 1990 (12), 1991 (2), 1992 (2), 1993 (6), 1994 (16), 1995 (7). Total: 45.

GRAY, CHRIS   G   DOLPHINS

PERSONAL: Born June 19, 1970, in Birmingham, Ala. ... 6-4/296. ... Full name: Christopher William Gray.
HIGH SCHOOL: Homewood (Ala.).
COLLEGE: Auburn (degree in marketing).
TRANSACTIONS/CAREER NOTES: Selected by Miami Dolphins in fifth round (132nd pick overall) of 1993 NFL draft. ... Signed by Dolphins (July 12, 1993). ... On injured reserve with ankle injury (November 15, 1995-remainder of season).
PLAYING EXPERIENCE: Miami NFL, 1993-1995. ... Games: 1993 (5), 1994 (16), 1995 (10). Total: 31.
PRO STATISTICS: 1994—Recovered one fumble.

GRAY, DERWIN   DB   COLTS

PERSONAL: Born April 9, 1971, in San Antonio. ... 5-11/203. ... Full name: Derwin Lamont Gray.
HIGH SCHOOL: Judson (Converse, Texas).
COLLEGE: Brigham Young.
TRANSACTIONS/CAREER NOTES: Selected by Indianapolis Colts in fourth round (92nd pick overall) of 1993 NFL draft. ... Signed by Colts (July 20, 1993). ... Granted free agency (February 16, 1996).

G

PLAYING EXPERIENCE: Indianapolis NFL, 1993-1995. ... Games: 1993 (11), 1994 (16), 1995 (16). Total: 43.
CHAMPIONSHIP GAME EXPERIENCE: Played in AFC championship game (1995 season).
PRO STATISTICS: 1993—Recovered one fumble. 1994—Ran four yards with lateral from kickoff return. 1995—Intercepted one pass for 10 yards and recovered one fumble.

GRAY, MEL   KR   OILERS

PERSONAL: Born March 16, 1961, in Williamsburg, Va. ... 5-9/171.
HIGH SCHOOL: Lafayette (Williamsburg, Va.).
JUNIOR COLLEGE: Coffeyville (Kan.) Community College.
COLLEGE: Purdue.
TRANSACTIONS/CAREER NOTES: Selected by Chicago Blitz in seventh round (132nd pick overall) of 1984 USFL draft. ... USFL rights traded by Blitz to Los Angeles Express for WR Kris Haines (February 11, 1984). ... Signed by Express (February 16, 1984). ... On developmental squad for four games (February 24-March 9 and May 26-June 9, 1984). ... Selected by New Orleans Saints in second round (42nd pick overall) of 1984 NFL supplemental draft. ... Traded by Express to Arizona Outlaws for DB Dwight Drane, DB John Warren, G Wayne Jones, LB Howard Carson and TE Ken O'Neal to Arizona Outlaws for past considerations (August 1, 1985). ... Granted free agency when USFL suspended operations (August 7, 1986). ... Signed by Saints (August 18, 1986). ... Granted roster exemption (August 18-29, 1986). ... Granted unconditional free agency (February 1, 1989). ... Signed by Detroit Lions (March 1, 1989). ... Granted free agency (February 1, 1992). ... Re-signed by Lions (1992). ... On injured reserve with knee injury (December 22, 1992-remainder of season). ... Granted unconditional free agency (February 17, 1994). ... Re-signed by Lions (April 29, 1994). ... Granted unconditional free agency (February 17, 1995). ... Signed by Houston Oilers (March 3, 1995).
CHAMPIONSHIP GAME EXPERIENCE: Played in NFC championship game (1991 season).
HONORS: Named kick returner on THE SPORTING NEWS NFL All-Pro team (1986, 1990, 1991, 1993 and 1994). ... Named punt returner on THE SPORTING NEWS NFL All-Pro team (1987, 1991 and 1992). ... Played in Pro Bowl (1990, 1991 and 1994 seasons). ... Named to play in Pro Bowl (1992 season); replaced by Johnny Bailey due to injury.
RECORDS: Holds NFL career records for most kickoff returns—362; most yards by kickoff return—8,833; and most yards by combined kick return—11,220. ... Shares NFL career records for most touchdowns by kickoff return—6; and most touchdowns by combined kick return—9.
PRO STATISTICS: USFL: 1984—Attempted one pass with one completion for 29 yards, fumbled 10 times and recovered two fumbles. 1985—Fumbled seven times and recovered one fumble. NFL: 1987—Fumbled three times and recovered one fumble. 1988—Fumbled five times and recovered two fumbles. 1990—Fumbled four times and recovered three fumbles. 1991—Fumbled three times and recovered two fumbles. 1993—Fumbled three times. 1994—Fumbled three times and recovered two fumbles for 13 yards. 1995—Fumbled five times and recovered one fumble.

Year—Team	G	RUSHING Att.	Yds.	Avg.	TD	RECEIVING No.	Yds.	Avg.	TD	PUNT RETURNS No.	Yds.	Avg.	TD	KICKOFF RETURNS No.	Yds.	Avg.	TD	TOTALS TD	2pt.	Pts.
1984—Los Angeles USFL	15	133	625	4.7	3	27	288	10.7	1	0	0	...	0	20	332	16.6	0	4	0	24
1985—Los Angeles USFL	16	125	526	4.2	1	20	101	5.1	0	0	0	...	0	11	203	18.5	0	1	0	6
1986—New Orleans NFL	16	6	29	4.8	0	2	45	22.5	0	0	0	...	0	31	866	27.9	*1	1	...	6
1987—New Orleans NFL	12	8	37	4.6	1	6	30	5.0	0	24	352	*14.7	0	30	636	21.2	0	1	...	6
1988—New Orleans NFL	14	0	0	...	0	0	0	...	0	25	305	12.2	1	32	670	20.9	0	1	...	6
1989—Detroit NFL	10	3	22	7.3	0	2	47	23.5	0	11	76	6.9	0	24	640	26.7	0	0	...	0
1990—Detroit NFL	16	0	0	...	0	0	0	...	0	34	361	10.6	0	41	939	22.9	0	0	...	0
1991—Detroit NFL	16	2	11	5.5	0	3	42	14.0	0	25	385	*15.4	1	36	*929	*25.8	0	1	...	6
1992—Detroit NFL	15	0	0	...	0	0	0	...	0	18	175	9.7	1	*42	1006	24.0	1	2	0	12
1993—Detroit NFL	11	0	0	...	0	0	0	...	0	23	197	8.6	0	28	688	*24.6	†1	1	0	6
1994—Detroit NFL	16	0	0	...	0	0	0	...	0	21	233	11.1	0	45	1276	*28.4	*3	3	0	18
1995—Houston NFL	15	0	0	...	0	0	0	...	0	30	303	10.1	0	53	1183	22.3	0	0	0	0
USFL totals (2 years)	31	258	1151	4.5	4	47	389	8.3	1	0	0	...	0	31	535	17.3	0	5	0	30
NFL totals (10 years)	141	19	99	5.2	1	13	164	12.6	0	211	2387	11.3	3	362	8833	24.4	6	9	0	54
Pro totals (12 years)	172	277	1250	4.5	5	60	553	9.2	1	370	2387	11.3	3	393	9368	23.8	6	14	0	84

GRBAC, ELVIS   QB   49ERS

PERSONAL: Born August 13, 1970, in Cleveland. ... 6-5/232. .. Name pronounced GER-bach
HIGH SCHOOL: St. Joseph (Cleveland).
COLLEGE: Michigan (degree in communications, 1993).
TRANSACTIONS/CAREER NOTES: Selected by San Francisco 49ers in eighth round (219th pick overall) of 1993 NFL draft. ... Signed by 49ers (July 13, 1993).
CHAMPIONSHIP GAME EXPERIENCE: Member of 49ers for NFC championship game (1993 season); inactive. ... Member of 49ers for NFC championship game (1994 season); did not play. ... Member of Super Bowl championship team (1994 season).
PRO STATISTICS: 1994—Fumbled five times. 1995—Fumbled twice and recovered two fumbles for minus one yard.
STATISTICAL PLATEAUS: 300-yard passing games: 1995 (3).
MISCELLANEOUS: Regular-season record as starting NFL quarterback: 3-2 (.600).

Year Team	G	PASSING Att.	Cmp.	Pct.	Yds.	TD	Int.	Avg.	Rat.	RUSHING Att.	Yds.	Avg.	TD	TOTALS TD	2pt.	Pts.
1993—San Francisco NFL					Did not play.											
1994—San Francisco NFL	11	50	35	70.0	393	2	1	7.86	98.2	13	1	.1	0	0	0	0
1995—San Francisco NFL	16	183	127	69.4	1469	8	5	8.03	96.6	20	33	1.7	2	0	0	0
Pro totals (2 years)	27	233	162	69.5	1862	10	6	7.99	96.9	33	34	1.0	2	0	0	0

GREEN, CHRIS   S

PERSONAL: Born February 26, 1968, in Lawrenceburg, Ind. ... 5-11/188. ... Full name: Chris Allen Green.
HIGH SCHOOL: Lawrenceburg (Ind.).
COLLEGE: Illinois (degree in speech communications).
TRANSACTIONS/CAREER NOTES: Selected by Miami Dolphins in seventh round (191st pick overall) of 1991 NFL draft. ... Signed by Dolphins (July 12, 1991). ... On injured reserve with torn knee ligament (October 7, 1992-remainder of season). ... Granted unconditional free agency (February 17, 1995). ... Signed by Buffalo Bills (June 5, 1995). ... Released by Bills (February 16, 1996).

G

			INTERCEPTIONS		
Year Team	G	No.	Yds.	Avg.	TD
1991—Miami NFL	16	0	0	...	0
1992—Miami NFL	4	0	0	...	0
1993—Miami NFL	14	2	0	0.0	0
1994—Miami NFL	16	0	0	...	0
1995—Buffalo NFL	16	0	0	...	0
Pro totals (5 years)	66	2	0	0.0	0

GREEN, DARRELL   CB   REDSKINS

PERSONAL: Born February 15, 1960, in Houston. ... 5-8/180.
HIGH SCHOOL: Jesse H. Jones Senior (Houston).
COLLEGE: Texas A&I.
TRANSACTIONS/CAREER NOTES: Selected by Denver Gold in 10th round (112th pick overall) of 1983 USFL draft. ... Selected by Washington Redskins in first round (28th pick overall) of 1983 NFL draft. ... Signed by Redskins (June 10, 1983). ... On injured reserve with broken hand (December 13, 1988-remainder of season). ... On injured reserve with broken bone in wrist (October 24, 1989-remainder of season). ... Granted free agency (February 1, 1992). ... Re-signed by Redskins (August 25, 1992). ... On injured reserve with broken forearm (September 16-November 23, 1992). ... Granted unconditional free agency (February 17, 1995). ... Re-signed by Redskins (March 10, 1995).
CHAMPIONSHIP GAME EXPERIENCE: Played in NFC championship game (1983, 1986, 1987 and 1991 seasons). ... Played in Super Bowl XVIII (1983 season). ... Member of Super Bowl championship team (1987 and 1991 seasons).
HONORS: Played in Pro Bowl (1984, 1986, 1987, 1990 and 1991 seasons). ... Named cornerback on The Sporting News NFL All-Pro team (1991).
POSTSEASON RECORDS: Shares NFL postseason career record for most touchdowns by punt return—1 (January 10, 1988, at Chicago).
PRO STATISTICS: 1983—Recovered one fumble. 1985—Rushed once for six yards and recovered one fumble. 1986—Recovered one fumble. 1987—Recovered one fumble for 26 yards and a touchdown. 1988—Credited with a sack and recovered one fumble. 1989—Recovered one fumble. 1993—Recovered one fumble for 78 yards and a touchdown.
MISCELLANEOUS: Active NFC leader for career interceptions (40). ... Holds Washington Redskins all-time record for most interceptions (40).

		INTERCEPTIONS				PUNT RETURNS				TOTALS			
Year Team	G	No.	Yds.	Avg.	TD	No.	Yds.	Avg.	TD	TD	2pt.	Pts.	Fum.
1983—Washington NFL	16	2	7	3.5	0	4	29	7.3	0	0	...	0	1
1984—Washington NFL	16	5	91	18.2	1	2	13	6.5	0	1	...	6	0
1985—Washington NFL	16	2	0	0.0	0	16	214	13.4	0	0	...	0	2
1986—Washington NFL	16	5	9	1.8	0	12	120	10.0	0	0	...	0	1
1987—Washington NFL	12	3	65	21.7	0	5	53	10.6	0	1	...	6	0
1988—Washington NFL	15	1	12	12.0	0	9	103	11.4	0	0	...	0	1
1989—Washington NFL	7	2	0	0.0	0	1	11	11.0	0	0	...	0	1
1990—Washington NFL	16	4	20	5.0	1	1	6	6.0	0	1	...	6	0
1991—Washington NFL	16	5	47	9.4	0	0	0	...	0	0	...	0	0
1992—Washington NFL	8	1	15	15.0	0	0	0	...	0	0	...	0	0
1993—Washington NFL	16	4	10	2.5	0	1	27	27.0	0	1	...	6	0
1994—Washington NFL	16	3	32	10.7	1	0	0	...	0	1	0	6	0
1995—Washington NFL	16	3	42	14.0	0	0	0	...	0	1	0	6	0
Pro totals (13 years)	186	40	350	8.8	4	51	576	11.3	0	6	0	36	6

GREEN, DAVID   RB   PATRIOTS

PERSONAL: Born April 18, 1972, in Mount Kisco, N.Y. ... 5-11/193.
HIGH SCHOOL: Fox Lane (Bedford, N.Y.).
COLLEGE: Boston College.
TRANSACTIONS/CAREER NOTES: Signed as non-drafted free agent by New England Patriots (April 24, 1995). ... Released by Patriots (August 22, 1995). ... Re-signed by Patriots to practice squad (August 28, 1995). ... Activated (August 30, 1995). ... On injured reserve with knee injury (September 13, 1995-remainder of season).
PLAYING EXPERIENCE: New England NFL, 1995. ... Games: 1995 (2).

GREEN, ERIC   TE   DOLPHINS

PERSONAL: Born June 22, 1967, in Savannah, Ga. ... 6-5/280. ... Full name: Bernard Eric Green.
HIGH SCHOOL: A.E. Beach (Savannah, Ga.).
COLLEGE: Liberty, Va. (degree in finance, 1991).
TRANSACTIONS/CAREER NOTES: Selected by Pittsburgh Steelers in first round (21st pick overall) of 1990 NFL draft. ... Signed by Steelers (September 10, 1990). ... Granted roster exemption (September 10-24, 1990). ... On injured reserve with ankle injury (November 23, 1991-remainder of season). ... On injured reserve with shoulder injury (September 9-October 5, 1992). ... On practice squad (October 5-10, 1992). ... On reserve/suspended list for substance abuse (November 9-December 21, 1992). ... Granted roster exemption (December 21-27, 1992). ... Designated by Steelers as franchise player (February 15, 1994). ... Free agency status changed by Steelers from franchise to unconditional (February 15, 1995). ... Signed by Miami Dolphins (March 10, 1995).
CHAMPIONSHIP GAME EXPERIENCE: Played in AFC championship game (1994 season).
HONORS: Played in Pro Bowl (1993 and 1994 seasons).
PRO STATISTICS: 1990—Returned one kickoff for 16 yards and recovered one fumble.
STATISTICAL PLATEAUS: 100-yard receiving games: 1990 (1), 1991 (1), 1993 (2). Total: 4.

		RECEIVING				TOTALS			
Year Team	G	No.	Yds.	Avg.	TD	TD	2pt.	Pts.	Fum.
1990—Pittsburgh NFL	13	34	387	11.4	7	7	...	42	1
1991—Pittsburgh NFL	11	41	582	14.2	6	6	...	30	2
1992—Pittsburgh NFL	7	14	152	10.9	2	2	...	12	0

G

		RECEIVING				TOTALS			
Year Team	G	No.	Yds.	Avg.	TD	TD	2pt.	Pts.	Fum.
1993—Pittsburgh NFL	16	63	942	15.0	5	5	...	30	3
1994—Pittsburgh NFL	15	46	618	13.4	4	4	0	24	2
1995—Miami NFL	14	43	499	11.6	3	3	1	20	0
Pro totals (6 years)	76	241	3180	13.2	27	27	1	158	8

GREEN, HAROLD   RB

PERSONAL: Born January 29, 1968, in Ladson, S.C. ... 6-2/222.
HIGH SCHOOL: Stratford (Goose Creek, S.C.).
COLLEGE: South Carolina.
TRANSACTIONS/CAREER NOTES: Selected by Cincinnati Bengals in second round (38th pick overall) of 1990 NFL draft. ... Signed by Bengals (August 1, 1990). ... Designated by Bengals as transition player (February 25, 1993). ... Free agency status changed by Bengals from transitional to unconditional (February 16, 1996).
HONORS: Played in Pro Bowl (1992 season).
PRO STATISTICS: 1990—Recovered two fumbles. 1992—Recovered one fumble. 1994—Recovered one fumble. 1995—Recovered one fumble.
STATISTICAL PLATEAUS: 100-yard rushing games: 1991 (3), 1992 (5). Total: 8.

		RUSHING				RECEIVING				KICKOFF RETURNS				TOTALS			
Year Team	G	Att.	Yds.	Avg.	TD	No.	Yds.	Avg.	TD	No.	Yds.	Avg.	TD	TD	2pt.	Pts.	Fum.
1990—Cincinnati NFL	12	83	353	4.3	1	12	90	7.5	1	0	0	...	0	2	...	12	2
1991—Cincinnati NFL	14	158	731	4.6	2	16	136	8.5	0	4	66	16.5	0	2	...	12	2
1992—Cincinnati NFL	16	265	1170	4.4	2	41	214	5.2	0	0	0	...	0	2	...	12	1
1993—Cincinnati NFL	15	215	589	2.7	0	22	115	5.2	0	0	0	...	0	0	...	0	3
1994—Cincinnati NFL	14	76	223	2.9	1	27	267	9.9	1	5	113	22.6	0	2	0	12	1
1995—Cincinnati NFL	15	171	661	3.9	2	27	182	6.7	1	0	0	...	0	3	0	18	2
Pro totals (6 years)	86	968	3727	3.9	8	145	1004	6.9	3	9	179	19.9	0	11	0	66	11

GREEN, ROBERT   RB   BEARS

PERSONAL: Born September 10, 1970, in Washington, D.C. ... 5-8/212. ... Full name: Robert David Green.
HIGH SCHOOL: Friendly (Md.) Senior.
COLLEGE: William & Mary.
TRANSACTIONS/CAREER NOTES: Signed as non-drafted free agent by Washington Redskins for 1992 season. ... Claimed on waivers by Chicago Bears (August 31, 1993). ... On injured reserve with broken leg (December 5, 1995-remainder of season).
PRO STATISTICS: 1994—Recovered one fumble. 1995—Recovered one fumble.

		RUSHING				RECEIVING				KICKOFF RETURNS				TOTALS			
Year Team	G	Att.	Yds.	Avg.	TD	No.	Yds.	Avg.	TD	No.	Yds.	Avg.	TD	TD	2pt.	Pts.	Fum.
1992—Washington NFL	15	8	46	5.8	0	1	5	5.0	0	1	9	9.0	0	0	...	0	0
1993—Chicago NFL	16	15	29	1.9	0	13	63	4.9	0	9	141	15.7	0	0	...	0	0
1994—Chicago NFL	15	25	122	4.9	0	24	199	8.3	2	6	77	12.8	0	2	0	12	1
1995—Chicago NFL	12	107	570	5.3	3	28	246	8.8	0	3	29	9.7	0	3	0	18	2
Pro totals (4 years)	58	155	767	5.0	3	66	513	7.8	2	19	256	13.5	0	5	0	30	3

GREEN, ROGERICK   CB

PERSONAL: Born December 15, 1969, in San Antonio. ... 6-0/184.
HIGH SCHOOL: West Campus (San Antonio).
COLLEGE: Kansas State.
TRANSACTIONS/CAREER NOTES: Selected by Tampa Bay Buccaneers in fifth round (118th pick overall) of 1992 NFL draft. ... Signed by Buccaneers (July 15, 1992). ... On injured reserve with elbow injury (September 1-October 24, 1992). ... On injured reserve with knee injury (October 26, 1992-remainder of season). ... On injured reserve with knee injury (August 30, 1993-entire season). ... Selected by Jacksonville Jaguars from Buccaneers in NFL expansion draft (February 15, 1995). ... Released by Jaguars (August 19, 1995). ... Re-signed by Jaguars (August 31, 1995). ... Granted unconditional free agency (February 16, 1996).
PLAYING EXPERIENCE: Tampa Bay NFL, 1992 and 1994; Jacksonville NFL, 1995. ... Games: 1992 (1), 1994 (11), 1995(14). Total: 26.
PRO STATISTICS: 1994—Returned two kickoffs for 33 yards.

GREEN, VICTOR   CB   JETS

PERSONAL: Born December 8, 1969, in Americus, Ga. ... 5-9/195. ... Full name: Victor Bernard Green. ... Cousin of Tommy Sims, defensive back, Indianapolis Colts (1986).
HIGH SCHOOL: Americus (Ga.).
JUNIOR COLLEGE: Copiah-Lincoln (Miss.) Junior College.
COLLEGE: Akron (degree in criminal justice, 1993).
TRANSACTIONS/CAREER NOTES: Signed as non-drafted free agent by New York Jets (April 29, 1993). ... Released by Jets (August 30, 1993). ... Re-signed by Jets to practice squad (September 1, 1993). ... Activated (September 28, 1993).
PLAYING EXPERIENCE: New York Jets NFL, 1993-1995. ... Games: 1993 (11), 1994 (16), 1995 (16). Total: 43.
PRO STATISTICS: 1994—Credited with one sack and recovered one fumble. 1995—Credited with two sacks, intercepted one pass for two yards and recovered one fumble.

G

GREEN, WILLIE   WR   PANTHERS

PERSONAL: Born April 2, 1966, in Athens, Ga. ... 6-4/185. ... Full name: Willie Aaron Green.

HIGH SCHOOL: Clarke Central (Athens, Ga.), then Tennessee Military Academy.
COLLEGE: Mississippi.
TRANSACTIONS/CAREER NOTES: Selected by Detroit Lions in eighth round (194th pick overall) of 1990 NFL draft. ... On injured reserve with shoulder injury (September 5, 1990-entire season). ... Granted free agency (February 1, 1992). ... Re-signed by Lions (August 11, 1992). ... On suspended list (December 7-14, 1992). ... Released by Lions (June 9, 1994). ... Signed by Tampa Bay Buccaneers (July 5, 1994). ... Released by Buccaneers (October 11, 1994). ... Signed by Carolina Panthers (December 15, 1994).
CHAMPIONSHIP GAME EXPERIENCE: Played in NFC championship game (1991 season).
STATISTICAL PLATEAUS: 100-yard receiving games: 1992 (2), 1993 (1), 1995 (4). Total: 7.
MISCELLANEOUS: Holds Carolina Panthers all-time record for most touchdowns (6).

Year Team		RECEIVING				TOTALS			
	G	No.	Yds.	Avg.	TD	TD	2pt.	Pts.	Fum.
1990—Detroit NFL				Did not play—injured.					
1991—Detroit NFL	16	39	592	15.2	7	7	...	42	0
1992—Detroit NFL	15	33	586	17.8	5	5	...	30	1
1993—Detroit NFL	16	28	462	16.5	2	2	...	12	0
1994—Tampa Bay NFL	5	9	150	16.7	0	0	0	0	0
1995—Carolina NFL	16	47	882	18.8	6	6	0	36	1
Pro totals (5 years)	68	156	2672	17.1	20	20	0	120	2

GREENE, ANDREW G DOLPHINS

PERSONAL: Born September 24, 1969, in Kingston, Jamaica. ... 6-3/304.
HIGH SCHOOL: Pickering (Ajax, Ont.).
COLLEGE: Indiana.
TRANSACTIONS/CAREER NOTES: Selected by Miami Dolphins in second round (53rd pick overall) of 1995 NFL draft. ... Signed by Dolphins (June 30, 1995).
PLAYING EXPERIENCE: Miami NFL, 1995. ... Games: 1995 (6).

GREENE, KEVIN LB PANTHERS

PERSONAL: Born July 31, 1962, in New York. ... 6-3/247. ... Full name: Kevin Darwin Greene.
HIGH SCHOOL: South (Granite City, Ill.).
COLLEGE: Auburn.
TRANSACTIONS/CAREER NOTES: Selected by Birmingham Stallions in 1985 USFL territorial draft. ... Selected by Los Angeles Rams in fifth round (113th pick overall) of 1985 NFL draft. ... Signed by Rams (July 12, 1985). ... Crossed picket line during players strike (October 14, 1987). ... Granted free agency (February 1, 1990). ... Re-signed by Rams (September 1, 1990). ... Granted roster exemption (September 1-7, 1990). ... Granted unconditional free agency (March 1, 1993). ... Signed by Pittsburgh Steelers (April 3, 1993). ... Granted unconditional free agency (February 16, 1996). ... Signed by Carolina Panthers (May 3, 1996).
CHAMPIONSHIP GAME EXPERIENCE: Played in NFC championship game (1985 and 1989 seasons). ... Played in AFC championship game (1994 and 1995 seasons). ... Played in Super Bowl XXX (1995 season).
HONORS: Named outside linebacker on THE SPORTING NEWS NFL All-Pro team (1989 and 1994). ... Played in Pro Bowl (1989, 1994 and 1995 seasons).
PRO STATISTICS: 1986—Recovered one fumble for 13 yards. 1987—Intercepted one pass for 25 yards. 1988—Credited with one safety and intercepted one pass for 10 yards. 1989—Recovered two fumbles. 1990—Recovered four fumbles. 1991—Credited with one safety. 1992—Credited with a safety and recovered four fumbles for two yards. 1993—Recovered three fumbles for five yards. 1994—Recovered three fumbles. 1995—Intercepted one pass for no yards.

Year Team	G	SACKS
1985—Los Angeles Rams NFL	15	0.0
1986—Los Angeles Rams NFL	16	7.0
1987—Los Angeles Rams NFL	9	6.5
1988—Los Angeles Rams NFL	16	16.5
1989—Los Angeles Rams NFL	16	16.5
1990—Los Angeles Rams NFL	15	13.0
1991—Los Angeles Rams NFL	16	3.0
1992—Los Angeles Rams NFL	16	10.0
1993—Pittsburgh NFL	16	12.5
1994—Pittsburgh NFL	16	*14.0
1995—Pittsburgh NFL	16	9.0
Pro totals (11 years)	167	108.0

GREENE, TRACY TE STEELERS

PERSONAL: Born November 5, 1972, in Monroe, La. ... 6-5/270. ... Full name: Tracy Lamar Greene.
HIGH SCHOOL: Grambling (La.) State University High.
COLLEGE: Grambling State.
TRANSACTIONS/CAREER NOTES: Selected by Kansas City Chiefs in seventh round (219th pick overall) of 1994 NFL draft. ... Signed by Chiefs (June 8, 1994). ... Traded by Chiefs to Pittsburgh Steelers for seventh-round pick (C Ben Lynch) in 1996 draft (August 27, 1995).
CHAMPIONSHIP GAME EXPERIENCE: Played in AFC championship game (1995 season). ... Member of Steelers for Super Bowl XXX (1995 season); inactive.
PRO STATISTICS: 1995—Returned one kickoff for seven yards.

Year Team		RECEIVING				TOTALS			
	G	No.	Yds.	Avg.	TD	TD	2pt.	Pts.	Fum.
1994—Kansas City NFL	7	6	69	11.5	1	1	0	6	0
1995—Pittsburgh NFL	16	0	0	...	0	0	0	0	0
Pro totals (2 years)	23	6	69	11.5	1	1	0	6	0

G

GREENWOOD, CARL   CB   JETS

PERSONAL: Born March 11, 1972, in Fort Ord, Calif. ... 5-11/186. ... Full name: Carlanditt Keith Greenwood.
HIGH SCHOOL: Mary Carroll (Corpus Christi, Texas).
COLLEGE: UCLA.
TRANSACTIONS/CAREER NOTES: Selected by New York Jets in fifth round (142nd pick overall) of 1995 NFL draft. ... Signed by Jets (May 15, 1995).
PLAYING EXPERIENCE: New York Jets NFL, 1995. ... Games: 1995 (10).

GRIFFIN, DON   CB   RAVENS

PERSONAL: Born March 17, 1964, in Camilla, Ga. ... 6-0/176. ... Full name: Donald Frederick Griffin. ... Brother of James Griffin, safety, Cincinnati Bengals and Detroit Lions (1983-1989).
HIGH SCHOOL: Mitchell-Baker (Camilla, Ga.).
COLLEGE: Middle Tennessee State.
TRANSACTIONS/CAREER NOTES: Selected by Memphis Showboats in 1986 USFL territorial draft. ... Selected by San Francisco 49ers in sixth round (162nd pick overall) of 1986 NFL draft. ... Signed by 49ers (July 21, 1986). ... Granted free agency (February 1, 1991). ... Re-signed by 49ers (June 2, 1991). ... Released by 49ers (August 30, 1993). ... Re-signed by 49ers (August 31, 1993). ... Granted unconditional free agency (February 17, 1994). ... Signed by Cleveland Browns (April 19, 1994). ... Browns franchise moved to Baltimore and renamed Ravens for 1996 season (March 11, 1996).
CHAMPIONSHIP GAME EXPERIENCE: Played in NFC championship game (1988-1990, 1992 and 1993 seasons). ... Member of Super Bowl championship team (1988 and 1989 seasons).
PRO STATISTICS: 1986—Returned five kickoffs for 97 yards and recovered two fumbles. 1987—Recovered one fumble for seven yards. 1989—Recovered one fumble. 1990—Returned one kickoff for 15 yards and recovered two fumbles. 1991—Recovered three fumbles for 99 yards and a touchdown. 1994—Recovered three fumbles for 15 yards.

		INTERCEPTIONS				SACKS	PUNT RETURNS				TOTALS			
Year Team	G	No.	Yds.	Avg.	TD	No.	No.	Yds.	Avg.	TD	TD	2pt.	Pts.	Fum.
1986—San Francisco NFL	16	3	0	0.0	0	1.0	38	377	9.9	1	1	...	6	3
1987—San Francisco NFL	12	5	1	.2	0	0.0	9	79	8.8	0	0	...	0	0
1988—San Francisco NFL	10	0	0	...	0	1.0	4	28	7.0	0	0	...	0	0
1989—San Francisco NFL	16	2	6	3.0	0	0.0	1	9	9.0	0	0	...	0	0
1990—San Francisco NFL	16	3	32	10.7	0	0.0	16	105	6.6	0	0	...	0	1
1991—San Francisco NFL	16	1	0	0.0	0	0.0	0	0	...	0	1	...	6	0
1992—San Francisco NFL	16	5	4	.8	0	0.0	6	69	11.5	0	0	...	0	1
1993—San Francisco NFL	12	3	6	2.0	0	0.0	0	0	...	0	0	...	0	0
1994—Cleveland NFL	15	2	2	1.0	0	4.0	0	0	...	0	0	0	0	1
1995—Cleveland NFL	16	1	0	0.0	0	0.0	0	0	...	0	0	0	0	0
Pro totals (10 years)	145	25	51	2.1	0	6.0	74	667	9.0	1	2	0	12	6

GRIFFITH, HOWARD   FB   PANTHERS

PERSONAL: Born November 17, 1967, in Chicago. ... 6-0/240. ... Full name: Howard Thomas Griffith.
HIGH SCHOOL: Percy L. Julian (Chicago).
COLLEGE: Illinois.
TRANSACTIONS/CAREER NOTES: Selected by Indianapolis Colts in ninth round (237th pick overall) of 1991 NFL draft. ... Signed by Colts (July 12, 1991). ... Released by Colts (August 26, 1991). ... Signed by Buffalo Bills to practice squad (September 4, 1991). ... Released by Bills (August 31, 1992). ... Re-signed by Bills to practice squad (September 2, 1992). ... Released by Bills (October 21, 1992). ... Signed by San Diego Chargers to practice squad (October 23, 1992). ... Released by Chargers (October 28, 1992). ... Re-signed by Chargers to practice squad (October 30, 1992). ... Released by Chargers (December 9, 1992). ... Re-signed by Chargers to practice squad (December 14, 1992). ... Granted free agency after 1992 season. ... Re-signed by Chargers for 1993 season. ... Released by Chargers (August 30, 1993). ... Signed by Los Angeles Rams (September 2, 1993). ... Selected by Carolina Panthers from Rams in NFL expansion draft (February 15, 1995). ... Granted free agency (February 16, 1996).
PRO STATISTICS: 1995—Recovered one fumble.

		RUSHING				RECEIVING				KICKOFF RETURNS				TOTALS			
Year Team	G	Att.	Yds.	Avg.	TD	No.	Yds.	Avg.	TD	No.	Yds.	Avg.	TD	TD	2pt.	Pts.	Fum.
1991—Buffalo NFL						Did not play.											
1992—San Diego NFL						Did not play.											
1993—Los Angeles Rams NFL	15	0	0	...	0	0	0	...	0	8	169	21.1	0	0	...	0	0
1994—Los Angeles Rams NFL	16	9	30	3.3	0	16	113	7.1	1	2	35	17.5	0	1	0	6	0
1995—Carolina NFL	15	65	197	3.0	1	11	63	5.7	1	0	0	...	0	2	0	12	1
Pro totals (3 years)	46	74	227	3.1	1	27	176	6.5	2	10	204	20.4	0	3	0	18	1

GRIFFITH, RICH   TE   JAGUARS

PERSONAL: Born July 31, 1969, in Tucson, Ariz. ... 6-5/256. ... Full name: Richard Pope Griffith.
HIGH SCHOOL: Catalina (Tucson, Ariz.).
COLLEGE: Arizona.
TRANSACTIONS/CAREER NOTES: Selected by New England Patriots in fifth round (138th pick overall) of 1993 NFL draft. ... Signed by Patriots (July 16, 1993). ... Released by Patriots (August 20, 1994). ... Signed by Jacksonville Jaguars (January 6, 1995).
PRO STATISTICS: 1995—Returned one kickoff for nine yards.

		RECEIVING				TOTALS			
Year Team	G	No.	Yds.	Avg.	TD	TD	2pt.	Pts.	Fum.
1993—New England NFL	3	0	0	...	0	0	0	0	0
1994—					Did not play.				
1995—Jacksonville NFL	16	16	243	15.2	0	0	0	0	0
Pro totals (3 years)	19	16	243	15.2	0	0	0	0	0

G

GRIFFITH, ROBERT   S   VIKINGS

PERSONAL: Born November 30, 1970, in Lonham, Md. ... 5-11/193. ... Full name: Robert Otis Griffith.
HIGH SCHOOL: Mount Miguel (Spring Valley, Calif.).
COLLEGE: San Diego State.
TRANSACTIONS/CAREER NOTES: Signed by Sacramento Gold Miners of CFL to practice squad (August 8, 1993). ... Granted free agency after 1993 season. ... Signed by Minnesota Vikings (April 21, 1994).
PLAYING EXPERIENCE: Minnesota NFL, 1994 and 1995. ... Games: 1994 (15), 1995 (16). Total: 31.
PRO STATISTICS: 1995—Credited with ½ sack.

GROCE, CLIF   RB   COLTS

PERSONAL: Born July 30, 1972, in College Station, Texas. ... 5-11/242. ... Full name: Clifton Allen Groce.
HIGH SCHOOL: A&M Consolidated (College Station, Texas).
COLLEGE: Texas A&M.
TRANSACTIONS/CAREER NOTES: Signed as non-drafted free agent by Indianapolis Colts (April 27, 1995). ... Released by Colts (August 22, 1995). ... Re-signed by Colts to practice squad (August 28, 1995). ... Activated (December 7, 1995).
PLAYING EXPERIENCE: Indianapolis NFL, 1995. ... Games: 1995 (1).
CHAMPIONSHIP GAME EXPERIENCE: Played in AFC championship game (1995 season).

GROW, MONTY   S   JAGUARS

PERSONAL: Born September 4, 1971, in Inverness, Fla. ... 6-4/214. ... Full name: Monty Roy Grow.
HIGH SCHOOL: Citrus (Inverness, Fla.).
COLLEGE: Florida.
TRANSACTIONS/CAREER NOTES: Signed as non-drafted free agent by Kansas City Chiefs (May 2, 1994). ... Selected by Jacksonville Jaguars from Chiefs in NFL expansion draft (February 15, 1995). ... On injured reserve with knee injury (September 27, 1995-remainder of season).
PRO STATISTICS: 1994—Fumbled once.

			INTERCEPTIONS		
Year Team	G	No.	Yds.	Avg.	TD
1994—Kansas City NFL	15	1	21	21.0	0
1995—Jacksonville NFL	4	1	2	2.0	0
Pro totals (2 years)	19	2	23	11.5	0

GRUBER, PAUL   OT   BUCCANEERS

PERSONAL: Born February 24, 1965, in Madison, Wis. ... 6-5/296. ... Full name: Paul Blake Gruber.
HIGH SCHOOL: Sauk Prairie (Prairie du Sac, Wis.).
COLLEGE: Wisconsin (degree in communication arts, 1988).
TRANSACTIONS/CAREER NOTES: Selected by Tampa Bay Buccaneers in first round (fourth pick overall) of 1988 NFL draft. ... Signed by Buccaneers (August 7, 1988). ... Designated by Buccaneers as franchise player (February 25, 1993). ... Re-signed by Buccaneers (October 20, 1993). ... Granted roster exemption (October 20-23, 1993).
PLAYING EXPERIENCE: Tampa Bay NFL, 1988-1995. ... Games: 1988 (16), 1989 (16), 1990 (16), 1991 (16), 1992 (16), 1993 (10), 1994 (16), 1995 (16). Total: 122.
HONORS: Named offensive tackle on THE SPORTING NEWS college All-America first team (1987).
PRO STATISTICS: 1988—Recovered two fumbles. 1990—Recovered one fumble. 1991—Recovered one fumble. 1992—Recovered one fumble. 1994—Recovered one fumble. 1995—Recovered two fumbles.

GRUNHARD, TIM   C   CHIEFS

PERSONAL: Born May 17, 1968, in Chicago. ... 6-2/299. ... Full name: Timothy Gerard Grunhard.
HIGH SCHOOL: St. Laurence (Burbank, Ill.).
COLLEGE: Notre Dame (degree in political science).
TRANSACTIONS/CAREER NOTES: Selected by Kansas City Chiefs in second round (40th pick overall) of 1990 NFL draft. ... Signed by Chiefs (July 22, 1990).
PLAYING EXPERIENCE: Kansas City NFL, 1990-1995. ... Games: 1990 (14), 1991 (16), 1992 (12), 1993 (16), 1994 (16), 1995 (16). Total: 90.
CHAMPIONSHIP GAME EXPERIENCE: Played in AFC championship game (1993 season).
PRO STATISTICS: 1991—Recovered one fumble. 1992—Recovered two fumbles. 1993—Fumbled once. 1995—Recovered one fumble.

GULIFORD, ERIC   WR

PERSONAL: Born October 25, 1969, in Kansas City, Kan. ... 5-8/165. ... Full name: Eric Andre Guliford.
HIGH SCHOOL: Peoria (Ariz.).
COLLEGE: Arizona State.
TRANSACTIONS/CAREER NOTES: Signed as non-drafted free agent by Minnesota Vikings (May 3, 1993). ... Selected by Carolina Panthers from Vikings in NFL expansion draft (February 15, 1995). ... On injured reserve with hamstring injury (December 13, 1995-remainder of season). ... Granted unconditional free agency (February 16, 1996).
PRO STATISTICS: 1995—Attempted two passes with one completion and one interception, rushed twice for two yards and recovered one fumble.

		RECEIVING				PUNT RETURNS				KICKOFF RETURNS				TOTALS			
Year Team	G	No.	Yds.	Avg.	TD	No.	Yds.	Avg.	TD	No.	Yds.	Avg.	TD	TD	2pt.	Pts.	Fum.
1993—Minnesota NFL	10	1	45	45.0	0	29	212	7.3	0	5	101	20.2	0	0	...	0	1

G

Year Team	G	RECEIVING No.	Yds.	Avg.	TD	PUNT RETURNS No.	Yds.	Avg.	TD	KICKOFF RETURNS No.	Yds.	Avg.	TD	TOTALS TD	2pt.	Pts.	Fum.
1994—Minnesota NFL..................	7	0	0	...	0	5	14	2.8	0	0	0	...	0	0	0	0	1
1995—Carolina NFL	14	29	444	15.3	1	43	475	11.1	†1	0	0	...	0	2	0	12	1
Pro totals (3 years)	31	30	489	16.3	1	77	701	9.1	1	5	101	20.2	0	2	0	12	3

GUNN, MARK   DE   EAGLES

PERSONAL: Born July 24, 1968, in Cleveland. ... 6-5/297.
HIGH SCHOOL: Glenville (Ohio).
JUNIOR COLLEGE: Merced (Calif.) Junior College.
COLLEGE: Pittsburgh.
TRANSACTIONS/CAREER NOTES: Selected by New York Jets in fourth round (94th pick overall) of 1991 NFL draft. ... Signed by Jets (June 18, 1991). ... Granted free agency (February 17, 1994). ... Re-signed by Jets (June 24, 1994). ... Released by Jets (November 8, 1994). ... Signed by New Orleans Saints (November 22, 1994). ... Granted unconditional free agency (February 17, 1995). ... Signed by Philadelphia Eagles (March 22, 1995). ... Granted free agency (February 16, 1996).
PLAYING EXPERIENCE: New York Jets NFL, 1991-1994; Philadelphia NFL, 1995. ... Games: 1991 (15), 1992 (16), 1993 (12), 1994 (3), 1995 (12). Total: 58.
PRO STATISTICS: 1992—Credited with two sacks. 1995—Credited with ½ sack and recovered one fumble.

GUYTON, MYRON   S

PERSONAL: Born August 26, 1967, in Metcalf, Ga. ... 6-1/205. ... Full name: Myron Mynard Guyton. ... Related to William Andrews, running back, Atlanta Falcons (1979-1983 and 1986).
HIGH SCHOOL: Central (Thomasville, Ga.).
COLLEGE: Eastern Kentucky.
TRANSACTIONS/CAREER NOTES: Selected by New York Giants in eighth round (218th pick overall) of 1989 NFL draft. ... Signed by Giants (July 25, 1989). ... Granted free agency (February 1, 1991). ... Re-signed by Giants (August 7, 1991). ... On injured reserve with back injury (September 9-December 6, 1992). ... Granted free agency (March 1, 1993). ... Re-signed by Giants (July 9, 1993). ... Granted unconditional free agency (February 17, 1994). ... Signed by New England Patriots (February 28, 1994). ... Released by Patriots (March 26, 1996).
CHAMPIONSHIP GAME EXPERIENCE: Played in NFC championship game (1990 season). ... Member of Super Bowl championship team (1990 season).
PRO STATISTICS: 1989—Recovered three fumbles for four yards. 1990—Recovered two fumbles. 1991—Recovered one fumble. 1993—Recovered one fumble. 1994—Returned one kickoff for minus one yard and recovered three fumbles for 34 yards.

Year Team	G	INTERCEPTIONS No.	Yds.	Avg.	TD
1989—New York Giants NFL..	16	2	27	13.5	0
1990—New York Giants NFL..	16	1	0	0.0	0
1991—New York Giants NFL..	16	0	0	...	0
1992—New York Giants NFL..	4	0	0	...	0
1993—New York Giants NFL..	16	2	34	17.0	0
1994—New England NFL	16	2	18	9.0	0
1995—New England NFL	14	3	68	22.7	0
Pro totals (7 years)	98	10	147	14.7	0

HABIB, BRIAN   G   BRONCOS

PERSONAL: Born December 2, 1964, in Ellensburg, Wash. ... 6-7/292. ... Full name: Brian Richard Habib.
HIGH SCHOOL: Ellensburg (Wash.).
COLLEGE: Washington.
TRANSACTIONS/CAREER NOTES: Selected by Minnesota Vikings in 10th round (264th pick overall) of 1988 NFL draft. ... Signed by Vikings (July 19, 1988). ... On injured reserve with shoulder injury (September 3-December 24, 1988). ... Granted free agency (February 1, 1991). ... Re-signed by Vikings (July 18, 1991). ... Granted free agency (February 1, 1992). ... Re-signed by Vikings (July 24, 1992). ... Granted unconditional free agency (March 1, 1993). ... Signed by Denver Broncos (March 8, 1993).
PLAYING EXPERIENCE: Minnesota NFL, 1989-1992; Denver NFL, 1993-1995. ... Games: 1989 (16), 1990 (16), 1991 (16), 1992 (16), 1993 (16), 1994 (16), 1995 (16). Total: 112.
PRO STATISTICS: 1994—Recovered one fumble.

HAGER, BRITT   LB   BRONCOS

PERSONAL: Born February 20, 1966, in Odessa, Texas. ... 6-1/225. ... Full name: Britt Harley Hager. ... Name pronounced HAY-ghurr.
HIGH SCHOOL: Permian (Odessa, Texas).
COLLEGE: Texas.
TRANSACTIONS/CAREER NOTES: Selected by Philadelphia Eagles in third round (81st pick overall) of 1989 NFL draft. ... Signed by Eagles (August 7, 1989). ... Granted free agency (February 1, 1992). ... Re-signed by Eagles (August 11, 1992). ... On injured reserve with back injury (November 18, 1992-remainder of season). ... Granted free agency (March 1, 1993). ... Re-signed by Eagles (July 21, 1993). ... Granted unconditional free agency (February 17, 1995). ... Signed by Denver Broncos (March 6, 1995).
PRO STATISTICS: 1989—Recovered two fumbles for nine yards. 1990—Returned one kickoff for no yards. 1991—Recovered one fumble. 1994—Recovered one fumble.

Year Team	G	INTERCEPTIONS No.	Yds.	Avg.	TD	SACKS No.
1989—Philadelphia NFL..	16	0	0	...	0	0.0
1990—Philadelphia NFL..	16	0	0	...	0	0.0
1991—Philadelphia NFL..	10	0	0	...	0	0.0

Year	Team	G	No.	Yds.	Avg.	TD	No.
			INTERCEPTIONS				SACKS
1992—Philadelphia NFL		10	0	0	...	0	0.0
1993—Philadelphia NFL		16	1	19	19.0	0	1.0
1994—Philadelphia NFL		16	1	0	0.0	0	1.0
1995—Denver NFL		16	1	19	19.0	0	0.0
Pro totals (7 years)		100	3	38	12.7	0	2.0

HALEY, CHARLES   DE   COWBOYS

PERSONAL: Born January 6, 1964, in Gladys, Va. ... 6-5/255. ... Full name: Charles Lewis Haley.
HIGH SCHOOL: William Campbell (Naruna, Va.).
COLLEGE: James Madison.
TRANSACTIONS/CAREER NOTES: Selected by San Francisco 49ers in fourth round (96th pick overall) of 1986 NFL draft. ... Signed by 49ers (May 27, 1986). ... On reserve/did not report list (July 24-August 23, 1989). ... Granted free agency (February 1, 1990). ... Re-signed by 49ers (August 23, 1990). ... Traded by 49ers to Dallas Cowboys for second-round pick (traded to Los Angeles Raiders) in 1993 draft (August 27, 1992). ... Granted unconditional free agency (March 1, 1993). ... Re-signed by Cowboys (March 16, 1993).
CHAMPIONSHIP GAME EXPERIENCE: Played in NFC championship game (1988-1990 and 1992-1995 seasons). ... Member of Super Bowl championship team (1988, 1989, 1992, 1993 and 1995 seasons).
HONORS: Played in Pro Bowl (1988, 1990, 1991, 1994 and 1995 seasons). ... Named defensive end on THE SPORTING NEWS NFL All-Pro team (1994).
POSTSEASON RECORDS: Holds Super Bowl career records for most games played on winning team—5; and most sacks—4.5. ... Shares Super Bowl record for most games played—5 (1988, 1989, 1992, 1993 and 1995 seasons).
PRO STATISTICS: 1986—Intercepted one pass for eight yards, fumbled once and recovered two fumbles for three yards. 1988—Credited with one safety and recovered two fumbles. 1989—Recovered one fumble for three yards and a touchdown. 1990—Recovered one fumble. 1991—Recovered one fumble for three yards. 1993—Recovered one fumble. 1994—Intercepted one pass for one yard.

Year	Team	G	SACKS
1986—San Francisco NFL		16	12.0
1987—San Francisco NFL		12	6.5
1988—San Francisco NFL		16	11.5
1989—San Francisco NFL		16	10.5
1990—San Francisco NFL		16	16.0
1991—San Francisco NFL		14	7.0
1992—Dallas NFL		15	6.0
1993—Dallas NFL		14	4.0
1994—Dallas NFL		16	12.5
1995—Dallas NFL		13	10.5
Pro totals (10 years)		148	96.5

HALL, COURTNEY   C   CHARGERS

PERSONAL: Born August 26, 1968, in Los Angeles. ... 6-2/281. ... Full name: Courtney Caesar Hall.
HIGH SCHOOL: Wilmington (Calif.)-Phineas Banning.
COLLEGE: Rice.
TRANSACTIONS/CAREER NOTES: Selected by San Diego Chargers in second round (37th pick overall) of 1989 NFL draft. ... Signed by Chargers (July 24, 1989). ... Granted free agency (February 1, 1992). ... Re-signed by Chargers (July 23, 1992). ... Granted unconditional free agency (February 17, 1994). ... Re-signed by Chargers (March 9, 1994).
PLAYING EXPERIENCE: San Diego NFL, 1989-1995. ... Games: 1989 (16), 1990 (16), 1991 (16), 1992 (16), 1993 (16), 1994 (15), 1995 (16). Total: 111.
CHAMPIONSHIP GAME EXPERIENCE: Played in AFC championship game (1994 season). ... Played in Super Bowl XXIX (1994 season).
PRO STATISTICS: 1989—Fumbled once for minus 29 yards. 1991—Recovered two fumbles. 1995—Recovered one fumble.

HALL, DANA   S   JAGUARS

PERSONAL: Born July 8, 1969, in Bellflower, Calif. ... 6-2/206. ... Full name: Dana Eric Hall.
HIGH SCHOOL: Genesha (Pomona, Calif.).
COLLEGE: Washington (degree in political science, 1992).
TRANSACTIONS/CAREER NOTES: Selected by San Francisco 49ers in first round (18th pick overall) of 1992 NFL draft. ... Signed by 49ers (July 20, 1992). ... Granted unconditional free agency (February 17, 1995). ... Signed by Cleveland Browns (April 28, 1995). ... Granted unconditional free agency (February 16, 1996). ... Signed by Jacksonville Jaguars (March 13, 1996).
CHAMPIONSHIP GAME EXPERIENCE: Played in NFC championship game (1992-1994 seasons). ... Member of Super Bowl championship team (1994 season).
PRO STATISTICS: 1992—Credited with one sack and recovered one fumble. 1995—Credited with one sack.

Year	Team	G	No.	Yds.	Avg.	TD
			INTERCEPTIONS			
1992—San Francisco NFL		15	2	34	17.0	0
1993—San Francisco NFL		13	0	0	...	0
1994—San Francisco NFL		16	2	0	0.0	0
1995—Cleveland NFL		15	2	41	20.5	0
Pro totals (4 years)		59	6	75	12.5	0

HALL, DARRYL   S

PERSONAL: Born August 1, 1966, in Oscoda, Mich. ... 6-2/210.
HIGH SCHOOL: Lompoc (Calif.) Senior.

H

COLLEGE: Washington.

TRANSACTIONS/CAREER NOTES: Signed as non-drafted free agent by Seattle Seahawks (April 27, 1989). ... Released by Seahawks (August 9, 1989). ... Signed by Calgary Stampeders of CFL (June 1990). ... Granted free agency (February 1993). ... Signed by Denver Broncos (April 29, 1993). ... Released by Broncos (June 8, 1995). ... Signed by San Francisco 49ers (June 26, 1995). ... Released by 49ers (August 30, 1995). ... Re-signed by 49ers (September 27, 1995). ... Granted unconditional free agency (February 16, 1996).

CHAMPIONSHIP GAME EXPERIENCE: Played in Grey Cup, CFL championship game (1991 and 1992 seasons).

PRO STATISTICS: CFL: 1990—Recovered one fumble. 1991—Recovered two fumbles for 16 yards.

			INTERCEPTIONS		
Year Team	G	No.	Yds.	Avg.	TD
1990—Calgary CFL	18	3	23	7.7	0
1991—Calgary CFL	18	2	21	10.5	0
1992—Calgary CFL	18	5	202	40.4	1
1993—Denver NFL	16	1	0	0.0	0
1994—Denver NFL	16	0	0	...	0
1995—San Francisco NFL	12	0	0	...	0
CFL totals (3 years)	54	10	246	24.6	1
NFL totals (3 years)	44	1	0	0.0	0
Pro totals (6 years)	98	11	246	22.4	1

HALL, LEMANSKI   LB   OILERS

PERSONAL: Born November 24, 1970, in Valley, Ala. ... 6-0/229.
HIGH SCHOOL: Valley (Valley, Ala.).
COLLEGE: Alabama.
TRANSACTIONS/CAREER NOTES: Selected by Houston Oilers in seventh round (220th pick overall) of 1994 NFL draft. ... Signed by Oilers (June 20, 1994); did not play. ... Released by Oilers (August 28, 1994). ... Re-signed by Oilers to practice squad (August 30, 1994). ... Activated (December 23, 1994). ... Assigned by Oilers to Frankfurt Galaxy in 1995 World League enhancement allocation program (February 20, 1995). ... Assigned by Oilers to Amsterdam Admirals in 1996 World League enhancement allocation program (February 19, 1996).
PLAYING EXPERIENCE: Houston NFL, 1995. ... Games: 1995 (12).

HALL, RAY   DT   JAGUARS

PERSONAL: Born March 2, 1971, in Seattle. ... 6-4/294. ... Full name: Hayward Ray Hall. ... Nephew of Terry Metcalf, running back, St. Louis Cardinals, Toronto Argonauts of CFL and Washington Redskins (1973-1981); and cousin of Eric Metcalf, wide receiver, Atlanta Falcons.
HIGH SCHOOL: Thomas (Seattle).
COLLEGE: Washington State.
TRANSACTIONS/CAREER NOTES: Signed as non-drafted free agent by Philadelphia Eagles (April 1994). ... Released by Eagles (August 23, 1994). ... Re-signed by Eagles to practice squad (October 26, 1994). ... Granted free agency (December 31, 1994). ... Signed by Jacksonville Jaguars (January 6, 1995).
PLAYING EXPERIENCE: Jacksonville NFL, 1995. ... Games: 1995 (12).

HALL, RHETT   DT   EAGLES

PERSONAL: Born December 5, 1968, in San Jose, Calif. ... 6-2/276. ... Full name: Rhett Floyd Hall.
HIGH SCHOOL: Live Oak (Morgan Hill, Calif.).
JUNIOR COLLEGE: Gavilan College (Calif.).
COLLEGE: California (degree in social sciences).
TRANSACTIONS/CAREER NOTES: Selected by Tampa Bay Buccaneers in sixth round (147th pick overall) of 1991 NFL draft. ... Signed by Buccaneers (July 18, 1991). ... Released by Buccaneers (August 31, 1992). ... Re-signed by Buccaneers (September 1, 1992). ... Released by Buccaneers (September 2, 1992). ... Re-signed by Buccaneers (September 4, 1992). ... Released by Buccaneers (September 23, 1992). ... Re-signed by Buccaneers (December 9, 1992). ... Released by Buccaneers (August 30, 1993). ... Re-signed by Buccaneers (August 31, 1993). ... Released by Buccaneers (September 11, 1993). ... Re-signed by Buccaneers (November 23, 1993). ... Granted free agency (February 17, 1994). ... Signed by San Francisco 49ers (June 1, 1994). ... Released by 49ers (September 7, 1994). ... Re-signed by 49ers (September 14, 1994). ... Granted unconditional free agency (February 17, 1995). ... Signed by Philadelphia Eagles (March 9, 1995).
CHAMPIONSHIP GAME EXPERIENCE: Played in NFC championship game (1994 season). ... Member of Super Bowl championship team (1994 season).
PRO STATISTICS: 1994—Recovered one fumble.

Year Team	G	SACKS
1991—Tampa Bay NFL	16	1.0
1992—Tampa Bay NFL	4	0.0
1993—Tampa Bay NFL	1	0.0
1994—San Francisco NFL	12	4.0
1995—Philadelphia NFL	2	1.0
Pro totals (5 years)	35	6.0

HALL, RON   TE

PERSONAL: Born March 15, 1964, in Fort Huachuca, Ariz. ... 6-4/245. ... Full name: Ronald Edwin Hall.
HIGH SCHOOL: San Pasqual (Escondido, Calif.).
COLLEGE: California State Poly, then Hawaii.
TRANSACTIONS/CAREER NOTES: Selected by Tampa Bay Buccaneers in fourth round (87th pick overall) of 1987 NFL draft. ... Signed by Buccaneers (July 18, 1987). ... On injured reserve with knee injury (December 8, 1992-remainder of season). ... Granted unconditional free agency (February 17, 1994). ... Signed by Detroit Lions (March 21, 1994). ... On injured reserve with foot injury (December 22, 1994-remainder of season). ... On injured reserve with broken leg (November 1, 1995-remainder of season). ... Granted unconditional free agency (February 16, 1996).
PRO STATISTICS: 1989—Recovered one fumble. 1990—Returned one kickoff for no yards. 1991—Returned one kickoff for one yard.

H

STATISTICAL PLATEAUS: 100-yard receiving games: 1988 (1).

Year Team	G	RECEIVING No.	Yds.	Avg.	TD	TOTALS TD	2pt.	Pts.	Fum.
1987—Tampa Bay NFL	11	16	169	10.6	1	1	...	6	0
1988—Tampa Bay NFL	15	39	555	14.2	0	0	...	0	0
1989—Tampa Bay NFL	16	30	331	11.0	2	2	...	12	0
1990—Tampa Bay NFL	16	31	464	15.0	2	2	...	12	0
1991—Tampa Bay NFL	15	31	284	9.2	0	0	...	0	1
1992—Tampa Bay NFL	12	39	351	9.0	4	4	...	24	0
1993—Tampa Bay NFL	16	23	268	11.7	1	1	...	6	0
1994—Detroit NFL	13	10	106	10.6	0	0	0	0	1
1995—Detroit NFL	6	11	81	7.4	0	0	0	0	0
Pro totals (9 years)	120	230	2609	11.4	10	10	0	60	2

HALL, TRAVIS — DL — FALCONS

PERSONAL: Born August 3, 1972, in Kenai, Alaska. ... 6-5/278.
HIGH SCHOOL: West Jordan (Utah).
COLLEGE: Brigham Young.
TRANSACTIONS/CAREER NOTES: Selected by Atlanta Falcons in sixth round (181st pick overall) of 1995 NFL draft. ... Signed by Falcons (June 30, 1995).
PLAYING EXPERIENCE: Atlanta NFL, 1995. ... Games: 1995 (1).

HALLER, ALAN — CB

PERSONAL: Born August 9, 1970, in Lansing, Mich. ... 5-11/186. ... Full name: Alan Glenn Haller.
HIGH SCHOOL: Sexton (Lansing, Mich.).
COLLEGE: Michigan State.
TRANSACTIONS/CAREER NOTES: Selected by Pittsburgh Steelers in fifth round (123rd pick overall) of 1992 NFL draft. ... Signed by Steelers (July 18, 1992). ... Released by Steelers (September 16, 1992). ... Signed by Steelers to practice squad (September 17, 1992). ... Activated (November 6, 1992). ... Claimed on waivers by Cleveland Browns (November 18, 1992). ... On injured reserve with hamstring injury (December 16, 1992-remainder of season). ... On injured reserve (August 24-30, 1993). ... Released by Browns (August 30, 1993). ... Signed by Steelers (October 20, 1993). ... Released by Steelers (October 26, 1993). ... Re-signed by Steelers (December 8, 1993). ... Released by Steelers (August 23, 1994). ... Signed by Carolina Panthers (March 7, 1995). ... Released by Panthers (August 27, 1995). ... Re-signed by Panthers (September 6, 1995). ... Released by Panthers (September 26, 1995).
PLAYING EXPERIENCE: Pittsburgh (3)-Cleveland (3) NFL, 1992; Pittsburgh NFL, 1993; Carolina NFL, 1995. ... Games: 1992 (6), 1993 (4), 1995 (2). Total: 12.

HALLOCK, TY — TE — JAGUARS

PERSONAL: Born April 30, 1971, in Greenville, Mich. ... 6-3/249. ... Full name: Ty Edward Hallock.
HIGH SCHOOL: Greenville (Mich.).
COLLEGE: Michigan State.
TRANSACTIONS/CAREER NOTES: Selected by Detroit Lions in seventh round (174th pick overall) of 1993 NFL draft. ... Signed by Lions (July 15, 1993). ... Released by Lions (August 30, 1993). ... Re-signed by Lions to practice squad (August 31, 1993). ... Activated (September 3, 1993). ... Traded by Lions to Jacksonville Jaguars for CB Corey Raymond (May 30, 1995). ... On reserve/retired list (July 10, 1995-February 12, 1996). ... Re-signed by Jaguars off reserved/retired list (February 12, 1996).
PRO STATISTICS: 1993—Returned one kickoff for 11 yards.

Year Team	G	RECEIVING No.	Yds.	Avg.	TD	TOTALS TD	2pt.	Pts.	Fum.
1993—Detroit NFL	16	8	88	11.0	2	2	...	12	0
1994—Detroit NFL	15	7	75	10.7	0	0	0	0	0
1995—Jacksonville NFL				Did not play.					
Pro totals (2 years)	31	15	163	10.9	2	2	0	12	0

HAMILTON, KEITH — DT — GIANTS

PERSONAL: Born May 25, 1971, in Paterson, N.J. ... 6-6/285. ... Full name: Keith Lamarr Hamilton.
HIGH SCHOOL: Heritage (Lynchburg, Va.).
COLLEGE: Pittsburgh.
TRANSACTIONS/CAREER NOTES: Selected after junior season by New York Giants in fourth round (99th pick overall) of 1992 NFL draft. ... Signed by Giants (July 21, 1992).
PRO STATISTICS: 1992—Recovered one fumble for four yards. 1993—Credited with one safety and recovered one fumble for 10 yards. 1994—Recovered three fumbles. 1995—Fumbled once and recovered three fumbles for 87 yards.

Year Team	G	SACKS
1992—New York Giants NFL	16	3.5
1993—New York Giants NFL	16	11.5
1994—New York Giants NFL	15	6.5
1995—New York Giants NFL	14	2.0
Pro totals (4 years)	61	23.5

HAMMONDS, SHELLY — CB — VIKINGS

PERSONAL: Born February 13, 1971, in Barnwell, S.C. ... 5-10/189. ... Full name: Shelton Cornelius Hammonds.

H

HIGH SCHOOL: Barnwell (S.C.).
COLLEGE: Penn State.
TRANSACTIONS/CAREER NOTES: Selected by Minnesota Vikings in fifth round (134th pick overall) of 1994 NFL draft. ... Signed by Vikings (July 11, 1994). ... Released by Vikings (August 29, 1994). ... Re-signed by Vikings to practice squad (August 31, 1994). ... Released by Vikings (August 27, 1995). ... Re-signed by Vikings to practice squad (August 28, 1995). ... Activated (September 21, 1995). ... Released by Vikings (October 9, 1995). ... Re-signed by Vikings to practice squad (October 10, 1995).
PLAYING EXPERIENCE: Minnesota NFL, 1995. ... Games: 1995 (1).

HAMPTON, RODNEY — RB — GIANTS

PERSONAL: Born April 3, 1969, in Houston, Texas. ... 5-11/230.
HIGH SCHOOL: Kashmere Senior (Houston).
COLLEGE: Georgia.
TRANSACTIONS/CAREER NOTES: Selected after junior season by New York Giants in first round (24th pick overall) of 1990 NFL draft. ... Signed by Giants (July 26, 1990). ... Deactivated for NFC championship game and Super Bowl XXV after 1990 season due to broken leg (January 1991). ... Designated by Giants as transition player (February 16, 1996). ... Tendered offer sheet by San Francisco 49ers (March 2, 1996). ... Offer matched by Giants (March 4, 1996).
HONORS: Played in Pro Bowl (1992 and 1993 seasons).
PRO STATISTICS: 1991—Recovered one fumble. 1992—Recovered two fumbles. 1993—Recovered one fumble. 1994—Recovered one fumble. 1995—Recovered one fumble.
STATISTICAL PLATEAUS: 100-yard rushing games: 1990 (1), 1991 (3), 1992 (2), 1993 (5), 1994 (4), 1995 (2). Total: 17.
MISCELLANEOUS: Holds New York Giants all-time record for most yards rushing (5,989 yards).

		RUSHING				RECEIVING				KICKOFF RETURNS				TOTALS			
Year Team	G	Att.	Yds.	Avg.	TD	No.	Yds.	Avg.	TD	No.	Yds.	Avg.	TD	TD	2pt.	Pts.	Fum.
1990—New York Giants NFL	15	109	455	4.2	2	32	274	8.6	2	20	340	17.0	0	4	...	24	2
1991—New York Giants NFL	14	256	1059	4.1	10	43	283	6.6	0	10	204	20.4	0	10	...	60	5
1992—New York Giants NFL	16	257	1141	4.4	14	28	215	7.7	0	0	0	...	0	14	...	84	1
1993—New York Giants NFL	12	292	1077	3.7	5	18	210	11.7	0	0	0	...	0	5	...	30	2
1994—New York Giants NFL	14	327	1075	3.3	6	14	103	7.4	0	0	0	...	0	6	1	38	0
1995—New York Giants NFL	16	306	1182	3.9	10	24	142	5.9	0	0	0	...	0	10	1	62	5
Pro totals (6 years)	87	1547	5989	3.9	47	159	1227	7.7	2	30	544	18.1	0	49	2	298	15

HANKS, MERTON — CB — 49ERS

PERSONAL: Born March 12, 1968, in Dallas. ... 6-2/185. ... Full name: Merton Edward Hanks.
HIGH SCHOOL: Lake Highlands (Dallas).
COLLEGE: Iowa (degree in liberal arts, 1990).
TRANSACTIONS/CAREER NOTES: Selected by San Francisco 49ers in fifth round (122nd pick overall) of 1991 NFL draft. ... Signed by 49ers (July 10, 1991).
CHAMPIONSHIP GAME EXPERIENCE: Played in NFC championship game (1992-1994 seasons). ... Member of Super Bowl championship team (1994 season).
HONORS: Named free safety on THE SPORTING NEWS NFL All-Pro team (1994 and 1995). ... Played in Pro Bowl (1994 and 1995 seasons).
PRO STATISTICS: 1991—Recovered two fumbles. 1992—Returned one punt for 48 yards. 1993—Recovered one fumble. 1994—Credited with ½ sack, recovered two fumbles and fumbled once. 1995—Returned one punt for no yards and recovered two fumbles for 69 yards and a touchdown.

		INTERCEPTIONS			
Year Team	G	No.	Yds.	Avg.	TD
1991—San Francisco NFL	13	0	0	...	0
1992—San Francisco NFL	16	2	5	2.5	0
1993—San Francisco NFL	16	3	104	34.7	1
1994—San Francisco NFL	16	7	93	13.3	0
1995—San Francisco NFL	16	5	31	6.2	0
Pro totals (5 years)	77	17	233	13.7	1

HANNAH, SHANE — G — COWBOYS

PERSONAL: Born October 21, 1971, in Dayton, Ohio. ... 6-5/345.
HIGH SCHOOL: Valley View (Germantown, Ohio).
COLLEGE: Michigan State.
TRANSACTIONS/CAREER NOTES: Selected by Dallas Cowboys in second round (63rd pick overall) of 1995 NFL draft. ... Signed by Cowboys (July 17, 1995). ... On injured reserve with knee injury (August 27, 1995-entire season).

HANNAH, TRAVIS — WR/KR

PERSONAL: Born January 31, 1970, in Los Angeles. ... 5-7/161. ... Full name: Travis Lamont Hannah. ... Cousin of Stephen Baker, wide receiver, New York Giants (1987-1992).
HIGH SCHOOL: Hawthorne (Calif.).
COLLEGE: Southern California (degree in public administration, 1993).
TRANSACTIONS/CAREER NOTES: Selected by Houston Oilers in fourth round (102nd pick overall) of 1993 NFL draft. ... Signed by Oilers (July 16, 1993). ... Granted unconditional free agency (February 16, 1996).
PRO STATISTICS: 1995—Rushed once for five yards and recovered one fumble.

		RECEIVING				PUNT RETURNS				KICKOFF RETURNS				TOTALS			
Year Team	G	No.	Yds.	Avg.	TD	No.	Yds.	Avg.	TD	No.	Yds.	Avg.	TD	TD	2pt.	Pts.	Fum.
1993—Houston NFL	12	0	0	...	0	0	0	...	0	0	0	...	0	0	...	0	0

H

Year—Team	G	No.	Yds.	Avg.	TD	No.	Yds.	Avg.	TD	No.	Yds.	Avg.	TD	TD	2pt.	Pts.	Fum.
			RECEIVING				PUNT RETURNS				KICKOFF RETURNS				TOTALS		
1994—Houston NFL	9	3	24	8.0	0	9	58	6.4	0	5	116	23.2	0	0	0	0	1
1995—Houston NFL	16	10	142	14.2	0	5	36	7.2	0	0	0	...	0	0	0	0	0
Pro totals (3 years)	37	13	166	12.8	0	14	94	6.7	0	5	116	23.2	0	0	0	0	1

HANSEN, BRIAN — P — JETS

PERSONAL: Born October 26, 1960, in Hawarden, Iowa. ... 6-4/215. ... Full name: Brian Dean Hansen.
HIGH SCHOOL: West Sioux Community (Hawarden, Iowa).
COLLEGE: Sioux Falls (S.D.) College.
TRANSACTIONS/CAREER NOTES: Selected by New Orleans Saints in ninth round (237th pick overall) of 1984 NFL draft. ... Released by Saints (September 5, 1989). ... Signed by New England Patriots (May 3, 1990). ... Granted unconditional free agency (February 1, 1991). ... Signed by Cleveland Browns (April 1, 1991). ... Granted unconditional free agency (February 1-April 1, 1992). ... Re-signed by Browns for 1992 season. ... Granted unconditional free agency (February 17, 1994). ... Signed by New York Jets (April 19, 1994).
HONORS: Played in Pro Bowl (1984 season).
PRO STATISTICS: 1984—Rushed twice for minus 27 yards. 1985—Attempted one pass with one completion for eight yards. 1986—Rushed once for no yards, fumbled once and recovered one fumble. 1987—Rushed twice for minus six yards. 1988—Rushed once for 10 yards. 1990—Rushed once for no yards, fumbled once and recovered two fumbles for minus 18 yards. 1991—Attempted one pass with one completion for 11 yards and a touchdown, rushed twice for minus three yards and recovered one fumble. 1992—Fumbled once and recovered one fumble.

					PUNTING			
Year—Team	G	No.	Yds.	Avg.	Net avg.	In. 20	Blk.	
1984—New Orleans NFL	16	69	3020	43.8	33.3	9	1	
1985—New Orleans NFL	16	89	3763	42.3	36.5	14	0	
1986—New Orleans NFL	16	81	3456	42.7	36.6	17	1	
1987—New Orleans NFL	12	52	2104	40.5	35.6	19	0	
1988—New Orleans NFL	16	72	2913	40.5	34.3	19	1	
1990—New England NFL	16	*90	*3752	41.7	33.6	18	2	
1991—Cleveland NFL	16	80	3397	42.5	36.1	20	0	
1992—Cleveland NFL	16	74	3083	41.7	36.1	28	1	
1993—Cleveland NFL	16	82	3632	44.3	35.6	15	2	
1994—New York Jets NFL	16	84	3534	42.1	36.1	25	0	
1995—New York Jets NFL	16	*99	*4090	41.3	31.9	23	1	
Pro totals (11 years)	172	872	36744	42.1	35.0	207	9	

HANSEN, PHIL — DE — BILLS

PERSONAL: Born May 20, 1968, in Ellendale, N.D. ... 6-5/278.
HIGH SCHOOL: Oakes (N.D.).
COLLEGE: North Dakota State (degree in agricultural economics).
TRANSACTIONS/CAREER NOTES: Selected by Buffalo Bills in second round (54th pick overall) of 1991 NFL draft. ... Signed by Bills (July 10, 1991). ... Granted free agency (February 17, 1994). ... Re-signed by Bills (April 29, 1994).
CHAMPIONSHIP GAME EXPERIENCE: Played in AFC championship game (1991-1993 seasons). ... Played in Super Bowl XXVI (1991 season), Super Bowl XXVII (1992 season) and Super Bowl XXVIII (1993 season).
PRO STATISTICS: 1991—Recovered one fumble. 1995—Recovered one fumble.

Year—Team	G	SACKS
1991—Buffalo NFL	14	2.0
1992—Buffalo NFL	16	8.0
1993—Buffalo NFL	11	3.5
1994—Buffalo NFL	16	5.5
1995—Buffalo NFL	16	10.0
Pro totals (5 years)	73	29.0

HANSHAW, TIM — G — 49ERS

PERSONAL: Born April 27, 1970, in Spokane, Wash. ... 6-5/300.
HIGH SCHOOL: West Valley (Spokane, Wash.).
COLLEGE: Brigham Young.
TRANSACTIONS/CAREER NOTES: Selected by San Francisco 49ers in fourth round (127th pick overall) of 1995 NFL draft. ... Signed by 49ers (July 17, 1995). ... Inactive for 16 games (1995).

HANSON, JASON — K — LIONS

PERSONAL: Born June 17, 1970, in Spokane, Wash. ... 5-11/183. ... Full name: Jason Douglas Hanson.
HIGH SCHOOL: Mead (Spokane, Wash.).
COLLEGE: Washington State (bachelor of science degree).
TRANSACTIONS/CAREER NOTES: Selected by Detroit Lions in second round (56th pick overall) of 1992 NFL draft. ... Signed by Lions (July 23, 1992). ... Designated by Lions as transition player (February 15, 1994).
HONORS: Named kicker on THE SPORTING NEWS college All-America first team (1989). ... Named kicker on THE SPORTING NEWS NFL All-Pro team (1993).
PRO STATISTICS: 1995—Punted once for 34 yards.

Year—Team	G	XPM	XPA	FGM	FGA	Lg.	50+	Pts.
				KICKING				
1992—Detroit NFL	16	30	30	21	26	52	2-5	93

H

Year—Team	G	XPM	XPA	FGM	FGA	Lg.	50+	Pts.
1993—Detroit NFL	16	28	28	34	43	53	3-7	130
1994—Detroit NFL	16	39	40	18	27	49	0-5	93
1995—Detroit NFL	16	*48	†48	28	34	56	1-1	132
Pro totals (4 years)	64	145	146	101	130	56	6-18	448

HARBAUGH, JIM   QB   COLTS

PERSONAL: Born December 23, 1963, in Toledo, Ohio. ... 6-3/215. ... Full name: James Joseph Harbaugh. ... Son of Jack Harbaugh, head coach, Western Kentucky University; and cousin of Mike Gottfried, ESPN college football analyst; and former head coach, Murray State University, University of Cincinnati, University of Kansas and University of Pittsburgh.
HIGH SCHOOL: Pioneer (Ann Arbor, Mich.), then Palo Alto (Calif.).
COLLEGE: Michigan (degree in communications, 1987).
TRANSACTIONS/CAREER NOTES: Selected by Chicago Bears in first round (26th pick overall) of 1987 NFL draft. ... Signed by Bears (August 3, 1987). ... On injured reserve with separated shoulder (December 19, 1990-remainder of season). ... Granted free agency (February 1, 1991). ... Re-signed by Bears (July 22, 1991). ... Granted unconditional free agency (March 1, 1993). ... Re-signed by Bears (March 19, 1993). ... Released by Bears (March 16, 1994). ... Signed by Indianapolis Colts (April 7, 1994). ... Designated by Colts as franchise player (February 16, 1996).
CHAMPIONSHIP GAME EXPERIENCE: Member of Bears for NFC championship game (1988 season); did not play. ... Played in AFC championship game (1995 season).
HONORS: Played in Pro Bowl (1995 season).
PRO STATISTICS: 1988—Fumbled once. 1989—Fumbled twice. 1990—Fumbled eight times and recovered three fumbles for minus four yards. 1991—Fumbled six times. 1992—Fumbled six times and recovered three fumbles. 1993—Caught one pass for one yard, led league with 15 fumbles and recovered four fumbles for minus one yard. 1994—Fumbled once. 1995—Caught one pass for minus nine yards, fumbled four times and recovered one fumble for minus 20 yards.
STATISTICAL PLATEAUS: 300-yard passing games: 1991 (1), 1992 (1), 1995 (1). Total: 3.
MISCELLANEOUS: Regular-season record as starting NFL quarterback: 46-40 (.535).

		PASSING								RUSHING				TOTALS		
Year—Team	G	Att.	Cmp.	Pct.	Yds.	TD	Int.	Avg.	Rat.	Att.	Yds.	Avg.	TD	TD	2pt.	Pts.
1987—Chicago NFL	6	11	8	72.7	62	0	0	5.64	86.2	4	15	3.8	0	0	...	0
1988—Chicago NFL	10	97	47	48.5	514	0	2	5.30	55.9	19	110	5.8	1	1	...	6
1989—Chicago NFL	12	178	111	62.4	1204	5	9	6.77	70.5	45	276	6.1	3	3	...	18
1990—Chicago NFL	14	312	180	57.7	2178	10	6	6.98	81.9	51	321	6.3	4	4	...	24
1991—Chicago NFL	16	478	275	57.5	3121	15	16	6.53	73.7	70	338	4.8	2	2	...	12
1992—Chicago NFL	16	358	202	56.4	2486	13	12	6.95	76.2	47	272	5.8	1	1	...	6
1993—Chicago NFL	15	325	200	61.5	2002	7	11	6.16	72.1	60	277	4.6	4	4	...	24
1994—Indianapolis NFL	12	202	125	61.9	1440	9	6	7.13	85.8	39	223	5.7	0	0	0	0
1995—Indianapolis NFL	15	314	200	63.7	2575	17	5	*8.20	*100.7	52	235	4.5	2	0	0	0
Pro totals (9 years)	116	2275	1348	59.3	15582	76	67	6.85	78.9	387	2067	5.4	17	15	0	90

HARDY, ADRIAN   CB/KR

PERSONAL: Born August 16, 1970, in New Orleans. ... 5-11/194. ... Full name: Adrian Paul Hardy.
HIGH SCHOOL: Redeemer (New Orleans).
COLLEGE: Northwestern (La.) State.
TRANSACTIONS/CAREER NOTES: Selected by San Francisco 49ers in second round (48th pick overall) of 1993 NFL draft. ... Signed by 49ers (July 12, 1993). ... Claimed on waivers by Cincinnati Bengals (September 16, 1994). ... Released by Bengals (August 27, 1995). ... Re-signed by Bengals (September 25, 1995). ... Released by Bengals (March 22, 1996).
CHAMPIONSHIP GAME EXPERIENCE: Member of 49ers for NFC championship game (1993 season); inactive.

		KICKOFF RETURNS				TOTALS			
Year—Team	G	No.	Yds.	Avg.	TD	TD	2pt.	Pts.	Fum.
1993—San Francisco NFL	10	0	0	...	0	0	...	0	0
1994—San Francisco NFL	2	0	0	...	0	0	0	0	0
—Cincinnati NFL	14	8	185	23.1	0	0	0	0	0
1995—Cincinnati NFL	10	0	0	...	0	0	0	0	0
Pro totals (3 years)	36	8	185	23.1	0	0	0	0	0

HARDY, DARRYL   LB   COWBOYS

PERSONAL: Born November 22, 1968, in Cincinnati. ... 6-2/230. ... Full name: Darryl Gerrod Hardy.
HIGH SCHOOL: Princeton (Cincinnati).
COLLEGE: Tennessee.
TRANSACTIONS/CAREER NOTES: Selected by Atlanta Falcons in 10th round (270th pick overall) of 1992 NFL draft. ... Released by Falcons (August 31, 1992). ... Re-signed by Falcons to practice squad (September 2, 1992). ... Released by Falcons (August 24, 1993). ... Signed by Dallas Cowboys (July 16, 1994). ... Claimed on waivers by Arizona Cardinals (August 4, 1994). ... Released by Cardinals (August 27, 1994). ... Re-signed by Cardinals to practice squad (August 30, 1994). ... Activated (December 24, 1994); did not play. ... Claimed on waivers by Dallas Cowboys (October 3, 1995).
PLAYING EXPERIENCE: Arizona (4)-Dallas (5) NFL, 1995. ... Games: 1995 (9).
CHAMPIONSHIP GAME EXPERIENCE: Member of Cowboys for NFC championship game (1995 season); inactive.

HARLOW, PAT   OT   RAIDERS

H

PERSONAL: Born March 16, 1969, in Norco, Calif. ... 6-6/290. ... Full name: Patrick Christopher Harlow.
HIGH SCHOOL: Norco (Calif.).
COLLEGE: Southern California (degree in public administration).

TRANSACTIONS/CAREER NOTES: Selected by New England Patriots in first round (11th pick overall) of 1991 NFL draft. ... Signed by Patriots (July 15, 1991). ... Granted free agency (February 17, 1994). ... Re-signed by Patriots (April 2, 1994). ... Traded by Patriots to Oakland Raiders for second-round pick (traded to Oakland) in 1996 NFL draft (April 17, 1996).
PLAYING EXPERIENCE: New England NFL, 1991-1995. ... Games: 1991 (16), 1992 (16), 1993 (16), 1994 (16), 1995 (10). Total: 74.

HARMON, ANDY   DT   EAGLES

PERSONAL: Born April 6, 1969, in Centerville, Ohio ... 6-4/278. ... Full name: Andrew Phillip Harmon.
HIGH SCHOOL: Centerville (Ohio).
COLLEGE: Kent.
TRANSACTIONS/CAREER NOTES: Selected by Philadelphia Eagles in sixth round (157th pick overall) of 1991 NFL draft. ... Signed by Eagles (July 12, 1991).
PRO STATISTICS: 1992—Recovered one fumble. 1993—Recovered two fumbles. 1994—Intercepted one pass for no yards and recovered two fumbles. 1995—Recovered one fumble.

Year Team	G	SACKS
1991—Philadelphia NFL	16	0.0
1992—Philadelphia NFL	16	7.0
1993—Philadelphia NFL	16	11.5
1994—Philadelphia NFL	16	9.0
1995—Philadelphia NFL	15	11.0
Pro totals (5 years)	79	38.5

HARMON, RONNIE   RB   OILERS

PERSONAL: Born May 7, 1964, in Queens, N.Y. ... 5-11/200. ... Full name: Ronnie Keith Harmon. ... Brother of Derrick Harmon, running back, San Francisco 49ers (1984-1986); and brother of Kevin Harmon, running back, Seattle Seahawks (1988 and 1989).
HIGH SCHOOL: Bayside (Queens, N.Y.).
COLLEGE: Iowa.
TRANSACTIONS/CAREER NOTES: Selected by Buffalo Bills in first round (16th pick overall) of 1986 NFL draft. ... Signed by Bills (August 13, 1986). ... Granted roster exemption (August 13-25, 1986). ... Granted unconditional free agency (February 1, 1990). ... Signed by San Diego Chargers (March 23, 1990). ... Designated by Chargers as transition player (February 25, 1993). ... Free agency status changed by Chargers from transitional to unconditional (February 16, 1996). ... Signed by Houston Oilers (May 3, 1996).
CHAMPIONSHIP GAME EXPERIENCE: Played in AFC championship game (1988 and 1994 seasons). ... Played in Super Bowl XXIX (1994 season).
HONORS: Named running back on THE SPORTING NEWS college All-America second team (1984). ... Played in Pro Bowl (1992 season).
PRO STATISTICS: 1992—Recovered two fumbles. 1994—Recovered one fumble.
STATISTICAL PLATEAUS: 100-yard rushing games: 1987 (1). ... 100-yard receiving games: 1990 (1).

		RUSHING				RECEIVING				KICKOFF RETURNS				TOTALS			
Year Team	G	Att.	Yds.	Avg.	TD	No.	Yds.	Avg.	TD	No.	Yds.	Avg.	TD	TD	2pt.	Pts.	Fum.
1986—Buffalo NFL	14	54	172	3.2	0	22	185	8.4	1	18	321	17.8	0	1	...	6	2
1987—Buffalo NFL	12	116	485	4.2	2	56	477	8.5	2	1	30	30.0	0	4	...	24	2
1988—Buffalo NFL	16	57	212	3.7	1	37	427	11.5	3	11	249	22.6	0	4	...	24	2
1989—Buffalo NFL	15	17	99	5.8	0	29	363	12.5	4	18	409	22.7	0	4	...	24	2
1990—San Diego NFL	16	66	363	5.5	0	46	511	11.1	2	0	0	...	0	2	...	12	1
1991—San Diego NFL	16	89	544	6.1	1	59	555	9.4	1	2	25	12.5	0	2	...	12	1
1992—San Diego NFL	16	55	235	4.3	3	79	914	11.6	1	7	96	13.7	0	4	...	24	4
1993—San Diego NFL	16	46	216	4.7	0	73	671	9.2	2	1	18	18.0	0	2	...	12	0
1994—San Diego NFL	16	25	94	3.8	1	58	615	10.6	1	9	157	17.4	0	2	3	18	0
1995—San Diego NFL	16	51	187	3.7	1	63	673	10.7	5	4	25	6.3	0	6	0	42	1
Pro totals (10 years)	153	576	2607	4.5	9	522	5391	10.3	22	71	1330	18.7	0	31	3	198	16

HARPER, ALVIN   WR   BUCCANEERS

PERSONAL: Born July 6, 1968, in Lake Wells, Fla. ... 6-4/218. ... Full name: Alvin Craig Harper.
HIGH SCHOOL: Frostproof (Fla.).
COLLEGE: Tennessee (degree in psychology).
TRANSACTIONS/CAREER NOTES: Selected by Dallas Cowboys in first round (12th pick overall) of 1991 NFL draft. ... Signed by Cowboys (April 22, 1991). ... Granted free agency (February 17, 1994). ... Re-signed by Cowboys (June 1, 1994). ... Granted unconditional free agency (February 17, 1995). ... Signed by Tampa Bay Buccaneers (March 8, 1995).
CHAMPIONSHIP GAME EXPERIENCE: Played in NFC championship game (1992-1994 seasons). ... Member of Super Bowl championship team (1992 and 1993 seasons).
POSTSEASON RECORDS: Holds NFL postseason career records for highest average gain (minimum 20 receptions)—27.3; and longest reception (from Troy Aikman)—94 yards (January 8, 1995, vs. Green Bay).
PRO STATISTICS: 1992—Rushed once for 15 yards and intercepted one pass for one yard. 1993—Attempted one pass with one completion for 46 yards.
STATISTICAL PLATEAUS: 100-yard receiving games: 1991 (1), 1993 (2), 1994 (3), 1995 (1). Total: 7.

		RECEIVING				TOTALS			
Year Team	G	No.	Yds.	Avg.	TD	TD	2pt.	Pts.	Fum.
1991—Dallas NFL	15	20	326	16.3	1	1	...	6	0
1992—Dallas NFL	16	35	562	16.1	4	4	...	24	1
1993—Dallas NFL	16	36	777	21.6	5	5	...	30	1
1994—Dallas NFL	16	33	821	*24.9	8	8	0	48	2
1995—Tampa Bay NFL	13	46	633	13.8	2	2	0	12	0
Pro totals (5 years)	76	170	3119	18.4	20	20	0	120	4

H

HARPER, DWAYNE CB CHARGERS

PERSONAL: Born March 29, 1966, in Orangeburg, S.C. ... 5-11/175. ... Full name: Dwayne Anthony Harper.
HIGH SCHOOL: Orangeburg (S.C.)-Wilkinson.
COLLEGE: South Carolina State.
TRANSACTIONS/CAREER NOTES: Selected by Seattle Seahawks in 11th round (299th pick overall) of 1988 NFL draft. ... Signed by Seahawks (July 16, 1988). ... Granted free agency (February 1, 1992). ... Re-signed by Seahawks (August 10, 1992). ... Granted unconditional free agency (February 17, 1994). ... Signed by San Diego Chargers (March 3, 1994).
CHAMPIONSHIP GAME EXPERIENCE: Played in AFC championship game (1994 season). ... Played in Super Bowl XXIX (1994 season).
PRO STATISTICS: 1988—Credited with one sack and recovered one fumble. 1989—Recovered one fumble. 1991—Returned one punt for five yards. 1992—Fumbled once and recovered two fumbles for 52 yards and one touchdown. 1993—Recovered one fumble. 1995—Recovered one fumble for one yard.

			INTERCEPTIONS		
Year Team	G	No.	Yds.	Avg.	TD
1988—Seattle NFL	16	0	0	...	0
1989—Seattle NFL	16	2	15	7.5	0
1990—Seattle NFL	16	3	69	23.0	0
1991—Seattle NFL	16	4	84	21.0	0
1992—Seattle NFL	16	3	74	24.7	0
1993—Seattle NFL	14	1	0	0.0	0
1994—San Diego NFL	16	3	28	9.3	0
1995—San Diego NFL	16	4	12	3.0	0
Pro totals (8 years)	126	20	282	14.1	0

HARPER, ROGER S COWBOYS

PERSONAL: Born October 26, 1970, in Columbus, Ohio. ... 6-2/223.
HIGH SCHOOL: Independence (Columbus, Ohio).
COLLEGE: Ohio State.
TRANSACTIONS/CAREER NOTES: Selected after junior season by Atlanta Falcons in second round (38th pick overall) of 1993 NFL draft. ... Signed by Falcons (July 23, 1993). ... On injured reserve with arm injury (November 16, 1994-remainder of season). ... Granted free agency (February 16, 1996). ... Re-signed by Falcons (April 1996). ... Traded by Falcons to Dallas Cowboys for fourth- (DB Juran Bolden) and fifth-round (DE Gary Bandy) picks in 1996 draft (April 19, 1996).
PRO STATISTICS: 1993—Fumbled once and recovered one fumble.

			INTERCEPTIONS			SACKS
Year Team	G	No.	Yds.	Avg.	TD	No.
1993—Atlanta NFL	16	0	0	...	0	0.0
1994—Atlanta NFL	10	1	22	22.0	0	1.0
1995—Atlanta NFL	16	1	0	0.0	0	0.0
Pro totals (3 years)	42	2	22	11.0	0	1.0

HARPER, SHAWN OT COLTS

PERSONAL: Born July 9, 1968, in Columbus, Ohio. ... 6-3/290.
HIGH SCHOOL: Independence (Columbus, Ohio).
JUNIOR COLLEGE: North Iowa Area Community College.
COLLEGE: Indiana.
TRANSACTIONS/CAREER NOTES: Signed as non-drafted free agent by Los Angeles Rams (April 1993). ... Released by Rams (August 24, 1993). ... Signed as non-drafted free agent by Houston Oilers (June 23, 1994). ... Released by Oilers (August 22, 1994). ... Signed by Indianapolis Colts (July 22, 1995).
PLAYING EXPERIENCE: Indianapolis NFL, 1995. ... Games: 1995 (8).
CHAMPIONSHIP GAME EXPERIENCE: Member of Colts for AFC championship game (1995 season); inactive.

HARRELL, GARY WR GIANTS

PERSONAL: Born January 23, 1972, in Miami. ... 5-7/170. ... Nickname: The Flea.
HIGH SCHOOL: Northwest Christian (Miami).
COLLEGE: Howard.
TRANSACTIONS/CAREER NOTES: Signed as non-drafted free agent by New York Giants (July 14, 1994). ... Released by Giants (August 28, 1994). ... Re-signed by Giants to practice squad (August 30, 1994). ... Activated (December 16, 1994); did not play.
PLAYING EXPERIENCE: New York Giants NFL, 1995. ... Games: 1995 (4).
PRO STATISTICS: 1995—Returned 12 punts for 76 yards and returned one kickoff for 23 yards.

HARRIS, BERNARDO LB PACKERS

PERSONAL: Born October 15, 1971, in Chapel Hill, N.C. ... 6-2/243. ... Full name: Bernardo Jamaine Harris.
HIGH SCHOOL: Chapel Hill (N.C.).
COLLEGE: North Carolina.
TRANSACTIONS/CAREER NOTES: Signed as non-drafted free agent by Kansas City Chiefs (June 2, 1994). ... Released by Chiefs (August 2, 1995). ... Signed by Green Bay Packers (January 20, 1995).
PLAYING EXPERIENCE: Green Bay NFL, 1995. ... Games: 1995 (11).
CHAMPIONSHIP GAME EXPERIENCE: Played in NFC championship game (1995 season).

H

HARRIS, COREY   CB   SEAHAWKS

PERSONAL: Born October 25, 1969, in Indianapolis. ... 5-11/199. ... Full name: Corey Lamont Harris.
HIGH SCHOOL: Ben Davis (Indianapolis).
COLLEGE: Vanderbilt (degree in human resources).
TRANSACTIONS/CAREER NOTES: Selected by Houston Oilers in third round (77th pick overall) of 1992 NFL draft. ... Signed by Oilers (August 5, 1992). ... Claimed on waivers by Green Bay Packers (October 14, 1992). ... Granted free agency (February 17, 1995). ... Tendered offer sheet by Seattle Seahawks (March 3, 1995). ... Packers declined to match offer (March 10, 1995).
PRO STATISTICS: 1992—Rushed twice for 10 yards. 1993—Caught two passes for 11 yards. 1994—Recovered one fumble. 1995—Recovered one fumble for 57 yards and a touchdown.
MISCELLANEOUS: Played wide receiver (1992 and 1993).

		INTERCEPTIONS				PUNT RETURNS				KICKOFF RETURNS				TOTALS			
Year Team	G	No.	Yds.	Avg.	TD	No.	Yds.	Avg.	TD	No.	Yds.	Avg.	TD	TD	2pt.	Pts.	Fum.
1992—Houston NFL	5	0	0	...	0	6	17	2.8	0	0	0	...	0	0	...	0	0
—Green Bay NFL	10	0	0	...	0	0	0	...	0	33	691	20.9	0	0	...	0	0
1993—Green Bay NFL	11	0	0	...	0	0	0	...	0	16	482	30.1	0	0	...	0	0
1994—Green Bay NFL	16	0	0	...	0	0	0	...	0	29	618	21.3	0	0	0	0	1
1995—Seattle NFL	16	3	-5	-1.7	0	0	0	...	0	19	397	20.9	0	1	0	6	0
Pro totals (4 years)	58	3	-5	-1.7	0	6	17	2.8	0	97	2188	22.6	0	1	0	6	1

HARRIS, JACKIE   TE   BUCCANEERS

PERSONAL: Born January 4, 1968, in Pine Bluff, Ark. ... 6-4/239. ... Full name: Jackie Bernard Harris.
HIGH SCHOOL: Pine Bluff (Ark.).
COLLEGE: Northeast Louisiana.
TRANSACTIONS/CAREER NOTES: Selected by Green Bay Packers in fourth round (102nd pick overall) of 1990 NFL draft. ... Signed by Packers (July 22, 1990). ... Granted free agency (February 1, 1992). ... Re-signed by Packers (August 14, 1992). ... Designated by Packers as transition player (February 25, 1993). ... Tendered offer sheet by Tampa Bay Buccaneers (June 15, 1994). ... Packers declined to match offer (June 22, 1994). ... On injured reserve with shoulder injury (November 22, 1994-remainder of season).
PRO STATISTICS: 1991—Rushed once for one yard and recovered one fumble.
STATISTICAL PLATEAUS: 100-yard receiving games: 1993 (1), 1995 (2). Total: 3.

		RECEIVING				TOTALS			
Year Team	G	No.	Yds.	Avg.	TD	TD	2pt.	Pts.	Fum.
1990—Green Bay NFL	16	12	157	13.1	0	0	...	0	0
1991—Green Bay NFL	16	24	264	11.0	3	3	...	18	1
1992—Green Bay NFL	16	55	595	10.8	2	2	...	12	1
1993—Green Bay NFL	12	42	604	14.4	4	4	...	24	0
1994—Tampa Bay NFL	9	26	337	13.0	3	3	1	20	0
1995—Tampa Bay NFL	16	62	751	12.1	1	1	0	6	2
Pro totals (6 years)	85	221	2708	12.3	13	13	1	80	4

HARRIS, JAMES   DE

PERSONAL: Born May 13, 1968, in East St. Louis, Ill. ... 6-6/255. ... Full name: James Edward Harris.
HIGH SCHOOL: East St. Louis (Ill.) Senior.
COLLEGE: Temple.
TRANSACTIONS/CAREER NOTES: Signed as non-drafted free agent by Seattle Seahawks (April 30, 1992). ... Released by Seahawks (August 24, 1992). ... Signed by Minnesota Vikings to practice squad (September 1992). ... On injured reserve (October 29, 1992-remainder of season). ... Granted free agency after 1992 season. ... Re-signed by Vikings (February 19, 1993). ... On physically unable to perform list with foot injury (July 24-September 10, 1995). ... Granted unconditional free agency (February 16, 1996).
PRO STATISTICS: 1994—Recovered three fumbles for 18 yards and one touchdown, intercepted one pass for 21 yards and fumbled twice. 1995—Recovered one fumble.

Year Team	G	SACKS
1993—Minnesota NFL	6	0.0
1994—Minnesota NFL	16	3.0
1995—Minnesota NFL	12	1.0
Pro totals (3 years)	34	4.0

HARRIS, ODIE   S

PERSONAL: Born April 1, 1966, in Bryan, Texas. ... 6-0/190. ... Full name: Odie Lazar Harris Jr. ... Cousin of Gerald Carter, wide receiver, New York Jets and Tampa Bay Buccaneers (1980-1987).
HIGH SCHOOL: Bryan (Texas).
COLLEGE: Sam Houston State.
TRANSACTIONS/CAREER NOTES: Signed as non-drafted free agent by Tampa Bay Buccaneers (April 29, 1988). ... Granted unconditional free agency (February 1, 1991). ... Signed by Dallas Cowboys (March 20, 1991). ... Claimed on waivers by Cleveland Browns (August 28, 1991). ... Granted unconditional free agency (February 1-April 1, 1992). ... Re-signed by Browns for 1992 season. ... Released by Browns (September 11, 1992). ... Re-signed by Browns (October 14, 1992). ... Claimed on waivers by Phoenix Cardinals (November 2, 1992). ... Granted unconditional free agency (March 1, 1993). ... Re-signed by Cardinals (April 20, 1993). ... Released by Cardinals (August 30, 1993). ... Re-signed by Cardinals (August 31, 1993). ... Granted unconditional free agency (February 17, 1994). ... Cardinals franchise renamed Arizona Cardinals for 1994 season. ... Re-signed by Cardinals (June 9, 1994). ... Granted unconditional free agency (February 17, 1995). ... Signed by Houston Oilers (July 21, 1995). ... Granted unconditional free agency (February 16, 1996).
PRO STATISTICS: 1988—Recovered one fumble. 1991—Recovered one fumble. 1994—Recovered one fumble.

H

Year Team		INTERCEPTIONS			
	G	No.	Yds.	Avg.	TD
1988—Tampa Bay NFL	16	2	26	13.0	0
1989—Tampa Bay NFL	16	1	19	19.0	0
1990—Tampa Bay NFL	16	0	0	...	0
1991—Cleveland NFL	16	0	0	...	0
1992—Cleveland NFL	4	0	0	...	0
—Phoenix NFL	8	0	0	...	0
1993—Phoenix NFL	16	0	0	...	0
1994—Arizona NFL	13	0	0	...	0
1995—Houston NFL	16	2	0	0.0	0
Pro totals (8 years)	121	5	45	9.0	0

HARRIS, RAYMONT   RB   BEARS

PERSONAL: Born December 23, 1970, in Lorain, Ohio. ... 6-0/225. ... Full name: Raymont LeShawn Harris.
HIGH SCHOOL: Admiral King (Lorain, Ohio).
COLLEGE: Ohio State.
TRANSACTIONS/CAREER NOTES: Selected by Chicago Bears in fourth round (114th pick overall) of 1994 NFL draft. ... Signed by Bears (June 21, 1994). ... On injured reserve with broken collarbone (November 29, 1995-remainder of season).
PRO STATISTICS: 1994—Recovered three fumbles.

Year Team		RUSHING				RECEIVING				KICKOFF RETURNS				TOTALS			
	G	Att.	Yds.	Avg.	TD	No.	Yds.	Avg.	TD	No.	Yds.	Avg.	TD	TD	2pt.	Pts.	Fum.
1994—Chicago NFL	16	123	464	3.8	1	39	236	6.1	0	1	18	18.0	0	1	0	6	1
1995—Chicago NFL	1	0	0	...	0	1	4	4.0	0	0	0	...	0	0	0	0	0
Pro totals (2 years)	17	123	464	3.8	1	40	240	6.0	0	1	18	18.0	0	1	0	6	1

HARRIS, ROBERT   DE   GIANTS

PERSONAL: Born June 13, 1969, in Riviera Beach, Fla. ... 6-4/295. ... Full name: Robert Lee Harris.
HIGH SCHOOL: Sun Coast (Riviera Beach, Fla.).
COLLEGE: Southern (La.).
TRANSACTIONS/CAREER NOTES: Selected by Minnesota Vikings in second round (39th pick overall) of 1992 NFL draft. ... Signed by Vikings (July 20, 1992). ... On injured reserve with knee injury (September 30-November 12, 1992). ... Granted free agency (February 17, 1995). ... Tendered offer sheet by New York Giants (March 13, 1995). ... Vikings declined to match offer (March 20, 1995).
PRO STATISTICS: 1995—Recovered two fumbles for five yards.

Year Team	G	SACKS
1992—Minnesota NFL	7	0.0
1993—Minnesota NFL	16	1.0
1994—Minnesota NFL	11	2.0
1995—New York Giants NFL	15	5.0
Pro totals (4 years)	49	8.0

HARRIS, RONNIE   WR   SEAHAWKS

PERSONAL: Born June 4, 1970, in Granada Hills, Calif. ... 5-11/175. ... Full name: Ronnie James Harris.
HIGH SCHOOL: Valley Christian (San Jose, Calif.).
COLLEGE: Oregon.
TRANSACTIONS/CAREER NOTES: Signed as non-drafted free agent by New England Patriots (April 30, 1993). ... Released by Patriots (August 23, 1993). ... Re-signed by Patriots to practice squad (August 31, 1993). ... Activated (December 3, 1993). ... Released by Patriots (August 20, 1994). ... Re-signed by Patriots to practice squad (August 30, 1994). ... Activated (October 15, 1994). ... Released by Patriots (October 19, 1994). ... Re-signed by Patriots to practice squad (October 19, 1994). ... Released by Patriots (November 23, 1994). ... Signed by Seattle Seahawks to practice squad (November 29, 1994). ... Activated (December 11, 1994).
RECORDS: Shares NFL single-game record for most combined kick returns—13 (December 5, 1993, at Pittsburgh).
PRO STATISTICS: 1993—Recovered one fumble.

Year Team		RECEIVING				PUNT RETURNS				KICKOFF RETURNS				TOTALS			
	G	No.	Yds.	Avg.	TD	No.	Yds.	Avg.	TD	No.	Yds.	Avg.	TD	TD	2pt.	Pts.	Fum.
1993—New England NFL	5	0	0	...	0	23	201	8.7	0	6	90	15.0	0	0	...	0	2
1994—New England NFL	1	1	11	11.0	0	3	26	8.7	0	0	0	...	0	0	0	0	1
—Seattle NFL	1	0	0	...	0	0	0	...	0	0	0	...	0	0	0	0	0
1995—Seattle NFL	13	0	0	...	0	3	23	7.7	0	1	29	29.0	0	0	0	0	0
Pro totals (3 years)	20	1	11	11.0	0	29	250	8.6	0	7	119	17.0	0	0	0	0	3

HARRIS, SEAN   LB   BEARS

PERSONAL: Born February 25, 1972, in Tucson, Ariz. ... 6-3/244. ... Full name: Sean Eugene Harris.
HIGH SCHOOL: Tucson (Ariz.).
COLLEGE: Arizona.
TRANSACTIONS/CAREER NOTES: Selected by Chicago Bears in third round (83rd pick overall) of 1995 NFL draft. ... Signed by Bears (July 18, 1995).
PLAYING EXPERIENCE: Chicago NFL, 1995. ... Games: 1995 (11).

H

HARRIS, TIM   DE

PERSONAL: Born September 10, 1964, in Birmingham, Ala. ... 6-6/258. ... Full name: Timothy David Harris.

HIGH SCHOOL: Woodlawn (Birmingham, Ala.) and Catholic (Memphis).
COLLEGE: Memphis State.
TRANSACTIONS/CAREER NOTES: Selected by Memphis Showboats in 1986 USFL territorial draft. ... Selected by Green Bay Packers in fourth round (84th pick overall) of 1986 NFL draft. ... Signed by Packers (May 17, 1986). ... Granted free agency (February 1, 1991). ... Traded by Packers to San Francisco 49ers for second-round pick (traded to Dallas) in 1993 draft (September 30, 1991). ... Activated (October 12, 1991). ... Granted unconditional free agency (March 1, 1993). ... Signed by Philadelphia Eagles (April 22, 1993). ... On injured reserve with elbow injury (December 17, 1993-remainder of season). ... Released by Eagles (July 22, 1994). ... Signed by 49ers (November 22, 1994). ... Granted unconditional free agency (February 17, 1995). ... Re-signed by 49ers (August 29, 1995). ... Released by 49ers (February 5, 1996).
CHAMPIONSHIP GAME EXPERIENCE: Played in NFC championship game (1992 and 1994 seasons). ... Member of Super Bowl championship team (1994 season).
HONORS: Named outside linebacker on THE SPORTING NEWS NFL All-Pro team (1989). ... Played in Pro Bowl (1989 season).
RECORDS: Shares NFL single-season record for most safeties—2 (1988).
PRO STATISTICS: 1986—Recovered one fumble. 1988—Returned blocked punt 10 yards for a touchdown and credited with two safeties. 1989—Recovered three fumbles. 1990—Recovered two fumbles for 28 yards. 1991—Recovered one fumble. 1992—Recovered one fumble.

Year Team	G	SACKS
1986—Green Bay NFL	16	8.0
1987—Green Bay NFL	12	7.0
1988—Green Bay NFL	16	13.5
1989—Green Bay NFL	16	19.5
1990—Green Bay NFL	16	7.0
1991—San Francisco NFL	11	3.0
1992—San Francisco NFL	16	17.0
1993—Philadelphia NFL	4	0.0
1994—San Francisco NFL	5	2.0
1995—San Francisco NFL	10	4.0
Pro totals (10 years)	**122**	**81.0**

HARRISON, MARTIN   DE

PERSONAL: Born September 20, 1967, in Livermore, Calif. ... 6-5/251. ... Full name: Martin Allen Harrison.
HIGH SCHOOL: Newport (Bellevue, Wash.).
COLLEGE: Washington (degree in sociology, 1990).
TRANSACTIONS/CAREER NOTES: Selected by San Francisco 49ers in 10th round (276th pick overall) of 1990 NFL draft. ... Signed by 49ers (July 18, 1990). ... On injured reserve with shoulder injury (September 18-December 13, 1990). ... Released by 49ers (December 13, 1990). ... Re-signed by 49ers (1991). ... Released by 49ers (August 26, 1991). ... Re-signed by 49ers to practice squad (August 28, 1991). ... Granted free agency after 1991 season. ... Re-signed by 49ers (March 25, 1992). ... Released by 49ers (August 31, 1992). ... Re-signed by 49ers (September 1, 1992). ... Granted unconditional free agency (February 17, 1994). ... Re-signed by 49ers (June 1, 1994). ... Released by 49ers (August 27, 1994). ... Signed by Minnesota Vikings (September 12, 1994). ... Granted unconditional free agency (February 17, 1995). ... Re-signed by Vikings (March 27, 1995). ... Granted unconditional free agency (February 16, 1996).
CHAMPIONSHIP GAME EXPERIENCE: Played in NFC championship game (1992 season). ... Member of 49ers for NFC championship game (1993 season); inactive.
PRO STATISTICS: 1995—Intercepted one pass for 15 yards.

Year Team	G	SACKS
1990—San Francisco NFL	2	0.0
1991—San Francisco NFL	Did not play.	
1992—San Francisco NFL	16	3.5
1993—San Francisco NFL	11	6.0
1994—Minnesota NFL	13	0.0
1995—Minnesota NFL	11	4.5
Pro totals (5 years)	**53**	**14.0**

HARRISON, NOLAN   DT   RAIDERS

PERSONAL: Born January 25, 1969, in Chicago. ... 6-5/285.
HIGH SCHOOL: Homewood-Flossmoor (Ill.).
COLLEGE: Indiana (degree in criminal justice, 1991).
TRANSACTIONS/CAREER NOTES: Selected by Los Angeles Raiders in sixth round (146th pick overall) of 1991 NFL draft. ... Signed by Raiders (1991). ... Raiders franchise moved to Oakland (July 21, 1995).
PRO STATISTICS: 1992—Credited with one safety. 1993—Recovered one fumble for five yards. 1994—Recovered two fumbles.

Year Team	G	SACKS
1991—Los Angeles Raiders NFL	14	1.0
1992—Los Angeles Raiders NFL	14	2.5
1993—Los Angeles Raiders NFL	16	3.0
1994—Los Angeles Raiders NFL	16	5.0
1995—Oakland NFL	7	0.0
Pro totals (5 years)	**67**	**11.5**

HARRISON, RODNEY   S   CHARGERS

H

PERSONAL: Born December 15, 1972, in Markham, Ill. ... 6-0/201. ... Full name: Rodney Scott Harrison.
HIGH SCHOOL: Marian Catholic (Chicago Heights, Ill.).
COLLEGE: Western Illinois.
TRANSACTIONS/CAREER NOTES: Selected after junior season by San Diego Chargers in fifth round (145th pick overall) of 1994 NFL draft. ... Signed by Chargers (June 29, 1994).
CHAMPIONSHIP GAME EXPERIENCE: Played in AFC championship game (1994 season). ... Played in Super Bowl XXIX (1994 season).
PRO STATISTICS: 1994—Recovered one fumble.

Year Team	G	No.	Yds.	Avg.	TD
			INTERCEPTIONS		
1994—San Diego NFL	15	0	0	...	0
1995—San Diego NFL	11	5	22	4.4	0
Pro totals (2 years)	26	5	22	4.4	0

HARTLEY, FRANK   TE   RAVENS

PERSONAL: Born December 15, 1967, in Chicago. ... 6-2/268.
HIGH SCHOOL: Bogan (Chicago).
COLLEGE: Illinois (degree in political science).
TRANSACTIONS/CAREER NOTES: Signed as non-drafted free agent by Los Angeles Rams to practice squad (December 4, 1991). ... Granted free agency after 1991 season. ... Re-signed by Rams (May 4, 1992). ... Released by Rams (August 31, 1992). ... Signed by San Francisco 49ers to practice squad (September 23, 1992). ... Released by 49ers (October 5, 1992). ... Signed by Atlanta Falcons (May 26, 1993). ... Released by Falcons (August 30, 1993). ... Signed by Cleveland Browns (February 21, 1994). ... Released by Browns (August 23, 1994). ... Re-signed by Browns (October 10, 1994). ... Browns franchise moved to Baltimore and renamed Ravens for 1996 season (March 11, 1996).
PRO STATISTICS: 1995—Recovered one fumble.

Year Team	G	No.	Yds.	Avg.	TD	TD	2pt.	Pts.	Fum.
			RECEIVING				TOTALS		
1994—Cleveland NFL	10	3	13	4.3	1	1	0	6	0
1995—Cleveland NFL	15	11	137	12.5	1	1	0	6	1
Pro totals (2 years)	25	14	150	10.7	2	2	0	12	1

HARVEY, KEN   LB   REDSKINS

PERSONAL: Born May 6, 1965, in Austin, Texas. ... 6-2/245. ... Full name: Kenneth Ray Harvey.
HIGH SCHOOL: Lanier (Austin, Texas).
JUNIOR COLLEGE: Laney College (Calif.).
COLLEGE: California.
TRANSACTIONS/CAREER NOTES: Selected by Phoenix Cardinals in first round (12th pick overall) of 1988 NFL draft. ... Signed by Cardinals (June 17, 1988). ... Granted free agency (February 1, 1992). ... Re-signed by Cardinals (July 28, 1992). ... On injured reserve with knee injury (November 18, 1992-remainder of season). ... Designated by Cardinals as transition player (February 25, 1993). ... Free agency status changed by Cardinals from transitional to unconditional (February 17, 1994). ... Signed by Washington Redskins (March 5, 1994).
HONORS: Played in Pro Bowl (1994 and 1995 seasons).
PRO STATISTICS: 1988—Credited with a safety. 1990—Recovered one fumble. 1991—Recovered two fumbles. 1992—Recovered two fumbles. 1994—Recovered one fumble. 1995—Recovered two fumbles.

Year Team	G	SACKS
1988—Phoenix NFL	16	6.0
1989—Phoenix NFL	16	7.0
1990—Phoenix NFL	16	10.0
1991—Phoenix NFL	16	9.0
1992—Phoenix NFL	10	6.0
1993—Phoenix NFL	16	9.5
1994—Washington NFL	16	13.5
1995—Washington NFL	16	7.5
Pro totals (8 years)	122	68.5

HARVEY, RICHARD   LB   SAINTS

PERSONAL: Born September 11, 1966, in Pascagoula, Miss. ... 6-1/242. ... Full name: Richard Clemont Harvey. ... Son of Richard Harvey Sr., defensive back, Philadelphia Eagles and New Orleans Saints (1970 and 1971).
HIGH SCHOOL: Pascagoula (Miss.).
COLLEGE: Tulane.
TRANSACTIONS/CAREER NOTES: Selected by Buffalo Bills in 11th round (305th pick overall) of 1989 NFL draft. ... On injured reserve with shoulder injury (September 4, 1989-entire season). ... Granted unconditional free agency (February 1, 1990). ... Signed by New England Patriots (March 23, 1990). ... Released by Patriots (September 2, 1991). ... Signed by Bills (February 3, 1992). ... Selected by Ohio Glory in first round of 1992 World League supplemental draft. ... Granted unconditional free agency (February 17, 1994). ... Signed by Denver Broncos (May 9, 1994). ... Granted unconditional free agency (February 17, 1995). ... Signed by New Orleans Saints (April 3, 1995).
PLAYING EXPERIENCE: New England NFL, 1990 and 1991; Buffalo NFL, 1992 and 1993; Denver NFL, 1994; New Orleans NFL, 1995. ... Games: 1990 (16), 1991 (1), 1992 (12), 1993 (15), 1994 (16), 1995 (16). Total: 76.
CHAMPIONSHIP GAME EXPERIENCE: Member of Bills for AFC championship game (1992 season); inactive. ... Member of Bills for Super Bowl XXVII (1992 season); inactive. ... Played in AFC championship game (1993 season). ... Played in Super Bowl XXVIII (1993 season).
PRO STATISTICS: 1992—Recovered one fumble. 1994—Recovered one fumble. 1995—Credited with two sacks.

HASELRIG, CARLTON   G

PERSONAL: Born January 22, 1966, in Johnstown, Pa. ... 6-1/295. ... Full name: Carlton Lee Haselrig.
HIGH SCHOOL: Greater Johnstown (Pa.).
COLLEGE: Pittsburgh-Johnstown (did not play football; degree in communications, 1989).
TRANSACTIONS/CAREER NOTES: Selected by Pittsburgh Steelers in 12th round (312th pick overall) of 1989 NFL draft. ... Released by Steelers (September 5, 1989). ... Signed by Steelers to developmental squad (September 6, 1989). ... Released by Steelers (January 29, 1990). ... Re-signed by Steelers (February 23, 1990). ... On reserve/non-football injury list (September 29-November 8, 1993). ... Activated (November 15, 1993). ... On reserve/left camp list (August 23, 1994-entire season). ... Released by Steelers (June 16, 1995). ... Signed by New York Jets (July 20, 1995). ... On suspended list for violating league substance abuse policy (December 4, 1995-remainder of season).
PLAYING EXPERIENCE: Pittsburgh NFL, 1990-1993; New York Jets NFL, 1995. ... Games: 1990 (16), 1991 (16), 1992 (16), 1993 (9), 1995

H

(11). Total: 68.
HONORS: Played in Pro Bowl (1992 season).
PRO STATISTICS: 1991—Recovered one fumble for two yards. 1992—Recovered one fumble for four yards.

HASSELBACH, HARALD　　　　DL　　　　BRONCOS

PERSONAL: Born September 22, 1967, in Amsterdam, Holland. ... 6-6/280.
HIGH SCHOOL: South Delta (Delta, B.C.).
COLLEGE: Washington.
TRANSACTIONS/CAREER NOTES: Selected by Calgary Stampeders in fifth round (34th pick overall) of 1989 CFL draft. ... Granted free agency after 1993 season. ... Signed by Denver Broncos (April 11, 1994).
CHAMPIONSHIP GAME EXPERIENCE: Played in Grey Cup, CFL championship game (1992).
PRO STATISTICS: CFL: 1992—Recovered two fumbles. 1993—Recovered four fumbles for 16 yards, intercepted one pass for no yards and fumbled once. NFL: 1995—Recovered four fumbles.

Year　Team	G	SACKS
1990—Calgary CFL	3	0.0
1991—Calgary CFL	11	3.0
1992—Calgary CFL	18	4.0
1993—Calgary CFL	18	7.0
1994—Denver NFL	16	2.0
1995—Denver NFL	16	4.0
CFL totals (4 years)	50	14.0
NFL totals (2 years)	32	6.0
Pro totals (6 years)	82	20.0

HASTINGS, ANDRE　　　　WR/KR　　　　STEELERS

PERSONAL: Born November 7, 1970, in Macon, Ga. ... 6-1/190. ... Full name: Andre Orlando Hastings.
HIGH SCHOOL: Morrow (Ga.).
COLLEGE: Georgia.
TRANSACTIONS/CAREER NOTES: Selected after junior season by Pittsburgh Steelers in third round (76th pick overall) of 1993 NFL draft. ... Signed by Steelers (July 18, 1993). ... Granted free agency (February 16, 1996).
CHAMPIONSHIP GAME EXPERIENCE: Played in AFC championship game (1994 and 1995 seasons). ... Played in Super Bowl XXX (1995 season).
PRO STATISTICS: 1995—Rushed once for 14 yards.

		RECEIVING				PUNT RETURNS				KICKOFF RETURNS				TOTALS			
Year　Team	G	No.	Yds.	Avg.	TD	No.	Yds.	Avg.	TD	No.	Yds.	Avg.	TD	TD	2pt.	Pts.	Fum.
1993—Pittsburgh NFL	6	3	44	14.7	0	0	0	...	0	12	177	14.8	0	0	...	0	0
1994—Pittsburgh NFL	16	20	281	14.1	2	0	0	...	0	0	0	...	0	2	0	12	0
1995—Pittsburgh NFL	16	48	502	10.5	1	48	474	9.9	†1	0	0	...	0	2	0	12	1
Pro totals (3 years)	38	71	827	11.7	3	48	474	9.9	1	12	177	14.8	0	4	0	24	1

HASTY, JAMES　　　　CB　　　　CHIEFS

PERSONAL: Born May 23, 1965, in Seattle. ... 6-0/207. ... Full name: James Edward Hasty.
HIGH SCHOOL: Franklin (Seattle).
COLLEGE: Central Washington, then Washington State (degree in liberal arts and business, 1988).
TRANSACTIONS/CAREER NOTES: Selected by New York Jets in third round (74th pick overall) of 1988 NFL draft. ... Signed by Jets (July 12, 1988). ... Designated by Jets as transition player (February 25, 1993). ... Tendered offer sheet by Cincinnati Bengals (April 29, 1993). ... Offer matched by Jets (May 4, 1993). ... Granted unconditional free agency (February 17, 1995). ... Signed by Kansas City Chiefs (March 29, 1995).
PRO STATISTICS: 1988—Recovered three fumbles for 35 yards. 1989—Fumbled once and recovered two fumbles for two yards. 1990—Returned one punt for no yards, fumbled once and recovered three fumbles. 1991—Recovered four fumbles for seven yards. 1992—Recovered two fumbles. 1993—Recovered two fumbles for 28 yards. 1994—Recovered two fumbles. 1995—Recovered one fumble for 20 yards.

		INTERCEPTIONS				SACKS
Year　Team	G	No.	Yds.	Avg.	TD	No.
1988—New York Jets NFL	15	5	20	4.0	0	1.0
1989—New York Jets NFL	16	5	62	12.4	1	0.0
1990—New York Jets NFL	16	2	0	0.0	0	0.0
1991—New York Jets NFL	16	3	39	13.0	0	0.0
1992—New York Jets NFL	16	2	18	9.0	0	0.0
1993—New York Jets NFL	16	2	22	11.0	0	0.0
1994—New York Jets NFL	16	5	90	18.0	0	3.0
1995—Kansas City NFL	16	3	89	29.7	1	0.0
Pro totals (8 years)	127	27	340	12.6	2	4.0

HAUCK, TIM　　　　S　　　　BRONCOS

PERSONAL: Born December 20, 1966, in Butte, Mont. ... 5-10/185. ... Full name: Timothy Christian Hauck. ... Name pronounced HOWK.
HIGH SCHOOL: Sweet Grass County (Big Timber, Mont.).
COLLEGE: Pacific (Ore.), then Montana.
TRANSACTIONS/CAREER NOTES: Signed as non-drafted free agent by New England Patriots (May 1, 1990). ... Released by Patriots (August 26, 1990). ... Signed by Patriots to practice squad (October 1, 1990). ... Activated (October 27, 1990). ... Granted unconditional free agency (February 1, 1991). ... Signed by Green Bay Packers (April 1, 1991). ... Granted unconditional free agency (February 1-April 1, 1992). ... Re-signed by Packers for 1992 season. ... Granted free agency (March 1, 1993). ... Re-signed by Packers (July 13, 1993). ... Granted unconditional free agency (February 17, 1994). ... Re-signed by Packers (July 20, 1994). ... Granted unconditional free agency (February 17, 1995).

H

... Signed by Denver Broncos (March 6, 1995).
PLAYING EXPERIENCE: New England NFL, 1990; Green Bay NFL, 1991-1994; Denver NFL, 1995. ... Games: 1990 (10), 1991 (16), 1992 (16), 1993 (13), 1994 (13), 1995 (16). Total: 84.
PRO STATISTICS: 1991—Recovered one fumble. 1992—Returned one punt for two yards. 1993—Recovered one fumble.

HAWKINS, COURTNEY   WR   BUCCANEERS

PERSONAL: Born December 12, 1969, in Flint, Mich. ... 5-9/183. ... Full name: Courtney Tyrone Hawkins Jr. ... Cousin of Roy Marble, guard/forward, Atlanta Hawks and Denver Nuggets of NBA (1990-91 and 1993-94).
HIGH SCHOOL: Beecher (Flint, Mich.).
COLLEGE: Michigan State.
TRANSACTIONS/CAREER NOTES: Selected by Tampa Bay Buccaneers in second round (44th pick overall) of 1992 NFL draft. ... Signed by Buccaneers (July 16, 1992). ... On injured reserve with knee injury (December 16, 1994-remainder of season). ... Granted free agency (February 17, 1995). ... Re-signed by Buccaneers (July 21, 1995). ... Granted unconditional free agency (February 16, 1996). ... Re-signed by Buccaneers (April 27, 1996).
PRO STATISTICS: 1992—Recovered one fumble. 1995—Rushed four times for five yards.
STATISTICAL PLATEAUS: 100-yard receiving games: 1992 (1), 1993 (2). Total: 3.

		RECEIVING				PUNT RETURNS				KICKOFF RETURNS				TOTALS			
Year Team	G	No.	Yds.	Avg.	TD	No.	Yds.	Avg.	TD	No.	Yds.	Avg.	TD	TD	2pt.	Pts.	Fum.
1992—Tampa Bay NFL	16	20	336	16.8	2	13	53	4.1	0	9	118	13.1	0	2	...	12	2
1993—Tampa Bay NFL	16	62	933	15.1	5	15	166	11.1	0	0	0	...	0	5	...	30	2
1994—Tampa Bay NFL	13	37	438	11.8	5	5	28	5.6	0	0	0	...	0	5	0	30	0
1995—Tampa Bay NFL	16	41	493	12.0	0	0	0	...	0	0	0	...	0	0	0	0	1
Pro totals (4 years)	61	160	2200	13.8	12	33	247	7.5	0	9	118	13.1	0	12	0	72	5

HAWKINS, GARLAND   DE

PERSONAL: Born February 19, 1970, in Washington, D.C. ... 6-3/253. ... Full name: Garland Anthony Hawkins.
HIGH SCHOOL: DeMatha Catholic (Hyattsville, Md.).
COLLEGE: Syracuse.
TRANSACTIONS/CAREER NOTES: Signed as non-drafted free agent by Chicago Bears (April 29, 1993). ... Released by Bears (August 24, 1993). ... Re-signed by Bears (April 27, 1994). ... On injured reserve with shoulder injury (August 8, 1994-entire season). ... Released by Bears (September 22, 1995).
PLAYING EXPERIENCE: Chicago NFL, 1995. ... Games: 1995 (1).

HAWTHORNE, ED   NT   DOLPHINS

PERSONAL: Born July 30, 1970, in St. Louis. ... 6-1/305.
HIGH SCHOOL: Parkway West (Ballwin, Mo.).
COLLEGE: Minnesota.
TRANSACTIONS/CAREER NOTES: Signed as non-drafted free agent by Miami Dolphins (April 27, 1995).
PLAYING EXPERIENCE: Miami NFL, 1995. ... Games: 1995 (1).

HAYDEN, AARON   RB   CHARGERS

PERSONAL: Born April 13, 1973, in Detroit. ... 6-0/218. ... Full name: Aaron Chautezz Hayden. ... Name pronounced HEY-den.
HIGH SCHOOL: Mumford (Detroit).
COLLEGE: Tennessee.
TRANSACTIONS/CAREER NOTES: Selected by San Diego Chargers in fourth round (104th pick overall) of 1995 NFL draft. ... Signed by Chargers (July 17, 1995). ...On physically unable to perform list with leg injury (August 22-November 10, 1995).
STATISTICAL PLATEAUS: 100-yard rushing games: 1995 (1).

		RUSHING				RECEIVING				TOTALS			
Year Team	G	Att.	Yds.	Avg.	TD	No.	Yds.	Avg.	TD	TD	2pt.	Pts.	Fum.
1995—San Diego NFL	6	128	470	3.7	3	5	53	10.6	0	3	0	18	0

HAYES, JONATHAN   TE   STEELERS

PERSONAL: Born August 11, 1962, in South Fayette, Pa. ... 6-5/248. ... Full name: Jonathan Michael Hayes. ... Brother of Jay Hayes, defensive end, Michigan Panthers, San Antonio Gunslingers and Memphis Showboats of USFL (1984 and 1985).
HIGH SCHOOL: South Fayette (McDonald, Pa.).
COLLEGE: Iowa (degree in sociology, 1986).
TRANSACTIONS/CAREER NOTES: Selected by Kansas City Chiefs in second round (41st pick overall) of 1985 NFL draft. ... Signed by Chiefs (June 19, 1985). ... On injured reserve with shoulder injury (September 4-October 6, 1990). ... Granted free agency (February 1, 1992). ... Re-signed by Chiefs (May 26, 1992). ... Released by Chiefs (April 28, 1994). ... Signed by Pittsburgh Steelers (July 1, 1994).
CHAMPIONSHIP GAME EXPERIENCE: Played in AFC championship game (1993, 1994 and 1995 seasons). ... Played in Super Bowl XXX (1995 season).
PRO STATISTICS: 1985—Returned one kickoff for no yards. 1987—Recovered one fumble.
STATISTICAL PLATEAUS: 100-yard receiving games: 1987 (1).

		RECEIVING				TOTALS			
Year Team	G	No.	Yds.	Avg.	TD	TD	2pt.	Pts.	Fum.
1985—Kansas City NFL	16	5	39	7.8	1	1	...	6	0
1986—Kansas City NFL	16	8	69	8.6	0	0	...	0	0

H

Year Team	G	RECEIVING				TOTALS			
		No.	Yds.	Avg.	TD	TD	2pt.	Pts.	Fum.
1987—Kansas City NFL	12	21	272	13.0	2	2	...	12	0
1988—Kansas City NFL	16	22	233	10.6	1	1	...	6	0
1989—Kansas City NFL	16	18	229	12.7	2	2	...	12	1
1990—Kansas City NFL	12	9	83	9.2	1	1	...	6	0
1991—Kansas City NFL	16	19	208	11.0	2	2	...	12	1
1992—Kansas City NFL	16	9	77	8.6	2	2	...	12	0
1993—Kansas City NFL	16	24	331	13.8	1	1	...	6	1
1994—Pittsburgh NFL	16	5	50	10.0	1	1	0	6	1
1995—Pittsburgh NFL	16	11	113	10.3	0	0	0	0	0
Pro totals (11 years)	168	151	1704	11.3	13	13	0	78	4

HAYES, MELVIN — OT — JETS

PERSONAL: Born April 28, 1973, in New Orleans. ... 6-6/329. ... Full name: Melvin Anthony Hayes.
HIGH SCHOOL: John Curtis (New Orleans).
COLLEGE: Mississippi State.
TRANSACTIONS/CAREER NOTES: Selected by New York Jets in fourth round (106th pick overall) of 1995 NFL draft. ... Signed by Jets (June 14, 1995). ... On physically unable to perform list with ankle injury (August 21-November 3, 1995).
PLAYING EXPERIENCE: New York Jets NFL, 1995. ... Games: 1995 (3).

HAYNES, MICHAEL — WR — SAINTS

PERSONAL: Born December 24, 1965, in New Orleans. ... 6-0/184. ... Full name: Michael David Haynes.
HIGH SCHOOL: Joseph S. Clark (New Orleans).
JUNIOR COLLEGE: Eastern Arizona Junior College.
COLLEGE: Northern Arizona.
TRANSACTIONS/CAREER NOTES: Selected by Atlanta Falcons in seventh round (166th pick overall) of 1988 NFL draft. ... Signed by Falcons (July 18, 1988). ... Designated by Falcons as transition player (February 17, 1994). ... Tendered offer sheet by New Orleans Saints (March 7, 1994). ... Falcons declined to match offer (March 14, 1994).
PRO STATISTICS: 1988—Returned six kickoffs for 113 yards. 1989—Rushed four times for 35 yards. 1994—Rushed four times for 43 yards.
STATISTICAL PLATEAUS: 100-yard receiving games: 1989 (1), 1991 (5), 1992 (2), 1993 (1). Total: 9.

Year Team	G	RECEIVING				TOTALS			
		No.	Yds.	Avg.	TD	TD	2pt.	Pts.	Fum.
1988—Atlanta NFL	15	13	232	17.9	4	4	...	24	1
1989—Atlanta NFL	13	40	681	17.0	4	4	...	24	0
1990—Atlanta NFL	13	31	445	14.4	0	0	...	0	0
1991—Atlanta NFL	16	50	1122	*22.4	11	11	...	66	0
1992—Atlanta NFL	14	48	808	16.8	10	10	...	60	0
1993—Atlanta NFL	16	72	778	10.8	4	4	...	24	1
1994—New Orleans NFL	16	77	985	12.8	5	5	0	30	1
1995—New Orleans NFL	16	41	597	14.6	4	4	0	24	0
Pro totals (8 years)	119	372	5648	15.2	42	42	0	252	3

HAYWORTH, TRACY — LB — FALCONS

PERSONAL: Born December 18, 1967, in Winchester, Tenn. ... 6-3/260. ... Full name: Tracy Keith Hayworth.
HIGH SCHOOL: Franklin County (Winchester, Tenn.).
COLLEGE: Tennessee (degree in education).
TRANSACTIONS/CAREER NOTES: Selected by Detroit Lions in seventh round (174th pick overall) of 1990 NFL draft. ... Signed by Lions (July 20, 1990). ... Granted free agency (February 1, 1992). ... Re-signed by Lions (July 27, 1992). ... On injured reserve with knee injury (October 13, 1992-remainder of season). ... On physically unable to perform list (July 18-August 2, 1993). ... Granted unconditional free agency (February 17, 1995). ... Re-signed by Lions (March 23, 1995). ... Released by Lions (March 11, 1996). ... Signed by Atlanta Falcons (May 13, 1996).
CHAMPIONSHIP GAME EXPERIENCE: Played in NFC championship game (1991 season).
PRO STATISTICS: 1990—Recovered one fumble. 1991—Intercepted one pass for no yards and recovered two fumbles for 28 yards and a touchdown. 1995—Recovered one fumble.

Year Team	G	SACKS
1990—Detroit NFL	16	4.0
1991—Detroit NFL	16	2.0
1992—Detroit NFL	4	0.0
1993—Detroit NFL	11	2.0
1994—Detroit NFL	9	1.0
1995—Detroit NFL	16	1.0
Pro totals (6 years)	72	10.0

HEARST, GARRISON — RB — CARDINALS

H

PERSONAL: Born January 4, 1971, in Lincolnton, Ga. ... 5-11/215. ... Full name: Gerald Garrison Hearst.
HIGH SCHOOL: Lincoln County (Lincolnton, Ga.).
COLLEGE: Georgia.
TRANSACTIONS/CAREER NOTES: Selected after junior season by Phoenix Cardinals in first round (third pick overall) of 1993 NFL draft. ... Signed by Cardinals (August 28, 1993). ... On injured reserve with knee injury (November 4, 1993-remainder of season). ... Cardinals franchise renamed Arizona Cardinals for 1994 season. ... On physically unable to perform list with knee injury (August 23-October 13, 1994). ... Granted free agency (February 16, 1996). ... Re-signed by Cardinals (May 23, 1996).

HONORS: Doak Walker Award winner (1992). ... Named running back on THE SPORTING NEWS college All-America first team (1992).
PRO STATISTICS: 1993—Had only pass attempt intercepted. 1994—Attempted one pass with one completion for 10 yards and a touchdown. 1995—Attempted two passes with one completion for 16 yards and recovered two fumbles.
STATISTICAL PLATEAUS: 100-yard rushing games: 1995 (3).

		RUSHING				RECEIVING				TOTALS			
Year Team	G	Att.	Yds.	Avg.	TD	No.	Yds.	Avg.	TD	TD	2pt.	Pts.	Fum.
1993—Phoenix NFL	6	76	264	3.5	1	6	18	3.0	0	1	...	6	2
1994—Arizona NFL	8	37	169	4.6	1	6	49	8.2	0	1	0	6	0
1995—Arizona NFL	16	284	1070	3.8	1	29	243	8.4	1	2	0	12	12
Pro totals (3 years)	30	397	1503	3.8	3	41	310	7.6	1	4	0	24	14

HEBERT, BOBBY   QB   FALCONS

PERSONAL: Born August 19, 1960, in Baton Rouge, La. ... 6-4/215. ... Full name: Bobby Joseph Hebert Jr. ... Brother of Billy Bob Hebert, wide receiver, Calgary Stampeders of CFL (1989). ... Name pronounced AY-bear.
HIGH SCHOOL: South Lafourche (Galliano, La.).
COLLEGE: Northwestern (La.) State (degree in business administration, 1983).
TRANSACTIONS/CAREER NOTES: Selected by Michigan Panthers in third round (34th pick overall) of 1983 USFL draft. ... Signed by Panthers (January 22, 1983). ... On reserve/did not report list (January 23-February 16, 1984). ... Protected in merger of Panthers and Oakland Invaders (December 6, 1984). ... Granted free agency (July 15, 1985). ... Signed by New Orleans Saints (August 7, 1985). ... On injured reserve with broken foot (September 22-November 8, 1986). ... On reserve/asked to re-sign list (February 1, 1990-June 3, 1991). ... Re-signed by Saints (June 4, 1991). ... Granted unconditional free agency (March 1, 1993). ... Signed by Atlanta Falcons (April 21, 1993). ... Released by Falcons (March 30, 1994). ... Re-signed by Falcons (April 18, 1994). ... Granted unconditional free agency (February 17, 1995). ... Re-signed by Falcons (March 27, 1995). ... Granted unconditional free agency (February 16, 1996). ... Re-signed by Falcons (May 6, 1996).
CHAMPIONSHIP GAME EXPERIENCE: Played in USFL championship game (1983 and 1985 seasons).
HONORS: Named USFL Player of the Year by THE SPORTING NEWS (1983). ... Named quarterback on THE SPORTING NEWS USFL All-Star team (1983). ... Played in Pro Bowl (1993 season).
PRO STATISTICS: USFL: 1983—Fumbled eight times and recovered two fumbles. 1984—Fumbled eight times and recovered three fumbles. 1985— Fumbled five times and recovered three fumbles for minus two yards. NFL: 1985—Caught one pass for seven yards and a touchdown, fumbled once and recovered one fumble. 1986—Caught one pass for one yard and fumbled three times. 1987—Fumbled four times and recovered two fumbles. 1988—Caught two passes for no yards, fumbled nine times and recovered one fumble. 1991—Fumbled five times and recovered two fumbles for minus 19 yards. 1992—Fumbled three times and recovered one fumble. 1993—Fumbled 11 times and recovered three fumbles for minus nine yards. 1994—Fumbled twice.
STATISTICAL PLATEAUS: USFL: 300-yard passing games: 1983 (1), 1984 (3), 1985 (5). Total: 9. ... NFL: 300-yard passing games: 1989 (1), 1991 (1), 1992 (2), 1993 (2). Total: 6.
MISCELLANEOUS: Regular-season record as starting NFL quarterback: 53-34 (.609).

		PASSING								RUSHING				TOTALS		
Year Team	G	Att.	Cmp.	Pct.	Yds.	TD	Int.	Avg.	Rat.	Att.	Yds.	Avg.	TD	TD	2pt.	Pts.
1983—Michigan USFL	18	451	257	57.0	3568	*27	17	*7.91	86.8	28	35	1.3	3	3	1	20
1984—Michigan USFL	17	500	272	54.4	3758	24	22	7.52	76.4	18	76	4.2	1	1	0	6
1985—Oakland USFL	18	456	244	53.5	3811	30	19	8.36	86.1	12	31	2.6	1	1	0	6
—New Orleans NFL	6	181	97	53.6	1208	5	4	6.68	74.6	12	26	2.2	0	1	...	6
1986—New Orleans NFL	5	79	41	51.9	498	2	8	6.30	40.5	5	14	2.8	0	0	...	0
1987—New Orleans NFL	12	294	164	55.8	2119	15	9	7.21	82.9	13	95	7.3	0	0	...	0
1988—New Orleans NFL	16	478	280	58.6	3156	20	15	6.60	79.3	37	79	2.1	0	0	...	0
1989—New Orleans NFL	14	353	222	62.9	2686	15	15	7.61	82.7	25	87	3.5	0	0	...	0
1990—New Orleans NFL							Did not play.									
1991—New Orleans NFL	9	248	149	60.1	1676	9	8	6.76	79.0	18	56	3.1	0	0	...	0
1992—New Orleans NFL	16	422	249	59.0	3287	19	16	7.79	82.9	32	95	3.0	0	0	...	0
1993—Atlanta NFL	14	430	263	61.2	2978	24	17	6.93	84.0	24	49	2.0	0	0	...	0
1994—Atlanta NFL	8	103	52	50.5	610	2	6	5.92	51.0	9	43	4.8	0	0	0	0
1995—Atlanta NFL	4	45	28	62.2	313	2	1	6.96	88.5	5	-1	-0.2	0	0	0	0
USFL totals (3 years)	53	1407	773	54.9	11137	81	58	7.92	82.9	58	142	2.5	5	5	1	32
NFL totals (10 years)	104	2633	1545	58.7	18531	113	99	7.04	78.9	180	543	3.0	0	1	0	6
Pro totals (13 years)	157	4040	2318	57.4	29668	194	157	7.34	80.3	238	685	2.9	5	6	1	38

HEBRON, VAUGHN   RB   EAGLES

PERSONAL: Born October 7, 1970, in Baltimore. ... 5-8/195. ... Full name: Vaughn Harlen Hebron.
HIGH SCHOOL: Cardinal Gibbons (Baltimore).
COLLEGE: Virginia Tech.
TRANSACTIONS/CAREER NOTES: Signed as non-drafted free agent by Philadelphia Eagles (April 29, 1993). ... On injured reserve with knee injury (August 22, 1995-entire season). ... Granted unconditional free agency (February 16, 1996). ... Re-signed by Eagles (April 18, 1996).
PRO STATISTICS: 1993—Recovered one fumble.

		RUSHING				RECEIVING				KICKOFF RETURNS				TOTALS		
Year Team	G	Att.	Yds.	Avg.	TD	No.	Yds.	Avg.	TD	No.	Yds.	Avg.	TD	TD	2pt.	Pts. Fum.
1993—Philadelphia NFL	16	84	297	3.5	3	11	82	7.5	0	3	35	11.7	0	3	...	18 5
1994—Philadelphia NFL	16	82	325	4.0	2	18	137	7.6	0	21	443	21.1	0	2	0	12 0
1995—Philadelphia NFL							Did not play-injured									
Pro totals (2 years)	32	166	622	3.8	5	29	219	7.6	0	24	478	19.9	0	5	0	30 5

HECK, ANDY   OT   BEARS

PERSONAL: Born January 1, 1967, in Fargo, N.D. ... 6-6/296. ... Full name: Andrew Robert Heck.
HIGH SCHOOL: W.T. Woodson (Fairfax, Va.).
COLLEGE: Notre Dame (degree in American studies, 1989).

H

TRANSACTIONS/CAREER NOTES: Selected by Seattle Seahawks in first round (15th pick overall) of 1989 NFL draft. ... Signed by Seahawks (July 31, 1989). ... On injured reserve with ankle injury (October 21-November 20, 1992); on practice squad (November 18-20, 1992). ... Designated by Seahawks as transition player (February 25, 1993). ... Tendered offer sheet by Chicago Bears (February 21, 1994). ... Seahawks declined to match offer (March 1, 1994).

PLAYING EXPERIENCE: Seattle NFL, 1989-1993; Chicago NFL, 1994 and 1995. ... Games: 1989 (16), 1990 (16), 1991 (16), 1992 (13), 1993 (16), 1994 (14), 1995 (16). Total: 107.

HONORS: Named offensive tackle on THE SPORTING NEWS college All-America first team (1988).

PRO STATISTICS: 1989—Recovered one fumble. 1990—Recovered one fumble. 1993—Recovered two fumbles.

HELLER, RON   OT

PERSONAL: Born August 25, 1962, in East Meadow, N.Y. ... 6-5/298. ... Full name: Ronald Ramon Heller.
HIGH SCHOOL: Farmingdale (N.Y.).
COLLEGE: Penn State (degree in administration of justice, 1984).
TRANSACTIONS/CAREER NOTES: Selected by Philadelphia Stars in 1984 USFL territorial draft. ... Selected by Tampa Bay Buccaneers in fourth round (112th pick overall) of 1984 NFL draft. ... Signed by Buccaneers (June 6, 1984). ... Granted free agency (February 1, 1988). ... Re-signed by Buccaneers and traded to Seattle Seahawks for DE Randy Edwards and sixth-round pick (LB Derrick Little) in 1989 draft (May 4, 1988). ... Traded by Seahawks to Philadelphia Eagles for fourth-round pick (DB James Henry) in 1989 draft (August 22, 1988). ... Granted free agency (February 1, 1990). ... Re-signed by Eagles (August 18, 1990). ... Granted unconditional free agency (March 1, 1993). ... Signed by Miami Dolphins (April 20, 1993). ... Released by Dolphins (August 30, 1995). ... Re-signed by Dolphins (August 31, 1995). ... On injured reserve with knee injury (November 2, 1995-remainder of season). ... Announced retirement (June 3, 1996).
PLAYING EXPERIENCE: Tampa Bay NFL, 1984-1987; Philadelphia NFL, 1988-1992; Miami NFL, 1993-1995. ... Games: 1984 (14), 1985 (16), 1986 (16), 1987 (12), 1988 (15), 1989 (16), 1990 (16), 1991 (16), 1992 (12), 1993 (16), 1994 (16), 1995 (7). Total: 172.
PRO STATISTICS: 1986—Caught one pass for one yard and a touchdown and recovered one fumble. 1988—Recovered two fumbles. 1991—Recovered one fumble. 1992—Recovered two fumbles.

HELLESTRAE, DALE   G/C   COWBOYS

PERSONAL: Born July 11, 1962, in Phoenix. ... 6-5/286. ... Full name: Dale Robert Hellestrae. ... Name pronounced hell-us-TRAY.
HIGH SCHOOL: Saguaro (Scottsdale, Ariz.).
COLLEGE: Southern Methodist (degree in business administration).
TRANSACTIONS/CAREER NOTES: Selected by Houston Gamblers in 1985 USFL territorial draft. ... Selected by Buffalo Bills in fourth round (112th pick overall) of 1985 NFL draft. ... Signed by Bills (July 19, 1985). ... On injured reserve with broken thumb (October 4, 1985-remainder of season). ... On injured reserve with broken wrist (September 17-November 15, 1986). ... On injured reserve with hip injury (September 1, 1987-entire season). ... Granted unconditional free agency (February 1, 1989). ... Signed by Los Angeles Raiders (February 24, 1989). ... On injured reserve with broken leg (August 29, 1989-entire season). ... Traded by Raiders to Dallas Cowboys for seventh-round pick (traded to Chicago) in 1991 draft (August 20, 1990). ... Granted unconditional free agency (February 1-April 1, 1991). ... Re-signed by Cowboys for 1991 season. ... Granted unconditional free agency (February 1-April 1, 1992). ... Re-signed by Cowboys for 1992 season. ... Released by Cowboys (August 31, 1992). ... Re-signed by Cowboys (September 2, 1992). ... Granted unconditional free agency (March 1, 1993). ... Re-signed by Cowboys (June 2, 1993). ... Released by Cowboys (August 30, 1993). ... Re-signed by Cowboys (August 31, 1993). ... Granted unconditional free agency (February 17, 1994). ... Re-signed by Cowboys (July 14, 1994). ... Granted unconditional free agency (February 16, 1996). ... Re-signed by Cowboys (April 8, 1996).
PLAYING EXPERIENCE: Buffalo NFL, 1985, 1986 and 1988; Dallas NFL, 1990-1995. ... Games: 1985 (4), 1986 (8), 1988 (16), 1990 (16), 1991 (16), 1992 (16), 1993 (16), 1994 (16), 1995 (16). Total: 124.
CHAMPIONSHIP GAME EXPERIENCE: Played in AFC championship game (1988 season). ... Played in NFC championship game (1992-1995 seasons). ... Member of Super Bowl championship team (1992, 1993 and 1995 seasons).
PRO STATISTICS: 1986—Fumbled once for minus 14 yards.

HEMPSTEAD, HESSLEY   G   LIONS

PERSONAL: Born January 29, 1972, in Upland, Calif. ... 6-1/295.
HIGH SCHOOL: Upland (Calif.).
COLLEGE: Kansas.
TRANSACTIONS/CAREER NOTES: Selected by Detroit Lions in seventh round (228th pick overall) of 1995 NFL draft. ... Signed by Lions (July 19, 1995).
PLAYING EXPERIENCE: Detroit NFL, 1995. ... Games: 1995 (2).

HENDERSON, JEROME   CB   EAGLES

PERSONAL: Born August 8, 1969, in Statesville, N.C. ... 5-10/188. ... Full name: Jerome Virgil Henderson.
HIGH SCHOOL: West Iredel (Statesville, N.C.).
COLLEGE: Clemson.
TRANSACTIONS/CAREER NOTES: Selected by New England Patriots in second round (41st pick overall) of 1991 NFL draft. ... Signed by Patriots (July 15, 1991). ... Released by Patriots (October 11, 1993). ... Signed by Buffalo Bills (October 15, 1993). ... Granted free agency (February 17, 1994). ... Re-signed by Bills (May 27, 1994). ... Granted unconditional free agency (February 17, 1995). ... Signed by Philadelphia Eagles (March 22, 1995).
CHAMPIONSHIP GAME EXPERIENCE: Member of Bills for AFC championship game (1993 season); inactive. ... Played in Super Bowl XXVIII (1993 season).
PRO STATISTICS: 1991—Recovered one fumble. 1995—Recovered one fumble in end zone for touchdown.

Year Team		INTERCEPTIONS				PUNT RETURNS				TOTALS		
	G	No.	Yds.	Avg.	TD	No.	Yds.	Avg.	TD	TD	2pt.	Pts.	Fum.
1991—New England NFL	16	2	2	1.0	0	27	201	7.4	0	0	...	0	2
1992—New England NFL	16	3	43	14.3	0	0	0	...	0	0	...	0	0
1993—New England NFL	1	0	0	...	0	0	0	...	0	0	...	0	0
—Buffalo NFL	2	0	0	...	0	0	0	...	0	0	...	0	0

H

Year Team	G	INTERCEPTIONS				PUNT RETURNS				TOTALS			
		No.	Yds.	Avg.	TD	No.	Yds.	Avg.	TD	TD	2pt.	Pts.	Fum.
1994—Buffalo NFL	12	0	0	...	0	0	0	...	0	0	0	0	0
1995—Philadelphia NFL	15	0	0	...	0	0	0	...	0	1	0	6	0
Pro totals (5 years)	62	5	45	9.0	0	27	201	7.5	0	1	0	6	2

HENDERSON, WILLIAM — FB — PACKERS

PERSONAL: Born February 19, 1971, in Chester, Va. ... 6-1/248. ... Full name: William Terrelle Henderson.
HIGH SCHOOL: Thomas Dale (Chester, Va.).
COLLEGE: North Carolina.
TRANSACTIONS/CAREER NOTES: Selected by Green Bay Packers in third round (66th pick overall) of 1995 NFL draft. ... Signed by Packers (July 17, 1995).
CHAMPIONSHIP GAME EXPERIENCE: Played in NFC championship game (1995 season).

Year Team	G	RUSHING				RECEIVING				TOTALS			
		Att.	Yds.	Avg.	TD	No.	Yds.	Avg.	TD	TD	2pt.	Pts.	Fum.
1995—Green Bay NFL	15	7	35	5.0	0	3	21	7.0	0	0	0	0	0

HENDRICKSON, STEVE — RB/LB

PERSONAL: Born August 30, 1966, in Richmond, Calif. ... 6-0/250. ... Full name: Steven Daniel Hendrickson.
HIGH SCHOOL: Napa (Calif.).
COLLEGE: California.
TRANSACTIONS/CAREER NOTES: Selected by San Francisco 49ers in sixth round (167th pick overall) of 1989 NFL draft. ... Signed by 49ers (July 19, 1989). ... Released by 49ers (September 27, 1989). ... Re-signed by 49ers (September 29, 1989). ... Claimed on waivers by Dallas Cowboys (October 3, 1989). ... Released by Cowboys (November 1, 1989). ... Signed by 49ers to developmental squad (November 4, 1989). ... Activated (November 10, 1989). ... Released by 49ers (September 3, 1990). ... Signed by San Diego Chargers (September 19, 1990). ... Granted free agency (February 1, 1991). ... Re-signed by Chargers (July 15, 1991). ... Granted unconditional free agency (February 1, 1992). ... Re-signed by Chargers (February 2, 1992). ... Granted unconditional free agency (February 17, 1994). ... Signed by Los Angeles Raiders (June 27, 1994). ... Released by Raiders (August 1994). ... Signed by Chargers (August 29, 1994). ... Granted unconditional free agency (February 17, 1995). ... Signed by Arizona Cardinals (July 10, 1995). ... Released by Cardinals (August 22, 1995). ... Signed by Philadelphia Eagles (September 21, 1995). ... Released by Eagles (October 13, 1995). ... Signed by Houston Oilers (November 21, 1995). ... Granted unconditional free agency (February 16, 1996).
CHAMPIONSHIP GAME EXPERIENCE: Played in NFC championship game (1989 season). ... Member of Super Bowl championship team (1989 season). ... Played in AFC championship game (1994 season). ... Played in Super Bowl XXIX (1994 season).
PRO STATISTICS: 1991—Recovered one fumble. 1993—Intercepted one pass for 16 yards and recovered one fumble. 1994—Recovered one fumble.

Year Team	G	RUSHING				RECEIVING				KICKOFF RETURNS				TOTALS			
		Att.	Yds.	Avg.	TD	No.	Yds.	Avg.	TD	No.	Yds.	Avg.	TD	TD	2pt.	Pts.	Fum.
1989—San Francisco NFL	11	0	0	...	0	0	0	...	0	0	0	...	0	0	...	0	0
—Dallas NFL	4	0	0	...	0	0	0	...	0	0	0	...	0	0	...	0	0
1990—San Diego NFL	14	0	0	...	0	1	12	12.0	0	0	0	...	0	0	...	0	0
1991—San Diego NFL	15	1	3	3.0	1	4	36	9.0	1	0	0	...	0	2	...	12	0
1992—San Diego NFL	16	0	0	...	0	0	0	...	0	2	14	7.0	0	0	...	0	0
1993—San Diego NFL	16	1	0	0.0	0	0	0	...	0	2	25	12.5	0	0	...	0	0
1994—San Diego NFL	16	1	3	3.0	0	0	0	...	0	0	0	...	0	0	0	0	0
1995—Philadelphia NFL	3	0	0	...	0	0	0	...	0	0	0	...	0	0	0	0	0
—Houston NFL	5	0	0	...	0	0	0	...	0	0	0	...	0	0	0	0	0
Pro totals (7 years)	100	3	6	2.0	1	5	48	9.6	1	4	39	9.8	0	2	0	12	0

HENDRIX, DAVID — S — CHARGERS

PERSONAL: Born May 29, 1972, in Jesup, Ga. ... 6-1/213. ... Full name: David Tyrone Hendrix.
HIGH SCHOOL: Meadowcreek (Norcross, Ga.).
COLLEGE: Georgia Tech.
TRANSACTIONS/CAREER NOTES: Signed as non-drafted free agent by San Diego Chargers (April 28, 1995). ... Released by Chargers (August 27, 1995). ... Re-signed by Chargers to practice squad (August 29, 1995). ... Activated (October 17, 1995).
PLAYING EXPERIENCE: San Diego NFL, 1995. ... Game: 1995 (5).

HENNINGS, CHAD — DT — COWBOYS

PERSONAL: Born October 20, 1965, in Elberton, Iowa. ... 6-6/288. ... Full name: Chad William Hennings.
HIGH SCHOOL: Benton Community (Van Horne, Iowa).
COLLEGE: Air Force (degree in management).
TRANSACTIONS/CAREER NOTES: Selected by Dallas Cowboys in 11th round (290th pick overall) of 1988 NFL draft.... Signed by Cowboys (November 22, 1988).... Served in military (1988-1992).... Granted unconditional free agency (February 17, 1994).... Re-signed by Cowboys (1994).
CHAMPIONSHIP GAME EXPERIENCE: Played in NFC championship game (1992, 1994 and 1995 seasons). ... Member of Cowboys for NFC championship game (1993 season); inactive. ... Member of Super Bowl championship team (1992, 1993 and 1995 seasons).
HONORS: Outland Trophy winner (1987). ... Named defensive lineman on THE SPORTING NEWS college All-America first team (1987).
POSTSEASON RECORDS: Shares Super Bowl single-game record for most sacks—2 (January 28, 1996, vs. Pittsburgh).
PRO STATISTICS: 1993—Returned one kickoff for seven yards. 1994—Recovered one fumble. 1995—Recovered one fumble.

Year Team	G	SACKS
1992—Dallas NFL	8	0.0
1993—Dallas NFL	13	0.0

H

Year Team	G	SACKS
1994—Dallas NFL	16	7.0
1995—Dallas NFL	16	5.5
Pro totals (4 years)	53	12.5

HENRY, KEVIN — DE — STEELERS

PERSONAL: Born October 23, 1968, in Mound Bayou, Miss. ... 6-4/282. ... Full name: Kevin Lerell Henry. ... Name pronounced KEE-vin.
HIGH SCHOOL: John F. Kennedy (Mound Bayou, Miss.).
COLLEGE: Mississippi State.
TRANSACTIONS/CAREER NOTES: Selected by Pittsburgh Steelers in fourth round (108th pick overall) of 1993 NFL draft. ... Signed by Steelers (July 9, 1993). ... Granted free agency (February 16, 1996).
PLAYING EXPERIENCE: Pittsburgh NFL, 1993-1995. ... Games: 1993 (12), 1994 (16), 1995 (14). Total: 42.
CHAMPIONSHIP GAME EXPERIENCE: Played in AFC championship game (1994 and 1995 seasons). ... Played in Super Bowl XXX (1995 season).
PRO STATISTICS: 1993—Credited with one sack and intercepted one pass for 10 yards. 1994—Recovered one fumble. 1995—Credited with two sacks.

HENTRICH, CRAIG — P — PACKERS

PERSONAL: Born May 18, 1971, in Alton, Ill. ... 6-3/200. ... Full name: Craig Anthony Hentrich. ... Name pronounced HEN-trick.
HIGH SCHOOL: Marquette (Alton, Ill.).
COLLEGE: Notre Dame.
TRANSACTIONS/CAREER NOTES: Selected by New York Jets in eighth round (200th pick overall) of 1993 NFL draft. ... Signed by Jets (July 14, 1993). ... Released by Jets (August 24, 1993). ... Signed by Green Bay Packers to practice squad (September 7, 1993). ... Activated (January 14, 1994); did not play.
CHAMPIONSHIP GAME EXPERIENCE: Played in NFC championship game (1995 season).

		PUNTING						KICKING						
Year Team	G	No.	Yds.	Avg.	Net avg.	In. 20	Blk.	XPM	XPA	FGM	FGA	Lg.	50+	Pts.
1993—Green Bay NFL								Did not play.						
1994—Green Bay NFL	16	81	3351	41.4	35.5	24	0	0	0	0	0	...	0-0	0
1995—Green Bay NFL	16	65	2740	42.2	34.6	26	2	5	5	3	5	49	0-0	14
Pro totals (2 years)	32	146	6091	41.7	35.1	50	2	5	5	3	5	49	0-0	14

HERROD, JEFF — LB — COLTS

PERSONAL: Born July 29, 1966, in Birmingham, Ala. ... 6-0/245. ... Full name: Jeff Sylvester Herrod.
HIGH SCHOOL: Banks (Birmingham, Ala.).
COLLEGE: Mississippi.
TRANSACTIONS/CAREER NOTES: Selected by Indianapolis Colts in ninth round (243rd pick overall) of 1988 NFL draft. ... Signed by Colts (July 13, 1988). ... Granted free agency (February 1, 1990). ... Re-signed by Colts (September 12, 1990). ... Activated (September 14, 1990). ... Released by Colts (July 19, 1995). ... Re-signed by Colts (July 20, 1995).
CHAMPIONSHIP GAME EXPERIENCE: Played in AFC championship game (1995 season).
HONORS: Named linebacker on THE SPORTING NEWS college All-America second team (1986).
PRO STATISTICS: 1991—Recovered three fumbles. 1993—Recovered one fumble in end zone for a touchdown.

		INTERCEPTIONS				SACKS
Year Team	G	No.	Yds.	Avg.	TD	No.
1988—Indianapolis NFL	16	0	0	...	0	1.0
1989—Indianapolis NFL	15	0	0	...	0	2.0
1990—Indianapolis NFL	13	1	12	12.0	0	4.0
1991—Indianapolis NFL	14	1	25	25.0	0	2.5
1992—Indianapolis NFL	16	1	4	4.0	0	2.0
1993—Indianapolis NFL	14	1	29	29.0	0	2.0
1994—Indianapolis NFL	15	0	0	...	0	1.0
1995—Indianapolis NFL	16	0	0	...	0	0.0
Pro totals (8 years)	119	4	70	17.5	0	14.5

HERVEY, EDWARD — WR — COWBOYS

PERSONAL: Born May 4, 1973, in Compton, Calif. ... 6-3/179.
HIGH SCHOOL: Compton (Calif.).
JUNIOR COLLEGE: Pasadena (Calif.) City College.
COLLEGE: Southern California.
TRANSACTIONS/CAREER NOTES: Selected by Dallas Cowboys in fifth round (166th pick overall) of 1995 NFL draft. ... Signed by Cowboys (July 17, 1995). ... Inactive for 16 games (1995).
CHAMPIONSHIP GAME EXPERIENCE: Member of Cowboys for NFC championship game (1995 season); inactive.

HESTER, JESSIE — WR

PERSONAL: Born January 21, 1963, in Belle Glade, Fla. ... 5-11/175. ... Full name: Jessie Lee Hester.
HIGH SCHOOL: Central (Belle Glade, Fla.).
COLLEGE: Florida State.
TRANSACTIONS/CAREER NOTES: Selected by Tampa Bay Bandits in 1985 USFL territorial draft. ... Selected by Los Angeles Raiders in first

H

round (23rd pick overall) of 1985 NFL draft. ... Signed by Raiders (July 23, 1985). ... Traded by Raiders to Atlanta Falcons for fifth-round pick in 1989 draft (August 22, 1988). ... Released by Falcons (August 30, 1989). ... Signed by Indianapolis Colts (March 23, 1990). ... Granted free agency (February 1, 1991). ... Re-signed by Colts (July 26, 1991). ... Released by Colts (February 17, 1994). ... Signed by Los Angeles Rams (June 8, 1994). ... Granted free agency (February 17, 1995). ... Tendered offer sheet by Seattle Seahawks (March 22, 1995). ... Offer matched by Rams (March 29, 1995). ... Rams franchise moved to St. Louis (April 12, 1995). ... Released by Rams (April 16, 1996).

PRO STATISTICS: 1985—Recovered one fumble. 1990—Recovered two fumbles. 1991—Recovered one fumble.

STATISTICAL PLATEAUS: 100-yard receiving games: 1986 (1), 1990 (1), 1991 (1), 1992 (1), 1993 (1). Total: 5.

		RUSHING				RECEIVING				TOTALS			
Year Team	G	Att.	Yds.	Avg.	TD	No.	Yds.	Avg.	TD	TD	2pt.	Pts.	Fum.
1985—Los Angeles Raiders NFL	16	1	13	13.0	1	32	665	20.8	4	5	...	30	0
1986—Los Angeles Raiders NFL	13	0	0	...	0	23	632	27.5	6	6	...	36	1
1987—Los Angeles Raiders NFL	10	0	0	...	0	1	30	30.0	0	0	...	0	0
1988—Atlanta NFL	16	1	3	3.0	0	12	176	14.7	0	0	...	0	1
1990—Indianapolis NFL	16	4	9	2.3	0	54	924	17.1	6	6	...	36	0
1991—Indianapolis NFL	16	0	0	...	0	60	753	12.6	5	5	...	30	3
1992—Indianapolis NFL	16	0	0	...	0	52	792	15.2	1	1	...	6	0
1993—Indianapolis NFL	16	0	0	...	0	64	835	13.1	1	1	...	6	1
1994—Los Angeles Rams NFL	16	2	28	14.0	0	45	644	14.3	3	3	0	18	1
1995—St. Louis NFL	12	0	0	...	0	30	399	13.3	3	3	0	18	0
Pro totals (10 years)	147	8	53	6.6	1	373	5850	15.7	29	30	0	180	7

HEYWARD, CRAIG FB FALCONS

PERSONAL: Born September 26, 1966, in Passaic, N.J. ... 5-11/265. ... Full name: Craig William Heyward. ... Nickname: Ironhead.

HIGH SCHOOL: Passaic (N.J.).

COLLEGE: Pittsburgh.

TRANSACTIONS/CAREER NOTES: Selected by New Orleans Saints in first round (24th pick overall) of 1988 NFL draft. ... Signed by Saints (July 8, 1988). ... Granted free agency (February 1, 1991). ... Re-signed by Saints (July 12, 1991). ... On injured reserve with foot injury (November 6-December 11, 1991). ... On suspended list (December 11, 1991-remainder of season). ... Granted unconditional free agency (March 1, 1993). ... Signed by Chicago Bears (April 11, 1993). ... Released by Bears (April 26, 1994). ... Signed by Atlanta Falcons (June 21, 1994).

HONORS: Named running back on THE SPORTING NEWS college All-America first team (1987).

PRO STATISTICS: 1988—Recovered one fumble. 1989—Recovered one fumble. 1990—Attempted one pass without a completion. 1991—Attempted one pass with one completion for 44 yards. 1992—Returned one kickoff for 14 yards and recovered one fumble. 1993—Returned one kickoff for 12 yards. 1994—Returned one kickoff for seven yards and recovered two fumbles. 1995—Recovered three fumbles.

STATISTICAL PLATEAUS: 100-yard rushing games: 1988 (1), 1990 (2), 1995 (3). Total: 6.

		RUSHING				RECEIVING				TOTALS			
Year Team	G	Att.	Yds.	Avg.	TD	No.	Yds.	Avg.	TD	TD	2pt.	Pts.	Fum.
1988—New Orleans NFL	11	74	355	4.8	1	13	105	8.1	0	1	...	6	0
1989—New Orleans NFL	16	49	183	3.7	1	13	69	5.3	0	1	...	6	2
1990—New Orleans NFL	16	129	599	4.6	4	18	121	6.7	0	4	...	24	3
1991—New Orleans NFL	7	76	260	3.4	4	4	34	8.5	1	5	...	30	0
1992—New Orleans NFL	16	104	416	4.0	3	19	159	8.4	0	3	...	18	1
1993—Chicago NFL	16	68	206	3.0	0	16	132	8.3	0	0	...	0	1
1994—Atlanta NFL	16	183	779	4.3	7	32	335	10.5	1	8	0	48	5
1995—Atlanta NFL	16	236	1083	4.6	6	37	350	9.5	2	8	0	48	3
Pro totals (8 years)	114	919	3881	4.2	26	152	1305	8.6	4	30	0	180	15

HICKMAN, KEVIN TE LIONS

PERSONAL: Born August 20, 1971, in Cherry Hill, N.J. ... 6-4/258.

HIGH SCHOOL: Holy Cross (Delran, N.J.), then Marine Military Academy (Harlingen, Texas).

COLLEGE: Navy.

TRANSACTIONS/CAREER NOTES: Selected by Detroit Lions in sixth round (186th pick overall) of 1995 NFL draft. ... Signed by Lions (July 19, 1995). ... On injured reserve with knee injury (December 21, 1995-remainder of season).

PLAYING EXPERIENCE: Detroit NFL, 1995. ... Games: 1995 (6).

HICKS, CLIFFORD S/CB

PERSONAL: Born August 18, 1964, in San Diego. ... 5-9/190. ... Full name: Clifford Wendell Hicks Jr.

HIGH SCHOOL: Kearny (San Diego).

JUNIOR COLLEGE: San Diego Mesa College.

COLLEGE: Oregon.

TRANSACTIONS/CAREER NOTES: Selected by Los Angeles Rams in third round (74th pick overall) of 1987 NFL draft. ... Signed by Rams (July 23, 1987). ... On injured reserve with broken leg (August 29-November 4, 1988). ... On injured reserve with knee injury (December 29, 1989-remainder of 1989 season playoffs). ... On physically unable to perform list (August 28-November 6, 1990). ... Released by Rams (November 23, 1990). ... Signed by Buffalo Bills (December 4, 1990). ... Granted unconditional free agency (February 1-April 1, 1991). ... Re-signed by Bills for 1991 season. ... On injured reserve with broken leg (September 1-October 3, 1992). ... Granted unconditional free agency (March 1, 1993). ... Signed by New York Jets (April 30, 1993). ... Granted unconditional free agency (February 17, 1994). ... Signed by Rams (April 15, 1994). ... Released by Rams (August 23, 1994). ... Signed by Jets (August 30, 1994). ... Granted unconditional free agency (February 17, 1995). ... Signed by San Francisco 49ers (April 13, 1995). ... Released by 49ers (August 22, 1995). ... Signed by Denver Broncos (November 14, 1995). ... Granted unconditional free agency (February 16, 1996).

CHAMPIONSHIP GAME EXPERIENCE: Played in AFC championship game (1990-1992 seasons). ... Played in Super Bowl XXV (1990 season), Super Bowl XXVI (1991 season) and Super Bowl XXVII (1992 season).

PRO STATISTICS: 1990—Credited with one sack. 1992—Credited with one sack. 1993—Recovered one fumble. 1994—Recovered two fumbles.

H

Year Team	G	INTERCEPTIONS				PUNT RETURNS				KICKOFF RETURNS				TOTALS			
		No.	Yds.	Avg.	TD	No.	Yds.	Avg.	TD	No.	Yds.	Avg.	TD	TD	2pt.	Pts.	Fum.
1987—Los Angeles Rams NFL	11	1	9	9.0	0	13	110	8.5	0	4	119	29.8	0	0	...	0	1
1988—Los Angeles Rams NFL	7	0	0	...	0	25	144	5.8	0	0	0	...	0	0	...	0	1
1989—Los Angeles Rams NFL	15	2	27	13.5	0	4	39	9.8	0	0	0	...	0	0	...	0	0
1990—Los Angeles Rams NFL	1	0	0	...	0	1	0	0.0	0	0	0	...	0	0	...	0	0
—Buffalo NFL	4	1	0	0.0	0	0	0	...	0	0	0	...	0	0	...	0	0
1991—Buffalo NFL	16	1	0	0.0	0	12	203	16.9	0	0	0	...	0	0	...	0	1
1992—Buffalo NFL	12	0	0	...	0	29	289	10.0	0	1	5	5.0	0	0	...	0	2
1993—New York Jets NFL	10	0	0	...	0	17	157	9.2	0	0	0	...	0	0	...	0	2
1994—New York Jets NFL	16	0	0	...	0	38	342	9.0	0	2	30	15.0	0	0	0	0	5
1995—Denver NFL	6	0	0	...	0	0	0	...	0	0	0	...	0	0	0	0	0
Pro totals (9 years)	98	5	36	7.2	0	139	1284	9.2	0	7	154	22.0	0	0	0	0	12

HIGGS, MARK — RB

PERSONAL: Born April 11, 1966, in Chicago. ... 5-7/199. ... Full name: Mark Deyon Higgs.
HIGH SCHOOL: Owensboro (Ky.).
COLLEGE: Kentucky.
TRANSACTIONS/CAREER NOTES: Selected by Dallas Cowboys in eighth round (205th pick overall) of 1988 NFL draft. ... Signed by Cowboys (July 6, 1988). ... Granted unconditional free agency (February 1, 1989). ... Signed by Philadelphia Eagles (March 2, 1989). ... Granted unconditional free agency (February 1, 1990). ... Signed by Miami Dolphins (April 1, 1990). ... On injured reserve with hamstring injury (December 7, 1990-remainder of season). ... Granted unconditional free agency (February 1-April 1, 1991). ... Re-signed by Dolphins for 1991 season. ... Granted free agency (February 1, 1992). ... Re-signed by Dolphins (July 14, 1992). ... Released by Dolphins (November 15, 1994). ... Signed by Arizona Cardinals (November 17, 1994). ... Granted unconditional free agency (February 17, 1995). ... Re-signed by Cardinals (March 9, 1995). ... Released by Cardinals (December 1, 1995).
PRO STATISTICS: 1989—Recovered one fumble. 1990—Returned blocked punt 19 yards for a touchdown.
STATISTICAL PLATEAUS: 100-yard rushing games: 1991 (3), 1992 (2), 1993 (2). Total: 7.

Year Team	G	RUSHING				RECEIVING				KICKOFF RETURNS				TOTALS			
		Att.	Yds.	Avg.	TD	No.	Yds.	Avg.	TD	No.	Yds.	Avg.	TD	TD	2pt.	Pts.	Fum.
1988—Dallas NFL	5	0	0	...	0	0	0	...	0	2	31	15.5	0	0	...	0	0
1989—Philadelphia NFL	15	49	184	3.8	0	3	9	3.0	0	16	293	18.3	0	0	...	0	3
1990—Miami NFL	12	10	67	6.7	0	0	0	...	0	10	210	21.0	0	1	...	6	1
1991—Miami NFL	14	231	905	3.9	4	11	80	7.3	0	0	0	...	0	4	...	24	3
1992—Miami NFL	16	256	915	3.6	7	16	142	8.9	0	0	0	...	0	7	...	42	5
1993—Miami NFL	16	186	693	3.7	3	10	72	7.2	0	0	0	...	0	3	...	18	1
1994—Miami NFL	5	19	68	3.6	0	0	0	...	0	0	0	...	0	0	0	0	1
—Arizona NFL	6	43	127	3.0	0	0	0	...	0	2	25	12.5	0	0	...	0	0
1995—Arizona NFL	1	0	0	...	0	0	0	...	0	2	26	13.0	0	0	0	0	0
Pro totals (8 years)	90	794	2959	3.7	14	40	303	7.6	0	32	585	18.3	0	15	0	90	14

HILL, ERIC — LB — CARDINALS

PERSONAL: Born November 14, 1966, in Galveston, Texas. ... 6-2/255.
HIGH SCHOOL: Ball (Galveston, Texas).
COLLEGE: Louisiana State.
TRANSACTIONS/CAREER NOTES: Selected by Phoenix Cardinals in first round (10th pick overall) of 1989 NFL draft. ... Signed by Cardinals (August 18, 1989). ... Granted free agency (March 1, 1993). ... Re-signed by Cardinals (September 4, 1993). ... Activated (September 26, 1993). ... Designated by Cardinals as transition player (February 15, 1994). ... Cardinals franchise renamed Arizona Cardinals for 1994 season.
PRO STATISTICS: 1989—Recovered one fumble. 1991—Recovered one fumble for 85 yards and a touchdown. 1992—Fumbled once and recovered one fumble for minus two yards. 1993—Recovered one fumble.

Year Team	G	SACKS
1989—Phoenix NFL	15	1.0
1990—Phoenix NFL	16	1.5
1991—Phoenix NFL	16	1.0
1992—Phoenix NFL	16	0.0
1993—Phoenix NFL	13	1.0
1994—Arizona NFL	16	1.5
1995—Arizona NFL	14	2.0
Pro totals (7 years)	106	8.0

HILL, GREG — RB — CHIEFS

PERSONAL: Born February 23, 1972, in Dallas. ... 5-11/207. ... Full name: Gregory Lamonte' Hill.
HIGH SCHOOL: David W. Carter (Dallas).
COLLEGE: Texas A&M.
TRANSACTIONS/CAREER NOTES: Selected after junior season by Kansas City Chiefs in first round (25th pick overall) of 1994 NFL draft. ... Signed by Chiefs (August 2, 1994).
HONORS: Named running back on The Sporting News college All-America second team (1992).
STATISTICAL PLATEAUS: 100-yard rushing games: 1995 (2).

Year Team	G	RUSHING				RECEIVING				TOTALS			
		Att.	Yds.	Avg.	TD	No.	Yds.	Avg.	TD	TD	2pt.	Pts.	Fum.
1994—Kansas City NFL	16	141	574	4.1	1	16	92	5.8	0	1	0	6	1
1995—Kansas City NFL	16	155	667	4.3	1	7	45	6.4	0	1	0	6	2
Pro totals (2 years)	32	296	1241	4.2	2	23	137	6.0	0	2	0	12	3

H

HILL, JEFF   WR/KR   BENGALS

PERSONAL: Born September 24, 1972, in Mount Healthy, Ohio. ... 5-11/178.
HIGH SCHOOL: Mount Healthy (Ohio).
COLLEGE: Purdue.
TRANSACTIONS/CAREER NOTES: Signed as non-drafted free agent by Cincinnati Bengals (April 29, 1994). ... Released by Bengals (August 28, 1994). ... Re-signed by Bengals to practice squad (August 30, 1994). ... Activated (December 5, 1994).
PRO STATISTICS: 1995—Rushed once for minus three yards and caught four passes for 44 yards.

		KICKOFF RETURNS				TOTALS			
Year Team	G	No.	Yds.	Avg.	TD	TD	2pt.	Pts.	Fum.
1994—Cincinnati NFL	1	4	97	24.3	0	0	0	0	0
1995—Cincinnati NFL	16	17	454	26.7	0	0	0	0	0
Pro totals (2 years)	17	21	551	26.2	0	0	0	0	0

HILL, RANDAL   WR

PERSONAL: Born September 21, 1969, in Miami. ... 5-10/180. ... Full name: Randal Thrill Hill.
HIGH SCHOOL: Miami Killian.
COLLEGE: Miami, Fla. (degree in sociology).
TRANSACTIONS/CAREER NOTES: Selected by Miami Dolphins in first round (23rd pick overall) of 1991 NFL draft. ... Signed by Dolphins (August 6, 1991). ... Traded by Dolphins to Phoenix Cardinals for first-round pick (CB Troy Vincent) in 1992 draft (September 3, 1991). ... Granted free agency (February 17, 1994). ... Cardinals franchise renamed Arizona Cardinals for 1994 season. ... Re-signed by Cardinals (June 16, 1994). ... Granted unconditional free agency (February 17, 1995). ... Signed by Dolphins (March 7, 1995). ... Granted unconditional free agency (February 16, 1996).
PRO STATISTICS: 1992—Rushed once for four yards.
STATISTICAL PLATEAUS: 100-yard receiving games: 1992 (1).

		RECEIVING				KICKOFF RETURNS				TOTALS			
Year Team	G	No.	Yds.	Avg.	TD	No.	Yds.	Avg.	TD	TD	2pt.	Pts.	Fum.
1991—Miami NFL	1	0	0	...	0	1	33	33.0	0	0	...	0	0
—Phoenix NFL	15	43	495	11.5	1	8	113	14.1	0	1	...	6	0
1992—Phoenix NFL	16	58	861	14.8	3	0	0	...	0	3	...	18	2
1993—Phoenix NFL	16	35	519	14.8	4	0	0	...	0	4	...	24	0
1994—Arizona NFL	14	38	544	14.3	0	0	0	...	0	0	0	0	0
1995—Miami NFL	12	12	260	21.7	0	12	287	23.9	0	0	0	0	0
Pro totals (5 years)	74	186	2679	14.4	8	21	433	20.6	0	8	0	48	2

HILL, SEAN   CB   DOLPHINS

PERSONAL: Born August 14, 1971, in Dowagiac, Mich. ... 5-10/179. ... Full name: Sean Terrell Hill.
HIGH SCHOOL: Widefield (Security, Mich.).
COLLEGE: Montana State.
TRANSACTIONS/CAREER NOTES: Selected by Miami Dolphins in seventh round (214th pick overall) of 1994 NFL draft. ... Signed by Dolphins (July 18, 1994).
PLAYING EXPERIENCE: Miami NFL, 1994 and 1995. ... Games: 1994 (16), 1995 (16). Total: 32.
PRO STATISTICS: 1995—Returned one kickoff for 38 yards.

HILL, TRAVIS   LB

PERSONAL: Born October 3, 1969, in Texas City, Texas. ... 6-2/240. ... Full name: Travis LaVell Hill. ... Cousin of Anthony Dickerson, linebacker, Dallas Cowboys (1980-1984).
HIGH SCHOOL: Pearland (Texas).
COLLEGE: Nebraska.
TRANSACTIONS/CAREER NOTES: Selected by Cleveland Browns in seventh round (180th pick overall) of 1993 NFL draft. ...Signed by Browns for 1993 season. ... On physically unable to perform list with knee injury (August 24, 1993-entire season). ... Traded by Browns to Carolina Panthers for WR/KR Michael Bates (August 29, 1995). ...Claimed on waivers by Browns (October 4, 1995). ... Released by Browns (November 8, 1995).
PLAYING EXPERIENCE: Cleveland NFL, 1994; Carolina (3)-Cleveland (4) NFL, 1995. ... Games: 1994 (14), 1995 (7). Total: 21.
HONORS: Named linebacker on THE SPORTING NEWS college All-America second team (1992).
PRO STATISTICS: 1994—Recovered blocked punt in end zone for a touchdown.

HILLIARD, RANDY   CB

PERSONAL: Born February 6, 1967, in Metairie, La. ... 5-11/165.
HIGH SCHOOL: East Jefferson (Metairie, La.).
COLLEGE: Northwestern (La.) State.
TRANSACTIONS/CAREER NOTES: Selected by Cleveland Browns in sixth round (157th pick overall) of 1990 NFL draft. ... Signed by Browns (July 22, 1990). ... Granted free agency (February 1, 1992). ... Re-signed by Browns (July 28, 1992). ... Granted free agency (March 1, 1993). ... Re-signed by Browns (July 19, 1993). ... Granted unconditional free agency (February 17, 1994). ... Signed by Denver Broncos (May 16, 1994). ... Granted unconditional free agency (February 16, 1996).
PRO STATISTICS: 1991—Recovered one fumble. 1992—Recovered one fumble.

		INTERCEPTIONS				SACKS
Year Team	G	No.	Yds.	Avg.	TD	No.
1990—Cleveland NFL	15	0	0	...	0	0.0

H

Year Team	G	INTERCEPTIONS				SACKS
		No.	Yds.	Avg.	TD	No.
1991—Cleveland NFL	14	1	19	19.0	0	2.0
1992—Cleveland NFL	16	0	0	...	0	1.0
1993—Cleveland NFL	12	1	54	54.0	0	0.0
1994—Denver NFL	15	2	8	4.0	0	0.0
1995—Denver NFL	12	0	0	...	0	0.0
Pro totals (6 years)	84	4	81	20.3	0	3.0

HINTON, CHRIS G

PERSONAL: Born July 31, 1961, in Chicago. ... 6-4/300. ... Full name: Christopher Jerrod Hinton.
HIGH SCHOOL: Wendell Phillips (Chicago).
COLLEGE: Northwestern (degree in sociology).
TRANSACTIONS/CAREER NOTES: Selected by Chicago Blitz in 1983 USFL territorial draft. ... Selected by Denver Broncos in first round (fourth pick overall) of 1983 NFL draft. ... Rights traded by Broncos with QB Mark Herrmann and first-round pick (OG Ron Solt) in 1984 draft to Baltimore Colts for rights to QB John Elway (May 2, 1983). ... Signed by Colts (May 12, 1983). ... Colts franchise moved to Indianapolis (March 31, 1984). ... On injured reserve with fractured fibula (October 8, 1984-remainder of season). ... Traded by Indianapolis Colts with WR Andre Rison, fifth-round pick (OT Reggie Redding) in 1990 draft and first-round pick (WR Mike Pritchard) in 1991 draft to Atlanta Falcons for first-round (QB Jeff George) and fourth-round (WR Stacey Simmons) picks in 1990 draft (April 20, 1990). ... On reserve/did not report list (July 27-August 28, 1990). ... Granted roster exemption (August 28-30, 1990). ... Designated by Falcons as transition player (February 25, 1993). ... On reserve/did not report list (July 23-August 30, 1993). ... Granted roster exemption (August 30-September 3, 1993). ... Free agency status changed by Falcons from transitional to unconditional (February 17, 1994). ... Signed by Minnesota Vikings (March 1, 1994). ... On injured reserve with knee injury (November 20, 1995-remainder of season). ... Released by Vikings (February 9, 1996).
PLAYING EXPERIENCE: Baltimore NFL, 1983; Indianapolis NFL, 1984-1989; Atlanta NFL, 1990-1993; Minnesota NFL, 1994 and 1995. ... Games: 1983 (16), 1984 (6), 1985 (16), 1986 (16), 1987 (12), 1988 (14), 1989 (14), 1990 (15), 1991 (16), 1992 (16), 1993 (16), 1994 (16), 1995 (4). Total: 177.
HONORS: Named offensive tackle on THE SPORTING NEWS college All-America first team (1982). ... Played in Pro Bowl (1983, 1985-1989 and 1991 seasons). ... Named offensive tackle on THE SPORTING NEWS NFL All-Pro team (1987).
PRO STATISTICS: 1983—Recovered one fumble. 1986—Recovered two fumbles. 1987—Recovered one fumble. 1988—Caught one pass for one yard. 1989—Recovered two fumbles. 1990—Recovered one fumble. 1992—Caught one pass for minus two yards. 1993—Caught one pass for minus eight yards.

HITCHCOCK, JIMMY CB PATRIOTS

PERSONAL: Born November 9, 1971, in Concord, N.C. ... 5-10/188. ... Full name: Jimmy Davis Hitchcock Jr.
HIGH SCHOOL: Concord (N.C.).
COLLEGE: North Carolina.
TRANSACTIONS/CAREER NOTES: Selected by New England Patriots in third round (88th pick overall) of 1995 NFL draft. ... Signed by Patriots (July 19, 1995).
PLAYING EXPERIENCE: New England NFL, 1995. ... Games: 1995 (8).

HOAGE, TERRY S CARDINALS

PERSONAL: Born April 11, 1962, in Ames, Iowa. ... 6-2/201. ... Full name: Terrell Lee Hoage. ... Name pronounced HOGUE.
HIGH SCHOOL: Huntsville (Texas).
COLLEGE: Georgia (degree in genetics, 1984).
TRANSACTIONS/CAREER NOTES: Selected by Jacksonville Bulls in 1984 USFL territorial draft. ... Selected by New Orleans Saints in third round (68th pick overall) of 1984 NFL draft. ... Signed by Saints (July 25, 1984). ... Released by Saints (August 26, 1986). ... Signed by Philadelphia Eagles (September 3, 1986). ... On injured reserve with calf injury (September 15-November 9, 1989). ... On developmental squad (November 9-13, 1989). ... Granted free agency (February 1, 1990). ... Re-signed by Eagles (August 16, 1990). ... Granted unconditional free agency (February 1, 1991). ... Signed by Washington Redskins (March 28, 1991). ... On injured reserve with broken arm (October 1991-January 1992). ... On injured reserve with arm injury (September 1, 1992-entire season). ... Released by Redskins (August 24, 1993). ... Signed by San Francisco 49ers (September 22, 1993). ... Released by 49ers (November 21, 1993). ... Signed by Houston Oilers (December 15, 1993). ... Granted unconditional free agency (February 17, 1994). ... Signed by Arizona Cardinals (June 3, 1994).
CHAMPIONSHIP GAME EXPERIENCE: Member of Super Bowl championship team (1991 season).
HONORS: Named defensive back on THE SPORTING NEWS college All-America first team (1983).
PRO STATISTICS: 1984—Recovered one fumble. 1985—Recovered two fumbles. 1986—Recovered two fumbles. 1987—Recovered two fumbles. 1988—Rushed once for 38 yards and a touchdown. 1994—Recovered two fumbles for four yards. 1995—Recovered two fumbles.

Year Team	G	INTERCEPTIONS				SACKS
		No.	Yds.	Avg.	TD	No.
1984—New Orleans NFL	14	0	0		0	0.0
1985—New Orleans NFL	16	4	79	19.8	†1	1.0
1986—Philadelphia NFL	16	1	18	18.0	0	0.0
1987—Philadelphia NFL	11	2	3	1.5	0	1.0
1988—Philadelphia NFL	16	8	116	14.5	0	2.0
1989—Philadelphia NFL	6	0	0	...	0	0.0
1990—Philadelphia NFL	16	1	0	0.0	0	1.0
1991—Washington NFL	6	0	0	...	0	0.0
1992—Washington NFL			Did not play—injured.			
1993—San Francisco NFL	4	0	0	...	0	0.0
—Houston NFL	3	0	0	...	0	0.0
1994—Arizona NFL	16	3	64	21.3	0	1.0
1995—Arizona NFL	12	2	0	0.0	0	1.0
Pro totals (11 years)	136	21	280	13.3	1	7.0

H

HOARD, LEROY   RB   RAVENS

PERSONAL: Born May 15, 1968, in New Orleans. ... 5-11/225.
HIGH SCHOOL: St. Augustine (New Orleans).
COLLEGE: Michigan.
TRANSACTIONS/CAREER NOTES: Selected after junior season by Cleveland Browns in second round (45th pick overall) of 1990 NFL draft. ... Signed by Browns (July 29, 1990). ... Granted free agency (March 1, 1993). ... Re-signed by Browns (1993). ... On physically unable to perform list with rib injury (July 22-24, 1995). ... On injured reserve with rib injury (December 16, 1995-remainder of season). ... Browns franchise moved to Baltimore and renamed Ravens for 1996 season (March 11, 1996).
HONORS: Played in Pro Bowl (1994 season).
PRO STATISTICS: 1991—Recovered one fumble for four yards. 1992—Recovered one fumble. 1993—Attempted one pass without a completion.
STATISTICAL PLATEAUS: 100-yard rushing games: 1994 (2). ... 100-yard receiving games: 1991 (1).

			RUSHING				RECEIVING				KICKOFF RETURNS				TOTALS		
Year Team	G	Att.	Yds.	Avg.	TD	No.	Yds.	Avg.	TD	No.	Yds.	Avg.	TD	TD	2pt.	Pts.	Fum.
1990—Cleveland NFL	14	58	149	2.6	3	10	73	7.3	0	2	18	9.0	0	3	...	18	6
1991—Cleveland NFL	16	37	154	4.2	2	48	567	11.8	9	0	0	...	0	11	...	66	1
1992—Cleveland NFL	16	54	236	4.4	0	26	310	11.9	1	2	34	17.0	0	1	...	6	3
1993—Cleveland NFL	16	56	227	4.1	0	35	351	10.0	0	13	286	22.0	0	0	...	0	4
1994—Cleveland NFL	16	209	890	4.3	5	45	445	9.9	4	2	30	15.0	0	9	0	54	8
1995—Cleveland NFL	12	136	547	4.0	0	13	103	7.9	0	1	13	13.0	0	0	0	0	5
Pro totals (6 years)	90	550	2203	4.0	10	177	1849	10.5	14	20	381	19.1	0	24	0	144	27

HOBBS, DARYL   WR   RAIDERS

PERSONAL: Born May 23, 1968, in Victoria, Texas ... 6-2/180. ... Full name: Daryl Ray Hobbs.
HIGH SCHOOL: University (Los Angeles).
JUNIOR COLLEGE: Santa Monica (Calif.) College.
COLLEGE: Pacific.
TRANSACTIONS/CAREER NOTES: Signed as non-drafted free agent by Los Angeles Raiders (1992). ... Released by Raiders (August 31, 1992). ... Re-signed by Raiders to practice squad (September 2, 1992). ... Granted free agency after 1992 season. ... Re-signed by Raiders for 1993 season. ... Raiders franchise moved to Oakland (July 21, 1995).
PRO STATISTICS: 1995—Attempted one pass without a completion, returned one punt for 10 yards and returned one kickoff for 20 yards.
STATISTICAL PLATEAUS: 100-yard receiving games: 1995 (1).

		RECEIVING				TOTALS		
Year Team	G	No.	Yds.	Avg.	TD	TD	2pt.	Pts.	Fum.
1992—Los Angeles Raiders NFL				Did not play.					
1993—Los Angeles Raiders NFL	3	0	0	...	0	0	...	0	0
1994—Los Angeles Raiders NFL	10	5	52	10.4	0	0	0	0	0
1995—Oakland NFL	16	38	612	16.1	3	3	0	18	0
Pro totals (3 years)	29	43	664	15.5	3	3	0	18	0

HOBERT, BILLY JOE   QB   RAIDERS

PERSONAL: Born January 8, 1971, in ... 6-3/225.
HIGH SCHOOL: Puyallup (Wash.).
COLLEGE: Washington.
TRANSACTIONS/CAREER NOTES: Selected after junior season by Los Angeles Raiders in third round (58th pick overall) of 1993 NFL draft. ... Raiders franchise moved to Oakland (July 21, 1995).
MISCELLANEOUS: Regular-season record as starting NFL quarterback: 0-2 (.000).

		PASSING								RUSHING				TOTAL		
Year Team	G	Att.	Cmp.	Pct.	Yds.	TD	Int.	Avg.	Rat.	Att.	Yds.	Avg.	TD	TD	2pt.	Pts.
1993—Los Angeles Raiders NFL					Did not play.											
1994—Los Angeles Raiders NFL					Did not play.											
1995—Oakland NFL	4	80	44	55.0	540	6	4	6.75	80.2	3	5	1.7	0	0	0	0

HODSON, TOMMY   QB   SAINTS

PERSONAL: Born January 28, 1967, in Mathews, La. ... 6-3/195. ... Full name: Thomas Paul Hodson.
HIGH SCHOOL: Central Lafourche (Mathews, La.).
COLLEGE: Louisiana State (degree in finance).
TRANSACTIONS/CAREER NOTES: Selected by New England Patriots in third round (59th pick overall) of 1990 NFL draft. ... Signed by Patriots (July 19, 1990). ... On injured reserve with thumb injury (November 10, 1992-remainder of season). ... Granted free agency (March 1, 1993). ... Re-signed by Patriots (July 26, 1993). ... Released by Patriots (August 23, 1993). ... Signed by Miami Dolphins (October 13, 1993). ... Released by Dolphins (November 10, 1993). ... Signed by Dallas Cowboys (November 22, 1994). ... Released by Cowboys (November 29, 1994). ... Signed by New Orleans Saints (April 27, 1995). ... Granted unconditional free agency (February 16, 1996). ... Re-signed by Saints (April 22, 1996).
PRO STATISTICS: 1992—Caught one pass for minus six yards and recovered one fumble.
MISCELLANEOUS: Regular-season record as starting NFL quarterback: 1-11 (.083).

		PASSING								RUSHING				TOTALS		
Year Team	G	Att.	Cmp.	Pct.	Yds.	TD	Int.	Avg.	Rat.	Att.	Yds.	Avg.	TD	TD	2pt.	Pts.
1990—New England NFL	7	156	85	54.5	968	4	5	6.21	68.5	12	79	6.6	0	0	...	0
1991—New England NFL	16	68	36	52.9	345	1	4	5.07	47.7	4	0	0.0	0	0	...	0
1992—New England NFL	9	91	50	55.0	496	2	2	5.45	68.8	5	11	2.2	0	0	...	0
1993—Miami NFL					Did not play.											

H

Year Team	G	Att.	Cmp.	Pct.	Yds.	TD	Int.	Avg.	Rat.	Att.	Yds.	Avg.	TD	TD	2pt.	Pts.
					PASSING					RUSHING				TOTALS		
1994—Dallas NFL							Did not play.									
1995—New Orleans NFL	4	5	3	60.0	14	0	0	2.80	64.6	0	0	...	0	0	0	0
Pro totals (4 years)	36	320	174	54.4	1823	7	11	5.70	64.1	21	90	4.3	0	0	0	0

HOLECEK, JOHN — LB — BILLS

PERSONAL: Born May 7, 1972, in Steger, Ill. ... 6-2/238. ... Name pronounced hol-e-SECK.
HIGH SCHOOL: Marian Catholic (Chicago Heights, Ill.).
COLLEGE: Illinois.
TRANSACTIONS/CAREER NOTES: Selected by Buffalo Bills in fifth round (144th pick overall) of 1995 NFL draft. ... Signed by Bills (June 12, 1995). ... On physically unable to perform list (August 22-November 21, 1995).
PLAYING EXPERIENCE: Buffalo NFL, 1995. ... Games: 1995 (1).

HOLLAND, DARIUS — DT — PACKERS

PERSONAL: Born November 10, 1973, in Petersburg, Va. ... 6-4/305.
HIGH SCHOOL: Mayfield (Las Cruces, N.M.).
COLLEGE: Colorado.
TRANSACTIONS/CAREER NOTES: Selected by Green Bay Packers in third round (65th pick overall) of 1995 NFL draft. ... Signed by Packers (July 18, 1995).
CHAMPIONSHIP GAME EXPERIENCE: Played in NFC championship game (1995 season).

Year Team	G	SACKS
1995—Green Bay NFL	14	1.5

HOLLIDAY, COREY — WR — STEELERS

PERSONAL: Born January 31, 1971, in Richmond, Va. ... 6-2/208. ... Full name: Corey Lamont Holliday.
HIGH SCHOOL: Huguenot (Richmond, Va.).
COLLEGE: North Carolina (degree in business administration).
TRANSACTIONS/CAREER NOTES: Signed as non-drafted free agent by Pittsburgh Steelers (April 29, 1994). ... Released by Steelers (August 22, 1994). ... Re-signed by Steelers to practice squad (November 16, 1994). ... Granted free agency (February 17, 1995). ... Re-signed by Steelers (February 17, 1995). ... Released by Steelers (September 12, 1995). ... Re-signed by Steelers to practice squad (September 14, 1995). ... Released by Steelers (September 22, 1995). ... Re-signed by Steelers (September 23, 1995). ... Released by Steelers (October 3, 1995). ... Re-signed by Steelers to practice squad (October 5, 1995).
PLAYING EXPERIENCE: Pittsburgh NFL, 1995. ... Games: 1995 (3).
CHAMPIONSHIP GAME EXPERIENCE: Played in AFC championship game (1995 season). ... Played in Super Bowl XXX (1995 season).

HOLLIER, DWIGHT — LB — DOLPHINS

PERSONAL: Born April 21, 1969, in Hampton, Va. ... 6-2/250. ... Full name: Dwight Leon Hollier.
HIGH SCHOOL: Kecoughtan (Hampton, Va.).
COLLEGE: North Carolina (degree in speech communications and psychology).
TRANSACTIONS/CAREER NOTES: Selected by Miami Dolphins in fourth round (97th pick overall) of 1992 NFL draft. ... Signed by Dolphins (July 10, 1992). ... Granted free agency (February 17, 1995). ... Re-signed by Dolphins (May 9, 1995).
PLAYING EXPERIENCE: Miami NFL, 1992-1995. ... Games: 1992 (16), 1993 (16), 1994 (11), 1995 (16). Total: 59.
CHAMPIONSHIP GAME EXPERIENCE: Played in AFC championship game (1992 season).
PRO STATISTICS: 1992—Recovered three fumbles and credited with one sack. 1993—Recovered one fumble. 1994—Intercepted one pass for 36 yards. 1995—Recovered one fumble.

HOLLINQUEST, LAMONT — LB — PACKERS

PERSONAL: Born October 24, 1970, in Lynwood, Calif. ... 6-3/243. ... Cousin of Charlie Smith, wide receiver, Philadelphia Eagles and Boston/New Orleans Breakers of USFL (1974-1981, 1983 and 1984).
HIGH SCHOOL: Pius X (Downey, Calif.).
COLLEGE: Southern California.
TRANSACTIONS/CAREER NOTES: Selected by Washington Redskins in eighth round (212th pick overall) of 1993 NFL draft. ... Signed by Redskins (July 15, 1993). ... Claimed on waivers by Cincinnati Bengals (December 21, 1994). ... Released by Bengals (August 21, 1995). ... Signed by Green Bay Packers (January 18, 1996).
PRO STATISTICS: 1994—Credited with ½ sack and recovered one fumble.

Year Team	G	No.	Yds.	Avg.	TD
		INTERCEPTIONS			
1993—Washington NFL	16	0	0	...	0
1994—Washington NFL	14	1	39	39.0	0
1995—		Did not play.			
Pro totals (2 years)	30	1	39	39.0	0

HOLLIS, MIKE — K — JAGUARS

PERSONAL: Born May 22, 1972, in Kellog, Idaho. ... 5-7/180. ... Full name: Michael Shane Hollis.

H

HIGH SCHOOL: Central Valley (Veradale, Wash.).
COLLEGE: Idaho.
TRANSACTIONS/CAREER NOTES: Signed as non-drafted free agent by San Diego Chargers (May 6, 1994). ... Released by Chargers (August 22, 1994). ... Signed by Jacksonville Jaguars (June 5, 1995).

				KICKING				
Year Team	G	XPM	XPA	FGM	FGA	Lg.	50+	Pts.
1995—Jacksonville NFL	16	27	28	20	27	53	2-3	87

HOLMAN, RODNEY   TE

PERSONAL: Born April 20, 1960, in Ypsilanti, Mich. ... 6-3/238. ... Cousin of Preston Pearson, running back, Baltimore Colts, Pittsburgh Steelers and Dallas Cowboys (1967-1980).
HIGH SCHOOL: Ypsilanti (Mich.).
COLLEGE: Tulane (received undergraduate degree, 1981).
TRANSACTIONS/CAREER NOTES: Selected by Cincinnati Bengals in third round (82nd pick overall) of 1982 NFL draft. ... Granted free agency (February 1, 1992). ... Re-signed by Bengals (July 27, 1992). ... Released by Bengals (February 20, 1993). ... Signed by Detroit Lions (March 23, 1993). ... Released by Lions (August 30, 1993). ... Re-signed by Lions (August 31, 1993). ... Granted unconditional free agency (February 17, 1994). ... Re-signed by Lions (July 26, 1994). ... Released by Lions (March 7, 1996).
CHAMPIONSHIP GAME EXPERIENCE: Played in AFC championship game (1988 season). ... Played in Super Bowl XXIII (1988 season).
HONORS: Played in Pro Bowl (1988-1990 seasons).
PRO STATISTICS: 1984—Recovered one fumble. 1985—Recovered one fumble. 1986—Returned one kickoff for 18 yards. 1987—Recovered one fumble. 1988—Recovered one fumble. 1991—Returned one kickoff for 15 yards. 1994—Recovered two fumbles for minus four yards.
STATISTICAL PLATEAUS: 100-yard receiving games: 1986 (1), 1990 (1). Total: 2.

		RECEIVING				TOTALS			
Year Team	G	No.	Yds.	Avg.	TD	TD	2pt.	Pts.	Fum.
1982—Cincinnati NFL	9	3	18	6.0	1	1	...	6	0
1983—Cincinnati NFL	16	2	15	7.5	0	0	...	0	0
1984—Cincinnati NFL	16	21	239	11.4	1	1	...	6	1
1985—Cincinnati NFL	16	38	479	12.6	7	7	...	42	1
1986—Cincinnati NFL	16	40	570	14.3	2	2	...	12	1
1987—Cincinnati NFL	12	28	438	15.6	2	2	...	12	0
1988—Cincinnati NFL	16	39	527	13.5	3	3	...	18	2
1989—Cincinnati NFL	16	50	736	14.7	9	9	...	54	0
1990—Cincinnati NFL	16	40	596	14.9	5	5	...	30	1
1991—Cincinnati NFL	16	31	445	14.4	2	2	...	12	1
1992—Cincinnati NFL	16	26	266	10.2	2	2	...	12	0
1993—Detroit NFL	16	25	244	9.8	2	2	...	12	1
1994—Detroit NFL	15	17	163	9.6	0	0	0	0	1
1995—Detroit NFL	16	5	35	7.0	0	0	0	0	0
Pro totals (14 years)	212	365	4771	13.1	36	36	0	216	9

HOLMBERG, ROB   LB   RAIDERS

PERSONAL: Born May 6, 1971, in Mt. Pleasant, Pa. ... 6-3/230. ... Full name: Robert Anthony Holmberg.
HIGH SCHOOL: Mt. Pleasant (Pa.).
COLLEGE: Penn State.
TRANSACTIONS/CAREER NOTES: Selected by Los Angeles Raiders in seventh round (217th pick overall) of 1994 NFL draft. ... Signed by Raiders (1994). ... Raiders franchise moved to Oakland (July 21, 1995).
PLAYING EXPERIENCE: Los Angeles Raiders NFL, 1994; Oakland NFL, 1995. ... Games: 1994 (16), 1995 (16). Total: 32.
PRO STATISTICS: 1995—Credited with one sack and recovered one fumble.

HOLMES, CLAYTON   CB/KR

PERSONAL: Born August 23, 1969, in Florence, S.C. ... 5-10/181. ... Full name: Clayton Antwan Holmes.
HIGH SCHOOL: Wilson (Florence, S.C.).
JUNIOR COLLEGE: North Greenville College (S.C.).
COLLEGE: Carson-Newman College (Tenn.).
TRANSACTIONS/CAREER NOTES: Selected by Dallas Cowboys in third round (58th pick overall) of 1992 NFL draft. ... Signed by Cowboys (April 26, 1992). ... On injured reserve with knee injury (August 23, 1993-remainder of season). ... Granted free agency (February 17, 1995). ... Re-signed by Cowboys (May 23, 1995). ... On suspended list for violating league substance abuse policy (November 3, 1995-remainder of season). ... Released by Cowboys (February 9, 1996).
CHAMPIONSHIP GAME EXPERIENCE: Played in NFC championship game (1992 and 1994 seasons). ... Member of Super Bowl championship team (1992 season).
PRO STATISTICS: 1992—Recovered one fumble. 1994—Ran three yards with lateral from interception. 1995—Intercepted one pass for no yards and recovered one fumble.

		PUNT RETURNS				KICKOFF RETURNS				TOTALS			
Year Team	G	No.	Yds.	Avg.	TD	No.	Yds.	Avg.	TD	TD	2pt.	Pts.	Fum.
1992—Dallas NFL	15	0	0	...	0	3	70	23.3	0	0	...	0	0
1993—Dallas NFL						Did not play—injured.							
1994—Dallas NFL	16	5	55	11.0	0	4	89	22.3	0	0	0	0	1
1995—Dallas NFL	8	4	35	8.8	0	5	134	26.8	0	0	0	0	1
Pro totals (3 years)	39	9	90	10.0	0	12	293	24.4	0	0	0	0	2

H

HOLMES, DARICK   RB   BILLS

PERSONAL: Born July 1, 1971, in Pasadena, Calif. ... 6-0/226.
HIGH SCHOOL: John Muir (Pasadena, Calif.).
JUNIOR COLLEGE: Sacramento City College.
COLLEGE: Portland State.
TRANSACTIONS/CAREER NOTES: Selected by Buffalo Bills in seventh round (244th pick overall) of 1995 NFL draft. ... Signed by Bills (June 19, 1995).
PRO STATISTICS: 1995—Recovered one fumble.

Year Team	G	RUSHING				RECEIVING				KICKOFF RETURNS				TOTALS			
		Att.	Yds.	Avg.	TD	No.	Yds.	Avg.	TD	No.	Yds.	Avg.	TD	TD	2pt.	Pts.	Fum.
1995—Buffalo NFL	16	172	698	4.1	4	24	214	8.9	0	39	799	20.5	0	4	0	24	4

HOLMES, LESTER   G   EAGLES

PERSONAL: Born September 27, 1969, in Tylertown, Miss. ... 6-3/305.
HIGH SCHOOL: Tylertown (Miss.).
COLLEGE: Jackson State.
TRANSACTIONS/CAREER NOTES: Selected by Philadelphia Eagles in first round (19th pick overall) of 1993 NFL draft. ... Signed by Eagles (August 2, 1993). ... On injured reserve with knee injury (November 28, 1995-remainder of season). ... Granted free agency (February 16, 1996).
PLAYING EXPERIENCE: Philadelphia NFL, 1993-1995. ... Games: 1993 (12), 1994 (16), 1995 (2). Total: 30.
PRO STATISTICS: 1993—Recovered one fumble. 1994—Recovered three fumbles.

HOLT, PIERCE   DL

PERSONAL: Born January 1, 1962, in Marlin, Texas. ... 6-4/275.
HIGH SCHOOL: Lamar (Rosenberg, Texas).
COLLEGE: Angelo State, Texas. (degree in physical education and history, 1988).
TRANSACTIONS/CAREER NOTES: Selected by San Francisco 49ers in second round (39th pick overall) of 1988 NFL draft. ... Signed by 49ers (July 17, 1988). ... On injured reserve with toe injury (August 30-October 24, 1988). ... Designated by 49ers as transition player (February 25, 1993). ... Tendered offer sheet by Atlanta Falcons (March 17, 1993). ... 49ers declined to match offer (March 24, 1993). ... Granted unconditional free agency (February 16, 1996).
CHAMPIONSHIP GAME EXPERIENCE: Played in NFC championship game (1988-1990 and 1992 seasons). ... Member of Super Bowl championship team (1988 and 1989 seasons).
HONORS: Played in Pro Bowl (1992 season).
PRO STATISTICS: 1988—Recovered one fumble. 1989—Recovered one fumble. 1990—Recovered two fumbles. 1994—Recovered one fumble.

Year Team	G	SACKS
1988—San Francisco NFL	9	5.0
1989—San Francisco NFL	16	10.5
1990—San Francisco NFL	16	5.5
1991—San Francisco NFL	13	3.0
1992—San Francisco NFL	16	5.5
1993—Atlanta NFL	16	6.5
1994—Atlanta NFL	12	0.0
1995—Atlanta NFL	11	1.0
Pro totals (8 years)	109	37.0

HOMCO, THOMAS   LB   RAMS

PERSONAL: Born January 8, 1970, in Hammond, Ind. ... 6-1/245. ... Full name: Thomas Ross Homco.
HIGH SCHOOL: Highland (Ind.).
COLLEGE: Northwestern.
TRANSACTIONS/CAREER NOTES: Signed as non-drafted free agent by Los Angeles Rams (April 30, 1992). ... Released by Rams (August 31, 1992). ... Re-signed by Rams to practice squad (September 2, 1992). ... Granted free agency after 1992 season. ... Re-signed by Rams for 1993 season. ... Released by Rams (August 30, 1993). ... Re-signed by Rams (August 31, 1993). ... Rams franchise moved to St. Louis (April 12, 1995). ... On injured reserve with knee injury (November 22, 1995-remainder of season).
PLAYING EXPERIENCE: Los Angeles Rams NFL, 1993 and 1994; St. Louis NFL, 1995. ... Games: 1993 (16), 1994 (15), 1995 (11). Total: 42.
PRO STATISTICS: 1993—Intercepted one pass for six yards.

HOPKINS, BRAD   OT   OILERS

PERSONAL: Born September 5, 1970, in Columbia, S.C. ... 6-3/306.
HIGH SCHOOL: Moline (Ill.).
COLLEGE: Illinois (degree in speech communications, 1993).
TRANSACTIONS/CAREER NOTES: Selected by Houston Oilers in first round (13th pick overall) of 1993 NFL draft. ... Signed by Oilers (August 10, 1993).
PLAYING EXPERIENCE: Houston NFL, 1993-1995. ... Games: 1993 (16), 1994 (16), 1995 (16). Total: 48.
PRO STATISTICS: 1994—Recovered one fumble. 1995—Recovered three fumbles.

H

HORAN, MIKE — P — GIANTS

PERSONAL: Born February 1, 1959, in Orange, Calif. ... 5-11/192. ... Full name: Michael William Horan. ... Name pronounced hor-RAN.
HIGH SCHOOL: Sunny Hills (Fullerton, Calif.).
JUNIOR COLLEGE: Fullerton (Calif.) College.
COLLEGE: Long Beach State (degree in mechanical engineering).
TRANSACTIONS/CAREER NOTES: Selected by Atlanta Falcons in ninth round (235th pick overall) of 1982 NFL draft. ... Released by Falcons (September 4, 1982). ... Signed by Green Bay Packers (March 15, 1983). ... Released by Packers after failing physical (May 6, 1983). ... Signed by Buffalo Bills (May 25, 1983). ... Released by Bills (August 22, 1983). ... Signed by Philadelphia Eagles (May 7, 1984). ... Released by Eagles (August 28, 1986). ... Signed by Minnesota Vikings (October 31, 1986). ... Active for one game with Vikings (1986); did not play. ... Released by Vikings (November 3, 1986). ... Signed by Denver Broncos (November 25, 1986). ... Granted unconditional free agency (February 1-April 1, 1991). ... Re-signed by Broncos for 1991 season. ... Granted unconditional free agency (February 1-April 1, 1992). ... Re-signed by Broncos for 1992 season. ... On injured reserve with knee injury (October 22, 1992-remainder of season). ... Released by Broncos (August 30, 1993). ... Signed by New York Giants (November 9, 1993). ... Granted unconditional free agency (February 16, 1996). ... Re-signed by Giants (May 6, 1996).
CHAMPIONSHIP GAME EXPERIENCE: Played in AFC championship game (1986, 1987, 1989 and 1991 seasons). ... Played in Super Bowl XXI (1986 season), Super Bowl XXII (1987 season) and Super Bowl XXIV (1989 season).
HONORS: Named punter on THE SPORTING NEWS NFL All-Pro team (1988). ... Played in Pro Bowl (1988 season).
POSTSEASON RECORDS: Shares NFL postseason career record for longest punt—76 yards (January 12, 1991, at Buffalo).
PRO STATISTICS: 1985—Rushed once for 12 yards. 1986—Rushed once for no yards, fumbled once and recovered one fumble for minus 12 yards. 1991—Rushed twice for nine yards and recovered one fumble. 1995—Rushed once for no yards, fumbled once and recovered one fumble for minus 18 yards.

			PUNTING				
Year Team	G	No.	Yds.	Avg.	Net avg.	In. 20	Blk.
1984—Philadelphia NFL	16	92	3880	42.2	35.6	21	0
1985—Philadelphia NFL	16	91	3777	41.5	34.2	20	0
1986—Denver NFL	4	13	571	43.9	34.5	8	0
1987—Denver NFL	12	44	1807	41.1	33.1	11	*2
1988—Denver NFL	16	65	2861	44.0	*37.8	19	0
1989—Denver NFL	16	77	3111	40.4	34.3	24	0
1990—Denver NFL	15	58	2575	*44.4	*38.9	14	1
1991—Denver NFL	16	72	3012	41.8	36.7	24	1
1992—Denver NFL	7	37	1681	45.4	40.2	7	1
1993—New York Giants NFL	8	44	1882	42.8	*39.9	13	0
1994—New York Giants NFL	16	85	3521	41.4	35.3	25	*2
1995—New York Giants NFL	16	72	3063	42.5	36.2	15	0
Pro totals (12 years)	158	750	31741	42.3	36.2	201	7

HOSKINS, DERRICK — S — RAIDERS

PERSONAL: Born November 14, 1970, in Meridian, Miss. ... 6-2/200.
HIGH SCHOOL: Neshoba Central (Philadelphia, Miss.).
COLLEGE: Southern Mississippi.
TRANSACTIONS/CAREER NOTES: Selected by Los Angeles Raiders in fifth round (128th pick overall) of 1992 NFL draft. ... Signed by Raiders (1992). ... Raiders franchise moved to Oakland (July 21, 1995).
PRO STATISTICS: 1993—Recovered one fumble. 1994—Recovered one fumble.

		INTERCEPTIONS			
Year Team	G	No.	Yds.	Avg.	TD
1992—Los Angeles Raiders NFL	16	0	0	...	0
1993—Los Angeles Raiders NFL	16	2	34	17.0	0
1994—Los Angeles Raiders NFL	15	0	0	...	0
1995—Oakland NFL	13	1	26	26.0	0
Pro totals (4 years)	60	3	60	20.0	0

HOSTETLER, JEFF — QB — RAIDERS

PERSONAL: Born April 22, 1961, in Hollsopple, Pa. ... 6-3/220. ... Son-in-law of Don Nehlen, head football coach, West Virginia University.
HIGH SCHOOL: Conemaugh Valley (Johnstown, Pa.).
COLLEGE: Penn State, then West Virginia.
TRANSACTIONS/CAREER NOTES: Selected by Pittsburgh Maulers in 1984 USFL territorial draft. ... Selected by New York Giants in third round (59th pick overall) of 1984 NFL draft. ... USFL rights traded by Maulers with rights to CB Dwayne Woodruff to Arizona Wranglers for draft pick (May 2, 1984). ... Signed by Giants (June 12, 1984). ... Active for 16 games with Giants (1984); did not play. ... On injured reserve with pulled hamstring (December 14, 1984-remainder of season). ... On injured reserve with leg injury (December 6, 1986-remainder of season). ... On injured reserve with kidney injury (September 7-November 7, 1987). ... Crossed picket line during players strike (October 14, 1987). ... Active for two games with Giants (1987); did not play. ... Granted free agency (February 1, 1991). ... Re-signed by Giants (July 16, 1991). ... On injured reserve with back injury (December 11, 1991-remainder of season). ... Granted unconditional free agency (March 1, 1993). ... Signed by Los Angeles Raiders (March 24, 1993). ... Raiders franchise moved to Oakland (July 21, 1995). ... Granted free agency (February 16, 1996). ... Re-signed by Raiders (April 2, 1996).
CHAMPIONSHIP GAME EXPERIENCE: Played in NFC championship game (1990 season). ... Member of Super Bowl championship team (1990 season).
HONORS: Played in Pro Bowl (1994 season).
PRO STATISTICS: 1988—Caught one pass for 10 yards, fumbled once and recovered one fumble. 1989—Fumbled twice and recovered one fumble. 1990—Fumbled four times and recovered five fumbles for minus four yards. 1991—Fumbled seven times and recovered six fumbles for minus nine yards. 1992—Fumbled six times. 1993—Fumbled six times and recovered two fumbles for minus one yard. 1994—Fumbled 10 times. 1995—Fumbled five times and recovered one fumble for minus 15 yards.
STATISTICAL PLATEAUS: 300-yard passing games: 1991 (1), 1993 (2), 1994 (3), 1995 (1). Total: 7.

H

MISCELLANEOUS: Regular-season record as starting NFL quarterback: 42-25 (.627).

Year Team	G	Att.	Cmp.	Pct.	Yds.	TD	Int.	Avg.	Rat.	Att.	Yds.	Avg.	TD	TD	2pt.	Pts.
					PASSING						RUSHING				TOTALS	
1984—New York Giants NFL							Did not play.									
1985—New York Giants NFL	5	0	0	...	0	0	0	...	...	0	0	...	0	0	...	0
1986—New York Giants NFL	13	0	0	...	0	0	0	...	...	1	1	1.0	0	0	...	0
1987—New York Giants NFL							Did not play.									
1988—New York Giants NFL	16	29	16	55.2	244	1	2	8.41	65.9	5	-3	-0.6	0	0	...	0
1989—New York Giants NFL	16	39	20	51.3	294	3	2	7.54	80.5	11	71	6.5	2	2	...	12
1990—New York Giants NFL	16	87	47	54.0	614	3	1	7.06	83.2	39	190	4.9	2	2	...	12
1991—New York Giants NFL	12	285	179	62.8	2032	5	4	7.13	84.1	42	273	6.5	2	2	...	12
1992—New York Giants NFL	13	192	103	53.7	1225	8	3	6.38	80.8	35	172	4.9	3	3	...	18
1993—Los Angeles Raiders NFL	15	419	236	56.3	3242	14	10	7.74	82.5	55	202	3.7	5	5	...	30
1994—Los Angeles Raiders NFL	16	455	263	57.8	3334	20	16	7.33	80.8	46	159	3.5	2	2	0	12
1995—Oakland NFL	11	286	172	60.1	1998	12	9	6.99	82.2	31	119	3.8	0	0	0	0
Pro totals (10 years)	133	1792	1036	57.8	12983	66	47	7.25	81.8	265	1184	4.5	16	16	0	96

HOUSTON, BOBBY — LB — JETS

PERSONAL: Born October 26, 1967, in Washington, D.C. ... 6-2/245.
HIGH SCHOOL: DeMatha Catholic (Hyattsville, Md.).
COLLEGE: North Carolina State (degree in accounting).
TRANSACTIONS/CAREER NOTES: Selected by Green Bay Packers in third round (75th pick overall) of 1990 NFL draft. ... Signed by Packers (July 23, 1990). ... On reserve/non-football injury list with pneumonia (September 22-December 19, 1990). ... Claimed on waivers by Atlanta Falcons (December 21, 1990). ... On inactive list for two games with Falcons (1990). ... Granted unconditional free agency (February 1, 1991). ... Signed by New York Jets (March 27, 1991). ... Granted unconditional free agency (February 17, 1995). ... Re-signed by Jets (February 17, 1995).
PRO STATISTICS: 1991—Recovered one fumble. 1993—Recovered one fumble. 1994—Recovered one fumble. 1995—Recovered three fumbles.

Year Team	G	No.	Yds.	Avg.	TD	No.
			INTERCEPTIONS			SACKS
1990—Green Bay NFL	1	0	0	...	0	0.0
1991—New York Jets NFL	15	0	0	...	0	1.0
1992—New York Jets NFL	16	1	20	20.0	1	4.0
1993—New York Jets NFL	16	1	0	0.0	0	3.0
1994—New York Jets NFL	16	0	0	...	0	3.5
1995—New York Jets NFL	16	0	0	...	0	3.0
Pro totals (6 years)	80	2	20	10.0	1	14.5

HOWARD, DANA — LB — RAMS

PERSONAL: Born February 25, 1972, in East St. Louis, Ill. ... 6-0/238.
HIGH SCHOOL: East St. Louis (Ill.).
COLLEGE: Illinois.
TRANSACTIONS/CAREER NOTES: Selected by Dallas Cowboys in fifth round (168th pick overall) of 1995 NFL draft. ... Signed by Cowboys (July 17, 1995). ... Released by Cowboys (August 27, 1995). ... Claimed on waivers by St. Louis Rams (August 28, 1995).
HONORS: Named linebacker on THE SPORTING NEWS college All-America second team (1993). ... Butkus Award winner (1994). ... Named linebacker on THE SPORTING NEWS college All-America first team (1994).
PLAYING EXPERIENCE: St. Louis NFL, 1995. ... Games: 1995 (6).
PRO STATISTICS: 1995—Recovered one fumble.

HOWARD, DESMOND — WR

PERSONAL: Born May 15, 1970, in Cleveland. ... 5-9/180. ... Full name: Desmond Kevin Howard.
HIGH SCHOOL: St. Joseph (Cleveland).
COLLEGE: Michigan (degree in communication studies).
TRANSACTIONS/CAREER NOTES: Selected by Washington Redskins in first round (fourth pick overall) of 1992 NFL draft. ... Signed by Redskins (August 25, 1992). ... On injured reserve with separated shoulder (December 29, 1992-remainder of 1992 season playoffs). ... Selected by Jacksonville Jaguars from Redskins in NFL expansion draft (February 15, 1995). ... Granted unconditional free agency (February 16, 1996).
HONORS: Heisman Trophy winner (1991). ... Named College Football Player of the Year by THE SPORTING NEWS (1991). ... Maxwell Award winner (1991). ... Named wide receiver on THE SPORTING NEWS college All-America first team (1991).
PRO STATISTICS: 1992—Fumbled once.
STATISTICAL PLATEAUS: 100-yard receiving games: 1994 (2).

Year Team	G	Att.	Yds.	Avg.	TD	No.	Yds.	Avg.	TD	No.	Yds.	Avg.	TD	No.	Yds.	Avg.	TD	TD	2pt.	Pts.
		RUSHING				RECEIVING				PUNT RETURNS				KICKOFF RETURNS				TOTALS		
1992—Washington NFL	16	3	14	4.7	0	3	20	6.7	0	6	84	14.0	1	22	462	21.0	0	1	...	6
1993—Washington NFL	16	2	17	8.5	0	23	286	12.4	0	4	25	6.3	0	21	405	19.3	0	0	...	0
1994—Washington NFL	16	1	4	4.0	0	40	727	18.2	5	0	0	...	0	0	0	...	0	5	1	32
1995—Jacksonville NFL	13	1	8	8.0	0	26	276	10.6	1	24	246	10.3	0	10	178	17.8	0	1	0	6
Pro totals (4 years)	61	7	43	6.2	0	92	1309	14.2	6	34	355	10.5	1	53	1045	19.7	0	7	1	44

H

HOWARD, ERIK — DT/DE — JETS

PERSONAL: Born November 12, 1964, in Pittsfield, Mass. ... 6-4/275.

HIGH SCHOOL: Bellarmine College Prep (San Jose, Calif.).
COLLEGE: Washington State.
TRANSACTIONS/CAREER NOTES: Selected by New York Giants in second round (46th pick overall) of 1986 NFL draft. ... Selected by Baltimore Stars in first round (seventh pick overall) of 1986 USFL draft. ... Signed by Giants (July 30, 1986). ... On injured reserve with hand injury (October 9-December 6, 1986). ... Granted free agency (February 1, 1990). ... Re-signed by Giants (August 22, 1990). ... On injured reserve with back injury (September 26-December 8, 1991). ... Granted free agency (February 1, 1992). ... Re-signed by Giants (August 26, 1992). ... Granted roster exemption (August 26-September 5, 1992). ... Granted unconditional free agency (February 17, 1995). ... Signed by New York Jets (April 23, 1995).
CHAMPIONSHIP GAME EXPERIENCE: Played in NFC championship game (1986 and 1990 seasons). ... Member of Super Bowl championship team (1986 and 1990 seasons).
HONORS: Played in Pro Bowl (1990 season).
PRO STATISTICS: 1987—Recovered one fumble. 1988—Recovered two fumbles. 1989—Recovered one fumble. 1991—Recovered one fumble. 1992—Recovered three fumbles for seven yards. 1994—Recovered one fumble. 1995—Recovered one fumble.

Year Team	G	SACKS
1986—New York Giants NFL	8	2.0
1987—New York Giants NFL	12	5.5
1988—New York Giants NFL	16	3.0
1989—New York Giants NFL	16	5.5
1990—New York Giants NFL	16	3.0
1991—New York Giants NFL	6	1.5
1992—New York Giants NFL	16	0.0
1993—New York Giants NFL	16	3.5
1994—New York Giants NFL	16	6.5
1995—New York Jets NFL	16	2.5
Pro totals (10 years)	138	33.0

HUDSON, CHRIS   S   JAGUARS

PERSONAL: Born October 6, 1971, in Houston. ... 5-10/203.
HIGH SCHOOL: E.E. Worthing (Houston).
COLLEGE: Colorado.
TRANSACTIONS/CAREER NOTES: Selected by Jacksonville Jaguars in third round (71st pick overall) of 1995 NFL draft. ... Signed by Jaguars (June 1, 1995). ... On injured reserve with groin injury (September 28, 1995-remainder of season).
PLAYING EXPERIENCE: Jacksonville NFL, 1995. ... Games: 1995 (1).
HONORS: Jim Thorpe Award winner (1994).

HUDSON, JOHN   C/G   JETS

PERSONAL: Born January 29, 1968, in Memphis. ... 6-2/276. ... Full name: John Lewis Hudson.
HIGH SCHOOL: Henry County (Paris, Tenn.).
COLLEGE: Auburn.
TRANSACTIONS/CAREER NOTES: Selected by Philadelphia Eagles in 11th round (294th pick overall) of 1990 NFL draft. ... Signed by Eagles (July 31, 1990). ... On physically unable to perform list with knee laceration (August 2, 1990-entire season). ... Granted unconditional free agency (February 1-April 1, 1992). ... Re-signed by Eagles (July 23, 1992). ... On injured reserve with broken hand (September 28, 1992-remainder of season). ... Granted free agency (March 1, 1993). ... Re-signed by Eagles (May 12, 1993). ... Granted unconditional free agency (February 17, 1994). ... Re-signed by Eagles (April 7, 1994). ... Granted unconditional free agency (February 16, 1996). ... Signed by New York Jets (February 26, 1996).
PLAYING EXPERIENCE: Philadelphia NFL, 1991-1995. ... Games: 1991 (16), 1992 (3), 1993 (16), 1994 (16), 1995 (16). Total: 67.
PRO STATISTICS: 1991—Fumbled once. 1993—Fumbled once.

HUGHES, DANAN   WR/KR   CHIEFS

PERSONAL: Born December 11, 1970, in Bayonne, N.J. ... 6-2/211. ... Full name: Robert Danan Hughes. ... Name pronounced DAY-nin.
HIGH SCHOOL: Bayonne (N.J.).
COLLEGE: Iowa (degree in communications).
TRANSACTIONS/CAREER NOTES: Selected by Kansas City Chiefs in seventh round (186th pick overall) of 1993 NFL draft. ... Signed by Chiefs (May 27, 1993). ... Released by Chiefs (September 6, 1993). ... Re-signed by Chiefs to practice squad (September 8, 1993). ... Activated (November 17, 1993). ... Granted free agency (February 16, 1996). ... Re-signed by Chiefs (May 6, 1996).
CHAMPIONSHIP GAME EXPERIENCE: Played in AFC championship game (1993 season).
PRO STATISTICS: 1995—Rushed once for five yards.

		RECEIVING				PUNT RETURNS				KICKOFF RETURNS				TOTALS		
Year Team	G	No.	Yds.	Avg.	TD	No.	Yds.	Avg.	TD	No.	Yds.	Avg.	TD	TD	2pt.	Pts. Fum.
1993—Kansas City NFL	6	0	0	...	0	3	49	16.3	0	14	266	19.0	0	0	...	0 0
1994—Kansas City NFL	16	7	80	11.4	0	27	192	7.1	0	9	190	21.1	0	0	0	0 0
1995—Kansas City NFL	16	14	103	7.4	1	3	9	3.0	0	1	18	18.0	0	1	0	6 0
Pro totals (3 years)	38	21	183	8.7	1	33	250	7.6	0	24	474	19.8	0	1	0	6 0

HUGHES, TYRONE   CB/KR   SAINTS

PERSONAL: Born January 14, 1970, in New Orleans. ... 5-9/175. ... Full name: Tyrone Christopher Hughes.
HIGH SCHOOL: St. Augustine (New Orleans).
COLLEGE: Nebraska.
TRANSACTIONS/CAREER NOTES: Selected by New Orleans Saints in fifth round (137th pick overall) of 1993 NFL draft. ... Signed by Saints (July 16, 1993).

H

HONORS: Played in Pro Bowl (1993 season).
RECORDS: Holds NFL single-season record for most yards by kickoff return—1,617 (1995). ... Holds NFL single-game records for most yards by kickoff return—304; and most yards by combined kick return—347 (October 23, 1994, vs. Los Angeles Rams). ... Shares NFL single-game records for most touchdowns by kickoff return—2; and most touchdowns by combined kick return—2 (October 23, 1994, vs. Los Angeles Rams).
PRO STATISTICS: 1994—Rushed twice for six yards and recovered three fumbles for 128 yards and two touchdowns.

			INTERCEPTIONS				PUNT RETURNS				KICKOFF RETURNS				TOTALS			
Year	Team	G	No.	Yds.	Avg.	TD	No.	Yds.	Avg.	TD	No.	Yds.	Avg.	TD	TD	2pt.	Pts.	Fum.
1993—New Orleans NFL		16	0	0	...	0	37	*503	*13.6	†2	30	753	25.1	†1	3	...	18	0
1994—New Orleans NFL		15	2	31	15.5	0	21	143	6.8	0	*63	*1556	24.7	2	4	0	24	7
1995—New Orleans NFL		16	2	19	9.5	0	28	262	9.4	0	*66	*1617	24.5	0	0	0	0	2
Pro totals (3 years)		47	4	50	12.5	0	86	908	10.6	2	159	3926	24.7	3	7	0	42	9

HULL, KENT   C   BILLS

PERSONAL: Born January 13, 1961, in Pontotoc, Miss. ... 6-5/278. ... Full name: James Kent Hull.
HIGH SCHOOL: Greenwood (Miss.).
COLLEGE: Mississippi State (degree in business administration, 1984).
TRANSACTIONS/CAREER NOTES: Selected by New Jersey Generals in seventh round (75th pick overall) of 1983 USFL draft. ... Signed by Generals (January 19, 1983). ... Granted free agency when USFL suspended operations (August 7, 1986). ... Signed by Buffalo Bills (August 18, 1986). ... Granted roster exemption (August 18-22, 1986). ... On physically unable to perform list (July 16-September 24, 1993).
PLAYING EXPERIENCE: New Jersey USFL, 1983-1985; Buffalo NFL, 1986-1995. ... Games: 1983 (18), 1984 (18), 1985 (18), 1986 (16), 1987 (12), 1988 (16), 1989 (16), 1990 (16), 1991 (16), 1992 (14), 1994 (16), 1995 (16). Total USFL: 54. Total NFL: 154. Total Pro: 208.
CHAMPIONSHIP GAME EXPERIENCE: Played in AFC championship game (1988 and 1990-1993 seasons). ... Played in Super Bowl XXV (1990 season), Super Bowl XXVI (1991 season), Super Bowl XXVII (1992 season) and Super Bowl XXVIII (1993 season).
HONORS: Named center on THE SPORTING NEWS USFL All-Star team (1985). ... Played in Pro Bowl (1988-1990 seasons). ... Named center on THE SPORTING NEWS NFL All-Pro team (1989 and 1990).
PRO STATISTICS: 1989—Recovered two fumbles. 1991—Recovered one fumble. 1992—Recovered two fumbles. 1994—Fumbled once. 1995—Fumbled once and recovered one fumble for minus one yard.

HUMPHREY, RONALD   RB/KR   COLTS

PERSONAL: Born March 3, 1969, in Marland, Texas. ... 5-10/211. ... Full name: Ronald Lynn Humphrey.
HIGH SCHOOL: Forest Brook (Houston).
COLLEGE: Mississippi Valley State.
TRANSACTIONS/CAREER NOTES: Selected by Indianapolis Colts in eighth round (212th pick overall) of 1992 NFL draft. ... Signed by Colts (July 22, 1992). ... Released by Colts (August 25, 1992). ... Re-signed by Colts to practice squad (September 2, 1992). ... Granted free agency after 1992 season. ... Re-signed by Colts (February 4, 1993). ... On injured reserve with hand injury (August 30, 1993-entire season). ... Granted free agency (February 16, 1996).
CHAMPIONSHIP GAME EXPERIENCE: Played in AFC championship game (1995 season).

			RUSHING				RECEIVING				KICKOFF RETURNS				TOTALS		
Year	Team	G	Att.	Yds.	Avg.	TD	No.	Yds.	Avg.	TD	No.	Yds.	Avg.	TD	TD	2pt.	Pts. Fum.
1992—Indianapolis NFL							Did not play.										
1993—Indianapolis NFL							Did not play—injured.										
1994—Indianapolis NFL		15	18	85	4.7	0	3	19	6.3	0	35	783	22.4	1	1	0	6 4
1995—Indianapolis NFL		11	2	6	3.0	0	2	11	5.5	0	21	453	21.6	0	0	0	0 1
Pro totals (2 years)		26	20	91	4.6	0	5	30	6.0	0	56	1236	22.1	1	1	0	6 5

HUMPHRIES, STAN   QB   CHARGERS

PERSONAL: Born April 14, 1965, in Shreveport, La. ... 6-2/223. ... Full name: William Stanley Humphries.
HIGH SCHOOL: Southwood (Shreveport, La.).
COLLEGE: Louisiana State, then Northeast Louisiana.
TRANSACTIONS/CAREER NOTES: Selected by Washington Redskins in sixth round (159th pick overall) of 1988 NFL draft. ... Signed by Redskins (July 13, 1988). ... On non-football injury list with blood disorder (September 3, 1988-entire season). ... On injured reserve with sprained knee (November 17, 1990-January 11, 1991). ... Active for two games (1991); did not play. ... Traded by Redskins to San Diego Chargers for third-round pick (P Ed Bunn) in 1993 draft (August 13, 1992).
CHAMPIONSHIP GAME EXPERIENCE: Member of Redskins for NFC championship game (1991 season); inactive. ... Member of Super Bowl championship team (1991 season). ... Played in AFC championship game (1994 season). ... Played in Super Bowl XXIX (1994 season).
RECORDS: Shares NFL record for longest pass completion (to Tony Martin)—99 yards, touchdown (September 18, 1994, at Seattle).
PRO STATISTICS: 1989—Fumbled once and recovered one fumble. 1992—Fumbled nine times and recovered three fumbles. 1993—Fumbled twice and recovered one fumble. 1994—Fumbled six times and recovered two fumbles for minus nine yards. 1995—Caught one pass for minus four yards, fumbled nine times and recovered seven fumbles for minus 11 yards.
STATISTICAL PLATEAUS: 300-yard passing games: 1992 (1), 1994 (1), 1995 (2). Total: 4.
MISCELLANEOUS: Regular-season record as starting NFL quarterback: 40-20 (.667).

			PASSING									RUSHING				TOTALS		
Year	Team	G	Att.	Cmp.	Pct.	Yds.	TD	Int.	Avg.	Rat.	Att.	Yds.	Avg.	TD	TD	2pt.	Pts.
1988—Washington NFL							Did not play.										
1989—Washington NFL		2	10	5	50.0	91	1	1	9.10	75.4	5	10	2.0	0	0	...	0
1990—Washington NFL		7	156	91	58.3	1015	3	10	6.51	57.5	23	106	4.6	2	2	...	12
1991—Washington NFL							Did not play.										
1992—San Diego NFL		16	454	263	57.9	3356	16	18	7.39	76.4	28	79	2.8	4	4	...	24
1993—San Diego NFL		12	324	173	53.4	1981	12	10	6.12	71.5	8	37	4.6	0	0	...	0
1994—San Diego NFL		15	453	264	58.3	3209	17	12	7.08	81.6	19	19	1.0	0	0	0	0
1995—San Diego NFL		15	478	282	59.0	3381	17	14	7.07	80.4	33	53	1.6	1	1	0	6
Pro totals (6 years)		67	1875	1078	57.5	13033	66	65	6.95	76.2	116	304	2.6	7	7	0	42

HUNTER, EARNEST   RB/KR   RAVENS

PERSONAL: Born December 21, 1970, in Longview, Texas. ... 5-8/201.
HIGH SCHOOL: Longview (Texas).
JUNIOR COLLEGE: Navarro College (Texas).
COLLEGE: Southeastern Oklahoma State.
TRANSACTIONS/CAREER NOTES: Signed as non-drafted free agent by Cleveland Browns (May 2, 1995). ... Browns franchise moved to Baltimore and renamed Ravens for 1996 season (March 11, 1996).
PRO STATISTICS: 1995—Fumbled four times.

		RUSHING				RECEIVING				PUNT RETURNS				KICKOFF RETURNS				TOTALS		
Year Team	G	Att.	Yds.	Avg.	TD	No.	Yds.	Avg.	TD	No.	Yds.	Avg.	TD	No.	Yds.	Avg.	TD	TD	2pt.	Pts.
1995—Cleveland NFL	10	30	100	3.3	0	5	42	8.4	0	3	40	13.3	0	23	508	22.1	0	0	0	0

HUNTER, PATRICK   CB

PERSONAL: Born October 24, 1964, in San Francisco. ... 5-11/186. ... Full name: Patrick Edward Hunter. ... Cousin of Louis Wright, cornerback, Denver Broncos (1975-1986).
HIGH SCHOOL: South San Francisco.
COLLEGE: Nevada.
TRANSACTIONS/CAREER NOTES: Selected by Seattle Seahawks in third round (68th pick overall) of 1986 NFL draft. ... Signed by Seahawks (July 16, 1986). ... On non-football injury list with lacerated kidney (November 1-December 10, 1988). ... Granted free agency (February 1, 1990). ... Re-signed by Seahawks (July 18, 1990). ... Granted unconditional free agency (February 17, 1995). ... Signed by Arizona Cardinals (March 20, 1995). ... On injured reserve with knee injury (November 8, 1995-remainder of season). ... Released by Cardinals (March 21, 1996).
PRO STATISTICS: 1988—Returned one punt for no yards and fumbled once. 1989—Credited with one sack. 1990—Recovered one fumble for 13 yards. 1992—Recovered one fumble for two yards. 1993—Recovered three fumbles.

		INTERCEPTIONS			
Year Team	G	No.	Yds.	Avg.	TD
1986—Seattle NFL	16	0	0	...	0
1987—Seattle NFL	11	1	3	3.0	0
1988—Seattle NFL	10	0	0	...	0
1989—Seattle NFL	16	0	0	...	0
1990—Seattle NFL	16	1	0	0.0	0
1991—Seattle NFL	15	1	32	32.0	1
1992—Seattle NFL	16	2	0	0.0	0
1993—Seattle NFL	15	4	54	13.5	0
1994—Seattle NFL	5	3	85	28.3	0
1995—Arizona NFL	5	2	21	10.5	0
Pro totals (10 years)	125	14	195	13.9	1

HUNTER, TOREY   CB   OILERS

PERSONAL: Born February 10, 1972, in Tacoma, Wash. ... 5-9/176. ... Full name: Torey Hayward Hunter.
HIGH SCHOOL: Curtis (Tacoma, Wash.).
COLLEGE: Washington State.
TRANSACTIONS/CAREER NOTES: Selected by Houston Oilers in third round (95th pick overall) of 1995 NFL draft. ... Signed by Oilers (June 30, 1995). ... Assigned by Oilers to Amsterdam Admirals in 1996 World League enhancement allocation program (February 19, 1996).
PLAYING EXPERIENCE: Houston NFL, 1995. ... Games: 1995 (12).

HUNTINGTON, GREG   G   JAGUARS

PERSONAL: Born September 22, 1970, in Mountain Brook, Ala. ... 6-3/293. ... Full name: Gregory Gerard Huntington.
HIGH SCHOOL: Moeller (Cincinnati).
COLLEGE: Penn State.
TRANSACTIONS/CAREER NOTES: Selected by Washington Redskins in fifth round (128th pick overall) of 1993 NFL draft. ... Signed by Redskins for 1993 season. ... Released by Redskins (August 28, 1994). ... Signed by Jacksonville Jaguars (December 15, 1994). ... Released by Jaguars (November 21, 1995). ... Re-signed by Jaguars (December 26, 1995).
PLAYING EXPERIENCE: Washington NFL, 1993; Jacksonville NFL, 1995. ... Games: 1993 (9), 1995 (4). Total: 13.

HURST, MAURICE   CB

PERSONAL: Born September 17, 1967, in New Orleans. ... 5-10/185. ... Full name: Maurice Roy Hurst.
HIGH SCHOOL: Fortier (New Orleans).
COLLEGE: Southern (La.).
TRANSACTIONS/CAREER NOTES: Selected by New England Patriots in fourth round (96th pick overall) of 1989 NFL draft. ... Signed by Patriots (July 19, 1989). ... Granted free agency (February 1, 1991). ... Re-signed by Patriots (August 23, 1991). ... Activated (August 30, 1991). ... Granted free agency (March 1, 1993). ... Re-signed by Patriots (August 11, 1993). ... Designated by Patriots as transition player (February 15, 1994). ... Released by Patriots (November 20, 1995). ... Claimed on waivers by St. Louis Rams (November 21, 1995). ... Released by Rams after failing physical (November 23, 1995).
PRO STATISTICS: 1989—Returned one punt for six yards. 1990—Fumbled once.

		INTERCEPTIONS				SACKS
Year Team	G	No.	Yds.	Avg.	TD	No.
1989—New England NFL	16	5	31	6.2	1	0.0

H

Year Team	G	INTERCEPTIONS				SACKS
		No.	Yds.	Avg.	TD	No.
1990—New England NFL	16	4	61	15.3	0	0.0
1991—New England NFL	15	3	21	7.0	0	0.0
1992—New England NFL	16	3	29	9.7	0	0.0
1993—New England NFL	16	4	53	13.3	0	1.0
1994—New England NFL	16	7	68	9.7	0	2.0
1995—New England NFL	10	1	0	0.0	0	0.0
Pro totals (7 years)	105	27	263	9.8	1	3.0

HUSTED, MICHAEL K BUCCANEERS

PERSONAL: Born June 16, 1970, in El Paso, Texas. ... 6-0/195. ... Full name: Michael James Husted.
HIGH SCHOOL: Hampton (Va.).
COLLEGE: Virginia (degree in sociology).
TRANSACTIONS/CAREER NOTES: Signed as non-drafted free agent by Tampa Bay Buccaneers (May 3, 1993). ... Granted free agency (February 16, 1996). ... Tendered offer sheet by San Francisco 49ers (February 21, 1996). ... Offer matched by Buccaneers (February 28, 1996).
PRO STATISTICS: 1994—Punted twice for 53 yards.

Year Team	G	KICKING						
		XPM	XPA	FGM	FGA	Lg.	50+	Pts.
1993—Tampa Bay NFL	16	27	27	16	22	57	3-5	75
1994—Tampa Bay NFL	16	20	20	23	35	53	1-5	89
1995—Tampa Bay NFL	16	25	25	19	26	53	3-3	82
Pro totals (3 years)	48	72	72	58	83	57	7-13	246

HUTTON, TOM P EAGLES

PERSONAL: Born July 8, 1972, in Memphis. ... 6-1/193. ... Full name: William Thomas Hutton.
HIGH SCHOOL: Memphis University.
COLLEGE: Tennessee.
TRANSACTIONS/CAREER NOTES: Signed as non-drafted free agent by Philadelphia Eagles (April 26, 1995).
PRO STATISTICS: 1995—Rushed once for no yards and fumbled once for minus 19 yards.

Year Team	G	PUNTING					
		No.	Yds.	Avg.	Net avg.	In. 20	Blk.
1995—Philadelphia NFL	16	85	3682	43.3	33.7	20	1

INGRAM, MARK WR

PERSONAL: Born August 23, 1965, in Rockford, Ill. ... 5-11/194. ... Cousin of Steve Atwater, safety, Denver Broncos.
HIGH SCHOOL: Northwestern (Flint, Mich.).
COLLEGE: Michigan State.
TRANSACTIONS/CAREER NOTES: Selected by New York Giants in first round (28th pick overall) of 1987 NFL draft. ... Signed by Giants (July 31, 1987). ... On injured reserve with broken collarbone (September 26-December 3, 1988). ... Granted free agency (February 1, 1991). ... Re-signed by Giants (August 29, 1991). ... Activated (September 2, 1991). ... On injured reserve with knee injury (November 3-December 6, 1992). ... Granted unconditional free agency (March 1, 1993). ... Signed by Miami Dolphins (March 18, 1993). ... Traded by Dolphins to Green Bay Packers for fourth-round pick (traded to Green Bay) in 1995 draft (March 21, 1995). ... Granted unconditional free agency (February 16, 1996).
CHAMPIONSHIP GAME EXPERIENCE: Played in NFC championship game (1990 and 1995 seasons). ... Member of Super Bowl championship team (1990 season).
PRO STATISTICS: 1989—Rushed once for one yard and recovered two fumbles. 1990—Rushed once for four yards. 1991— Attempted one pass without a completion, returned eight punts for 49 yards and recovered one fumble. 1992—Recovered one fumble. 1993—Recovered one fumble. 1994—Recovered one fumble. 1995—Rushed once for minus three yards and returned one punt for no yards.
STATISTICAL PLATEAUS: 100-yard receiving games: 1991 (2), 1993 (1), 1994 (1). Total: 4.

Year Team	G	RECEIVING				KICKOFF RETURNS				TOTALS			
		No.	Yds.	Avg.	TD	No.	Yds.	Avg.	TD	TD	2pt.	Pts.	Fum.
1987—New York Giants NFL	9	2	32	16.0	0	6	114	19.0	0	0	...	0	0
1988—New York Giants NFL	7	13	158	12.2	1	8	129	16.1	0	1	...	6	0
1989—New York Giants NFL	16	17	290	17.1	1	22	332	15.1	0	1	...	6	2
1990—New York Giants NFL	16	26	499	19.2	5	3	42	14.0	0	5	...	30	1
1991—New York Giants NFL	16	51	824	16.2	3	8	125	15.6	0	3	...	18	3
1992—New York Giants NFL	12	27	408	15.1	1	0	0	...	0	1	...	6	0
1993—Miami NFL	16	44	707	16.1	6	0	0	...	0	6	...	36	3
1994—Miami NFL	15	44	506	11.5	6	1	0	0.0	0	6	0	36	1
1995—Green Bay NFL	16	39	469	12.0	3	0	0	...	0	3	0	18	1
Pro totals (9 years)	123	263	3893	14.8	26	48	742	15.5	0	26	0	156	11

INGRAM, STEPHEN OT/G BUCCANEERS

PERSONAL: Born May 8, 1971, in Seat Pleasant, Md. ... 6-4/311.
HIGH SCHOOL: DuVal (Seat Pleasant, Md.).
COLLEGE: Maryland.
TRANSACTIONS/CAREER NOTES: Selected by Tampa Bay Buccaneers in seventh round (215th pick overall) of 1995 NFL draft. ... Signed by Buccaneers (May 3, 1995).
PLAYING EXPERIENCE: Tampa Bay NFL, 1995. ... Games: 1995 (2).

IRELAND, DARWIN   LB

PERSONAL: Born May 26, 1971, in Pine Bluff, Ark. ... 5-11/240.
HIGH SCHOOL: Dollarway (Pine Bluff, Ark.).
COLLEGE: Arkansas.
TRANSACTIONS/CAREER NOTES: Signed as non-drafted free agent by Chicago Bears (April 28, 1994). ... Released by Bears (August 23, 1994). ... Re-signed by Bears to practice squad (August 30, 1994). ... Activated (October 7, 1994). ... Released by Bears (October 10, 1994). ... Re-signed by Bears to practice squad (October 11, 1994). ... Activated (October 28, 1994). ... Released by Bears (November 17, 1994). ... Re-signed by Bears to practice squad (November 21, 1994). ... Granted free agency after 1994 season. ... Re-signed by Bears (March 2, 1995). ... Released by Bears (August 27, 1995). ... Re-signed by Bears to practice squad (August 29, 1995). ... Activated (September 9, 1995). ... On injured reserve with hamstring injury (September 12-November 29, 1995). ... Released by Bears (November 29, 1995).
PLAYING EXPERIENCE: Chicago NFL, 1994 and 1995. ... Games: 1994 (2), 1995 (1). Total: 3.

IRVIN, KEN   CB   BILLS

PERSONAL: Born July 11, 1972, in Lindale, Ga. ... 5-10/182.
HIGH SCHOOL: Pepperell (Lindale, Ga.).
COLLEGE: Memphis.
TRANSACTIONS/CAREER NOTES: Selected by Buffalo Bills in fourth round (109th pick overall) of 1995 NFL draft. ... Signed by Bills (July 10, 1995).
PLAYING EXPERIENCE: Buffalo NFL, 1995. ... Games: 1995 (16).
PRO STATISTICS: 1995—Returned one kickoff for 12 yards.

IRVIN, MICHAEL   WR   COWBOYS

PERSONAL: Born March 5, 1966, in Fort Lauderdale. ... 6-2/205. ... Full name: Michael Jerome Irvin.
HIGH SCHOOL: St. Thomas Aquinas (Fort Lauderdale).
COLLEGE: Miami, Fla. (degree in business management, 1988).
TRANSACTIONS/CAREER NOTES: Selected by Dallas Cowboys in first round (11th pick overall) of 1988 NFL draft. ... Signed by Cowboys (July 9, 1988). ... On injured reserve with knee injury (October 17, 1989-remainder of season). ... On injured reserve with knee injury (September 4-October 7, 1990). ... Granted free agency (February 1, 1992). ... Re-signed by Cowboys (September 3, 1992). ... Designated by Cowboys as transition player (February 25, 1993).
CHAMPIONSHIP GAME EXPERIENCE: Played in NFC championship game (1992-1995 seasons). ... Member of Super Bowl championship team (1992, 1993 and 1995 seasons).
HONORS: Named wide receiver on THE SPORTING NEWS college All-America second team (1986). ... Named wide receiver on THE SPORTING NEWS NFL All-Pro team (1991). ... Played in Pro Bowl (1991-1995 seasons). ... Named Outstanding Player of Pro Bowl (1991 season).
RECORDS: Holds NFL single-season record for most games with 100 or more yards receiving—11 (1995). ... Shares NFL record for most consecutive games with 100 or more yards receiving—7 (1995).
PRO STATISTICS: 1988—Rushed once for two yards. 1989—Rushed once for six yards and recovered one fumble. 1991—Recovered one fumble. 1992—Rushed once for minus nine yards and recovered one fumble. 1993—Rushed twice for six yards.
STATISTICAL PLATEAUS: 100-yard receiving games: 1988 (1), 1989 (1), 1991 (7), 1992 (6), 1993 (5), 1994 (5), 1995 (11). Total: 36.
MISCELLANEOUS: Holds Dallas Cowboys all-time record for most yards receiving (8,538 yards).

| | | RECEIVING | | | | TOTALS | | | |
Year Team	G	No.	Yds.	Avg.	TD	TD	2pt.	Pts.	Fum.
1988—Dallas NFL	14	32	654	20.4	5	5	...	30	0
1989—Dallas NFL	6	26	378	14.5	2	2	...	12	0
1990—Dallas NFL	12	20	413	20.7	5	5	...	30	0
1991—Dallas NFL	16	93	*1523	16.4	8	8	...	48	3
1992—Dallas NFL	16	78	1396	17.9	7	7	...	42	1
1993—Dallas NFL	16	88	1330	15.1	7	7	...	42	0
1994—Dallas NFL	16	79	1241	15.7	6	6	0	36	0
1995—Dallas NFL	16	111	1603	14.4	10	10	0	60	1
Pro totals (8 years)	112	527	8538	16.2	50	50	0	300	5

IRVING, TERRY   LB   CARDINALS

PERSONAL: Born July 3, 1971, in Galveston, Texas. ... 6-0/224. ... Full name: Terry Duane Irving.
HIGH SCHOOL: Ball (Galveston, Texas).
COLLEGE: McNeese State.
TRANSACTIONS/CAREER NOTES: Selected by Arizona Cardinals in fourth round (115th pick overall) of 1994 NFL draft. ... Signed by Cardinals (July 15, 1994).
PLAYING EXPERIENCE: Arizona NFL, 1994 and 1995. ... Games: 1994 (16), 1995 (16). Total: 32.
PRO STATISTICS: 1994—Recovered one fumble. 1995—Credited with one sack and recovered three fumbles for minus two yards.

ISMAIL, QADRY   WR/KR   VIKINGS

PERSONAL: Born November 8, 1970, in Newark, N.J. ... 6-0/196. ... Full name: Qadry Rahmadan Ismail. ... Brother of Rocket Ismail, wide receiver/kick returner, Los Angeles Raiders. ... Name pronounced KAH-dree ISS-mile.
HIGH SCHOOL: Elmer L. Meyers (Wilkes-Barre, Pa.).
COLLEGE: Syracuse.
TRANSACTIONS/CAREER NOTES: Selected by Minnesota Vikings in second round (52nd pick overall) of 1993 NFL draft. ... Signed by Vikings (July 20, 1993).

HONORS: Named kick returner on THE SPORTING NEWS college All-America second team (1991).
PRO STATISTICS: 1994—Recovered one fumble.
STATISTICAL PLATEAUS: 100-yard receiving games: 1994 (2), 1995 (1). Total: 3.

Year Team	G	RUSHING				RECEIVING				KICKOFF RETURNS				TOTALS			
		Att.	Yds.	Avg.	TD	No.	Yds.	Avg.	TD	No.	Yds.	Avg.	TD	TD	2pt.	Pts.	Fum.
1993—Minnesota NFL	15	3	14	4.7	0	19	212	11.2	1	42	902	21.5	0	1	...	6	1
1994—Minnesota NFL	16	0	0	...	0	45	696	15.5	5	35	807	23.1	0	5	0	30	2
1995—Minnesota NFL	16	1	7	7.0	0	32	597	18.7	3	42	1037	24.7	0	3	0	18	3
Pro totals (3 years)	47	4	21	5.3	0	96	1505	15.7	9	119	2746	23.1	0	9	0	54	6

ISMAIL, ROCKET   WR/KR   RAIDERS

PERSONAL: Born November 18, 1969, in Elizabeth, N.J. ... 5-11/175. ... Full name: Raghib Ramadian Ismail. ... Brother of Qadry Ismail, wide receiver/kick returner, Minnesota Vikings. ... Name pronounced rahg-HEEB ISS-mile.
HIGH SCHOOL: Elmer L. Meyers (Wilkes-Barre, Pa.).
COLLEGE: Notre Dame (degree in sociology, 1994).
TRANSACTIONS/CAREER NOTES: Signed after junior season by Toronto Argonauts of CFL (April 21, 1991). ... Selected by Los Angeles Raiders in fourth round (100th pick overall) of 1991 NFL draft. ... Granted free agency from Argonauts (February 15, 1993). ... Signed by Raiders (August 30, 1993). ... Activated (September 12, 1993). ... Raiders franchise moved to Oakland (July 21, 1995). ... Granted free agency (February 16, 1996).
CHAMPIONSHIP GAME EXPERIENCE: Played in Grey Cup, CFL championship game (1991).
HONORS: Named kick returner on THE SPORTING NEWS college All-America first team (1989). ... Named College Football Player of the Year by THE SPORTING NEWS (1990). ... Named wide receiver on THE SPORTING NEWS college All-America first team (1990).
PRO STATISTICS: CFL: 1991—Returned two unsuccessful field-goals for 90 yards, attempted one pass without a completion, fumbled eight times and recovered two fumbles. 1992—Fumbled seven times and recovered two fumbles. NFL: 1993—Recovered one fumble. 1995—Fumbled four times and recovered one fumble.
STATISTICAL PLATEAUS: 100-yard receiving games: 1995 (1).

Year Team	G	RUSHING				RECEIVING				PUNT RETURNS				KICKOFF RETURNS				TOTALS		
		Att.	Yds.	Avg.	TD	No.	Yds.	Avg.	TD	No.	Yds.	Avg.	TD	No.	Yds.	Avg.	TD	TD	2pt.	Pts.
1991—Toronto CFL	17	36	271	7.5	3	64	1300	20.3	9	48	602	12.5	1	31	786	25.4	0	13	1	80
1992—Toronto CFL	16	34	154	4.5	3	36	651	18.1	4	59	614	10.4	1	43	*1139	26.5	0	8	0	48
1993—LA Raiders NFL	13	4	-5	-1.3	0	26	353	13.6	1	0	0	...	0	25	605	24.2	0	1	...	6
1994—LA Raiders NFL	16	4	31	7.8	0	34	513	15.1	5	0	0	...	0	43	923	21.5	0	5	0	30
1995—Oakland NFL	16	6	29	4.8	0	28	491	17.5	3	0	0	...	0	36	706	19.6	0	3	0	18
CFL totals (2 years)	33	70	425	6.1	6	100	1951	19.5	13	107	1216	11.4	2	74	1925	26.0	0	21	1	128
NFL totals (3 years)	45	14	55	3.9	0	88	1357	15.4	9	0	0	...	0	104	2234	21.5	0	9	0	54
Pro totals (5 years)	78	84	480	5.7	6	188	3308	17.6	22	107	1216	11.4	2	178	4159	23.4	0	30	1	182

ISRAEL, STEVE   CB

PERSONAL: Born March 16, 1969, in Lawnside, N.J. ... 5-11/186. ... Full name: Steven Douglas Israel.
HIGH SCHOOL: Haddon Heights (N.J.).
COLLEGE: Pittsburgh (degree in economics).
TRANSACTIONS/CAREER NOTES: Selected by Los Angeles Rams in second round (30th pick overall) of 1992 NFL draft. ... Signed by Rams (August 23, 1992). ... Granted roster exemption (August 25-September-4, 1992). ... Claimed on waivers by Green Bay Packers (August 7, 1995). ... Released by Packers (August 25, 1995). ... Signed by San Francisco 49ers (October 3, 1995). ... Granted unconditional free agency (February 16, 1996).
PRO STATISTICS: 1992—Recovered one fumble.

Year Team	G	KICKOFF RETURNS				TOTALS			
		No.	Yds.	Avg.	TD	TD	2pt.	Pts.	Fum.
1992—Los Angeles Rams NFL	16	1	-3	-3.0	0	0	...	0	0
1993—Los Angeles Rams NFL	16	5	92	18.4	0	0	0	0	0
1994—Los Angeles Rams NFL	10	0	0	...	0	0	0	0	0
1995—San Francisco NFL	8	0	0	...	0	0	0	0	0
Pro totals (4 years)	50	6	89	14.8	0	0	0	0	0

JACKE, CHRIS   K   PACKERS

PERSONAL: Born March 12, 1966, in Richmond, Va. ... 6-0/205. ... Full name: Christopher Lee Jacke. ... Name pronounced JACK-ee.
HIGH SCHOOL: J.J. Pearce (Richardson, Texas).
COLLEGE: Texas-El Paso (degree in business, 1989).
TRANSACTIONS/CAREER NOTES: Selected by Green Bay Packers in sixth round (142nd pick overall) of 1989 NFL draft. ... Signed by Packers (July 28, 1989). ... Granted free agency (February 1, 1991). ... Re-signed by Packers (August 26, 1991).
CHAMPIONSHIP GAME EXPERIENCE: Played in NFC championship game (1995 season).

Year Team	G	KICKING						
		XPM	XPA	FGM	FGA	Lg.	50+	Pts.
1989—Green Bay NFL	16	42	42	22	28	52	1-3	108
1990—Green Bay NFL	16	28	29	23	30	53	2-4	97
1991—Green Bay NFL	16	31	31	18	24	53	1-1	85
1992—Green Bay NFL	16	30	30	22	29	53	2-3	96
1993—Green Bay NFL	16	35	35	31	37	54	6-7	128
1994—Green Bay NFL	16	41	43	19	26	50	1-3	98
1995—Green Bay NFL	14	43	43	17	23	51	3-4	94
Pro totals (7 years)	110	250	253	152	197	54	16-25	706

JACKSON, AL   CB   JAGUARS

PERSONAL: Born September 7, 1971, in Pensacola, Fla. ... 5-10/191.
HIGH SCHOOL: Pine Forest (Pensacola, Fla.).
COLLEGE: Georgia.
TRANSACTIONS/CAREER NOTES: Signed as non-drafted free agent by Philadelphia Eagles (April 27, 1994). ... Selected by Jacksonville Jaguars from Eagles in NFL expansion draft (February 15, 1995). ... On injured reserve with knee injury (August 31, 1995-entire season).
PLAYING EXPERIENCE: Philadelphia NFL, 1994. ... Games: 1994 (11).

JACKSON, ALFRED   CB   VIKINGS

PERSONAL: Born July 10, 1967, in Tulare, Calif. ... 6-0/183. ... Full name: Alfred Melvin Jackson Jr.
HIGH SCHOOL: Tulare (Calif.).
COLLEGE: San Diego State.
TRANSACTIONS/CAREER NOTES: Selected by Los Angeles Rams in fifth round (135th pick overall) of 1989 NFL draft. ... Signed by Rams (July 14, 1989). ... On injured reserve with groin injury (October 18-December 1, 1989). ... Released by Rams (November 3, 1990). ... Re-signed by Rams (February 27, 1991). ... Released by Rams (August 26, 1991). ... Re-signed by Rams (August 27, 1991). ... On injured reserve with ankle injury (August 27-September 11, 1991). ... Released by Rams (September 11, 1991). ... Signed by Cleveland Browns (November 14, 1991). ... Granted unconditional free agency (February 1-April 1, 1992). ... Re-signed by Browns for 1992 season. ... Released by Browns (October 10, 1992). ... Signed by Miami Dolphins (December 2, 1992). ... Released by Dolphins (December 5, 1992). ... Re-signed by Browns (December 16, 1992). ... Granted unconditional free agency (March 1, 1993). ... Signed by Winnipeg Blue Bombers (August 1993). ... Signed by Minnesota Vikings (March 23, 1995).
PLAYING EXPERIENCE: Los Angeles Rams NFL, 1989 and 1990; Cleveland NFL, 1991 and 1992; Winnipeg CFL, 1993 and 1994; Minnesota NFL, 1995. ... Games: 1989 (7), 1990 (5), 1991 (6), 1992 (5), 1993 (12), 1994 (13), 1995 (8). Total CFL: 25. Total NFL: 31. Total: 56.
CHAMPIONSHIP GAME EXPERIENCE: Played in NFC championship game (1989 season).
PRO STATISTICS: NFL: 1991—Intercepted one pass for no yards and recovered two fumbles. 1995—Intercepted two passes for 46 yards and one touchdown. CFL: 1993—Caught 13 passes for 194 yards and two touchdowns and returned six punts for 32 yards. CFL: 1994—Caught 41 passes for 901 yards and seven touchdowns and returned on punt for nine yards.

JACKSON, CALVIN   CB   DOLPHINS

PERSONAL: Born October 28, 1972, in Miami. ... 5-9/185. ... Full name: Calvin Bernard Jackson.
HIGH SCHOOL: Dillard (Fort Lauderdale).
COLLEGE: Auburn.
TRANSACTIONS/CAREER NOTES: Signed as non-drafted free agent by Miami Dolphins (July 21, 1994). ... Released by Dolphins (August 22, 1994). ... Re-signed by Dolphins to practice squad (August 29, 1994). ... Activated (September 17, 1994). ... Released by Dolphins (October 26, 1994). ... Re-signed by Dolphins to practice squad (October 27, 1994). ... On practice squad injured reserve with knee injury (December 24, 1994-remainder of season). ... Granted free agency after 1994 season. ... Re-signed by Dolphins (February 21, 1995). ... Released by Dolphins (August 27, 1995). ... Re-signed by Dolphins to practice squad (August 30, 1995). ... Activated (September 9, 1995).
PLAYING EXPERIENCE: Miami NFL, 1994 and 1995. ... Games: 1994 (2), 1995 (9). Total: 11.
PRO STATISTICS: 1995—Intercepted one pass for 23 yards.

JACKSON, GREG   S

PERSONAL: Born August 20, 1966, in Hialeah, Fla. ... 6-
HIGH SCHOOL: American (Miami).
COLLEGE: Louisiana State.
TRANSACTIONS/CAREER NOTES: Selected by New York ... 24, 1989). ... Granted free agency (February 1, 1992)- ... (February 17, 1994). ... Signed by Philadelphia Eagles (
CHAMPIONSHIP GAME EXPERIENCE: Played in NFC c... (1990 season).
PRO STATISTICS: 1989—Recovered one fumble. 1991- ... three yards. 1995—Recovered three fumbles for 45 yard...

Year Team			
1989—New York Giants NFL			
1990—New York Giants NFL			
1991—New York Giants NFL			
1992—New York Giants NFL			
1993—New York Giants NFL			
1994—Philadelphia NFL			
1995—Philadelphia NFL			
Pro totals (7 years)			

JACKSON, JACK   EARS

PERSONAL: Born November 11, 1972, in Moss Point, Mi...
HIGH SCHOOL: Moss Point (Miss.).
COLLEGE: Florida.
TRANSACTIONS/CAREER NOTES: Selected after junior se... Signed by Bears (June 27, 1995). ... On injured reserve w...

Where are they now? — The United States Football League ceased to exist 11 years ago, but there are still 18 refugees who play in the NFL. The Oilers have two of them – offensive tackle **Irv Eatman** and return specialist **Mel Gray**. There are two former Oilers – Philadelphia defensive end **William Fuller** and Oakland punter **Jeff Gossett**. Of those USFL products, 13 have combined for 48 Pro Bowl appearances. Five played for the two-time USFL champion Philadelphia Stars. The Stars' coach was **Jim Mora**, and the general manager was **Carl Peterson**.

The other USFL alums are Dallas running back **Herschel Walker**, Dallas guard **Nate Newton**, Green Bay defensive end **Reggie White**, Detroit receiver **Aubrey Matthews**, Denver offensive tackle **Gary Zimmerman**, Denver offensive tackle **Broderick Thompson**, Kansas City linebacker **George Jamison**, Atlanta quarterback **Bobby Hebert**, Carolina linebacker **Sam Mills**, San Francisco quarterback **Steve Young**, St. Louis punter **Sean Landeta**, San Francisco linebacker **Gary Plummer**, Buffalo quarterback **Jim Kelly** and Buffalo center **Kent Hull**.

HONORS: Named wide receiver on THE SPORTING NEWS college All-America first team (1994).

JACKSON, JOHN — OT — STEELERS

PERSONAL: Born January 4, 1965, in Camp Kwe, Okinawa, Japan. ... 6-6/297.
HIGH SCHOOL: Woodward (Cincinnati).
COLLEGE: Eastern Kentucky.
TRANSACTIONS/CAREER NOTES: Selected by Pittsburgh Steelers in 10th round (252nd pick overall) of 1988 NFL draft. ... Signed by Steelers (May 17, 1988).
PLAYING EXPERIENCE: Pittsburgh NFL, 1988-1995. ... Games: 1988 (16), 1989 (14), 1990 (16), 1991 (16), 1992 (16), 1993 (16), 1994 (16), 1995 (11). Total: 121.
CHAMPIONSHIP GAME EXPERIENCE: Played in AFC championship game (1994 and 1995 seasons). ... Played in Super Bowl XXX (1995 season).
PRO STATISTICS: 1988—Returned one kickoff for 10 yards. 1991—Recovered one fumble. 1993—Recovered one fumble. 1994—Recovered two fumbles.

JACKSON, KEITH — TE

PERSONAL: Born April 19, 1965, in Little Rock, Ark. ... 6-2/258. ... Full name: Keith Jerome Jackson.
HIGH SCHOOL: Parkview (Little Rock, Ark.).
COLLEGE: Oklahoma (degree in communications, 1988).
TRANSACTIONS/CAREER NOTES: Selected by Philadelphia Eagles in first round (13th pick overall) of 1988 NFL draft. ... Signed by Eagles (August 10, 1988). ... On reserve/did not report list (August 28-September 21, 1990). ... Granted free agency (February 1, 1992). ... Granted unconditional free agency (September 24, 1992). ... Signed by Miami Dolphins (September 29, 1992). ... Traded by Dolphins with fourth-round pick (traded to Miami) in 1995 draft to Green Bay Packers for second-round pick (OG Andrew Greene) in 1995 draft (March 29, 1995). ... Activated (October 28, 1995). ... Granted unconditional free agency (February 16, 1996).
CHAMPIONSHIP GAME EXPERIENCE: Played in AFC championship game (1992 season). ... Played in NFC championship game (1995 season).
HONORS: Named tight end on THE SPORTING NEWS college All-America first team (1986). ... Named tight end on THE SPORTING NEWS college All-America second team (1987). ... Named NFL Rookie of the Year by THE SPORTING NEWS (1988). ... Named tight end on THE SPORTING NEWS NFL All-Pro team (1988-1990 and 1992). ... Played in Pro Bowl (1988-1990 seasons). ... Named to play in Pro Bowl (1992 season); replaced by Shannon Sharpe due to injury.
PRO STATISTICS: 1994—Recovered one fumble.
STATISTICAL PLATEAUS: 100-yard receiving games: 1989 (1), 1994 (1). Total: 2.

| | | | RECEIVING | | | | TOTALS | | | |
Year Team	G	No.	Yds.	Avg.	TD	TD	2pt.	Pts.	Fum.
1988—Philadelphia NFL	16	81	869	10.7	6	6	...	36	3
1989—Philadelphia NFL	14	63	648	10.3	3	3	...	18	1
1990—Philadelphia NFL	14	50	670	13.4	6	6	...	36	1
1991—Philadelphia NFL	16	48	569	11.9	5	5	...	30	2
1992—Miami NFL	13	48	594	12.4	5	5	...	30	2
1993—Miami NFL	15	39	613	15.7	6	6	...	36	2
1994—Miami NFL	16	59	673	11.4	7	7	1	44	2
1995—Green Bay NFL	9	13	142	10.9	1	1	0	6	0
Pro totals (8 years)	113	401	4778	11.9	39	39	1	236	13

JACKSON, MICHAEL — WR — RAVENS

PERSONAL: Born April 12, 1969, in Tangipahoa, La. ... 6-4/195. ... Full name: Michael Dwayne Jackson.
HIGH SCHOOL: Kentwood (La.).
COLLEGE: Southern Mississippi.
TRANSACTIONS/CAREER NOTES: Selected by Cleveland Browns in sixth round (141st pick overall) of 1991 NFL draft. ... Granted free agency (February 17, 1994). ... Re-signed by Browns (1994). ... Browns franchise moved to Baltimore and renamed Ravens for 1996 season (March 11, 1996).
PRO STATISTICS: 1993—Attempted one pass with one completion for 25 yards and recovered one fumble. 1994—Attempted two passes without a completion. 1995—Had only pass attempt intercepted and recovered one fumble. Total: 4.
STATISTICAL PLATEAUS: 100-yard receiving games: 1993 (2), 1995 (2). Total: 4.

| | | RUSHING | | | | RECEIVING | | | | TOTALS | | | |
Year Team	G	Att.	Yds.	Avg.	TD	No.	Yds.	Avg.	TD	TD	2pt.	Pts.	Fum.
1991—Cleveland NFL	16	0	0	...	0	17	268	15.8	2	0	...	0	0
1992—Cleveland NFL	16	1	21	21.0	0	47	755	16.1	7	7	...	42	0
1993—Cleveland NFL	15	1	1	1.0	0	41	756	18.4	8	8	...	48	1
1994—Cleveland NFL	9	0	0	...	0	21	304	14.5	2	2	0	12	0
1995—Cleveland NFL	13	0	0	...	0	44	714	16.2	9	9	0	54	1
Pro totals (5 years)	69	2	22	11.0	0	170	2797	16.5	28	26	0	156	2

JACKSON, RICKEY — LB

PERSONAL: Born March 20, 1958, in Pahokee, Fla. ... 6-2/243. ... Full name: Rickey Anderson Jackson.
HIGH SCHOOL: Pahokee (Fla.).
COLLEGE: Pittsburgh.
TRANSACTIONS/CAREER NOTES: Selected by New Orleans Saints in second round (51st pick overall) of 1981 NFL draft. ... Granted free agency (February 1, 1990). ... Re-signed by Saints (July 25, 1990). ... Granted free agency (February 1, 1992). ... Re-signed by Saints (July

24, 1992). ... Granted unconditional free agency (February 17, 1994). ... Signed by San Francisco 49ers (August 2, 1994). ... Granted uncon-ditional free agency (February 17, 1995). ... Re-signed by 49ers (June 19, 1995). ... Granted unconditional free agency (February 16, 1996). ... Signed by Saints (June 6, 1996). ... Announced retirement (June 6, 1996).

CHAMPIONSHIP GAME EXPERIENCE: Played in NFC championship game (1994 season). ... Member of Super Bowl championship team (1994 season).

HONORS: Played in Pro Bowl (1983-1986, 1992 and 1993 seasons). ... Named outside linebacker on THE SPORTING NEWS NFL All-Pro team (1987 and 1993).

PRO STATISTICS: 1981—Recovered one fumble. 1982—Recovered two fumbles. 1983—Fumbled once and recovered two fumbles for minus two yards. 1984—Fumbled once and recovered four fumbles for four yards. 1986—Recovered one fumble. 1988—Credited with a safety. 1990—Recovered seven fumbles. 1991—Recovered four fumbles for four yards. 1992—Recovered three fumbles for 15 yards. 1993—Recovered three fumbles for three yards. 1994—Recovered two fumbles for five yards.

MISCELLANEOUS: Holds New Orleans Saints all-time record for most sacks (115).

			INTERCEPTIONS			SACKS
Year Team	G	No.	Yds.	Avg.	TD	No.
1981—New Orleans NFL	16	0	0	...	0	...
1982—New Orleans NFL	9	1	32	32.0	0	4.5
1983—New Orleans NFL	16	1	0	0.0	0	12.0
1984—New Orleans NFL	16	1	14	14.0	0	12.0
1985—New Orleans NFL	16	0	0	...	0	11.0
1986—New Orleans NFL	16	1	1	1.0	0	9.0
1987—New Orleans NFL	12	2	4	2.0	0	9.5
1988—New Orleans NFL	16	1	16	16.0	0	7.0
1989—New Orleans NFL	14	0	0	...	0	7.5
1990—New Orleans NFL	16	0	0	...	0	6.0
1991—New Orleans NFL	16	0	0	...	0	11.5
1992—New Orleans NFL	16	0	0	...	0	13.5
1993—New Orleans NFL	16	0	0	...	0	11.5
1994—San Francisco NFL	16	0	0	...	0	3.5
1995—San Francisco NFL	16	1	1	1.0	0	9.5
Pro totals (15 years)	227	8	68	8.5	0	128.0

JACKSON, STEVE® — CB — OILERS

PERSONAL: Born April 8, 1969, in Houston. ... 5-8/182. ... Full name: Steven Wayne Jackson.
HIGH SCHOOL: Klein Forest (Houston).
COLLEGE: Purdue.
TRANSACTIONS/CAREER NOTES: Selected by Houston Oilers in third round (71st pick overall) of 1991 NFL draft. ... Signed by Oilers (July 11, 1991). ... Granted free agency (February 17, 1994). ... Re-signed by Oilers (June 10, 1994).
PRO STATISTICS: 1991—Returned one punt for no yards and recovered two fumbles.

		INTERCEPTIONS				SACKS	KICKOFF RETURNS				TOTALS			
Year Team	G	No.	Yds.	Avg.	TD	No.	No.	Yds.	Avg.	TD	TD	2pt.	Pts.	Fum.
1991—Houston NFL	15	0	0	...	0	1.0	0	0	...	0	0	...	0	0
1992—Houston NFL	16	3	18	6.0	0	1.0	0	0	...	0	0	...	0	0
1993—Houston NFL	16	5	54	10.8	1	0.0	0	0	...	0	1	...	6	0
1994—Houston NFL	11	1	0	0.0	0	1.0	14	285	20.4	0	0	0	0	0
1995—Houston NFL	10	2	0	0.0	0	1.0	0	0	...	0	0	0	0	0
Pro totals (5 years)	68	11	72	6.6	1	4.0	14	285	20.4	0	1	0	6	0

JACKSON, WILLIE — WR/KR — JAGUARS

PERSONAL: Born August 16, 1971, in Gainesville, Fla. ... 6-1/203. ... Full name: Willie Bernard Jackson.
HIGH SCHOOL: P.K. Yonge Laboratory (Gainesville, Fla.).
COLLEGE: Florida.
TRANSACTIONS/CAREER NOTES: Selected by Dallas Cowboys in fourth round (109th pick overall) of 1994 NFL draft. ... Signed by Cowboys (July 16, 1994). ... Inactive for 16 games (1994). ... Selected by Jacksonville Jaguars from Cowboys in NFL expansion draft (February 15, 1995).
CHAMPIONSHIP GAME EXPERIENCE: Member of Cowboys for NFC championship game (1994 season); inactive.
PRO STATISTICS: 1995—Returned one punt for minus two yards recovered one fumble.
STATISTICAL PLATEAUS: 100-yard receiving games: 1995 (1).
MISCELLANEOUS: Holds Jacksonville Jaguars all-time record for most yards receiving (589) and shares all-time record for most touchdowns (5).

		RECEIVING				KICKOFF RETURNS				TOTALS			
Year Team	G	No.	Yds.	Avg.	TD	No.	Yds.	Avg.	TD	TD	2pt.	Pts.	Fum.
1994—Dallas NFL			Did not play.											
1995—Jacksonville NFL	14	53	589	11.1	5	19	404	21.3	0	5	1	32	2

JACOBS, RAY — LB — BRONCOS

PERSONAL: Born August 18, 1972, in Hamstead, N.C. ... 6-2/244. ... Full name: Ray Anthony Jacobs.
HIGH SCHOOL: Topsail (Hamstead, N.C.).
COLLEGE: North Carolina.
TRANSACTIONS/CAREER NOTES: Signed as non-drafted free agent by Denver Broncos (May 2, 1994).
PLAYING EXPERIENCE: Denver NFL, 1994 and 1995. ... Games: 1994 (16), 1995 (15). Total: 31.

PRO STATISTICS: 1995—Recovered one fumble.

JACOBS, TIM   CB

PERSONAL: Born April 5, 1970, in Washington, D.C. ... 5-10/185.
HIGH SCHOOL: Eleanor Roosevelt (Greenbelt, Md.).
COLLEGE: Delaware.
TRANSACTIONS/CAREER NOTES: Signed as non-drafted free agent by Cleveland Browns (April 27, 1993). ... Released by Browns (August 30, 1993). ... Re-signed by Browns to practice squad (August 31, 1993). ... Activated (November 27, 1993). ... Granted unconditional free agency (February 16, 1996).

			INTERCEPTIONS		
Year Team	G	No.	Yds.	Avg.	TD
1993—Cleveland NFL	2	0	0	...	0
1994—Cleveland NFL	9	2	9	4.5	0
1995—Cleveland NFL	14	0	0	...	0
Pro totals (3 years)	25	2	9	4.5	0

JAEGER, JEFF   K   RAIDERS

PERSONAL: Born November 26, 1964, in Tacoma, Wash. ... 5-11/190. ... Full name: Jeff Todd Jaeger. ... Name pronounced JAY-ger.
HIGH SCHOOL: Kent (Wash.)-Meridian.
COLLEGE: Washington.
TRANSACTIONS/CAREER NOTES: Selected by Cleveland Browns in third round (82nd pick overall) of 1987 NFL draft. ... Signed by Browns (July 26, 1987). ... Crossed picket line during players strike (October 14, 1987). ... On injured reserve with foot injury (August 26, 1988-entire season). ... Granted unconditional free agency (February 1, 1989). ... Signed by Los Angeles Raiders (March 20, 1989). ... Granted free agency (February 1, 1991). ... Re-signed by Raiders (July 13, 1991). ... Released by Raiders (August 30, 1993). ... Re-signed by Raiders (August 31, 1993). ... Raiders franchise moved to Oakland (July 21, 1995).
CHAMPIONSHIP GAME EXPERIENCE: Played in AFC championship game (1990 season).
HONORS: Played in Pro Bowl (1991 season).
RECORDS: Shares NFL single-season record for most field goals made—35 (1993).
PRO STATISTICS: 1987—Attempted one pass without a completion and recovered one fumble.

				KICKING				
Year Team	G	XPM	XPA	FGM	FGA	Lg.	50+	Pts.
1987—Cleveland NFL	10	33	33	14	22	48	0-1	75
1988—Cleveland NFL				Did not play—injured.				
1989—Los Angeles Raiders NFL	16	34	34	23	34	50	1-2	103
1990—Los Angeles Raiders NFL	16	40	42	15	20	50	1-2	85
1991—Los Angeles Raiders NFL	16	29	30	29	34	53	2-4	116
1992—Los Angeles Raiders NFL	16	28	28	15	26	54	3-6	73
1993—Los Angeles Raiders NFL	16	27	29	*35	*44	53	4-7	*132
1994—Los Angeles Raiders NFL	16	31	31	22	28	51	2-2	97
1995—Oakland NFL	11	22	22	13	18	46	0-1	61
Pro totals (8 years)	117	244	249	166	226	54	13-25	742

JAMES, JESSE   C   RAMS

PERSONAL: Born September 16, 1971, in Mobile, Ala. ... 6-4/311.
HIGH SCHOOL: Williamson (Mobile, Ala.).
COLLEGE: Mississippi State.
TRANSACTIONS/CAREER NOTES: Selected by St. Louis Rams in second round (62nd pick overall) of 1995 NFL draft. ... Signed by Rams (July 11, 1995).
PLAYING EXPERIENCE: St. Louis NFL, 1995. ... Games: 1995 (1).

JAMISON, GEORGE   LB   CHIEFS

PERSONAL: Born September 30, 1962, in Bridgeton, N.J. ... 6-1/235. ... Cousin of Anthony (Bubba) Green, defensive tackle, Baltimore Colts (1981); and cousin of Larry Milbourne, major league infielder with six teams (1975-1984).
HIGH SCHOOL: Bridgeton (N.J.).
COLLEGE: Cincinnati.
TRANSACTIONS/CAREER NOTES: Selected by Philadelphia Stars in second round (34th pick overall) of 1984 USFL draft. ... Signed by Stars (January 17, 1984). ... On developmental squad for two games (February 24-March 2; and June 21, 1984-remainder of season). ... Selected by Detroit Lions in second round (47th pick overall) of 1984 NFL supplemental draft. ... Stars franchise moved to Baltimore (November 1, 1984). ... On developmental squad for one game (May 3-10, 1985). ... Granted free agency when USFL suspended operations (August 7, 1986). ... Signed by Lions (August 17, 1986). ... On injured reserve with Achilles' tendon injury (August 30, 1986-entire season). ... On injured reserve with knee injury (December 21, 1989-remainder of season). ... Granted free agency (February 1, 1992). ... Re-signed by Lions (July 23, 1992). ... Granted unconditional free agency (February 17, 1994). ... Signed by Kansas City Chiefs (July 15, 1994).
CHAMPIONSHIP GAME EXPERIENCE: Played in USFL championship game (1984 and 1985 seasons). ... Played in NFC championship game (1991 season).
PRO STATISTICS: 1987—Credited with one safety. 1988—Recovered three fumbles for four yards and one touchdown. 1990—Recovered one fumble. 1991—Fumbled once and recovered one fumble. 1992—Recovered one fumble. 1993—Returned one kickoff. 1994—Recovered three fumbles for 22 yards. 1995—Recovered two fumbles.

			INTERCEPTIONS			SACKS
Year Team	G	No.	Yds.	Avg.	TD	No.
1984—Philadelphia USFL	15	0	0	...	0	4.0

| Year | Team | G | INTERCEPTIONS | | | | SACKS |
			No.	Yds.	Avg.	TD	No.
1985—Baltimore USFL		17	1	16	16.0	0	5.0
1986—Detroit NFL			Did not play—injured.				
1987—Detroit NFL		12	0	0	...	0	1.0
1988—Detroit NFL		16	3	56	18.7	1	5.5
1989—Detroit NFL		10	0	0	...	0	2.0
1990—Detroit NFL		14	0	0	...	0	2.0
1991—Detroit NFL		16	3	52	17.3	0	4.0
1992—Detroit NFL		16	0	0	...	0	2.0
1993—Detroit NFL		16	2	48	24.0	1	2.0
1994—Kansas City NFL		13	0	0	...	0	1.0
1995—Kansas City NFL		14	0	0	...	0	0.0
USFL totals (2 years)		32	1	16	16.0	0	9.0
NFL totals (9 years)		127	8	156	19.5	2	19.5
Pro totals (11 years)		159	9	172	19.1	2	28.5

JAX, GARTH   LB   CARDINALS

PERSONAL: Born September 16, 1963, in Houston. ... 6-2/250. ... Full name: James Garth Jax.
HIGH SCHOOL: Strake Jesuit Preparatory (Houston).
COLLEGE: Florida State (degree in criminology, 1986).
TRANSACTIONS/CAREER NOTES: Selected by Tampa Bay Bandits in 1986 USFL territorial draft. ... Selected by Dallas Cowboys in 11th round (296th pick overall) of 1986 NFL draft. ... Signed by Cowboys (July 1, 1986). ... Released by Cowboys (September 1, 1986). ... Re-signed by Cowboys (September 8, 1986). ... On injured reserve with fractured wrist (November 2, 1987-remainder of season). ... Granted unconditional free agency (February 1, 1989). ... Signed by Phoenix Cardinals (April 1, 1989). ... Granted free agency (February 1, 1991). ... Re-signed by Cardinals (July 16, 1991). ... On injured reserve with neck injury (November 21, 1991-remainder of season). ... Granted unconditional free agency (February 1-April 1, 1992). ... Re-signed by Cardinals for 1992 season. ... Granted unconditional free agency (March 1, 1993). ... Re-signed by Cardinals (July 21, 1993). ... Granted unconditional free agency (February 17, 1994). ... Cardinals franchise renamed Arizona Cardinals for 1994 season. ... Re-signed by Cardinals (June 7, 1994). ... Granted unconditional free agency (February 17, 1995). ... Re-signed by Cardinals (April 13, 1995).
PLAYING EXPERIENCE: Dallas NFL, 1986-1988; Phoenix NFL, 1989-1993; Arizona NFL, 1994 and 1995. ... Games: 1986 (16), 1987 (3), 1988 (16), 1989 (16), 1990 (16), 1991 (12), 1992 (16), 1993 (16), 1994 (16), 1995 (16). Total: 143.
PRO STATISTICS: 1988—Recovered one fumble. 1990—Credited with three sacks, intercepted two passes for five yards and returned two kickoffs for 17 yards.

JEFFCOAT, JIM   DE   BILLS

PERSONAL: Born April 1, 1961, in Long Branch, N.J. ... 6-5/280. ... Full name: James Wilson Jeffcoat Jr.
HIGH SCHOOL: Regional (Matawan, N.J.).
COLLEGE: Arizona State (degree in communications, 1983).
TRANSACTIONS/CAREER NOTES: Selected by Arizona Wranglers in 1983 USFL territorial draft. ... Selected by Dallas Cowboys in first round (23rd pick overall) of 1983 NFL draft. ... Signed by Cowboys (May 24, 1983). ... Granted free agency (February 1, 1992). ... Re-signed by Cowboys (August 6, 1992). ... Granted unconditional free agency (February 17, 1995). ... Signed by Buffalo Bills (February 22, 1995).
CHAMPIONSHIP GAME EXPERIENCE: Played in NFC championship game (1992-1994 seasons). ... Member of Super Bowl championship team (1992 and 1993 seasons).
PRO STATISTICS: 1984—Recovered fumble in end zone for a touchdown. 1985—Recovered two fumbles. 1986—Recovered two fumbles for eight yards. 1987—Recovered two fumbles for eight yards. 1989—Recovered three fumbles for 77 yards and one touchdown. 1990—Recovered one fumble for 28 yards.

| Year | Team | G | INTERCEPTIONS | | | | SACKS |
			No.	Yds.	Avg.	TD	No.
1983—Dallas NFL		16	0	0	...	0	2.0
1984—Dallas NFL		16	0	0	...	0	11.5
1985—Dallas NFL		16	1	65	65.0	†1	12.0
1986—Dallas NFL		16	0	0	...	0	14.0
1987—Dallas NFL		12	1	26	26.0	1	5.0
1988—Dallas NFL		16	0	0	...	0	6.5
1989—Dallas NFL		16	0	0	...	0	11.5
1990—Dallas NFL		16	0	0	...	0	3.5
1991—Dallas NFL		16	0	0	...	0	4.0
1992—Dallas NFL		16	0	0	...	0	10.5
1993—Dallas NFL		16	0	0	...	0	6.0
1994—Dallas NFL		16	0	0	...	0	8.0
1995—Buffalo NFL		16	0	0	...	0	2.5
Pro totals (13 years)		204	2	91	45.5	2	97.0

JEFFERSON, GREG   DE   EAGLES

PERSONAL: Born August 31, 1971, in Orlando. ... 6-3/257.
HIGH SCHOOL: Bartow (Fla.).
COLLEGE: Central Florida.
TRANSACTIONS/CAREER NOTES: Selected by Philadelphia Eagles in third round (72nd pick overall) of 1995 NFL draft. ... Signed by Eagles (June 29, 1995). ... On injured reserve with knee injury (September 21, 1995-remainder of season).
PLAYING EXPERIENCE: Philadelphia NFL, 1995. ... Games: 1995 (3).

JEFFERSON, KEVIN — LB — BENGALS

PERSONAL: Born January 14, 1974, in Greensburg, Pa. ... 6-2/232.
HIGH SCHOOL: Hempfield Area (Greensburg, Pa.).
COLLEGE: Lehigh.
TRANSACTIONS/CAREER NOTES: Signed as non-drafted free agent by Cincinnati Bengals (April 28, 1994). ... Released by Bengals (August 28, 1994). ... Re-signed by Bengals to practice squad (August 30, 1994). ... Activated (October 4, 1994).
PLAYING EXPERIENCE: Cincinnati NFL, 1994 and 1995. ... Games: 1994 (6), 1995 (16). Total: 22.
PRO STATISTICS: 1995—Recovered one fumble for six yards.

JEFFERSON, SHAWN — WR — PATRIOTS

PERSONAL: Born February 22, 1969, in Jacksonville. ... 5-11/180. ... Full name: Vanchi LaShawn Jefferson.
HIGH SCHOOL: Raines (Jacksonville).
COLLEGE: Central Florida.
TRANSACTIONS/CAREER NOTES: Selected by Houston Oilers in ninth round (240th pick overall) of 1991 NFL draft. ... Signed by Oilers (July 15, 1991). ... Traded by Oilers with first-round pick (DE Chris Mims) in 1992 draft to San Diego Chargers for DL Lee Williams (August 22, 1991). ... Granted free agency (March 1, 1993). ... Re-signed by Chargers (July 15, 1993). ... Granted free agency (February 17, 1994). ... Re-signed by Chargers (May 2, 1994). ... Released by Chargers (February 29, 1996). ... Signed by New England Patriots (March 13, 1996).
CHAMPIONSHIP GAME EXPERIENCE: Played in AFC championship game (1994 season). ... Played in Super Bowl XXIX (1994 season).
STATISTICAL PLATEAUS: 100-yard receiving games: 1995 (1).

Year Team	G	RUSHING				RECEIVING				TOTALS			
		Att.	Yds.	Avg.	TD	No.	Yds.	Avg.	TD	TD	2pt.	Pts.	Fum.
1991—San Diego NFL	16	1	27	27.0	0	12	125	10.4	1	1	...	6	0
1992—San Diego NFL	16	0	0	...	0	29	377	13.0	2	2	...	12	0
1993—San Diego NFL	16	5	53	10.6	0	30	391	13.0	2	2	...	12	0
1994—San Diego NFL	16	3	40	13.3	0	43	627	14.6	3	3	0	18	0
1995—San Diego NFL	16	2	1	0.5	0	48	621	12.9	2	2	0	12	0
Pro totals (5 years)	80	11	121	11.0	0	162	2141	13.2	10	10	0	60	0

JEFFIRES, HAYWOOD — WR

PERSONAL: Born December 12, 1964, in Greensboro, N.C. ... 6-2/201. ... Full name: Haywood Franklin Jeffires. ... Name pronounced JEFF-rees.
HIGH SCHOOL: Page (Greensboro, N.C.).
COLLEGE: North Carolina State (degree in recreation administration, 1987).
TRANSACTIONS/CAREER NOTES: Selected by Houston Oilers in first round (20th pick overall) of 1987 NFL draft. ... Signed by Oilers (July 22, 1987). ... Crossed picket line during players strike (October 14, 1987). ... On injured reserve with ankle injury (August 29-December 10, 1988). ... Granted free agency (February 1, 1991). ... Re-signed by Oilers (July 21, 1991). ... Granted unconditional free agency (February 17, 1994). ... Re-signed by Oilers (May 13, 1994). ... Granted unconditional free agency (February 28, 1995). ... Re-signed by Oilers (June 30, 1995). ... Released by Oilers (February 15, 1996).
HONORS: Played in Pro Bowl (1991-1993 seasons).
PRO STATISTICS: 1991—Recovered one fumble.
STATISTICAL PLATEAUS: 100-yard receiving games: 1990 (1), 1991 (2), 1992 (1), 1993 (1), 1994 (1). Total: 6.

Year Team	G	RECEIVING				TOTALS			
		No.	Yds.	Avg.	TD	TD	2pt.	Pts.	Fum.
1987—Houston NFL	9	7	89	12.7	0	0	...	0	0
1988—Houston NFL	2	2	49	24.5	1	1	...	6	0
1989—Houston NFL	16	47	619	13.2	2	2	...	12	0
1990—Houston NFL	16	74	1048	14.2	8	8	...	48	0
1991—Houston NFL	16	*100	1181	11.8	7	7	...	42	3
1992—Houston NFL	16	90	913	10.1	9	9	...	54	1
1993—Houston NFL	16	66	753	11.4	6	6	...	36	5
1994—Houston NFL	16	68	783	11.5	6	6	3	42	0
1995—Houston NFL	16	61	684	11.2	8	8	0	48	0
Pro totals (9 years)	123	515	6119	11.9	47	47	3	288	9

JEFFRIES, DAMEIAN — DE — SAINTS

PERSONAL: Born May 7, 1973, in Sylacauga, Ala. ... 6-4/277.
HIGH SCHOOL: B.B. Comer (Sylacauga, Ala.).
COLLEGE: Alabama.
TRANSACTIONS/CAREER NOTES: Selected by New Orleans Saints in fourth round (108th pick overall) of 1995 NFL draft. ... Signed by Saints (July 14, 1995).
PLAYING EXPERIENCE: New Orleans NFL, 1995. ... Games: 1995 (2).

JEFFRIES, GREG — CB — LIONS

PERSONAL: Born October 16, 1971, in High Point, N.C. ... 5-9/184. ... Full name: Greg Lemont Jeffries.
HIGH SCHOOL: T.W. Andrews (High Point, N.C.).
COLLEGE: Virginia.
TRANSACTIONS/CAREER NOTES: Selected by Detroit Lions in sixth round (147th pick overall) of 1993 NFL draft. ... Signed by Lions (July 17, 1993).
PLAYING EXPERIENCE: Detroit NFL, 1993-1995. ... Games: 1993 (7), 1994 (16), 1995 (14). Total: 37.

PRO STATISTICS: 1993—Recovered one fumble. 1995—Credited with ½ sack.

JENKINS, CARLOS   LB   RAMS

PERSONAL: Born July 12, 1968, in Palm Beach, Fla. ... 6-3/217. ... Full name: Carlos Edward Jenkins.
HIGH SCHOOL: Santaluces Community (Lantana, Fla.).
COLLEGE: Michigan State.
TRANSACTIONS/CAREER NOTES: Selected by Minnesota Vikings in third round (65th pick overall) of 1991 NFL draft. ... Signed by Vikings (July 22, 1991). ... On injured reserve with foot injury (August 27-September 24 and October 16, 1991-remainder of season). ... Granted free agency (February 17, 1994). ... Re-signed by Vikings (May 20, 1994). ... Granted unconditional free agency (February 17, 1995). ... Signed by Los Angeles Rams (March 30, 1995). ... Rams franchise moved to St. Louis (April 12, 1995).
PRO STATISTICS: 1992—Recovered one fumble for 22 yards and a touchdown. 1993—Recovered one fumble. 1994—Recovered two fumbles. 1995—Recovered one fumble.

		INTERCEPTIONS			SACKS
Year Team	G	No.	Yds.	Avg.	TD	No.
1991—Minnesota NFL	3	0	0	...	0	0.0
1992—Minnesota NFL	16	1	19	19.0	1	4.0
1993—Minnesota NFL	16	2	7	3.5	0	2.5
1994—Minnesota NFL	16	0	0	...	0	1.0
1995—St. Louis NFL	16	0	0	...	0	1.5
Pro totals (5 years)	67	3	26	8.7	1	9.0

JENKINS, JAMES   TE   REDSKINS

PERSONAL: Born August 17, 1967, in Staten Island, N.Y. ... 6-2/241.
HIGH SCHOOL: Staten Island (N.Y.) Academy.
COLLEGE: Rutgers.
TRANSACTIONS/CAREER NOTES: Signed as non-drafted free agent by Washington Redskins (April 25, 1991). ... Released by Redskins (August 26, 1991). ... Re-signed by Redskins to practice squad (August 27, 1991). ... Activated (November 30, 1991). ... Released by Redskins (August 31, 1992). ... Re-signed by Redskins (September 1, 1992). ... On injured reserve with back injury (September-November 28, 1992). ... On injured reserve with shoulder injury (December 28, 1993-remainder of season). ... Granted free agency (February 17, 1995). ... Re-signed by Redskins (July 19, 1995).
CHAMPIONSHIP GAME EXPERIENCE: Played in NFC championship game (1991 season). ... Member of Super Bowl championship team (1991 season).
PRO STATISTICS: 1994—Returned one kickoff for four yards. 1995—Returned one kickoff for 12 yards and recovered one fumble.

		RECEIVING				TOTALS			
Year Team	G	No.	Yds.	Avg.	TD	TD	2pt.	Pts.	Fum.
1991—Washington NFL	4	0	0	...	0	0	...	0	0
1992—Washington NFL	5	0	0	...	0	0	...	0	0
1993—Washington NFL	15	0	0	...	0	0	...	0	0
1994—Washington NFL	16	8	32	4.0	4	4	0	24	0
1995—Washington NFL	16	1	2	2.0	0	0	0	0	0
Pro totals (5 years)	56	9	34	3.8	4	4	0	24	0

JENKINS, ROBERT   OT   RAIDERS

PERSONAL: Born December 30, 1963, in San Francisco. ... 6-5/285. ... Full name: Robert Lloyd Jenkins. ... Formerly known as Robert Cox.
HIGH SCHOOL: Dublin (Calif.).
JUNIOR COLLEGE: Chabot College (Calif.).
COLLEGE: UCLA.
TRANSACTIONS/CAREER NOTES: Selected by Arizona Outlaws in 1986 USFL territorial draft. ... Selected by Los Angeles Rams in sixth round (144th pick overall) of 1986 NFL draft. ... Signed by Rams (July 22, 1986). ... On injured reserve with ankle injury (August 27, 1986-entire season). ... Granted free agency (February 1, 1991). ... Re-signed by Rams (July 28, 1991). ... On injured reserve with hyperextended toe (September 18-October 26, 1991). ... Released by Rams (November 23, 1993). ... Signed by Los Angeles Raiders (July 22, 1994). ... Raiders franchise moved to Oakland (July 21, 1995).
PLAYING EXPERIENCE: Los Angeles Rams NFL, 1987-1993; Los Angeles Raiders NFL, 1994; Oakland NFL, 1995. ... Games: 1987 (10), 1988 (16), 1989 (16), 1990 (11), 1991 (12), 1992 (9), 1993 (8), 1994 (10), 1995 (15). Total: 107.
CHAMPIONSHIP GAME EXPERIENCE: Played in NFC championship game (1989 season).
PRO STATISTICS: 1987—Returned one kickoff for 12 yards.

JENKINS, TREZELLE   OT   CHIEFS

PERSONAL: Born March 13, 1973, in Chicago. ... 6-7/322. ... Name pronounced TRUH-zell.
HIGH SCHOOL: Morgan Park (Chicago).
COLLEGE: Michigan.
TRANSACTIONS/CAREER NOTES: Selected after junior season by Kansas City Chiefs in first round (31st pick overall) of 1995 NFL draft. ... Signed by Chiefs (April 25, 1995).
PLAYING EXPERIENCE: Kansas City NFL, 1995. ... Games: 1995 (1).

JENNINGS, KEITH   TE   BEARS

PERSONAL: Born May 19, 1966, in Summerville, S.C. ... 6-4/270. ... Full name: Keith O'Neal Jennings. ... Brother of Stanford Jennings, running back, Cincinnati Bengals, New Orleans Saints and Tampa Bay Buccaneers (1984-1992).

HIGH SCHOOL: Summerville (S.C.).
COLLEGE: Clemson.
TRANSACTIONS/CAREER NOTES: Selected by Dallas Cowboys in fifth round (113th pick overall) of 1989 NFL draft. ... Signed by Cowboys (August 2, 1989). ... Released by Cowboys (September 5, 1989). ... Re-signed by Cowboys to developmental squad (September 6, 1989). ... Activated (October 18, 1989). ... Released by Cowboys (September 3, 1990). ... Signed by WLAF (January 31, 1991). ... Selected by Montreal Machine in first round (first tight end) of 1991 WLAF positional draft. ... Released by Machine (April 16, 1991). ... Signed by Denver Broncos (July 3, 1991). ... Released by Broncos (August 26, 1991). ... Signed by Chicago Bears (October 9, 1991). ... Granted free agency (February 1, 1992). ... Re-signed by Bears (March 30, 1992). ... Granted free agency (February 17, 1994). ... Re-signed by Bears (May 6, 1994). ... Released by Bears (August 28, 1994). ... Re-signed by Bears (October 24, 1994). ... Granted unconditional free agency (February 17, 1995). ... Re-signed by Bears (March 6, 1995).
PRO STATISTICS: 1993—Recovered one fumble.

			RECEIVING				TOTALS			
Year Team	G	No.	Yds.	Avg.	TD	TD	2pt.	Pts.	Fum.
1989—Dallas NFL	10	6	47	7.8	0	0	...	0	0
1990—				Did not play.					
1991—Montreal W.L.	4	4	54	13.5	1	1	0	6	0
—Chicago NFL	10	8	109	13.6	0	0	...	0	0
1992—Chicago NFL	16	23	264	11.5	1	1	...	6	0
1993—Chicago NFL	13	14	150	10.7	0	0	...	0	1
1994—Chicago NFL	9	11	75	6.8	3	3	0	18	0
1995—Chicago NFL	16	25	217	8.7	6	6	0	36	0
W.L. totals (1 year)	4	4	54	13.5	1	1	0	6	0
NFL totals (6 years)	74	87	862	9.9	10	10	0	60	1
Pro totals (6 years)	78	91	916	10.1	11	11	0	66	1

JERVEY, TRAVIS   RB   PACKERS

PERSONAL: Born May 5, 1972, in Isle of Palm, S.C. ... 5-11/225. ... Full name: Travis Richard Jervey.
HIGH SCHOOL: Wando (Mount Pleasant, S.C.).
COLLEGE: The Citadel.
TRANSACTIONS/CAREER NOTES: Selected by Green Bay Packers in fifth round (170th pick overall) of 1995 NFL draft. ... Signed by Packers (May 23, 1995).
CHAMPIONSHIP GAME EXPERIENCE: Played in NFC championship game (1995 season).
PLAYING EXPERIENCE: Green Bay NFL, 1995. ... Games: 1995 (16).
PRO STATISTICS: 1995—Returned eight kickoffs for 165 yards and recovered one fumble.

JETT, JAMES   WR   RAIDERS

PERSONAL: Born December 28, 1970, in Charlestown, W.Va. ... 5-10/165.
HIGH SCHOOL: Jefferson (Shenandoah Junction, W.Va.).
COLLEGE: West Virginia.
TRANSACTIONS/CAREER NOTES: Signed as non-drafted free agent by Los Angeles Raiders (May 1993). ... Raiders franchise moved to Oakland (July 21, 1995).
PRO STATISTICS: 1993—Rushed once for no yards. 1994—Recovered two fumbles for 15 yards.
STATISTICAL PLATEAUS: 100-yard receiving games: 1993 (2).

			RECEIVING				TOTALS			
Year Team	G	No.	Yds.	Avg.	TD	TD	2pt.	Pts.	Fum.
1993—Los Angeles Raiders NFL	16	33	771	*23.4	3	3	...	18	1
1994—Los Angeles Raiders NFL	16	15	253	16.9	0	0	0	0	0
1995—Oakland NFL	16	13	179	13.8	1	1	0	6	1
Pro totals (3 years)	48	61	1203	19.7	4	4	0	24	2

JETT, JOHN   P   COWBOYS

PERSONAL: Born November 11, 1968, in Richmond, Va. ... 6-0/194.
HIGH SCHOOL: Northumberland (Heathsville, Va.).
COLLEGE: East Carolina.
TRANSACTIONS/CAREER NOTES: Signed as non-drafted free agent by Minnesota Vikings (June 22, 1992). ... Released by Vikings (August 25, 1992). ... Signed by Dallas Cowboys (March 10, 1993). ... Granted unconditional free agency (February 16, 1996). ... Re-signed by Cowboys (April 16, 1996).
CHAMPIONSHIP GAME EXPERIENCE: Played in NFC championship game (1993-1995 seasons). ... Member of Super Bowl championship team (1993 and 1995 seasons).

				PUNTING			
Year Team	G	No.	Yds.	Avg.	Net avg.	In. 20	Blk.
1992—				Did not play.			
1993—Dallas NFL	16	56	2342	41.8	37.7	22	0
1994—Dallas NFL	16	70	2935	41.9	35.4	26	0
1995—Dallas NFL	16	53	2166	40.9	34.5	17	0
Pro totals (3 years)	48	179	7443	41.6	35.9	65	0

JOHNSON, A.J.   CB

PERSONAL: Born June 22, 1967, in Lompoc, Calif. ... 5-8/175. ... Full name: Anthony Sean Johnson.
HIGH SCHOOL: Samuel Clemens (Schertz, Texas).

COLLEGE: Southwest Texas State.
TRANSACTIONS/CAREER NOTES: Selected by Washington Redskins in sixth round (149th pick overall) of 1989 NFL draft. ... Signed by Redskins (July 23, 1989). ... On physically unable to perform list with knee injury (August 28-December 1, 1990). ... On injured reserve with broken wrist (August 27-October 5, 1991). ... Released by Redskins (August 29, 1994). ... Re-signed by Redskins (August 31, 1994). ... Granted unconditional free agency (February 17, 1995). ... Signed by Kansas City Chiefs (June 13, 1995). ... Released by Chiefs (August 22, 1995). ... Signed by San Diego Chargers (August 24, 1995). ... Released by Chargers (September 14, 1995).
CHAMPIONSHIP GAME EXPERIENCE: Played in NFC championship game (1991 season). ... Member of Super Bowl championship team (1991 season).
PRO STATISTICS: 1991—Credited with one sack and recovered one fumble for 10 yards. 1993—Recovered one fumble.

		INTERCEPTIONS				KICKOFF RETURNS				TOTALS			
Year Team	G	No.	Yds.	Avg.	TD	No.	Yds.	Avg.	TD	TD	2pt.	Pts.	Fum.
1989—Washington NFL	16	4	94	23.5	1	24	504	21.0	0	1	...	6	0
1990—Washington NFL	5	1	0	0.0	0	0	0	...	0	0	...	0	0
1991—Washington NFL	11	0	0	...	0	0	0	...	0	0	...	0	0
1992—Washington NFL	14	3	38	12.7	0	0	0	...	0	0	...	0	0
1993—Washington NFL	13	1	69	69.0	1	0	0	...	0	1	...	6	0
1994—Washington NFL	11	0	0	...	0	0	0	...	0	0	...	0	0
1995—San Diego NFL	1	0	0	...	0	0	0	...	0	0	0	0	0
Pro totals (7 years)	71	9	201	22.3	2	24	504	21.0	0	2	0	12	0

JOHNSON, ANTHONY　　　FB　　　PANTHERS

PERSONAL: Born October 25, 1967, in Indianapolis. ... 6-0/225. ... Full name: Anthony Scott Johnson.
HIGH SCHOOL: John Adams (South Bend, Ind.).
COLLEGE: Notre Dame.
TRANSACTIONS/CAREER NOTES: Selected by Indianapolis Colts in second round (36th pick overall) of 1990 NFL draft. ... Signed by Colts (July 27, 1990). ... On injured reserve with eye injury (November 5, 1991-remainder of season). ... Granted unconditional free agency (February 17, 1994). ... Signed by New York Jets (June 21, 1994). ... Granted unconditional free agency (February 17, 1995). ... Signed by Chicago Bears (March 21, 1995). ... Released by Bears (November 6, 1995). ... Claimed on waivers by Carolina Panthers (November 7, 1995).
PRO STATISTICS: 1992—Attempted one pass without a completion and recovered four fumbles. 1993—Had only pass attempt intercepted and recovered two fumbles. 1994—Returned one punt for three yards.
STATISTICAL PLATEAUS: 100-yard receiving games: 1991 (1), 1992 (1). Total: 2.

		RUSHING				RECEIVING				TOTALS			
Year Team	G	Att.	Yds.	Avg.	TD	No.	Yds.	Avg.	TD	TD	2pt.	Pts.	Fum.
1990—Indianapolis NFL	16	0	0	...	0	5	32	6.4	2	2	...	12	0
1991—Indianapolis NFL	9	22	94	4.3	0	42	344	8.2	0	0	...	0	2
1992—Indianapolis NFL	15	178	592	3.3	0	49	517	10.6	3	3	...	18	6
1993—Indianapolis NFL	13	95	331	3.5	1	55	443	8.1	0	1	...	6	5
1994—New York Jets NFL	15	5	12	2.4	0	5	31	6.2	0	0	0	0	0
1995—Chicago NFL	8	6	30	5.0	0	13	86	6.6	0	0	0	0	2
—Carolina NFL	7	24	110	4.6	1	16	121	7.6	0	1	0	6	0
Pro totals (6 years)	83	330	1169	3.6	2	185	1574	8.5	5	7	0	42	15

JOHNSON, BILL　　　DL　　　STEELERS

PERSONAL: Born December 9, 1968, in Chicago. ... 6-4/300. ... Full name: William Edward Johnson.
HIGH SCHOOL: Neal F. Simeon (Chicago).
COLLEGE: Michigan State.
TRANSACTIONS/CAREER NOTES: Selected by Cleveland Browns in third round (65th pick overall) of 1992 NFL draft. ... Signed by Browns (July 19, 1992). ... Granted free agency (February 17, 1995). ... Re-signed by Browns (April 13, 1995). ... Claimed on waivers by Cincinnati Bengals (August 1, 1995); released after failing physical. ... Signed by Pittsburgh Steelers (October 25, 1995).
CHAMPIONSHIP GAME EXPERIENCE: Played in AFC championship game (1995 season). ... Played in Super Bowl XXX (1995 season).
PRO STATISTICS: 1994—Recovered one fumble. 1995—Recovered one fumble.

Year Team	G	SACKS
1992—Cleveland NFL	16	2.0
1993—Cleveland NFL	10	1.0
1994—Cleveland NFL	14	1.0
1995—Pittsburgh NFL	9	0.0
Pro totals (4 years)	49	4.0

JOHNSON, BRAD　　　QB　　　VIKINGS

PERSONAL: Born September 13, 1968, in Marietta, Ga. ... 6-5/223. ... Full name: James Bradley Johnson.
HIGH SCHOOL: Charles D. Owen (Swannanoa, N.C.).
COLLEGE: Florida State (degree in physical education).
TRANSACTIONS/CAREER NOTES: Selected by Minnesota Vikings in ninth round (227th pick overall) of 1992 NFL draft. ... Signed by Vikings (July 17, 1992). ... Active for one game (1992); did not play. ... Inactive for 16 games (1993). ... Granted free agency (February 17, 1995). ... Assigned by Vikings to London Monarchs in 1995 World League enhancement allocation program (February 20, 1995). ... Re-signed by Vikings (March 27, 1995).
PRO STATISTICS: 1995—Fumbled twice.

		PASSING								RUSHING				TOTALS		
Year Team	G	Att.	Cmp.	Pct.	Yds.	TD	Int.	Avg.	Rat.	Att.	Yds.	Avg.	TD	TD	2pt.	Pts.
1992—Minnesota NFL							Did not play.									
1993—Minnesota NFL							Did not play.									
1994—Minnesota NFL	4	37	22	59.5	150	0	0	4.06	68.5	2	-2	-1.0	0	0	0	0

Year Team	G	PASSING								RUSHING				TOTALS		
		Att.	Cmp.	Pct.	Yds.	TD	Int.	Avg.	Rat.	Att.	Yds.	Avg.	TD	TD	2pt.	Pts.
1995—London W.L.	...	328	194	59.2	2227	13	14	6.79	75.1	24	99	4.1	1	1	1	8
—Minnesota NFL	5	36	25	69.4	272	0	2	7.56	68.3	9	-9	-1.0	0	0	0	0
W.L. totals (1 year)	...	328	194	592	2227	13	14	6.79	75.1	24	99	4.1	1	1	1	8
NFL totals (2 years)	9	73	47	644	422	0	2	5.78	68.4	11	-11	-1.0	0	0	0	0
Pro totals (2 years)	...	401	241	60.1	2649	13	16	6.61	73.9	35	88	2.5	1	1	1	8

JOHNSON, CHARLES — WR — STEELERS

PERSONAL: Born January 3, 1972, in San Bernardino, Calif. ... 6-0/193. ... Full name: Charles Everett Johnson.
HIGH SCHOOL: Cajun (San Berardino, Calif.).
COLLEGE: Colorado.
TRANSACTIONS/CAREER NOTES: Selected by Pittsburgh Steelers in first round (17th pick overall) of 1994 NFL draft. ... Signed by Steelers (July 21, 1994). ... On injured reserve with knee injury (December 23, 1995-remainder of season).
CHAMPIONSHIP GAME EXPERIENCE: Played in AFC championship game (1994 season).
HONORS: Named wide receiver on THE SPORTING NEWS college All-America second team (1993).
PRO STATISTICS: 1994—Fumbled twice. 1995—Recovered one fumble.
STATISTICAL PLATEAUS: 100-yard receiving games: 1994 (1).

Year Team	G	RUSHING				RECEIVING				PUNT RETURNS				KICKOFF RETURNS				TOTALS		
		Att.	Yds.	Avg.	TD	No.	Yds.	Avg.	TD	No.	Yds.	Avg.	TD	No.	Yds.	Avg.	TD	TD	2pt.	Pts.
1994—Pittsburgh NFL	16	4	-1	-0.3	0	38	577	15.2	3	15	90	6.0	0	16	345	21.6	0	3	0	18
1995—Pittsburgh NFL	15	1	-10	-10.0	0	38	432	11.4	0	0	0	...	0	2	47	23.5	0	0	0	0
Pro totals (2 years)	31	5	-11	-2.2	0	76	1009	13.3	3	15	90	6.0	0	18	392	21.8	0	3	0	18

JOHNSON, D.J. — CB — FALCONS

PERSONAL: Born July 14, 1966, in Louisville, Ky. ... 6-0/190. ... Full name: David Allen Johnson.
HIGH SCHOOL: Male (Louisville, Ky.).
COLLEGE: Kentucky (degree in journalism, 1989).
TRANSACTIONS/CAREER NOTES: Selected by Pittsburgh Steelers in seventh round (174th pick overall) of 1989 NFL draft. ... Signed by Steelers (July 24, 1989). ... Granted unconditional free agency (February 17, 1994). ... Signed by Atlanta Falcons (March 7, 1994).
PRO STATISTICS: 1990—Recovered one fumble for nine yards. 1992—Credited with one sack and recovered two fumbles. 1994—Recovered two fumbles for 15 yards.

Year Team	G	INTERCEPTIONS			
		No.	Yds.	Avg.	TD
1989—Pittsburgh NFL	16	1	0	0.0	0
1990—Pittsburgh NFL	16	2	60	30.0	1
1991—Pittsburgh NFL	16	1	0	0.0	0
1992—Pittsburgh NFL	15	5	67	13.4	0
1993—Pittsburgh NFL	16	3	51	17.0	0
1994—Atlanta NFL	16	5	0	0.0	0
1995—Atlanta NFL	13	2	4	2.0	0
Pro totals (7 years)	108	19	182	9.6	1

JOHNSON, ELLIS — DT — COLTS

PERSONAL: Born October 30, 1973, in Wildwood, Fla. ... 6-2/298.
HIGH SCHOOL: Wildwood (Fla.).
COLLEGE: Florida.
TRANSACTIONS/CAREER NOTES: Selected by Indianapolis Colts in first round (15th pick overall) of 1995 NFL draft. ... Signed by Colts (June 7, 1995).
CHAMPIONSHIP GAME EXPERIENCE: Played in AFC championship game (1995 season).

Year Team	G	SACKS
1995—Indianapolis NFL	16	4.5

JOHNSON, FILMEL — CB

PERSONAL: Born December 24, 1970, in Detroit. ... 5-10/187.
HIGH SCHOOL: Saint Mary's Preparatory (Orchard Lake, Mich.).
COLLEGE: Illinois.
TRANSACTIONS/CAREER NOTES: Selected by Buffalo Bills in seventh round (221st pick overall) of 1994 NFL draft. ... Signed by Bills (July 8, 1994). ... Released by Bills (August 28, 1994). ... Re-signed by Bills to practice squad (August 29, 1994). ... Active for one game (1994); did not play. ... Released by Bills (August 27, 1995). ... Re-signed by Bills to practice squad (September 5, 1995). ... Activated (December 16, 1995). ... Granted unconditional free agency (February 16, 1996).
PLAYING EXPERIENCE: Buffalo NFL, 1995. ... Games: 1995 (2).

JOHNSON, JIMMIE — TE — EAGLES

PERSONAL: Born October 6, 1966, in Augusta, Ga. ... 6-2/257.
HIGH SCHOOL: T.W. Josey (Augusta, Ga.).
COLLEGE: Howard (degree in consumer studies, 1989).
TRANSACTIONS/CAREER NOTES: Selected by Washington Redskins in 12th round (316th pick overall) of 1989 NFL draft. ... Signed by

Redskins (July 23, 1989). ... On injured reserve with pinched nerve in neck (October 12, 1991-remainder of season). ... Granted unconditional free agency (February 1, 1992). ... Signed by Detroit Lions (April 1, 1992). ... On active/non-football injury list (July 16-August 23, 1993). ... On reserve/non-football injury list (August 23-October 15, 1993). ... Released by Lions (November 29, 1993). ... Signed by Kansas City Chiefs (1994). ... Released by Chiefs (August 29, 1994). ... Re-signed by Chiefs (October 12, 1994). ... Released by Chiefs (March 30, 1995). ... Signed by Philadelphia Eagles (August 2, 1995). ... Granted unconditional free agency (February 16, 1996). ... Re-signed by Eagles (April 18, 1996).

PRO STATISTICS: 1992—Returned one kickoff for no yards.

			RECEIVING			TOTALS			
Year Team	G	No.	Yds.	Avg.	TD	TD	2pt.	Pts.	Fum.
1989—Washington NFL	16	4	84	21.0	0	0	...	0	0
1990—Washington NFL	16	15	218	14.5	2	2	...	12	1
1991—Washington NFL	6	3	7	2.3	2	2	...	12	0
1992—Detroit NFL	16	6	34	5.7	0	0	...	0	0
1993—Detroit NFL	6	2	18	9.0	0	0	...	0	0
1994—Kansas City NFL	7	2	7	3.5	0	0	0	0	0
1995—Philadelphia NFL	16	6	37	6.2	0	0	0	0	0
Pro totals (7 years)	83	38	405	10.7	4	4	0	24	1

J

JOHNSON, JOE — DT — SAINTS

PERSONAL: Born July 11, 1972, in St. Louis. ... 6-4/270.
HIGH SCHOOL: Jennings (Mo.).
COLLEGE: Louisville.
TRANSACTIONS/CAREER NOTES: Selected after junior season by New Orleans Saints in first round (13th pick overall) of 1994 NFL draft. ... Signed by Saints (June 7, 1994).
PRO STATISTICS: 1994—Recovered one fumble.

Year Team	G	SACKS
1994—New Orleans NFL	15	1.0
1995—New Orleans NFL	14	5.5
Pro totals (2 years)	29	6.5

JOHNSON, JOHN — LB

PERSONAL: Born May 8, 1968, in LaGrange, Ga. ... 6-3/247. ... Full name: John Vernard Johnson.
HIGH SCHOOL: LaGrange (Ga.).
COLLEGE: Clemson.
TRANSACTIONS/CAREER NOTES: Selected by San Francisco 49ers in second round (53rd pick overall) of 1991 NFL draft. ... Signed by 49ers (July 10, 1991). ... On injured reserve with neck injury (November 9, 1991-remainder of season). ... Granted unconditional free agency (February 1-April 1, 1992). ... Re-signed by 49ers (June 10, 1994). ... Claimed on waivers by Cincinnati Bengals (June 13, 1994). ... Released by Bengals (October 4, 1994). ... Signed by Kansas City Chiefs (February 28, 1995). ... Released by Chiefs (July 19, 1995). ... Signed by New Orleans Saints (July 24, 1995). ... Released by Saints (August 28, 1995). ... Re-signed by Saints (September 6, 1995). ... Released by Saints (October 21, 1995).
CHAMPIONSHIP GAME EXPERIENCE: Played in NFC championship game (1992 and 1993 seasons).
PRO STATISTICS: 1993—Recovered one fumble for seven yards.

		INTERCEPTIONS				SACKS
Year Team	G	No.	Yds.	Avg.	TD	No.
1991—San Francisco NFL	9	0	0	...	0	0.0
1992—San Francisco NFL	16	1	56	56.0	1	1.0
1993—San Francisco NFL	15	1	0	0.0	0	2.0
1994—Cincinnati NFL	5	0	0	...	0	0.0
1995—New Orleans NFL	1	0	0	...	0	0.0
Pro totals (5 years)	46	2	56	28.0	1	3.0

JOHNSON, JOHNNY — RB — 49ERS

PERSONAL: Born June 11, 1968, in Santa Clara, Calif. ... 6-3/220.
HIGH SCHOOL: Santa Cruz (Calif.).
COLLEGE: San Jose State.
TRANSACTIONS/CAREER NOTES: Selected by Phoenix Cardinals in seventh round (169th pick overall) of 1990 NFL draft. ... Signed by Cardinals (July 25, 1990). ... Granted free agency (February 1, 1992). ... Re-signed by Cardinals (August 30, 1992). ... Granted roster exemption (August 30-September 11, 1992). ... Traded by Cardinals with first-round pick (LB Marvin Jones) in 1993 draft to New York Jets for first-round pick (RB Garrison Hearst) in 1993 draft (April 25, 1993). ... Released by Jets (June 27, 1995). ... Signed by San Francisco 49ers (March 28, 1996).
HONORS: Played in Pro Bowl (1990 season).
PRO STATISTICS: 1990—Had only pass attempt intercepted and recovered one fumble. 1993—Recovered two fumbles.
STATISTICAL PLATEAUS: 100-yard rushing games: 1990 (3), 1992 (3), 1993 (2), 1994 (2). Total: 10.

		RUSHING				RECEIVING				TOTALS			
Year Team	G	Att.	Yds.	Avg.	TD	No.	Yds.	Avg.	TD	TD	2pt.	Pts.	Fum.
1990—Phoenix NFL	14	234	926	4.0	5	25	241	9.6	0	5	...	30	7
1991—Phoenix NFL	15	196	666	3.4	4	29	225	7.8	2	6	...	36	2
1992—Phoenix NFL	12	178	734	4.1	6	14	103	7.4	0	6	...	36	2
1993—New York Jets NFL	15	198	821	4.2	3	67	641	9.6	1	4	...	24	5
1994—New York Jets NFL	16	240	931	3.9	3	42	303	7.2	2	5	0	30	4
1995—							Did not play.						
Pro totals (5 years)	72	1046	4078	3.9	21	177	1513	8.6	5	26	0	156	20

JOHNSON, KESHON — CB

PERSONAL: Born July 17, 1970, in Fresno, Calif. ... 5-10/183. ... Full name: Keshon Lorenzo Johnson. ... Name pronounced KEY-shawn
HIGH SCHOOL: Edison (Fresno, Calif.).
JUNIOR COLLEGE: Fresno (Calif.) City College.
COLLEGE: Arizona.
TRANSACTIONS/CAREER NOTES: Selected by Chicago Bears in seventh round (173rd pick overall) of 1993 NFL draft. ... Signed by Bears (July 6, 1993). ... Claimed on waivers by Green Bay Packers (November 1, 1994). ... Released by Packers (April 27, 1995). ... Claimed on waivers by Detroit Lions (May 8, 1995). ... Released by Lions (September 7, 1995). ... Signed by Bears (September 27, 1995). ... Granted unconditional free agency (February 16, 1996).
PRO STATISTICS: 1994—Recovered one fumble.

| | | INTERCEPTIONS | | | |
Year Team	G	No.	Yds.	Avg.	TD
1993—Chicago NFL	15	0	0	...	0
1994—Chicago NFL	6	0	0	...	0
—Green Bay NFL	7	1	3	3.0	0
1995—Chicago NFL	12	0	0	...	0
Pro totals (3 years)	40	1	3	3.0	0

JOHNSON, KEVIN — DT — EAGLES

PERSONAL: Born October 30, 1970, in Los Angeles. ... 6-1/306.
HIGH SCHOOL: Westchester (Los Angeles).
JUNIOR COLLEGE: Harbor Junior College (Calif.).
COLLEGE: Texas Southern.
TRANSACTIONS/CAREER NOTES: Selected by New England Patriots in fourth round (86th pick overall) of 1993 NFL draft. ... Signed by Patriots (June 30, 1993). ... Released by Patriots (August 23, 1993). ... Signed by Minnesota Vikings to practice squad (September 1, 1993). ... Released by Vikings (September 27, 1993). ... Signed by Oakland Raiders (June 1995). ... Claimed on waivers by Philadelphia Eagles (August 29, 1995).
PRO STATISTICS: 1995—Recovered one fumble for 37 yards and a touchdown.

Year Team	G	SACKS
1993—	Did not play.	
1994—	Did not play.	
1995—Philadelphia NFL	11	6.0

JOHNSON, LEE — P — BENGALS

PERSONAL: Born November 27, 1961, in Dallas. ... 6-2/200.
HIGH SCHOOL: McCullough (The Woodlands, Texas).
COLLEGE: Brigham Young.
TRANSACTIONS/CAREER NOTES: Selected by Houston Gamblers in ninth round (125th pick overall) of 1985 USFL draft. ... Selected by Houston Oilers in fifth round (138th pick overall) of 1985 NFL draft. ... Signed by Oilers (June 25, 1985). ... Crossed picket line during players strike (October 14, 1987). ... Claimed on waivers by Buffalo Bills (December 2, 1987). ... Claimed on waivers by Cleveland Browns (December 10, 1987). ... Claimed on waivers by Cincinnati Bengals (September 23, 1988). ... Granted free agency (February 1, 1991). ... Re-signed by Bengals (1991). ... Granted unconditional free agency (March 1, 1993). ... Re-signed by Bengals (May 10, 1993).
CHAMPIONSHIP GAME EXPERIENCE: Played in AFC championship game (1987 and 1988 seasons). ... Played in Super Bowl XXIII (1988 season).
POSTSEASON RECORDS: Holds Super Bowl career record for longest punt—63 yards (January 22, 1989, vs. San Francisco).
PRO STATISTICS: 1985—Rushed once for no yards, fumbled twice and recovered one fumble for seven yards. 1987—Had 32.8-yard net punting average. 1988—Had 33.4-yard net punting average. 1989—Rushed once for minus seven yards. 1990—Attempted one pass with one completion for four yards and a touchdown. 1991—Attempted one pass with one completion for three yards, rushed once for minus two yards and fumbled once. 1993—Attempted one pass without a completion. 1994—Attempted one pass with one completion for seven yards and one touchdown. 1995—Attempted one pass with one completion for five yards, rushed once for minus 16 yards and fumbled once.

| | | | PUNTING | | | | | | KICKING | | | | | |
Year Team	G	No.	Yds.	Avg.	Net avg.	In. 20	Blk.	XPM	XPA	FGM	FGA	Lg.	50+	Pts.
1985—Houston NFL	16	83	3464	41.7	35.7	22	0	0	0	0	0	...	0-0	0
1986—Houston NFL	16	88	3623	41.2	35.7	26	0	0	0	0	0	...	0-0	0
1987—Houston NFL	9	25	1008	40.3	...	5	1	0	0	0	0	...	0-0	0
—Cleveland NFL	3	9	317	35.2	32.3	3	0	0	0	0	0	...	0-0	0
1988—Cleveland NFL	3	31	1237	39.9	...	6	0	0	0	1	2	50	1-2	3
—Cincinnati NFL	12	14	594	42.4	...	4	0	0	0	0	0	...	0-0	0
1989—Cincinnati NFL	16	61	2446	40.1	30.2	14	2	0	1	0	0	...	0-0	0
1990—Cincinnati NFL	16	64	2705	42.3	34.3	12	0	0	0	0	1	0	0-0	0
1991—Cincinnati NFL	16	64	2795	43.7	34.7	15	0	0	0	1	3	53	1-3	3
1992—Cincinnati NFL	16	76	3196	42.1	35.9	15	0	0	0	0	1	0	0-1	0
1993—Cincinnati NFL	16	90	3954	43.9	36.6	24	0	0	0	0	0	...	0-0	0
1994—Cincinnati NFL	16	79	3461	43.8	35.3	19	1	0	0	0	0	...	0-0	0
1995—Cincinnati NFL	16	68	2861	42.1	38.6	26	0	0	0	0	0	...	0-0	0
Pro totals (12 years)	171	752	31661	42.1	35.5	191	4	0	1	2	7	53	2-6	6

JOHNSON, LeSHON — RB — CARDINALS

PERSONAL: Born January 15, 1971, in Tulsa, Okla. ... 5-11/195. ... Full name: LeShon Eugene Johnson.
HIGH SCHOOL: Haskell (Okla.).
COLLEGE: Northeastern Oklahoma A&M, then Northern Illinois.

TRANSACTIONS/CAREER NOTES: Selected by Green Bay Packers in third round (84th pick overall) of 1994 NFL draft. ... Signed by Packers (July 19, 1994). ... On injured reserve with knee injury (January 3, 1995-remainder of 1994 playoffs). ... On physically unable to perform list with knee injury (August 27-October 21, 1995). ... Claimed on waivers by Arizona Cardinals (November 29, 1995).
HONORS: Named running back on THE SPORTING NEWS college All-America first team (1993).
PRO STATISTICS: 1995—Recovered one fumble.

Year Team	G	RUSHING				RECEIVING				KICKOFF RETURNS				TOTALS			
		Att.	Yds.	Avg.	TD	No.	Yds.	Avg.	TD	No.	Yds.	Avg.	TD	TD	2pt.	Pts.	Fum.
1994—Green Bay NFL	12	26	99	3.8	0	13	168	12.9	0	0	0	...	0	0	0	0	0
1995—Green Bay NFL	2	2	-2	-1.0	0	0	0	...	0	0	0	...	0	0	0	0	0
—Arizona NFL	3	0	0	...	0	0	0	...	0	11	259	23.6	0	0	0	0	1
Pro totals (2 years)	17	28	97	3.5	0	13	168	12.9	0	11	259	23.6	0	0	0	0	1

JOHNSON, LONNIE   TE   BILLS   J

PERSONAL: Born February 14, 1971, in Miami. ... 6-3/240.
HIGH SCHOOL: Senior (Miami).
COLLEGE: Florida State.
TRANSACTIONS/CAREER NOTES: Selected by Buffalo Bills in second round (61st pick overall) of 1994 NFL draft. ... Signed by Bills (July 15, 1994).
PRO STATISTICS: 1995—Recovered one fumble.

Year Team	G	RECEIVING				TOTALS			
		No.	Yds.	Avg.	TD	TD	2pt.	Pts.	Fum.
1994—Buffalo NFL	10	3	42	14.0	0	0	0	0	0
1995—Buffalo NFL	16	49	504	10.3	1	1	0	6	0
Pro totals (2 years)	26	52	546	10.5	1	1	0	6	0

JOHNSON, MELVIN   S   BUCCANEERS

PERSONAL: Born April 15, 1972, in Cincinnati. ... 6-0/191. ... Full name: Melvin Carlton Johnson III.
HIGH SCHOOL: St. Xavier (Cincinnati).
COLLEGE: Kentucky.
TRANSACTIONS/CAREER NOTES: Selected by Tampa Bay Buccaneers in second round (43rd pick overall) of 1995 NFL draft. ... Signed by Buccaneers (May 10, 1995).

Year Team	G	INTERCEPTIONS			
		No.	Yds.	Avg.	TD
1995—Tampa Bay NFL	11	1	0	0.0	0

JOHNSON, MIKE   LB

PERSONAL: Born November 26, 1962, in Southport, N.C. ... 6-1/230.
HIGH SCHOOL: DeMatha Catholic (Hyattsville, Md.).
COLLEGE: Virginia Tech.
TRANSACTIONS/CAREER NOTES: Selected by Pittsburgh Maulers in 1984 USFL territorial draft. ... USFL rights traded by Maulers with DE Mark Buben, rights to LB Al Chesley and draft pick to Philadelphia Stars for rights to LB Ron Crosby (February 1, 1984). ... Signed by Stars (February 20, 1984). ... Granted roster exemption (February 20-March 2, 1984). ... Selected by Cleveland Browns in first round (18th pick overall) of 1984 NFL supplemental draft. ... Stars franchise moved to Baltimore (November 1, 1984). ... Granted free agency when USFL suspended operations (August 7, 1986). ... Signed by Browns (August 12, 1986). ... Granted roster exemption (August 12-22, 1986). ... Granted free agency (February 1, 1990). ... Re-signed by Browns (August 31, 1990). ... Granted roster exemption (September 3-8, 1990). ... Granted free agency (February 1, 1991). ... Re-signed by Browns (May 14, 1991). ... On injured reserve with broken foot (September 25-December 21, 1991). ... Designated by Browns as transition player (February 25, 1993). ... Free agency status changed by Browns from transitional to unconditional (February 17, 1994). ... Signed by Detroit Lions (April 22, 1994). ... Granted unconditional free agency (February 17, 1995). ... Re-signed by Lions (March 31, 1995). ... Released by Lions (April 25, 1996).
CHAMPIONSHIP GAME EXPERIENCE: Played in USFL championship game (1984 and 1985 seasons). ... Played in AFC championship game (1986, 1987 and 1989 seasons).
HONORS: Played in Pro Bowl (1990 season).
PRO STATISTICS: USFL: 1984—Recovered one fumble for eight yards. 1985—Recovered two fumbles. NFL: 1986—Recovered two fumbles. 1987—Recovered one fumble. 1992—Recovered five fumbles (including one in end zone for a touchdown). 1994—Recovered one fumble. 1995—Recovered four fumbles for six yards.

Year Team	G	INTERCEPTIONS				SACKS
		No.	Yds.	Avg.	TD	No.
1984—Philadelphia USFL	17	0	0	...	0	2.0
1985—Baltimore USFL	18	0	0	...	0	3.5
1986—Cleveland NFL	16	0	0	...	0	0.0
1987—Cleveland NFL	11	1	3	3.0	0	2.0
1988—Cleveland NFL	16	2	36	18.0	0	0.0
1989—Cleveland NFL	16	3	43	14.3	0	1.0
1990—Cleveland NFL	16	1	64	64.0	1	2.0
1991—Cleveland NFL	5	1	0	0.0	0	0.0
1992—Cleveland NFL	16	1	0	0.0	0	2.0
1993—Cleveland NFL	16	1	0	0.0	0	4.0
1994—Detroit NFL	16	1	48	48.0	1	1.5
1995—Detroit NFL	16	2	23	11.5	0	2.0
USFL totals (2 years)	35	0	0	...	0	55
NFL totals (10 years)	144	13	217	16.7	2	145
Pro totals (12 years)	179	13	217	16.7	2	20.0

JOHNSON, NORM K STEELERS

PERSONAL: Born May 31, 1960, in Inglewood, Calif. ... 6-2/202.
HIGH SCHOOL: Pacifica (Garden Grove, Calif.).
COLLEGE: UCLA.
TRANSACTIONS/CAREER NOTES: Signed as non-drafted free agent by Seattle Seahawks (May 4, 1982). ... Crossed picket line during players strike (October 14, 1987). ... Granted free agency (February 1, 1991). ... Re-signed by Seahawks (July 19, 1991). ... Released by Seahawks (August 26, 1991). ... Signed by Atlanta Falcons (September 9, 1991). ... Granted free agency (February 1, 1992). ... Re-signed by Falcons (1992). ... Released by Falcons (July 20, 1995). ... Signed by Pittsburgh Steelers (August 22, 1995).
CHAMPIONSHIP GAME EXPERIENCE: Played in AFC championship game (1983 and 1995 seasons). ... Played in Super Bowl XXX (1995 season).
HONORS: Named kicker on THE SPORTING NEWS NFL All-Pro team (1984). ... Played in Pro Bowl (1984 and 1993 seasons).
PRO STATISTICS: 1982—Attempted one pass with one completion for 27 yards. 1991—Punted once for 21 yards. 1992—Punted once for 37 yards.

		KICKING						
Year Team	G	XPM	XPA	FGM	FGA	Lg.	50+	Pts.
1982—Seattle NFL	9	13	14	10	14	48	0-1	43
1983—Seattle NFL	16	49	50	18	25	54	1-3	103
1984—Seattle NFL	16	50	51	20	24	50	1-3	110
1985—Seattle NFL	16	40	41	14	25	51	1-3	82
1986—Seattle NFL	16	42	42	22	35	54	5-7	108
1987—Seattle NFL	13	40	40	15	20	49	0-1	85
1988—Seattle NFL	16	39	39	22	28	47	0-0	105
1989—Seattle NFL	16	27	27	15	25	50	1-5	72
1990—Seattle NFL	16	33	34	23	32	51	1-3	102
1991—Atlanta NFL	14	38	39	19	23	50	1-2	95
1992—Atlanta NFL	16	39	39	18	22	54	4-4	93
1993—Atlanta NFL	15	34	34	26	27	54	2-2	112
1994—Atlanta NFL	16	32	32	21	25	50	1-5	95
1995—Pittsburgh NFL	16	39	39	*34	*41	50	1-1	141
Pro totals (14 years)	211	515	521	277	366	54	19-40	1346

JOHNSON, PAT S DOLPHINS

PERSONAL: Born June 10, 1972, in Mineral Point, Mo. ... 6-1/204. ... Full name: John Patrick Johnson.
HIGH SCHOOL: Potosi (Mo.).
COLLEGE: Purdue.
TRANSACTIONS/CAREER NOTES: Signed as non-drafted free agent by Atlanta Falcons (May 2, 1994). ... Claimed on waivers by Miami Dolphins (July 13, 1994). ... Released by Dolphins (August 22, 1994). ... Re-signed by Dolphins to practice squad (August 29, 1994). ... Granted free agency after 1994 season. ... Re-signed by Dolphins (February 16, 1995).
PLAYING EXPERIENCE: Miami NFL, 1995. ... Games: 1995 (14).
PRO STATISTICS: 1995—Recovered one fumble for 37 yards and a touchdown.

JOHNSON, PEPPER LB RAVENS

PERSONAL: Born July 29, 1964, in Detroit. ... 6-3/248.
HIGH SCHOOL: MacKenzie (Detroit).
COLLEGE: Ohio State.
TRANSACTIONS/CAREER NOTES: Selected by New Jersey Generals in 1986 USFL territorial draft. ... Selected by New York Giants in second round (51st pick overall) of 1986 NFL draft. ... Signed by Giants (July 30, 1986). ... Granted free agency (February 1, 1989). ... Re-signed by Giants (September 14, 1989). ... Granted roster exemption (September 14-23, 1989). ... Granted free agency (February 1, 1991). ... Re-signed by Giants (August 14, 1991). ... Designated by Giants as transition player (February 25, 1993). ... Claimed on waivers by Cleveland Browns (September 1, 1993). ... Granted unconditional free agency (February 17, 1994). ... Re-signed by Browns (June 3, 1994). ... Browns franchise moved to Baltimore and renamed Ravens for 1996 season (March 11, 1996).
CHAMPIONSHIP GAME EXPERIENCE: Played in NFC championship game (1986 and 1990 seasons). ... Member of Super Bowl championship team (1986 and 1990 seasons).
HONORS: Named inside linebacker on THE SPORTING NEWS NFL All-Pro team (1990). ... Played in Pro Bowl (1990 and 1994 seasons).
PRO STATISTICS: 1987—Recovered one fumble. 1988—Recovered one fumble. 1989—Recovered one fumble. 1990—Recovered one fumble. 1992—Fumbled once and recovered two fumbles. 1994—Recovered one fumble for 10 yards.

		INTERCEPTIONS				SACKS
Year Team	G	No.	Yds.	Avg.	TD	No.
1986—New York Giants NFL	16	1	13	13.0	0	2.0
1987—New York Giants NFL	12	0	0	...	0	1.0
1988—New York Giants NFL	16	1	33	33.0	1	4.0
1989—New York Giants NFL	14	3	60	20.0	1	1.0
1990—New York Giants NFL	16	1	0	0.0	0	3.5
1991—New York Giants NFL	16	2	5	2.5	0	6.5
1992—New York Giants NFL	16	2	42	21.0	0	1.0
1993—Cleveland NFL	16	0	0	...	0	1.0
1994—Cleveland NFL	16	0	0	...	0	2.5
1995—Cleveland NFL	16	2	22	11.0	0	2.0
Pro totals (10 years)	154	12	175	14.6	2	24.5

JOHNSON, RAYLEE DE CHARGERS

PERSONAL: Born June 1, 1970, in Fordyce, Ark. ... 6-3/265. ... Full name: Raylee Terrell Johnson.

J

HIGH SCHOOL: Fordyce (Ark.).
COLLEGE: Arkansas.
TRANSACTIONS/CAREER NOTES: Selected by San Diego Chargers in fourth round (95th pick overall) of 1993 NFL draft. ... Signed by Chargers (July 15, 1993).
CHAMPIONSHIP GAME EXPERIENCE: Played in AFC championship game (1994 season). ... Played in Super Bowl XXIX (1994 season).

Year Team	G	SACKS
1993—San Diego NFL	9	0.0
1994—San Diego NFL	15	1.5
1995—San Diego NFL	16	3.0
Pro totals (3 years)	40	4.5

JOHNSON, REGGIE — TE — CHIEFS

PERSONAL: Born January 27, 1968, in Pensacola, Fla. ... 6-2/256.
HIGH SCHOOL: Escambia (Pensacola, Fla.).
COLLEGE: Florida State (degree in criminology, 1991).
TRANSACTIONS/CAREER NOTES: Selected by Denver Broncos in second round (30th pick overall) of 1991 NFL draft. ... Signed by Broncos (July 19, 1991). ... Granted free agency (February 17, 1994). ... Re-signed by Broncos (June 16, 1994). ... Claimed on waivers by Cincinnati Bengals (August 25, 1994). ... Released by Bengals (August 26, 1994). ... Signed by Green Bay Packers (September 27, 1994). ... Granted unconditional free agency (February 17, 1995). ... Signed by Philadelphia Eagles (March 20, 1995). ... Released by Eagles (August 29, 1995). ... Re-signed by Eagles (October 25, 1995). ... Granted unconditional free agency (February 16, 1996). ... Signed by Kansas City Chiefs (May 24, 1996).
CHAMPIONSHIP GAME EXPERIENCE: Member of Broncos for AFC championship game (1991 season); did not play.
POSTSEASON RECORDS: Shares NFL postseason career and single-games records for most two-point conversions—1 (January 7, 1996, vs. Dallas).
PRO STATISTICS: 1991—Recovered one fumble. 1992—Rushed twice for seven yards, returned two kickoffs for 47 yards and recovered one fumble.

Year Team	G	No.	Yds.	Avg.	TD	TD	2pt.	Pts.	Fum.
		RECEIVING				TOTALS			
1991—Denver NFL	16	6	73	12.2	1	0	...	0	0
1992—Denver NFL	15	10	139	13.9	1	1	...	6	0
1993—Denver NFL	13	20	243	12.2	1	1	...	6	1
1994—Green Bay NFL	9	7	79	11.3	0	0	0	0	0
1995—Philadelphia NFL	9	5	68	13.6	2	2	0	12	0
Pro totals (5 years)	62	48	602	12.6	5	4	0	24	1

JOHNSON, ROB — QB — JAGUARS

PERSONAL: Born March 18, 1973, in Newport Beach, Calif. ... 6-3/222. ... Brother of Bret Johnson, quarterback, Toronto Argonauts of CFL (1995).
HIGH SCHOOL: El Toro (Calif.).
COLLEGE: Southern California.
TRANSACTIONS/CAREER NOTES: Selected by Jacksonville Jaguars in fourth round (99th pick overall) of 1995 NFL draft. ... Signed by Jaguars (June 1, 1995).
MISCELLANEOUS: Selected by Minnesota Twins organization in 16th round of free-agent draft (June 4, 1991); did not sign.

Year Team	G	Att.	Cmp.	Pct.	Yds.	TD	Int.	Avg.	Rat.	Att.	Yds.	Avg.	TD	TD	2pt.	Pts.
		PASSING								RUSHING				TOTALS		
1995—Jacksonville NFL	1	7	3	42.9	24	0	1	3.43	12.5	3	17	5.7	0	0	0	0

JOHNSON, TED — LB — PATRIOTS

PERSONAL: Born December 4, 1972, in Alameda, Calif. ... 6-3/240.
HIGH SCHOOL: Carlsbad (Calif.).
COLLEGE: Colorado.
TRANSACTIONS/CAREER NOTES: Selected by New England Patriots in second round (57th pick overall) of 1995 NFL draft. ... Signed by Patriots (July 18, 1995).
HONORS: Named linebacker on THE SPORTING NEWS college All-America second team (1994).
PRO STATISTICS: 1995—Recovered two fumbles.

Year Team	G	SACKS
1995—New England NFL	12	0.5

JOHNSON, TIM — DT

PERSONAL: Born January 29, 1965, in Sarasota, Fla. ... 6-3/286.
HIGH SCHOOL: Sarasota (Fla.).
COLLEGE: Penn State (degree in hotel, restaurant and institutional management, 1987).
TRANSACTIONS/CAREER NOTES: Selected by Pittsburgh Steelers in sixth round (141st pick overall) of 1987 NFL draft. ... Signed by Steelers (July 26, 1987). ... Traded by Steelers to Washington Redskins for fourth-round pick (TE Adrian Cooper) in 1991 draft (August 23, 1990). ... Granted unconditional free agency (March 1, 1993). ... Re-signed by Redskins for 1993 season. ... Granted unconditional free agency (February 16, 1996).
CHAMPIONSHIP GAME EXPERIENCE: Played in NFC championship game (1991 season). ... Member of Super Bowl championship team (1991 season).
PRO STATISTICS: 1990—Recovered one fumble. 1991—Intercepted one pass for 14 yards. 1992—Recovered one fumble. 1993—

Year Team	G	SACKS
1987—Pittsburgh NFL	12	0.0
1988—Pittsburgh NFL	15	4.0
1989—Pittsburgh NFL	14	4.5
1990—Washington NFL	16	3.0
1991—Washington NFL	16	3.5
1992—Washington NFL	16	6.0
1993—Washington NFL	15	4.0
1994—Washington NFL	14	1.0
1995—Washington NFL	14	3.0
Pro totals (9 years)	132	29.0

JOHNSON, TOMMY　　　　CB　　　　JAGUARS

PERSONAL: Born December 5, 1971, in Rome, Ga. ... 5-10/183. ... Full name: Tommy Postell Johnson.
HIGH SCHOOL: Niceville (Fla.).
COLLEGE: Alabama.
TRANSACTIONS/CAREER NOTES: Signed as non-drafted free agent by Jacksonville Jaguars (April 24, 1995). ... Released by Jaguars (August 19, 1995). ... Re-signed by Jaguars to practice squad (August 28, 1995). ... Activated (November 17, 1995).
PLAYING EXPERIENCE: Jacksonville NFL, 1995. ... Games: 1995 (1).

JOHNSON, TRACY　　　　FB　　　　BUCCANEERS

PERSONAL: Born November 29, 1966, in Concord, N.C. ... 6-0/242. ... Full name: Tracy Illya Johnson.
HIGH SCHOOL: A.L. Brown (Kannapolis, N.C.).
COLLEGE: Clemson.
TRANSACTIONS/CAREER NOTES: Selected by Houston Oilers in 10th round (271st pick overall) of 1989 NFL draft. ... Signed by Oilers (July 27, 1989). ... Granted unconditional free agency (February 1, 1990). ... Signed by Atlanta Falcons (March 30, 1990). ... Granted unconditional free agency (February 1, 1992). ... Signed by Seattle Seahawks (April 1, 1992). ... Released by Seahawks (February 6, 1996). ... Signed by Tampa Bay Buccaneers (March 23, 1996).
PRO STATISTICS: 1991—Recovered one fumble. 1992—Recovered one fumble for 10 yards.

		RUSHING				RECEIVING				KICKOFF RETURNS				TOTALS			
Year Team	G	Att.	Yds.	Avg.	TD	No.	Yds.	Avg.	TD	No.	Yds.	Avg.	TD	TD	2pt.	Pts.	Fum.
1989—Houston NFL	16	4	16	4.0	0	1	8	8.0	0	13	224	17.2	0	0	...	0	1
1990—Atlanta NFL	16	30	106	3.5	3	10	79	7.9	1	2	2	1.0	0	4	...	24	1
1991—Atlanta NFL	16	8	26	3.3	0	3	27	9.0	0	0	0	...	0	0	...	0	0
1992—Seattle NFL	16	3	26	8.7	0	0	0	...	0	1	15	15.0	0	0	...	0	0
1993—Seattle NFL	16	2	8	4.0	0	3	15	5.0	1	0	0	...	0	1	...	6	0
1994—Seattle NFL	16	12	44	3.7	2	10	91	9.1	0	0	0	...	0	2	0	12	1
1995—Seattle NFL	15	1	2	2.0	1	1	-2	-2.0	0	0	0	...	0	1	0	6	0
Pro totals (7 years)	111	60	228	3.8	6	28	218	7.8	2	16	241	15.1	0	8	0	48	3

JOHNSON, TRE'　　　　OT　　　　REDSKINS

PERSONAL: Born August 30, 1971, in Manhattan, N.Y. ... 6-2/338. ... Full name: Edward Stanton Johnson III. ... Name pronounced TRAY
HIGH SCHOOL: Peekskill (N.Y.).
COLLEGE: Temple (degree in social administration, 1993).
TRANSACTIONS/CAREER NOTES: Selected by Washington Redskins in second round (31st pick overall) of 1994 NFL draft. ... Signed by Redskins (July 22, 1994).
PLAYING EXPERIENCE: Washington NFL, 1994 and 1995. ... Games: 1994 (14), 1995 (10). Total: 24.
PRO STATISTICS: 1994—Ran four yards with lateral from kickoff return.

JOHNSON, TYRONE　　　　WR　　　　FALCONS

PERSONAL: Born September 4, 1971, in Aurora, Colo. ... 5-11/171.
HIGH SCHOOL: Rangeview (Aurora, Colo.).
COLLEGE: Western State (Colo.).
TRANSACTIONS/CAREER NOTES: Signed as non-drafted free agent by New Orleans Saints (April 28, 1994). ... Released by Saints (August 27, 1995). ... Selected by Scottish Claymores in 1996 World League draft (February 22, 1996). ... Signed by Atlanta Falcons (February 26, 1996).

		RECEIVING				KICKOFF RETURNS				TOTALS			
Year Team	G	No.	Yds.	Avg.	TD	No.	Yds.	Avg.	TD	TD	2pt.	Pts.	Fum.
1994—New Orleans NFL	1	0	0	...	0	0	0	...	0	0	0	0	0
1995—Rhein W.L.	...	29	463	16.0	0	1	14	14.0	0	0	0	0	...
Pro totals (2 years)	...	29	463	16.0	0	1	14	14.0	0	0	0	0	...

JOHNSON, VANCE　　　　WR

PERSONAL: Born March 13, 1963, in Trenton, N.J. ... 5-11/185. ... Full name: Vance Edward Johnson.
HIGH SCHOOL: Cholla (Tucson, Ariz.).
COLLEGE: Arizona.
TRANSACTIONS/CAREER NOTES: Selected by Arizona Outlaws in 1985 USFL territorial draft. ... Selected by Denver Broncos in second round

(31st pick overall) of 1985 NFL draft. ... Signed by Broncos (July 16, 1985). ... On injured reserve with knee injury (September 9-October 10, 1986). ... On injured reserve with knee injury (August 27-September 28, 1991). ... On injured reserve with shoulder injury (September 1-30, 1992). ... Traded by Broncos to Minnesota Vikings for conditional draft pick (August 24, 1993). ... Released by Vikings (August 30, 1993). ... Signed by Broncos (September 7, 1993). ... On injured reserve with ankle injury (November 30, 1993-remainder of season). ... Granted unconditional free agency (February 17, 1994). ... Signed by San Diego Chargers (March 24, 1994). ... Released by Chargers (August 22, 1994). ... Signed by Broncos (April 18, 1995). ... Granted unconditional free agency (February 16, 1996).
CHAMPIONSHIP GAME EXPERIENCE: Played in AFC championship game (1986, 1989 and 1991 seasons). ... Played in Super Bowl XXI (1986 season), Super Bowl XXII (1987 season) and Super Bowl XXIV (1989 season).
PRO STATISTICS: 1985—Attempted one pass without a completion, fumbled five times and recovered two fumbles. 1986—Attempted one pass without a completion and fumbled once. 1987—Attempted one pass without a completion and fumbled once. 1989—Attempted one pass without a completion. 1990—Fumbled once. 1991—Fumbled once and recovered one fumble. 1992—Fumbled once.J207
STATISTICAL PLATEAUS: 100-yard receiving games: 1985 (1), 1987 (1), 1988 (1), 1989 (3), 1990 (2), 1993 (1). Total: 9.

Year Team	G	RUSHING				RECEIVING				PUNT RETURNS				KICKOFF RETURNS				TOTALS		
		Att.	Yds.	Avg.	TD	No.	Yds.	Avg.	TD	No.	Yds.	Avg.	TD	No.	Yds.	Avg.	TD	TD	2pt.	Pts.
1985—Denver NFL	16	10	36	3.6	0	51	721	14.1	3	30	260	8.7	0	30	740	24.7	0	3	...	18
1986—Denver NFL	12	5	15	3.0	0	31	363	11.7	2	3	36	12.0	0	2	21	10.5	0	2	...	12
1987—Denver NFL	11	1	-8	-8.0	0	42	684	16.3	7	1	9	9.0	0	7	140	20.0	0	7	...	42
1988—Denver NFL	16	1	1	1.0	0	68	896	13.2	5	0	0	...	0	0	0	...	0	5	...	30
1989—Denver NFL	16	0	0	...	0	76	1095	14.4	7	12	118	9.8	0	0	0	...	0	7	...	42
1990—Denver NFL	16	0	0	...	0	54	747	13.8	3	11	92	8.4	0	6	126	21.0	0	3	...	18
1991—Denver NFL	10	0	0	...	0	21	208	9.9	3	24	174	7.3	0	0	0	...	0	3	...	18
1992—Denver NFL	11	0	0	...	0	24	294	12.3	2	0	0	...	0	0	0	...	0	2	...	12
1993—Denver NFL	10	0	0	...	0	36	517	14.4	5	0	0	...	0	0	0	...	0	5	...	30
1994—										Did not play.										
1995—Denver NFL	10	0	0	...	0	12	170	14.2	0	0	0	...	0	0	0	...	0	0	0	0
Pro totals (10 years)	128	17	44	2.6	0	415	5695	13.7	37	81	689	8.5	0	45	1027	22.8	0	37	0	222

J

JOHNSTON, DARYL — FB — COWBOYS

PERSONAL: Born February 10, 1966, in Youngstown, N.Y. ... 6-2/242. ... Full name: Daryl Peter Johnston.
HIGH SCHOOL: Lewiston-Porter Central (Youngstown, N.Y.).
COLLEGE: Syracuse (degree in economics, 1989).
TRANSACTIONS/CAREER NOTES: Selected by Dallas Cowboys in second round (39th pick overall) of 1989 NFL draft. ... Signed by Cowboys (July 24, 1989). ... Granted free agency (March 1, 1993). ... Re-signed by Cowboys (July 16, 1993). ... Granted unconditional free agency (February 17, 1994). ... Re-signed by Cowboys (April 7, 1994).
CHAMPIONSHIP GAME EXPERIENCE: Played in NFC championship game (1992-1995 seasons). ... Member of Super Bowl championship team (1992, 1993 and 1995 seasons).
HONORS: Played in Pro Bowl (1993 and 1994 seasons).
PRO STATISTICS: 1990—Recovered one fumble. 1992—Recovered one fumble. 1993—Recovered one fumble. 1995—Recovered one fumble.

Year Team	G	RUSHING				RECEIVING				TOTALS			
		Att.	Yds.	Avg.	TD	No.	Yds.	Avg.	TD	TD	2pt.	Pts.	Fum.
1989—Dallas NFL	16	67	212	3.2	0	16	133	8.3	3	3	...	18	3
1990—Dallas NFL	16	10	35	3.5	1	14	148	10.6	1	2	...	12	1
1991—Dallas NFL	16	17	54	3.2	0	28	244	8.7	1	1	...	6	0
1992—Dallas NFL	16	17	61	3.6	0	32	249	7.8	2	2	...	12	0
1993—Dallas NFL	16	24	74	3.1	3	50	372	7.4	1	4	...	24	1
1994—Dallas NFL	16	40	138	3.5	2	44	325	7.4	2	4	0	24	2
1995—Dallas NFL	16	25	111	4.4	2	30	248	8.3	1	3	0	18	1
Pro totals (7 years)	112	200	685	3.4	8	214	1719	8.0	11	19	0	114	8

JONASSEN, ERIC — OT — EAGLES

PERSONAL: Born August 16, 1968, in Baltimore. ... 6-5/310. ... Full name: Eric Gustav Jonassen.
HIGH SCHOOL: Mount St. Joseph (Baltimore).
COLLEGE: Penn State, then Bloomsburg (Pa.).
TRANSACTIONS/CAREER NOTES: Selected by San Diego Chargers in fifth round (140th pick overall) of 1992 NFL draft. ... Signed by Chargers (July 16, 1992). ... On injured reserve (September 1-28, 1992). ... On practice squad (September 28, 1992-remainder of season). ... Granted free agency after 1992 season. ... Re-signed by Chargers for 1993 season. ... Granted free agency (February 17, 1995). ... Rights relinquished by Chargers (June 15, 1995). ... Signed by Atlanta Falcons (June 30, 1995). ... Released by Falcons (August 21, 1995). ... Signed by Chargers (June 14, 1995). ... Released by Chargers (June 15, 1995). ... Selected by Frankfurt Galaxy in 1996 World League draft (February 21, 1996). ... Signed by Philadelphia Eagles (April 9, 1996).
PLAYING EXPERIENCE: San Diego NFL, 1993 and 1994. ... Games: 1993 (16), 1994 (16). Total: 32.
CHAMPIONSHIP GAME EXPERIENCE: Played in AFC championship game (1994 season). ... Played in Super Bowl XXIX (1994 season).

JONES, AARON — DE — DOLPHINS

PERSONAL: Born December 18, 1966, in Orlando. ... 6-5/267. ... Full name: Aaron Delmas Jones II.
HIGH SCHOOL: Apopka (Fla.).
COLLEGE: Eastern Kentucky.
TRANSACTIONS/CAREER NOTES: Selected by Pittsburgh Steelers in first round (18th pick overall) of 1988 NFL draft. ... Signed by Steelers (July 15, 1988). ... On injured reserve with knee injury (December 16, 1988-remainder of season). ... On injured reserve with foot injury (October 25, 1990-remainder of season). ... Granted free agency (February 1, 1992). ... Re-signed by Steelers (June 22, 1992). ... Granted unconditional free agency (March 1, 1993). ... Signed by New England Patriots (March 18, 1993). ... Released by Patriots (August 30, 1993). ... Re-signed by Patriots (August 31, 1993). ... Granted unconditional free agency (February 17, 1995). ... Re-signed by Patriots (March 29,

1995). ... Released by Patriots (February 20, 1996). ... Signed by Miami Dolphins (April 4, 1996).

PRO STATISTICS: 1990—Intercepted one pass for three yards and recovered one fumble. 1992—Recovered one fumble. 1994—Fumbled once and recovered three fumbles for 28 yards.

Year Team	G	SACKS
1988—Pittsburgh NFL	15	1.5
1989—Pittsburgh NFL	16	2.0
1990—Pittsburgh NFL	7	2.0
1991—Pittsburgh NFL	16	2.0
1992—Pittsburgh NFL	13	2.0
1993—New England NFL	11	3.5
1994—New England NFL	16	4.0
1995—New England NFL	10	1.0
Pro totals (8 years)	**104**	**18.0**

JONES, BRENT   TE   49ERS

PERSONAL: Born February 12, 1963, in Santa Clara, Calif. ... 6-4/230. ... Full name: Brent Michael Jones. ... Son of Mike Jones, selected by Oakland Raiders in 21st round of 1961 AFL draft and by Pittsburgh Steelers in 20th round of 1961 NFL draft.

HIGH SCHOOL: Leland (San Jose, Calif.).

COLLEGE: Santa Clara (degree in economics, 1986).

TRANSACTIONS/CAREER NOTES: Selected by Pittsburgh Steelers in fifth round (135th pick overall) of 1986 NFL draft. ... Signed by Steelers (July 30, 1986). ... On injured reserve with neck injury (August 19-September 23, 1986). ... Released by Steelers (September 24, 1986). ... Signed by San Francisco 49ers (December 24, 1986). ... On injured reserve with neck injury (September 1-December 5, 1987). ... Crossed picket line during players strike (October 14, 1987). ... On injured reserve with knee injury (August 29-October 5, 1988). ... Re-signed by 49ers (October 7, 1988). ... Granted unconditional free agency (February 1-April 1, 1989). ... Re-signed by 49ers (April 28, 1989). ... On injured reserve with knee injury (September 11-November 2, 1991). ... Granted free agency (February 1, 1992). ... Re-signed by 49ers (August 4, 1992).

CHAMPIONSHIP GAME EXPERIENCE: Played in NFC championship game (1988-1990 and 1992-1994 seasons). ... Member of Super Bowl championship team (1988, 1989 and 1994 seasons).

HONORS: Played in Pro Bowl (1992-1995 seasons).

PRO STATISTICS: 1990—Recovered two fumbles. 1991—Recovered one fumble. 1993—Recovered two fumbles. 1994—Recovered one fumble. 1995—Fumbled three times and recovered one fumble.

STATISTICAL PLATEAUS: 100-yard receiving games: 1990 (1).

Year Team	G	RECEIVING				TOTALS			
		No.	Yds.	Avg.	TD	TD	2pt.	Pts.	Fum.
1986—					Did not play.				
1987—San Francisco NFL	4	2	35	17.5	0	0	...	0	0
1988—San Francisco NFL	11	8	57	7.1	2	2	...	12	0
1989—San Francisco NFL	16	40	500	12.5	4	4	...	24	0
1990—San Francisco NFL	16	56	747	13.3	5	5	...	30	2
1991—San Francisco NFL	10	27	417	15.4	0	0	...	0	2
1992—San Francisco NFL	15	45	628	14.0	4	4	...	24	1
1993—San Francisco NFL	16	68	735	10.8	3	3	...	18	2
1994—San Francisco NFL	15	49	670	13.7	9	9	1	56	1
1995—San Francisco NFL	16	60	595	9.9	3	3	0	18	3
Pro totals (9 years)	**119**	**355**	**4384**	**12.4**	**30**	**30**	**1**	**182**	**11**

JONES, BRIAN   LB   SAINTS

PERSONAL: Born January 22, 1968, in Iowa City, Iowa. ... 6-1/250. ... Full name: Brian Keith Jones.

HIGH SCHOOL: Dunbar (Lubbock, Texas).

COLLEGE: UCLA, then Texas.

TRANSACTIONS/CAREER NOTES: Selected by Los Angeles Raiders in eighth round (213th pick overall) of 1991 NFL draft. ... Released by Raiders (August 26, 1991). ... Signed by Indianapolis Colts to practice squad (September 9, 1991). ... Activated (October 4, 1991). ... Granted unconditional free agency (February 1, 1992). ... Signed by Miami Dolphins (April 1, 1992). ... Released by Dolphins (July 20, 1992). ... Selected by Scottish Claymores in 33rd round (197th pick overall) of 1995 World League Draft. ... Signed by New Orleans Saints (July 31, 1995).

PLAYING EXPERIENCE: Indianapolis NFL, 1991; New Orleans NFL, 1995. ... Games: 1991 (11), 1995 (16). Total: 27.

PRO STATISTICS: W.L.: 1995—Credited with 1½ sacks. NFL:1995—Credited with one sack and recovered one fumble.

MISCELLANEOUS: Games played statistics not available; W.L., 1995.

JONES, CALVIN   RB   RAIDERS

PERSONAL: Born November 27, 1970, in Omaha, Neb. ... 5-11/205.

HIGH SCHOOL: Omaha (Neb.) Central.

COLLEGE: Nebraska.

TRANSACTIONS/CAREER NOTES: Selected after junior season by Los Angeles Raiders in third round (80th pick overall) of 1994 NFL draft. ... Signed by Raiders (July 14, 1994). ... Raiders franchise moved to Oakland (July 21, 1995).

PRO STATISTICS: 1995—Returned five kickoffs for 92 yards.

Year Team	G	RUSHING				RECEIVING				TOTALS			
		Att.	Yds.	Avg.	TD	No.	Yds.	Avg.	TD	TD	2pt.	Pts.	Fum.
1994—Los Angeles Raiders NFL	7	22	93	4.2	0	2	6	3.0	0	0	0	0	0
1995—Oakland NFL	8	5	19	3.8	0	0	0	...	0	0	0	0	1
Pro totals (2 years)	**15**	**27**	**112**	**4.2**	**0**	**2**	**6**	**3.0**	**0**	**0**	**0**	**0**	**1**

JONES CHRIS T.   WR   EAGLES

PERSONAL: Born August 7, 1971, in West Palm Beach, Fla. ... 6-3/209. ... Full name: Chris Todd Jones.
HIGH SCHOOL: Cardinal Newman (West Palm Beach, Fla.).
COLLEGE: Miami (Fla.).
TRANSACTIONS/CAREER NOTES: Selected by Philadelphia Eagles in third round (78th pick overall) of 1995 NFL draft. ... Signed by Eagles (July 12, 1995).

		RECEIVING				KICKOFF RETURNS				TOTALS		
Year Team	G	No.	Yds.	Avg.	TD	No.	Yds.	Avg.	TD	TD	2pt.	Pts.	Fum.
1995—Philadelphia NFL	12	5	61	10.2	0	2	46	23	0	0	0	0	0

JONES, CLARENCE   OT   SAINTS

J

PERSONAL: Born May 6, 1968, in Brooklyn, N.Y. ... 6-6/280.
HIGH SCHOOL: Central Islip (N.Y.).
COLLEGE: Maryland.
TRANSACTIONS/CAREER NOTES: Selected by New York Giants in fourth round (111th pick overall) of 1991 NFL draft. ... Placed on injured reserve (October 1991). ... Activated (November 1991). ... Granted free agency (February 17, 1994). ... Released by Giants (May 6, 1994). ... Signed by Los Angeles Rams (June 1, 1994). ... Rams franchise moved to St. Louis (April 12, 1995). ... Granted unconditional free agency (February 16, 1996). ... Signed by New Orleans Saints (February 19, 1996).
PLAYING EXPERIENCE: New York Giants NFL, 1991-1993; Los Angeles Rams NFL, 1994; St. Louis NFL, 1995. ... Games: 1991 (3), 1992 (3), 1993 (4), 1994 (16), 1995 (13). Total: 39.

JONES DAN   OT

PERSONAL: Born July 22, 1970, in Malden, Mass. ... 6-7/298.
HIGH SCHOOL: Malden (Mass.).
COLLEGE: Maine.
TRANSACTIONS/CAREER NOTES: Signed as non-drafted free agent by Cincinnati Bengals (May 14, 1993). ... Released by Bengals (August 30, 1993). ... Re-signed by Bengals (September 1, 1993). ... Released by Bengals (August 20, 1995). ... Re-signed by Bengals (October 30, 1995). ... Released by Bengals (March 25, 1996).
PLAYING EXPERIENCE: Cincinnati NFL, 1993-1995. ... Games: 1993 (15), 1994 (14), 1995 (5). Total: 34.

JONES DANTE   LB

PERSONAL: Born March 23, 1965, in Dallas. ... 6-2/235. ... Full name: Dante Delaneo Jones. ... Name pronounced DON-tay
HIGH SCHOOL: Skyline (Dallas).
COLLEGE: Oklahoma (degree in political science, 1988).
TRANSACTIONS/CAREER NOTES: Selected by Chicago Bears in second round (51st pick overall) of 1988 NFL draft. ... Signed by Bears (July 21, 1988). ... On injured reserve with hamstring injury (September 29-November 8, 1989). ... On injured reserve with knee injury (September 4-December 19, 1990). ... Granted free agency (February 1, 1992). ... Re-signed by Bears (July 25, 1992). ... On injured reserve with hamstring injury (December 11, 1992-remainder of season). ... Granted unconditional free agency (February 17, 1994). ... Re-signed by Bears (May 10, 1994). ... Released by Bears (March 7, 1995). ... Signed by Denver Broncos (June 5, 1995). ... Released by Broncos (November 14, 1995).
CHAMPIONSHIP GAME EXPERIENCE: Played in NFC championship game (1988 season).
PRO STATISTICS: 1993—Recovered three fumbles for 32 yards and one touchdown. 1994—Recovered two fumbles.

		INTERCEPTIONS				SACKS
Year Team	G	No.	Yds.	Avg.	TD	No.
1988—Chicago NFL	13	0	0	...	0	0.0
1989—Chicago NFL	10	0	0	...	0	0.0
1990—Chicago NFL	2	0	0	...	0	2.0
1991—Chicago NFL	16	0	0	...	0	0.0
1992—Chicago NFL	13	0	0	...	0	0.0
1993—Chicago NFL	16	4	52	13.0	0	1.0
1994—Chicago NFL	15	0	0	...	0	0.0
1995—Denver NFL	5	0	0	...	0	0.0
Pro totals (8 years)	90	4	52	13.0	0	3.0

JONES DONTA   LB   STEELERS

PERSONAL: Born August 27, 1972, in Washington, D.C. ... 6-2/226. ... Full name: Markeysia Donta Jones. ... Name pronounced DON-tay.
HIGH SCHOOL: McDonough (Pomfret, Md.).
COLLEGE: Nebraska (degree in accounting and business administration, 1994).
TRANSACTIONS/CAREER NOTES: Selected by Pittsburgh Steelers in fourth round (125th pick overall) of 1995 NFL draft. ... Signed by Steelers (July 19, 1995).
CHAMPIONSHIP GAME EXPERIENCE: Played in AFC championship game (1995 season). ... Played in Super Bowl XXX (1995 season).
PLAYING EXPERIENCE: Pittsburgh NFL, 1995. ... Games: 1995 (16).

JONES, ERNEST　　　　　DE　　　　　BRONCOS

PERSONAL: Born April 1, 1971, in Utica, N.Y. ... 6-2/270. ... Full name: Ernest Lee Jones.
HIGH SCHOOL: Utica (N.Y.) Senior Academy.
COLLEGE: Oregon.
TRANSACTIONS/CAREER NOTES: Selected by Los Angeles Rams in third round (100th pick overall) of 1994 NFL draft. ... Signed by Rams (June 20, 1994). ... On injured reserve with knee injury (August 28, 1994-entire season). ... Released by Rams (August 21, 1995). ... Signed by New Orleans Saints to practice squad (August 28, 1995). ... Activated (October 21, 1995). ... Released by Saints (October 30, 1995). ... Re-signed by Saints to practice squad (November 1, 1995). ... Granted free agency (February 16, 1996). ... Signed by Denver Broncos (March 25, 1996).
PLAYING EXPERIENCE: New Orleans NFL, 1995. ... Games: 1995 (1).

JONES, GARY　　　　　S　　　　　JETS

PERSONAL: Born November 30, 1967, in San Augustine, Texas. ... 6-1/217. ... Full name: Gary DeWayne Jones.
HIGH SCHOOL: John Tyler (Tyler, Texas).
COLLEGE: Texas A&M.
TRANSACTIONS/CAREER NOTES: Selected by Pittsburgh Steelers in ninth round (239th pick overall) of 1990 NFL draft. ... Signed by Steelers (July 18, 1990). ... On injured reserve with forearm injury (August 27-October 17, 1991). ... On injured reserve with knee injury (August 25, 1992-entire season). ... Granted unconditional free agency (February 17, 1995). ... Signed by New York Jets (March 7, 1995).
CHAMPIONSHIP GAME EXPERIENCE: Member of Steelers for AFC championship game (1994 season); inactive.
PRO STATISTICS: 1993—Recovered one fumble. 1994—Recovered one fumble.

		INTERCEPTIONS			
Year　Team	G	No.	Yds.	Avg.	TD
1990—Pittsburgh NFL	16	0	0	...	0
1991—Pittsburgh NFL	9	1	0	0.0	0
1992—Pittsburgh NFL	Did not play—injured.				
1993—Pittsburgh NFL	13	2	11	5.5	0
1994—Pittsburgh NFL	14	1	0	0.0	0
1995—New York Jets NFL	11	2	51	25.5	1
Pro totals (5 years)	63	6	62	10.3	1

JONES, HENRY　　　　　S　　　　　BILLS

PERSONAL: Born December 29, 1967, in St. Louis. ... 5-11/197.
HIGH SCHOOL: St. Louis University.
COLLEGE: Illinois (degree in psychology, 1990).
TRANSACTIONS/CAREER NOTES: Selected by Buffalo Bills in first round (26th pick overall) of 1991 NFL draft. ... Signed by Bills (August 30, 1991). ... Activated (September 7, 1991). ... Designated by Bills as transition player (February 15, 1994).
CHAMPIONSHIP GAME EXPERIENCE: Played in AFC championship game (1991-1993 seasons). ... Played in Super Bowl XXVI (1991 season), Super Bowl XXVII (1992 season) and Super Bowl XXVIII (1993 season).
HONORS: Named strong safety on THE SPORTING NEWS NFL All-Pro team (1992). ... Played in Pro Bowl (1992 season).
RECORDS: Shares NFL single-game record for most touchdowns scored by interception—2 (September 20, 1992, vs. Indianapolis).
PRO STATISTICS: 1991—Recovered one fumble. 1992—Recovered two fumbles. 1993—Credited with one safety and recovered two fumbles. 1994—Recovered one fumble. 1995—Recovered one fumble.

		INTERCEPTIONS				SACKS
Year　Team	G	No.	Yds.	Avg.	TD	No.
1991—Buffalo NFL	15	0	0	...	0	0.0
1992—Buffalo NFL	16	*8	*263	32.9	2	0.0
1993—Buffalo NFL	16	2	92	46.0	1	2.0
1994—Buffalo NFL	16	2	45	22.5	0	1.0
1995—Buffalo NFL	13	1	10	10.0	0	0.0
Pro totals (5 years)	76	13	410	31.5	3	3.0

JONES, JAMES　　　　　DT　　　　　BRONCOS

PERSONAL: Born February 6, 1969, in Davenport, Iowa. ... 6-2/290. ... Full name: James Alfie Jones.
HIGH SCHOOL: Davenport (Iowa) Central.
COLLEGE: Northern Iowa (degree in science, 1992).
TRANSACTIONS/CAREER NOTES: Selected by Cleveland Browns in third round (57th pick overall) of 1991 NFL draft. ... Signed by Browns (1991). ... Granted unconditional free agency (February 17, 1995). ... Signed by Denver Broncos (February 24, 1995).
PRO STATISTICS: 1991—Credited with one safety, intercepted one pass for 20 yards and a touchdown and recovered three fumbles for 15 yards. 1992—Recovered one fumble. 1993—Rushed twice for two yards and one touchdown. 1994—Rushed once for no yards, caught one pass for one yard and recovered two fumbles. 1995—Recovered two fumbles.

Year　Team	G	SACKS
1991—Cleveland NFL	16	1.0
1992—Cleveland NFL	16	4.0
1993—Cleveland NFL	16	5.5
1994—Cleveland NFL	16	3.0
1995—Denver NFL	16	1.0
Pro totals (5 years)	80	14.5

JONES, JEFF OT LIONS

PERSONAL: Born May 30, 1972, in Killeen, Texas. ... 6-6/310. ... Full name: Jeff Raymond Jones.
HIGH SCHOOL: Killeen (Texas).
COLLEGE: Texas A&M.
TRANSACTIONS/CAREER NOTES: Signed as non-drafted free agent by Detroit Lions (May 3, 1995).
PLAYING EXPERIENCE: Detroit NFL, 1995. ... Games: 1995 (1).

JONES, JIMMIE DT RAMS

PERSONAL: Born January 9, 1966, in Lakeland, Fla. ... 6-4/285. ... Full name: Jimmie Sims Jones.
HIGH SCHOOL: Okeechobee (Fla.).
COLLEGE: Miami (Fla.).
TRANSACTIONS/CAREER NOTES: Selected by Dallas Cowboys in third round (63rd pick overall) of 1990 NFL draft. ... Signed by Cowboys (August 3, 1990). ... Granted unconditional free agency (February 17, 1994). ... Signed by Los Angeles Rams (March 4, 1994). ... Rams franchise moved to St. Louis (April 12, 1995).
CHAMPIONSHIP GAME EXPERIENCE: Played in NFC championship game (1992 and 1993 seasons). ... Member of Super Bowl championship team (1992 and 1993 seasons).
POSTSEASON RECORDS: Shares Super Bowl career and single-game records for most fumbles recovered—2; and most touchdowns by fumble recovery—1 (January 31, 1993, vs. Buffalo).
PRO STATISTICS: 1991—Recovered two fumbles for 15 yards. 1994—Recovered one fumble.

Year Team	G	SACKS
1990—Dallas NFL	16	7.5
1991—Dallas NFL	16	2.0
1992—Dallas NFL	16	4.0
1993—Dallas NFL	15	5.5
1994—Los Angeles Rams NFL	14	5.0
1995—St. Louis NFL	16	0.0
Pro totals (6 years)	93	24.0

JONES, MARVIN LB JETS

PERSONAL: Born June 28, 1972, in Miami. ... 6-2/249. ... Full name: Marvin Maurice Jones.
HIGH SCHOOL: Miami Northwestern.
COLLEGE: Florida State.
TRANSACTIONS/CAREER NOTES: Selected after junior season by New York Jets in first round (fourth pick overall) of 1993 NFL draft. ... Signed by Jets (August 5, 1993). ... On injured reserve with hip injury (November 16, 1993-remainder of season).
PLAYING EXPERIENCE: New York Jets NFL, 1993-1995. ... Games: 1993 (9), 1994 (15), 1995 (10). Total: 34.
HONORS: Butkus Award winner (1992). ... Named College Football Player of the Year by THE SPORTING NEWS (1992). ... Named linebacker on THE SPORTING NEWS college All-America first team (1992).
PRO STATISTICS: 1993—Recovered one fumble.

Year Team	G	SACKS
1993—New York Jets NFL	9	0.0
1994—New York Jets NFL	15	0.5
1995—New York Jets NFL	10	1.5
Pro totals (3 years)	34	2.0

JONES, MIKE LB RAIDERS

PERSONAL: Born April 15, 1969, in Kansas City, Mo. ... 6-1/230. ... Full name: Michael Anthony Jones.
HIGH SCHOOL: Southwest (Kansas City, Mo.).
COLLEGE: Missouri.
TRANSACTIONS/CAREER NOTES: Signed as non-drafted free agent by Los Angeles Raiders (April 1991). ... Assigned by Raiders to Sacramento Surge in 1992 World League enhancement allocation program (February 20, 1992). ... Raiders franchise moved to Oakland (July 21, 1995).
PLAYING EXPERIENCE: Los Angeles Raiders NFL, 1991-1994; Sacramento W.L., 1992; Oakland NFL, 1995. ... Games: 1991 (16), 1992 W.L. (7), 1992 NFL (16), 1993 (16), 1994 (16), 1995 (16). Total W.L.: 7. Total NFL: 80. Total Pro: 87.
PRO STATISTICS: W.L.: 1992—Credited with two sacks. NFL: 1995—Intercepted one pass for 23 yards, recovered two fumbles for 52 yards and a touchdown.

JONES, MIKE DE PATRIOTS

PERSONAL: Born August 25, 1969, in Columbia, S.C. ... 6-4/295. ... Full name: Michael David Jones.
HIGH SCHOOL: C.A. Johnson (Columbia, S.C.).
COLLEGE: North Carolina State.
TRANSACTIONS/CAREER NOTES: Selected by Phoenix Cardinals in second round (32nd pick overall) of 1991 NFL draft. ... Signed by Cardinals (July 15, 1991). ... Granted free agency (February 17, 1994). ... Signed by New England Patriots (June 7, 1994).
PRO STATISTICS: 1994—Recovered one fumble.

Year Team	G	SACKS
1991—Phoenix NFL	16	0.0
1992—Phoenix NFL	15	6.0
1993—Phoenix NFL	16	3.0
1994—New England NFL	16	6.0

Year Team	G	SACKS
1995—New England NFL	13	3.0
Pro totals (5 years)	76	18.0

JONES, REGGIE   WR   PANTHERS

PERSONAL: Born May 5, 1971, in Kansas City, Kan. ... 6-0/175.
HIGH SCHOOL: Wyandotte (Kansas City, Kan.).
JUNIOR COLLEGE: Butler County (Kan.) Community College.
COLLEGE: Louisiana State (did not play football).
TRANSACTIONS/CAREER NOTES: Signed as non-drafted free agent by Washington Redskins (April 27, 1995). ... Released by Redskins (August 22, 1995). ... Signed by Carolina Panthers to practice squad (September 4, 1995). ... Activated (October 21, 1995).
PLAYING EXPERIENCE: Carolina NFL, 1995. ... Games: 1995 (1).

JONES, ROBERT   LB   RAMS

PERSONAL: Born September 27, 1969, in Blackstone, Va. ... 6-2/244. ... Full name: Robert Lee Jones.
HIGH SCHOOL: Nottoway (Va.), then Fork Union (Va.) Military Academy.
COLLEGE: East Carolina.
TRANSACTIONS/CAREER NOTES: Selected by Dallas Cowboys in first round (24th pick overall) of 1992 NFL draft. ... Signed by Cowboys (April 26, 1992). ... Granted unconditional free agency (February 16, 1996). ... Signed by St. Louis Rams (March 4, 1996).
PLAYING EXPERIENCE: Dallas NFL, 1992-1995. ... Games: 1992 (15), 1993 (13), 1994 (16), 1995 (12). Total: 56.
CHAMPIONSHIP GAME EXPERIENCE: Played in NFC championship game (1992-1995 seasons). ... Member of Super Bowl championship team (1992, 1993 and 1995 seasons).
HONORS: Named linebacker on THE SPORTING NEWS college All-America second team (1990). ... Named linebacker on THE SPORTING NEWS college All-America first team (1991).
PRO STATISTICS: 1992—Credited with one sack and recovered one fumble. 1993—Returned one kickoff for 12 yards. 1994—Returned one kickoff for eight yards and recovered one fumble. 1995—Credited with one sack.

JONES, ROD   CB   BENGALS

PERSONAL: Born March 31, 1964, in Dallas. ... 6-0/185. ... Full name: Roderick Wayne Jones.
HIGH SCHOOL: South Oak Cliff (Dallas).
COLLEGE: Southern Methodist.
TRANSACTIONS/CAREER NOTES: Selected by Tampa Bay Buccaneers in first round (25th pick overall) of 1986 NFL draft. ... Signed by Buccaneers (June 19, 1986). ... Granted free agency (February 1, 1990). ... Re-signed by Buccaneers (August 12, 1990). ... Traded by Buccaneers to Cincinnati Bengals for DE Jim Skow (September 1, 1990). ... On injured reserve with arm injury (September 25, 1991-remainder of season). ... Granted free agency (February 1, 1992). ... Re-signed by Bengals (July 27, 1992).
PRO STATISTICS: 1986—Recovered one fumble. 1987—Recovered one fumble for eight yards. 1990—Recovered one fumble for one yard. 1992—Recovered one fumble. 1993—Recovered one fumble. 1995—Recovered one fumble.

		INTERCEPTIONS			
Year Team	G	No.	Yds.	Avg.	TD
1986—Tampa Bay NFL	16	1	0	0.0	0
1987—Tampa Bay NFL	11	2	9	4.5	0
1988—Tampa Bay NFL	14	1	0	0.0	0
1989—Tampa Bay NFL	16	0	0	...	0
1990—Cincinnati NFL	16	0	0	...	0
1991—Cincinnati NFL	4	0	0	...	0
1992—Cincinnati NFL	16	2	14	7.0	0
1993—Cincinnati NFL	16	1	0	0.0	0
1994—Cincinnati NFL	16	0	0	...	0
1995—Cincinnati NFL	13	1	24	24.0	0
Pro totals (10 years)	138	8	47	5.9	0

JONES, ROGER   CB   BENGALS

PERSONAL: Born April 22, 1969, in Cleveland. ... 5-9/175. ... Full name: Roger Carver Jones.
HIGH SCHOOL: Pearl-Cohn (Nashville).
COLLEGE: Tennessee State.
TRANSACTIONS/CAREER NOTES: Signed as non-drafted free agent by Indianapolis Colts (April 23, 1991). ... Released by Colts (August 19, 1991). ... Signed by Tampa Bay Buccaneers to practice squad (October 1, 1991). ... Activated (November 8, 1991). ... Granted unconditional free agency (February 1-April 1, 1992). ... Re-signed by Buccaneers for 1992 season. ... On injured reserve with leg injury (September 4-October 30, 1992). ... Claimed on waivers by Cincinnati Bengals (August 29, 1994). ... Granted unconditional free agency (February 16, 1996). ... Re-signed by Bengals (March 14, 1996).
PRO STATISTICS: 1991—Recovered one fumble. 1992—Recovered two fumbles for 26 yards and a touchdown. 1993—Recovered three fumbles for 12 yards. 1994—Returned one punt for no yards and fumbled once. 1995—Intercepted one pass for 17 yards and a touchdown.

Year Team	G	SACKS
1991—Tampa Bay NFL	6	0.0
1992—Tampa Bay NFL	9	0.0
1993—Tampa Bay NFL	16	1.0
1994—Cincinnati NFL	16	1.5
1995—Cincinnati NFL	16	2.0
Pro totals (5 years)	63	4.5

JONES, RONDELL   S   BRONCOS

PERSONAL: Born May 7, 1971, in Sunderland, Mass. ... 6-2/210. ... Full name: Rondell Tony Jones.
HIGH SCHOOL: Northern (Owings, Md.).
COLLEGE: North Carolina.
TRANSACTIONS/CAREER NOTES: Selected by Denver Broncos in third round (69th pick overall) of 1993 NFL draft. ... Signed by Broncos (July 15, 1993). ... Granted free agency (February 16, 1996).
PRO STATISTICS: 1994—Recovered one fumble.

| | | | INTERCEPTIONS | | |
| | | | | | |
Year Team	G	No.	Yds.	Avg.	TD
1993—Denver NFL	16	0	0	...	0
1994—Denver NFL	16	2	9	4.5	0
1995—Denver NFL	14	0	0	...	0
Pro totals (3 years)	46	2	9	4.5	0

J

JONES, SEAN   DE   PACKERS

PERSONAL: Born December 19, 1962, in Kingston, Jamaica. ... 6-7/283. ... Full name: Dwight Sean Jones. ... Brother of Max Jones, linebacker, Birmingham Stallions of USFL (1984).
HIGH SCHOOL: Kimberly Academy (Montclair, N.J.).
COLLEGE: Northeastern.
TRANSACTIONS/CAREER NOTES: Selected by Washington Federals in fifth round (91st pick overall) of 1984 USFL draft. ... Selected by Los Angeles Raiders in second round (51st pick overall) of 1984 NFL draft. ... Signed by Raiders (July 12, 1984). ... Traded by Raiders with second-round (DB Quintin Jones) and third-round (traded to San Diego) picks in 1988 draft to Houston Oilers for first-round (CB Terry McDaniel), third-round (traded to New York Jets) and fourth-round (traded to San Francisco) picks in 1988 draft (April 21, 1988). ... Granted free agency (February 1, 1990). ... Re-signed by Oilers (August 24, 1990). ... Granted free agency (February 1, 1991). ... Re-signed by Oilers (August 30, 1991). ... Reported to camp (September 9, 1992). ... Activated (September 11, 1992). ... Granted unconditional free agency (February 17, 1994). ... Signed by Green Bay Packers (April 18, 1994).
CHAMPIONSHIP GAME EXPERIENCE: Played in NFC championship game (1995 season).
HONORS: Played in Pro Bowl (1993 season).
PRO STATISTICS: 1985—Recovered one fumble. 1987—Recovered two fumbles. 1989—Recovered two fumbles. 1990—Recovered one fumble. 1992—Intercepted one pass for no yards. 1993—Recovered two fumbles. 1994—Recovered three fumbles. 1995—Recovered one fumble in end zone for a touchdown.

Year Team	G	SACKS
1984—Los Angeles Raiders NFL	16	1.0
1985—Los Angeles Raiders NFL	15	8.5
1986—Los Angeles Raiders NFL	16	15.5
1987—Los Angeles Raiders NFL	12	6.0
1988—Houston NFL	16	7.5
1989—Houston NFL	16	6.0
1990—Houston NFL	16	12.5
1991—Houston NFL	16	10.0
1992—Houston NFL	15	8.5
1993—Houston NFL	16	13.0
1994—Green Bay NFL	16	10.5
1995—Green Bay NFL	16	9.0
Pro totals (12 years)	186	108.0

JONES, SELWYN   CB

PERSONAL: Born May 13, 1970, in Houston. ... 6-0/185. ... Full name: Selwyn Aldridge Jones.
HIGH SCHOOL: Willowridge (Sugar Land, Texas).
COLLEGE: Colorado State.
TRANSACTIONS/CAREER NOTES: Selected by Cleveland Browns in seventh round (177th pick overall) of 1992 NFL draft. ... Signed by Browns (July 14, 1992). ... On injured reserve with hip injury (August 25, 1992-entire season). ... Claimed on waivers by New Orleans Saints (October 11, 1994). ... Granted free agency (February 17, 1995). ... Re-signed by Saints (May 31, 1995). ... On injured reserve with leg injury (August 22-29, 1995). ... Released by Saints (August 29, 1995). ... Signed by Seattle Seahawks (September 5, 1995). ... Granted unconditional free agency (February 16, 1996).
PRO STATISTICS: 1993—Recovered one fumble.

| | | | INTERCEPTIONS | | |
| | | | | | |
Year Team	G	No.	Yds.	Avg.	TD
1992—Cleveland NFL			Did not play.		
1993—Cleveland NFL	11	3	0	0.0	0
1994—New Orleans NFL	5	0	0	...	0
1995—Seattle NFL	15	1	0	0.0	0
Pro totals (3 years)	31	4	0	0.0	0

JONES, TONY   WR   CARDINALS

PERSONAL: Born December 30, 1965, in Grapeland, Texas. ... 5-7/145. ... Full name: Anthony Bernard Jones.
HIGH SCHOOL: Grapeland (Texas).
COLLEGE: Texas.

TRANSACTIONS/CAREER NOTES: Selected by Houston Oilers in sixth round (153rd pick overall) of 1990 NFL draft. ... Signed by Oilers (July 22, 1990). ... Granted unconditional free agency (February 1, 1992). ... Signed by Atlanta Falcons (March 30, 1992). ... On injured reserve with ankle injury (October 7-November 9 and December 22, 1992-remainder of season). ... Released by Falcons (August 23, 1993). ... Signed by Oilers (October 27, 1993). ... Granted unconditional free agency (February 17, 1994). ... Signed by Falcons (1994). ... Released by Falcons (June 27, 1994). ... Signed by Arizona Cardinals (November 22, 1995). ... Released by Cardinals (December 13, 1995). ... Re-signed by Cardinals (April 19, 1996).

PRO STATISTICS: 1990—Rushed once for minus two yards. 1992—Recovered one fumble for one yard.

			RECEIVING				TOTALS			
Year Team	G	No.	Yds.	Avg.	TD	TD	2pt.	Pts.	Fum.
1990—Houston NFL	15	30	409	13.6	6	6	...	36	0
1991—Houston NFL	16	19	251	13.2	2	2	...	12	1
1992—Atlanta NFL	10	14	138	9.9	1	1	...	6	0
1993—Houston NFL	2	0	0	0	0	0	...	0	0
1994—					Did not play.				
1995—Arizona NFL	2	0	0	...	0	0	0	0	0
Pro totals (5 years)	45	63	798	12.7	9	9	0	54	1

JONES, TONY   OT   RAVENS

PERSONAL: Born May 24, 1966, in Royston, Ga. ... 6-5/295. ... Full name: Tony Edward Jones.
HIGH SCHOOL: Franklin County (Carnesville, Ga.).
JUNIOR COLLEGE: Angelina College (Texas).
COLLEGE: Western Carolina (degree in management, 1989).
TRANSACTIONS/CAREER NOTES: Signed as non-drafted free agent by Cleveland Browns (May 2, 1988). ... On injured reserve with toe injury (August 29-October 22, 1988). ... On injured reserve with toe injury (September 20-November 7, 1989). ... Granted free agency (February 1, 1992). ... Re-signed by Browns (July 29, 1992). ... Browns franchise moved to Baltimore and renamed Ravens for 1996 season (March 11, 1996).
PLAYING EXPERIENCE: Cleveland NFL, 1988-1995. ... Games: 1988 (4), 1989 (9), 1990 (16), 1991 (16), 1992 (16), 1993 (16), 1994 (16), 1995 (16). Total: 109.
CHAMPIONSHIP GAME EXPERIENCE: Played in AFC championship game (1989 season).
PRO STATISTICS: 1989—Recovered one fumble. 1991—Recovered one fumble. 1994—Recovered one fumble. 1995—Recovered one fumble.

JORDAN, ANDREW   TE   VIKINGS

PERSONAL: Born June 21, 1972, in Charlotte. ... 6-4/258.
HIGH SCHOOL: West Charlotte (N.C.).
COLLEGE: Western Carolina.
TRANSACTIONS/CAREER NOTES: Selected by Minnesota Vikings in sixth round (179th pick overall) of 1994 NFL draft. ... Signed by Vikings (June 17, 1994).
PRO STATISTICS: 1994—Returned one kickoff for eight yards and recovered a fumble.

			RECEIVING				TOTALS			
Year Team	G	No.	Yds.	Avg.	TD	TD	2pt.	Pts.	Fum.
1994—Minnesota NFL	16	35	336	9.6	0	0	1	2	1
1995—Minnesota NFL	13	27	185	6.9	2	2	0	12	1
Pro totals (2 years)	29	62	521	8.4	2	0	1	14	2

JORDAN, CHARLES   WR/KR   DOLPHINS

PERSONAL: Born October 9, 1969, in Los Angeles. ... 5-11/183.
HIGH SCHOOL: Morningside (Inglewood, Calif.).
COLLEGE: Long Beach (Calif.) City College.
TRANSACTIONS/CAREER NOTES: Signed as non-drafted free agent by Los Angeles Raiders (May 4, 1993). ... On inactive list for six games (1993). ... On injured reserve (October 27, 1993-remainder of season. ... Traded by Raiders to Green Bay Packers for fifth-round pick (traded to Washington) in 1995 draft (August 28, 1994). ... Granted free agency (February 16, 1996). ... Tendered offer sheet by Miami Dolphins (March 7, 1996). ... Packers declined to match offer (March 13, 1996).
CHAMPIONSHIP GAME EXPERIENCE: Member of Packers for NFC championship game (1995 season); inactive.
PRO STATISTICS: 1994—Rushed once for five yards. 1995—Recovered one fumble.

		RECEIVING				PUNT RETURNS				KICKOFF RETURNS				TOTALS			
Year Team	G	No.	Yds.	Avg.	TD	No.	Yds.	Avg.	TD	No.	Yds.	Avg.	TD	TD	2pt.	Pts.	Fum.
1993—Los Angeles Raiders NFL....								Did not play.									
1994—Green Bay NFL	10	0	0	...	0	1	0	0.0	0	5	115	23.0	0	0	0	0	1
1995—Green Bay NFL	6	7	117	16.7	2	21	213	10.1	0	21	444	21.1	0	2	0	12	1
Pro totals (2 years)	16	7	117	16.7	2	22	213	9.7	0	26	559	21.5	0	2	0	12	2

JORDAN, RANDY   RB/KR   JAGUARS

PERSONAL: Born June 6, 1970, in Henderson, N.C. ... 5-10/216. ... Full name: Randy Loment Jordan.
HIGH SCHOOL: Warren County (Warrenton, N.C.).
COLLEGE: North Carolina.
TRANSACTIONS/CAREER NOTES: Signed as non-drafted free agent by Los Angeles Raiders (May 1993). ... Released by Raiders (August 25, 1993). ... Re-signed by Raiders to practice squad (August 31, 1993). ... Activated (October 30, 1993). ... Released by Raiders (August 28,

1994). ... Signed by Jacksonville Jaguars (December 15, 1994).
PRO STATISTICS: 1995—Returned two kickoffs for 41 yards.

		RUSHING				RECEIVING				TOTALS			
Year Team	G	Att.	Yds.	Avg.	TD	No.	Yds.	Avg.	TD	TD	2pt.	Pts.	Fum.
1993—Los Angeles Raiders NFL	10	12	33	2.8	0	4	42	10.5	0	0	...	0	2
1994—							Did not play.						
1995—Jacksonville NFL	12	21	62	3.0	0	5	89	17.8	1	1	0	6	0
Pro totals (2 years)	22	33	95	2.9	0	9	131	14.6	1	1	0	6	2

JOSEPH, DWAYNE — CB — BEARS

PERSONAL: Born June 2, 1972, in Miami. ... 5-9/180. ... Full name: Dwayne Leonard Joseph.
HIGH SCHOOL: Carol City (Miami).
COLLEGE: Syracuse.
TRANSACTIONS/CAREER NOTES: Signed as non-drafted free agent by Chicago Bears (July 14, 1994). ... Released by Bears (August 31, 1994). ... Re-signed by Bears to practice squad (November 2, 1994). ... Granted free agency after 1994 season. ... Re-signed by Bears (February 16, 1995).

		INTERCEPTIONS			
Year Team	G	No.	Yds.	Avg.	TD
1994—Chicago NFL			Did not play.		
1995—Chicago NFL	16	2	31	15.5	0

JOSEPH, JAMES — RB — BENGALS

PERSONAL: Born October 28, 1967, in Phenix City, Ala. ... 6-2/222.
HIGH SCHOOL: Central (Phenix City, Ala.).
COLLEGE: Auburn.
TRANSACTIONS/CAREER NOTES: Selected by Philadelphia Eagles in seventh round (188th pick overall) of 1991 NFL draft. ... Signed by Eagles (July 14, 1991). ... Granted unconditional free agency (February 17, 1995). ... Signed by Cincinnati Bengals (March 22, 1995).
PRO STATISTICS: 1994—Returned one kickoff for 11 yards and recovered one fumble. 1995—Returned one kickoff for 17 yards and recovered three fumbles for two yards.
STATISTICAL PLATEAUS: 100-yard receiving games: 1993 (1).

		RUSHING				RECEIVING				TOTALS			
Year Team	G	Att.	Yds.	Avg.	TD	No.	Yds.	Avg.	TD	TD	2pt.	Pts.	Fum.
1991—Philadelphia NFL	16	135	440	3.3	3	10	64	6.4	0	3	...	18	2
1992—Philadelphia NFL	16	0	0	...	0	0	0	...	0	0	...	0	0
1993—Philadelphia NFL	16	39	140	3.6	0	29	291	10.0	1	1	...	6	0
1994—Philadelphia NFL	14	60	203	3.4	1	43	344	8.0	2	3	0	18	1
1995—Cincinnati NFL	16	16	40	2.5	0	20	118	5.9	0	0	0	0	1
Pro totals (5 years)	78	250	823	3.3	4	102	817	8.0	3	7	0	42	4

JOSEPH, VANCE — DB — JETS

PERSONAL: Born September 20, 1972, in Marrero, La. ... 6-0/202.
HIGH SCHOOL: Archbishop Shaw (Marrero, La.).
COLLEGE: Colorado (degree in business).
TRANSACTIONS/CAREER NOTES: Signed as non-drafted free agent by New York Jets (April 28, 1995). ... Released by Jets (August 27, 1995). ... Re-signed by Jets to practice squad (August 28, 1995). ... Activated (September 20, 1995).

		INTERCEPTIONS			
Year Team	G	No.	Yds.	Avg.	TD
1995—New York Jets NFL	13	2	39	19.5	0

JOURDAIN, YONEL — RB/KR — BILLS

PERSONAL: Born April 20, 1971, in Brooklyn, N.Y. ... 5-11/204. ... Name pronounced ya-NEL.
HIGH SCHOOL: Evanston (Ill.).
COLLEGE: Southern Illinois.
TRANSACTIONS/CAREER NOTES: Signed as non-drafted free agent by Buffalo Bills (May 7, 1993). ... Released by Bills (August 24, 1993). ... Re-signed by Bills to practice squad (September 1, 1993). ... Granted free agency after 1993 season. ... Re-signed by Bills (February 17, 1994).
PRO STATISTICS: 1995—Returned one punt for no yards and recovered two fumbles.

		RUSHING				RECEIVING				KICKOFF RETURNS				TOTALS			
Year Team	G	Att.	Yds.	Avg.	TD	No.	Yds.	Avg.	TD	No.	Yds.	Avg.	TD	TD	2pt.	Pts.	Fum.
1993—Buffalo NFL								Did not play.									
1994—Buffalo NFL	9	17	56	3.3	0	10	56	5.6	0	27	601	22.3	0	0	0	0	1
1995—Buffalo NFL	8	8	31	3.9	0	1	7	7.0	0	19	348	18.3	0	0	0	0	2
Pro totals (2 years)	17	25	87	3.5	0	11	63	5.7	0	46	949	20.6	0	0	0	0	3

JOYCE, MATT — G — SEAHAWKS

PERSONAL: Born March 30, 1972, in St. Petersburg, Fla. ... 6-7/316.

HIGH SCHOOL: New York Military Academy (Cornwall Hudson, N.Y.).
COLLEGE: Richmond.
TRANSACTIONS/CAREER NOTES: Signed as non-drafted free agent by Dallas Cowboys (May 2, 1994). ... Claimed on waivers by Cincinnati Bengals (August 28, 1994); released after failing physical. ... Signed by Cowboys to practice squad (September 5, 1994). ... Granted free agency after 1994 season. ... Signed by Seattle Seahawks (March 1, 1995).
PLAYING EXPERIENCE: Seattle NFL, 1995. ... Games: 1995 (16).
PRO STATISTICS: 1995—Recovered one fumble.

OYNER, SETH — LB — CARDINALS

PERSONAL: Born November 18, 1964, in Spring Valley, N.Y. ... 6-2/235.
HIGH SCHOOL: Spring Valley (N.Y.).
COLLEGE: Texas-El Paso.
TRANSACTIONS/CAREER NOTES: Selected by Philadelphia Eagles in eighth round (208th pick overall) of 1986 NFL draft. ... Signed by Eagles (July 17, 1986). ... Released by Eagles (September 1, 1986). ... Re-signed by Eagles (September 17, 1986). ... Granted free agency (February 1, 1991). ... Re-signed by Eagles (August 28, 1991). ... Activated (August 30, 1991). ... Designated by Eagles as transition player (February 25, 1993). ... Free agency status changed by Eagles from transitional to unconditional (February 17, 1994). ... Signed by Arizona Cardinals (April 17, 1994).
HONORS: Played in Pro Bowl (1991, 1993 and 1994 seasons).
RECORDS: Shares NFL single-season records for most touchdowns by fumble recovery—2 (1991); and most touchdowns by recovery of opponents' fumbles—2 (1991).
PRO STATISTICS: 1987—Recovered two fumbles for 18 yards and one touchdown. 1988—Fumbled once and recovered one fumble. 1990—Fumbled once. 1991—Recovered four fumbles for 47 yards and two touchdowns. 1992—Recovered one fumble. 1995—Fumbled once and recovered three fumbles.

		INTERCEPTIONS				SACKS
Year Team	G	No.	Yds.	Avg.	TD	No.
1986—Philadelphia NFL	14	1	4	4.0	0	2.0
1987—Philadelphia NFL	12	2	42	21.0	0	4.0
1988—Philadelphia NFL	16	4	96	24.0	0	3.5
1989—Philadelphia NFL	14	1	0	0.0	0	4.5
1990—Philadelphia NFL	16	1	9	9.0	0	7.5
1991—Philadelphia NFL	16	3	41	13.7	0	6.5
1992—Philadelphia NFL	16	4	88	22.0	2	6.5
1993—Philadelphia NFL	16	1	6	6.0	0	2.0
1994—Arizona NFL	16	3	2	.7	0	6.0
1995—Arizona NFL	16	3	9	3.0	0	1.0
Pro totals (10 years)	152	23	297	12.9	2	43.5

JUNKIN, TREY — TE

PERSONAL: Born January 23, 1961, in Conway, Ark. ... 6-2/241. ... Full name: Abner Kirk Junkin. ... Brother of Mike Junkin, linebacker, Cleveland Browns and Kansas City Chiefs (1987-1989).
HIGH SCHOOL: Northeast (North Little Rock, Ark.).
COLLEGE: Louisiana Tech.
TRANSACTIONS/CAREER NOTES: Selected by Buffalo Bills in fourth round (93rd pick overall) of 1983 NFL draft. ... Released by Bills (September 12, 1984). ... Signed by Washington Redskins (September 25, 1984). ... Rights relinquished by Redskins (February 1, 1985). ... Signed by Los Angeles Raiders (March 10, 1985). ... On injured reserve with knee injury (September 24, 1986-remainder of season). ... Released by Raiders (September 3, 1990). ... Signed by Seattle Seahawks (October 3, 1990). ... Granted unconditional free agency (February 1-April 1, 1991). ... Re-signed by Seahawks (July 9, 1991). ... Granted unconditional free agency (February 1-April 1, 1992). ... Re-signed by Seahawks for 1992 season. ... Granted unconditional free agency (March 1, 1993). ... Re-signed by Seahawks (March 11, 1993). ... Released by Seahawks (August 30, 1993). ... Re-signed by Seahawks (August 31, 1993). ... Granted unconditional free agency (February 17, 1994). ... Re-signed by Seahawks (May 31, 1994). ... Granted unconditional free agency (February 17, 1995). ... Re-signed by Seahawks (March 20, 1995). ... Granted unconditional free agency (February 16, 1996).
PRO STATISTICS: 1983—Recovered one fumble. 1984—Recovered one fumble. 1989—Returned one kickoff for no yards.

		RECEIVING				TOTALS			
Year Team	G	No.	Yds.	Avg.	TD	TD	2pt.	Pts.	Fum.
1983—Buffalo NFL	16	0	0	...	0	0	...	0	0
1984—Buffalo NFL	2	0	0	...	0	0	...	0	0
—Washington NFL	12	0	0	...	0	0	...	0	0
1985—Los Angeles Raiders NFL	16	2	8	4.0	1	1	...	6	0
1986—Los Angeles Raiders NFL	3	2	38	19.0	0	0	...	0	0
1987—Los Angeles Raiders NFL	12	2	15	7.5	0	0	...	0	0
1988—Los Angeles Raiders NFL	16	4	25	6.3	2	2	...	12	0
1989—Los Angeles Raiders NFL	16	3	32	10.7	2	2	...	12	0
1990—Seattle NFL	12	0	0	...	0	0	...	0	0
1991—Seattle NFL	16	0	0	...	0	0	...	0	0
1992—Seattle NFL	16	3	25	8.3	1	1	...	6	0
1993—Seattle NFL	16	0	0	...	0	0	...	0	0
1994—Seattle NFL	16	1	1	1.0	1	1	0	6	0
1995—Seattle NFL	16	0	0	...	0	0	0	0	0
Pro totals (13 years)	185	17	144	8.5	7	7	0	42	0

JURKOVIC, JOHN — NT — JAGUARS

PERSONAL: Born August 18, 1967, in Friedrischafen, West Germany. ... 6-2/295. ... Full name: John Ivan Jurkovic.

HIGH SCHOOL: Thornton Fractional North (Calumet City, Ill.).
COLLEGE: Eastern Illinois (degree in business).
TRANSACTIONS/CAREER NOTES: Signed as non-drafted free agent by Miami Dolphins (April 27, 1990). ... Released by Dolphins (August 28, 1990). ... Re-signed by Dolphins to practice squad (October 3, 1990). ... Granted free agency after 1990 season. ... Signed by Green Bay Packers (March 8, 1991). ... Released by Packers (August 26, 1991). ... Re-signed by Packers to practice squad (August 28, 1991). ... Activated (November 22, 1991). ... Granted unconditional free agency (February 1-April 1, 1992). ... Re-signed by Packers (April 2, 1992). ... Granted unconditional free agency (February 16, 1996). ... Signed by Jacksonville Jaguars (April 13, 1996).
CHAMPIONSHIP GAME EXPERIENCE: Played in NFC championship game (1995 season).
PRO STATISTICS: 1992—Returned three kickoffs for 39 yards. 1993—Returned two kickoffs for 22 yards. 1994—Returned four kickoffs for 57 yards. 1995—Returned one kickoff for 17 yards.

Year Team	G	SACKS
1991—Green Bay NFL	5	0.0
1992—Green Bay NFL	16	2.0
1993—Green Bay NFL	16	5.5
1994—Green Bay NFL	16	0.0
1995—Green Bay NFL	16	0.0
Pro totals (5 years)	**69**	**7.5**

JUSTIN, PAUL   QB   COLTS

PERSONAL: Born May 19, 1968, in Schaumburg, Ill. ... 6-4/215. ... Full name: Paul Donald Justin.
HIGH SCHOOL: Schaumburg (Ill.).
COLLEGE: Arizona State.
TRANSACTIONS/CAREER NOTES: Selected by Chicago Bears in seventh round (190th pick overall) of 1991 NFL draft. ... Released by Bears (August 27, 1991). ... Signed by Bears to practice squad (August 28, 1991). ... Released by Bears (August 31, 1992). ... Signed by Indianapolis Colts (April 11, 1994). ... Released by Colts (April 11, 1994). ... Re-signed by Colts to practice squad (August 29, 1994). ... Granted free agency after 1994 season. ... Re-signed by Colts (January 12, 1995). ... Assigned by Colts to Frankfurt Galaxy in 1995 World League enhancement allocation program (February 20, 1995). ... Re-signed by Colts (April 28, 1995).
CHAMPIONSHIP GAME EXPERIENCE: Member of Colts for AFC championship game (1995 season); inactive.
PRO STATISTICS: 1995—Fumbled once and recovered one fumbled for minus one yard.
MISCELLANEOUS: Regular-season record as starting NFL quarterback: 0-1 (.000).

Year Team	G	Att.	Cmp.	Pct.	Yds.	TD	Int.	Avg.	Rat.	Att.	Yds.	Avg.	TD	TD	2pt.	Pts.
1991—Chicago NFL							Did not play.									
1992—Chicago NFL							Did not play.									
1993—							Did not play.									
1994—Indianapolis NFL							Did not play.									
1995—Frankfurt W.L.	...	279	172	61.7	2394	17	12	8.58	91.6	14	50	3.6	0	0	0	0
—Indianapolis NFL	3	36	20	55.6	212	0	2	5.89	49.8	3	1	0.3	0	0	0	0
W.L. totals (1 year)	...	279	172	617	2394	17	12	8.58	91.6	14	50	3.6	0	0	0	0
NFL totals (1 year)	3	36	20	55.6	212	0	2	5.89	49.8	3	1	0.3	0	0	0	0
Pro totals (1 year)	...	**315**	**192**	**61.0**	**2606**	**17**	**14**	**8.27**	**86.8**	**17**	**51**	**3.0**	**0**	**0**	**0**	**0**

KALIS, TODD   G

PERSONAL: Born May 10, 1965, in Stillwater, Minn. ... 6-6/296. ... Full name: Todd Alexander Kalis. ... Name pronounced KA-lis.
HIGH SCHOOL: Thunderbird (Phoenix).
COLLEGE: Arizona State.
TRANSACTIONS/CAREER NOTES: Selected by Minnesota Vikings in fourth round (108th pick overall) of 1988 NFL draft. ... Signed by Vikings (July 21, 1988). ... Granted free agency (February 1, 1991). ... Re-signed by Vikings (July 23, 1991). ... Granted free agency (February 1, 1992). ... Re-signed by Vikings (August 4, 1992). ... On injured reserve (August 31, 1992-entire season). ... Granted unconditional free agency (February 17, 1994). ... Signed by Pittsburgh Steelers (May 20, 1994). ... On injured reserve with ankle injury (November 22, 1994-remainder of season). ... Released by Steelers (August 27, 1995). ... Signed by Cincinnati Bengals (August 29, 1995). ... Released by Bengals (March 25, 1996).
PLAYING EXPERIENCE: Minnesota NFL, 1988-1991 and 1993; Pittsburgh NFL, 1994; Cincinnati NFL, 1995. ... Games: 1988 (14), 1989 (16), 1990 (15), 1991 (16), 1993 (16), 1994 (11), 1995 (15). Total: 103.

KASAY, JOHN   K   PANTHERS

PERSONAL: Born October 27, 1969, in Athens, Ga. ... 5-10/198. ... Full name: John David Kasay. ... Son of John Kasay, strength and conditioning coach, University of Georgia. ... Name pronounced KAY-see.
HIGH SCHOOL: Clarke Central (Athens, Ga.).
COLLEGE: Georgia (degree in journalism).
TRANSACTIONS/CAREER NOTES: Selected by Seattle Seahawks in fourth round (98th pick overall) of 1991 NFL draft. ... Signed by Seahawks (July 19, 1991). ... Granted free agency (February 17, 1994). ... Re-signed by Seahawks (July 19, 1994). ... Granted unconditional free agency (February 17, 1995). ... Signed by Carolina Panthers (February 20, 1995).
PRO STATISTICS: 1993—Recovered one fumble. 1995—Punted once for 32 yards.

				KICKING					
Year Team	G	XPM	XPA	FGM	FGA	Lg.	50+	Pts.	
1991—Seattle NFL	16	27	28	25	31	54	2-3	102	
1992—Seattle NFL	16	14	14	14	22	43	0-0	56	
1993—Seattle NFL	16	29	29	23	28	55	3-5	98	
1994—Seattle NFL	16	25	26	20	24	50	1-2	85	
1995—Carolina NFL	16	27	28	26	33	52	1-1	105	
Pro totals (5 years)	**80**	**122**	**125**	**108**	**138**	**55**	**7-11**	**446**	

KAUFMAN, NAPOLEON　　　　RB/KR　　　　RAIDERS

PERSONAL: Born June 7, 1973, in Kansas City, Mo. ... 5-9/185.
HIGH SCHOOL: Lompoc (Calif.).
COLLEGE: Washington.
TRANSACTIONS/CAREER NOTES: Selected by Los Angeles Raiders in first round (18th pick overall) of 1995 NFL draft. ... Signed by Raiders (May 24, 1995). ... Raiders franchise moved to Oakland (July 21, 1995).
HONORS: Named running back on THE SPORTING NEWS college All-America second team (1994).

		RUSHING				RECEIVING				KICKOFF RETURNS				TOTALS			
Year Team	G	Att.	Yds.	Avg.	TD	No.	Yds.	Avg.	TD	No.	Yds.	Avg.	TD	TD	2pt.	Pts.	Fum.
1995—Oakland NFL	16	108	490	4.5	1	9	62	6.9	0	22	572	26.0	1	2	0	12	0

KEIM, MIKE　　　　OT　　　　SEAHAWKS

PERSONAL: Born November 12, 1965, in Anaheim, Calif. ... 6-7/302. ... Name pronounced KHYME.
HIGH SCHOOL: Round Valley (Springerville, Ariz.).
COLLEGE: Brigham Young.
TRANSACTIONS/CAREER NOTES: Signed as non-drafted free agent by New Orleans Saints (May 4, 1991). ... Released by Saints (August 26, 1991). ... Re-signed by Saints to practice squad (September 2, 1991). ... Activated (December 20, 1991). ... Granted unconditional free agency (February 1-April 1, 1992). ... Re-signed by Saints for 1992 season. ... Released by Saints (August 31, 1992). ... Re-signed by Saints to practice squad (September 2, 1992). ... Signed by Seattle Seahawks off Saints practice squad (December 9, 1992). ... Granted free agency (February 16, 1996).
PLAYING EXPERIENCE: New Orleans NFL, 1991; Seattle NFL, 1992-1995. ... Games: 1991 (1), 1992 (1), 1993 (3); 1994 (16), 1995 (7). Total: 28.

KEITH, CRAIG　　　　TE　　　　DOLPHINS

PERSONAL: Born April 27, 1971, in Raleigh, N.C. ... 6-3/262. ... Full name: Craig Carlton Keith.
HIGH SCHOOL: Millbrook (Raleigh, N.C.).
COLLEGE: Lenoir-Rhyne (N.C.).
TRANSACTIONS/CAREER NOTES: Selected by Pittsburgh Steelers in seventh round (189th pick overall) of 1993 NFL draft. ... Signed by Steelers (June 3, 1993). ... Traded by Steelers to Jacksonville Jaguars for seventh-round pick (traded to Kansas City) in 1996 draft (August 26, 1995). ... Granted free agency (February 16, 1996). ... Released by Jaguars (April 24, 1996). ... Signed by Miami Dolphins (April 26, 1996).
PLAYING EXPERIENCE: Pittsburgh NFL, 1993 and 1994; Jacksonville NFL, 1995. ... Games: 1993 (1), 1994 (16), 1995 (11). Total: 28.
CHAMPIONSHIP GAME EXPERIENCE: Member of Steelers for AFC championship game (1994 season); inactive.
PRO STATISTICS: 1994—Caught one pass for two yards. 1995—Caught three passes for 20 yards.

KELLY, JIM　　　　QB　　　　BILLS

PERSONAL: Born February 14, 1960, in Pittsburgh. ... 6-3/226. ... Full name: James Edward Kelly. ... Brother of Pat Kelly, linebacker, Birmingham Vulcans of WFL (1975).
HIGH SCHOOL: East Brady (Pa.).
COLLEGE: Miami, Fla. (degree in business management, 1982).
TRANSACTIONS/CAREER NOTES: Selected by Chicago Blitz in 14th round (163rd pick overall) of 1983 USFL draft. ... Selected by Buffalo Bills in first round (14th pick overall) of 1983 NFL draft. ... USFL rights traded by Blitz with RB Mark Rush to Houston Gamblers for first-, third-, eighth- and 10th-round picks in 1984 draft (June 9, 1983). ... Signed by Gamblers (June 9, 1983). ... On developmental squad for four games (June 1-29, 1985). ... Traded by Gamblers with DB Luther Bradley, DB Will Lewis, DB Mike Mitchell, DB Durwood Roquemore, DE Pete Catan, QB Todd Dillon, DT Tony Fitzpatrick, DT Van Hughes, DT Hosea Taylor, RB Sam Harrell, LB Andy Hawkins, LB Ladell Wills, WR Richard Johnson, WR Scott McGhee, WR Gerald McNeil, WR Ricky Sanders, WR Clarence Verdin, G Rich Kehr, C Billy Kidd, OT Chris Riehm and OT Tommy Robison to New Jersey Generals for past considerations (March 7, 1986). ... Granted free agency when USFL suspended operations (August 7, 1986). ... Signed by Bills (August 18, 1986). ... Granted roster exemption (August 18-29, 1986). ... On injured reserve with knee injury (December 16, 1994-remainder of season).
CHAMPIONSHIP GAME EXPERIENCE: Played in AFC championship game (1988 and 1990-1993 seasons). ... Played in Super Bowl XXV (1990 season), Super Bowl XXVI (1991 season), Super Bowl XXVII (1992 season) and Super Bowl XXVIII (1993 season).
HONORS: Named USFL Rookie of the Year by THE SPORTING NEWS (1984). ... Named quarterback on THE SPORTING NEWS USFL All-Star team (1985). ... Played in Pro Bowl (1987, 1990 and 1991 seasons). ... Named to play in Pro Bowl (1988 season); replaced by Dave Krieg due to injury. ... Named Outstanding Player of Pro Bowl (1990 season). ... Named quarterback on THE SPORTING NEWS NFL All-Pro team (1991). ... Named to play in Pro Bowl (1992 season); replaced by Neil O'Donnell due to injury.
POSTSEASON RECORDS: Holds Super Bowl career record for most passes attempted—145; and most passes intercepted—7. ... Holds Super Bowl single-game records for most passes completed—31 (January 30, 1994, vs. Dallas); most passes attempted—58 (January 26, 1992, vs. Washington); and most passes intercepted—4 (January 26, 1992, vs. Washington). ... Shares Super Bowl single-game record for most fumbles—3 (January 26, 1992, vs. Washington). ... Hold NFL postseason career record for most passes intercepted—27.
PRO STATISTICS: USFL: 1984—Caught one pass for minus 13 yards, fumbled nine times and recovered four fumbles. 1985—Caught one pass for three yards, fumbled 10 times and recovered three fumbles. NFL: 1986—Fumbled seven times and recovered two fumbles. 1987—Caught one pass for 35 yards, fumbled six times and recovered two fumbles. 1988—Caught one pass for five yards and fumbled five times. 1989—Fumbled six times and recovered three fumbles for minus six yards. 1990—Fumbled four times and recovered two fumbles for minus eight yards. 1991—Fumbled six times and recovered two fumbles for minus four yards. 1992—Fumbled eight times. 1993—Fumbled seven times and recovered three fumbles for minus 17 yards. 1994—Fumbled 11 times and recovered two fumbles for minus 19 yards. 1995—Fumbled seven times and recovered two fumbles.
STATISTICAL PLATEAUS: USFL: 300-yard passing games: 1984 (9), 1985 (7). Total: 16. ... NFL: 300-yard passing games: 1986 (2), 1987 (3), 1988 (2), 1989 (2), 1990 (1), 1991 (6), 1992 (4), 1993 (1), 1994 (2), 1995 (1). Total: 24.
MISCELLANEOUS: Regular-season record as starting NFL quarterback: 93-54 (.633). ... Holds Buffalo Bills all-time records for most yards passing (32,657) and most touchdown passes (223).

K

Year—Team	G	PASSING								RUSHING				TOTALS		
		Att.	Cmp.	Pct.	Yds.	TD	Int.	Avg.	Rat.	Att.	Yds.	Avg.	TD	TD	2pt.	Pts.
1984—Houston USFL	18	*587	*370	63.0	*5219	*44	*26	8.89	98.2	85	493	5.8	5	5	1	32
1985—Houston USFL	14	*567	*360	63.5	*4623	*39	19	8.15	*97.9	28	170	6.1	1	1	0	6
1986—Buffalo NFL	16	480	285	59.4	3593	22	17	7.49	83.3	41	199	4.9	0	0	...	0
1987—Buffalo NFL	12	419	250	59.7	2798	19	11	6.68	83.8	29	133	4.6	0	0	...	0
1988—Buffalo NFL	16	452	269	59.5	3380	15	17	7.48	78.2	35	154	4.4	0	0	...	0
1989—Buffalo NFL	13	391	228	58.3	3130	25	18	8.01	86.2	29	137	4.7	2	2	...	12
1990—Buffalo NFL	14	346	219	*63.3	2829	24	9	8.18	*101.2	22	63	2.9	0	0	...	0
1991—Buffalo NFL	15	474	304	64.1	3844	*33	17	8.11	97.6	20	45	2.3	1	1	...	6
1992—Buffalo NFL	16	462	269	58.2	3457	23	*19	7.48	81.2	31	53	1.7	1	1	...	6
1993—Buffalo NFL	16	470	288	61.3	3382	18	18	7.20	79.9	36	102	2.8	0	0	...	0
1994—Buffalo NFL	14	448	285	63.6	3114	22	17	6.95	84.6	25	77	3.1	1	1	0	6
1995—Buffalo NFL	15	458	255	55.7	3130	22	13	6.84	81.1	17	20	1.2	0	0	0	0
USFL totals (2 years)	32	1154	730	63.3	9842	83	45	8.53	98.1	113	663	5.9	6	6	1	38
NFL totals (10 years)	147	4400	2652	60.3	32657	223	156	7.42	85.4	285	983	3.5	5	5	0	30
Pro totals (12 years)	179	5554	3382	60.9	42499	306	201	7.65	88.0	398	1646	4.1	11	11	1	68

KELLY, JOE — LB

PERSONAL: Born December 11, 1964, in Sun Valley, Calif. ... 6-2/235. ... Full name: Joseph Winston Kelly. ... Son of Joe Kelly Sr., former player with Ottawa Rough Riders of CFL; and nephew of Bob Kelly, NFL tackle with four teams (1961-1964 and 1967-1969).

HIGH SCHOOL: Jefferson (Los Angeles).

COLLEGE: Washington (degree in criminal justice, 1986).

TRANSACTIONS/CAREER NOTES: Selected by Cincinnati Bengals in first round (11th pick overall) of 1986 NFL draft. ... Signed by Bengals (August 29, 1986). ... Granted roster exemption (August 29-September 3, 1986). ... Traded by Bengals with OT Scott Jones to New York Jets for rights to WR Reggie Rembert (August 27, 1990). ... On injured reserve with knee injury (December 21, 1990-remainder of season). ... On injured reserve with ankle injury (November 13, 1992-remainder of season). ... Granted unconditional free agency (March 1, 1993). ... Signed by Los Angeles Raiders (April 13, 1993). ... Released by Raiders (April 20, 1994). ... Signed by Los Angeles Rams (May 19, 1994). ... Granted free agency (February 17, 1995). ... Signed by Green Bay Packers (August 25, 1995). ... On injured reserve with toe injury (January 5, 1996-remainder of 1995 playoffs). ... Released by Packers (February 5, 1996).

CHAMPIONSHIP GAME EXPERIENCE: Played in AFC championship game (1988 season). ... Played in Super Bowl XXIII (1988 season).

PRO STATISTICS: 1986—Recovered one fumble. 1989—Recovered three fumbles for 23 yards. 1990—Recovered one fumble. 1991—Fumbled once. 1993—Recovered one fumble. 1994—Recovered one fumble.

Year—Team	G	INTERCEPTIONS				SACKS
		No.	Yds.	Avg.	TD	No.
1986—Cincinnati NFL	16	1	6	6.0	0	1.0
1987—Cincinnati NFL	10	0	0	...	0	1.0
1988—Cincinnati NFL	16	0	0	...	0	0.0
1989—Cincinnati NFL	16	1	25	25.0	0	1.0
1990—New York Jets NFL	12	0	0	...	0	0.0
1991—New York Jets NFL	16	2	6	3.0	0	0.0
1992—New York Jets NFL	9	0	0	...	0	0.0
1993—Los Angeles Raiders NFL	16	0	0	...	0	1.0
1994—Los Angeles Rams NFL	16	1	31	31.0	0	2.0
1995—Green Bay NFL	13	1	0	0.0	0	0.0
Pro totals (10 years)	140	6	68	11.3	0	6.0

KELLY, TODD — DE — BENGALS

PERSONAL: Born November 27, 1970, in Hampton, Va. ... 6-2/259. ... Full name: Todd Eric Kelly.

HIGH SCHOOL: Bethel (Hampton, Va.).

COLLEGE: Tennessee.

TRANSACTIONS/CAREER NOTES: Selected by San Francisco 49ers in first round (27th pick overall) of 1993 NFL draft. ... Signed by 49ers (July 16, 1993). ... Claimed on waivers by Cincinnati Bengals (July 25, 1995).

CHAMPIONSHIP GAME EXPERIENCE: Played in NFC championship game (1993 season). ... Member of 49ers for NFC championship game (1994 season); inactive. ... Member of Super Bowl championship team (1994 season).

PRO STATISTICS: 1995—Recovered one fumble.

Year—Team	G	SACKS
1993—San Francisco NFL	14	1.0
1994—San Francisco NFL	11	3.5
1995—Cincinnati NFL	16	1.0
Pro totals (3 years)	41	5.5

KENNARD, DEREK — C

PERSONAL: Born September 9, 1962, in Stockton, Calif. ... 6-3/300. ... Full name: Derek Craig Kennard.

HIGH SCHOOL: Edison (Stockton, Calif.).

COLLEGE: Nevada.

TRANSACTIONS/CAREER NOTES: Selected by Los Angeles Express in third round (52nd pick overall) of 1984 USFL draft. ... Signed by Express (March 22, 1984). ... Granted roster exemption (March 22, 1984). ... Activated (April 13, 1984). ... On developmental squad for two games (April 13-28, 1984). ... Selected by St. Louis Cardinals in second round (45th pick overall) of 1984 NFL supplemental draft. ... On developmental squad for four games with Express (March 15-April 13, 1985). ... Released by Express (August 1, 1985). ... Re-signed by Express (August 2, 1985). ... Released by Express (April 29, 1986). ... Signed by Cardinals (May 29, 1986). ... Cardinals franchise moved to Phoenix (March 15, 1988). ... On non-football injury list (October 19-November 1, 1989). ... Traded by Cardinals with a fifth-round pick (WR

Torrance Small) in 1992 draft to New Orleans Saints for CB Robert Massey (August 19, 1991). ... On injured reserve with chest muscle injury (September 17, 1991-remainder of season). ... Granted free agency (February 1, 1992). ... Re-signed by Saints (July 17, 1992). ... Granted unconditional free agency (February 17, 1994). ... Signed by Dallas Cowboys (April 18, 1994). ... Granted unconditional free agency (February 17, 1995). ... Re-signed by Cowboys (August 2, 1995). ... On reserve/left camp list (August 4-September 18, 1995). ... Released by Cowboys (February 9, 1996).

PLAYING EXPERIENCE: Los Angeles USFL, 1984 and 1985; St. Louis NFL, 1986 and 1987; Phoenix NFL, 1988-1990; New Orleans NFL, 1991-1993; Dallas NFL, 1994 and 1995. ... Games: 1984 (6), 1985 (14), 1986 (15), 1987 (12), 1988 (16), 1989 (14), 1990 (16), 1991 (3), 1992 (16), 1993 (16), 1994 (16), 1995 (9). Total USFL: 20. Total NFL: 133. Total Pro: 153.

CHAMPIONSHIP GAME EXPERIENCE: Played in NFC championship game (1994 and 1995 seasons). ... Member of Super Bowl championship team (1995 season).

PRO STATISTICS: USFL: 1985—Returned one kickoff for no yards and recovered one fumble. NFL: 1987—Fumbled twice for minus four yards. 1992—Returned one kickoff for 11 yards and recovered one fumble. 1994—Caught one pass for minus three yards and fumbled once. 1995—Fumbled once and recovered one fumble for minus one yards.

KENNEDY, CORTEZ — DT — SEAHAWKS

PERSONAL: Born August 23, 1968, in Osceola, Ark. ... 6-3/293.
HIGH SCHOOL: Rivercrest (Wilson, Ark.).
JUNIOR COLLEGE: Northwest Mississippi Community College.
COLLEGE: Miami, Fla. (degree in criminal justice).
TRANSACTIONS/CAREER NOTES: Selected by Seattle Seahawks in first round (third pick overall) of 1990 NFL draft. ... Signed by Seahawks (September 3, 1990). ... Granted roster exemption (September 3-9, 1990).
HONORS: Named defensive tackle on THE SPORTING NEWS college All-America first team (1989). ... Played in Pro Bowl (1991-1995 seasons). ... Named defensive tackle on THE SPORTING NEWS NFL All-Pro team (1992 and 1993).
PRO STATISTICS: 1990—Recovered one fumble. 1991—Recovered one fumble. 1992—Fumbled once and recovered one fumble for 19 yards. 1993—Recovered one fumble. 1994—Recovered one fumble.

Year Team	G	SACKS
1990—Seattle NFL	16	1.0
1991—Seattle NFL	16	6.5
1992—Seattle NFL	16	14.0
1993—Seattle NFL	16	6.5
1994—Seattle NFL	16	4.0
1995—Seattle NFL	16	6.5
Pro totals (6 years)	96	38.5

KENNEDY, LINCOLN — G/OT — RAIDERS

PERSONAL: Born February 12, 1971, in York, Pa. ... 6-6/350. ... Full name: Tamerlane Lincoln Kennedy.
HIGH SCHOOL: Samuel F. B. Morse (San Diego).
COLLEGE: Washington (degree in speech and drama, 1993).
TRANSACTIONS/CAREER NOTES: Selected by Atlanta Falcons in first round (ninth pick overall) of 1993 NFL draft. ... Signed by Falcons (August 2, 1993). ... Granted free agency (February 16, 1996). ... Traded by Falcons to Oakland Raiders for undisclosed pick in 1997 draft (May 13, 1996).
PLAYING EXPERIENCE: Atlanta NFL, 1993-1995. ... Games: 1993 (16), 1994 (16), 1995 (16). Total: 48.
HONORS: Named offensive tackle on THE SPORTING NEWS college All-America first team (1992).
PRO STATISTICS: 1993—Recovered one fumble. 1994—Recovered one fumble.

KERNER, MARLON — CB — BILLS

PERSONAL: Born March 18, 1973, in Columbus, Ohio. ... 5-10/187.
HIGH SCHOOL: Brookhaven (Columbus, Ohio.).
COLLEGE: Ohio State.
TRANSACTIONS/CAREER NOTES: Selected by Buffalo Bills in third round (76th pick overall) of 1995 NFL draft. ... Signed by Bills (July 10, 1995).
PLAYING EXPERIENCE: Buffalo NFL, 1995. ... Games: 1995 (14).

KIDD, CARL — CB — RAIDERS

PERSONAL: Born June 14, 1973, in Pine Bluff, Ark. ... 6-1/205.
HIGH SCHOOL: Dollarway (Pine Bluff, Ark.).
JUNIOR COLLEGE: Northeastern Oklahoma A&M.
COLLEGE: Arkansas.
TRANSACTIONS/CAREER NOTES: Signed as non-drafted free agent by Oakland Raiders (June 1995)
PLAYING EXPERIENCE: Oakland NFL, 1995. ... Games: 1995 (13).

KIDD, JOHN — P — DOLPHINS

PERSONAL: Born August 22, 1961, in Springfield, Ill. ... 6-3/214. ... Full name: Max John Kidd.
HIGH SCHOOL: Findlay (Ohio).
COLLEGE: Northwestern (degree in industrial engineering and management science, 1984).
TRANSACTIONS/CAREER NOTES: Selected by Chicago Blitz in 1984 USFL territorial draft. ... Selected by Buffalo Bills in fifth round (128th pick over-

all) of 1984 NFL draft. ... Signed by Bills (June 1, 1984). ... Granted unconditional free agency (February 1, 1990). ... Signed by San Diego Chargers (March 15, 1990). ... Granted free agency (February 1, 1992). ... Re-signed by Chargers (July 23, 1992). ... Granted unconditional free agency (March 1, 1993). ... Re-signed by Chargers (July 23, 1993). ... Granted unconditional free agency (February 17, 1994). ... Re-signed by Chargers (August 20, 1994). ... On injured reserve with hamstring injury (September 12-22, 1994). ... Released by Chargers (September 22, 1994). ... Signed by Miami Dolphins (November 30, 1994). ... Granted unconditional free agency (February 17, 1995). ... Re-signed by Dolphins (April 18, 1995).

CHAMPIONSHIP GAME EXPERIENCE: Played in AFC championship game (1988 season).

PRO STATISTICS: 1986—Rushed once for no yards and recovered one fumble. 1987—Attempted one pass without a completion. 1990—Fumbled once and recovered one fumble. 1992—Rushed twice for minus 13 yards, fumbled once and recovered one fumble for minus nine yards. 1993—Rushed three times for minus 13 yards and a touchdown.

				PUNTING			
Year Team	G	No.	Yds.	Avg.	Net avg.	In. 20	Blk.
1984—Buffalo NFL	16	88	3696	42.0	32.7	16	2
1985—Buffalo NFL	16	92	3818	41.5	35.9	33	0
1986—Buffalo NFL	16	75	3031	40.4	34.5	14	0
1987—Buffalo NFL	12	64	2495	39.0	34.5	20	0
1988—Buffalo NFL	16	62	2451	39.5	35.3	13	0
1989—Buffalo NFL	16	65	2564	39.4	32.2	15	2
1990—San Diego NFL	16	61	2442	40.0	36.6	14	1
1991—San Diego NFL	16	76	3064	40.3	34.8	22	1
1992—San Diego NFL	16	68	2899	42.6	36.4	22	0
1993—San Diego NFL	14	57	2431	42.6	35.9	16	0
1994—San Diego NFL	2	7	246	35.1	32.3	1	0
—Miami NFL	4	14	602	43.0	29.1	2	0
1995—Miami NFL	16	57	2433	42.7	36.3	15	0
Pro totals (12 years)	176	786	32172	40.9	34.8	203	6

KIMBROUGH, TONY   WR   JAGUARS

PERSONAL: Born September 17, 1970, in Weir, Miss. ... 6-2/192.
HIGH SCHOOL: Weir (Miss.) Consolidated.
COLLEGE: Jackson State.
TRANSACTIONS/CAREER NOTES: Selected by Denver Broncos in seventh round (182nd pick overall) of 1993 NFL draft. ... Signed by Broncos (June 15, 1993). ... Released by Broncos (July 10, 1995). ... Signed by Carolina Panthers (July 11, 1995). ... Released by Panthers (August 21, 1995). ... Re-signed by Panthers (Janaury 25, 1996).

		RECEIVING				TOTALS			
Year Team	G	No.	Yds.	Avg.	TD	TD	2pt.	Pts.	Fum.
1993—Denver NFL	15	8	79	9.9	0	0	...	0	0
1994—Denver NFL	12	2	20	10.0	0	0	0	0	0
1995—	—				Did not play.				
Pro totals (2 years)	27	10	99	9.9	0	0	0	0	0

KINCHEN, BRIAN   TE   RAVENS

PERSONAL: Born August 6, 1965, in Baton Rouge, La. ... 6-2/240. ... Full name: Brian Douglas Kinchen. ... Brother of Todd Kinchen, wide receiver/kick returner, St. Louis Rams.
HIGH SCHOOL: University (Baton Rouge, La.).
COLLEGE: Louisiana State.
TRANSACTIONS/CAREER NOTES: Selected by Miami Dolphins in 12th round (320th pick overall) of 1988 NFL draft. ... Signed by Dolphins (June 6, 1988). ... On injured reserve with hamstring injury (October 4, 1990-remainder of season). ... Granted unconditional free agency (February 1, 1991). ... Signed by Green Bay Packers (April 1, 1991). ... Released by Packers (August 26, 1991). ... Signed by Cleveland Browns (September 13, 1991). ... Granted unconditional free agency (February 1-April 1, 1992). ... Re-signed by Browns for 1992 season. ... Granted unconditional free agency (February 17, 1994). ... Re-signed by Browns (March 4, 1994). ... Granted unconditional free agency (February 16, 1996). ... Browns franchise moved to Baltimore and renamed Ravens for 1996 season (March 11, 1996). ... Re-signed by Ravens (April 3, 1996).

PRO STATISTICS: 1995—Recovered one fumble.

		RECEIVING				KICKOFF RETURNS				TOTALS			
Year Team	G	No.	Yds.	Avg.	TD	No.	Yds.	Avg.	TD	TD	2pt.	Pts.	Fum.
1988—Miami NFL	16	1	3	3.0	0	0	0	...	0	0	...	0	0
1989—Miami NFL	16	1	12	12.0	0	2	26	13.0	0	0	...	0	2
1990—Miami NFL	4	0	0	...	0	1	16	16.0	0	0	...	0	0
1991—Cleveland NFL	14	0	0	...	0	0	0	...	0	0	...	0	1
1992—Cleveland NFL	16	0	0	...	0	0	0	...	0	0	...	0	0
1993—Cleveland NFL	16	29	347	12.0	2	1	0	0.0	0	2	...	12	1
1994—Cleveland NFL	16	24	232	9.7	1	3	38	12.7	0	1	0	6	1
1995—Cleveland NFL	13	20	216	10.8	0	0	0	...	0	0	0	0	1
Pro totals (8 years)	111	75	810	10.8	3	7	80	11.4	0	3	0	18	6

KINCHEN, TODD   WR/KR   RAMS

PERSONAL: Born January 7, 1969, in Baton Rouge, La. ... 5-11/187. ... Full name: Todd Whittington Kinchen. ... Brother of Brian Kinchen, tight end, Baltimore Ravens.
HIGH SCHOOL: Trafton Academy (Baton Rouge, La.).
COLLEGE: Louisiana State.
TRANSACTIONS/CAREER NOTES: Selected by Los Angeles Rams in third round (60th pick overall) of 1992 NFL draft. ... Signed by Rams (July 13, 1992). ... On injured reserve with knee injury (November 23, 1993-remainder of season). ... On physically unable to perform list

(July 22-28, 1994). ... Released by Rams (September 6, 1994). ... Re-signed by Rams (September 21, 1994). ... Granted free agency (February 17, 1995). ... Rams franchise moved to St. Louis (April 12, 1995). ... Re-signed by Rams (June 16, 1995).
RECORDS: Shares NFL single-game records for most touchdowns by punt return—2; and most touchdowns by combined kick return—2 (December 27, 1992, vs. Atlanta).
PRO STATISTICS: 1993—Fumbled once. 1994—Fumbled five times. 1995—Attempted one pass without a completion, fumbled eight times and recovered one fumble.

			RUSHING			RECEIVING				PUNT RETURNS				KICKOFF RETURNS				TOTALS		
Year Team	G	Att.	Yds.	Avg.	TD	No.	Yds.	Avg.	TD	No.	Yds.	Avg.	TD	No.	Yds.	Avg.	TD	TD	2pt.	Pts.
1992—L.A. Rams NFL	14	0	0	...	0	0	0	...	0	4	103	25.8	†2	4	63	15.8	0	2	...	12
1993—L.A. Rams NFL	6	2	10	5.0	0	8	137	17.1	1	7	32	4.6	0	6	96	16.0	0	1	...	6
1994—L.A. Rams NFL	13	1	44	44.0	1	23	352	15.3	3	16	158	9.9	0	21	510	24.3	0	4	0	24
1995—St. Louis NFL	16	4	16	4.0	0	36	419	11.6	4	*53	416	7.9	0	35	743	21.2	0	4	0	24
Pro totals (4 years)	49	7	70	10.0	1	67	908	13.6	8	80	709	8.9	2	66	1412	21.4	0	11	0	66

KING, ED   G   SAINTS

PERSONAL: Born December 3, 1969, in Fort Benning, Ga. ... 6-4/300. ... Full name: Ed E'Dainia King.
HIGH SCHOOL: Central (Phenix City, Ala.).
COLLEGE: Auburn.
TRANSACTIONS/CAREER NOTES: Selected after junior season by Cleveland Browns in second round (29th pick overall) of 1991 NFL draft. ... Signed by Browns (July 16, 1991). ... Granted free agency (February 17, 1994). ... Signed by Green Bay Packers (June 2, 1994). ... Released by Packers (August 28, 1994). ... Selected by Barcelona Dragons in ninth round (54th pick overall) of 1995 World League Draft. ... Signed by New Orleans Saints (July 19, 1995).
PLAYING EXPERIENCE: Cleveland NFL, 1991-1993; New Orleans NFL, 1995. ... Games: 1991 (16), 1992 (16), 1993 (6), 1995 (1). Total: 39.
HONORS: Named guard on THE SPORTING NEWS college All-America second team (1990).
PRO STATISTICS: 1991—Recovered one fumble.

KING, JOE   S   RAIDERS

PERSONAL: Born May 7, 1968, in Dallas. ... 6-2/195.
HIGH SCHOOL: South Oak Cliff (Dallas).
COLLEGE: Oklahoma State.
TRANSACTIONS/CAREER NOTES: Signed as non-drafted free agent by Cincinnati Bengals (1991). ... Released by Bengals (August 26, 1991). ... Re-signed by Bengals (August 27, 1991). ... Claimed on waivers by Cleveland Browns and signed to practice squad (October 16, 1991). ... Activated (October 19, 1991). ... Released by Browns (November 13, 1991). ... Re-signed by Browns to practice squad (November 14, 1991). ... Activated (November 16, 1991). ... Released by Browns (November 22, 1991). ... Re-signed by Browns to practice squad (November 23, 1991). ... Activated (December 13, 1991). ... Granted unconditional free agency (February 1, 1992). ... Signed by Tampa Bay Buccaneers (March 12, 1992). ... Released by Buccaneers (August 31, 1992). ... Re-signed by Buccaneers (September 9, 1992). ... Released by Buccaneers (September 29, 1992). ... Re-signed by Buccaneers (October 9, 1992). ... Released by Buccaneers (June 27, 1994). ... Signed by Los Angeles Raiders (July 1994). ... Released by Raiders (August 23, 1994). ... Re-signed by Raiders (May 1995). ... Raiders franchise moved to Oakland (July 21, 1995).
PRO STATISTICS: 1993—Recovered two fumbles.

		INTERCEPTIONS				KICKOFF RETURNS				TOTALS			
Year Team	G	No.	Yds.	Avg.	TD	No.	Yds.	Avg.	TD	TD	2pt.	Pts.	Fum.
1991—Cincinnati NFL	6	0	0	...	0	3	34	11.3	0	0	...	0	0
—Cleveland NFL	7	0	0	...	0	0	0	...	0	0	...	0	0
1992—Tampa Bay NFL	14	2	24	12.0	0	0	0	...	0	0	...	0	0
1993—Tampa Bay NFL	15	3	29	9.7	0	0	0	...	0	0	...	0	0
1994—				Did not play.									
1995—Oakland NFL	16	0	0	...	0	0	0	...	0	0	0	0	0
Pro totals (4 years)	58	5	53	10.6	0	3	34	11.3	0	0	0	0	0

KING, SHAWN   DE   PANTHERS

PERSONAL: Born June 24, 1972, in West Monroe, La. ... 6-3/278.
HIGH SCHOOL: West Monroe (La.).
COLLEGE: Louisiana State, then Northeast Louisiana.
TRANSACTIONS/CAREER NOTES: Selected by Carolina Panthers in second round (36th pick overall) of 1995 NFL draft. ... Signed by Panthers (July 15, 1995).

Year Team	G	SACKS
1995—Carolina NFL	14	2.0

KIRBY, TERRY   RB   DOLPHINS

PERSONAL: Born January 20, 1970, in Hampton, Va. ... 6-1/218. ... Full name: Terry Gayle Kirby. ... Brother of Wayne Kirby, outfielder, Cleveland Indians; and cousin of Chris Slade, linebacker, New England Patriots.
HIGH SCHOOL: Tabb (Va.).
COLLEGE: Virginia (degree in psychology).
TRANSACTIONS/CAREER NOTES: Selected by Miami Dolphins in third round (78th pick overall) of 1993 NFL draft. ... Signed by Dolphins (July 19, 1993). ... On injured reserve with knee injury (September 26, 1994-remainder of season). ... Granted free agency (February 16, 1996).
PRO STATISTICS: 1993—Recovered four fumbles. 1995—Attempted one pass with one completion for 31 yards and a touchdown.
STATISTICAL PLATEAUS: 100-yard rushing games: 1994 (1). ... 100-yard receiving games: 1993 (2).

		RUSHING				RECEIVING				KICKOFF RETURNS				TOTALS			
Year Team	G	Att.	Yds.	Avg.	TD	No.	Yds.	Avg.	TD	No.	Yds.	Avg.	TD	TD	2pt.	Pts.	Fum.
1993—Miami NFL	16	119	390	3.3	3	75	874	11.7	3	4	85	21.3	0	6	...	36	5
1994—Miami NFL	4	60	233	3.9	2	14	154	11.0	0	0	0	...	0	2	1	14	2
1995—Miami NFL	16	108	414	3.8	4	66	618	9.4	3	0	0	...	0	7	0	42	2
Pro totals (3 years)	36	287	1037	3.6	9	155	1646	10.6	6	4	85	21.3	0	15	1	92	9

KIRK, RANDY   LB   49ERS

PERSONAL: Born December 27, 1964, in San Jose, Calif. ... 6-2/231. ... Full name: Randall Scott Kirk.
HIGH SCHOOL: Bellarmine College Prep (San Jose, Calif.).
JUNIOR COLLEGE: De Anza College (Calif.).
COLLEGE: San Diego State.
TRANSACTIONS/CAREER NOTES: Signed as non-drafted free agent by New York Giants (May 10, 1987). ... Released by Giants (August 31, 1987). ... Signed as replacement player by San Diego Chargers (September 24, 1987). ... Granted unconditional free agency (February 1, 1989). ... Signed by Phoenix Cardinals (March 31, 1989). ... On injured reserve with broken ankle (October 16, 1989-remainder of season). ... On injured reserve with foot injury (August 27-September 18, 1990). ... Released by Cardinals (September 18, 1990). ... Signed by Washington Redskins (November 7, 1990). ... Released by Redskins (November 13, 1990). ... Signed by Cleveland Browns (July 27, 1991). ... On injured reserve with back injury (September 13-November 19, 1991). ... Claimed on waivers by Chargers (November 19, 1991). ... Granted unconditional free agency (February 1, 1992). ... Signed by Cincinnati Bengals (March 3, 1992). ... Granted unconditional free agency (February 17, 1994). ... Signed by Cardinals (March 7, 1994). ... Cardinals franchise renamed Arizona Cardinals for 1994 season. ... Granted unconditional free agency (February 16, 1996). ... Signed by San Francisco 49ers (March 25, 1996).
PLAYING EXPERIENCE: San Diego NFL, 1987 and 1988; Phoenix NFL, 1989; Washington NFL, 1990; Cleveland (2)-San Diego (5) NFL, 1991; Cleveland NFL, 1992; Cincinnati NFL, 1993; Arizona NFL, 1994 and 1995. ... Games: 1987 (13), 1988 (16), 1989 (6), 1990 (1), 1991 (7), 1992 (15), 1993 (16), 1994 (16), 1995 (16). Total: 106.
PRO STATISTICS: 1987—Credited with one sack. 1988—Recovered one fumble. 1992—Recovered two fumbles for seven yards.

KIRKLAND, LEVON   LB   STEELERS

PERSONAL: Born February 17, 1969, in Lamar, S.C. ... 6-1/264. ... Full name: Lorenzo Levon Kirkland. ... Name pronounced luh-VON.
HIGH SCHOOL: Lamar (S.C.).
COLLEGE: Clemson.
TRANSACTIONS/CAREER NOTES: Selected by Pittsburgh Steelers in second round (38th pick overall) of 1992 NFL draft. ... Signed by Steelers (July 25, 1992).
CHAMPIONSHIP GAME EXPERIENCE: Played in AFC championship game (1994 and 1995 seasons). ... Played in Super Bowl XXX (1995 season).
HONORS: Named linebacker on The Sporting News college All-America first team (1991).
PRO STATISTICS: 1993—Recovered two fumbles for 24 yards and one touchdown. 1995—Recovered two fumbles.

		INTERCEPTIONS				SACKS
Year Team	G	No.	Yds.	Avg.	TD	No.
1992—Pittsburgh NFL	16	0	0	...	0	0.0
1993—Pittsburgh NFL	16	0	0	...	0	1.0
1994—Pittsburgh NFL	16	2	0	0.0	0	3.0
1995—Pittsburgh NFL	16	0	0	...	0	1.0
Pro totals (4 years)	64	2	0	0.0	0	5.0

KLEIN, PERRY   QB   FALCONS

PERSONAL: Born March 25, 1971, in Santa Monica, Calif. ... 6-2/218. ... Full name: Perry Sandor Klein.
HIGH SCHOOL: Carson (Calif.).
COLLEGE: California, then C.W. Post (N.Y.).
TRANSACTIONS/CAREER NOTES: Selected by Atlanta Falcons in fourth round (111th pick overall) of 1994 NFL draft. ... Signed by Falcons (July 5, 1994). ... Active for three games (1995); did not play.
PLAYING EXPERIENCE: Atlanta NFL, 1994. ... Games: 1994 (2).
PRO STATISTICS: 1994—Attempted one pass without a completion.

KLINE, ALAN   OT   SAINTS

PERSONAL: Born May 25, 1971, in Tiffin, Ohio. ... 6-5/290.
HIGH SCHOOL: Columbian (Tiffin, Ohio).
COLLEGE: Ohio State.
TRANSACTIONS/CAREER NOTES: Signed as non-drafted free agent by New Orleans Saints (April 28, 1994). ... Released by Saints (August 28, 1994). ... Re-signed by Saints to practice squad (August 30, 1994). ... Activated (December 22, 1994); did not play.
PLAYING EXPERIENCE: New Orleans NFL, 1995. ... Games: 1995 (3).

KLINGBEIL, CHUCK   NT   DOLPHINS

PERSONAL: Born November 2, 1965, in Houghton, Mich. ... 6-1/288. ... Name pronounced KLING-bile.
HIGH SCHOOL: Houghton (Mich.).
COLLEGE: Northern Michigan.
TRANSACTIONS/CAREER NOTES: Signed as non-drafted free agent by Saskatchewan Roughriders of CFL (March 1989). ... Granted free agency (February 1991). ... Signed by Miami Dolphins (April 4, 1991). ... Granted unconditional free agency (February 1, 1992). ... Re-signed

K

by Dolphins for 1992 season. ... Granted free agency (February 17, 1994). ... Re-signed by Dolphins (July 18, 1994). ... Granted unconditional free agency (February 17, 1995). ... Re-signed by Dolphins (April 18, 1995). ... Released by Dolphins (June 6, 1996).
CHAMPIONSHIP GAME EXPERIENCE: Played in Grey Cup, CFL championship game (1989 season). ... Played in AFC championship game (1992 season).
PRO STATISTICS: CFL: 1990—Recovered one fumble. NFL: 1991—Recovered one fumble in end zone for a touchdown.

Year Team	G	SACKS
1989—Saskatchewan CFL	5	1.0
1990—Saskatchewan CFL	18	7.0
1991—Miami NFL	15	5.0
1992—Miami NFL	15	1.0
1993—Miami NFL	16	1.5
1994—Miami NFL	16	0.0
1995—Miami NFL	16	0.0
CFL totals (2 years)	23	8.0
NFL totals (5 years)	78	7.5
Pro totals (7 years)	101	15.5

KLINGLER, DAVID   QB   RAIDERS

PERSONAL: Born February 17, 1969, in Stratford, Texas. ... 6-2/205.
HIGH SCHOOL: Stratford (Houston).
COLLEGE: Houston (degree in marketing, 1991).
TRANSACTIONS/CAREER NOTES: Selected by Cincinnati Bengals in first round (sixth pick overall) of 1992 NFL draft. ... Signed by Bengals (August 30, 1992). ... Granted unconditional free agency (February 16, 1996). ... Signed by Oakland Raiders (June 8, 1996).
PRO STATISTICS: 1992—Fumbled seven times. 1993—Fumbled seven times and recovered two fumbles for minus 10 yards. 1994—Caught one pass for minus six yards, fumbled seven times and recovered one fumble.
MISCELLANEOUS: Regular-season record as starting NFL quarterback: 4-20 (.167).

Year Team	G	PASSING								RUSHING				TOTALS		
		Att.	Cmp.	Pct.	Yds.	TD	Int.	Avg.	Rat.	Att.	Yds.	Avg.	TD	TD	2pt.	Pts.
1992—Cincinnati NFL	4	98	47	48.0	530	3	2	5.41	66.3	11	53	4.8	0	0	...	0
1993—Cincinnati NFL	14	343	190	55.4	1935	6	9	5.64	66.6	41	282	6.9	0	0	...	0
1994—Cincinnati NFL	10	231	131	56.7	1327	6	9	5.75	65.7	17	85	5.0	0	0	0	0
1995—Cincinnati NFL	3	15	7	46.7	88	1	1	5.87	59.9	0	0	...	0	0	0	0
Pro totals (4 years)	31	687	375	54.6	3880	16	21	5.65	66.1	69	420	6.1	0	0	0	0

KOONCE, GEORGE   LB   PACKERS

PERSONAL: Born October 15, 1968, in New Bern, N.C. ... 6-1/243. ... Full name: George Earl Koonce Jr.
HIGH SCHOOL: West Craven (Vanceboro, N.C.).
COLLEGE: Chowan College (N.C.), then East Carolina.
TRANSACTIONS/CAREER NOTES: Signed as non-drafted free agent by Atlanta Falcons (1991). ... Released by Falcons (August 26, 1991). ... Selected by Ohio Glory in 13th round (143rd pick overall) of 1992 World League draft. ... Signed by Green Bay Packers (June 2, 1992). ... On injured reserve with shoulder injury (January 3, 1994-entire 1993 playoffs). ... Granted free agency (February 17, 1995). ... Re-signed by Packers (June 2, 1995).
CHAMPIONSHIP GAME EXPERIENCE: Played in NFC championship game (1995 season).
PRO STATISTICS: W.L.: 1992—Recovered two fumbles for 35 yards. NFL: 1992—Recovered one fumble. 1993—Recovered one fumble. 1994—Recovered two fumbles. 1995—Intercepted one pass for 12 yards.

Year Team	G	SACKS
1992—Ohio W.L.	10	2.5
—Green Bay NFL	16	1.5
1993—Green Bay NFL	15	3.0
1994—Green Bay NFL	16	1.0
1995—Green Bay NFL	16	1.0
W.L. totals (1 year)	10	2.5
NFL totals (4 years)	63	6.5
Pro totals (4 years)	73	9.0

KOPP, JEFF   LB   DOLPHINS

PERSONAL: Born July 8, 1971, in Danville, Calif. ... 6-3/243.
HIGH SCHOOL: San Ramon (Danville, Calif.).
COLLEGE: Southern California.
TRANSACTIONS/CAREER NOTES: Selected by Miami Dolphins in sixth round (194th pick overall) of 1995 NFL draft.
PLAYING EXPERIENCE: Miami NFL, 1995. ... Games: 1995 (16).

KOSAR, BERNIE   QB   DOLPHINS

PERSONAL: Born November 25, 1963, in Boardman, Ohio. ... 6-5/214. ... Full name: Bernie Joseph Kosar Jr.
HIGH SCHOOL: Boardman (Ohio).
COLLEGE: Miami, Fla. (degree in finance and economics, 1985).
TRANSACTIONS/CAREER NOTES: Selected by Cleveland Browns in first round of 1985 NFL supplemental draft (July 2, 1985). ... Signed by Browns (July 2, 1985). ... On injured reserve with elbow injury (September 10-October 21, 1988). ... On injured reserve with broken ankle (September 16-November 28, 1992). ... Released by Browns (November 8, 1993). ... Signed by Dallas Cowboys (November 10, 1993). ...

K

Granted unconditional free agency (February 17, 1994). ... Signed by Miami Dolphins (April 13, 1994). ... Granted unconditional free agency (February 16, 1996). ... Re-signed by Dolphins (June 3, 1996).
CHAMPIONSHIP GAME EXPERIENCE: Played in AFC championship game (1986, 1987 and 1989 seasons). ... Played in NFC championship game (1993 season). ... Member of Super Bowl championship team (1993 season).
HONORS: Named quarterback on THE SPORTING NEWS college All-America second team (1984). ... Played in Pro Bowl (1987 season).
RECORDS: Holds NFL career records for lowest percentage of passes intercepted—2.54; and most consecutive pass attempts without an interception—308 (1990-1991).
POSTSEASON RECORDS: Holds NFL postseason single-game records for most yards passing—489; and most passes attempted—64 (January 3, 1987, OT, vs. New York Jets).
PRO STATISTICS: 1985—Fumbled 14 times and recovered two fumbles for minus 25 yards. 1986—Caught one pass for one yard, fumbled seven times and recovered three fumbles for minus 15 yards. 1987—Fumbled twice and recovered one fumble for minus three yards. 1988—Recovered two fumbles. 1989—Caught one pass for minus seven yards, fumbled twice and recovered two fumbles for minus one yard. 1990—Fumbled six times and recovered one fumble for minus nine yards. 1991—Caught one pass for one yard, fumbled 10 times and recovered two fumbles for minus 18 yards. 1992—Fumbled once. 1993—Fumbled six times. 1995—Fumbled three times and recovered one fumble for minus seven yards.
STATISTICAL PLATEAUS: 300-yard passing games: 1986 (2), 1987 (2), 1988 (2), 1989 (1), 1990 (1), 1991 (2), 1995 (1). Total: 11.
MISCELLANEOUS: Regular-season record as starting NFL quarterback: 53-54-1 (.495).

				PASSING						RUSHING				TOTALS		
Year	Team	G	Att.	Cmp.	Pct.	Yds.	TD	Int.	Avg.	Rat.	Att.	Yds.	Avg.	TD	TD	2pt.	Pts.
1985—Cleveland NFL		12	248	124	50.0	1578	8	7	6.36	69.3	26	-12	-0.5	1	1	...	6
1986—Cleveland NFL		16	531	310	58.4	3854	17	10	7.26	83.8	24	19	0.8	0	0	...	0
1987—Cleveland NFL		12	389	241	62.0	3033	22	9	7.80	95.4	15	22	1.5	1	1	...	6
1988—Cleveland NFL		9	259	156	60.2	1890	10	7	7.30	84.3	12	-1	-0.1	1	1	...	6
1989—Cleveland NFL		16	513	303	59.1	3533	18	14	6.89	80.3	30	70	2.3	1	1	...	6
1990—Cleveland NFL		13	423	230	54.4	2562	10	15	6.06	65.7	10	13	1.3	0	0	...	0
1991—Cleveland NFL		16	494	307	62.2	3487	18	9	7.06	87.8	26	74	2.9	0	0	...	0
1992—Cleveland NFL		7	155	103	66.5	1160	8	7	7.48	87.0	5	12	2.4	0	0	...	0
1993—Cleveland NFL		7	138	79	57.3	807	5	3	5.85	77.2	14	19	1.4	0	0	...	0
—Dallas NFL		4	63	36	57.1	410	3	0	6.51	92.7	9	7	0.8	0	0	...	0
1994—Miami NFL		2	12	7	58.3	80	1	1	6.67	71.5	1	17	17.0	0	0	0	0
1995—Miami NFL		9	108	74	68.5	699	3	5	6.47	76.1	7	19	2.7	1	1	0	6
Pro totals (11 years)		123	3333	1970	59.1	23093	123	87	6.93	81.6	179	259	1.5	5	5	0	30

KOWALKOWSKI, SCOTT   LB

PERSONAL: Born August 23, 1968, in Royal Oak, Mich. ... 6-2/228. ... Full name: Scott Thomas Kowalkowski. ... Son of David Kowalkowski, guard, Detroit Lions and Green Bay Packers (1966-1977). ... Name pronounced KO-wal-KOW-skee.
HIGH SCHOOL: St. Mary's Prep (Orchard Lake, Mich.).
COLLEGE: Notre Dame (degree in American studies).
TRANSACTIONS/CAREER NOTES: Selected by Philadelphia Eagles in eighth round (217th pick overall) of 1991 NFL draft. ... Signed by Eagles (July 10, 1991). ... On injured reserve with ankle injury (August 30-November 23, 1993). ... Released by Eagles (November 23, 1993). ... Signed by Detroit Lions (1994). ... Granted unconditional free agency (February 17, 1995). ... Re-signed by Lions (March 24, 1995). ... Granted unconditional free agency (February 16, 1996).
PLAYING EXPERIENCE: Philadelphia NFL, 1991 and 1992; Detroit NFL, 1994 and 1995. ... Games: 1991 (16), 1992 (16), 1994 (16), 1995 (16). Total: 64.
PRO STATISTICS: 1991—Recovered one fumble.

KOZERSKI, BRUCE   G   BENGALS

PERSONAL: Born April 2, 1962, in Plains, Pa. ... 6-4/287.
HIGH SCHOOL: James M. Coughlin (Wilkes-Barre, Pa.).
COLLEGE: Holy Cross (degree in physics, 1984).
TRANSACTIONS/CAREER NOTES: Selected by Houston Gamblers in 12th round (245th pick overall) of 1984 USFL draft. ... Selected by Cincinnati Bengals in ninth round (231st pick overall) of 1984 NFL draft. ... Signed by Bengals (June 10, 1984). ... On injured reserve with pinched nerve in neck (November 14-December 11, 1987). ... Granted free agency (February 1, 1992). ... Re-signed by Bengals (August 30, 1992). ... On injured reserve with ankle injury (December 18, 1995-remainder of season).
PLAYING EXPERIENCE: Cincinnati NFL, 1984-1995. ... Games: 1984 (16), 1985 (14), 1986 (16), 1987 (8), 1988 (16), 1989 (15), 1990 (16), 1991 (16), 1992 (16), 1993 (15), 1994 (16), 1995 (8). Total: 172.
CHAMPIONSHIP GAME EXPERIENCE: Played in AFC championship game (1988 season). ... Played in Super Bowl XXIII (1988 season).
PRO STATISTICS: 1987—Recovered one fumble. 1989—Recovered one fumble. 1991—Recovered one fumble. 1993—Fumbled three times and recovered one fumble for minus 14 yards.

KOZLOWSKI, BRIAN   TE   GIANTS

PERSONAL: Born October 4, 1970, in Rochester, N.Y. ... 6-3/255. ... Full name: Brian Scott Kozlowski.
HIGH SCHOOL: Webster (N.Y.).
COLLEGE: Connecticut.
TRANSACTIONS/CAREER NOTES: Signed as non-drafted free agent by New York Giants (May 1, 1993). ... Released by Giants (August 16, 1993). ... Re-signed by Giants to practice squad (December 8, 1993). ... Granted free agency after 1993 season. ... Re-signed by Giants (March 1, 1994).
PRO STATISTICS: 1995—Recovered one fumble.

			RECEIVING				KICKOFF RETURNS				TOTALS			
Year	Team	G	No.	Yds.	Avg.	TD	No.	Yds.	Avg.	TD	TD	2pt.	Pts.	Fum.
1993—New York Giants NFL							Did not play.							
1994—New York Giants NFL		16	1	5	5.0	0	2	21	10.5	0	0	0	0	0

Year Team	G	No.	RECEIVING Yds.	Avg.	TD	No.	KICKOFF RETURNS Yds.	Avg.	TD	TD	TOTALS 2pt.	Pts.	Fum.
1995—New York Giants NFL	16	2	17	8.5	0	5	75	15.0	0	0	0	0	1
Pro totals (2 years)	32	3	22	7.3	0	7	96	13.7	0	0	0	0	1

KRAGEN, GREG   NT   PANTHERS

PERSONAL: Born March 4, 1962, in Chicago. ... 6-3/267. ... Full name: Greg John Kragen.
HIGH SCHOOL: Amador (Pleasanton, Calif.).
COLLEGE: Utah State.
TRANSACTIONS/CAREER NOTES: Selected by Oklahoma Outlaws in 15th round (296th pick overall) of 1984 USFL draft. ... Signed as non-drafted free agent by Denver Broncos (May 2, 1984). ... Released by Broncos (August 27, 1984). ... Re-signed by Broncos (January 20, 1985). ... Released by Broncos (April 22, 1994). ... Signed by Kansas City Chiefs (August 18, 1994). ... Selected by Carolina Panthers from Chiefs in NFL expansion draft (February 15, 1995).
CHAMPIONSHIP GAME EXPERIENCE: Played in AFC championship game (1986, 1987, 1989 and 1991 seasons). ... Played in Super Bowl XXI (1986 season), Super Bowl XXII (1987 season) and Super Bowl XXIV (1989 season).
HONORS: Played in Pro Bowl (1989 season).
PRO STATISTICS: 1986—Recovered three fumbles. 1987—Recovered one fumble. 1988—Recovered one fumble. 1989—Recovered four fumbles for 17 yards and a touchdown. 1990—Recovered two fumbles. 1993—Recovered one fumble. 1995—Intercepted one pass for 29 yards and recovered two fumbles for three yards and a touchdown.

Year Team	G	SACKS
1985—Denver NFL	16	2.0
1986—Denver NFL	16	0.0
1987—Denver NFL	12	2.0
1988—Denver NFL	16	2.5
1989—Denver NFL	14	2.0
1990—Denver NFL	16	2.0
1991—Denver NFL	16	3.5
1992—Denver NFL	16	5.5
1993—Denver NFL	14	3.0
1994—Kansas City NFL	16	0.0
1995—Carolina NFL	16	1.0
Pro totals (11 years)	168	23.5

KRAMER, ERIK   QB   BEARS

PERSONAL: Born November 6, 1964, in Encino, Calif. ... 6-1/200. ... Full name: William Erik Kramer.
HIGH SCHOOL: Conoga Park (Calif.).
JUNIOR COLLEGE: Los Angeles Pierce Community College.
COLLEGE: North Carolina State.
TRANSACTIONS/CAREER NOTES: Signed as non-drafted free agent by New Orleans Saints (May 6, 1987). ... Released by Saints (August 31, 1987). ... Signed as replacement player by Atlanta Falcons (September 24, 1987). ... Released by Falcons (September 1, 1988). ... Signed by Calgary Stampeders of CFL (September 28, 1988). ... Released by Stampeders (July 4, 1989). ... Signed by Detroit Lions (March 21, 1990). ... On injured reserve with shoulder injury (September 4-December 28, 1990). ... Released by Lions (December 28, 1990). ... Re-signed by Lions (March 6, 1991). ... Granted free agency (March 1, 1993). ... Tendered offer sheet by Dallas Cowboys (April 1993). ... Offer matched by Lions (April 23, 1993). ... Granted unconditional free agency (February 17, 1994). ... Signed by Chicago Bears (February 21, 1994).
CHAMPIONSHIP GAME EXPERIENCE: Played in NFC championship game (1991 season).
PRO STATISTICS: CFL: 1988—Fumbled seven times. NFL: 1991—Fumbled eight times and recovered four fumbles for minus five yards. 1992—Fumbled four times and recovered one fumble for minus one yard. 1993—Fumbled three times and recovered two fumbles for minus five yards. 1995—Fumbled six times and recovered two fumbles for minus 13 yards.
STATISTICAL PLATEAUS: 300-yard passing games: 1987 (1), 1992 (1), 1994 (1), 1995 (3). Total: 6.
MISCELLANEOUS: Regular-season record as starting NFL quarterback: 21-17 (.553).

Year Team	G	Att.	Cmp.	Pct.	PASSING Yds.	TD	Int.	Avg.	Rat.	Att.	RUSHING Yds.	Avg.	TD	TD	TOTALS 2pt.	Pts.
1987—Atlanta NFL	3	92	45	48.9	559	4	5	6.08	60.0	2	10	5.0	0	0	...	0
1988—Calgary CFL	6	153	62	40.5	964	5	13	6.30	37.6	12	17	1.4	1	1	0	6
1989—						Did not play.										
1990—Detroit NFL						Did not play.										
1991—Detroit NFL	13	265	136	51.3	1635	11	8	6.17	71.8	35	26	0.7	1	1	...	6
1992—Detroit NFL	7	106	58	54.7	771	4	8	7.27	59.1	12	34	2.8	0	0	...	0
1993—Detroit NFL	5	138	87	63.0	1002	8	3	7.26	95.1	10	5	0.5	0	0	...	0
1994—Chicago NFL	6	158	99	62.7	1129	8	8	7.15	79.9	6	-2	-0.3	0	0	0	0
1995—Chicago NFL	16	522	315	60.3	3838	29	10	7.35	93.5	35	39	1.1	1	1	0	6
CFL totals (1 year)	6	153	62	40.5	964	5	13	6.30	37.6	12	17	1.4	1	1	0	6
NFL totals (6 years)	50	1281	740	57.8	8934	64	42	6.98	82.3	100	112	1.1	2	2	0	12
Pro totals (7 years)	56	1434	802	55.9	9898	69	55	6.90	77.5	112	129	1.2	3	3	0	18

KRATCH, BOB   G   PATRIOTS

PERSONAL: Born January 6, 1966, in Brooklyn, N.Y. ... 6-3/288.
HIGH SCHOOL: Mahwah (N.J.).
COLLEGE: Iowa (degree in communications, 1989).
TRANSACTIONS/CAREER NOTES: Selected by New York Giants in third round (64th pick overall) of 1989 NFL draft. ... Signed by Giants (July 24, 1989). ... On injured reserve with broken finger (September 5-October 17, 1989). ... On developmental squad (October 18-21, 1989). ... Granted free agency (February 1, 1992). ... Re-signed by Giants (July 31, 1992). ... Granted unconditional free agency (February 17, 1994). ... Signed by New England Patriots (February 19, 1994).
PLAYING EXPERIENCE: New York Giants NFL, 1989-1993; New England NFL, 1994 and 1995. ... Games: 1989 (4), 1990 (14), 1991 (15),

K

1992 (16), 1993 (16), 1994 (16), 1995 (16). Total: 97.
CHAMPIONSHIP GAME EXPERIENCE: Played in NFC championship game (1990 season). ... Member of Super Bowl championship team (1990 season).

KRIEG, DAVE　　　　　　　　　QB　　　　　　　　　BEARS

PERSONAL: Born October 20, 1958, in Iola, Wis. ... 6-1/202. ... Name pronounced CRAIG.
HIGH SCHOOL: D.C. Everest (Schofield, Wis.).
COLLEGE: Milton College, Wis. (degree in marketing management, 1980).
TRANSACTIONS/CAREER NOTES: Signed as non-drafted free agent by Seattle Seahawks (May 6, 1980). ... On injured reserve with separated shoulder (September 19-November 12, 1988). ... On injured reserve with thumb injury (September 3-October 18, 1991). ... Granted unconditional free agency (February 1, 1992). ... Signed by Kansas City Chiefs (March 19, 1992). ... Granted unconditional free agency (February 17, 1994). ... Signed by Detroit Lions (April 22, 1994). ... Granted unconditional free agency (February 17, 1995). ... Signed by Arizona Cardinals (March 11, 1995). ... Released by Cardinals (April 8, 1996). ... Signed by Chicago Bears (May 21, 1996).
CHAMPIONSHIP GAME EXPERIENCE: Played in AFC championship game (1983 and 1993 seasons).
HONORS: Played in Pro Bowl (1984, 1988 and 1989 seasons).
RECORDS: Holds NFL career record for most fumbles—144. ... Holds NFL single-season record for most own fumbles recovered—9 (1989). ... Shares NFL single-season records for most fumbles—18 (1989); and most fumbles recovered, own and opponents—9 (1989).
PRO STATISTICS: 1981—Fumbled four times. 1982—Fumbled five times and recovered two fumbles for minus 14 yards. 1983—Caught one pass for 11 yards, fumbled 10 times and recovered two fumbles. 1984—Fumbled 11 times and recovered three fumbles for minus 24 yards. 1985—Fumbled 11 times and recovered three fumbles for minus two yards. 1986—Fumbled 10 times and recovered one fumble for minus five yards. 1987—Fumbled 11 times and recovered five fumbles for minus two yards. 1988—Fumbled six times. 1989—Led league with 18 fumbles and recovered nine fumbles for minus 20 yards. 1990—Caught one pass for minus six yards, fumbled 16 times and recovered two fumbles. 1991—Fumbled six times. 1992—Fumbled 10 times and recovered six fumbles for minus 15 yards. 1993—Fumbled six times and recovered one fumble. 1994—Fumbled four times and recovered two fumbles for minus one yard. 1995—Lead league with 16 fumbles and recovered seven fumbles for minus 13 yards.
STATISTICAL PLATEAUS: 300-yard passing games: 1983 (1), 1984 (3), 1985 (2), 1986 (1), 1988 (1), 1989 (1), 1990 (1), 1991 (1), 1992 (2), 1994 (1), 1995 (4). Total: 18.
MISCELLANEOUS: Regular-season record as starting NFL quarterback: 92-71 (.564). ... Shares active NFC lead for career touchdown passes (247). ... Holds Seattle Seahawks all-time records for most yards passing (26,132) and most touchdown passes (195).

Year Team	G	Att.	Cmp.	Pct.	Yds.	TD	Int.	Avg.	Rat.	Att.	Yds.	Avg.	TD	TD	2pt.	Pts.
1980—Seattle NFL	1	2	0	0.0	0	0	0	.00	39.6	0	0	0	0	0	...	0
1981—Seattle NFL	7	112	64	57.1	843	7	5	7.53	83.3	11	56	5.1	1	1	...	6
1982—Seattle NFL	3	78	49	62.8	501	2	2	6.42	79.1	6	-3	-0.5	0	0	...	0
1983—Seattle NFL	9	243	147	60.5	2139	18	11	8.80	95.0	16	55	3.4	2	2	...	12
1984—Seattle NFL	16	480	276	57.5	3671	32	*24	7.65	83.3	46	186	4.0	3	3	...	18
1985—Seattle NFL	16	532	285	53.6	3602	27	20	6.77	76.2	35	121	3.5	1	1	...	6
1986—Seattle NFL	15	375	225	60.0	2921	21	11	7.79	91.0	35	122	3.5	1	1	...	6
1987—Seattle NFL	12	294	178	60.5	2131	23	15	7.25	87.6	36	155	4.3	2	2	...	12
1988—Seattle NFL	9	228	134	58.8	1741	18	8	7.64	94.6	24	64	2.7	0	0	...	0
1989—Seattle NFL	15	499	286	57.3	3309	21	20	6.63	74.8	40	160	4.0	0	0	...	0
1990—Seattle NFL	16	448	265	59.2	3194	15	20	7.13	73.6	32	115	3.6	0	0	...	0
1991—Seattle NFL	10	285	187	*65.6	2080	11	12	7.30	82.5	13	59	4.5	0	0	...	0
1992—Kansas City NFL	16	413	230	55.7	3115	15	12	7.54	79.9	37	74	2.0	2	2	...	12
1993—Kansas City NFL	12	189	105	55.6	1238	7	3	6.55	81.4	21	24	1.1	0	0	...	0
1994—Detroit NFL	14	212	131	61.8	1629	14	3	7.68	101.7	23	35	1.5	0	0	0	0
1995—Arizona NFL	16	521	304	58.4	3554	16	21	6.82	72.6	19	29	1.5	0	0	0	0
Pro totals (16 years)	187	4911	2866	58.4	35668	247	187	7.26	81.9	394	1252	3.2	12	12	0	72

KUBERSKI, BOB　　　　　　　　DT　　　　　　　　PACKERS

PERSONAL: Born April 5, 1971, in Chester, Pa. ... 6-4/300. ... Full name: Robert Kenneth Kuberski Jr.
HIGH SCHOOL: Ridley (Folsom, Pa.).
COLLEGE: Navy.
TRANSACTIONS/CAREER NOTES: Selected by Green Bay Packers in seventh round (183rd pick overall) of 1993 NFL draft. ... Signed by Packers (June 7, 1993). ... On reserve/military list (August 23, 1993-April 19, 1995).
PLAYING EXPERIENCE: Green Bay NFl, 1995. ... Games: 1995 (9).
CHAMPIONSHIP GAME EXPERIENCE: Played in NFC championship game (1995 season).

KYLE, JASON　　　　　　　　　LB　　　　　　　　SEAHAWKS

PERSONAL: Born May 12, 1972, in Mesa, Ariz. ... 6-3/242.
HIGH SCHOOL: McClintock (Tempe, Ariz.).
COLLEGE: Arizona State.
TRANSACTIONS/CAREER NOTES: Selected by Seattle Seahawks in fourth round (126th pick overall) of 1995 NFL draft. ... Signed by Seahawks (July 16, 1995).
PLAYING EXPERIENCE: Seattle NFL, 1995. ... Games: 1995 (16).
PRO STATISTICS: 1995—Credited with two sacks.

KYSAR, JEFF　　　　　　　　　OT　　　　　　　　RAIDERS

PERSONAL: Born June 14, 1972, in Norman, Okla. ... 6-7/320. ... Full name: Jeffrey John Charles Kysar.
HIGH SCHOOL: Serra (San Diego).

COLLEGE: Arizona State.
TRANSACTIONS/CAREER NOTES: Selected by Los Angeles Raiders in fifth round (154th pick overall) of 1995 NFL draft. ... Signed by Raiders (July 21, 1995). ... Raiders franchise moved to Oakland (July 21, 1995).
PLAYING EXPERIENCE: Oakland NFL, 1995. ... Games: 1995 (1).

LaBOUNTY, MATT   DE   PACKERS

PERSONAL: Born January 3, 1969, in San Francisco. ... 6-3/278. ... Full name: Matthew James LaBounty.
HIGH SCHOOL: San Marin (Novato, Calif.).
COLLEGE: Oregon.
TRANSACTIONS/CAREER NOTES: Selected by San Francisco 49ers in 12th round (327th pick overall) of 1992 NFL draft. ... Signed by 49ers (July 13, 1992). ... Released by 49ers (August 31, 1992). ... Re-signed by 49ers to practice squad (September 1, 1992). ... Granted free agency after 1992 season. ... Re-signed by 49ers for 1993 season. ... Released by 49ers (October 17, 1993). ... Re-signed by 49ers to practice squad (October 20, 1993). ... Activated (December 2, 1993). ... Claimed on waivers by Green Bay Packers (December 8, 1993). ... On injured reserve with back injury (August 23, 1994-entire season).
PLAYING EXPERIENCE: San Francisco NFL, 1993; Green Bay NFL, 1995. ... Games: 1993 (6), 1995 (14). Total: 20.
CHAMPIONSHIP GAME EXPERIENCE: Played in NFC championship game (1995 season).
PRO STATISTICS: 1995—Credited with three sacks.

LaCHAPELLE, SEAN   WR   CHIEFS

PERSONAL: Born July 29, 1970, in Sacramento. ... 6-3/205. ... Full name: Sean Paul LaChapelle.
HIGH SCHOOL: Vintage (Napa Valley, Calif.).
COLLEGE: UCLA.
TRANSACTIONS/CAREER NOTES: Selected by Los Angeles Rams in fifth round (122nd pick overall) of 1993 NFL draft. ... Signed by Rams (June 4, 1993). ... Released by Rams (August 22, 1994). ... Signed by Kansas City Chiefs (February 28, 1995). ... Released by Chiefs (August 22, 1995). ... Re-signed by Chiefs (March 1996). ... Assigned by Chiefs to Scottish Claymores in 1996 World League enhancement allocation program (February 19, 1996).

		RECEIVING					TOTALS		
Year Team	G	No.	Yds.	Avg.	TD	TD	2pt.	Pts.	Fum.
1993—Los Angeles Rams NFL	10	2	23	11.5	0	0	0	0	0
1994—					Did not play.				
1995—					Did not play.				

LACHEY, JIM   OT

PERSONAL: Born June 4, 1963, in St. Henry, Ohio. ... 6-6/294. ... Full name: James Michael Lachey. ... Name pronounced luh-SHAY.
HIGH SCHOOL: St. Henry (Ohio).
COLLEGE: Ohio State (degree in marketing, 1985).
TRANSACTIONS/CAREER NOTES: Selected by New Jersey Generals in 1985 USFL territorial draft. ... Selected by San Diego Chargers in first round (12th pick overall) of 1985 NFL draft. ... Signed by Chargers (July 28, 1985). ... Traded by Chargers to Los Angeles Raiders for OT John Clay, third-round pick (traded to New York Giants) in 1989 draft and conditional pick in 1990 draft (July 30, 1988). ... Traded by Raiders with second-round (traded to Dallas), fourth-round (WR Erik Affholter) and fifth-round (DE Lybrant Robinson) picks in 1989 draft and fourth-round (DB Rico Labbe) and fifth-round picks in 1990 draft to Washington Redskins for QB Jay Schroeder and second-round pick in 1989 draft (September 7, 1988). ... Granted free agency (February 1, 1992). ... Re-signed by Redskins (August 25, 1992). ... On injured reserve with sprained knee (October 15-November 28, 1992). ... Designated by Redskins as transition player (February 25, 1993). ... On injured reserve (August 24, 1993-entire season). ... On injured reserve with leg injury (December 22, 1994-remainder of season). ... On injured reserve with shoulder injury (September 27, 1995-remainder of season). ... Announced retirement (June 6, 1996).
PLAYING EXPERIENCE: San Diego NFL, 1985-1987; Los Angeles Raiders (1)-Washington (15) NFL, 1988; Washington NFL, 1989-1992, 1994 and 1995. ... Games: 1985 (16), 1986 (16), 1987 (12), 1988 (16), 1989 (14), 1990 (16), 1991 (15), 1992 (10), 1994 (13), 1995 (3). Total: 131.
CHAMPIONSHIP GAME EXPERIENCE: Played in NFC championship game (1991 season). ... Member of Super Bowl championship team (1991 season).
HONORS: Named offensive guard on THE SPORTING NEWS college All-America second team (1984). ... Played in Pro Bowl (1987, 1990 and 1991 seasons). ... Named offensive tackle on THE SPORTING NEWS NFL All-Pro team (1989-1991).
PRO STATISTICS: 1988—Recovered one fumble. 1989—Recovered one fumble. 1990—Recovered one fumble.

LACINA, CORBIN   G   BILLS

PERSONAL: Born November 2, 1970, in Woodbury, Minn. ... 6-4/297.
HIGH SCHOOL: Cretin-Derham Hall (St. Paul, Minn.).
COLLEGE: Augustana (S.D.).
TRANSACTIONS/CAREER NOTES: Selected by Buffalo Bills in sixth round (167th pick overall) of 1993 NFL draft. ... Signed by Bills (July 12, 1993). ... Released by Bills (August 30, 1993). ... Re-signed by Bills to practice squad (September 1, 1993). ... Activated (December 30, 1993); did not play. ... On injured reserve with foot injury (December 22, 1994-remainder of season).
PLAYING EXPERIENCE: Buffalo NFL, 1994 and 1995. ... Games: 1994 (11), 1995 (16). Total: 27.
CHAMPIONSHIP GAME EXPERIENCE: Member of Bills for AFC championship game (1993 season); inactive. ... Member of Bills for Super Bowl XXVIII (1993 season); inactive.

LAGEMAN, JEFF   DE   JAGUARS

PERSONAL: Born July 18, 1967, in Fairfax, Va. ... 6-6/268. ... Full name: Jeffrey David Lageman. ... Name pronounced LOG-a-man.
HIGH SCHOOL: Park View (Sterling, Va.).
COLLEGE: Virginia (degree in economics, 1989).

TRANSACTIONS/CAREER NOTES: Selected by New York Jets in first round (14th pick overall) of 1989 NFL draft. ... Signed by Jets (August 24, 1989). ... On injured reserve with knee injury (September 15, 1992-remainder of season). ... Granted unconditional free agency (February 17, 1995). ... Signed by Jacksonville Jaguars (March 14, 1995). ... On injured reserve with foot injury (December 19, 1995-remainder of season).
PRO STATISTICS: 1989—Rushed once for minus five yards. 1993—Intercepted one pass for 15 yards. 1994—Recovered three fumbles. 1995—Recovered one fumble.

Year Team	G	SACKS
1989—New York Jets NFL	16	4.5
1990—New York Jets NFL	16	4.0
1991—New York Jets NFL	16	10.0
1992—New York Jets NFL	2	1.0
1993—New York Jets NFL	16	8.5
1994—New York Jets NFL	16	6.5
1995—Jacksonville NFL	11	3.0
Pro totals (7 years)	93	37.5

LAKE, CARNELL   S   STEELERS

PERSONAL: Born July 15, 1967, in Salt Lake City. ... 6-1/210. ... Full name: Carnell Augustino Lake.
HIGH SCHOOL: Culver City (Calif.).
COLLEGE: UCLA.
TRANSACTIONS/CAREER NOTES: Selected by Pittsburgh Steelers in second round (34th pick overall) of 1989 NFL draft. ... Signed by Steelers (July 23, 1989). ... Granted free agency (February 1, 1992). ... Re-signed by Steelers (August 21, 1992). ... Granted roster exemption (August 21-28, 1992). ... Designated by Steelers as franchise player (February 15, 1995).
CHAMPIONSHIP GAME EXPERIENCE: Played in AFC championship game (1994 and 1995 seasons). ... Played in Super Bowl XXX (1995 season).
HONORS: Named linebacker on THE SPORTING NEWS college All-America second team (1987). ... Played in Pro Bowl (1994 and 1995 seasons).
POSTSEASON RECORDS: Shares NFL postseason single-game record for most safeties—1 (January 7, 1995, vs. Cleveland).
PRO STATISTICS: 1989—Recovered six fumbles for two yards. 1990—Recovered one fumble. 1992—Recovered one fumble for 12 yards. 1993—Recovered two fumbles. 1994—Recovered one fumble. 1995—Recovered one fumble.

Year Team	G	INTERCEPTIONS No.	Yds.	Avg.	TD	SACKS No.
1989—Pittsburgh NFL	15	1	0	0.0	0	1.0
1990—Pittsburgh NFL	16	1	0	0.0	0	1.0
1991—Pittsburgh NFL	16	0	0	...	0	1.0
1992—Pittsburgh NFL	16	0	0	...	0	2.0
1993—Pittsburgh NFL	14	4	31	7.8	0	5.0
1994—Pittsburgh NFL	16	1	2	2.0	0	1.0
1995—Pittsburgh NFL	16	1	32	32.0	1	1.5
Pro totals (7 years)	109	8	65	8.1	1	12.5

LAND, DAN   CB

PERSONAL: Born July 3, 1965, in Donalsonville, Ga. ... 6-0/195.
HIGH SCHOOL: Seminole County (Donalsonville, Ga.).
COLLEGE: Albany (Ga.) State.
TRANSACTIONS/CAREER NOTES: Signed as non-drafted free agent by Tampa Bay Buccaneers (May 4, 1987). ... Released by Buccaneers (September 7, 1987). ... Re-signed as replacement player by Buccaneers (September 24, 1987). ... Released by Buccaneers (October 19, 1987). ... Signed by Atlanta Falcons for 1988 season (December 5, 1987). ... Released by Falcons (August 30, 1988). ... Signed by Los Angeles Raiders (January 10, 1989). ... Released by Raiders (September 5, 1989). ... Re-signed by Raiders (October 4, 1989). ... Granted free agency (February 1, 1991). ... Re-signed by Raiders (1991). ... Assigned by Raiders to New York/New Jersey Knights in 1992 World League enhancement allocation program (February 20, 1992). ... Released by Raiders (August 30, 1993). ... Re-signed by Raiders (August 31, 1993). ... Released by Raiders (August 27, 1995). ... Re-signed by Raiders (August 30, 1995). ... Raiders franchise moved to Oakland (July 21, 1995). ... Granted unconditional free agency (February 16, 1996).
PLAYING EXPERIENCE: Tampa Bay NFL, 1987; Los Angeles Raiders NFL, 1989-1994; New York/New Jersey W.L., 1992; Oakland NFL, 1995. ... Games: 1987 (3), 1989 (10), 1990 (16), 1991 (16), 1992 WL (10), 1992 NFL (16), 1993 (15), 1994 (16), 1995 (16). Total W.L.: 10. Total NFL: 108. Total Pro: 118.
CHAMPIONSHIP GAME EXPERIENCE: Played in AFC championship game (1990 season).
PRO STATISTICS: NFL: 1987—Rushed nine times for 20 yards. 1992—Returned two kickoffs for 27 yards, intercepted one pass for no yards and fumbled once. W.L.: 1992—Rushed once for 16 yards, credited with one sack and intercepted one pass for 11 yards.

LANDETA, SEAN   P   RAMS

PERSONAL: Born January 6, 1962, in Baltimore. ... 6-0/210. ... Full name: Sean Edward Landeta.
HIGH SCHOOL: Loch Raven (Baltimore).
COLLEGE: Towson State.
TRANSACTIONS/CAREER NOTES: Selected by Philadelphia Stars in 14th round (161st pick overall) of 1983 USFL draft. ... Signed by Stars (January 24, 1983). ... Stars franchise moved to Baltimore (November 1, 1984). ... Granted free agency (August 1, 1985). ... Signed by New York Giants (August 5, 1985). ... On injured reserve with back injury (September 7, 1988-remainder of season). ... Granted free agency (February 1, 1990). ... Re-signed by Giants (July 23, 1990). ... On injured reserve with knee injury (November 25, 1992-remainder of season). ... Granted unconditional free agency (March 1, 1993). ... Re-signed by Giants (March 18, 1993). ... Released by Giants (November 9, 1993). ... Signed by Los Angeles Rams (November 12, 1993). ... Granted unconditional free agency (February 17, 1994). ... Re-signed by Rams (May 10, 1994). ... Granted unconditional free agency (February 17, 1995). ... Rams franchise moved to St. Louis (April 12, 1995). ... Re-signed by Rams (May 8, 1995).
CHAMPIONSHIP GAME EXPERIENCE: Played in USFL championship game (1983-1985 seasons). ... Played in NFC championship game (1986 and 1990 seasons). ... Member of Super Bowl championship team (1986 and 1990 season).
HONORS: Named punter on THE SPORTING NEWS USFL All-Star team (1983 and 1984). ... Named punter on THE SPORTING NEWS NFL All-Pro team (1986, 1989 and 1990). ... Played in Pro Bowl (1986 and 1990 seasons).

L

PRO STATISTICS: USFL: 1983—Rushed once for minus five yards, fumbled once and recovered one fumble. 1984—Recovered one fumble. NFL: 1985—Attempted one pass without a completion.

				PUNTING			
Year Team	G	No.	Yds.	Avg.	Net avg.	In. 20	Blk.
1983—Philadelphia USFL	18	86	3601	41.9	36.5	31	0
1984—Philadelphia USFL	18	53	2171	41.0	*38.1	18	0
1985—Baltimore USFL	18	65	2718	41.8	33.3	18	0
—New York Giants NFL	16	81	3472	42.9	36.4	20	0
1986—New York Giants NFL	16	79	3539	44.8	37.1	24	0
1987—New York Giants NFL	12	65	2773	42.7	31.0	13	1
1988—New York Giants NFL	1	6	222	37.0	35.8	1	0
1989—New York Giants NFL	16	70	3019	43.1	*37.8	19	0
1990—New York Giants NFL	16	75	3306	44.1	37.3	24	0
1991—New York Giants NFL	15	64	2768	43.3	35.3	16	0
1992—New York Giants NFL	11	53	2317	43.7	31.5	13	*2
1993—New York Giants NFL	8	33	1390	42.1	35.0	11	1
—Los Angeles Rams NFL	8	42	1825	43.5	32.9	7	0
1994—Los Angeles Rams NFL	16	78	3494	*44.8	34.3	23	0
1995—St. Louis NFL	16	83	3679	44.3	36.7	23	0
USFL totals (3 years)	54	204	8490	41.6	35.9	67	0
NFL totals (11 years)	151	729	31804	43.6	35.3	194	4
Pro totals (13 years)	205	933	40294	43.2	35.4	261	4

LANE, MAX   OT   PATRIOTS

PERSONAL: Born February 22, 1971, in Norborne, Mo. ... 6-6/295. ... Full name: Max Aaron Lane.
HIGH SCHOOL: Norborne (Mo.), then Naval Academy Preparatory (Newport, R.I.).
COLLEGE: Navy.
TRANSACTIONS/CAREER NOTES: Selected by New England Patriots in sixth round (168th pick overall) of 1994 NFL draft. ... Signed by Patriots (June 1, 1994).
PLAYING EXPERIENCE: New England NFL, 1994 and 1995. ... Games: 1994 (14), 1995 (16). Total: 30.
PRO STATISTICS: 1995—Recovered one fumble for 30 yards.

LANG, DAVID   RB

PERSONAL: Born March 28, 1968, in San Bernardino, Calif. ... 5-11/213.
HIGH SCHOOL: Eisenhower (Rialto, Calif.).
COLLEGE: Northern Arizona.
TRANSACTIONS/CAREER NOTES: Selected by Los Angeles Rams in 12th round (328th pick overall) of 1990 NFL draft. ... Released by Rams prior to 1990 season. ... Re-signed by Rams (March 4, 1991). ... Granted unconditional free agency (February 17, 1994). ... Re-signed by Rams (June 1, 1994). ... Granted unconditional free agency (February 17, 1995). ... Signed by Dallas Cowboys (April 28, 1995). ... Granted unconditional free agency (February 16, 1996).
CHAMPIONSHIP GAME EXPERIENCE: Played in NFC championship game (1995 season). ... Member of Super Bowl championship team (1995 season).
PRO STATISTICS: 1991—Fumbled once. 1992—Recovered two fumbles.

		RUSHING				RECEIVING				KICKOFF RETURNS				TOTALS			
Year Team	G	Att.	Yds.	Avg.	TD	No.	Yds.	Avg.	TD	No.	Yds.	Avg.	TD	TD	2pt.	Pts.	Fum.
1991—Los Angeles Rams NFL	16	0	0	...	0	0	0	...	0	12	194	16.2	0	0	...	0	0
1992—Los Angeles Rams NFL	16	33	203	6.2	5	18	283	15.7	1	13	228	17.5	0	6	...	36	5
1993—Los Angeles Rams NFL	6	9	29	3.2	0	4	45	11.3	0	0	0	...	0	0	...	0	0
1994—Los Angeles Rams NFL	13	6	34	5.7	0	8	60	7.5	0	27	626	23.2	0	0	0	0	2
1995—Dallas NFL	16	1	7	7.0	0	0	0	...	0	0	0	...	0	0	0	0	0
Pro totals (5 years)	67	49	273	5.6	5	30	388	12.9	1	52	1048	20.2	0	6	0	36	7

LANGHAM, ANTONIO   CB   RAVENS

PERSONAL: Born July 31, 1972, in Town Creek, Ala. ... 6-0/180. ... Full name: Collie Antonio Langham.
HIGH SCHOOL: Hazelwood (Town Creek, Ala.).
COLLEGE: Alabama.
TRANSACTIONS/CAREER NOTES: Selected by Cleveland Browns in first round (ninth pick overall) of 1994 NFL draft. ... Signed by Browns (August 4, 1994). ... Browns franchise moved to Baltimore and renamed Ravens for 1996 season (March 11, 1996).
HONORS: Jim Thorpe Award winner (1993). ... Named defensive back on THE SPORTING NEWS college All-America first team (1993).
PRO STATISTICS: 1994—Fumbled once.

		INTERCEPTIONS			
Year Team	G	No.	Yds.	Avg.	TD
1994—Cleveland NFL	16	2	2	1.0	0
1995—Cleveland NFL	16	2	29	14.5	0
Pro totals (2 years)	32	4	31	7.8	0

LARO, GORDON   TE

PERSONAL: Born April 17, 1972, in Lynn, Mass. ... 6-3/253. ... Full name: Gordon Edward Laro.
HIGH SCHOOL: Lynn (Mass.) English.
COLLEGE: Michigan, then Boston College (degree in sociology).
TRANSACTIONS/CAREER NOTES: Signed as non-drafted free agent by Jacksonville Jaguars (April 24, 1995). ... Released by Jaguars (September 13, 1995).

PLAYING EXPERIENCE: Jacksonville NFL, 1995. ... Games: 1995 (2).
PRO STATISTICS: 1995—Caught one pass for six yards.

LASSIC, DERRICK   RB   49ERS

PERSONAL: Born January 26, 1970, in Haverstraw, N.Y. ... 5-10/188. ... Full name: Derrick Owens Lassic.
HIGH SCHOOL: North Rockland (Haverstraw, N.Y.).
COLLEGE: Alabama.
TRANSACTIONS/CAREER NOTES: Selected by Dallas Cowboys in fourth round (94th pick overall) of 1993 NFL draft. ... Signed by Cowboys (July 16, 1993). ... On injured reserve with knee injury (December 5, 1994-remainder of season). ... Selected by Carolina Panthers from Cowboys in NFL expansion draft (February 15, 1995). ... Released by Panthers (August 27, 1995). ... Signed by San Francisco 49ers (March 8, 1996).
CHAMPIONSHIP GAME EXPERIENCE: Played in NFC championship game (1993 season). ... Member of Super Bowl championship team (1993 season).
PRO STATISTICS: 1993—Recovered one fumble.

		RUSHING				RECEIVING				TOTALS			
Year Team	G	Att.	Yds.	Avg.	TD	No.	Yds.	Avg.	TD	TD	2pt.	Pts.	Fum.
1993—Dallas NFL	10	75	269	3.6	3	9	37	4.1	0	3	...	18	2
1994—Dallas NFL						Did not play—injured.							
1995—						Did not play.							

LASSITER, KWAMIE   DB   CARDINALS

PERSONAL: Born December 3, 1969, in Newport News, Va. ... 5-11/180.
HIGH SCHOOL: Menchville (Newport News, Va.).
JUNIOR COLLEGE: Butler County (Kan.) Community College.
COLLEGE: Kansas.
TRANSACTIONS/CAREER NOTES: Signed as non-drafted free agent by Arizona Cardinals (April 28, 1995). ... On injured reserve with ankle injury (October 5, 1995-remainder of season).
PLAYING EXPERIENCE: Arizona NFL, 1995. ... Games: 1995 (5).
PRO STATISTICS: 1995—Rushed once for one yard.

LATHON, LAMAR   LB   PANTHERS

PERSONAL: Born December 23, 1967, in Wharton, Texas. ... 6-3/260. ... Full name: Lamar Lavantha Lathon. ... Name pronounced LAY-thin.
HIGH SCHOOL: Wharton (Texas).
COLLEGE: Houston.
TRANSACTIONS/CAREER NOTES: Selected by Houston Oilers in first round (15th pick overall) of 1990 NFL draft. ... Signed by Oilers (July 18, 1990). ... On injured reserve with shoulder injury (September 19-October 19, 1990). ... On injured reserve with knee injury (November 24, 1992-January 2, 1993). ... Granted unconditional free agency (February 17, 1995). ... Signed by Carolina Panthers (March 1, 1995).
PRO STATISTICS: 1990—Recovered one fumble. 1993—Recovered one fumble. 1994—Credited with one safety and recovered one fumble. 1995—Recovered one fumble.
MISCELLANEOUS: Holds Carolina Panthers all-time record for most sacks (8).

		INTERCEPTIONS				SACKS
Year Team	G	No.	Yds.	Avg.	TD	No.
1990—Houston NFL	11	0	0	...	0	0.0
1991—Houston NFL	16	3	77	25.7	1	2.0
1992—Houston NFL	11	0	0	...	0	1.5
1993—Houston NFL	13	0	0	...	0	2.0
1994—Houston NFL	16	0	0	...	0	8.5
1995—Carolina NFL	15	0	0	...	0	8.0
Pro totals (6 years)	82	3	77	25.7	1	22.0

LAW, TY   CB   PATRIOTS

PERSONAL: Born February 10, 1974, in Aliquippa, Pa. ... 5-11/196.
HIGH SCHOOL: Aliquippa (Pa.).
COLLEGE: Michigan.
TRANSACTIONS/CAREER NOTES: Selected after junior season by New England Patriots in first round (23rd pick overall) of 1995 NFL draft. ... Signed by Patriots (July 20, 1995).

		INTERCEPTIONS			
Year Team	G	No.	Yds.	Avg.	TD
1995—New England NFL	14	3	47	15.7	0

LEASY, WESLEY   LB   CARDINALS

PERSONAL: Born September 7, 1971, in Vicksburg, Miss. ... 6-2/234. ... Name pronounced LEE-see.
HIGH SCHOOL: Greenville (Miss.).
COLLEGE: Mississippi State.
TRANSACTIONS/CAREER NOTES: Selected by Arizona Cardinals in seventh round (224th pick overall) of 1995 NFL draft. ... Signed by Cardinals (July 24, 1995).
PLAYING EXPERIENCE: Arizona NFL, 1995. ... Games: 1995 (12).

L

Le BEL, HARPER   TE   FALCONS

PERSONAL: Born July 14, 1963, in Granada Hills, Calif. ... 6-4/255. ... Full name: Brian Harper Le Bel.
HIGH SCHOOL: Notre Dame (Sherman Oaks, Calif.).
COLLEGE: Colorado State.
TRANSACTIONS/CAREER NOTES: Selected by Kansas City Chiefs in 12th round (321st pick overall) of 1985 NFL draft. ... Signed by Chiefs (July 18, 1985). ... Released by Chiefs (August 12, 1985). ... Signed by San Francisco 49ers for 1986 (December 20, 1985). ... Released by 49ers after failing physical (April 7, 1986). ... Signed as replacement player by San Diego Chargers (September 29, 1987). ... Released by Chargers (October 20, 1987). ... Signed by Dallas Cowboys (April 27, 1988). ... Released by Cowboys (August 2, 1988). ... Signed by Tampa Bay Buccaneers (August 15, 1988). ... Released by Buccaneers (August 23, 1988). ... Signed by Seattle Seahawks (August 8, 1989). ... Granted unconditional free agency (February 1, 1990). ... Signed by Philadelphia Eagles (March 30, 1990). ... Granted unconditional free agency (February 1, 1991). ... Signed by Atlanta Falcons (April 1, 1991). ... On injured reserve with wrist injury (September 18, 1991-remainder of season). ... Granted unconditional free agency (February 1-April 1, 1992). ... Re-signed by Falcons for 1992 season. ... Granted free agency (March 1, 1993). ... Re-signed by Falcons (June 11, 1993). ... Granted unconditional free agency (February 17, 1994). ... Re-signed by Falcons (March 30, 1994). ... Granted unconditional free agency (February 17, 1995). ... Re-signed by Falcons (March 22, 1995).
PLAYING EXPERIENCE: Seattle NFL, 1989; Philadelphia NFL, 1990; Atlanta NFL, 1991-1995. ... Games: 1989 (16), 1990 (16), 1991 (3), 1992 (16), 1993 (16), 1994 (16), 1995 (16). Total: 99.
PRO STATISTICS: 1989—Fumbled once for minus 25 yards. 1990—Caught one pass for nine yards and fumbled once. 1992—Fumbled once for minus 37 yards. 1993—Fumbled once. 1995—Fumbled once for minus eight yards.

LEE, AMP   RB   VIKINGS

PERSONAL: Born October 1, 1971, in Chipley, Fla. ... 5-11/197. ... Full name: Anthonia Wayne Lee.
HIGH SCHOOL: Chipley (Fla.).
COLLEGE: Florida State.
TRANSACTIONS/CAREER NOTES: Selected after junior season by San Francisco 49ers in second round (45th pick overall) of 1992 NFL draft. ... Signed by 49ers (July 18, 1992). ... Released by 49ers (May 4, 1994). ... Signed by Minnesota Vikings (May 24, 1994). ... On physically unable to perform list (July 13-20, 1994).
CHAMPIONSHIP GAME EXPERIENCE: Played in NFC championship game (1992 and 1993 seasons).
PRO STATISTICS: 1992—Recovered three fumbles. 1994—Recovered one fumble. 1995—Returned five punts for 50 yards and recovered two fumbles.
STATISTICAL PLATEAUS: 100-yard rushing games: 1992 (1).

		RUSHING				RECEIVING				KICKOFF RETURNS				TOTALS			
Year Team	G	Att.	Yds.	Avg.	TD	No.	Yds.	Avg.	TD	No.	Yds.	Avg.	TD	TD	2pt.	Pts.	Fum.
1992—San Francisco NFL	16	91	362	4.0	2	20	102	5.1	2	14	276	19.7	0	4	...	24	1
1993—San Francisco NFL	15	72	230	3.2	1	16	115	7.2	2	10	160	16.0	0	3	...	18	1
1994—Minnesota NFL	13	29	104	3.6	0	45	368	8.2	2	3	42	14.0	0	2	0	12	1
1995—Minnesota NFL	16	69	371	5.4	2	71	558	7.9	1	5	100	20.0	0	3	0	18	3
Pro totals (4 years)	60	261	1067	4.1	5	152	1143	7.5	7	32	578	18.1	0	12	0	72	6

LEE, KEVIN   WR   PATRIOTS

PERSONAL: Born January 1, 1971, in Mobile, Ala. ... 6-1/194.
HIGH SCHOOL: Vigor (Prichard, Ala.).
COLLEGE: Alabama.
TRANSACTIONS/CAREER NOTES: Selected by New England Patriots in second round (35th pick overall) of 1994 NFL draft. ... Signed by Patriots (June 2, 1994). ... On injured reserve with jaw injury (August 20, 1994-entire season).
PLAYING EXPERIENCE: New England Nfl, 1995. ... Games: 1995 (7).
PRO STATISTICS: 1995—Rushed once for four yards and returned one kickoff for 14 yards.

LEE, SHAWN   DT   CHARGERS

PERSONAL: Born October 24, 1966, in Brooklyn, N.Y. ... 6-2/300. ... Full name: Shawn Swaboda Lee.
HIGH SCHOOL: Erasmus Hall (Brooklyn, N.Y.).
COLLEGE: North Alabama.
TRANSACTIONS/CAREER NOTES: Selected by Tampa Bay Buccaneers in sixth round (163rd pick overall) of 1988 NFL draft. ... Signed by Buccaneers (July 10, 1988). ... Granted unconditional free agency (February 1-April 1, 1990). ... Re-signed by Buccaneers (July 20, 1990). ... Claimed on waivers by Atlanta Falcons (August 29, 1990). ... Traded by Falcons to Miami Dolphins for conditional pick in 1991 draft (September 3, 1990). ... On injured reserve with ankle injury (September 29-October 27, 1990). ... Granted free agency (February 1, 1991). ... Re-signed by Dolphins (August 21, 1991). ... Activated (August 23, 1991). ... On injured reserve with knee injury (September 17, 1991-remainder of season). ... Granted free agency (February 1, 1992). ... Re-signed by Dolphins (July 22, 1992). ... Released by Dolphins (August 31, 1992). ... Signed by San Diego Chargers (October 28, 1992). ... Granted unconditional free agency (March 1, 1993). ... Re-signed by Chargers (April 23, 1993).
CHAMPIONSHIP GAME EXPERIENCE: Member of Chargers for AFC championship game (1994 season); inactive. ... Played in Super Bowl XXIX (1994 season).
PRO STATISTICS: 1991—Intercepted one pass for 14 yards. 1992—Recovered one fumble. 1993—Recovered one fumble. 1994—Recovered one fumble. 1995—Recovered one fumble.

Year Team	G	SACKS
1988—Tampa Bay NFL	15	2.0
1989—Tampa Bay NFL	15	1.0
1990—Miami NFL	13	1.5
1991—Miami NFL	3	0.0
1992—San Diego NFL	9	0.5
1993—San Diego NFL	16	3.0
1994—San Diego NFL	15	6.5

Year	Team	G	SACKS
1995—San Diego NFL		16	8.0
Pro totals (8 years)		102	22.5

LEEUWENBURG, JAY   G/C   COLTS

PERSONAL: Born June 18, 1969, in St. Louis. ... 6-3/290. ... Full name: Jay Robert Leeuwenburg. ... Son of Richard Leeuwenburg, tackle, Chicago Bears (1965).
HIGH SCHOOL: Kirkwood (Mo.).
COLLEGE: Colorado (degree in English).
TRANSACTIONS/CAREER NOTES: Selected by Kansas City Chiefs in ninth round (244th pick overall) of 1992 NFL draft. ... Signed by Chiefs (July 20, 1992). ... Claimed on waivers by Chicago Bears (September 2, 1992). ... Granted free agency (February 17, 1995). ... Re-signed by Bears (April 12, 1995). ... Granted unconditional free agency (February 16, 1996). ... Signed by Indianapolis Colts (February 21, 1996).
PLAYING EXPERIENCE: Chicago NFL, 1992-1995. ... Games: 1992 (12), 1993 (16), 1994 (16), 1995 (16). Total: 60.
HONORS: Named center on THE SPORTING NEWS college All-America first team (1991).
PRO STATISTICS: 1992—Returned one kickoff for 12 yards. 1995—Recovered one fumble.

LEGETTE, TYRONE   CB

PERSONAL: Born February 15, 1970, in Columbia, S.C. ... 5-9/177. ... Name pronounced luh-GET.
HIGH SCHOOL: Spring Valley (Columbia, S.C.).
COLLEGE: Nebraska.
TRANSACTIONS/CAREER NOTES: Selected by New Orleans Saints in third round (72nd pick overall) of 1992 NFL draft. ... Signed by Saints (July 26, 1992). ... On injured reserve with hamstring injury (November 3, 1992-remainder of season). ... Granted free agency (February 17, 1995). ... Re-signed by Saints (July 23, 1995). ... Granted unconditional free agency (February 16, 1996).
PLAYING EXPERIENCE: New Orleans NFL, 1992-1995. ... Games: 1992 (8), 1993 (14), 1994 (15), 1995 (16). Total: 53.
PRO STATISTICS: 1994—Credited with one sack, returned one punt for no yards and fumbled once. 1995—Credited with one sack, intercepted one pass for 43 yards and returned one punt for six yards.

LESTER, TIM   FB   STEELERS

PERSONAL: Born June 15, 1968, in Miami. ... 5-9/227. ... Full name: Tim Lee Lester.
HIGH SCHOOL: Miami Southridge Senior.
COLLEGE: Eastern Kentucky.
TRANSACTIONS/CAREER NOTES: Selected by Los Angeles Rams in 10th round (255th pick overall) of 1992 NFL draft. ... Signed by Rams (July 13, 1992). ... Released by Rams (September 4, 1992). ... Re-signed by Rams to practice squad (September 7, 1992). ... Activated (October 7, 1992). ... Released by Rams (August 29, 1995). ... Signed by Pittsburgh Steelers (October 3, 1995).
CHAMPIONSHIP GAME EXPERIENCE: Played in AFC championship game (1995 season). ... Played in Super Bowl XXX (1995 season).
PRO STATISTICS: 1994—Returned one kickoff for eight yards and recovered one fumble.

			RUSHING				RECEIVING				TOTALS		
Year	Team	G	Att.	Yds.	Avg.	TD	No.	Yds.	Avg.	TD	TD	2pt.	Pts.	Fum.
1992—Los Angeles Rams NFL		11	0	0	...	0	0	0	...	0	0	...	0	0
1993—Los Angeles Rams NFL		16	11	74	6.7	0	18	154	8.6	0	0	...	0	0
1994—Los Angeles Rams NFL		14	7	14	2.0	0	1	1	1.0	0	0	0	0	1
1995—Pittsburgh NFL		6	5	9	1.8	1	0	0	...	0	1	0	6	0
Pro totals (4 years)		47	23	97	4.2	1	19	155	8.2	0	1	0	6	1

LETT, LEON   DL   COWBOYS

PERSONAL: Born October 12, 1968, in Mobile, Ala. ... 6-6/288. ... Nickname: The Big Cat.
HIGH SCHOOL: Fairhope (Ala.).
JUNIOR COLLEGE: Hinds Community College (Miss.).
COLLEGE: Emporia (Kan.) State.
TRANSACTIONS/CAREER NOTES: Selected by Dallas Cowboys in seventh round (173rd pick overall) of 1991 NFL draft. ... Signed by Cowboys (July 14, 1991). ... On injured reserve with back injury (August 27-November 21, 1991). ... On suspended list for violating league substance abuse policy (November 3-24, 1995).
CHAMPIONSHIP GAME EXPERIENCE: Played in NFC championship game (1992-1995 seasons). ... Member of Super Bowl championship team (1992, 1993 and 1995 seasons).
HONORS: Played in Pro Bowl (1994 season).
POSTSEASON RECORDS: Holds Super Bowl career record for most yards by fumble recovery—64. ... Holds Super Bowl single-game record for most yards by fumble recovery—64 (January 31, 1993).
PRO STATISTICS: 1992—Recovered one fumble. 1993—Fumbled once. 1995—Recovered two fumbles.

Year	Team	G	SACKS
1991—Dallas NFL		5	0.0
1992—Dallas NFL		16	3.5
1993—Dallas NFL		11	0.0
1994—Dallas NFL		16	4.0
1995—Dallas NFL		12	3.0
Pro totals (5 years)		60	10.5

LEVENS, DORSEY   RB   PACKERS

PERSONAL: Born May 21, 1970, in Syracuse, N.Y. ... 6-1/240. ... Full name: Hebert Dorsey Levens.

HIGH SCHOOL: Nottingham (Syracuse, N.Y.).
COLLEGE: Georgia Tech.
TRANSACTIONS/CAREER NOTES: Selected by Green Bay Packers in fifth round (149th pick overall) of 1994 NFL draft. ... Signed by Packers (June 9, 1994).
CHAMPIONSHIP GAME EXPERIENCE: Played in NFC championship game (1995 season).

			RUSHING			RECEIVING				KICKOFF RETURNS				TOTALS			
Year Team	G	Att.	Yds.	Avg.	TD	No.	Yds.	Avg.	TD	No.	Yds.	Avg.	TD	TD	2pt.	Pts.	Fum.
1994—Green Bay NFL	14	5	15	3.0	0	1	9	9.0	0	2	31	15.5	0	0	0	0	0
1995—Green Bay NFL	15	36	120	3.3	3	48	434	9.0	4	0	0	...	0	7	0	42	0
Pro totals (2 years)	29	41	135	3.3	3	49	443	9.1	4	2	31	15.5	0	7	0	42	0

LEVY, CHUCK   WR/KR   CARDINALS

PERSONAL: Born January 7, 1972, in Torrance, Calif. ... 6-0/197.
HIGH SCHOOL: Lynwood (Calif.).
COLLEGE: Arizona.
TRANSACTIONS/CAREER NOTES: Selected after junior season by Arizona Cardinals in second round (38th pick overall) of 1994 NFL draft. ... Signed by Cardinals (August 10, 1994). ... Suspended by NFL for violating league substance abuse policy (August 25, 1995-entire season). ... Applied to NFL for reinstatement prior to 1996 season.
PRO STATISTICS: 1994—Recovered one fumble.

			RUSHING			RECEIVING				KICKOFF RETURNS				TOTALS			
Year Team	G	Att.	Yds.	Avg.	TD	No.	Yds.	Avg.	TD	No.	Yds.	Avg.	TD	TD	2pt.	Pts.	Fum.
1994—Arizona NFL	11	3	15	5.0	0	4	35	8.8	0	26	513	19.7	0	0	0	0	0
1995—Arizona NFL									Did not play.								

LEWIS, ALBERT   CB   RAIDERS

PERSONAL: Born October 6, 1960, in Mansfield, La. ... 6-2/195. ... Full name: Albert Ray Lewis.
HIGH SCHOOL: DeSoto (Mansfield, La.).
COLLEGE: Grambling State (degree in political science, 1983).
TRANSACTIONS/CAREER NOTES: Selected by Philadelphia Stars in 15th round (175th pick overall) of 1983 USFL draft. ... Selected by Kansas City Chiefs in third round (61st pick overall) of 1983 NFL draft. ... Signed by Chiefs (May 19, 1983). ... On injured reserve with knee injury (December 10, 1984-remainder of season). ... On reserve/did not report list (July 24-September 17, 1990). ... On injured reserve with knee injury (December 14, 1991-remainder of season). ... On injured reserve with forearm injury (November 11, 1992-remainder of season). ... On practice squad (December 16-23, 1992). ... Granted unconditional free agency (February 17, 1994). ... Signed by Los Angeles Raiders (March 15, 1994). ... Raiders franchise moved to Oakland (July 21, 1995).
CHAMPIONSHIP GAME EXPERIENCE: Played in AFC championship game (1993 season).
HONORS: Played in Pro Bowl (1987, 1989 and 1990 seasons). ... Named to play in Pro Bowl (1988 season); replaced by Eric Thomas due to injury. ... Named cornerback on THE SPORTING NEWS NFL All-Pro team (1989 and 1990).
PRO STATISTICS: 1983—Recovered two fumbles. 1985—Recovered one fumble in end zone for a touchdown. 1986—Recovered two fumbles. 1987—Recovered one fumble. 1988—Credited with one safety and recovered one fumble. 1990—Recovered three fumbles for one yard. 1993—Recovered blocked punt in end zone for a touchdown and recovered two fumbles. 1995—Recovered one fumble for 29 yards.

		INTERCEPTIONS				SACKS
Year Team	G	No.	Yds.	Avg.	TD	No.
1983—Kansas City NFL	16	4	42	10.5	0	0.0
1984—Kansas City NFL	15	4	57	14.3	0	1.0
1985—Kansas City NFL	16	8	59	7.4	0	1.5
1986—Kansas City NFL	15	4	18	4.5	0	1.0
1987—Kansas City NFL	12	1	0	0.0	0	0.0
1988—Kansas City NFL	14	1	19	19.0	0	0.0
1989—Kansas City NFL	16	4	37	9.3	0	1.0
1990—Kansas City NFL	15	2	15	7.5	0	0.0
1991—Kansas City NFL	8	3	21	7.0	0	0.0
1992—Kansas City NFL	9	1	0	0.0	0	0.0
1993—Kansas City NFL	14	6	61	10.2	0	0.0
1994—Los Angeles Raiders NFL	14	0	0	...	0	1.0
1995—Oakland NFL	16	0	0	...	0	1.0
Pro totals (13 years)	180	38	329	8.7	0	6.5

LEWIS, DARRYLL   CB   OILERS

PERSONAL: Born December 16, 1968, in Bellflower, Calif. ... 5-9/183. ... Full name: Darryll Lamont Lewis.
HIGH SCHOOL: Nogales (West Covina, Calif.).
COLLEGE: Arizona.
TRANSACTIONS/CAREER NOTES: Selected by Houston Oilers in second round (38th pick overall) of 1991 NFL draft. ... Signed by Oilers (July 19, 1991). ... On injured reserve with knee injury (October 25, 1993). ... Granted free agency (February 17, 1994). ... Re-signed by Oilers (July 17, 1994). ... Granted unconditional free agency (February 17, 1995). ... Re-signed by Oilers (March 9, 1995).
HONORS: Jim Thorpe Award winner (1990). ... Named defensive back on THE SPORTING NEWS college All-America first team (1990). ... Played in Pro Bowl (1995 season).
PRO STATISTICS: 1991—Recovered one fumble. 1992—Recovered one fumble.

		INTERCEPTIONS				SACKS	KICKOFF RETURNS				TOTALS			
Year Team	G	No.	Yds.	Avg.	TD	No.	No.	Yds.	Avg.	TD	TD	2pt.	Pts.	Fum.
1991—Houston NFL	16	1	33	33.0	1	1.0	0	0	...	0	0	...	0	0
1992—Houston NFL	13	0	0	...	0	1.0	8	171	21.4	0	0	...	0	0
1993—Houston NFL	4	1	47	47.0	1	0.0	0	0	...	0	1	...	6	0

Year Team	G	No.	INTERCEPTIONS Yds.	Avg.	TD	SACKS No.	No.	KICKOFF RETURNS Yds.	Avg.	TD	TD	TOTALS 2pt.	Pts.	Fum.
1994—Houston NFL	16	5	57	11.4	0	0.0	0	0	...	0	0	0	0	0
1995—Houston NFL	16	6	145	24.2	1	1.0	0	0	...	0	1	0	6	0
Pro totals (5 years)	65	13	282	21.7	3	3.0	8	171	21.4	0	2	0	12	0

LEWIS, MO   LB   JETS

PERSONAL: Born October 21, 1969, in Atlanta. ... 6-3/250.
HIGH SCHOOL: J.C. Murphy (Atlanta).
COLLEGE: Georgia.
TRANSACTIONS/CAREER NOTES: Selected by New York Jets in third round (62nd pick overall) of 1991 NFL draft. ... Signed by Jets (July 18, 1991).
PRO STATISTICS: 1991—Recovered one fumble. 1992—Recovered four fumbles for 22 yards. 1994—Recovered one fumble for 11 yards.

Year Team	G	No.	INTERCEPTIONS Yds.	Avg.	TD	SACKS No.
1991—New York Jets NFL	16	0	0	...	0	2.0
1992—New York Jets NFL	16	1	1	1.0	0	2.0
1993—New York Jets NFL	16	2	4	2.0	0	4.0
1994—New York Jets NFL	16	4	106	26.5	2	6.0
1995—New York Jets NFL	16	2	22	11.0	1	5.0
Pro totals (5 years)	80	9	133	14.8	3	19.0

LEWIS, NATE   WR/KR

PERSONAL: Born October 19, 1966, in Moultrie, Ga. ... 5-11/198.
HIGH SCHOOL: Colquitt County (Moultrie, Ga.).
COLLEGE: Oregon Tech.
TRANSACTIONS/CAREER NOTES: Selected by San Diego Chargers in seventh round (187th pick overall) of 1990 NFL draft. ... Signed by Chargers (July 11, 1990). ... Traded by Chargers to Los Angeles Rams for fourth-round pick (RB Aaron Hayden) in 1995 draft (March 18, 1994). ... Released by Rams (August 23, 1994). ... Signed by Chicago Bears (August 28, 1994). ... Granted free agency (February 17, 1995). ... Signed by Atlanta Falcons (April 6, 1995). ... Released by Falcons (August 27, 1995). ... Signed by Bears (September 27, 1995). ... Granted unconditional free agency (February 16, 1996).
PRO STATISTICS: 1990—Fumbled three times and recovered two fumbles. 1991—Recovered one fumble for two yards. 1992—Fumbled once and recovered two fumbles. 1993—Fumbled twice and recovered two fumbles. 1994—Fumbled once.
STATISTICAL PLATEAUS: 100-yard receiving games: 1993 (1). Total: 1.

Year Team	G	RUSHING Att.	Yds.	Avg.	TD	RECEIVING No.	Yds.	Avg.	TD	PUNT RETURNS No.	Yds.	Avg.	TD	KICKOFF RETURNS No.	Yds.	Avg.	TD	TOTALS TD	2pt.	Pts.
1990—San Diego NFL	12	4	25	6.3	1	14	192	13.7	1	13	117	9.0	†1	17	383	22.5	0	3	...	18
1991—San Diego NFL	16	3	10	3.3	0	42	554	13.2	3	5	59	11.8	0	23	578	25.1	†1	4	...	24
1992—San Diego NFL	15	2	7	3.5	0	34	580	17.1	4	13	127	9.8	0	19	402	21.2	0	4	...	24
1993—San Diego NFL	15	3	2	.7	0	38	463	12.2	4	3	17	5.7	0	33	684	20.7	0	4	...	24
1994—Chicago NFL	13	0	0	...	0	2	13	6.5	1	1	7	7.0	0	35	874	25.0	0	1	0	6
1995—Chicago NFL	11	0	0	...	0	0	0	...	0	0	0	...	0	42	904	21.5	0	0	0	0
Pro totals (6 years)	82	12	44	3.7	1	130	1802	13.9	13	35	327	9.4	1	169	3825	22.6	1	16	0	96

LEWIS, ROD   TE   OILERS

PERSONAL: Born June 9, 1971, in Washington, D.C. ... 6-5/254. ... Full name: Roderick Albert Lewis.
HIGH SCHOOL: Bishop Dunne (Dallas).
COLLEGE: Arizona.
TRANSACTIONS/CAREER NOTES: Selected by Houston Oilers in fifth round (157th pick overall) of 1994 NFL draft. ... Signed by Oilers (July 16, 1994).
PRO STATISTICS: 1995—Returned one kickoff for five yards.

Year Team	G	RECEIVING No.	Yds.	Avg.	TD	TD	TOTALS 2pt.	Pts.	Fum.
1994—Houston NFL	3	4	48	12.0	0	0	0	0	0
1995—Houston NFL	16	16	116	7.3	0	0	0	0	0
Pro totals (2 years)	19	20	164	8.2	0	0	0	0	0

LEWIS, RON   G   REDSKINS

PERSONAL: Born November 17, 1972, in Los Angeles. ... 6-3/299.
HIGH SCHOOL: Dorsey (Los Angeles).
JUNIOR COLLEGE: West Los Angeles Community College.
COLLEGE: Washington State.
TRANSACTIONS/CAREER NOTES: Signed as non-drafted free agent by Washington Redskins (June 9, 1995). ... Released by Redskins (August 27, 1995). ... Re-signed by Redskins to practice squad (August 28, 1995). ... Activated (September 19, 1995).
PLAYING EXPERIENCE: Washington NFL, 1995. ... Games: 1995 (4).

LEWIS, THOMAS   WR   GIANTS

PERSONAL: Born January 10, 1972, in Akron, Ohio. ... 6-1/195.

COLLEGE: Indiana.
TRANSACTIONS/CAREER NOTES: Selected after junior season by New York Giants in first round (24th pick overall) of 1994 NFL draft. ... Signed by Giants (July 22, 1994). ... On non-football injury list (July 22-August 2, 1994). ... On injured reserve with knee injury (December 16, 1994-remainder of season).
PRO STATISTICS: 1994—Recovered two fumbles.
STATISTICAL PLATEAUS: 100-yard receiving games: 1994 (1).

Year Team	G	RECEIVING				PUNT RETURNS				KICKOFF RETURNS				TOTALS			
		No.	Yds.	Avg.	TD	No.	Yds.	Avg.	TD	No.	Yds.	Avg.	TD	TD	2pt.	Pts.	Fum.
1994—New York Giants NFL	9	4	46	11.5	0	5	64	12.8	0	26	509	19.6	0	0	0	0	2
1995—New York Giants NFL	8	12	208	17.3	1	6	46	7.7	0	9	257	28.6	1	2	0	12	1
Pro totals (2 years)	17	16	254	15.9	1	11	110	10.0	0	35	766	21.9	1	2	0	12	3

LEWIS, VERNON   CB   PATRIOTS

PERSONAL: Born October 27, 1970, in Houston. ... 5-10/192.
HIGH SCHOOL: Kashmere Senior (Houston).
COLLEGE: Pittsburgh.
TRANSACTIONS/CAREER NOTES: Signed as non-drafted free agent by New England Patriots (April 30, 1993). ... Granted free agency (February 16, 1996). ...Re-signed by Patriots (June 1, 1996).
PLAYING EXPERIENCE: New England NFL, 1993-1995. ... Games: 1993 (10), 1994 (11), 1995 (16). Total: 37.
PRO STATISTICS: 1995—Credited with 1½ sacks and recovered one fumble.

LINCOLN, JEREMY   CB   BEARS

PERSONAL: Born April 7, 1969, in Toledo, Ohio. ... 5-10/180. ... Full name: Jeremy Arlo Lincoln.
HIGH SCHOOL: DeVilbiss (Toledo, Ohio).
COLLEGE: Tennessee.
TRANSACTIONS/CAREER NOTES: Selected by Chicago Bears in third round (80th pick overall) of 1992 NFL draft. ... Signed by Bears (July 23, 1992). ... On injured reserve with knee injury (September 1, 1992-entire season). ... Granted free agency (February 17, 1995). ... Re-signed by Bears (July 17, 1995).
PRO STATISTICS: 1995—Credited with one sack.

Year Team	G	INTERCEPTIONS			
		No.	Yds.	Avg.	TD
1992—Chicago NFL			Did not play.		
1993—Chicago NFL	16	3	109	36.3	1
1994—Chicago NFL	15	1	5	5.0	0
1995—Chicago NFL	16	1	32	32.0	0
Pro totals (3 years)	47	5	146	29.2	1

LINDSAY, EVERETT   G/C   VIKINGS

PERSONAL: Born September 18, 1970, in Burlington, Iowa. ... 6-4/305. ... Full name: Everett Eric Lindsay.
HIGH SCHOOL: Millbrook (Raleigh, N.C.).
COLLEGE: Mississippi (degree in general business).
TRANSACTIONS/CAREER NOTES: Selected by Minnesota Vikings in fifth round (133rd pick overall) of 1993 NFL draft. ... Signed by Vikings (July 14, 1993). ... On injured reserve with shoulder injury (December 22, 1993-remainder of season). ... On injured reserve with shoulder injury (August 23, 1994-entire season).
PLAYING EXPERIENCE: Minnesota NFL, 1993 and 1995. ... Games: 1993 (12), 1995 (16). Total: 28.
HONORS: Named offensive tackle on THE SPORTING NEWS college All-America second team (1992).

LINGNER, ADAM   C

PERSONAL: Born November 2, 1960, in Indianapolis. ... 6-4/268. ... Full name: Adam James Lingner.
HIGH SCHOOL: Alleman (Rock Island, Ill.).
COLLEGE: Illinois.
TRANSACTIONS/CAREER NOTES: Selected by Chicago Blitz in 1983 USFL territorial draft. ... Selected by Kansas City Chiefs in ninth round (231st pick overall) of 1983 NFL draft. ... Signed by Chiefs (June 1, 1983). ... Released by Chiefs (November 24, 1986). ... Signed by New England Patriots (November 28, 1986). ... Active for one game with Patriots (1986); did not play. ... Released by Patriots (December 2, 1986). ... Signed by Denver Broncos (May 1, 1987). ... Claimed on waivers by Buffalo Bills (August 27, 1987). ... Claimed on waivers by Chiefs (August 23, 1988). ... Granted unconditional free agency (February 1, 1989). ... Signed by Bills (March 16, 1989). ... Granted unconditional free agency (February 1-April 1, 1991). ... Re-signed by Bills for 1991 season. ... Granted unconditional free agency (February 1-April 1, 1992). ... Re-signed by Bills for 1992 season. ... Granted unconditional free agency (March 1, 1993). ... Re-signed by Bills for 1993 season. ... Granted unconditional free agency (February 17, 1995). ... Re-signed by Bills (March 27, 1995). ... Granted unconditional free agency (February 16, 1996). ... Announced retirement (May 4, 1996).
PLAYING EXPERIENCE: Kansas City NFL, 1983-1985 and 1988; Kansas City (12)-New England (0) NFL, 1986; Buffalo NFL, 1987, 1989-1995. ... Games: 1983 (16), 1984 (16), 1985 (16), 1986 (12), 1987 (12), 1988 (16), 1989 (16), 1990 (16), 1991 (16), 1992 (16), 1993 (16), 1994 (16), 1995 (16). Total: 200.
CHAMPIONSHIP GAME EXPERIENCE: Played in AFC championship game (1990-1993 seasons). ... Played in Super Bowl XXV (1990 season), Super Bowl XXVI (1991 season), Super Bowl XXVII (1992 season) and Super Bowl XXVIII (1993 season).
PRO STATISTICS: 1987—Recovered one fumble.

LLOYD, GREG   LB   STEELERS

PERSONAL: Born May 26, 1965, in Miami. ... 6-2/228. ... Full name: Gregory Lenard Lloyd.
HIGH SCHOOL: Peach County (Ga.).
COLLEGE: Fort Valley (Ga.) State College.
TRANSACTIONS/CAREER NOTES: Selected by Pittsburgh Steelers in sixth round (150th pick overall) of 1987 NFL draft. ... Signed by Steelers (May 19, 1987). ... On injured reserve with knee injury (August 31, 1987-entire season). ... On injured reserve with knee injury (August 30-October 22, 1988).
CHAMPIONSHIP GAME EXPERIENCE: Played in AFC championship game (1994 and 1995 seasons). ... Played in Super Bowl XXX (1995 season).
HONORS: Played in Pro Bowl (1991-1995 seasons). ... Named outside linebacker on THE SPORTING NEWS NFL All-Pro team (1994 and 1995).
PRO STATISTICS: 1988—Recovered one fumble. 1989—Fumbled once and recovered three fumbles. 1991—Fumbled once and recovered two fumbles. 1992—Fumbled once and recovered four fumbles. 1993—Recovered one fumble. 1994—Recovered one fumble.

| | | INTERCEPTIONS | | | | SACKS |
Year Team	G	No.	Yds.	Avg.	TD	No.
1987—Pittsburgh NFL			Did not play—injured.			
1988—Pittsburgh NFL	9	0	0	...	0	0.5
1989—Pittsburgh NFL	16	3	49	16.3	0	7.0
1990—Pittsburgh NFL	15	1	9	9.0	0	4.5
1991—Pittsburgh NFL	16	1	0	0.0	0	8.0
1992—Pittsburgh NFL	16	1	35	35.0	0	6.5
1993—Pittsburgh NFL	15	0	0	...	0	6.0
1994—Pittsburgh NFL	15	1	8	8.0	0	10.0
1995—Pittsburgh NFL	16	3	85	28.3	0	6.5
Pro totals (8 years)	118	10	186	18.6	0	49.0

LODISH, MIKE   NT   BRONCOS

PERSONAL: Born August 11, 1967, in Detroit. ... 6-3/280. ... Full name: Michael Timothy Lodish. ... Name pronounced LO-dish.
HIGH SCHOOL: Brother Rice (Birmingham, Mich.).
COLLEGE: UCLA (degree in history and business administration, 1990).
TRANSACTIONS/CAREER NOTES: Selected by Buffalo Bills in 10th round (265th pick overall) of 1990 NFL draft. ... Signed by Bills (July 26, 1990). ... Granted free agency (February 1, 1992). ... Re-signed by Bills (July 23, 1992). ... Granted unconditional free agency (February 17, 1995). ... Signed by Denver Broncos (April 4, 1995).
CHAMPIONSHIP GAME EXPERIENCE: Played in AFC championship game (1990-1993 seasons). ... Played in Super Bowl XXV (1990 season), Super Bowl XXVI (1991 season), Super Bowl XXVII (1992 season) and Super Bowl XXVIII (1993 season).
PRO STATISTICS: 1992—Recovered one fumble for 18 yards and a touchdown. 1993—Recovered one fumble. 1994—Recovered one fumble in end zone for a touchdown.

Year Team	G	SACKS
1990—Buffalo NFL	12	2.0
1991—Buffalo NFL	16	1.5
1992—Buffalo NFL	16	0.0
1993—Buffalo NFL	15	0.5
1994—Buffalo NFL	15	0.0
1995—Denver NFL	16	0.0
Pro totals (6 years)	90	4.0

LOFTON, STEVE   CB   PANTHERS

PERSONAL: Born November 26, 1968, in Jacksonville, Texas. ... 5-9/177. ... Full name: Steven Lynn Lofton.
HIGH SCHOOL: Alto (Texas).
COLLEGE: Texas A&M.
TRANSACTIONS/CAREER NOTES: Signed as non-drafted free agent by WLAF (January 31, 1991). ... Selected by Montreal Machine in third round (34th defensive back) of 1991 WLAF positional draft. ... Signed by Phoenix Cardinals (July 9, 1991). ... On injured reserve with hamstring injury (October 12-December 2, 1991). ... On practice squad (December 2, 1992-remainder of season). ... Cardinals franchise renamed Arizona Cardinals for 1994 season. ... Claimed on waivers by Cincinnati Bengals (August 4, 1994). ... Released by Bengals (August 7, 1994). ... Signed by Carolina Panthers (April 11, 1995).
PRO STATISTICS: W.L.: 1991—Recovered one fumble. NFL: 1993—Returned one kickoff for 18 yards.

| | | INTERCEPTIONS | | | |
Year Team	G	No.	Yds.	Avg.	TD
1991—Montreal W.L.	10	2	16	8.0	0
—Phoenix NFL	11	0	0	...	0
1992—Phoenix NFL	4	0	0	...	0
1993—Phoenix NFL	13	0	0	...	0
1994—			Did not play.		
1995—Carolina NFL	10	0	0	...	0
W.L. totals (1 year)	10	2	16	8.0	0
NFL totals (4 years)	38	0	0	...	0
Pro totals (4 years)	48	2	16	8.0	0

LOGAN, ERNIE   DE   JAGUARS

PERSONAL: Born May 18, 1968, in Fort Bragg, N.C. ... 6-3/283. ... Full name: Ernest Edward Logan.
HIGH SCHOOL: Pine Forest (Fayetteville, N.C.).
COLLEGE: East Carolina.

TRANSACTIONS/CAREER NOTES: Selected by Atlanta Falcons in ninth round (226th pick overall) of 1991 NFL draft. ... Released by Falcons (August 19, 1991). ... Signed by Cleveland Browns (August 21, 1991). ... Released by Browns (September 8, 1993). ... Signed by Falcons (October 7, 1993). ... Granted free agency (February 17, 1994). ... Re-signed by Falcons (April 28, 1994). ... Released by Falcons (August 22, 1994). ... Signed by Jacksonville Jaguars (December 15, 1994).
PRO STATISTICS: 1991—Recovered one fumble.

Year Team	G	SACKS
1991—Cleveland NFL	15	0.5
1992—Cleveland NFL	16	1.0
1993—Atlanta NFL	8	1.0
1994—	Did not play.	
1995—Jacksonville NFL	15	3.0
Pro totals (4 years)	54	5.5

LOGAN, JAMES   LB   SEAHAWKS

PERSONAL: Born December 6, 1972, in Opp, Ala. ... 6-2/214.
HIGH SCHOOL: Opp (Ala.).
JUNIOR COLLEGE: Jones County Junior College (Miss.).
COLLEGE: Memphis.
TRANSACTIONS/CAREER NOTES: Signed as non-drafted free agent by Houston Oilers (May 3, 1995). ... Released by Oilers (August 27, 1995). ... Re-signed by Oilers (August 30, 1995). ... Activated (September 15, 1995). ... Claimed on waivers by Cincinnati Bengals (October 18, 1995). ... Claimed on waivers by Seattle Seahawks (October 31, 1995).
PLAYING EXPERIENCE: Houston (3)-Cincinnati (1)-Seattle (6) NFL, 1995. ... Games: 1995 (10).

LOGAN, MARC   FB   REDSKINS

PERSONAL: Born May 9, 1965, in Lexington, Ky. ... 6-0/212. ... Full name: Marc Anthony Logan. ... Cousin of Dermontti Dawson, center, Pittsburgh Steelers.
HIGH SCHOOL: Bryan Station (Lexington, Ky.).
COLLEGE: Kentucky (degree in political science, 1987).
TRANSACTIONS/CAREER NOTES: Selected by Cincinnati Bengals in fifth round (130th pick overall) of 1987 NFL draft. ... Signed by Bengals (July 7, 1987). ... Released by Bengals (September 7, 1987). ... Re-signed as replacement player by Bengals (September 25, 1987). ... Claimed on waivers by Cleveland Browns (October 20, 1987). ... Released by Browns (November 5, 1987). ... Re-signed by Browns for 1988 (November 7, 1987). ... Released by Browns (August 24, 1988). ... Signed by Bengals (October 4, 1988). ... Granted unconditional free agency (February 1, 1989). ... Signed by Miami Dolphins (February 16, 1989). ... On injured reserve with knee injury (October 25-December 6, 1989). ... Granted free agency (February 1, 1991). ... Re-signed by Dolphins (August 20, 1991). ... Activated (August 23, 1991). ... Granted unconditional free agency (February 1, 1992). ... Signed by San Francisco 49ers (April 1, 1992). ... Granted unconditional free agency (March 1, 1993). ... Re-signed by 49ers (July 20, 1993). ... Released by 49ers (August 30, 1993). ... Re-signed by 49ers (August 31, 1993). ... Released by 49ers (July 28, 1994). ... Re-signed by 49ers (July 29, 1994). ... Released by 49ers (March 10, 1995). ... Signed by Washington Redskins (April 25, 1995).
CHAMPIONSHIP GAME EXPERIENCE: Member of Bengals for AFC championship game (1988 season); inactive. ... Played in Super Bowl XXIII (1988 season). ... Played in NFC championship game (1992-1994 seasons). ... Member of Super Bowl championship team (1994 season).
POSTSEASON RECORDS: Shares NFL postseason single-game record for most kickoff returns—8 (January 12, 1991, at Buffalo).
PRO STATISTICS: 1989—Returned blocked punt two yards for a touchdown, fumbled once and recovered two fumbles for minus one yard. 1990—Recovered one fumble. 1993—Recovered one fumble.
STATISTICAL PLATEAUS: 100-yard rushing games: 1987 (1).

		RUSHING				RECEIVING				KICKOFF RETURNS				TOTALS			
Year Team	G	Att.	Yds.	Avg.	TD	No.	Yds.	Avg.	TD	No.	Yds.	Avg.	TD	TD	2pt.	Pts.	Fum.
1987—Cincinnati NFL	3	37	203	5.5	1	3	14	4.7	0	3	31	10.3	0	1	...	6	0
1988—Cincinnati NFL	9	2	10	5.0	0	2	20	10.0	0	4	80	20.0	0	0	...	0	1
1989—Miami NFL	10	57	201	3.5	0	5	34	6.8	0	24	613	25.5	†1	2	...	12	1
1990—Miami NFL	16	79	317	4.0	2	7	54	7.7	0	20	367	18.4	0	2	...	12	4
1991—Miami NFL	16	4	5	1.3	0	0	0	...	0	12	191	15.9	0	0	...	0	1
1992—San Francisco NFL	16	8	44	5.5	1	2	17	8.5	0	22	478	21.7	0	1	...	6	0
1993—San Francisco NFL	14	58	280	4.8	7	37	348	9.4	0	0	0	...	0	7	...	42	2
1994—San Francisco NFL	10	33	143	4.3	1	16	97	6.1	1	0	0	...	0	2	0	12	0
1995—Washington NFL	16	23	72	3.1	1	25	276	11.0	2	0	0	...	0	3	0	18	1
Pro totals (9 years)	110	301	1275	4.2	13	97	860	8.9	3	85	1760	20.7	1	18	0	108	10

LOHMILLER, CHIP   K   RAMS

PERSONAL: Born July 16, 1966, in Woodbury, Minn. ... 6-3/215.
HIGH SCHOOL: Woodbury (Minn.).
COLLEGE: Minnesota.
TRANSACTIONS/CAREER NOTES: Selected by Washington Redskins in second round (55th pick overall) of 1988 NFL draft. ... Signed by Redskins (July 17, 1988). ... Designated by Redskins as transition player (February 25, 1993). ... Released by Redskins (August 8, 1995). ... Signed by New Orleans Saints (August 13, 1995). ... Released by Saints (October 30, 1995). ... Signed by St. Louis Rams (April 6, 1996).
CHAMPIONSHIP GAME EXPERIENCE: Played in NFC championship game (1991 season). ... Member of Super Bowl championship team (1991 season).
HONORS: Named kicker on The Sporting News college All-America second team (1987). ... Played in Pro Bowl (1991 season). ... Named kicker on The Sporting News NFL All-Pro team (1991).
PRO STATISTICS: 1988—Punted six times for 208 yards.

		KICKING						
Year Team	G	XPM	XPA	FGM	FGA	Lg.	50+	Pts.
1988—Washington NFL	16	40	41	19	26	46	0-0	97
1989—Washington NFL	16	41	41	29	*40	48	0-1	128

		KICKING						
Year Team	G	XPM	XPA	FGM	FGA	Lg.	50+	Pts.
1990—Washington NFL	16	41	41	30	*40	56	3-8	131
1991—Washington NFL	16	†56	56	*31	*43	53	2-5	*149
1992—Washington NFL	16	30	30	*30	*40	53	2-2	†120
1993—Washington NFL	16	24	26	16	28	51	1-6	72
1994—Washington NFL	16	30	32	20	28	54	1-3	90
1995—New Orleans NFL	8	11	13	8	14	51	1-2	35
Pro totals (8 years)	120	273	280	183	259	56	10-27	822

LONDON, ANTONIO   LB   LIONS

PERSONAL: Born April 14, 1971, in Tullahoma, Tenn. ... 6-2/234. ... Full name: Antonio Monte London.
HIGH SCHOOL: Tullahoma (Tenn.).
COLLEGE: Alabama.
TRANSACTIONS/CAREER NOTES: Selected by Detroit Lions in third round (62nd pick overall) of 1993 NFL draft.... Signed by Lions (July 17, 1993).

Year Team	G	SACKS
1993—Detroit NFL	14	1.0
1994—Detroit NFL	16	0.0
1995—Detroit NFL	15	7.0
Pro totals (3 years)	45	8.0

LONEKER, KEITH   G   RAMS

PERSONAL: Born June 21, 1971, in Roselle Park, N.J. ... 6-3/330. ... Full name: Keith Joseph Loneker.
HIGH SCHOOL: Roselle Park (N.J.).
COLLEGE: Kansas.
TRANSACTIONS/CAREER NOTES: Signed as non-drafted free agent by Los Angeles Rams (May 3, 1993). ... On injured reserve with knee injury (December 31, 1993-remainder of season). ... On injured reserve with arch injury (September 21, 1994-remainder of season). ... Rams franchise moved to St. Louis (April 12, 1995).
PLAYING EXPERIENCE: Los Angeles Rams NFL, 1993 and 1994; St. Louis NFL, 1995. ... Games: 1993 (4), 1994 (2), 1995 (13). Total: 19.

LOUCHIEY, COREY   OT   BILLS

PERSONAL: Born October 10, 1971, in Greenville, S.C. ... 6-7/305. ... Pronounced LOU-chee
HIGH SCHOOL: Carolina (Greenville, S.C.).
COLLEGE: Tennessee (did not play football), then South Carolina.
TRANSACTIONS/CAREER NOTES: Selected by Buffalo Bills in third round (98th pick overall) of 1994 NFL draft. ... Signed by Bills (July 15, 1994). ... Active for four games (1994); did not play.
PLAYING EXPERIENCE: Buffalo NFL, 1995. ... Games: 1995 (13).

LOVE, DUVAL   G   CARDINALS

PERSONAL: Born June 24, 1963, in Los Angeles. ... 6-3/288. ... Full name: Duval Lee Love.
HIGH SCHOOL: Fountain Valley (Calif.).
COLLEGE: UCLA.
TRANSACTIONS/CAREER NOTES: Selected by Memphis Showboats in 1985 USFL territorial draft. ... Selected by Los Angeles Rams in 10th round (274th pick overall) of 1985 NFL draft. ... Signed by Rams (July 16, 1985). ... On injured reserve with shoulder injury (September 2-October 4, 1985). ... On injured reserve with pinched nerve in neck (November 15, 1985-remainder of season). ... On injured reserve with knee injury (September 8-October 24, 1987). ... Granted free agency (February 1, 1991). ... Re-signed by Rams (June 24, 1991). ... Granted unconditional free agency (February 1, 1992). ... Signed by Pittsburgh Steelers (March 15, 1992). ... Granted unconditional free agency (February 17, 1995). ... Signed by Arizona Cardinals (April 4, 1995).
PLAYING EXPERIENCE: Los Angeles Rams NFL, 1985-1991; Pittsburgh NFL, 1992-1994; Arizona NFL, 1995. ... Games: 1985 (6), 1986 (16), 1987 (10), 1988 (15), 1989 (15), 1990 (16), 1991 (16), 1992 (16), 1993 (16), 1994 (16), 1995 (16). Total: 158.
CHAMPIONSHIP GAME EXPERIENCE: Played in NFC championship game (1989 season). ... Played in AFC championship game (1994 season).
HONORS: Played in Pro Bowl (1994 season).
PRO STATISTICS: 1986—Returned one kickoff for minus six yards and fumbled once. 1988—Recovered one fumble. 1990—Recovered two fumbles. 1991—Recovered two fumbles. 1992—Recovered one fumble for seven yards. 1995—Recovered one fumble.

LOVE, SEAN   G   PANTHERS

PERSONAL: Born September 6, 1968, in Tamaqua, Pa. ... 6-3/304. ... Full name: Sean Fitzgerald Love.
HIGH SCHOOL: Marion (Tamaqua, Pa.).
COLLEGE: Penn State.
TRANSACTIONS/CAREER NOTES: Selected after junior season by Dallas Cowboys in 10th round (264th pick overall) of 1991 NFL draft. ... Released by Cowboys (August 11, 1991). ... Claimed on waivers by New York Giants (August 14, 1991). ... Released by Giants (August 26, 1991). ... Selected by Sacramento Surge in 14th round (145th pick overall) of 1992 World League draft. ... Released by Surge (March 1, 1992). ... Signed by Buffalo Bills (July 7, 1992). ... Released by Bills (August 25, 1992). ... Re-signed by Bills to practice squad (September 1, 1992). ... Released by Bills (October 21, 1992). ... Re-signed by Bills (March 11, 1993). ... Released by Bills (August 30, 1993). ... Signed by Tampa Bay Buccaneers (August 31, 1993). ... Released by Buccaneers (October 18, 1993). ... Re-signed by Buccaneers to practice squad (October 19, 1993). ... Activated (November 17, 1993). ... Released by Buccaneers (August 22, 1995). ... Signed by Carolina Panthers (June

L

9, 1995). ... Granted free agency (February 16, 1996). ... Re-signed by Panthers (March 20, 1996).
PLAYING EXPERIENCE: Tampa Bay NFL, 1993 and 1994; Carolina NFL, 1995. ... Games: 1993 (2), 1994 (6), 1995 (11). Total: 19.

LOVILLE, DEREK   RB   49ERS

PERSONAL: Born July 4, 1968, in San Francisco. ... 5-10/205. ... Full name: Derek Kevin Loville. ... Name pronounced luh-VILL.
HIGH SCHOOL: Riordan (San Francisco).
COLLEGE: Oregon (degree in American studies).
TRANSACTIONS/CAREER NOTES: Signed as non-drafted free agent by Seattle Seahawks (May 9, 1990). ... Granted unconditional free agency (February 1-April 1, 1991). ... Re-signed by Seahawks for 1991 season. ... Granted unconditional free agency (February 1, 1992). ... Signed by Los Angeles Rams (March 27, 1992). ... Released by Rams (August 31, 1992). ... Signed by San Francisco 49ers (March 22, 1993). ... On injured reserve (August 30-November 10, 1993). ... Released by 49ers (November 10, 1993). ... Re-signed by 49ers (June 1, 1994). ... Granted unconditional free agency (February 17, 1995). ... Re-signed by 49ers (March 1, 1995).
CHAMPIONSHIP GAME EXPERIENCE: Played in NFC championship game (1994 season). ... Member of Super Bowl championship team (1994 season).
PRO STATISTICS: 1990—Fumbled once. 1991—Recovered one fumble. 1995—Fumbled once.

		RUSHING				RECEIVING				PUNT RETURNS				KICKOFF RETURNS				TOTALS		
Year Team	G	Att.	Yds.	Avg.	TD	No.	Yds.	Avg.	TD	No.	Yds.	Avg.	TD	No.	Yds.	Avg.	TD	TD	2pt.	Pts.
1990—Seattle NFL	11	7	12	1.7	0	0	0	...	0	0	0	...	0	18	359	19.9	0	0	...	0
1991—Seattle NFL	16	22	69	3.1	0	0	0	...	0	3	16	5.3	0	18	412	22.9	0	0	...	0
1992—										Did not play.										
1993—San Francisco NFL										Did not play.										
1994—San Francisco NFL	14	31	99	3.2	0	2	26	13.0	0	0	0	...	0	2	34	17.0	0	0	0	0
1995—San Francisco NFL	16	218	723	3.3	10	87	662	7.6	3	0	0	...	0	0	0	...	0	13	1	80
Pro totals (4 years)	57	278	903	3.3	10	89	688	7.7	3	3	16	5.3	0	38	805	21.2	0	13	1	80

LOWDERMILK, KIRK   C

PERSONAL: Born April 10, 1963, in Canton, Ohio. ... 6-4/280. ... Full name: Robert Kirk Lowdermilk. ... Brother-in-law of Rich Karlis, kicker, Denver Broncos, Minnesota Vikings and Detroit Lions (1982-1990).
HIGH SCHOOL: Salem (Ohio).
COLLEGE: Ohio State.
TRANSACTIONS/CAREER NOTES: Selected by New Jersey Generals in 1985 USFL territorial draft. ... Selected by Minnesota Vikings in third round (59th pick overall) of 1985 NFL draft. ... Signed by Vikings (August 12, 1985). ... On injured reserve with knee injury (September 2-October 11, 1986). ... Granted free agency (February 1, 1988). ... Re-signed by Vikings (August 23, 1988). ... On injured reserve with fractured thumb (September 27-October 29, 1988). ... Granted free agency (February 1, 1990). ... Re-signed by Vikings (September 12, 1990). ... Granted roster exemption (September 12-15, 1990). ... Granted free agency (February 1, 1991). ... Re-signed by Vikings (May 22, 1991). ... Granted unconditional free agency (March 1, 1993). ... Signed by Indianapolis Colts (March 29, 1993). ... Granted unconditional free agency (February 16, 1996).
PLAYING EXPERIENCE: Minnesota NFL, 1985-1992; Indianapolis NFL, 1993-1995. ... Games: 1985 (16), 1986 (11), 1987 (12), 1988 (12), 1989 (16), 1990 (15), 1991 (16), 1992 (16), 1993 (16), 1994 (16), 1995 (16). Total: 162.
CHAMPIONSHIP GAME EXPERIENCE: Played in NFC championship game (1987 season). ... Played in AFC championship game (1995 season).
PRO STATISTICS: 1989—Recovered one fumble. 1990—Recovered one fumble. 1991—Fumbled once and recovered one fumble for minus 22 yards. 1993—Recovered one fumble. 1994—Fumbled once.

LOWERY, NICK   K   JETS

PERSONAL: Born May 27, 1956, in Munich, Germany. ... 6-4/215. ... Full name: Dominic Gerald Lowery.
HIGH SCHOOL: Albans (Washington, D.C.).
COLLEGE: Dartmouth (degree in government, 1978).
TRANSACTIONS/CAREER NOTES: Signed as non-drafted free agent by New York Jets (May 17, 1978). ... Released by Jets (August 21, 1978). ... Signed by New England Patriots (September 19, 1978). ... Released by Patriots (October 6, 1978). ... Signed by Cincinnati Bengals (July 2, 1979). ... Released by Bengals (August 13, 1979). ... Signed by Washington Redskins (August 18, 1979). ... Released by Redskins (August 20, 1979). ... Re-signed by Redskins (August 25, 1979). ... Released by Redskins (August 27, 1979). ... Signed by Kansas City Chiefs (February 16, 1980). ... Granted free agency (February 1, 1992). ... Re-signed by Chiefs (August 21, 1992). ... Released by Chiefs (June 8, 1994). ... Signed by Jets (June 22, 1994).
CHAMPIONSHIP GAME EXPERIENCE: Played in AFC championship game (1993 season).
HONORS: Played in Pro Bowl (1981, 1990 and 1992 seasons). ... Named kicker on THE SPORTING NEWS NFL All-Pro team (1990).
RECORDS: Holds NFL career record for highest field-goal percentage—80.44. ... Holds NFL record for most seasons with 100 or more points—11 (1981, 1983-1986 and 1988-1993).
PRO STATISTICS: 1981—Recovered one fumble. 1992—Punted four times for 141 yards.

		KICKING						
Year Team	G	XPM	XPA	FGM	FGA	Lg.	50+	Pts.
1978—New England NFL	2	7	7	0	1	0	0-1	7
1979—				Did not play.				
1980—Kansas City NFL	16	37	37	20	26	57	4-7	97
1981—Kansas City NFL	16	37	38	26	36	52	1-7	115
1982—Kansas City NFL	9	17	17	19	*24	48	0-3	74
1983—Kansas City NFL	16	44	45	24	30	58	2-4	116
1984—Kansas City NFL	16	35	35	23	33	52	2-5	104
1985—Kansas City NFL	16	35	35	24	27	58	3-5	107
1986—Kansas City NFL	16	43	43	19	26	47	0-1	100
1987—Kansas City NFL	12	26	26	19	23	54	2-2	83
1988—Kansas City NFL	16	23	23	27	32	51	3-3	104
1989—Kansas City NFL	16	34	35	24	33	50	1-3	106

Year Team	G	KICKING							
		XPM	XPA	FGM	FGA	Lg.	50+	Pts.
1990—Kansas City NFL	16	37	38	*34	37	48	0-1	*139
1991—Kansas City NFL	16	35	35	25	30	48	0-2	110
1992—Kansas City NFL	15	39	39	22	24	52	1-1	105
1993—Kansas City NFL	16	37	37	23	29	52	1-1	106
1994—New York Jets NFL	16	26	27	20	23	49	0-0	86
1995—New York Jets NFL	14	24	24	17	21	50	2-4	75
Pro totals (17 years)	244	536	541	366	455	58	22-50	1634

LUMPKIN, SEAN   S

PERSONAL: Born January 4, 1970, in Golden Valley, Minn. ... 6-0/206. ... Full name: Sean Franklin Lumpkin.
HIGH SCHOOL: Benilde-St. Margaret (St. Louis Park, Minn.).
COLLEGE: Minnesota.
TRANSACTIONS/CAREER NOTES: Selected by New Orleans Saints in fourth round (106th pick overall) of 1992 NFL draft. ... Signed by Saints (July 7, 1992). ... Granted free agency (February 17, 1995). ... Re-signed by Saints (May 31, 1995). ... Granted unconditional free agency (February 16, 1996).
PLAYING EXPERIENCE: New Orleans NFL, 1992-1995. ... Games: 1992 (16), 1993 (12), 1994 (16), 1995 (16). Total: 60.
PRO STATISTICS: 1992—Recovered one fumble. 1994—Intercepted one pass for one yard and recovered one fumble. 1995—Intercepted one pass for 47 yards and a touchdown.

LUNDY, DENNIS   RB/KR   BEARS

PERSONAL: Born July 6, 1972, in Tampa. ... 5-8/187. ... Full name: Dennis Leonard Lundy.
HIGH SCHOOL: Chamberlain (Tampa).
COLLEGE: Northwestern.
TRANSACTIONS/CAREER NOTES: Signed as non-drafted free agent by Houston Oilers (May 3, 1995). ... Released by Oilers (August 22, 1995). ... Re-signed by Oilers (September 6, 1995). ... Activated (September 29, 1995). ... Released by Oilers (November 21, 1995). ... Re-signed by Oilers (November 30, 1995). ... Released by Oilers (December 6, 1995). ... Claimed on waivers by Chicago Bears (December 6, 1995).
PLAYING EXPERIENCE: Houston (7)-Chicago (2) NFL, 1995. ... Games: 1995 (9).
PRO STATISTICS: 1995—Caught one pass for 11 yards and returned two kickoffs for 28 yards. 1995—Caught one pass for 11 yards and returned three kickoffs for 39 yards.

L

LUTZ, DAVID   G/OT

PERSONAL: Born December 20, 1959, in Monroe, N.C. ... 6-6/305. ... Full name: David Graham Lutz. ... Name pronounced LOOTS.
HIGH SCHOOL: Bowman (Wadesboro, N.C.).
COLLEGE: Georgia Tech.
TRANSACTIONS/CAREER NOTES: Selected by Oakland Invaders in third round (31st pick overall) of 1983 USFL draft. ... Selected by Kansas City Chiefs in second round (34th pick overall) of 1983 NFL draft. ... Signed by Chiefs (June 1, 1983). ... On injured reserve with knee injury (September 4-November 9, 1984). ... On injured reserve with knee injury (October 7-November 28, 1986). ... Granted free agency (February 1, 1990). ... Re-signed by Chiefs (August 15, 1990). ... Granted unconditional free agency (March 1, 1993). ... Signed by Detroit Lions (March 30, 1993). ... Granted unconditional free agency (February 17, 1995). ... Re-signed by Lions (April 24, 1995). ... Released by Lions (March 11, 1996).
PLAYING EXPERIENCE: Kansas City NFL, 1983-1992; Detroit NFL, 1993-1995. ... Games: 1983 (16), 1984 (7), 1985 (16), 1986 (9), 1987 (12), 1988 (15), 1989 (16), 1990 (16), 1991 (16), 1992 (16), 1993 (16), 1994 (16), 1995 (16). Total: 187.
PRO STATISTICS: 1985—Recovered one fumble. 1989—Recovered one fumble. 1991—Recovered one fumble. 1992—Recovered one fumble.

LYGHT, TODD   CB   RAMS

PERSONAL: Born February 9, 1969, in Kwajalein, Marshall Islands. ... 6-0/186. ... Full name: Todd William Lyght.
HIGH SCHOOL: Powers (Flint, Mich.).
COLLEGE: Notre Dame.
TRANSACTIONS/CAREER NOTES: Selected by Los Angeles Rams in first round (fifth pick overall) of 1991 NFL draft. ... Signed by Rams (August 16, 1991). ... On injured reserve with shoulder injury (September 22-October 22, 1992). ... On injured reserve with knee injury (November 23, 1993-remainder of season). ... Designated by Rams as transition player (February 15, 1994). ... Rams franchise moved to St. Louis (April 12, 1995). ... Tendered offer sheet by Jacksonville Jaguars (April 12, 1996). ... Offer matched by Rams (April 15, 1996).
HONORS: Named defensive back on THE SPORTING NEWS college All-America first team (1989). ... Named defensive back on THE SPORTING NEWS college All-America second team (1990).
PRO STATISTICS: 1991—Fumbled once and recovered one fumble. 1993—Recovered one fumble for 13 yards. 1994—Returned one punt for 29 yards and recovered one fumble for 74 yards and a touchdown. 1995—Ran 16 yards with lateral from punt return.

Year Team	G	INTERCEPTIONS			
		No.	Yds.	Avg.	TD
1991—Los Angeles Rams NFL	12	1	0	0.0	0
1992—Los Angeles Rams NFL	12	3	80	26.7	0
1993—Los Angeles Rams NFL	9	2	0	0.0	0
1994—Los Angeles Rams NFL	16	1	14	14.0	0
1995—St. Louis NFL	16	4	34	8.5	1
Pro totals (5 years)	65	11	128	11.6	1

LYLE, KEITH   S   RAMS

PERSONAL: Born April 17, 1972, in Washington, D.C. ... 6-2/204. ... Full name: Keith Allen Lyle. ... Son of Garry Lyle, free safety, Chicago

Bears (1968-1974).
HIGH SCHOOL: George C. Marshall (Falls Church, Va.).
COLLEGE: Virginia.
TRANSACTIONS/CAREER NOTES: Selected by Los Angeles Rams in third round (71st pick overall) of 1994 NFL draft. ... Signed by Rams (July 8, 1994). ... Rams franchise moved to St. Louis (April 12, 1995).
PRO STATISTICS: 1995—Rushed once for four yards.

			INTERCEPTIONS			
Year Team	G	No.	Yds.	Avg.	TD	
1994—Los Angeles Rams NFL	16	2	1	.5	0	
1995—St. Louis NFL	16	3	42	14.0	0	
Pro totals (2 years)	32	5	43	8.6	0	

LYLE, RICK   DL   RAVENS

PERSONAL: Born February 26, 1971, in Monroe, La. ... 6-5/280. ... Full name: Rick James Earl Lyle.
HIGH SCHOOL: Hickman Mills (Kansas City, Mo.).
COLLEGE: Missouri.
TRANSACTIONS/CAREER NOTES: Signed as non-drafted free agent by Cleveland Browns (May 2, 1994). ... On injured reserve with back injury (September 2, 1995-entire season). ... Browns franchise moved to Baltimore and renamed Ravens for 1996 season (March 11, 1996).
PLAYING EXPERIENCE: Cleveland NFL, 1994. ... Games: 1994 (3).

LYNCH, ERIC   RB   LIONS

PERSONAL: Born May 16, 1970, in Woodhaven, Mich. ... 5-10/224.
HIGH SCHOOL: Woodhaven (Flat Rock, Mich.).
COLLEGE: Grand Valley State (Mich.).
TRANSACTIONS/CAREER NOTES: Signed as non-drafted free agent by Detroit Lions (May 1, 1992). ... Released by Lions (August 31, 1992). ... Re-signed by Lions to practice squad (September 1, 1992). ... Activated (September 25, 1992). ... Released by Lions (September 29, 1992). ... Re-signed by Lions to practice squad (October 1, 1992). ... Activated (December 22, 1992). ... Released by Lions (August 30, 1993). ... Re-signed by Lions to practice squad (August 31, 1993). ... Activated (December 3, 1993). ... Granted free agency (February 17, 1995). ... Re-signed by Lions (April 5, 1995).
STATISTICAL PLATEAUS: 100-yard rushing games: 1993 (1).

		RUSHING				RECEIVING				KICKOFF RETURNS				TOTALS			
Year Team	G	Att.	Yds.	Avg.	TD	No.	Yds.	Avg.	TD	No.	Yds.	Avg.	TD	TD	2pt.	Pts.	Fum.
1992—Detroit NFL	1	0	0	...	0	0	0	...	0	0	0	...	0	0	...	0	0
1993—Detroit NFL	4	53	207	3.9	2	13	82	6.3	0	1	22	22.0	0	2	...	12	1
1994—Detroit NFL	12	1	0	0.0	0	2	18	9.0	0	9	105	11.7	0	0	0	0	0
1995—Detroit NFL	4	0	0	...	0	0	0	...	0	0	0	...	0	0	0	0	0
Pro totals (4 years)	21	54	207	3.8	2	15	100	6.7	0	10	127	12.7	0	2	0	12	1

LYNCH, JOHN   S   BUCCANEERS

PERSONAL: Born September 25, 1971, in Hinsdale, Ill. ... 6-2/210. ... Full name: John Terrence Lynch. ... Son of John Lynch, linebacker, Pittsburgh Steelers (1969).
HIGH SCHOOL: Torrey Pines (Encinitas, Calif.).
COLLEGE: Stanford.
TRANSACTIONS/CAREER NOTES: Selected by Tampa Bay Buccaneers in third round (82nd pick overall) of 1993 NFL draft. ... Signed by Buccaneers (June 1, 1993). ... On injured reserve with knee injury (December 12, 1995-remainder of season). ... Granted free agency (February 16, 1996).

			INTERCEPTIONS			
Year Team	G	No.	Yds.	Avg.	TD	
1993—Tampa Bay NFL	15	0	0	...	0	
1994—Tampa Bay NFL	16	0	0	...	0	
1995—Tampa Bay NFL	9	3	3	1.0	0	
Pro totals (3 years)	40	3	3	1.0	0	

LYNCH, LORENZO   S   RAIDERS

PERSONAL: Born April 6, 1963, in Oakland. ... 5-11/200.
HIGH SCHOOL: Oakland.
COLLEGE: Sacramento State.
TRANSACTIONS/CAREER NOTES: Signed as non-drafted free agent by Dallas Cowboys (April 30, 1987). ... Released by Cowboys (July 27, 1987). ... Signed by Chicago Bears (July 31, 1987). ... Released by Bears (September 1, 1987). ... Re-signed as replacement player by Bears (September 24, 1987). ... On injured reserve with dislocated shoulder (October 16, 1987-remainder of season). ... On injured reserve with hamstring injury (August 29-October 14, 1988). ... Granted unconditional free agency (February 1, 1990). ... Signed by Phoenix Cardinals (March 30, 1990). ... Granted free agency (February 1, 1992). ... Re-signed by Cardinals (July 19, 1992). ... Granted unconditional free agency (February 17, 1994). ... Cardinals franchise renamed Arizona Cardinals for 1994 season. ... Re-signed by Cardinals (June 2, 1994). ... Granted unconditional free agency (February 17, 1995). ... Re-signed by Cardinals (February 27, 1995). ... Released by Cardinals (March 6, 1996). ... Signed by Oakland Raiders (March 8, 1996).
CHAMPIONSHIP GAME EXPERIENCE: Played in NFC championship game (1988 season).
PRO STATISTICS: 1991—Recovered one fumble for 17 yards. 1992—Recovered one fumble. 1993—Credited with one sack and recovered three fumbles for 55 yards and a touchdown. 1994—Credited with ½ sack. 1995—Credited with one sack and recovered one fumble.

Year Team		INTERCEPTIONS			
	G	No.	Yds.	Avg.	TD
1987—Chicago NFL	2	0	0	...	0
1988—Chicago NFL	9	0	0	...	0
1989—Chicago NFL	16	3	55	18.3	0
1990—Phoenix NFL	16	0	0	...	0
1991—Phoenix NFL	16	3	59	19.7	1
1992—Phoenix NFL	16	0	0	...	0
1993—Phoenix NFL	16	3	13	4.3	0
1994—Arizona NFL	15	2	35	17.5	0
1995—Arizona NFL	12	1	72	72.0	1
Pro totals (9 years)	118	12	234	19.5	2

LYNN, ANTHONY   RB   49ERS

PERSONAL: Born December 21, 1968, in McKinney, Texas. ... 6-3/230. ... Full name: Anthony Ray Lynn.
HIGH SCHOOL: Celina (Texas).
COLLEGE: Texas Tech.
TRANSACTIONS/CAREER NOTES: Signed as non-drafted free agent by New York Giants (May 5, 1992). ... Released by Giants (August 31, 1992). ... Signed by Denver Broncos (April 21, 1993). ... Released by Broncos (August 23, 1994). ... Signed by San Francisco 49ers (March 28, 1995).
PLAYING EXPERIENCE: Denver NFL, 1993; San Francisco NFL, 1995. ... Games: 1993 (13), 1995 (6). Total: 19.
PRO STATISTICS: 1995—Rushed twice for 11 yards.

LYONS, MITCH   TE   FALCONS

PERSONAL: Born May 13, 1970, in Grand Rapids, Mich. ... 6-4/265. ... Full name: Mitchell Warren Lyons.
HIGH SCHOOL: Forest Hills Northern (Grand Rapids, Mich.).
COLLEGE: Michigan State.
TRANSACTIONS/CAREER NOTES: Selected by Atlanta Falcons in sixth round (151st pick overall) of 1993 NFL draft. ... Signed by Falcons (May 26, 1993). ... Granted free agency (February 16, 1996).

Year Team		RECEIVING				TOTALS			
	G	No.	Yds.	Avg.	TD	TD	2pt.	Pts.	Fum.
1993—Atlanta NFL	16	8	63	7.9	0	0	...	0	0
1994—Atlanta NFL	7	7	54	7.7	0	0	0	0	0
1995—Atlanta NFL	14	5	83	16.6	0	0	0	0	0
Pro totals (3 years)	37	20	200	10.0	0	0	0	0	0

MACK, MILTON   CB   SAINTS

PERSONAL: Born September 20, 1963, in Jackson, Miss. ... 5-11/195. ... Full name: Milton Jerome Mack. ... Cousin of Cedric Mack, cornerback with four NFL teams (1983-1993).
HIGH SCHOOL: Callaway (Jackson, Miss.).
COLLEGE: Alcorn State.
TRANSACTIONS/CAREER NOTES: Selected by New Orleans Saints in fifth round (123rd pick overall) of 1987 NFL draft. ... Signed by Saints (July 24, 1987). ... Crossed picket line during players strike (October 14, 1987). ... On injured reserve with hamstring injury (January 2, 1991-remainder of 1990 season playoffs). ... On injured reserve with hamstring injury (October 11-December 6, 1991). ... Granted unconditional free agency (February 1, 1992). ... Signed by Tampa Bay Buccaneers (March 12, 1992). ... Released by Buccaneers (August 26, 1994). ... Signed by Detroit Lions (August 30, 1994). ... Granted unconditional free agency (February 17, 1995). ... Signed by Saints (February 26, 1996).
PRO STATISTICS: 1988—Credited with one sack. 1989—Credited with one sack. 1990—Returned one kickoff for 17 yards.

Year Team		INTERCEPTIONS			
	G	No.	Yds.	Avg.	TD
1987—New Orleans NFL	13	4	32	8.0	0
1988—New Orleans NFL	14	1	19	19.0	0
1989—New Orleans NFL	16	2	0	0.0	0
1990—New Orleans NFL	16	0	0	...	0
1991—New Orleans NFL	8	0	0	...	0
1992—Tampa Bay NFL	16	3	0	0.0	0
1993—Tampa Bay NFL	12	1	27	27.0	1
1994—Detroit NFL	16	1	0	0.0	0
1995—			Did not play.		
Pro totals (8 years)	111	12	78	6.5	1

MADDOX, MARK   LB   BILLS

PERSONAL: Born March 23, 1968, in Milwaukee. ... 6-1/233. ... Full name: Mark Anthony Maddox.
HIGH SCHOOL: James Madison (Milwaukee).
COLLEGE: Northern Michigan.
TRANSACTIONS/CAREER NOTES: Selected by Buffalo Bills in ninth round (249th pick overall) of 1991 NFL draft. ... Signed by Bills (June 18, 1991). ... On injured reserve (August 27, 1991-entire season). ... On injured reserve (October 10, 1995-remainder of season). ... Granted unconditional free agency (February 16, 1996). ... Re-signed by Bills (March 4, 1996).
PLAYING EXPERIENCE: Buffalo NFL, 1992-1995. ... Games: 1992 (15), 1993 (11), 1994 (15), 1995 (4). Total: 45.
CHAMPIONSHIP GAME EXPERIENCE: Played in AFC championship game (1992 and 1993 season). ... Played in Super Bowl XXVII (1992 season) and Super Bowl XXVIII (1993 season).
PRO STATISTICS: 1993—Recovered two fumbles. 1994—Intercepted one pass for 11 yards and recovered one fumble.

L
M

MADDOX, TOMMY — QB — GIANTS

PERSONAL: Born September 2, 1971, in Shreveport, La. ... 6-4/218. ... Full name: Thomas Alfred Maddox.
HIGH SCHOOL: L.D. Bell (Hurst, Texas).
COLLEGE: UCLA.
TRANSACTIONS/CAREER NOTES: Selected after sophomore season by Denver Broncos in first round (25th pick overall) of 1992 NFL draft. ... Signed by Broncos (July 22, 1992). ... Traded by Broncos to Los Angeles Rams for fourth-round pick (LB Ken Brown) in 1995 draft (August 27, 1994). ... Granted free agency (February 17, 1995). ... Rams franchise moved to St. Louis (April 12, 1995). ... Re-signed by Rams (July 7, 1995). ... Released by Rams (August 27, 1995). ... Signed by New York Giants (August 30, 1995).
PRO STATISTICS: 1992—Fumbled four times and recovered two fumbles. 1995—Fumbled once.
MISCELLANEOUS: Regular-season record as starting NFL quarterback: 0-4 (.000).

				PASSING						RUSHING				TOTALS		
Year Team	G	Att.	Cmp.	Pct.	Yds.	TD	Int.	Avg.	Rat.	Att.	Yds.	Avg.	TD	TD	2pt.	Pts.
1992—Denver NFL	13	121	66	54.6	757	5	9	6.26	56.4	9	20	2.2	0	0	...	0
1993—Denver NFL	16	1	1	100.0	1	1	0	1.00	118.8	2	-2	-1.0	0	0	...	0
1994—Los Angeles Rams NFL	5	19	10	52.6	141	0	2	7.42	37.3	1	1	1.0	0	0	0	0
1995—New York Giants NFL	16	23	6	26.1	49	0	3	2.13	0.0	1	4	4.0	0	0	0	0
Pro totals (4 years)	50	164	83	50.6	948	6	14	5.78	45.0	13	23	1.8	0	0	0	0

MAHLUM, ERIC — G — COLTS

PERSONAL: Born December 6, 1970, in San Diego. ... 6-4/290.
HIGH SCHOOL: Pacific Grove (Calif.).
COLLEGE: California.
TRANSACTIONS/CAREER NOTES: Selected by Indianapolis Colts in second round (32nd pick overall) of 1994 NFL draft. ... Signed by Colts (July 22, 1994).
PLAYING EXPERIENCE: Indianapolis NFL, 1994 and 1995. ... Games: 1994 (16), 1995 (7). Total: 23.
CHAMPIONSHIP GAME EXPERIENCE: Played in AFC championship game (1995 season).
PRO STATISTICS: 1995—Recovered two fumbles.

MAJKOWSKI, DON — QB — LIONS

PERSONAL: Born February 25, 1964, in Buffalo. ... 6-3/208. ... Full name: Donald Vincent Majkowski. ... Grandson of Edward Majkowski, minor league pitcher (1931 and 1940). ... Name pronounced muh-KOW-skee.
HIGH SCHOOL: Depew (N.Y.), then Fork Union (Va.) Military Academy.
COLLEGE: Virginia (degree in sports management, 1987).
TRANSACTIONS/CAREER NOTES: Selected by Green Bay Packers in 10th round (255th pick overall) of 1987 NFL draft. ... Signed by Packers (July 25, 1987). ... Granted free agency (February 1, 1990). ... Re-signed by Packers (September 4, 1990). ... Activated (September 8, 1990). ... On injured reserve with shoulder injury (December 14, 1990-remainder of season). ... Granted free agency (February 1, 1991). ... Re-signed by Packers (July 15, 1991). ... Granted free agency (February 1, 1992). ... Re-signed by Packers (June 11, 1992). ... Granted unconditional free agency (March 1, 1993). ... Signed by Indianapolis Colts (July 20, 1993). ... Released by Colts (July 13, 1994). ... Re-signed by Colts (July 20, 1994). ... Granted unconditional free agency (February 17, 1995). ... Signed by Detroit Lions (April 18, 1995).
HONORS: Named to play in Pro Bowl (1989 season); replaced by Jim Everett due to injury.
PRO STATISTICS: 1987—Fumbled five times. 1988—Fumbled eight times and recovered three fumbles. 1989—Fumbled 15 times and recovered six fumbles for minus 13 yards. 1990—Fumbled six times and recovered three fumbles for minus 10 yards. 1991—Fumbled 10 times and recovered four fumbles for minus three yards. 1992—Fumbled four times and recovered three fumbles. 1993—Fumbled once. 1994—Fumbled five times and recovered two fumbles for minus 14 yards.
STATISTICAL PLATEAUS: 300-yard passing games: 1987 (1), 1988 (1), 1989 (6), 1990 (1). Total: 9.
MISCELLANEOUS: Regular-season record as starting NFL quarterback: 25-29-1 (.464).

				PASSING						RUSHING				TOTALS		
Year Team	G	Att.	Cmp.	Pct.	Yds.	TD	Int.	Avg.	Rat.	Att.	Yds.	Avg.	TD	TD	2pt.	Pts.
1987—Green Bay NFL	7	127	55	43.3	875	5	3	6.89	70.2	15	127	8.5	0	0	...	0
1988—Green Bay NFL	13	336	178	53.0	2119	9	11	6.31	67.8	47	225	4.8	1	1	...	6
1989—Green Bay NFL	16	*599	*353	58.9	*4318	27	20	7.21	82.3	75	358	4.8	5	5	...	30
1990—Green Bay NFL	9	264	150	56.8	1925	10	12	7.29	73.5	29	186	6.4	1	1	...	6
1991—Green Bay NFL	9	226	115	50.9	1362	3	8	6.03	59.3	25	108	4.3	2	2	...	12
1992—Green Bay NFL	14	55	38	69.1	271	2	2	4.93	77.2	8	33	4.1	0	0	...	0
1993—Indianapolis NFL	3	24	13	54.2	105	0	1	4.38	48.1	2	4	2.0	0	0	...	0
1994—Indianapolis NFL	9	152	84	55.3	1010	6	7	6.65	69.8	24	34	1.4	3	3	0	18
1995—Detroit NFL	5	20	15	75.0	161	1	0	8.05	114.8	9	1	0.1	0	0	0	0
Pro totals (9 years)	85	1803	1001	55.5	12146	63	64	6.74	73.3	234	1076	4.6	12	12	0	72

MALAMALA, SIUPELI — G/OT — JETS

PERSONAL: Born January 15, 1969, in Tofoa, Tonga. ... 6-5/315. ... Name pronounced see-uh-pell-ee ma-la-ma-la.
HIGH SCHOOL: Kalahoe (Kailua, Hawaii).
COLLEGE: Washington.
TRANSACTIONS/CAREER NOTES: Selected by New York Jets in third round (68th pick overall) of 1992 NFL draft. ... Signed by Jets (July 14, 1992). ... On injured reserve with shoulder injury (August 31-September 29, 1992). ... On practice squad (September 29-October 9, 1992). ... Granted free agency (February 17, 1995). ... Re-signed by Jets (March 29, 1995). ... On injured reserve with knee injury (October 31, 1995-remainder of season).
PLAYING EXPERIENCE: New York Jets NFL, 1992-1995. ... Games: 1992 (9), 1993 (15), 1994 (12), 1995 (6). Total: 42.
PRO STATISTICS: 1993—Recovered one fumble.

MALONE, VAN   S   LIONS

PERSONAL: Born July 1, 1970, in Houston. ... 5-11/186. ... Full name: Van Buren Malone.
HIGH SCHOOL: Waltrip (Houston.).
COLLEGE: Texas.
TRANSACTIONS/CAREER NOTES: Selected by Detroit Lions in second round (57th pick overall) of 1994 NFL draft. ... Signed by Lions (July 19, 1994).
PRO STATISTICS: 1995—Intercepted one pass for no yards.

| | | KICKOFF RETURNS | | | | TOTALS | | | |
Year Team	G	No.	Yds.	Avg.	TD	TD	2pt.	Pts.	Fum.
1994—Detroit NFL	16	3	38	12.7	0	0	0	0	1
1995—Detroit NFL	16	0	0	...	0	0	0	0	0
Pro totals (2 years)	32	3	38	12.7	0	0	0	0	1

MAMULA, MIKE   DE   EAGLES

PERSONAL: Born August 14, 1973, in Lackawanna, N.Y. ... 6-4/252. ... Full name: Michael Brian Mamula. ... Name pronounced ma-MOO-lah.
HIGH SCHOOL: Lackawanna (N.Y.) Secondary.
COLLEGE: Boston College.
TRANSACTIONS/CAREER NOTES: Selected after junior season by Philadelphia Eagles in first round (seventh pick overall) of 1995 NFL draft. ... Signed by Eagles (July 19, 1995).
PRO STATISTICS: 1995—Recovered one fumblefor 25 yards.

Year Team	G	SACKS
1995—Philadelphia NFL	14	5.5

MANDARICH, TONY   OL   COLTS

PERSONAL: Born September 23, 1966, in Oakville, Ont. ... 6-5/303. ... Full name: Tony Joseph Mandarich. ... Brother of John Mandarich, former defensive tackle, Edmonton Eskimos and Ottawa Rough Riders of CFL (1984-1990).
HIGH SCHOOL: White Oaks (Ont.) and Roosevelt (Kent, O.).
COLLEGE: Michigan State (degree in telecommunications, 1990).
TRANSACTIONS/CAREER NOTES: Selected by Green Bay Packers in first round (second pick overall) of 1989 NFL draft. ... Signed by Packers (September 5, 1989). ... Granted roster exemption (September 5-18, 1989). ... On reserve/non-football illness list with thyroid injury (September 1, 1992-entire season). ... Granted unconditional free agency (March 1, 1993). ... Signed by Indianapolis Colts (March 22, 1996).
PLAYING EXPERIENCE: Green Bay NFL, 1989-1991. ... Games: 1989 (14), 1990 (16), 1991 (15). Total: 45.
HONORS: Named offensive tackle on THE SPORTING NEWS college All-America second team (1987). ... Named offensive tackle on THE SPORTING NEWS college All-America first team (1988).
PRO STATISTICS: 1989—Returned one kickoff for no yards. 1990—Recovered one fumble.

MANGUM, JOHN   S   BEARS

PERSONAL: Born March 16, 1967, in Magee, Miss. ... 5-10/186. ... Full name: John Wayne Mangum Jr. ... Son of John Mangum, defensive tackle, Boston Patriots of AFL (1966 and 1967).
HIGH SCHOOL: Magee (Miss.).
COLLEGE: Alabama (degree In finance).
TRANSACTIONS/CAREER NOTES: Selected by Chicago Bears in sixth round (144th pick overall) of 1990 NFL draft. ... Signed by Bears (July 24, 1990). ... Released by Bears (September 3, 1990). ... Signed by Tampa Bay Buccaneers to practice squad (October 1, 1990). ... Signed by Bears off Buccaneers practice squad (October 23, 1990). ... On injured reserve with knee injury (September 1992-remainder of season). ... Granted free agency (March 1, 1993). ... Re-signed by Bears (May 17, 1993). ... Granted unconditional free agency (February 17, 1995). ... Re-signed by Bears (March 2, 1995).
PLAYING EXPERIENCE: Chicago NFL, 1990-1995. ... Games: 1990 (10), 1991 (16), 1992 (5), 1993 (12), 1994 (16), 1995 (11). Total: 70.
PRO STATISTICS: 1990—Credited with one sack and recovered one fumble. 1991—Intercepted one pass for five yards and recovered two fumbles. 1993—Intercepted one pass for no yards and returned one kickoff for no yards. 1994—Credited with ½ sack. 1995—Credited with one sack and intercepted one pass for two yards.

MANUSKY, GREG   LB

PERSONAL: Born August 12, 1966, in Wilkes-Barre, Pa. ... 6-1/243.
HIGH SCHOOL: Dallas (Pa.).
COLLEGE: Colgate (degree in education, 1988).
TRANSACTIONS/CAREER NOTES: Signed as non-drafted free agent by Washington Redskins (May 3, 1988). ... On injured reserve with thigh injury (August 29-November 4, 1988). ... Granted unconditional free agency (February 1, 1991). ... Signed by Minnesota Vikings (March 27, 1991). ... On injured reserve with kidney injury (November 24-December 23, 1992). ... Granted unconditional free agency (March 1, 1993). ... Re-signed by Vikings for 1993 season. ... Released by Vikings (August 30, 1993). ... Re-signed by Vikings (August 31, 1993). ... Released by Vikings (August 22, 1994). ... Signed by Kansas City Chiefs (August 31, 1994). ... Granted unconditional free agency (February 16, 1996).
PLAYING EXPERIENCE: Washington NFL, 1988-1990; Minnesota NFL, 1991-1993; Kansas City NFL, 1994 and 1995. ... Games: 1988 (7), 1989 (16), 1990 (16), 1991 (16), 1992 (16), 1993 (16), 1994 (16), 1995 (16). Total: 114.
PRO STATISTICS: 1989—Recovered one fumble. 1994—Recovered two fumbles.

MARINO, DAN   QB   DOLPHINS

PERSONAL: Born September 15, 1961, in Pittsburgh. ... 6-4/224. ... Full name: Daniel Constantine Marino Jr. ... Brother-in-law of Bill Maas,

nose tackle, Kansas City Chiefs and Green Bay Packers (1984-1993).
HIGH SCHOOL: Central Catholic (Pittsburgh).
COLLEGE: Pittsburgh (degree in communications).
TRANSACTIONS/CAREER NOTES: Selected by Los Angeles Express in first round (first pick overall) of 1983 USFL draft. ... Selected by Miami Dolphins in first round (27th pick overall) of 1983 NFL draft. ... Signed by Dolphins (July 9, 1983). ... Left Dolphins camp voluntarily (July 25-August 31, 1985). ... Granted roster exemption (September 1-5, 1985). ... On injured reserve with Achilles tendon injury (October 13, 1993-remainder of season).
CHAMPIONSHIP GAME EXPERIENCE: Played in AFC championship game (1984, 1985 and 1992 seasons). ... Played in Super Bowl XIX (1984 season).
HONORS: Named quarterback on THE SPORTING NEWS college All-America first team (1981). ... Named NFL Rookie of the Year by THE SPORTING NEWS (1983). ... Named to play in Pro Bowl (1983 season); replaced by Bill Kenney due to injury. ... Named NFL Player of the Year by THE SPORTING NEWS (1984). ... Named quarterback on THE SPORTING NEWS NFL All-Pro team (1984-1986). ... Played in Pro Bowl (1984 and 1992 seasons). ... Named to play in Pro Bowl (1985 season); replaced by Ken O'Brien due to injury. ... Named to play in Pro Bowl (1986 season); replaced by Boomer Esiason due to injury. ... Named to play in Pro Bowl (1987 season); replaced by Jim Kelly due to injury. ... Named to play in Pro Bowl (1991 season); replaced by John Elway due to injury. Elway replaced by Ken O'Brien due to injury. ... Named to play in Pro Bowl (1994 season); replaced by Jeff Hostetler due to injury. ... Named to play in Pro Bowl (1995 season); replaced by Steve Bono due to injury.
RECORDS: Holds NFL career records for most touchdown passes—352; most yards passing—48,841; most passes attempted—6,531; most passes completed—3,913; most games with 400 or more yards passing—12; and most games with four or more touchdown passes—18. ... Holds NFL records for most seasons with 4,000 or more yards passing—6; most seasons with 3,000 or more yards passing—11; most consecutive seasons with 3,000 or more yards passing—9 (1984-1992); most games with 300 or more yards passing—52; and most consecutive games with four or more touchdown passes—4 (November 26-December 17, 1984). ... Holds NFL single-season records for most yards passing—5,084 (1984); most touchdown passes—48 (1984); most games with 400 or more yards passing—4 (1984); most games with four or more touchdown passes—6 (1984); and most consecutive games with four or more touchdown passes—4 (1984). ... Holds NFL rookie-season records for highest pass completion percentage—58.45 (1983); highest passer rating—96.0 (1983); and lowest percentage of passes intercepted—2.03 (1983). ... Shares NFL career records for most seasons leading league in pass attempts—4; most seasons leading league in pass completions—5; most seasons leading league in yards passing—5; most consecutive seasons leading league in pass completions—3 (1984-1986); and most consecutive games with 400 or more yards passing—2 (December 2 and 9, 1984). ... Shares NFL single-season record for most games with 300 or more yards passing—9 (1984).
POSTSEASON RECORDS: Holds NFL postseason career record for most consecutive games with one or more touchdown passes—13. ... Shares NFL postseason single-game record for pass attempts—64 (December 30, 1995, vs. Buffalo).
PRO STATISTICS: 1983—Fumbled five times and recovered two fumbles. 1984—Fumbled six times and recovered two fumbles for minus three yards. 1985—Fumbled nine times and recovered two fumbles for minus four yards. 1986—Fumbled eight times and recovered four fumbles for minus 12 yards. 1987—Fumbled five times and recovered four fumbles for minus 25 yards. 1988—Fumbled 10 times and recovered eight fumbles for minus 31 yards. 1989—Fumbled seven times. 1990—Fumbled three times and recovered two fumbles. 1991—Fumbled six times and recovered three fumbles for minus eight yards. 1992—Fumbled five times and recovered two fumbles for minus 12 yards. 1993—Fumbled four times and recovered two fumbles for minus 13 yards. 1994—Fumbled nine times and recovered three fumbles for minus four yards. 1995—Caught one pass for minus six yards, fumbled seven times and recovered three fumbles for minus 14 yards.
STATISTICAL PLATEAUS: 300-yard passing games: 1983 (1), 1984 (9), 1985 (6), 1986 (6), 1987 (4), 1988 (6), 1989 (5), 1990 (1), 1991 (3), 1992 (3), 1994 (5), 1995 (3). Total: 52.
MISCELLANEOUS: Selected by Kansas City Royals organization in fourth round of free-agent baseball draft (June 5, 1979); did not sign. Regular-season record as starting NFL quarterback: 116-68 (.630). ... Active AFC leader for career passing yards (48,841) and touchdown passes (352). ... Holds Miami Dolphins all-time records for most yards passing (48,841) and most touchdown passes (352).

Year Team	G	PASSING								RUSHING				TOTALS		
		Att.	Cmp.	Pct.	Yds.	TD	Int.	Avg.	Rat.	Att.	Yds.	Avg.	TD	TD	2pt.	Pts.
1983—Miami NFL	11	296	173	58.5	2210	20	6	7.47	96.0	28	45	1.6	2	2	...	12
1984—Miami NFL	16	*564	*362	64.2	*5084	*48	17	*9.02	*108.9	28	-7	-0.3	0	0	...	0
1985—Miami NFL	16	567	*336	59.3	*4137	*30	21	7.30	84.1	26	-24	-0.9	0	0	...	0
1986—Miami NFL	16	*623	*378	60.7	*4746	*44	23	7.62	92.5	12	-3	-0.3	0	0	...	0
1987—Miami NFL	12	444	263	59.2	3245	26	13	7.31	89.2	12	-5	-0.4	1	1	...	6
1988—Miami NFL	16	*606	*354	58.4	*4434	28	23	7.32	80.8	20	-17	-0.9	0	0	...	0
1989—Miami NFL	16	550	308	56.0	3997	24	22	7.27	76.9	14	-7	-0.5	2	2	...	12
1990—Miami NFL	16	531	306	57.6	3563	21	11	6.71	82.6	16	29	1.8	0	0	...	0
1991—Miami NFL	16	549	318	57.9	3970	25	13	7.23	85.8	27	32	1.2	1	1	...	6
1992—Miami NFL	16	*554	*330	59.6	*4116	24	16	7.43	85.1	20	66	3.3	0	0	...	0
1993—Miami NFL	5	150	91	60.7	1218	8	3	8.12	95.9	9	-4	-0.4	1	1	...	6
1994—Miami NFL	16	615	385	62.6	4453	30	17	7.24	89.2	22	-6	-0.3	1	1	0	6
1995—Miami NFL	14	482	309	64.1	3668	24	15	7.61	90.8	11	14	1.3	0	0	0	0
Pro totals (13 years)	186	6531	3913	59.9	48841	352	200	7.48	88.4	245	113	0.5	8	8	0	48

MARION, BROCK — S — COWBOYS

PERSONAL: Born June 11, 1970, in Bakersfield, Calif. ... 5-11/189. ... Full name: Brock Elliot Marion. ... Son of Jerry Marion, wide receiver, Pittsburgh Steelers (1967); and nephew of Brent McClanahan, running back, Minnesota Vikings (1973-79).
HIGH SCHOOL: West (Bakersfield, Calif.).
COLLEGE: Nevada.
TRANSACTIONS/CAREER NOTES: Selected by Dallas Cowboys in seventh round (196th overall) of 1993 NFL draft. ... Signed by Cowboys (July 14, 1993). ... Granted free agency (February 16, 1996).
CHAMPIONSHIP GAME EXPERIENCE: Played in NFC championship game (1993-1995 seasons). ... Member of Super Bowl championship team (1993 and 1995 seasons).
PRO STATISTICS: 1993—Recovered one fumble. 1994—Credited with one sack and returned two kickoffs for 39 yards. 1995—Returned one kickoff for 16 yards.

Year Team	G	INTERCEPTIONS			
		No.	Yds.	Avg.	TD
1993—Dallas NFL	15	1	2	2.0	0
1994—Dallas NFL	14	1	11	11.0	0
1995—Dallas NFL	16	6	40	6.7	1
Pro totals (3 years)	45	8	53	6.6	1

MARSH, CURTIS — WR/KR — JAGUARS

PERSONAL: Born November 24, 1970, in Simi Valley, Calif. ... 6-2/201. ... Full name: Curtis Joseph Marsh.
HIGH SCHOOL: Simi Valley (Calif.).
JUNIOR COLLEGE: Moorpark (Calif.) Community College.
COLLEGE: Utah.
TRANSACTIONS/CAREER NOTES: Selected by Jacksonville Jaguars in seventh round (219th pick overall) of 1995 NFL draft. ... Signed by Jaguars (June 1, 1995). ... Released by Jaguars (August 27, 1995). ... Re-signed by Jaguars to practice squad (August 28, 1995). ... Activated (October 17, 1995).
PRO STATISTICS: 1995—Recovered one fumble.

		RECEIVING				KICKOFF RETURNS				TOTALS		
Year Team	G	No.	Yds.	Avg.	TD	No.	Yds.	Avg.	TD	TD	2pt.	Pts. Fum.
1995—Jacksonville NFL	9	7	127	18.1	0	15	323	21.5	0	0	0	0 2

MARSHALL, ANTHONY — S — BEARS

PERSONAL: Born September 16, 1970, in Mobile, Ala. ... 6-1/205. ... Full name: Anthony Dewayne Marshall.
HIGH SCHOOL: LeFlore (Mobile, Ala.).
COLLEGE: Louisiana State.
TRANSACTIONS/CAREER NOTES: Signed as non-drafted free agent by Chicago Bears (April 28, 1994). ... Released by Bears (August 28, 1994). ... Re-signed by Bears to practice squad (August 30, 1994). ... Activated (December 9, 1994).
PLAYING EXPERIENCE: Chicago NFL, 1994 and 1995. ... Games: 1994 (3), 1995 (16). Total: 19.
PRO STATISTICS: 1995—Intercepted one pass for no yards and returned one blocked punt 11 yards for a touchdown.

MARSHALL, ARTHUR — WR/KR

PERSONAL: Born April 29, 1969, in Fort Gordon, Ga. ... 5-11/186. ... Full name: Arthur James Marshall.
HIGH SCHOOL: Hephzibah (Ga.).
COLLEGE: Georgia (degree in real estate).
TRANSACTIONS/CAREER NOTES: Signed as non-drafted free agent by Denver Broncos (April 30, 1992). ... Traded by Broncos to New York Giants for seventh-round pick (OL Tom Nalen) in 1994 draft (April 25, 1994). ... Granted free agency (February 17, 1995). ... Re-signed by Giants (June 12, 1995). ... Granted unconditional free agency (February 16, 1996).
PRO STATISTICS: 1992—Attempted one pass with one completion for 81 yards and a touchdown, fumbled three times and recovered one fumble. 1993—Attempted one pass for 30 yards and a touchdown. 1994—Fumbled once. 1995—Fumbled once.
STATISTICAL PLATEAUS: 100-yard receiving games: 1992 (1).

		RUSHING				RECEIVING				PUNT RETURNS				KICKOFF RETURNS				TOTALS		
Year Team	G	Att.	Yds.	Avg.	TD	No.	Yds.	Avg.	TD	No.	Yds.	Avg.	TD	No.	Yds.	Avg.	TD	TD	2pt.	Pts.
1992—Denver NFL	16	11	56	5.1	0	26	493	19.0	1	33	349	10.6	0	8	132	16.5	0	1	...	6
1993—Denver NFL	16	0	0	...	0	28	360	12.9	2	0	0	...	0	0	0	...	0	2	...	12
1994—New York Giants NFL	16	2	8	4.0	0	16	219	13.7	0	1	1	1.0	0	15	249	16.6	0	0	0	0
1995—New York Giants NFL	15	1	1	1.0	0	17	195	11.5	1	12	96	8.0	0	0	0	...	0	1	0	6
Pro totals (4 years)	63	14	65	4.7	0	87	1267	14.6	4	46	446	9.7	0	23	381	16.6	0	4	0	24

MARSHALL, WILBER — LB

PERSONAL: Born April 18, 1962, in Titusville, Fla. ... 6-1/231. ... Full name: Wilber Buddyhia Marshall.
HIGH SCHOOL: Astronaut (Titusville, Fla.).
COLLEGE: Florida.
TRANSACTIONS/CAREER NOTES: Selected by Tampa Bay Bandits in 1984 USFL territorial draft. ... Selected by Chicago Bears in first round (11th pick overall) of 1984 NFL draft. ... Signed by Bears (June 19, 1984). ... Granted free agency (February 1, 1988). ... Tendered offer sheet by Washington Redskins (March 15, 1988); Bears declined to match offer and received first-round pick (WR Wendell Davis) in 1988 draft and first-round pick (DE Trace Armstrong) in 1989 draft. ... Designated by Redskins as franchise player (February 25, 1993). ... Signed by Houston Oilers (July 2, 1993); Redskins received third-round pick (OG Joe Patton) in 1994 draft and fifth-round pick (TE Jamie Asher) in 1995 draft as compensation. ... Granted free agency (February 17, 1994). ... Signed by Arizona Cardinals (August 12, 1994). ... Granted unconditional free agency (February 17, 1995). ... Signed by New York Jets (August 25, 1995). ... Released by Jets (February 27, 1996).
CHAMPIONSHIP GAME EXPERIENCE: Played in NFC championship game (1984, 1985 and 1991 seasons). ... Member of Super Bowl championship team (1985 and 1991 seasons).
HONORS: Named linebacker on THE SPORTING NEWS college All-America second team (1983). ... Named outside linebacker on THE SPORTING NEWS NFL All-Pro team (1986). ... Played in Pro Bowl (1986, 1987 and 1992 seasons).
PRO STATISTICS: 1985—Ran two yards with lateral from kickoff return and recovered one fumble for eight yards. 1986—Recovered three fumbles for 12 yards and a touchdown. 1987—Rushed once for one yard and recovered one fumble. 1989—Recovered two fumbles for six yards. 1990—Recovered one fumble for four yards. 1991—Recovered one fumble. 1992—Recovered three fumbles for 35 yards. 1993—Recovered one fumble. 1994—Ran 14 yards with lateral from interception and recovered one fumble. 1995—Recovered two fumbles for 11 yards.

		INTERCEPTIONS				SACKS
Year Team	G	No.	Yds.	Avg.	TD	No.
1984—Chicago NFL	15	0	0	...	0	0.0
1985—Chicago NFL	16	4	23	5.8	0	6.0
1986—Chicago NFL	16	5	68	13.6	1	5.5
1987—Chicago NFL	12	0	0	...	0	5.0
1988—Washington NFL	16	3	61	20.3	0	4.0
1989—Washington NFL	16	1	18	18.0	0	4.0
1990—Washington NFL	16	1	6	6.0	0	5.0
1991—Washington NFL	16	5	75	15.0	1	5.5

M

Year Team	G	INTERCEPTIONS No.	Yds.	Avg.	TD	SACKS No.
1992—Washington NFL	16	2	20	10.0	1	6.0
1993—Houston NFL	10	0	0	...	0	2.0
1994—Arizona NFL	15	0	0	...	0	1.0
1995—New York Jets NFL	15	2	20	10.0	0	1.0
Pro totals (12 years)	179	23	291	12.7	3	45.0

MARTIN, CURTIS   RB   PATRIOTS

PERSONAL: Born May 1, 1973, in Pittsburgh. ... 5-11/203.
HIGH SCHOOL: Allderdice (Pittsburgh).
COLLEGE: Pittsburgh.
TRANSACTIONS/CAREER NOTES: Selected after junior season by New England Patriots in third round (74th pick overall) of 1995 NFL draft. ... Signed by Patriots (July 18, 1995).
HONORS: Named NFL Rookie of the Year by THE SPORTING NEWS (1995). ... Played in Pro Bowl (1995 season).
PRO STATISTICS: 1995—Recovered three fumbles.
STATISTICAL PLATEAUS: 100-yard rushing games: 1995 (9).

Year Team	G	RUSHING Att.	Yds.	Avg.	TD	RECEIVING No.	Yds.	Avg.	TD	TOTALS TD	2pt.	Pts.	Fum.
1995—New England NFL	16	368	1487	4.0	14	30	261	8.7	1	15	1	92	5

MARTIN, EMERSON   G   STEELERS

PERSONAL: Born May 6, 1970, in Elizabethtown, N.C. ... 6-3/302. ... Full name: Emerson Floyd Martin.
HIGH SCHOOL: East Bladen (Elizabethtown, N.C.).
COLLEGE: Catawba (N.C.), then Hampton (Va.).
TRANSACTIONS/CAREER NOTES: Signed as non-drafted free agent by Kansas City Chiefs (May 2, 1994). ... Released by Chiefs (August 29, 1994). ... Re-signed by Chiefs to practice squad (September 7, 1994). ... Released by Chiefs (September 28, 1994). ... Re-signed by Chiefs to practice squad (October 12, 1994). ... Granted free agency after 1994 season. ... Signed by Carolina Panthers (January 10, 1995). ... Released by Panthers (September 15, 1995). ... Re-signed by Panthers to practice squad (September 21, 1995). ... Released by Panthers (October 10, 1995). ... Signed by Pittsburgh Steelers to practice squad (October 24, 1995).
PLAYING EXPERIENCE: Carolina NFL, 1995. ... Games: 1995 (2).

MARTIN, KELVIN   WR/KR

M

PERSONAL: Born May 14, 1965, in San Diego. ... 5-9/162. ... Full name: Kelvin Brian Martin.
HIGH SCHOOL: Ribault (Jacksonville).
COLLEGE: Boston College (degree in speech communication, 1987).
TRANSACTIONS/CAREER NOTES: Selected by Dallas Cowboys in fourth round (95th pick overall) of 1987 NFL draft. ... Signed by Cowboys (July 13, 1987). ... On injured reserve with leg injury (September 15-November 14, 1987). ... Crossed picket line during players strike (October 14, 1987). ... On injured reserve with knee injury (November 21, 1989-remainder of season). ... Granted unconditional free agency (March 1, 1993). ... Signed by Seattle Seahawks (April 1, 1993). ... Selected by Jacksonville Jaguars from Seahawks in NFL expansion draft (February 15, 1995). ... Released by Jaguars (May 30, 1995). ... Signed by Philadelphia Eagles (June 12, 1995). ... On injured reserve with foot injury (December 13, 1995-remainder of season). ... Granted unconditional free agency (February 16, 1996).
CHAMPIONSHIP GAME EXPERIENCE: Played in NFC championship game (1992 season). ... Member of Super Bowl championship team (1992 season).
HONORS: Named wide receiver on THE SPORTING NEWS college All-America first team (1985).
PRO STATISTICS: 1987—Fumbled once. 1988—Fumbled twice. 1990—Fumbled twice and recovered one fumble. 1991—Fumbled twice and recovered one fumble. 1992—Fumbled twice. 1993—Fumbled once and recovered one fumble. 1994—Fumbled twice and recovered one fumble. 1995—Fumbled twice.
STATISTICAL PLATEAUS: 100-yard receiving games: 1994 (1).

Year Team	G	RUSHING Att.	Yds.	Avg.	TD	RECEIVING No.	Yds.	Avg.	TD	PUNT RETURNS No.	Yds.	Avg.	TD	KICKOFF RETURNS No.	Yds.	Avg.	TD	TOTALS TD	2pt.	Pts.
1987—Dallas NFL	7	0	0	...	0	5	103	20.6	0	22	216	9.8	0	12	237	19.8	0	0	...	0
1988—Dallas NFL	16	4	-4	-1.0	0	49	622	12.7	3	44	360	8.2	0	12	210	17.5	0	3	...	18
1989—Dallas NFL	11	0	0	...	0	46	644	14.0	2	4	32	8.0	0	0	0	...	0	2	...	12
1990—Dallas NFL	16	4	-2	-0.5	0	64	732	11.4	0	5	46	9.2	0	0	0	...	0	0	...	0
1991—Dallas NFL	16	0	0	...	0	16	243	15.2	0	21	244	11.6	1	3	47	15.7	0	1	...	6
1992—Dallas NFL	16	2	13	6.5	0	32	359	11.2	3	42	*532	12.7	†2	24	503	21.0	0	5	...	30
1993—Seattle NFL	16	1	0	0.0	0	57	798	14.0	5	32	270	8.4	0	3	38	12.7	0	5	...	30
1994—Seattle NFL	16	0	0	...	0	56	681	12.2	1	33	280	8.5	0	2	30	15.0	0	1	0	6
1995—Philadelphia NFL	9	0	0	...	0	17	206	12.1	0	17	214	12.6	0	20	388	19.4	0	0	0	0
Pro totals (9 years)	123	11	7	0.6	0	342	4388	12.8	14	220	2194	10.0	3	76	1453	19.1	0	17	0	102

MARTIN, TONY   WR   CHARGERS

PERSONAL: Born September 5, 1965, in Miami. ... 6-0/181. ... Full name: Tony Derrick Martin.
HIGH SCHOOL: Miami Northwestern.
COLLEGE: Bishop (Texas), then Mesa State (Colo.).
TRANSACTIONS/CAREER NOTES: Selected by New York Jets in fifth round (126th pick overall) of 1989 NFL draft. ... Released by Jets (September 4, 1989). ... Signed by Miami Dolphins to developmental squad (September 5, 1989). ... Activated (December 23, 1989). ... On inactive list for one game (1989). ... Granted free agency (February 1, 1992). ... Re-signed by Dolphins (March 10, 1992). ... Traded by Dolphins to San Diego Chargers for fourth-round pick (traded to Arizona) in 1994 draft (March 24, 1994).
CHAMPIONSHIP GAME EXPERIENCE: Played in AFC championship game (1992 and 1994 seasons). ... Played in Super Bowl XXIX (1994 season).

RECORDS: Shares NFL record for longest pass reception (from Stan Humphries)—99 yards, touchdown (September 18, 1994, at Seattle).
PRO STATISTICS: 1990—Fumbled four times and recovered two fumbles. 1991—Fumbled twice. 1992—Attempted one pass without a completion, fumbled twice and recovered one fumble. 1993—Fumbled once. 1994—Attempted one pass without a completion and fumbled twice. 1995—Attempted one pass without a completion and fumbled three times.
STATISTICAL PLATEAUS: 100-yard receiving games: 1991 (2), 1993 (1), 1994 (2), 1995 (4). Total: 9.

		RUSHING				RECEIVING				PUNT RETURNS				KICKOFF RETURNS				TOTALS		
Year Team	G	Att.	Yds.	Avg.	TD	No.	Yds.	Avg.	TD	No.	Yds.	Avg.	TD	No.	Yds.	Avg.	TD	TD	2pt.	Pts.
1990—Miami NFL	16	1	8	8.0	0	29	388	13.4	2	26	140	5.4	0	0	0	...	0	2	...	12
1991—Miami NFL	16	0	0	...	0	27	434	16.1	2	1	10	10.0	0	0	0	...	0	2	...	12
1992—Miami NFL	16	1	-2	-2.0	0	33	553	16.8	2	1	0	0.0	0	0	0	...	0	2	...	12
1993—Miami NFL	12	1	6	6.0	0	20	347	17.4	3	0	0	...	0	0	0	...	0	3	...	18
1994—San Diego NFL	16	2	-9	-4.5	0	50	885	17.7	7	0	0	...	0	8	167	20.9	0	7	0	42
1995—San Diego NFL	16	0	0	...	0	90	1224	13.6	6	0	0	...	0	0	0	...	0	6	0	36
Pro totals (6 years)	92	5	3	0.6	0	249	3831	15.4	22	28	150	5.4	0	8	167	20.9	0	22	0	132

MARTIN, WAYNE   DT   SAINTS

PERSONAL: Born October 26, 1965, in Forrest City, Ark. ... 6-5/275. ... Full name: Gerald Wayne Martin.
HIGH SCHOOL: Cross Country (Cherry Valley, Ark.).
COLLEGE: Arkansas (degree in criminal justice, 1990).
TRANSACTIONS/CAREER NOTES: Selected by New Orleans Saints in first round (19th pick overall) of 1989 NFL draft. ... Signed by Saints (August 10, 1989). ... On injured reserve with knee injury (December 19, 1990-remainder of season). ... Granted free agency (March 1, 1993). ... Tendered offer sheet by Washington Redskins (April 8, 1993). ... Offer matched by Saints (April 14, 1993).
HONORS: Named defensive lineman on THE SPORTING NEWS college All-America first team (1988). ... Played in Pro Bowl (1994 season).
PRO STATISTICS: 1989—Recovered two fumbles. 1991—Recovered one fumble. 1992—Recovered two fumbles. 1993—Recovered two fumbles for seven yards. 1995—Intercepted one pass for 12 yards and recovered one fumble.

Year Team	G	SACKS
1989—New Orleans NFL	16	2.5
1990—New Orleans NFL	11	4.0
1991—New Orleans NFL	16	3.5
1992—New Orleans NFL	16	15.5
1993—New Orleans NFL	16	5.0
1994—New Orleans NFL	16	10.0
1995—New Orleans NFL	16	13.0
Pro totals (7 years)	107	53.5

MARTS, LONNIE   LB   BUCCANEERS

PERSONAL: Born November 10, 1968, in New Orleans. ... 6-2/236.
HIGH SCHOOL: St. Augustine (New Orleans).
COLLEGE: Tulane (degree in sociology).
TRANSACTIONS/CAREER NOTES: Signed as non-drafted free agent by Kansas City Chiefs (May 1, 1990). ... On injured reserve with ankle injury (September 8, 1990-entire season). ... Granted unconditional free agency (February 17, 1994). ... Signed by Tampa Bay Buccaneers (March 21, 1994).
CHAMPIONSHIP GAME EXPERIENCE: Played in AFC championship game (1993 season).
PRO STATISTICS: 1991—Recovered one fumble. 1992—Recovered one fumble for two yards. 1993—Returned one kickoff for no yards and recovered one fumble. 1994—Recovered two fumbles. 1995—Recovered one fumble.

		INTERCEPTIONS				SACKS
Year Team	G	No.	Yds.	Avg.	TD	No.
1990—Kansas City NFL		Did not play—injured.				
1991—Kansas City NFL	16	0	0	...	0	1.0
1992—Kansas City NFL	15	1	36	36.0	1	0.0
1993—Kansas City NFL	16	1	20	20.0	0	2.0
1994—Tampa Bay NFL	16	0	0	...	0	0.0
1995—Tampa Bay NFL	15	1	8	8.0	0	0.0
Pro totals (5 years)	78	2	28	14.0	0	3.0

MARYLAND, RUSSELL   DT   RAIDERS

PERSONAL: Born March 22, 1969, in Chicago. ... 6-1/279.
HIGH SCHOOL: Whitney-Young (Chicago).
COLLEGE: Miami, Fla. (degree in psychology, 1990).
TRANSACTIONS/CAREER NOTES: Selected by Dallas Cowboys in first round (first pick overall) of 1991 NFL draft. ... Signed by Cowboys (April 22, 1991). ... Granted unconditional free agency (February 16, 1996). ... Signed by Oakland Raiders (February 21, 1996).
CHAMPIONSHIP GAME EXPERIENCE: Played in NFC championship game (1992-1995 seasons). ... Member of Super Bowl championship team (1992, 1993 and 1995 seasons).
HONORS: Named defensive tackle on THE SPORTING NEWS college All-America second team (1989). ... Outland Trophy winner (1990). ... Named defensive lineman on THE SPORTING NEWS college All-America first team (1990). ... Played in Pro Bowl (1993 season).
PRO STATISTICS: 1992—Recovered two fumbles for 26 yards and a touchdown. 1993—Recovered two fumbles. 1994—Recovered one fumble.

Year Team	G	SACKS
1991—Dallas NFL	16	4.5
1992—Dallas NFL	14	2.5
1993—Dallas NFL	16	2.5
1994—Dallas NFL	16	3.0
1995—Dallas NFL	13	2.0
Pro totals (5 years)	75	14.5

M

MASON, EDDIE   LB   JETS

PERSONAL: Born January 9, 1972, in Siler City, N.C. ... 6-0/230. ... Full name: Eddie Lee Mason.
HIGH SCHOOL: Jordan-Matthews (Siler City, N.C.).
COLLEGE: North Carolina.
TRANSACTIONS/CAREER NOTES: Selected by New York Jets in sixth round (178th pick overall) of 1995 NFL draft. ... Signed by Jets (June 14, 1995).
PLAYING EXPERIENCE: New York Jets NFL, 1995. ... Games: (15).

MASSEY, ROBERT   CB   JAGUARS

PERSONAL: Born February 17, 1967, in Rock Hill, S.C. ... 5-11/195. ... Full name: Robert Lee Massey.
HIGH SCHOOL: Garinger (Charlotte).
COLLEGE: North Carolina Central (degree in history, 1990).
TRANSACTIONS/CAREER NOTES: Selected by New Orleans Saints in second round (46th pick overall) of 1989 NFL draft. ... Signed by Saints (July 30, 1989). ... Granted free agency (February 1, 1991). ... Rights traded by Saints to Phoenix Cardinals for G Derek Kennard and fifth-round pick in 1992 draft (August 19, 1991). ... On injured reserve with viral hepatitis (October 2-30, 1991). ... Granted free agency (March 1, 1993). ... Re-signed by Cardinals (September 24, 1993). ... Granted roster exemption (September 25-October 19, 1994). ... Granted unconditional free agency (February 17, 1994). ... Signed by Detroit Lions (March 12, 1994). ... Released by Lions (March 29, 1996). ... Signed by Jacksonville Jaguars (April 24, 1996).
HONORS: Played in Pro Bowl (1992 season).
RECORDS: Shares NFL single-game record for most touchdowns scored by interception—2 (October 4, 1992, vs. Washington).
PRO STATISTICS: 1989—Ran 54 yards with a lateral from punt return. 1990—Recovered two fumbles. 1991—Recovered one fumble for two yards. 1993—Recovered two fumbles. 1994—Returned one punt for three yards and fumbled once.

		INTERCEPTIONS			
Year Team	G	No.	Yds.	Avg.	TD
1989—New Orleans NFL	16	5	26	5.2	0
1990—New Orleans NFL	16	0	0	...	0
1991—Phoenix NFL	12	0	0	...	0
1992—Phoenix NFL	15	5	147	29.4	*3
1993—Phoenix NFL	10	0	0	...	0
1994—Detroit NFL	16	4	25	6.3	0
1995—Detroit NFL	16	0	0	...	0
Pro totals (7 years)	101	14	198	14.2	3

MASTON, LE'SHAI   RB   JAGUARS

PERSONAL: Born October 7, 1970, in Dallas. ... 6-0/229. ... Full name: Le'Shai Edwoin Maston. ... Name pronounced le-SHAY
HIGH SCHOOL: David W. Carter (Dallas).
COLLEGE: Baylor.
TRANSACTIONS/CAREER NOTES: Signed as non-drafted free agent by Houston Oilers (June 30, 1993). ... Released by Oilers (August 30, 1993). ... Re-signed by Oilers to practice squad (August 31, 1993). ... Activated (September 10, 1993). ... Selected by Jacksonville Jaguars from Oilers in NFL expansion draft (February 15, 1995). ... Granted free agency (February 16, 1996).
PRO STATISTICS: 1995—Returned one kickoff for five yards and recovered one fumble for four yards.

		RUSHING				RECEIVING				TOTALS			
Year Team	G	Att.	Yds.	Avg.	TD	No.	Yds.	Avg.	TD	TD	2pt.	Pts.	Fum.
1993—Houston NFL	10	1	10	10.0	0	1	14	14.0	0	0	...	0	1
1994—Houston NFL	5	0	0	...	0	2	12	6.0	0	0	0	0	0
1995—Jacksonville NFL	16	41	186	4.5	0	18	131	7.3	0	0	0	0	3
Pro totals (3 years)	31	42	196	4.7	0	21	157	7.5	0	0	0	0	4

MATHEWS, JASON   OT   COLTS

PERSONAL: Born February 9, 1971, in Orange, Texas. ... 6-5/288.
HIGH SCHOOL: Bridge City (Texas).
COLLEGE: Texas A&M.
TRANSACTIONS/CAREER NOTES: Selected by Indianapolis Colts in third round (67th pick overall) of 1994 NFL draft. ... Signed by Colts (July 23, 1994).
PLAYING EXPERIENCE: Indianapolis NFL, 1994 and 1995. ... Games: 1994 (10), 1995 (16). Total: 26.
CHAMPIONSHIP GAME EXPERIENCE: Played in AFC championship game (1995 season).

MATHIS, TERANCE   WR/KR   FALCONS

PERSONAL: Born June 7, 1967, in Detroit. ... 5-10/180.
HIGH SCHOOL: Redan (Stone Mountain, Ga.).
COLLEGE: New Mexico.
TRANSACTIONS/CAREER NOTES: Selected by New York Jets in sixth round (140th pick overall) of 1990 NFL draft. ... Signed by Jets (July 12, 1990). ... Granted unconditional free agency (February 17, 1994). ... Signed by Atlanta Falcons (May 3, 1994). ... Granted unconditional free agency (February 16, 1996). ... Re-signed by Falcons (April 30, 1996).
HONORS: Named wide receiver on THE SPORTING NEWS college All-America first team (1989). ... Played in Pro Bowl (1994 season).
PRO STATISTICS: 1990—Fumbled once. 1991—Fumbled four times and recovered one fumble. 1992—Fumbled twice and recovered one fumble. 1993—Fumbled five times and recovered one fumble. 1994—Recovered one fumble. 1995—Fumbled once.
STATISTICAL PLATEAUS: 100-yard receiving games: 1992 (1), 1994 (5), 1995 (2). Total: 8.

Year Team	G	RUSHING				RECEIVING				PUNT RETURNS				KICKOFF RETURNS				TOTALS		
		Att.	Yds.	Avg.	TD	No.	Yds.	Avg.	TD	No.	Yds.	Avg.	TD	No.	Yds.	Avg.	TD	TD	2pt.	Pts.
1990—New York Jets NFL.....	16	2	9	4.5	0	19	245	12.9	0	11	165	15.0	†1	43	787	18.3	0	1	...	6
1991—New York Jets NFL.....	16	1	19	19.0	0	28	329	11.8	1	23	157	6.8	0	29	599	20.7	0	1	...	6
1992—New York Jets NFL.....	16	3	25	8.3	1	22	316	14.4	3	2	24	12.0	0	28	492	17.6	0	4	...	24
1993—New York Jets NFL.....	16	2	20	10.0	1	24	352	14.7	0	14	99	7.1	0	7	102	14.6	0	1	...	6
1994—Atlanta NFL...............	16	0	0	...	0	111	1342	12.1	11	0	0	...	0	0	0	...	0	11	2	70
1995—Atlanta NFL...............	14	0	0	...	0	78	1039	13.3	9	0	0	...	0	0	0	...	0	9	3	60
Pro totals (6 years)	94	8	73	9.1	2	282	3623	12.9	24	50	445	8.9	1	107	1980	18.5	0	27	5	172

MATICH, TREVOR   C

PERSONAL: Born October 9, 1961, in Sacramento. ... 6-4/297. ... Full name: Trevor Anthony Matich.
HIGH SCHOOL: Rio Americano (Sacramento).
COLLEGE: Brigham Young.
TRANSACTIONS/CAREER NOTES: Selected by Houston Gamblers in 10th round (139th pick overall) of 1985 USFL draft. ... Selected by New England Patriots in first round (28th pick overall) of 1985 NFL draft. ... Signed by Patriots (July 30, 1985). ... On injured reserve with ankle injury (October 12, 1985-remainder of season. ... On injured reserve with broken foot (September 7-November 7, 1987). ... Released by Patriots (September 7, 1989). ... Signed by Detroit Lions (September 14, 1989). ... Granted unconditional free agency (February 1, 1990). ... Signed by New York Jets (March 19, 1990). ... Granted unconditional free agency (February 1-April 1, 1991). ... Re-signed by Jets for 1991 season. ... Granted unconditional free agency (February 1, 1992). ... Signed by Indianapolis Colts (March 20, 1992). ... Granted unconditional free agency (February 17, 1994). ... Signed by Washington Redskins (April 8, 1994). ... Granted unconditional free agency (February 16, 1996).
PLAYING EXPERIENCE: New England NFL, 1985-1988; Detroit NFL, 1989; New York Jets NFL, 1990 and 1991; Indianapolis NFL, 1992 and 1993; Washington NFL, 1994 and 1995. ... Games: 1985 (1), 1986 (11), 1987 (6), 1988 (8), 1989 (11), 1990 (16), 1991 (15), 1992 (16), 1993 (16), 1994 (16), 1995 (16). Total: 132.
PRO STATISTICS: 1990—Recovered one fumble. 1991—Caught three passes for 23 yards and one touchdown. 1995—Fumbled once for minus two yards.

MATTHEWS, AUBREY   WR   LIONS

PERSONAL: Born September 15, 1962, in Pascagoula, Miss. ... 5-7/165. ... Full name: Aubrey Derron Matthews.
HIGH SCHOOL: Moss Point (Miss.).
JUNIOR COLLEGE: Gulf Coast Community College (Fla.).
COLLEGE: Delta State (Miss.).
TRANSACTIONS/CAREER NOTES: Signed by Jacksonville Bulls of USFL (January 10, 1984). ... On developmental squad for two games (April 10-25, 1984). ... On developmental squad for one game (June 10-15, 1985). ... Granted free agency when USFL suspended operations (August 7, 1986). ... Signed by Atlanta Falcons (August 18, 1986). ... Granted roster exemption (August 18-22, 1986). ... On injured reserve with hamstring injury (August 26-November 28, 1986). ... Released by Falcons (September 29, 1988). ... Signed by Green Bay Packers (November 2, 1988). ... Granted unconditional free agency (February 1, 1990). ... Signed by Detroit Lions (March 2, 1990). ... On injured reserve with knee injury (September 2, 1991-January 3, 1992). ... Granted unconditional free agency (February 1-April 1, 1992). ... Re-signed by Lions for 1992 season. ... Granted unconditional free agency (March 1, 1993). ... Re-signed by Lions (July 17, 1993). ... Granted unconditional free agency (February 17, 1994). ... Re-signed by Lions (July 15, 1994).
CHAMPIONSHIP GAME EXPERIENCE: Played in NFC championship game (1991 season).
PRO STATISTICS: USFL: 1984—Recovered four fumbles. 1985—Recovered two fumbles. NFL: 1987—Recovered one fumble. 1988—Returned six punts for 26 yards.
STATISTICAL PLATEAUS: 100-yard receiving games: 1987 (1).

Year Team	G	RUSHING				RECEIVING				KICKOFF RETURNS				TOTALS		
		Att.	Yds.	Avg.	TD	No.	Yds.	Avg.	TD	No.	Yds.	Avg.	TD	TD	2pt.	Pts. Fum.
1984—Jacksonville USFL...............	16	3	5	1.7	0	27	406	15.0	1	29	623	21.5	0	1	0	6 5
1985—Jacksonville USFL...............	16	0	0	...	0	25	271	10.8	5	19	366	19.3	0	5	0	30 2
1986—Atlanta NFL	4	1	12	12.0	0	1	25	25.0	0	3	42	14.0	0	0	...	0 0
1987—Atlanta NFL	12	1	-4	-4.0	0	32	537	16.8	3	0	0	...	0	3	...	18 2
1988—Atlanta NFL	4	0	0	...	0	5	64	12.8	0	0	0	...	0	0	...	0 0
—Green Bay NFL	7	3	3	1.0	0	15	167	11.1	2	0	0	...	0	2	...	12 0
1989—Green Bay NFL	13	0	0	...	0	18	200	11.1	0	0	0	...	0	0	...	0 0
1990—Detroit NFL..........................	13	0	0	...	0	30	349	11.6	1	0	0	...	0	1	...	6 2
1991—Detroit NFL..........................	1	0	0	...	0	3	21	7.0	0	0	0	...	0	0	...	0 0
1992—Detroit NFL..........................	13	0	0	...	0	9	137	15.2	0	0	0	...	0	0	...	0 0
1993—Detroit NFL..........................	14	2	7	3.5	0	11	171	15.6	0	0	0	...	0	0	...	0 0
1994—Detroit NFL..........................	14	0	0	...	0	29	359	12.4	3	0	0	...	0	3	0	18 1
1995—Detroit NFL..........................	11	0	0	...	0	4	41	10.3	0	0	0	...	0	0	...	0 0
USFL totals (2 years)................	32	3	5	1.7	0	52	677	13.0	6	48	989	20.6	0	6	0	36 7
NFL totals (10 years).................	106	7	18	2.6	0	157	2071	13.2	9	3	42	14.0	0	9	0	54 5
Pro totals (12 years).................	138	10	23	2.3	0	209	2748	13.2	15	51	1031	20.2	0	15	0	90 12

MATTHEWS, BRUCE   G/C   OILERS

PERSONAL: Born August 8, 1961, in Arcadia, Calif. ... 6-5/298. ... Full name: Bruce Rankin Matthews. ... Son of Clay Matthews Sr., end, San Francisco 49ers (1950 and 1953-1955); and brother of Clay Matthews Jr., linebacker, Atlanta Falcons.
HIGH SCHOOL: Arcadia (Calif.).
COLLEGE: Southern California (degree in industrial engineering, 1983).
TRANSACTIONS/CAREER NOTES: Selected by Los Angeles Express in 1983 USFL territorial draft. ... Selected by Houston Oilers in first round (ninth pick overall) of 1983 NFL draft. ... Signed by Oilers (July 24, 1983). ... Granted free agency (February 1, 1987). ... On reserve/unsigned list (August 31-November 3, 1987). ... Re-signed by Oilers (November 4, 1987). ... Granted roster exemption (November 4-7, 1987). ... Granted unconditional free agency (February 17, 1995). ... Re-signed by Oilers (August 8, 1995).
PLAYING EXPERIENCE: Houston NFL, 1983-1995. ... Games: 1983 (16), 1984 (16), 1985 (16), 1986 (16), 1987 (8), 1988 (16), 1989 (16), 1990 (16), 1991 (16), 1992 (16), 1993 (16), 1994 (16), 1995 (16). Total: 200.

HONORS: Named guard on THE SPORTING NEWS college All-America first team (1982). ... Named guard on THE SPORTING NEWS NFL All-Pro team (1988-1990 and 1992). ... Played in Pro Bowl (1988-1994 seasons). ... Named center on THE SPORTING NEWS NFL All-Pro team (1993). ... Named to play in Pro Bowl (1995 season); replaced by Will Shields due to injury.

PRO STATISTICS: 1985—Recovered three fumbles. 1986—Recovered one fumble for seven yards. 1989—Fumbled twice and recovered one fumble for minus 29 yards. 1990—Recovered one fumble. 1991—Fumbled once and recovered one fumble for minus three yards. 1994—Fumbled twice.

MATTHEWS, CLAY — LB — FALCONS

PERSONAL: Born March 15, 1956, in Palo Alto, Calif. ... 6-2/245. ... Full name: William Clay Matthews Jr. ... Son of Clay Matthews Sr., end, San Francisco 49ers (1950 and 1953-1955); and brother of Bruce Matthews, guard/center, Houston Oilers.

HIGH SCHOOL: Arcadia (Calif.) and New Trier East (Winnetka, Ill.).

COLLEGE: Southern California (degree in business administration, 1978).

TRANSACTIONS/CAREER NOTES: Selected by Cleveland Browns in first round (12th pick overall) of 1978 NFL draft. ... On injured reserve with broken ankle (September 16-December 31, 1982). ... Granted free agency (February 1, 1990). ... Re-signed by Browns (August 30, 1990). ... Granted roster exemption (September 3-8, 1990). ... Granted free agency (February 1, 1991). ... Re-signed by Browns (1991). ... Granted free agency (February 1, 1992). ... Re-signed by Browns (August 1, 1992). ... Granted unconditional free agency (March 1, 1993). ... Re-signed by Browns (July 29, 1993). ... Granted unconditional free agency (February 17, 1994). ... Signed by Atlanta Falcons (June 22, 1994). ... Granted unconditional free agency (February 16, 1996). ... Re-signed by Falcons (May 14, 1996).

CHAMPIONSHIP GAME EXPERIENCE: Played in AFC championship game (1986, 1987 and 1989 seasons).

HONORS: Named linebacker on THE SPORTING NEWS college All-America first team (1977). ... Named outside linebacker on THE SPORTING NEWS NFL All-Pro team (1984). ... Played in Pro Bowl (1985 and 1987-1989 seasons).

PRO STATISTICS: 1979—Recovered two fumbles. 1980—Recovered one fumble. 1981—Recovered two fumbles for 16 yards. 1984—Recovered one fumble. 1985—Recovered one fumble for 15 yards. 1987—Recovered two fumbles. 1988—Recovered two fumbles. 1989—Fumbled once and recovered two fumbles for minus two yards and a touchdown. 1995—Recovered one fumble.

MISCELLANEOUS: Holds Cleveland Browns all-time record for most sacks (63.5).

		INTERCEPTIONS				SACKS
Year Team	G	No.	Yds.	Avg.	TD	No.
1978—Cleveland NFL	15	1	5	5.0	0	...
1979—Cleveland NFL	16	1	30	30.0	0	...
1980—Cleveland NFL	14	1	6	6.0	0	...
1981—Cleveland NFL	16	2	14	7.0	0	...
1982—Cleveland NFL	2	0	0	...	0	0.0
1983—Cleveland NFL	16	0	0	...	0	7.0
1984—Cleveland NFL	16	0	0	...	0	12.0
1985—Cleveland NFL	14	0	0	...	0	6.0
1986—Cleveland NFL	16	2	12	6.0	0	1.0
1987—Cleveland NFL	12	3	62	20.7	1	3.0
1988—Cleveland NFL	16	0	0	...	0	6.0
1989—Cleveland NFL	16	1	25	25.0	0	4.0
1990—Cleveland NFL	16	0	0	...	0	3.5
1991—Cleveland NFL	15	1	35	35.0	0	6.5
1992—Cleveland NFL	16	1	6	6.0	0	9.0
1993—Cleveland NFL	16	1	10	10.0	0	5.5
1994—Atlanta NFL	15	0	0	...	0	1.0
1995—Atlanta NFL	16	2	1	.5	0	0.0
Pro totals (18 years)	263	16	206	12.9	1	64.5

MATTHEWS, SHANE — QB

PERSONAL: Born June 1, 1970, in Pascagoula, Miss. ... 6-3/196. ... Full name: Michael Shane Matthews.

HIGH SCHOOL: Pascagoula (Miss.).

COLLEGE: Florida.

TRANSACTIONS/CAREER NOTES: Signed as non-drafted free agent by Chicago Bears (April 29, 1993). ... Active for two games (1994); did not play. ... Released by Bears (September 15, 1995). ... Re-signed by Bears (February 12, 1996). ... Released by Bears (June 7, 1996).

MAUMALANGA, CHRIS — DT — CARDINALS

PERSONAL: Born December 15, 1971, in Redwood City, Calif. ... 6-2/292. ... Name pronounced MAL-ma-longa.

HIGH SCHOOL: Bishop Montgomery (Torrance, Calif.).

COLLEGE: Kansas.

TRANSACTIONS/CAREER NOTES: Selected by New York Giants in fourth round (128th pick overall) of 1994 NFL draft. ... Signed by Giants (July 18, 1994). ... Released by Giants (August 27, 1995). ... Signed by Arizona Cardinals (September 15, 1995). ... Released by Cardinals (September 25, 1995). ... Re-signed by Cardinals (October 2, 1995).

PLAYING EXPERIENCE: New York Giants NFL, 1994; Arizona NFL, 1995. ... 1994 (7), 1995 (6). Total: 13.

MAWAE, KEVIN — C — SEAHAWKS

PERSONAL: Born January 23, 1971, in Leesville, La. ... 6-4/296. ... Full name: Kevin James Mawae. ... Name pronounced ma-WHY.

HIGH SCHOOL: Leesville (La.).

COLLEGE: Louisiana State.

TRANSACTIONS/CAREER NOTES: Selected by Seattle Seahawks in second round (36th pick overall) of 1994 NFL draft. ... Signed by Seahawks (July 21, 1994).

PLAYING EXPERIENCE: Seattle NFL, 1994 and 1995. ... Games: 1994 (14), 1995 (16). Total: 30.

PRO STATISTICS: 1994—Recovered one fumble.

M

MAXIE, BRETT   S   PANTHERS

PERSONAL: Born January 13, 1962, in Dallas. ... 6-2/210. ... Full name: Brett Derrell Maxie.
HIGH SCHOOL: James Madison (Dallas).
COLLEGE: Texas Southern.
TRANSACTIONS/CAREER NOTES: Signed as non-drafted free agent by New Orleans Saints (June 21, 1985). ... Released by Saints (September 2, 1985). ... Re-signed by Saints (September 3, 1985). ... Granted free agency (February 1, 1990). ... Re-signed by Saints (August 13, 1990). ... Granted free agency (February 1, 1992). ... Re-signed by Saints (August 22, 1992). ... On injured reserve with knee injury (November 19, 1992-remainder of season). ... On injured reserve with knee injury (September 14, 1993-remainder of season). ... Granted unconditional free agency (February 17, 1994). ... Signed by Atlanta Falcons (September 27, 1994). ... Granted unconditional free agency (February 17, 1995). ... Signed by Carolina Panthers (March 9, 1995).
PRO STATISTICS: 1985—Recovered one fumble. 1986—Recovered one fumble. 1987—Credited with a safety and returned one punt for 12 yards. 1989—Recovered one fumble. 1991—Recovered one fumble. 1992—Recovered one fumble. 1995—Recovered one fumble.
MISCELLANEOUS: Holds Carolina Panthers all-time record for most interceptions (6).

		INTERCEPTIONS				SACKS
Year Team	G	No.	Yds.	Avg.	TD	No.
1985—New Orleans NFL	16	0	0	...	0	0.0
1986—New Orleans NFL	15	2	15	7.5	0	0.0
1987—New Orleans NFL	12	3	17	5.7	0	2.0
1988—New Orleans NFL	16	0	0	...	0	0.0
1989—New Orleans NFL	16	3	41	13.7	1	0.0
1990—New Orleans NFL	16	2	88	44.0	1	0.0
1991—New Orleans NFL	16	3	33	11.0	1	0.0
1992—New Orleans NFL	10	2	12	6.0	0	1.0
1993—New Orleans NFL	1	0	0	...	0	0.0
1994—Atlanta NFL	4	0	0	...	0	0.0
1995—Carolina NFL	16	6	59	9.8	0	0.0
Pro totals (11 years)	138	21	265	12.6	3	3.0

MAY, CHAD   QB   VIKINGS

PERSONAL: Born September 28, 1971, in West Covina, Calif. ... 6-1/219.
HIGH SCHOOL: Damien (La Verne, Calif.).
COLLEGE: Cal State Fullerton, then Kansas State.
TRANSACTIONS/CAREER NOTES: Selected by Minnesota Vikings in fourth round (111th pick overall) of 1995 NFL draft. ... Signed by Vikings (July 24, 1995). ... Inactive for 16 games (1995).

MAY, DEEMS   TE   CHARGERS

PERSONAL: Born March 6, 1969, in Lexington, N.C. ... 6-4/263. ... Full name: Bert Deems May Jr.
HIGH SCHOOL: Lexington (N.C.) Senior.
COLLEGE: North Carolina (degree in political science).
TRANSACTIONS/CAREER NOTES: Selected by San Diego Chargers in seventh round (174th pick overall) of 1992 NFL draft. ... Signed by Chargers (July 16, 1992). ... On injured reserve with foot injury (November 2, 1994-remainder of season). ... Granted free agency (February 17, 1995). ... Re-signed by Chargers (May 19, 1995). ... On physically unable to perform list with foot injury (July 18-October 10, 1995).
PLAYING EXPERIENCE: San Diego NFL, 1992-1995. ... Games: 1992 (16), 1993 (15), 1994 (5), 1995 (5). Total: 41.
PRO STATISTICS: 1994—Caught two passes for 22 yards.

MAY, SHERIDAN   FB   JETS

PERSONAL: Born August 10, 1973, in Tacoma, Wash. ... 6-0/215.
HIGH SCHOOL: Spanaway (Wash.) Lake.
COLLEGE: Idaho.
TRANSACTIONS/CAREER NOTES: Signed as non-drafted free agent by New York Jets (April 28, 1995). ... Released by Jets (August 27, 1995). ... Re-signed by Jets to practice squad (November 22, 1995). ... Activated (November 24, 1995).
PLAYING EXPERIENCE: New York Jets NFL, 1995. ... Games: 1995 (5).
PRO STATISTICS: 1995—Rushed twice for five yards.

MAYBERRY, TONY   C   BUCCANEERS

PERSONAL: Born December 8, 1967, in Wurzburg, West Germany. ... 6-4/292. ... Full name: Eino Anthony Mayberry.
HIGH SCHOOL: Hayfield (Alexandria, Va.).
COLLEGE: Wake Forest (degree in sociology).
TRANSACTIONS/CAREER NOTES: Selected by Tampa Bay Buccaneers in fourth round (108th pick overall) of 1990 NFL draft. ... Signed by Buccaneers (July 19, 1990). ... Granted free agency (March 1, 1993). ... Tendered offer sheet by New England Patriots (March 11, 1993). ... Offer matched by Buccaneers (March 18, 1993). ... Granted unconditional free agency (February 16, 1996). ... Re-signed by Buccaneers (February 27, 1996).
PLAYING EXPERIENCE: Tampa Bay NFL, 1990-1995. ... Games: 1990 (16), 1991 (16), 1992 (16), 1993 (16), 1994 (16), 1995 (16). Total: 96.
PRO STATISTICS: 1991—Fumbled three times for minus 17 yards. 1993—Fumbled once and recovered one fumble for minus six yards. 1994—Recovered one fumble.

MAYFIELD, COREY   DT   JAGUARS

PERSONAL: Born February 25, 1970, in Tyler, Texas. ... 6-3/302. ... Full name: Arthur Corey Mayfield.

M

HIGH SCHOOL: Robert E. Lee (Tyler, Texas).

COLLEGE: Oklahoma.

TRANSACTIONS/CAREER NOTES: Selected by San Francisco 49ers in 10th round (269th pick overall) of 1992 NFL draft. ... Signed by 49ers (July 16, 1992). ... Released by 49ers (August 25, 1992). ... Signed by Tampa Bay Buccaneers to practice squad (September 9, 1992). ... Activated (October 2, 1992). ... Released by Buccaneers (August 30, 1993). ... Signed by New Orleans Saints (April 14, 1994). ... Released by Saints (August 23, 1994). ... Signed by Jacksonville Jaguars (February 8, 1995).

PLAYING EXPERIENCE: Tampa Bay NFL, 1992; Jacksonville NFL, 1995. ... Games: 1992 (11), 1995 (16). Total: 27.

PRO STATISTICS: 1992—Returned two kickoffs for 22 yards. 1995—Credited with 1½ sacks and recovered one fumble.

MAYHEW, MARTIN   CB   BUCCANEERS

PERSONAL: Born October 8, 1965, in Daytona Beach, Fla. ... 5-8/178.

HIGH SCHOOL: Florida (Tallahassee, Fla.).

COLLEGE: Florida State (degree in management, 1987).

TRANSACTIONS/CAREER NOTES: Selected by Buffalo Bills in 10th round (262nd pick overall) of 1988 NFL draft. ... Signed by Bills (July 15, 1988). ... On injured reserve with broken hand (August 17, 1988-entire season). ... Granted unconditional free agency (February 1, 1989). ... Signed by Washington Redskins (March 7, 1989). ... Granted free agency (February 1, 1991). ... Re-signed by Redskins (1991). ... On injured reserve with broken forearm (November 18, 1992-January 1, 1993). ... Granted unconditional free agency (March 1, 1993). ... Signed by Tampa Bay Buccaneers (March 30, 1993).

CHAMPIONSHIP GAME EXPERIENCE: Played in NFC championship game (1991 season). ... Member of Super Bowl championship team (1991 season).

PRO STATISTICS: 1989—Returned one punt for no yards and fumbled once. 1991—Recovered one fumble. 1992—Recovered one fumble. 1994—Recovered one fumble. 1995—Recovered one fumble for 78 yards.

| | | | INTERCEPTIONS | | |
Year Team	G	No.	Yds.	Avg.	TD
1988—Buffalo NFL			Did not play—injured.		
1989—Washington NFL	16	0	0	...	0
1990—Washington NFL	16	7	20	2.9	0
1991—Washington NFL	16	3	31	10.3	1
1992—Washington NFL	10	3	58	19.3	0
1993—Tampa Bay NFL	15	0	0	...	0
1994—Tampa Bay NFL	16	2	4	2.0	0
1995—Tampa Bay NFL	13	5	81	16.2	0
Pro totals (7 years)	102	20	194	9.7	1

MAYS, ALVOID   CB   STEELERS

PERSONAL: Born July 10, 1966, in Palmetto, Fla. ... 5-9/180.

HIGH SCHOOL: Manatee (Bradenton, Fla.).

COLLEGE: West Virginia.

TRANSACTIONS/CAREER NOTES: Selected by Houston Oilers in eighth round (217th pick overall) of 1989 NFL draft. ... Released by Oilers (August 30, 1989). ... Signed by Washington Redskins (May 17, 1990). ... Released by Redskins (September 3, 1990). ... Re-signed by Redskins (September 5, 1990). ... Granted unconditional free agency (February 1-April 1, 1991). ... Re-signed by Redskins for 1991 season. ... Granted unconditional free agency (February 1-April 1, 1992). ... Re-signed by Redskins for 1992 season. ... On injured reserve with knee injury (September 27, 1994-remainder of season). ... Granted unconditional free agency (February 17, 1995). ... Signed by Pittsburgh Steelers (May 18, 1995).

PLAYING EXPERIENCE: Washington NFL, 1990-1994; Pittsburgh NFL, 1995. ... Games: 1990 (15), 1991 (13), 1992 (16), 1993 (15), 1994 (2), 1995 (13). Total: 74.

CHAMPIONSHIP GAME EXPERIENCE: Played in NFC championship game (1991 season). ... Member of Super Bowl championship team (1991 season). ... Member of Steelers for AFC championship game (1995 season); inactive. ... Played in Super Bowl XXX (1995 season).

PRO STATISTICS: 1990—Recovered one fumble. 1991—Intercepted one pass for no yards and recovered one fumble. 1992—Intercepted two passes for 18 yards and credited with a sack. 1993—Returned one punt for no yards and fumbled once. 1995—Intercepted two passes for 35 yards and a touchdown.

McAFEE, FRED   RB   STEELERS

PERSONAL: Born June 20, 1968, in Philadelphia, Miss. ... 5-10/193. ... Full name: Fred Lee McAfee.

HIGH SCHOOL: Philadelphia (Miss.).

COLLEGE: Mississippi College (degree in business).

TRANSACTIONS/CAREER NOTES: Selected by New Orleans Saints in sixth round (154th pick overall) of 1991 NFL draft. ... Signed by Saints (July 14, 1991). ... Released by Saints (August 26, 1991). ... Signed by Saints to practice squad (August 28, 1991). ... Activated (October 18, 1991). ... On injured reserve with shoulder injury (December 15, 1992-remainder of season). ... Granted free agency (February 17, 1994). ... Signed by Arizona Cardinals (August 2, 1994). ... Released by Cardinals (October 31, 1994). ... Signed by Pittsburgh Steelers (November 9, 1994). ... Granted unconditional free agency (February 16, 1996). ... Re-signed by Steelers (April 12, 1996).

CHAMPIONSHIP GAME EXPERIENCE: Played in AFC championship game (1994 and 1995 seasons). ... Played in Super Bowl XXX (1995 season).

PRO STATISTICS: 1995—Recovered one fumble.

STATISTICAL PLATEAUS: 100-yard rushing games: 1991 (1).

| | | RUSHING | | | | RECEIVING | | | | KICKOFF RETURNS | | | | TOTALS | | | |
Year Team	G	Att.	Yds.	Avg.	TD	No.	Yds.	Avg.	TD	No.	Yds.	Avg.	TD	TD	2pt.	Pts.	Fum.
1991—New Orleans NFL	9	109	494	4.5	2	1	8	8.0	0	1	14	14.0	0	2	...	12	2
1992—New Orleans NFL	14	39	114	2.9	1	1	16	16.0	0	19	393	20.7	0	1	...	6	0
1993—New Orleans NFL	15	51	160	3.1	1	1	3	3.0	0	28	580	20.7	0	1	...	6	3
1994—Arizona NFL	7	2	-5	-2.5	1	1	4	4.0	0	7	113	16.1	0	1	0	6	1
—Pittsburgh NFL	6	16	56	3.5	1	0	0	...	0	0	0	...	0	1	0	6	0
1995—Pittsburgh NFL	16	39	156	4.0	1	15	88	5.9	0	5	56	11.2	0	1	0	6	0
Pro totals (5 years)	67	256	975	3.8	7	19	119	6.3	0	60	1156	19.3	0	7	0	42	6

M

McBRIDE, OSCAR — TE — CARDINALS

PERSONAL: Born July 23, 1972, in Gainesville, Fla. ... 6-5/266.
HIGH SCHOOL: Chiefland (Fla.).
COLLEGE: Notre Dame (degree in government, 1993).
TRANSACTIONS/CAREER NOTES: Signed as non-drafted free agent by Arizona Cardinals (April 28, 1995).... Granted free agency after 1995 season.... Re-signed by Cardinals (April 25, 1996).

| | | RECEIVING | | | | TOTALS | | | |
Year Team	G	No.	Yds.	Avg.	TD	TD	2pt.	Pts.	Fum.
1995—Arizona NFL	16	13	112	8.6	2	2	0	12	0

McBURROWS, GERALD — S — RAMS

PERSONAL: Born October 7, 1973, in Detroit. ... 5-11/195.
HIGH SCHOOL: Martin Luther King (Detroit).
COLLEGE: Kansas.
TRANSACTIONS/CAREER NOTES: Selected by St. Louis Rams in seventh round (214th pick overall) of 1995 NFL draft. ... Signed by Rams (June 16, 1995).
PLAYING EXPERIENCE: St. Louis NFL, 1995. ... Games: 1995 (14).
PRO STATISTICS: Credited with one sack.

McCAFFREY, ED — WR — BRONCOS

PERSONAL: Born August 17, 1968, in Allentown, Pa. ... 6-5/215.
HIGH SCHOOL: Allentown (Pa.) Central Catholic.
COLLEGE: Stanford.
TRANSACTIONS/CAREER NOTES: Selected by New York Giants in third round (83rd pick overall) of 1991 NFL draft. ... Signed by Giants (July 23, 1991). ... Granted free agency (February 17, 1994). ... Signed by San Francisco 49ers (July 24, 1994). ... Granted unconditional free agency (February 17, 1995). ... Signed by Denver Broncos (March 7, 1995).
CHAMPIONSHIP GAME EXPERIENCE: Played in NFC championship game (1994 season). ... Member of Super Bowl championship team (1994 season).
HONORS: Named wide receiver on THE SPORTING NEWS college All-America second team (1990).
PRO STATISTICS: 1995—Rushed once for minus one yard.
STATISTICAL PLATEAUS: 100-yard receiving games: 1992 (1).

| | | RECEIVING | | | | TOTALS | | | |
Year Team	G	No.	Yds.	Avg.	TD	TD	2pt.	Pts.	Fum.
1991—New York Giants NFL	16	16	146	9.1	0	0	...	0	0
1992—New York Giants NFL	16	49	610	12.5	5	5	...	30	2
1993—New York Giants NFL	16	27	335	12.4	2	2	...	12	0
1994—San Francisco NFL	16	11	131	11.9	2	2	0	12	0
1995—Denver NFL	16	39	477	12.2	2	2	1	14	1
Pro totals (5 years)	80	142	1699	12.0	11	11	1	68	3

McCANTS, KEITH — DE

PERSONAL: Born April 19, 1968, in Mobile, Ala. ... 6-3/265. ... Full name: Alvin Keith McCants.
HIGH SCHOOL: Murphy (Mobile, Ala.).
COLLEGE: Alabama.
TRANSACTIONS/CAREER NOTES: Selected after junior season by Tampa Bay Buccaneers in first round (fourth pick overall) of 1990 NFL draft. ... Signed by Buccaneers (July 11, 1990). ... Claimed on waivers by New England Patriots (August 25, 1993). ... Released by Patriots (August 30, 1993). ... Signed by Houston Oilers (September 2, 1993). ... Granted unconditional free agency (February 17, 1994). ... Re-signed by Oilers (June 17, 1994). ... Released by Oilers (November 2, 1994). ... Signed by Arizona Cardinals (November 3, 1994). ... Granted unconditional free agency (February 17, 1995). ... Signed by Los Angeles Rams (April 6, 1995). ... Released by Rams (July 14, 1995). ... Signed by Cardinals (July 19, 1995). ... Granted unconditional free agency (February 16, 1996).
HONORS: Named linebacker on THE SPORTING NEWS college All-America first team (1989).
PRO STATISTICS: 1990—Recovered one fumble. 1991—Recovered one fumble. 1992—Recovered one fumble. 1994—Intercepted one pass for 46 yards and a touchdown and recovered one fumble. 1995—Recovered two fumbles for 16 yards and one touchdown.

Year Team	G	SACKS
1990—Tampa Bay NFL	15	2.0
1991—Tampa Bay NFL	16	5.0
1992—Tampa Bay NFL	16	5.0
1993—Houston NFL	13	0.0
1994—Houston NFL	4	0.0
—Arizona NFL	8	1.0
1995—Arizona NFL	16	0.5
Pro totals (6 years)	88	13.5

McCARDELL, KEENAN — WR — JAGUARS

PERSONAL: Born January 6, 1970, in Houston. ... 6-1/175. ... Full name: Keenan Wayne McCardell.
HIGH SCHOOL: Waltrip (Houston).
COLLEGE: UNLV.
TRANSACTIONS/CAREER NOTES: Selected by Washington Redskins in 12th round (326th pick overall) of 1991 NFL draft. ... On injured

M

reserve with knee injury (August 20, 1991-entire season). ... Granted unconditional free agency (February 1, 1992). ... Signed by Cleveland Browns (March 24, 1992). ... Released by Browns (September 1, 1992). ... Re-signed by Browns to practice squad (September 3, 1992). ... Activated (October 6, 1992). ... Released by Browns (October 13, 1992). ... Re-signed by Browns to practice squad (October 14, 1992). ... Activated (November 14, 1992). ... Released by Browns (November 19, 1992). ... Re-signed by Browns to practice squad (November 20, 1992). ... Activated (December 26, 1992). ... Released by Browns (September 22, 1993). ... Signed by Chicago Bears to practice squad (November 2, 1993). ... Signed by Browns off Bears practice squad (November 24, 1993). ... Granted free agency (February 17, 1994). ... Re-signed by Browns (March 4, 1994). ... Granted unconditional free agency (February 16, 1996). ... Signed by Jacksonville Jaguars (March 2, 1996).

PRO STATISTICS: 1995—Returned 13 punts for 93 yards and returned nine kickoffs for 161 yards.

STATISTICAL PLATEAUS: 100-yard receiving games: 1995 (1).

		RECEIVING				TOTALS			
Year Team	G	No.	Yds.	Avg.	TD	TD	2pt.	Pts.	Fum.
1991—Washington NFL				Did not play—injured.					
1992—Cleveland NFL	2	1	8	8.0	0	0	...	0	0
1993—Cleveland NFL	6	13	234	18.0	4	4	...	24	0
1994—Cleveland NFL	13	10	182	18.2	0	0	0	0	0
1995—Cleveland NFL	16	56	709	12.7	4	4	0	24	0
Pro totals (4 years)	37	80	1133	14.2	8	8	0	48	0

McCLESKEY, J.J.　　　　　S　　　　　SAINTS

PERSONAL: Born April 10, 1970, in Knoxville, Tenn. ... 5-7/177. ... Full name: Tommy Joe McCleskey.

HIGH SCHOOL: Karns Comprehensive (Knoxville, Tenn.).

COLLEGE: Tennessee.

TRANSACTIONS/CAREER NOTES: Signed as non-drafted free agent by New Orleans Saints (May 7, 1993). ... Released by Saints (August 24, 1993). ... Re-signed by Saints to practice squad (August 31, 1993). ... Activated (December 23, 1993). ... Released by Saints (August 23, 1994). ... Re-signed by Saints (September 20, 1994).

PLAYING EXPERIENCE: New Orleans NFL, 1994 and 1995. ... Games: 1994 (13), 1995 (14). Total: 27.

PRO STATISTICS: 1994—Recovered one fumble. 1995—Intercepted one pass for no yards, returned one kickoff for no yards and recovered one fumble.

McCOLLUM, ANDY　　　　　C/G　　　　　SAINTS

PERSONAL: Born June 6, 1970, in Akron, Ohio. ... 6-5/295. ... Full name: Andrew Jon McCollum.

HIGH SCHOOL: Revere (Richfield, Ohio).

COLLEGE: Toledo.

TRANSACTIONS/CAREER NOTES: Played in Arena Football League with Milwaukee Mustangs (1994). ... Signed by Cleveland Browns (June 1994). ... Released by Browns (August 28, 1994). ... Re-signed by Browns to practice squad (August 30, 1994). ... Signed by New Orleans Saints off Browns practice squad (November 15, 1994). ... Assigned by Saints to Barcelona Dragons in 1995 World League enhancement allocation program (February 20, 1995).

PLAYING EXPERIENCE: New Orleans NFL, 1995. ... Games: 1995 (11).

M

McCORMACK, HURVIN　　　　　DT　　　　　COWBOYS

PERSONAL: Born April 6, 1972, in Brooklyn, N.Y. ... 6-5/274.

HIGH SCHOOL: New Dorp (Staten Island, N.Y.).

COLLEGE: Indiana.

TRANSACTIONS/CAREER NOTES: Signed as non-drafted free agent by Dallas Cowboys (April 28, 1994).

PLAYING EXPERIENCE: Dallas NFL, 1994 and 1995. ... Games: 1994 (4), 1995 (15). Total: 19.

CHAMPIONSHIP GAME EXPERIENCE: Member of Cowboys for NFC championship game (1994 season); did not play. ... Played in NFC championship game (1995 season). ... Member of Super Bowl championship team (1995 season).

PRO STATISTICS: Credited with two sacks.

McCORVEY, KEZ　　　　　WR　　　　　LIONS

PERSONAL: Born January 23, 1972, in Gautier, Miss. ... 6-0/180.

HIGH SCHOOL: Pascagoula (Miss.).

COLLEGE: Florida State.

TRANSACTIONS/CAREER NOTES: Selected by Detroit Lions in fifth round (156th pick overall) of 1995 NFL draft. ... Signed by Lions (July 19, 1995).

PLAYING EXPERIENCE: Detroit NFL, 1995. ... Games: 1995 (1).

McCOY, TONY　　　　　NT　　　　　COLTS

PERSONAL: Born June 10, 1969, in Orlando. ... 6-0/282. ... Full name: Anthony Bernard McCoy.

HIGH SCHOOL: Maynard Evans (Orlando).

COLLEGE: Florida.

TRANSACTIONS/CAREER NOTES: Selected by Indianapolis Colts in fourth round (105th pick overall) of 1992 NFL draft. ... Signed by Colts (July 17, 1992). ... Granted free agency (February 17, 1995). ... Re-signed by Colts (June 7, 1995).

CHAMPIONSHIP GAME EXPERIENCE: Played in AFC championship game (1995 season).

PRO STATISTICS: 1992—Recovered one fumble. 1994—Recovered one fumble.

Year Team	G	SACKS
1992—Indianapolis NFL	16	1.0

Year Team	G	SACKS
1993—Indianapolis NFL	6	0.0
1994—Indianapolis NFL	15	6.0
1995—Indianapolis NFL	16	2.5
Pro totals (4 years)	53	9.5

McCRARY, FRED   FB   EAGLES

PERSONAL: Born September 19, 1972, in Naples, Fla. ... 6-0/219. ... Full name: Freddy Demetrius McCrary.
HIGH SCHOOL: Naples (Fla.).
COLLEGE: Mississippi State.
TRANSACTIONS/CAREER NOTES: Selected by Philadelphia Eagles in sixth round (208th pick overall) of 1995 NFL draft. ... Signed by Eagles (June 27, 1995).

		RUSHING				RECEIVING				KICKOFF RETURNS				TOTALS			
Year Team	G	Att.	Yds.	Avg.	TD	No.	Yds.	Avg.	TD	No.	Yds.	Avg.	TD	TD	2pt.	Pts.	Fum.
1991—Philadelphia NFL	13	3	1	0.3	1	9	60	6.7	0	1	1	1.0	0	1	0	6	0

McCRARY, MICHAEL   DE   SEAHAWKS

PERSONAL: Born July 7, 1970, in Vienna, Va. ... 6-4/267.
HIGH SCHOOL: George C. Marshall (Falls Church, Va.).
COLLEGE: Wake Forest.
TRANSACTIONS/CAREER NOTES: Selected by Seattle Seahawks in seventh round (170th pick overall) of 1993 NFL draft. ... Signed by Seahawks (July 13, 1993). ... Granted free agency (February 16, 1996).

Year Team	G	SACKS
1993—Seattle NFL	15	4.0
1994—Seattle NFL	16	1.5
1995—Seattle NFL	11	1.0
Pro totals (3 years)	42	6.5

McDANIEL, ED   LB   VIKINGS

PERSONAL: Born February 23, 1969, in Batesburg, S.C. ... 5-11/230.
HIGH SCHOOL: Batesburg (S.C.)-Leesville.
COLLEGE: Clemson.
TRANSACTIONS/CAREER NOTES: Selected by Minnesota Vikings in fifth round (125th pick overall) of 1992 NFL draft.... Signed by Vikings (July 20, 1992). ... Released by Vikings (August 31, 1992). ... Re-signed by Vikings to practice squad (September 1, 1992).... Activated (November 5, 1992).
PRO STATISTICS: 1995—Recovered one fumble.

		INTERCEPTIONS				SACKS
Year Team	G	No.	Yds.	Avg.	TD	No.
1992—Minnesota NFL	8	0	0	...	0	0.0
1993—Minnesota NFL	7	0	0	...	0	0.0
1994—Minnesota NFL	16	1	0	0.0	0	1.5
1995—Minnesota NFL	16	1	3	3.0	0	4.5
Pro totals (4 years)	47	2	3	1.5	0	6.0

McDANIEL, RANDALL   G   VIKINGS

PERSONAL: Born December 19, 1964, in Phoenix. ... 6-3/277. ... Full name: Randall Cornell McDaniel.
HIGH SCHOOL: Agua Fria Union (Avondale, Ariz.).
COLLEGE: Arizona State (degree in physical education, 1988).
TRANSACTIONS/CAREER NOTES: Selected by Minnesota Vikings in first round (19th pick overall) of 1988 NFL draft. ... Signed by Vikings (July 22, 1988). ... Granted free agency (February 1, 1991). ... Re-signed by Vikings (July 22, 1991). ... Designated by Vikings as transition player (February 25, 1993). ... Free agency status changed by Vikings from transitional to unconditional (February 17, 1994). ... Re-signed by Vikings (April 21, 1994).
PLAYING EXPERIENCE: Minnesota NFL, 1988-1995. ... Games: 1988 (16), 1989 (14), 1990 (16), 1991 (16), 1992 (16), 1993 (16), 1994 (16), 1995 (16). Total: 126.
HONORS: Named guard on THE SPORTING NEWS college All-America second team (1987). ... Played in Pro Bowl (1989-1995 seasons). ... Named guard on THE SPORTING NEWS NFL All-Pro team (1991-1994).
PRO STATISTICS: 1991—Recovered one fumble. 1994—Recovered one fumble.

McDANIEL, TERRY   CB   RAIDERS

PERSONAL: Born February 8, 1965, in Saginaw, Mich. ... 5-10/180. ... Full name: Terence Lee McDaniel.
HIGH SCHOOL: Saginaw (Mich.).
COLLEGE: Tennessee.
TRANSACTIONS/CAREER NOTES: Selected by Los Angeles Raiders in first round (ninth pick overall) of 1988 NFL draft. ... Signed by Raiders (July 13, 1988). ... On injured reserve with broken leg (September 14, 1988-remainder of season). ... Granted free agency (February 1, 1992). ... Re-signed by Raiders (August 12, 1992). ... Designated by Raiders as transition player (February 25, 1993). ... Raiders franchise moved to Oakland (July 21, 1995).
CHAMPIONSHIP GAME EXPERIENCE: Played in AFC championship game (1990 season).

HONORS: Named defensive back on THE SPORTING NEWS college All-America second team (1987). ... Played in Pro Bowl (1992-1995 seasons).
PRO STATISTICS: 1990—Recovered two fumbles for 44 yards and one touchdown. 1991—Recovered one fumble. 1992—Recovered one fumble for 40 yards. 1994—Recovered three fumbles for 48 yards and one touchdown.

		INTERCEPTIONS				SACKS
Year Team	G	No.	Yds.	Avg.	TD	No.
1988—Los Angeles Raiders NFL	2	0	0	...	0	0.0
1989—Los Angeles Raiders NFL	16	3	21	7.0	0	1.0
1990—Los Angeles Raiders NFL	16	3	20	6.7	0	2.0
1991—Los Angeles Raiders NFL	16	0	0	...	0	0.0
1992—Los Angeles Raiders NFL	16	4	180	45.0	0	0.0
1993—Los Angeles Raiders NFL	16	5	87	17.4	1	0.0
1994—Los Angeles Raiders NFL	16	7	103	14.7	2	0.0
1995—Oakland NFL	16	6	46	7.7	1	0.0
Pro totals (8 years)	114	28	457	16.3	4	3.0

McDANIELS, PELLOM DE CHIEFS

PERSONAL: Born February 21, 1968, in San Jose, Calif. ... 6-3/292.
HIGH SCHOOL: Silver Creek (San Jose, Calif.).
COLLEGE: Oregon State (degree in communications and political science).
TRANSACTIONS/CAREER NOTES: Selected by Birmingham Fire in fifth round of 1991 World League draft. ... Signed as free agent by Philadelphia Eagles (June 19, 1991). ... Released by Eagles (August 12, 1991). ... Signed by Kansas City Chiefs (June 5, 1992). ... Released by Chiefs (August 31, 1992). ... Re-signed by Chiefs to practice squad (September 2, 1992). ... Released by Chiefs (September 16, 1992). ... Re-signed by Chiefs for 1993 season. ... On injured reserve with shoulder injury (December 20, 1994-remainder of season).
CHAMPIONSHIP GAME EXPERIENCE: Played in AFC championship game (1993 season).
PRO STATISTICS: 1994—Recovered one fumble. 1995—Returned one kickoff for no yards.

Year Team	G	SACKS
1991—Birmingham W.L.	10	3.0
1992—Birmingham W.L.	10	3.5
1993—Kansas City NFL	10	0.0
1994—Kansas City NFL	12	2.0
1995—Kansas City NFL	16	2.0
W.L. totals (2 years)	20	6.5
NFL totals (3 years)	38	4.0
Pro totals (5 years)	58	10.5

McDONALD, DEVON LB COLTS

PERSONAL: Born November 8, 1969, in Kingston, Jamaica. ... 6-4/228. ... Full name: Devon Linton McDonald. ... Twin brother of Ricardo McDonald, linebacker, Cincinnati Bengals.
HIGH SCHOOL: John F. Kennedy (Paterson, N.J.).
COLLEGE: Notre Dame.
TRANSACTIONS/CAREER NOTES: Selected by Indianapolis Colts in fourth round (107th pick overall) of 1993 NFL draft. ... Signed by Colts (July 22, 1993). ... Granted free agency (February 16, 1996).
PLAYING EXPERIENCE: Indianapolis NFL, 1993-1995. ... Games: 1993 (16), 1994 (16), 1995 (15). Total: 47.
CHAMPIONSHIP GAME EXPERIENCE: Played in AFC championship game (1995 season).
PRO STATISTICS: 1994—Credited with one sack and recovered one fumble.

McDONALD, RICARDO LB BENGALS

PERSONAL: Born November 8, 1969, in Kingston, Jamaica. ... 6-2/235. ... Full name: Ricardo Milton McDonald. ... Twin brother of Devon McDonald, linebacker, Indianapolis Colts.
HIGH SCHOOL: Eastside (Paterson, N.J.).
COLLEGE: Pittsburgh.
TRANSACTIONS/CAREER NOTES: Selected by Cincinnati Bengals in fourth round (88th pick overall) of 1992 NFL draft. ... Signed by Bengals (July 24, 1992). ... On injured reserve with knee injury (December 24, 1993-remainder of season). ... Granted free agency (February 17, 1995). ... Re-signed by Bengals (March 6, 1996). ... Granted unconditional free agency (February 16, 1996). ... Re-signed by Bengals (March 8, 1996).
PRO STATISTICS: 1992—Recovered one fumble for four yards and intercepted one pass for no yards. 1995—Recovered one fumble.

Year Team	G	SACKS
1992—Cincinnati NFL	16	0.0
1993—Cincinnati NFL	14	1.0
1994—Cincinnati NFL	13	1.0
1995—Cincinnati NFL	16	5.0
Pro totals (4 years)	59	7.0

McDONALD, TIM S 49ERS

PERSONAL: Born January 6, 1965, in Fresno, Calif. ... 6-2/215.
HIGH SCHOOL: Edison (Fresno, Calif.).
COLLEGE: Southern California.
TRANSACTIONS/CAREER NOTES: Selected by St. Louis Cardinals in second round (34th pick overall) of 1987 NFL draft. ... Signed by Cardinals (August 2, 1987). ... On injured reserve with broken ankle (September 1-December 12, 1987). ... Cardinals franchise moved to Phoenix (March 15, 1988). ... Granted free agency (February 1, 1990). ... Re-signed by Cardinals (August 21, 1990). ... On injured reserve with broken leg and ankle (December 3, 1991-remainder of season). ... Designated by Cardinals as franchise player (February 25, 1993). ...

M

Signed by San Francisco 49ers (April 7, 1993); Cardinals received first-round pick (OT Ernest Dye) in 1993 draft as compensation.
CHAMPIONSHIP GAME EXPERIENCE: Played in NFC championship game (1993 and 1994 seasons). ... Member of Super Bowl championship team (1994 season).
HONORS: Named defensive back on THE SPORTING NEWS college All-America second team (1984). ... Named defensive back on THE SPORTING NEWS college All-America first team (1985). ... Played in Pro Bowl (1989 and 1992-1995 seasons). ... Named to play in Pro Bowl (1991 season); replaced by Shaun Gayle due to injury.
PRO STATISTICS: 1988—Recovered one fumble for nine yards. 1989—Recovered one fumble for one yard. 1990—Recovered one fumble. 1991—Recovered one fumble. 1992—Recovered three fumbles for two yards. 1993—Recovered one fumble for 15 yards. 1994—Recovered one fumble for 49 yards and a touchdown.

		INTERCEPTIONS				SACKS
Year Team	G	No.	Yds.	Avg.	TD	No.
1987—St. Louis NFL	3	0	0	...	0	0.0
1988—Phoenix NFL	16	2	11	5.5	0	2.0
1989—Phoenix NFL	16	7	140	20.0	1	0.0
1990—Phoenix NFL	16	4	63	15.8	0	0.0
1991—Phoenix NFL	13	5	36	7.2	0	0.0
1992—Phoenix NFL	16	2	35	17.5	0	0.5
1993—San Francisco NFL	16	3	23	7.7	0	0.0
1994—San Francisco NFL	16	2	79	39.5	1	0.0
1995—San Francisco NFL	16	4	135	33.8	†2	0.0
Pro totals (9 years)	128	29	522	18.0	4	2.5

McDOWELL, ANTHONY   FB   REDSKINS

PERSONAL: Born November 12, 1968, in Killeen, Texas. ... 5-11/240. ... Full name: Anthony Leguinn McDowell.
HIGH SCHOOL: Killeen (Texas).
COLLEGE: Texas Tech.
TRANSACTIONS/CAREER NOTES: Selected by Tampa Bay Buccaneers in eighth round (200th pick overall) of 1992 NFL draft. ... Signed by Buccaneers (July 23, 1992). ... Released by Buccaneers (September 1, 1992). ... Re-signed by Buccaneers to practice squad (September 2, 1992). ... Activated (October 2, 1992). ... On injured reserve with ankle injury (November 17, 1993-remainder of season). ... Granted free agency (February 17, 1995). ... Re-signed by Buccaneers (July 5, 1995). ... Released by Buccaneers (August 21, 1995). ... Signed by Washington Redskins (January 30, 1996).
PRO STATISTICS: 1993—Recovered one fumble. 1994—Recovered one fumble.

		RUSHING				RECEIVING				TOTALS			
Year Team	G	Att.	Yds.	Avg.	TD	No.	Yds.	Avg.	TD	TD	2pt.	Pts.	Fum.
1992—Tampa Bay NFL	12	14	81	5.8	0	27	258	9.6	2	2	...	12	1
1993—Tampa Bay NFL	4	2	6	3.0	0	8	26	3.3	1	1	...	6	2
1994—Tampa Bay NFL	14	21	58	2.8	0	29	193	6.7	1	1	0	6	0
Pro totals (3 years)	30	37	145	3.9	0	64	477	7.5	4	4	0	24	3

McDOWELL, BUBBA   S   PANTHERS

M

PERSONAL: Born November 4, 1966, in Fort Gaines, Ga. ... 6-1/206.
HIGH SCHOOL: Merritt Island (Fla.).
COLLEGE: Miami, Fla. (degree in business management, 1989).
TRANSACTIONS/CAREER NOTES: Selected by Houston Oilers in third round (77th pick overall) of 1989 NFL draft. ... Signed by Oilers (July 28, 1989). ... Granted free agency (February 1, 1992). ... Re-signed by Oilers (April 21, 1992). ... Released by Oilers (March 28, 1995). ... Signed by Carolina Panthers (April 24, 1995).
PRO STATISTICS: 1989—Credited with one safety, fumbled once and recovered one fumble. 1990—Recovered one fumble. 1991—Recovered blocked punt in end zone for a touchdown and recovered two fumbles. 1994—Recovered one fumble. 1995—Recovered one fumble.

		INTERCEPTIONS				SACKS
Year Team	G	No.	Yds.	Avg.	TD	No.
1989—Houston NFL	16	4	65	16.3	0	1.0
1990—Houston NFL	15	2	11	5.5	0	0.5
1991—Houston NFL	16	4	31	7.8	0	1.0
1992—Houston NFL	16	3	52	17.3	1	1.5
1993—Houston NFL	14	3	31	10.3	0	1.0
1994—Houston NFL	9	0	0	...	0	0.0
1995—Carolina NFL	16	1	33	33.0	0	0.0
Pro totals (7 years)	102	17	223	13.1	1	5.0

McDUFFIE, O.J.   WR/KR   DOLPHINS

PERSONAL: Born December 2, 1969, in Marion, Ohio. ... 5-10/188. ... Full name: Otis James McDuffie.
HIGH SCHOOL: Hawken (Gates Mills, Ohio).
COLLEGE: Penn State (degree in labor and industrial relations).
TRANSACTIONS/CAREER NOTES: Selected by Miami Dolphins in first round (25th pick overall) of 1993 NFL draft. ... Signed by Dolphins (July 18, 1993).
HONORS: Named wide receiver on THE SPORTING NEWS college All-America second team (1992).
POSTSEASON RECORDS: Shares NFL postseason career and single-game records for most two-point conversions—1 (December 30, 1995, vs. Buffalo).
PRO STATISTICS: 1993—Fumbled four times and recovered one fumble. 1994—Fumbled three times. 1995—Fumbled four times and recovered two fumbles.
STATISTICAL PLATEAUS: 100-yard receiving games: 1994 (1).

Year Team	G	RUSHING Att.	Yds.	Avg.	TD	RECEIVING No.	Yds.	Avg.	TD	PUNT RETURNS No.	Yds.	Avg.	TD	KICKOFF RETURNS No.	Yds.	Avg.	TD	TOTALS TD	2pt.	Pts.
1993—Miami NFL	16	1	-4	-4.0	0	19	197	10.4	0	28	317	11.3	†2	32	755	23.6	0	2	...	12
1994—Miami NFL	15	5	32	6.4	0	37	488	13.2	3	32	228	7.1	0	36	767	21.3	0	3	0	18
1995—Miami NFL	16	3	6	2.0	0	62	819	13.2	8	24	163	6.8	0	23	564	24.5	0	8	1	50
Pro totals (3 years)	47	9	34	3.8	0	118	1504	12.8	11	84	708	8.4	2	91	2086	22.9	0	13	1	80

McELROY, RAY   CB/KR   COLTS

PERSONAL: Born July 31, 1972, in Bellwood, Ill. ... 5-11/195.
HIGH SCHOOL: Proviso West (Hillside, Ill.).
COLLEGE: Eastern Illinois.
TRANSACTIONS/CAREER NOTES: Selected by Indianapolis Colts in fourth round (114th pick overall) of 1995 NFL draft. ... Signed by Colts (July 12, 1995).
PLAYING EXPERIENCE: Indianapolis NFL, 1995. ... Games: 1995 (16).
CHAMPIONSHIP GAME EXPERIENCE: Played in AFC championship game (1995 season).

McELROY, REGGIE   OT   BRONCOS

PERSONAL: Born March 4, 1960, in Beaumont, Texas ... 6-6/290. ... Full name: Reginald Lee McElroy.
HIGH SCHOOL: Charlton Pollard (Beaumont, Texas).
COLLEGE: West Texas State (degree in physical education).
TRANSACTIONS/CAREER NOTES: Selected by New York Jets in second round (51st pick overall) of 1982 NFL draft. ... On injured reserve with knee injury (August 24, 1982-entire season). ... Granted free agency (February 1, 1985). ... Re-signed by Jets (September 10, 1985). ... Granted roster exemption (September 10-14, 1985). ... On injured reserve with knee injury (October 22-December 12, 1986). ... On injured reserve with knee injury (December 17, 1986-remainder of season). ... On physically unable to perform list with knee injury (September 6-November 9, 1987). ... On injured reserve with knee injury (December 19, 1989-remainder of season). ... Released by Jets (June 21, 1990). ... Signed by Los Angeles Raiders (March 20, 1991). ... Granted unconditional free agency (February 1-April 1, 1992). ... Re-signed by Raiders for 1992 season. ... Granted unconditional free agency (March 1, 1993). ... Signed by Kansas City Chiefs (June 1, 1993). ... Released by Chiefs (1994). ... Signed by Minnesota Vikings (August 2, 1994). ... Granted unconditional free agency (February 17, 1995). ... Signed by Denver Broncos (May 3, 1995). ... Granted unconditional free agency (February 16, 1996). ... Re-signed by Broncos (April 10, 1996).
PLAYING EXPERIENCE: New York Jets NFL, 1983-1989; Los Angeles Raiders NFL, 1991 and 1992; Kansas City NFL, 1993; Minnesota NFL, 1994; Denver NFL, 1995. ... Games: 1983 (16), 1984 (16), 1985 (13), 1986 (8), 1987 (8), 1988 (16), 1989 (15), 1991 (16), 1992 (16), 1993 (8), 1994 (10), 1995 (16). Total: 158.
CHAMPIONSHIP GAME EXPERIENCE: Member of Chiefs for AFC championship game (1993 season); inactive.
PRO STATISTICS: 1983—Returned one kickoff for seven yards. 1986—Recovered one fumble for minus two yards. 1988—Recovered one fumble.

McGEE, TIM   WR   BENGALS

M

PERSONAL: Born August 7, 1964, in Cleveland. ... 5-10/183. ... Full name: Timothy Dwayne Hatchett McGee.
HIGH SCHOOL: John Hay (Cleveland).
COLLEGE: Tennessee.
TRANSACTIONS/CAREER NOTES: Selected by Memphis Showboats in 1986 USFL territorial draft. ... Selected by Cincinnati Bengals in first round (21st pick overall) of 1986 NFL draft. ... USFL rights traded by Showboats to Jacksonville Bulls for rights to C Leonard Burton and OT Doug Williams (May 6, 1986). ... Signed by Bengals (July 26, 1986). ... On injured reserve with hamstring injury (September 19-October 21, 1987). ... Granted unconditional free agency (March 1, 1993). ... Signed by Washington Redskins (April 5, 1993). ... Released by Redskins (March 8, 1994). ... Signed by Bengals (April 11, 1994). ... Granted free agency (February 17, 1995). ... Re-signed by Bengals (April 28, 1995). ... On injured reserve with concussion (August 22, 1995-entire season). ... Granted free agency (February 16, 1996).
CHAMPIONSHIP GAME EXPERIENCE: Played in AFC championship game (1988 season). ... Played in Super Bowl XXIII (1988 season).
HONORS: Named wide receiver on THE SPORTING NEWS college All-America second team (1985).
PRO STATISTICS: 1986—Returned three punts for 21 yards and recovered one fumble. 1988—Recovered one fumble. 1992—Recovered two fumbles.
STATISTICAL PLATEAUS: 100-yard receiving games: 1987 (2), 1988 (1), 1989 (4), 1990 (2), 1991 (1). Total: 10.

Year Team	G	RUSHING Att.	Yds.	Avg.	TD	RECEIVING No.	Yds.	Avg.	TD	KICKOFF RETURNS No.	Yds.	Avg.	TD	TOTALS TD	2pt.	Pts.	Fum.
1986—Cincinnati NFL	16	4	10	2.5	0	16	276	17.3	1	43	*1007	23.4	0	1	...	6	0
1987—Cincinnati NFL	11	1	-10	-10.0	0	23	408	17.7	1	15	242	16.1	0	1	...	6	0
1988—Cincinnati NFL	16	0	0	...	0	36	686	19.1	6	0	0	...	0	6	...	36	0
1989—Cincinnati NFL	16	2	36	18.0	0	65	1211	18.6	8	0	0	...	0	8	...	48	0
1990—Cincinnati NFL	16	0	0	...	0	43	737	17.1	1	0	0	...	0	1	...	6	1
1991—Cincinnati NFL	16	0	0	...	0	51	802	15.7	4	0	0	...	0	4	...	24	1
1992—Cincinnati NFL	16	0	0	...	0	35	408	11.7	3	0	0	...	0	3	...	18	0
1993—Washington NFL	13	0	0	...	0	39	500	12.8	3	0	0	...	0	3	...	18	0
1994—Cincinnati NFL	14	1	-18	-18.0	0	13	175	13.5	1	0	0	...	0	1	0	6	0
1995—Cincinnati NFL									Did not play.								
Pro totals (9 years)	134	8	18	2.3	0	321	5203	16.2	28	58	1249	21.5	0	28	0	168	2

McGEE, TONY   TE   BENGALS

PERSONAL: Born April 21, 1971, in Terre Haute, Ind. ... 6-3/246.
HIGH SCHOOL: South Vigo (Terre Haute, Ind.).
COLLEGE: Michigan.
TRANSACTIONS/CAREER NOTES: Selected by Cincinnati Bengals in second round (37th pick overall) of 1993 NFL draft. ... Signed by Bengals (July 20, 1993). ... Granted free agency (February 16, 1996).
PRO STATISTICS: 1994—Returned one kickoff for four yards.

STATISTICAL PLATEAUS: 100-yard receiving games: 1993 (1), 1995 (1). Total: 2.

		RECEIVING				TOTALS			
Year Team	G	No.	Yds.	Avg.	TD	TD	2pt.	Pts.	Fum.
1993—Cincinnati NFL	15	44	525	11.9	0	0	...	0	1
1994—Cincinnati NFL	16	40	492	12.3	1	1	0	6	0
1995—Cincinnati NFL	16	55	754	13.7	4	4	0	24	2
Pro totals (3 years)	47	139	1771	12.8	5	5	0	30	3

McGHEE, KANAVIS   LB

PERSONAL: Born October 4, 1968, in Houston. ... 6-4/257.
HIGH SCHOOL: Phillis Wheatley (Houston).
COLLEGE: Colorado.
TRANSACTIONS/CAREER NOTES: Selected by New York Giants in second round (55th pick overall) of 1991 NFL draft. ... Signed by Giants (July 24, 1991). ... Granted free agency (February 17, 1994). ... Free agency status changed from restricted to unconditional (May 10, 1994). ... Signed by Cincinnati Bengals (July 7, 1994). ... Released by Bengals (September 20, 1994). ... Signed by Houston Oilers (July 19, 1995). ... Granted unconditional free agency (February 16, 1996).
PLAYING EXPERIENCE: New York Giants NFL, 1991-1993; Cincinnati NFL, 1994; Houston NFL, 1995. ... Games: 1991 (16), 1992 (14), 1993 (10), 1994 (1), 1995 (9). Total: 50.
HONORS: Named defensive lineman on THE SPORTING NEWS college All-America second team (1988).
PRO STATISTICS: 1993—Credited with 1½ sacks. 1995—Credited with 1½ sacks.

McGILL, LENNY   CB   FALCONS

PERSONAL: Born May 31, 1971, in Long Beach, Calif. ... 6-1/198. ... Full name: Charles Leonard McGill.
HIGH SCHOOL: Orange Glen (Escondido, Calif.).
COLLEGE: Arizona State.
TRANSACTIONS/CAREER NOTES: Signed as non-drafted free agent by Green Bay Packers (May 2, 1994). ... On injured reserve with torn knee ligament (November 1, 1994-remainder of season). ... Traded by Packers to Atlanta Falcons for RB Robert Baldwin (June 6, 1996).
CHAMPIONSHIP GAME EXPERIENCE: Played in NFC championship game (1995 season).
PRO STATISTICS: 1995—Recovered one fumble.

		INTERCEPTIONS			
Year Team	G	No.	Yds.	Avg.	TD
1994—Green Bay NFL	6	2	16	8.0	0
1995—Green Bay NFL	15	0	0	...	0
Pro totals (2 years)	21	2	16	8.0	0

McGINEST, WILLIE   LB   PATRIOTS

PERSONAL: Born December 11, 1971, in Long Beach, Calif. ... 6-5/255.
HIGH SCHOOL: L.B. Polytechnic (Long Beach, Calif.).
COLLEGE: Southern California.
TRANSACTIONS/CAREER NOTES: Selected by New England Patriots in first round (fourth pick overall) of 1994 NFL draft. ... Signed by Patriots (May 17, 1994).
PRO STATISTICS: 1994—Recovered two fumbles.

Year Team	G	SACKS
1994—New England NFL	16	4.5
1995—New England NFL	16	11.0
Pro totals (2 years)	32	15.5

McGLOCKTON, CHESTER   DT   RAIDERS

PERSONAL: Born September 16, 1969, in Whiteville, N.C. ... 6-4/310.
HIGH SCHOOL: Whiteville (N.C.).
COLLEGE: Clemson.
TRANSACTIONS/CAREER NOTES: Selected after junior season by Los Angeles Raiders in first round (16th pick overall) of 1992 NFL draft. ... Signed by Raiders for 1992 season. ... On injured reserve (January 11, 1994-remainder of 1993 playoffs). ... Raiders franchise moved to Oakland (July 21, 1995).
HONORS: Named defensive tackle on THE SPORTING NEWS NFL All-Pro team (1994). ... Played in Pro Bowl (1994 and 1995 seasons).
PRO STATISTICS: 1993—Intercepted one pass for 19 yards. 1994—Recovered one fumble. 1995—Recovered two fumbles.

Year Team	G	SACKS
1992—Los Angeles Raiders NFL	10	3.0
1993—Los Angeles Raiders NFL	16	7.0
1994—Los Angeles Raiders NFL	16	9.5
1995—Oakland NFL	16	7.5
Pro totals (4 years)	58	27.0

McGRUDER, MIKE   CB   PATRIOTS

PERSONAL: Born May 6, 1964, in Cleveland HeightsOhio ... 5-10/178. ... Full name: Michael J.P. McGruder.
HIGH SCHOOL: Cleveland Heights (Ohio).
COLLEGE: Kent (degree in business management).

TRANSACTIONS/CAREER NOTES: Signed as non-drafted free agent by Ottawa Rough Riders of CFL (May 1985). ... Released by Rough Riders (July 1985). ... Signed by Saskatchewan Roughriders of CFL (April 1986). ... Granted free agency (March 1, 1989). ... Signed by Green Bay Packers (April 26, 1989). ... Released by Packers (September 19, 1989). ... Re-signed by Packers to developmental squad (September 22, 1989). ... Released by Packers (January 29, 1990). ... Signed by Miami Dolphins (April 3, 1990). ... On injured reserve with shoulder injury (September 14, 1990-remainder of season). ... Granted unconditional free agency (February 1-April 1, 1991). ... Re-signed by Dolphins for 1991 season. ... Granted free agency (February 1, 1992). ... Re-signed by Dolphins (July 20, 1992). ... Released by Dolphins (August 31, 1992). ... Signed by San Francisco 49ers (October 6, 1992). ... Granted unconditional free agency (February 17, 1994). ... Signed by Tampa Bay Buccaneers (June 2, 1994). ... Granted unconditional free agency (February 16, 1996). ... Signed by New England Patriots (April 5, 1996).
CHAMPIONSHIP GAME EXPERIENCE: Played in NFC championship game (1992 and 1993 seasons).
PRO STATISTICS: CFL: 1986—Recovered one fumble and ran minus four yards with lateral from punt return. 1987—Recovered four fumbles for 26 yards. 1988—Recovered two fumbles for 20 yards and one touchdown. NFL: 1989—Recovered one fumble. 1991—Recovered one fumble. 1992—Recovered one fumble for seven yards. 1995—Recovered one fumble.

				INTERCEPTIONS		
Year Team	G	No.	Yds.	Avg.	TD	
1986—Saskatchewan CFL	14	5	35	7.0	0	
1987—Saskatchewan CFL	14	5	26	5.2	0	
1988—Saskatchewan CFL	18	7	89	12.7	0	
1989—Green Bay NFL	2	0	0	...	0	
1990—Miami NFL	1	0	0	...	0	
1991—Miami NFL	16	0	0	...	0	
1992—San Francisco NFL	9	0	0	...	0	
1993—San Francisco NFL	16	5	89	17.8	1	
1994—Tampa Bay NFL	15	1	0	0.0	0	
1995—Tampa Bay NFL	16	0	0	...	0	
CFL totals (3 years)	46	17	150	8.8	0	
NFL totals (7 years)	75	6	89	14.8	1	
Pro totals (10 years)	121	23	239	10.4	1	

McGWIRE, DAN   QB   DOLPHINS

PERSONAL: Born December 18, 1967, in Pomona, Calif. ... 6-8/240. ... Full name: Daniel Scott McGwire. ... Brother of Mark McGwire, first baseman, Oakland Athletics.
HIGH SCHOOL: Claremont (Calif.).
COLLEGE: Iowa, then San Diego State (degree in public administration).
TRANSACTIONS/CAREER NOTES: Selected by Seattle Seahawks in first round (16th pick overall) of 1991 NFL draft. ... Signed by Seahawks (July 15, 1991). ... On injured reserve with hip injury (October 14, 1992-remainder of season). ... Granted free agency (February 17, 1994). ... Re-signed by Seahawks (May 20, 1994). ... Granted unconditional free agency (February 17, 1995). ... Signed by Miami Dolphins (April 24, 1995).
PRO STATISTICS: 1992—Fumbled once. 1994—Fumbled nine times and recovered three fumbles for minus seven yards.
MISCELLANEOUS: Regular-season record as starting NFL quarterback: 2-3 (.400).

M

			PASSING							RUSHING				TOTALS		
Year Team	G	Att.	Cmp.	Pct.	Yds.	TD	Int.	Avg.	Rat.	Att.	Yds.	Avg.	TD	TD	2pt.	Pts.
1991—Seattle NFL	1	7	3	42.9	27	0	1	3.86	14.3	0	0	...	0	0	...	0
1992—Seattle NFL	2	30	17	56.7	116	0	3	3.87	25.8	3	13	4.3	0	0	...	0
1993—Seattle NFL	2	5	3	60.0	24	1	0	4.80	111.7	1	-1	-1.0	0	0	...	0
1994—Seattle NFL	7	105	51	48.6	578	1	2	5.51	60.7	10	-6	-0.6	0	0	0	0
1995—Miami NFL	1	1	0	0.0	0	0	0	0.00	39.6	0	0	...	0	0	0	0
Pro totals (5 years)	13	148	74	50.0	745	2	6	5.03	52.3	14	6	0.4	0	0	0	0

McHALE, TOM   G

PERSONAL: Born February 25, 1963, in Gaithersburg, Md. ... 6-4/290.
HIGH SCHOOL: Gaithersburg (Md.).
COLLEGE: Cornell.
TRANSACTIONS/CAREER NOTES: Signed as non-drafted free agent by Tampa Bay Buccaneers (May 4, 1987). ... On injured reserve with back injury (September 7-November 28, 1987). ... On injured reserve with knee injury (September 24-November 23, 1990). ... Granted free agency (February 1, 1992). ... Re-signed by Buccaneers (August 19, 1992). ... Granted roster exemption (August 19-28, 1992). ... Released by Buccaneers (August 30, 1993). ... Signed by Philadelphia Eagles (September 8, 1993). ... Granted unconditional free agency (February 17, 1994). ... Re-signed by Eagles (September 24, 1994). ... Granted unconditional free agency (February 17, 1994). ... Signed by Atlanta Falcons (July 17, 1995). ... Released by Falcons (August 27, 1995). ... Signed by Miami Dolphins (September 2, 1995). ... Released by Dolphins (February 15, 1996).
PLAYING EXPERIENCE: Tampa Bay NFL, 1987-1992; Philadelphia NFL, 1993 and 1994; Miami NFL, 1995. ... Games: 1987 (3), 1988 (10), 1989 (15), 1990 (7), 1991 (15), 1992 (9), 1993 (8), 1994 (13), 1995 (7). Total: 87.
PRO STATISTICS: 1987—Recovered one fumble. 1988—Fumbled once for minus four yards.

McINTOSH, TODDRICK   DE   PACKERS

PERSONAL: Born January 22, 1972, in Tallahassee, Fla. ... 6-3/270.
HIGH SCHOOL: L.V. Berkner (Richardson, Texas).
COLLEGE: Florida State.
TRANSACTIONS/CAREER NOTES: Selected by Dallas Cowboys in seventh round (216th pick overall) of 1994 NFL draft. ... Signed by Cowboys (July 17, 1994). ... Claimed on waivers by Tampa Bay Buccaneers (November 22, 1994). ... Claimed on waivers by New Orleans Saints (December 21, 1995). ... Traded by Saints to Green Bay Packers for future considerations (May 10, 1996).
PLAYING EXPERIENCE: Tampa Bay NFL, 1994 and 1995. ... Games: 1994 (4), 1995 (11). Total: 15.
PRO STATISTICS: 1995—Credited with two sacks.

McINTYRE, GUY　　　　　　　　　　G

PERSONAL: Born February 17, 1961, in Thomasville, Ga. ... 6-3/275. ... Full name: Guy Maurice McIntyre. ... Cousin of Lomas Brown, offensive tackle, Arizona Cardinals; and cousin of Eric Curry, defensive end, Tampa Bay Buccaneers.
HIGH SCHOOL: Thomasville (Ga.).
COLLEGE: Georgia.
TRANSACTIONS/CAREER NOTES: Selected by Jacksonville Bulls in 1984 USFL territorial draft. ... Selected by San Francisco 49ers in third round (73rd pick overall) of 1984 NFL draft. ... Signed by 49ers (May 8, 1984). ... On injured reserve with foot injury (October 31, 1987-remainder of season). ... On reserve/did not report list (July 30-August 27, 1990). ... Granted unconditional free agency (February 17, 1994). ... Signed by Green Bay Packers (July 14, 1994). ... Granted unconditional free agency (February 17, 1995). ... Signed by Philadelphia Eagles (August 7, 1995). ... Granted unconditional free agency (February 16, 1996).
PLAYING EXPERIENCE: San Francisco NFL, 1984-1993; Green Bay NFL, 1994; Philadelphia NFL, 1995. ... Games: 1984 (15), 1985 (15), 1986 (16), 1987 (3), 1988 (16), 1989 (16), 1990 (16), 1991 (16), 1992 (16), 1993 (16), 1994 (10), 1995 (16). Total: 171.
CHAMPIONSHIP GAME EXPERIENCE: Played in NFC championship game (1984, 1988-1990, 1992 and 1993 seasons). ... Member of Super Bowl championship team (1984, 1988 and 1989 seasons).
HONORS: Played in Pro Bowl (1989-1993 seasons).
PRO STATISTICS: 1984—Returned one kickoff for no yards. 1985—Recovered one fumble in end zone for a touchdown. 1988—Caught one pass for 17 yards and a touchdown. 1991—Recovered one fumble. 1992—Recovered one fumble. 1993—Recovered two fumbles.

McIVER, EVERETT　　　　　　　G　　　　　　　　JETS

PERSONAL: Born August 5, 1970, in Fayetteville, N.C. ... 6-6/315.
HIGH SCHOOL: 71st Senior (Fayetteville, N.C.).
COLLEGE: Elizabeth (N.C.) City State.
TRANSACTIONS/CAREER NOTES: Signed as non-drafted free agent by San Diego Chargers (April 27, 1993). ... Claimed on waivers by Dallas Cowboys (July 27, 1993). ... Released by Cowboys (August 30, 1993). ... Re-signed by Cowboys to practice squad (August 31, 1993). ... Released by Cowboys (December 7, 1993). ... Signed by New York Jets to practice squad (December 10, 1993). ... Activated (January 2, 1994). ... Assigned by Jets to London Monarchs in 1996 World League enhancement allocation program (February 19, 1996).
PLAYING EXPERIENCE: New York Jets NFL, 1994 and 1995. ... Games: 1994 (4), 1995 (14). Total: 18.

McKENZIE, RALEIGH　　　　　　C　　　　　　　EAGLES

PERSONAL: Born February 8, 1963, in Knoxville, Tenn. ... 6-2/283. ... Twin brother of Reggie McKenzie, linebacker, Los Angeles Raiders, Phoenix Cardinals, San Francisco 49ers and Montreal Machine of World League (1985-1988, 1990 and 1992).
HIGH SCHOOL: Austin-East (Knoxville, Tenn.).
COLLEGE: Tennessee.
TRANSACTIONS/CAREER NOTES: Selected by Washington Redskins in 11th round (290th pick overall) of 1985 NFL draft. ... Signed by Redskins (June 20, 1985). ... Granted free agency (February 1, 1992). ... Re-signed by Redskins for 1992 season. ... Granted unconditional free agency (February 17, 1995). ... Signed by Philadelphia Eagles (March 28, 1995).
PLAYING EXPERIENCE: Washington NFL, 1985-1994; Philadelphia NFL, 1995. ... Games: 1985 (6), 1986 (15), 1987 (12), 1988 (16), 1989 (15), 1990 (16), 1991 (16), 1992 (16), 1993 (16), 1994 (16), 1995 (16). Total: 160.
CHAMPIONSHIP GAME EXPERIENCE: Played in NFC championship game (1986, 1987 and 1991 seasons). ... Member of Super Bowl championship team (1987 and 1991 seasons).
PRO STATISTICS: 1994—Recovered one fumble. 1995—Recovered one fumble.

McKENZIE, RICH　　　　　　　LB　　　　　　PATRIOTS

PERSONAL: Born April 15, 1971, in Fort Lauderdale. ... 6-2/258. ... Full name: Richard Anthony McKenzie.
HIGH SCHOOL: Boyd Anderson (Fort Lauderdale).
COLLEGE: Penn State.
TRANSACTIONS/CAREER NOTES: Selected by Cleveland Browns in sixth round (153rd pick overall) of 1993 NFL draft. ... Signed by Browns (1993). ... Released by Browns (September 1, 1993). ... Re-signed by Browns to practice squad (September 6, 1993). ... Activated (December 23, 1993); did not play. ... On reserve/non-football injury list with sinus problem (August 2, 1994-February 6, 1995). ... Signed by New England Patriots (April 17, 1996).
PLAYING EXPERIENCE: Cleveland NFL, 1995 (8).
PRO STATISTICS: 1995—Credited with 1½ sacks and recovered one fumble for three yards.

McKNIGHT, JAMES　　　　　　WR　　　　　SEAHAWKS

PERSONAL: Born June 17, 1972, in Orlando. ... 6-0/186.
HIGH SCHOOL: ApoKa (Fla.).
COLLEGE: Liberty (Va.).
TRANSACTIONS/CAREER NOTES: Signed as non-drafted free agent by Seattle Seahawks (April 29, 1994). ... Released by Seahawks (August 28, 1994). ... Re-signed by Seahawks to practice squad (August 29, 1994). ... Activated (November 19, 1994).
PRO STATISTICS: 1995—Returned one kickoff for four yards and recovered one fumble.

| Year　Team | | RECEIVING | | | | TOTALS | | | |
	G	No.	Yds.	Avg.	TD	TD	2pt.	Pts.	Fum.
1994—Seattle NFL	2	1	25	25.0	1	1	0	6	0
1995—Seattle NFL	16	6	91	15.2	0	0	0	0	1
Pro totals (2 years)	18	7	116	16.6	1	1	0	6	1

M

McKYER, TIM   CB

PERSONAL: Born September 5, 1963, in Orlando. ... 6-0/178. ... Full name: Timothy Bernard McKyer.
HIGH SCHOOL: Lincoln (Port Arthur, Texas).
COLLEGE: Texas-Arlington.
TRANSACTIONS/CAREER NOTES: Selected by San Francisco 49ers in third round (64th pick overall) of 1986 NFL draft. ... Signed by 49ers (July 20, 1986). ... On suspended list (October 7-24, 1989). ... Traded by 49ers to Miami Dolphins for 11th-round pick (S Anthony Shelton) in 1990 draft and second-round pick (traded to Cincinnati) in 1991 draft (April 22, 1990). ... Granted free agency (February 1, 1991). ... Traded by Dolphins to Atlanta Falcons for third-round pick (RB Aaron Craver) in 1991 draft (April 22, 1991). ... Granted unconditional free agency (March 1, 1993). ... Signed by Detroit Lions (August 20, 1993). ... Granted unconditional free agency (February 17, 1994). ... Signed by Pittsburgh Steelers (August 24, 1994). ... Selected by Carolina Panthers from Steelers in NFL expansion draft (February 15, 1995). ... Granted unconditional free agency (February 16, 1996).
CHAMPIONSHIP GAME EXPERIENCE: Played in NFC championship game (1988 and 1989 seasons). ... Member of Super Bowl championship team (1988 and 1989 seasons). ... Played in AFC championship game (1994 season).
PRO STATISTICS: 1986—Returned one kickoff for 15 yards and returned one punt for five yards. 1991—Ran six yards with lateral from fumble recovery. 1992—Credited with one sack. 1993—Recovered one fumble for 23 yards. 1995—Recovered two fumbles.

		INTERCEPTIONS			
Year Team	G	No.	Yds.	Avg.	TD
1986—San Francisco NFL	16	6	33	5.5	1
1987—San Francisco NFL	12	2	0	0.0	0
1988—San Francisco NFL	16	7	11	1.6	0
1989—San Francisco NFL	7	1	18	18.0	0
1990—Miami NFL	16	4	40	10.0	0
1991—Atlanta NFL	16	6	24	4.0	0
1992—Atlanta NFL	16	1	0	0.0	0
1993—Detroit NFL	15	2	10	5.0	0
1994—Pittsburgh NFL	16	0	0	...	0
1995—Carolina NFL	16	3	99	33.0	1
Pro totals (10 years)	146	32	235	7.4	2

McLAUGHLIN, STEVE   K   FALCONS

PERSONAL: Born October 2, 1971, in Tucson, Ariz. ... 6-0/167. ... Full name: Steven John McLaughlin. ... Name pronounced mick-LAW-flin.
HIGH SCHOOL: Sahuaro (Tucson, Ariz.).
COLLEGE: Arizona.
TRANSACTIONS/CAREER NOTES: Selected by St. Louis Rams in third round (82nd pick overall) of 1995 NFL draft. ... Signed by Rams (July 17, 1995). ... Released by Rams (October 30, 1995). ... Signed by Atlanta Falcons (April 24, 1996).
HONORS: Lou Groza Award winner (1994). ... Named kicker on THE SPORTING NEWS college All-America first team (1994).

		KICKING						
Year Team	G	XPM	XPA	FGM	FGA	Lg.	50+	Pts.
1995—St. Louis NFL	8	17	17	8	16	45	0-1	41

McLEMORE, TOM   DL   COLTS

PERSONAL: Born March 14, 1970, in Shreveport, La. ... 6-5/250. ... Full name: Thomas Tyree McLemore.
HIGH SCHOOL: Huntington (Shreveport, La.).
COLLEGE: Southern (La.).
TRANSACTIONS/CAREER NOTES: Selected by Detroit Lions in third round (81st pick overall) of 1992 NFL draft. ... Signed by Lions (July 23, 1992). ... On injured reserve with shoulder injury (September 1-October 7, 1992). ... Claimed on waivers by Cleveland Browns (August 31, 1993). ... Released by Browns (October 10, 1993). ... Re-signed by Browns (October 27, 1993). ... Released by Browns (November 9, 1993). ... Re-signed by Browns (November 19, 1993). ... Granted unconditional free agency (February 17, 1995). ... Signed by Indianapolis Colts (April 28, 1995). ... On injured reserve with foot injury (October 6, 1995).
PLAYING EXPERIENCE: Detroit NFL, 1992; Cleveland NFL, 1993 and 1994; Indianapolis NFL, 1995. ... Games: 1992 (11), 1993 (4), 1994 (2), 1995 (1). Total: 18.
PRO STATISTICS: 1992—Caught two passes for 12 yards.
MISCELLANEOUS: Played tight end (1992-1995).

McMAHON, JIM   QB   PACKERS

PERSONAL: Born August 21, 1959, in Jersey City, N.J. ... 6-1/195. ... Full name: James Robert McMahon.
HIGH SCHOOL: Roy (Utah).
COLLEGE: Brigham Young.
TRANSACTIONS/CAREER NOTES: Selected by Chicago Bears in first round (fifth pick overall) of 1982 NFL draft. ... On injured reserve with lacerated kidney (November 9, 1984-remainder of season). ... On injured reserve with shoulder injury (November 28, 1986-remainder of season). ... On injured reserve with shoulder injury (September 7-October 22, 1987). ... On injured reserve with knee injury (November 5-December 9, 1988). ... Traded by Bears to San Diego Chargers for second-round pick (LB Ron Cox) in 1990 draft (August 18, 1989). ... Granted free agency (February 1, 1990). ... Rights relinquished by Chargers (April 26, 1990). ... Signed by Philadelphia Eagles (July 10, 1990). ... Granted unconditional free agency (February 1-April 1, 1991). ... Re-signed by Eagles (July 15, 1991). ... Granted unconditional free agency (February 1-April 1, 1992). ... Re-signed by Eagles for 1992 season. ... Granted unconditional free agency (March 1, 1993). ... Signed by Minnesota Vikings (March 30, 1993). ... Released by Vikings (March 14, 1994). ... Signed by Arizona Cardinals (June 2, 1994). ... Granted unconditional free agency (February 17, 1995). ... Signed by Cleveland Browns (August 9, 1995). ... Released by Browns (August 27, 1995). ... Re-signed by Browns (October 5, 1995). ... Claimed on waivers by Green Bay Packers (November 28, 1995). ... Granted unconditional free agency (February 16, 1996). ... Re-signed by Packers (April 11, 1996).
CHAMPIONSHIP GAME EXPERIENCE: Played in NFC championship game (1985 and 1988 seasons). ... Member of Super Bowl championship

M

team (1985 season). ... Member of Packers for NFC championship game (1995 season); did not play.
HONORS: Davey O'Brien Award winner (1981). ... Played in Pro Bowl (1985 season).
POSTSEASON RECORDS: Shares Super Bowl single-game record for most rushing touchdowns—2 (January 26, 1986, vs. New England).
PRO STATISTICS: 1982—Punted once for 59 yards and fumbled once. 1983—Caught one pass for 18 yards and a touchdown, punted once for 36 yards, fumbled four times and recovered three fumbles. 1984—Caught one pass for 42 yards and fumbled once. 1985—Caught one pass for 13 yards and a touchdown and fumbled four times. 1986—Fumbled once. 1987—Fumbled twice. 1988—Fumbled six times and recovered three fumbles. 1989—Caught one pass for four yards, fumbled three times and recovered one fumble. 1991—Caught one pass for minus five yards, fumbled twice and recovered two fumbles. 1993—Fumbled four times and recovered one fumble for minus seven yards. 1994—Fumbled once.
STATISTICAL PLATEAUS: 300-yard passing games: 1987 (1), 1989 (1), 1991 (1). Total: 3.
MISCELLANEOUS: Regular-season record as starting NFL quarterback: 67-30 (.691).

					PASSING						RUSHING				TOTALS		
Year Team	G	Att.	Cmp.	Pct.	Yds.	TD	Int.	Avg.	Rat.	Att.	Yds.	Avg.	TD	TD	2pt.	Pts.
1982—Chicago NFL	8	210	120	57.1	1501	9	7	7.15	79.9	24	105	4.4	1	1	...	6
1983—Chicago NFL	14	295	175	59.3	2184	12	13	7.40	77.6	55	307	5.6	2	3	...	18
1984—Chicago NFL	9	143	85	59.4	1146	8	2	8.01	97.8	39	276	7.1	2	2	...	12
1985—Chicago NFL	13	313	178	56.9	2392	15	11	7.64	82.6	47	252	5.4	3	4	...	24
1986—Chicago NFL	6	150	77	51.3	995	5	8	6.63	61.4	22	152	6.9	1	1	...	6
1987—Chicago NFL	7	210	125	59.5	1639	12	8	7.81	87.4	22	88	4.0	2	2	...	12
1988—Chicago NFL	9	192	114	59.4	1346	6	7	7.01	76.0	26	104	4.0	4	4	...	24
1989—San Diego NFL	12	318	176	55.4	2132	10	10	6.71	73.5	29	141	4.9	0	0	...	0
1990—Philadelphia NFL	5	9	6	66.7	63	0	0	7.00	86.8	3	1	.3	0	0	...	0
1991—Philadelphia NFL	12	311	187	60.1	2239	12	11	7.20	80.3	22	55	2.5	1	1	...	6
1992—Philadelphia NFL	4	43	22	51.2	279	1	2	6.49	60.1	6	23	3.8	0	0	...	0
1993—Minnesota NFL	12	331	200	60.4	1968	9	8	5.95	76.2	33	96	2.9	0	0	...	0
1994—Arizona NFL	2	43	23	53.5	219	1	3	5.09	46.6	6	32	5.3	0	0	0	0
1995—Green Bay NFL	1	1	1	100.0	6	0	0	6.00	91.7	0	0	...	0	0	0	0
Pro totals (14 years)	114	2569	1489	58.0	18109	100	90	7.05	78.1	334	1632	4.9	16	18	0	108

McMANUS, TOM   LB   JAGUARS

PERSONAL: Born July 30, 1970, in Buffalo Grove, Ill. ... 6-2/252. ... Full name: Thomas Edward McManus.
HIGH SCHOOL: Wheeling (Ill.).
COLLEGE: Boston College.
TRANSACTIONS/CAREER NOTES: Signed as non-drafted free agent by New Orleans Saints (May 7, 1993). ... Released by Saints (August 24, 1993). ... Signed by Jacksonville Jaguars (February 1, 1995).
PLAYING EXPERIENCE: Jacksonville NFL, 1995. ... Games: 1995 (14).

McMILLAN, ERIK   S   BRONCOS

M

PERSONAL: Born May 3, 1965, in St. Louis. ... 6-2/200. ... Full name: Erik Charles McMillan. ... Son of Ernie McMillan, offensive tackle, St. Louis Cardinals and Green Bay Packers (1961-1975) and assistant coach, Packers and Cardinals (1979-1983 and 1985); and cousin of Howard Richards, offensive lineman, Dallas Cowboys and Seattle Seahawks (1981-1987).
HIGH SCHOOL: John F. Kennedy (Silver Spring, Md.).
COLLEGE: Missouri (degree in business management, 1988), then Fordham (master's degree in education administration, 1991).
TRANSACTIONS/CAREER NOTES: Selected by New York Jets in third round (63rd pick overall) of 1988 NFL draft. ... Signed by Jets (July 6, 1988). ... On injured reserve with sprained arch (December 17, 1988-remainder of season). ... Granted unconditional free agency (March 1, 1993). ... Signed by Philadelphia Eagles (April 22, 1993). ... Released by Eagles (August 30, 1993). ... Re-signed by Eagles (September 1, 1993). ... Released by Eagles (October 24, 1993). ... Signed by Cleveland Browns (November 9, 1993). ... Released by Browns (November 30, 1993). ... Signed by Kansas City Chiefs (December 29, 1993). ... Released by Chiefs (January 19, 1994). ... Signed by Denver Broncos (April 9, 1996).
HONORS: Played in Pro Bowl (1988 and 1989 seasons).
RECORDS: Shares NFL single-season records for most touchdowns by fumble recovery—2 (1989); most touchdowns by recovery of opponents' fumbles—2 (1989).
PRO STATISTICS: 1989—Recovered two fumbles for 119 yards and two touchdowns. 1990—Fumbled three times and recovered one fumble for one yard. 1991—Recovered one fumble. 1992—Recovered two fumbles.

		INTERCEPTIONS				SACKS	KICKOFF RETURNS				TOTALS			
Year Team	G	No.	Yds.	Avg.	TD	No.	No.	Yds.	Avg.	TD	TD	2pt.	Pts.	Fum.
1988—New York Jets NFL	13	8	168	21.0	*2	0.0	0	0	...	0	2	...	12	1
1989—New York Jets NFL	16	6	180	30.0	1	2.0	0	0	...	0	3	...	18	0
1990—New York Jets NFL	16	5	92	18.4	0	0.0	0	0	...	0	0	...	0	3
1991—New York Jets NFL	16	3	168	56.0	*2	1.0	0	0	...	0	2	...	12	0
1992—New York Jets NFL	15	0	0	...	0	2.0	22	420	19.1	0	0	...	0	1
1993—Philadelphia NFL	6	0	0	...	0	0.0	0	0	...	0	0	...	0	0
—Cleveland NFL	3	0	0	...	0	0.0	0	0	...	0	0	...	0	0
—Kansas City NFL	1	0	0	...	0	0.0	0	0	...	0	0	...	0	0
1994—						Did not play.								
1995—						Did not play.								
Pro totals (6 years)	86	22	608	27.6	5	5.0	22	420	19.1	0	7	0	42	5

McMILLIAN, HENRY   DT   SEAHAWKS

PERSONAL: Born October 17, 1971, in Folkston, Ga. ... 6-3/275. ... Full name: Henry James McMillian.
HIGH SCHOOL: Folkston (Ga.).
COLLEGE: Florida.

McMILLIAN, MARK   CB   SAINTS

PERSONAL: Born April 29, 1970, in Los Angeles. ... 5-7/148. ... Nephew of Gary Davis, running back, Miami Dolphins, Cleveland Browns and Tampa Bay Buccaneers (1976-1981). ... Name pronounced mik-MILL-en.
HIGH SCHOOL: John F. Kennedy (Granada Hills, Calif.).
JUNIOR COLLEGE: Glendale (Calif.) College.
COLLEGE: Alabama.
TRANSACTIONS/CAREER NOTES: Selected by Philadelphia Eagles in 10th round (272nd pick overall) of 1992 NFL draft. ... Signed by Eagles (July 20, 1992). ... Granted unconditional free agency (February 16, 1996). ... Signed by New Orleans Saints (February 29, 1996).
PRO STATISTICS: 1993—Fumbled once and recovered one fumble. 1994—Recovered one fumble. 1995—Recovered two fumbles for minus one yard.

		INTERCEPTIONS			
Year Team	G	No.	Yds.	Avg.	TD
1992—Philadelphia NFL	16	1	0	0.0	0
1993—Philadelphia NFL	16	2	25	12.5	0
1994—Philadelphia NFL	16	2	2	1.0	0
1995—Philadelphia NFL	16	3	27	9.0	0
Pro totals (4 years)	64	8	54	6.8	0

McMURTRY, GREG   WR   REDSKINS

PERSONAL: Born October 15, 1967, in Brockton, Mass. ... 6-2/210. ... Full name: Greg Wendell McMurtry.
HIGH SCHOOL: Brockton (Mass.).
COLLEGE: Michigan (degree in general studies).
TRANSACTIONS/CAREER NOTES: Selected by New England Patriots in third round (80th pick overall) of 1990 NFL draft. ... On injured reserve with ankle injury (December 21, 1991-remainder of season). ... Granted free agency (February 1, 1992). ... Re-signed by Patriots (June 5, 1992). ... Granted unconditional free agency (February 17, 1994). ... Signed by Los Angeles Rams (May 10, 1994). ... Claimed on waivers by Chicago Bears (August 23, 1994). ... Granted unconditional free agency (February 17, 1995). ... Re-signed by Bears (March 10, 1995). ... Released by Bears (August 22, 1995). ... Signed by Washington Redskins (January 30, 1996).
PRO STATISTICS: 1992—Rushed twice for three yards and attempted one pass without a completion. 1993—Recovered one fumble.
STATISTICAL PLATEAUS: 100-yard receiving games: 1991 (1).

		RECEIVING				TOTALS			
Year Team	G	No.	Yds.	Avg.	TD	TD	2pt.	Pts.	Fum.
1990—New England NFL	13	22	240	10.9	0	0	...	0	1
1991—New England NFL	15	41	614	15.0	2	2	...	12	1
1992—New England NFL	16	35	424	12.1	1	1	...	6	0
1993—New England NFL	14	22	241	11.0	1	1	...	6	1
1994—Chicago NFL	9	8	112	14.0	1	1	0	6	0
1995—					Did not play.				
Pro totals (5 years)	67	128	1631	12.8	5	5	0	30	3

McNABB, DEXTER   FB   SAINTS

PERSONAL: Born July 9, 1969, in De Funiak Springs, Fla. ... 6-2/250. ... Full name: Dexter Eugene McNabb.
HIGH SCHOOL: Walton Senior (De Funiak Springs, Fla.).
COLLEGE: Florida.
TRANSACTIONS/CAREER NOTES: Selected by Green Bay Packers in fifth round (119th pick overall) of 1992 NFL draft. ... Signed by Packers (July 20, 1992). ... Released by Packers (August 28, 1994). ... Signed by Jacksonville Jaguars (December 30, 1994). ... Released by Jaguars (August 27, 1995). ... Signed by Philadelphia Eagles (September 12, 1995). ... Released by Eagles (October 21, 1995). ... Signed by New Orleans Saints (February 26, 1996).

		RUSHING				KICKOFF RETURNS				TOTALS			
Year Team	G	Att.	Yds.	Avg.	TD	No.	Yds.	Avg.	TD	TD	2pt.	Pts.	Fum.
1992—Green Bay NFL	16	2	11	5.5	0	1	15	15.0	0	0	...	0	0
1993—Green Bay NFL	16	0	0	...	0	0	0	...	0	0	...	0	0
1995—Philadelphia NFL	1	0	0	...	0	0	0	...	0	0	0	0	0
Pro totals (3 years)	33	2	11	5.5	0	1	15	15.0	0	0	0	0	0

McNAIR, STEVE   QB   OILERS

PERSONAL: Born February 14, 1973, in Mount Olive, Miss. ... 6-2/224. ... Brother of Fred McNair, quarterback, Florida Bobcats of Arena Football League. ...Nickname: Air McNair.
HIGH SCHOOL: Mount Olive (Miss.).
COLLEGE: Alcorn State.
TRANSACTIONS/CAREER NOTES: Selected by Houston Oilers in first round (third pick overall) of 1995 NFL draft. ... Signed by Oilers (July 25, 1995).
HONORS: Walter Payton Award winner (1994).
PRO STATISTICS: 1995—Fumbled three times and recovered two fumbles for minus two yards.
MISCELLANEOUS: Regular-season record as starting NFL quarterback: 2-0 (1.000).

M

Year Team	G	Att.	Cmp.	Pct.	Yds.	TD	Int.	Avg.	Rat.	Att.	Yds.	Avg.	TD	TD	2pt.	Pts.
				PASSING							RUSHING				TOTALS	
1995—Houston NFL	4	80	41	51.3	569	3	1	7.11	81.7	11	38	3.5	0	0	0	0

McNAIR, TODD — RB/KR

PERSONAL: Born October 7, 1965, in Camden, N.J. ... 6-1/202. ... Full name: Todd Darren McNair.
HIGH SCHOOL: Pennsauken (N.J.).
COLLEGE: Temple (degree in sociology).
TRANSACTIONS/CAREER NOTES: Selected by Kansas City Chiefs in eighth round (220th pick overall) of 1989 NFL draft. ... Signed by Chiefs (July 12, 1989). ... Released by Chiefs (September 5, 1989). ... Re-signed by Chiefs to developmental squad (September 6, 1989). ... Activated (September 22, 1989). ... Granted free agency (February 1, 1991). ... Re-signed by Chiefs (August 29, 1991). ... Granted roster exemption (August 29-September 7, 1991). ... Granted free agency (March 1, 1993). ... Re-signed by Chiefs (August 1993). ... Activated (September 6, 1993). ... Granted unconditional free agency (February 17, 1994). ... Signed by Houston Oilers (August 1, 1994). ... Granted unconditional free agency (February 17, 1995). ... Re-signed by Oilers (June 2, 1995). ... Released by Oilers (February 15, 1996).
CHAMPIONSHIP GAME EXPERIENCE: Played in AFC championship game (1993 season).
PRO STATISTICS: 1990—Recovered one fumble. 1991—Recovered two fumbles. 1992—Recovered one fumble. 1994—Recovered one fumble.
STATISTICAL PLATEAUS: 100-yard receiving games: 1990 (1).

Year Team	G	Att.	Yds.	Avg.	TD	No.	Yds.	Avg.	TD	No.	Yds.	Avg.	TD	TD	2pt.	Pts.	Fum.
		RUSHING				RECEIVING				KICKOFF RETURNS				TOTALS			
1989—Kansas City NFL	14	23	121	5.3	0	34	372	10.9	1	13	257	19.8	0	1	...	6	1
1990—Kansas City NFL	15	14	61	4.4	0	40	507	12.7	2	14	227	16.2	0	2	...	12	1
1991—Kansas City NFL	14	10	51	5.1	0	37	342	9.2	1	4	66	16.5	0	1	...	6	2
1992—Kansas City NFL	16	21	124	5.9	1	44	380	8.6	1	2	20	10.0	0	2	...	12	1
1993—Kansas City NFL	15	51	278	5.5	2	10	74	7.4	0	1	28	28.0	0	2	...	12	2
1994—Houston NFL	16	0	0	...	0	8	78	9.8	0	23	481	20.9	0	0	0	0	0
1995—Houston NFL	15	19	136	7.2	0	60	501	8.4	1	0	0	...	0	1	0	6	1
Pro totals (7 years)	105	138	771	5.6	3	233	2254	9.7	6	57	1079	18.9	0	9	0	54	8

McNEIL, RYAN — CB — LIONS

PERSONAL: Born October 4, 1970, in Fort Pierce, Fla. ... 6-2/192. ... Full name: Ryan Darrell McNeil.
HIGH SCHOOL: Fort Pierce (Fla.) Westwood.
COLLEGE: Miami (Fla.).
TRANSACTIONS/CAREER NOTES: Selected by Detroit Lions in second round (33rd pick overall) of 1993 NFL draft. ... Signed by Lions (August 25, 1993).
HONORS: Named defensive back on THE SPORTING NEWS college All-America second team (1992).
PRO STATISTICS: 1995—Recovered two fumbles.

Year Team	G	No.	Yds.	Avg.	TD
		INTERCEPTIONS			
1993—Detroit NFL	16	2	19	9.5	0
1994—Detroit NFL	14	1	14	14.0	0
1995—Detroit NFL	16	2	26	13.0	0
Pro totals (3 years)	46	5	59	11.8	0

McRAE, CHARLES — OT/G — RAIDERS

PERSONAL: Born September 16, 1968, in Clinton, Tenn. ... 6-7/306. ... Full name: Charles Edward McRae.
HIGH SCHOOL: Clinton (Tenn.).
COLLEGE: Tennessee (degree in history).
TRANSACTIONS/CAREER NOTES: Selected by Tampa Bay Buccaneers in first round (seventh pick overall) of 1991 NFL draft. ... Signed by Buccaneers (August 14, 1991). ... Granted unconditional free agency (February 16, 1996). ... Signed by Oakland Raiders (March 5, 1996).
PLAYING EXPERIENCE: Tampa Bay NFL, 1991-1995. ... Games: 1991 (16), 1992 (16), 1993 (13), 1994 (15), 1995 (11). Total: 71.

MEANS, NATRONE — RB — JAGUARS

PERSONAL: Born April 26, 1972, in Harrisburg, N.C. ... 5-10/245. ... Full name: Natrone Jermaine Means. ... Name pronounced NAY-trone.
HIGH SCHOOL: Central Cabarrus (Concord, N.C.).
COLLEGE: North Carolina.
TRANSACTIONS/CAREER NOTES: Selected after junior season by San Diego Chargers in second round (41st pick overall) of 1993 NFL draft. ... Signed by Chargers (July 18, 1993). ... Claimed on waivers by Jacksonville Jaguars (March 11, 1996).
CHAMPIONSHIP GAME EXPERIENCE: Played in AFC championship game (1994 season). ... Played in Super Bowl XXIX (1994 season).
HONORS: Played in Pro Bowl (1994 season).
PRO STATISTICS: 1993—Attempted one pass without a completion, returned two kickoffs for 22 yards and recovered one fumble. 1994—Attempted one pass without a completion.
STATISTICAL PLATEAUS: 100-yard rushing games: 1993 (2), 1994 (6), 1995 (3). Total: 11.

Year Team	G	Att.	Yds.	Avg.	TD	No.	Yds.	Avg.	TD	TD	2pt.	Pts.	Fum.
		RUSHING				RECEIVING				TOTALS			
1993—San Diego NFL	16	160	645	4.0	8	10	59	5.9	0	8	...	48	1
1994—San Diego NFL	16	343	1350	3.9	12	39	235	6.0	0	12	0	72	5
1995—San Diego NFL	10	186	730	3.9	5	7	46	6.6	0	5	0	30	2
Pro totals (3 years)	42	689	2725	4.0	25	56	340	6.1	0	25	0	150	8

M

MEGGETT, DAVE　　　RB/KR　　　PATRIOTS

PERSONAL: Born April 30, 1966, in Charleston, S.C. ... 5-7/195. ... Full name: David Lee Meggett.
HIGH SCHOOL: Bonds-Wilson (North Charleston, S.C.).
COLLEGE: Morgan State, then Towson State.
TRANSACTIONS/CAREER NOTES: Selected by New York Giants in fifth round (132nd pick overall) of 1989 NFL draft. ... Signed by Giants (July 24, 1989). ... Granted free agency (February 1, 1991). ... Re-signed by Giants (August 29, 1991). ... Activated (September 2, 1991). ... Granted free agency (March 1, 1993). ... Re-signed by Giants (July 28, 1993). ... Granted unconditional free agency (February 17, 1995). ... Signed by New England Patriots (March 3, 1995).
CHAMPIONSHIP GAME EXPERIENCE: Played in NFC championship game (1990 season). ... Member of Super Bowl championship team (1990 season).
HONORS: Walter Payton Award winner (1988). ... Played in Pro Bowl (1989 season). ... Named punt returner on THE SPORTING NEWS NFL All-Pro team (1990).
POSTSEASON RECORDS: Shares Super Bowl single-game record for most fair catches—3 (January 27, 1991, vs. Buffalo).
PRO STATISTICS: 1989—Fumbled eight times and recovered three fumbles. 1990—Fumbled three times and recovered two fumbles. 1991—Attempted one pass without a completion, fumbled eight times and recovered three fumbles. 1992—Fumbled five times and recovered three fumbles. 1993—Attempted two passes with two completions for 63 yards and two touchdowns, fumbled once and recovered one fumble. 1994—Attempted two passes with one completion for 16 yards and a touchdown, fumbled six times and recovered five fumbles. 1995—Attempted one pass without a completion and fumbled five times.

Year　Team	G	RUSHING				RECEIVING				PUNT RETURNS				KICKOFF RETURNS				TOTALS		
		Att.	Yds.	Avg.	TD	No.	Yds.	Avg.	TD	No.	Yds.	Avg.	TD	No.	Yds.	Avg.	TD	TD	2pt.	Pts.
1989—New York Giants NFL .	16	28	117	4.2	0	34	531	15.6	4	46	*582	12.7	†1	27	577	21.4	0	5	...	30
1990—New York Giants NFL .	16	22	164	7.5	0	39	410	10.5	1	*43	*467	10.9	†1	21	492	23.4	0	2	...	12
1991—New York Giants NFL .	16	29	153	5.3	1	50	412	8.2	3	28	287	10.3	1	25	514	20.6	0	5	...	30
1992—New York Giants NFL .	16	32	167	5.2	0	38	229	6.0	2	27	240	8.9	0	20	455	22.8	1	3	...	18
1993—New York Giants NFL .	16	69	329	4.8	0	38	319	8.4	0	32	331	10.3	1	24	403	16.8	0	1	...	6
1994—New York Giants NFL .	16	91	298	3.3	4	32	293	9.2	0	26	323	12.4	†2	29	548	18.9	0	6	0	36
1995—New England NFL.......	16	60	250	4.2	2	52	334	6.4	0	45	383	8.5	0	38	964	25.4	0	2	2	16
Pro totals (7 years)	112	331	1478	4.5	7	283	2528	8.9	10	247	2613	10.6	6	184	3953	21.5	1	24	2	148

MERRITT, DAVID　　　LB

PERSONAL: Born September 8, 1971, in Raleigh, N.C. ... 6-1/237. ... Full name: David Lee Merritt.
HIGH SCHOOL: Millbrook (Raleigh, N.C.).
COLLEGE: North Carolina State.
TRANSACTIONS/CAREER NOTES: Selected by Miami Dolphins in seventh round (191st pick overall) of 1993 NFL draft. ... Signed by Dolphins (July 15, 1993). ... Released by Dolphins (October 8, 1993). ... Re-signed by Dolphins to practice squad (October 9, 1993). ... Signed by Phoenix Cardinals off Dolphins practice squad (November 17, 1993). ... Cardinals franchise renamed Arizona Cardinals for 1994 season. ... Granted unconditional free agency (February 16, 1996).
PLAYING EXPERIENCE: Miami (4)-Phoenix (3) NFL, 1993; Arizona NFL, 1994 and 1995. ... Games: 1993 (7), 1994 (16), 1995 (15). Total: 38.
PRO STATISTICS: 1994—Recovered one fumble.

METCALF, ERIC　　　WR/KR　　　FALCONS

PERSONAL: Born January 23, 1968, in Seattle. ... 5-10/190. ... Full name: Eric Quinn Metcalf. ... Son of Terry Metcalf, running back, St. Louis Cardinals, Toronto Argonauts of CFL and Washington Redskins (1973-1981); and cousin of Ray Hall, defensive tackle, Jacksonville Jaguars.
HIGH SCHOOL: Bishop Dennis J. O'Connell (Arlington, Va.).
COLLEGE: Texas (degree in liberal arts, 1990).
TRANSACTIONS/CAREER NOTES: Selected by Cleveland Browns in first round (13th pick overall) of 1989 NFL draft. ... Signed by Browns (August 20, 1989). ... Granted free agency (February 1, 1991). ... Re-signed by Browns (1991). ... On injured reserve with shoulder injury (November 2, 1991-remainder of season). ... Granted free agency (February 1, 1992). ... Re-signed by Browns (August 30, 1992). ... Granted roster exemption (August 30-September 5, 1992). ... Traded by Browns with first-round pick (DB Devin Bush) in 1995 draft to Atlanta Falcons for first-round pick (traded to San Francisco in 1995 draft (March 25, 1995).
CHAMPIONSHIP GAME EXPERIENCE: Played in AFC championship game (1989 season).
HONORS: Named all-purpose player on THE SPORTING NEWS college All-America second team (1987). ... Named punt returner on THE SPORTING NEWS NFL All-Pro team (1993 and 1994). ... Played in Pro Bowl (1993 and 1994 seasons).
RECORDS: Shares NFL single-game records for most touchdowns by punt return—2; and most touchdowns by combined kick return—2 (October 24, 1993, vs. Pittsburgh).
POSTSEASON RECORDS: Shares NFL postseason career record for most touchdowns by kickoff return—1 (January 6, 1990, vs. Buffalo).
PRO STATISTICS: 1989—Attempted two passes with one completion for 32 yards and a touchdown and fumbled five times. 1990—Fumbled eight times and recovered one fumble. 1991—Fumbled once. 1992—Attempted one pass without a completion, fumbled six times and recovered two fumbles. 1993—Fumbled five times. 1994—Attempted one pass without a completion and fumbled six times. 1995—Attempted one pass without a completion, fumbled four times and recovered two fumbles.
STATISTICAL PLATEAUS: 100-yard receiving games: 1992 (1), 1993 (1), 1995 (2). Total: 4.

Year　Team	G	RUSHING				RECEIVING				PUNT RETURNS				KICKOFF RETURNS				TOTALS		
		Att.	Yds.	Avg.	TD	No.	Yds.	Avg.	TD	No.	Yds.	Avg.	TD	No.	Yds.	Avg.	TD	TD	2pt.	Pts.
1989—Cleveland NFL	16	187	633	3.4	6	54	397	7.4	4	0	0	...	0	31	718	23.2	0	10	...	60
1990—Cleveland NFL	16	80	248	3.1	1	57	452	7.9	1	0	0	...	0	*52	*1052	20.2	*2	4	...	24
1991—Cleveland NFL	8	30	107	3.6	0	29	294	10.1	0	12	100	8.3	0	23	351	15.3	0	0	...	0
1992—Cleveland NFL	16	73	301	4.1	1	47	614	13.1	5	*44	429	9.8	1	9	157	17.4	0	7	...	42
1993—Cleveland NFL	16	129	611	4.7	1	63	539	8.6	2	36	464	12.9	†2	15	318	21.2	0	5	...	30
1994—Cleveland NFL	16	93	329	3.5	2	47	436	9.3	3	35	348	9.9	†2	9	210	23.3	0	7	0	42
1995—Atlanta NFL................	16	28	133	4.8	1	104	1189	11.4	8	39	383	9.8	†1	12	278	23.2	0	10	0	60
Pro totals (7 years)	104	620	2362	3.8	12	401	3921	9.8	23	166	1724	10.4	6	151	3084	20.4	2	43	0	258

METZELAARS, PETE   TE   LIONS

PERSONAL: Born May 24, 1960, in Three Rivers, Mich. ... 6-7/254. ... Full name: Peter Henry Metzelaars. ... Name pronounced METZ-eh-lars.
HIGH SCHOOL: Central (Portage, Mich.).
COLLEGE: Wabash, Ind. (degree in economics, 1982).
TRANSACTIONS/CAREER NOTES: Selected by Seattle Seahawks in third round (75th pick overall) of 1982 NFL draft. ... On injured reserve with knee injury (October 17-December 1, 1984). ... Traded by Seahawks to Buffalo Bills for WR Byron Franklin (August 20, 1985). ... Granted unconditional free agency (February 1-April 1, 1992). ... Re-signed by Bills (1992). ... Granted unconditional free agency (March 1, 1993). ... Re-signed by Bills (May 21, 1993). ... Granted unconditional free agency (February 17, 1995). ... Signed by Carolina Panthers (March 8, 1995). ... Released by Panthers (February 14, 1996). ... Signed by Detroit Lions (May 7, 1996).
CHAMPIONSHIP GAME EXPERIENCE: Played in AFC championship game (1983, 1988 and 1990-1993 seasons). ... Played in Super Bowl XXV (1990 season), Super Bowl XXVI (1991 season), Super Bowl XXVII (1992 season) and Super Bowl XXVIII (1993 season).
PRO STATISTICS: 1982—Recovered one fumble. 1983—Returned one kickoff for no yards. 1985—Recovered one fumble for two yards. 1986—Recovered one fumble in end zone for a touchdown. 1987—Recovered one fumble. 1988—Recovered one fumble.
STATISTICAL PLATEAUS: 100-yard receiving games: 1986 (1), 1992 (1). Total: 2.

| | | RECEIVING | | | | TOTALS | | | |
Year Team	G	No.	Yds.	Avg.	TD	TD	2pt.	Pts.	Fum.
1982—Seattle NFL	9	15	152	10.1	0	0	...	0	2
1983—Seattle NFL	16	7	72	10.3	1	1	...	6	0
1984—Seattle NFL	9	5	80	16.0	0	0	...	0	1
1985—Buffalo NFL	16	12	80	6.7	1	1	...	6	0
1986—Buffalo NFL	16	49	485	9.9	3	4	...	24	2
1987—Buffalo NFL	12	28	290	10.4	0	0	...	0	3
1988—Buffalo NFL	16	33	438	13.3	1	1	...	6	0
1989—Buffalo NFL	16	18	179	9.9	2	2	...	12	0
1990—Buffalo NFL	16	10	60	6.0	1	1	...	6	1
1991—Buffalo NFL	16	5	54	10.8	2	2	...	12	0
1992—Buffalo NFL	16	30	298	9.9	6	6	...	36	0
1993—Buffalo NFL	16	68	609	9.0	4	4	...	24	1
1994—Buffalo NFL	16	49	428	8.7	5	5	0	30	0
1995—Carolina NFL	14	20	171	8.6	3	3	0	18	0
Pro totals (14 years)	204	349	3396	9.7	29	30	0	180	10

MIANO, RICH   S

PERSONAL: Born September 3, 1962, in Newton, Mass. ... 6-1/200. ... Full name: Richard James Miano. ... Name pronounced mee-ON-oh.
HIGH SCHOOL: Kaiser (Honolulu).
COLLEGE: Hawaii.
TRANSACTIONS/CAREER NOTES: Selected by Denver Gold in ninth round (132nd pick overall) of 1985 USFL draft. ... Selected by New York Jets in sixth round (166th pick overall) of 1985 NFL draft. ... Signed by Jets (July 16, 1985). ... Released by Jets (September 2, 1985). ... Re-signed by Jets (September 3, 1985). ... On injured reserve with knee injury (September 19, 1989-remainder of season). ... On physically unable to perform list with knee injury (August 27, 1990-November 14, 1990). ... Released by Jets (November 14, 1990). ... Signed by Philadelphia Eagles (May 16, 1991). ... Granted free agency (February 1, 1992). ... Re-signed by Eagles (August 3, 1992). ... Granted unconditional free agency (February 17, 1994). ... Re-signed by Eagles (July 11, 1994). ... Granted unconditional free agency (February 17, 1995). ... Signed by Atlanta Falcons (March 28, 1995). ... Granted unconditional free agency (February 16, 1996).
PRO STATISTICS: 1987—Returned blocked field-goal attempt 67 yards for a touchdown. 1988—Credited with ½ sack. 1992—Recovered two fumbles. 1993—Recovered one fumble.

| | | INTERCEPTIONS | | | |
Year Team	G	No.	Yds.	Avg.	TD
1985—New York Jets NFL	16	2	9	4.5	0
1986—New York Jets NFL	14	0	0	...	0
1987—New York Jets NFL	12	3	24	8.0	0
1988—New York Jets NFL	16	2	0	0.0	0
1989—New York Jets NFL	2	0	0	...	0
1990—			Did not play.		
1991—Philadelphia NFL	16	3	30	10.0	0
1992—Philadelphia NFL	16	1	39	39.0	0
1993—Philadelphia NFL	16	4	26	6.5	0
1994—Philadelphia NFL	16	0	0	...	0
1995—Atlanta NFL	11	0	0	...	0
Pro totals (10 years)	135	15	128	8.5	0

MICKELL, DARREN   DE   SAINTS

PERSONAL: Born August 3, 1970, in Miami. ... 6-4/291.
HIGH SCHOOL: Senior (Miami).
COLLEGE: Florida.
TRANSACTIONS/CAREER NOTES: Selected by Kansas City Chiefs in second round of 1992 NFL supplemental draft (second of two supplemental drafts in 1992). ... Signed by Chiefs (September 16, 1992). ... Granted roster exemption (September 16-29, 1992). ... On injured reserve with knee injury (September 30-November 11, 1992). ... On practice squad (November 11-December 26, 1992). ... Granted unconditional free agency (February 16, 1996). ... Signed by New Orleans Saints (March 12, 1996).
CHAMPIONSHIP GAME EXPERIENCE: Played in AFC championship game (1993 season).
PRO STATISTICS: 1993—Recovered one fumble. 1994—Recovered one fumble. 1995—Recovered one fumble.

Year Team	G	SACKS
1992—Kansas City NFL	1	0.0
1993—Kansas City NFL	16	1.0

M

1994—Kansas City NFL	16	7.0
1995—Kansas City NFL	12	5.5
Pro totals (4 years)	45	13.5

MICKENS, TERRY | WR | PACKERS

PERSONAL: Born February 21, 1971, in Tallahassee, Fla. ... 6-0/198. ... Full name: Terry KaJuan Mickens.
HIGH SCHOOL: Leon (Tallahassee, Fla.).
COLLEGE: Florida A&M.
TRANSACTIONS/CAREER NOTES: Selected by Green Bay Packers in fifth round (146th pick overall) of 1994 NFL draft. ... Signed by Packers (July 7, 1994).
CHAMPIONSHIP GAME EXPERIENCE: Played in NFC championship game (1995 season).
PRO STATISTICS: 1995—Returned one kickoff for no yards.

		RECEIVING				TOTALS			
Year Team	G	No.	Yds.	Avg.	TD	TD	2pt.	Pts.	Fum.
1994—Green Bay NFL	12	4	31	7.8	0	0	0	0	0
1995—Green Bay NFL	16	3	50	16.7	0	0	0	0	0
Pro totals (2 years)	28	7	81	11.6	0	0	0	0	0

MIDDLETON, RON | TE

PERSONAL: Born July 17, 1965, in Atmore, Ala. ... 6-2/262. ... Full name: Ronald Allen Middleton.
HIGH SCHOOL: Escambia County (Atmore, Ala.).
COLLEGE: Auburn.
TRANSACTIONS/CAREER NOTES: Selected by Birmingham Stallions in 1986 USFL territorial draft. ... Signed as non-drafted free agent by Atlanta Falcons (May 3, 1986). ... Released by Falcons (August 30, 1988). ... Signed by Washington Redskins (September 13, 1988). ... Released by Redskins (October 3, 1988). ... Re-signed by Redskins (November 14, 1988). ... Released by Redskins (December 12, 1988). ... Re-signed by Redskins (December 13, 1988). ... Claimed on waivers by Tampa Bay Buccaneers (August 30, 1989). ... Released by Buccaneers (September 4, 1989). ... Re-signed by Buccaneers (September 5, 1989). ... Released by Buccaneers (September 12, 1989). ... Signed by Cleveland Browns (October 11, 1989). ... Released by Browns (November 21, 1989). ... Re-signed by Browns (November 27, 1989). ... Granted unconditional free agency (February 1, 1990). ... Signed by Redskins (March 15, 1990). ... Released by Redskins (August 22, 1994). ... Signed by Los Angeles Rams (August 29, 1994). ... Granted unconditional free agency (February 17, 1995). ... Signed by San Diego Chargers (July 18, 1995). ... Released by Chargers (August 28, 1995). ... Re-signed by Chargers (September 14, 1995). ... Released by Chargers (October 17, 1995).
CHAMPIONSHIP GAME EXPERIENCE: Played in AFC championship game (1989 season). ... Played in NFC championship game (1991 season). ... Member of Super Bowl championship team (1991 season).
PRO STATISTICS: 1990—Returned one kickoff for seven yards. 1993—Recovered one fumble.

		RECEIVING				TOTALS			
Year Team	G	No.	Yds.	Avg.	TD	TD	2pt.	Pts.	Fum.
1986—Atlanta NFL	16	6	31	5.2	0	0	...	0	0
1987—Atlanta NFL	12	1	1	1.0	0	0	...	0	0
1988—Washington NFL	2	0	0	...	0	0	...	0	0
1989—Cleveland NFL	9	1	5	5.0	1	1	...	6	0
1990—Washington NFL	16	0	0	...	0	0	...	0	0
1991—Washington NFL	12	3	25	8.3	0	0	...	0	0
1992—Washington NFL	16	7	50	7.1	0	0	...	0	0
1993—Washington NFL	16	24	154	6.4	2	2	...	12	0
1994—Los Angeles Rams NFL	16	0	0	...	0	0	0	0	0
1995—San Diego NFL	3	0	0	...	0	0	0	0	0
Pro totals (10 years)	118	42	266	6.3	3	3	0	18	0

MILBURN, GLYN | WR/RB | LIONS

PERSONAL: Born February 19, 1971, in Santa Monica, Calif. ... 5-8/177. ... Full name: Glyn Curt Milburn. ... Cousin of Rod Milburn, gold medalist in 110-meter high hurdles in 1972 Summer Olympics.
HIGH SCHOOL: Santa Monica (Calif.).
COLLEGE: Oklahoma, then Stanford.
TRANSACTIONS/CAREER NOTES: Selected by Denver Broncos in second round (43rd pick overall) of 1993 NFL draft. ... Signed by Broncos (July 15, 1993). ... Traded by Broncos to Detroit Lions for second (traded to Baltimore)- and seventh-round (P Brian Gragert) picks in 1996 NFL draft.
HONORS: Named kick returner on THE SPORTING NEWS NFL All-Pro team (1995). ... Played in Pro Bowl (1995 season).
RECORDS: Holds NFL single-game record for most combined net yards gained—404 (December 10, 1995).
PRO STATISTICS: 1993—Fumbled nine times and recovered one fumble. 1994—Fumbled four times and recovered one fumble. 1995—Fumbled twice.
STATISTICAL PLATEAUS: 100-yard rushing games: 1995 (1).

		RUSHING				RECEIVING				PUNT RETURNS				KICKOFF RETURNS				TOTALS		
Year Team	G	Att.	Yds.	Avg.	TD	No.	Yds.	Avg.	TD	No.	Yds.	Avg.	TD	No.	Yds.	Avg.	TD	TD	2pt.	Pts.
1993—Denver NFL	16	52	231	4.4	0	38	300	7.9	3	40	425	10.6	0	12	188	15.7	0	3	...	18
1994—Denver NFL	16	58	201	3.5	1	77	549	7.1	3	41	379	9.2	0	37	793	21.4	0	4	0	24
1995—Denver NFL	16	49	266	5.4	0	22	191	8.7	0	31	354	11.4	0	47	1269	27.0	0	0	0	0
Pro totals (3 years)	48	159	698	4.4	1	137	1040	7.6	6	112	1158	10.3	0	96	2250	23.4	0	7	0	42

MILLEN, HUGH | QB | SAINTS

PERSONAL: Born November 22, 1963, in Des Moines, Iowa. ... 6-5/216.
HIGH SCHOOL: Roosevelt (Seattle).

JUNIOR COLLEGE: Santa Rosa (Calif.) Community College.
COLLEGE: Washington.
TRANSACTIONS/CAREER NOTES: Selected by Los Angeles Rams in third round (71st pick overall) of 1986 NFL draft. ... Signed by Rams (July 17, 1986). ... On injured reserve with broken ankle (August 19, 1986-entire season). ... On injured reserve with knee injury (September 7-December 4, 1987). ... Claimed on waivers by Atlanta Falcons (August 30, 1988). ... Granted free agency (February 1, 1990). ... Re-signed by Falcons (July 27, 1990). ... Released by Falcons (September 11, 1990). ... Re-signed by Falcons (October 17, 1990). ... Granted unconditional free agency (February 1, 1991). ... Signed by New England Patriots (April 1, 1991). ... Granted free agency (February 1, 1992). ... Re-signed by Patriots (July 16, 1992). ... On injured reserve with shoulder injury (December 10, 1992-remainder of season). ... Traded by Patriots to Dallas Cowboys for eighth-round pick (LB Marty Moore) in 1994 draft (April 26, 1993). ... Released by Cowboys (August 30, 1993). ... Re-signed by Cowboys (September 1, 1993). ... Released by Cowboys (November 10, 1993). ... Signed by Miami Dolphins (November 15, 1993). ... Granted unconditional free agency (February 17, 1994). ... Signed by Denver Broncos (July 10, 1994). ... Released by Broncos. (February 28, 1996 ... Signed by New Orleans Saints (April 22, 1996).
PRO STATISTICS: 1989—Fumbled once. 1989—Fumbled twice and recovered one fumble for minus 11 yards. 1990—Fumbled three times. 1991—Fumbled 10 times and recovered four fumbles for minus 17 yards. 1992—Fumbled eight times. 1994—Fumbled twice. 1995—Fumbled once.
STATISTICAL PLATEAUS: 300-yard passing games: 1991 (3).
MISCELLANEOUS: Regular-season record as starting NFL quarterback: 7-18 (.280).

				PASSING						RUSHING				TOTALS		
Year Team	G	Att.	Cmp.	Pct.	Yds.	TD	Int.	Avg.	Rat.	Att.	Yds.	Avg.	TD	TD	2pt.	Pts.
1986—Los Angeles Rams NFL.......						Did not play—injured.										
1987—Los Angeles Rams NFL.......	1	1	1	100.0	0	0	0	.00	79.2	0	0	...	0	0	...	0
1988—Atlanta NFL	3	31	17	54.8	215	0	2	6.94	49.8	1	7	7.0	0	0	...	0
1989—Atlanta NFL	5	50	31	62.0	432	1	2	8.64	79.8	1	0	0.0	0	0	...	0
1990—Atlanta NFL	3	63	34	54.0	427	1	0	6.78	80.6	7	-12	-1.7	0	0	...	0
1991—New England NFL...............	13	409	246	60.2	3073	9	18	7.51	72.5	31	92	3.0	1	1	...	6
1992—New England NFL...............	7	203	124	61.1	1203	8	10	5.93	70.3	17	108	6.4	0	0	...	0
1993—Dallas NFL.........................						Did not play.										
1994—Denver NFL	5	131	81	61.8	893	2	3	6.82	77.6	5	57	11.4	0	0	0	0
1995—Denver NFL	3	40	26	65.0	197	1	0	4.93	85.1	3	8	2.7	0	0	0	0
Pro totals (8 years)..................	40	928	560	60.4	6440	22	35	6.94	73.5	65	260	4.0	1	1	0	6

MILLER, ANTHONY   WR   BRONCOS

PERSONAL: Born April 15, 1965, in Los Angeles. ... 5-11/190. ... Full name: Lawrence Anthony Miller.
HIGH SCHOOL: John Muir (Pasadena, Calif.).
JUNIOR COLLEGE: Pasadena (Calif.) College.
COLLEGE: San Diego State, then Tennessee.
TRANSACTIONS/CAREER NOTES: Selected by San Diego Chargers in first round (15th pick overall) of 1988 NFL draft. ... Signed by Chargers (July 12, 1988). ... On injured reserve with leg injury (December 7, 1991-remainder of season). ... Designated by Chargers as transition player (February 15, 1994). ... Tendered offer sheet by Denver Broncos (March 18, 1994). ... Chargers declined to match offer (March 24, 1994).
HONORS: Played in Pro Bowl (1989, 1990, 1992, 1993 and 1995 seasons).
PRO STATISTICS: 1990—Recovered one fumble. 1991—Recovered one fumble. 1992—Recovered one fumble in end zone for a touchdown. 1995—Recovered one fumble for nine yards.
STATISTICAL PLATEAUS: 100-yard receiving games: 1989 (5), 1990 (2), 1991 (2), 1992 (4), 1993 (6), 1994 (4), 1995 (3). Total: 26.

		RUSHING				RECEIVING				KICKOFF RETURNS				TOTALS			
Year Team	G	Att.	Yds.	Avg.	TD	No.	Yds.	Avg.	TD	No.	Yds.	Avg.	TD	TD	2pt.	Pts.	Fum.
1988—San Diego NFL..................	16	7	45	6.4	0	36	526	14.6	3	25	648	25.9	†1	4	...	24	1
1989—San Diego NFL..................	16	4	21	5.3	0	75	1252	16.7	10	21	533	25.4	†1	11	...	66	1
1990—San Diego NFL..................	16	3	13	4.3	0	63	933	14.8	7	1	13	13.0	0	7	...	42	2
1991—San Diego NFL..................	13	0	0	...	0	44	649	14.8	3	0	0	...	0	3	...	18	1
1992—San Diego NFL..................	16	1	-1	-1.0	0	72	1060	14.7	7	1	33	33.0	0	8	...	48	0
1993—San Diego NFL..................	16	1	0	0.0	0	84	1162	13.8	7	2	42	21.0	0	7	...	42	0
1994—Denver NFL	16	1	3	3.0	0	60	1107	18.5	5	0	0	...	0	5	1	32	0
1995—Denver NFL	14	1	5	5.0	0	59	1079	18.3	14	0	0	...	0	14	0	84	1
Pro totals (8 years)..................	123	18	86	4.8	0	493	7768	15.8	56	50	1269	25.4	2	59	1	356	6

M

MILLER, BRONZELL   DE/LB   JAGUARS

PERSONAL: Born October 12, 1971, in Federal Way, Wash. ... 6-3/247. ... Full name: Bronzell LaJames Miller.
HIGH SCHOOL: Federal Way (Wash.).
JUNIOR COLLEGE: Eastern Arizona Junior College.
COLLEGE: Utah.
TRANSACTIONS/CAREER NOTES: Selected by St. Louis Rams in seventh round (239th pick overall) of 1995 NFL draft. ... Signed by Rams (June 16, 1995). ... Released by Rams (August 23, 1995). ... Re-signed by Rams (August 24, 1995). ... Released by Rams (August 27, 1995). ... Re-signed by Rams to practice squad (August 28, 1995). ... Signed by Jacksonville Jaguars off Rams practice squad (November 28, 1995).
PLAYING EXPERIENCE: Jacksonville NFL, 1995. ... Games: 1995 (3).

MILLER, CHRIS   QB

PERSONAL: Born August 9, 1965, in Pomona, Calif. ... 6-2/212. ... Full name: Christopher James Miller.
HIGH SCHOOL: Sheldon (Eugene, Ore.).
COLLEGE: Oregon.
TRANSACTIONS/CAREER NOTES: Selected by Atlanta Falcons in first round (13th pick overall) of 1987 NFL draft. ... Signed by Falcons (October 30, 1987). ... Granted roster exemption (October 30-November 9, 1987). ... On injured reserve with broken collarbone (December 4, 1990-remainder of season). ... On injured reserve with knee injury (November 1, 1992-remainder of season). ... On injured reserve with knee injury (October 7, 1993-remainder of season). ... Granted unconditional free agency (February 17, 1994). ... Signed by Los Angeles Rams (March 7, 1994). ... Rams franchise moved to St. Louis (April 12, 1995). ... On injured reserve with concussion (December 14, 1995-remainder of season). ... Released by Rams (March 11, 1996).

HONORS: Played in Pro Bowl (1991 season).
PRO STATISTICS: 1988—Fumbled twice and recovered one fumble. 1989—Successful on 25-yard field-goal attempt, fumbled 13 times and recovered five fumbles for minus three yards. 1990—Fumbled 11 times and recovered four fumbles for minus nine yards. 1991—Fumbled five times. 1992—Fumbled six times and recovered one fumble for minus one yard. 1993—Fumbled twice. 1994—Fumbled seven times and recovered three fumbles for minus five yards. 1995—Fumbled four times and recovered two fumbles for minus six yards.
STATISTICAL PLATEAUS: 300-yard passing games: 1989 (3), 1990 (2), 1991 (2), 1992 (1), 1994 (1), 1995 (2). Total: 11.
MISCELLANEOUS: Regular-season record as starting NFL quarterback: 32-57 (.360).

		PASSING								RUSHING				TOTALS		
Year Team	G	Att.	Cmp.	Pct.	Yds.	TD	Int.	Avg.	Rat.	Att.	Yds.	Avg.	TD	TD	2pt.	Pts.
1987—Atlanta NFL	3	92	39	42.4	552	1	9	6.00	26.4	4	21	5.3	0	0	...	0
1988—Atlanta NFL	13	351	184	52.4	2133	11	12	6.08	67.3	31	138	4.5	1	1	...	6
1989—Atlanta NFL	15	526	280	53.2	3459	16	10	6.58	76.1	10	20	2.0	0	0	...	3
1990—Atlanta NFL	12	388	222	57.2	2735	17	14	7.05	78.7	26	99	3.8	1	1	...	6
1991—Atlanta NFL	15	413	220	53.3	3103	26	18	7.51	80.6	32	229	7.2	0	0	...	0
1992—Atlanta NFL	8	253	152	60.1	1739	15	6	6.87	90.7	23	89	3.9	0	0	...	0
1993—Atlanta NFL	3	66	32	48.5	345	1	3	5.23	50.4	2	11	5.5	0	0	...	0
1994—Los Angeles Rams NFL	13	317	173	54.6	2104	16	14	6.64	73.6	20	100	5.0	0	0	0	0
1995—St. Louis NFL	13	405	232	57.3	2623	18	15	6.48	76.2	22	67	3.1	0	0	0	0
Pro totals (9 years)	95	2811	1534	54.6	18793	121	101	6.69	74.8	170	774	4.6	2	2	0	15

MILLER, COREY — LB — GIANTS

PERSONAL: Born October 25, 1968, in Pageland, S.C. ... 6-2/245.
HIGH SCHOOL: Central (Pageland, S.C.).
COLLEGE: South Carolina.
TRANSACTIONS/CAREER NOTES: Selected by New York Giants in sixth round (167th pick overall) of 1991 NFL draft. ... Signed by Giants (July 15, 1991). ... Granted free agency (February 17, 1994). ... Re-signed by Giants (July 22, 1994). ... Granted unconditional free agency (February 17, 1995). ... Re-signed by Giants (March 9, 1995).
PRO STATISTICS: 1991—Recovered one fumble. 1993—Recovered two fumbles and fumbled once. 1994—Recovered one fumble.

		INTERCEPTIONS				SACKS
Year Team	G	No.	Yds.	Avg.	TD	No.
1991—New York Giants NFL	16	0	0	...	0	2.5
1992—New York Giants NFL	16	2	10	5.0	0	2.0
1993—New York Giants NFL	16	2	18	9.0	0	6.5
1994—New York Giants NFL	15	2	6	3.0	0	0.0
1995—New York Giants NFL	14	0	0	...	0	0.0
Pro totals (5 years)	77	6	34	5.7	0	11.0

MILLER, JAMIR — LB — CARDINALS

PERSONAL: Born November 19, 1973, in Philadelphia. ... 6-4/242. ... Full name: Jamir Malik Miller.
HIGH SCHOOL: El Cerrito (Calif.).
COLLEGE: UCLA.
TRANSACTIONS/CAREER NOTES: Selected after junior season by Arizona Cardinals in first round (10th pick overall) of 1994 NFL draft. ... Signed by Cardinals (August 12, 1994). ... On suspended list for violating league substance abuse policy (September 4-October 3, 1995).
HONORS: Named linebacker on The Sporting News college All-America first team (1993).
PRO STATISTICS: 1995—Fumbled once and recovered two fumbles for 26 yards.

Year Team	G	SACKS
1994—Arizona NFL	16	3.0
1995—Arizona NFL	10	1.0
Pro totals (2 years)	26	4.0

MILLER, JEFF — OT — PACKERS

PERSONAL: Born November 23, 1972, in Vero Beach, Fla. ... 6-3/295.
HIGH SCHOOL: Vero Beach (Fla.).
JUNIOR COLLEGE: Northwest Mississippi Community College.
COLLEGE: Mississippi.
TRANSACTIONS/CAREER NOTES: Selected by Green Bay Packers in fourth round (117th pick overall) of 1995 NFL draft. ... Signed by Packers (July 17, 1995). ... On injured reserve witrh knee injury (August 21, 1995-entire season).

MILLER, JIM — QB — STEELERS

PERSONAL: Born February 9, 1971, in Grosse Pointe, Mich. ... 6-2/210. ... Full name: James Donald Miller.
HIGH SCHOOL: Kettering (Detroit).
COLLEGE: Michigan State.
TRANSACTIONS/CAREER NOTES: Selected by Pittsburgh Steelers in sixth round (178th pick overall) of 1994 NFL draft. ... Signed by Steelers (May 12, 1994). ... Assigned by Steelers to Frankfurt Galaxy in 1995 World League enhancement allocation program (February 20, 1995).
CHAMPIONSHIP GAME EXPERIENCE: Member of Steelers for AFC championship game (1994 and 1995 seasons); inactive. ... Member of Steelers for Super Bowl XXX (1995 season); inactive.
PRO STATISTICS: 1995—Fumbled once.

		PASSING								RUSHING				TOTALS		
Year Team	G	Att.	Cmp.	Pct.	Yds.	TD	Int.	Avg.	Rat.	Att.	Yds.	Avg.	TD	TD	2pt.	Pts.
1995—Frankfurt W.L.	...	43	23	53.5	236	1	1	5.49	67.6	3	-2	-0.7	0	0	0	0

M

Year Team	G	PASSING								RUSHING				TOTALS		
		Att.	Cmp.	Pct.	Yds.	TD	Int.	Avg.	Rat.	Att.	Yds.	Avg.	TD	TD	2pt.	Pts.
—Pittsburgh NFL	3	56	32	57.1	397	2	5	7.09	53.9	1	2	2.0	0	0	0	0
W.L. totals (1 year)	...	43	23	535	236	1	1	5.49	67.6	3	-2	-0.7	0	0	0	0
NFL totals (1 year)	3	56	32	572	397	2	5	7.09	53.9	1	2	2.0	0	0	0	0
Pro totals (2 years)	...	99	55	55.6	633	3	6	6.39	59.9	4	0	0.0	0	0	0	0

MILLER, LES   DE   PANTHERS

PERSONAL: Born March 1, 1965, in Arkansas City, Kan. ... 6-7/285.
HIGH SCHOOL: Arkansas City (Kan.).
COLLEGE: Fort Hays State (Kan.).
TRANSACTIONS/CAREER NOTES: Signed as non-drafted free agent by New Orleans Saints (May 11, 1987). ... Released by Saints (September 7, 1987). ... Signed as replacement player by San Diego Chargers (September 24, 1987). ... On injured reserve with back injury (December 22, 1990-remainder of season). ... Granted unconditional free agency (February 1, 1991). ... Signed by Saints (April 1, 1991). ... Granted unconditional free agency (March 1, 1993). ... Re-signed by Saints (March 9, 1993). ... Released by Saints (October 25, 1994). ... Signed by Chargers (November 2, 1994). ... Granted unconditional free agency (February 17, 1995). ... Signed by Saints (August 16, 1995). ... Released by Saints (August 27, 1995). ... Signed by Carolina Panthers for 1996 season.
CHAMPIONSHIP GAME EXPERIENCE: Member of Chargers for AFC championship game (1994 season); did not play. ... Played in Super Bowl XXIX (1994 season).
RECORDS: Shares NFL single-season records for most touchdowns by fumble recovery—2 (1990); and most touchdowns by recovery of opponents' fumbles—2 (1990).
PRO STATISTICS: 1987—Recovered two fumbles (including one in end zone for a touchdown). 1989—Recovered one fumble. 1990—Recovered three fumbles for one yard (including two in end zone for touchdowns). 1992—Recovered one fumble.

Year Team	G	SACKS
1987—San Diego NFL	9	3.0
1988—San Diego NFL	13	0.0
1989—San Diego NFL	14	2.5
1990—San Diego NFL	14	1.0
1991—New Orleans NFL	16	1.0
1992—New Orleans NFL	16	1.0
1993—New Orleans NFL	13	2.5
1994—New Orleans NFL	8	0.0
—San Diego NFL	4	0.5
1995—	Did not play.	
Pro totals (8 years)	107	11.5

MILLER, SCOTT   WR   DOLPHINS

PERSONAL: Born October 20, 1968, in Phoenix. ... 5-11/185. ... Full name: Scott Patrick Miller.
HIGH SCHOOL: El Toro (Calif.).
JUNIOR COLLEGE: Saddleback Community College (Calif.).
COLLEGE: UCLA.
TRANSACTIONS/CAREER NOTES: Selected by Miami Dolphins in ninth round (246th pick overall) of 1991 NFL draft. ... Signed by Dolphins (July 11, 1991). ... Released by Dolphins (March 3, 1994). ... Re-signed by Dolphins (May 31, 1994). ... On physically unable to perform list with knee injury (August 21, 1995-entire season).
CHAMPIONSHIP GAME EXPERIENCE: Played in AFC championship game (1992 season).
PRO STATISTICS: 1991—Recovered three fumbles. 1992—Recovered one fumble. 1993—Returned two kickoffs for 22 yards. 1994—Returned one kickoff for 13 yards.

Year Team	G	RECEIVING				PUNT RETURNS				TOTALS			
		No.	Yds.	Avg.	TD	No.	Yds.	Avg.	TD	TD	2pt.	Pts.	Fum.
1991—Miami NFL	16	4	49	12.3	0	28	248	8.9	0	0	...	0	4
1992—Miami NFL	15	0	0	...	0	24	175	7.3	0	0	...	0	2
1993—Miami NFL	3	2	15	7.5	0	0	0	...	0	0	...	0	0
1994—Miami NFL	9	6	94	15.7	1	1	13	13.0	0	1	0	6	0
1995—Miami NFL						Did not play—injured.							
Pro totals (4 years)	43	12	158	13.2	1	53	436	8.2	0	1	0	6	6

MILLS, ERNIE   WR   STEELERS

PERSONAL: Born October 28, 1968, in Dunnellon, Fla. ... 5-11/192. ... Full name: Ernest Lee Mills III.
HIGH SCHOOL: Dunnellon (Fla.) Senior.
COLLEGE: Florida.
TRANSACTIONS/CAREER NOTES: Selected by Pittsburgh Steelers in third round (73rd pick overall) of 1991 NFL draft. ... Signed by Steelers (August 13, 1991). ... Granted free agency (February 17, 1994). ... Re-signed by Steelers (June 1, 1994).
CHAMPIONSHIP GAME EXPERIENCE: Played in AFC championship game (1994 and 1995 seasons). ... Played in Super Bowl XXX (1995 season).
PRO STATISTICS: 1991—Recovered punt return in end zone for a touchdown, returned one punt for no yards and recovered one fumble. 1995—Recovered one fumble.

Year Team	G	RUSHING				RECEIVING				KICKOFF RETURNS				TOTALS			
		Att.	Yds.	Avg.	TD	No.	Yds.	Avg.	TD	No.	Yds.	Avg.	TD	TD	2pt.	Pts.	Fum.
1991—Pittsburgh NFL	16	0	0	...	0	3	79	26.3	1	11	284	25.8	0	2	...	12	0
1992—Pittsburgh NFL	16	1	20	20.0	0	30	383	12.8	3	1	11	11.0	0	3	...	18	2
1993—Pittsburgh NFL	14	3	12	4.0	0	29	386	13.3	1	0	0	...	0	1	...	6	0
1994—Pittsburgh NFL	15	3	18	6.0	0	19	384	20.2	1	2	6	3.0	0	1	0	6	1
1995—Pittsburgh NFL	16	5	39	7.8	0	39	679	17.4	8	54	1306	24.2	0	8	0	48	2
Pro totals (5 years)	77	12	89	7.4	0	120	1911	15.9	14	68	1607	23.6	0	15	0	90	5

MILLS, JOHN HENRY   LB   OILERS

PERSONAL: Born October 31, 1969, in Jacksonville. ... 6-0/222. .
HIGH SCHOOL: Godby (Tallahassee, Fla.).
COLLEGE: Wake Forest (degree in speech communications, 1993).
TRANSACTIONS/CAREER NOTES: Selected by Houston Oilers in fifth round (131st pick overall) of 1993 NFL draft. ... Signed by Oilers (July 16, 1993). ... Released by Oilers (August 30, 1993). ... Re-signed by Oilers (August 31, 1993). ... Granted free agency (February 16, 1996).
PRO STATISTICS: 1994—Caught one pass for four yards.

		KICKOFF RETURNS				TOTALS			
Year Team	G	No.	Yds.	Avg.	TD	TD	2pt.	Pts.	Fum.
1993—Houston NFL	16	11	230	20.9	0	0	...	0	0
1994—Houston NFL	16	15	282	18.8	0	0	0	0	1
1995—Houston NFL	16	0	0	...	0	0	0	0	1
Pro totals (3 years)	48	26	512	19.7	0	0	0	0	1

MILLS, LAMAR   DT   BUCCANEERS

PERSONAL: Born January 26, 1971, in Detroit. ... 6-4/307.
HIGH SCHOOL: St. Martin DePorres (Detroit).
COLLEGE: Indiana.
TRANSACTIONS/CAREER NOTES: Signed as non-drafted free agent by Washington Redskins (April 28, 1994). ... Released by Redskins (August 29, 1995). ... Signed by Tampa Bay Buccaneers (February 15, 1996).
PLAYING EXPERIENCE: Washington NFL, 1994. ... Games: 1994 (13).

MILLS, SAM   LB   PANTHERS

PERSONAL: Born June 3, 1959, in Neptune, N.J. ... 5-9/232. ... Full name: Samuel Davis Mills Jr.
HIGH SCHOOL: Long Branch (N.J.).
COLLEGE: Montclair (N.J.) State.
TRANSACTIONS/CAREER NOTES: Signed as non-drafted free agent by Cleveland Browns (May 3, 1981). ... Released by Browns (August 24, 1981). ... Signed by Toronto Argonauts of CFL (March 1982). ... Released by Argonauts (June 30, 1982). ... Signed by Philadelphia Stars of USFL (October 21, 1982). ... Stars franchise moved to Baltimore (November 1, 1984). ... Granted free agency (August 7, 1985). ... Re-signed by Stars (August 7, 1985). ... Granted free agency when USFL suspended operations (August 7, 1986). ... Signed by New Orleans Saints (August 12, 1986). ... Granted roster exemption (August 12-22, 1986). ... Granted unconditional free agency (February 17, 1995). ... Signed by Carolina Panthers (March 9, 1995).
CHAMPIONSHIP GAME EXPERIENCE: Played in USFL championship game (1983-1985 seasons).
HONORS: Named inside linebacker on THE SPORTING NEWS USFL All-Star team (1983 and 1985). ... Played in Pro Bowl (1987, 1988, 1991 and 1992 seasons). ... Named inside linebacker on THE SPORTING NEWS NFL All-Pro team (1991 and 1992).
PRO STATISTICS: USFL: 1983—Recovered five fumbles for eight yards. 1984—Recovered three fumbles for two yards. 1985—Recovered two fumbles. NFL: 1986—Recovered one fumble. 1987—Recovered three fumbles. 1988—Recovered four fumbles. 1989—Recovered one fumble. 1990—Recovered one fumble. 1991—Recovered two fumbles. 1992—Recovered three fumbles for 76 yards and a touchdown. 1993—Recovered one fumble for 30 yards and a touchdown. 1994—Recovered one fumble. 1995—Recovered four fumbles for seven yards.

		INTERCEPTIONS				SACKS
Year Team	G	No.	Yds.	Avg.	TD	No.
1981—			Did not play.			
1982—			Did not play.			
1983—Philadelphia USFL	18	3	13	4.3	0	3.5
1984—Philadelphia USFL	18	3	24	8.0	0	5.0
1985—Baltimore USFL	18	3	32	10.7	1	5.5
1986—New Orleans NFL	16	0	0	...	0	0.0
1987—New Orleans NFL	12	0	0	...	0	0.0
1988—New Orleans NFL	16	0	0	...	0	0.0
1989—New Orleans NFL	16	0	0	...	0	3.0
1990—New Orleans NFL	16	0	0	...	0	0.5
1991—New Orleans NFL	16	2	13	6.5	0	1.0
1992—New Orleans NFL	16	1	10	10.0	0	3.0
1993—New Orleans NFL	9	0	0	...	0	2.0
1994—New Orleans NFL	16	1	10	10.0	0	1.0
1995—Carolina NFL	16	5	58	11.6	1	4.5
USFL totals (3 years)	54	9	69	7.7	1	140
NFL totals (10 years)	149	9	91	10.1	1	150
Pro totals (13 years)	203	18	160	8.9	2	29.0

MILNER, BILLY   OT   DOLPHINS

PERSONAL: Born June 21, 1972, in Atlanta. ... 6-5/293.
HIGH SCHOOL: Northside (Atlanta).
JUNIOR COLLEGE: Southwest Mississippi Community College.
COLLEGE: Houston.
TRANSACTIONS/CAREER NOTES: Selected by Miami Dolphins in first round (25th pick overall) of 1995 NFL draft. ... Signed by Dolphins (July 16, 1995).
PLAYING EXPERIENCE: Miami NFL, 1995. ... Games: 1995 (16).
PRO STATISTICS: 1995—Returned one kickoff for 13 yards and recovered two fumbles.

M

MILSTEAD, ROD   G   49ERS

PERSONAL: Born November 10, 1969, in Washington, D.C. ... 6-2/278. ... Full name: Roderick Leon Milstead Jr.
HIGH SCHOOL: Lackey (Indian Head, Md.).
COLLEGE: Delaware State (degree in sociology and criminal justice).
TRANSACTIONS/CAREER NOTES: Selected by Dallas Cowboys in fifth round (121st pick overall) of 1992 NFL draft. ... Traded by Cowboys to Cleveland Browns for eighth-round pick in 1993 draft (August 24, 1992). ... On injured reserve with back injury (September 3, 1992-entire season). ... Released by Browns (August 30, 1993). ... Re-signed by Browns (October 6, 1993). ... Released by Browns (November 27, 1993). ... Re-signed by Browns (November 30, 1993). ... Released by Browns (August 28, 1994). ... Signed by San Francisco 49ers (September 14, 1994).
PLAYING EXPERIENCE: San Francisco NFL, 1994 and 1995. ... Games: 1994 (5), 1995 (16). Total: 21.
CHAMPIONSHIP GAME EXPERIENCE: Member of 49ers for NFC championship game (1994 season); inactive. ... Member of Super Bowl championship team (1994 season).

MIMS, CHRIS   DE   CHARGERS

PERSONAL: Born September 29, 1970, in Los Angeles. ... 6-5/290. ... Full name: Christopher Eddie Mims.
HIGH SCHOOL: Dorsey (Los Angeles).
JUNIOR COLLEGE: Los Angeles Pierce Junior College, then Los Angeles Southwest Community College.
COLLEGE: Tennessee.
TRANSACTIONS/CAREER NOTES: Selected by San Diego Chargers in first round (23rd pick overall) of 1992 NFL draft. ... Signed by Chargers (June 5, 1992).
CHAMPIONSHIP GAME EXPERIENCE: Played in AFC championship game (1994 season). ... Played in Super Bowl XXIX (1994 season).
PRO STATISTICS: 1992—Credited with one safety and recovered one fumble. 1993—Recovered two fumbles. 1994—Recovered two fumbles. 1995—Recovered one fumble.

Year Team	G	SACKS
1992—San Diego NFL	16	10.0
1993—San Diego NFL	16	7.0
1994—San Diego NFL	16	11.0
1995—San Diego NFL	15	2.0
Pro totals (4 years)	63	30.0

MINCY, CHARLES   S

PERSONAL: Born December 16, 1969, in Los Angeles. ... 5-11/197. ... Full name: Charles Anthony Mincy.
HIGH SCHOOL: Dorsey (Los Angeles).
JUNIOR COLLEGE: Pasadena (Calif.) City College.
COLLEGE: Washington.
TRANSACTIONS/CAREER NOTES: Selected by Kansas City Chiefs in fifth round (133rd pick overall) of 1991 NFL draft. ... Signed by Chiefs (July 17, 1991). ... On injured reserve with ankle/toe injury (August 30-December 25, 1991). ... Did not play during regular season (1991); played in two playoff games. ... Granted free agency (February 17, 1994). ... Re-signed by Chiefs (June 17, 1994). ... Granted unconditional free agency (February 17, 1995). ... Signed by Minnesota Vikings (March 6, 1995). ... Released by Vikings (February 9, 1996).
CHAMPIONSHIP GAME EXPERIENCE: Played in AFC championship game (1993 season).
PRO STATISTICS: 1992—Recovered one fumble for 30 yards and a touchdown. 1993—Recovered two fumbles. 1995—Recovered two fumbles for 10 yards.

Year Team	G	INTERCEPTIONS				PUNT RETURNS				TOTALS			
		No.	Yds.	Avg.	TD	No.	Yds.	Avg.	TD	TD	2pt.	Pts.	Fum.
1991—Kansas City NFL					Did not play.								
1992—Kansas City NFL	16	4	128	32.0	2	1	4	4.0	0	3	...	18	0
1993—Kansas City NFL	16	5	44	8.8	0	2	9	4.5	0	0	...	0	0
1994—Kansas City NFL	16	3	49	16.3	0	0	0	...	0	0	0	0	0
1995—Minnesota NFL	16	3	37	12.3	0	4	22	5.5	0	0	0	0	0
Pro totals (4 years)	64	15	258	17.2	2	7	35	5.0	0	3	0	18	0

MINIEFIELD, KEVIN   DB   BEARS

PERSONAL: Born March 2, 1970, in Phoenix. ... 5-9/180. ... Full name: Kevin Lamar Miniefield.
HIGH SCHOOL: Camelback (Phoenix).
COLLEGE: Arizona State.
TRANSACTIONS/CAREER NOTES: Selected by Detroit Lions in eighth round (201st pick overall) of 1993 NFL draft. ... Signed by Lions (July 17, 1993). ... Released by Lions (August 30, 1993). ... Re-signed by Lions to practice squad (August 31, 1993). ... Signed by Chicago Bears off Lions practice squad (October 13, 1993).
PRO STATISTICS: 1994—Recovered one fumble for minus five yards.

Year Team	G	INTERCEPTIONS			
		No.	Yds.	Avg.	TD
1993—Chicago NFL	8	0	0	...	0
1994—Chicago NFL	12	0	0	...	0
1995—Chicago NFL	15	3	37	12.3	0
Pro totals (3 years)	35	3	37	12.3	0

MINTER, BARRY   LB   BEARS

PERSONAL: Born January 28, 1970, in Mt. Pleasant, Texas. ... 6-2/240. ... Full name: Barry Antoine Minter.

M

HIGH SCHOOL: Mount Pleasant (Texas).
COLLEGE: Tulsa.
TRANSACTIONS/CAREER NOTES: Selected by Dallas Cowboys in sixth round (168th pick overall) of 1993 NFL draft. ... Signed by Cowboys (July 14, 1993). ... Traded by Cowboys with LB Vinson Smith and sixth-round pick (DE Carl Reeves) in 1995 draft to Chicago Bears for TE Kelly Blackwell, S Markus Paul and LB John Roper (August 17, 1993). ... Granted free agency (February 16, 1996).
PLAYING EXPERIENCE: Chicago NFL, 1993-1995. ... Games: 1993 (2), 1994 (13), 1995 (16). Total: 31.
PRO STATISTICS: 1994—Recovered one fumble. 1995—Intercepted one pass for two yards and a touchdown.

MIRER, RICK — QB — SEAHAWKS

PERSONAL: Born March 19, 1970, in Goshen, Ind. ... 6-2/214.
HIGH SCHOOL: Goshen (Ind.).
COLLEGE: Notre Dame.
TRANSACTIONS/CAREER NOTES: Selected by Seattle Seahawks in first round (second pick overall) of 1993 NFL draft. ... Signed by Seahawks (August 2, 1993). ... On injured reserve with thumb injury (December 20, 1994-remainder of season).
RECORDS: Holds NFL rookie-season records for most yards passing—2,833 (1993); most passes attempted—486 (1993); and most passes completed—274 (1993).
PRO STATISTICS: 1993—Fumbled 13 times and recovered five fumbles for minus 14 yards. 1994—Fumbled twice and recovered one fumble for minus seven yards. 1995—Fumbled five times and recovered one fumble for minus one yard.
MISCELLANEOUS: Regular-season record as starting NFL quarterback: 18-24 (.429).

					PASSING						RUSHING				TOTALS		
Year Team	G	Att.	Cmp.	Pct.	Yds.	TD	Int.	Avg.	Rat.	Att.	Yds.	Avg.	TD	TD	2pt.	Pts.
1993—Seattle NFL	16	486	274	56.4	2833	12	17	5.83	67.0	68	343	5.0	3	3	...	18
1994—Seattle NFL	13	381	195	51.2	2151	11	7	5.65	70.2	34	153	4.5	0	0	...	0
1995—Seattle NFL	15	391	209	53.5	2564	13	20	6.56	63.7	43	193	4.5	1	1	...	6
Pro totals (3 years)	44	1258	678	53.9	7548	36	44	6.00	67.0	145	689	4.8	4	4	0	24

MITCHELL, BRIAN — FB/KR — REDSKINS

PERSONAL: Born August 18, 1968, in Fort Polk, La. ... 5-10/221. ... Full name: Brian Keith Mitchell.
HIGH SCHOOL: Plaquemine (La.).
COLLEGE: Southwestern Louisiana.
TRANSACTIONS/CAREER NOTES: Selected by Washington Redskins in fifth round (130th pick overall) of 1990 NFL draft. ... Signed by Redskins (July 22, 1990). ... Granted free agency (February 1, 1992). ... Re-signed by Redskins for 1992 season. ... Granted unconditional free agency (February 17, 1994). ... Re-signed by Redskins (May 24, 1994). ... Granted free agency (February 17, 1995). ... Re-signed by Redskins (March 27, 1995).
CHAMPIONSHIP GAME EXPERIENCE: Played in NFC championship game (1991 season). ... Member of Super Bowl championship team (1991 season).
HONORS: Named punt returner on THE SPORTING NEWS NFL All-Pro team (1995). ... Played in Pro Bowl (1995 season).
RECORDS: Holds NFL single-season record for most yards by combined kick return—1,930 (1994).
PRO STATISTICS: 1990—Attempted six passes with three completions for 40 yards and fumbled twice. 1991—Fumbled eight times and recovered one fumble. 1992—Attempted one pass without a completion, fumbled four times and recovered two fumbles. 1993—Attempted two passes with one completion for 50 yards and an interception, fumbled three times and recovered one fumble. 1994—Had only pass attempt intercepted and fumbled four times. 1995—Fumbled twice and recovered one fumble.
STATISTICAL PLATEAUS: 100-yard rushing games: 1993 (1).

		RUSHING				RECEIVING				PUNT RETURNS				KICKOFF RETURNS				TOTALS		
Year Team	G	Att.	Yds.	Avg.	TD	No.	Yds.	Avg.	TD	No.	Yds.	Avg.	TD	No.	Yds.	Avg.	TD	TD	2pt.	Pts.
1990—Washington NFL	15	15	81	5.4	1	2	5	2.5	0	12	107	8.9	0	18	365	20.3	0	1	...	6
1991—Washington NFL	16	3	14	4.7	0	0	0	...	0	45	*600	13.3	*2	29	583	20.1	0	2	...	12
1992—Washington NFL	16	6	70	11.7	0	3	30	10.0	0	29	271	9.3	1	23	492	21.4	0	1	...	6
1993—Washington NFL	16	63	246	3.9	3	20	157	7.9	0	29	193	6.7	0	33	678	20.6	0	3	...	18
1994—Washington NFL	16	78	311	4.0	0	26	236	9.1	1	32	452	*14.1	†2	58	1478	25.5	0	3	1	20
1995—Washington NFL	16	46	301	6.5	1	38	324	8.5	1	25	315	12.6	†1	55	1408	25.6	0	3	0	18
Pro totals (6 years)	95	211	1023	4.9	5	89	752	8.5	2	172	1938	11.3	6	216	5004	23.2	0	13	1	80

MITCHELL, DERRELL — WR/KR — FALCONS

PERSONAL: Born September 16, 1971, in Miami. ... 5-9/190. ... Full name: Derrell Lavoice Mitchell.
HIGH SCHOOL: Northwestern (Miami).
JUNIOR COLLEGE: Joliet (Ill.) Junior College.
COLLEGE: Texas Tech.
TRANSACTIONS/CAREER NOTES: Selected by New Orleans Saints in sixth round (176th pick overall) of 1994 NFL draft. ... Signed by Saints (June 16, 1994). ... Assigned by Saints to Scottish Claymores in 1995 World League enhancement allocation program (February 20, 1995). ... Released by Saints (August 22, 1995). ... Signed by Atlanta Falcons (January 16, 1996).
PRO STATISTICS: 1994—Recovered one fumble.

		RECEIVING				PUNT RETURNS				KICKOFF RETURNS				TOTALS			
Year Team	G	No.	Yds.	Avg.	TD	No.	Yds.	Avg.	TD	No.	Yds.	Avg.	TD	TD	2pt.	Pts.	Fum.
1994—New Orleans NFL	14	1	13	13.0	0	3	9	3.0	0	6	129	21.5	0	0	0	0	0
1995—Scottish W.L.	...	11	145	13.2	1	0	0	...	0	0	0	...	0	1	0	6	0
W.L. totals (1 year)	...	11	145	13.2	1	0	0	...	0	0	0	...	0	1	0	6	0
NFL totals (1 year)	14	1	13	13.0	0	3	9	3.0	0	6	129	21.5	0	0	0	0	0
Pro totals (2 years)	...	12	158	13.2	1	3	9	3.0	0	6	129	21.5	0	1	0	6	0

M

MITCHELL, JOHNNY — TE

PERSONAL: Born January 20, 1971, in Chicago. ... 6-3/241.
HIGH SCHOOL: Neal F. Simeon (Chicago).
COLLEGE: Nebraska.
TRANSACTIONS/CAREER NOTES: Selected after sophomore season by New York Jets in first round (15th pick overall) of 1992 NFL draft. ... Signed by Jets (July 14, 1992). ... On injured reserve with shoulder injury (September 8-October 11, 1992). ... Designated by Jets as transition player (February 15, 1994). ... Free agency status changed by Jets from transitional to franchise player (February 16, 1996). ... Granted unconditional free agency (April 23, 1996).
PRO STATISTICS: 1994—Recovered one fumble for four yards.
STATISTICAL PLATEAUS: 100-yard receiving games: 1993 (1), 1994 (1), 1995 (1). Total: 3.

		RECEIVING				TOTALS			
Year Team	G	No.	Yds.	Avg.	TD	TD	2pt.	Pts.	Fum.
1992—New York Jets NFL	11	16	210	13.1	1	1	...	6	0
1993—New York Jets NFL	14	39	630	16.2	6	6	...	36	0
1994—New York Jets NFL	16	58	749	12.9	4	4	0	24	1
1995—New York Jets NFL	12	45	497	11.0	5	5	0	30	2
Pro totals (4 years)	53	158	2086	13.2	16	16	0	96	3

MITCHELL, KEVIN — LB — 49ERS

PERSONAL: Born January 1, 1971, in Harrisburg, Pa. ... 6-1/260. ... Full name: Kevin Danyelle Mitchell. ... Cousin of Troy Drayton, tight end, St. Louis Rams.
HIGH SCHOOL: Harrisburg (Pa.).
COLLEGE: Syracuse.
TRANSACTIONS/CAREER NOTES: Selected by San Francisco 49ers in second round (53rd pick overall) of 1994 NFL draft. ... Signed by 49ers (July 20, 1994).
PLAYING EXPERIENCE: San Francisco NFL, 1994 and 1995. ... Games: 1994 (16), 1995 (15). Total: 31.
CHAMPIONSHIP GAME EXPERIENCE: Played in NFC championship game (1994 season). ... Member of Super Bowl championship team (1994 season).
HONORS: Named defensive lineman on The Sporting News college All-America second team (1992 and 1993).

MITCHELL, PETE — TE — JAGUARS

PERSONAL: Born October 9, 1971, in Bloomfield Hills, Mich. ... 6-2/243. ... Full name: Peter Clark Mitchell.
HIGH SCHOOL: Brother Rice (Bloomfield Hills, Mich.).
COLLEGE: Boston College (degree in communications).
TRANSACTIONS/CAREER NOTES: Selected by Miami Dolphins in fourth round (122nd pick overall) of 1995 NFL draft. ... Signed by Dolphins (July 14, 1995). ... Traded by Dolphins to Jacksonville Jaguars for WR Mike Williams (August 27, 1995).
HONORS: Named tight end on The Sporting News college All-America first team (1993 and 1994).
STATISTICAL PLATEAUS: 100-yard receiving games: 1995 (1).

		RECEIVING				TOTALS			
Year Team	G	No.	Yds.	Avg.	TD	TD	2pt.	Pts.	Fum.
1995—Jacksonville NFL	16	41	527	12.9	2	2	0	12	0

M

MITCHELL, SCOTT — QB — LIONS

PERSONAL: Born January 2, 1968, in Salt Lake City. ... 6-6/230. ... Full name: William Scott Mitchell.
HIGH SCHOOL: Springville (Utah).
COLLEGE: Utah.
TRANSACTIONS/CAREER NOTES: Selected after junior season by Miami Dolphins in fourth round (93rd pick overall) of 1990 NFL draft. ... Signed by Dolphins (July 20, 1990). ... On inactive list for all 16 games (1990). ... Granted free agency (February 1, 1992). ... Assigned by Dolphins to Orlando Thunder in 1992 World League enhancement allocation program (February 20, 1992). ... Re-signed by Dolphins (February 21, 1992). ... Granted unconditional free agency (February 17, 1994). ... Signed by Detroit Lions (March 6, 1994). ... On injured reserve with wrist injury (November 8, 1994-remainder of season).
CHAMPIONSHIP GAME EXPERIENCE: Played in AFC championship game (1992 season).
PRO STATISTICS: W.L.: 1992—Fumbled six times and recovered two fumbles for minus 19 yards. ... NFL: 1993—Fumbled once and recovered one fumble for minus four yards. 1994—Fumbled eight times and recovered two fumbles for minus five yards. 1995—Fumbled eight times and recovered one fumble.
STATISTICAL PLATEAUS: 300-yard passing games: 1993 (1), 1995 (5). Total: 6.
MISCELLANEOUS: Regular-season record as starting NFL quarterback: 17-15 (.531).

		PASSING								RUSHING				TOTALS		
Year Team	G	Att.	Cmp.	Pct.	Yds.	TD	Int.	Avg.	Rat.	Att.	Yds.	Avg.	TD	TD	2pt.	Pts.
1990—Miami NFL							Did not play.									
1991—Miami NFL	2	0	0	...	0	0	0	...	...	0	0	...	0	0	...	0
1992—Orlando W.L.	10	*361	*201	55.7	2213	12	7	6.13	77.0	21	45	2.1	1	1	0	6
—Miami NFL	16	8	2	25.0	32	0	1	4.00	4.2	8	10	1.3	0	0	...	0
1993—Miami NFL	13	233	133	57.1	1773	12	8	7.61	84.2	21	89	4.2	0	0	...	0
1994—Detroit NFL	9	246	119	48.4	1456	10	11	5.92	62.0	15	24	1.6	1	1	0	6
1995—Detroit NFL	16	583	346	59.4	4338	32	12	7.44	92.3	36	104	2.9	4	4	0	24
W.L.totals (1 year)	10	361	201	557	2213	12	7	6.13	77.0	21	45	2.2	1	1	0	6
NFL totals (5 years)	56	1070	600	561	7599	54	32	7.10	82.8	80	227	2.8	5	5	0	30
Pro totals (5 years)	66	1431	801	56.0	9812	66	39	6.86	81.3	101	272	2.7	6	6	0	36

MITCHELL, SHANNON   TE   CHARGERS

PERSONAL: Born March 28, 1972, in Alcoa, Tenn. ... 6-2/245. ... Full name: Shannon Lamont Mitchell.
HIGH SCHOOL: Alcoa (Tenn.).
COLLEGE: Georgia.
TRANSACTIONS/CAREER NOTES: Signed as non-drafted free agent by San Diego Chargers (April 28, 1994).
CHAMPIONSHIP GAME EXPERIENCE: Played in AFC championship game (1994 season). ... Played in Super Bowl XXIX (1994 season).
PRO STATISTICS: 1994—Returned one kickoff for 18 yards.

			RECEIVING				TOTALS			
Year Team	G	No.	Yds.	Avg.	TD	TD	2pt.	Pts.	Fum.
1994—San Diego NFL	16	11	105	9.6	0	0	0	0	0
1995—San Diego NFL	16	3	31	10.3	1	1	0	6	0
Pro totals (2 years)	32	14	136	9.7	1	1	0	6	0

MOHR, CHRIS   P   BILLS

PERSONAL: Born May 11, 1966, in Atlanta. ... 6-5/215. ... Full name: Christopher Garrett Mohr. ... Name pronounced MORE.
HIGH SCHOOL: Briarwood Academy (Thomson, Ga.).
COLLEGE: Alabama (degree in criminal justice).
TRANSACTIONS/CAREER NOTES: Selected by Tampa Bay Buccaneers in sixth round (146th pick overall) of 1989 NFL draft. ... Signed by Buccaneers (July 15, 1989). ... Released by Buccaneers (September 2, 1990). ... Signed by WLAF (January 31, 1991). ... Selected by Montreal Machine in first round (eighth punter) of 1991 WLAF positional draft. ... Signed by Buffalo Bills (June 6, 1991). ... Granted unconditional free agency (February 17, 1994). ... Re-signed by Bills (March 3, 1994).
CHAMPIONSHIP GAME EXPERIENCE: Played in AFC championship game (1991-1993 seasons). ... Played in Super Bowl XXVI (1991 season), Super Bowl XXVII (1992 season) and Super Bowl XXVIII (1993 season).
HONORS: Named punter on All-World League team (1991).
PRO STATISTICS: NFL: 1989—Converted one extra point. 1991—Attempted one pass with one completion for minus nine yards. 1992—Rushed once for 11 yards and recovered one fumble. 1993—Fumbled once and recovered one fumble. 1994—Rushed once for minus nine yards. ... W.L.: 1991—Had only pass attempt intercepted and rushed three times for minus four yards.

				PUNTING			
Year Team	G	No.	Yds.	Avg.	Net avg.	In. 20	Blk.
1989—Tampa Bay NFL	16	84	3311	39.4	32.1	10	2
1990—				Did not play.			
1991—Montreal W.L.	10	57	2436	*42.7	34.0	13	2
—Buffalo NFL	16	54	2085	38.6	36.1	12	0
1992—Buffalo NFL	15	60	2531	42.2	36.8	12	0
1993—Buffalo NFL	16	74	2991	40.4	36.0	19	0
1994—Buffalo NFL	16	67	2799	41.8	36.0	13	0
1995—Buffalo NFL	16	86	3473	40.4	36.2	23	0
W.L. totals (1 year)	10	57	2436	42.7	34.0	13	2
NFL totals (6 years)	95	425	17190	40.5	35.4	89	2
Pro totals (6 years)	105	482	19626	40.7	35.2	102	4

MONK, ART   WR

PERSONAL: Born December 5, 1957, in White Plains, N.Y. ... 6-3/210.
HIGH SCHOOL: White Plains (N.Y.).
COLLEGE: Syracuse.
TRANSACTIONS/CAREER NOTES: Selected by Washington Redskins in first round (18th pick overall) of 1980 NFL draft. ... On injured reserve with broken foot (January 7, 1983-remainder of 1982 season playoffs). ... On injured reserve with knee injury (September 2-30, 1983). ... On injured reserve with knee injury (December 9, 1987-January 30, 1988). ... Granted unconditional free agency (March 1, 1993). ... Re-signed by Redskins (July 15, 1993). ... Granted unconditional free agency (February 17, 1994). ... Signed by New York Jets (June 3, 1994). ... Granted unconditional free agency (February 17, 1995). ... Signed by Philadelphia Eagles (November 27, 1995). ... On injured reserve (January 5, 1996). ... Granted unconditional free agency (February 16, 1996).
CHAMPIONSHIP GAME EXPERIENCE: Played in NFC championship game (1983, 1986 and 1991 seasons). ... Played in Super Bowl XVIII (1983 season). ... Member of Super Bowl championship team (1987 and 1991 seasons).
HONORS: Named wide receiver on THE SPORTING NEWS NFL All-Pro team (1984 and 1985). ... Played in Pro Bowl (1984-1986 seasons).
RECORDS: Holds NFL career record for most consecutive games with one or more reception—183 (January 2, 1983-December 24, 1995).
PRO STATISTICS: 1980—Returned one kickoff for 10 yards. 1983—Attempted one pass with one completion for 46 yards. 1986—Recovered two fumbles. 1988—Attempted one pass without a completion and recovered one fumble. 1990—Recovered one fumble.
STATISTICAL PLATEAUS: 100-yard receiving games: 1980 (1), 1981 (2), 1982 (2), 1983 (3), 1984 (5), 1985 (6), 1986 (4), 1988 (1), 1989 (4), 1990 (1), 1991 (3), 1994 (1). Total: 33.
MISCELLANEOUS: Holds Washington Redskins all-time record for most yards receiving (12,026).

		RUSHING				RECEIVING				TOTALS			
Year Team	G	Att.	Yds.	Avg.	TD	No.	Yds.	Avg.	TD	TD	2pt.	Pts.	Fum.
1980—Washington NFL	16	0	0	...	0	58	797	13.7	3	3	...	18	0
1981—Washington NFL	16	1	-5	-5.0	0	56	894	16.0	6	6	...	36	0
1982—Washington NFL	9	7	21	3.0	0	35	447	12.8	1	1	...	6	3
1983—Washington NFL	12	3	-19	-6.3	0	47	746	15.9	5	5	...	30	0
1984—Washington NFL	16	2	18	9.0	0	*106	1372	12.9	7	7	...	42	1
1985—Washington NFL	15	7	51	7.3	0	91	1226	13.5	2	2	...	12	2
1986—Washington NFL	16	4	27	6.8	0	73	1068	14.6	4	4	...	24	2
1987—Washington NFL	9	6	63	10.5	0	38	483	12.7	6	6	...	36	0
1988—Washington NFL	16	7	46	6.6	0	72	946	13.1	5	5	...	30	0
1989—Washington NFL	16	3	8	2.7	0	86	1186	13.8	8	8	...	48	2
1990—Washington NFL	16	7	59	8.4	0	68	770	11.3	5	5	...	30	0

M

Year Team	G	RUSHING Att.	Yds.	Avg.	TD	RECEIVING No.	Yds.	Avg.	TD	TOTALS TD	2pt.	Pts.	Fum.
1991—Washington NFL	16	9	19	2.1	0	71	1049	14.8	8	8	...	48	2
1992—Washington NFL	16	6	45	7.5	0	46	644	14.0	3	3	...	18	1
1993—Washington NFL	16	1	-1	-1.0	0	41	398	9.7	2	2	...	12	0
1994—New York Jets NFL	16	0	0	...	0	46	581	12.6	3	3	0	18	0
1995—Philadelphia NFL	3	0	0	...	0	6	114	19.0	0	0	0	0	0
Pro totals (16 years)	224	63	332	5.3	0	940	12721	13.5	68	68	0	408	13

MONTGOMERY, ALTON   S   FALCONS

PERSONAL: Born June 16, 1968, in Griffin, Ga. ... 6-0/205.
HIGH SCHOOL: Griffin (Ga.).
JUNIOR COLLEGE: Northwest Mississippi Community College.
COLLEGE: Houston.
TRANSACTIONS/CAREER NOTES: Selected by Denver Broncos in second round (52nd pick overall) of 1990 NFL draft. ... Signed by Broncos (July 1990). ... On injured reserve with knee injury (October 29-December 1, 1992). ... Granted free agency (March 1, 1993). ... Traded by Broncos to Atlanta Falcons for third-round (S Rondell Jones) and seventh-round (TE Clarence Williams) picks in 1993 draft (April 13, 1993). ... Signed by Falcons (April 1993). ... On injured reserve with kidney injury (December 9, 1994-remainder of season). ... Granted unconditional free agency (February 17, 1995). ... Re-signed by Falcons (April 21, 1995).
CHAMPIONSHIP GAME EXPERIENCE: Played in AFC championship game (1991 season).
PRO STATISTICS: 1990—Recovered two fumbles. 1991—Recovered one fumble. 1992—Fumbled once and recovered two fumbles for 66 yards. 1995—Credited with three sacks.

Year Team	G	INTERCEPTIONS No.	Yds.	Avg.	TD	KICKOFF RETURNS No.	Yds.	Avg.	TD	TOTALS TD	2pt.	Pts.	Fum.
1990—Denver NFL	15	2	43	21.5	0	14	286	20.4	0	0	...	0	1
1991—Denver NFL	16	0	0	...	0	26	488	18.8	0	0	...	0	1
1992—Denver NFL	12	0	0	...	0	21	466	22.2	0	0	...	0	1
1993—Atlanta NFL	8	0	0	...	0	2	53	26.5	0	0	...	0	0
1994—Atlanta NFL	2	0	0	...	0	2	58	29.0	0	0	0	0	0
1995—Atlanta NFL	15	1	71	71.0	1	0	0	...	0	1	0	6	0
Pro totals (6 years)	68	3	114	38.0	1	65	1351	20.8	0	1	0	6	3

MONTGOMERY, GLENN   DT   SEAHAWKS

PERSONAL: Born March 31, 1967, in New Orleans. ... 6-0/282. ... Full name: Glenn Steven Montgomery.
HIGH SCHOOL: West Jefferson (Harvey, La.).
COLLEGE: Houston.
TRANSACTIONS/CAREER NOTES: Selected by Houston Oilers in fifth round (131st pick overall) of 1989 NFL draft. ... Signed by Oilers (July 27, 1989). ... Granted free agency (February 1, 1991). ... Re-signed by Oilers (July 26, 1991). ... Designated by Oilers as transition player (February 15, 1994). ... Traded by Oilers with first-round pick (traded to Detroit) in 1996 draft to Seattle Seahawks for first-round pick (RB Eddie George) in 1996 draft (April 20, 1996).
PRO STATISTICS: 1989—Returned one kickoff for no yards. 1991—Returned one kickoff for 13 yards and recovered one fumble. 1992—Recovered two fumbles. 1993—Recovered three fumbles. 1994—Recovered three fumbles for minus two yards. 1995—Recovered two fumbles.

Year Team	G	SACKS
1989—Houston NFL	15	1.5
1990—Houston NFL	15	0.5
1991—Houston NFL	16	0.0
1992—Houston NFL	16	0.5
1993—Houston NFL	16	6.0
1994—Houston NFL	14	3.0
1995—Houston NFL	15	2.0
Pro totals (7 years)	107	13.5

M

MONTGOMERY, GREG   P   RAVENS

PERSONAL: Born October 29, 1964, in Morristown, N.J. ... 6-4/215. ... Full name: Gregory Hugh Montgomery Jr.
HIGH SCHOOL: Red Bank Regional (Little Silver, N.J.).
COLLEGE: Penn State, then Michigan State (degree in communications/sales, 1988).
TRANSACTIONS/CAREER NOTES: Selected by Houston Oilers in third round (72nd pick overall) of 1988 NFL draft. ... Signed by Oilers (August 3, 1988). ... Granted free agency (February 1, 1991). ... Re-signed by Oilers (September 6, 1991). ... Granted unconditional free agency (February 17, 1994). ... Signed by Detroit Lions (May 6, 1994). ... Granted unconditional free agency (February 17, 1995). ... Signed by Baltimore Ravens (April 3, 1996).
HONORS: Named punter on THE SPORTING NEWS NFL All-Pro team (1993). ... Played in Pro Bowl (1993 season).
PRO STATISTICS: 1989—Rushed three times for 17 yards and fumbled once. 1992—Rushed twice for minus 14 yards and fumbled once and recovered one fumble for minus 15 yards.

Year Team	G	PUNTING No.	Yds.	Avg.	Net avg.	In. 20	Blk.
1988—Houston NFL	16	65	2523	38.8	34.1	12	0
1989—Houston NFL	16	56	2422	43.3	36.1	15	2
1990—Houston NFL	16	34	1530	45.0	36.6	7	0
1991—Houston NFL	15	48	2105	43.9	36.8	13	2
1992—Houston NFL	16	53	2487	*46.9	37.3	14	*2
1993—Houston NFL	15	54	2462	*45.6	39.1	13	0
1994—Detroit NFL	16	63	2782	44.2	34.2	19	1
Pro totals (7 years)	110	373	16311	43.7	36.2	93	7

MONTREUIL, MARK CB CHARGERS

PERSONAL: Born December 29, 1971, in Montreal. ... 6-2/200. ... Full name: Mark Allen Montreuil. ... Name pronounced mon-TROY.
HIGH SCHOOL: Beaconsfield (Montreal).
COLLEGE: Concordia (Canada).
TRANSACTIONS/CAREER NOTES: Selected by Toronto Argonauts in first round (third pick overall) of 1995 CFL draft. ... Selected by San Diego Chargers in seventh round (237th pick overall) of 1995 NFL draft. ... Signed by Chargers (July 12, 1995). ... Assigned by Chargers to London Monarchs in 1996 World League enhancement allocation program (February 19, 1996).
PLAYING EXPERIENCE: San Diego NFL, 1995. ... Games: 1995 (16).
PRO STATISTICS: 1995—Recovered one fumble.

MOON, WARREN QB VIKINGS

PERSONAL: Born November 18, 1956, in Los Angeles. ... 6-3/213. ... Full name: Harold Warren Moon.
HIGH SCHOOL: Hamilton (Los Angeles).
COLLEGE: Washington.
TRANSACTIONS/CAREER NOTES: Signed as free agent by Edmonton Eskimos of CFL (March 1978). ... USFL rights traded by Memphis Showboats to Los Angeles Express for future draft pick (August 30, 1983). ... Granted free agency (March 1, 1984). ... Signed by Houston Oilers (March 1, 1984). ... On injured reserve with fractured scapula (September 5-October 15, 1988). ... Traded by Oilers to Minnesota Vikings for third-round pick (WR Malcolm Seabron) in 1994 draft and third-round pick (RB Rodney Thomas) in 1995 draft (April 14, 1994).
CHAMPIONSHIP GAME EXPERIENCE: Played in Grey Cup, CFL championship game (1978-1982 seasons).
HONORS: Played in Pro Bowl (1988-1995 seasons). ... Named quarterback on THE SPORTING NEWS NFL All-Pro team (1990).
RECORDS: Holds NFL single-season record for most passes completed—404 (1991). ... Shares NFL single-season records for most games with 300 or more yards passing—9 (1990); and most fumbles—18 (1990). ... Shares NFL single-game record for most times sacked—12 (September 29, 1985, vs. Dallas).
POSTSEASON RECORDS: Holds NFL postseason career records for most fumbles—16; and most own fumbles recovered—8. ... Holds NFL postseason single-game records for most passes completed—36 (January 3, 1993, OT, at Buffalo); and most fumbles—5 (January 16, 1994, vs. Kansas City).
PRO STATISTICS: CFL: 1978—Fumbled once. 1979—Fumbled once. 1981—Fumbled once. 1982—Fumbled once and recovered one fumble. 1983—Fumbled seven times. NFL: 1984—Led league with 17 fumbles and recovered seven fumbles for minus one yard. 1985—Fumbled 12 times and recovered five fumbles for minus eight yards. 1986—Fumbled 11 times and recovered three fumbles for minus four yards. 1987—Fumbled eight times and recovered six fumbles for minus seven yards. 1988—Fumbled eight times and recovered four fumbles for minus 12 yards. 1989—Fumbled 11 times and recovered six fumbles for minus 13 yards. 1990—Led league with 18 fumbles and recovered four fumbles. 1991—Fumbled 11 times and recovered four fumbles for minus four yards. 1992—Fumbled seven times. 1993—Fumbled 13 times and recovered five fumbles for minus seven yards. 1994—Fumbled nine times and recovered two fumbles for minus five yards. 1995—Fumbled 13 times and recovered five fumbles for minus 12 yards.
STATISTICAL PLATEAUS: 300-yard passing games: 1984 (4), 1985 (3), 1986 (3), 1987 (2), 1989 (4), 1990 (9), 1991 (6), 1992 (4), 1993 (3), 1994 (6), 1995 (4). Total: 48.
MISCELLANEOUS: Regular-season record as starting NFL quarterback: 87-83 (.512). ... Active NFC leader for career passing yards (42,177) and shares lead for career touchdown passes (247). ... Holds Houston Oilers all-time records for most yards passing (33,685) and most touchdown passes (196).

Year Team	G	Att.	Cmp.	Pct.	Yds.	TD	Int.	Avg.	Rat.	Att.	Yds.	Avg.	TD	TD	2pt.	Pts.
				PASSING							RUSHING				TOTALS	
1978—Edmonton CFL	15	173	89	51.5	1112	5	7	6.43	64.5	30	114	3.8	1	1	0	6
1979—Edmonton CFL	16	274	149	54.4	2382	20	12	8.69	89.7	56	150	2.7	2	2	0	12
1980—Edmonton CFL	16	331	181	54.7	3127	25	11	9.45	98.3	55	352	6.4	3	3	0	18
1981—Edmonton CFL	15	378	237	62.7	3959	27	12	10.47	108.6	50	298	6.0	3	3	0	18
1982—Edmonton CFL	16	562	333	59.3	5000	36	16	8.90	98.0	54	259	4.8	4	4	0	24
1983—Edmonton CFL	16	664	380	57.2	5648	31	19	8.51	88.9	85	527	6.2	3	3	0	18
1984—Houston NFL	16	450	259	57.6	3338	12	14	7.42	76.9	58	211	3.6	1	1	...	6
1985—Houston NFL	14	377	200	53.1	2709	15	19	7.19	68.5	39	130	3.3	0	0	...	0
1986—Houston NFL	15	488	256	52.5	3489	13	*26	7.15	62.3	42	157	3.7	2	2	...	12
1987—Houston NFL	12	368	184	50.0	2806	21	18	7.63	74.2	34	112	3.3	3	3	...	18
1988—Houston NFL	11	294	160	54.4	2327	17	8	7.92	88.4	33	88	2.7	5	5	...	30
1989—Houston NFL	16	464	280	60.3	3631	23	14	7.83	88.9	70	268	3.8	4	4	...	24
1990—Houston NFL	15	*584	*362	62.0	*4689	*33	13	8.03	96.8	55	215	3.9	2	2	...	12
1991—Houston NFL	16	*655	*404	61.7	*4690	23	*21	7.16	81.7	33	68	2.1	2	2	...	12
1992—Houston NFL	11	346	224	64.7	2521	18	12	7.29	89.3	27	147	5.4	1	1	...	6
1993—Houston NFL	15	520	303	58.3	3485	21	21	6.70	75.2	48	145	3.0	1	1	...	6
1994—Minnesota NFL	15	601	371	61.7	4264	18	19	7.10	79.9	27	55	2.0	0	0	0	0
1995—Minnesota NFL	16	606	*377	62.2	4228	33	14	6.98	91.5	33	82	2.5	0	0	0	0
CFL totals (6 years)	94	2382	1369	57.5	21228	144	77	8.91	93.8	330	1700	5.2	16	16	0	96
NFL totals (12 years)	172	5753	3380	58.8	42177	247	199	7.33	81.5	499	1678	3.4	21	21	0	126
Pro totals (18 years)	266	8135	4749	58.4	63405	391	276	7.80	85.1	829	3378	4.1	37	37	0	222

MOORE, BRANDON OT CARDINALS

PERSONAL: Born June 21, 1970, in Ardmore, Pa. ... 6-7/295. ... Full name: Brandon Christopher Moore. ... Son of Richard Moore, defensive tackle, Green Bay Packers (1969 and 1970).
HIGH SCHOOL: Archbishop Carroll (Radnor, Pa.).
COLLEGE: Duke.
TRANSACTIONS/CAREER NOTES: Signed as non-drafted free agent by Miami Dolphins (April 29, 1993). ... Released by Dolphins (July 14, 1993). ... Signed by New England Patriots (July 18, 1993). ... Released by Patriots (December 6, 1995). ... Claimed on waivers by Arizona Cardinals (December 6,1995). ... Granted free agency (February 16, 1996).
PLAYING EXPERIENCE: New England NFL, 1993-1995. ... Games: 1993 (16), 1994 (4), 1995 (6). Total: 26.

MOORE, DARRYL　　　　　　　　G　　　　　　　　BUCCANEERS

PERSONAL: Born January 27, 1969, in Minden, La. ... 6-3/293.
HIGH SCHOOL: Minden (La.).
JUNIOR COLLEGE: Tyler (Texas) Junior College.
COLLEGE: Texas-El Paso.
TRANSACTIONS/CAREER NOTES: Selected by Washington Redskins in eighth round (224th pick overall) of 1992 NFL draft. ... Signed by Redskins for 1992 season. ... On physically unable to perform list for 1992 season. ... Traded by Redskins to Green Bay Packers for conditional fifth-round pick in 1995 draft (August 28, 1994). ... Released by Packers (August 30, 1994). ... Signed by Carolina Panthers (December 15, 1994). ... Released by Panthers (August 17, 1995). ... Signed by Tampa Bay Buccaneers (December 29, 1995).
PLAYING EXPERIENCE: Washington NFL, 1993. ... Games: 1993 (12).

MOORE, DAVE　　　　　　　TE/FB　　　　　　BUCCANEERS

PERSONAL: Born November 11, 1969, in Morristown, N.J. ... 6-2/243. ... Full name: David Edward Moore.
HIGH SCHOOL: Roxbury (Succasunna, N.J.).
COLLEGE: Pittsburgh (degree in justice administration).
TRANSACTIONS/CAREER NOTES: Selected by Miami Dolphins in seventh round (191st pick overall) of 1992 NFL draft. ... Signed by Dolphins (July 15, 1992). ... Released by Dolphins (August 31, 1992). ... Signed by Dolphins to practice squad (September 1, 1992). ... Released by Dolphins (September 16, 1992). ... Re-signed by Dolphins to practice squad (October 21, 1992). ... Activated (October 24, 1992). ... Released by Dolphins (October 28, 1992). ... Re-signed by Dolphins to practice squad (October 28, 1992). ... Released by Dolphins (November 18, 1992). ... Signed by Tampa Bay Buccaneers to practice squad (November 24, 1992). ... Activated (December 4, 1992). ... Granted free agency (February 16, 1996). ... Re-signed by Buccaneers (June 3, 1996).
PRO STATISTICS: 1993—Attempted one pass without a completion and recovered one fumble. 1995—Rushed once for four yards.

		RECEIVING				TOTALS			
Year　Team	G	No.	Yds.	Avg.	TD	TD	2pt.	Pts.	Fum.
1992—Miami NFL	1	0	0	...	0	0	...	0	0
—Tampa Bay NFL	4	1	10	10.0	0	0	...	0	0
1993—Tampa Bay NFL	15	4	47	11.8	1	1	...	6	0
1994—Tampa Bay NFL	15	4	57	14.3	0	0	0	0	0
1995—Tampa Bay NFL	16	13	102	7.9	0	0	0	0	0
Pro totals (4 years)	51	22	216	9.8	1	1	0	6	0

MOORE, DERRICK　　　　　　RB　　　　　　　　LIONS

PERSONAL: Born October 13, 1967, in Albany, Ga. ... 6-1/227.
HIGH SCHOOL: Monroe Comprehensive (Albany, Ga.).
COLLEGE: Troy (Ala.) State, then Northeastern Oklahoma State.
TRANSACTIONS/CAREER NOTES: Selected by Atlanta Falcons in eighth round (216th pick overall) of 1992 NFL draft. ... Signed by Falcons (July 27, 1992). ... On injured reserve (September 2-October 16, 1992). ... Released by Falcons (October 16, 1992). ... Re-signed by Falcons to practice squad (November 11, 1992). ... On injured reserve (November 18-December 17, 1992). ... Released by Falcons (December 17, 1992). ... Re-signed by Falcons to practice squad (December 17, 1992). ... Activated (December 26, 1992). ... Claimed on waivers by Detroit Lions (September 1, 1994). ... Granted free agency (February 17, 1995). ... Re-signed by Lions (April 17, 1995). ... Traded by Lions to San Francisco 49ers for fifth-round pick (OT Ronald Cherry) in 1995 draft (April 17, 1995). ... Released by 49ers (August 19, 1995). ... Signed by Carolina Panthers (August 29, 1995). ... Granted unconditional free agency (February 16, 1996). ...Signed by Lions (May 21, 1996).
PRO STATISTICS: 1993—Recovered three fumbles.
STATISTICAL PLATEAUS: 100-yard rushing games: 1993 (1), 1995 (2). Total: 3.
MISCELLANEOUS: Holds Carolina Panthers all-time record for most yards rushing (740).

		RUSHING				RECEIVING				KICKOFF RETURNS				TOTALS			
Year　Team	G	Att.	Yds.	Avg.	TD	No.	Yds.	Avg.	TD	No.	Yds.	Avg.	TD	TD	2pt.	Pts.	Fum.
1993—Detroit NFL	13	88	405	4.6	3	21	169	8.1	1	1	68	68.0	0	4	...	24	4
1994—Detroit NFL	16	27	52	1.9	4	1	10	10.0	0	10	113	11.3	0	4	0	24	2
1995—Carolina NFL	13	195	740	3.8	4	4	12	3.0	0	0	0	...	0	4	0	24	4
Pro totals (3 years)	42	310	1197	3.9	11	26	191	7.4	1	11	181	16.5	0	12	0	72	10

MOORE, ERIC　　　　　　　　G

PERSONAL: Born January 21, 1965, in Berkeley, Mo. ... 6-5/290. ... Full name: Eric Patrick Moore. ... Cousin of Dwight Scales, wide receiver with four NFL teams (1976-1979 and 1981-1984).
HIGH SCHOOL: Berkeley (Mo.).
COLLEGE: Northeastern Oklahoma A&M, then Indiana (degree in general studies and criminal justice, 1988).
TRANSACTIONS/CAREER NOTES: Selected by New York Giants in first round (10th pick overall) of 1988 NFL draft. ... Signed by Giants (August 1, 1988). ... Granted free agency (February 1, 1992). ... Re-signed by Giants (September 7, 1992). ... Granted roster exemption for one game (September 1992). ... On suspended list for steroid use (August 29-October 4, 1993). ... Granted unconditional free agency (February 17, 1994). ... Signed by Cincinnati Bengals (April 4, 1994). ... On injured reserve with leg injury (December 21, 1994-remainder of season). ... Granted free agency (February 17, 1995). ... Tendered offer sheet by New Orleans Saints (July 25, 1995). ... Offer matched by Bengals (July 28, 1995). ... Released by Bengals (August 20, 1995). ... Signed by Cleveland Browns (August 30, 1995). ... Released by Browns (October 5, 1995). ... Signed by Miami Dolphins (November 2, 1995). ... Granted unconditional free agency (February 16, 1996).
PLAYING EXPERIENCE: New York Giants NFL, 1988-1993; Cincinnati NFL, 1994; Cleveland (1)-Miami (2) NFL, 1995. ... Games: 1988 (11), 1989 (16), 1990 (15), 1991 (16), 1992 (10), 1993 (7), 1994 (6), 1995 (3). Total: 84.
CHAMPIONSHIP GAME EXPERIENCE: Played in NFC championship game (1990 season). ... Member of Super Bowl championship team (1990 season).
PRO STATISTICS: 1989—Recovered three fumbles.

M

MOORE, HERMAN   WR   LIONS

PERSONAL: Born October 20, 1969, in Danville, Va. ... 6-3/210. ... Full name: Herman Joseph Moore.
HIGH SCHOOL: George Washington (Danville, Va.).
COLLEGE: Virginia (degree in rhetoric and communication studies, 1991).
TRANSACTIONS/CAREER NOTES: Selected after junior season by Detroit Lions in first round (10th pick overall) of 1991 NFL draft. ... Signed by Lions (July 19, 1991). ... On injured reserve with quadricep injury (September 11-October 9, 1992). ... On practice squad (October 9-14, 1992). ... Designated by Lions as transition player (February 25, 1993).
CHAMPIONSHIP GAME EXPERIENCE: Played in NFC championship game (1991 season).
HONORS: Named wide receiver on THE SPORTING NEWS college All-America first team (1990). ... Played in Pro Bowl (1994 and 1995 seasons). ... Named wide receiver on THE SPORTING NEWS NFL All-Pro team (1995).
RECORDS: Holds NFL single-season record for most pass receptions—123 (1995).
POSTSEASON RECORDS: Shares NFL postseason career and single-game records for most two-point conversions—1 (December 30, 1995, vs. Philadelphia).
STATISTICAL PLATEAUS: 100-yard receiving games: 1992 (3), 1993 (3), 1994 (3), 1995 (10). Total: 19.

		RECEIVING				TOTALS			
Year Team	G	No.	Yds.	Avg.	TD	TD	2pt.	Pts.	Fum.
1991—Detroit NFL	13	11	135	12.3	0	0	...	0	0
1992—Detroit NFL	12	51	966	18.9	4	4	...	24	0
1993—Detroit NFL	15	61	935	15.3	6	6	...	36	2
1994—Detroit NFL	16	72	1173	16.3	11	11	0	66	1
1995—Detroit NFL	16	*123	1686	13.7	14	14	0	84	2
Pro totals (5 years)	72	318	4895	15.4	35	35	0	210	5

MOORE, MARTY   LB   PATRIOTS

PERSONAL: Born March 19, 1971, in Phoenix. ... 6-1/244. ... Full name: Martin Neff Moore.
HIGH SCHOOL: Highlands (Fort Thomas, Ky.).
COLLEGE: Kentucky.
TRANSACTIONS/CAREER NOTES: Selected by New England Patriots in seventh round (222nd pick overall) of 1994 NFL draft. ... Signed by Patriots (June 1, 1994).
PLAYING EXPERIENCE: New England NFL, 1994 and 1995. ... Games: 1994 (16), 1995 (16). Total: 32.

MOORE, ROB   WR   CARDINALS

PERSONAL: Born September 27, 1968, in New York. ... 6-3/205.
HIGH SCHOOL: Hempstead (N.Y.).
COLLEGE: Syracuse (degree in psychology, 1990).
TRANSACTIONS/CAREER NOTES: Selected by New York Jets in first round of 1990 NFL supplemental draft. ... Signed by Jets (July 22, 1990). ... Designated by Jets as transition player (February 25, 1993). ... Free agency status changed by Jets from transitional to restricted (February 17, 1994). ... Re-signed by Jets (July 12, 1994). ... Designated by Jets as franchise player (February 15, 1995). ... Traded by Jets to Arizona Cardinals for RB Ronald Moore and first-round (DE Hugh Douglas) and fourth-round (OT Melvin Hayes) picks in 1995 draft (April 21, 1995).
HONORS: Named wide receiver on THE SPORTING NEWS college All-America first team (1989). ... Played in Pro Bowl (1994 season).
PRO STATISTICS: 1994—Recovered one fumble. 1995—Attempted two passes with one completion for 33 yards and an interception.
STATISTICAL PLATEAUS: 100-yard receiving games: 1990 (1), 1993 (2), 1994 (2), 1995 (3). Total: 8.

		RUSHING				RECEIVING				TOTALS			
Year Team	G	Att.	Yds.	Avg.	TD	No.	Yds.	Avg.	TD	TD	2pt.	Pts.	Fum.
1990—New York Jets NFL	15	2	-4	-2.0	0	44	692	15.7	6	6	...	36	1
1991—New York Jets NFL	16	0	0	...	0	70	987	14.1	5	5	...	30	2
1992—New York Jets NFL	16	1	21	21.0	0	50	726	14.5	4	4	...	24	0
1993—New York Jets NFL	13	1	-6	-6.0	0	64	843	13.2	1	1	...	6	2
1994—New York Jets NFL	16	1	-3	-3.0	0	78	1010	13.0	6	6	2	40	0
1995—Arizona NFL	15	0	0	...	0	63	907	14.4	5	5	1	32	0
Pro totals (6 years)	91	5	8	1.6	0	369	5165	14.0	27	27	3	168	5

MOORE, RONALD   RB/KR   JETS

PERSONAL: Born November 26, 1970, in Spencer, Okla. ... 5-10/225.
HIGH SCHOOL: Star Spencer (Okla.).
COLLEGE: Pittsburg (Kan.) State.
TRANSACTIONS/CAREER NOTES: Selected by Phoenix Cardinals in fourth round (87th pick overall) of 1993 NFL draft. ... Signed by Cardinals (July 22, 1993). ... Cardinals franchise renamed Arizona Cardinals for 1994 season. ... Traded by Cardinals with first-round (DE Hugh Douglas) and fourth-round (OT Melvin Hayes) picks in 1995 draft to New York Jets for WR Rob Moore (April 21, 1995).
HONORS: Harlon Hill Trophy winner (1992).
PRO STATISTICS: 1993—Returned one kickoff for nine yards and recovered one fumble. 1994—Attempted one pass without a completion and recovered one fumble. 1995—Recovered one fumble.
STATISTICAL PLATEAUS: 100-yard rushing games: 1993 (3), 1994 (1). Total: 4.

		RUSHING				RECEIVING				KICKOFF RETURNS				TOTALS			
Year Team	G	Att.	Yds.	Avg.	TD	No.	Yds.	Avg.	TD	No.	Yds.	Avg.	TD	TD	2pt.	Pts.	Fum.
1993—Phoenix NFL	16	263	1018	3.9	9	3	16	5.3	0	1	9	9.0	0	9	...	54	3
1994—Arizona NFL	16	232	780	3.4	4	8	52	6.5	1	0	0	...	0	5	1	32	2
1995—New York Jets NFL	15	43	121	2.8	0	8	50	6.3	0	8	166	20.8	0	0	0	0	3
Pro totals (3 years)	47	538	1919	3.6	13	19	118	6.2	1	9	175	19.5	0	14	1	86	8

MOORE, STEVON   S   RAVENS

PERSONAL: Born February 9, 1967, in Wiggins, Miss. ... 5-11/210. ... Full name: Stevon Nathaniel Moore. ... Name pronounced Stee-von.
HIGH SCHOOL: Stone County (Wiggins, Miss.).
COLLEGE: Mississippi.
TRANSACTIONS/CAREER NOTES: Selected by New York Jets in seventh round (181st pick overall) of 1989 NFL draft. ... Signed by Jets (July 22, 1989). ... On injured reserve with knee injury (August 28, 1989-entire season). ... Granted unconditional free agency (February 1, 1990). ... Signed by Miami Dolphins (March 30, 1990). ... On physically unable to perform list with knee injury (July 21-August 27, 1990). ... On physically unable to perform list with knee injury (August 28-October 18, 1990). ... On injured reserve with hamstring injury (November 8-December 8, 1990). ... On injured reserve with knee injury (August 27, 1991-entire season). ... Granted unconditional free agency (February 1, 1992). ... Signed by Cleveland Browns (March 25, 1992). ... On injured reserve with separated shoulder (December 15, 1992-remainder of season). ... Browns franchise moved to Baltimore and renamed Ravens for 1996 season (March 11, 1996).
PRO STATISTICS: 1990—Recovered one fumble. 1992—Recovered three fumbles for 115 yards and one touchdown. 1993—Recovered one fumble for 22 yards and a touchdown. 1994—Recovered five fumbles for three yards.

		INTERCEPTIONS				SACKS
Year Team	G	No.	Yds.	Avg.	TD	No.
1990—Miami NFL	7	0	0	...	0	0.0
1991—Miami		Did not play—injured.				
1992—Cleveland NFL	14	0	0	...	0	2.0
1993—Cleveland NFL	16	0	0	...	0	0.0
1994—Cleveland NFL	16	0	0	...	0	0.0
1995—Cleveland NFL	16	5	55	11.0	0	1.0
Pro totals (5 years)	69	5	55	11.0	0	3.0

MOORE, WILL   WR   PATRIOTS

PERSONAL: Born February 21, 1970, in Dallas. ... 6-2/180.
HIGH SCHOOL: David D. Carter (Dallas).
COLLEGE: Texas Southern.
TRANSACTIONS/CAREER NOTES: Signed as free agent by Calgary Stampeders of CFL (April 1992). ... Granted free agency (February 1995). ... Signed by New England Patriots (April 3, 1995).
PRO STATISTICS: CFL: 1994—Attempted two passes with two completions for 52 yards and returned two kickoffs for two yards.

		RECEIVING				TOTALS			
Year Team	G	No.	Yds.	Avg.	TD	TD	2pt.	Pts.	Fum.
1992—Calgary CFL	1	3	38	12.7	0	0	0	0	0
1993—Calgary CFL	18	73	1083	14.8	12	12	0	72	2
1994—Calgary CFL	16	44	792	18.0	11	11	0	66	0
1995—New England NFL	14	43	502	11.7	1	1	0	6	0
CFL totals (3 years)	35	120	1913	15.9	23	23	0	138	2
NFL totals (1 year)	14	43	502	11.7	1	1	0	6	0
Pro totals (4 years)	49	163	2415	14.8	24	24	0	144	2

MORGAN, ANTHONY   WR

PERSONAL: Born November 15, 1967, in Cleveland. ... 6-1/200. ... Full name: Anthony Eugene Morgan.
HIGH SCHOOL: John Adams (Cleveland).
COLLEGE: Tennessee.
TRANSACTIONS/CAREER NOTES: Selected by Chicago Bears in fifth round (134th pick overall) of 1991 NFL draft. ... Signed by Bears (July 15, 1991). ... On injured reserve with knee injury (September 2-30, 1992). ... Released by Bears (August 30, 1993). ... Re-signed by Bears (August 31, 1993). ... Claimed on waivers by Green Bay Packers (November 3, 1993). ... Granted unconditional free agency (February 17, 1995). ... Re-signed by Packers (April 28, 1995). ... Granted unconditional free agency (February 16, 1996).
CHAMPIONSHIP GAME EXPERIENCE: Played in NFC championship game (1995 season).
PRO STATISTICS: 1991—Fumbled once. 1994—Fumbled once.
STATISTICAL PLATEAUS: 100-yard receiving games: 1994 (1).

		RUSHING				RECEIVING				PUNT RETURNS				KICKOFF RETURNS				TOTALS		
Year Team	G	Att.	Yds.	Avg.	TD	No.	Yds.	Avg.	TD	No.	Yds.	Avg.	TD	No.	Yds.	Avg.	TD	TD	2pt.	Pts.
1991—Chicago NFL	14	3	18	6.0	0	13	211	16.2	2	3	19	6.3	0	8	133	16.6	0	2	...	12
1992—Chicago NFL	12	3	68	22.7	0	14	323	23.1	2	3	21	7.0	0	4	71	17.8	0	2	...	12
1993—Chicago NFL	1	0	0	...	0	0	0	...	0	0	0	...	0	0	0	...	0	0	...	0
—Green Bay NFL	2	0	0	...	0	1	8	8.0	0	0	0	...	0	0	0	...	0	0	...	0
1994—Green Bay NFL	16	0	0	...	0	28	397	14.2	4	0	0	...	0	0	0	...	0	4	0	24
1995—Green Bay NFL	16	0	0	...	0	31	344	11.1	4	0	0	...	0	3	46	15.3	0	4	0	24
Pro totals (5 years)	61	6	86	14.3	0	87	1283	14.8	12	6	40	6.7	0	15	250	16.7	0	12	0	72

MORRIS, BAM   RB   STEELERS

PERSONAL: Born January 13, 1972, in Cooper, Texas. ... 6-0/246. ... Brother of Ron Morris, wide receiver, Chicago Bears (1987-1992); and cousin of Terry Norris, World Boxing Council and International Boxing Federation junior middleweight champion.
HIGH SCHOOL: Cooper (Texas).
COLLEGE: Texas Tech.
TRANSACTIONS/CAREER NOTES: Selected after junior season by Pittsburgh Steelers in third round (91st pick overall) of 1994 NFL draft. ... Signed by Steelers (July 15, 1994).
CHAMPIONSHIP GAME EXPERIENCE: Played in AFC championship game (1994 and 1995 seasons). ... Played in Super Bowl XXX (1995 season).
HONORS: Doak Walker Award winner (1993). ... Named running back on The Sporting News college All-America second team (1993).
PRO STATISTICS: 1994—Recovered one fumble.

M

STATISTICAL PLATEAUS: 100-yard rushing games: 1994 (2), 1995 (2). Total: 4.

Year Team	G	RUSHING				RECEIVING				KICKOFF RETURNS				TOTALS			
		Att.	Yds.	Avg.	TD	No.	Yds.	Avg.	TD	No.	Yds.	Avg.	TD	TD	2pt.	Pts.	Fum.
1994—Pittsburgh NFL	15	198	836	4.2	7	22	204	9.3	0	4	114	28.5	0	7	0	42	3
1995—Pittsburgh NFL	13	148	559	3.8	9	8	36	4.5	0	0	0	...	0	9	0	54	3
Pro totals (2 years)	28	346	1395	4.0	16	30	240	8.0	0	4	114	28.5	0	16	0	96	6

MORRIS, MIKE C VIKINGS

PERSONAL: Born February 22, 1961, in Centerville, Iowa. ... 6-5/275. ... Full name: Michael Stephen Morris.
HIGH SCHOOL: Centerville (Iowa).
COLLEGE: Northeast Missouri State (degree in psychology and physical education).
TRANSACTIONS/CAREER NOTES: Signed as non-drafted free agent by Arizona Outlaws of USFL (November 1, 1984). ... Released by Outlaws (February 11, 1985). ... Signed by Denver Broncos (May 8, 1986). ... Released by Broncos (July 21, 1986). ... Signed by St. Louis Cardinals (May 20, 1987). ... Crossed picket line during players strike (October 7, 1987). ... Cardinals franchise moved to Phoenix (March 15, 1988). ... On injured reserve with knee injury (August 23, 1988-entire season). ... Granted unconditional free agency (February 1, 1989). ... Signed by Washington Redskins (March 20, 1989). ... Claimed on waivers by Kansas City Chiefs (August 30, 1989). ... Released by Chiefs (October 11, 1989). ... Signed by New England Patriots (October 13, 1989). ... Granted unconditional free agency (February 1, 1990). ... Signed by Chiefs (April 1, 1990). ... Released by Chiefs (July 28, 1990). ... Signed by Seattle Seahawks (preseason, 1990). ... Released by Seahawks (October 4, 1990). ... Signed by Cleveland Browns (October 16, 1990). ... Granted unconditional free agency (February 1-April 1, 1991). ... Re-signed by Browns (1991). ... Released by Browns (July 22, 1991). ... Signed by Minnesota Vikings (August 10, 1991). ... Released by Vikings (August 26, 1991). ... Re-signed by Vikings (August 29, 1991). ... Granted unconditional free agency (February 1-April 1, 1992). ... Re-signed by Vikings for 1992 season. ... Granted unconditional free agency (February 17, 1994). ... Re-signed by Vikings (May 17, 1994). ... Granted unconditional free agency (February 17, 1995). ... Re-signed by Vikings (March 27, 1995).
PLAYING EXPERIENCE: St. Louis NFL, 1987; Kansas City (5)-New England (11) NFL, 1989; Seattle (4)-Cleveland (10) NFL, 1990; Minnesota NFL, 1991-1995. ... Games: 1987 (14), 1989 (16), 1990 (14), 1991 (16), 1992 (16), 1993 (16), 1994 (16), 1995 (16). Total: 124.
PRO STATISTICS: 1990—Fumbled once for minus 23 yards.

MORRISON, DARRYL S REDSKINS

PERSONAL: Born May 19, 1971, in Phoenix. ... 5-11/200. ... Full name: Darryl Lamon Morrison.
HIGH SCHOOL: Central, then Camelback (Phoenix).
JUNIOR COLLEGE: Phoenix College.
COLLEGE: Arizona.
TRANSACTIONS/CAREER NOTES: Selected by Washington Redskins in sixth round (155th pick overall) of 1993 NFL draft. ... Signed by Redskins (July 15, 1993). ... Released by Redskins (August 30, 1993). ... Re-signed by Redskins to practice squad (August 31, 1993). ... Activated (December 4, 1993).
PLAYING EXPERIENCE: Washington NFL, 1993-1995. ... Games: 1993 (4), 1994 (16), 1995 (16). Total: 36.
PRO STATISTICS: 1994—Recovered two fumbles for 32 yards and a touchdown. 1995—Recovered one fumble.

M

MORRISON, STEVE LB COLTS

PERSONAL: Born December 28, 1971, in Birmingham, Mich. ... 6-3/246.
HIGH SCHOOL: Brother Rice (Bloomfield Hills, Mich.).
COLLEGE: Michigan.
TRANSACTIONS/CAREER NOTES: Signed as non-drafted free agent by Indianapolis Colts (April 27, 1995).
PLAYING EXPERIENCE: Indianapolis NFL, 1995. ... Games: 1995 (10).
CHAMPIONSHIP GAME EXPERIENCE: Member of Colts for AFC championship game (1995 season); inactive.
PRO STATISTICS: 1995—Returned two kickoffs for six yards.

MORTON, JOHNNIE WR/KR LIONS

PERSONAL: Born October 7, 1971, in Inglewood, Calif. ... 6-0/190. ... Full name: Johnnie James Morton.
HIGH SCHOOL: South Torrance (Calif.).
COLLEGE: Southern California.
TRANSACTIONS/CAREER NOTES: Selected by Detroit Lions in first round (21st pick overall) of 1994 NFL draft. ... Signed by Lions (July 18, 1994).
HONORS: Named wide receiver on THE SPORTING NEWS college All-America first team (1993).
PRO STATISTICS: 1994—Recovered one fumble. 1995—Rushed three times for 33 yards.
STATISTICAL PLATEAUS: 100-yard receiving games: 1995 (1).

Year Team	G	RECEIVING				PUNT RETURNS				KICKOFF RETURNS				TOTALS			
		No.	Yds.	Avg.	TD	No.	Yds.	Avg.	TD	No.	Yds.	Avg.	TD	TD	2pt.	Pts.	Fum.
1994—Detroit NFL	14	3	39	13.0	1	0	0	...	0	4	143	35.8	1	2	0	12	1
1995—Detroit NFL	16	44	590	13.4	8	7	48	6.9	0	18	390	21.7	0	8	0	48	1
Pro totals (2 years)	30	47	629	13.4	9	7	48	6.9	0	22	533	24.2	1	10	0	60	2

MORTON, MIKE LB RAIDERS

PERSONAL: Born March 28, 1972, in Kannapolis, N.C. ... 6-4/230. ... Full name: Michael Anthony Morton Jr.
HIGH SCHOOL: A.L. Brown (Kannapolis, N.C.).
COLLEGE: North Carolina.
TRANSACTIONS/CAREER NOTES: Selected by Los Angeles Raiders in fourth round (118th pick overall) of 1995 NFL draft. ... Signed by Raiders (July 21, 1995). ... Raiders franchise moved to Oakland (July 21, 1995).

PLAYING EXPERIENCE: Oakland NFL, 1995. ... Games: 1995 (2).
PRO STATISTICS: 1995—Recovered one fumble.

MOSS, BRENT   RB   RAMS

PERSONAL: Born January 30, 1972, in Racine, Wis. ... 5-9/211.
HIGH SCHOOL: Washington Park (Racine, Wis.).
COLLEGE: Wisconsin.
TRANSACTIONS/CAREER NOTES: Signed as non-drafted free agent by Miami Dolphins (April 28, 1995). ... Released by Dolphins (August 27, 1995). ... Signed by St. Louis Rams to practice squad (September 4, 1995). ... Activated (October 16, 1995).

		RUSHING				RECEIVING				TOTALS		
Year Team	G	Att.	Yds.	Avg.	TD	No.	Yds.	Avg.	TD	TD	2pt.	Pts.	Fum.
1995—St. Louis Rams NFL	4	22	90	4.1	0	1	-3	-3.0	0	0	0	0	0

MOSS, WINSTON   LB   SEAHAWKS

PERSONAL: Born December 24, 1965, in Miami. ... 6-3/245. ... Brother of Anthony Moss, linebacker, New York Giants (1991).
HIGH SCHOOL: Southridge (Miami).
COLLEGE: Miami (Fla.).
TRANSACTIONS/CAREER NOTES: Selected by Tampa Bay Buccaneers in second round (50th pick overall) of 1987 NFL draft. ... Signed by Buccaneers (July 18, 1987). ... Granted free agency (February 1, 1990). ... Re-signed by Buccaneers (July 27, 1990). ... Traded by Buccaneers to Los Angeles Raiders for third-round (RB Robert Wilson) and fifth-round (G Tim Ryan) picks in 1991 draft (April 22, 1991). ... Granted free agency (February 1, 1992). ... Re-signed by Raiders (August 26, 1992). ... Granted roster exemption (August 26-28, 1992). ... Granted unconditional free agency (February 17, 1995). ... Signed by Seattle Seahawks (March 15, 1995).
PRO STATISTICS: 1987—Recovered one fumble in end zone for a touchdown. 1990—Intercepted one pass for 31 yards and recovered one fumble. 1991—Recovered two fumbles. 1995—Intercepted one pass for no yards and recovered two fumbles.

Year Team	G	SACKS
1987—Tampa Bay NFL	12	1.5
1988—Tampa Bay NFL	16	0.0
1989—Tampa Bay NFL	16	5.5
1990—Tampa Bay NFL	16	3.5
1991—Los Angeles Raiders NFL	16	3.0
1992—Los Angeles Raiders NFL	15	2.0
1993—Los Angeles Raiders NFL	16	0.0
1994—Los Angeles Raiders NFL	16	2.0
1995—Seattle NFL	16	2.0
Pro totals (9 years)	139	19.5

MOSS, ZEFROSS   OT   LIONS

PERSONAL: Born August 17, 1966, in Holt, Ala. ... 6-6/324.
HIGH SCHOOL: Holt (Ala.).
COLLEGE: Alabama State.
TRANSACTIONS/CAREER NOTES: Signed as non-drafted free agent by Dallas Cowboys (April 29, 1988). ... Released by Cowboys (August 24, 1988). ... Re-signed by Cowboys (December 8, 1988). ... Traded by Cowboys to Indianapolis Colts for 10th-round pick (traded to Minnesota) in 1990 draft (August 22, 1989). ... On injured reserve with ankle injury (December 20, 1991-remainder of season). ... Granted unconditional free agency (February 17, 1995). ... Signed by Detroit Lions (April 28, 1995).
PLAYING EXPERIENCE: Indianapolis NFL, 1989-1994; Detroit NFL, 1995. ... Games: 1989 (16), 1990 (16), 1991 (11), 1992 (13), 1993 (16), 1994 (11), 1995 (14). Total: 97.

MOTEN, ERIC   G/OT   CHARGERS

PERSONAL: Born April 11, 1968, in Cleveland. ... 6-2/306. ... Full name: Eric Dean Moten.
HIGH SCHOOL: Shaw (East Cleveland, Ohio).
COLLEGE: Michigan State.
TRANSACTIONS/CAREER NOTES: Selected by San Diego Chargers in second round (47th pick overall) of 1991 NFL draft. ... Signed by Chargers (July 22, 1991). ... On injured reserve with knee injury (October 7, 1993-remainder of season). ... Granted free agency (February 17, 1994). ... Re-signed by Chargers (July 20, 1994). ... On physically unable to perform list (July 20-August 22, 1994). ... On physically unable to perform list (August 22, 1994-entire season).
PLAYING EXPERIENCE: San Diego NFL, 1991-1993 and 1995. ... Games: 1991 (16), 1992 (16), 1993 (4), 1995 (16). Total: 52.
PRO STATISTICS: 1995—Recovered one fumble.

MULLEN, RODERICK   DB   PACKERS

PERSONAL: Born December 5, 1972, in Baton Rouge, La. ... 6-1/204.
HIGH SCHOOL: West Feleciana (St. Francisville, La.).
COLLEGE: Grambling State.
TRANSACTIONS/CAREER NOTES: Selected by New York Giants in fifth round (153rd pick overall) of 1995 NFL draft. ... Signed by Giants (July 23, 1995). ... Released by Giants (August 29, 1995). ... Signed by Green Bay Packers (October 18, 1995).
PLAYING EXPERIENCE: Green Bay NFL, 1995. ... Games: 1995 (8). Total: 8.
CHAMPIONSHIP GAME EXPERIENCE: Played in NFC championship game (1995 season).

MURRAY, EDDIE   K   REDSKINS

PERSONAL: Born August 29, 1956, in Halifax, Nova Scotia. ... 5-11/195. ... Full name: Edward Peter Murray. ... Cousin of Mike Rogers, center, Edmonton Oilers, New England/Hartford Whalers and New York Rangers of World Hockey Association and NHL (1974-75 through 1985-86).
HIGH SCHOOL: Spectrum (Victoria, B.C.).
COLLEGE: Tulane (degree in education, 1980).
TRANSACTIONS/CAREER NOTES: Selected by Detroit Lions in seventh round (166th pick overall) of 1980 NFL draft. ... On suspended list (September 10-November 20, 1982). ... On injured reserve with hip injury (October 12-November 20, 1990). ... Granted unconditional free agency (February 1-April 1, 1991). ... Re-signed by Lions for 1991 season. ... Granted unconditional free agency (February 1-April 1, 1992). ... Rights relinquished by Lions (April 29, 1992). ... Signed by Kansas City Chiefs (October 24, 1992). ... Released by Chiefs (October 28, 1992). ... Signed by Tampa Bay Buccaneers (November 10, 1992). ... Granted unconditional free agency (March 1, 1993). ... Re-signed by Buccaneers (1993). ... Released by Buccaneers (August 23, 1993). ... Signed by Dallas Cowboys (September 14, 1993). ... Granted unconditional free agency (February 17, 1994). ... Signed by Philadelphia Eagles (March 22, 1994). ... Released by Eagles (July 23, 1995). ... Signed by Washington Redskins (August 8, 1995). ... Granted unconditional free agency (February 16, 1996). ... Re-signed by Redskins (May 14, 1996).
CHAMPIONSHIP GAME EXPERIENCE: Played in NFC championship game (1991 and 1993 seasons). ... Member of Super Bowl championship team (1993 season).
HONORS: Played in Pro Bowl (1980 and 1989 seasons). ... Named Outstanding Player of Pro Bowl (1980 season).
PRO STATISTICS: 1986—Punted once for 37 yards. 1987—Punted four times for 155 yards (38.8-yard average).

					KICKING				
Year Team	G	XPM	XPA	FGM	FGA	Lg.	50+	Pts.
1980—Detroit NFL	16	35	36	*27	*42	52	1-4	116
1981—Detroit NFL	16	46	46	25	35	53	3-4	†121
1982—Detroit NFL	7	16	16	11	12	49	0-0	49
1983—Detroit NFL	16	38	38	25	32	54	3-4	113
1984—Detroit NFL	16	31	31	20	27	52	1-4	91
1985—Detroit NFL	16	31	33	26	31	51	2-3	109
1986—Detroit NFL	16	31	32	18	25	52	2-5	85
1987—Detroit NFL	12	21	21	20	32	53	1-2	81
1988—Detroit NFL	16	22	23	20	21	48	0-1	82
1989—Detroit NFL	16	36	36	20	21	50	1-1	96
1990—Detroit NFL	11	34	34	13	19	47	0-2	73
1991—Detroit NFL	16	40	40	19	28	50	2-4	97
1992—Kansas City NFL	1	0	0	1	1	52	1-1	3
—Tampa Bay NFL	7	13	13	4	8	47	0-0	25
1993—Dallas NFL	14	38	38	28	33	52	3-5	122
1994—Philadelphia NFL	16	33	33	21	25	42	0-0	96
1995—Washington NFL	16	33	33	27	36	52	1-2	114
Pro totals (16 years)	228	498	503	325	428	54	21-42	1473

MURRELL, ADRIAN   RB   JETS

M

PERSONAL: Born October 16, 1970, in Lafayette, La. ... 5-11/214. ... Full name: Adrian Bryan Murrell.
HIGH SCHOOL: Leilehua (Wahiawa, Hawaii).
COLLEGE: West Virginia.
TRANSACTIONS/CAREER NOTES: Selected by New York Jets in fifth round (120th pick overall) of 1993 NFL draft. ... Signed by Jets (July 22, 1993). ... Granted free agency (February 16, 1996). ... Re-signed by Jets (April 21, 1996).
PRO STATISTICS: 1993—Recovered two fumbles. 1995—Recovered two fumbles.
STATISTICAL PLATEAUS: 100-yard rushing games: 1995 (1).

		RUSHING				RECEIVING				KICKOFF RETURNS				TOTALS			
Year Team	G	Att.	Yds.	Avg.	TD	No.	Yds.	Avg.	TD	No.	Yds.	Avg.	TD	TD	2pt.	Pts.	Fum.
1993—New York Jets NFL	16	34	157	4.6	1	5	12	2.4	0	23	342	14.9	0	1	...	6	4
1994—New York Jets NFL	10	33	160	4.9	0	7	76	10.9	0	14	268	19.1	0	0	0	0	1
1995—New York Jets NFL	15	192	795	4.1	1	71	465	6.6	2	1	5	5.0	0	3	0	18	2
Pro totals (3 years)	41	259	1112	4.3	2	83	553	6.7	2	38	615	16.2	0	4	0	24	7

MUSGRAVE, BILL   QB   BRONCOS

PERSONAL: Born November 11, 1967, in Grand Junction, Colo. ... 6-3/215. ... Full name: William Scott Musgrave.
HIGH SCHOOL: Grand Junction (Colo.).
COLLEGE: Oregon (degree in finance).
TRANSACTIONS/CAREER NOTES: Selected by Dallas Cowboys in fourth round (106th pick overall) of 1991 NFL draft. ... Signed by Cowboys (July 14, 1991). ... Released by Cowboys (August 26, 1991). ... Signed by San Francisco 49ers to practice squad (August 28, 1991). ... Activated (November 9, 1991). ... Granted unconditional free agency (February 1-April 1, 1992). ... Re-signed by 49ers for 1992 season. ... Active for one game (1992); did not play. ... On injured reserve with knee injury (December 15, 1992-remainder of season). ... Released by 49ers (June 10, 1994). ... Re-signed by 49ers (July 21, 1994). ... Granted unconditional free agency (February 17, 1995). ... Signed by Denver Broncos (March 7, 1995).
CHAMPIONSHIP GAME EXPERIENCE: Member of 49ers for NFC championship game (1993 season); inactive. ... Member of 49ers for NFC championship game (1994 season); inactive. ... Member of Super Bowl championship team (1994 season).
PRO STATISTICS: 1995—Fumbled once.

		PASSING								RUSHING				TOTALS		
Year Team	G	Att.	Cmp.	Pct.	Yds.	TD	Int.	Avg.	Rat.	Att.	Yds.	Avg.	TD	TD	2pt.	Pts.
1991—San Francisco NFL	1	5	4	80.0	33	1	0	6.60	133.8	0	0	...	0	0	...	0
1992—San Francisco NFL						Did not play.										
1993—San Francisco NFL	1	0	0	...	0	0	0	...	...	3	-3	-1.0	0	0	...	0
1994—San Francisco NFL						Did not play.										
1995—Denver NFL	4	12	8	66.7	93	0	0	7.75	89.9	4	-4	-1.0	0	0	0	0
Pro totals (3 years)	6	17	12	70.6	126	1	0	7.41	111.4	7	-7	-1.0	0	0	0	0

MUSTAFAA, NAJEE   CB   RAIDERS

PERSONAL: Born June 20, 1964, in East Point, Ga. ... 6-1/190. ... Formerly known as Reggie Rutland. ... Name pronounced NAH-jee.
HIGH SCHOOL: Russell (East Point, Ga.).
COLLEGE: Georgia Tech.
TRANSACTIONS/CAREER NOTES: Selected by Minnesota Vikings in fourth round (100th pick overall) of 1987 NFL draft. ... Signed by Vikings (July 17, 1987). ... On injured reserve with ankle injury (November 18-December 25, 1987). ... Granted free agency (February 1, 1990). ... Re-signed by Vikings (August 1, 1990). ... Granted free agency (February 1, 1991). ... Re-signed by Vikings (August 20, 1991). ... On injured reserve (September 1, 1992-entire season). ... Granted unconditional free agency (March 1, 1993). ... Signed by Cleveland Browns (March 17, 1993). ... Released by Browns (July 20, 1994). ... Signed by Miami Dolphins (September 29, 1994). ... Announced retirement (October 6, 1994). ... Released by Dolphins from reserve/retired list (February 24, 1995). ... Signed by Los Angeles Raiders (April 5, 1995). ... Raiders franchise moved to Oakland (July 21, 1995).
CHAMPIONSHIP GAME EXPERIENCE: Played in NFC championship game (1987 season).
PRO STATISTICS: 1988—Fumbled once and recovered two fumbles for 17 yards. 1989—Recovered two fumbles for 27 yards and a touchdown.

			INTERCEPTIONS		
Year Team	G	No.	Yds.	Avg.	TD
1987—Minnesota NFL	7	0	0	...	0
1988—Minnesota NFL	16	3	63	21.0	0
1989—Minnesota NFL	16	2	7	3.5	0
1990—Minnesota NFL	16	2	21	10.5	0
1991—Minnesota NFL	13	3	104	34.7	1
1992—Minnesota NFL			Did not play—injured.		
1993—Cleveland NFL	14	1	97	97.0	1
1994—Miami NFL			Did not play.		
1995—Oakland NFL	15	0	0	...	0
Pro totals (7 years)	97	11	292	26.6	2

MYLES, GODFREY   LB   COWBOYS

PERSONAL: Born September 22, 1968, in Miami. ... 6-1/242. ... Full name: Godfrey Clarence Myles. ... Cousin of Oliver Gibson, defensive tackle, Pittsburgh Steelers.
HIGH SCHOOL: Miami Carol City Senior.
COLLEGE: Florida (degree in sociology).
TRANSACTIONS/CAREER NOTES: Selected by Dallas Cowboys in third round (63rd pick overall) of 1991 NFL draft. ... Signed by Cowboys (July 15, 1991). ... On injured reserve with shoulder injury (September 25, 1991-remainder of season). ... On physically unable to perform list (August 23-October 28, 1993). ... Granted free agency (February 17, 1994). ... Re-signed by Cowboys (June 6, 1994).
PLAYING EXPERIENCE: Dallas NFL, 1991-1995. ... Games: 1991 (3), 1992 (16), 1993 (10), 1994 (15), 1995 (16). Total: 60.
CHAMPIONSHIP GAME EXPERIENCE: Played in NFC championship game (1992-1995 seasons). ... Member of Super Bowl championship team (1992, 1993 and 1995 seasons).
PRO STATISTICS: 1992—Intercepted one pass for 13 yards. 1995—Intercepted one pass for 15 yards and recovered two fumbles.

MYSLINSKI, TOM   OL   STEELERS

PERSONAL: Born December 7, 1968, in Rome, N.Y. ... 6-3/287. ... Full name: Thomas Joseph Myslinski.
HIGH SCHOOL: Free Academy (Rome, N.Y.).
COLLEGE: Tennessee.
TRANSACTIONS/CAREER NOTES: Selected by Dallas Cowboys in fourth round (109th pick overall) of 1992 NFL draft. ... Signed by Cowboys (July 15, 1992). ... Released by Cowboys (August 31, 1992). ... Re-signed by Cowboys to practice squad (September 1, 1992). ... Signed by Cleveland Browns off Cowboys practice squad (September 8, 1992). ... Inactive for three games with Browns (1992). ... Released by Browns (October 9, 1992). ... Re-signed by Browns to practice squad (October 14, 1992). ... Released by Browns (October 17, 1992). ... Signed by Washington Redskins to practice squad (October 21, 1992). ... Activated (November 11, 1992). ... Released by Redskins (November 28, 1992). ... Signed by Buffalo Bills (April 6, 1993). ... Released by Bills (August 30, 1993). ... Re-signed by Bills (August 31, 1993). ... Released by Bills (November 15, 1993). ... Signed by Chicago Bears (November 30, 1993). ... Selected by Jacksonville Jaguars from Bears in NFL expansion draft (February 15, 1995). ... Granted free agency (February 17, 1995). ... Signed by Jaguars (April 19, 1995). ... Granted free agency (February 16, 1996). ... Signed by Pittsburgh Steelers (April 24, 1996).
PLAYING EXPERIENCE: Washington NFL, 1992; Buffalo (1)-Chicago (1) NFL, 1993; Chicago NFL, 1994; Jacksonville NFL, 1995. ... Games: 1992 (1), 1993 (2), 1994 (4), 1995 (9). Total: 16.

NAGLE, BROWNING   QB   FALCONS

PERSONAL: Born April 29, 1968, in Philadelphia. ... 6-3/225.
HIGH SCHOOL: Pinellas Park Senior (Largo, Fla.).
COLLEGE: West Virginia, then Louisville.
TRANSACTIONS/CAREER NOTES: Selected by New York Jets in second round (34th pick overall) of 1991 NFL draft. ... Signed by Jets (June 27, 1991). ... Granted free agency (February 17, 1994). ... Re-signed by Jets (May 2, 1994). ... Released by Jets (May 6, 1994). ... Signed by Indianapolis Colts (July 8, 1994). ... Released by Colts (June 2, 1995). ... Signed by Atlanta Falcons (June 28, 1995). ... Released by Falcons (October 10, 1995). ... Re-signed by Falcons (October 17, 1995). ... Inactive for 15 games (1995).
PRO STATISTICS: 1992—Fumbled 12 times and recovered three fumbles for minus 14 yards. 1994—Fumbled twice.
STATISTICAL PLATEAUS: 300-yard passing games: 1992 (1).
MISCELLANEOUS: Selected by California Angels organization in free-agent baseball draft (June 3, 1991); did not sign. ... Regular-season record as starting NFL quarterback: 4-10 (.286).

		PASSING							RUSHING				TOTALS		
Year Team	G	Att.	Cmp.	Pct.	Yds.	TD	Int.	Avg.	Rat.	Att.	Yds.	Avg.	TD	TD	2pt.	Pts.
1991—New York Jets NFL	1	2	1	50.0	10	0	0	5.00	64.6	1	-1	-1.0	0	0	...	0
1992—New York Jets NFL	14	387	192	49.6	2280	7	17	5.89	55.7	24	57	2.4	0	0	...	0

M

N

Year	Team		G	PASSING							RUSHING				TOTALS		
				Att.	Cmp.	Pct.	Yds.	TD	Int.	Avg.	Rat.	Att.	Yds.	Avg.	TD	TD	2pt.	Pts.
1993—New York Jets NFL			3	14	6	42.9	71	0	0	5.07	58.9	0	0	...	0	0	...	0
1994—Indianapolis NFL			1	21	8	38.1	69	0	1	3.29	27.7	1	12	12.0	0	0	0	0
1995—Atlanta NFL											Did not play.							
Pro totals (5 years)			20	424	207	48.8	2430	7	18	5.73	54.5	26	68	2.6	0	0	0	0

NALEN, TOM   OL   BRONCOS

PERSONAL: Born May 13, 1971, in Foxboro, Mass. ... 6-2/280. ... Full name: Thomas Andrew Nalen.
HIGH SCHOOL: Foxboro (Mass.).
COLLEGE: Boston College.
TRANSACTIONS/CAREER NOTES: Selected by Denver Broncos in seventh round (218th pick overall) of 1994 NFL draft. ... Signed by Broncos (July 15, 1994). ... Released by Broncos (September 2, 1994). ... Re-signed by Broncos to practice squad (September 6, 1994). ... Activated (October 7, 1994).
PLAYING EXPERIENCE: Denver NFL, 1994 and 1995. ... Games: 1994 (7), 1995 (15). Total: 22.

NASH, JOE   DT

PERSONAL: Born October 11, 1960, in Boston. ... 6-3/278. ... Full name: Joseph Andrew Nash.
HIGH SCHOOL: Boston College High.
COLLEGE: Boston College (degree in sociology, 1982).
TRANSACTIONS/CAREER NOTES: Signed as non-drafted free agent by Seattle Seahawks (April 30, 1982). ... On inactive list (September 12 and 19, 1982). ... Granted unconditional free agency (February 1-April 1, 1992). ... Re-signed by Seahawks (May 1, 1992). ... Granted unconditional free agency (February 17, 1994). ... Re-signed by Seahawks (July 12, 1994). ... Granted unconditional free agency (February 17, 1995). ... Re-signed by Seahawks (June 8, 1995). ... Granted unconditional free agency (February 16, 1996).
CHAMPIONSHIP GAME EXPERIENCE: Played in AFC championship game (1983 season).
HONORS: Played in Pro Bowl (1984 season).
PRO STATISTICS: 1984—Recovered three fumbles (including one in end zone for a touchdown). 1986—Recovered two fumbles. 1988—Recovered one fumble. 1990—Recovered one fumble. 1993—Intercepted one pass for 13 yards and a touchdown.

Year Team	G	SACKS
1982—Seattle NFL	7	1.0
1983—Seattle NFL	16	3.0
1984—Seattle NFL	16	7.0
1985—Seattle NFL	16	9.0
1986—Seattle NFL	16	5.0
1987—Seattle NFL	12	3.5
1988—Seattle NFL	15	2.0
1989—Seattle NFL	16	8.0
1990—Seattle NFL	16	1.0
1991—Seattle NFL	16	0.0
1992—Seattle NFL	16	4.5
1993—Seattle NFL	16	0.5
1994—Seattle NFL	16	2.0
1995—Seattle NFL	16	1.0
Pro totals (14 years)	210	47.5

NEAL, LORENZO   FB   SAINTS

PERSONAL: Born December 27, 1970, in Hanford, Calif. ... 5-11/240. ... Full name: Lorenzo LaVon Neal.
HIGH SCHOOL: Lemoore (Calif.).
COLLEGE: Fresno State.
TRANSACTIONS/CAREER NOTES: Selected by New Orleans Saints in fourth round (89th pick overall) of 1993 NFL draft. ... Signed by Saints (July 15, 1993). ... On injured reserve with ankle injury (September 15, 1993-remainder of season). ... Granted free agency (February 16, 1996).
PRO STATISTICS: 1994—Returned one kickoff for 17 yards. 1995—Returned two kickoffs for 28 yards.

Year Team	G	RUSHING				RECEIVING				TOTALS			
		Att.	Yds.	Avg.	TD	No.	Yds.	Avg.	TD	TD	2pt.	Pts.	Fum.
1993—New Orleans NFL	2	21	175	8.3	1	0	0	...	0	1	1	6	1
1994—New Orleans NFL	16	30	90	3.0	1	2	9	4.5	0	1	0	6	1
1995—New Orleans NFL	16	5	3	.6	0	12	123	10.3	1	1	0	6	2
Pro totals (3 years)	34	56	268	4.8	2	14	132	9.4	1	3	0	18	4

NEAL, RANDY   LB   BENGALS

PERSONAL: Born December 29, 1972, in Hackensack, N.J. ... 6-3/236. ... Full name: Randy Peter Neal.
HIGH SCHOOL: Hackensack (N.J.).
COLLEGE: Virginia.
TRANSACTIONS/CAREER NOTES: Signed as non-drafted free agent by Cleveland Browns (May 2, 1995). ... Released by Browns (August 18, 1995). ... Signed by Green Bay Packers to practice squad (August 29, 1995). ... Signed by Cincinnati Bengals off Packers practice squad (November 22, 1995).
PLAYING EXPERIENCE: Cincinnati NFL, 1995. ... Games: 1995 (2).

NED, DERRICK   FB

PERSONAL: Born January 5, 1969, in Eunice, La. ... 6-1/220.

HIGH SCHOOL: Eunice (La.).
COLLEGE: Grambling State.
TRANSACTIONS/CAREER NOTES: Signed as non-drafted free agent by Houston Oilers (July 21, 1992). ... Released by Oilers (August 24, 1992). ... Signed by New Orleans Saints to practice squad (September 2, 1992). ... Released by Saints (November 19, 1992). ... Re-signed by Saints to practice squad (November 25, 1992). ... Granted free agency after 1992 season. ... Re-signed by Saints (March 8, 1993). ... Released by Saints (August 30, 1993). ... Re-signed by Saints to practice squad (August 31, 1993). ... Activated (September 14, 1993). ... Released by Saints (August 28, 1995). ... Re-signed by Saints (September 6, 1995). ... Granted unconditional free agency (February 16, 1996).

		RUSHING				RECEIVING				KICKOFF RETURNS				TOTALS			
Year Team	G	Att.	Yds.	Avg.	TD	No.	Yds.	Avg.	TD	No.	Yds.	Avg.	TD	TD 2pt.	Pts. Fum.		
1992—New Orleans NFL							Did not play.										
1993—New Orleans NFL	14	9	71	7.9	1	9	54	6.0	0	0	0	...	0	1	...	6	1
1994—New Orleans NFL	16	11	36	3.3	0	13	86	6.6	0	7	77	11.0	0	0	0	0	1
1995—New Orleans NFL	12	3	1	.3	0	3	9	3.0	0	2	33	16.5	0	0	0	0	1
Pro totals (3 years)	42	23	108	4.7	1	25	149	6.0	0	9	110	12.2	0	1	0	6	3

NEWBERRY, TOM　　　　　　　G

PERSONAL: Born December 20, 1962, in Onalaska, Wis. ... 6-2/285.
HIGH SCHOOL: Onalaska (Wis.).
COLLEGE: Wisconsin-La Crosse (degree in geography, 1986).
TRANSACTIONS/CAREER NOTES: Selected by Los Angeles Rams in second round (50th pick overall) of 1986 NFL draft. ... Signed by Rams (July 18, 1986). ... On reserve/did not report list (August 22, 1988). ... Activated (August 23, 1988). ... Granted free agency (February 1, 1991). ... Re-signed by Rams (August 8, 1991). ... Granted unconditional free agency (February 17, 1995). ... Signed by Pittsburgh Steelers (April 6, 1995). ... Announced retirement (June 3, 1996).
PLAYING EXPERIENCE: Los Angeles Rams NFL, 1986-1994; Pittsburgh NFL, 1995. ... Games: 1986 (16), 1987 (12), 1988 (16), 1989 (16), 1990 (15), 1991 (16), 1992 (16), 1993 (9), 1994 (15), 1995 (16). Total: 147.
CHAMPIONSHIP GAME EXPERIENCE: Played in NFC championship game (1989 season). ... Played in AFC championship game (1995 season). ... Played in Super Bowl XXX (1995 season).
HONORS: Named guard on THE SPORTING NEWS NFL All-Pro team (1988 and 1989). ... Played in Pro Bowl (1988 season). ... Named to play in Pro Bowl (1989 season); did not play.
PRO STATISTICS: 1986—Recovered one fumble in end zone for a touchdown. 1992—Recovered one fumble. 1993—Recovered one fumble. 1994—Recovered one fumble. 1995—Recovered one fumble.

NEWMAN, ANTHONY　　　　　　S　　　　　　　　　SAINTS

PERSONAL: Born November 21, 1965, in Bellingham, Wash. ... 6-0/200.
HIGH SCHOOL: Beaverton (Ore.).
COLLEGE: Oregon.
TRANSACTIONS/CAREER NOTES: Selected by Los Angeles Rams in second round (35th pick overall) of 1988 NFL draft. ... Signed by Rams (July 11, 1988). ... On injured reserve with fractured elbow (December 21, 1989-remainder of season). ... Granted free agency (February 1, 1992). ... Re-signed by Rams (July 21, 1992). ... Released by Rams (August 27, 1995). ... Signed by New Orleans Saints (August 28, 1995). ... Granted unconditional free agency (February 16, 1996). ... Re-signed by Saints (March 6, 1996).
PRO STATISTICS: 1988—Recovered one fumble. 1990—Recovered one fumble. 1991—Credited with a sack and recovered one fumble for 17 yards and a touchdown. 1992—Recovered three fumbles. 1994—Recovered one fumble. 1995—Caught one pass for 18 yards.
MISCELLANEOUS: Selected by Toronto Blue Jays organization in 26th round of free-agent baseball draft (June 4, 1984); did not sign. ... Selected by Cleveland Indians organization in secondary phase of free-agent baseball draft (January 9, 1985); did not sign. ... Selected by Texas Rangers organization in secondary phase of free-agent baseball draft (June 3, 1985); did not sign.

		INTERCEPTIONS			
Year Team	G	No.	Yds.	Avg.	TD
1988—Los Angeles Rams NFL	16	2	27	13.5	0
1989—Los Angeles Rams NFL	15	0	0	...	0
1990—Los Angeles Rams NFL	16	2	0	0.0	0
1991—Los Angeles Rams NFL	16	1	58	58.0	0
1992—Los Angeles Rams NFL	16	4	33	8.3	0
1993—Los Angeles Rams NFL	16	0	0	...	0
1994—Los Angeles Rams NFL	16	2	46	23.0	1
1995—New Orleans NFL.................................	12	0	0	...	0
Pro totals (8 years)	123	11	164	14.9	1

N

NEWSOME, CRAIG　　　　　　CB　　　　　　　　PACKERS

PERSONAL: Born August 10, 1971, in San Bernardino, Calif. ... 5-11/188.
HIGH SCHOOL: Eisenhower (Rialto, Calif.).
JUNIOR COLLEGE: San Bernadino (Calif.) Valley.
COLLEGE: Arizona State.
TRANSACTIONS/CAREER NOTES: Selected by Green Bay Packers in first round (32nd pick overall) of 1995 NFL draft. ... Signed by Packers (May 23, 1995).
CHAMPIONSHIP GAME EXPERIENCE: Played in NFC championship game (1995 season).

		INTERCEPTIONS			
Year Team	G	No.	Yds.	Avg.	TD
1995—Green Bay NFL.................................	16	1	3	3.0	0

NEWTON, NATE　　　　　　　G　　　　　　　　　COWBOYS

PERSONAL: Born December 20, 1961, in Orlando. ... 6-3/320. ... Brother of Tim Newton, defensive tackle, Minnesota Vikings, Tampa Bay

Buccaneers and Kansas City Chiefs (1985-1991 and 1993).
HIGH SCHOOL: Jones (Orlando).
COLLEGE: Florida A&M.
TRANSACTIONS/CAREER NOTES: Selected by Tampa Bay Bandits in 1983 USFL territorial draft. ... Signed as non-drafted free agent by Washington Redskins (May 5, 1983). ... Released by Redskins (August 29, 1983). ... Signed by Bandits (November 6, 1983). ... Granted free agency when USFL suspended operations (August 7, 1986). ... Signed by Dallas Cowboys (August 14, 1986). ... Granted roster exemption (August 14-21, 1986). ... Crossed picket line during players strike (October 24, 1987). ... Granted unconditional free agency (February 17, 1994). ... Re-signed by Cowboys (April 7, 1994).
PLAYING EXPERIENCE: Tampa Bay USFL, 1984 and 1985; Dallas NFL, 1986-1995. ... Games: 1984 (18), 1985 (18), 1986 (11), 1987 (11), 1988 (15), 1989 (16), 1990 (16), 1991 (14), 1992 (15), 1993 (16), 1994 (16), 1995 (16). Total USFL: 36. Total NFL: 146. Total Pro: 182.
CHAMPIONSHIP GAME EXPERIENCE: Played in NFC championship game (1992-1995 seasons). ... Member of Super Bowl championship team (1992, 1993 and 1995 seasons).
HONORS: Played in Pro Bowl (1992-1995 seasons). ... Named guard on The Sporting News NFL All-Pro team (1995).
PRO STATISTICS: 1988—Caught one pass for two yards. 1990—Recovered two fumbles. 1991—Recovered one fumble. 1992—Recovered one fumble.

NICKERSON, HARDY   LB   BUCCANEERS

PERSONAL: Born September 1, 1965, in Los Angeles. ... 6-2/229. ... Full name: Hardy Otto Nickerson.
HIGH SCHOOL: Verbum Dei (Los Angeles).
COLLEGE: California.
TRANSACTIONS/CAREER NOTES: Selected by Pittsburgh Steelers in fifth round (122nd pick overall) of 1987 NFL draft. ... Signed by Steelers (July 26, 1987). ... On injured reserve with ankle and knee injuries (November 3-December 16, 1989). ... Granted free agency (February 1, 1992). ... Re-signed by Steelers (June 15, 1992). ... Granted unconditional free agency (March 1, 1993). ... Signed by Tampa Bay Buccaneers (March 18, 1993). ... Granted unconditional free agency (February 16, 1996). ... Re-signed by Buccaneers (February 22, 1996).
HONORS: Named linebacker on The Sporting News college All-America second team (1985). ... Named inside linebacker on The Sporting News NFL All-Pro team (1993). ... Played in Pro Bowl (1993 season).
PRO STATISTICS: 1987—Recovered one fumble. 1988—Intercepted one pass for no yards and recovered one fumble. 1992—Recovered two fumbles for 44 yards. 1993—Intercepted one pass for six yards and recovered one fumble. 1994—Intercepted two passes for nine yards. 1995—Recovered three fumbles.

Year Team	G	SACKS
1987—Pittsburgh NFL	12	0.0
1988—Pittsburgh NFL	15	3.5
1989—Pittsburgh NFL	10	1.0
1990—Pittsburgh NFL	16	2.0
1991—Pittsburgh NFL	16	1.0
1992—Pittsburgh NFL	15	2.0
1993—Tampa Bay NFL	16	1.0
1994—Tampa Bay NFL	14	1.0
1995—Tampa Bay NFL	16	1.5
Pro totals (9 years)	130	13.0

NORGARD, ERIK   G/C   OILERS

PERSONAL: Born November 4, 1965, in Bellevue, Wash. ... 6-1/282. ... Full name: Erik Christian Norgard.
HIGH SCHOOL: Arlington (Wash.).
COLLEGE: Colorado (degree in communications, 1989).
TRANSACTIONS/CAREER NOTES: Signed as non-drafted free agent by Houston Oilers (May 12, 1989). ... Released by Oilers (August 30, 1989). ... Re-signed by Oilers to developmental squad (September 6, 1989). ... Released by Oilers (January 2, 1990). ... Re-signed by Oilers (March 8, 1990). ... Released by Oilers (August 26, 1991). ... Re-signed by Oilers (August 27, 1991). ... On injured reserve with shoulder injury (August 29, 1991-entire season). ... Granted unconditional free agency (February 1-April 1, 1992). ... Assigned by Oilers to San Antonio Riders in 1992 World League enhancement allocation program. ... Re-signed by Oilers for 1992 season. ... Released by Oilers (August 31, 1992). ... Re-signed by Oilers (September 11, 1992). ... Granted unconditional free agency (February 17, 1994). ... Re-signed by Oilers (March 9, 1994). ... Released by Oilers (July 14, 1995). ... Signed by Atlanta Falcons (August 2, 1995); released after failing physical. ... Signed by Oilers (August 8, 1995).
PLAYING EXPERIENCE: Houston NFL, 1990 and 1992-1995; San Antonio W.L., 1992. ... Games: 1990 (16), 1992 W.L. (10), 1992 NFL (15), 1993 (16), 1994 (16), 1995 (15). W.L.: 10. Total NFL: 78. Total Pro: 88.
PRO STATISTICS: NFL: 1990—Returned two kickoffs for no yards. 1993—Caught one pass for 13 yards and recovered one fumble. W.L.: 1992—Caught two passes for 22 yards.

NORTON, KEN   LB   49ERS

PERSONAL: Born September 29, 1966, in Jacksonville, Ill. ... 6-2/241. ... Full name: Kenneth Howard Norton Jr. ... Son of Ken Norton Sr., former world heavyweight boxing champion.
HIGH SCHOOL: Westchester (Los Angeles).
COLLEGE: UCLA.
TRANSACTIONS/CAREER NOTES: Selected by Dallas Cowboys in second round (41st pick overall) of 1988 NFL draft. ... Signed by Cowboys (July 13, 1988). ... On injured reserve with broken arm (August 23-December 3, 1988). ... On injured reserve with knee injury (December 24, 1990-remainder of season). ... Granted free agency (February 1, 1992). ... Re-signed by Cowboys (August 12, 1992). ... Granted unconditional free agency (February 17, 1994). ... Signed by San Francisco 49ers (April 20, 1994).
CHAMPIONSHIP GAME EXPERIENCE: Played in NFC championship game (1992-1994 seasons). ... Member of Super Bowl championship team (1992-1994 seasons).
HONORS: Named linebacker on The Sporting News college All-America first team (1987). ... Played in Pro Bowl (1993 and 1995 seasons).
POSTSEASON RECORDS: Shares Super Bowl career record for most touchdowns by fumble recovery—1 (January 31, 1993, vs. Buffalo).
PRO STATISTICS: 1988—Recovered one fumble. 1990—Recovered two fumbles. 1992—Recovered two fumbles. 1993—Recovered one fumble for three yards.

Year Team	G	INTERCEPTIONS No.	Yds.	Avg.	TD	SACKS No.
1988—Dallas NFL	3	0	0	...	0	0.0
1989—Dallas NFL	13	0	0	...	0	2.5
1990—Dallas NFL	15	0	0	...	0	2.5
1991—Dallas NFL	16	0	0	...	0	0.0
1992—Dallas NFL	16	0	0	...	0	0.0
1993—Dallas NFL	16	1	25	25.0	0	2.0
1994—San Francisco NFL	16	1	0	0.0	0	0.0
1995—San Francisco NFL	16	3	102	34.0	†2	1.0
Pro totals (8 years)	111	5	127	25.4	2	8.0

NOTTAGE, DEXTER　　　　DE　　　　REDSKINS

PERSONAL: Born November 14, 1970, in Miami. ... 6-4/290.
HIGH SCHOOL: Hollywood (Fla.) Hills.
COLLEGE: Florida A&M.
TRANSACTIONS/CAREER NOTES: Selected by Washington Redskins in sixth round (163rd pick overall) of 1994 NFL draft. ... Signed by Redskins (June 2, 1994).
PRO STATISTICS: 1995—Recovered three fumbles.

Year Team	G	SACKS
1994—Washington NFL	15	1.0
1995—Washington NFL	16	0.0
Pro totals (2 years)	31	1.0

NOVACEK, JAY　　　　TE　　　　COWBOYS

PERSONAL: Born October 24, 1962, in Martin, S.D. ... 6-4/234. ... Full name: Jay McKinley Novacek.
HIGH SCHOOL: Gothenburg (Neb.).
COLLEGE: Wyoming (degree in industrial education, 1986).
TRANSACTIONS/CAREER NOTES: Selected by Houston Gamblers in fifth round (69th pick overall) of 1985 USFL draft. ... Selected by St. Louis Cardinals in sixth round (158th pick overall) of 1985 NFL draft. ... Signed by Cardinals (July 21, 1985). ... On injured reserve with broken thumb (August 19-October 17, 1986). ... On injured reserve with knee injury (December 10, 1986-remainder of season). ... On injured reserve with broken bone in elbow (November 3-December 5, 1987). ... Cardinals franchise moved to Phoenix (March 15, 1988). ... Granted unconditional free agency (February 1, 1990). ... Signed by Dallas Cowboys (March 5, 1990). ... Granted free agency (February 1, 1992). ... Re-signed by Cowboys (August 30, 1992). ... Granted roster exemption (August 30-September 2, 1992). ... Granted unconditional free agency (February 17, 1995). ... Re-signed by Cowboys (March 13, 1995).
CHAMPIONSHIP GAME EXPERIENCE: Played in NFC championship game (1992-1995 seasons). ... Member of Super Bowl championship team (1992, 1993 and 1995 seasons).
HONORS: Played in Pro Bowl (1991-1994 seasons). ... Named to play in Pro Bowl (1995 season); replaced by Brent Jones due to injury.
PRO STATISTICS: 1985—Returned one kickoff for 20 yards. 1988—Rushed once for 10 yards and recovered one fumble. 1989—Recovered one fumble. 1991—Recovered one fumble. 1993—Rushed once for two yards and a touchdown, returned one kickoff for minus one yard and recovered one fumble.
STATISTICAL PLATEAUS: 100-yard receiving games: 1987 (1), 1988 (1), 1990 (1), 1991 (2), 1993 (1). Total: 6.

Year Team	G	RECEIVING No.	Yds.	Avg.	TD	TOTALS TD	2pt.	Pts.	Fum.
1985—St. Louis NFL	16	1	4	4.0	0	0	...	0	0
1986—St. Louis NFL	8	1	2	2.0	0	0	...	0	0
1987—St. Louis NFL	7	20	254	12.7	3	3	...	18	1
1988—Phoenix NFL	16	38	569	15.0	4	4	...	24	0
1989—Phoenix NFL	16	23	225	9.8	1	1	...	6	0
1990—Dallas NFL	16	59	657	11.1	4	4	...	24	1
1991—Dallas NFL	16	59	664	11.3	4	4	...	24	3
1992—Dallas NFL	16	68	630	9.3	6	6	...	36	0
1993—Dallas NFL	16	44	445	10.1	1	2	...	12	3
1994—Dallas NFL	16	47	475	10.1	2	2	0	12	0
1995—Dallas NFL	15	62	705	11.4	5	5	1	32	1
Pro totals (11 years)	158	422	4630	11.0	30	31	1	188	9

NOVAK, JEFF　　　　G/OT　　　　JAGUARS

PERSONAL: Born July 27, 1967, in Cook County, Ill. ... 6-5/295. ... Full name: Jeff Ladd Novak.
HIGH SCHOOL: Clear Lake (Houston).
COLLEGE: Southwest Texas State (degree in hospital administration).
TRANSACTIONS/CAREER NOTES: Selected by San Diego Chargers in seventh round (172nd pick overall) of 1990 NFL draft. ... Released by Chargers (August 30, 1990). ... Selected by Montreal Machine in first round of 1991 World League draft. ... Signed by New York Giants (June 1, 1992). ... Released by Giants (August 31, 1992). ... Re-signed by Giants to practice squad (September 2, 1992). ... On injured reserve with hand injury (October 12, 1992-remainder of season). ... Granted free agency after 1992 season. ... Re-signed by Giants (March 5, 1993). ... Released by Giants (August 30, 1993). ... Re-signed by Giants to practice squad (August 31, 1993). ... Signed by Miami Dolphins off Giants practice squad (December 15, 1993). ... Selected by Jacksonville Jaguars from Dolphins in NFL expansion draft (February 15, 1995).
PLAYING EXPERIENCE: Montreal W.L., 1991 and 1992; Miami NFL, 1994; Jacksonville NFL, 1995. ... Games: 1991 (9), 1992 (10), 1994 (6), 1995 (16). W.L.: 19. Total NFL: 22. Total Pro: 41.

NOVITSKY, CRAIG　　　　C/OT　　　　SAINTS

PERSONAL: Born May 12, 1971, in Washington, D.C. ... 6-5/295. ... Full name: Craig Aaron Novitsky.

N

HIGH SCHOOL: Potomac Senior (Dumfries, Va.).
COLLEGE: UCLA.
TRANSACTIONS/CAREER NOTES: Selected by New Orleans Saints in fifth round (143rd pick overall) of 1994 NFL draft. ... Signed by Saints (June 7, 1994).
PLAYING EXPERIENCE: New Orleans NFL, 1994 and 1995. ... Games: 1994 (9), 1995 (16). Total: 25.

NUNN, FREDDIE JOE   LB   COLTS

PERSONAL: Born April 9, 1962, in Noxubee County, Miss. ... 6-5/258. .
HIGH SCHOOL: Nanih Waiya (Louisville, Miss.).
COLLEGE: Mississippi.
TRANSACTIONS/CAREER NOTES: Selected by Birmingham Stallions in 1985 USFL territorial draft. ... Selected by St. Louis Cardinals in first round (18th pick overall) of 1985 NFL draft. ... Signed by Cardinals (August 5, 1985). ... Cardinals franchise moved to Phoenix (March 15, 1988). ... On non-football injury list with substance abuse problem (September 26-October 23, 1989). ... Reinstated and granted roster exemption (October 24-27, 1989). ... Granted free agency (February 1, 1990). ... Re-signed by Cardinals (July 30, 1990). ... Granted free agency (February 1, 1991). ... Re-signed by Cardinals (July 26, 1991). ... On injured reserve with knee injury (November 18-December 18, 1992); on practice squad (December 16-18, 1992). ... Granted unconditional free agency (February 17, 1994). ... Signed by Indianapolis Colts (September 21, 1994). ... Granted unconditional free agency (February 17, 1995). ... Re-signed by Colts (July 5, 1995). ... Granted unconditional free agency (February 16, 1996). ... Re-signed by Colts (April 27, 1996).
CHAMPIONSHIP GAME EXPERIENCE: Played in AFC championship game (1995 season).
PRO STATISTICS: 1985—Recovered two fumbles. 1986—Recovered one fumble. 1988—Recovered two fumbles for eight yards. 1989—Recovered one fumble. 1990—Recovered one fumble. 1991—Recovered two fumbles for one yard. 1992—Recovered one fumble. 1993—Recovered one fumble.

Year Team	G	SACKS
1985—St. Louis NFL	16	3.0
1986—St. Louis NFL	16	7.0
1987—St. Louis NFL	12	11.0
1988—Phoenix NFL	16	14.0
1989—Phoenix NFL	12	5.0
1990—Phoenix NFL	16	9.0
1991—Phoenix NFL	16	7.0
1992—Phoenix NFL	11	4.0
1993—Phoenix NFL	16	6.5
1994—Indianapolis NFL	11	1.0
1995—Indianapolis NFL	10	0.0
Pro totals (11 years)	**152**	**67.5**

NUTTEN, TOM   C   BILLS

PERSONAL: Born June 8, 1971, in Magog, Quebec. ... 6-4/295. ... Name pronounced NEW-ton.
HIGH SCHOOL: Champlain Regional (Lennoxville, Quebec).
COLLEGE: Western Michigan.
TRANSACTIONS/CAREER NOTES: Selected by Hamilton Tiger-Cats in first round (first pick overall) of 1995 CFL draft. ... Selected by Buffalo Bills in seventh round (221st pick overall) of 1995 NFL draft. ... Signed by Bills (June 12, 1995). ... Released by Bills (August 27, 1995). ... Re-signed by Bills to practice squad (August 29, 1995). ... Activated (October 10, 1995).
PLAYING EXPERIENCE: Buffalo NFL, 1995. ... Games: 1995 (1).

OATES, BART   C

PERSONAL: Born December 16, 1958, in Mesa, Ariz. ... 6-4/275. ... Full name: Bart Steven Oates. ... Brother of Brad Oates, offensive tackle with five NFL teams and Philadelphia Stars of USFL (1976-1981, 1983 and 1984).
HIGH SCHOOL: Albany (Ga.).
COLLEGE: Brigham Young (degree in accounting).
TRANSACTIONS/CAREER NOTES: Selected by Philadelphia Stars in second round (17th pick overall) of 1983 USFL draft. ... Signed by Stars (January 24, 1983). ... On developmental squad for one game (April 28-May 6, 1983). ... Stars franchise moved to Baltimore (November 1, 1984). ... Released by Stars (August 27, 1985). ... Signed by New York Giants (August 28, 1985). ... Granted free agency (February 1, 1992). ... Re-signed by Giants (July 22, 1992). ... Released by Giants (August 30, 1993). ... Re-signed by Giants (August 31, 1993). ... Granted unconditional free agency (February 17, 1994). ... Signed by San Francisco 49ers (July 15, 1994). ... Released by 49ers (March 25, 1996). ... Signed by Giants and announced retirement (March 26, 1996).
PLAYING EXPERIENCE: Philadelphia USFL, 1983 and 1984; Baltimore USFL, 1985; New York Giants NFL, 1985-1993; San Francisco NFL, 1994 and 1995. ... Games: 1983 (17), 1984 (17), 1985 USFL (18), 1985 NFL (16), 1986 (16), 1987 (12), 1988 (16), 1989 (16), 1990 (16), 1991 (16), 1992 (16), 1993 (16), 1994 (16), 1995 (16). Total USFL: 52. Total NFL: 172. Total Pro: 224.
CHAMPIONSHIP GAME EXPERIENCE: Played in USFL championship game (1983-1985 seasons). ... Played in NFC championship game (1986, 1990 and 1994 seasons). ... Member of Super Bowl championship team (1986, 1990 and 1994 seasons).
HONORS: Named center on THE SPORTING NEWS USFL All-Star team (1983). ... Played in Pro Bowl (1990, 1991 and 1993-1995 seasons).
PRO STATISTICS: USFL: 1984—Rushed once for five yards and recovered two fumbles. 1985—Recovered one fumble for four yards. NFL: 1985—Recovered two fumbles. 1986—Fumbled once for minus four yards. 1987—Recovered one fumble. 1988—Fumbled once for minus 10 yards. 1989—Fumbled once. 1990—Fumbled once for minus 19 yards. 1992—Fumbled twice for minus 29 yards.

OBEE, TERRY   WR   PANTHERS

PERSONAL: Born June 15, 1968, in Vallejo, Calif. ... 5-10/189.
HIGH SCHOOL: John F. Kennedy (Richmond, Calif.).
COLLEGE: Oregon (degree in marketing/management).
TRANSACTIONS/CAREER NOTES: Signed as non-drafted free agent by Seattle Seahawks (1990). ... Released by Seahawks (September 3,

1990). ... Re-signed by Seahawks to practice squad (1990). ... Granted free agency after 1990 season. ... Signed as free agent by Minnesota Vikings (March 29, 1991). ... Released by Vikings (August 26, 1991). ... Re-signed by Vikings to practice squad (August 27, 1991). ... Activated (November 2, 1991). ... Released by Vikings (November 16, 1991). ... Re-signed by Vikings to practice squad (November 19, 1991). ... Activated (December 20, 1991). ... Granted unconditional free agency (February 1-April 1, 1992). ... Re-signed by Vikings for 1992 season. ... Released by Vikings (August 31, 1992). ... Signed by Seahawks to practice squad (December 16, 1992). ... Granted free agency after 1993 season. ... Signed by Chicago Bears (April 19, 1993). ... On injured reserve with leg injury (August 23, 1994-entire season). ... Released by Bears (August 22, 1995). ... Signed by Carolina Panthers (April 22, 1996).
PRO STATISTICS: 1993—Recovered one fumble.

			RECEIVING				PUNT RETURNS				KICKOFF RETURNS				TOTALS			
Year Team	G	No.	Yds.	Avg.	TD	No.	Yds.	Avg.	TD	No.	Yds.	Avg.	TD	TD	2pt.	Pts.	Fum.
1990—Seattle NFL.........................								Did not play.									
1991—Minnesota NFL...................	1	0	0	...	0	0	0		0	0	0	...	0	0	...	0	0
1992—								Did not play.									
1993—Chicago NFL......................	16	26	351	13.5	3	35	289	8.3	0	9	159	17.7	0	3	...	18	1
1994—Chicago NFL......................								Did not play—injured.									
1995—								Did not play.									
Pro totals (2 years)...................	17	26	351	13.5	3	35	289	8.3	0	9	159	17.7	0	3	0	18	1

ODEN, DERRICK   LB

PERSONAL: Born September 29, 1970, in Los Angeles. ... 5-11/230.
HIGH SCHOOL: Hillcrest (Evergreen, Ala.).
COLLEGE: Alabama.
TRANSACTIONS/CAREER NOTES: Selected by Philadelphia Eagles in sixth round (163rd pick overall) of 1993 NFL draft. ... Signed by Eagles (May 11, 1993). ... Re-signed by Eagles (July 21, 1995). ... Granted unconditional free agency (February 16, 1996).
PLAYING EXPERIENCE: Philadelphia NFL, 1993-1995. ... Games: 1993 (12), 1994 (11), 1995 (12). Total: 35.

ODOMES, NATE   CB   SEAHAWKS

PERSONAL: Born August 25, 1965, in Columbus, Ga. ... 5-10/188. ... Full name: Nathaniel Bernard Odomes. ... Name pronounced O-dums.
HIGH SCHOOL: Carver (Columbus, Ga.).
COLLEGE: Wisconsin.
TRANSACTIONS/CAREER NOTES: Selected by Buffalo Bills in second round (29th pick overall) of 1987 NFL draft. ... Signed by Bills (July 22, 1987). ... Granted free agency (February 1, 1991). ... Re-signed by Bills (1991). ... Granted unconditional free agency (February 17, 1994). On non-football/injury list with knee injury (July 21, 1994-entire season). ... Signed by Seattle Seahawks (February 24, 1994). ... On injured reserve with knee injury (August 16, 1995-remainder of season).
CHAMPIONSHIP GAME EXPERIENCE: Played in AFC championship game (1988 and 1990-1993 seasons). ... Played in Super Bowl XXV (1990 season), Super Bowl XXVI (1991 season), Super Bowl XXVII (1992 season) and Super Bowl XXVIII (1993 season).
HONORS: Played in Pro Bowl (1992 and 1993 seasons).
PRO STATISTICS: 1987—Recovered two fumbles. 1990—Recovered three fumbles for 49 yards and a touchdown. 1991—Recovered one fumble. 1992—Recovered one fumble for 12 yards. 1993—Recovered one fumble for 25 yards and a touchdown.

		INTERCEPTIONS				SACKS	PUNT RETURNS				TOTALS			
Year Team	G	No.	Yds.	Avg.	TD	No.	No.	Yds.	Avg.	TD	TD	2pt.	Pts.	Fum.
1987—Buffalo NFL	12	0	0	...	0	0.0	0	0	...	0	0	...	0	0
1988—Buffalo NFL	16	1	0	0.0	0	0.0	0	0	...	0	0	...	0	0
1989—Buffalo NFL	16	5	20	4.0	0	1.0	0	0	...	0	0	...	0	0
1990—Buffalo NFL	16	1	0	0.0	0	0.0	1	9	9.0	0	1	...	6	0
1991—Buffalo NFL	16	5	120	24.0	1	1.0	1	9	9.0	0	1	...	6	1
1992—Buffalo NFL	16	5	19	3.8	0	1.0	0	0	...	0	0	...	0	0
1993—Buffalo NFL	16	†9	65	7.2	0	0.0	0	0	...	0	1	...	6	0
1994—Seattle NFL............................							Did noy play—injured.							
1995—Seattle NFL............................							Did not play—injured.							
Pro totals (7 years)............................	108	26	224	8.6	1	3.0	2	18	9.0	0	3	0	18	1

O'DONNELL, NEIL   QB   JETS

PERSONAL: Born July 3, 1966, in Morristown, N.J. ... 6-3/226. ... Full name: Neil Kennedy O'Donnell.
HIGH SCHOOL: Madison (N.J)-Boro.
COLLEGE: Maryland (degree in economics, 1990).
TRANSACTIONS/CAREER NOTES: Selected by Pittsburgh Steelers in third round (70th pick overall) of 1990 NFL draft. ... Signed by Steelers (August 8, 1990). ... Active for three games (1990); did not play. ... Granted free agency (March 1, 1993). ... Tendered offer sheet by Tampa Bay Buccaneers (April 2, 1993). ... Offer matched by Steelers (April 12, 1993). ... Granted unconditional free agency (February 16, 1996). ... Signed by New York Jets (February 29, 1996).
CHAMPIONSHIP GAME EXPERIENCE: Played in AFC championship game (1994 and 1995 seasons). ... Played in Super Bowl XXX (1995 season).
HONORS: Played in Pro Bowl (1992 season).
POSTSEASON RECORDS: Holds NFL postseason single-game record for most passes attempted without an interception—54 (January 15, 1995, vs. San Diego).
PRO STATISTICS: 1991—Fumbled 11 times and recovered two fumbles for minus three yards. 1992—Fumbled six times and recovered four fumbles for minus 20 yards. 1993—Fumbled five times. 1994—Fumbled four times and recovered one fumble. 1995—Fumbled twice and recovered one fumble.
STATISTICAL PLATEAUS: 300-yard passing games: 1991 (1), 1993 (1), 1995 (4). Total: 6.
MISCELLANEOUS: Regular-season record as starting NFL quarterback: 39-22 (.639).

		PASSING								RUSHING				TOTALS		
Year Team	G	Att.	Cmp.	Pct.	Yds.	TD	Int.	Avg.	Rat.	Att.	Yds.	Avg.	TD	TD	2pt.	Pts.
1990—Pittsburgh NFL....................						Did not play.										
1991—Pittsburgh NFL....................	12	286	156	54.6	1963	11	7	6.86	78.8	18	82	4.6	1	1	...	6

O

Year Team	G	Att.	Cmp.	Pct.	PASSING Yds.	TD	Int.	Avg.	Rat.	RUSHING Att.	Yds.	Avg.	TD	TOTALS TD	2pt.	Pts.
1992—Pittsburgh NFL	12	313	185	59.1	2283	13	9	7.29	83.6	27	5	.2	1	1	...	6
1993—Pittsburgh NFL	16	486	270	55.6	3208	14	7	6.60	79.5	26	111	4.3	0	0	...	0
1994—Pittsburgh NFL	14	370	212	57.3	2443	13	9	6.60	78.9	31	80	2.6	1	1	0	6
1995—Pittsburgh NFL	12	416	246	59.1	2970	17	7	7.14	87.7	24	45	1.9	0	0	0	0
Pro totals (5 years)	66	1871	1069	57.1	12867	68	39	6.88	81.8	126	323	2.6	3	3	0	18

O'DWYER, MATT   G   JETS

PERSONAL: Born September 1, 1972, in Lincolnshire, Ill. ... 6-5/308. ... Full name: Matthew Phillip O'Dwyer.
HIGH SCHOOL: Adlai E. Stevenson (Prairie View, Ill.).
COLLEGE: Northwestern.
TRANSACTIONS/CAREER NOTES: Selected by New York Jets in second round (33rd pick overall) of 1995 NFL draft. ... Signed by Jets (July 20, 1995).
PLAYING EXPERIENCE: New York Jets NFL, 1995. ... Games: 1995 (12).

OGLESBY, ALFRED   DT

PERSONAL: Born January 27, 1967, in Weimar, Texas. ... 6-4/290. ... Full name: Alfred Lee Oglesby.
HIGH SCHOOL: Weimar (Texas).
COLLEGE: Houston.
TRANSACTIONS/CAREER NOTES: Selected by Miami Dolphins in third round (66th pick overall) of 1990 NFL draft. ... On injured reserve with knee injury (November 27, 1991-remainder of season). ... Released by Dolphins (October 21, 1992). ... Signed by Green Bay Packers (November 10, 1992). ... Released by Packers (August 30, 1993). ... Signed by New York Jets (December 8, 1993). ... Released by Jets (December 14, 1993). ... Re-signed by Jets (May 18, 1994). ... Released by Jets (September 19, 1995). ... Signed by Cincinnati Bengals (September 20, 1995). ... Released by Bengals (March 25, 1996).
PRO STATISTICS: 1990—Recovered one fumble.

Year Team	G	SACKS
1990—Miami NFL	13	2.5
1991—Miami NFL	12	0.0
1992—Miami NFL	6	0.0
—Green Bay NFL	7	0.0
1993—	Did not play.	
1994—New York Jets NFL	15	0.5
1995—Cincinnati NFL	6	1.0
Pro totals (5 years)	59	4.0

OLDHAM, CHRIS   CB   STEELERS

PERSONAL: Born October 26, 1968, in Sacramento. ... 5-9/193. ... Full name: Christopher Martin Oldham.
HIGH SCHOOL: O. Perry Walker (New Orleans).
COLLEGE: Oregon (degree in communications).
TRANSACTIONS/CAREER NOTES: Selected by Detroit Lions in fourth round (105th pick overall) of 1990 NFL draft. ... Signed by Lions (July 19, 1990). ... Released by Lions (August 26, 1991). ... Signed by Buffalo Bills (September 25, 1991). ... Released by Bills (October 8, 1991). ... Signed by Phoenix Cardinals (October 15, 1991). ... Released by Cardinals (November 13, 1991). ... Signed by San Diego Chargers (February 15, 1992). ... Assigned by Chargers to San Antonio Riders in 1992 World League enhancement allocation program (February 20, 1992). ... Released by Chargers (August 25, 1992). ... Signed by Cardinals (December 22, 1992). ... Granted unconditional free agency (February 17, 1994). ... Cardinals franchise renamed Arizona Cardinals for 1994 season. ... Re-signed by Cardinals (June 7, 1994). ... Granted unconditional free agency (February 17, 1995). ... Signed by Pittsburgh Steelers (April 12, 1995).
CHAMPIONSHIP GAME EXPERIENCE: Played in AFC championship game (1995 season). ... Played in Super Bowl XXX (1995 season).
PRO STATISTICS: W.L.: 1992—Credited with one sack and recovered one fumble. NFL: 1993—Credited with one sack. 1995—Recovered one fumble for 23 yards and a touchdown.

Year Team	G	INTERCEPTIONS No.	Yds.	Avg.	TD	KICKOFF RETURNS No.	Yds.	Avg.	TD	TOTALS TD	2pt.	Pts.	Fum.
1990—Detroit NFL	16	1	28	28.0	0	13	234	18.0	0	0	...	0	2
1991—Buffalo NFL	2	0	0	...	0	0	0	...	0	0	...	0	0
—Phoenix NFL	2	0	0	...	0	0	0	...	0	0	...	0	0
1992—San Antonio W.L.	9	3	52	17.3	*1	1	11	11.0	0	1	0	6	0
—Phoenix NFL	1	0	0	...	0	0	0	...	0	0	...	0	0
1993—Phoenix NFL	16	1	0	0.0	0	0	0	...	0	0	...	0	0
1994—Arizona NFL	11	0	0	...	0	0	0	...	0	0	0	0	0
1995—Pittsburgh NFL	15	1	12	12.0	0	0	0	...	0	1	0	6	0
W.L. totals (1 year)	9	3	52	17.3	1	1	11	11.0	0	1	0	6	0
NFL totals (6 years)	63	3	40	13.3	0	13	234	18.0	0	1	0	6	2
Pro totals (6 years)	72	6	92	15.3	1	14	245	17.5	0	2	0	12	2

OLIVE, BOBBY   WR   COLTS

PERSONAL: Born April 22, 1969, in Paris, Tenn. ... 5-11/170. ... Full name: Bobby Leo Olive Jr.
HIGH SCHOOL: Frederick Douglass (Atlanta).
COLLEGE: Ohio State.
TRANSACTIONS/CAREER NOTES: Selected by Kansas City Chiefs in 11th round (300th pick overall) of 1991 NFL draft. ... Signed by Chiefs (July 17, 1991). ... Released by Chiefs (August 26, 1991). ... Signed by Atlanta Falcons (March 10, 1992). ... Released by Falcons (August 25, 1992). ... Signed by Cleveland Browns (1994). ... Released by Browns (August 12, 1994). ... Selected by Frankfurt Galaxy in 15th round

(86th pick overall) of 1995 World League Draft. ... Signed by Washington Redskins (July 17, 1995). ... Released by Redskins (August 27, 1995). ... Re-signed by Redskins to practice squad (August 28, 1995). ... Signed by Indianapolis Colts off Redskins practice squad (September 14, 1995).
PRO STATISTICS: WL: 1995—Rushed once for four yards.
CHAMPIONSHIP GAME EXPERIENCE: Member of Colts for AFC championship game (1995 season); inactive.

		RECEIVING				PUNT RETURNS				KICKOFF RETURNS				TOTALS			
Year Team	G	No.	Yds.	Avg.	TD	No.	Yds.	Avg.	TD	No.	Yds.	Avg.	TD	TD	2pt.	Pts.	Fum.
1995—Frankfurt WL	...	57	899	15.8	2	5	45	9.0	0	6	60	10.0	0	2	1	14	...
—Indianapolis NFL	1	0	0	...	0	0	0	...	0	0	0	...	0	0	0	0	0
Pro totals (1 year)	...	57	899	15.8	2	5	45	9.0	0	6	60	10.0	0	2	1	14	...

OLIVER, JIMMY WR CHARGERS

PERSONAL: Born January 30, 1973, in Dallas. ... 5-10/173.
HIGH SCHOOL: W.H. Adamson (Dallas).
COLLEGE: Texas Christian.
TRANSACTIONS/CAREER NOTES: Selected by San Diego Chargers in second round (61st pick overall) of 1995 NFL draft. ... Signed by Chargers (June 15, 1995). ... Inactive for nine games (1995). ... On injured reserve with shoulder injury (November 10, 1995-remainder of season).

OLIVER, LOUIS S DOLPHINS

PERSONAL: Born March 9, 1966, in Belle Glade, Fla. ... 6-2/224.
HIGH SCHOOL: Glades Central (Belle Glade, Fla.).
COLLEGE: Florida (degree in criminology and law, 1989).
TRANSACTIONS/CAREER NOTES: Selected by Miami Dolphins in first round (25th pick overall) of 1989 NFL draft. ... Signed by Dolphins (August 9, 1989). ... Granted free agency (March 1, 1993). ... Re-signed by Dolphins (July 27, 1993). ... Designated by Dolphins as transition player (February 15, 1994). ... Free agency status changed by Dolphins from transitional to unconditional (March 9, 1994). ... Signed by Cincinnati Bengals (March 15, 1994). ... On injured reserve with leg injury (November 30, 1994-remainder of season). ... Released by Bengals (May 9, 1995). ... Signed by Dolphins (May 16, 1995). ... On physically unable to perform list with foot injury (July 20-August 7, 1995).
CHAMPIONSHIP GAME EXPERIENCE: Played in AFC championship game (1992 season).
HONORS: Named defensive back on THE SPORTING NEWS college All-America first team (1987 and 1988).
RECORDS: Shares NFL record for longest interception return—103 yards, touchdown (October 4, 1992, at Buffalo).
PRO STATISTICS: 1990—Credited with one sack. 1991—Recovered one fumble. 1992—Recovered one fumble. 1993—Recovered one fumble. 1994—Credited with one sack and fumbled once.

		INTERCEPTIONS			
Year Team	G	No.	Yds.	Avg.	TD
1989—Miami NFL	15	4	32	8.0	0
1990—Miami NFL	16	5	87	17.4	0
1991—Miami NFL	16	5	80	16.0	0
1992—Miami NFL	16	5	200	40.0	1
1993—Miami NFL	11	2	60	30.0	1
1994—Cincinnati NFL	12	3	36	12.0	0
1995—Miami NFL	15	0	0	...	0
Pro totals (7 years)	101	24	495	20.6	2

OLIVER, MUHAMMAD CB REDSKINS

PERSONAL: Born March 12, 1969, in Brooklyn, N.Y. ... 5-11/185. ... Full name: Muhammad Ramadan Oliver.
HIGH SCHOOL: North (Phoenix).
JUNIOR COLLEGE: Glendale (Ariz.) Community College.
COLLEGE: Oregon (degree in sociology).
TRANSACTIONS/CAREER NOTES: Selected by Denver Broncos in ninth round (249th pick overall) of 1992 NFL draft. ... Signed by Broncos (July 16, 1992). ... On injured reserve with knee injury (September 23-November 7, 1992). ... On practice squad (November 7, 1992-remainder of season). ... Claimed on waivers by Kansas City Chiefs (August 31, 1993). ... Released by Chiefs (September 15, 1993). ... Signed by Green Bay Packers (September 20, 1993). ... Released by Packers (October 25, 1993). ... Signed by Miami Dolphins (December 22, 1993). ... Granted free agency (February 17, 1995). ... Signed by Washington Redskins (April 26, 1995). ... On injured reserve with knee injury (September 7, 1995-remainder of season). ... Granted unconditional free agency (February 16, 1996). ... Re-signed by Redskins (April 4, 1996).
PLAYING EXPERIENCE: Denver NFL, 1992; Kansas City (2)-Green Bay (2) NFL, 1993; Miami NFL, 1994; Washington NFL, 1995. ... Games: 1992 (3), 1993 (4), 1994 (13), 1995 (1). Total: 21.
PRO STATISTICS: 1992—Returned one kickoff for 20 yards. 1994—Intercepted one pass for no yards.

OLSAVSKY, JERRY LB

PERSONAL: Born March 29, 1967, in Youngstown, Ohio. ... 6-1/224. ... Full name: Jerome Donald Olsavsky. ... Name pronounced ol-SAV-skee.
HIGH SCHOOL: Chaney (Youngstown, Ohio).
COLLEGE: Pittsburgh (degree in information science).
TRANSACTIONS/CAREER NOTES: Selected by Pittsburgh Steelers in 10th round (258th pick overall) of 1989 NFL draft. ... Signed by Steelers (July 18, 1989). ... On injured reserve with foot injury (November 6-December 27, 1992); on practice squad (December 2-27, 1992). ... On injured reserve with knee injury (October 26, 1993-remainder of season). ... Released by Steelers (February 17, 1994). ... Re-signed by Steelers (November 16, 1994). ... Granted unconditional free agency (February 16, 1996).
PLAYING EXPERIENCE: Pittsburgh NFL, 1989-1995. ... Games: 1989 (16), 1990 (15), 1991 (16), 1992 (7), 1993 (7), 1994 (1), 1995 (15). Total: 77.

O

CHAMPIONSHIP GAME EXPERIENCE: Member of Steelers for AFC championship game (1994 season); inactive. ... Played in AFC championship game (1995 season). ... Played in Super Bowl XXX (1995 season).
PRO STATISTICS: 1989—Credited with one sack. 1995—Credited with one sack.

O'NEAL, BRIAN   FB   49ERS

PERSONAL: Born February 25, 1970, in Cincinnati. ... 6-0/233.
HIGH SCHOOL: Purcell Marian (Cincinnati).
COLLEGE: Penn State.
TRANSACTIONS/CAREER NOTES: Signed as non-drafted free agent by Philadelphia Eagles (April 27, 1994). ... Selected by Carolina Panthers from Eagles in NFL expansion draft (February 15, 1995). ... Released by Panthers (August 30, 1995). ... Signed by San Francisco 49ers (November 1, 1995).
PLAYING EXPERIENCE: Philadelphia NFL, 1994; San Francisco NFL, 1995. ... Games: 1994 (14), 1995 (3). Total: 17.
PRO STATISTICS: 1994—Returned one kickoff for no yards, returned one punt for no yards and fumbled once.

O'NEAL, LESLIE   DE   RAMS

PERSONAL: Born May 7, 1964, in Pulaski County, Ark. ... 6-4/265. ... Full name: Leslie Cornelius O'Neal.
HIGH SCHOOL: Hall (Little Rock, Ark.).
COLLEGE: Oklahoma State.
TRANSACTIONS/CAREER NOTES: Selected by New Jersey Generals in 1986 USFL territorial draft. ... Selected by San Diego Chargers in first round (eighth pick overall) of 1986 NFL draft. ... Signed by Chargers (August 5, 1986). ... On injured reserve with knee injury (December 4, 1986-remainder of season). ... On physically unable to perform list with knee injury (August 30, 1987-entire season). ... On physically unable to perform list with knee injury (July 23-August 21, 1988). ... On physically unable to perform list with knee injury (August 22-October 15, 1988). ... Granted free agency (February 1, 1990). ... Re-signed by Chargers (August 21, 1990). ... Granted free agency (February 1, 1992). ... Re-signed by Chargers (July 23, 1992). ... Designated by Chargers as franchise player (February 25, 1993). ... Free agency status changed by Chargers from franchise player to restricted free agent (June 15, 1993). ... Re-signed by Chargers (August 19, 1993). ... Granted unconditional free agency (February 16, 1996). ... Signed by St. Louis Rams (March 1, 1996).
CHAMPIONSHIP GAME EXPERIENCE: Played in AFC championship game (1994 season). ... Played in Super Bowl XXIX (1994 season).
HONORS: Named defensive lineman on THE SPORTING NEWS college All-America first team (1984 and 1985). ... Played in Pro Bowl (1989, 1990 and 1992-1995 seasons).
RECORDS: Holds NFL rookie-season record for most sacks—12.5 (1986).
PRO STATISTICS: 1986—Intercepted two passes for 22 yards and one touchdown and recovered two fumbles. 1989—Recovered two fumbles for 10 yards. 1990—Fumbled once and recovered two fumbles for 10 yards. 1992—Recovered one fumble. 1993—Recovered one fumble for 13 yards. 1994—Recovered one fumble.
MISCELLANEOUS: Holds San Diego Chargers all-time record for most sacks (105.5).

Year Team	G	SACKS
1986—San Diego NFL	13	12.5
1987—San Diego NFL	Did not play.	
1988—San Diego NFL	9	4.0
1989—San Diego NFL	16	12.5
1990—San Diego NFL	16	13.5
1991—San Diego NFL	16	9.0
1992—San Diego NFL	15	17.0
1993—San Diego NFL	16	12.0
1994—San Diego NFL	16	12.5
1995—San Diego NFL	16	12.5
Pro totals (9 years)	**133**	**105.5**

O'NEILL, PAT   P   JETS

PERSONAL: Born February 9, 1971, in Scott Air Force Base, Ill. ... 6-1/200. ... Full name: Patrick James O'Neill.
HIGH SCHOOL: Red Land (Lewisberry, Pa.).
COLLEGE: Syracuse.
TRANSACTIONS/CAREER NOTES: Selected by New England Patriots in fifth round (135th pick overall) of 1994 NFL draft. ... Signed by Patriots (May 27, 1994). ... Released by Patriots (October 31, 1995). ... Signed by Chicago Bears (November 15, 1995). ... Released by Bears (December 5, 1995). ... Signed by New York Jets (December 12, 1995).
PRO STATISTICS: 1994—Missed only extra-point attempt.

Year Team	G	No.	Yds.	Avg.	Net avg.	In. 20	Blk.
				PUNTING			
1994—New England NFL	16	69	2841	41.2	35.7	25	0
1995—New England NFL	8	41	1514	36.9	30.9	14	0
—Chicago NFL	1	3	89	29.7	26.7	0	0
Pro totals (2 years)	**25**	**113**	**4444**	**39.3**	**33.7**	**39**	**0**

ORLANDO, BO   S   BENGALS

PERSONAL: Born April 3, 1966, in Berwick, Pa. ... 5-10/180. ... Full name: Joseph John Orlando.
HIGH SCHOOL: Berwick (Pa.) Area Senior.
COLLEGE: West Virginia.
TRANSACTIONS/CAREER NOTES: Selected by Houston Oilers in sixth round (157th pick overall) of 1989 NFL draft. ... Signed by Oilers (July 26, 1989). ... Released by Oilers (September 5, 1989). ... Re-signed by Oilers to developmental squad (September 8, 1989). ... Released by Oilers (January 2, 1990). ... Re-signed by Oilers (April 17, 1990). ... Granted free agency (February 1, 1992). ... Re-signed by Oilers (August 11, 1992). ... On injured reserve with knee injury (September 11-November 24, 1992). ... Granted unconditional free agency (February 17,

1995). ... Signed by San Diego Chargers (April 18, 1995). ... Granted unconditional free agency (February 16, 1996). ... Signed by Cincinnati Bengals (March 5, 1996).

PRO STATISTICS: 1991—Recovered two fumbles. 1995—Ran 37 yards with lateral from interception return.

			INTERCEPTIONS		
Year Team	G	No.	Yds.	Avg.	TD
1989—Houston NFL			Did not play.		
1990—Houston NFL	16	0	0	...	0
1991—Houston NFL	16	4	18	4.5	0
1992—Houston NFL	6	0	0	...	0
1993—Houston NFL	16	3	68	22.7	1
1994—Houston NFL	16	0	0	...	0
1995—San Diego NFL	16	0	37	...	0
Pro totals (6 years)	86	7	123	17.6	1

OSHODIN, WILLIE   DE

PERSONAL: Born September 16, 1969, in Benin City, Nigeria. ... 6-4/265. ... Full name: William Ehizela Oshodin.
HIGH SCHOOL: Georgetown Prep (Rockville, Md.).
COLLEGE: Villanova (degree in international business, 1992).
TRANSACTIONS/CAREER NOTES: Signed as non-drafted free agent by Denver Broncos (April 30, 1992). ... Released by Broncos (August 27, 1995). ... Re-signed by Broncos (December 5, 1995). ... On injured reserve with knee injury (December 20, 1995-remainder of season)... Granted unconditional free agency (February 16, 1996).
PLAYING EXPERIENCE: Denver NFL, 1993-1995. ... Games: 1993 (15), 1994 (13), 1995 (2). Total: 30.
PRO STATISTICS: 1993—Credited with one sack.

OSTROSKI, JERRY   G   BILLS

PERSONAL: Born July 12, 1970, in Collegeville, Pa. ... 6-4/310.
HIGH SCHOOL: Owen J. Roberts (Pottstown, Pa.).
COLLEGE: Tulsa.
TRANSACTIONS/CAREER NOTES: Selected by Kansas City Chiefs in 10th round (271st pick overall) of 1992 NFL draft. ... Signed by Chiefs (July 21, 1992). ... Released by Chiefs (August 25, 1992). ... Signed by Atlanta Falcons (May 7, 1993). ... Released by Falcons (August 24, 1993). ... Signed by Buffalo Bills to practice squad (November 18, 1993). ... Released by Bills (August 28, 1994). ... Re-signed by Bills to practice squad (August 29, 1994). ... Activated (November 30, 1994).
PLAYING EXPERIENCE: Buffalo NFL, 1994 and 1995. ... Games: 1994 (4), 1995 (16). Total: 20.

OTTIS, BRAD   DE   RAMS

PERSONAL: Born August 2, 1972, in Wahoo, Neb. ... 6-4/272. ... Full name: Brad Allen Ottis. ... Name pronounced Ah-tis.
HIGH SCHOOL: Fremont (Neb.) Bergan.
COLLEGE: Wayne State (Neb.).
TRANSACTIONS/CAREER NOTES: Selected by Los Angeles Rams in second round (56th pick overall) of 1994 NFL draft. ... Signed by Rams (June 23, 1994). ... Rams franchise moved to St. Louis (April 12, 1995).

Year Team	G	SACKS
1994—Los Angeles Rams NFL	13	1.0
1995—St. Louis NFL	12	0.0
Pro totals (2 years)	25	1.0

OWENS, DAN   DE   FALCONS

PERSONAL: Born March 16, 1967, in Whittier, Calif. ... 6-3/280. ... Full name: Daniel William Owens.
HIGH SCHOOL: La Habra (Calif.).
COLLEGE: Southern California (bachelor of arts degree).
TRANSACTIONS/CAREER NOTES: Selected by Detroit Lions in second round (35th pick overall) of 1990 NFL draft. ... Signed by Lions (July 26, 1990). ... Granted free agency (March 1, 1993). ... Re-signed by Lions (August 14, 1993). ... Granted unconditional free agency (February 17, 1995). ... Re-signed by Lions (March 13, 1995). ... Granted unconditional free agency (February 16, 1996). ... Signed by Atlanta Falcons (March 27, 1996).
CHAMPIONSHIP GAME EXPERIENCE: Played in NFC championship game (1991 season).
PRO STATISTICS: 1991—Recovered two fumbles. 1992—Recovered one fumble. 1993—Intercepted one pass for one yard and recovered two fumbles for 17 yards. 1995—Returned one kickoff for nine yards.

Year Team	G	SACKS
1990—Detroit NFL	16	3.0
1991—Detroit NFL	16	5.5
1992—Detroit NFL	16	2.0
1993—Detroit NFL	15	3.0
1994—Detroit NFL	16	3.0
1995—Detroit NFL	16	0.0
Pro totals (6 years)	95	16.5

O

OWENS, RICH   DE   REDSKINS

PERSONAL: Born May 22, 1972, in Philadelphia. ... 6-6/270.
HIGH SCHOOL: Lincoln (Philadelphia).

COLLEGE: Lehigh.
TRANSACTIONS/CAREER NOTES: Selected by Washington Redskins in fifth round (152nd pick overall) of 1995 NFL draft. ... Signed by Redskins (May 23, 1995).
PLAYING EXPERIENCE: Washington NFL, 1995. ... Games: 1995 (10).
PRO STATISTICS: Credited with three sacks.

PAHUKOA, JEFF G/OT FALCONS

PERSONAL: Born February 9, 1969, in Vancouver, Wash. ... 6-2/298. ... Full name: Jeff Kalani Pahukoa. ... Brother of Shane Pahukoa, safety, New Orleans Saints. ... Name pronounced POW-uh-KOH-uh.
HIGH SCHOOL: Marysville (Wash.)-Pilchuk.
COLLEGE: Washington.
TRANSACTIONS/CAREER NOTES: Selected by Los Angeles Rams in 12th round (311th pick overall) of 1991 NFL draft. ... Signed by Rams (July 2, 1991). ... Released by Rams (August 20, 1991). ... Re-signed by Rams to practice squad (September 25, 1991). ... Activated (September 26, 1991). ... Released by Rams (October 25, 1991). ... Re-signed by Rams to practice squad (October 29, 1991). ... Activated (November 20, 1991). ... Granted unconditional free agency (February 1-April 1, 1992). ... Re-signed by Rams for 1992 season. ... Granted free agency (February 17, 1994). ... Re-signed by Rams (May 2, 1994). ... Released by Rams (August 22, 1994). ... Signed by Atlanta Falcons (February 13, 1995).
PLAYING EXPERIENCE: Los Angeles Rams NFL, 1991-1993; Atlanta NFL, 1995. ... Games: 1991 (7), 1992 (16), 1993 (16), 1995 (6). Total: 45.

PAHUKOA, SHANE S SAINTS

PERSONAL: Born November 25, 1970, in Vancouver, Wash. ... 6-2/202. ... Brother of Jeff Pahukoa, guard/offensive tackle, Atlanta Falcons. ... Name pronounced POW-uh-KOH-uh.
HIGH SCHOOL: Marysville (Wash.)-Pilchuk.
COLLEGE: Washington.
TRANSACTIONS/CAREER NOTES: Signed as non-drafted free agent by New Orleans Saints (May 7, 1993). ... Released by Saints (August 24, 1993). ... Re-signed by Saints to practice squad (December 13, 1993). ... Granted free agency after 1993 season. ... Re-signed by Saints (April 28, 1994). ... On injured reserve with left knee injury (August 23, 1994-entire season). ... On injured reserve with knee injury (December 21, 1995-remainder of season).

		INTERCEPTIONS			
Year Team	G	No.	Yds.	Avg.	TD
1993—New Orleans NFL		Did not play.			
1994—New Orleans NFL		Did not play—injured.			
1995—New Orleans NFL	15	2	12	6.0	0

PALELEI, SIULAGI G RAVENS

PERSONAL: Born October 15, 1970, in Nu'uuli, American Samoa. ... 6-3/320. ... Full name: Siulagi Jack Palelei. ... Name pronounced SEE-oo-lon-nee pah-le-LAY.
HIGH SCHOOL: Blue Springs (Mo.).
COLLEGE: Purdue, then UNLV.
TRANSACTIONS/CAREER NOTES: Selected by Pittsburgh Steelers in fifth round (135th pick overall) of 1993 NFL draft. ... Signed by Steelers (July 9, 1993). ... Inactive for 16 games (1994). ... On reserve/non-football injury list (August 21-November 3, 1995). ... Claimed on waivers by Cleveland Browns (November 28, 1995). ... Browns franchise moved to Baltimore and renamed Ravens for 1996 season (March 11, 1996).
PLAYING EXPERIENCE: Pittsburgh NFL, 1993 and 1995. ... Games: 1993 (3), 1995 (1). Total: 4.
CHAMPIONSHIP GAME EXPERIENCE: Member of Steelers for AFC championship game (1994 season); inactive.

PALMER, DAVID RB/WR/PR VIKINGS

PERSONAL: Born November 19, 1972, in Birmingham, Ala. ... 5-8/169.
HIGH SCHOOL: Jackson-Olin (Birmingham, Ala.).
COLLEGE: Alabama.
TRANSACTIONS/CAREER NOTES: Selected after junior season by Minnesota Vikings in second round (40th pick overall) of 1994 NFL draft. ... Signed by Vikings (July 19, 1994).
HONORS: Named kick returner on THE SPORTING NEWS college All-America first team (1993).
PRO STATISTICS: 1994—Fumbled twice. 1995—Fumbled once.

		RUSHING				RECEIVING				PUNT RETURNS				KICKOFF RETURNS				TOTALS		
Year Team	G	Att.	Yds.	Avg.	TD	No.	Yds.	Avg.	TD	No.	Yds.	Avg.	TD	No.	Yds.	Avg.	TD	TD	2pt.	Pts.
1994—Minnesota NFL	13	1	1	1.0	0	6	90	15.0	0	30	193	6.4	0	0	0	...	0	0	0	0
1995—Minnesota NFL	14	7	15	2.1	0	12	100	8.3	0	26	342	*13.2	†1	17	354	20.8	0	1	0	6
Pro totals (2 years)	27	8	16	2.0	0	18	190	10.6	0	56	535	9.6	1	17	354	20.8	0	1	0	6

PALMER, STERLING DE REDSKINS

PERSONAL: Born February 4, 1971, in Fort Lauderdale. ... 6-5/277.
HIGH SCHOOL: St. Thomas Aquinas (Fort Lauderdale).
COLLEGE: Florida State.
TRANSACTIONS/CAREER NOTES: Selected after junior season by Washington Redskins in fourth round (101st pick overall) of 1993 NFL draft. ... Signed by Redskins (July 15, 1993). ... On injured reserve with knee injury (December 8, 1995-remainder of season). ... Granted free agency (February 16, 1996). ... Re-signed by Redskins (April 3, 1996).
PRO STATISTICS: 1995—Recovered one fumble.

O
P

Year—Team	G	SACKS
1993—Washington NFL	14	4.5
1994—Washington NFL	16	1.0
1995—Washington NFL	13	4.5
Pro totals (3 years)	43	10.0

PANOS, JOE   G/C   EAGLES

PERSONAL: Born January 24, 1971, in Brookfield, Wis. ... 6-2/293.
HIGH SCHOOL: East (Brookfield, Wis.).
COLLEGE: Wisconsin.
TRANSACTIONS/CAREER NOTES: Selected by Philadelphia Eagles in third round (77th pick overall) of 1994 NFL draft. ... Signed by Eagles (July 11, 1994). ... On injured reserve with shoulder injury (November 12, 1995-remainder of season).
PLAYING EXPERIENCE: Philadelphia NFL, 1994 and 1995. ... Games: 1994 (16), 1995 (9). Total: 25.

PARKER, ANTHONY   CB   RAMS

PERSONAL: Born February 11, 1966, in Sylacauga, Ala. ... 5-10/181. ... Full name: Will Anthony Parker. ... Son of Billy Parker, second baseman/third baseman, California Angels (1971-73).
HIGH SCHOOL: McClintock (Tempe, Ariz.).
COLLEGE: Arizona State (degree in physical education, 1989).
TRANSACTIONS/CAREER NOTES: Signed as non-drafted free agent by Indianapolis Colts (April 21, 1989). ... On injured reserve with hamstring injury (September 5-November 17, 1989). ... Granted unconditional free agency (February 1, 1990). ... Released by Jets (March 31, 1990). ... Released by Jets (September 4, 1990). ... Signed by WLAF (January 31, 1991). ... Selected by New York/New Jersey Knights in first round (second defensive back) of 1991 WLAF positional draft. ... Signed by Phoenix Cardinals (July 9, 1991). ... Released by Cardinals (August 13, 1991). ... Signed by Kansas City Chiefs to practice squad (September 11, 1991). ... Activated (September 15, 1991). ... Released by Chiefs (September 25, 1991). ... Re-signed by Chiefs to practice squad (October 1, 1991). ... Activated (December 14, 1991). ... Granted unconditional free agency (February 1, 1992). ... Signed by Minnesota Vikings (March 26, 1992). ... Granted free agency (February 17, 1994). ... Re-signed by Vikings (May 7, 1994). ... Granted unconditional free agency (February 17, 1995). ... Signed by Los Angeles Rams (April 4, 1995). ... Rams franchise moved to St. Louis (April 12, 1995).
HONORS: Named cornerback on All-World League team (1991).
PRO STATISTICS: 1992—Returned two kickoffs for 30 yards and recovered two fumbles for 58 yards and a touchdown. 1994—Recovered one fumble for 23 yards and a touchdown. 1995—Recovered four fumbles for 35 yards and a touchdown.
MISCELLANEOUS: Only player in NFL history to score a defensive touchdown in three consecutive games (1994).

		INTERCEPTIONS				PUNT RETURNS				TOTALS			
Year—Team	G	No.	Yds.	Avg.	TD	No.	Yds.	Avg.	TD	TD	2pt.	Pts.	Fum.
1989—Indianapolis NFL	1	0	0	...	0	0	0	...	0	0	...	0	0
1990—						Did not play.							
1991—New York/New Jersey W.L.	10	*11	*270	24.6	*2	0	0	...	0	2	0	12	0
—Kansas City NFL	2	0	0	...	0	0	0	...	0	0	...	0	0
1992—Minnesota NFL	16	3	23	7.7	0	33	336	10.2	0	1	...	6	2
1993—Minnesota NFL	14	1	1	1.0	0	9	64	7.1	0	0	...	0	0
1994—Minnesota NFL	15	4	99	24.8	2	4	31	7.8	0	3	0	18	1
1995—St. Louis NFL	16	2	-5	-2.5	0	0	0	...	0	1	0	6	0
W.L. totals (1 year)	10	11	270	24.6	2	0	0	...	0	2	0	12	0
NFL totals (6 years)	64	10	118	11.8	2	46	431	9.4	0	5	0	30	3
Pro totals (6 years)	74	21	388	18.5	4	46	431	9.4	0	7	0	42	3

PARKER, GLENN   G/OT   BILLS

PERSONAL: Born April 22, 1966, in Westminster, Calif. ... 6-5/305. ... Full name: Glenn Andrew Parker.
HIGH SCHOOL: Edison (Huntington Beach, Calif.).
COLLEGE: Arizona.
TRANSACTIONS/CAREER NOTES: Selected by Buffalo Bills in third round (69th pick overall) of 1990 NFL draft. ... Signed by Bills (July 26, 1990). ... Granted free agency (March 1, 1993). ... Re-signed by Bills (March 11, 1993).
PLAYING EXPERIENCE: Buffalo NFL, 1990-1995. ... Games: 1990 (16), 1991 (16), 1992 (13), 1993 (16), 1994 (16), 1995 (13). Total: 90.
CHAMPIONSHIP GAME EXPERIENCE: Played in AFC championship game (1990, 1992 and 1993 seasons). ... Member of Bills for AFC championship game (1991 season); inactive. ... Played in Super Bowl XXV (1990 season), Super Bowl XXVI (1991 season), Super Bowl XXVII (1992 season) and Super Bowl XXVIII (1993 season).
PRO STATISTICS: 1992—Recovered one fumble. 1995—Recovered one fumble.

PARKER, VAUGHN   G/OT   CHARGERS

PERSONAL: Born June 5, 1971, in Buffalo. ... 6-3/296. ... Full name: Vaughn Antoine Parker.
HIGH SCHOOL: Saint Joseph's Collegiate Institute (Buffalo).
COLLEGE: UCLA.
TRANSACTIONS/CAREER NOTES: Selected by San Diego Chargers in second round (63rd pick overall) of 1994 NFL draft. ... Signed by Chargers (July 12, 1994).
PLAYING EXPERIENCE: San Diego NFL, 1994 and 1995. ... Games: 1994 (6), 1995 (15). Total: 21.
CHAMPIONSHIP GAME EXPERIENCE: Played in AFC championship game (1994 season). ... Played in Super Bowl XXIX (1994 season).
PRO STATISTICS: 1994—Returned one kickoff for one yard.

P

PARMALEE, BERNIE — RB — DOLPHINS

PERSONAL: Born September 16, 1967, in Jersey City, N.J. ... 5-11/196.
HIGH SCHOOL: Lincoln (Jersey City, N.J.).
COLLEGE: Ball State.
TRANSACTIONS/CAREER NOTES: Signed as non-drafted free agent by Miami Dolphins (May 1, 1992). ... Released by Dolphins (August 31, 1992). ... Signed by Dolphins to practice squad (September 1, 1992). ... Activated (October 21, 1992). ... Deactivated for remainder of 1992 playoffs (January 16, 1993). ... Granted free agency (February 17, 1995). ... Re-signed by Dolphins (March 31, 1995).
PRO STATISTICS: 1994—Recovered three fumbles for 20 yards.
STATISTICAL PLATEAUS: 100-yard rushing games: 1994 (3), 1995 (3). Total: 6.

		RUSHING				RECEIVING				KICKOFF RETURNS				TOTALS			
Year Team	G	Att.	Yds.	Avg.	TD	No.	Yds.	Avg.	TD	No.	Yds.	Avg.	TD	TD	2pt.	Pts.	Fum.
1992—Miami NFL	10	6	38	6.3	0	0	0	...	0	14	289	20.6	0	0	...	0	3
1993—Miami NFL	16	4	16	4.0	0	1	1	1.0	0	0	0	...	0	0	...	0	0
1994—Miami NFL	15	216	868	4.0	6	34	249	7.3	1	2	0	0.0	0	7	1	44	5
1995—Miami NFL	16	236	878	3.7	9	39	345	8.9	1	0	0	...	0	10	0	60	5
Pro totals (4 years)	57	462	1800	3.9	15	74	595	8.1	2	16	289	18.1	0	17	1	104	13

PARRELLA, JOHN — DT — CHARGERS

PERSONAL: Born November 22, 1969, in Topeka, Kan. ... 6-3/290. ... Full name: John Lorin Parrella.
HIGH SCHOOL: Central Catholic (Grand Island, Neb.).
COLLEGE: Nebraska.
TRANSACTIONS/CAREER NOTES: Selected by Buffalo Bills in second round (55th pick overall) of 1993 NFL draft. ... Signed by Bills (July 12, 1993). ... Released by Bills (August 28, 1994). ... Signed by San Diego Chargers (September 12, 1994). ... Granted free agency (February 16, 1996).
CHAMPIONSHIP GAME EXPERIENCE: Member of Bills for AFC championship game (1993 season); inactive. ... Member of Bills for Super Bowl XXVIII (1993 season); inactive. ... Played in AFC championship game (1994 season). ... Played in Super Bowl XXIX (1994 season).

Year Team	G	SACKS
1993—Buffalo NFL	10	1.0
1994—San Diego NFL	13	1.0
1995—San Diego NFL	16	2.0
Pro totals (3 years)	39	4.0

PARRISH, JAMES — OT — STEELERS

PERSONAL: Born May 19, 1968, in Baltimore. ... 6-6/310. ... Full name: James Herbert Parrish Jr.
HIGH SCHOOL: Dundalk (Baltimore).
COLLEGE: Temple (degree in physical education).
TRANSACTIONS/CAREER NOTES: Signed as non-drafted free agent by Miami Dolphins (April 26, 1991). ... On physically unable to perform list with knee injury (August 20, 1991-entire season). ... Granted unconditional free agency (February 1, 1992). ... Signed by San Diego Chargers (February 19, 1992). ... Assigned by Chargers to London Monarchs in 1992 World League enhancement allocation program (February 20, 1992). ... Signed as free agent by Barcelona Dragons of World League (April 21, 1992). ... Released by Chargers (August 31, 1992). ... Signed by San Francisco 49ers (May 3, 1993). ... Released by 49ers (September 7, 1993). ... Signed by Indianapolis Colts (September 8, 1993). ... Released by Colts (October 12, 1993). ... Signed by 49ers to practice squad (November 8, 1993). ... Released by 49ers (December 1, 1993). ... Signed by Dallas Cowboys to practice squad (December 7, 1993). ... Activated (December 22, 1993). ... Released by Cowboys (August 17, 1994). ... Re-signed by Cowboys (October 25, 1994). ... Released by Cowboys (November 1, 1994). ... Signed by Pittsburgh Steelers (February 22, 1995).
PLAYING EXPERIENCE: London (5)-Barcelona (1) W.L., 1992; Dallas NFL, 1993; Pittsburgh NFL, 1995. ... Games: 1992 (6), 1993 (1), 1995 (16). Total WL: 6. Total NFL: 17. Total Pro: 23.
CHAMPIONSHIP GAME EXPERIENCE: Member of Cowboys for NFC championship game (1993 season); inactive. ... Member of Super Bowl championship team (1993 season). ... Played in AFC championship game (1995 season). ... Played in Super Bowl XXX (1995 season).

PARTEN, TY — DE

PERSONAL: Born October 13, 1969, in Washington, D.C. ... 6-4/272. ... Full name: Ty Danile Parten.
HIGH SCHOOL: Horizon (Scottsdale, Ariz.).
COLLEGE: Arizona.
TRANSACTIONS/CAREER NOTES: Selected by Cincinnati Bengals in third round (63rd pick overall) of 1993 draft. ... Signed by Bengals (July 19, 1993). ... On injured reserve with left thumb injury (November 29, 1993-remainder of season). ... Released by Bengals (September 20, 1995). ... Selected by Scottish Claymores in 1996 World League draft (February 22, 1996).
PLAYING EXPERIENCE: Cincinnati NFL, 1993-1995. ... Games: 1993 (11), 1994 (14), 1995 (1). Total: 26.

PATRICK, GARIN — OL

PERSONAL: Born August 31, 1971, in Canton, Ohio. ... 6-3/269.
HIGH SCHOOL: St. Thomas Aquinas (Louisville, Ohio).
COLLEGE: Louisville.
TRANSACTIONS/CAREER NOTES: Signed as non-drafted free agent by Indianapolis Colts (July 22, 1994). ... Released by Colts (August 23, 1994). ... Re-signed by Colts (January 3, 1995). ... Released by Colts (October 10, 1995). ... Re-signed by Colts to practice squad (October 11, 1995). ... Granted free agency after 1995 season.
PLAYING EXPERIENCE: Indianapolis NFL, 1995. ... Games: 1995 (5).

P

PATTON, JOE   G   REDSKINS

PERSONAL: Born January 5, 1972, in Birmingham, Ala. ... 6-5/290.
HIGH SCHOOL: Jones Valley (Birmingham, Ala.).
COLLEGE: Alabama A&M.
TRANSACTIONS/CAREER NOTES: Selected by Washington Redskins in third round (97th pick overall) of 1994 NFL draft. ... Signed by Redskins (July 19, 1994).
PLAYING EXPERIENCE: Washington NFL, 1994 and 1995. ... Games: 1994 (2), 1995 (16). Total: 18.
PRO STATISTICS: 1995—Recovered one fumble.

PATTON, MARVCUS   LB   REDSKINS

PERSONAL: Born May 1, 1967, in Los Angeles. ... 6-2/240. ... Full name: Marvcus Raymond Patton.
HIGH SCHOOL: Leuzinger (Lawndale, Calif.).
COLLEGE: UCLA (degree in political science, 1990).
TRANSACTIONS/CAREER NOTES: Selected by Buffalo Bills in eighth round (208th pick overall) of 1990 NFL draft. ... Signed by Bills (July 27, 1990). ... On injured reserve with broken leg (January 26, 1991-remainder of 1990 season playoffs). ... Granted free agency (February 1, 1992). ... Re-signed by Bills (July 23, 1992). ... Granted unconditional free agency (February 17, 1995). ... Signed by Washington Redskins (February 22, 1995).
CHAMPIONSHIP GAME EXPERIENCE: Played in AFC championship game (1991-1993 seasons). ... Played in Super Bowl XXVI (1991 season), Super Bowl XXVII (1992 season) and Super Bowl XXVIII (1993 season).
PRO STATISTICS: 1993—Intercepted two passes for no yards and recovered three fumbles for five yards. 1994—Fumbled once and recovered one fumble. 1995—Intercepted two passes for seven yards and recovered one fumble.

Year Team	G	SACKS
1990—Buffalo NFL	16	0.5
1991—Buffalo NFL	16	0.0
1992—Buffalo NFL	16	2.0
1993—Buffalo NFL	16	1.0
1994—Buffalo NFL	16	0.0
1995—Washington NFL	16	2.0
Pro totals (6 years)	96	5.5

PAUL, TITO   DB   CARDINALS

PERSONAL: Born May 24, 1972, in Kissimmee, Fla. ... 6-0/195. ... Cousin of Markus Paul, safety, Chicago Bears and Tampa Bay Buccaneers (1989-1993).
HIGH SCHOOL: Kissimmee (Fla.)-Osceola.
COLLEGE: Ohio State.
TRANSACTIONS/CAREER NOTES: Selected by Arizona Cardinals in fifth round (167th pick overall) of 1995 NFL draft. ... Signed by Cardinals (July 20, 1995).
PLAYING EXPERIENCE: Arizona NFL, 1995. ... Games: 1995 (14).
PRO STATISTICS: 1995—Intercepted one pass for four yards.

PAUP, BRYCE   LB   BILLS

PERSONAL: Born February 29, 1968, in Scranton, Iowa. ... 6-5/247. ... Full name: Bryce Eric Paup.
HIGH SCHOOL: Scranton (Iowa).
COLLEGE: Northern Iowa (degree in business).
TRANSACTIONS/CAREER NOTES: Selected by Green Bay Packers in sixth round (159th pick overall) of 1990 NFL draft. ... Signed by Packers (July 22, 1990). ... On injured reserve with hand injury (September 4-November 17, 1990). ... On injured reserve with calf injury (December 12, 1991-remainder of season). ... Granted free agency (February 1, 1992). ... Re-signed by Packers (August 13, 1992). ... Granted unconditional free agency (February 17, 1995). ... Signed by Buffalo Bills (March 9, 1995).
HONORS: Played in Pro Bowl (1994 and 1995 seasons). ... Named linebacker on THE SPORTING NEWS NFL All-Pro team (1995).
PRO STATISTICS: 1991—Credited with one safety. 1992—Recovered two fumbles. 1994—Recovered two fumbles. 1995—Recovered one fumble.

Year Team	G	INTERCEPTIONS No.	Yds.	Avg.	TD	SACKS No.
1990—Green Bay NFL	5	0	0	...	0	0.0
1991—Green Bay NFL	12	0	0	...	0	7.5
1992—Green Bay NFL	16	0	0	...	0	6.5
1993—Green Bay NFL	15	1	8	8.0	0	11.0
1994—Green Bay NFL	16	3	47	15.7	1	7.5
1995—Buffalo NFL	15	2	0	0.0	0	*17.5
Pro totals (6 years)	79	6	55	9.2	1	50.0

PEETE, RODNEY   QB   EAGLES

PERSONAL: Born March 16, 1966, in Mesa, Ariz. ... 6-0/225. ... Son of Willie Peete, running backs coach, Chicago Bears; and cousin of Calvin Peete, professional golfer.
HIGH SCHOOL: Sahuaro (Tucson, Ariz.), then Shawnee Mission South (Overland Park, Kan.).
COLLEGE: Southern California (degree in communications, 1989).
TRANSACTIONS/CAREER NOTES: Selected by Detroit Lions in sixth round (141st pick overall) of 1989 NFL draft. ... Signed by Lions (July 13, 1989). ... On injured reserve with Achilles' tendon injury (October 30, 1991-remainder of season). ... Granted free agency (February 1,

P

1992). ... Re-signed by Lions (July 30, 1992). ... Granted unconditional free agency (February 17, 1994). ... Signed by Dallas Cowboys (May 4, 1994). ... Granted unconditional free agency (February 17, 1995). ... Signed by Philadelphia Eagles (April 22, 1995). ... Granted unconditional free agency (February 16, 1996). ... Re-signed by Eagles (March 14, 1996).

CHAMPIONSHIP GAME EXPERIENCE: Member of Cowboys for NFC championship game (1994 season); did not play.

HONORS: Named quarterback on THE SPORTING NEWS college All-America second team (1988).

PRO STATISTICS: 1989—Fumbled nine times and recovered three fumbles. 1990—Fumbled nine times and recovered one fumble. 1991—Fumbled twice and recovered one fumble for minus one yard. 1992—Fumbled six times and recovered two fumbles for minus seven yards. 1993—Fumbled 11 times and recovered four fumbles for minus eight yards. 1994—Fumbled three times and recovered two fumbles for minus one yard. 1995—Fumbled 13 times and recovered five fumbles.

STATISTICAL PLATEAUS: 300-yard passing games: 1990 (1), 1992 (1). Total: 2.

MISCELLANEOUS: Selected by Toronto Blue Jays organization in 30th round of free-agent baseball draft (June 4, 1984); did not sign. ... Selected by Oakland Athletics organization in 14th round of free-agent baseball draft (June 1, 1988); did not sign. ... Selected by Athletics organization in 13th round of free-agent baseball draft (June 5, 1989); did not sign. ... Regular-season record as starting NFL quarterback: 31-29 (.517).

					PASSING						RUSHING				TOTALS		
Year Team	G	Att.	Cmp.	Pct.	Yds.	TD	Int.	Avg.	Rat.	Att.	Yds.	Avg.	TD	TD	2pt.	Pts.
1989—Detroit NFL	8	195	103	52.8	1479	5	9	7.59	67.0	33	148	4.5	4	4	...	24
1990—Detroit NFL	11	271	142	52.4	1974	13	8	7.29	79.8	47	363	7.7	6	6	...	36
1991—Detroit NFL	8	194	116	59.8	1339	5	9	6.90	69.9	25	125	5.0	2	2	...	12
1992—Detroit NFL	10	213	123	57.8	1702	9	9	7.99	80.0	21	83	4.0	0	0	...	0
1993—Detroit NFL	10	252	157	62.3	1670	9	14	6.63	66.4	45	165	3.7	1	1	...	6
1994—Dallas NFL	7	56	33	58.9	470	4	1	8.39	102.5	9	-2	-0.2	0	0	0	0
1995—Philadelphia NFL	15	375	215	57.3	2326	8	14	6.20	67.3	32	147	4.6	1	1	0	6
Pro totals (7 years)	69	1556	889	57.1	10960	50	64	7.04	72.6	212	1029	4.9	14	14	0	84

PEGRAM, ERRIC — RB — STEELERS

PERSONAL: Born January 7, 1969, in Dallas. ... 5-10/195. ... Full name: Erric Demont Pegram. ... Name pronounced PEE-grum.

HIGH SCHOOL: Hillcrest (Dallas).

COLLEGE: North Texas.

TRANSACTIONS/CAREER NOTES: Selected by Atlanta Falcons in sixth round (145th pick overall) of 1991 NFL draft. ... Signed by Falcons (July 20, 1991). ... Granted free agency (February 17, 1994). ... Re-signed by Falcons (June 3, 1994). ... Granted unconditional free agency (February 17, 1995). ... Signed by Pittsburgh Steelers (April 27, 1995).

CHAMPIONSHIP GAME EXPERIENCE: Played in AFC championship game (1995 season). ... Played in Super Bowl XXX (1995 season).

PRO STATISTICS: 1992—Recovered three fumbles for one yard. 1993—Recovered four fumbles. 1995—Recovered one fumble.

STATISTICAL PLATEAUS: 100-yard rushing games: 1993 (4), 1995 (2). Total: 6.

		RUSHING				RECEIVING				KICKOFF RETURNS				TOTALS			
Year Team	G	Att.	Yds.	Avg.	TD	No.	Yds.	Avg.	TD	No.	Yds.	Avg.	TD	TD	2pt.	Pts.	Fum.
1991—Atlanta NFL	16	101	349	3.5	1	1	-1	-1.0	0	16	260	16.3	0	1	...	6	1
1992—Atlanta NFL	16	21	89	4.2	0	2	25	12.5	0	9	161	17.9	0	0	...	0	0
1993—Atlanta NFL	16	292	1185	4.1	3	33	302	9.2	0	4	63	15.8	0	3	...	18	6
1994—Atlanta NFL	13	103	358	3.5	1	16	99	6.2	0	9	145	16.1	0	1	0	6	2
1995—Pittsburgh NFL	15	213	813	3.8	5	26	206	7.9	1	4	85	21.3	0	6	1	38	9
Pro totals (5 years)	76	730	2794	3.8	10	78	631	8.1	1	42	714	17.0	0	11	1	68	18

PELFREY, DOUG — K — BENGALS

PERSONAL: Born September 25, 1970, in Fort Thomas, Ky. ... 5-11/185. ... Full name: Thomas Douglas Pelfrey.

HIGH SCHOOL: Scott (Covington, Ky.).

COLLEGE: Kentucky (degree in biology, 1993).

TRANSACTIONS/CAREER NOTES: Selected by Cincinnati Bengals in eighth round (202nd pick overall) of 1993 NFL draft. ... Signed by Bengals (July 19, 1993). ... Granted free agency (February 16, 1996). ... Re-signed by Bengals (June 7, 1996).

PRO STATISTICS: 1995—Punted twice for 52 yards.

		KICKING						
Year Team	G	XPM	XPA	FGM	FGA	Lg.	50+	Pts.
1993—Cincinnati NFL	15	13	16	24	31	53	2-3	85
1994—Cincinnati NFL	16	24	25	28	33	54	2-4	108
1995—Cincinnati NFL	16	34	34	29	36	51	1-2	121
Pro totals (3 years)	47	71	75	81	100	54	5-9	314

PENN, CHRIS — WR/KR — CHIEFS

PERSONAL: Born April 20, 1971, in Lenapah, Okla. ... 6-0/198. ... Full name: Christopher Anthony Penn.

HIGH SCHOOL: Oklahoma Union (Lenapah Okla.).

COLLEGE: Northeastern Oklahoma A&M, then Tulsa.

TRANSACTIONS/CAREER NOTES: Selected by Kansas City Chiefs in third round (96th pick overall) of 1994 NFL draft. ... Signed by Chiefs (June 2, 1994).

		RECEIVING				PUNT RETURNS				KICKOFF RETURNS				TOTALS			
Year Team	G	No.	Yds.	Avg.	TD	No.	Yds.	Avg.	TD	No.	Yds.	Avg.	TD	TD	2pt.	Pts.	Fum.
1994—Kansas City NFL	8	3	24	8.0	0	0	0	...	0	9	194	21.6	0	0	0	0	0
1995—Kansas City NFL	2	1	12	12.0	0	4	12	3.0	0	2	26	13.0	0	0	0	0	0
Pro totals (2 years)	10	4	36	9.0	0	4	12	3.0	0	11	220	20.0	0	0	0	0	0

P

PERRIMAN, BRETT   WR   LIONS

PERSONAL: Born October 10, 1965, in Miami. ... 5-9/180.
HIGH SCHOOL: Northwestern (Miami).
COLLEGE: Miami (Fla.).
TRANSACTIONS/CAREER NOTES: Selected by New Orleans Saints in second round (52nd pick overall) of 1988 NFL draft. ... Signed by Saints (May 19, 1988). ... Granted free agency (February 1, 1991). ... Traded by Saints to Detroit Lions for fifth-round pick (WR Torrance Small) in 1992 draft (August 21, 1991). ... Activated (September 2, 1991). ... Granted free agency (February 1, 1992). ... Re-signed by Lions (1992). ... Granted unconditional free agency (February 17, 1994). ... Re-signed by Lions (March 11, 1994).
CHAMPIONSHIP GAME EXPERIENCE: Played in NFC championship game (1991 season).
PRO STATISTICS: 1989—Returned one punt for 10 yards. 1990—Recovered one fumble. 1992—Returned four kickoffs for 59 yards. 1994—Attempted one pass without a completion. 1995—Returned five punts for 50 yards, returned five kickoffs for 65 yards and recovered one fumble.
STATISTICAL PLATEAUS: 100-yard receiving games: 1991 (1), 1992 (2), 1994 (1), 1995 (8). Total: 12.

| | | RUSHING | | | | RECEIVING | | | | TOTALS | | | |
Year Team	G	Att.	Yds.	Avg.	TD	No.	Yds.	Avg.	TD	TD	2pt.	Pts.	Fum.
1988—New Orleans NFL	16	3	17	5.7	0	16	215	13.4	2	2	...	12	1
1989—New Orleans NFL	14	1	-10	-10.0	0	20	356	17.8	0	0	...	0	0
1990—New Orleans NFL	16	0	0	...	0	36	382	10.6	2	2	...	12	2
1991—Detroit NFL	15	4	10	2.5	0	52	668	12.9	1	1	...	6	0
1992—Detroit NFL	16	0	0	...	0	69	810	11.7	4	4	...	24	1
1993—Detroit NFL	15	4	16	4.0	0	49	496	10.1	2	2	...	12	1
1994—Detroit NFL	16	9	86	9.6	0	56	761	13.6	4	4	2	28	1
1995—Detroit NFL	16	5	48	9.6	0	108	1488	13.8	9	9	1	56	1
Pro totals (8 years)	124	26	167	6.4	0	406	5176	12.8	24	24	3	150	7

PERRY, DARREN   S   STEELERS

PERSONAL: Born December 29, 1968, in Chesapeake, Va. ... 5-11/196.
HIGH SCHOOL: Deep Creek (Chesapeake, Va.).
COLLEGE: Penn State.
TRANSACTIONS/CAREER NOTES: Selected by Pittsburgh Steelers in eighth round (203rd pick overall) of 1992 NFL draft. ... Signed by Steelers (July 16, 1992). ... Granted free agency (February 17, 1995). ... Re-signed by Steelers (June 15, 1995).
CHAMPIONSHIP GAME EXPERIENCE: Played in AFC championship game (1994 and 1995 seasons). ... Played in Super Bowl XXX (1995 season).
HONORS: Named defensive back on THE SPORTING NEWS college All-America second team (1991).
PRO STATISTICS: 1992—Recovered one fumble. 1994—Recovered two fumbles. 1995—Fumbled once and recovered two fumbles.

| | | INTERCEPTIONS | | | |
Year Team	G	No.	Yds.	Avg.	TD
1992—Pittsburgh NFL	16	6	69	11.5	0
1993—Pittsburgh NFL	16	4	61	15.3	0
1994—Pittsburgh NFL	16	7	112	16.0	0
1995—Pittsburgh NFL	16	4	71	17.8	0
Pro totals (4 years)	64	21	313	14.9	0

PERRY, GERALD   OT   RAIDERS

PERSONAL: Born November 12, 1964, in Columbia, S.C. ... 6-6/290.
HIGH SCHOOL: Dreher (Columbia, S.C.).
JUNIOR COLLEGE: Northwest Mississippi Community College.
COLLEGE: Southern (La.).
TRANSACTIONS/CAREER NOTES: Selected by Denver Broncos in second round (45th pick overall) of 1988 NFL draft. ... Signed by Broncos (July 15, 1988). ... On reserve/left squad list (December 6, 1990-remainder of season). ... Traded by Broncos with 12th-round pick (OL Jeff Pahukoa) in 1991 draft to Los Angeles Rams for RB Gaston Green and fourth-round pick (WR Derek Russell) in 1991 draft (April 22, 1991). ... On injured reserve with knee injury (November 19, 1991-remainder of season). ... Granted unconditional free agency (March 1, 1993). ... Signed by Los Angeles Raiders (March 4, 1993). ... Designated by Raiders as transition player (February 15, 1994). ... Raiders franchise moved to Oakland (July 21, 1995).
PLAYING EXPERIENCE: Denver NFL, 1988-1990; Los Angeles Rams NFL, 1991 and 1992; Los Angeles Raiders NFL, 1993 and 1994; Oakland NFL, 1995. ... Games: 1988 (16), 1989 (16), 1990 (8), 1991 (11), 1992 (16), 1993 (15), 1994 (12), 1995 (3). Total: 97.
CHAMPIONSHIP GAME EXPERIENCE: Played in AFC championship game (1989 season). ... Played in Super Bowl XXIV (1989 season).
PRO STATISTICS: 1989—Recovered one fumble. 1993—Recovered one fumble.

PERRY, MARLO   LB   BILLS

PERSONAL: Born August 25, 1972, in Forest, Miss. ... 6-4/250. ... Full name: Malcolm Marlo Perry.
HIGH SCHOOL: Scott Central (Forest, Miss.).
COLLEGE: Jackson State.
TRANSACTIONS/CAREER NOTES: Selected by Buffalo Bills in third round (81st pick overall) of 1994 NFL draft. ... Signed by Bills (July 18, 1994).
PLAYING EXPERIENCE: Buffalo NFL, 1994 and 1995. ... Games: 1994 (2), 1995 (16). Total: 18.

P

PERRY, MICHAEL DEAN   DT   BRONCOS

PERSONAL: Born August 27, 1965, in Aiken, S.C. ... 6-1/285. . ... Brother of William Perry, defensive tackle, London Monarchs of World League.
HIGH SCHOOL: South Aiken (S.C.).
COLLEGE: Clemson.
TRANSACTIONS/CAREER NOTES: Selected by Cleveland Browns in second round (50th pick overall) of 1988 NFL draft. ... Signed by Browns (July 23, 1988). ... Granted free agency (February 1, 1991). ... Re-signed by Browns (August 27, 1991). ... Released by Browns (February 16, 1995). ... Signed by Denver Broncos (February 28, 1995).
CHAMPIONSHIP GAME EXPERIENCE: Played in AFC championship game (1989 season).
HONORS: Named defensive lineman on THE SPORTING NEWS college All-America second team (1987). ... Played in Pro Bowl (1989-1991, 1993 and 1994 seasons). ... Named defensive tackle on THE SPORTING NEWS NFL All-Pro team (1989-1993).
PRO STATISTICS: 1988—Returned one kickoff for 13 yards and recovered two fumbles for 10 yards and one touchdown. 1989—Recovered two fumbles. 1990—Recovered one fumble. 1993—Recovered two fumbles for four yards.

Year Team	G	SACKS
1988—Cleveland NFL	16	6.0
1989—Cleveland NFL	16	7.0
1990—Cleveland NFL	16	11.5
1991—Cleveland NFL	16	8.5
1992—Cleveland NFL	14	8.5
1993—Cleveland NFL	16	6.0
1994—Cleveland NFL	15	4.0
1995—Denver NFL	14	6.0
Pro totals (8 years)	**123**	**57.5**

PERRY, TODD   G   BEARS

PERSONAL: Born November 28, 1970, in Elizabethtown, Ky. ... 6-5/310. ... Full name: Todd Joseph Perry.
HIGH SCHOOL: Elizabethtown (Ky.).
COLLEGE: Kentucky.
TRANSACTIONS/CAREER NOTES: Selected by Chicago Bears in fourth round (97th pick overall) of 1993 NFL draft. ... Signed by Bears (June 16, 1993).
PLAYING EXPERIENCE: Chicago NFL, 1993-1995. ... Games: 1993 (13), 1994 (15), 1995 (15). Total: 43.

PETERSON, ANDREW   OT   PANTHERS

PERSONAL: Born June 11, 1972, in Greenock, Scotland. ... 6-5/308.
HIGH SCHOOL: South Kitsap (Port Orchard, Wash.).
COLLEGE: Washington..
TRANSACTIONS/CAREER NOTES: Selected by Carolina Panthers in fifth round (171st pick overall) of 1995 NFL draft.... Signed by Panthers (July 14, 1995).
PLAYING EXPERIENCE: Carolina NFL, 1995. ... Games: 1995 (4).

PETERSON, TODD   K   SEAHAWKS

PERSONAL: Born February 4, 1970, in Valdosta, Ga. ... 5-10/173. ... Full name: Joseph Todd Peterson.
HIGH SCHOOL: Valdosta (Ga.).
COLLEGE: Navy, then Georgia (degree in finance).
TRANSACTIONS/CAREER NOTES: Selected by New York Giants in seventh round (177th pick overall) of 1993 NFL draft. ... Signed by Giants (July 19, 1993). ... Released by Giants (August 24, 1993). ... Signed by New England Patriots to practice squad (November 30, 1993). ... Released by Patriots (December 6, 1993). ... Signed by Atlanta Falcons (May 3, 1994). ... Released by Falcons (August 29, 1994). ... Signed by Arizona Cardinals (October 12, 1994). ... Released by Cardinals (October 24, 1994). ... Signed by Seattle Seahawks (January 17, 1995).

Year Team	G	XPM	XPA	FGM	FGA	Lg.	50+	Pts.
1993—				Did not play.				
1994—Arizona NFL	2	4	4	2	4	35	0-0	10
1995—Seattle NFL	16	40	40	23	28	49	0-2	109
Pro totals (2 years)	**18**	**44**	**44**	**25**	**32**	**49**	**0-2**	**119**

PETERSON, TONY   LB   49ERS

PERSONAL: Born January 23, 1972, in Cleveland. ... 6-0/223. ... Full name: Anthony Wayne Peterson.
HIGH SCHOOL: Ringgold (Monongahela, Pa.).
COLLEGE: Notre Dame.
TRANSACTIONS/CAREER NOTES: Selected by San Francisco 49ers in fifth round (153rd pick overall) of 1994 NFL draft. ... Signed by 49ers (July 20, 1994). ... On injured reserve with hamstring injury (January 18, 1995-remainder of 1994 playoffs).
PLAYING EXPERIENCE: San Francisco NFL, 1994 and 1995. ... Games: 1994 (15), 1995 (15). Total: 30.
CHAMPIONSHIP GAME EXPERIENCE: Member of 49ers for NFC championship game (1994 season); inactive.

P

PHIFER, ROMAN   LB   RAMS

PERSONAL: Born March 5, 1968, in Plattsburgh, N.Y. ... 6-2/230. ... Full name: Roman Zubinsky Phifer.

HIGH SCHOOL: South Mecklenburg (Charlotte).

COLLEGE: UCLA.

TRANSACTIONS/CAREER NOTES: Selected by Los Angeles Rams in second round (31st pick overall) of 1991 NFL draft. ... Signed by Rams (July 19, 1991). ... On injured reserve with broken leg (November 26, 1991-remainder of season). ... Granted unconditional free agency (February 17, 1995). ... Re-signed by Rams (March 22, 1995). ... Rams franchise moved to St. Louis (April 12, 1995).

PRO STATISTICS: 1992—Recovered two fumbles. 1993—Recovered two fumbles for 10 yards. 1995—Fumbled once.

			INTERCEPTIONS			SACKS
Year Team	G	No.	Yds.	Avg.	TD	No.
1991—Los Angeles Rams NFL	16	0	0	...	0	2.0
1992—Los Angeles Rams NFL	16	1	3	3.0	0	0.0
1993—Los Angeles Rams NFL	16	0	0	...	0	0.0
1994—Los Angeles Rams NFL	16	2	7	3.5	0	1.5
1995—St. Louis NFL	16	3	52	17.3	0	3.0
Pro totals (5 years)	76	6	62	10.3	0	6.5

PHILCOX, TODD QB JAGUARS

PERSONAL: Born September 25, 1966, in Norwalk, Conn. ... 6-4/225. ... Full name: Todd Stuart Philcox.

HIGH SCHOOL: Norwalk (Conn.).

COLLEGE: Syracuse (degree in finance, 1988).

TRANSACTIONS/CAREER NOTES: Signed as non-drafted free agent by Cincinnati Bengals (May 1989).... Released by Bengals (September 5, 1989). ... Re-signed by Bengals to developmental squad (September 6, 1989). ... Released by Bengals (January 29, 1990). ... Re-signed by Bengals (May 1990). ... Granted unconditional free agency (February 1, 1991). ... Signed by Cleveland Browns (April 1, 1991). ... Granted unconditional free agency (February 1-April 1, 1992). ... Re-signed by Browns for 1992 season.... On injured reserve with broken thumb (September 22-November 14, 1992). ... Re-signed by Browns (March 1, 1993).... Re-signed by Browns (July 24, 1993).... Released by Browns (August 30, 1993).... Re-signed by Browns (September 1, 1993).... Granted unconditional free agency (February 17, 1994).... Signed by Bengals (October 25, 1994).... Released by Bengals (November 8, 1994).... Signed by Miami Dolphins (February 21, 1995).... Released by Dolphins (April 24, 1995).... Signed by Tampa Bay Buccaneers (April 27, 1995).... Released by Buccaneers (August 27, 1995).... Re-signed by Buccaneers (August 29, 1995).... Granted unconditional free agency (February 16, 1996).... Signed by Jacksonville Jaguars (April 11, 1996).

STATISTICAL PLATEAUS: 300-yard passing games: 1993 (1).

MISCELLANEOUS: Regular-season record as starting NFL quarterback: 2-3 (.400).

		PASSING								RUSHING				TOTALS		
Year Team	G	Att.	Cmp.	Pct.	Yds.	TD	Int.	Avg.	Rat.	Att.	Yds.	Avg.	TD	TD	2pt.	Pts.
1989—Cincinnati NFL								Did not play.								
1990—Cincinnati NFL	2	2	0	0.0	0	0	1	0.00	0.0	0	0	...	0	0	...	0
1991—Cleveland NFL	4	8	4	50.0	49	0	1	6.13	29.7	1	-1	-1.0	0	0	...	0
1992—Cleveland NFL	2	27	13	48.2	217	3	1	8.04	97.3	0	0	...	0	0	...	0
1993—Cleveland NFL	5	108	52	48.2	699	4	7	6.47	54.5	2	3	1.5	1	1	...	6
1994—Cincinnati NFL								Did not play.								
1995—Tampa Bay NFL								Did not play.								
Pro totals (4 years)	13	145	69	47.6	965	7	10	6.66	56.8	3	2	0.7	1	1	0	6

PHILION, ED DT BILLS

PERSONAL: Born March 27, 1970, in Windsor, Ont. ... 6-2/277.

COLLEGE: Ferris State (Mich.).

TRANSACTIONS/CAREER NOTES: Signed as non-drafted free agent by Buffalo Bills (May 6, 1994). ... On injured reserve (December 17, 1994-remainder of season).

PLAYING EXPERIENCE: Buffalo NFL, 1994 and 1995. ... Games: 1994 (4), 1995 (2). Total: 6.

PHILLIPS, ANTHONY CB FALCONS

PERSONAL: Born October 5, 1970, in Galveston, Texas. ... 6-2/207. ... Full name: Anthony Dwayne Phillips.

HIGH SCHOOL: Ball (Galveston, Texas).

JUNIOR COLLEGE: Trinity Valley Community College (Texas).

COLLEGE: Texas A&M-Kingsville.

TRANSACTIONS/CAREER NOTES: Selected by Atlanta Falcons in third round (72nd pick overall) of 1994 NFL draft. ... Signed by Falcons (July 19, 1994). ... On suspended list (August 11-12, 1995). ... On injured reserve with broken right leg (November 17, 1995-remainder of season).

		INTERCEPTIONS			
Year Team	G	No.	Yds.	Avg.	TD
1994—Atlanta NFL	5	1	0	0.0	0
1995—Atlanta NFL	6	1	43	43.0	0
Pro totals (2 years)	11	2	43	21.5	0

PHILLIPS, BOBBY RB VIKINGS

PERSONAL: Born December 8, 1969, in Richmond, Va. ... 5-9/187.

HIGH SCHOOL: John Marshall (Richmond, Va.).

COLLEGE: Virginia Union.

TRANSACTIONS/CAREER NOTES: Signed as non-drafted free agent by Minnesota Vikings (May 2, 1995). ... Signed by Frankfurt Galaxy of WLAF (April 10, 1996).

		RUSHING				KICKOFF RETURNS				TOTALS		
Year Team	G	Att.	Yds.	Avg.	TD	No.	Yds.	Avg.	TD	TD	2pt.	Pts.Fum.
1995—Minnesota NFL	8	14	26	1.9	0	4	60	15.0	0	0	0	0 1

P

PHILLIPS, JOE DT CHIEFS

PERSONAL: Born July 15, 1963, in Portland, Ore. ... 6-5/310. ... Full name: Joseph Gordon Phillips.
HIGH SCHOOL: Columbia River (Vancouver, Wash.).
JUNIOR COLLEGE: Chemeketa Community College (Ore.).
COLLEGE: Oregon State, then Southern Methodist (degree in economics, 1986).
TRANSACTIONS/CAREER NOTES: Selected by Minnesota Vikings in fourth round (93rd pick overall) of 1986 NFL draft. ... Signed by Vikings (July 28, 1986). ... Released by Vikings (September 7, 1987). ... Signed as replacement player by San Diego Chargers (September 24, 1987). ... Granted free agency (February 1, 1988). ... Re-signed by Chargers (August 29, 1988). ... On reserve/non-football injury list with head injuries (September 26, 1990-remainder of season). ... Granted free agency (February 1, 1992). ... Rights relinquished by Chargers (September 21, 1992). ... Signed by Kansas City Chiefs (September 30, 1992). ... Granted unconditional free agency (February 17, 1994). ... Re-signed by Chiefs (March 29, 1994).
CHAMPIONSHIP GAME EXPERIENCE: Played in AFC championship game (1993 season).
PRO STATISTICS: 1986—Recovered one fumble. 1991—Recovered one fumble. 1992—Recovered one fumble. 1994—Recovered one fumble. 1995—Intercepted one pass for two yards and recovered one fumble.

Year Team	G	SACKS
1986—Minnesota NFL	16	0.0
1987—San Diego NFL	13	5.0
1988—San Diego NFL	16	2.0
1989—San Diego NFL	16	1.0
1990—San Diego NFL	3	0.5
1991—San Diego NFL	16	1.0
1992—Kansas City NFL	12	2.5
1993—Kansas City NFL	16	1.5
1994—Kansas City NFL	16	3.0
1995—Kansas City NFL	16	4.5
Pro totals (10 years)	**140**	**21.0**

PHILYAW, DINO RB PANTHERS

PERSONAL: Born October 30, 1970, in Kenansville, N.C. ... 5-10/199. ... Full name: Delvic Dyvon Philyaw.
HIGH SCHOOL: Southern Wayne (Dudley, N.C.).
JUNIOR COLLEGE: Taft (Calif.) Junior College.
COLLEGE: Oregon.
TRANSACTIONS/CAREER NOTES: Selected by New England Patriots in sixth round (195th pick overall) of 1995 NFL draft. ... Signed by Patriots (July 10, 1995). ... Released by Patriots (August 30, 1995). ... Re-signed by Patriots to practice squad (September 1, 1995). ... Signed by Carolina Panthers off Patriots practice squad (November 8, 1995).
PLAYING EXPERIENCE: Carolina NFL, 1995. ... Games: 1995 (1).
PRO STATISTICS: 1995—Returned one kickoff for 23 yards.

PICKENS, BRUCE CB RAIDERS

PERSONAL: Born May 9, 1968, in Kansas City, Mo. ... 5-11/190. ... Full name: Bruce Evon Pickens.
HIGH SCHOOL: Westport (Kansas City, Mo.).
JUNIOR COLLEGE: Coffeyville (Kan.) Community College.
COLLEGE: Nebraska.
TRANSACTIONS/CAREER NOTES: Selected by Atlanta Falcons in first round (third pick overall) of 1991 NFL draft. ... Signed by Falcons (October 1, 1991). ... Activated (October 16, 1991). ... Traded by Falcons to Green Bay Packers for undisclosed draft pick (October 12, 1993); in separate deal, Falcons traded RB Eric Dickerson to Packers for RB John Stephens (October 12, 1993); Dickerson failed physical and was returned to Falcons (October 15, 1993); deal completed with Falcons retaining Stephens and Packers retaining Pickens (October 15, 1993). ... Released by Packers (November 29, 1993). ... Signed by Kansas City Chiefs (December 10, 1993). ... Released by Chiefs (August 17, 1994). ... Signed by Los Angeles Raiders (March 28, 1995). ... Raiders franchise moved to Oakland (July 21, 1995).
PRO STATISTICS: 1992—Credited with one sack. 1995—Recovered one fumble for 10 yards.

		INTERCEPTIONS			
Year Team	G	No.	Yds.	Avg.	TD
1991—Atlanta NFL	7	0	0	...	0
1992—Atlanta NFL	16	2	16	8.0	0
1993—Atlanta NFL	4	0	0	...	0
—Green Bay NFL	2	0	0	...	0
—Kansas City NFL	3	0	0	...	0
1994—			Did not play.		
1995—Oakland NFL	16	0	0	...	0
Pro totals (4 years)	**48**	**2**	**16**	**8.0**	**0**

PICKENS, CARL WR BENGALS

PERSONAL: Born March 23, 1970, in Murphy, N.C. ... 6-2/206. ... Full name: Carl McNally Pickens.
HIGH SCHOOL: Murphy (N.C.).
COLLEGE: Tennessee.
TRANSACTIONS/CAREER NOTES: Selected after junior season by Cincinnati Bengals in second round (31st pick overall) of 1992 NFL draft. ... Signed by Bengals (August 4, 1992). ... Granted free agency (February 17, 1995). ... Tendered offer sheet by Arizona Cardinals (March 17, 1995). ... Offer matched by Bengals (March 24, 1995).
HONORS: Named wide receiver on THE SPORTING NEWS college All-America first team (1991). ... Played in Pro Bowl (1995 season).
PRO STATISTICS: 1992—Recovered two fumbles. 1993—Attempted one pass without a completion. 1994—Recovered one fumble. 1995—Rushed once for six yards.

P

Year Team	G	RECEIVING				PUNT RETURNS				TOTALS			
		No.	Yds.	Avg.	TD	No.	Yds.	Avg.	TD	TD	2pt.	Pts.	Fum.
1992—Cincinnati NFL	16	26	326	12.5	1	18	229	12.7	1	2	...	12	3
1993—Cincinnati NFL	13	43	565	13.1	6	4	16	4.0	0	6	...	36	1
1994—Cincinnati NFL	15	71	1127	15.9	11	9	62	6.9	0	11	0	66	1
1995—Cincinnati NFL	16	99	1234	12.5	†17	5	-2	-0.4	0	17	0	102	1
Pro totals (4 years)	60	239	3252	13.6	35	36	305	8.5	1	36	0	216	6

PIERCE, AARON — TE — GIANTS

PERSONAL: Born September 6, 1969, in Seattle. ... 6-5/250.
HIGH SCHOOL: Franklin (Seattle).
COLLEGE: Washington.
TRANSACTIONS/CAREER NOTES: Selected by New York Giants in third round (69th pick overall) of 1992 NFL draft. ... Signed by Giants (July 21, 1992). ... On injured reserve with wrist injury (September 1-December 26, 1992); on practice squad (October 7-November 4, 1992). ... Granted free agency (February 17, 1995). ... Re-signed by Giants (April 5, 1995).
PRO STATISTICS: 1995—Rushed once for six yards and recovered one fumble.

Year Team	G	RECEIVING				TOTALS			
		No.	Yds.	Avg.	TD	TD	2pt.	Pts.	Fum.
1992—New York Giants NFL	1	0	0	...	0	0	...	0	0
1993—New York Giants NFL	13	12	212	17.7	0	0	...	0	2
1994—New York Giants NFL	16	20	214	10.7	4	4	0	24	0
1995—New York Giants NFL	16	33	310	9.4	0	0	0	0	0
Pro totals (4 years)	46	65	736	11.3	4	4	0	24	2

PIERSON, PETE — OT — BUCCANEERS

PERSONAL: Born February 4, 1971, in Portland, Ore. ... 6-5/295. ... Full name: Peter Samuel Pierson.
HIGH SCHOOL: David Douglas (Portland, Ore.).
COLLEGE: Washington (degree in political science, 1994).
TRANSACTIONS/CAREER NOTES: Selected by Tampa Bay Buccaneers in fifth round (136th pick overall) of 1994 NFL draft. ... Signed by Buccaneers (July 6, 1994). ... Released by Buccaneers (August 28, 1994). ... Re-signed by Buccaneers to practice squad (September 2, 1994). ... Activated (November 22, 1994); did not play.
PLAYING EXPERIENCE: Tampa Bay NFL, 1995. ... Games: 1995 (12).
PRO STATISTICS: 1995—Recovered one fumble.

PIKE, MARK — DE — BILLS

PERSONAL: Born December 27, 1963, in Elizabethtown, Ky. ... 6-4/272. ... Full name: Mark Harold Pike.
HIGH SCHOOL: Dixie Heights (Edgewood, Ky.).
COLLEGE: Georgia Tech.
TRANSACTIONS/CAREER NOTES: Selected by Jacksonville Bulls in 1986 USFL territorial draft. ... Selected by Buffalo Bills in seventh round (178th pick overall) of 1986 NFL draft. ... Signed by Bills (July 20, 1986). ... On injured reserve with shoulder injury (August 26, 1986-entire season). ... On injured reserve with leg injury (September 16-November 14, 1987). ... On injured reserve with foot injury (December 8, 1987-remainder of season). ... Granted free agency (February 1, 1991). ... Re-signed by Bills (1991). ... Granted unconditional free agency (February 1-April 1, 1992). ... Re-signed by Bills for 1992 season. ... Granted unconditional free agency (March 1, 1993). ... Re-signed by Bills (May 26, 1993). ... Granted unconditional free agency (February 17, 1995). ... Re-signed by Bills (March 14, 1995).
PLAYING EXPERIENCE: Buffalo NFL, 1987-1995. ... Games: 1987 (3), 1988 (16), 1989 (16), 1990 (16), 1991 (16), 1992 (16), 1993 (14), 1994 (16), 1995 (16). Total: 129.
CHAMPIONSHIP GAME EXPERIENCE: Played in AFC championship game (1988 and 1990-1993 seasons). ... Played in Super Bowl XXV (1990 season), Super Bowl XXVI (1991 season), Super Bowl XXVII (1992 season) and Super Bowl XXVIII (1993 season).
PRO STATISTICS: 1988—Returned one kickoff for five yards. 1989—Recovered one fumble. 1992—Credited with one sack. 1994—Returned two kickoffs for nine yards. 1995—Returned one kickoff for 20 yards.

PINKNEY, LOVELL — TE — RAMS

PERSONAL: Born August 18, 1972, in Washington, D.C. ... 6-4/248.
HIGH SCHOOL: Anacostia (Washington, D.C.).
COLLEGE: Texas.
TRANSACTIONS/CAREER NOTES: Selected after junior season by St. Louis Rams in fourth round (115th pick overall) of 1995 NFL draft. ... Signed by Rams (July 17, 1995).
PLAYING EXPERIENCE: St. Louis NFL, 1995. ... Games: 1995 (8).
PRO STATISTICS: 1995—Caught one pass for 13 yards and returned one kickoff for 26 yards.

PITTS, MIKE — DT

PERSONAL: Born September 25, 1960, in Baltimore. ... 6-5/277. ... Cousin of Rick Porter, running back, Detroit Lions, Baltimore Colts, Buffalo Bills and Memphis Showboats of USFL (1982, 1983, 1985 and 1987).
HIGH SCHOOL: Polytechnic (Baltimore).
COLLEGE: Alabama.

P

TRANSACTIONS/CAREER NOTES: Selected by Birmingham Stallions in 1983 USFL territorial draft. ... Selected by Atlanta Falcons in first round (16th pick overall) of 1983 NFL draft. ... Signed by Falcons (July 16, 1983). ... On injured reserve with knee injury (December 6, 1984-remainder of season). ... Granted free agency (February 1, 1987). ... Re-signed by Falcons and traded to Philadelphia Eagles for DE Greg Brown (September 7, 1987). ... Granted roster exemption (September 7-11, 1987). ... On injured reserve with knee injury (September 19-December 21, 1990). ... Granted free agency (February 1, 1991). ... Re-signed by Eagles (August 15, 1991). ... On injured reserve with back injury (September 1-October 14, 1992). ... Granted unconditional free agency (March 1, 1993). ... Signed by New England Patriots (June 7, 1993). ... Released by Patriots (August 30, 1993). ... Re-signed by Patriots (August 31, 1993). ... Granted unconditional free agency (February 17, 1994). ... Re-signed by Patriots (March 4, 1994). ... Granted unconditional free agency (February 17, 1995). ... Re-signed by Patriots (April 7, 1995). ... Released by Patriots (August 27, 1995).

HONORS: Named defensive end on THE SPORTING NEWS college All-America first team (1982).

PRO STATISTICS: 1983—Recovered one fumble for 26 yards. 1984—Recovered two fumbles. 1985—Intercepted one pass for one yard, fumbled once and recovered one fumble for six yards. 1986—Recovered two fumbles for 22 yards and one touchdown. 1987—Recovered four fumbles for 21 yards. 1989—Recovered two fumbles. 1991—Recovered one fumble. 1994—Recovered two fumbles for eight yards.

Year Team	G	SACKS
1983—Atlanta NFL	16	7.0
1984—Atlanta NFL	14	5.5
1985—Atlanta NFL	16	7.0
1986—Atlanta NFL	16	5.5
1987—Philadelphia NFL	12	2.0
1988—Philadelphia NFL	16	1.5
1989—Philadelphia NFL	16	7.0
1990—Philadelphia NFL	4	3.0
1991—Philadelphia NFL	16	2.0
1992—Philadelphia NFL	11	4.0
1993—New England NFL	16	3.0
1994—New England NFL	16	1.0
1995—	Did not play.	
Pro totals (12 years)	**169**	**48.5**

PLANANSKY, JOE   TE   DOLPHINS

PERSONAL: Born October 21, 1971, in Hemingford, Neb. ... 6-4/254.
HIGH SCHOOL: Hemingford (Neb.).
COLLEGE: Chadron (Neb.) State.
TRANSACTIONS/CAREER NOTES: Signed as non-drafted free agent by Miami Dolphins (April 24, 1995). ... Released by Dolphins (August 27, 1995). ... Re-signed by Dolphins to practice squad (August 30, 1995). ... Activated (October 21, 1995). ... Released by Dolphins (November 2, 1995). ... Re-signed by Dolphins to practice squad (November 3, 1995).
PLAYING EXPERIENCE: Miami NFL, 1995. ... Games: 1995 (2).

PLEASANT, ANTHONY   DE   RAVENS

PERSONAL: Born January 27, 1968, in Century, Fla. ... 6-5/280. ... Full name: Anthony Devon Pleasant.
HIGH SCHOOL: Century (Fla.).
COLLEGE: Tennessee State.
TRANSACTIONS/CAREER NOTES: Selected by Cleveland Browns in third round (73rd pick overall) of 1990 NFL draft. ... Signed by Browns (July 22, 1990). ... Browns franchise moved to Baltimore and renamed Ravens for 1996 season (March 11, 1996).
PRO STATISTICS: 1991—Recovered one fumble for four yards. 1993—Credited with one safety.

Year Team	G	SACKS
1990—Cleveland NFL	16	3.5
1991—Cleveland NFL	16	2.5
1992—Cleveland NFL	16	4.0
1993—Cleveland NFL	16	11.0
1994—Cleveland NFL	14	4.5
1995—Cleveland NFL	16	8.0
Pro totals (6 years)	**94**	**33.5**

PLUMMER, GARY   LB   49ERS

PERSONAL: Born January 26, 1960, in Fremont, Calif. ... 6-2/247. ... Full name: Gary Lee Plummer.
HIGH SCHOOL: Mission San Jose (Fremont, Calif.).
JUNIOR COLLEGE: Ohlone (Calif.) College.
COLLEGE: California.
TRANSACTIONS/CAREER NOTES: Selected by Oakland Invaders in 1983 USFL territorial draft. ... Signed by Invaders (January 26, 1983). ... On developmental squad for one game (March 30-April 6, 1984). ... Protected in merger of Invaders and Michigan Panthers (December 6, 1984). ... Claimed on waivers by Tampa Bay Bandits (August 3, 1985). ... Granted free agency when USFL suspended operations (August 7, 1986). ... Signed by San Diego Chargers (August 18, 1986). ... Granted roster exemption (August 18-22, 1986). ... On injured reserve with broken wrist (October 27-November 28, 1987). ... Granted free agency (February 1, 1992). ... Re-signed by Chargers (July 27, 1992). ... Granted unconditional free agency (March 1, 1993). ... Re-signed by Chargers (July 23, 1993). ... Granted unconditional free agency (February 17, 1994). ... Signed by San Francisco 49ers (March 24, 1994).
CHAMPIONSHIP GAME EXPERIENCE: Played in USFL championship game (1985 season). ... Played in NFC championship game (1994 season). ... Member of Super Bowl championship team (1994 season).
PRO STATISTICS: USFL: 1983—Recovered one fumble. 1984—Recovered one fumble. 1985—Returned three kickoffs for 31 yards and recovered one fumble. NFL: 1986—Returned one kickoff for no yards and recovered two fumbles. 1989—Rushed once for six yards and recovered one fumble. 1990—Caught one pass for two yards and a touchdown and rushed twice for three yards and one touchdown. 1991—Recovered one fumble. 1992—Recovered two fumbles. 1994—Recovered one fumble.

P

Year Team	G	INTERCEPTIONS No.	Yds.	Avg.	TD	SACKS No.
1983—Oakland USFL	18	3	20	6.7	0	0.0
1984—Oakland USFL	17	2	11	5.5	0	1.0
1985—Oakland USFL	18	1	46	46.0	0	1.0
1986—San Diego NFL	15	0	0	...	0	2.5
1987—San Diego NFL	8	1	2	2.0	0	0.0
1988—San Diego NFL	16	0	0	...	0	0.0
1989—San Diego NFL	16	0	0	...	0	0.0
1990—San Diego NFL	16	0	0	...	0	0.0
1991—San Diego NFL	16	0	0	...	0	1.0
1992—San Diego NFL	16	2	40	20.0	0	0.0
1993—San Diego NFL	16	2	7	3.5	0	0.0
1994—San Francisco NFL	16	1	1	1.0	0	0.0
1995—San Francisco NFL	16	0	0	...	0	1.0
USFL totals (3 years)	53	6	77	12.8	0	2.0
NFL totals (10 years)	151	6	50	8.3	0	4.5
Pro totals (13 years)	204	12	127	10.6	0	6.5

POLLACK, FRANK — G/OT — 49ERS

PERSONAL: Born November 5, 1967, in Camp Springs, Md. ... 6-5/285. ... Full name: Frank Steven Pollack.
HIGH SCHOOL: Greenway (Phoenix).
COLLEGE: Northern Arizona (degree in advertising, 1990).
TRANSACTIONS/CAREER NOTES: Selected by San Francisco 49ers in sixth round (165th pick overall) of 1990 NFL draft. ... Signed by 49ers (July 18, 1990). ... Granted unconditional free agency (February 1-April 1, 1991). ... Re-signed by 49ers for 1991 season. ... Granted unconditional free agency (February 1, 1992). ... Signed by Denver Broncos (March 20, 1992). ... On injured reserve with back injury (August 24, 1992-entire season). ... Released by Broncos (August 18, 1993). ... Signed by 49ers (May 18, 1994). ... Granted unconditional free agency (February 17, 1995). ... Re-signed by 49ers (May 15, 1995). ... Granted unconditional free agency (February 16, 1996). ... Selected by Scottish Claymores in 1996 World League draft (February 22, 1996). ... Re-signed by 49ers (June 3, 1996).
PLAYING EXPERIENCE: San Francisco NFL, 1990, 1991, 1994 and 1995. ... Games: 1990 (15), 1991 (15), 1994 (12), 1995 (15). Total: 57.
CHAMPIONSHIP GAME EXPERIENCE: Played in NFC championship game (1990 season). ... Member of 49ers for NFC championship game (1994 season); inactive. ... Member of Super Bowl championship team (1994 season).

POLLARD, MARCUS — TE — COLTS

PERSONAL: Born February 8, 1972, in Lanett, Ala. ... 6-4/245.
HIGH SCHOOL: Valley (Ala.).
JUNIOR COLLEGE: Seward County (Kan.) Community College (did not play football).
COLLEGE: Bradley (did not play football).
TRANSACTIONS/CAREER NOTES: Signed as non-drafted free agent by Indianapolis Colts (January 24, 1995). ... Released by Colts (August 22, 1995). ... Re-signed by Colts to practice squad (August 28, 1995). ... Activated (October 10, 1995).
PLAYING EXPERIENCE: Indianapolis NFL, 1995. ... Games: 1995 (8).
CHAMPIONSHIP GAME EXPERIENCE: Played in AFC championship game (1995 season).
MISCELLANEOUS: Played basketball during college.

POLLARD, TRENT — OT — BENGALS

PERSONAL: Born November 20, 1972, in Seattle. ... 6-4/330. ... Full name: Trent Deshawn Pollard.
HIGH SCHOOL: Rainier (Wash.).
COLLEGE: Eastern Washington.
TRANSACTIONS/CAREER NOTES: Selected by Cincinnati Bengals in fifth round (132nd pick overall) of 1994 NFL draft. ... Signed by Bengals (May 9, 1994).
PLAYING EXPERIENCE: Cincinnati NFL, 1994 and 1995. ... Games: 1994 (8) and 1995 (9). Total: 17.

POOLE, TYRONE — CB/KR — PANTHERS

PERSONAL: Born February 3, 1972, in LaGrange, Ga. ... 5-8/188.
HIGH SCHOOL: LaGrange (Ga.).
COLLEGE: Fort Valley (Ga.) State.
TRANSACTIONS/CAREER NOTES: Selected by Carolina Panthers in first round (22nd pick overall) of 1995 NFL draft. ... Signed by Panthers (July 15, 1995).

Year Team	G	INTERCEPTIONS No.	Yds.	Avg.	TD	SACKS No.
1995—Carolina NFL	16	2	8	4.0	0	2.0

POPE, MARQUEZ — S/CB — 49ERS

PERSONAL: Born October 29, 1970, in Nashville. ... 5-11/193. ... Full name: Marquez Phillips Pope. ... Name pronounced MARK-ez
HIGH SCHOOL: Polytechnic (Long Beach, Calif.).
COLLEGE: Fresno State.
TRANSACTIONS/CAREER NOTES: Selected by San Diego Chargers in second round (33rd pick overall) of 1992 NFL draft. ... Signed by Chargers (July 16, 1992). ... On reserve/non-football illness list with virus (September 1-28, 1992). ... On practice squad (September 28-

P

November 7, 1992). ... Traded by Chargers to Los Angeles Rams for sixth-round pick in 1995 draft (April 11, 1994). ... Granted free agency (February 17, 1995). ... Tendered offer sheet by San Francisco 49ers (April 9, 1995). ... Rams declined to match offer (April 12, 1995); received second-round pick (OL Jesse James) in 1995 draft as compensation.

PRO STATISTICS: 1993—Credited with ½ sack.

			INTERCEPTIONS		
Year Team	G	No.	Yds.	Avg.	TD
1992—San Diego NFL	7	0	0	...	0
1993—San Diego NFL	16	2	14	7.0	0
1994—Los Angeles Rams NFL	16	3	66	22.0	0
1995—San Francisco NFL	16	1	-7	-7.0	0
Pro totals (4 years)	55	6	73	12.2	0

POPSON, TED   TE   49ERS

PERSONAL: Born September 10, 1966, in Granada Hills, Calif. ... 6-4/250.
HIGH SCHOOL: Tahoe Truckee (Truckee, Calif.).
JUNIOR COLLEGE: Marin Community College (Calif.).
COLLEGE: Portland State.
TRANSACTIONS/CAREER NOTES: Selected by New York Giants in 11th round (306th pick overall) of 1991 NFL draft. ... Selected by London Monarchs in 1992 World League draft. ... Released by Giants (August 31, 1992). ... Re-signed by Giants to practice squad (September 2, 1992). ... Released by Giants (October 7, 1992). ... Signed by San Francisco 49ers (April 30, 1993). ... Released by 49ers (August 27, 1993). ... Re-signed by 49ers to practice squad (August 31, 1993). ... Granted free agency after 1993 season. ... Re-signed by 49ers (February 15, 1994).
CHAMPIONSHIP GAME EXPERIENCE: Played in NFC championship game (1994 season). ... Member of Super Bowl championship team (1994 season).
PRO STATISTICS: W.L.: 1992—Returned three kickoffs for 31 yards.

		RECEIVING				TOTALS				
Year Team	G	No.	Yds.	Avg.	TD	TD	2pt.	Pts.	Fum.
1991—New York Giants NFL					Did not play.				
1992—London W.L.	10	4	24	6.0	0	0	0	0	0
1993—San Francisco NFL					Did not play.				
1994—San Francisco NFL	16	13	141	10.9	0	0	0	0	0
1995—San Francisco NFL	12	16	128	8.0	0	0	0	0	1
W.L. totals (1 year)	10	4	24	6.0	0	0	0	0	0
NFL totals (2 years)	28	29	269	9.3	0	0	0	0	1
Pro totals (3 years)	38	33	293	8.9	0	0	0	0	1

PORCHER, ROBERT   DE   LIONS

PERSONAL: Born July 30, 1969, in Wando, S.C. ... 6-3/270. ... Name pronounced por-SHAY.
HIGH SCHOOL: Cainhoy (Huger, S.C.).
COLLEGE: Tennessee State, then South Carolina State.
TRANSACTIONS/CAREER NOTES: Selected by Detroit Lions in first round (26th pick overall) of 1992 NFL draft. ... Signed by Lions (July 25, 1992). ... Granted unconditional free agency (February 16, 1996). ... Re-signed by Lions (March 29, 1996).
PRO STATISTICS: 1994—Recovered one fumble.

Year Team	G	SACKS
1992—Detroit NFL	16	1.0
1993—Detroit NFL	16	8.5
1994—Detroit NFL	15	3.0
1995—Detroit NFL	16	5.0
Pro totals (4 years)	63	17.5

PORT, CHRIS   G/OT

PERSONAL: Born November 2, 1967, in Wanaque, N.J. ... 6-5/295. ... Full name: Christopher Charles Port.
HIGH SCHOOL: Don Bosco (Ramsey, N.J.).
COLLEGE: Duke (degree in history).
TRANSACTIONS/CAREER NOTES: Selected by New Orleans Saints in 12th round (320th pick overall) of 1990 NFL draft. ... Signed by Saints (July 16, 1990). ... Released by Saints (September 3, 1990). ... Re-signed by Saints to practice squad (October 1, 1990). ... Granted free agency after 1990 season. ... Re-signed by Saints (February 15, 1991). ... Granted free agency (February 17, 1994). ... Re-signed by Saints (May 4, 1994). ... On injured reserve with neck injury (December 1, 1995-remainder of season). ... Released by Saints (February 21, 1996).
PLAYING EXPERIENCE: New Orleans NFL, 1991-1995. ... Games: 1991 (14), 1992 (16), 1993 (15), 1994 (16), 1995 (8). Total: 69.
PRO STATISTICS: 1993—Recovered one fumble.

PORTER, RUFUS   LB   SAINTS

PERSONAL: Born May 18, 1965, in Amite, La. ... 6-1/230.
HIGH SCHOOL: Capitol (Baton Rouge, La.).
COLLEGE: Southern (La.).
TRANSACTIONS/CAREER NOTES: Signed as non-drafted free agent by Seattle Seahawks (May 11, 1988). ... On injured reserve with groin injury (December 5, 1990-remainder of season). ... On injured reserve with Achilles' tendon injury (November 10, 1993-remainder of season). ... Granted unconditional free agency (February 17, 1995). ... Signed by New Orleans Saints (March 10, 1995).
HONORS: Played in Pro Bowl (1988 and 1989 seasons).
PRO STATISTICS: 1988—Recovered one fumble. 1990—Recovered four fumbles for 11 yards. 1991—Intercepted one pass for no yards.

P

1994—Intercepted one pass for 33 yards. 1995—Recovered one fumble for 13 yards.

Year Team	G	SACKS
1988—Seattle NFL	16	0.0
1989—Seattle NFL	16	10.5
1990—Seattle NFL	12	5.0
1991—Seattle NFL	15	10.0
1992—Seattle NFL	16	9.5
1993—Seattle NFL	7	1.0
1994—Seattle NFL	16	1.5
1995—New Orleans NFL	13	3.0
Pro totals (8 years)	111	40.5

POTTS, ROOSEVELT   RB   COLTS

PERSONAL: Born January 8, 1971, in Rayville, La. ... 6-0/260. ... Full name: Roosevelt Bernard Potts. ... Cousin of Reggie Burnette, linebacker, Green Bay Packers and Tampa Bay Buccaneers (1991-1993).
HIGH SCHOOL: Rayville (La.).
COLLEGE: Northeast Louisiana.
TRANSACTIONS/CAREER NOTES: Selected by Indianapolis Colts in second round (49th pick overall) of 1993 NFL draft. ... Signed by Colts (July 20, 1993). ... On injured reserve with knee injury (December 19, 1995-remainder of season). ... Granted free agency (February 16, 1996).
PRO STATISTICS: 1993—Recovered two fumbles. 1994—Recovered one fumble.
STATISTICAL PLATEAUS: 100-yard rushing games: 1993 (2).

Year Team	G	RUSHING				RECEIVING				TOTALS			
		Att.	Yds.	Avg.	TD	No.	Yds.	Avg.	TD	TD	2pt.	Pts.	Fum.
1993—Indianapolis NFL	16	179	711	4.0	0	26	189	7.3	0	0	...	0	8
1994—Indianapolis NFL	16	77	336	4.4	1	26	251	9.7	1	2	0	12	5
1995—Indianapolis NFL	15	65	309	4.8	0	21	228	10.9	1	1	0	6	0
Pro totals (3 years)	47	321	1356	4.2	1	73	668	9.2	2	3	0	18	13

POUNDS, DARRYL   CB   REDSKINS

PERSONAL: Born July 21, 1972, in Fort Worth, Texas. ... 5-10/177.
HIGH SCHOOL: South Pike (Magnolia, Miss.).
COLLEGE: Nicholls State.
TRANSACTIONS/CAREER NOTES: Selected by Washington Redskins in third round (68th pick overall) of 1995 NFL draft. ... Signed by Redskins (May 26, 1995). ... On physically unable to perform list with bulging disks (August 22-October 17, 1995).
PRO STATISTICS: 1995—Fumbled once.

Year Team	G	INTERCEPTIONS			
		No.	Yds.	Avg.	TD
1995—Washington NFL	9	1	26	26.0	0

POWELL, KEITH   DE   BUCCANEERS

PERSONAL: Born June 5, 1969, in Biloxi, Miss. ... 6-3/265.
HIGH SCHOOL: Jersey Village (Houston).
COLLEGE: Texas-El Paso.
TRANSACTIONS/CAREER NOTES: Signed as non-drafted free agent by Dallas Cowboys (May 5, 1991). ... Released by Cowboys (August 20, 1991). ... Signed by British Columbia Lions of CFL (August 31, 1991). ... Traded by Lions with DB Patrick Wayne to Toronto Argonauts for a player to be named later (August 1993). ... Released by Argonauts (November 1993). ... Signed by Cowboys (April 22, 1994). ... Released by Cowboys (August 23, 1994). ... Signed by Tampa Bay Buccaneers to practice squad (August 30, 1994). ... Activated (September 17, 1994). ... On injured reserve with knee injury (November 17, 1995-remainder of season).
PRO STATISTICS: CFL: 1992—Recovered one fumble for three yards. 1993—Recovered one fumble.

Year Team	G	SACKS
1991—British Columbia CFL	9	1.0
1992—British Columbia CFL	14	8.0
1993—British Columbia CFL	4	1.0
—Toronto CFL	6	2.0
1994—Tampa Bay NFL	5	0.0
1995—Tampa Bay NFL	3	1.0
CFL totals (3 years)	33	12.0
NFL totals (2 years)	8	1.0
Pro totals (5 years)	41	13.0

POWELL, CRAIG   LB   RAVENS

PERSONAL: Born November 13, 1971, in Youngstown, Ohio. ... 6-4/230.
HIGH SCHOOL: Rayen (Youngstown, Ohio).
COLLEGE: Ohio State.
TRANSACTIONS/CAREER NOTES: Selected after junior season by Cleveland Browns in first round (30th pick overall) of 1995 NFL draft. ... Signed by Browns (July 31, 1995). ... On injured reserve with knee injury (October 4, 1995-remainder of season). ... Browns franchise moved to Baltimore and renamed Ravens for 1996 season (March 11, 1996).
PLAYING EXPERIENCE: Cleveland NFL, 1995. ... Games: 1995 (3).

P

POWERS, RICKY   RB   RAVENS

PERSONAL: Born November 30, 1970, in Akron, Ohio. ... 6-0/213.
HIGH SCHOOL: Akron (Ohio) Buchtel.
COLLEGE: Michigan.
TRANSACTIONS/CAREER NOTES: Signed by Cleveland Browns as non-drafted free agent (February 14, 1995). ... Released by Browns (August 27, 1995). ... Re-signed by Browns to practice squad (August 30, 1995). ... Released by Browns (September 26, 1995). ... Re-signed by Browns to practice squad (October 13, 1995). ... Activated (December 8, 1995). ... Browns franchise moved to Baltimore and renamed Ravens for 1996 season (March 11, 1996).

		RUSHING				RECEIVING				KICKOFF RETURNS				TOTALS			
Year Team	G	Att.	Yds.	Avg.	TD	No.	Yds.	Avg.	TD	No.	Yds.	Avg.	TD	TD	2pt.	Pts.	Fum.
1995—Cleveland NFL	3	14	51	3.6	0	1	6	6.0	0	3	54	18.0	0	0	0	0	0

PRESIDENT, ANDRE   TE   BEARS

PERSONAL: Born June 16, 1971, in Fort Worth, Texas. ... 6-3/255.
HIGH SCHOOL: Everman (Texas).
JUNIOR COLLEGE: Lamar (Colo.) Community College.
COLLEGE: Angelo State (Texas).
TRANSACTIONS/CAREER NOTES: Signed as non-drafted free agent by New England Patriots (April 24, 1995). ... Released by Patriots (September 28, 1995). ... Re-signed by Patriots to practice squad (October 5, 1995). ... Signed by Chicago Bears off Patriots practice squad (October 19, 1995).
PLAYING EXPERIENCE: New England (1)-Chicago (2) NFL, 1995. ... Games: 1995 (3).

PRESTON, ROELL   WR   FALCONS

PERSONAL: Born June 23, 1972, in Miami. ... 5-10/187. ... Name pronounced ROW-ell.
HIGH SCHOOL: Hialeah (Fla.).
JUNIOR COLLEGE: Northwest Mississippi Community College.
COLLEGE: Mississippi.
TRANSACTIONS/CAREER NOTES: Selected by Atlanta Falcons in fifth round (145th pick overall) of 1995 NFL draft. ... Signed by Falcons (July 13, 1995).

		RECEIVING				KICKOFF RETURNS				TOTALS			
Year Team	G	No.	Yds.	Avg.	TD	No.	Yds.	Avg.	TD	TD	2pt.	Pts.	Fum.
1995—Atlanta NFL	14	7	129	18.4	1	30	627	20.9	0	1	0	6	1

PRICE, JIM   TE

PERSONAL: Born October 2, 1966, in Englewood, N.J. ... 6-4/247.
HIGH SCHOOL: Montville (N.J.).
COLLEGE: Stanford.
TRANSACTIONS/CAREER NOTES: Signed as non-drafted free agent by Los Angeles Rams (May 8, 1990). ... On injured reserve with ham-string injury (September 7-30, 1990). ... Released by Rams (October 1, 1990). ... Re-signed by Rams to practice squad (October 3, 1990). ... Granted free agency after 1990 season. ... Re-signed by Rams (February 9, 1991). ... On injured reserve with broken leg (November 26, 1991-remainder of season). ... Traded by Rams to Dallas Cowboys for undisclosed pick in 1994 draft (October 5, 1993). ... On injured reserve (November 10, 1993-remainder of season). ... Granted unconditional free agency (February 17, 1994). ... Signed by St. Louis Rams (April 28, 1995). ... Granted unconditional free agency (February 16, 1996).
PRO STATISTICS: 1991—Recovered one fumble. 1992—Recovered two fumbles.

		RECEIVING				TOTALS			
Year Team	G	No.	Yds.	Avg.	TD	TD	2pt.	Pts.	Fum.
1990—Los Angeles Rams NFL					Did not play.				
1991—Los Angeles Rams NFL	12	35	410	11.7	2	2	...	12	2
1992—Los Angeles Rams NFL	15	34	324	9.5	2	2	...	12	2
1993—Dallas NFL	3	1	4	4.0	0	0		0	0
1994—					Did not play.				
1995—St. Louis NFL	13	4	29	7.3	0	0	0	0	0
Pro totals (4 years)	43	74	767	10.4	4	4	0	24	4

PRICE, SHAWN   DE   BILLS

PERSONAL: Born March 28, 1970, in Jacksonville. ... 6-5/260. ... Full name: Shawn Sterling Price.
HIGH SCHOOL: North Tahoe (Nev.).
JUNIOR COLLEGE: Sierra College (Calif.).
COLLEGE: Pacific.
TRANSACTIONS/CAREER NOTES: Signed as non-drafted free agent by Tampa Bay Buccaneers (April 29, 1993). ... Released by Buccaneers (August 30, 1993). ... Re-signed by Buccaneers to practice squad (August 31, 1993). ... Activated (November 5, 1993). ... Selected by Carolina Panthers from Buccaneers in NFL expansion draft (February 15, 1995). ... Granted unconditional free agency (February 16, 1996). ... Signed by Buffalo Bills (April 12, 1996).

Year Team	G	SACKS
1993—Tampa Bay NFL	9	3.0
1994—Tampa Bay NFL	6	0.0
1995—Carolina NFL	16	1.0
Pro totals (3 years)	31	4.0

P

PRIMUS, GREG — WR

PERSONAL: Born October 20, 1970, in Denver. ... 5-11/190. ... Name pronounced PREE-mus.
HIGH SCHOOL: George Washington (Denver).
COLLEGE: Colorado State (degree in microbiology).
TRANSACTIONS/CAREER NOTES: Signed as non-drafted free agent by Denver Broncos (April 27, 1993). ... Released by Broncos (August 23, 1993). ... Re-signed by Broncos to practice squad (November 30, 1993). ... Granted free agency after 1993 season. ... Signed by Chicago Bears (April 5, 1994). ... Released by Bears (August 24, 1994). ... Re-signed by Bears to practice squad (August 30, 1994). ... Activated (November 17, 1994). ... Released by Bears (October 19, 1995).
PLAYING EXPERIENCE: Chicago NFL, 1994 and 1995. ... Games: 1994 (3), 1995 (4). Total: 7.
PRO STATISTICS: 1994—Caught three passes for 25 yards. 1995—Returned two kickoffs for 39 yards.

PRIOR, ANTHONY — DB — BENGALS

PERSONAL: Born March 27, 1970, in Mira Loma, Calif. ... 5-11/185.
HIGH SCHOOL: Rubidoux (Riverside, Calif.).
COLLEGE: Washington State.
TRANSACTIONS/CAREER NOTES: Selected by New York Giants in ninth round (238th pick overall) of 1992 NFL draft. ... Signed by Giants (July 21, 1992). ... Released by Giants (August 25, 1992). ... Signed by New York Jets to practice squad (September 9, 1992). ... Released by Jets (September 29, 1992). ... Re-signed by Jets for 1993 season. ... Re-signed by Jets (March 29, 1995). ... Released by Jets (March 1, 1996). ... Signed by Cincinnati Bengals (March 12, 1996).
PRO STATISTICS: 1993—Recovered one fumble.

		KICKOFF RETURNS				TOTALS		
Year—Team	G	No.	Yds.	Avg.	TD	TD	2pt.	Pts.	Fum.
1992—New York Jets NFL					Did not play.				
1993—New York Jets NFL	16	9	126	14.0	0	0	...	0	0
1994—New York Jets NFL	13	16	316	19.8	0	0	0	0	0
1995—New York Jets NFL	11	0	0	...	0	0	0	0	0
Pro totals (3 years)	40	25	442	17.7	0	0	0	0	0

PRIOR, MIKE — S — PACKERS

PERSONAL: Born November 14, 1963, in Chicago Heights, Ill. ... 6-0/208. ... Full name: Michael Robert Prior.
HIGH SCHOOL: Marian Catholic (Chicago Heights, Ill.).
COLLEGE: Illinois State (degree in business administration, 1985).
TRANSACTIONS/CAREER NOTES: Selected by Memphis Showboats in fourth round (60th pick overall) of 1985 USFL draft. ... Selected by Tampa Bay Buccaneers in seventh round (176th pick overall) of 1985 NFL draft. ... Signed by Buccaneers (June 10, 1985). ... On injured reserve with fractured wrist (August 25-September 28, 1986). ... Released by Buccaneers (September 29, 1986). ... Signed by Indianapolis Colts (May 11, 1987). ... Released by Colts (August 31, 1987). ... Re-signed as replacement player by Colts (September 23, 1987). ... On injured reserve with abdomen injury (October 11-December 6, 1991). ... Granted unconditional free agency (March 1, 1993). ... Signed by Green Bay Packers (April 16, 1993). ... Released by Packers (July 27, 1994). ... Re-signed by Packers (July 27, 1994). ... Granted unconditional free agency (February 17, 1995). ... Re-signed by Packers (April 28, 1995).
CHAMPIONSHIP GAME EXPERIENCE: Played in NFC championship game (1995 season).
PRO STATISTICS: 1985—Recovered two fumbles. 1987—Credited with one sack and recovered three fumbles. 1988—Credited with one sack and recovered one fumble for 12 yards. 1989—Recovered one fumble for 10 yards. 1990—Caught one pass for 40 yards and recovered two fumbles for six yards. 1991—Recovered one fumble. 1992—Caught one pass for 17 yards and recovered one fumble. 1993—Recovered two fumbles. 1995—Credited with 1½ sacks and recovered one fumble.
MISCELLANEOUS: Selected by Baltimore Orioles organization in 18th round of free-agent baseball draft (June 4, 1984); did not sign. ... Selected by Los Angeles Dodgers organization in fourth round of free-agent baseball draft (June 3, 1985); did not sign.

		INTERCEPTIONS				PUNT RETURNS				KICKOFF RETURNS				TOTALS		
Year—Team	G	No.	Yds.	Avg.	TD	No.	Yds.	Avg.	TD	No.	Yds.	Avg.	TD	TD	2pt.	Pts.	Fum.
1985—Tampa Bay NFL	16	0	0	...	0	13	105	8.1	0	10	131	13.1	0	0	...	0	4
1986—										Did not play.							
1987—Indianapolis NFL	13	6	57	9.5	0	0	0	...	0	3	47	15.7	0	0	...	0	0
1988—Indianapolis NFL	16	3	46	15.3	0	1	0	0.0	0	0	0	...	0	0	...	0	1
1989—Indianapolis NFL	16	6	88	14.7	1	0	0	...	0	0	0	...	0	1	...	6	0
1990—Indianapolis NFL	16	3	66	22.0	0	2	0	0.0	0	0	0	...	0	0	...	0	1
1991—Indianapolis NFL	9	3	50	16.7	0	0	0	...	0	0	0	...	0	0	...	0	0
1992—Indianapolis NFL	16	6	44	7.3	0	1	7	7.0	0	0	0	...	0	0	...	0	0
1993—Green Bay NFL	16	1	1	1.0	0	17	194	11.4	0	0	0	...	0	0	...	0	3
1994—Green Bay NFL	16	0	0	...	0	8	62	7.8	0	0	0	...	0	0	0	0	3
1995—Green Bay NFL	16	1	9	9.0	0	1	10	10.0	0	0	0	...	0	0	0	0	0
Pro totals (10 years)	150	29	361	12.5	1	43	378	8.8	0	13	178	13.7	0	1	0	6	12

PRITCHARD, MIKE — WR

PERSONAL: Born October 26, 1969, in Shaw A.F.B., S.C. ... 5-10/190. ... Full name: Michael Robert Pritchard.
HIGH SCHOOL: Rancho (North Las Vegas, Nev.).
COLLEGE: Colorado.
TRANSACTIONS/CAREER NOTES: Selected by Atlanta Falcons in first round (13th pick overall) of 1991 NFL draft. ... Signed by Falcons (July 24, 1991). ... Traded by Falcons with seventh-round pick (WR Byron Chamberlain) in 1995 draft to Denver Broncos for first-round pick (traded to Minnesota) in 1995 draft (April 24, 1994). ... On injured reserve with kidney injury (November 2, 1994-remainder of season). ... Released by Broncos (June 3, 1996).
PRO STATISTICS: 1991—Returned one kickoff for 18 yards.
STATISTICAL PLATEAUS: 100-yard receiving games: 1992 (1), 1994 (2). Total: 3.

P

Year	Team	G	RUSHING				RECEIVING				TOTALS			
			Att.	Yds.	Avg.	TD	No.	Yds.	Avg.	TD	2pt.	Pts.	Fum.
1991—Atlanta NFL		16	0	0	...	0	50	624	12.5	2	2	...	12	2
1992—Atlanta NFL		16	5	37	7.4	0	77	827	10.7	5	5	...	30	3
1993—Atlanta NFL		15	2	4	2.0	0	74	736	10.0	7	7	...	42	1
1994—Denver NFL		3	0	0	...	0	19	271	14.3	1	1	0	6	1
1995—Denver NFL		15	6	17	2.8	0	33	441	13.4	3	3	0	18	1
Pro totals (5 years)		65	13	58	4.5	0	253	2899	11.5	18	18	0	108	8

PRITCHETT, KELVIN   DT   JAGUARS

PERSONAL: Born October 24, 1969, in Atlanta. ... 6-3/290. ... Full name: Kelvin Bratodd Pritchett.
HIGH SCHOOL: Therrell (Atlanta).
COLLEGE: Mississippi.
TRANSACTIONS/CAREER NOTES: Selected by Dallas Cowboys in first round (20th pick overall) of 1991 NFL draft. ... Rights traded by Cowboys to Detroit Lions for second-round (LB Dixon Edwards), third-round (G James Richards) and fourth-round (DE Tony Hill) picks in 1991 draft (April 21, 1991). ... Granted free agency (February 17, 1994). ... Re-signed by Lions (August 12, 1994). ... Granted unconditional free agency (February 17, 1995). ... Signed by Jacksonville Jaguars (March 11, 1995).
CHAMPIONSHIP GAME EXPERIENCE: Played in NFC championship game (1991 season).
PRO STATISTICS: 1994—Recovered one fumble.

Year	Team	G	SACKS
1991—Detroit NFL		16	1.5
1992—Detroit NFL		16	6.5
1993—Detroit NFL		16	4.0
1994—Detroit NFL		16	5.5
1995—Jacksonville NFL		16	1.5
Pro totals (5 years)		80	19.0

PROBY, BRYAN   DT   CHIEFS

PERSONAL: Born November 30, 1971, in Compton, Calif. ... 6-5/285. ... Full name: Bryan Craig Proby. ... Name pronounced PRO-bee.
HIGH SCHOOL: Banning (Los Angeles).
JUNIOR COLLEGE: Southwest Community College (Calif.).
COLLEGE: Arizona State.
TRANSACTIONS/CAREER NOTES: Selected by Kansas City Chiefs in sixth round (202nd pick overall) of 1995 NFL draft. ... Signed by Chiefs (June 22, 1995). ... Assigned by Chiefs to Scottish Claymores in 1996 World League enhancement allocation program (February 19, 1996).
PLAYING EXPERIENCE: Kansas City NFL. ... Games: 1995 (3).

PROEHL, RICKY   WR   SEAHAWKS

PERSONAL: Born March 7, 1968, in Belle Mead, N.J. ... 6-0/189. ... Full name: Richard Scott Proehl.
HIGH SCHOOL: Hillsborough (N.J.).
COLLEGE: Wake Forest.
TRANSACTIONS/CAREER NOTES: Selected by Phoenix Cardinals in third round (58th pick overall) of 1990 NFL draft. ... Signed by Cardinals (July 23, 1990). ... Granted free agency (March 1, 1993). ... Tendered offer sheet by New England Patriots (April 13, 1993). ... Offer matched by Cardinals (April 19, 1993). ... Cardinals franchise renamed Arizona Cardinals for 1994 season. ... Traded by Cardinals to Seattle Seahawks for fourth-round pick (traded to New York Jets) in 1995 draft (April 3, 1995).
PRO STATISTICS: 1991—Recovered one fumble. 1992—Had only pass attempt intercepted and fumbled five times. 1993—Fumbled once. 1994—Fumbled twice and recovered two fumbles.
STATISTICAL PLATEAUS: 100-yard receiving games: 1990 (2), 1991 (1), 1992 (3), 1993 (1). Total: 7.

Year	Team	G	RUSHING				RECEIVING				PUNT RETURNS				KICKOFF RETURNS				TOTALS		
			Att.	Yds.	Avg.	TD	No.	Yds.	Avg.	TD	No.	Yds.	Avg.	TD	No.	Yds.	Avg.	TD	TD	2pt.	Pts.
1990—Phoenix NFL		16	1	4	4.0	0	56	802	14.3	4	1	2	2.0	0	4	53	13.3	0	4	...	24
1991—Phoenix NFL		16	3	21	7.0	0	55	766	13.9	2	4	26	6.5	0	0	0	...	0	2	...	12
1992—Phoenix NFL		16	3	23	7.7	0	60	744	12.4	3	0	0	...	0	0	0	...	0	3	...	18
1993—Phoenix NFL		16	8	47	5.9	0	65	877	13.5	7	0	0	...	0	0	0	...	0	7	...	42
1994—Arizona NFL		16	0	0	...	0	51	651	12.8	5	0	0	...	0	0	0	...	0	5	0	30
1995—Seattle NFL		8	0	0	...	0	5	29	5.8	0	0	0	...	0	0	0	...	0	0	0	0
Pro totals (6 years)		88	15	95	6.3	0	292	3869	13.3	21	5	28	5.6	0	4	53	13.3	0	21	0	126

PUPUNU, ALFRED   TE   CHARGERS

PERSONAL: Born October 17, 1969, in Tonga. ... 6-2/265. ... Full name: Alfred Sione Pupunu. ... Name pronounced puh-POO-noo.
HIGH SCHOOL: Salt Lake City South.
JUNIOR COLLEGE: Dixie College (Utah).
COLLEGE: Weber State.
TRANSACTIONS/CAREER NOTES: Signed as non-drafted free agent by Kansas City Chiefs (May 2, 1992). ... Claimed on waivers by San Diego Chargers (September 1, 1992). ... Granted unconditional free agency (February 16, 1996). ... Re-signed by Chargers (February 29, 1996).
CHAMPIONSHIP GAME EXPERIENCE: Played in AFC championship game (1994 season). ... Played in Super Bowl XXIX (1994 season).
POSTSEASON RECORDS: Shares Super Bowl career and single-game records for most two-point conversions—1 (January 29, 1995, vs. San Francisco). ... Shares NFL postseason career and single-game records for most two-point conversions—1 (January 29, 1995, vs. San Francisco).
PRO STATISTICS: 1993—Recovered one fumble.

Year	Team	G	RECEIVING				TOTALS			
			No.	Yds.	Avg.	TD	TD	2pt.	Pts.	Fum.
1992—San Diego NFL		15	0	0	...	0	0	...	0	0

Year Team	G	RECEIVING No.	Yds.	Avg.	TD	TOTALS TD	2pt.	Pts.	Fum.
1993—San Diego NFL	16	13	142	10.9	0	0	...	0	0
1994—San Diego NFL	13	21	214	10.2	2	2	0	12	0
1995—San Diego NFL	15	35	315	9.0	0	0	0	0	1
Pro totals (4 years)	59	69	671	9.7	2	2	0	12	1

PYNE, JIM　　　　　　　C　　　　　　BUCCANEERS

PERSONAL: Born November 23, 1971, in Milford, Mass. ... 6-2/282. ... Son of George Pyne III, tackle, Boston Patriots of AFL (1965); and grandson of George Pyne Jr., tackle, Providence Steamrollers of NFL (1931).
HIGH SCHOOL: Milford (Mass.).
COLLEGE: Virginia Tech.
TRANSACTIONS/CAREER NOTES: Selected by Tampa Bay Buccaneers in seventh round (200th pick overall) of 1994 NFL draft. ... Signed by Buccaneers (July 14, 1994). ... Active for four games; did not play (1994).
PLAYING EXPERIENCE: Tampa Bay NFL, 1995. ... Games: 1995 (15).
HONORS: Named offensive lineman on The Sporting News college All-America first team (1993).
PRO STATISTICS: 1995—Recovered one fumble.

QUERY, JEFF　　　　　　　WR

PERSONAL: Born March 7, 1967, in Decatur, Ill. ... 6-0/165. ... Full name: Jeff Lee Query.
HIGH SCHOOL: Maroa (Ill.)-Forsyth.
COLLEGE: Millikin, Ill. (degree in physical education).
TRANSACTIONS/CAREER NOTES: Selected by Green Bay Packers in fifth round (124th pick overall) of 1989 NFL draft. ... Signed by Packers (July 19, 1989). ... Granted free agency (February 1, 1991). ... Re-signed by Packers (July 15, 1991). ... Granted unconditional free agency (February 1, 1992). ... Signed by Houston Oilers (March 13, 1992). ... Released by Oilers (August 28, 1992). ... Signed by Cincinnati Bengals (September 25, 1992). ... On injured reserve with ankle injury (December 19, 1992-remainder of season). ... Granted free agency (March 1, 1993). ... Re-signed by Bengals (June 22, 1993). ... Released by Bengals (October 10, 1995). ... Signed by Washington Redskins (November 7, 1995). ... Released by Redskins (December 5, 1995). ... Signed by Packers (March 1, 1996). ... Released by Packers (April 1, 1996).
PRO STATISTICS: 1989—Fumbled once and recovered one fumble. 1990—Fumbled three times and recovered three fumbles for one touchdown. 1991—Fumbled once and recovered one fumble. 1993—Fumbled once.

Year Team	G	RUSHING Att.	Yds.	Avg.	TD	RECEIVING No.	Yds.	Avg.	TD	PUNT RETURNS No.	Yds.	Avg.	TD	KICKOFF RETURNS No.	Yds.	Avg.	TD	TOTALS TD	2pt.	Pts.
1989—Green Bay NFL	16	0	0	...	0	23	350	15.2	2	30	247	8.2	0	6	125	20.8	0	2	...	12
1990—Green Bay NFL	16	3	39	13.0	0	34	458	13.5	2	32	308	9.6	0	0	0	...	0	3	...	18
1991—Green Bay NFL	16	0	0	...	0	7	94	13.4	0	14	157	11.2	0	0	0	...	0	0	...	0
1992—Cincinnati NFL	10	1	1	1.0	0	16	265	16.6	3	0	0	...	0	1	13	13.0	0	3	...	18
1993—Cincinnati NFL	16	2	13	6.5	0	56	654	11.7	4	0	0	...	0	0	0	...	0	4	...	24
1994—Cincinnati NFL	10	0	0	...	0	5	44	8.8	0	0	0	...	0	0	0	...	0	0	0	0
1995—Cincinnati NFL	1	0	0	...	0	0	0	...	0	0	0	...	0	0	0	...	0	0	0	0
—Washington NFL	1	0	0	...	0	0	0	...	0	0	0	...	0	0	0	...	0	0	0	0
Pro totals (7 years)	86	6	53	8.8	0	141	1865	13.2	11	76	712	9.4	0	7	138	19.7	0	12	0	72

RADECIC, SCOTT　　　　　　LB

PERSONAL: Born June 14, 1962, in Pittsburgh. ... 6-3/243. ... Full name: J. Scott Radecic. ... Brother of Keith Radecic, center, St. Louis Cardinals (1987). ... Name pronounced RAD-uh-sek.
HIGH SCHOOL: Brentwood (Pittsburgh).
COLLEGE: Penn State.
TRANSACTIONS/CAREER NOTES: Selected by Philadelphia Stars in 1984 USFL territorial draft. ... Selected by Kansas City Chiefs in second round (34th pick overall) of 1984 NFL draft. ... Signed by Chiefs (July 12, 1984). ... Claimed on waivers by Buffalo Bills (September 8, 1987). ... Claimed on waivers by Indianapolis Colts (September 5, 1990). ... Released by Colts (March 30, 1994). ... Re-signed by Colts (July 25, 1994). ... Granted unconditional free agency (February 17, 1995). ... Re-signed by Colts (April 29, 1995). ... Released by Colts (May 29, 1996).
CHAMPIONSHIP GAME EXPERIENCE: Played in AFC championship game (1988 and 1995 seasons).
PRO STATISTICS: 1985—Recovered one fumble. 1986—Recovered one fumble. 1987—Returned one kickoff for 14 yards and recovered two fumbles. 1988—Recovered two fumbles. 1992—Recovered one fumble. 1993—Returned one kickoff for 10 yards. 1994—Returned one kickoff for 17 yards. 1995—Returned one kickoff for minus five yards.

Year Team	G	INTERCEPTIONS No.	Yds.	Avg.	TD	SACKS No.
1984—Kansas City NFL	16	2	54	27.0	1	0.0
1985—Kansas City NFL	16	1	21	21.0	0	3.0
1986—Kansas City NFL	16	1	20	20.0	0	1.0
1987—Buffalo NFL	12	2	4	2.0	0	0.0
1988—Buffalo NFL	16	0	0	...	0	1.5
1989—Buffalo NFL	16	0	0	...	0	1.5
1990—Indianapolis NFL	15	0	0	...	0	0.0
1991—Indianapolis NFL	14	1	26	26.0	0	0.0
1992—Indianapolis NFL	16	1	0	0.0	0	0.0
1993—Indianapolis NFL	16	0	0	...	0	0.0
1994—Indianapolis NFL	16	0	0	...	0	0.0
1995—Indianapolis NFL	13	0	0	...	0	0.0
Pro totals (12 years)	182	8	125	15.6	1	7.0

RANDLE, JOHN   DT   VIKINGS

PERSONAL: Born December 12, 1967, in Hearne, Texas. ... 6-1/277. ... Brother of Ervin Randle, linebacker, Tampa Bay Buccaneers and Kansas City Chiefs (1985-1992).
HIGH SCHOOL: Hearne (Texas).
JUNIOR COLLEGE: Trinity Valley Community College (Texas).
COLLEGE: Texas A&I.
TRANSACTIONS/CAREER NOTES: Signed as non-drafted free agent by Minnesota Vikings (May 4, 1990). ... Designated by Vikings as transition player (January 15, 1994).
HONORS: Played in Pro Bowl (1993-1995 seasons). ... Named defensive tackle on THE SPORTING NEWS NFL All-Pro team (1994 and 1995).
PRO STATISTICS: 1992—Recovered one fumble. 1994—Recovered two fumbles.

Year Team	G	SACKS
1990—Minnesota NFL	16	1.0
1991—Minnesota NFL	16	9.5
1992—Minnesota NFL	16	11.5
1993—Minnesota NFL	16	12.5
1994—Minnesota NFL	16	13.5
1995—Minnesota NFL	16	10.5
Pro totals (6 years)	96	58.5

RANDOLPH, THOMAS   CB   GIANTS

PERSONAL: Born October 5, 1970, in Norfolk, Va. ... 5-9/178.
HIGH SCHOOL: Manhattan (Kan.).
COLLEGE: Kansas State.
TRANSACTIONS/CAREER NOTES: Selected by New York Giants in second round (47th pick overall) of 1994 NFL draft. ... Signed by Giants (July 17, 1994).
PRO STATISTICS: 1995—Recovered one fumble.

Year Team	G	INTERCEPTIONS No.	Yds.	Avg.	TD
1994—New York Giants NFL	16	1	0	0.0	0
1995—New York Giants NFL	16	2	15	7.5	0
Pro totals (2 years)	32	3	15	5.0	0

RASBY, WALTER   TE   PANTHERS

PERSONAL: Born September 7, 1972, in Washington, D.C. ... 6-3/247.
HIGH SCHOOL: Washington (N.C.).
COLLEGE: Wake Forest.
TRANSACTIONS/CAREER NOTES: Signed as non-drafted free agent by Pittsburgh Steelers (April 29, 1994). ... Released by Steelers (August 27, 1995). ... Signed by Carolina Panthers (October 17, 1995).
PLAYING EXPERIENCE: Pittsburgh NFL, 1994; Carolina NFL, 1995. ... Games: 1994 (2), 1995 (9). Total: 11.
CHAMPIONSHIP GAME EXPERIENCE: Played in AFC championship game (1994 season).
PRO STATISTICS: 1995—Credited with one two-point conversion and caught five passes for 47 yards.

RASHEED, KENYON   FB   JETS

PERSONAL: Born August 23, 1970, in Kansas City, Mo. ... 5-10/235. ... Name pronounced ken-YON rah-SHEED.
HIGH SCHOOL: Rockhurst (Kansas City, Mo.).
COLLEGE: Oklahoma.
TRANSACTIONS/CAREER NOTES: Signed as non-drafted free agent by New York Giants (May 1, 1993). ... Released by Giants (August 27, 1995). ... Signed by New York Jets (November 30, 1995).

Year Team	G	RUSHING Att.	Yds.	Avg.	TD	RECEIVING No.	Yds.	Avg.	TD	TOTALS TD	2pt.	Pts.	Fum.
1993—New York Giants NFL	5	9	42	4.7	1	1	3	3.0	0	1	...	6	0
1994—New York Giants NFL	16	17	44	2.6	0	10	97	9.7	0	0	0	0	0
1995—New York Jets NFL	3	1	3	3.0	0	2	15	7.5	0	0	0	0	0
Pro totals (3 years)	24	27	89	3.3	1	13	115	8.9	0	1	0	6	1

RAVOTTI, ERIC   LB   STEELERS

PERSONAL: Born March 16, 1971, in Freeport, Pa. ... 6-3/246. ... Full name: Eric Allen Ravotti.
HIGH SCHOOL: Freeport (Pa.) Area.
COLLEGE: Penn State.
TRANSACTIONS/CAREER NOTES: Selected by Pittsburgh Steelers in sixth round (180th pick overall) of 1994 NFL draft. ... Signed by Steelers (May 6, 1994).
PLAYING EXPERIENCE: Pittsburgh NFL, 1994 and 1995. ... Games: 1994 (2), 1995 (6). Total: 8.
CHAMPIONSHIP GAME EXPERIENCE: Member of Steelers for AFC championship game (1994 and 1995 seasons); inactive.

RAY, TERRY   S   PATRIOTS

PERSONAL: Born October 12, 1969, in Belgium. ... 6-1/205. ... Brother of Darrol Ray, safety, New York Jets (1980-1984).

HIGH SCHOOL: C.E. Ellison (Killeen, Texas).
COLLEGE: Oklahoma.
TRANSACTIONS/CAREER NOTES: Selected by Atlanta Falcons in sixth round (158th pick overall) of 1992 NFL draft. ... Signed by Falcons (July 27, 1993). ... Claimed on waivers by New England Patriots (August 31, 1993). ... Granted free agency (February 17, 1995). ... Re-signed by Patriots (April 21, 1995).
PRO STATISTICS: 1992—Recovered one fumble. 1995—Recovered two fumbles.

		INTERCEPTIONS			
Year Team	G	No.	Yds.	Avg.	TD
1992—Atlanta NFL	10	0	0	...	0
1993—New England NFL	15	1	0	0.0	0
1994—New England NFL	16	1	2	2.0	0
1995—New England NFL	16	1	21	21.0	0
Pro totals (4 years)	57	3	23	7.7	0

RAYMER, CORY   C   REDSKINS

PERSONAL: Born March 3, 1973, in Fond du Lac, Wis. ... 6-2/302.
HIGH SCHOOL: Goodrich (Fond du Lac, Wis.).
COLLEGE: Wisconsin.
TRANSACTIONS/CAREER NOTES: Selected by Washington Redskins in second round (37th pick overall) of 1995 NFL draft. ... Signed by Redskins (July 24, 1995).
PLAYING EXPERIENCE: Washington NFL, 1995. ... Games: 1995 (3).
HONORS: Named offensive lineman on THE SPORTING NEWS college All-America first team (1994).

RAYMOND, COREY   CB

PERSONAL: Born July 28, 1969, in New Iberia, La. ... 5-11/185.
HIGH SCHOOL: New Iberia (La.).
COLLEGE: Louisiana State.
TRANSACTIONS/CAREER NOTES: Signed as non-drafted free agent by New York Giants (May 5, 1992). ... Selected by Jacksonville Jaguars from Giants in NFL expansion draft (February 15, 1995). ... Granted free agency (February 17, 1995). ... Traded by Jaguars to Detroit Lions for TE Ty Hallock (May 30, 1995). ... Granted unconditional free agency (February 16, 1996).
PRO STATISTICS: 1992—Credited with one sack. 1995—Credited with two sacks and recovered one fumble for nine yards.

		INTERCEPTIONS			
Year Team	G	No.	Yds.	Avg.	TD
1992—New York Giants NFL	16	0	0	...	0
1993—New York Giants NFL	16	2	11	5.5	0
1994—New York Giants NFL	16	1	0	0.0	0
1995—Detroit NFL	16	6	44	7.3	0
Pro totals (4 years)	64	9	55	6.1	0

REDMON, ANTHONY   G   CARDINALS

PERSONAL: Born April 9, 1971, in Brewton, Ala. ... 6-4/308. ... Full name: Kendrick Anthony Redmon.
HIGH SCHOOL: T. R. Miller (Brewton, Ala.).
COLLEGE: Auburn.
TRANSACTIONS/CAREER NOTES: Selected by Arizona Cardinals in fifth round (139th pick overall) of 1994 NFL draft. ... Signed by Cardinals (June 13, 1994).
PLAYING EXPERIENCE: Arizona NFL, 1994 and 1995. ... Games: 1994 (6), 1995 (12). Total: 18.

REECE, JOHN   CB   RAMS

PERSONAL: Born January 24, 1971, in Crowell, Texas. ... 6-0/203.
HIGH SCHOOL: Jersey Village (Houston).
COLLEGE: Nebraska.
TRANSACTIONS/CAREER NOTES: Selected by Arizona Cardinals in fourth round (113th pick overall) of 1994 NFL draft. ... Signed by Cardinals (July 29, 1994). ... Claimed on waivers by Indianapolis Colts (August 23, 1994). ... Released by Colts (August 28, 1994). ... Signed by Kansas City Chiefs to practice squad (September 2, 1994). ... Released by Chiefs (November 9, 1994). ... Signed by Los Angeles Raiders to practice squad (November 16, 1994). ... Granted free agency after 1994 season. ... Signed by Chiefs (February 28, 1995). ... Claimed on waivers by St. Louis Rams (July 25, 1995). ... Released by Rams (August 31, 1995). ... Re-signed by Rams (August 30, 1995). ... Released by Rams (November 9, 1995). ... Re-signed by Rams to practice squad (November 10, 1995). ... Activated (December 6, 1995). ... On injured reserve with sprained left knee (December 20, 1995-remainder of season). ... Assigned by Rams to Amsterdam Admirals in 1996 World League enhancement allocation program (February 19, 1996).
PLAYING EXPERIENCE: St. Louis NFL, 1995. ... Games: 1995 (5).

REED, ANDRE   WR   BILLS

PERSONAL: Born January 29, 1964, in Allentown, Pa. ... 6-2/190. ... Full name: Andre Darnell Reed.
HIGH SCHOOL: Louis E. Dieruff (Allentown, Pa.).
COLLEGE: Kutztown (Pa.) State.
TRANSACTIONS/CAREER NOTES: Selected by Orlando Renegades in third round (39th pick overall) of 1985 USFL draft. ... Selected by Buffalo

Bills in fourth round (86th pick overall) of 1985 NFL draft. ... Signed by Bills (July 19, 1985). ... Granted unconditional free agency (February 16, 1996). ... Re-signed by Bills (May 6, 1996).

CHAMPIONSHIP GAME EXPERIENCE: Played in AFC championship game (1988 and 1990-1993 seasons). ... Played in Super Bowl XXV (1990 season), Super Bowl XXVI (1991 season), Super Bowl XXVII (1992 season) and Super Bowl XXVIII (1993 season).

HONORS: Played in Pro Bowl (1988-1990, 1992 and 1994 seasons). ... Member of Pro Bowl squad (1991 season); did not play. ... Named to play in Pro Bowl (1993 season); replaced by Haywood Jeffires due to injury.

POSTSEASON RECORDS: Shares NFL postseason single-game record for most touchdown receptions—3 (January 3, 1993, OT, vs. Houston).

PRO STATISTICS: 1985—Returned five punts for 12 yards and recovered two fumbles. 1986—Recovered two fumbles for two yards. 1990—Recovered one fumble. 1994—Attempted one pass with one completion for 32 yards and recovered two fumbles.

STATISTICAL PLATEAUS: 100-yard receiving games: 1985 (1), 1987 (2), 1988 (3), 1989 (6), 1990 (2), 1991 (4), 1992 (2), 1993 (2), 1994 (5). Total: 27.

MISCELLANEOUS: Holds Buffalo Bills all-time record for most yards receiving (9,848).

R

Year Team	G	RUSHING Att.	Yds.	Avg.	TD	RECEIVING No.	Yds.	Avg.	TD	TOTALS TD	2pt.	Pts.	Fum.
1985—Buffalo NFL	16	3	-1	-.3	1	48	637	13.3	4	5	...	30	1
1986—Buffalo NFL	15	3	-8	-2.7	0	53	739	13.9	7	7	...	42	2
1987—Buffalo NFL	12	1	1	1.0	0	57	752	13.2	5	5	...	30	0
1988—Buffalo NFL	15	6	64	10.7	0	71	968	13.6	6	6	...	36	1
1989—Buffalo NFL	16	2	31	15.5	0	88	1312	14.9	9	9	...	54	4
1990—Buffalo NFL	16	3	23	7.7	0	71	945	13.3	8	8	...	48	1
1991—Buffalo NFL	16	12	136	11.3	0	81	1113	13.7	10	10	...	60	1
1992—Buffalo NFL	16	8	65	8.1	0	65	913	14.1	3	3	...	18	4
1993—Buffalo NFL	15	9	21	2.3	0	52	854	16.4	6	6	...	36	3
1994—Buffalo NFL	16	10	87	8.7	0	90	1303	14.5	8	8	0	48	3
1995—Buffalo NFL	6	7	48	6.9	0	24	312	13.0	3	3	0	18	2
Pro totals (11 years)	159	64	467	7.3	1	700	9848	14.1	69	70	0	420	22

REED, JAKE   WR   VIKINGS

PERSONAL: Born September 28, 1967, in Covington, Ga. ... 6-3/216. ... Brother of Dale Carter, cornerback, Kansas City Chiefs.

HIGH SCHOOL: Newton County (Covington, Ga.).

COLLEGE: Grambling State (degree in criminal justice).

TRANSACTIONS/CAREER NOTES: Selected by Minnesota Vikings in third round (68th pick overall) of 1991 NFL draft. ... Signed by Vikings (July 22, 1991). ... On injured reserve with ankle injury (November 2, 1991-remainder of season). ... Granted free agency (February 17, 1994). ... Re-signed by Vikings (May 6, 1994). ... Granted unconditional free agency (February 17, 1995). ... Re-signed by Vikings (February 28, 1995).

PRO STATISTICS: 1992—Returned one kickoff for one yard. 1995—Recovered one fumble.

STATISTICAL PLATEAUS: 100-yard receiving games: 1994 (3), 1995 (3). Total: 6.

Year Team	G	RECEIVING No.	Yds.	Avg.	TD	TOTALS TD	2pt.	Pts.	Fum.
1991—Minnesota NFL	1	0	0	...	0	0	...	0	0
1992—Minnesota NFL	16	6	142	23.7	0	0	...	0	0
1993—Minnesota NFL	10	5	65	13.0	0	0	...	0	0
1994—Minnesota NFL	16	85	1175	13.8	4	4	0	24	3
1995—Minnesota NFL	16	72	1167	16.2	9	9	0	54	1
Pro totals (5 years)	59	168	2549	15.2	13	13	0	78	4

REED, MICHAEL   CB   PANTHERS

PERSONAL: Born August 16, 1972, in Wilmington, Del. ... 5-9/180. ... Full name: Michael Jerome Reed.

HIGH SCHOOL: Salesianum School (Wilmington, Del.).

COLLEGE: Boston College.

TRANSACTIONS/CAREER NOTES: Selected by Carolina Panthers in seventh round (249th pick overall) of 1995 NFL draft. ... Signed by Panthers (June 6, 1995). ... On injured reserve with knee injury (September 4, 1995-remainder of season).

PLAYING EXPERIENCE: Carolina NFL, 1995. ... Games: 1995 (1).

REEVES, BRYAN   WR/KR   REDSKINS

PERSONAL: Born July 10, 1970, in Los Angeles. ... 5-11/195. ... Brother of Dwayne O'Steen, defensive back, Oakland Raiders (1980 and 1981).

HIGH SCHOOL: Carson (Calif.).

JUNIOR COLLEGE: El Camino Junior College (Calif).

COLLEGE: Arizona State (did not play football), then Nevada.

TRANSACTIONS/CAREER NOTES: Signed as non-drafted free agent by Arizona Cardinals (May 10, 1994). ... Released by Cardinals (October 30, 1995). ... Signed by Washington Redskins (January 30, 1996).

PRO STATISTICS: 1994—Recovered two fumbles.

Year Team	G	RUSHING Att.	Yds.	Avg.	TD	RECEIVING No.	Yds.	Avg.	TD	PUNT RETURNS No.	Yds.	Avg.	TD	KICKOFF RETURNS No.	Yds.	Avg.	TD	TOTALS TD	2pt.	Pts.
1994—Arizona NFL	14	1	-1	-1.0	0	14	202	14.4	1	1	1	1.0	0	3	83	27.7	0	1	0	6
1995—Arizona NFL	5	0	0	...	0	6	62	10.3	0	4	41	10.3	0	0	0	...	0	0	0	0
Pro totals (2 years)	19	1	-1	-1.0	0	20	264	13.2	1	5	42	8.4	0	3	83	27.7	0	1	0	6

REEVES, WALTER   TE   CHARGERS

PERSONAL: Born December 16, 1965, in Eufaula, Ala. ... 6-4/270. ... Full name: Walter James Reeves.
HIGH SCHOOL: Eufaula (Ala.).
COLLEGE: Auburn.
TRANSACTIONS/CAREER NOTES: Selected by Phoenix Cardinals in second round (40th pick overall) of 1989 NFL draft. ... Signed by Cardinals (July 25, 1989). ... Granted unconditional free agency (February 17, 1994). ... Signed by Cleveland Browns (March 20, 1994). ... On injured reserve with back injury (October 10, 1994-remainder of season). ... Released by Browns (November 4, 1995). ... Signed by San Diego Chargers (February 21, 1996).
HONORS: Named tight end on THE SPORTING NEWS college All-America first team (1988).
PRO STATISTICS: 1989—Recovered one fumble for two yards and returned one kickoff for five yards. 1990—Recovered one fumble. 1991— Recovered one fumble. 1992—Recovered two fumbles. 1993—Recovered one fumble.

| | | | RECEIVING | | | | TOTALS | | |
Year Team	G	No.	Yds.	Avg.	TD	TD	2pt.	Pts.	Fum.
1989—Phoenix NFL	16	1	5	5.0	0	0	...	0	0
1990—Phoenix NFL	16	18	126	7.0	0	0	...	0	1
1991—Phoenix NFL	15	8	45	5.6	0	0	...	0	1
1992—Phoenix NFL	16	6	28	4.7	0	0	...	0	0
1993—Phoenix NFL	16	9	67	7.4	1	1	...	6	0
1994—Cleveland NFL	5	6	61	10.2	1	1	0	6	0
1995—Cleveland NFL	5	6	12	2.0	1	1	0	6	0
Pro totals (7 years)	89	54	344	6.4	3	3	0	18	2

REICH, FRANK   QB   JETS

PERSONAL: Born December 4, 1961, in Freeport, N.Y. ... 6-4/210. ... Full name: Frank Michael Reich. ... Name pronounced RIKE.
HIGH SCHOOL: Cedar Crest (Lebanon, Pa.).
COLLEGE: Maryland (degree in finance, 1984).
TRANSACTIONS/CAREER NOTES: Selected by Tampa Bay Bandits in 1985 USFL territorial draft. ... Selected by Buffalo Bills in third round (57th pick overall) of 1985 NFL draft. ... Signed by Bills (August 1, 1985). ... On injured reserve with Achilles' heel injury (September 3-December 6, 1985). ... Active for 12 games with Bills (1987); did not play. ... Granted unconditional free agency (February 17, 1995). ... Signed by Carolina Panthers (March 27, 1995). ... Granted unconditional free agency (February 16, 1996). ... Signed by New York Jets (April 11, 1996).
CHAMPIONSHIP GAME EXPERIENCE: Member of Bills for AFC championship game (1988 season); did not play. ... Played in AFC championship game (1990-1993 seasons). ... Played in Super Bowl XXV (1990 season), Super Bowl XXVI (1991 season), Super Bowl XXVII (1992 season) and Super Bowl XXVIII (1993 season).
POSTSEASON RECORDS: Shares Super Bowl single-game record for most fumbles—3 (January 31, 1993, vs. Dallas).
PRO STATISTICS: 1986—Fumbled once. 1989—Fumbled twice. 1990—Fumbled once. 1992—Fumbled three times and recovered two fumbles for minus four yards. 1994—Fumbled once and recovered one fumble. 1995—Fumbled three times and recovered one fumble.
STATISTICAL PLATEAUS: 300-yard passing games: 1995 (1).
MISCELLANEOUS: Regular-season record as starting NFL quarterback: 4-7 (.364).

| | | PASSING | | | | | | | RUSHING | | | | TOTALS | | |
Year Team	G	Att.	Cmp.	Pct.	Yds.	TD	Int.	Avg.	Rat.	Att.	Yds.	Avg.	TD	TD	2pt.	Pts.
1985—Buffalo NFL	1	1	1	100.0	19	0	0	19.00	118.8	0	0	...	0	0	...	0
1986—Buffalo NFL	3	19	9	47.4	104	0	2	5.47	24.8	1	0	0.0	0	0	...	0
1987—Buffalo NFL							Did not play.									
1988—Buffalo NFL	3	0	0	...	0	0	0	...	...	3	-3	-1.0	0	0	...	0
1989—Buffalo NFL	7	87	53	60.9	701	7	2	8.06	103.7	9	30	3.3	0	0	...	0
1990—Buffalo NFL	16	63	36	57.1	469	2	0	7.45	91.3	15	24	1.6	0	0	...	0
1991—Buffalo NFL	16	41	27	65.9	305	6	2	7.44	107.2	13	6	0.5	0	0	...	0
1992—Buffalo NFL	16	47	24	51.1	221	0	2	4.70	46.5	9	-9	-1.0	0	0	...	0
1993—Buffalo NFL	15	26	16	61.5	153	2	0	5.89	103.5	6	-6	-1.0	0	0	...	0
1994—Buffalo NFL	16	93	56	60.2	568	1	4	6.11	63.4	6	3	0.5	0	0	0	0
1995—Carolina NFL	3	84	37	44.1	441	2	2	5.25	58.7	1	3	3.0	0	0	0	0
Pro totals (10 years)	96	461	259	56.2	2981	20	14	6.47	77.7	63	48	0.8	0	0	0	0

REID, JIM   OT/G   OILERS

PERSONAL: Born February 13, 1971, in Newport News, Va. ... 6-6/306. ... Full name: James Jarrett Reid.
HIGH SCHOOL: Hampton Roads Academy (Newport News, Va.).
COLLEGE: Virginia.
TRANSACTIONS/CAREER NOTES: Selected by Houston Oilers in fifth round (161st pick overall) of 1994 NFL draft. ... Signed by Oilers (June 15, 1994). ... Assigned by Oilers to Amsterdam Admirals in 1995 World League enhancement allocation program (February 20, 1995).
PLAYING EXPERIENCE: Houston NFL, 1995. ... Games: 1995 (6).

RENFRO, LEONARD   DT   REDSKINS

PERSONAL: Born June 29, 1970, in Detroit. ... 6-3/308.
HIGH SCHOOL: St. Mary's Prep (Orchard Lake, Mich.).
COLLEGE: Colorado.
TRANSACTIONS/CAREER NOTES: Selected after junior season by Philadelphia Eagles in first round (24th pick overall) of 1993 NFL draft. ... Signed by Eagles (May 2, 1993). ... Released by Eagles (August 29, 1995). ... Signed by Washington Redskins (March 1, 1996).
PLAYING EXPERIENCE: Philadelphia NFL, 1993 and 1994. ... Games: 1993 (14), 1994 (9). Total: 23.

PERSONAL: Born February 24, 1963, in Bogota, Colombia. ... 5-11/225. Name pronounced fwad ruh-VEZ.
HIGH SCHOOL: Sunset (Miami).
COLLEGE: Tennessee.
TRANSACTIONS/CAREER NOTES: Selected by Memphis Showboats in 1985 USFL territorial draft. ... Selected by Miami Dolphins in seventh round (195th pick overall) of 1985 NFL draft. ... Signed by Dolphins (July 20, 1985). ... On injured reserve with pulled thigh (October 19-November 26, 1988). ... On injured reserve with groin injury (September 4-October 24, 1989). ... Released by Dolphins (October 25, 1989). ... Signed by San Diego Chargers (April 3, 1990). ... Released by Chargers (October 1, 1990). ... Signed by Minnesota Vikings (November 3, 1990). ... Granted unconditional free agency (February 1-April 1, 1991). ... Re-signed by Vikings for 1991 season. ... Granted unconditional free agency (February 1-April 1, 1992). ... Re-signed by Vikings for 1992 season. ... Granted unconditional free agency (February 17, 1994). ... Re-signed by Vikings (May 31, 1994).
CHAMPIONSHIP GAME EXPERIENCE: Played in AFC championship game (1985 season).
HONORS: Played in Pro Bowl (1994 season).
RECORDS: Holds NFL record for most consecutive field goals—30 (October 10, 1994-September 17, 1995).

Year Team	G	XPM	XPA	FGM	FGA	Lg.	50+	Pts.
1985—Miami NFL	16	50	52	22	27	49	0-3	116
1986—Miami NFL	16	*52	55	14	22	52	1-2	94
1987—Miami NFL	11	28	30	9	11	48	0-0	55
1988—Miami NFL	11	31	32	8	12	45	0-2	55
1989—Miami NFL				Did not play—injured.				
1990—San Diego NFL	4	7	8	2	7	42	0-0	13
—Minnesota NFL	9	19	19	11	12	45	0-0	52
1991—Minnesota NFL	16	34	35	17	24	50	2-5	85
1992—Minnesota NFL	16	45	45	19	25	52	3-4	102
1993—Minnesota NFL	16	27	28	26	35	51	1-6	105
1994—Minnesota NFL	16	30	30	*34	*39	51	1-3	132
1995—Minnesota NFL	16	44	44	26	36	51	1-4	122
Pro totals (10 years)	147	367	378	188	250	52	9-29	931

PERSONAL: Born January 19, 1965, in Sacramento. ... 5-11/190. ... Full name: Derrick Scott Reynolds. ... Cousin of Jerry Royster, manager, Las Vegas Stars of San Diego Padres organization; and infielder with five major league teams (1973-1988).
HIGH SCHOOL: Luther Burbank (Sacramento).
COLLEGE: Washington State.
TRANSACTIONS/CAREER NOTES: Selected by Tampa Bay Buccaneers in second round (36th pick overall) of 1987 NFL draft. ... Signed by Buccaneers (July 18, 1987). ... Granted roster exemption (beginning of 1990 season-September 14, 1990). ... Granted free agency (February 1, 1992). ... Re-signed by Buccaneers (August 18, 1992). ... Designated by Buccaneers as transition player (February 25, 1993). ... Free agency status changed by Buccaneers from transitional to unconditional (February 17, 1994). ... Signed by New England Patriots (April 11, 1994).
PRO STATISTICS: 1988—Recovered two fumbles. 1989—Returned blocked punt 33 yards for a touchdown and recovered two fumbles. 1990—Recovered two fumbles. 1992—Recovered two fumbles for 11 yards and one touchdown. 1994—Recovered three fumbles for 25 yards and one touchdown. 1995—Recovered one fumble.

Year Team	G	INTERCEPTIONS No.	Yds.	Avg.	TD	SACKS No.
1987—Tampa Bay NFL	12	0	0	...	0	0.0
1988—Tampa Bay NFL	16	4	7	1.8	0	0.0
1989—Tampa Bay NFL	16	5	87	17.4	1	0.0
1990—Tampa Bay NFL	15	3	70	23.3	0	0.0
1991—Tampa Bay NFL	16	2	7	3.5	0	1.0
1992—Tampa Bay NFL	16	2	0	0.0	0	1.0
1993—Tampa Bay NFL	14	1	3	3.0	0	1.0
1994—New England NFL	15	1	11	11.0	1	2.0
1995—New England NFL	16	3	6	2.0	0	2.5
Pro totals (9 years)	136	21	191	9.1	2	7.5

PERSONAL: Born November 9, 1971, in Ocala, Fla. ... 6-2/212.
HIGH SCHOOL: Vanguard (Ocala, Fla.).
COLLEGE: Minnesota, then Northeast Louisiana (did not play football), then Arkansas-Monticello (did not play football), then Rowan College of New Jersey (did not play football).
TRANSACTIONS/CAREER NOTES: Signed as non-drafted free agent by New Orleans Saints (April 28, 1994). ... On injured reserve with ankle injury (November 9, 1994-remainder of season).
PLAYING EXPERIENCE: New Orleans NFL, 1994 and 1995. ... Games: 1994 (7), 1995 (8). Total: 15.
PRO STATISTICS: 1995—Caught four passes for 50 yards.

PERSONAL: Born December 11, 1970, in Pembroke Pines, Fla. ... 5-11/211. ... Full name: Errict Undra Rhett.
HIGH SCHOOL: McArthur (Hollywood, Fla.).
COLLEGE: Florida (degree in commercial management).

TRANSACTIONS/CAREER NOTES: Selected by Tampa Bay Buccaneers in second round (34th pick overall) of 1994 NFL draft. ... Signed by Buccaneers (August 9, 1994).
HONORS: Named running back on The Sporting News college All-America second team (1993).
PRO STATISTICS: 1994—Recovered one fumble. 1995—Recovered one fumble.
STATISTICAL PLATEAUS: 100-yard rushing games: 1994 (4), 1995 (4). Total: 8.

		RUSHING				RECEIVING				TOTALS			
Year Team	G	Att.	Yds.	Avg.	TD	No.	Yds.	Avg.	TD	TD	2pt.	Pts.	Fum.
1994—Tampa Bay NFL	16	284	1011	3.6	7	22	119	5.4	0	7	1	44	2
1995—Tampa Bay NFL	16	332	1207	3.6	11	14	110	7.9	0	11	0	66	2
Pro totals (2 years)	32	616	2218	3.6	18	36	229	6.4	0	18	1	110	4

RICE, JERRY　　　　　WR　　　　　49ERS

PERSONAL: Born October 13, 1962, in Starkville, Miss. ... 6-2/200. ... Full name: Jerry Lee Rice.
HIGH SCHOOL: B.L. Moor (Crawford, Miss.).
COLLEGE: Mississippi Valley State.
TRANSACTIONS/CAREER NOTES: Selected by Birmingham Stallions in first round (first pick overall) of 1985 USFL draft. ... Selected by San Francisco 49ers in first round (16th pick overall) of 1985 NFL draft. ... Signed by 49ers (July 23, 1985). ... Granted free agency (February 1, 1992). ... Re-signed by 49ers (August 25, 1992).
CHAMPIONSHIP GAME EXPERIENCE: Played in NFC championship game (1988-1990 and 1992-1994 seasons). ... Member of Super Bowl championship team (1988, 1989 and 1994 seasons).
HONORS: Named wide receiver on The Sporting News college All-America first team (1984). ... Named wide receiver on The Sporting News NFL All-Pro team (1986-1995). ... Played in Pro Bowl (1986, 1987, 1989-1993 and 1995 seasons). ... Named NFL Player of the Year by The Sporting News (1987 and 1990). ... Named Most Valuable Player of Super Bowl XXIII (1988 season). ... Named to play in Pro Bowl (1988 season); replaced by J.T. Smith due to injury. ... Named to play in Pro Bowl (1994 season); replaced by Herman Moore due to injury. ... Named Outstanding Player of Pro Bowl (1995 season).
RECORDS: Holds NFL career records for most touchdowns—156; most touchdown receptions—146; most receiving yards—15,123; most pass receptions—942; most seasons with 1,000 or more yards receiving—10; most games with 100 or more yards receiving—58; and most consecutive games with one or more touchdown reception—13 (December 19, 1986-December 27, 1987). ... Holds NFL single-season record for most yards receiving—1,848 (1995); and most touchdown receptions—22 (1987). ... Shares NFL single-game record for most touchdown receptions—5 (October 14, 1990, at Atlanta).
POSTSEASON RECORDS: Holds Super Bowl career records for most points—42; most touchdowns—7; most touchdown receptions—7; most receptions—28; most combined yards—527; and most yards receiving—512. ... Holds Super Bowl single-game records for most touchdowns receptions—3 (January 28, 1990, vs. Denver and January 29, 1995, vs. San Diego); and most yards receiving—215 (January 22, 1989, vs. Cincinnati). ... Shares Super Bowl single-game records for most points—18; most touchdowns—3 (January 28, 1990, vs. Denver and January 29, 1995, vs. San Diego); and most receptions—11 (January 22, 1989, vs. Cincinnati). ... Holds NFL postseason career records for most touchdowns—17; most touchdown receptions—17; most receptions—111; most yards receiving—1,656; and most games with 100 or more yards receiving—7. ... Shares NFL postseason career record for most consecutive games with 100 or more yards receiving—3. ... Shares NFL postseason single-game record for most touchdown receptions—3 (January 28, 1990, vs. Denver; January 1, 1989, vs. Minnesota; and January 29, 1995, vs. San Diego).
PRO STATISTICS: 1985—Returned one kickoff for six yards. 1986—Attempted two passes with one completion for 16 yards and recovered three fumbles. 1987—Recovered one fumble. 1988—Attempted three passes with one completion for 14 yards and one interception and recovered one fumble. 1993—Recovered one fumble. 1995—Recovered one fumble in end zone for a touchdown.
STATISTICAL PLATEAUS: 100-yard receiving games: 1985 (2), 1986 (6), 1987 (4), 1988 (5), 1989 (8), 1990 (7), 1991 (4), 1992 (3), 1993 (5), 1994 (5), 1995 (9). Total: 58.
MISCELLANEOUS: Active NFC leader for career receiving yards (15,123) and touchdowns (156). ... Holds San Francisco 49ers all-time records for most yards receiving (15,123 yards) and most touchdowns (156).

		RUSHING				RECEIVING				TOTALS			
Year Team	G	Att.	Yds.	Avg.	TD	No.	Yds.	Avg.	TD	TD	2pt.	Pts.	Fum.
1985—San Francisco NFL	16	6	26	4.3	1	49	927	18.9	3	4	...	24	1
1986—San Francisco NFL	16	10	72	7.2	1	86	*1570	18.3	*15	16	...	96	2
1987—San Francisco NFL	12	8	51	6.4	1	65	1078	16.6	*22	*23	...	*138	2
1988—San Francisco NFL	16	13	107	8.2	1	64	1306	20.4	9	10	...	60	2
1989—San Francisco NFL	16	5	33	6.6	0	82	*1483	18.1	*17	17	...	102	0
1990—San Francisco NFL	16	2	0	0.0	0	*100	*1502	15.0	*13	13	...	78	1
1991—San Francisco NFL	16	1	2	2.0	0	80	1206	15.1	*14	14	...	84	1
1992—San Francisco NFL	16	9	58	6.4	1	84	1201	14.3	10	11	...	66	2
1993—San Francisco NFL	16	3	69	23.0	1	98	*1503	15.3	*15	*16	...	96	3
1994—San Francisco NFL	16	7	93	13.3	2	112	*1499	13.4	13	15	1	92	1
1995—San Francisco NFL	16	5	36	7.2	1	122	*1848	15.2	15	17	1	104	3
Pro totals (11 years)	172	69	547	7.9	9	942	15123	16.1	146	156	2	940	18

RICHARD, STANLEY　　　　　S　　　　　REDSKINS

PERSONAL: Born October 21, 1967, in Miniola, Texas. ... 6-2/197. ... Full name: Stanley Palmer Richard.
HIGH SCHOOL: Hawkins (Texas).
COLLEGE: Texas.
TRANSACTIONS/CAREER NOTES: Selected by San Diego Chargers in first round (ninth pick overall) of 1991 NFL draft. ... Signed by Chargers (August 5, 1991). ... Granted free agency (February 17, 1994). ... Re-signed by Chargers (May 2, 1994). ... Granted unconditional free agency (February 17, 1995). ... Signed by Washington Redskins (March 10, 1995).
CHAMPIONSHIP GAME EXPERIENCE: Played in AFC championship game (1994 season). ... Played in Super Bowl XXIX (1994 season).
PRO STATISTICS: 1992—Recovered one fumble. 1993—Recovered one fumble. 1995—Recovered one fumble.

		INTERCEPTIONS				SACKS
Year Team	G	No.	Yds.	Avg.	TD	No.
1991—San Diego NFL	15	2	5	2.5	0	0.0

| Year Team | G | INTERCEPTIONS | | | | SACKS |
		No.	Yds.	Avg.	TD	No.
1992—San Diego NFL	14	3	26	8.7	0	0.0
1993—San Diego NFL	16	1	-2	-2.0	0	2.0
1994—San Diego NFL	16	4	224	56.0	2	0.0
1995—Washington NFL	16	3	24	8.0	0	0.0
Pro totals (5 years)	77	13	277	21.3	2	2.0

RICHARDS, DAVE   G   FALCONS

PERSONAL: Born April 11, 1966, in Staten Island, N.Y. ... 6-5/310. ... Full name: David Reed Richards.
HIGH SCHOOL: Highland Park (Dallas).
COLLEGE: Southern Methodist, then UCLA.
TRANSACTIONS/CAREER NOTES: Selected by San Diego Chargers in fourth round (98th pick overall) of 1988 NFL draft. ... Signed by Chargers (July 13, 1988). ... Granted free agency (February 1, 1990). ... Re-signed by Chargers (August 2, 1990). ... Granted free agency (February 1, 1991). ... Re-signed by Chargers (July 30, 1991). ... Granted free agency (February 1, 1992). ... Re-signed by Chargers (July 28, 1992). ... Granted unconditional free agency (March 1, 1993). ... Signed by Detroit Lions (April 6, 1993). ... Released by Lions (July 18, 1994). ... Signed by Atlanta Falcons (August 30, 1994).
PLAYING EXPERIENCE: San Diego NFL, 1988-1992; Detroit NFL, 1993; Atlanta NFL, 1994 and 1995. ... Games: 1988 (16), 1989 (16), 1990 (16), 1991 (16), 1992 (16), 1993 (15), 1994 (15), 1995 (14). Total: 124.
PRO STATISTICS: 1988—Recovered one fumble. 1993—Recovered one fumble. 1994—Recovered one fumble. 1995—Recovered one fumble.

RICHARDSON, BUCKY   QB   CHIEFS

PERSONAL: Born February 7, 1969, in Baton Rouge, La. ... 6-1/228. ... Full name: John Powell Richardson.
HIGH SCHOOL: Broadmoor (Baton Rouge, La.).
COLLEGE: Texas A&M (degree in kinesiology, 1992).
TRANSACTIONS/CAREER NOTES: Selected by Houston Oilers in eighth round (220th pick overall) of 1992 NFL draft.... Signed by Oilers (July 10, 1992).... Released by Oilers (August 1, 1995).... Claimed on waivers by New England Patriots (August 3, 1995).... Released by Patriots (August 19, 1995).... Signed by Dallas Cowboys (August 23, 1995).... Released by Cowboys (August 27, 1995).... Signed by Kansas City Chiefs (March 13, 1996).
PRO STATISTICS: 1994—Fumbled seven times and recovered three fumbles for minus two yards.
MISCELLANEOUS: Regular-season record as starting NFL quarterback: 1-3 (.250).

| Year Team | G | PASSING | | | | | | | | RUSHING | | | | TOTALS | | |
		Att.	Cmp.	Pct.	Yds.	TD	Int.	Avg.	Rat.	Att.	Yds.	Avg.	TD	TD	2pt.	Pts.
1992—Houston NFL	7	0	0	...	0	0	0	...	...	1	-1	-1.0	0	0	...	0
1993—Houston NFL	2	4	3	75.0	55	0	0	13.75	116.7	2	9	4.5	0	0	...	0
1994—Houston NFL	7	181	94	51.9	1202	6	6	6.64	70.3	30	217	7.2	1	1	0	6
1995—								Did not play.								
Pro totals (3 years)	16	185	97	52.4	1257	6	6	6.80	71.4	33	225	6.8	1	1	0	6

RICHARDSON, C.J.   S   CARDINALS

PERSONAL: Born June 10, 1972, in Dallas. ... 5-10/209. ... Full name: Carl Ray Richardson Jr.
HIGH SCHOOL: H. Grady Spruce (Dallas).
COLLEGE: Miami, Fla. (degree in criminal justice).
TRANSACTIONS/CAREER NOTES: Selected by Houston Oilers in seventh round (211th pick overall) of 1995 NFL draft. ... Signed by Oilers (July 10, 1995). ... Released by Oilers (August 27, 1995). ... Re-signed by Oilers (August 30, 1995). ... Signed by Arizona Cardinals off Oilers practice squad (November 8, 1995).
PLAYING EXPERIENCE: Arizona NFL, 1995. ... Games: 1995 (1).
HONORS: Named defensive back on THE SPORTING NEWS college All-America second team (1994).

RICHARDSON, TONY   RB   CHIEFS

PERSONAL: Born December 17, 1971, in Frankfurt, Germany. ... 6-1/232. ... Full name: Antonio Richardson.
HIGH SCHOOL: Daleville (Ala.).
COLLEGE: Auburn.
TRANSACTIONS/CAREER NOTES: Signed as non-drafted free agent by Dallas Cowboys (April 28, 1994). ... Released by Cowboys (August 28, 1994). ... Re-signed by Cowboys to practice squad (August 30, 1994). ... Granted free agency after 1994 season. ... Signed by Kansas City Chiefs (February 28, 1995).
PLAYING EXPERIENCE: Kansas City NFL, 1995. ... Games: 1995 (14).
PRO STATISTICS: 1995—Rushed eight times for 18 yards.

RIDDICK, LOUIS   S   FALCONS

PERSONAL: Born March 15, 1969, in Quakertown, Pa. ... 6-2/215. ... Full name: Louis Angelo Riddick. ... Brother of Robb Riddick, running back, Buffalo Bills (1981, 1983, 1984 and 1986-1988); and cousin of Tim Lewis, defensive back/kick returner, Green Bay Packers (1983-1986).
HIGH SCHOOL: Pennridge (Perkasie, Pa.).
COLLEGE: Pittsburgh (degree in economics, 1991).
TRANSACTIONS/CAREER NOTES: Selected by San Francisco 49ers in ninth round (248th pick overall) of 1991 NFL draft. ... Signed by 49ers (July 11, 1991). ... Released by 49ers (August 20, 1991). ... Selected by Sacramento Surge in 19th round (200th pick overall) of 1992 World League draft. ... Signed by Atlanta Falcons (June 25, 1992). ... Released by Falcons (August 31, 1993). ... Signed by Cleveland Browns (September 8, 1993). ... Granted free agency (February 17, 1995). ... Re-signed by Browns (March 31, 1995). ... Granted unconditional free

agency (February 16, 1996). ... Signed by Falcons (April 11, 1996).
PRO STATISTICS: W.L.: 1992—Intercepted one pass for three yards and recovered one fumble. NFL: 1993—Credited with one safety. 1995—Caught one pass for 25 yards.

Year Team	G	SACKS
1992—Sacramento W.L.	10	1.0
—Atlanta NFL	16	1.0
1993—Cleveland NFL	15	0.0
1994—Cleveland NFL	16	0.0
1995—Cleveland NFL	16	0.0
W.L. totals (1 year)	10	1.0
NFL totals (4 years)	63	1.0
Pro totals (4 years)	73	2.0

RIESENBERG, DOUG　　　　OT

PERSONAL: Born July 22, 1965, in Moscow, Idaho. ... 6-5/288.
HIGH SCHOOL: Moscow (Idaho).
COLLEGE: California.
TRANSACTIONS/CAREER NOTES: Selected by New York Giants in sixth round (168th pick overall) of 1987 NFL draft. ... Signed by Giants (July 27, 1987). ... Granted free agency (February 1, 1992). ... Re-signed by Giants (July 21, 1992). ... Granted unconditional free agency (February 17, 1994). ... Re-signed by Giants (April 5, 1994). ... Released by Giants (June 7, 1996).
PLAYING EXPERIENCE: New York Giants NFL, 1987-1995. ... Games: 1987 (8), 1988 (16), 1989 (16), 1990 (16), 1991 (15), 1992 (16), 1993 (16), 1994 (16), 1995 (16). Total: 135.
CHAMPIONSHIP GAME EXPERIENCE: Played in NFC championship game (1990 season). ... Member of Super Bowl championship team (1990 season).
PRO STATISTICS: 1988—Recovered one fumble. 1989—Recovered two fumbles. 1992—Recovered two fumbles. 1994—Recovered one fumble. 1995—Recovered one fumble.

RILEY, PATRICK　　　　DE　　　　BEARS

PERSONAL: Born March 8, 1972, in Marrero, La. ... 6-5/286.
HIGH SCHOOL: Archbishop Shaw (Marrero, La.).
COLLEGE: Miami (Fla.).
TRANSACTIONS/CAREER NOTES: Selected by Chicago Bears in second round (52nd pick overall) of 1995 NFL draft. ... Signed by Bears (July 21, 1995).
PLAYING EXPERIENCE: Chicago NFL, 1995. ... Games: 1995 (1).

RISON, ANDRE　　　　WR　　　　RAVENS

PERSONAL: Born March 18, 1967, in Flint, Mich. ... 6-1/188. ... Full name: Andre Previn Rison. ... Name pronounced RYE-zun.
HIGH SCHOOL: Northwestern (Flint, Mich.).
COLLEGE: Michigan State.
TRANSACTIONS/CAREER NOTES: Selected by Indianapolis Colts in first round (22nd pick overall) of 1989 NFL draft. ... Signed by Colts (May 2, 1989). ... Traded by Colts with OT Chris Hinton, fifth-round pick (OT Reggie Redding) in 1990 draft and first-round pick (WR Mike Pritchard) in 1991 draft to Atlanta Falcons for first-round (QB Jeff George) and fourth-round (WR Stacey Simmons) picks in 1990 draft (April 20, 1990). ... Granted roster exemption for one game (September 1992). ... Designated by Falcons as transition player (February 25, 1993). ... On reserve/did not report list (July 23-August 20, 1993). ... Granted roster exemption (August 20-26, 1993). ... On suspended list (November 21-22, 1994). ... Free agency status changed by Falcons from transitional to unconditional (February 17, 1995). ... Signed by Cleveland Browns (March 24, 1995). ... Browns franchise moved to Baltimore and renamed Ravens for 1996 season (March 11, 1996).
HONORS: Named wide receiver on THE SPORTING NEWS NFL All-Pro team (1990). ... Played in Pro Bowl (1990-1993 seasons). ... Named Outstanding Player of Pro Bowl (1993 season).
PRO STATISTICS: 1989—Rushed three times for 18 yards and returned two punts for 20 yards. 1990—Returned two punts for 10 yards. 1991—Rushed once for minus nine yards. 1995—Rushed twice for no yards and recovered one fumble.
STATISTICAL PLATEAUS: 100-yard receiving games: 1989 (3), 1990 (5), 1991 (1), 1992 (2), 1993 (4), 1994 (3), 1995 (2). Total: 20.
MISCELLANEOUS: Holds Atlanta Falcons all-time record for most touchdowns (56).

		RECEIVING				KICKOFF RETURNS				TOTALS			
Year Team	G	No.	Yds.	Avg.	TD	No.	Yds.	Avg.	TD	TD	2pt.	Pts.	Fum.
1989—Indianapolis NFL	16	52	820	15.8	4	8	150	18.8	0	4	...	24	1
1990—Atlanta NFL	16	82	1208	14.7	10	0	0	...	0	10	...	60	2
1991—Atlanta NFL	16	81	976	12.1	12	0	0	...	0	12	...	72	1
1992—Atlanta NFL	15	93	1119	12.0	11	0	0	...	0	11	...	66	2
1993—Atlanta NFL	16	86	1242	14.4	*15	0	0	...	0	15	...	90	2
1994—Atlanta NFL	15	81	1088	13.4	8	0	0	...	0	8	1	50	1
1995—Cleveland NFL	16	47	701	14.9	3	0	0	...	0	3	0	18	1
Pro totals (7 years)	110	522	7154	13.7	63	8	150	18.8	0	63	1	380	10

RITCHER, JIM　　　　G

PERSONAL: Born May 21, 1958, in Hinckley, Ohio. ... 6-3/273. ... Full name: James Alexander Ritcher. ... Name pronounced RICH-er.
HIGH SCHOOL: Highland (Granger, Ohio).
COLLEGE: North Carolina State (degree in sociology).
TRANSACTIONS/CAREER NOTES: Selected by Buffalo Bills in first round (16th pick overall) of 1980 NFL draft. ... Granted unconditional free agency (February 17, 1994). ... Signed by Atlanta Falcons (August 10, 1994). ... Granted unconditional free agency (February 17, 1995). ... Re-signed by Falcons (August 21, 1995). ... Granted unconditional free agency (February 16, 1996).
PLAYING EXPERIENCE: Buffalo NFL, 1980-1993; Atlanta NFL, 1994 and 1995. ... Games: 1980 (14), 1981 (14), 1982 (9), 1983 (16), 1984

(14), 1985 (16), 1986 (16), 1987 (12), 1988 (16), 1989 (16), 1990 (16), 1991 (16), 1992 (16), 1993 (12), 1994 (2), 1995 (13). Total: 218.
CHAMPIONSHIP GAME EXPERIENCE: Played in AFC championship game (1988 and 1990-1993 seasons). ... Played in Super Bowl XXV (1990 season), Super Bowl XXVI (1991 season), Super Bowl XXVII (1992 season), and Super Bowl XXVIII (1993 season).
HONORS: Outland Trophy winner (1979). ... Named center on THE SPORTING NEWS college All-America first team (1979). ... Played in Pro Bowl (1991 and 1992 seasons).
PRO STATISTICS: 1986—Recovered one fumble. 1990—Recovered one fumble. 1992—Recovered one fumble.

RIVERS, REGGIE — RB — BRONCOS

PERSONAL: Born February 22, 1968, in Dayton, Ohio. ... 6-1/215.
HIGH SCHOOL: Randolph (Universal City, Texas).
COLLEGE: Southwest Texas State (degree in journalism, 1991).
TRANSACTIONS/CAREER NOTES: Signed as non-drafted free agent by Denver Broncos (April 26, 1991). ... Granted unconditional free agency (February 1-April 1, 1992). ... Re-signed by Broncos for 1992 season. ... Granted unconditional free agency (February 17, 1995). ... Re-signed by Broncos (March 31, 1995).
CHAMPIONSHIP GAME EXPERIENCE: Played in AFC championship game (1991 season).
PRO STATISTICS: 1992—Recovered one fumble. 1993—Credited with one safety and recovered one fumble. 1994—Attempted one pass without a completion and recovered one fumble.

		RUSHING				RECEIVING				TOTALS			
Year Team	G	Att.	Yds.	Avg.	TD	No.	Yds.	Avg.	TD	TD	2pt.	Pts.	Fum.
1991—Denver NFL	16	2	5	2.5	0	0	0	...	0	0	...	0	0
1992—Denver NFL	16	74	282	3.8	3	45	449	10.0	1	4	...	24	2
1993—Denver NFL	16	15	50	3.3	1	6	59	9.8	1	2	...	14	0
1994—Denver NFL	16	43	83	1.9	2	20	136	6.8	0	2	0	12	1
1995—Denver NFL	16	2	2	1.0	0	3	32	10.7	0	0	0	0	0
Pro totals (5 years)	80	136	422	3.1	6	74	676	9.1	2	8	0	50	3

RIVERS, RON — RB — LIONS

PERSONAL: Born November 13, 1971, in Elizabeth, N.J. ... 5-8/205. ... Full name: Ronald Leroy Rivers.
HIGH SCHOOL: San Gorgonio (San Bernardino, Calif.).
COLLEGE: Fresno State.
TRANSACTIONS/CAREER NOTES: Signed as non-drafted free agent by San Diego Chargers (May 2, 1994). ... Released by Chargers (August 29, 1994). ... Signed by Detroit Lions to practice squad (September 21, 1994). ... Activated (December 22, 1994); did not play.
POSTSEASON RECORDS: Shares NFL postseason career and single-game records for most two-point conversions—1. (December 30, 1995, vs. Philadelphia).
PLAYING EXPERIENCE: Detroit NFL, 1995. ... Games: 1995 (16).
PRO STATISTICS: 1995—Caught one pass for five yards, fumbled twice and recovered one fumble.

		RUSHING				RECEIVING				KICKOFF RETURNS				TOTALS		
Year Team	G	Att.	Yds.	Avg.	TD	No.	Yds.	Avg.	TD	No.	Yds.	Avg.	TD	TD	2pt.	Pts.	Fum.
1995—Detroit NFL	16	18	73	4.1	1	1	5	5.0	0	19	420	22.1	0	1	0	6	2

ROAF, WILLIE — OT — SAINTS

PERSONAL: Born April 18, 1970, in Pine Bluff, Ark. ... 6-5/300. ... Full name: William Layton Roaf.
HIGH SCHOOL: Pine Bluff (Ark.).
COLLEGE: Louisiana Tech.
TRANSACTIONS/CAREER NOTES: Selected by New Orleans Saints in first round (eighth pick overall) of 1993 NFL draft. ... Signed by Saints (July 15, 1993). ... Designated by Saints as transition player (February 15, 1994).
PLAYING EXPERIENCE: New Orleans NFL, 1993-1995. ... Games: 1993 (16), 1994 (16), 1995 (16). Total: 48.
HONORS: Named offensive tackle on THE SPORTING NEWS college All-America second team (1992). ... Named offensive tackle on THE SPORTING NEWS NFL All-Pro team (1994 and 1995). ... Played in Pro Bowl (1994 and 1995 seasons).
PRO STATISTICS: 1994—Recovered one fumble.

ROAN, MICHAEL — TE — OILERS

PERSONAL: Born August 29, 1972, in Iowa City, Iowa. ... 6-3/251.
HIGH SCHOOL: Iowa City (Iowa).
COLLEGE: Wisconsin.
TRANSACTIONS/CAREER NOTES: Selected by Houston Oilers in fourth round (101st pick overall) of 1995 NFL draft. ... Signed by Oilers (July 10, 1995).
PLAYING EXPERIENCE: Houston NFL, 1995. ... Games: 1995 (5).
PRO STATISTICS: 1995—Caught eight passes for 46 yards, fumbled once and recovered one fumble.

ROBBINS, AUSTIN — DT — RAIDERS

PERSONAL: Born March 1, 1971, in Washington, D.C. ... 6-6/290. ... Full name: Austin Dion Robbins.
HIGH SCHOOL: Howard D. Woodson (Washington D.C.).
COLLEGE: North Carolina.
TRANSACTIONS/CAREER NOTES: Selected by Los Angeles Raiders in fourth round (120th pick overall) of 1994 NFL draft. ... Signed by Raiders (July 14, 1994). ... Raiders franchise moved to Oakland (July 21, 1995).
PLAYING EXPERIENCE: Los Angeles Raiders NFL, 1994; Oakland NFL, 1995. ... Games: 1994 (2), 1995 (16). Total: 18.

ROBBINS, BARRET   C   RAIDERS

PERSONAL: Born August 26, 1973, in Houston. ... 6-3/310.
HIGH SCHOOL: Sharpstown (Houston).
COLLEGE: Texas Christian.
TRANSACTIONS/CAREER NOTES: Selected by Los Angeles Raiders in second round (49th pick overall) of 1995 NFL draft. ... Signed by Raiders (June 20, 1995). ... Raiders franchise moved to Oakland (July 21, 1995).
PLAYING EXPERIENCE: Oakland NFL, 1995. ... Games: 1995 (16).

ROBERTS, RAY   OT   LIONS

R

PERSONAL: Born June 3, 1969, in Asheville, N.C. ... 6-6/308. ... Full name: Richard Ray Roberts Jr.
HIGH SCHOOL: Asheville (N.C.).
COLLEGE: Virginia (degree in communication studies, 1991).
TRANSACTIONS/CAREER NOTES: Selected by Seattle Seahawks in first round (10th pick overall) of 1992 NFL draft. ... Signed by Seahawks (August 1, 1992). ... Designated by Seahawks as transition player (February 15, 1994). ... On injured reserve with ankle/leg injury (December 11, 1994-remainder of season). ... Free agency status changed by Seahawks from transitional to unconditional (February 16, 1996). ... Signed by Detroit Lions (March 11, 1996).
PLAYING EXPERIENCE: Seattle NFL, 1992-1995. ... Games: 1992 (16), 1993 (16), 1994 (14), 1995 (11). Total: 57.
HONORS: Named offensive tackle on THE SPORTING NEWS college All-America second team (1991).
PRO STATISTICS: 1993—Caught one pass for four yards.

ROBERTS, TIM   DE

PERSONAL: Born April 14, 1969, in Atlanta. ... 6-6/318.
HIGH SCHOOL: Therrell (Atlanta).
COLLEGE: Southern Mississippi (degree in criminal justice, 1992).
TRANSACTIONS/CAREER NOTES: Selected by Houston Oilers in fifth round (136th pick overall) of 1992 NFL draft. ... Signed by Oilers (July 20, 1992). ... Granted free agency (February 17, 1995). ... Signed by New England Patriots (March 6, 1995). ... Granted unconditional free agency (February 16, 1996).
PLAYING EXPERIENCE: Houston NFL, 1992-1994; New England NFL, 1995. ... Games: 1992 (6), 1993 (6), 1994 (12), 1995 (13). Total: 37.
PRO STATISTICS: 1995—Credited with one sack.

ROBERTS, WILLIAM   G   PATRIOTS

PERSONAL: Born August 5, 1962, in Miami. ... 6-5/298. ... Full name: William Harold Roberts. ... Cousin of Reggie Sandilands, wide receiver, Memphis Showboats of USFL (1984).
HIGH SCHOOL: Carol City (Miami).
COLLEGE: Ohio State.
TRANSACTIONS/CAREER NOTES: Selected by New Jersey Generals in 1984 USFL territorial draft. ... Selected by New York Giants in first round (27th pick overall) of 1984 NFL draft. ... Signed by Giants (June 4, 1984). ... On injured reserve with knee injury (July 20, 1985-entire season). ... Granted free agency (February 1, 1991). ... Re-signed by Giants (August 29, 1991). ... Activated (September 2, 1991). ... Granted unconditional free agency (February 17, 1994). ... Re-signed by Giants (July 17, 1994). ... Released by Giants (May 17, 1995). ... Signed by New England Patriots (July 23, 1995). ... Granted unconditional free agency (February 16, 1996). ... Re-signed by Patriots (February 27, 1996).
PLAYING EXPERIENCE: New York Giants NFL, 1984 and 1986-1994; New England NFL, 1995. ... Games: 1984 (11), 1986 (16), 1987 (12), 1988 (16), 1989 (16), 1990 (16), 1991 (16), 1992 (16), 1993 (16), 1994 (16), 1995 (16). Total: 167.
CHAMPIONSHIP GAME EXPERIENCE: Played in NFC championship game (1986 and 1990 seasons). ... Member of Super Bowl championship team (1986 and 1990 seasons).
HONORS: Played in Pro Bowl (1990 season).
PRO STATISTICS: 1984—Recovered one fumble. 1988—Recovered two fumbles. 1993—Recovered one fumble.

ROBERTSON, MARCUS   S   OILERS

PERSONAL: Born October 2, 1969, in Pasadena, Calif. ... 5-11/197. ... Full name: Marcus Aaron Robertson.
HIGH SCHOOL: John Muir (Pasadena, Calif.).
COLLEGE: Iowa State.
TRANSACTIONS/CAREER NOTES: Selected by Houston Oilers in fourth round (102nd pick overall) of 1991 NFL draft. ... Signed by Oilers (July 16, 1991). ... On injured reserve with knee injury (December 30, 1993-remainder of season). ... Granted free agency (February 17, 1994). ... Re-signed by Oilers (July 11, 1994). ... On injured reserve with knee injury (November 30, 1995-remainder of season).
HONORS: Named free safety on THE SPORTING NEWS NFL All-Pro team (1993).
PRO STATISTICS: 1991—Credited with one sack, returned one punt for no yards and fumbled once. 1993—Recovered three fumbles for 107 yards and one touchdown. 1994—Returned one punt for no yards, fumbled once and recovered one fumble.

| | | INTERCEPTIONS | | | |
Year—Team	G	No.	Yds.	Avg.	TD
1991—Houston NFL	16	0	0	...	0
1992—Houston NFL	16	1	27	27.0	0
1993—Houston NFL	13	7	137	19.6	0
1994—Houston NFL	16	3	90	30.0	0
1995—Houston NFL	2	0	0	...	0
Pro totals (5 years)	63	10	227	22.7	0

ROBINSON, EDDIE — LB — JAGUARS

PERSONAL: Born April 13, 1970, in New Orleans. ... 6-1/245. ... Full name: Eddie Joseph Robinson.
HIGH SCHOOL: Brother Martin (New Orleans).
COLLEGE: Alabama State.
TRANSACTIONS/CAREER NOTES: Selected by Houston Oilers in second round (50th pick overall) of 1992 NFL draft. ... Signed by Oilers (July 16, 1992). ... Granted free agency (February 17, 1995). ... Re-signed by Oilers (July 1995). ... Granted unconditional free agency (February 16, 1996). ... Signed by Jacksonville Jaguars (March 1, 1996).
PRO STATISTICS: 1995—Intercepted one pass for 49 yards and a touchdown and recovered one fumble.

Year Team	G	SACKS
1992—Houston NFL	16	1.0
1993—Houston NFL	16	1.0
1994—Houston NFL	15	0.0
1995—Houston NFL	16	3.5
Pro totals (4 years)	63	5.5

ROBINSON, EUGENE — S — SEAHAWKS

PERSONAL: Born May 28, 1963, in Hartford, Conn. ... 6-0/195.
HIGH SCHOOL: Weaver (Hartford, Conn.).
COLLEGE: Colgate.
TRANSACTIONS/CAREER NOTES: Selected by New Jersey Generals in 1985 USFL territorial draft. ... Signed as non-drafted free agent by Seattle Seahawks (May 15, 1985). ... On injured reserve with Achilles' tendon injury (December 11, 1994-remainder of season).
HONORS: Played in Pro Bowl (1992 and 1993 seasons).
PRO STATISTICS: 1985—Returned one kickoff for 10 yards. 1986—Recovered three fumbles for six yards. 1987—Returned blocked punt eight yards for a touchdown and recovered one fumble. 1989—Fumbled once and recovered one fumble. 1990—Recovered four fumbles for 16 yards and a touchdown. 1991—Recovered one fumble. 1992—Recovered one fumble. 1993—Recovered two fumbles for seven yards. 1994—Recovered one fumble. 1995—Returned one punt for one yard and recovered one fumble.
MISCELLANEOUS: Active NFL and AFC leader for career interceptions (42).

Year Team	G	INTERCEPTIONS No.	Yds.	Avg.	TD	SACKS No.
1985—Seattle NFL	16	2	47	23.5	0	0.0
1986—Seattle NFL	16	3	39	13.0	0	0.0
1987—Seattle NFL	12	3	75	25.0	0	0.0
1988—Seattle NFL	16	1	0	0.0	0	1.0
1989—Seattle NFL	16	5	24	4.8	0	0.0
1990—Seattle NFL	16	3	89	29.7	0	0.0
1991—Seattle NFL	16	5	56	11.2	0	1.0
1992—Seattle NFL	16	7	126	18.0	0	0.0
1993—Seattle NFL	16	*9	80	8.9	0	2.0
1994—Seattle NFL	14	3	18	6.0	0	1.0
1995—Seattle NFL	16	1	32	32.0	0	0.0
Pro totals (11 years)	170	42	586	14.0	0	5.0

ROBINSON, GREG — RB — RAMS

PERSONAL: Born August 7, 1969, in Grenada, Miss. ... 5-10/205.
HIGH SCHOOL: Grenada (Miss.).
JUNIOR COLLEGE: Holmes (Miss.) Community College.
COLLEGE: Northeast Louisiana.
TRANSACTIONS/CAREER NOTES: Selected by Los Angeles Raiders in eighth round (208th pick overall) of 1993 NFL draft. ... Signed by Raiders (July 13, 1993). ... On injured reserve with knee injury (August 22, 1994-entire season). ... Traded by Raiders to Green Bay Packers for undisclosed draft pick (August 21, 1995); trade voided when Robinson failed physical. ... Released by Raiders (August 22, 1995). ... Signed by St. Louis Rams (November 1, 1995). ... Granted free agency (February 16, 1996).
PRO STATISTICS: 1993—Recovered one fumble.

Year Team	G	RUSHING Att.	Yds.	Avg.	TD	RECEIVING No.	Yds.	Avg.	TD	KICKOFF RETURNS No.	Yds.	Avg.	TD	TOTALS TD	2pt.	Pts.	Fum.
1993—Los Angeles Raiders NFL....	12	156	591	3.8	1	15	142	9.5	0	4	57	14.3	0	1	...	6	3
1994—Los Angeles Raiders NFL....							Did not play—injured.										
1995—St. Louis NFL	5	40	165	4.1	0	2	12	6.0	0	0	0	...	0	0	0	0	0
Pro totals (2 years)	17	196	756	3.9	1	17	154	9.1	0	4	57	14.3	0	1	0	6	3

ROBINSON, JEFF — DE — BRONCOS

PERSONAL: Born February 20, 1970, in Kennewick, Wash. ... 6-4/265.
HIGH SCHOOL: Joel E. Ferris (Spokane, Wash.).
COLLEGE: Idaho.
TRANSACTIONS/CAREER NOTES: Selected by Denver Broncos in fourth round (98th pick overall) of 1993 NFL draft. ... Signed by Broncos (July 13, 1993). ... Granted free agency (February 16, 1996).
PRO STATISTICS: 1993—Recovered one fumble for minus 10 yards. 1995—Returned one kickoff for 14 yards and recovered one fumble.

Year Team	G	SACKS
1993—Denver NFL	16	3.5
1994—Denver NFL	16	1.0
1995—Denver NFL	16	1.0
Pro totals (3 years)	48	5.5

ROBINSON, RAFAEL　　　　　　S　　　　　　OILERS

PERSONAL: Born June 19, 1969, in Marshall, Texas. ... 5-11/200. ... Full name: Eugene Rafael Robinson.
HIGH SCHOOL: Jefferson (Texas).
COLLEGE: Wisconsin.
TRANSACTIONS/CAREER NOTES: Signed as non-drafted free agent by Seattle Seahawks (May 1, 1992). ... Released by Seahawks (August 31, 1992). ... Signed by Seahawks to practice squad (September 2, 1992). ... Activated (September 26, 1992). ... Released by Seahawks (October 5, 1992). ... Re-signed by Seahawks to practice squad (October 6, 1992). ... Activated (October 14, 1992). ... Released by Seahawks (October 24, 1992). ... Re-signed by Seahawks to practice squad (October 26, 1992). ... Activated (December 9, 1992). ... Granted free agency (February 17, 1995). ... Re-signed by Seahawks (April 24, 1995). ... Granted unconditional free agency (February 16, 1996). ... Signed by Houston Oilers (March 26, 1996).
PLAYING EXPERIENCE: Seattle NFL, 1992-1995. ... Games: 1992 (6), 1993 (16), 1994 (16), 1995 (13). Total: 51.
PRO STATISTICS: 1993—Credited with 1½ sacks and recovered one fumble. 1994—Intercepted one pass for no yards and recovered one fumble.

R

ROBY, REGGIE　　　　　　P　　　　　　OILERS

PERSONAL: Born July 30, 1961, in Waterloo, Iowa. ... 6-2/253. ... Full name: Reginald Henry Roby. ... Brother of Mike Roby, first baseman/outfielder, San Francisco Giants organization (1967 and 1968).
HIGH SCHOOL: East (Waterloo, Iowa).
COLLEGE: Iowa.
TRANSACTIONS/CAREER NOTES: Selected by Chicago Blitz in 16th round (187th pick overall) of 1983 USFL draft. ... Selected by Miami Dolphins in sixth round (167th pick overall) of 1983 NFL draft. ... Signed by Dolphins (July 9, 1983). ... On injured reserve with knee, ankle and groin injuries (September 16-October 31, 1987). ... Crossed picket line during players strike (October 14, 1987). ... On injured reserve with knee injury (September 18-November 4, 1987). ... Released by Dolphins (August 30, 1993). ... Signed by Washington Redskins (September 7, 1993). ... Granted unconditional free agency (February 17, 1995). ... Signed by Tampa Bay Buccaneers (February 20, 1995). ... Released by Buccaneers (May 13, 1996). ... Signed by Houston Oilers (June 1, 1996).
CHAMPIONSHIP GAME EXPERIENCE: Played in AFC championship game (1984, 1985 and 1992 seasons). ... Played in Super Bowl XIX (1984 season).
HONORS: Named punter on THE SPORTING NEWS NFL All-Pro team (1984 and 1994). ... Played in Pro Bowl (1984, 1989 and 1994 seasons).
PRO STATISTICS: 1986—Rushed twice for minus eight yards, fumbled twice and recovered two fumbles for minus 11 yards. 1987—Rushed once for no yards and recovered one fumble. 1989—Rushed twice for no yards and recovered two fumbles. 1993—Rushed once for no yards and recovered one fumble. 1994—Fumbled once and recovered one fumble. 1995—Rushed once for no yards, attempted one pass with one completion for 48 yards.

| | | | | PUNTING | | | |
Year　Team	G	No.	Yds.	Avg.	Net avg.	In. 20	Blk.
1983—Miami NFL	16	74	3189	43.1	36.5	26	1
1984—Miami NFL	16	51	2281	44.7	*38.1	15	0
1985—Miami NFL	16	59	2576	43.7	34.7	19	0
1986—Miami NFL	15	56	2476	44.2	*37.4	13	0
1987—Miami NFL	10	32	1371	42.8	38.3	8	0
1988—Miami NFL	15	64	2754	43.0	35.3	18	0
1989—Miami NFL	16	58	2458	42.4	35.3	18	1
1990—Miami NFL	16	72	3022	42.0	35.6	20	0
1991—Miami NFL	16	54	2466	*45.7	36.4	17	1
1992—Miami NFL	9	35	1443	41.2	34.3	11	0
1993—Washington NFL	15	78	3447	44.2	37.2	25	0
1994—Washington NFL	16	82	3639	44.4	36.1	21	0
1995—Tampa Bay NFL	16	77	3296	42.8	36.2	23	1
Pro totals (13 years)	192	792	34418	43.5	36.2	234	4

RODENHAUSER, MARK　　　　　　C　　　　　　PANTHERS

PERSONAL: Born June 1, 1961, in Elmhurst, Ill. ... 6-5/280. ... Full name: Mark Todd Rodenhauser. ... Name pronounced RO-den-howser.
HIGH SCHOOL: Addison (Ill.) Trail.
COLLEGE: Illinois State (degree in industrial technology).
TRANSACTIONS/CAREER NOTES: Signed as non-drafted free agent by Michigan Panthers of USFL (January 15, 1984). ... Released by Panthers (February 13, 1984). ... Signed by Memphis Showboats of USFL (December 3, 1984). ... Released by Showboats (January 22, 1985). ... Signed by Chicago Bruisers of Arena Football League (June 29, 1987). ... Granted free agency (August 15, 1987). ... Signed as replacement player by Chicago Bears (September 24, 1987). ... Left camp voluntarily (August 16, 1988). ... Released by Bears (August 17, 1988). ... Signed by Minnesota Vikings (March 16, 1989). ... Granted unconditional free agency (February 1, 1990). ... Signed by San Diego Chargers (March 1, 1990). ... Granted unconditional free agency (February 1-April 1, 1991). ... Re-signed by Chargers (April 5, 1991). ... On injured reserve with foot injury (November 13, 1991-remainder of season). ... Granted unconditional free agency (February 1, 1992). ... Signed by Bears (March 6, 1992). ... Released by Bears (December 18, 1992). ... Signed by Detroit Lions (April 30, 1993). ... Granted unconditional free agency (February 17, 1994). ... Re-signed by Lions (August 15, 1994). ... Selected by Carolina Panthers from Lions in NFL expansion draft (February 15, 1995). ... Granted unconditional free agency (February 16, 1996). ... Re-signed by Panthers (March 4, 1996).
PLAYING EXPERIENCE: Chicago Bruisers, Arena Football, 1987; Chicago NFL, 1987 and 1992; Minnesota NFL, 1989; San Diego NFL, 1990 and 1991; Detroit NFL, 1993 and 1994; Carolina NFL, 1995. ... Games: 1987 Arena Football (4), 1987 NFL (9), 1989 (16), 1990 (16), 1991 (10), 1992 (13), 1993 (16), 1994 (16), 1995 (16). Arena League: 4. Total NFL: 112. Total Pro: 116.

ROGERS, SAM　　　　　　LB　　　　　　BILLS

PERSONAL: Born May 30, 1970, in Pontiac, Mich. ... 6-3/245. ... Full name: Sammy Lee Rogers.
HIGH SCHOOL: Saint Mary's Preparatory (Orchard Lake, Mich.).

JUNIOR COLLEGE: West Hills College (Calif.), then West Los Angeles College.
COLLEGE: Colorado.
TRANSACTIONS/CAREER NOTES: Selected by Buffalo Bills in second round (64th pick overall) of 1994 NFL draft. ... Signed by Bills (July 12, 1994).
PLAYING EXPERIENCE: Buffalo NFL, 1994 and 1995. ... Games: 1994 (14), 1995 (16). Total: 30.
PRO STATISTICS: 1995—Credited with two sacks and recovered one fumble.

ROGERS, TRACY — LB — CHIEFS

PERSONAL: Born August 13, 1967, in Taft, Calif. ... 6-2/244. ... Full name: Tracy Darin Rogers.
HIGH SCHOOL: Taft (Calif.) Union.
COLLEGE: Fresno State.
TRANSACTIONS/CAREER NOTES: Selected by Houston Oilers in seventh round (190th pick overall) of 1989 NFL draft. ... Released by Oilers (September 5, 1989). ... Re-signed by Oilers to developmental squad (September 8, 1989). ... Released by Oilers (January 2, 1990). ... Signed by Kansas City Chiefs (March 20, 1990). ... On injured reserve with knee injury (November 21, 1990-remainder of season). ... Granted unconditional free agency (February 1-April 1, 1991). ... Re-signed by Chiefs for 1991 season. ... On injured reserve with hamstring injury (September 4-October 12, 1991). ... On injured reserve with knee injury (January 2, 1992-remainder of 1991 season playoffs). ... Granted unconditional free agency (February 1-April 1, 1992). ... Re-signed by Chiefs for 1992 season. ... On physically unable to perform list with knee injury (August 25-November 3, 1992). ... Granted free agency (March 1, 1993). ... Re-signed by Chiefs for 1993 season. ... Granted unconditional free agency (February 17, 1994). ... Re-signed by Chiefs (July 18, 1994). ... Granted unconditional free agency (February 16, 1996). ... Re-signed by Chiefs (April 9, 1996).
PLAYING EXPERIENCE: Kansas City NFL, 1990-1995. ... Games: 1990 (10), 1991 (10), 1992 (8), 1993 (14), 1994 (14), 1995 (16). Total: 72.
CHAMPIONSHIP GAME EXPERIENCE: Played in AFC championship game (1993 season).
PRO STATISTICS: 1992—Recovered blocked punt in end zone for a touchdown. 1992—Recovered one fumble. 1993—Recovered one fumble.

ROMANOWSKI, BILL — LB — BRONCOS

PERSONAL: Born April 2, 1966, in Vernon, Conn. ... 6-4/241. ... Full name: William Thomas Romanowski.
HIGH SCHOOL: Rockville (Vernon, Conn.).
COLLEGE: Boston College (degree in general management, 1988).
TRANSACTIONS/CAREER NOTES: Selected by San Francisco 49ers in third round (80th pick overall) of 1988 NFL draft. ... Signed by 49ers (July 15, 1988). ... Granted free agency (February 1, 1991). ... Re-signed by 49ers (July 17, 1991). ... Granted unconditional free agency (March 1, 1993). ... Re-signed by 49ers (March 23, 1993). ... Traded by 49ers to Philadelphia Eagles for third-round (traded to Los Angeles Rams) and sixth-round (traded to Green Bay) picks in 1994 draft (April 24, 1994). ... Granted unconditional free agency (February 16, 1996). ... Signed by Denver Broncos (February 26, 1996).
CHAMPIONSHIP GAME EXPERIENCE: Played in NFC championship game (1988-1990, 1992 and 1993 seasons). ... Member of Super Bowl championship team (1988 and 1989 seasons).
PRO STATISTICS: 1988—Recovered one fumble. 1989—Returned one punt for no yards, fumbled once and recovered two fumbles. 1991—Recovered two fumbles. 1992—Recovered one fumble. 1993—Recovered one fumble. 1994—Recovered one fumble. 1995—Recovered one fumble.

| | | | INTERCEPTIONS | | | | SACKS |
Year Team	G	No.	Yds.	Avg.	TD		No.
1988—San Francisco NFL	16	0	0	...	0		0.0
1989—San Francisco NFL	16	1	13	13.0	0		1.0
1990—San Francisco NFL	16	0	0	...	0		1.0
1991—San Francisco NFL	16	1	7	7.0	0		1.0
1992—San Francisco NFL	16	0	0	...	0		1.0
1993—San Francisco NFL	16	0	0	...	0		3.0
1994—Philadelphia NFL	16	2	8	4.0	0		2.5
1995—Philadelphia NFL	16	2	5	2.5	0		1.0
Pro totals (8 years)	128	6	33	5.5	0		10.5

ROSS, DOMINIQUE — RB — COWBOYS

PERSONAL: Born January 12, 1972, in Jacksonville. ... 6-0/203.
HIGH SCHOOL: Raines (Jacksonville).
COLLEGE: Valdosta (Ga.) State.
TRANSACTIONS/CAREER NOTES: Signed as non-drafted free agent by Dallas Cowboys (April 25, 1995). ... Released by Cowboys (August 22, 1995). ... Re-signed by Cowboys to practice squad (August 30, 1995). ... Activated (December 21, 1995).
PLAYING EXPERIENCE: Dallas NFL, 1995. ... Games: 1995 (1).
CHAMPIONSHIP GAME EXPERIENCE: Member of Cowboys for NFC championship game (1995 season); inactive. ... Member of Super Bowl championship team (1995 season).

ROSS, JERMAINE — WR — RAMS

PERSONAL: Born April 27, 1971, in Jeffersonville, Ind. ... 6-0/192. ... Full name: Jermaine Lewis Ross.
HIGH SCHOOL: Jeffersonville (Ind.).
COLLEGE: Purdue.
TRANSACTIONS/CAREER NOTES: Signed as non-drafted free agent by Los Angeles Rams (April 29, 1994). ... Released by Rams (August 22, 1994). ... Re-signed by Rams to practice squad (August 29, 1994). ... Activated (November 30, 1994). ... Rams franchise moved to St. Louis (April 12, 1995). ... On injured reserve with right knee injury (August 21, 1995-entire season).

| | | RECEIVING | | | | TOTALS | | | |
Year Team	G	No.	Yds.	Avg.	TD	TD	2pt.	Pts.	Fum.
1994—Los Angeles Rams NFL	4	1	36	36.0	1	1	0	6	0
1995—St. Louis NFL				Did not play—injured.					

ROSS, KEVIN   S   CHARGERS

PERSONAL: Born January 16, 1962, in Camden, N.J. ... 5-9/185. ... Full name: Kevin Lesley Ross.
HIGH SCHOOL: Paulsboro (N.J.).
COLLEGE: Temple.
TRANSACTIONS/CAREER NOTES: Selected by Philadelphia Stars in 1984 USFL territorial draft. ... Selected by Kansas City Chiefs in seventh round (173rd pick overall) of 1984 NFL draft. ... Signed by Chiefs (June 21, 1984). ... Crossed picket line during players strike (October 14, 1987). ... Granted roster exemption (September 3-8, 1990). ... Granted unconditional free agency (February 17, 1994). ... Signed by Atlanta Falcons (March 17, 1994). ... Released by Falcons (January 2, 1996). ... Signed by San Diego Chargers (March 4, 1996).
CHAMPIONSHIP GAME EXPERIENCE: Played in AFC championship game (1993 season).
HONORS: Played in Pro Bowl (1989 and 1990 seasons).
PRO STATISTICS: 1984—Recovered one fumble. 1985—Recovered one fumble. 1986—Recovered three fumbles for 33 yards and one touchdown. 1987—Returned blocked field-goal attempt 65 yards for a touchdown. 1989—Returned two punts for no yards and fumbled once. 1990—Returned blocked punt four yards for a touchdown and recovered three fumbles. 1991—Recovered one fumble for 13 yards. 1992—Recovered two fumbles. 1993—Recovered one fumble for 22 yards. 1995—Returned blocked field-goal attempt 83 yards for a touchdown and recovered two fumbles.

| | | INTERCEPTIONS | | | | SACKS |
Year Team	G	No.	Yds.	Avg.	TD	No.
1984—Kansas City NFL	16	6	124	20.7	1	0.0
1985—Kansas City NFL	16	3	47	15.7	0	0.0
1986—Kansas City NFL	16	4	66	16.5	0	2.0
1987—Kansas City NFL	12	3	40	13.3	0	1.0
1988—Kansas City NFL	15	1	0	0.0	0	0.0
1989—Kansas City NFL	15	4	29	7.3	0	0.0
1990—Kansas City NFL	16	5	97	19.4	0	0.0
1991—Kansas City NFL	14	1	0	0.0	0	0.0
1992—Kansas City NFL	16	1	99	99.0	1	0.5
1993—Kansas City NFL	15	2	49	24.5	0	0.5
1994—Atlanta NFL	16	3	26	8.7	0	1.0
1995—Atlanta NFL	16	3	70	23.3	0	0.0
Pro totals (12 years)	183	36	647	18.0	2	5.0

ROUEN, TOM   P   BRONCOS

PERSONAL: Born June 9, 1968, in Hinsdale, Ill. ... 6-3/215. ... Name pronounced RUIN
HIGH SCHOOL: Heritage (Littleton, Colo.).
COLLEGE: Colorado State, then Colorado.
TRANSACTIONS/CAREER NOTES: Signed as non-drafted free agent by New York Giants (April 29, 1991). ... Released by Giants (August 19, 1991). ... Selected by Ohio Glory in fourth round (44th pick overall) of 1992 World League draft. ... Signed by Los Angeles Rams (July 1992). ... Released by Rams (August 24, 1992). ... Signed by Denver Broncos (April 29, 1993).
HONORS: Named punter on The Sporting News college All-America second team (1989).
PRO STATISTICS: 1993—Rushed once for no yards.

| | | PUNTING | | | | | |
Year Team	G	No.	Yds.	Avg.	Net avg.	In. 20	Blk.
1992—Ohio W.L.	10	48	1992	41.5	36.1	14	1
1993—Denver NFL	16	67	3017	45.0	37.1	17	1
1994—Denver NFL	16	76	3258	42.9	*37.1	23	0
1995—Denver NFL	16	52	2192	42.2	37.6	22	1
W.L. totals (1 year)	10	48	1992	41.5	36.1	14	1
NFL totals (3 years)	48	195	8467	43.4	37.2	62	2
Pro totals (4 years)	58	243	10459	43.1	37.0	76	3

ROUSE, WARDELL   LB   BUCCANEERS

PERSONAL: Born June 9, 1972, in Clewiston, Fla. ... 6-2/235.
HIGH SCHOOL: Clewiston (Fla.).
JUNIOR COLLEGE: Itawamba Community College (Miss.).
COLLEGE: Clemson.
TRANSACTIONS/CAREER NOTES: Selected by Tampa Bay Buccaneers in sixth round (179th pick overall) of 1995 NFL draft. ... Signed by Buccaneers (May 3, 1995).

Year Team	G	SACKS
1995—Tampa Bay NFL	16	0.5

ROYAL, ANDRE   LB   PANTHERS

PERSONAL: Born December 1, 1972, in Northport, Ala. ... 6-2/220.
HIGH SCHOOL: Tuscaloosa County (Northport, Ala.).
COLLEGE: Alabama.
TRANSACTIONS/CAREER NOTES: Signed as non-drafted free agent by Cleveland Browns (May 2, 1995). ... Released by Browns (August 21, 1995). ... Signed by Carolina Panthers to practice squad (August 30, 1995). ... Activated (September 26, 1995).
PLAYING EXPERIENCE: Carolina NFL, 1995. ... Games: 1995 (12).

R

ROYALS, MARK — P — LIONS

PERSONAL: Born June 22, 1964, in Hampton, Va. ... 6-5/215. ... Full name: Mark Alan Royals.
HIGH SCHOOL: Mathews (Va.).
COLLEGE: Chowan College (N.C.), then Appalachian State (degree in political science).
TRANSACTIONS/CAREER NOTES: Signed as non-drafted free agent by Dallas Cowboys (June 6, 1986). ... Released by Cowboys (August 8, 1986). ... Signed as replacement player by St. Louis Cardinals (September 30, 1987). ... Released by Cardinals (December 12, 1987). ... Signed as replacement player by Philadelphia Eagles (October 14, 1987). ... Released by Eagles (November 1987). ... Signed by Cardinals (December 12, 1987). ... Released by Cardinals (July 27, 1988). ... Signed by Miami Dolphins (May 2, 1989). ... Released by Dolphins (August 28, 1989). ... Signed by Tampa Bay Buccaneers (April 24, 1990). ... Granted unconditional free agency (February 1, 1992). ... Signed by Pittsburgh Steelers (March 15, 1992). ... Granted unconditional free agency (February 17, 1995). ... Signed by Detroit Lions (April 26, 1995). ... Granted free agency (February 16, 1996).
CHAMPIONSHIP GAME EXPERIENCE: Played in AFC championship game (1994 season).
PRO STATISTICS: 1987—Had 25.8-yard net punting average. 1992—Attempted one pass with one completion for 44 yards. 1994—Rushed once for minus 13 yards. 1995—Rushed once for minus seven yards.

						PUNTING		
Year Team	G	No.	Yds.	Avg.	Net avg.	In. 20	Blk.
1986—			Did not play.				
1987—St. Louis NFL	1	6	222	37.0	...	2	0
—Philadelphia NFL	1	5	209	41.8	...	1	0
1988—			Did not play.				
1989—			Did not play.				
1990—Tampa Bay NFL	16	72	2902	40.3	34.0	8	0
1991—Tampa Bay NFL	16	84	3389	40.3	32.3	22	0
1992—Pittsburgh NFL	16	73	3119	42.7	35.6	22	1
1993—Pittsburgh NFL	16	89	3781	42.5	34.2	28	0
1994—Pittsburgh NFL	16	97	3849	39.7	35.7	35	0
1995—Detroit NFL	16	57	2393	42.0	31.0	15	2
Pro totals (7 years)	98	483	19864	41.1	33.8	133	3

RUBLEY, T.J. — QB — BRONCOS

PERSONAL: Born November 29, 1968, in Davenport, Iowa. ... 6-3/212. ... Full name: Theron Joseph Rubley.
HIGH SCHOOL: Davenport (Iowa.) West.
COLLEGE: Tulsa.
TRANSACTIONS/CAREER NOTES: Selected by Los Angeles Rams in ninth round (228th pick overall) of 1992 NFL draft. ... Signed by Rams (July 13, 1992). ... On injured reserve (August 23-November 29, 1994). ... Released by Rams (November 29, 1994). ... Signed by Green Bay Packers (March 30, 1995). ... Released by Packers (December 12, 1995). ... Signed by Denver Broncos (April 3, 1996).
PRO STATISTICS: 1993—Recovered two fumbles for minus 18 yards. 1995—Fumbled once.
MISCELLANEOUS: Regular-season record as starting NFL quarterback: 2-5 (.286).

		PASSING								RUSHING				TOTALS		
Year Team	G	Att.	Cmp.	Pct.	Yds.	TD	Int.	Avg.	Rat.	Att.	Yds.	Avg.	TD	TD	2pt.	Pts.
1993—Los Angeles Rams NFL	9	189	108	57.1	1338	8	6	7.08	80.1	29	102	3.5	0	0	...	0
1994—Los Angeles Rams NFL					Did not play.											
1995—Green Bay NFL	1	6	4	66.7	39	0	1	6.50	45.1	2	6	3.0	0	0	0	0
Pro totals (2 years)	10	195	112	57.4	1377	8	7	7.06	78.1	31	108	3.5	0	0	0	0

RUCCI, TODD — G — PATRIOTS

PERSONAL: Born July 14, 1970, in Upper Darby, Pa. ... 6-5/291.
HIGH SCHOOL: Upper Darby (Pa.).
COLLEGE: Penn State.
TRANSACTIONS/CAREER NOTES: Selected by New England Patriots in second round (51st pick overall) of 1993 NFL draft. ... Signed by Patriots (July 22, 1993). ... On injured reserve with pectoral muscle injury (September 19, 1993-remainder of season).
PLAYING EXPERIENCE: New England NFL, 1993-1995. ... Games: 1993 (2), 1994 (13), 1995 (6). Total: 21.

RUCKER, KEITH — DT — BENGALS

PERSONAL: Born November 20, 1968, in University Park, Ill. ... 6-4/332.
HIGH SCHOOL: Shaker Heights (Cleveland).
COLLEGE: Eastern Michigan, then Ohio Wesleyan.
TRANSACTIONS/CAREER NOTES: Signed as non-drafted free agent by Phoenix Cardinals (May 8, 1992). ... Released by Cardinals (September 11, 1992). ... Re-signed by Cardinals to practice squad (September 14, 1992). ... Activated (September 16, 1992). ... Released by Cardinals (July 7, 1994). ... Signed by Cincinnati Bengals (July 11, 1994).
PRO STATISTICS: 1993—Recovered one fumble.

Year Team	G	SACKS
1992—Phoenix NFL	14	2.0
1993—Phoenix NFL	16	0.0
1994—Cincinnati NFL	16	2.0
1995—Cincinnati NFL	15	2.0
Pro totals (4 years)	61	6.0

R

RUDDY, TIM   C   DOLPHINS

PERSONAL: Born April 27, 1972, in Scranton, Pa. ... 6-3/290. ... Full name: Timothy Daniel Ruddy.
HIGH SCHOOL: Dunmore (Pa.).
COLLEGE: Notre Dame.
TRANSACTIONS/CAREER NOTES: Selected by Miami Dolphins in second round (65th pick overall) of 1994 NFL draft. ... Signed by Dolphins (July 18, 1994).
PLAYING EXPERIENCE: Miami NFL, 1994 and 1995. ... Games: 1994 (16), 1995 (16). Total: 32.
PRO STATISTICS: 1995—Fumbled once.

RUDOLPH, COLEMAN   DE   GIANTS

R

PERSONAL: Born October 22, 1970, in Valdosta, Ga. ... 6-4/262. ... Full name: Coleman Harris Rudolph. ... Son of Jack Rudolph, linebacker, Boston Patriots and Miami Dolphins of AFL (1960 and 1962-1966).
HIGH SCHOOL: Valdosta (Ga.).
COLLEGE: Georgia Tech.
TRANSACTIONS/CAREER NOTES: Selected by New York Jets in second round (36th pick overall) of 1993 NFL draft. ... Signed by Jets (July 13, 1993). ... Claimed on waivers by New York Giants (September 21, 1994).
PLAYING EXPERIENCE: New York Jets NFL, 1993; New York Giants NFL, 1994 and 1995. ... Games: 1993 (4), 1994 (12), 1995 (16). Total: 32.
PRO STATISTICS: 1995—Credited with four sacks.
HONORS: Named defensive lineman on THE SPORTING NEWS college All-America first team (1992).

RUDOLPH, JOE   G   EAGLES

PERSONAL: Born July 21, 1972, in Belle Vernon, Pa. ... 6-1/285.
HIGH SCHOOL: Belle Vernon (Pa.).
COLLEGE: Wisconsin.
TRANSACTIONS/CAREER NOTES: Signed as non-drafted free agent by Philadelphia Eagles (April 26, 1995). ... Released by Eagles (August 27, 1995). ... Re-signed by Eagles (October 4, 1995). ... Released by Eagles (December 22, 1995). ... Re-signed by Eagles to practice squad (December 22, 1995). ... Activated (January 5, 1996).
PLAYING EXPERIENCE: Philadelphia NFL, 1995. ... Games: 1995 (4).

RUETTGERS, KEN   OT   PACKERS

PERSONAL: Born August 20, 1962, in Bakersfield, Calif. ... 6-6/292. ... Name pronounced RUTT-gers.
HIGH SCHOOL: Garces Memorial (Bakersfield, Calif.).
COLLEGE: Southern California (degree in business administration, 1985).
TRANSACTIONS/CAREER NOTES: Selected by Green Bay Packers in first round (seventh pick overall) of 1985 NFL draft. ... Signed by Packers (August 12, 1985). ... Granted free agency (February 1, 1990). ... Re-signed by Packers (August 15, 1990). ... On injured reserve with knee injury (October 22-December 1, 1990). ... On injured reserve with hamstring injury (November 13, 1991-remainder of season). ... Granted free agency (February 1, 1992). ... Re-signed by Packers (August 18, 1992). ... Designated by Packers as transition player (February 25, 1993).
PLAYING EXPERIENCE: Green Bay NFL, 1985-1995. ... Games: 1985 (15), 1986 (16), 1987 (12), 1988 (15), 1989 (16), 1990 (11), 1991 (4), 1992 (16), 1993 (16), 1994 (16), 1995 (15). Total: 152.
CHAMPIONSHIP GAME EXPERIENCE: Played in NFC championship game (1995 season).
PRO STATISTICS: 1986—Recovered one fumble. 1988—Recovered one fumble. 1989—Recovered two fumbles. 1990—Recovered one fumble. 1991—Recovered one fumble. 1993—Recovered two fumbles. 1994—Recovered one fumble. 1995—Recovered two fumbles.

RUSSELL, DEREK   WR/KR   OILERS

PERSONAL: Born June 22, 1969, in Little Rock, Ark. ... 6-0/195. ... Full name: Derek Dwayne Russell. ... Cousin of Sidney Moncrief, guard, Milwaukee Bucks and Atlanta Hawks (1979-1989 and 1990-91).
HIGH SCHOOL: Little Rock (Ark.) Central.
COLLEGE: Arkansas.
TRANSACTIONS/CAREER NOTES: Selected by Denver Broncos in fourth round (89th pick overall) of 1991 NFL draft. ... Signed by Broncos (July 12, 1991). ... On injured reserve with thumb injury (December 1, 1992-remainder of season). ... Granted unconditional free agency (February 17, 1995). ... Signed by Houston Oilers (June 2, 1995).
CHAMPIONSHIP GAME EXPERIENCE: Played in AFC championship game (1991 season).
PRO STATISTICS: 1993—Recovered one fumble in end zone for a touchdown.
STATISTICAL PLATEAUS: 100-yard receiving games: 1993 (2).

		RECEIVING				KICKOFF RETURNS				TOTALS		
Year Team	G	No.	Yds.	Avg.	TD	No.	Yds.	Avg.	TD	TD	2pt.	Pts.	Fum.
1991—Denver NFL	13	21	317	15.1	1	7	120	17.1	0	1	...	6	0
1992—Denver NFL	12	12	140	11.7	0	7	154	22.0	0	0	...	0	0
1993—Denver NFL	13	44	719	16.3	3	18	374	20.8	0	4	...	24	1
1994—Denver NFL	12	25	342	13.7	1	5	105	21.0	0	1	0	6	0
1995—Houston NFL	11	24	321	13.4	0	0	0	...	0	0	0	0	0
Pro totals (5 years)	61	126	1839	14.6	5	37	753	20.4	0	6	0	36	1

RUSSELL, LEONARD   RB   CHARGERS

PERSONAL: Born November 17, 1969, in Long Beach, Calif. ... 6-2/240. ... Full name: Leonard James Russell.
HIGH SCHOOL: Long Beach (Calif.) Polytechnic.
JUNIOR COLLEGE: Mount San Antonio College (Calif.).
COLLEGE: Arizona State.
TRANSACTIONS/CAREER NOTES: Selected after junior season by New England Patriots in first round (14th pick overall) of 1991 NFL draft. ... Signed by Patriots (July 23, 1991). ... On injured reserve with rib injury (December 24, 1992-remainder of season). ... Granted free agency (February 17, 1994). ... Rights relinquished by Patriots (August 10, 1994). ... Signed by Denver Broncos (August 12, 1994). ... On injured reserve with shoulder injury (December 15, 1994-remainder of season). ... Granted unconditional free agency (February 17, 1995). ... Signed by St. Louis Rams (June 1, 1995). ... Released by Rams (December 14, 1995). ... Signed by San Diego Chargers (April 3, 1996).
PRO STATISTICS: 1993—Recovered two fumbles for 22 yards.
STATISTICAL PLATEAUS: 100-yard rushing games: 1991 (2), 1993 (3), 1994 (2). Total: 7.

		RUSHING				RECEIVING				TOTALS			
Year Team	G	Att.	Yds.	Avg.	TD	No.	Yds.	Avg.	TD	TD	2pt.	Pts.	Fum.
1991—New England NFL	16	266	959	3.6	4	18	81	4.5	0	4	...	24	8
1992—New England NFL	11	123	390	3.2	2	11	24	2.2	0	2	...	12	3
1993—New England NFL	16	300	1088	3.6	7	26	245	9.4	0	7	...	42	4
1994—Denver NFL	14	190	620	3.3	9	38	227	6.0	0	9	0	54	4
1995—St. Louis NFL	13	66	203	3.1	0	16	89	5.6	0	0	0	0	2
Pro totals (5 years)	70	945	3260	3.5	22	109	666	6.1	0	22	0	132	21

RYPIEN, MARK   QB   RAMS

PERSONAL: Born October 2, 1962, in Calgary, Alberta. ... 6-4/231. ... Full name: Mark Robert Rypien. ... Brother of Tim Rypien, catcher, Toronto Blue Jays organization (1984-1986); and cousin of Shane Churla, forward, New York Rangers of NHL. ... Name pronounced RIP-in.
HIGH SCHOOL: Shadle Park (Spokane, Wash.).
COLLEGE: Washington State.
TRANSACTIONS/CAREER NOTES: Selected by Washington Redskins in sixth round (146th pick overall) of 1986 NFL draft. ... Signed by Redskins (July 18, 1986). ... On injured reserve with knee injury (September 5, 1986-entire season). ... On injured reserve with back injury (September 7-November 28, 1987). ... Active for one game with Redskins (1987); did not play. ... On injured reserve with knee injury (September 26-November 17, 1990). ... Granted free agency (February 1, 1991). ... Re-signed by Redskins (July 24, 1991). ... Granted free agency (February 1, 1992). ... Re-signed by Redskins (August 11, 1992). ... Released by Redskins (April 13, 1994). ... Signed by Cleveland Browns (May 10, 1994). ... Granted unconditional free agency (February 17, 1995). ... Signed by St. Louis Rams (May 8, 1995). ... Granted free agency (February 16, 1996).
CHAMPIONSHIP GAME EXPERIENCE: Played in NFC championship game (1991 season). ... Member of Super Bowl championship team (1987 and 1991 seasons).
HONORS: Played in Pro Bowl (1989 and 1991 seasons). ... Named Most Valuable Player of Super Bowl XXVI (1991 season).
PRO STATISTICS: 1988—Fumbled six times. 1989—Fumbled 14 times and recovered two fumbles. 1990—Fumbled twice. 1991—Fumbled nine times and recovered three fumbles for minus five yards. 1992—Fumbled four times and recovered two fumbles. 1993—Fumbled seven times. 1994—Fumbled twice. 1995—Fumbled once.
STATISTICAL PLATEAUS: 300-yard passing games: 1988 (2), 1989 (5), 1990 (1), 1991 (2), 1995 (3). Total: 13.
MISCELLANEOUS: Regular-season record as starting NFL quarterback: 47-31 (.603).

		PASSING								RUSHING				TOTALS		
Year Team	G	Att.	Cmp.	Pct.	Yds.	TD	Int.	Avg.	Rat.	Att.	Yds.	Avg.	TD	TD	2pt.	Pts.
1986—Washington NFL						Did not play—injured.										
1987—Washington NFL						Did not play.										
1988—Washington NFL	9	208	114	54.8	1730	18	13	8.32	85.2	9	31	3.4	1	1	...	6
1989—Washington NFL	14	476	280	58.8	3768	22	13	7.92	88.1	26	56	2.2	1	1	...	6
1990—Washington NFL	10	304	166	54.6	2070	16	11	6.81	78.4	15	4	0.3	0	0	...	0
1991—Washington NFL	16	421	249	59.1	3564	28	11	8.47	97.9	15	6	0.4	1	1	...	6
1992—Washington NFL	16	479	269	56.2	3282	13	17	6.85	71.7	36	50	1.4	2	2	...	12
1993—Washington NFL	12	319	166	52.0	1514	4	10	4.75	56.3	9	4	0.4	3	3	...	18
1994—Cleveland NFL	6	128	59	46.1	694	4	3	5.42	63.7	7	4	0.6	0	0	0	0
1995—St. Louis NFL	11	217	129	59.5	1448	9	8	6.67	77.9	9	10	1.1	0	0	0	0
Pro totals (8 years)	94	2552	1432	56.1	18070	114	86	7.08	79.2	126	165	1.3	8	8	0	48

SABB, DWAYNE   LB   PATRIOTS

PERSONAL: Born October 9, 1969, in Union City, N.J. ... 6-4/248. ... Full name: Dwayne Irving Sabb.
HIGH SCHOOL: Hudson Catholic (Jersey City, N.J.).
COLLEGE: New Hampshire.
TRANSACTIONS/CAREER NOTES: Selected by New England Patriots in fifth round (116th pick overall) of 1992 NFL draft. ... Signed by Patriots (July 15, 1992). ... Granted free agency (February 17, 1995). ... Re-signed by Patriots (May 24, 1995).
PRO STATISTICS: 1993—Returned two kickoffs for no yards.

		INTERCEPTIONS				SACKS
Year Team	G	No.	Yds.	Avg.	TD	No.
1992—New England NFL	16	0	0	...	0	1.0
1993—New England NFL	14	0	0	...	0	2.0
1994—New England NFL	16	2	6	3.0	0	3.5
1995—New England NFL	12	0	0	...	0	0.0
Pro totals (4 years)	58	2	6	3.0	0	6.5

R
S

SADOWSKI, TROY   TE   BENGALS

PERSONAL: Born December 8, 1965, in Atlanta. ... 6-5/250. ... Full name: Troy Robert Sadowski.
HIGH SCHOOL: Chamblee (Ga.).
COLLEGE: Georgia.
TRANSACTIONS/CAREER NOTES: Selected by Atlanta Falcons in sixth round (145th pick overall) of 1989 NFL draft. ... Released by Falcons (August 30, 1989). ... Re-signed by Falcons to developmental squad (December 6, 1989). ... Released by Falcons (January 9, 1990). ... Re-signed by Falcons (February 20, 1990). ... Released by Falcons (September 3, 1990). ... Re-signed by Falcons (September 4, 1990). ... Granted unconditional free agency (February 1, 1991). ... Signed by Kansas City Chiefs (April 2, 1991). ... Released by Chiefs (December 17, 1991). ... Signed by New York Jets (March 23, 1992). ... Released by Jets (October 25, 1992). ... Re-signed by Jets (April 20, 1993). ... Released by Jets (August 24, 1993). ... Re-signed by Jets (September 28, 1993). ... Granted unconditional free agency (February 17, 1994). ... Signed by Cincinnati Bengals (April 26, 1994).
PRO STATISTICS: 1993—Returned one kickoff for no yards. 1994—Recovered one fumble. 1995—Recovered one fumble.

		RECEIVING				TOTALS			
Year Team	G	No.	Yds.	Avg.	TD	TD	2pt.	Pts.	Fum.
1990—Atlanta NFL	13	0	0	...	0	0	...	0	0
1991—Kansas City NFL	14	0	0	...	0	0	...	0	0
1992—New York Jets NFL	6	1	20	20.0	0	0	...	0	0
1993—New York Jets NFL	13	2	14	7.0	0	0	...	0	0
1994—Cincinnati NFL	15	11	54	4.9	0	0	0	0	0
1995—Cincinnati NFL	12	5	37	7.4	0		0		0
Pro totals (6 years)	73	18	105	5.8	0	0	0	0	0

SAGAPOLUTELE, PIO   DL   PATRIOTS

PERSONAL: Born November 28, 1969, in American Samoa. ... 6-6/297. ... Full name: Pio Alika Sagapolutele. ... Name pronounced SAANG-uh-POO-luh-tel-ee.
HIGH SCHOOL: Maryknoll (Honolulu).
COLLEGE: San Diego State (degree in criminal justice, 1991).
TRANSACTIONS/CAREER NOTES: Selected by Cleveland Browns in fourth round (85th pick overall) of 1991 NFL draft. ... Granted free agency (February 17, 1994). ... Re-signed by Browns (May 11, 1994). ... Granted unconditional free agency (February 17, 1995). ... Re-signed by Browns (April 17, 1995). ... Granted unconditional free agency (February 16, 1996). ... Signed by New England Patriots (March 20, 1996).
PLAYING EXPERIENCE: Cleveland NFL, 1991-1995. ... Games: 1991 (15), 1992 (14), 1993 (8), 1994 (11), 1995 (15). Total: 63.
PRO STATISTICS: 1991—Credited with 1½ sacks.

SALAAM, RASHAAN   RB   BEARS

PERSONAL: Born October 8, 1974, in San Diego. ... 6-1/226. ... Son of Sulton Salaam (formerly known as Teddy Washington), running back, Cincinnati Bengals of American Football League (1968). ... Name pronounced rah-SHAHN sah-LAHM.
HIGH SCHOOL: La Jolla (Calif.) Country Day.
COLLEGE: Colorado.
TRANSACTIONS/CAREER NOTES: Selected after junior season by Chicago Bears in first round (21st pick overall) of 1995 NFL draft. ... Signed by Bears (August 3, 1995).
HONORS: Heisman Trophy winner (1994). ... Named College Football Player of the Year by THE SPORTING NEWS (1994). ... Doak Walker Award winner (1994). ... Named running back on THE SPORTING NEWS college All-America first team (1994).
PRO STATISTICS: 1995—Recovered one fumble.
STATISTICAL PLATEAUS: 100-yard rushing games: 1995 (5).

		RUSHING				RECEIVING				TOTALS			
Year Team	G	Att.	Yds.	Avg.	TD	No.	Yds.	Avg.	TD	TD	2pt.	Pts.	Fum.
1995—Chicago NFL	16	296	1074	3.6	10	7	56	8.0	0	10	0	60	9

SALEAUMUA, DAN   DT   CHIEFS

PERSONAL: Born November 25, 1964, in San Diego. ... 6-0/315. ... Full name: Raymond Daniel Saleaumua. ... Name pronounced SOL-ee-uh-MOO-uh.
HIGH SCHOOL: Sweetwater (National City, Calif.).
COLLEGE: Arizona State.
TRANSACTIONS/CAREER NOTES: Selected by Detroit Lions in seventh round (175th pick overall) of 1987 NFL draft. ... Signed by Lions (July 25, 1987). ... On injured reserve with hamstring injury (September 7-October 31, 1987). ... Granted unconditional free agency (February 1, 1989). ... Signed by Kansas City Chiefs (March 20, 1989). ... Designated by Chiefs as transition player (February 25, 1993). ... Free agency status changed by Chiefs from transitional to unconditional (February 17, 1994). ... Re-signed by Chiefs (August 23, 1994).
CHAMPIONSHIP GAME EXPERIENCE: Played in AFC championship game (1993 season).
HONORS: Played in Pro Bowl (1995 season).
PRO STATISTICS: 1987—Returned three kickoffs for 57 yards. 1988—Returned one kickoff for no yards and fumbled once. 1989—Intercepted one pass for 21 yards, returned one kickoff for eight yards and recovered five fumbles for two yards. 1990—Recovered six fumbles (including one in end zone for a touchdown). 1991—Credited with one safety and recovered two fumbles. 1992—Recovered one fumble. 1993—Intercepted one pass for 13 yards and recovered one fumble for 16 yards and a touchdown. 1994—Recovered one fumble. 1995—Intercepted one pass for no yards and recovered one fumble.

Year Name	G	SACKS
1987—Detroit NFL	9	2.0
1988—Detroit NFL	16	2.0
1989—Kansas City NFL	16	2.0
1990—Kansas City NFL	16	7.0
1991—Kansas City NFL	16	1.5

Year Name	G	SACKS
1992—Kansas City NFL	16	6.0
1993—Kansas City NFL	16	3.5
1994—Kansas City NFL	14	1.0
1995—Kansas City NFL	16	7.0
Pro totals (9 years)	135	32.0

SALISBURY, SEAN — QB — CHARGERS

PERSONAL: Born March 9, 1963, in Escondido, Calif. ... 6-5/225. ... Full name: Richard Sean Salisbury.
HIGH SCHOOL: Orange Glen (Escondido, Calif.).
COLLEGE: Southern California (degree in broadcasting, 1986).
TRANSACTIONS/CAREER NOTES: Selected by New Jersey Generals in 1986 USFL territorial draft. ... Signed as non-drafted free agent by Seattle Seahawks (May 12, 1986). ... On injured reserve with shoulder injury (October 22, 1986-remainder of season). ... Released by Seahawks (September 1, 1987). ... Signed as replacement player by Indianapolis Colts (October 14, 1987). ... Released by Colts (July 23, 1988). ... Signed by Winnipeg Blue Bombers of CFL (September 13, 1988). ... Released by Blue Bombers (November 2, 1989). ... Signed by Minnesota Vikings (March 17, 1990). ... Granted free agency (February 1, 1992). ... Re-signed by Vikings (July 21, 1992). ... Granted unconditional free agency (March 1, 1993). ... Re-signed by Vikings (April 14, 1993). ... Granted unconditional free agency (February 17, 1994). ... Signed by Houston Oilers (April 28, 1994). ... Released by Oilers (September 2, 1994). ... Signed by Vikings (September 3, 1994). ... Granted unconditional free agency (February 17, 1995). ... Signed by San Diego Chargers (February 21, 1996).
CHAMPIONSHIP GAME EXPERIENCE: Played in Grey Cup, CFL championship game (1988 season).
PRO STATISTICS: NFL: 1987—Fumbled once. 1992—Fumbled four times and recovered three fumbles for minus five yards. 1993—Fumbled three times and recovered one fumble for minus nine yards. CFL: 1988—Fumbled once and recovered one fumble. 1989—Caught one pass for 13 yards, fumbled nine times and recovered three fumbles.
STATISTICAL PLATEAUS: 300-yard passing games: 1993 (2).
MISCELLANEOUS: Regular-season record as starting NFL quarterback: 5-4 (.556).

		PASSING								RUSHING				TOTALS		
Year Team	G	Att.	Cmp.	Pct.	Yds.	TD	Int.	Avg.	Rat.	Att.	Yds.	Avg.	TD	TD	2pt.	Pts.
1986—Seattle NFL							Did not play.									
1987—Indianapolis NFL	2	12	8	66.7	68	0	2	5.67	41.7	0	0	...	0	0	0	0
1988—Winnipeg CFL	7	202	100	49.5	1566	11	5	7.75	83.5	3	9	3.0	0	0	0	0
1989—Winnipeg CFL	17	595	293	49.2	4049	26	26	6.81	67.8	24	54	2.3	0	0	0	0
1990—Minnesota NFL							Did not play.									
1991—Minnesota NFL							Did not play.									
1992—Minnesota NFL	10	175	97	55.4	1203	5	2	6.88	81.7	11	0	0.0	0	0	...	0
1993—Minnesota NFL	11	195	115	59.0	1413	9	6	7.25	84.0	10	-1	-0.1	0	0	...	0
1994—Minnesota NFL	1	34	16	47.1	156	0	1	4.59	48.2	3	2	0.7	0	0	...	0
1995—							Did not play.									
CFL totals (2 years)	24	797	393	49.3	5615	37	31	7.05	71.8	27	63	2.3	0	0	0	0
NFL totals (4 years)	24	416	236	56.7	2840	14	11	6.83	78.0	24	1	0.1	0	0	0	0
Pro totals (6 years)	48	1213	629	51.9	8455	51	42	6.97	73.9	51	64	1.3	0	0	0	0

SAMUELS, TERRY — TE

PERSONAL: Born September 27, 1970, in Louisville, Ky. ... 6-2/254.
HIGH SCHOOL: Louisville (Ky.) Male.
COLLEGE: Kentucky.
TRANSACTIONS/CAREER NOTES: Selected by Arizona Cardinals in sixth round (172nd pick overall) of 1994 NFL draft. ... Signed by Cardinals (June 14, 1994). ... Released by Cardinals (October 9, 1995).
PRO STATISTICS: 1994—Rushed once for one yard and returned one kickoff for six yards.

		RECEIVING				TOTALS			
Year Team	G	No.	Yds.	Avg.	TD	TD	2pt.	Pts.	Fum.
1994—Arizona NFL	16	8	57	7.1	0	0	0	0	0
1995—Arizona NFL	4	2	19	9.5	0	0	0	0	0
Pro totals (2 years)	20	10	76	7.6	0	0	0	0	0

SANDERS, BARRY — RB — LIONS

PERSONAL: Born July 16, 1968, in Wichita, Kan. ... 5-8/203.
HIGH SCHOOL: North (Wichita, Kan.).
COLLEGE: Oklahoma State.
TRANSACTIONS/CAREER NOTES: Selected after junior season by Detroit Lions in first round (third pick overall) of 1989 NFL draft. ... Signed by Lions (September 7, 1989).
CHAMPIONSHIP GAME EXPERIENCE: Played in NFC championship game (1991 season).
HONORS: Named kick returner on THE SPORTING NEWS college All-America first team (1987). ... Heisman Trophy winner (1988). ... Named College Football Player of the Year by THE SPORTING NEWS (1988). ... Maxwell Award winner (1988). ... Named running back on THE SPORTING NEWS college All-America first team (1988). ... Named NFL Rookie of the Year by THE SPORTING NEWS (1989). ... Named running back on THE SPORTING NEWS NFL All-Pro team (1989-1991 and 1993-1995). ... Played in Pro Bowl (1989-1992, 1994 and 1995 seasons). ... Named to play in Pro Bowl (1993 season); replaced by Ricky Watters due to injury.
RECORDS: Shares NFL record for most consecutive seasons with 1,000 or more yards rushing—7 (1989-1995).
PRO STATISTICS: 1989—Returned five kickoffs for 118 yards. 1990—Recovered two fumbles. 1991—Recovered one fumble. 1992—Attempted one pass without a completion and recovered two fumbles. 1993—Recovered three fumbles. 1995—Attempted two passes with one completion for 11 yards and recovered one fumble.
STATISTICAL PLATEAUS: 100-yard rushing games: 1989 (7), 1990 (4), 1991 (8), 1992 (7), 1993 (4), 1994 (10), 1995 (7). Total: 47. ... 100-yard receiving games: 1990 (1).
MISCELLANEOUS: Active NFC leader for career rushing yards (10,172). ... Holds Detroit Lions all-time records for most yards rushing

(10,172 yards) and most touchdowns (80).

Year Team	G	RUSHING Att.	Yds.	Avg.	TD	RECEIVING No.	Yds.	Avg.	TD	TOTALS TD	2pt.	Pts.	Fum.
1989—Detroit NFL	15	280	1470	5.3	14	24	282	11.8	0	14	...	84	10
1990—Detroit NFL	16	255	*1304	5.1	13	36	480	13.3	3	*16	...	96	4
1991—Detroit NFL	15	342	1548	4.5	*16	41	307	7.5	1	*17	...	102	5
1992—Detroit NFL	16	312	1352	4.3	9	29	225	7.8	1	10	...	60	6
1993—Detroit NFL	11	243	1115	4.6	3	36	205	5.7	0	3	...	18	3
1994—Detroit NFL	16	331	*1883	*5.7	7	44	283	6.4	1	8	0	48	0
1995—Detroit NFL	16	314	1500	4.8	11	48	398	8.3	1	12	0	72	3
Pro totals (7 years)	105	2077	10172	4.9	73	258	2180	8.5	7	80	0	480	31

SANDERS, CHRIS — WR — OILERS

PERSONAL: Born May 8, 1972, in Denver. ... 6-0/184.
HIGH SCHOOL: Montbello (Denver).
COLLEGE: Ohio State.
TRANSACTIONS/CAREER NOTES: Selected by Houston Oilers in third round (67th pick overall) of 1995 NFL draft. ... Signed by Oilers (July 20, 1995).
STATISTICAL PLATEAUS: 100-yard receiving games: 1995 (1).

Year Team	G	RUSHING Att.	Yds.	Avg.	TD	RECEIVING No.	Yds.	Avg.	TD	TOTALS TD	2pt.	Pts.	Fum.
1995—Houston NFL	16	2	-19	-9.5	0	35	823	*23.5	9	9	0	54	0

SANDERS, DEION — CB/KR — COWBOYS

PERSONAL: Born August 9, 1967, in Fort Myers, Fla. ... 6-1/185. ... Full name: Deion Luwynn Sanders.
HIGH SCHOOL: North Fort Myers (Fla.).
COLLEGE: Florida State.
TRANSACTIONS/CAREER NOTES: Selected by Atlanta Falcons in first round (fifth pick overall) of 1989 NFL draft. ... Signed by Falcons (September 7, 1989). ... On reserve/did not report list (July 27-August 13, 1990). ... Granted roster exemption for one game (September 1992). ... On reserve/did not report list (July 23-October 14, 1993). ... Designated by Falcons as transition player (February 15, 1994). ... Free agency status changed by Falcons from transitional to unconditional (April 28, 1994). ... Signed by San Francisco 49ers (September 15, 1994). ... Granted unconditional free agency (February 17, 1995). ... Signed by Dallas Cowboys (September 9, 1995). ... Activated (September 22, 1995).
CHAMPIONSHIP GAME EXPERIENCE: Played in NFC championship game (1994 and 1995 seasons). ... Member of Super Bowl championship team (1994 and 1995 seasons).
HONORS: Named defensive back on THE SPORTING NEWS college All-America first team (1986-1988). ... Jim Thorpe Award winner (1988). ... Named cornerback on THE SPORTING NEWS NFL All-Pro team (1991-1995). ... Played in Pro Bowl (1991-1994 seasons). ... Named kick returner on THE SPORTING NEWS NFL All-Pro team (1992).
PRO STATISTICS: 1989—Caught one pass for minus eight yards and recovered one fumble. 1990—Recovered two fumbles. 1991—Credited with a sack, caught one pass for 17 yards and recovered one fumble. 1992—Rushed once for minus four yards, caught three passes for 45 yards and one touchdown and recovered two fumbles. 1993—Attempted one pass without a completion and caught six passes for 106 yards and one touchdown. 1994—Recovered one fumble. 1995—Rushed twice for nine yards and caught two passes for 25 yards.
MISCELLANEOUS: Only person in history to play in both the World Series (1992) and Super Bowl (1994 and 1995 seasons).

Year Team	G	INTERCEPTIONS No.	Yds.	Avg.	TD	PUNT RETURNS No.	Yds.	Avg.	TD	KICKOFF RETURNS No.	Yds.	Avg.	TD	TOTALS TD	2pt.	Pts.	Fum.
1989—Atlanta NFL	15	5	52	10.4	0	28	307	11.0	†1	35	725	20.7	0	1	...	6	2
1990—Atlanta NFL	16	3	153	51.0	2	29	250	8.6	†1	39	851	21.8	0	3	...	18	4
1991—Atlanta NFL	15	6	119	19.8	1	21	170	8.1	0	26	576	22.2	†1	2	...	12	1
1992—Atlanta NFL	13	3	105	35.0	0	13	41	3.2	0	40	*1067	26.7	*2	3	...	18	3
1993—Atlanta NFL	11	7	91	13.0	0	2	21	10.5	0	7	169	24.1	0	1	...	6	0
1994—San Francisco NFL	14	6	*303	50.5	†3	0	0	...	0	0	0	...	0	3	0	18	0
1995—Dallas NFL	9	2	34	17.0	0	1	54	54.0	0	1	15	15.0	0	0	0	0	0
Pro totals (7 years)	93	32	857	26.8	6	94	843	9.0	2	148	3403	23.0	3	13	0	78	10

RECORD AS BASEBALL PLAYER

TRANSACTIONS/CAREER NOTES: Threw left, batted left. ... Selected by Kansas City Royals organization in sixth round of free-agent draft (June 3, 1985); did not sign. ... Selected by New York Yankees organization in 30th round of free-agent draft (June 1, 1988). ... On disqualified list (August 1-September 24, 1990). ... Released by Yankees organization (September 24, 1990). ... Signed by Atlanta Braves (January 29, 1991). ... Placed on Richmond temporary inactive list (August 1, 1991) ... On disqualified list (April 29-May 21, 1993) ... On disabled list (August 22-September 6, 1993). ... Traded by Braves to Cincinnati Reds for OF Roberto Kelly and P Roger Etheridge (May 29, 1994).
STATISTICAL NOTES: Led N.L in caught stealing with 16 in 1994.

Year Team (League)	Pos.	G	BATTING AB	R	H	2B	3B	HR	RBI	Avg.	BB	SO	SB	FIELDING PO	A	E	Avg.
1988—GC Yankees (GCL)	OF	17	75	7	21	4	2	0	6	.280	2	10	11	33	1	2	.944
—Fort Lauder (FSL)	OF	6	21	5	9	2	0	0	2	.429	1	3	2	22	2	0	1.000
—Columbus (Int'l)	OF	5	20	3	3	1	0	0	0	.150	1	4	1	13	0	0	1.000
1989—Alb/Colon. (East)	OF	33	119	28	34	2	2	1	6	.286	11	20	17	79	3	0	1.000
—New York (A.L.)	OF	14	47	7	11	2	0	2	7	.234	3	8	1	30	1	1	.969
—Columbus (Int'l)	OF	70	259	38	72	12	7	5	30	.278	22	46	16	165	0	4	.967
1990—New York (A.L.)	OF-DH	57	133	24	21	2	2	3	9	.158	13	27	8	69	2	2	.973
—Columbus (Int'l)	OF	22	84	21	27	7	1	2	10	.321	17	15	9	49	1	0	1.000
1991—Atlanta (N.L.)■	OF	54	110	16	21	1	2	4	13	.191	12	23	11	57	3	3	.952
—Richmond (Int'l)	OF	29	130	20	34	6	3	5	16	.262	10	28	12	73	1	1	.987
1992—Atlanta (N.L.)	OF	97	303	54	92	6	*14	8	28	.304	18	52	26	174	4	3	.983
1993—Atlanta (N.L.)	OF	95	272	42	75	18	6	6	28	.276	16	42	19	137	1	2	.986

S

BATTING / FIELDING

Year Team (League)	Pos.	G	AB	R	H	2B	3B	HR	RBI	Avg.	BB	SO	SB	PO	A	E	Avg.
1994—Atlanta (N.L.)	OF	46	191	32	55	10	0	4	21	.288	16	28	19	99	0	2	.980
—Cincinnati (N.L.)■	OF	46	184	26	51	7	4	0	7	.277	16	35	19	110	2	0	1.000
1995—Cincinnati (N.L.)	OF	33	129	19	31	2	3	1	10	.240	9	18	16	88	2	3	.968
—Chatt. (South)	OF	2	7	1	4	0	0	1	2	.571	0	1	1	3	1	0	1.000
—San Franc. (N.L.)■	OF	52	214	29	61	9	5	5	18	.285	18	42	8	127	0	2	.984
American League totals (2 years)		71	180	31	32	4	2	5	16	.178	16	35	9	99	3	3	.971
National League totals (5 years)		423	1403	218	386	53	34	28	125	.275	105	240	118	792	12	15	.982
Major League totals (7 years)		494	1583	249	418	57	36	33	141	.264	121	275	127	891	15	18	.981

CHAMPIONSHIP SERIES RECORD

Year Team (League)	Pos.	G	AB	R	H	2B	3B	HR	RBI	Avg.	BB	SO	SB	PO	A	E	Avg.
1992—Atlanta (N.L.)	OF-PH	4	5	0	0	0	0	0	0	.000	0	3	0	1	0	0	1.000
1993—Atlanta (N.L.)	PH-OF-PR	5	3	0	0	0	0	0	0	.000	0	1	0	0	0	0	...
Championship series totals (2 years)		9	8	0	0	0	0	0	0	.000	0	4	0	1	0	0	1.000

WORLD SERIES RECORD

Year Team (League)	Pos.	G	AB	R	H	2B	3B	HR	RBI	Avg.	BB	SO	SB	PO	A	E	Avg.
1992—Atlanta (N.L.)	OF	4	15	4	8	2	0	0	1	.533	2	1	5	5	1	0	1.000

SANDERS, FRANK   WR   CARDINALS

PERSONAL: Born February 17, 1973, in Fort Lauderdale. ... 6-1/202. ... Full name: Frank Vondel Sanders.
HIGH SCHOOL: Dillard (Fort Lauderdale).
COLLEGE: Auburn.
TRANSACTIONS/CAREER NOTES: Selected by Arizona Cardinals in second round (47th pick overall) of 1995 NFL draft. ... Signed by Cardinals (July 17, 1995).
HONORS: Named wide receiver on THE SPORTING NEWS college All-America second team (1994).
STATISTICAL PLATEAUS: 100-yard receiving games: 1995 (2).

		RUSHING				RECEIVING				TOTALS			
Year Team	G	Att.	Yds.	Avg.	TD	No.	Yds.	Avg.	TD	TD	2pt.	Pts.	Fum.
1995—Arizona NFL	16	1	1	1.0	0	52	883	17.0	2	2	2	16	0

SANDERS, GLENELL   LB

PERSONAL: Born November 4, 1966, in Clinton, La. ... 6-1/240.
HIGH SCHOOL: Clinton (La.).
COLLEGE: Louisiana Tech.
TRANSACTIONS/CAREER NOTES: Signed as non-drafted free agent by Chicago Bears (April 28, 1990). ... Released by Bears (September 3, 1990). ... Re-signed by Bears to practice squad (December 19, 1990). ... Activated (December 21, 1990). ... Granted unconditional free agency (February 1, 1991). ... Signed by Los Angeles Rams (March 29, 1991). ... Released by Rams (August 31, 1992). ... Signed by Buffalo Bills (March 30, 1993). ... Released by Bills (August 24, 1993). ... Signed by Denver Broncos (March 18, 1994). ... Released by Broncos (September 6, 1994). ... Signed by Indianapolis Colts (April 27, 1995). ... Released by Colts (November 14, 1995).
PLAYING EXPERIENCE: Chicago NFL, 1990; Los Angeles Rams NFL, 1991; Denver NFL, 1994; Indianapolis NFL, 1995. ... Games: 1990 (2), 1991 (16), 1994 (1), 1995 (9). Total: 28.
PRO STATISTICS: 1991—Returned one kickoff for two yards. 1995—Recovered one fumble.

SANDERS, RICKY   WR   FALCONS

PERSONAL: Born August 30, 1962, in Temple, Texas. ... 5-11/180. ... Full name: Ricky Wayne Sanders.
HIGH SCHOOL: Belton (Texas).
COLLEGE: Southwest Texas State.
TRANSACTIONS/CAREER NOTES: Selected by Houston Gamblers in 1984 USFL territorial draft. ... Signed by Gamblers (January 26, 1984). ... Selected by New England Patriots in first round (16th pick overall) of 1984 NFL supplemental draft. ... On developmental squad for eight games with Gamblers (March 7-May 6, 1985). ... Traded by Gamblers with DB Luther Bradley, DB Will Lewis, DB Mike Mitchell, DB Durwood Roquemore, DE Pete Catan, QB Jim Kelly, QB Todd Dillon, DT Tony Fitzpatrick, DT Van Hughes, DT Hosea Taylor, RB Sam Harrell, LB Andy Hawkins, LB Ladell Wills, WR Richard Johnson, WR Scott McGhee, WR Gerald McNeil, WR Clarence Verdin, G Rich Kehr, C Billy Kidd, OT Chris Riehm and OT Tommy Robison to New Jersey Generals for past considerations (March 7, 1986). ... Granted free agency when USFL suspended operations (August 7, 1986). ... Patriots rights traded to Washington Redskins for third-round pick (traded to Los Angeles Raiders) in 1987 draft (August 11, 1986). ... Signed by Redskins (August 13, 1986). ... Granted roster exemption (August 13-25, 1986). ... On injured reserve with pulled hamstring and calf muscle (September 2-October 11, 1986). ... Granted free agency (February 1, 1992). ... Re-signed by Redskins (July 21, 1992). ... Granted unconditional free agency (February 17, 1994). ... Signed by Atlanta Falcons (July 19, 1994). ... Granted unconditional free agency (February 17, 1995). ... Signed by Miami Dolphins (July 13, 1995). ... Released by Dolphins (October 10, 1995). ... Signed by Falcons (October 25, 1995).
CHAMPIONSHIP GAME EXPERIENCE: Played in NFC championship game (1986, 1987 and 1991 seasons). ... Member of Super Bowl championship team (1987 and 1991 seasons).
POSTSEASON RECORDS: Shares Super Bowl career record for longest pass reception (from Doug Williams)—80 yards (January 31, 1988, vs. Denver). ... Holds Super Bowl single-game record for most combined yards—235 (January 31, 1988, vs. Denver).
PRO STATISTICS: USFL: 1984—Fumbled three times and recovered two fumbles. 1985—Attempted one pass without a completion. NFL: 1989—Attempted one pass with one completion for 32 yards. 1993—Fumbled once and recovered one fumble. 1994—Recovered one fumble.
STATISTICAL PLATEAUS: USFL: 100-yard receiving games: 1984 (3), 1985 (2). Total: 5. ... NFL: 100-yard receiving games: 1987 (1), 1988 (4), 1989 (3), 1990 (1), 1992 (1). Total: 10.

Year Team	G	RUSHING				RECEIVING				PUNT RETURNS				KICKOFF RETURNS				TOTALS		
		Att.	Yds.	Avg.	TD	No.	Yds.	Avg.	TD	No.	Yds.	Avg.	TD	No.	Yds.	Avg.	TD	TD	2pt.	Pts.
1984—Houston USFL	18	10	58	5.8	0	101	1378	13.6	11	19	148	7.8	0	2	28	14.0	0	11	0	66
1985—Houston USFL	10	5	32	6.4	0	48	538	11.2	7	0	0	...	0	0	0	...	0	7	1	44
1986—Washington NFL	10	0	0	...	0	14	286	20.4	2	0	0	...	0	0	0	...	0	2	...	12
1987—Washington NFL	12	1	-4	-4.0	0	37	630	17.0	3	0	0	...	0	4	118	29.5	0	3	...	18
1988—Washington NFL	16	2	14	7.0	0	73	1148	15.7	12	0	0	...	0	19	362	19.1	0	12	...	72
1989—Washington NFL	16	4	19	4.8	0	80	1138	14.2	4	2	12	6.0	0	9	134	14.9	0	4	...	24
1990—Washington NFL	16	4	17	4.3	0	56	727	13.0	3	1	22	22.0	0	0	0	...	0	3	...	18
1991—Washington NFL	16	7	47	6.7	0	45	580	12.9	5	0	0	...	0	0	0	...	0	6	...	36
1992—Washington NFL	15	4	-6	-1.5	0	51	707	13.9	3	0	0	...	0	0	0	...	0	3	...	18
1993—Washington NFL	16	1	7	7.0	0	58	638	11.0	4	0	0	...	0	0	0	...	0	4	...	24
1994—Atlanta NFL	14	0	0	...	0	67	599	8.9	1	0	0	...	0	0	0	...	0	1	0	6
1995—Atlanta NFL	3	0	0	...	0	2	24	12.0	0	0	0	...	0	0	0	...	0	0	0	0
USFL totals (2 years)	28	15	90	6.0	0	149	1916	12.9	18	19	148	7.8	0	2	28	14.0	0	18	1	110
NFL totals (10 years)	134	23	94	4.1	1	483	6477	13.4	37	3	34	11.3	0	32	614	19.2	0	38	0	228
Pro totals (12 years)	162	38	184	4.9	1	632	8393	13.3	55	22	182	8.3	0	34	642	18.9	0	56	1	338

SAPOLU, JESSE　　　G　　　49ERS

PERSONAL: Born March 10, 1961, in Laie, Western Samoa. ... 6-4/278. ... Full name: Manase Jesse Sapolu.
HIGH SCHOOL: Farrington (Honolulu).
COLLEGE: Hawaii.
TRANSACTIONS/CAREER NOTES: Selected by Oakland Invaders in 17th round (199th pick overall) of 1983 USFL draft. ... Selected by San Francisco 49ers in 11th round (289th pick overall) of 1983 NFL draft. ... Signed by 49ers (July 10, 1983). ... On physically unable to perform list with fractured foot (July 19-August 12, 1984). ... On physically unable to perform list with fractured foot (August 13-November 8, 1984). ... On injured reserve with fractured foot (November 16, 1984-remainder of season). ... On injured reserve with broken foot (August 12, 1985-entire season). ... On injured reserve with broken leg (July 30, 1986-entire season). ... On reserve/did not report list (July 30-August 27, 1990).
PLAYING EXPERIENCE: San Francisco NFL, 1983, 1984 and 1987-1995. ... Games: 1983 (16), 1984 (1), 1987 (12), 1988 (16), 1989 (16), 1990 (16), 1991 (16), 1992 (16), 1993 (16), 1994 (13), 1995 (16). Total: 154.
CHAMPIONSHIP GAME EXPERIENCE: Played in NFC championship game (1983, 1988-1990 and 1992-1994 seasons). ... Member of Super Bowl championship team (1988, 1989 and 1994 seasons).
HONORS: Played in Pro Bowl (1993 and 1994 seasons).
PRO STATISTICS: 1994—Recovered one fumble.

SAPP, WARREN　　　DT　　　BUCCANEERS

PERSONAL: Born December 19, 1972, in Plymouth, Fla. ... 6-2/281.
HIGH SCHOOL: Apopka (Fla.).
COLLEGE: Miami (Fla.).
TRANSACTIONS/CAREER NOTES: Selected after junior season by Tampa Bay Buccaneers in first round (12th pick overall) of 1995 NFL draft. ... Signed by Buccaneers (April 27, 1995).
HONORS: Lombardi Award winner (1994). ... Named defensive lineman on The Sporting News college All-America first team (1994).
PRO STATISTICS: 1995—Intercepted one pass for five yards and a touchdown.

Year Team	G	SACKS
1995—Tampa Bay NFL	16	3.0

SARGENT, KEVIN　　　G/G　　　BENGALS

PERSONAL: Born March 31, 1969, in Bremerton, Wash. ... 6-6/284.
HIGH SCHOOL: Bremerton (Wash.).
COLLEGE: Eastern Washington.
TRANSACTIONS/CAREER NOTES: Signed as non-drafted free agent by Cincinnati Bengals (1992). ... On injured reserve with fractured right forearm (December 3, 1993-remainder of season).
PLAYING EXPERIENCE: Cincinnati NFL, 1992-1995. ... Games: 1992 (16), 1993 (1), 1994 (15), 1995 (15). Total: 47.
PRO STATISTICS: 1992—Recovered two fumbles. 1995—Recovered one fumble.

SASA, DON　　　DT　　　CHARGERS

PERSONAL: Born September 16, 1972, in American Samoa. ... 6-3/286. ... Name pronounced SAW-sa.
HIGH SCHOOL: Long Beach (Calif.) Poly.
JUNIOR COLLEGE: Long Beach (Calif.) City College.
COLLEGE: Washington State.
TRANSACTIONS/CAREER NOTES: Selected by San Diego Chargers in third round (93rd pick overall) of 1995 NFL draft. ... Signed by Chargers (July 17, 1995). ... On injured reserve with knee injury (October 17, 1995-remainder of season).
PLAYING EXPERIENCE: San Diego NFL, 1995. ... Games: 1995 (5).

SAUERBRUN, TODD　　　P　　　BEARS

PERSONAL: Born January 20, 1971, in Setauket, N.Y. ... 5-10/206. ... Name pronounced SOW-er-bruhn.
HIGH SCHOOL: Ward Melville (Setauket, N.Y.).
COLLEGE: West Virginia.
TRANSACTIONS/CAREER NOTES: Selected by Chicago Bears in second round (56th pick overall) of 1995 NFL draft. ... Signed by Bears (July

20, 1995).

HONORS: Named punter on The Sporting News college All-America first team (1994).

Year Team	G	No.	Yds.	Avg.	Net avg.	In. 20	Blk.
				PUNTING			
1995—Chicago NFL	15	55	2080	37.8	31.1	16	0

SAUNDERS, CEDRIC — TE — BUCCANEERS

PERSONAL: Born September 30, 1972, in Sarasota, Fla. ... 6-3/240.
HIGH SCHOOL: Sarasota (Fla.).
COLLEGE: Ohio State.
TRANSACTIONS/CAREER NOTES: Signed as non-drafted free agent by Tampa Bay Buccaneers (April 27, 1994). ... Released by Buccaneers (August 23, 1994). ... Re-signed by Buccaneers (January 24, 1995). ... Released by Buccaneers (August 27, 1995). ... Re-signed by Buccaneers to practice squad (August 28, 1995). ... Activated (November 17, 1995).
PLAYING EXPERIENCE: Tampa Bay NFL, 1995. ... Games: 1995 (3).

SAVAGE, SEBASTIAN — S

PERSONAL: Born December 12, 1969, in Carlisle, S.C. ... 5-10/187.
HIGH SCHOOL: Union (S.C.).
COLLEGE: North Carolina State.
TRANSACTIONS/CAREER NOTES: Selected by Buffalo Bills in fifth round (139th pick overall) of 1993 NFL draft. ... Signed by Bills (July 13, 1993). ... Released by Bills (August 24, 1993). ... Re-signed by Bills to practice squad (September 3, 1993). ... Granted free agency after 1993 season. ... Signed by Denver Broncos (March 15, 1994). ... Released by Broncos (August 26, 1994). ... Signed by Washington Redskins to practice squad (September 6, 1994). ... Activated (September 16, 1994). ... Released by Redskins (September 20, 1994). ... Re-signed by Redskins to practice squad (September 22, 1994). ... Activated (December 23, 1994). ... Released by Redskins (August 27, 1995). ... Re-signed by Redskins (September 7, 1995). ... Released by Redskins (September 19, 1995). ... Selected by Rhein Fire in 1996 World League draft (February 22, 1996).
PLAYING EXPERIENCE: Washington NFL, 1994 and 1995. ... Games: 1994 (1), 1995 (2). Total: 3.

SAWYER, COREY — CB — BENGALS

PERSONAL: Born October 4, 1971, in Key West, Fla. ... 5-11/171.
HIGH SCHOOL: Key West (Fla.).
COLLEGE: Florida State.
TRANSACTIONS/CAREER NOTES: Selected after junior season by Cincinnati Bengals in fourth round (104th pick overall) of 1994 NFL draft. ... Signed by Bengals (July 22, 1994).
HONORS: Named defensive back on The Sporting News college All-America first team (1993).
PRO STATISTICS: 1994—Recovered one fumble. 1995—Credited with two sacks.

Year Team	G	INTERCEPTIONS No.	Yds.	Avg.	TD	PUNT RETURNS No.	Yds.	Avg.	TD	KICKOFF RETURNS No.	Yds.	Avg.	TD	TOTALS TD	2pt.	Pts.	Fum.
1994—Cincinnati NFL	15	2	0	0.0	0	26	307	11.8	1	1	14	14.0	0	1	0	6	2
1995—Cincinnati NFL	12	2	61	30.5	0	9	58	6.4	0	2	50	25.0	0	0	0	0	1
Pro totals (2 years)	27	4	61	15.3	0	35	365	10.4	1	3	64	21.3	0	1	0	6	3

SAXON, JAMES — FB

PERSONAL: Born March 23, 1966, in Buford, S.C. ... 5-11/237. ... Full name: James Elijah Saxon.
HIGH SCHOOL: Battery Creek (Burton, S.C.).
JUNIOR COLLEGE: American River College (Calif.).
COLLEGE: San Jose State.
TRANSACTIONS/CAREER NOTES: Selected by Kansas City Chiefs in sixth round (139th pick overall) of 1988 NFL draft. ... Signed by Chiefs (July 19, 1988). ... On injured reserve with ankle injury (September 8-November 24, 1990). ... Granted unconditional free agency (February 1, 1992). ... Signed by Miami Dolphins (March 17, 1992). ... Granted unconditional free agency (February 17, 1994). ... Re-signed by Dolphins (April 25, 1994). ... Granted unconditional free agency (February 17, 1995). ... Signed by Kansas City Chiefs (June 19, 1995). ... Released by Chiefs (August 27, 1995). ... Signed by Philadelphia Eagles (October 23, 1995). ... Granted unconditional free agency (February 16, 1996).
CHAMPIONSHIP GAME EXPERIENCE: Played in AFC championship game (1992 season).
PRO STATISTICS: 1988—Recovered one fumble. 1989—Had only pass attempt intercepted.

Year Team	G	RUSHING Att.	Yds.	Avg.	TD	RECEIVING No.	Yds.	Avg.	TD	KICKOFF RETURNS No.	Yds.	Avg.	TD	TOTALS TD	2pt.	Pts.	Fum.
1988—Kansas City NFL	16	60	236	3.9	2	19	177	9.3	0	2	40	20.0	0	2	...	12	0
1989—Kansas City NFL	16	58	233	4.0	3	11	86	7.8	0	3	16	5.3	0	3	...	18	2
1990—Kansas City NFL	6	3	15	5.0	0	1	5	5.0	0	5	81	16.2	0	0	...	0	0
1991—Kansas City NFL	16	6	13	2.2	0	6	55	9.2	0	4	56	14.0	0	0	...	0	1
1992—Miami NFL	16	4	7	1.8	0	5	41	8.2	0	0	0	...	0	0	...	0	0
1993—Miami NFL	16	5	13	2.6	0	0	0	...	0	1	7	7.0	0	0	...	0	0
1994—Miami NFL	16	8	16	2.0	0	27	151	5.6	0	1	12	12.0	0	0	...	0	0
1995—Philadelphia NFL	9	1	0	0.0	0	0	0	...	0	1	3	3.0	0	0	...	0	0
Pro totals (8 years)	111	145	533	3.7	5	69	515	7.5	0	17	215	12.7	0	5	0	30	4

SAXON, MIKE — P — VIKINGS

PERSONAL: Born July 10, 1962, in Arcadia, Calif. ... 6-3/205. ... Full name: Michael Eric Saxon.

HIGH SCHOOL: Arcadia (Calif.).
JUNIOR COLLEGE: Pasadena (Calif.) City College.
COLLEGE: San Diego State.
TRANSACTIONS/CAREER NOTES: Selected by Arizona Wranglers in 13th round (265th pick overall) of 1984 USFL draft. ... Selected by Detroit Lions in 11th round (300th pick overall) of 1984 NFL draft. ... Signed by Lions (May 29, 1984). ... Released by Lions (August 27, 1984). ... Signed by Wranglers (November 7, 1984). ... Released by Wranglers (February 11, 1985). ... Signed by Dallas Cowboys (March 27, 1985). ... Granted unconditional free agency (February 1-April 1, 1992). ... Re-signed by Cowboys for 1992 season. ... Released by Cowboys (July 7, 1993). ... Signed by New England Patriots (July 26, 1993). ... Released by Patriots (August 20, 1994). ... Signed by Minnesota Vikings (August 30, 1994). ... Granted unconditional free agency (February 17, 1995). ... Re-signed by Vikings (March 7, 1995).
CHAMPIONSHIP GAME EXPERIENCE: Played in NFC championship game (1992 season). ... Member of Super Bowl championship team (1992 season).
PRO STATISTICS: 1989—Rushed once for one yard and attempted one pass with one completion for four yards. 1990—Rushed once for 20 yards. 1993—Rushed twice for two yards, fumbled once and recovered one fumble. 1994—Rushed once for no yards, attempted one pass without a completion and fumbled once.

				PUNTING			
Year Team	G	No.	Yds.	Avg.	Net avg.	In. 20	Blk.
1985—Dallas NFL	16	81	3396	41.9	35.5	20	1
1986—Dallas NFL	16	86	3498	40.7	34.4	28	1
1987—Dallas NFL	12	68	2685	39.5	34.2	20	0
1988—Dallas NFL	16	80	3271	40.9	34.2	24	0
1989—Dallas NFL	16	79	3233	40.9	34.3	19	2
1990—Dallas NFL	16	79	3413	43.2	35.6	20	0
1991—Dallas NFL	16	57	2426	42.6	36.8	16	0
1992—Dallas NFL	16	61	2620	43.0	33.5	19	0
1993—New England NFL	16	73	3096	42.4	34.8	25	*3
1994—Minnesota NFL	16	77	3301	42.9	36.2	28	0
1995—Minnesota NFL	16	72	2948	40.9	33.1	21	0
Pro totals (11 years)	172	813	33887	41.7	34.8	240	7

SCHLERETH, MARK   G   BRONCOS

PERSONAL: Born January 25, 1966, in Anchorage, Alaska. ... 6-3/278.
HIGH SCHOOL: Robert Service (Anchorage, Alaska).
COLLEGE: Idaho.
TRANSACTIONS/CAREER NOTES: Selected by Washington Redskins in 10th round (263rd pick overall) of 1989 NFL draft. ... Signed by Redskins (July 23, 1989). ... On injured reserve with knee injury (September 5-November 11, 1989). ... On injured reserve (November 16, 1993-remainder of season). ... Released by Redskins (September 2, 1994). ... Re-signed by Redskins (September 3, 1994). ... Granted unconditional free agency (February 17, 1995). ... Signed by Denver Broncos (March 27, 1995).
PLAYING EXPERIENCE: Washington NFL, 1989-1994; Denver NFL, 1995. ... Games: 1989 (6), 1990 (12), 1991 (16), 1992 (16), 1993 (9), 1994 (16), 1995 (16). Total: 91.
CHAMPIONSHIP GAME EXPERIENCE: Played in NFC championship game (1991 season). ... Member of Super Bowl championship team (1991 season).
HONORS: Played in Pro Bowl (1991 season).
PRO STATISTICS: 1989—Recovered one fumble. 1993—Recovered one fumble.

SCHLESINGER, COREY   FB   LIONS

PERSONAL: Born June 23, 1972, in Columbus, Neb. ... 6-0/230.
HIGH SCHOOL: Columbus (Neb.).
COLLEGE: Nebraska.
TRANSACTIONS/CAREER NOTES: Selected by Detroit Lions in sixth round (192nd pick overall) of 1995 NFL draft. ... Signed by Lions (July 19, 1995).
PLAYING EXPERIENCE: Detroit NFL, 1995. ... Games: 1995 (16).
PRO STATISTICS: 1995—Rushed once for one yard, caught one pass for two yards and recovered one fumble for 11 yards.

SCHREIBER, ADAM   C   GIANTS

PERSONAL: Born February 20, 1962, in Galveston, Texas. ... 6-4/298. ... Full name: Adam Blayne Schreiber.
HIGH SCHOOL: Butler (Huntsville, Ala.).
COLLEGE: Texas.
TRANSACTIONS/CAREER NOTES: Selected by Seattle Seahawks in ninth round (243rd pick overall) of 1984 NFL draft. ... Signed by Seahawks (June 20, 1984). ... Released by Seahawks (August 27, 1984). ... Re-signed by Seahawks (October 10, 1984). ... Released by Seahawks (August 29, 1985). ... Signed by New Orleans Saints (November 20, 1985). ... Released by Saints (September 1, 1986). ... Signed by Philadelphia Eagles (October 16, 1986). ... Claimed on waivers by New York Jets (October 19, 1988). ... Granted unconditional free agency (February 1, 1990). ... Signed by Minnesota Vikings (March 21, 1990). ... Granted unconditional free agency (February 1, 1992). ... Re-signed by Vikings for 1992 season. ... Granted unconditional free agency (March 1, 1993). ... Re-signed by Vikings (May 7, 1993). ... Released by Vikings (July 12, 1994). ... Signed by New York Giants (August 16, 1994). ... Granted unconditional free agency (February 17, 1995). ... Re-signed by Giants (May 8, 1995).
PLAYING EXPERIENCE: Seattle NFL, 1984; New Orleans NFL, 1985; Philadelphia NFL, 1986 and 1987; Philadelphia (6)-New York Jets (7) NFL, 1988; New York Jets NFL, 1989; Minnesota NFL, 1990-1993; New York Giants NFL, 1994 and 1995. ... Games: 1984 (6), 1985 (1), 1986 (9), 1987 (12), 1988 (13), 1989 (16), 1990 (16), 1991 (15), 1992 (16), 1993 (16), 1994 (16), 1995 (16). Total: 152.
PRO STATISTICS: 1990—Returned one kickoff for five yards. 1992—Recovered one fumble.

SCHULTZ, BILL   G/OT   BRONCOS

PERSONAL: Born May 1, 1967, in Granada Hills, Calif. ... 6-5/305.

HIGH SCHOOL: John F. Kennedy (Granada Hills, Calif.).
JUNIOR COLLEGE: Glendale (Calif.) College.
COLLEGE: Southern California.
TRANSACTIONS/CAREER NOTES: Selected by Indianapolis Colts in fourth round (94th pick overall) of 1990 NFL draft. ... Signed by Colts (July 23, 1990). ... On injured reserve with knee injury (September 11-October 11, 1991). ... On injured reserve with virus (December 13, 1991-remainder of season). ... On injured reserve with ankle injury (November 13-December 12, 1992); on practice squad (December 9-12, 1992). ... Granted free agency (March 1, 1993). ... Re-signed by Colts (July 18, 1993). ... Released by Colts (April 26, 1994). ... Signed by Los Angeles Rams (July 8, 1994). ... Released by Rams (August 28, 1994). ... Signed by Houston Oilers (September 7, 1994). ... On inactive list for 10 games (1994). ... Granted unconditional free agency (February 17, 1995). ... Signed by Denver Broncos (March 23, 1995). ... Released by Broncos (October 3, 1995). ... Re-signed by Broncos (October 30, 1995).
PLAYING EXPERIENCE: Indianapolis NFL, 1990-1993; Denver NFL, 1995. ... Games: 1990 (12), 1991 (10), 1992 (10), 1993 (14), 1995 (2). Total: 48.
PRO STATISTICS: 1991—Recovered two fumbles. 1992—Caught one pass for three yards and a touchdown.

SCHULZ, KURT S BILLS

PERSONAL: Born December 28, 1968, in Wenatchee, Wash. ... 6-1/208. ... Full name: Kurt Erich Schulz.
HIGH SCHOOL: Eisenhower (Yakima, Wash.).
COLLEGE: Eastern Washington.
TRANSACTIONS/CAREER NOTES: Selected by Buffalo Bills in seventh round (195th pick overall) of 1992 NFL draft. ... Signed by Bills (July 22, 1992). ... On injured reserve with knee injury (October 26-December 19, 1992).
CHAMPIONSHIP GAME EXPERIENCE: Played in AFC championship game (1993 season). ... Member of Bills for Super Bowl XXVII (1992 season); inactive. ... Played in Super Bowl XXVIII (1993 season).
PRO STATISTICS: 1992—Recovered two fumbles.

			INTERCEPTIONS		
Year Team	G	No.	Yds.	Avg.	TD
1992—Buffalo NFL	8	0	0	...	0
1993—Buffalo NFL	12	0	0	...	0
1994—Buffalo NFL	16	0	0	...	0
1995—Buffalo NFL	13	6	48	8.0	1
Pro totals (4 years)	49	6	48	8.0	1

SCHWANTZ, JIM LB COWBOYS

PERSONAL: Born January 23, 1970, in Arlington Heights, Ill. ... 6-2/232. ... Full name: James William Schwantz.
HIGH SCHOOL: William Fremd (Palatine, Ill).
COLLEGE: Purdue.
TRANSACTIONS/CAREER NOTES: Signed as non-drafted free agent by Chicago Bears (1992). ... Released by Bears (August 31, 1992). ... Re-signed by Bears to practice squad (September 1992). ... Activated (December 26, 1992). ... Released by Bears (August 30, 1993). ... Re-signed by Bears to practice squad (August 31, 1993). ... Traded by Bears to Dallas Cowboys for sixth-round pick (traded to St. Louis) in 1996 draft (August 28, 1994).
PLAYING EXPERIENCE: Chicago NFL, 1992; Dallas NFL, 1994 and 1995. ... Games: 1992 (1), 1994 (7), 1995 (16). Totals: 24.
CHAMPIONSHIP GAME EXPERIENCE: Member of Cowboys for NFC championship game (1994 season); inactive. ... Played in NFC championship game (1995 season). ... Member of Super Bowl championship team (1995 season).
PRO STATISTICS: 1995—Returned one kickoff for nine yards.

SCHWARTZ, BRYAN LB JAGUARS

PERSONAL: Born December 5, 1971, in St. Lawrence, S.D. ... 6-4/250.
HIGH SCHOOL: Miller (S.D.).
COLLEGE: Augustana (S.D.).
TRANSACTIONS/CAREER NOTES: Selected by Jacksonville Jaguars in second round (64th pick overall) of 1995 NFL draft. ... Signed by Jaguars (June 1, 1995).
PLAYING EXPERIENCE: Jacksonville NFL, 1995. ... Games: 1995 (14).
PRO STATISTICS: 1995—Recovered one fumble.

SCOTT, DARNAY WR/KR BENGALS

PERSONAL: Born July 7, 1972, in St. Louis. ... 6-1/180.
HIGH SCHOOL: Kearny (San Diego).
COLLEGE: San Diego State.
TRANSACTIONS/CAREER NOTES: Selected after junior season by Cincinnati Bengals in second round (30th pick overall) of 1994 NFL draft. ... Signed by Bengals (July 18, 1994).
PRO STATISTICS: 1994—Attempted one pass with one completion for 53 yards.
STATISTICAL PLATEAUS: 100-yard receiving games: 1994 (2), 1995 (1). Total: 3.

		RUSHING				RECEIVING				KICKOFF RETURNS				TOTALS			
Year Team	G	Att.	Yds.	Avg.	TD	No.	Yds.	Avg.	TD	No.	Yds.	Avg.	TD	TD	2pt.	Pts.	Fum.
1994—Cincinnati NFL	16	10	106	10.6	0	46	866	18.8	5	15	342	22.8	0	5	0	30	0
1995—Cincinnati NFL	16	5	11	2.2	0	52	821	15.8	5	0	0	...	0	5	0	30	0
Pro totals (2 years)	32	15	117	7.8	0	98	1687	17.2	10	15	342	22.8	0	10	0	60	0

SCOTT, TODD S BUCCANEERS

PERSONAL: Born January 23, 1968, in Galveston, Texas. ... 5-10/205. ... Full name: Todd Carlton Scott.

HIGH SCHOOL: Ball (Galveston, Texas).
COLLEGE: Southwestern Louisiana (degree in business management).
TRANSACTIONS/CAREER NOTES: Selected by Minnesota Vikings in sixth round (163rd pick overall) of 1991 NFL draft. ... Signed by Vikings (July 24, 1991). ... Granted unconditional free agency (February 17, 1995). ... Signed by New York Jets (March 21, 1995). ... Claimed on waivers by Tampa Bay Buccaneers (November 29, 1995).
HONORS: Played in Pro Bowl (1992 season).
PRO STATISTICS: 1992—Credited with one sack. 1993—Recovered one fumble.

		INTERCEPTIONS			
Year Team	G	No.	Yds.	Avg.	TD
1991—Minnesota NFL	16	0	0	...	0
1992—Minnesota NFL	16	5	79	15.8	1
1993—Minnesota NFL	13	2	26	13.0	0
1994—Minnesota NFL	15	0	0	...	0
1995—New York Jets NFL	10	0	0	...	0
—Tampa Bay NFL	1	0	0	...	0
Pro totals (5 years)	71	7	105	15.0	1

SCRAFFORD, KIRK   OT   49ERS

PERSONAL: Born March 16, 1967, in Billings, Mont. ... 6-6/275. ... Full name: Kirk Tippet Scrafford.
HIGH SCHOOL: Billings (Mont.) West.
COLLEGE: Montana.
TRANSACTIONS/CAREER NOTES: Signed as non-drafted free agent by Cincinnati Bengals (May 1990). ... On injured reserve with knee injury (September 4-November 23, 1990). ... On practice squad (November 23-December 22, 1990). ... On injured reserve with knee injury (August 27-October 15, 1991). ... Claimed on waivers by Seattle Seahawks (November 16, 1992). ... Released by Seahawks after failing physical (November 17, 1992). ... Signed by Bengals (November 1992). ... Claimed on waivers by Denver Broncos (August 17, 1993). ... Granted unconditional free agency (February 17, 1995). ... Signed by San Francisco 49ers (March 29, 1995).
PLAYING EXPERIENCE: Cincinnati NFL, 1990-1992; Denver NFL, 1993 and 1994; San Francisco NFL, 1995. ... Games: 1990 (2), 1991 (9), 1992 (8), 1993 (16), 1994 (16), 1995 (16). Total: 67.
PRO STATISTICS: 1994—Recovered one fumble.

SCROGGINS, TRACY   LB   LIONS

PERSONAL: Born September 11, 1969, in Checotah, Okla. ... 6-2/255.
HIGH SCHOOL: Checotah (Okla.).
JUNIOR COLLEGE: Coffeyville (Kan.) Community College.
COLLEGE: Tulsa.
TRANSACTIONS/CAREER NOTES: Selected by Detroit Lions in second round (53rd pick overall) of 1992 NFL draft. ... Signed by Lions (July 23, 1992). ... Granted free agency (February 17, 1995). ... Re-signed by Lions (May 17, 1995).
PRO STATISTICS: 1993—Intercepted one pass for no yards and recovered one fumble. 1994—Recovered one fumble. 1995—Recovered one fumble for 81 yards and a touchdown.

Year Team	G	SACKS
1992—Detroit NFL	16	7.5
1993—Detroit NFL	16	8.0
1994—Detroit NFL	16	2.5
1995—Detroit NFL	16	9.5
Pro totals (4 years)	64	27.5

SCURLOCK, MIKE   CB   RAMS

PERSONAL: Born February 26, 1972, in Casa Grande, Ariz. ... 5-10/197. ... Cousin of Randy Robbins, safety, Denver Broncos (1984-1991). ... Name pronounced SKER-lock.
HIGH SCHOOL: Sunnyside (Tucson, Ariz.), then Cholla (Tucson, Ariz.).
COLLEGE: Arizona.
TRANSACTIONS/CAREER NOTES: Selected by St. Louis Rams in fifth round (140th pick overall) of 1995 NFL draft. ... Signed by Rams (June 20, 1995). ... On injured reserve with sprained left knee (December 20, 1995-remainder of season).
PLAYING EXPERIENCE: St. Louis NFL, 1995. ... Games: 1995 (14).
PRO STATISTICS: 1995—Intercepted one pass for 13 yards and recovered one fumble.

SEABRON, MALCOLM   WR   OILERS

PERSONAL: Born December 29, 1972, in San Francisco. ... 6-0/194. ... Full name: Malcolm Gregory Seabron.
HIGH SCHOOL: C.K. McClatchy (Sacramento).
COLLEGE: Fresno State.
TRANSACTIONS/CAREER NOTES: Selected by Houston Oilers in third round (101st pick overall) of 1994 NFL draft. ... Signed by Oilers (June 17, 1994).

		RECEIVING				TOTALS			
Year Team	G	No.	Yds.	Avg.	TD	TD	2pt.	Pts.	Fum.
1994—Houston NFL	13	0	0	...	0	0	0	0	0
1995—Houston NFL	15	12	167	13.9	1	1	0	6	0
Pro totals (2 years)	28	12	167	13.9	1	1	0	6	0

SEALS, RAY — DE — STEELERS

PERSONAL: Born June 17, 1965, in Syracuse, N.Y. ... 6-3/306.
HIGH SCHOOL: Henninger (Syracuse, N.Y.).
COLLEGE: None.
TRANSACTIONS/CAREER NOTES: Played semipro football for Syracuse Express of Eastern Football League (1986 and 1987). ... Signed as non-drafted free agent by Tampa Bay Buccaneers for 1988 (November 18, 1987). ... On injured reserve with back injury (August 8, 1988-entire season). ... On injured reserve with broken bone in foot (September 20, 1989-remainder of season). ... Released by Buccaneers (November 2, 1990). ... Signed by Detroit Lions (November 8, 1990). ... On inactive list for two games with Lions (1990). ... Released by Lions (November 20, 1990). ... Signed by Indianapolis Colts (November 27, 1990). ... Active for one game with Colts (1990); did not play. ... Released by Colts (December 5, 1990). ... Signed by Buccaneers (March 6, 1991). ... On injured reserve with sprained ankle (November 14-December 13, 1991). ... Granted free agency (February 1, 1992). ... Re-signed by Buccaneers (July 28, 1992). ... On injured reserve with knee injury (November 25, 1992-remainder of season). ... Granted unconditional free agency (February 17, 1994). ... Signed by Pittsburgh Steelers (March 21, 1994).
CHAMPIONSHIP GAME EXPERIENCE: Played in AFC championship game (1994 and 1995 seasons). ... Played in Super Bowl XXX (1995 season).
PRO STATISTICS: 1991—Recovered two fumbles. 1993—Intercepted one pass in end zone for a touchdown and recovered one fumble. 1994—Recovered two fumbles. 1995—Intercepted one pass for no yards and recovered one fumble for four yards.

Year Team	G	SACKS
1988—Tampa Bay NFL	Did not play.	
1989—Tampa Bay NFL	2	0.0
1990—Tampa Bay NFL	8	0.0
1991—Tampa Bay NFL	10	0.0
1992—Tampa Bay NFL	11	5.0
1993—Tampa Bay NFL	16	8.5
1994—Pittsburgh NFL	13	7.0
1995—Pittsburgh NFL	16	8.5
Pro totals (7 years)	**76**	**29.0**

SEARCY, LEON — OT — JAGUARS

PERSONAL: Born December 21, 1969, in Washington, D.C. ... 6-3/304. ... Name pronounced SEER-see.
HIGH SCHOOL: Maynard Evans (Orlando).
COLLEGE: Miami, Fla. (degree in sociology, 1992).
TRANSACTIONS/CAREER NOTES: Selected by Pittsburgh Steelers in first round (11th pick overall) of 1992 NFL draft. ... Signed by Steelers (August 3, 1992). ... Granted unconditional free agency (February 16, 1996). ... Signed by Jacksonville Jaguars (February 18, 1996).
PLAYING EXPERIENCE: Pittsburgh NFL, 1992-1995. ... Games: 1992 (15), 1993 (16), 1994 (16), 1995 (16). Total: 63.
CHAMPIONSHIP GAME EXPERIENCE: Played in AFC championship game (1994 and 1995 seasons). ... Played in Super Bowl XXX (1995 season).
HONORS: Named offensive tackle on THE SPORTING NEWS college All-America second team (1991).
PRO STATISTICS: 1993—Recovered one fumble. 1995—Recovered one fumble.

SEAU, JUNIOR — LB — CHARGERS

PERSONAL: Born January 19, 1969, in Samoa. ... 6-3/250. ... Name pronounced SAY-ow.
HIGH SCHOOL: Oceanside (Calif.).
COLLEGE: Southern California.
TRANSACTIONS/CAREER NOTES: Selected after junior season by San Diego Chargers in first round (fifth pick overall) of 1990 NFL draft. ... Signed by Chargers (August 27, 1990).
CHAMPIONSHIP GAME EXPERIENCE: Played in AFC championship game (1994 season). ... Played in Super Bowl XXIX (1994 season).
HONORS: Named linebacker on THE SPORTING NEWS college All-America first team (1989). ... Played in Pro Bowl (1991-1995 seasons). ... Named inside linebacker on THE SPORTING NEWS NFL All-Pro team (1992-1995).
PRO STATISTICS: 1992—Recovered one fumble for 10 yards. 1993—Recovered one fumble for 21 yards. 1994—Recovered three fumbles. 1995—Recovered three fumbles for 30 yards and one touchdown.

Year Team	G	INTERCEPTIONS No.	Yds.	Avg.	TD	SACKS No.
1990—San Diego NFL	16	0	0	...	0	1.0
1991—San Diego NFL	16	0	0	...	0	7.0
1992—San Diego NFL	15	2	51	25.5	0	4.5
1993—San Diego NFL	16	2	58	29.0	0	0.0
1994—San Diego NFL	16	0	0	...	0	5.5
1995—San Diego NFL	16	2	5	2.5	0	2.0
Pro totals (6 years)	**95**	**6**	**114**	**19.0**	**0**	**20.0**

SEAY, MARK — WR — EAGLES

PERSONAL: Born April 11, 1967, in Los Angeles. ... 6-0/175. ... Full name: Mark Edward Seay.
HIGH SCHOOL: San Bernardino (Calif.).
COLLEGE: Long Beach State.
TRANSACTIONS/CAREER NOTES: Signed as non-drafted free agent by San Francisco 49ers (May 8, 1992). ... Released by 49ers (August 31, 1992). ... Re-signed by 49ers to practice squad (September 1, 1992). ... Granted free agency after 1992 season. ... Re-signed by 49ers (March 12, 1993). ... Claimed on waivers by San Diego Chargers (August 31, 1993). ... Granted unconditional free agency (February 16, 1996). ... Signed by Philadelphia Eagles (April 8, 1996).
CHAMPIONSHIP GAME EXPERIENCE: Played in AFC championship game (1994 season). ... Played in Super Bowl XXIX (1994 season).
POSTSEASON RECORDS: Shares Super Bowl and career and single-game records for most two-point conversions—1 (January 29, 1995,

vs. San Francisco). ... Shares NFL postseason career and single-game records for most two-point conversions—1 (January 29, 1995, vs. San Francisco).

STATISTICAL PLATEAUS: 100-yard receiving games: 1994 (1), 1995 (1). Total: 2.

		RECEIVING				TOTALS			
Year — Team	G	No.	Yds.	Avg.	TD	TD	2pt.	Pts.	Fum.
1993—San Diego NFL	1	0	0	...	0	0	...	0	0
1994—San Diego NFL	16	58	645	11.1	6	6	0	36	0
1995—San Diego NFL	16	45	537	11.9	3	3	1	20	0
Pro totals (3 years)	33	103	1182	11.5	9	9	1	56	0

SEHORN, JASON CB GIANTS

PERSONAL: Born April 15, 1971, in Mt. Shasta, Calif. ... 6-2/210.
HIGH SCHOOL: Mt. Shasta (Calif.).
COLLEGE: Southern California.
TRANSACTIONS/CAREER NOTES: Selected by New York Giants in second round (59th pick overall) of 1994 NFL draft. ... Signed by Giants (July 17, 1994).
PLAYING EXPERIENCE: New York Giants NFL, 1994 and 1995. ... Games: 1994 (8), 1995 (14). Total: 22.

SELBY, ROB G

PERSONAL: Born October 11, 1967, in Birmingham, Ala. ... 6-3/286. ... Full name: Robert Seth Selby Jr.
HIGH SCHOOL: Berry (Ala.).
COLLEGE: Auburn.
TRANSACTIONS/CAREER NOTES: Selected by Philadelphia Eagles in third round (76th pick overall) of 1991 NFL draft. ... Signed by Eagles (July 14, 1991). ... On injured reserve with knee injury (September 8, 1993-remainder of season). ... Granted free agency (February 17, 1994). ... Re-signed by Eagles (June 22, 1994). ... Granted unconditional free agency (February 17, 1995). ... Signed by Atlanta Falcons (May 18, 1995). ... Released by Falcons (August 27, 1995). ... Signed by Arizona Cardinals (October 17, 1995). ... Granted unconditional free agency (February 16, 1996).
PLAYING EXPERIENCE: Philadelphia NFL, 1991-1994; Arizona NFL, 1995. ... Games: 1991 (13), 1992 (16), 1993 (1), 1994 (2), 1995 (7). Total: 39.

SEMPLE, TONY G LIONS

PERSONAL: Born December 20, 1970, in Springfield, Ill. ... 6-4/286. ... Full name: Anthony Lee Semple.
HIGH SCHOOL: Lincoln Community (Ill.).
COLLEGE: Memphis State.
TRANSACTIONS/CAREER NOTES: Selected by Detroit Lions in fifth round (154th pick overall) of 1994 NFL draft. ... Signed by Lions (July 21, 1994). ... On injured reserve with knee injury (August 19, 1994-entire season).
PLAYING EXPERIENCE: Detroit NFL, 1995. ... Games: 1995 (16).

SHADE, SAM S BENGALS

PERSONAL: Born June 14, 1973, in Birmingham, Ala. ... 6-1/191.
HIGH SCHOOL: Wenonah (Birmingham, Ala.).
COLLEGE: Alabama.
TRANSACTIONS/CAREER NOTES: Selected by Cincinnati Bengals in fourth round (102nd pick overall) of 1995 NFL draft. ... Signed by Bengals (July 18, 1995).
PLAYING EXPERIENCE: Cincinnati NFL, 1995. ... Games: 1995 (16).

SHANKS, SIMON LB CARDINALS

PERSONAL: Born October 16, 1971, in Laurel, Miss. ... 6-1/215.
HIGH SCHOOL: R.H. Watkins (Laurel, Miss.).
JUNIOR COLLEGE: Coahoma Junior College (Okla.).
COLLEGE: Tennessee State.
TRANSACTIONS/CAREER NOTES: Signed as non-drafted free agent by Arizona Cardinals (April 27, 1995). ... Released by Cardinals (August 21, 1995). ... Re-signed by Cardinals (August 28, 1995). ... On injured reserve (December 19, 1995-remainder of season). ... Released by Cardinals (December 1995)... Re-signed by Cardinals (April 25, 1996).
PLAYING EXPERIENCE: Arizona NFL, 1995. ... Games: 1995 (15).
PRO STATISTICS: 1995—Recovered one fumble.

SHARPE, SHANNON TE BRONCOS

PERSONAL: Born June 26, 1968, in Chicago. ... 6-2/230. ... Brother of Sterling Sharpe, wide receiver, Green Bay Packers (1988-1994).
HIGH SCHOOL: Glennville (Ga.).
COLLEGE: Savannah (Ga.) State.
TRANSACTIONS/CAREER NOTES: Selected by Denver Broncos in seventh round (192nd pick overall) of 1990 NFL draft. ... Signed by Broncos (July 1990). ... Granted free agency (February 1, 1992). ... Re-signed by Broncos (July 31, 1992). ... Designated by Broncos as transition player (February 15, 1994).
CHAMPIONSHIP GAME EXPERIENCE: Played in AFC championship game (1991 season).

HONORS: Played in Pro Bowl (1992, 1993 and 1995 seasons). ... Named tight end on THE SPORTING NEWS NFL All-Pro team (1993). ... Named to play in Pro Bowl (1994 season); replaced by Eric Green due to injury.
POSTSEASON RECORDS: Shares NFL postseason single-game record for most receptions—13 (January 9, 1994, vs. Los Angeles Raiders).
PRO STATISTICS: 1991—Rushed once for 15 yards and recovered one fumble. 1992—Rushed twice for minus six yards. 1993—Returned one kickoff for no yards. 1995—Recovered one fumble.
STATISTICAL PLATEAUS: 100-yard receiving games: 1992 (2), 1993 (2), 1994 (1), 1995 (2). Total: 7.

		RECEIVING					TOTALS		
Year Team	G	No.	Yds.	Avg.	TD	TD	2pt.	Pts.	Fum.
1990—Denver NFL	16	7	99	14.1	1	1	...	6	1
1991—Denver NFL	16	22	322	14.6	1	1	...	6	0
1992—Denver NFL	16	53	640	12.1	2	2	...	12	1
1993—Denver NFL	16	81	995	12.3	9	9	...	54	1
1994—Denver NFL	15	87	1010	11.6	4	4	2	28	1
1995—Denver NFL	13	63	756	12.0	4	4	0	24	1
Pro totals (6 years)	92	313	3822	12.2	21	21	2	130	5

SHAW, TERRANCE   CB   CHARGERS

PERSONAL: Born November 11, 1973, in Marshall, Texas. ... 5-11/190.
HIGH SCHOOL: Marshall (Texas).
COLLEGE: Stephen F. Austin State.
TRANSACTIONS/CAREER NOTES: Selected by San Diego Chargers in second round (34th pick overall) of 1995 NFL draft. ... Signed by Chargers (June 15, 1995).

		INTERCEPTIONS		
Year Team	G	No.	Yds.	Avg.	TD
1995—San Diego NFL	16	1	31	31.0	0

SHELLEY, ELBERT   CB   FALCONS

PERSONAL: Born December 24, 1964, in Tyronza, Ark. ... 5-11/190. ... Full name: Elbert Vernell Shelley.
HIGH SCHOOL: Truman (Ark.).
COLLEGE: Arkansas State.
TRANSACTIONS/CAREER NOTES: Selected by Atlanta Falcons in 11th round (292nd pick overall) of 1987 NFL draft. ... Signed by Falcons (July 27, 1987). ... On injured reserve with neck injury (September 2-November 28, 1987). ... On injured reserve with wrist injury (September 15-October 14, 1988). ... On injured reserve with hamstring injury (December 2, 1989-remainder of season). ... Granted free agency (February 1, 1990). ... Re-signed by Falcons (July 10, 1990). ... Released by Falcons (September 3, 1990). ... Re-signed by Falcons (September 4, 1990). ... On injured reserve with hamstring injury (October 17-November 15, 1990). ... On injured reserve (September 4-October 18, 1991). ... Granted free agency (February 1, 1992). ... Re-signed by Falcons (August 4, 1992). ... Granted unconditional free agency (March 1, 1993). ... Re-signed by Falcons (July 23, 1993). ... Released by Falcons (August 30, 1993). ... Re-signed by Falcons (August 31, 1993). ... Granted unconditional free agency (February 17, 1994). ... Re-signed by Falcons (July 8, 1994). ... Granted unconditional free agency (February 17, 1995). ... Re-signed by Falcons (April 7, 1995). ... Granted unconditional free agency (February 16, 1996). ... Re-signed by Falcons (April 4, 1996).
PLAYING EXPERIENCE: Atlanta NFL, 1987-1995. ... Games: 1987 (4), 1988 (12), 1989 (10), 1990 (12), 1991 (11), 1992 (13), 1993 (16), 1994 (16), 1995 (13). Total: 107.
HONORS: Played in Pro Bowl (1992-1995 seasons).
PRO STATISTICS: 1988—Returned two kickoffs for five yards and fumbled once. 1989—Intercepted one pass for 31 yards. 1990—Recovered one fumble. 1991—Credited with two sacks. 1994—Recovered one fumble.

SHELLING, CHRISTOPHER   S   BENGALS

PERSONAL: Born November 3, 1972, in Columbus, Ga. ... 5-10/180.
HIGH SCHOOL: Baker (Columbus, Ga.).
COLLEGE: Auburn.
TRANSACTIONS/CAREER NOTES: Signed as non-drafted free agent by Cincinnati Bengals (April 26, 1995).
PLAYING EXPERIENCE: Cincinnati NFL, 1995. ... Games: 1995 (13).

SHEPHERD, LESLIE   WR   REDSKINS

PERSONAL: Born November 3, 1969, in Washington, D.C. ... 5-11/189. ... Full name: Leslie Glenard Shepherd.
HIGH SCHOOL: Forestville (Md.).
COLLEGE: Temple.
TRANSACTIONS/CAREER NOTES: Signed as non-drafted free agent by Tampa Bay Buccaneers (May 2, 1992). ... Released by Buccaneers (August 31, 1992). ... Signed by Pittsburgh Steelers (March 17, 1993). ... Released by Steelers (August 24, 1993). ... Re-signed by Steelers to practice squad (August 31, 1993). ... Granted free agency after 1993 season. ... Re-signed by Steelers (April 4, 1994). ... Claimed on waivers by Washington Redskins (September 4, 1994). ... Released by Redskins (September 16, 1994). ... Re-signed by Redskins to practice squad (September 20, 1994). ... Activated (December 2, 1994).
PRO STATISTICS: 1995—Rushed seven times for 63 yards and one touchdown, returned three kickoffs for 85 yards and recovered one fumble.
STATISTICAL PLATEAUS: 100-yard receiving games: 1995 (1).

		RECEIVING					TOTALS		
Year Team	G	No.	Yds.	Avg.	TD	TD	2pt.	Pts.	Fum.
1994—Washington NFL	3	1	8	8.0	0	0	0	0	0
1995—Washington NFL	14	29	486	16.8	2	3	0	18	0
Pro totals (2 years)	17	30	494	16.5	2	3	0	18	0

SHEPPARD, ASHLEY   LB   RAMS

PERSONAL: Born January 21, 1969, in Greenville, N.C. ... 6-3/240. ... Full name: Ashley Guy Sheppard.
HIGH SCHOOL: North Pitt (Bethel, N.C.), then Fork Union (Va.) Military Academy.
COLLEGE: Clemson.
TRANSACTIONS/CAREER NOTES: Selected by Minnesota Vikings in fourth round (106th pick overall) of 1993 NFL draft. ... Signed by Vikings (July 17, 1993). ... On injured reserve with ankle injury (December 22, 1993-remainder of season). ... Claimed on waivers by Jacksonville Jaguars (August 28, 1995). ... Released by Jaguars (September 18, 1995). ... Signed by Vikings (November 20, 1995). ... Released by Vikings (December 7, 1995). ... Signed by St. Louis Rams (December 13, 1995)
PRO STATISTICS: 1994—Recovered one fumble.

Year Team	G	SACKS
1993—Minnesota NFL	10	1.0
1994—Minnesota NFL	7	0.5
1995—Jacksonville NFL	2	0.0
—St. Louis NFL	2	0.0
Pro totals (3 years)	22	1.5

SHERRARD, MIKE   WR   BRONCOS

PERSONAL: Born June 21, 1963, in Oakland. ... 6-2/187. ... Full name: Michael Watson Sherrard.
HIGH SCHOOL: Chino (Calif.).
COLLEGE: UCLA (degree in history, 1986).
TRANSACTIONS/CAREER NOTES: Selected by Arizona Outlaws in 1986 USFL territorial draft. ... Selected by Dallas Cowboys in first round (18th pick overall) of 1986 NFL draft. ... Signed by Cowboys (August 7, 1986). ... On injured reserve with broken leg (September 1, 1987-entire season). ... On physically unable to perform list with leg injury (July 25, 1988-entire season). ... Granted unconditional free agency (February 1, 1989). ... Signed by San Francisco 49ers (March 30, 1989). ... On physically unable to perform list with leg injury (August 29, 1989-January 4, 1990). ... On injured reserve with broken leg (October 29, 1990-January 11, 1991). ... Granted free agency (February 1, 1992). ... Re-signed by 49ers (July 28, 1992). ... Granted unconditional free agency (March 1, 1993). ... Signed by New York Giants (April 2, 1993). ... On injured reserve with hip injury (October 29, 1993-remainder of season). ... Granted unconditional free agency (February 16, 1996). ... Signed by Denver Broncos (May 3, 1996).
CHAMPIONSHIP GAME EXPERIENCE: Played in NFC championship game (1989, 1990 and 1992 seasons). ... Member of Super Bowl championship team (1989 season).
HONORS: Named wide receiver on THE SPORTING NEWS college All-America second team (1983).
PRO STATISTICS: 1986—Rushed twice for 11 yards. 1992—Recovered two fumbles for 39 yards and one touchdown. 1994—Rushed once for minus 10 yards.
STATISTICAL PLATEAUS: 100-yard receiving games: 1986 (2), 1992 (1), 1993 (1), 1994 (2), 1995 (1). Total: 7.

		RECEIVING					TOTALS		
Year Team	G	No.	Yds.	Avg.	TD	TD	2pt.	Pts.	Fum.
1986—Dallas NFL	16	41	744	18.2	5	5	...	30	0
1987—Dallas NFL				Did not play—injured.					
1988—Dallas NFL				Did not play—injured.					
1989—San Francisco NFL				Did not play—injured.					
1990—San Francisco NFL	7	17	264	15.5	2	2	...	12	0
1991—San Francisco NFL	16	24	296	12.3	2	2	...	12	0
1992—San Francisco NFL	16	38	607	16.0	0	1	...	6	1
1993—New York Giants NFL	6	24	433	18.0	2	2	...	12	0
1994—New York Giants NFL	16	53	825	15.6	6	6	0	36	0
1995—New York Giants NFL	13	44	577	13.1	4	4	0	24	2
Pro totals (7 years)	90	241	3746	15.6	21	22	0	132	3

SHIELDS, WILL   G   CHIEFS

PERSONAL: Born September 15, 1971, in Fort Riley, Kan. ... 6-3/308. ... Full name: Will Herthie Shields.
HIGH SCHOOL: Lawton (Okla.).
COLLEGE: Nebraska (degree in communications).
TRANSACTIONS/CAREER NOTES: Selected by Kansas City Chiefs in the third round (74th pick overall) of 1993 NFL draft. ... Signed by Chiefs (May 3, 1993).
PLAYING EXPERIENCE: Kansas City NFL, 1993-1995. ... Games: 1993 (16), 1994 (16), 1995 (16). Total: 48.
CHAMPIONSHIP GAME EXPERIENCE: Played in AFC championship game (1993 season).
HONORS: Named guard on THE SPORTING NEWS college All-America second team (1991). ... Named guard on THE SPORTING NEWS college All-America first team (1992). ... Played in Pro Bowl (1995 season).
PRO STATISTICS: 1993—Recovered two fumbles. 1994—Recovered one fumble. 1995—Recovered one fumble.

SHULER, HEATH   QB   REDSKINS

PERSONAL: Born December 31, 1971, in Bryson City, N.C. ... 6-2/221. ... Full name: Joseph Heath Shuler.
HIGH SCHOOL: Swain County (Bryson City, N.C.).
COLLEGE: Tennessee.
TRANSACTIONS/CAREER NOTES: Selected after junior season by Washington Redskins in first round (third pick overall) of 1994 NFL draft. ... Signed by Redskins (August 3, 1994).
HONORS: Named quarterback on THE SPORTING NEWS college All-America second team (1993).
PRO STATISTICS: 1994—Fumbled three times. 1995—Fumbled once and recovered one fumble.
MISCELLANEOUS: Regular-season record as starting NFL quarterback: 4-9 (.308).

Year	Team						PASSING						RUSHING				TOTALS		
		G	Att.	Cmp.	Pct.	Yds.	TD	Int.	Avg.	Rat.	Att.	Yds.	Avg.	TD	TD	2pt.	Pts.
1994—Washington NFL		11	265	120	45.3	1658	10	12	6.26	59.6	26	103	4.0	0	0	0	0
1995—Washington NFL		7	125	66	52.8	745	3	7	5.96	55.6	18	57	3.2	0	0	0	0
Pro totals (2 years)		18	390	186	47.7	2403	13	19	6.16	58.3	44	160	3.6	0	0	0	0

SIGLAR, RICKY — OT — CHIEFS

PERSONAL: Born June 14, 1966, in Albuquerque, N.M. ... 6-7/316. ... Full name: Ricky Allan Siglar.
HIGH SCHOOL: Manzano (Albuquerque, N.M.).
JUNIOR COLLEGE: Arizona Western College.
COLLEGE: San Jose State.
TRANSACTIONS/CAREER NOTES: Signed as non-drafted free agent by Dallas Cowboys (March 24, 1989). ... Released by Cowboys (September 5, 1989). ... Signed by San Francisco 49ers to developmental squad (September 20, 1989). ... Released by 49ers (January 29, 1990). ... Re-signed by 49ers (February 5, 1990). ... Released by 49ers (August 20, 1991). ... Re-signed by 49ers (February 4, 1992). ... Released by 49ers (August 31, 1992). ... Signed by Kansas City Chiefs (April 1993). ... Granted free agency (February 17, 1995). ... Tendered offer sheet by Jacksonville Jaguars (March 3, 1995). ... Offer matched by Chiefs (March 10, 1995).
PLAYING EXPERIENCE: San Francisco NFL, 1990; Kansas City NFL, 1993-1995. ... Games: 1990 (15), 1993 (14), 1994 (16), 1995 (16). Total: 61.
CHAMPIONSHIP GAME EXPERIENCE: Played in NFC championship game (1990 season). ... Played in AFC championship game (1993 season).

S

SILVESTRI, DON — K — JETS

PERSONAL: Born December 25, 1968, in Perkasie, Pa. ... 6-4/210.
HIGH SCHOOL: Pennridge (Perkasie, Pa.).
COLLEGE: Pittsburgh.
TRANSACTIONS/CAREER NOTES: Signed as non-drafted free agent by Buffalo Bills (May 5, 1994). ... Released by Bills (August 22, 1994). ... Selected by London Monarchs in 1995 World League draft (February 21, 1995). ... Signed by New York Jets (June 19, 1995).

Year	Team			PUNTING						KICKING						
		G	No.	Yds.	Avg.	Net avg.	In. 20	Blk.	XPM	XPA	FGM	FGA	Lg.	50+	Pts.
1995—London W.L.		...	0	0	...	...	0	0	12	12	13	18	52	1-2	52
—New York Jets NFL		16	5	238	47.6	33.6	0	0	0	0	0	0	...	0-0	0
Pro totals (1 year)		...	5	238	47.6	33.6	0	0	12	12	13	18	52	1-2	52

SIMIEN, TRACY — LB — CHIEFS

PERSONAL: Born May 21, 1967, in Bay City, Texas. ... 6-1/255. ... Full name: Tracy Anthony Simien. ... Related to Elmo Wright, wide receiver, Kansas City Chiefs, Houston Oilers and New England Patriots (1971-1975).
HIGH SCHOOL: Sweeny (Texas).
COLLEGE: Texas Christian.
TRANSACTIONS/CAREER NOTES: Signed as non-drafted free agent by Pittsburgh Steelers (May 3, 1989). ... Released by Steelers (September 5, 1989). ... Re-signed by Steelers to developmental squad (September 6, 1989). ... On developmental squad (September 6, 1989-January 5, 1990). ... Played in one playoff game with Steelers (1989 season). ... Granted unconditional free agency (February 1, 1990). ... Signed by New Orleans Saints (March 30, 1990). ... Released by Saints (September 3, 1990). ... Signed by Kansas City Chiefs to practice squad (November 30, 1990). ... Granted free agency after 1990 season. ... Re-signed by Chiefs (February 2, 1991). ... Assigned by Chiefs to Montreal Machine in 1991 WLAF enhancement allocation program (March 4, 1991).
CHAMPIONSHIP GAME EXPERIENCE: Played in AFC championship game (1993 season).
HONORS: Named outside linebacker on All-World League team (1991).
PRO STATISTICS: W.L.: 1991—Recovered one fumble for five yards. NFL: 1991—Recovered one fumble. 1994—Recovered two fumbles. 1995—Recovered three fumbles.

Year	Team			INTERCEPTIONS			SACKS
		G	No.	Yds.	Avg.	TD	No.
1989—Pittsburgh NFL				Did not play.			
1990—				Did not play.			
1991—Montreal W.L.		10	0	0	...	0	5.0
—Kansas City NFL		15	0	0	...	0	2.0
1992—Kansas City NFL		15	3	18	6.0	0	1.0
1993—Kansas City NFL		16	0	0	...	0	0.0
1994—Kansas City NFL		15	0	0	...	0	0.0
1995—Kansas City NFL		16	0	0	...	0	1.0
W.L. totals (1 year)		10	0	0	...	0	50
NFL totals (5 years)		77	3	18	6.0	0	40
Pro totals (5 years)		87	3	18	6.0	0	9.0

SIMMONS, CLYDE — DE — CARDINALS

PERSONAL: Born August 4, 1964, in Lanes, S.C. ... 6-6/280.
HIGH SCHOOL: New Hanover (Wilmington, N.C.).
COLLEGE: Western Carolina.
TRANSACTIONS/CAREER NOTES: Selected by Philadelphia Eagles in ninth round (233rd pick overall) of 1986 NFL draft. ... Signed by Eagles (July 3, 1986). ... Granted free agency (February 1, 1991). ... Re-signed by Eagles (August 28, 1991). ... Activated (August 30, 1991). ... Designated by Eagles as transition player (February 15, 1994). ... Signed by Phoenix Cardinals (March 17, 1994); Eagles received second-round pick (DB Brian Dawkins) in 1996 draft as compensation. ... Cardinals franchise renamed Arizona Cardinals for 1994 season.
HONORS: Played in Pro Bowl (1991 and 1992 seasons). ... Named defensive end on THE SPORTING NEWS NFL All-Pro team (1991).
PRO STATISTICS: 1986—Returned one kickoff for no yards. 1987—Recovered one fumble. 1988—Credited with one safety, ran 15 yards with

blocked field-goal attempt and recovered three fumbles. 1989—Intercepted one pass for 60 yards and a touchdown. 1990—Recovered two fumbles for 28 yards and one touchdown. 1991—Recovered three fumbles (including one in end zone for a touchdown). 1992—Recovered one fumble. 1993—Intercepted one pass for no yards. 1995—Intercepted one pass for 25 yards and a touchdown and recovered one fumble for 12 yards.

Year	Team	G	SACKS
1986—Philadelphia NFL		16	2.0
1987—Philadelphia NFL		12	6.0
1988—Philadelphia NFL		16	8.0
1989—Philadelphia NFL		16	15.5
1990—Philadelphia NFL		16	7.5
1991—Philadelphia NFL		16	13.0
1992—Philadelphia NFL		16	*19.0
1993—Philadelphia NFL		16	5.0
1994—Arizona NFL		16	6.0
1995—Arizona NFL		16	11.0
Pro totals (10 years)		156	93.0

SIMMONS, ED   OT   REDSKINS

PERSONAL: Born December 31, 1963, in Seattle. ... 6-5/325.
HIGH SCHOOL: Nathan Hale (Seattle).
COLLEGE: Eastern Washington.
TRANSACTIONS/CAREER NOTES: Selected by Washington Redskins in sixth round (164th pick overall) of 1987 NFL draft. ... Signed by Redskins (July 24, 1987). ... On injured reserve with knee injury (November 23, 1987-remainder of season). ... On injured reserve with knee injury (December 11, 1990-remainder of season). ... On injured reserve with knee injury (September 11-November 1991).
PLAYING EXPERIENCE: Washington NFL, 1987-1995. ... Games: 1987 (5), 1988 (16), 1989 (16), 1990 (13), 1991 (6), 1992 (16), 1993 (13), 1994 (16), 1995 (16). Total: 117.
CHAMPIONSHIP GAME EXPERIENCE: Played in NFC championship game (1991 season). ... Member of Super Bowl championship team (1991 season).
PRO STATISTICS: 1993—Recovered one fumble. 1995—Recovered two fumbles.

SIMMONS, WAYNE   LB   PACKERS

PERSONAL: Born December 15, 1969, in Beauford, S.C. ... 6-2/248. ... Full name: Wayne General Simmons.
HIGH SCHOOL: Hilton Head (S.C.).
COLLEGE: Clemson (degree in finance).
TRANSACTIONS/CAREER NOTES: Selected by Green Bay Packers in first round (15th pick overall) of 1993 NFL draft. ... Signed by Packers (July 1, 1993).
CHAMPIONSHIP GAME EXPERIENCE: Played in NFC championship game (1995 season).
PRO STATISTICS: 1993—Credited with one sack and recovered one fumble. 1995—Recovered one fumble.

			INTERCEPTIONS				SACKS
Year	Team	G	No.	Yds.	Avg.	TD	No.
1993—Green Bay NFL		14	2	21	10.5	0	1.0
1994—Green Bay NFL		12	0	0	...	0	0.0
1995—Green Bay NFL		16	0	0	...	0	4.0
Pro totals (3 years)		42	2	21	10.5	0	5.0

SIMPSON, CARL   DT   BEARS

PERSONAL: Born April 18, 1970, in Baxley, Ga. ... 6-2/295. ... Full name: Carl Wilhelm Simpson.
HIGH SCHOOL: Appling County (Baxley, Ga.).
COLLEGE: Florida State (degree in criminology).
TRANSACTIONS/CAREER NOTES: Selected by Chicago Bears in second round (35th pick overall) of 1993 NFL draft. ... Signed by Bears (July 17, 1993).
PLAYING EXPERIENCE: Chicago NFL, 1993-1995. ... Games: 1993 (11), 1994 (15), 1995 (16). Total: 42.
PRO STATISTICS: 1993—Credited with ½ sack. 1995—Credited with one sack and recovered two fumbles for six yards.

SIMS, JOE   OT

PERSONAL: Born March 1, 1969, in Sudbury, Mass. ... 6-3/310. ... Full name: Joseph Anthony Sims.
HIGH SCHOOL: Lincoln-Sudbury (Mass.) Regional.
COLLEGE: Nebraska.
TRANSACTIONS/CAREER NOTES: Selected by Atlanta Falcons in 11th round (283rd pick overall) of 1991 NFL draft. ... Released by Falcons (August 26, 1991). ... Re-signed by Falcons to practice squad (August 28, 1991). ... Activated (November 9, 1991). ... Released by Falcons (August 29, 1992). ... Signed by Green Bay Packers (September 1, 1992). ... Granted unconditional free agency (February 17, 1995). ... Signed by Philadelphia Eagles (April 20, 1995). ... Traded by Eagles to Green Bay Packers for sixth-round pick (TE Tony Johnson) in 1996 draft (August 27, 1995). ... Released by Packers (October 21, 1995).
PLAYING EXPERIENCE: Atlanta NFL, 1991; Green Bay NFL, 1992-1995. ... Games: 1991 (6), 1992 (15), 1993 (13), 1994 (15), 1995 (4). Total: 53.
PRO STATISTICS: 1992—Returned one kickoff for 11 yards. 1994—Recovered one fumble.

SIMS, KEITH   G   DOLPHINS

PERSONAL: Born June 17, 1967, in Baltimore. ... 6-3/309.
HIGH SCHOOL: Watchung Hills Regional (Warren, N.J.).

COLLEGE: Iowa State (degree in industrial technology).
TRANSACTIONS/CAREER NOTES: Selected by Miami Dolphins in second round (39th pick overall) of 1990 NFL draft. ... Signed by Dolphins (July 30, 1990). ... On injured reserve with knee injury (October 12-November 18, 1991). ... Granted free agency (March 1, 1993). ... Re-signed by Dolphins (July 16, 1993). ... Granted unconditional free agency (February 16, 1996). ... Re-signed by Dolphins (March 8, 1996).
PLAYING EXPERIENCE: Miami NFL, 1990-1995. ... Games: 1990 (14), 1991 (12), 1992 (16), 1993 (16), 1994 (16), 1995 (16). Total: 90.
CHAMPIONSHIP GAME EXPERIENCE: Played in AFC championship game (1992 season).
HONORS: Played in Pro Bowl (1993-1995 seasons).
PRO STATISTICS: 1990—Returned one kickoff for nine yards and recovered one fumble. 1991—Caught one pass for nine yards. 1993—Recovered one fumble. 1994—Recovered two fumbles. 1995—Recovered one fumble.

SINCLAIR, MICHAEL   DE

PERSONAL: Born January 31, 1968, in Galveston, Texas. ... 6-4/267. ... Full name: Michael Glenn Sinclair.
HIGH SCHOOL: Charlton-Pollard (Beaumont, Texas).
COLLEGE: Eastern New Mexico (degree in physical education).
TRANSACTIONS/CAREER NOTES: Selected by Seattle Seahawks in sixth round (155th pick overall) of 1991 NFL draft. ... Signed by Seahawks (July 18, 1991). ... Released by Seahawks (August 26, 1991). ... Re-signed by Seahawks to practice squad (August 28, 1991). ... Activated (November 30, 1991). ... On injured reserve with back injury (December 14, 1991-remainder of season). ... Active for two games (1991); did not play. ... Assigned by Seahawks to Sacramento Surge in 1992 World League enhancement allocation program (February 20, 1992). ... On injured reserve with ankle injury (September 1-October 3, 1992). ... On injured reserve with thumb injury (November 10, 1993-remainder of season). ... Granted free agency (February 17, 1995). ... Re-signed by Seahawks (May 24, 1995). ... Granted unconditional free agency (February 16, 1996).
HONORS: Named defensive end on All-World League team (1992).
PRO STATISTICS: W.L.: 1992—Recovered one fumble. NFL: 1995—Recovered two fumbles.

Year Team	G	SACKS
1991—Seattle NFL	Did not play.	
1992—Sacramento W.L.	10	10.0
—Seattle NFL	12	1.0
1993—Seattle NFL	9	8.0
1994—Seattle NFL	12	4.5
1995—Seattle NFL	16	5.5
W.L. totals (1 year)	10	10.0
NFL totals (4 years)	49	19.0
Pro totals (4 years)	59	29.0

SINGLETON, CHRIS   LB   DOLPHINS

PERSONAL: Born February 20, 1967, in Parsippany, N.J. ... 6-2/246.
HIGH SCHOOL: Parsippany (N.J.) Hills.
COLLEGE: Arizona.
TRANSACTIONS/CAREER NOTES: Selected by New England Patriots in first round (eighth pick overall) of 1990 NFL draft. ... Signed by Patriots (September 3, 1990). ... Activated (September 17, 1990). ... Released by Patriots (November 2, 1993). ... Signed by Miami Dolphins (November 4, 1993). ... On injured reserve with leg injury (November 23, 1994-remainder of season). ... Granted unconditional free agency (February 17, 1995). ... Re-signed by Dolphins (March 16, 1995). ... On physically unable to perform list with ankle injury (July 17-August 14, 1995).
HONORS: Named outside linebacker on THE SPORTING NEWS college All-America second team (1989).
PRO STATISTICS: 1991—Recovered one fumble for 21 yards. 1992—Intercepted one pass for 82 yards and a touchdown. 1994—Recovered two fumbles. 1995—Intercepted one pass for three yards and recovered two fumbles.

Year Team	G	SACKS
1990—New England NFL	13	3.0
1991—New England NFL	12	1.0
1992—New England NFL	8	0.0
1993—New England NFL	8	0.0
—Miami NFL	9	0.0
1994—Miami NFL	11	2.0
1995—Miami NFL	15	1.0
Pro totals (6 years)	76	7.0

SINGLETON, NATE   WR   49ERS

PERSONAL: Born July 5, 1968, in New Orleans. ... 5-11/190. ... Nephew of Ron Singleton, offensive tackle, San Diego Chargers and San Francisco 49ers (1976-1980).
HIGH SCHOOL: Higgins (New Orleans).
COLLEGE: Grambling State.
TRANSACTIONS/CAREER NOTES: Selected by New York Giants in 11th round (292nd pick overall) of 1992 NFL draft. ... Signed by Giants (July 21, 1992). ... Released by Giants (August 24, 1992). ... Signed by San Francisco 49ers (May 3, 1993).
CHAMPIONSHIP GAME EXPERIENCE: Member of 49ers for NFC Championship game (1993 season); inactive. ... Played in NFC championship game (1994 season). ... Member of Super Bowl championship team (1994 season).
PRO STATISTICS: 1995—Recovered one fumble.

Year Team	G	RECEIVING				PUNT RETURNS				KICKOFF RETURNS				TOTALS			
		No.	Yds.	Avg.	TD	No.	Yds.	Avg.	TD	No.	Yds.	Avg.	TD	TD	2pt.	Pts.	Fum.
1992—							Did not play.										
1993—San Francisco NFL	6	8	126	15.8	1	0	0	...	0	0	0	...	0	1	...	6	0
1994—San Francisco NFL	16	21	294	14.0	2	2	13	6.5	0	2	23	11.5	0	2	0	12	0
1995—San Francisco NFL	6	8	108	13.5	1	5	27	5.4	0	0	0	...	0	1	0	6	1
Pro totals (3 years)	38	37	528	14.3	4	7	40	5.7	0	2	23	11.5	0	4	0	24	1

SIRAGUSA, TONY   NT   COLTS

PERSONAL: Born May 14, 1967, in Kenilworth, N.J. ... 6-3/315.
HIGH SCHOOL: David Brearley Regional (Kenilworth, N.J.).
COLLEGE: Pittsburgh.
TRANSACTIONS/CAREER NOTES: Signed as non-drafted free agent by Indianapolis Colts (April 30, 1990).
CHAMPIONSHIP GAME EXPERIENCE: Played in AFC championship game (1995 season).
PRO STATISTICS: 1990—Recovered one fumble. 1991—Recovered one fumble for five yards. 1992—Recovered one fumble. 1994—Recovered one fumble.

Year Team	G	SACKS
1990—Indianapolis NFL	13	1.0
1991—Indianapolis NFL	13	2.0
1992—Indianapolis NFL	16	3.0
1993—Indianapolis NFL	14	1.5
1994—Indianapolis NFL	16	5.0
1995—Indianapolis NFL	14	2.0
Pro totals (6 years)	86	14.5

SKREPENAK, GREG   OT   PANTHERS

PERSONAL: Born January 31, 1970, in Wilkes-Barre, Pa. ... 6-7/325.
HIGH SCHOOL: G.A.R. Memorial (Wilkes-Barre, Pa.).
COLLEGE: Michigan.
TRANSACTIONS/CAREER NOTES: Selected by Los Angeles Raiders in second round (32nd pick overall) of 1992 NFL draft. ... On injured reserve (December 1992-remainder of season). ... Inactive for 16 games (1993). ... Raiders franchise moved to Oakland (July 21, 1995). ... Granted unconditional free agency (February 16, 1996). ... Signed by Carolina Panthers (February 19, 1996).
PLAYING EXPERIENCE: Los Angeles Raiders NFL, 1992 and 1994; Oakland NFL, 1995. ... Games: 1992 (10), 1994 (12), 1995 (14). Total: 36.
HONORS: Named offensive tackle on THE SPORTING NEWS college All-America first team (1991).

SLADE, CHRIS   LB   PATRIOTS

PERSONAL: Born January 30, 1971, in Newport News, Va. ... 6-5/242. ... Full name: Christopher Carroll Slade. ... Cousin of Terry Kirby, running back, Miami Dolphins and cousin of Wayne Kirby, outfielder, Cleveland Indians.
HIGH SCHOOL: Tabb (Va.).
COLLEGE: Virginia.
TRANSACTIONS/CAREER NOTES: Selected by New England Patriots in second round (31st pick overall) of 1993 NFL draft. ... Signed by Patriots (July 24, 1993). ... Granted free agency (February 16, 1996). ... Re-signed by Patriots (May 28, 1996).
HONORS: Named defensive lineman on THE SPORTING NEWS college All-America first team (1992).
PRO STATISTICS: 1993—Recovered one fumble. 1995—Recovered two fumbles for 38 yards and one touchdown.

Year Team	G	SACKS
1993—New England NFL	16	9.0
1994—New England NFL	16	9.5
1995—New England NFL	16	4.0
Pro totals (3 years)	48	22.5

SLATER, JACKIE   OT

PERSONAL: Born May 27, 1954, in Jackson, Miss. ... 6-4/285. ... Full name: Jackie Ray Slater.
HIGH SCHOOL: Wingfield (Jackson, Miss.).
COLLEGE: Jackson State (bachelor of arts degree).
TRANSACTIONS/CAREER NOTES: Selected by Los Angeles Rams in third round (86th pick overall) of 1976 NFL draft. ... On injured reserve with knee injury (October 17, 1984-remainder of season). ... Crossed picket line during players strike (October 14, 1987). ... Granted free agency (February 1, 1992). ... Re-signed by Rams (July 24, 1992). ... On injured reserve with pectoral muscle injury (December 17, 1993-remainder of season). ... Granted unconditional free agency (February 17, 1994). ... Re-signed by Rams (June 1, 1994). ... Rams franchise moved to St. Louis (April 12, 1995). ... On physically unable to perform list with elbow injury (August 21-November 11, 1995). ... On injured reserve with elbow injury (November 14, 1995-remainder of season). ... Granted unconditional free agency (February 16, 1996).
PLAYING EXPERIENCE: Los Angeles Rams NFL, 1976-1994; St. Louis NFL, 1995. ... Games: 1976 (14), 1977 (14), 1978 (16), 1979 (16), 1980 (15), 1981 (11), 1982 (9), 1983 (16), 1984 (7), 1985 (16), 1986 (16), 1987 (12), 1988 (16), 1989 (16), 1990 (15), 1991 (13), 1992 (16), 1993 (8), 1994 (12), 1995 (1). Total: 259.
CHAMPIONSHIP GAME EXPERIENCE: Played in NFC championship game (1976, 1978, 1979, 1985 and 1989 seasons). ... Played in Super Bowl XIV (1979 season).
HONORS: Played in Pro Bowl (1983 and 1985-1990 seasons).
RECORDS: Holds NFL career record for most seasons with one club—20 (Los Angeles Rams, St. Louis Rams, 1976-1995).
PRO STATISTICS: 1978—Recovered one fumble. 1980—Recovered one fumble. 1983—Recovered one fumble for 13 yards. 1985—Recovered one fumble.

SLAUGHTER, WEBSTER   WR

PERSONAL: Born October 19, 1964, in Stockton, Calif. ... 6-1/175.
HIGH SCHOOL: Franklin (Stockton, Calif.).
JUNIOR COLLEGE: Delta College (Calif.).
COLLEGE: San Diego State.
TRANSACTIONS/CAREER NOTES: Selected by Cleveland Browns in second round (43rd pick overall) of 1986 NFL draft. ... Signed by Browns

S

(July 24, 1986). ... On injured reserve with broken arm (October 21-December 12, 1988). ... Granted free agency (February 1, 1992). ... Granted unconditional free agency (September 24, 1992). ... Signed by Houston Oilers (September 29, 1992). ... On injured reserve with knee injury (December 30, 1993-remainder of season). ... Released by Oilers (July 20, 1995). ... Re-signed by Oilers (June 6, 1994). ... Released by Oilers (July 20, 1995). ... Signed by Kansas City Chiefs (August 9, 1995). ... Released by Chiefs (February 15, 1996).
CHAMPIONSHIP GAME EXPERIENCE: Played in AFC championship game (1986, 1987 and 1989 seasons).
HONORS: Played in Pro Bowl (1989 season). ... Named to play in Pro Bowl (1993 season); did not play due to injury.
PRO STATISTICS: 1986—Recovered one fumble in end zone for a touchdown. 1992—Returned one kickoff for 21 yards and recovered two fumbles. 1994—Recovered one fumble.
STATISTICAL PLATEAUS: 100-yard receiving games: 1986 (1), 1987 (2), 1988 (1), 1989 (4), 1990 (3), 1991 (3), 1993 (2), 1994 (2). Total: 18.

			RUSHING				RECEIVING				PUNT RETURNS				TOTALS		
Year Team	G	Att.	Yds.	Avg.	TD	No.	Yds.	Avg.	TD	No.	Yds.	Avg.	TD	TD	2pt.	Pts.	Fum.
1986—Cleveland NFL	16	1	1	1.0	0	40	577	14.4	4	1	2	2.0	0	5	...	30	1
1987—Cleveland NFL	12	0	0	...	0	47	806	17.2	7	0	0	...	0	7	...	42	1
1988—Cleveland NFL	8	0	0	...	0	30	462	15.4	3	0	0	...	0	3	...	18	1
1989—Cleveland NFL	16	0	0	...	0	65	1236	19.0	6	0	0	...	0	6	...	36	2
1990—Cleveland NFL	16	5	29	5.8	0	59	847	14.4	4	0	0	...	0	4	...	24	2
1991—Cleveland NFL	16	0	0	...	0	64	906	14.2	3	17	112	6.6	0	3	...	18	1
1992—Houston NFL	12	3	20	6.7	0	39	486	12.5	4	20	142	7.1	0	4	...	24	3
1993—Houston NFL	14	0	0	...	0	77	904	11.7	5	0	0	...	0	5	...	30	4
1994—Houston NFL	16	0	0	...	0	68	846	12.4	2	0	0	...	0	2	0	12	2
1995—Kansas City NFL	16	0	0	...	0	34	514	15.1	4	0	0	...	0	4	0	24	0
Pro totals (10 years)	142	9	50	5.6	0	523	7584	14.5	42	38	256	6.7	0	43	0	258	17

S

SLOAN, DAVID — TE — LIONS

PERSONAL: Born June 8, 1972, in Fresno, Calif. ... 6-6/254. ... Full name: David Lyle Sloan.
HIGH SCHOOL: Sierra Joint Union (Tollhouse, Calif.).
JUNIOR COLLEGE: Fresno (Calif.) City College.
COLLEGE: New Mexico.
TRANSACTIONS/CAREER NOTES: Selected by Detroit Lions in third round (70th pick overall) of 1995 NFL draft. ... Signed by Lions (July 20, 1995).
PRO STATISTICS: 1995—Returned one kickoff for 14 yards.

		RECEIVING				TOTALS			
Year Team	G	No.	Yds.	Avg.	TD	TD	2pt.	Pts.	Fum.
1995—Detroit NFL	16	17	184	10.8	1	1	0	6	0

SMALL, TORRANCE — WR — SAINTS

PERSONAL: Born September 6, 1970, in Tampa. ... 6-3/201. ... Full name: Torrance Ramon Small.
HIGH SCHOOL: Thomas Jefferson (Tampa).
COLLEGE: Alcorn State.
TRANSACTIONS/CAREER NOTES: Selected by New Orleans Saints in fifth round (138th pick overall) of 1992 NFL draft. ... Signed by Saints (July 15, 1992). ... Released by Saints (September 3, 1992). ... Re-signed by Saints to practice squad (September 4, 1992). ... Activated (September 19, 1992). ... Granted free agency (February 17, 1995). ... Tendered offer sheet by Seattle Seahawks (March 8, 1995). ... Offer matched by Saints (March 15, 1995).
PRO STATISTICS: 1994—Recovered one fumble. 1995—Rushed six times for 75 yards and one touchdown and recovered one fumble.
STATISTICAL PLATEAUS: 100-yard receiving games: 1994 (1).

		RECEIVING				TOTALS			
Year Team	G	No.	Yds.	Avg.	TD	TD	2pt.	Pts.	Fum.
1992—New Orleans NFL	13	23	278	12.1	3	3	...	18	0
1993—New Orleans NFL	11	16	164	10.3	1	1	...	6	0
1994—New Orleans NFL	16	49	719	14.7	5	5	1	32	0
1995—New Orleans NFL	16	38	461	12.1	5	6	0	36	0
Pro totals (4 years)	56	126	1622	12.9	14	15	1	92	0

SMEENGE, JOEL — DE — JAGUARS

PERSONAL: Born April 1, 1968, in Holland, Mich. ... 6-6/260. ... Full name: Joel Andrew Smeenge. ... Name pronounced SMEN-ghee.
HIGH SCHOOL: Hudsonville (Mich.).
COLLEGE: Western Michigan.
TRANSACTIONS/CAREER NOTES: Selected by New Orleans Saints in third round (70th pick overall) of 1990 NFL draft. ... Signed by Saints (July 17, 1990). ... Granted free agency (March 1, 1993). ... Re-signed by Saints (July 9, 1993). ... Granted unconditional free agency (February 17, 1995). ... Signed by Jacksonville Jaguars (February 28, 1995).
PRO STATISTICS: 1991—Recovered one fumble. 1992—Recovered one fumble. 1995—Intercepted one pass for 12 yards and fumbled once.
MISCELLANEOUS: Holds Jacksonville Jaguars all-time record for most sacks (4).

Year Team	G	SACKS
1990—New Orleans NFL	15	0.0
1991—New Orleans NFL	14	0.0
1992—New Orleans NFL	11	0.5
1993—New Orleans NFL	16	1.0
1994—New Orleans NFL	16	0.0
1995—Jacksonville NFL	15	4.0
Pro totals (6 years)	87	5.5

SMITH, AL   LB   OILERS

PERSONAL: Born November 26, 1964, in Los Angeles. ... 6-1/244. ... Full name: Al Fredrick Smith. ... Brother of Aaron Smith, linebacker, Denver Broncos (1984).
HIGH SCHOOL: St. Bernard (Playa Del Rey, Calif.).
COLLEGE: Cal Poly Pomona, then Utah State (degree in sociology, 1987).
TRANSACTIONS/CAREER NOTES: Selected by Houston Oilers in sixth round (147th pick overall) of 1987 NFL draft. ... Signed by Oilers (July 31, 1987). ... Designated by Oilers as transition player (February 25, 1993). ... Free agency status changed by Oilers from transitional to unconditional (February 17, 1994). ... Re-signed by Oilers (May 17, 1994). ... On injured reserve with foot injury (September 29, 1995-remainder of season).
HONORS: Played in Pro Bowl (1991 and 1992 seasons).
PRO STATISTICS: 1988—Recovered one fumble. 1989—Recovered one fumble. 1990—Recovered one fumble. 1991—Recovered one fumble for 70 yards and a touchdown. 1992—Fumbled once. 1994—Recovered one fumble.

		INTERCEPTIONS				SACKS
Year Team	G	No.	Yds.	Avg.	TD	No.
1987—Houston NFL	12	0	0	...	0	0.0
1988—Houston NFL	16	0	0	...	0	0.0
1989—Houston NFL	15	0	0	...	0	0.0
1990—Houston NFL	15	0	0	...	0	1.0
1991—Houston NFL	16	1	16	16.0	0	1.0
1992—Houston NFL	16	1	26	26.0	0	1.0
1993—Houston NFL	16	0	0	...	0	0.0
1994—Houston NFL	16	0	0	...	0	2.5
1995—Houston NFL	2	0	0	...	0	0.0
Pro totals (9 years)	124	2	42	21.0	0	5.5

SMITH, ANTHONY   DE   RAIDERS

PERSONAL: Born June 28, 1967, in Elizabeth City, N.C. ... 6-3/265. ... Full name: Anthony Wayne Smith.
HIGH SCHOOL: Northeastern (Elizabeth City, N.C.).
COLLEGE: Alabama, then Arizona.
TRANSACTIONS/CAREER NOTES: Selected by Los Angeles Raiders in first round (11th pick overall) of 1990 NFL draft. ... On injured reserve (September 3, 1990-entire season). ... Raiders franchise moved to Oakland (July 21, 1995).
PRO STATISTICS: 1991—Recovered one fumble. 1994—Recovered one fumble for 25 yards and a touchdown. 1995—Recovered three fumbles for four yards.

Year Team	G	SACKS
1990—Los Angeles Raiders NFL	Did not play.	
1991—Los Angeles Raiders NFL	16	10.5
1992—Los Angeles Raiders NFL	15	13.0
1993—Los Angeles Raiders NFL	16	12.5
1994—Los Angeles Raiders NFL	16	6.0
1995—Oakland NFL	16	7.0
Pro totals (5 years)	79	49.0

SMITH, ARTIE   DE   BENGALS

PERSONAL: Born May 15, 1970, in Stillwater, Okla. ... 6-4/285. ... Full name: Artie Enlow Smith.
HIGH SCHOOL: Stillwater (Okla.).
COLLEGE: Louisiana Tech.
TRANSACTIONS/CAREER NOTES: Selected by San Francisco 49ers in fifth round (116th pick overall) of 1993 NFL draft. ... Signed by 49ers (July 14, 1993). ... Claimed on waivers by Cincinnati Bengals (September 16, 1994). ... Granted free agency (February 16, 1996). ... Re-signed by Bengals (May 4, 1996).
PLAYING EXPERIENCE: San Francisco NFL, 1993; San Francisco (2)-Cincinnati (7) NFL, 1994; Cincinnati NFL, 1995. ... Games: 1993 (16), 1994 (9), 1995 (16). Total: 41.
CHAMPIONSHIP GAME EXPERIENCE: Played in NFC championship game (1993 season).
PRO STATISTICS: 1993—Credited with 1½ sacks. 1995—Credited with two sacks.

SMITH, BEN   DB   CARDINALS

PERSONAL: Born May 14, 1967, in Warner Robins, Ga. ... 5-11/185.
HIGH SCHOOL: Warner Robins (Ga.).
COLLEGE: Georgia.
TRANSACTIONS/CAREER NOTES: Selected by Philadelphia Eagles in first round (22nd pick overall) of 1990 NFL draft. ... Signed by Eagles (August 15, 1990). ... On injured reserve with knee injury (November 12, 1991-remainder of season). ... On physically unable to perform list with knee injury (July 25, 1992-entire season). ... Traded by Eagles to Denver Broncos for third-round pick (WR Chris T. Jones) in 1995 draft (April 18, 1994). ... Granted unconditional free agency (February 17, 1995). ... Signed by Arizona Cardinals (August 28, 1995).

		INTERCEPTIONS			
Year Team	G	No.	Yds.	Avg.	TD
1990—Philadelphia NFL	16	3	1	.3	0
1991—Philadelphia NFL	10	2	6	3.0	0
1992—Philadelphia NFL	Did not play—injured.				
1993—Philadelphia NFL	13	0	0	...	0
1994—Denver NFL	14	1	0	0.0	0
1995—Arizona NFL	2	0	0	...	0
Pro totals (5 years)	55	6	7	1.2	0

SMITH, BRUCE   DE   BILLS

PERSONAL: Born June 18, 1963, in Norfolk, Va. ... 6-4/273. ... Full name: Bruce Bernard Smith.
HIGH SCHOOL: Booker T. Washington (Norfolk, Va.).
COLLEGE: Virginia Tech.
TRANSACTIONS/CAREER NOTES: Selected by Baltimore Stars in 1985 USFL territorial draft. ... Signed by Buffalo Bills (February 28, 1985). ... Selected officially by Bills in first round (first pick overall) of 1985 NFL draft. ... On non-football injury list with substance abuse problem (September 2-28, 1988). ... Granted free agency (February 1, 1989). ... Tendered offer sheet by Denver Broncos (March 23, 1989). ... Offer matched by Bills (March 29, 1989). ... On injured reserve with knee injury (October 12-November 30, 1991).
CHAMPIONSHIP GAME EXPERIENCE: Played in AFC championship game (1988 and 1990-1993 seasons). ... Played in Super Bowl XXV (1990 season), Super Bowl XXVI (1991 season), Super Bowl XXVII (1992 season) and Super Bowl XXVIII (1993 season).
HONORS: Named defensive lineman on THE SPORTING NEWS college All-America second team (1983 and 1984). ... Outland Trophy winner (1984). ... Named defensive end on THE SPORTING NEWS NFL All-Pro team (1987, 1988, 1990, 1992-1995). ... Played in Pro Bowl (1987-1990, 1994 and 1995 seasons). ... Named Outstanding Player of Pro Bowl (1987 season). ... Named to play in Pro Bowl (1992 season); replaced by Howie Long due to injury. ... Named to play in Pro Bowl (1993 season); replaced by Sean Jones due to injury.
POSTSEASON RECORDS: Shares Super Bowl single-game record for most safeties—1 (January 27, 1991, vs. New York Giants). ... Holds NFL postseason career record for most sacks—12. ... Shares NFL postseason single-game record for most safeties—1 (January 27, 1991, vs. New York Giants).
PRO STATISTICS: 1985—Rushed once for no yards and recovered four fumbles. 1987—Recovered two fumbles for 15 yards and one touchdown. 1988—Credited with one safety. 1993—Intercepted one pass for no yards and recovered one fumble. 1994—Intercepted one pass for no yards and recovered two fumbles. 1995—Recovered one fumble.
MISCELLANEOUS: Active AFC leader for career sacks (126.5). ... Holds Buffalo Bills all-time record for most sacks (126.5).

Year Team	G	SACKS
1985—Buffalo NFL	16	6.5
1986—Buffalo NFL	16	15.0
1987—Buffalo NFL	12	12.0
1988—Buffalo NFL	12	11.0
1989—Buffalo NFL	16	13.0
1990—Buffalo NFL	16	19.0
1991—Buffalo NFL	5	1.5
1992—Buffalo NFL	15	14.0
1993—Buffalo NFL	16	14.0
1994—Buffalo NFL	15	10.0
1995—Buffalo NFL	15	10.5
Pro totals (11 years)	**154**	**126.5**

SMITH, CEDRIC   FB   CARDINALS

PERSONAL: Born May 27, 1968, in Enterprise, Ala. ... 5-10/222. ... Full name: Cedric Delon Smith.
HIGH SCHOOL: Enterprise (Ala.).
COLLEGE: Florida (degree in rehabilitative counseling).
TRANSACTIONS/CAREER NOTES: Selected by Minnesota Vikings in fifth round (131st pick overall) of 1990 NFL draft. ... Signed by Vikings (July 27, 1990). ... Released by Vikings (August 26, 1991). ... Signed by New Orleans Saints (November 6, 1991). ... Released by Saints (November 9, 1991). ... Re-signed by Saints (November 11, 1991). ... Granted unconditional free agency (February 1-April 1, 1992). ... Re-signed by Saints for 1992 season. ... Released by Saints (August 26, 1992). ... Signed by Miami Dolphins (March 3, 1993). ... Released by Dolphins (August 24, 1993). ... Signed by Washington Redskins (April 11, 1994). ... Released by Redskins (August 28, 1994). ... Re-signed by Redskins (August 31, 1994). ... Released by Redskins (September 20, 1994). ... Re-signed by Redskins (October 4, 1994). ... Granted free agency (February 17, 1995). ... Re-signed by Redskins (March 24, 1995). ... Released by Redskins (October 17, 1995). ... Signed by Arizona Cardinals (April 23, 1996).
PRO STATISTICS: 1990—Returned one kickoff for 16 yards.

Year Team	G	RUSHING Att.	RUSHING Yds.	RUSHING Avg.	RUSHING TD	RECEIVING No.	RECEIVING Yds.	RECEIVING Avg.	RECEIVING TD	TOTALS TD	TOTALS 2pt.	TOTALS Pts.	TOTALS Fum.
1990—Minnesota NFL	15	9	19	2.1	0	0	0	...	0	0	...	0	0
1991—New Orleans NFL	6	0	0	...	0	0	0	...	0	0	...	0	0
1992—					Did not play.								
1993—					Did not play.								
1994—Washington NFL	14	10	48	4.8	0	15	118	7.9	1	1	0	6	1
1995—Washington NFL	6	3	13	4.3	0	0	0	...	0	0	0	0	0
Pro totals (4 years)	**41**	**22**	**80**	**3.6**	**0**	**15**	**118**	**7.9**	**1**	**1**	**0**	**6**	**1**

SMITH, CHUCK   LB/DE   FALCONS

PERSONAL: Born December 21, 1969, in Athens, Ga. ... 6-2/257. ... Full name: Charles Henry Smith III.
HIGH SCHOOL: Clarke Central (Athens, Ga.).
COLLEGE: Northeastern Oklahoma A&M, then Tennessee.
TRANSACTIONS/CAREER NOTES: Selected by Atlanta Falcons in second round (51st pick overall) of 1992 NFL draft. ... Signed by Falcons (July 27, 1992). ... On suspended list (July 25-August 15, 1994). ... On injured reserve with knee injury (December 21, 1994-remainder of season). ... Granted free agency (February 17, 1995). ... Re-signed by Falcons (July 14, 1995). ... Granted unconditional free agency (February 16, 1996). ... Re-signed by Falcons (February 27, 1996).
PRO STATISTICS: 1993—Recovered two fumbles. 1994—Intercepted one pass for 36 yards and a touchdown and recovered two fumbles. 1995—Recovered two fumbles.

Year Team	G	SACKS
1992—Atlanta NFL	16	2.0
1993—Atlanta NFL	15	3.5
1994—Atlanta NFL	15	11.0
1995—Atlanta NFL	14	5.5
Pro totals (4 years)	**60**	**22.0**

SMITH, DARRIN   LB   COWBOYS

PERSONAL: Born April 15, 1970, in Miami. ... 6-1/230. ... Full name: Darrin Andrew Smith.
HIGH SCHOOL: Norland (Miami).
COLLEGE: Miami, Fla. (degree in business management, 1991; master's degree in business administration, 1993).
TRANSACTIONS/CAREER NOTES: Selected by Dallas Cowboys in second round (54th pick overall) of 1993 NFL draft. ... Signed by Cowboys (July 21, 1993). ... On reserve/did not report list (July 20-October 14, 1995). ... Granted free agency (February 16, 1996).
CHAMPIONSHIP GAME EXPERIENCE: Played in NFC championship game (1993 and 1995 seasons). ... Member of Super Bowl championship team (1993 and 1995 seasons).
PRO STATISTICS: 1993—Recovered one fumble. 1994—Recovered two fumbles for 11 yards. 1995—Recovered one fumble for 63 yards.

		INTERCEPTIONS				SACKS
Year Team	G	No.	Yds.	Avg.	TD	No.
1993—Dallas NFL	16	0	0	...	0	1.0
1994—Dallas NFL	16	2	13	6.5	1	4.0
1995—Dallas NFL	9	0	0	...	0	3.0
Pro totals (3 years)	41	2	13	6.5	1	8.0

SMITH, EMMITT   RB   COWBOYS

PERSONAL: Born May 15, 1969, in Pensacola, Fla. ... 5-9/209.
HIGH SCHOOL: Escambia (Pensacola, Fla.).
COLLEGE: Florida (degree in public recreation, 1996).
TRANSACTIONS/CAREER NOTES: Selected after junior season by Dallas Cowboys in first round (17th pick overall) of 1990 NFL draft. ... Signed by Cowboys (September 4, 1990). ... Granted roster exemption (September 4-8, 1990). ... Granted free agency (March 1, 1993). ... Re-signed by Cowboys (September 16, 1993).
CHAMPIONSHIP GAME EXPERIENCE: Played in NFC championship game (1992-1995 seasons). ... Member of Super Bowl championship team (1992, 1993 and 1995 seasons).
HONORS: Named running back on THE SPORTING NEWS college All-America first team (1989). ... Played in Pro Bowl (1990-1992 and 1995 seasons). ... Named running back on THE SPORTING NEWS NFL All-Pro team (1992-1995). ... Named NFL Player of the Year by THE SPORTING NEWS (1993). ... Named Most Valuable Player of Super Bowl XXVIII (1993 season). ... Named to play in Pro Bowl (1993 season); replaced by Rodney Hampton due to injury. ... Named Sportsman of the Year by THE SPORTING NEWS (1994). ... Named to play in Pro Bowl (1994 season); replaced by Ricky Watters due to injury.
RECORDS: Holds NFL single-season records for most touchdowns—25 (1995); and most rushing touchdowns—25 (1995).
POSTSEASON RECORDS: Holds Super Bowl career record for most rushing touchdowns—5. ... Shares Super Bowl single-game record for most rushing touchdowns—2 (January 30, 1994, vs. Buffalo and January 28, 1996, vs. Pittsburgh). Shares NFL postseason career records for most games with 100 or more yards rushing—6; and most consecutive games with one or more rushing touchdowns—7.
PRO STATISTICS: 1991—Recovered one fumble. 1992—Recovered one fumble. 1993—Recovered three fumbles.
STATISTICAL PLATEAUS: 100-yard rushing games: 1990 (3), 1991 (8), 1992 (7), 1993 (7), 1994 (6), 1995 (11). Total: 42. ... 100-yard receiving games: 1990 (1), 1993 (1). Total: 2.
MISCELLANEOUS: Holds Dallas Cowboys all-time record for most touchdowns (100).

		RUSHING				RECEIVING				TOTALS			
Year Team	G	Att.	Yds.	Avg.	TD	No.	Yds.	Avg.	TD	TD	2pt.	Pts.	Fum.
1990—Dallas NFL	16	241	937	3.9	11	24	228	9.5	0	11	...	66	7
1991—Dallas NFL	16	*365	*1563	4.3	12	49	258	5.3	1	13	...	78	8
1992—Dallas NFL	16	373	*1713	4.6	*18	59	335	5.7	1	*19	...	114	4
1993—Dallas NFL	14	283	*1486	*5.3	9	57	414	7.3	1	10	...	60	4
1994—Dallas NFL	15	*368	1484	4.0	*21	50	341	6.8	1	*22	0	132	1
1995—Dallas NFL	16	*377	*1773	4.7	*25	62	375	6.1	0	*25	0	*150	7
Pro totals (6 years)	93	2007	8956	4.5	96	301	1951	6.5	4	100	0	600	31

SMITH, FERNANDO   DE   VIKINGS

PERSONAL: Born August 2, 1971, in Flint, Mich. ... 6-6/283. ... Full name: Fernando Dewitt Smith.
HIGH SCHOOL: Northwestern Community (Flint, Mich.).
COLLEGE: Jackson State.
TRANSACTIONS/CAREER NOTES: Selected by Minnesota Vikings in second round (55th pick overall) of 1994 NFL draft. ... Signed by Vikings (July 15, 1994).

Year Team	G	SACKS
1994—Minnesota NFL	7	0.0
1995—Minnesota NFL	12	2.5
Pro totals (2 years)	19	2.5

SMITH, FRANKIE   CB   PATRIOTS

PERSONAL: Born October 8, 1968, in Groesbeck, Texas. ... 5-9/182.
HIGH SCHOOL: Groesbeck (Texas).
COLLEGE: Baylor.
TRANSACTIONS/CAREER NOTES: Selected by Atlanta Falcons in fourth round (104th pick overall) of 1992 NFL draft. ... Signed by Falcons (July 7, 1992). ... Released by Falcons (August 25, 1992). ... Signed by Miami Dolphins (March 17, 1993). ... Released by Dolphins (October 22, 1993). ... Re-signed by Dolphins to practice squad (October 23, 1993). ... Activated (November 29, 1993). ... Released by Dolphins (February 15, 1996). ... Signed by New England Patriots (February 27, 1996).
PLAYING EXPERIENCE: Miami NFL, 1993-1995. ... Games: 1993 (5), 1994 (13), 1995 (11). Total: 29.
PRO STATISTICS: 1994—Credited with one sack.

S

SMITH, HERMAN   DE   BUCCANEERS

PERSONAL: Born January 25, 1971, in Ft. Lauderdale, Fla. ... 6-5/261.
COLLEGE: Portland State.
TRANSACTIONS/CAREER NOTES: Signed as non-drafted free agent by Tampa Bay Buccaneers (June 20, 1995). ... Released by Buccaneers (August 27, 1995). ... Re-signed by Buccaneers to practice squad (August 28, 1995). ... Activated (November 17, 1995).
PLAYING EXPERIENCE: Tampa Bay NFL, 1995. ... Games: 1995 (3).

SMITH, IRV   TE   SAINTS

PERSONAL: Born October 13, 1971, in Trenton, N.J. ... 6-3/246. ... Full name: Irvin Martin Smith. ... Brother of Ed Smith, infielder, Chicago Cubs organization (1994) and Cleveland Indians organization (1995).
HIGH SCHOOL: Township (Pemberton, N.J.).
COLLEGE: Notre Dame (degree in marketing).
TRANSACTIONS/CAREER NOTES: Selected by New Orleans Saints in first round (20th pick overall) of 1993 NFL draft. ... Signed by Saints (July 25, 1993).
PRO STATISTICS: 1993—Recovered one fumble. 1994—Returned two kickoffs for 10 yards. 1995—Returned one kickoff for six yards.

Year Team	G	RECEIVING					TOTALS			
		No.	Yds.	Avg.	TD	TD	2pt.	Pts.	Fum.
1993—New Orleans NFL	16	16	180	11.3	2	2	...	12	1
1994—New Orleans NFL	16	41	330	8.1	3	3	0	18	0
1995—New Orleans NFL	16	45	466	10.4	3	3	1	20	1
Pro totals (3 years)	48	102	976	9.6	8	8	1	50	2

SMITH, JIMMY   WR/KR   JAGUARS

PERSONAL: Born February 9, 1969, in Detroit. ... 6-1/207. ... Full name: Jimmy Lee Smith Jr.
HIGH SCHOOL: Callaway (Jackson, Miss.).
COLLEGE: Jackson State.
TRANSACTIONS/CAREER NOTES: Selected by Dallas Cowboys in second round (36th pick overall) of 1992 NFL draft. ... Signed by Cowboys (April 26, 1992). ... On injured reserve with fibula injury (September 2-October 7, 1992); on practice squad (September 28-October 7, 1992). ... On non-football injury list with appendicitis (September 2, 1993-remainder of season). ... Released by Cowboys (July 11, 1994). ... Signed by Philadelphia Eagles (July 19, 1994). ... Released by Eagles (August 29, 1994). ... Signed by Jacksonville Jaguars (February 28, 1995). ... Granted free agency (February 16, 1996). ... Re-signed by Jaguars (May 28, 1996).
CHAMPIONSHIP GAME EXPERIENCE: Played in NFC championship game (1992 season). ... Member of Super Bowl championship team (1992 season).
PRO STATISTICS: 1995—Recovered blocked punt in end zone for a touchdown and recovered one fumble.
MISCELLANEOUS: Shares Jacksonville Jaguars all-time record for most touchdowns (5).

Year Team	G	RECEIVING				KICKOFF RETURNS				TOTALS			
		No.	Yds.	Avg.	TD	No.	Yds.	Avg.	TD	TD	2pt.	Pts.	Fum.
1992—Dallas NFL	7	0	0	...	0	0	0	...	0	0		0	0
1993—Dallas NFL						Did not play.							
1994—Dallas NFL						Did not play.							
1995—Jacksonville NFL	16	22	288	13.1	3	24	540	22.5	1	5	0	30	2
Pro totals (2 years)	23	22	288	13.1	3	24	540	22.5	1	5	0	30	2

SMITH, KEVIN   TE   PACKERS

PERSONAL: Born July 25, 1969, in Bakersfield, Calif. ... 6-4/265. ... Full name: Kevin Linn Smith. ... Son of Charlie Smith, running back, Oakland Raiders and San Diego Chargers (1968-1975).
HIGH SCHOOL: Skyline (Oakland).
COLLEGE: UCLA.
TRANSACTIONS/CAREER NOTES: Selected by Los Angeles Raiders in seventh round (185th pick overall) of 1992 NFL draft. ... Released by Raiders (August 31, 1992). ... Re-signed by Raiders to practice squad (September 2, 1992). ... Activated (December 1992). ... Raiders franchise moved to Oakland (July 21, 1995). ... Released by Raiders (September 9, 1995). ... Signed by Green Bay Packers (December 12, 1995).
PLAYING EXPERIENCE: Los Angeles Raiders NFL, 1992-1994. ... Games: 1992 (1), 1993 (10), 1994 (3). Total: 14.
PRO STATISTICS: 1993—Returned two kickoffs for 15 yards. 1994—Rushed once for two yards and caught one pass for eight yards.

SMITH, KEVIN   CB   COWBOYS

PERSONAL: Born April 7, 1970, in Orange, Texas. ... 5-11/184. ... Full name: Kevin Rey Smith.
HIGH SCHOOL: West Orange-Stark (Orange, Texas).
COLLEGE: Texas A&M.
TRANSACTIONS/CAREER NOTES: Selected by Dallas Cowboys in first round (17th pick overall) of 1992 NFL draft. ... Signed by Cowboys (April 26, 1992). ... On injured reserve with Achilles' tendon injury (September 22, 1995-remainder of season).
CHAMPIONSHIP GAME EXPERIENCE: Played in NFC championship game (1992-1994 seasons). ... Member of Super Bowl championship team (1992, 1993 and 1995 seasons).
HONORS: Named defensive back on THE SPORTING NEWS college All-America first team (1991).
PRO STATISTICS: 1992—Returned one punt for 17 yards and returned one kickoff for nine yards. 1993—Returned one kickoff for 33 yards and recovered one fumble for 14 yards.

Year Team	G	INTERCEPTIONS			
		No.	Yds.	Avg.	TD
1992—Dallas NFL	16	2	10	5.0	0

S

Year Team	G	No.	Yds.	Avg.	TD
		INTERCEPTIONS			
1993—Dallas NFL	16	6	56	9.3	1
1994—Dallas NFL	16	2	11	5.5	0
1995—Dallas NFL	1	0	0	...	0
Pro totals (4 years)	49	10	77	7.7	1

SMITH, LAMAR   RB   SEAHAWKS

PERSONAL: Born November 29, 1970, in Fort Wayne, Ind. ... 5-11/223.
HIGH SCHOOL: South Side (Fort Wayne, Ind.).
COLLEGE: Houston.
TRANSACTIONS/CAREER NOTES: Selected by Seattle Seahawks in third round (73rd pick overall) of 1994 NFL draft. ... Signed by Seahawks (July 19, 1994). ... On non-football injury list with back injury (December 13, 1994-remainder of season).
PRO STATISTICS: 1995—Caught one pass for 10 yards and returned one kickoff for 20 yards.

Year Team	G	Att.	Yds.	Avg.	TD	TD	2pt.	Pts.	Fum.
		RUSHING				**TOTALS**			
1994—Seattle NFL	2	2	-1	-0.5	0	0	0	0	0
1995—Seattle NFL	12	36	215	6.0	0	0	0	0	1
Pro totals (2 years)	14	38	214	5.6	0	0	0	0	1

SMITH, LANCE   G   GIANTS

PERSONAL: Born January 1, 1963, in Kannapolis, N.C. ... 6-3/282.
HIGH SCHOOL: A.L. Brown (Kannapolis, N.C.).
COLLEGE: Louisiana State.
TRANSACTIONS/CAREER NOTES: Selected by Portland Breakers in 1985 USFL territorial draft. ... Selected by St. Louis Cardinals in third round (72nd pick overall) of 1985 NFL draft. ... Signed by Cardinals (July 21, 1985). ... Crossed picket line during players strike (October 2, 1987). ... Cardinals franchise moved to Phoenix (March 15, 1988). ... Granted free agency (February 1, 1991). ... Re-signed by Cardinals (July 23, 1991). ... Granted free agency (February 1, 1992). ... Re-signed by Cardinals (July 27, 1992). ... Granted unconditional free agency (February 17, 1994). ... Signed by New York Giants (April 5, 1994).
PLAYING EXPERIENCE: St. Louis NFL, 1985-1987; Phoenix NFL, 1988-1993; New York Giants NFL, 1994 and 1995. ... Games: 1985 (14), 1986 (15), 1987 (15), 1988 (16), 1989 (16), 1990 (16), 1991 (16), 1992 (16), 1993 (16), 1994 (13), 1995 (13). Total: 166.
HONORS: Named offensive tackle on THE SPORTING NEWS college All-America second team (1984).
PRO STATISTICS: 1985—Recovered one fumble. 1989—Recovered one fumble. 1991—Recovered two fumbles for five yards. 1992—Returned two kickoffs for 16 yards. 1993—Returned one kickoff for 11 yards and recovered two fumbles.

SMITH, NEIL   DE   CHIEFS

PERSONAL: Born April 10, 1966, in New Orleans. ... 6-4/273.
HIGH SCHOOL: McDonogh 35 (New Orleans).
COLLEGE: Nebraska.
TRANSACTIONS/CAREER NOTES: Selected by Kansas City Chiefs in first round (second pick overall) of 1988 NFL draft. ... Signed by Chiefs (July 19, 1988). ... Designated by Chiefs as franchise player (February 25, 1993).
CHAMPIONSHIP GAME EXPERIENCE: Played in AFC championship game (1993 season).
HONORS: Named defensive lineman on THE SPORTING NEWS college All-America first team (1987). ... Played in Pro Bowl (1991-1993 and 1995 seasons). ... Named to play in Pro Bowl (1994 season); replaced by Rob Burnett due to injury.
PRO STATISTICS: 1989—Recovered two fumbles for three yards and one touchdown. 1990—Recovered one fumble. 1991—Recovered two fumbles for 10 yards. 1992—Intercepted one pass for 22 yards and a touchdown and recovered two fumbles. 1993—Intercepted one pass for three yards and recovered three fumbles. 1994—Intercepted one pass for 41 yards and recovered one fumble for six yards. 1995—Recovered one fumble.

Year Team	G	SACKS
1988—Kansas City NFL	13	2.5
1989—Kansas City NFL	15	6.5
1990—Kansas City NFL	16	9.5
1991—Kansas City NFL	16	8.0
1992—Kansas City NFL	16	14.5
1993—Kansas City NFL	16	*15.0
1994—Kansas City NFL	14	11.5
1995—Kansas City NFL	16	12.0
Pro totals (8 years)	122	79.5

SMITH, OTIS   CB   JETS

PERSONAL: Born October 22, 1965, in New Orleans. ... 5-11/190.
JUNIOR COLLEGE: Taft (Calif.) College.
HIGH SCHOOL: East Jefferson (Metairie, La.).
COLLEGE: Missouri.
TRANSACTIONS/CAREER NOTES: Signed as non-drafted free agent by Philadelphia Eagles (April 25, 1990). ... On physically unable to perform list with appendectomy (August 2, 1990-entire season). ... Granted free agency (February 1, 1992). ... Re-signed by Eagles (August 11, 1992). ... Granted unconditional free agency (February 17, 1994). ... Re-signed by Eagles (April 25, 1994). ... Released by Eagles (March 22, 1995). ... Signed by New York Jets (April 13, 1995).
PRO STATISTICS: 1991—Recovered one fumble. 1994—Credited with one sack and returned one kickoff for 14 yards. 1995—Returned one kickoff for six yards.

Year Team		INTERCEPTIONS			
	G	No.	Yds.	Avg.	TD
1990—Philadelphia NFL			Did not play.		
1991—Philadelphia NFL	15	2	74	37.0	1
1992—Philadelphia NFL	16	1	0	0.0	0
1993—Philadelphia NFL	15	1	0	0.0	0
1994—Philadelphia NFL	16	0	0	...	0
1995—New York Jets NFL	11	6	101	16.8	1
Pro totals (5 years)	73	10	175	17.5	2

SMITH, RICO   WR   JETS

PERSONAL: Born January 14, 1969, in Compton, Calif. ... 6-0/185. ... Full name: Rico Louis Smith Jr.
HIGH SCHOOL: Paramount (Calif.).
JUNIOR COLLEGE: Cerritos College (Calif.).
COLLEGE: Colorado.
TRANSACTIONS/CAREER NOTES: Selected by Cleveland Browns in sixth round (143rd pick overall) of 1992 NFL draft. ... Signed by Browns (July 14, 1992). ... Granted free agency (February 17, 1995). ... Re-signed by Browns (March 7, 1995). ... Granted unconditional free agency (February 16, 1996). ... Signed by New York Jets (February 23, 1996).
PRO STATISTICS: 1993—Returned one kickoff for 13 yards.
STATISTICAL PLATEAUS: 100-yard receiving games: 1995 (1).

Year Team		RECEIVING				TOTALS			
	G	No.	Yds.	Avg.	TD	TD	2pt.	Pts.	Fum.
1992—Cleveland NFL	10	5	64	12.8	0	0	...	0	0
1993—Cleveland NFL	10	4	55	13.8	0	0	...	0	0
1994—Cleveland NFL	5	2	61	30.5	0	0	0	0	0
1995—Cleveland NFL	5	13	173	13.3	1	1	0	6	1
Pro totals (4 years)	30	24	353	14.7	1	1	0	6	1

SMITH, ROBERT   RB   VIKINGS

PERSONAL: Born March 4, 1972, in Euclid, Ohio. ... 6-1/205. ... Full name: Robert Scott Smith.
HIGH SCHOOL: Senior (Euclid, Ohio).
COLLEGE: Ohio State.
TRANSACTIONS/CAREER NOTES: Selected after sophomore season by Minnesota Vikings in first round (21st pick overall) of 1993 NFL draft. ... Signed by Vikings (July 16, 1993). ... On injured reserve with knee injury (December 7, 1993-remainder of season). ... On physically unable to perform list (July 13-19, 1994). ... Granted free agency (February 16, 1996).
PRO STATISTICS: 1993—Returned one punt for four yards.
STATISTICAL PLATEAUS: 100-yard rushing games: 1993 (1), 1995 (2). Total: 3.

Year Team		RUSHING				RECEIVING				KICKOFF RETURNS				TOTALS			
	G	Att.	Yds.	Avg.	TD	No.	Yds.	Avg.	TD	No.	Yds.	Avg.	TD	TD	2pt.	Pts.	Fum.
1993—Minnesota NFL	10	82	399	4.9	2	24	111	4.6	0	3	41	13.7	0	2	...	12	0
1994—Minnesota NFL	14	31	106	3.4	1	15	105	7.0	0	16	419	26.2	0	1	0	6	0
1995—Minnesota NFL	9	139	632	4.6	5	7	35	5.0	0	0	0	...	0	5	1	32	1
Pro totals (3 years)	33	252	1137	4.5	8	46	251	5.5	0	19	460	24.2	0	8	1	50	1

SMITH, ROD   WR   BRONCOS

PERSONAL: Born May 15, 1970, in Texarkana, Ark. ... 6-0/183.
HIGH SCHOOL: Arkansas (Texarkana, Ark.).
COLLEGE: Missouri Southern.
TRANSACTIONS/CAREER NOTES: Signed as non-drafted free agent by Denver Broncos (March 23, 1995).

Year Team		RECEIVING				KICKOFF RETURNS				TOTALS			
	G	No.	Yds.	Avg.	TD	No.	Yds.	Avg.	TD	TD	2pt.	Pts.	Fum.
1995—Denver NFL	16	6	152	25.3	1	4	54	13.5	0	1	0	6	0

SMITH, ROD   CB   VIKINGS

PERSONAL: Born March 12, 1970, in St. Paul, Minn. ... 5-11/187. ... Full name: Rodney Marc Smith.
HIGH SCHOOL: Roseville (Minn.).
COLLEGE: Notre Dame (degree in economics).
TRANSACTIONS/CAREER NOTES: Selected by New England Patriots in second round (35th pick overall) of 1992 NFL draft. ... Signed by Patriots (August 3, 1992). ... Selected by Carolina Panthers from Patriots in NFL expansion draft (February 15, 1995). ... Granted free agency (February 17, 1995). ... Signed by Panthers (May 5, 1995). ... Granted unconditional free agency (February 16, 1996). ... Signed by Minnesota Vikings (May 3, 1996).
PRO STATISTICS: 1993—Returned one punt for no yards. 1994—Credited with ½ sack.

Year Team		INTERCEPTIONS			
	G	No.	Yds.	Avg.	TD
1992—New England NFL	16	1	0	0.0	0
1993—New England NFL	16	0	0	...	0
1994—New England NFL	16	2	10	5.0	0
1995—Carolina NFL	16	0	0	...	0
Pro totals (4 years)	64	3	10	3.3	0

SMITH, STEVE — FB

PERSONAL: Born August 30, 1964, in Washington, D.C. ... 6-1/242. ... Full name: Steven Anthony Smith.
HIGH SCHOOL: DeMatha Catholic (Hyattsville, Md.).
COLLEGE: Penn State (degree in hotel, restaurant and institutional management, 1987).
TRANSACTIONS/CAREER NOTES: Selected by Los Angeles Raiders in third round (81st pick overall) of 1987 NFL draft. ... Signed by Raiders (July 22, 1987). ... On injured reserve with knee injury (September 16-October 24, 1987). ... On injured reserve with knee and ankle injuries (December 3, 1987-remainder of season). ... Granted free agency (February 1, 1990). ... Re-signed by Raiders (August 14, 1990). ... Granted unconditional free agency (March 1, 1993). ... Re-signed by Raiders (April 14, 1993). ... Released by Raiders (May 17, 1994). ... Signed by Seattle Seahawks (June 13, 1994). ... Announced retirement (June 6, 1996).
CHAMPIONSHIP GAME EXPERIENCE: Played in AFC championship game (1990 season).
PRO STATISTICS: 1987—Recovered one fumble. 1988—Recovered one fumble. 1989—Recovered one fumble. 1990—Recovered one fumble. 1991—Recovered two fumbles. 1993—Recovered three fumbles.
STATISTICAL PLATEAUS: 100-yard rushing games: 1989 (1). ... 100-yard receiving games: 1988 (1).

Year Team	G	RUSHING				RECEIVING				KICKOFF RETURNS				TOTALS			
		Att.	Yds.	Avg.	TD	No.	Yds.	Avg.	TD	No.	Yds.	Avg.	TD	TD	2pt.	Pts.	Fum.
1987—Los Angeles Raiders NFL....	7	5	18	3.6	0	3	46	15.3	0	0	0	...	0	0	...	0	0
1988—Los Angeles Raiders NFL....	16	38	162	4.3	3	26	299	11.5	6	3	46	15.3	0	9	...	54	1
1989—Los Angeles Raiders NFL....	16	117	471	4.0	1	19	140	7.4	0	2	19	9.5	0	1	...	6	2
1990—Los Angeles Raiders NFL....	16	81	327	4.0	2	4	30	7.5	3	0	0	...	0	5	...	30	3
1991—Los Angeles Raiders NFL....	16	62	265	4.3	1	15	130	8.7	1	1	0	0.0	0	2	...	12	4
1992—Los Angeles Raiders NFL....	16	44	129	2.9	1	28	217	7.8	1	0	0	...	0	1	...	6	0
1993—Los Angeles Raiders NFL....	16	47	156	3.3	0	18	187	10.4	0	0	0	...	0	0	...	0	1
1994—Seattle NFL......	16	26	80	3.1	2	11	142	12.9	1	0	0	...	0	3	...	18	0
1995—Seattle NFL......	9	9	19	2.1	0	7	59	8.4	1	1	11	11.0	0	0	0	0	0
Pro totals (9 years)	128	429	1627	3.8	9	131	1250	9.6	13	7	76	10.9	0	21	0	126	11

S

SMITH, THOMAS — CB — BILLS

PERSONAL: Born December 5, 1970, in Gates, N.C. ... 5-11/188. ... Full name: Thomas Lee Smith Jr. ... Cousin of Sam Perkins, forward/center, Seattle SuperSonics.
HIGH SCHOOL: Gates County (Gatesville, N.C.).
COLLEGE: North Carolina.
TRANSACTIONS/CAREER NOTES: Selected by Buffalo Bills in first round (28th pick overall) of 1993 NFL draft. ... Signed by Bills (July 16, 1993). ... Granted free agency (February 16, 1996). ... Re-signed by Bills (February 27, 1996).
PLAYING EXPERIENCE: Buffalo NFL, 1993-1995. ... Games: 1993 (16), 1994 (16), 1995 (16). Total: 48.
PRO STATISTICS: 1993—Recovered one fumble. 1994—Intercepted one pass for four yards. 1995—Intercepted two passes for 23 yards.

SMITH, TONY — RB/KR — PANTHERS

PERSONAL: Born June 29, 1970, in Chicago. ... 6-1/212.
HIGH SCHOOL: Warren Central (Vicksburg, Miss.).
COLLEGE: Southern Mississippi.
TRANSACTIONS/CAREER NOTES: Selected by Atlanta Falcons in first round (19th pick overall) of 1992 NFL draft. ... Signed by Falcons (July 30, 1992). ... On injured reserve with knee injury (December 22, 1992-remainder of season). ... Released by Falcons (September 27, 1994). ... Signed by Carolina Panthers (December 15, 1994). ... On injured reserve with broken leg (August 16, 1995-entire season).
PRO STATISTICS: 1992—Fumbled four times and recovered one fumble. 1993—Fumbled four times and recovered one fumble. 1994—Fumbled once.

Year Team	G	RUSHING				RECEIVING				PUNT RETURNS				KICKOFF RETURNS				TOTALS		
		Att.	Yds.	Avg.	TD	No.	Yds.	Avg.	TD	No.	Yds.	Avg.	TD	No.	Yds.	Avg.	TD	TD	2pt.	Pts.
1992—Atlanta NFL	14	87	329	3.8	2	2	14	7.0	0	16	155	9.7	0	7	172	24.6	0	2	...	12
1993—Atlanta NFL	15	0	0	...	0	0	0	...	0	32	255	8.0	0	38	948	25.0	†1	1	...	6
1994—Atlanta NFL	4	0	0	...	0	0	0	...	0	8	75	9.4	0	16	333	20.8	0	0	0	0
1995—Carolina NFL								Did not play—injured.												
Pro totals (3 years)	33	87	329	3.8	2	2	14	7.0	0	56	485	8.7	0	61	1453	23.8	1	3	0	18

SMITH, VERNICE — G

PERSONAL: Born October 24, 1965, in Orlando. ... 6-3/300. ... Full name: Vernice Carlton Smith.
HIGH SCHOOL: Oak Ridge (Orlando).
COLLEGE: Florida A&M.
TRANSACTIONS/CAREER NOTES: Signed as non-drafted free agent by Miami Dolphins (May 22, 1987). ... Released by Dolphins (September 7, 1987). ... Signed by Dallas Cowboys (March 8, 1988). ... Released by Cowboys (August 30, 1988). ... Signed by Cleveland Browns (March 24, 1989). ... Released by Browns (August 30, 1989). ... Signed by Phoenix Cardinals to developmental squad (September 14, 1989). ... Released by Cardinals (November 1, 1989). ... Re-signed by Cardinals to developmental squad (November 8, 1989). ... Released by Cardinals (January 3, 1990). ... Re-signed by Cardinals (off-season, 1990). ... Granted unconditional free agency (February 1-April 1, 1992). ... Re-signed by Cardinals for 1992 season. ... Granted free agency (March 1, 1993). ... Tendered offer sheet by Chicago Bears (April 24, 1993). ... Cardinals declined to match offer (April 25, 1993). ... Released by Bears (October 29, 1993). ... Signed by Washington Redskins (November 9, 1993). ... Released by Redskins (August 24, 1994). ... Re-signed by Redskins (August 25, 1994). ... Granted unconditional free agency (February 17, 1995). ... Re-signed by Redskins (June 6, 1995). ... Granted unconditional free agency (February 16, 1996).
PLAYING EXPERIENCE: Phoenix NFL, 1990-1992; Chicago (6)-Washington (8) NFL, 1993; Washington NFL, 1994 and 1995. ... Games: 1990 (11), 1991 (14), 1992 (12), 1993 (14), 1994 (4), 1995 (9). Total: 64.
PRO STATISTICS: 1995—Recovered one fumble.

SMITH, VINSON   LB   BEARS

PERSONAL: Born July 3, 1965, in Statesville, N.C. ... 6-2/247. ... Full name: Vinson Robert Smith.
HIGH SCHOOL: Statesville (N.C.).
COLLEGE: East Carolina (degree in communications, 1989).
TRANSACTIONS/CAREER NOTES: Signed as non-drafted free agent by Atlanta Falcons (May 2, 1988).... On injured reserve with elbow injury (August 29-November 4, 1988). ... On injured reserve with knee injury (December 10, 1988-remainder of season). ... Granted unconditional free agency (February 1, 1989). ... Signed by Pittsburgh Steelers (February 28, 1989). ... On injured reserve with broken foot (August 29, 1989-entire season). ... Granted unconditional free agency (February 1, 1990). ... Signed by Dallas Cowboys (March 3, 1990). ... Granted free agency (February 1, 1992). ... Re-signed by Cowboys (August 4, 1992). ... Traded by Cowboys with LB Barry Minter and sixth-round pick (DE Carl Reeves) in 1995 draft to Chicago Bears for TE Kelly Blackwell, S Markus Paul and LB John Roper (August 17, 1993).... Granted unconditional free agency (February 17, 1995).... Re-signed by Bears (March 2, 1995).
PLAYING EXPERIENCE: Atlanta NFL, 1988; Dallas NFL, 1990-1992; Chicago 1993-1995. ... Games: 1988 (3), 1990 (16), 1991 (13), 1992 (16), 1993 (16), 1994 (12), 1995 (16). Total: 92.
CHAMPIONSHIP GAME EXPERIENCE: Played in NFC championship game (1992 season). ... Member of Super Bowl championship team (1992 season).
PRO STATISTICS: 1990—Recovered two fumbles. 1992—Recovered two fumbles. 1995—Credited with four sacks, fumbled once and recovered one fumble.

Year Team	G	SACKS
1992—Dallas NFL	16	1.0
1993—Chicago NFL	16	0.0
1994—Chicago NFL	12	1.0
1995—Chicago NFL	16	4.0
Pro totals (4 years)	60	6.0

SOLOMON, ARIEL   C/G   VIKINGS

PERSONAL: Born July 16, 1968, in Brooklyn, N.Y. ... 6-5/290. ... Full name: Ariel Mace Solomon.
HIGH SCHOOL: Boulder (Colo.).
COLLEGE: Colorado (degree in economics).
TRANSACTIONS/CAREER NOTES: Selected by Pittsburgh Steelers in 10th round (269th pick overall) of 1991 NFL draft. ... Signed by Steelers (July 10, 1991). ... Released by Steelers (August 26, 1991). ... Re-signed by Steelers to practice squad (August 27, 1991). ... Activated (October 31, 1991). ... On injured reserve with knee injury (September 15-November 3, 1992). ... Signed by Minnesota Vikings (May 3, 1996).
PLAYING EXPERIENCE: Pittsburgh NFL, 1991-1995. ... Games: 1991 (5), 1992 (4), 1993 (16), 1994 (16), 1995 (4). Total: 45.
CHAMPIONSHIP GAME EXPERIENCE: Played in AFC championship game (1994 season). ... Member of Steelers for AFC championship game and Super Bowl XXX (1995 season); inactive.

SPARKS, PHILLIPPI   CB   GIANTS

PERSONAL: Born April 15, 1969, in Phoenix. ... 5-11/190. ... Full name: Phillippi Dwaine Sparks.
HIGH SCHOOL: Maryvale (Phoenix).
JUNIOR COLLEGE: Glendale (Ariz.) Community College.
COLLEGE: Arizona State.
TRANSACTIONS/CAREER NOTES: Selected by New York Giants in second round (41st pick overall) of 1992 NFL draft. ... Signed by Giants (July 21, 1992). ... Granted free agency (February 17, 1995). ... Re-signed by Giants (May 8, 1995).
PRO STATISTICS: 1992—Returned two kickoffs for 23 yards.

Year Team	G	No.	Yds.	Avg.	TD
			INTERCEPTIONS		
1992—New York Giants NFL	16	1	0	0.0	0
1993—New York Giants NFL	5	0	0	...	0
1994—New York Giants NFL	11	3	4	1.3	0
1995—New York Giants NFL	16	5	11	2.2	0
Pro totals (4 years)	48	9	15	1.7	0

SPELLMAN, ALONZO   DE   BEARS

PERSONAL: Born September 27, 1971, in Mount Holly, N.J. ... 6-4/290. ... Full name: Alonzo Robert Spellman.
HIGH SCHOOL: Rancocas Valley Regional (Mount Holly, N.J.).
COLLEGE: Ohio State.
TRANSACTIONS/CAREER NOTES: Selected after junior season by Chicago Bears in first round (22nd pick overall) of 1992 NFL draft. ... Signed by Bears (July 13, 1992). ... Designated by Bears as transition player (February 16, 1996). ... Tendered offer sheet by Jacksonville Jaguars (February 18, 1996). ... Offer matched by Bears (February 23, 1996).
PRO STATISTICS: 1994—Intercepted one pass for 31 yards. 1995—Recovered one fumble for four yards.

Year Team	G	SACKS
1992—Chicago NFL	15	4.0
1993—Chicago NFL	16	2.5
1994—Chicago NFL	16	7.0
1995—Chicago NFL	16	8.5
Pro totals (4 years)	63	22.0

SPENCER, DARRYL   WR

PERSONAL: Born March 21, 1970, in Merrit Island, Fla. ... 5-8/172. ... Full name: Darryl Eugene Spencer. ... Cousin of Mercury Morris, running back, Miami Dolphins and San Diego Chargers (1969-1976); cousin of Dennis McKinnon, wide receiver/kick returner, Chicago Bears

(1983-1988); and cousin of Tim Spencer, running back, Chicago Blitz, Arizona Wranglers and Memphis Showboats of USFL and San Diego Chargers (1983-1990).
HIGH SCHOOL: Merrit Island (Fla.).
COLLEGE: Miami (Fla.).
TRANSACTIONS/CAREER NOTES: Signed as non-drafted free agent by Atlanta Falcons (May 7, 1993). ... Released by Falcons (August 24, 1993). ... Re-signed by Falcons to practice squad (September 23, 1993). ... Granted free agency after 1993 season. ... Re-signed by Falcons (March 18, 1994). ... Released by Falcons (October 24, 1995).

		RECEIVING				TOTALS			
Year Team	G	No.	Yds.	Avg.	TD	TD	2pt.	Pts.	Fum.
1994—Atlanta NFL	8	2	51	25.5	0	0	0	0	0
1995—Atlanta NFL	5	5	60	12.0	0	0	0	0	0
Pro totals (2 years)	13	7	111	15.9	0	0	0	0	0

SPENCER, JIMMY   CB   BENGALS

PERSONAL: Born March 29, 1969, in Manning, S.C. ... 5-9/180. ... Full name: James Arthur Spencer Jr.
HIGH SCHOOL: Glades Central (Belle Glade, Fla.).
COLLEGE: Florida.
TRANSACTIONS/CAREER NOTES: Selected by Washington Redskins in eighth round (215th pick overall) of 1991 NFL draft. ... Released by Redskins (August 26, 1991). ... Signed by New Orleans Saints (April 2, 1992). ... Granted unconditional free agency (February 16, 1996). ... Signed by Cincinnati Bengals (March 21, 1996).
PRO STATISTICS: 1992—Recovered one fumble. 1993—Recovered three fumbles for 53 yards. 1994—Recovered one fumble.

		INTERCEPTIONS			
Year Team	G	No.	Yds.	Avg.	TD
1992—New Orleans NFL	16	0	0	...	0
1993—New Orleans NFL	16	0	0	...	0
1994—New Orleans NFL	16	5	24	4.8	0
1995—New Orleans NFL	16	4	11	2.8	0
Pro totals (4 years)	64	9	35	3.9	0

S

SPIELMAN, CHRIS   LB   BILLS

PERSONAL: Born October 11, 1965, in Canton, Ohio. ... 6-0/247. ... Full name: Charles Christopher Spielman.
HIGH SCHOOL: Washington (Massillon, Ohio).
COLLEGE: Ohio State.
TRANSACTIONS/CAREER NOTES: Selected by Detroit Lions in second round (29th pick overall) of 1988 NFL draft. ... Signed by Lions (July 15, 1988). ... On injured reserve with separated shoulder (September 19-October 26, 1990). ... Granted unconditional free agency (February 16, 1996). ... Signed by Buffalo Bills (March 8, 1996).
CHAMPIONSHIP GAME EXPERIENCE: Played in NFC championship game (1991 season).
HONORS: Named linebacker on THE SPORTING NEWS college All-America first team (1986 and 1987). ... Lombardi Award winner (1987). ... Played in Pro Bowl (1989-1991 and 1994 seasons). ... Named inside linebacker on THE SPORTING NEWS NFL All-Pro team (1994).
PRO STATISTICS: 1988—Recovered one fumble. 1989—Recovered two fumbles for 31 yards. 1990—Recovered two fumbles. 1991—Recovered three fumbles. 1992—Recovered one fumble. 1993—Recovered two fumbles. 1994—Recovered three fumbles for 25 yards and a touchdown. 1995—Recovered three fumbles for eight yards.

		INTERCEPTIONS				SACKS
Year Team	G	No.	Yds.	Avg.	TD	No.
1988—Detroit NFL	16	0	0	...	0	0.0
1989—Detroit NFL	16	0	0	...	0	5.0
1990—Detroit NFL	12	1	12	12.0	0	2.0
1991—Detroit NFL	16	0	0	...	0	1.0
1992—Detroit NFL	16	0	0	...	0	1.0
1993—Detroit NFL	16	2	-2	-1.0	0	0.5
1994—Detroit NFL	16	0	0	...	0	0.0
1995—Detroit NFL	16	1	4	4.0	0	1.0
Pro totals (8 years)	124	4	14	3.5	0	10.5

SPIKES, IRVING   RB/KR   DOLPHINS

PERSONAL: Born December 21, 1970, in Ocean Springs, Miss. ... 5-8/206.
HIGH SCHOOL: Ocean Springs (Miss.).
COLLEGE: Alabama, then Northeast Louisiana.
TRANSACTIONS/CAREER NOTES: Signed as non-drafted free agent by Miami Dolphins (April 28, 1994).

		RUSHING				RECEIVING				KICKOFF RETURNS				TOTALS			
Year Team	G	Att.	Yds.	Avg.	TD	No.	Yds.	Avg.	TD	No.	Yds.	Avg.	TD	TD	2pt.	Pts.	Fum.
1994—Miami NFL	12	70	312	4.5	2	4	16	4.0	0	19	434	22.8	0	2	0	12	1
1995—Miami NFL	9	32	126	3.9	1	5	18	3.6	1	18	378	21.0	0	2	0	12	0
Pro totals (2 years)	21	102	438	4.3	3	9	34	3.8	1	37	812	22.0	0	4	0	24	1

SPINDLER, MARC   DE/DT   JETS

PERSONAL: Born November 28, 1969, in West Scranton, Pa. ... 6-5/290. ... Full name: Marc Rudolph Spindler.
HIGH SCHOOL: West Scranton (Pa.).
COLLEGE: Pittsburgh.
TRANSACTIONS/CAREER NOTES: Selected after junior season by Detroit Lions in third round (62nd pick overall) of 1990 NFL draft. ... Signed

by Lions (July 24, 1990). ... On injured reserve with knee injury (September 27, 1990-remainder of season). ... On injured reserve with hamstring injury (September 18-October 14, 1992). ... Granted free agency (March 1, 1993). ... Re-signed by Lions (August 2, 1993). ... Granted unconditional free agency (February 17, 1995). ... Signed by Tampa Bay Buccaneers (April 25, 1995). ... Traded by Buccaneers with WR Charles Wilson to New York Jets for fourth-round pick (OT Jason Odom) in 1996 draft (August 27, 1995).

CHAMPIONSHIP GAME EXPERIENCE: Played in NFC championship game (1991 season).

HONORS: Named defensive tackle on THE SPORTING NEWS college All-America first team (1989).

PRO STATISTICS: 1991—Recovered one fumble. 1993—Recovered two fumbles.

Year Team	G	SACKS
1990—Detroit NFL	3	1.0
1991—Detroit NFL	16	3.5
1992—Detroit NFL	13	2.5
1993—Detroit NFL	16	2.0
1994—Detroit NFL	9	0.0
1995—New York Jets NFL	10	0.0
Pro totals (6 years)	67	9.0

SPITULSKI, BOB   LB

PERSONAL: Born September 10, 1969, in Toledo, Ohio. ... 6-3/246.
HIGH SCHOOL: Bishop Moore (Orlando).
COLLEGE: Central Florida.
TRANSACTIONS/CAREER NOTES: Selected by Seattle Seahawks in third round (66th pick overall) of 1992 NFL draft. ... Signed by Seahawks (July 21, 1992). ... On injured reserve with knee injury (September 30, 1992-remainder of season). ... On injured reserve with knee injury (October 19, 1993-remainder of season). ... Granted free agency (February 17, 1995). ... Re-signed by Seahawks (July 17, 1995). ... On injured reserve with knee injury (August 16, 1995-entire season). ... Granted unconditional free agency (February 16, 1996).

PRO STATISTICS: 1994—Intercepted one pass for seven yards.

Year Team	G	SACKS
1992—Seattle NFL	4	0.0
1993—Seattle NFL	6	0.0
1994—Seattle NFL	16	3.0
1995—Seattle NFL	Did not play.	
Pro totals (3 years)	26	3.0

STABLEIN, BRIAN   WR   COLTS

PERSONAL: Born April 14, 1970, in Erie, Pa. ... 6-1/190.
HIGH SCHOOL: McDowell (Erie, Pa.).
COLLEGE: Ohio State.
TRANSACTIONS/CAREER NOTES: Selected by Denver Broncos in eighth round (210nd pick overall) of 1993 NFL draft. ... Signed by Broncos (June 7, 1993). ... Released by Broncos (August 24, 1993). ... Signed by Indianapolis Colts to practice squad (September 7, 1993). ... Granted free agency after 1993 season. ... Re-signed by Colts (March 4, 1994).
PLAYING EXPERIENCE: Indianapolis NFL, 1995. ... Games: 1995 (15).
CHAMPIONSHIP GAME EXPERIENCE: Played in AFC championship game (1995 season).
PRO STATISTICS: 1995—Caught eight passes for 95 yards.

STAI, BRENDEN   G   STEELERS

PERSONAL: Born March 30, 1972, in Phoenix. ... 6-4/297. ... Name pronounced STY.
HIGH SCHOOL: Anaheim (Calif.) Esperanza.
COLLEGE: Nebraska.
TRANSACTIONS/CAREER NOTES: Selected by Pittsburgh Steelers in third round (91st pick overall) of 1995 NFL draft. ... Signed by Steelers (July 18, 1995).
PLAYING EXPERIENCE: Pittsburgh NFL, 1995. ... Games: 1995 (16).
CHAMPIONSHIP GAME EXPERIENCE: Played in AFC championship game (1995 season). ... Played in Super Bowl XXX (1995 season).
HONORS: Named offensive lineman on THE SPORTING NEWS college All-America second team (1994).

STALLINGS, RAMONDO   DE   BENGALS

PERSONAL: Born November 21, 1971, in Winston-Salem, N.C. ... 6-7/285. ... Full name: Ramondo Antonio Stallings.
HIGH SCHOOL: Ansonia (Conn.).
COLLEGE: San Diego State.
TRANSACTIONS/CAREER NOTES: Selected by Cincinnati Bengals in seventh round (195th pick overall) of 1994 NFL draft. ... Signed by Bengals (June 2, 1994). ... Released by Bengals (August 23, 1994). ... Re-signed by Bengals to practice squad (August 30, 1994). ... Activated (November 8, 1994).
PLAYING EXPERIENCE: Cincinnati NFL, 1994 and 1995. ... Games: 1994 (6), 1995 (13). Total: 19.
PRO STATISTICS: 1995—Credited with one sack, fumbled once and recovered one fumble.

STAMS, FRANK   LB

PERSONAL: Born July 17, 1966, in Akron, Ohio. ... 6-2/240. ... Full name: Frank Michael Stams Jr. ... Nephew of Steve Stonebreaker, linebacker, Minnesota Vikings, Baltimore Colts and New Orleans Saints (1962-1968); and cousin of Mike Stonebreaker, linebacker, New Orleans Saints (1994) and Frankfurt Galaxy of World League (1995).
HIGH SCHOOL: St. Vincent-St. Mary (Akron, Ohio).

S

COLLEGE: Notre Dame (bachelor of arts degree, 1989).
TRANSACTIONS/CAREER NOTES: Selected by Los Angeles Rams in second round (45th pick overall) of 1989 NFL draft. ... Signed by Rams (July 26, 1989). ... On injured reserve with leg injury (September 11-November 20, 1991). ... Traded by Rams to Cleveland Browns for eighth-round pick (P Jeff Buffaloe) in 1993 draft (August 24, 1992). ... On injured reserve with leg injury (September 11-October 6, 1992). ... Granted free agency (March 1, 1993). ... Re-signed by Browns (June 16, 1993). ... Granted unconditional free agency (February 17, 1994). ... Re-signed by Browns (May 3, 1994). ... Granted unconditional free agency (February 17, 1995). ... Signed by Carolina Panthers (March 8, 1995). ... Released by Panthers (August 27, 1995). ... Signed by Kansas City Chiefs (September 20, 1995). ... Released by Chiefs (October 31, 1995). ... Signed by Browns (November 8, 1995). ... On injured reserve with knee injury (December 22, 1995-remainder of season). ... Granted unconditional free agency (February 16, 1996).
PLAYING EXPERIENCE: Los Angeles Rams NFL, 1989-1991; Cleveland NFL, 1992-1994; Kansas City (1)-Cleveland (4) NFL, 1995. ... Games: 1989 (16), 1990 (14), 1991 (5), 1992 (12), 1993 (14), 1994 (16), 1995 (5). Total: 82.
CHAMPIONSHIP GAME EXPERIENCE: Played in NFC championship game (1989 season).
HONORS: Named defensive lineman on THE SPORTING NEWS college All-America second team (1988).
PRO STATISTICS: 1989—Intercepted one pass for 20 yards. 1994—Credited with two sacks and intercepted one pass for seven yards.

STANLEY, ISRAEL — DT — SAINTS

PERSONAL: Born April 21, 1970, in San Diego. ... 6-3/260. ... Full name: Israel Damon Stanley.
HIGH SCHOOL: Point Loma (San Diego).
COLLEGE: Arizona State.
TRANSACTIONS/CAREER NOTES: Signed as non-drafted free agent by San Diego Chargers (May 6, 1993). ... Released by Chargers (August 22, 1993). ... Re-signed by Chargers to practice squad (September 1, 1993). ... Activated (December 15, 1993); did not play. ... Released by Chargers (August 22, 1994). ... Signed by New Orleans Saints (March 7, 1995).
PRO STATISTICS: 1995—Recovered one fumble.

Year Team	G	SACKS
1993—San Diego	Did not play.	
1994—	Did not play.	
1995—New Orleans NFL	14	2.0

STARGELL, TONY — CB

PERSONAL: Born August 7, 1966, in LaGrange, Ga. ... 5-11/186.
HIGH SCHOOL: LaGrange (Ga.).
COLLEGE: Tennessee State (degree in health and physical education, 1990).
TRANSACTIONS/CAREER NOTES: Selected by New York Jets in third round (56th pick overall) of 1990 NFL draft. ... Signed by Jets (July 22, 1990). ... Claimed on waivers by Indianapolis Colts (August 31, 1992). ... Granted unconditional free agency (February 17, 1994). ... Signed by Tampa Bay Buccaneers (April 20, 1994). ... On injured reserve with knee injury (November 22, 1994-remainder of season). ... Released by Buccaneers (August 29, 1995). ... Re-signed by Buccaneers (August 31, 1995). ... Granted unconditional free agency (February 16, 1996).
PRO STATISTICS: 1990—Recovered one fumble. 1991—Recovered one fumble. 1993—Credited with one sack. 1994—Recovered one fumble for two yards.

		INTERCEPTIONS			
Year Team	G	No.	Yds.	Avg.	TD
1990—New York Jets NFL	16	2	-3	-1.5	0
1991—New York Jets NFL	16	0	0	...	0
1992—Indianapolis NFL	13	2	26	13.0	0
1993—Indianapolis NFL	16	0	0	...	0
1994—Tampa Bay NFL	10	1	0	0.0	0
1995—Tampa Bay NFL	14	0	0	...	0
Pro totals (6 years)	85	5	23	4.6	0

STARK, ROHN — P — STEELERS

PERSONAL: Born May 4, 1959, in Minneapolis. ... 6-3/203. ... Full name: Rohn Taylor Stark. ... Name pronounced RON.
HIGH SCHOOL: Pine River (Minn.).
COLLEGE: Florida State (degree in finance, 1982).
TRANSACTIONS/CAREER NOTES: Selected by Baltimore Colts in second round (34th pick overall) of 1982 NFL draft. ... Colts franchise moved to Indianapolis (March 31, 1984). ... Granted unconditional free agency (February 17, 1995). ... Signed by Pittsburgh Steelers (March 28, 1995).
CHAMPIONSHIP GAME EXPERIENCE: Played in AFC championship game (1995 season). ... Played in Super Bowl XXX (1995 season).
HONORS: Named punter on THE SPORTING NEWS college All-America first team (1980 and 1981). ... Played in Pro Bowl (1985, 1986, 1990 and 1992 seasons). ... Named punter on THE SPORTING NEWS NFL All-Pro team (1992).
PRO STATISTICS: 1982—Attempted one pass without a completion, rushed once for eight yards and fumbled once. 1983—Attempted one pass without a completion and rushed once for eight yards. 1984—Had only pass attempt intercepted, rushed twice for no yards and recovered one fumble. 1985—Attempted one pass without a completion and recovered one fumble. 1986—Fumbled once and recovered one fumble. 1989—Rushed once for minus 11 yards. 1990—Attempted one pass with one completion for 40 yards. 1991—Rushed once for minus 13 yards, fumbled once and recovered two fumbles. 1992—Attempted one pass with one completion for 17 yards. 1993—Rushed once for 11 yards.

		PUNTING					
Year Team	G	No.	Yds.	Avg.	Net avg.	In. 20	Blk.
1982—Baltimore NFL	9	46	2044	44.4	34.3	8	0
1983—Baltimore NFL	16	91	*4124	*45.3	36.3	20	0
1984—Indianapolis NFL	16	*98	4383	44.7	37.2	21	0
1985—Indianapolis NFL	16	78	3584	*45.9	34.2	12	†2
1986—Indianapolis NFL	16	76	3432	*45.2	37.2	22	0
1987—Indianapolis NFL	12	61	2440	40.0	30.9	12	†2
1988—Indianapolis NFL	16	64	2784	43.5	34.5	15	0
1989—Indianapolis NFL	16	79	3392	42.9	32.9	14	1
1990—Indianapolis NFL	16	71	3084	43.4	37.4	24	1

Year Team		PUNTING					
	G	No.	Yds.	Avg.	Net avg.	In. 20	Blk.
1991—Indianapolis NFL	16	82	3492	42.6	34.8	14	0
1992—Indianapolis NFL	16	83	3716	44.8	39.3	22	0
1993—Indianapolis NFL	16	83	3595	43.3	35.9	18	0
1994—Indianapolis NFL	16	73	3092	42.4	34.1	22	1
1995—Pittsburgh NFL	16	59	2368	40.1	33.3	20	0
Pro totals (14 years)	213	1044	45530	43.6	35.4	244	7

STAYSNIAK, JOE   G

PERSONAL: Born December 8, 1966, in Elyria, Ohio. ... 6-4/302. ... Full name: Joseph Andrew Staysniak.
HIGH SCHOOL: Midview (Grafton, Ohio).
COLLEGE: Ohio State (degree in marketing, 1990).
TRANSACTIONS/CAREER NOTES: Selected by San Diego Chargers in seventh round (185th pick overall) of 1990 NFL draft. ... Released by Chargers (preseason, 1990). ... Signed by Buffalo Bills to practice squad (November 28, 1990). ... Released by Bills (August 27, 1991). ... Re-signed by Bills to practice squad (1991). ... Activated (October 9, 1991). ... Granted unconditional free agency (February 1-April 1, 1992). ... Re-signed by Bills for 1992 season. ... Released by Bills (August 31, 1992). ... Signed by Kansas City Chiefs (September 16, 1992). ... Released by Chiefs (December 8, 1992). ... Signed by Indianapolis Colts (December 23, 1992). ... On inactive list for one game with Colts (1992). ... Granted unconditional free agency (February 16, 1996).
PLAYING EXPERIENCE: Buffalo NFL, 1991; Kansas City NFL, 1992; Indianapolis NFL, 1993-1995 . ... Games: 1991 (2), 1992 (6), 1993 (14), 1994 (16), 1995 (16). Total: 54.
CHAMPIONSHIP GAME EXPERIENCE: Member of Bills for AFC championship game (1991 season); did not play. ... Played in Super Bowl XXVI (1991 season). ... Played in AFC championship game (1995 season).
HONORS: Named offensive tackle on THE SPORTING NEWS college All-America second team (1989).
PRO STATISTICS: 1994—Recovered two fumbles for minus 18 yards and fumbled once.

STEED, JOEL   NT   STEELERS

PERSONAL: Born February 17, 1969, in Frankfurt, West Germany. ... 6-2/300. ... Full name: Joel Edward Steed.
HIGH SCHOOL: W.C. Hinkley (Aurora, Colo.).
COLLEGE: Colorado.
TRANSACTIONS/CAREER NOTES: Selected by Pittsburgh Steelers in third round (67th pick overall) of 1992 NFL draft. ... Signed by Steelers (July 27, 1992). ... On suspended list for anabolic steroid use (October 23-November 20, 1995).
CHAMPIONSHIP GAME EXPERIENCE: Played in AFC championship game (1994 and 1995 seasons). ... Played in Super Bowl XXX (1995 season).
HONORS: Named defensive lineman on THE SPORTING NEWS college All-America second team (1991).
PRO STATISTICS: 1993—Recovered one fumble.

Year Team	G	SACKS
1992—Pittsburgh NFL	11	0.0
1993—Pittsburgh NFL	14	1.5
1994—Pittsburgh NFL	16	2.0
1995—Pittsburgh NFL	12	1.0
Pro totals (4 years)	53	4.5

STENSTROM, STEVE   QB   BEARS

PERSONAL: Born December 23, 1971, in El Toro (Calif.). ... 6-1/200.
HIGH SCHOOL: El Toro (Calif.).
COLLEGE: Stanford (degree in public policy, 1994).
TRANSACTIONS/CAREER NOTES: Selected by Kansas City Chiefs in fourth round (134th pick overall) of 1995 NFL draft. ... Signed by Chiefs (September 11, 1995). ... Claimed on waivers by Chicago Bears (September 13, 1995). ... Activated (September 25, 1995). ... Active for 12 games during the 1995 season; did not play.

STEPHENS, DARNELL   LB   BUCCANEERS

PERSONAL: Born January 29, 1973, in San Antonio. ... 5-11/243.
HIGH SCHOOL: Judson (Converse, Texas).
COLLEGE: Clemson.
TRANSACTIONS/CAREER NOTES: Signed as non-drafted free agent by Tampa Bay Buccaneers (April 25, 1995).
PLAYING EXPERIENCE: Tampa Bay NFL, 1995. ... Games: 1995 (13).

STEPHENS, RICH   G   RAIDERS

PERSONAL: Born January 1, 1965, in St. Louis. ... 6-7/310. ... Full name: Richard Scott Stephens.
HIGH SCHOOL: Northwest (House Springs, Mo.).
COLLEGE: Tulsa.
TRANSACTIONS/CAREER NOTES: Selected by Cincinnati Bengals in ninth round (250th pick overall) of 1989 NFL draft. ... Released by Bengals prior to 1989 season. ... Signed by Washington Redskins to developmental squad (September 1989). ... Released by Redskins (October 1989). ... Signed by New York Jets to developmental squad (October 1989). ... Released by Jets (October 1989). ... Signed by WLAF (January 9, 1991). ... Selected by Sacramento Surge in second round (12th offensive lineman) of 1991 WLAF positional draft. ... Signed by Los Angeles Raiders (June 1991). ... Released by Raiders (August 26, 1991). ... Re-signed by Raiders (June 1992). ... Released by Raiders (August 31, 1992). ... Re-signed by Raiders to practice squad (September 2, 1992). ... Activated (October 24, 1992). ... Active for two games

(1992); did not play. ... Raiders franchise moved to Oakland (July 21, 1995). ... Granted free agency (February 16, 1996).
PLAYING EXPERIENCE: Sacramento W.L., 1991 and 1992; Los Angeles Raiders NFL, 1993; Oakland NFL, 1995. ... Games: 1991 (10), 1992 (10), 1993 (16), 1995 (13). Total W.L.: 20. Total NFL: 29. Total Pro: 49.

STEPHENS, ROD — LB — REDSKINS

PERSONAL: Born June 14, 1966, in Atlanta. ... 6-1/237. ... Full name: Rodrequis La'Vant Stephens.
HIGH SCHOOL: North Fulton (Atlanta).
COLLEGE: Georgia Tech.
TRANSACTIONS/CAREER NOTES: Signed as non-drafted free agent by Seattle Seahawks (April 26, 1989). ... Released by Seahawks (September 5, 1989). ... Re-signed by Seahawks to developmental squad (September 6, 1989). ... Activated (September 22, 1989). ... Released by Seahawks (November 13, 1989). ... Re-signed by Seahawks to developmental squad (November 14, 1989). ... Activated (December 1, 1989). ... Granted unconditional free agency (February 1, 1990). ... Signed by Denver Broncos (April 1, 1990). ... Released by Broncos (August 22, 1990). ... Signed by Seahawks (December 5, 1990). ... Granted unconditional free agency (February 1-April 1, 1991). ... Re-signed by Seahawks (July 18, 1991). ... Granted unconditional free agency (February 1-April 1, 1992). ... Re-signed by Seahawks (July 21, 1992). ... Granted free agency (March 1, 1993). ... Re-signed by Seahawks (July 22, 1993). ... Granted unconditional free agency (February 17, 1995). ... Signed by Washington Redskins (March 8, 1995).
PRO STATISTICS: 1991—Recovered one fumble. 1993—Recovered one fumble in end zone for a touchdown. 1994—Recovered two fumbles. 1995—Recovered one fumble.

Year Team	G	SACKS
1989—Seattle NFL	10	0.0
1990—Seattle NFL	4	0.0
1991—Seattle NFL	16	0.0
1992—Seattle NFL	16	0.0
1993—Seattle NFL	13	2.5
1994—Seattle NFL	16	2.5
1995—Washington NFL	16	0.0
Pro totals (7 years)	91	5.0

STEPHENS, SANTO — LB — JAGUARS

PERSONAL: Born June 16, 1969, in Washington, D.C. ... 6-4/244. ... Full name: Santo Sean Stephens.
HIGH SCHOOL: Forestville (Md.).
COLLEGE: Temple (degree in communications).
TRANSACTIONS/CAREER NOTES: Signed as non-drafted free agent by Kansas City Chiefs (May 12, 1992). ... Released by Chiefs (August 31, 1992). ... Re-signed by Chiefs to practice squad (September 2, 1992). ... Granted free agency after 1992 season. ... Re-signed by Chiefs for 1993 season. ... Claimed on waivers by Cincinnati Bengals (April 11, 1994). ... Selected by Jacksonville Jaguars from Bengals in NFL expansion draft (February 15, 1995). ... Granted free agency (February 16, 1996).
PLAYING EXPERIENCE: Kansas City NFL, 1993 and 1994; Jacksonville NFL, 1995. ... Games: 1993 (16), 1994 (14), 1995 (13). Total: 43.
CHAMPIONSHIP GAME EXPERIENCE: Played in AFC championship game (1993 season).

STEPNOSKI, MARK — C — OILERS

PERSONAL: Born January 20, 1967, in Erie, Pa. ... 6-2/269. ... Full name: Mark Matthew Stepnoski.
HIGH SCHOOL: Cathedral Prep (Erie, Pa.).
COLLEGE: Pittsburgh (degree in communications).
TRANSACTIONS/CAREER NOTES: Selected by Dallas Cowboys in third round (57th pick overall) of 1989 NFL draft. ... Signed by Cowboys (July 23, 1989). ... Granted free agency (February 1, 1992). ... Re-signed by Cowboys (September 5, 1992). ... Granted roster exemption (September 5-14, 1992). ... On injured reserve with knee injury (December 22, 1993-remainder of season). ... Granted unconditional free agency (February 17, 1994). ... Re-signed by Cowboys (June 29, 1994). ... Granted unconditional free agency (February 17, 1995). ... Signed by Houston Oilers (March 11, 1995).
PLAYING EXPERIENCE: Dallas NFL, 1989-1994; Houston NFL, 1995. ... Games: 1989 (16), 1990 (16), 1991 (16), 1992 (14), 1993 (13), 1994 (16), 1995 (16). Total: 107.
CHAMPIONSHIP GAME EXPERIENCE: Played in NFC championship game (1992 and 1994 seasons). ... Member of Super Bowl championship team (1992 and 1993 seasons).
HONORS: Named guard on THE SPORTING NEWS college All-America first team (1988). ... Played in Pro Bowl (1992, 1994 and 1995 seasons).
PRO STATISTICS: 1989—Recovered three fumbles. 1990—Returned one kickoff for 15 yards. 1992—Recovered one fumble. 1993—Fumbled once. 1994—Fumbled four times for minus three yards.

STEUSSIE, TODD — OT — VIKINGS

PERSONAL: Born December 1, 1970, in Canoga Park, Calif. ... 6-6/313. ... Full name: Todd Edward Steussie.
HIGH SCHOOL: Agoura (Calif.).
COLLEGE: California.
TRANSACTIONS/CAREER NOTES: Selected by Minnesota Vikings in first round (19th pick overall) of 1994 NFL draft. ... Signed by Vikings (July 13, 1994).
PLAYING EXPERIENCE: Minnesota NFL, 1994 and 1995. ... Games: 1994 (16), 1995 (16). Total: 32.
HONORS: Named offensive lineman on THE SPORTING NEWS college All-America second team (1993).
PRO STATISTICS: 1994—Recovered one fumble.

STEWART, JAMES — RB — VIKINGS

PERSONAL: Born December 8, 1971, in Vero Beach, Fla. ... 6-2/238.

S

HIGH SCHOOL: Vero Beach (Fla.).
COLLEGE: Miami (Fla.).
TRANSACTIONS/CAREER NOTES: Selected after junior season by Minnesota Vikings in fifth round (157th pick overall) of 1995 NFL draft. ... Signed by Vikings (July 22, 1995).
PRO STATISTICS: 1995—Recovered one fumble.

			RUSHING				RECEIVING				TOTALS		
Year Team	G	Att.	Yds.	Avg.	TD	No.	Yds.	Avg.	TD	TD	2pt.	Pts.	Fum.
1995—Minnesota NFL	4	31	144	4.7	0	1	3	3.0	0	0	0	0	2

STEWART, JAMES   RB   JAGUARS

PERSONAL: Born December 27, 1971, in Morristown, Tenn. ... 6-1/221. ... Full name: James Ottis Stewart.
HIGH SCHOOL: Morristown (Tenn.)-Hamblen West.
COLLEGE: Tennessee.
TRANSACTIONS/CAREER NOTES: Selected by Jacksonville Jaguars in first round (19th pick overall) of 1995 NFL draft. ... Signed by Jaguars (June 1, 1995).
MISCELLANEOUS: Holds Jacksonville Jaguars all-time record for most yards rushing (525).

			RUSHING				RECEIVING				TOTALS		
Year Team	G	Att.	Yds.	Avg.	TD	No.	Yds.	Avg.	TD	TD	2pt.	Pts.	Fum.
1995—Jacksonville NFL	14	137	525	3.8	2	21	190	9.1	1	3	0	18	1

STEWART, KORDELL   QB   STEELERS

PERSONAL: Born October 16, 1972, in New Orleans. ... 6-1/212. ... Nickname: Slash.
HIGH SCHOOL: John Ehret (Marrero, La.).
COLLEGE: Colorado.
TRANSACTIONS/CAREER NOTES: Selected by Pittsburgh Steelers in second round (60th pick overall) of 1995 NFL draft. ... Signed by Steelers (July 17, 1995).
CHAMPIONSHIP GAME EXPERIENCE: Played in AFC championship game (1995 season). ... Played in Super Bowl XXX (1995 season).
PRO STATISTICS: 1995—Compiled a quarterback rating of 136.9.

		PASSING							RUSHING				RECEIVING				TOTALS		
Year Team	G	Att.	Cmp.	Pct.	Yds.	TD	Int.	Avg.	Att.	Yds.	Avg.	TD	No.	Yds.	Avg.	TD	TD	2pt.	Pts.
1995—Pittsburgh NFL	10	7	5	71.4	60	1	0	8.57	15	86	5.7	1	14	235	16.8	1	3	0	18

STEWART, MICHAEL   S   DOLPHINS

PERSONAL: Born July 12, 1965, in Atascadero, Calif. ... 5-11/202. ... Full name: Michael Anthony Stewart.
HIGH SCHOOL: Bakersfield (Calif.).
JUNIOR COLLEGE: Bakersfield (Calif.) College.
COLLEGE: Fresno State.
TRANSACTIONS/CAREER NOTES: Selected by Los Angeles Rams in eighth round (213th pick overall) of 1987 NFL draft. ... Signed by Rams (July 6, 1987). ... Granted free agency (February 1, 1990). ... Re-signed by Rams (September 3, 1990). ... Activated (September 7, 1990). ... Granted free agency (February 1, 1992). ... Re-signed by Rams (August 24, 1992). ... Granted roster exemption (August 25-September 4, 1992). ... On injured reserve with broken forearm (October 22-December 5, 1992). ... Granted unconditional free agency (February 17, 1994). ... Signed by Miami Dolphins (March 9, 1994).
CHAMPIONSHIP GAME EXPERIENCE: Played in NFC championship game (1989 season).
PRO STATISTICS: 1987—Credited with one safety. 1988—Returned one kickoff for no yards and recovered two fumbles for 24 yards. 1989—Fumbled once and recovered three fumbles for four yards. 1990—Recovered two fumbles. 1992—Recovered one fumble. 1994—Recovered one fumble. 1995—Recovered one fumble.
MISCELLANEOUS: Selected by Milwaukee Brewers organization in 29th round of free-agent baseball draft (June 4, 1984); did not sign. ... Selected by Minnesota Twins organization in 26th round of free-agent baseball draft (June 2, 1986); did not sign. ... Selected by Toronto Blue Jays organization in 49th round of free-agent baseball draft (June 2, 1987); did not sign.

		INTERCEPTIONS				SACKS
Year Team	G	No.	Yds.	Avg.	TD	No.
1987—Los Angeles Rams NFL	12	0	0	...	0	0.0
1988—Los Angeles Rams NFL	16	2	61	30.5	0	1.0
1989—Los Angeles Rams NFL	16	2	76	38.0	1	0.0
1990—Los Angeles Rams NFL	16	0	0	...	0	0.0
1991—Los Angeles Rams NFL	16	2	8	4.0	0	1.0
1992—Los Angeles Rams NFL	11	0	0	...	0	2.0
1993—Los Angeles Rams NFL	16	1	30	30.0	0	1.0
1994—Miami NFL	16	3	11	3.7	0	0.0
1995—Miami NFL	16	1	0	0.0	0	0.0
Pro totals (9 years)	135	11	186	16.9	1	5.0

STOKES, FRED   DE   SAINTS

PERSONAL: Born March 14, 1964, in Vidalia, Ga. ... 6-3/274. ... Full name: Louis Fred Stokes.
HIGH SCHOOL: Vidalia (Ga.).
COLLEGE: Georgia Southern.
TRANSACTIONS/CAREER NOTES: Selected by Los Angeles Rams in 12th round (332nd pick overall) of 1987 NFL draft. ... Signed by Rams (July 18, 1987). ... On injured reserve with shoulder injury (September 7-November 7, 1987). ... On injured reserve with ankle injury (October

8, 1988-remainder of season). ... Granted unconditional free agency (February 1, 1989). ... Signed by Washington Redskins (March 20, 1989). ... Granted unconditional free agency (March 1, 1993). ... Signed by Rams (March 26, 1993). ... Rams franchise moved to St. Louis (April 12, 1995). ... Granted unconditional free agency (February 16, 1996). ... Signed by New Orleans Saints (February 23, 1996).

CHAMPIONSHIP GAME EXPERIENCE: Played in NFC championship game (1991 season). ... Member of Super Bowl championship team (1991 season).

PRO STATISTICS: 1988—Recovered two fumbles. 1989—Credited with a safety and recovered two fumbles for six yards. 1990—Recovered four fumbles for five yards. 1991—Intercepted one pass for no yards and recovered two fumbles for 10 yards. 1992—Recovered one fumble. 1993—Recovered two fumbles for 51 yards.

Year—Team	G	SACKS
1987—Los Angeles Rams NFL	8	0.5
1988—Los Angeles Rams NFL	5	1.0
1989—Washington NFL	16	3.0
1990—Washington NFL	16	7.5
1991—Washington NFL	16	6.5
1992—Washington NFL	16	3.5
1993—Los Angeles Rams NFL	15	9.5
1994—Los Angeles Rams NFL	16	2.0
1995—St. Louis NFL	14	3.5
Pro totals (9 years)	**122**	**37.0**

STOKES, J.J.　　　　WR　　　　49ERS

PERSONAL: Born October 6, 1972, in San Diego. ... 6-4/217. ... Full name: Jerel Jamal Stokes.
HIGH SCHOOL: Point Loma (San Diego).
COLLEGE: UCLA.
TRANSACTIONS/CAREER NOTES: Selected by San Francisco 49ers in first round (10th pick overall) of 1995 NFL draft. ... Signed by 49ers (July 27, 1995).
HONORS: Named wide receiver on THE SPORTING NEWS college All-America first team (1993).
STATISTICAL PLATEAUS: 100-yard receiving games: 1995 (1).

		RECEIVING				TOTALS			
Year—Team	G	No.	Yds.	Avg.	TD	TD	2pt.	Pts.	Fum.
1995—San Francisco NFL	12	38	517	13.6	4	4	0	24	0

STONE, DWIGHT　　　　WR/KR　　　　PANTHERS

PERSONAL: Born January 28, 1964, in Florala, Ala. ... 6-0/180.
HIGH SCHOOL: Florala (Ala.) and Marion (Ala.) Military Institute.
COLLEGE: Middle Tennessee State.
TRANSACTIONS/CAREER NOTES: Signed as non-drafted free agent by Pittsburgh Steelers (May 19, 1987). ... Crossed picket line during players strike (October 7, 1987). ... Granted free agency (February 1, 1992). ... Re-signed by Steelers (May 15, 1992). ... Released by Steelers (August 30, 1993). ... Re-signed by Steelers (August 31, 1993). ... Granted unconditional free agency (February 17, 1995). ... Signed by Carolina Panthers (May 16, 1995). ... Granted unconditional free agency (February 16, 1996). ... Re-signed by Panthers (March 14, 1996).
CHAMPIONSHIP GAME EXPERIENCE: Played in AFC championship game (1994 season).
PRO STATISTICS: 1987—Recovered one fumble. 1989—Recovered one fumble. 1990—Recovered two fumbles. 1993—Recovered one fumble.
STATISTICAL PLATEAUS: 100-yard receiving games: 1991 (1), 1992 (1), 1993 (1). Total: 3.

		RUSHING				RECEIVING				KICKOFF RETURNS				TOTALS			
Year—Team	G	Att.	Yds.	Avg.	TD	No.	Yds.	Avg.	TD	No.	Yds.	Avg.	TD	TD	2pt.	Pts.	Fum.
1987—Pittsburgh NFL	14	17	135	7.9	0	1	22	22.0	0	28	568	20.3	0	0	...	0	0
1988—Pittsburgh NFL	16	40	127	3.2	0	11	196	17.8	1	29	610	21.0	*1	2	...	12	5
1989—Pittsburgh NFL	16	10	53	5.3	0	7	92	13.1	0	7	173	24.7	0	0	...	0	2
1990—Pittsburgh NFL	16	2	-6	-3.0	0	19	332	17.5	1	5	91	18.2	0	1	...	6	1
1991—Pittsburgh NFL	16	1	2	2.0	0	32	649	20.3	5	6	75	12.5	0	5	...	30	0
1992—Pittsburgh NFL	15	12	118	9.8	0	34	501	14.7	3	12	219	18.3	0	3	...	18	0
1993—Pittsburgh NFL	16	12	121	10.1	1	41	587	14.3	2	11	168	15.3	0	3	...	18	
21994—Pittsburgh NFL	15	2	7	3.5	0	7	81	11.6	0	11	182	16.6	0	0	1	2	0
1995—Carolina NFL	16	1	3	3.0	0	0	0	...	0	12	269	22.4	0	0	0	0	0
Pro totals (9 years)	**140**	**97**	**560**	**5.8**	**1**	**152**	**2460**	**16.2**	**12**	**121**	**2355**	**19.5**	**1**	**14**	**1**	**86**	**10**

STONE, RON　　　　OT/G　　　　GIANTS

PERSONAL: Born July 20, 1971, in West Roxbury, Mass. ... 6-5/325.
HIGH SCHOOL: West Roxbury (Mass.).
COLLEGE: Boston College.
TRANSACTIONS/CAREER NOTES: Selected by Dallas Cowboys in fourth round (96th pick overall) of 1993 NFL draft. ... Signed by Cowboys (July 16, 1993). ... Active for four games with Cowboys (1993); did not play. ... Granted free agency (February 16, 1996). ... Tendered offer sheet by New York Giants (March 1, 1996). ... Cowboys declined to match offer (March 7, 1996).
PLAYING EXPERIENCE: Dallas NFL, 1994 and 1995. ... Games: 1994 (16), 1995 (16). Total: 32.
CHAMPIONSHIP GAME EXPERIENCE: Member of Cowboys for NFC championship game (1993 season); inactive. ... Played in NFC championship game (1994 and 1995 seasons). ... Member of Super Bowl championship team (1993 and 1995 seasons).
PRO STATISTICS: 1994—Recovered one fumble.

STOVER, MATT　　　　K　　　　RAVENS

PERSONAL: Born January 27, 1968, in Dallas. ... 5-11/178. ... Full name: John Matthew Stover.

S

HIGH SCHOOL: Lake Highlands (Dallas).
COLLEGE: Louisiana Tech (degree in marketing, 1991).
TRANSACTIONS/CAREER NOTES: Selected by New York Giants in 12th round (329th pick overall) of 1990 NFL draft. ... Signed by Giants (July 23, 1990). ... On injured reserve with leg injury (September 4, 1990-entire season). ... Granted unconditional free agency (February 1, 1991). ... Signed by Cleveland Browns (March 15, 1991). ... Granted free agency (March 1, 1993). ... Re-signed by Browns (July 24, 1993). ... Released by Browns (August 30, 1993). ... Re-signed by Browns (August 31, 1993). ... Granted unconditional free agency (February 17, 1994). ... Re-signed by Browns (March 4, 1994). ... Browns franchise moved to Baltimore and renamed Ravens for 1996 season (March 11, 1996).
PRO STATISTICS: 1992—Had only pass attempt intercepted.

				KICKING					
Year Team	G	XPM	XPA	FGM	FGA	Lg.	50+	Pts.	
1990—New York Giants NFL			Did not play—injured.						
1991—Cleveland NFL	16	33	34	16	22	55	2-2	81	
1992—Cleveland NFL	16	29	30	21	29	51	1-3	92	
1993—Cleveland NFL	16	36	36	16	22	53	1-4	84	
1994—Cleveland NFL	16	32	32	26	28	45	0-1	110	
1995—Cleveland NFL	16	26	26	29	33	47	0-1	113	
Pro totals (5 years)	80	156	158	108	134	55	4-11	480	

STOWE, TYRONNE — LB — SEAHAWKS

PERSONAL: Born May 30, 1965, in Passaic, N.J. ... 6-2/250. ... Full name: Tyronne Kevin Stowe.
HIGH SCHOOL: Passaic (N.J.).
COLLEGE: Rutgers.
TRANSACTIONS/CAREER NOTES: Signed as non-drafted free agent by San Diego Chargers (April 30, 1987). ... Released by Chargers (September 7, 1987). ... Signed as replacement player by Pittsburgh Steelers (September 24, 1987). ... Released by Steelers (October 22, 1988). ... Re-signed by Steelers (December 1, 1988). ... Granted unconditional free agency (February 1, 1991). ... Signed by Phoenix Cardinals (February 25, 1991). ... Granted unconditional free agency (March 1, 1993). ... Re-signed by Cardinals (April 8, 1993). ... Traded by Cardinals to Washington Redskins for seventh-round pick (WR Billy Williams) in 1995 draft (June 17, 1994). ... Granted free agency (February 17, 1995). ... Signed by Seattle Seahawks (March 29, 1995). ... On injured reserve with forearm injury (October 25, 1995-remainder of season).
PLAYING EXPERIENCE: Pittsburgh NFL, 1987-1990; Phoenix NFL, 1991-1993; Washington NFL, 1994; Seattle NFL, 1995. ... Games: 1987 (13), 1988 (10), 1989 (16), 1990 (16), 1991 (13), 1992 (15), 1993 (15), 1994 (16), 1995 (6). Total: 120.
PRO STATISTICS: 1990—Credited with one safety on blocked punt out of the end zone and recovered one fumble. 1991—Recovered one fumble. 1993—Credited with 1½ sacks. 1994—Intercepted one pass for two yards and fumbled once.

STOYANOVICH, PETE — K — DOLPHINS

PERSONAL: Born April 28, 1967, in Dearborn, Mich. ... 5-11/195. ... Name pronounced sto-YAWN-o-vich.
HIGH SCHOOL: Crestwood (Dearborn Heights, Mich.).
COLLEGE: Indiana (degree in public affairs, 1989).
TRANSACTIONS/CAREER NOTES: Selected by Miami Dolphins in eighth round (203rd pick overall) of 1989 NFL draft. ... Signed by Dolphins (July 27, 1989). ... Granted free agency (February 1, 1991). ... Re-signed by Dolphins (September 6, 1991). ... Activated (September 13, 1991). ... Granted unconditional free agency (February 17, 1994). ... Re-signed by Dolphins (February 21, 1994).
CHAMPIONSHIP GAME EXPERIENCE: Played in AFC championship game (1992 season).
HONORS: Named kicker on The Sporting News college All-America second team (1988). ... Named kicker on The Sporting News NFL All-Pro team (1992).
POSTSEASON RECORDS: Holds NFL postseason career record for longest field goal—58 yards (January 5, 1991, vs. Kansas City).

		PUNTING						KICKING						
Year Team	G	No.	Yds.	Avg.	Net avg.	In. 20	Blk.	XPM	XPA	FGM	FGA	Lg.	50+	Pts.
1989—Miami NFL	16	0	0	...	...	0	0	38	39	19	26	59	1-3	95
1990—Miami NFL	16	0	0	...	...	0	0	37	37	21	25	53	2-3	100
1991—Miami NFL	14	2	85	42.5	38.5	1	0	28	29	*31	37	53	3-5	121
1992—Miami NFL	16	2	90	45.0	45.0	0	0	34	36	*30	37	53	3-8	*124
1993—Miami NFL	16	0	0	...	...	0	0	37	37	24	32	52	2-2	109
1994—Miami NFL	16	0	0	...	...	0	0	35	35	24	31	50	1-2	107
1995—Miami NFL	16	0	0	...	...	0	0	37	37	27	34	51	2-5	118
Pro totals (7 years)	110	4	175	43.8	41.8	1	0	246	250	176	222	59	14-28	774

STRAHAN, MICHAEL — DE — GIANTS

PERSONAL: Born November 21, 1971, in Houston. ... 6-4/268. ... Full name: Michael Anthony Strahan. ... Nephew of Art Strahan, defensive tackle, Atlanta Falcons (1968).
HIGH SCHOOL: Westbury (Houston), then Mannheim (Germany) American.
COLLEGE: Texas Southern.
TRANSACTIONS/CAREER NOTES: Selected by New York Giants in second round (40th pick overall) of 1993 NFL draft. ... Signed by Giants (July 25, 1993). ... On injured reserve with foot injury (January 13, 1994-remainder of 1993 playoffs). ... Granted free agency (February 16, 1996).
PRO STATISTICS: 1995—Intercepted two passes for 56 yards.

Year Team	G	SACKS
1993—New York Giants NFL	9	1.0
1994—New York Giants NFL	15	4.5
1995—New York Giants NFL	15	7.5
Pro totals (3 years)	39	13.0

STRICKLAND, FRED — LB — COWBOYS

PERSONAL: Born August 15, 1966, in Ringwood, N.J. ... 6-2/250. ... Full name: Fredrick William Strickland Jr.

HIGH SCHOOL: Lakeland Regional (Wanaque, N.J.).
COLLEGE: Purdue.
TRANSACTIONS/CAREER NOTES: Selected by Los Angeles Rams in second round (47th pick overall) of 1988 NFL draft. ... Signed by Rams (July 10, 1988). ... On injured reserve with foot injury (October 16, 1990-remainder of season). ... Granted free agency (February 1, 1991). ... Re-signed by Rams (August 13, 1991). ... Granted unconditional free agency (March 1, 1993). ... Signed by Minnesota Vikings (May 7, 1993). ... Granted unconditional free agency (February 17, 1994). ... Signed by Green Bay Packers (June 24, 1994). ... Granted unconditional free agency (February 16, 1996). ... Signed by Dallas Cowboys (March 11, 1996).
CHAMPIONSHIP GAME EXPERIENCE: Played in NFC championship game (1989 and 1995 seasons).
PRO STATISTICS: 1988—Recovered two fumbles. 1989—Recovered one fumble for minus three yards. 1993—Recovered four fumbles for four yards. 1994—Recovered one fumble.

			INTERCEPTIONS			SACKS
Year Team	G	No.	Yds.	Avg.	TD	No.
1988—Los Angeles Rams NFL	16	0	0	...	0	4.0
1989—Los Angeles Rams NFL	12	2	56	28.0	0	2.0
1990—Los Angeles Rams NFL	5	0	0	...	0	0.0
1991—Los Angeles Rams NFL	14	0	0	...	0	1.0
1992—Los Angeles Rams NFL	16	0	0	...	0	0.0
1993—Minnesota NFL	16	0	0	...	0	0.0
1994—Green Bay NFL	16	1	7	7.0	0	0.0
1995—Green Bay NFL	14	0	0	...	0	0.0
Pro totals (8 years)	109	3	63	21.0	0	7.0

STRINGER, KOREY OT VIKINGS

PERSONAL: Born May 8, 1974, in Warren, Ohio. ... 6-4/339.
HIGH SCHOOL: Harding (Warren, Ohio).
COLLEGE: Ohio State.
TRANSACTIONS/CAREER NOTES: Selected after junior season by Minnesota Vikings in first round (24th pick overall) of 1995 NFL draft. ... Signed by Vikings (July 22, 1995).
PLAYING EXPERIENCE: Minnesota NFL, 1995. ... Games: 1995 (16).
HONORS: Named offensive lineman on THE SPORTING NEWS college All-America second team (1993). ... Named offensive lineman on THE SPORTING NEWS college All-America first team (1994).
PRO STATISTICS: 1995—Caught one pass for minus one yard and recovered two fumbles.

STROM, RICK QB LIONS

PERSONAL: Born March 11, 1965, in Pittsburgh. ... 6-2/197. ... Full name: Richard James Strom.
HIGH SCHOOL: Fox Chapel (Pittsburgh).
COLLEGE: Georgia Tech (degree in management).
TRANSACTIONS/CAREER NOTES: Signed as non-drafted free agent by Pittsburgh Steelers (April 26, 1988).... Released by Steelers (August 24, 1988). ... Re-signed by Steelers (February 24, 1989). ... Released by Steelers (September 5, 1989). ... Re-signed by Steelers to developmental squad (September 6, 1989). ... On developmental squad (September 6-October 14, 1989). ... Granted unconditional free agency (February 1-April 1, 1991). ... Re-signed by Steelers for 1991 season.... Released by Steelers (August 26, 1991). ... Re-signed by Steelers (September 24, 1991). ... Active for three games (1991); did not play. ... Granted unconditional free agency (February 1-April 1, 1992). ... Re-signed by Steelers for 1992 season.... Released by Steelers (August 31, 1992). ... Re-signed by Steelers (November 15, 1992). ... Active for four games (1992); did not play.... Released by Steelers (August 30, 1993).... Re-signed by Steelers (August 31, 1993)... On inactive list for 16 games (1993).... Granted unconditional free agency (February 17, 1994). ... Signed by Buffalo Bills (May 6, 1994).... Granted unconditional free agency (February 17, 1995).... Re-signed by Bills (March 14, 1995).... Signed by Detroit Lions (August 27, 1995).... Signed by Detroit Lions (February 29, 1996).... Released by Lions (March 29, 1996).... Re-signed by Lions (April 23, 1996).
PRO STATISTICS: 1989—Fumbled once for minus 18 yards. 1990—Fumbled once.

		PASSING								RUSHING				TOTALS		
Year Team	G	Att.	Cmp.	Pct.	Yds.	TD	Int.	Avg.	Rat.	Att.	Yds.	Avg.	TD	TD	2pt.	Pts.
1989—Pittsburgh NFL	3	1	0	0.00	0	0	0	0.00	39.6	4	-3	-0.8	0	0	...	0
1990—Pittsburgh NFL	6	21	14	66.7	162	0	1	7.71	69.9	4	10	2.5	0	0	...	0
1991—Pittsburgh NFL								Did not play.								
1992—Pittsburgh NFL								Did not play.								
1993—Pittsburgh NFL								Did not play.								
1994—Buffalo NFL								Did not play.								
1995—Detroit NFL								Did not play.								
Pro totals (3 years)	9	22	14	63.6	162	0	1	7.36	66.9	8	7	0.9	0	0	...	0

STRONG, MACK FB SEAHAWKS

PERSONAL: Born September 11, 1971, in Fort Benning, Ga. ... 6-0/224.
HIGH SCHOOL: Brookstone (Columbus, Ga.).
COLLEGE: Georgia.
TRANSACTIONS/CAREER NOTES: Signed as non-drafted free agent by Seattle Seahawks (April 28, 1993). ... Released by Seahawks (September 4, 1993). ... Re-signed by Seahawks to practice squad (September 6, 1993). ... Granted free agency (January 10, 1994). ... Re-signed by Seahawks (February 15, 1994).
PRO STATISTICS: 1995—Returned four kickoffs for 65 yards and recovered one fumble.

		RUSHING				RECEIVING				TOTALS			
Year Team	G	Att.	Yds.	Avg.	TD	No.	Yds.	Avg.	TD	TD	2pt.	Pts.	Fum.
1994—Seattle NFL	8	27	114	4.2	2	3	3	1.0	0	2	0	12	1
1995—Seattle NFL	16	8	23	2.9	1	12	117	9.8	3	4	0	24	2
Pro totals (2 years)	24	35	137	3.9	3	15	120	8.0	3	6	0	36	3

STRYZINSKI, DAN   P   FALCONS

PERSONAL: Born May 15, 1965, in Indianapolis. ... 6-2/200. ... Full name: Daniel Thomas Stryzinski. ... Name pronounced stri-ZIN-skee.
HIGH SCHOOL: Lincoln (Vincennes, Ind.).
COLLEGE: Indiana (bachelor of science degree in public finance and management, 1988).
TRANSACTIONS/CAREER NOTES: Signed as non-drafted free agent by Indianapolis Colts (July 1988). ... Released by Colts (August 23, 1988). ... Signed by Cleveland Browns (August 25, 1988). ... Released by Browns (August 30, 1988). ... Re-signed by Browns (off-season 1989). ... Released by Browns (August 30, 1989). ... Signed by New Orleans Saints to developmental squad (October 11, 1989). ... Granted free agency after 1989 season. ... Signed by Pittsburgh Steelers (March 14, 1990). ... Granted unconditional free agency (February 1, 1992). ... Signed by Tampa Bay Buccaneers (February 21, 1992). ... Granted unconditional free agency (February 17, 1995). ... Signed by Atlanta Falcons (February 20, 1995).
PRO STATISTICS: 1990—Rushed three times for 17 yards and recovered one fumble. 1991—Rushed four times for minus 11 yards, fumbled once and recovered two fumbles. 1992—Attempted two passes with two completions for 14 yards and rushed once for seven yards. 1994—Attempted once pass with one completion for 21 yards. 1995—Rushed once for no yards.

				PUNTING				
Year Team	G	No.	Yds.	Avg.	Net avg.	In. 20	Blk.	
1990—Pittsburgh NFL	16	65	2454	37.8	34.1	18	1	
1991—Pittsburgh NFL	16	74	2996	40.5	36.3	10	1	
1992—Tampa Bay NFL	16	74	3015	40.7	36.2	15	0	
1993—Tampa Bay NFL	16	*93	3772	40.6	35.3	24	1	
1994—Tampa Bay NFL	16	72	2800	38.9	35.9	20	0	
1995—Atlanta NFL	16	67	2759	41.2	36.2	21	0	
Pro totals (6 years)	96	445	17796	40.0	35.7	108	3	

STRZELCZYK, JUSTIN   G/OT   STEELERS

PERSONAL: Born August 18, 1968, in Seneca, N.Y. ... 6-6/302. ... Full name: Justin Conrad Strzelczyk. ... Name pronounced STREL-zik.
HIGH SCHOOL: West Seneca (N.Y.) West.
COLLEGE: Maine.
TRANSACTIONS/CAREER NOTES: Selected by Pittsburgh Steelers in 11th round (293rd pick overall) of 1990 NFL draft. ... Signed by Steelers (July 18, 1990).
PLAYING EXPERIENCE: Pittsburgh NFL, 1990-1995. ... Games: 1990 (16), 1991 (16), 1992 (16), 1993 (16), 1994 (16), 1995 (16). Total: 96.
CHAMPIONSHIP GAME EXPERIENCE: Played in AFC championship game (1994 and 1995 seasons). ... Played in Super Bowl XXX (1995 season).
PRO STATISTICS: 1993—Recovered one fumble.

STUBBLEFIELD, DANA   DT   49ERS

PERSONAL: Born November 14, 1970, in Cleves, Ohio. ... 6-2/290. ... Full name: Dana William Stubblefield.
HIGH SCHOOL: Taylor (North Bend, Ohio).
COLLEGE: Kansas.
TRANSACTIONS/CAREER NOTES: Selected by San Francisco 49ers in first round (26th pick overall) of 1993 NFL draft. ... Signed by 49ers (July 14, 1993).
CHAMPIONSHIP GAME EXPERIENCE: Played in NFC championship game (1993 and 1994 seasons). ... Member of Super Bowl championship team (1994 season).
HONORS: Played in Pro Bowl (1994 and 1995 seasons).
PRO STATISTICS: 1995—Intercepted one pass for 12 yards.

Year Name	G	SACKS
1993—San Francisco NFL	16	10.5
1994—San Francisco NFL	14	8.5
1995—San Francisco NFL	16	4.5
Pro totals (3 years)	46	23.5

STUBBS, DANIEL   DE   DOLPHINS

PERSONAL: Born January 3, 1965, in Long Branch, N.J. ... 6-4/272.
HIGH SCHOOL: Red Bank Regional (Little Silver, N.J.).
COLLEGE: Miami, Fla. (degree in criminal justice, 1988).
TRANSACTIONS/CAREER NOTES: Selected by San Francisco 49ers in second round (33rd pick overall) of 1988 NFL draft. ... Signed by 49ers (July 19, 1988). ... Traded by 49ers with RB Terrence Flagler and third-round (traded to Pittsburgh) and 11th-round (traded to Los Angeles Raiders) picks in 1990 draft to Dallas Cowboys for second-round (DL Dennis Brown) and third-round (WR Ronald Lewis) picks in 1990 draft (April 19, 1990). ... Granted free agency (February 1, 1991). ... Re-signed by Cowboys (August 10, 1991). ... Claimed on waivers by Cincinnati Bengals (November 6, 1991). ... Granted unconditional free agency (February 17, 1994). ... Re-signed by Bengals (June 14, 1994). ... Released by Bengals (August 16, 1994). ... Signed by Philadelphia Eagles (April 7, 1995). ... Granted unconditional free agency (February 16, 1996). ... Signed by Miami Dolphins (April 4, 1996).
CHAMPIONSHIP GAME EXPERIENCE: Played in NFC championship game (1988 season). ... Member of Super Bowl championship team (1988 season).
HONORS: Named defensive lineman on THE SPORTING NEWS college All-America second team (1986). ... Named defensive lineman on THE SPORTING NEWS college All-America first team (1987).
PRO STATISTICS: 1988—Recovered one fumble. 1990—Recovered two fumbles. 1991—Recovered one fumble. 1992—Recovered one fumble. 1993—Recovered one fumble. 1995—Recovered one fumble.

Year Name	G	SACKS
1988—San Francisco NFL	16	6.0
1989—San Francisco NFL	16	4.5
1990—Dallas NFL	16	7.5

Year Name	G	SACKS
1991—Dallas NFL	9	1.0
—Cincinnati NFL	7	3.0
1992—Cincinnati NFL	16	9.0
1993—Cincinnati NFL	16	5.0
1994—	Did not play.	
1995—Philadelphia NFL	16	5.5
Pro totals (7 years)	112	41.5

STUDSTILL, DARREN   S   JAGUARS

PERSONAL: Born August 9, 1970, in ... 6-1/186. ... Full name: Darren Henry Studstill.
HIGH SCHOOL: Palm Beach Gardens (Fla.).
COLLEGE: West Virginia.
TRANSACTIONS/CAREER NOTES: Selected by Dallas Cowboys in sixth round (191st pick overall) of 1994 NFL draft. ... Signed by Cowboys (July 15, 1994). ... Released by Cowboys (August 28, 1994). ... Re-signed by Cowboys to practice squad (August 30, 1994). ... Activated (November 30, 1994). ... Released by Cowboys (August 22, 1995). ... Signed by New York Jets to practice squad (October 4, 1995). ... Signed by Jacksonville Jaguars off Jets practice squad (October 10, 1995). ... Assigned by Jaguars to London Monarchs in 1996 World League enhancement allocation program (February 19, 1996).
PLAYING EXPERIENCE: Dallas NFL, 1994; Jacksonville NFL, 1995. ... Games: 1994 (1), 1995 (8). Total: 9.
CHAMPIONSHIP GAME EXPERIENCE: Member of Cowboys for NFC championship game (1994 season); inactive.

STURGIS, OSCAR   DE   COWBOYS   S

PERSONAL: Born January 12, 1971, in Hamlet, N.C. ... 6-5/280.
HIGH SCHOOL: Richmond County (N.C.).
COLLEGE: North Carolina.
TRANSACTIONS/CAREER NOTES: Selected by Dallas Cowboys in seventh round (236th pick overall) of 1995 NFL draft. ... Signed by Cowboys (July 17, 1995).
PLAYING EXPERIENCE: Dallas NFL, 1995. ... Games: 1995 (1).
CHAMPIONSHIP GAME EXPERIENCE: Member of Cowboys for NFC championship game (1995 season). ... Member of Super Bowl championship team (1995 season).

STYLES, LORENZO   LB   FALCONS

PERSONAL: Born January 31, 1974, in Columbus, Ohio. ... 6-1/244.
HIGH SCHOOL: Columbus (Ohio), then Farrell (Pa.).
COLLEGE: Ohio State.
TRANSACTIONS/CAREER NOTES: Selected after junior season by Atlanta Falcons in third round (77th pick overall) of 1995 NFL draft. ... Signed by Falcons (July 21, 1995).
PLAYING EXPERIENCE: Atlanta NFL, 1995. ... Games: 1995 (12).

SULLIVAN, MIKE   G/C   BEARS

PERSONAL: Born December 22, 1967, in Chicago. ... 6-3/292. ... Full name: Michael Gerald Sullivan.
HIGH SCHOOL: St. Francis De Sales (Chicago).
COLLEGE: Miami, Fla. (degree in business).
TRANSACTIONS/CAREER NOTES: Selected by Dallas Cowboys in sixth round (153rd pick overall) of 1991 NFL draft. ... Signed by Cowboys (July 15, 1991). ... Released by Cowboys (August 26, 1991). ... Re-signed by Cowboys to practice squad (August 28, 1991). ... Activated (November 11, 1991). ... Released by Cowboys (November 21, 1991). ... Re-signed by Cowboys to practice squad (November 26, 1991). ... Active for one game (1991); did not play. ... Granted free agency after 1991 season. ... Signed by Tampa Bay Buccaneers (March 10, 1992). ... Granted unconditional free agency (February 16, 1996). ... Signed by Chicago Bears (March 26, 1996).
PLAYING EXPERIENCE: Tampa Bay NFL, 1992-1995. ... Games: 1992 (9), 1993 (11), 1994 (16), 1995 (12). Total: 48.
HONORS: Named offensive tackle on THE SPORTING NEWS college All-America second team (1990).

SUTTER, EDDIE   LB

PERSONAL: Born October 3, 1969, in Peoria, Ill. ... 6-3/235. ... Full name: Edward Lee Sutter.
HIGH SCHOOL: Richwoods (Peoria, Ill.).
COLLEGE: Northwestern (degree in organizational studies).
TRANSACTIONS/CAREER NOTES: Signed as non-drafted free agent by Minnesota Vikings (May 1, 1992). ... Released by Vikings (August 25, 1992). ... Signed by Cleveland Browns to practice squad (September 9, 1992). ... Released by Browns (October 21, 1992). ... Re-signed by Browns to practice squad (October 23, 1992). ... Activated (November 20, 1992). ... On inactive list for one game (1992). ... Released by Browns (November 28, 1992). ... Re-signed by Browns to practice squad (December 1, 1992). ... Granted free agency after 1992 season. ... Signed by New England Patriots (February 22, 1993). ... Claimed on waivers by Browns (August 30, 1993). ... Browns franchise moved Baltimore and renamed Ravens for 1996 season (March 11, 1996). ... Granted unconditional free agency (February 16, 1996).
PLAYING EXPERIENCE: Cleveland NFL, 1993-1995. ... Games: 1993 (15), 1994 (16), 1995 (16). Total: 47.

SWANN, ERIC   DT   CARDINALS

PERSONAL: Born August 16, 1970, in Pinehurst, N.C. ... 6-5/295. ... Full name: Eric Jerrod Swann.
HIGH SCHOOL: Western Harnett (Lillington, N.C.).

COLLEGE: Wake Technical College, N.C. (did not play football).

TRANSACTIONS/CAREER NOTES: Played with Bay State Titans of Minor League Football System (1990). ... Selected by Phoenix Cardinals in first round (sixth pick overall) of 1991 NFL draft. ... Signed by Cardinals (April 24, 1991). ... On injured reserve with knee injury (August 27-September 27, 1991). ... On injured reserve with knee injury (November 17, 1993-remainder of season). ... Cardinals franchise renamed Arizona Cardinals for 1994 season. ... Designated by Cardinals as franchise player (February 16, 1996).

HONORS: Named defensive tackle on THE SPORTING NEWS NFL All-Pro team (1995). ... Played in Pro Bowl (1995 season).

PRO STATISTICS: 1992—Credited with one safety. 1993—Credited with one safety and recovered one fumble. 1994—Credited with one safety and recovered one fumble for 10 yards. 1995—Recovered two fumbles.

Year Name	G	SACKS
1991—Phoenix NFL	12	4.0
1992—Phoenix NFL	16	2.0
1993—Phoenix NFL	9	3.5
1994—Arizona NFL	16	7.0
1995—Arizona NFL	12	8.5
Pro totals (5 years)	65	25.0

SWAYNE, HARRY   OT

PERSONAL: Born February 2, 1965, in Philadelphia. ... 6-5/295.

HIGH SCHOOL: Cardinal Dougherty (Philadelphia).

COLLEGE: Rutgers.

TRANSACTIONS/CAREER NOTES: Selected by Tampa Bay Buccaneers in seventh round (190th pick overall) of 1987 NFL draft. ... Signed by Buccaneers (July 18, 1987). ... On injured reserve with fractured hand (September 8-October 31, 1987). ... On injured reserve with neck injury (November 18, 1988-remainder of season). ... Granted free agency (February 1, 1990). ... Re-signed by Buccaneers (July 19, 1990). ... Granted unconditional free agency (February 1, 1991). ... Signed by San Diego Chargers (April 1, 1991). ... On injured reserve with fractured leg (November 26, 1991-remainder of season). ... Designated by Chargers as transition player (February 25, 1993). ... Tendered offer sheet by Phoenix Cardinals (April 9, 1993). ... Offer matched by Chargers (April 15, 1993). ... On physically unable to perform list (July 24-August 21, 1995). ... Free agency status changed by Chargers from transitional to unconditional (February 16, 1996).

PLAYING EXPERIENCE: Tampa Bay NFL, 1987-1990; San Diego NFL, 1991-1995. ... Games: 1987 (8), 1988 (10), 1989 (16), 1990 (10), 1991 (12), 1992 (16), 1993 (11), 1994 (16), 1995 (16). Total: 115.

CHAMPIONSHIP GAME EXPERIENCE: Played in AFC championship game (1994 season). ... Played in Super Bowl XXIX (1994 season).

SWEENEY, JIM   C   SEAHAWKS

PERSONAL: Born August 8, 1962, in Pittsburgh. ... 6-4/284. ... Full name: James Joseph Sweeney.

HIGH SCHOOL: Seton LaSalle (Pittsburgh).

COLLEGE: Pittsburgh.

TRANSACTIONS/CAREER NOTES: Selected by Pittsburgh Maulers in 1984 USFL territorial draft. ... Selected by New York Jets in second round (37th pick overall) of 1984 NFL draft. ... Signed by Jets (July 12, 1984). ... Granted free agency (February 1, 1990). ... Re-signed by Jets (August 27, 1990). ... Released by Jets (August 30, 1993). ... Re-signed by Jets (August 31, 1993). ... Granted unconditional free agency (February 1, 1994). ... Re-signed by Jets (May 2, 1994). ... Granted unconditional free agency (February 17, 1995). ... Signed by Seattle Seahawks (March 23, 1995).

PLAYING EXPERIENCE: New York Jets NFL, 1984-1994; Seattle NFL, 1995. ... Games: 1984 (10), 1985 (16), 1986 (16), 1987 (12), 1988 (16), 1989 (16), 1990 (16), 1991 (16), 1992 (16), 1993 (16), 1994 (16), 1995 (16). Total: 182.

PRO STATISTICS: 1990—Recovered one fumble. 1994—Recovered one fumble.

SWILLING, PAT   LB   RAIDERS

PERSONAL: Born October 25, 1964, in Toccoa, Ga. ... 6-3/245. ... Full name: Patrick Travis Swilling.

HIGH SCHOOL: Stephens County (Toccoa, Ga.).

COLLEGE: Georgia Tech.

TRANSACTIONS/CAREER NOTES: Selected by Jacksonville Bulls in 1986 USFL territorial draft. ... Selected by New Orleans Saints in third round (60th pick overall) of 1986 NFL draft. ... Signed by Saints (July 21, 1986). ... Granted free agency (February 1, 1990). ... Re-signed by Saints (September 1, 1990). ... Granted free agency (February 1, 1992). ... Tendered offer sheet by Detroit Lions (March 23, 1992). ... Offer matched by Saints (March 30, 1992). ... Traded by Saints to Lions for first-round (OT Willie Roaf) and fourth-round (RB Lorenzo Neal) picks in 1993 draft (April 25, 1993). ... Granted unconditional free agency (February 17, 1995). ... Signed by Los Angeles Raiders (April 11, 1995). ... Raiders franchise moved to Oakland (July 21, 1995).

HONORS: Named defensive lineman on THE SPORTING NEWS college All-America second team (1985). ... Played in Pro Bowl (1990-1993 seasons). ... Named outside linebacker on THE SPORTING NEWS NFL All-Pro team (1991 and 1992).

PRO STATISTICS: 1987—Recovered three fumbles for one yard. 1988—Recovered one fumble. 1989—Recovered one fumble. 1991—Recovered one fumble for five yards. 1992—Recovered one fumble. 1993—Recovered one fumble. 1994—Recovered one fumble for five yards.

Year Team	G	INTERCEPTIONS No.	Yds.	Avg.	TD	SACKS No.
1986—New Orleans NFL	16	0	0	...	0	4.0
1987—New Orleans NFL	12	1	10	10.0	0	10.5
1988—New Orleans NFL	15	0	0	...	0	7.0
1989—New Orleans NFL	16	1	14	14.0	0	16.5
1990—New Orleans NFL	16	0	0	...	0	11.0
1991—New Orleans NFL	16	1	39	39.0	1	*17.0
1992—New Orleans NFL	16	0	0	...	0	10.5
1993—Detroit NFL	14	3	16	5.3	0	6.5
1994—Detroit NFL	16	0	0	...	0	3.5
1995—Oakland NFL	16	0	0	...	0	13.0
Pro totals (10 years)	153	6	79	13.2	1	99.5

PERSONAL: Born November 11, 1969, in Columbus, Ohio. ... 5-6/177. ... Brother-in-law of Duane Ferrell, forward, Indiana Pacers. ... Name pronounced SIDE-ner.
HIGH SCHOOL: East (Columbus, Ohio).
COLLEGE: Hawaii.
TRANSACTIONS/CAREER NOTES: Selected by Philadelphia Eagles in sixth round (160th pick overall) of 1992 NFL draft. ... Signed by Eagles (July 21, 1992). ... On injured reserve with knee injury (October 4, 1993-remainder of season). ... Granted free agency (February 17, 1995). ... Re-signed by Eagles (April 20, 1995). ... Released by Eagles (August 29, 1995). ... Signed by New York Jets (November 8, 1995).

		RECEIVING			PUNT RETURNS				KICKOFF RETURNS				TOTALS			
Year Team	G	No.	Yds.	Avg.	TD	No.	Yds.	Avg.	TD	No.	Yds.	Avg.	TD	TD 2pt.	Pts. Fum.
1992—Philadelphia NFL	15	0	0	...	0	7	52	7.4	0	17	368	21.7	0	0 ...	0 1
1993—Philadelphia NFL	4	2	42	21.0	0	0	0	...	0	9	158	17.6	0	0 ...	0 3
1994—Philadelphia NFL	16	1	10	10.0	0	40	381	9.5	0	20	392	19.6	0	0 0	0 2
1995—New York Jets NFL	6	0	0	...	0	17	178	10.5	0	4	80	20.0	0	0 0	0 0
Pro totals (4 years)	41	3	52	17.3	0	64	611	9.6	0	50	998	20.0	0	0 0	0 6

SZOTT, DAVID G CHIEFS

PERSONAL: Born December 12, 1967, in Passaic, N.J. ... 6-4/290. ... Full name: David Andrew Szott. ... Name pronounced ZOT.
HIGH SCHOOL: Clifton (N.J.).
COLLEGE: Penn State (degree in political science).
TRANSACTIONS/CAREER NOTES: Selected by Kansas City Chiefs in seventh round (180th pick overall) of 1990 NFL draft. ... Signed by Chiefs (July 25, 1990). ... Granted free agency (March 1, 1993). ... Re-signed by Chiefs for 1993 season.
PLAYING EXPERIENCE: Kansas City NFL, 1990-1995. ... Games: 1990 (16), 1991 (16), 1992 (16), 1993 (14), 1994 (16), 1995 (16). Total: 94.
CHAMPIONSHIP GAME EXPERIENCE: Played in AFC championship game (1993 season).
PRO STATISTICS: 1990—Recovered one fumble. 1991—Recovered one fumble.

TALLEY, BEN LB GIANTS

PERSONAL: Born July 14, 1972, in Griffin, Ga. ... 6-3/245. ... Full name: Benjamin Jermaine Talley.
HIGH SCHOOL: Griffin (Ga.).
COLLEGE: Tennessee.
TRANSACTIONS/CAREER NOTES: Selected by New York Giants in fourth round (133rd pick overall) of 1995 NFL draft. ... Signed by Giants (July 23, 1995).
PLAYING EXPERIENCE: New York Giants NFL, 1995. ... Games: 1995 (4).

TALLEY, DARRYL LB

PERSONAL: Born July 10, 1960, in Cleveland. ... 6-4/235. ... Full name: Darryl Victor Talley. ... Brother of John Talley, tight end, Cleveland Browns (1990 and 1991).
HIGH SCHOOL: Shaw (East Cleveland, Ohio).
COLLEGE: West Virginia (degree in physical education).
TRANSACTIONS/CAREER NOTES: Selected by New Jersey Generals in second round (24th pick overall) of 1983 USFL draft. ... Selected by Buffalo Bills in second round (39th pick overall) of 1983 NFL draft. ... Signed by Bills (June 14, 1983). ... Granted unconditional free agency (February 17, 1995). ... Signed by Atlanta Falcons (April 11, 1995). ... Released by Falcons (February 16, 1996).
CHAMPIONSHIP GAME EXPERIENCE: Played in AFC championship game (1988 and 1990-1993 seasons). ... Played in Super Bowl XXV (1990 season), Super Bowl XXVI (1991 season), Super Bowl XXVII (1992 season) and Super Bowl XXVIII (1993 season).
HONORS: Named linebacker on THE SPORTING NEWS college All-America first team (1982). ... Named outside linebacker on THE SPORTING NEWS NFL All-Pro team (1990 and 1993). ... Played in Pro Bowl (1990 and 1991 seasons).
PRO STATISTICS: 1983—Returned two kickoffs for nine yards and recovered two fumbles for six yards. 1984—Recovered one fumble. 1986—Recovered one fumble for 47 yards. 1987—Recovered one fumble for one yard. 1988—Recovered one fumble. 1990—Recovered one fumble for four yards. 1991—Recovered two fumbles. 1993—Recovered two fumbles for four yards. 1994—Recovered one fumble for two yards. 1995—Recovered two fumbles for 12 yards.

		INTERCEPTIONS				SACKS
Year Team	G	No.	Yds.	Avg.	TD	No.
1983—Buffalo NFL	16	0	0	...	0	5.0
1984—Buffalo NFL	16	1	0	0.0	0	5.0
1985—Buffalo NFL	16	0	0	...	0	2.0
1986—Buffalo NFL	16	0	0	...	0	3.0
1987—Buffalo NFL	12	0	0	...	0	1.0
1988—Buffalo NFL	16	0	0	...	0	2.5
1989—Buffalo NFL	16	0	0	...	0	6.0
1990—Buffalo NFL	16	2	60	30.0	1	4.0
1991—Buffalo NFL	16	5	45	9.0	0	4.0
1992—Buffalo NFL	16	0	0	...	0	4.0
1993—Buffalo NFL	16	3	74	24.7	1	2.0
1994—Buffalo NFL	16	0	0	...	0	0.0
1995—Atlanta NFL	16	0	0	...	0	0.0
Pro totals (13 years)	204	11	179	16.3	2	38.5

TAMM, RALPH G/C BRONCOS

PERSONAL: Born March 11, 1966, in Philadelphia. ... 6-4/280. ... Full name: Ralph Earl Tamm.

HIGH SCHOOL: Bensalem (Pa.).
COLLEGE: West Chester (Pa.).
TRANSACTIONS/CAREER NOTES: Selected by New York Jets in ninth round (230th pick overall) of 1988 NFL draft. ... On injured reserve (August 29, 1988-entire season). ... Granted unconditional free agency (February 1, 1989). ... Signed by Washington Redskins (1989). ... On injured reserve with shoulder injury (September 1989-entire season). ... Granted unconditional free agency (February 1, 1990). ... Signed by Cleveland Browns (March 21, 1990). ... Released by Browns (September 5, 1991). ... Signed by Redskins (September 11, 1991). ... Released by Redskins (November 1991). ... Signed by Cincinnati Bengals (December 9, 1991). ... Granted unconditional free agency (February 1, 1992). ... Signed by San Francisco 49ers (March 29, 1992). ... On injured reserve with knee injury (December 15, 1992-January 16, 1993). ... Released by 49ers (May 5, 1995). ... Signed by Denver Broncos (June 7, 1995).
PLAYING EXPERIENCE: Cleveland NFL, 1990; Cleveland (1)-Washington (2)-Cincinnati (1) NFL, 1991; San Francisco NFL, 1992-1994; Denver NFL, 1995. ... Games: 1990 (16), 1991 (4), 1992 (14), 1993 (16), 1994 (1), 1995 (13). Total: 64.
CHAMPIONSHIP GAME EXPERIENCE: Played in NFC championship game (1992-1994 seasons). ... Member of Super Bowl championship team (1994 season).
PRO STATISTICS: 1993—Recovered one fumble in end zone for a touchdown. 1995—Recovered one fumble.

TANUVASA, MAA — DT — BRONCOS

PERSONAL: Born November 6, 1970, in America Samoa. ... 6-2/277. ... Full name: Maa Junior Tanuvasa. ... Name pronounced MAW-aw TAW-noo-VA-suh.
HIGH SCHOOL: Mililani (Hawaii).
COLLEGE: Hawaii.
TRANSACTIONS/CAREER NOTES: Selected by Los Angeles Rams in eighth round (209th pick overall) of 1993 NFL draft. ... Signed by Rams for 1993 season. ... Released by Rams (August 23, 1994). ... Signed by Steelers to practice squad (December 1, 1994). ... Granted free agency after 1994 season. ... Signed by Denver Broncos (February 22, 1995). ... Released by Broncos (August 27, 1995). ... Re-signed by Broncos to practice squad (August 28, 1995). ... Activated (October 24, 1995).
PLAYING EXPERIENCE: Denver NFL, 1995. ... Games: 1995 (1).

TASKER, STEVE — WR — BILLS

PERSONAL: Born April 10, 1962, in Leoti, Kan. ... 5-9/183. ... Full name: Steven Jay Tasker.
HIGH SCHOOL: Wichita County (Leoti, Kan.).
JUNIOR COLLEGE: Dodge City (Kan.) Community College.
COLLEGE: Northwestern (degree in communication studies).
TRANSACTIONS/CAREER NOTES: Selected by Houston Oilers in ninth round (226th pick overall) of 1985 NFL draft. ... Signed by Oilers (June 14, 1985). ... On injured reserve with knee injury (October 23, 1985-remainder of season). ... On injured reserve with knee injury (September 15-November 5, 1986). ... Claimed on waivers by Buffalo Bills (November 5, 1986). ... Granted unconditional free agency (February 1-April 1, 1992). ... Re-signed by Bills for 1992 season. ... Granted unconditional free agency (February 17, 1994). ... Re-signed by Bills (April 7, 1994). ... On injured reserve with arm injury (December 22, 1994-remainder of season).
CHAMPIONSHIP GAME EXPERIENCE: Played in AFC championship game (1988 and 1990-1993 seasons). ... Played in Super Bowl XXV (1990 season), Super Bowl XXVI (1991 season), Super Bowl XXVII (1992 season) and Super Bowl XXVIII (1993 season).
HONORS: Played in Pro Bowl (1987 and 1990-1995 seasons). ... Named Outstanding Player of Pro Bowl (1992 season).
PRO STATISTICS: 1985—Rushed twice for 16 yards. 1987—Credited with one safety. 1990—Recovered two fumbles for five yards. 1992—Rushed once for nine yards and recovered one fumble. 1993—Recovered one fumble. 1995—Rushed eight times for 74 yards.

Year Team		RECEIVING				KICKOFF RETURNS				TOTALS			
	G	No.	Yds.	Avg.	TD	No.	Yds.	Avg.	TD	TD	2pt.	Pts.	Fum.
1985—Houston NFL	7	2	19	9.5	0	17	447	26.3	0	0	...	0	0
1986—Houston NFL	2	0	0	...	0	3	65	21.7	0	0	...	0	0
—Buffalo NFL	7	0	0	...	0	9	148	16.4	0	0		0	0
1987—Buffalo NFL	12	0	0	...	0	11	197	17.9	0	0	...	2	2
1988—Buffalo NFL	14	0	0	...	0	0	0	...	0	0		0	0
1989—Buffalo NFL	16	0	0	...	0	2	39	19.5	0	0		0	0
1990—Buffalo NFL	16	2	44	22.0	2	0	0	...	0	2	...	12	0
1991—Buffalo NFL	16	2	39	19.5	1	0	0	...	0	1	...	6	0
1992—Buffalo NFL	15	2	24	12.0	0	0	0	...	0	0	...	0	0
1993—Buffalo NFL	15	2	26	13.0	0	0	0	...	0	0	...	0	1
1994—Buffalo NFL	14	0	0	...	0	1	2	2.0	0	0	0	0	0
1995—Buffalo NFL	13	20	255	12.8	3	0	0	...	0	3	...	18	0
Pro totals (11 years)	147	30	407	13.6	6	43	898	20.9	0	6	0	38	3

TATE, DAVID — DB — COLTS

PERSONAL: Born November 22, 1964, in Denver. ... 6-1/212.
HIGH SCHOOL: Mullen (Denver).
COLLEGE: Colorado.
TRANSACTIONS/CAREER NOTES: Selected by Chicago Bears in eighth round (208th pick overall) of 1988 NFL draft. ... Signed by Bears (July 6, 1988). ... On injured reserve with knee injury (December 31, 1990-remainder of season playoffs). ... Granted unconditional free agency (March 1, 1993). ... Signed by New York Jets (May 4, 1993). ... Released by Jets (August 30, 1993). ... Signed by New York Giants (September 1, 1993). ... Granted unconditional free agency (February 17, 1994). ... Signed by Indianapolis Colts (July 20, 1994). ... Granted unconditional free agency (February 17, 1995). ... Re-signed by Colts (July 26, 1995).
CHAMPIONSHIP GAME EXPERIENCE: Played in NFC championship game (1988 season). ... Played in AFC championship game (1995 season).
PRO STATISTICS: 1989—Returned one kickoff for 12 yards. 1992—Recovered one fumble. 1993—Fumbled once. 1995—Recovered one fumble.

Year Team		INTERCEPTIONS			
	G	No.	Yds.	Avg.	TD
1988—Chicago NFL	16	4	35	8.8	0
1989—Chicago NFL	14	1	0	0.0	0

Year Team	G	INTERCEPTIONS			
		No.	Yds.	Avg.	TD
1990—Chicago NFL	16	0	0	...	0
1991—Chicago NFL	16	2	35	17.5	0
1992—Chicago NFL	16	0	0	...	0
1993—New York Giants NFL	14	1	12	12.0	0
1994—Indianapolis NFL	16	3	51	17.0	0
1995—Indianapolis NFL	16	0	0	...	0
Pro totals (8 years)	124	11	133	12.1	0

TAYLOR, AARON   G   PACKERS

PERSONAL: Born November 14, 1972, in San Francisco. ... 6-4/305. ... Full name: Aaron Matthew Taylor.
HIGH SCHOOL: De La Salle Catholic (Concord, Calif.).
COLLEGE: Notre Dame.
TRANSACTIONS/CAREER NOTES: Selected by Green Bay Packers in first round (16th pick overall) of 1994 NFL draft. ... Signed by Packers (July 26, 1994). ... On physically unable to perform list with knee injury (August 25, 1994-entire season). ... On injured reserve with knee injury (January 11, 1996-remainder of 1995 playoffs).
PLAYING EXPERIENCE: Green Bay NFL, 1995. ... Games: 1995 (16).
HONORS: Named offensive lineman on THE SPORTING NEWS college All-America first team (1992 and 1993). ... Lombardi Award winner (1993).
PRO STATISTICS: 1995—Recovered two fumbles.

TAYLOR, BOBBY   DB   EAGLES

PERSONAL: Born December 28, 1973, in Houston. ... 6-3/216. ... Son of Robert Taylor, silver medalist in 100-meter dash and member of gold-medal winning 400-meter relay team at 1972 Summer Olympics.
HIGH SCHOOL: Longview (Texas).
COLLEGE: Notre Dame.
TRANSACTIONS/CAREER NOTES: Selected after junior season by Philadelphia Eagles in second round (49th pick overall) of 1995 NFL draft. ... Signed by Eagles (July 19, 1995).
HONORS: Named defensive back on THE SPORTING NEWS college All-America first team (1993 and 1994).

Year Team	G	INTERCEPTIONS			
		No.	Yds.	Avg.	TD
1995—Philadelphia NFL	16	2	52	26.0	0

TAYLOR, JOHN   WR

PERSONAL: Born March 31, 1962, in Pennsauken, N.J. ... 6-1/185. ... Full name: John Gregory Taylor. ... Brother of Keith Taylor, safety, Indianapolis Colts, New Orleans Saints and Washington Redskins (1988-1995).
HIGH SCHOOL: Pennsauken (N.J.).
COLLEGE: Delaware State.
TRANSACTIONS/CAREER NOTES: Selected by San Francisco 49ers in third round (76th pick overall) of 1986 NFL draft. ... Selected by Baltimore Stars in second round (13th pick overall) of 1986 USFL draft. ... Signed by 49ers (July 21, 1986). ... On injured reserve with back injury (August 26, 1986-entire season). ... On non-football injury list with substance abuse problem (September 2-28, 1988). ... On injured reserve with broken fibula (October 17-November 14, 1992); on practice squad (November 11-14, 1992). ... Released by 49ers (June 27, 1995). ... Re-signed by 49ers (June 29, 1995). ... Released by 49ers (February 15, 1996).
CHAMPIONSHIP GAME EXPERIENCE: Played in NFC championship game (1988-1990 and 1992-1994 seasons). ... Member of Super Bowl championship team (1988, 1989 and 1994 seasons).
HONORS: Named punt returner on THE SPORTING NEWS NFL All-Pro team (1988). ... Played in Pro Bowl (1988 season). ... Named to play in Pro Bowl (1989 season); replaced by Mark Carrier due to injury.
POSTSEASON RECORDS: Holds Super Bowl career records for most yards by punt return—94; longest punt return—45 yards (January 22, 1989, vs. Cincinnati); and highest punt-return average (minimum 4 returns)—15.7. ... Shares Super Bowl career record for most punt returns—6. ... Holds Super Bowl single-game records for most yards by punt return—56 (January 22, 1989, vs. Cincinnati); and highest punt-return average (minimum 3 returns)—18.7 (January 22, 1989, vs. Cincinnati).
PRO STATISTICS: 1987—Recovered one fumble for 26 yards and a touchdown. 1988—Fumbled six times and recovered two fumbles. 1989—Fumbled three times. 1990—Fumbled twice. 1991—Fumbled once. 1993—Attempted one pass with one completion for 41 yards and fumbled once. 1994—Fumbled once. 1995—Attempted one pass with one completion for 21 yards and fumbled twice.
STATISTICAL PLATEAUS: 100-yard receiving games: 1989 (3), 1990 (2), 1991 (3), 1992 (1), 1993 (2), 1994 (1). Total: 12.

Year Team	G	RUSHING				RECEIVING				PUNT RETURNS				KICKOFF RETURNS				TOTALS		
		Att.	Yds.	Avg.	TD	No.	Yds.	Avg.	TD	No.	Yds.	Avg.	TD	No.	Yds.	Avg.	TD	TD	2pt.	Pts.
1986—San Francisco NFL							Did not play—injured.													
1987—San Francisco NFL	12	0	0	...	0	9	151	16.8	0	1	9	9.0	0	0	0	...	0	1	...	6
1988—San Francisco NFL	12	0	0	...	0	14	325	23.2	2	44	*556	*12.6	*2	12	225	18.8	0	4	...	24
1989—San Francisco NFL	15	1	6	6.0	0	60	1077	18.0	10	36	417	11.6	0	2	51	25.5	0	10	...	60
1990—San Francisco NFL	14	0	0	...	0	49	748	15.3	7	26	212	8.2	0	0	0	...	0	7	...	42
1991—San Francisco NFL	16	0	0	...	0	64	1011	15.8	9	31	267	8.6	0	0	0	...	0	9	...	54
1992—San Francisco NFL	9	1	10	10.0	0	25	428	17.1	3	0	0	...	0	0	0	...	0	3	...	18
1993—San Francisco NFL	16	2	17	8.5	0	56	940	16.8	5	0	0	...	0	0	0	...	0	5	...	30
1994—San Francisco NFL	15	2	-2	-1.0	0	41	531	13.0	5	0	0	...	0	0	0	...	0	5	0	30
1995—San Francisco NFL	12	0	0	...	0	29	387	13.3	2	11	56	5.1	0	0	0	...	0	2	0	12
Pro totals (9 years)	121	6	31	5.2	0	347	5598	16.1	43	149	1517	10.2	2	14	276	19.7	0	46	0	276

TAYLOR, KEITH   S

PERSONAL: Born December 21, 1964, in Pennsauken, N.J. ... 5-11/212. ... Full name: Keith Gerard Taylor. ... Brother of John Taylor, wide

receiver, San Francisco 49ers (1986-1995).
HIGH SCHOOL: Pennsauken (N.J.).
COLLEGE: Illinois.
TRANSACTIONS/CAREER NOTES: Selected by New Orleans Saints in fifth round (134th pick overall) of 1988 NFL draft. ... Signed by Saints (June 24, 1988). ... Released by Saints (August 30, 1988). ... Signed by Indianapolis Colts (November 30, 1988). ... Granted free agency (February 1, 1991). ... Re-signed by Colts (June 28, 1991). ... Granted unconditional free agency (February 1, 1992). ... Signed by Saints (April 1, 1992). ... Granted unconditional free agency (February 17, 1994). ... Signed by Washington Redskins (May 6, 1994). ... On injured reserve with Achilles' tendon injury (September 5, 1994-remainder of season). ... Granted unconditional free agency (February 16, 1996).
PRO STATISTICS: 1990—Recovered one fumble. 1991—Recovered one fumble for 13 yards. 1993—Recovered one fumble. 1995—Credited with one sack and recovered one fumble.

Year Team	G	INTERCEPTIONS			
		No.	Yds.	Avg.	TD
1988—Indianapolis NFL	3	0	0	...	0
1989—Indianapolis NFL	16	7	225	32.2	1
1990—Indianapolis NFL	16	2	51	25.5	0
1991—Indianapolis NFL	16	0	-2		0
1992—New Orleans NFL	16	2	20	10.0	0
1993—New Orleans NFL	16	2	32	16.0	0
1994—Washington NFL	1	0	0		0
1995—Washington NFL	16	0	0	...	0
Pro totals (8 years)	100	13	326	25.1	1

TAYLOR, TERRY   CB   FALCONS

PERSONAL: Born July 18, 1961, in Warren, Ohio. ... 5-10/185. ... Full name: Terry Lee Taylor. ... Cousin of Vince Marrow, tight end, Carolina Panthers; and cousin of Walter Poole, running back, Chicago Blitz and Houston Gamblers of USFL (1983 and 1984).
HIGH SCHOOL: Rayen (Youngstown, Ohio).
COLLEGE: Southern Illinois.
TRANSACTIONS/CAREER NOTES: Selected by Chicago Blitz in second round (25th pick overall) of 1984 USFL draft. ... Selected by Seattle Seahawks in first round (22nd pick overall) of 1984 NFL draft. ... Signed by Seahawks (July 10, 1984). ... On reserve/non-football injury list with substance abuse problem (August 31-September 16, 1988). ... Traded by Seahawks to Detroit Lions for FB James Jones (August 31, 1989). ... On suspended list for substance abuse (September 19, 1990-September 23, 1991). ... Activated (September 28, 1991). ... Granted unconditional free agency (February 1, 1992). ... Signed by Cleveland Browns (March 27, 1992). ... On injured reserve with neck injury (December 23, 1993-remainder of season). ... Granted unconditional free agency (February 17, 1994). ... Signed by Los Angeles Rams (June 3, 1994). ... Released by Rams (August 23, 1994). ... Signed by Seattle Seahawks (November 23, 1994). ... Granted unconditional free agency (February 17, 1995). ... Signed by Atlanta Falcons (May 2, 1995).
CHAMPIONSHIP GAME EXPERIENCE: Played in NFC championship game (1991 season).
PRO STATISTICS: 1985—Returned blocked punt for 15 yards and a touchdown. 1989—Recovered one fumble for 35 yards. 1991—Recovered one fumble. 1992—Recovered one fumble for seven yards. 1995—Recovered two fumbles for eight yards.

Year Team	G	INTERCEPTIONS			
		No.	Yds.	Avg.	TD
1984—Seattle NFL	16	3	63	21.0	0
1985—Seattle NFL	16	4	75	18.8	*1
1986—Seattle NFL	16	2	0	0.0	0
1987—Seattle NFL	12	1	11	11.0	0
1988—Seattle NFL	14	5	53	10.6	1
1989—Detroit NFL	15	1	0	0.0	0
1990—Detroit NFL	2	0	0	...	0
1991—Detroit NFL	11	4	26	6.5	0
1992—Cleveland NFL	16	1	0	0.0	0
1993—Cleveland NFL	10	0	0	...	0
1994—Seattle NFL	5	1	0	0.0	0
1995—Atlanta NFL	16	3	31	10.3	0
Pro totals (12 years)	149	25	259	10.4	2

TEAGUE, GEORGE   S   PACKERS

PERSONAL: Born February 18, 1971, in Lansing, Mich. ... 6-1/195. ... Full name: George Theo Teague. ... Name pronounced TEEG.
HIGH SCHOOL: Jeff Davis (Montgomery, Ala.).
COLLEGE: Alabama.
TRANSACTIONS/CAREER NOTES: Selected by Green Bay Packers in first round (29th pick overall) of 1993 NFL draft. ... Signed by Packers (July 9, 1993). ... Granted free agency (February 16, 1996). ... Re-signed by Packers (April 11, 1996).
CHAMPIONSHIP GAME EXPERIENCE: Played in NFC championship game (1995 season).
POSTSEASON RECORDS: Holds NFL postseason single-game record for longest interception return—101 yards, touchdown (January 8, 1994, at Detroit).
PRO STATISTICS: 1993—Returned one punt for minus one yard and recovered two fumbles. 1995—Recovered one fumble for four yards.

Year Team	G	INTERCEPTIONS			
		No.	Yds.	Avg.	TD
1993—Green Bay NFL	16	1	22	22.0	0
1994—Green Bay NFL	16	3	33	11.0	0
1995—Green Bay NFL	15	2	100	50.0	0
Pro totals (3 years)	47	6	155	25.8	0

TERRELL, PAT   S   PANTHERS

PERSONAL: Born March 18, 1968, in Memphis, Tenn. ... 6-2/210. ... Full name: Patrick Christopher Terrell. ... Name pronounced TAIR-el.

HIGH SCHOOL: Lakewood Senior (St. Petersburg, Fla.).
COLLEGE: Notre Dame (degree in business administration with emphasis in marketing).
TRANSACTIONS/CAREER NOTES: Selected by Los Angeles Rams in second round (49th pick overall) of 1990 NFL draft. ... Signed by Rams (August 1, 1990). ... Granted unconditional free agency (February 17, 1994). ... Signed by New York Jets (May 19, 1994). ... Released by Jets (August 21, 1995). ... Signed by Carolina Panthers (August 23, 1995). ... Granted unconditional free agency (February 16, 1996). ... Re-signed by Panthers (February 26, 1996).
PRO STATISTICS: 1990—Recovered one fumble. 1991—Recovered one fumble. 1995—Recovered one fumble.

		INTERCEPTIONS			
Year Team	G	No.	Yds.	Avg.	TD
1990—Los Angeles Rams NFL	15	1	6	6.0	0
1991—Los Angeles Rams NFL	16	1	4	4.0	0
1992—Los Angeles Rams NFL	15	0	0	...	0
1993—Los Angeles Rams NFL	13	2	1	0.5	0
1994—New York Jets NFL	16	0	0	...	0
1995—Carolina NFL	16	3	33	11.0	0
Pro totals (6 years)	91	7	44	6.3	0

TERRY, DOUG   S   CHIEFS

PERSONAL: Born December 12, 1969, in Dumas, Ark. ... 5-11/204. ... Full name: Douglas Maurice Terry.
HIGH SCHOOL: Liberal (Kan.).
COLLEGE: Kansas.
TRANSACTIONS/CAREER NOTES: Signed as non-drafted free agent by Kansas City Chiefs (April 12, 1992). ... On injured reserve with knee injury (December 30, 1993-rest of season). ... On physically unable to perform list (August 24-October 22, 1994). ... Granted unconditional free agency (February 16, 1996). ... Re-signed by Chiefs (April 23, 1996).
PLAYING ... 1993 (15), 1994 (10), 1995 (16). Total: 57.
PRO STAT ... ited with one sack. 1994—Recovered three fumbles for 12 yards.

TER...   KR   CARDINALS

PERSONA
HIGH SCH
COLLEGE
TRANSA ... zona Cardinals (May 2, 1995).... Granted free agency after 1995 season...
PRO STA

		KICKOFF RETURNS				TOTALS			
Year Te		No.	Yds.	Avg.	TD	TD	2pt.	Pts.	Fum.
1995—A		37	808	21.8	0	0	0	0	1

TES...   RAVENS

PERSON ... name: Vincent Frank Testaverde. ... Name pronounced TESS-tuh-VER-dee.
HIGH SC ... y Academy.
COLLEGE
TRANSA ..., 1987). ... Selected officially by Buccaneers in first round (first pick over... ember 20, 1989-remainder of season). ... Granted unconditional free agenc...). ... Browns franchise moved to Baltimore and renamed Ravens for 1996 s...
HONORS: ... ond team (1985). ... Heisman Trophy winner (1986). ... Named College Fo... Award winner (1986). ... Davey O'Brien Award winner (1986). ... Named quar... ack on THE SPORTING NEWS college All-America first team (1986).
PRO STATISTICS: 1987—Fumbled seven times and recovered four fumbles for minus three yards. 1988—Fumbled eight times and recovered two fumbles. 1989—Fumbled four times and recovered two fumbles. 1990—Caught one pass for three yards, fumbled 10 times and recovered three fumbles. 1991—Fumbled five times and recovered three fumbles. 1992—Fumbled four times and recovered four fumbles for minus eight yards. 1993—Fumbled four times. 1994—Fumbled three times and recovered two fumbles for two yards. 1995—Caught one pass for seven yards and fumbled four times for minus five yards.
STATISTICAL PLATEAUS: 300-yard passing games: 1987 (1), 1988 (4), 1989 (4), 1991 (1), 1992 (1), 1993 (1), 1995 (2). Total: 14. ... 100-yard rushing games: 1990 (1).
MISCELLANEOUS: Regular-season record as starting NFL quarterback: 40-63 (.388). ... Holds Tampa Bay Buccaneers all-time records for most yards passing (14,820) and most touchdown passes (77).

		PASSING								RUSHING				TOTALS		
Year Team	G	Att.	Cmp.	Pct.	Yds.	TD	Int.	Avg.	Rat.	Att.	Yds.	Avg.	TD	TD	2pt.	Pts.
1987—Tampa Bay NFL	6	165	71	43.0	1081	5	6	6.55	60.2	13	50	3.9	1	1	...	6
1988—Tampa Bay NFL	15	466	222	47.6	3240	13	*35	6.95	48.8	28	138	4.9	1	1	...	6
1989—Tampa Bay NFL	14	480	258	53.8	3133	20	22	6.53	68.9	25	139	5.6	0	0	...	0
1990—Tampa Bay NFL	14	365	203	55.6	2818	17	18	7.72	75.6	38	280	7.4	1	1	...	6
1991—Tampa Bay NFL	13	326	166	50.9	1994	8	15	6.12	59.0	32	101	3.2	0	0	...	0
1992—Tampa Bay NFL	14	358	206	57.5	2554	14	16	7.14	74.2	36	197	5.5	2	2	...	12
1993—Cleveland NFL	10	230	130	56.5	1797	14	9	7.81	85.7	18	74	4.1	0	0	...	0
1994—Cleveland NFL	14	376	207	55.1	2575	16	18	6.85	70.7	21	37	1.8	2	2	0	12
1995—Cleveland NFL	13	392	241	61.5	2883	17	10	7.36	87.8	18	62	3.4	2	2	0	12
Pro totals (9 years)	113	3158	1704	54.0	22075	124	149	6.99	69.6	229	1078	4.7	9	9	0	54

THARPE, LARRY   OT   PATRIOTS

PERSONAL: Born November 19, 1970, in Macon, Ga. ... 6-4/300.
HIGH SCHOOL: Southwest (Macon, Ga.).
COLLEGE: Tennessee State.
TRANSACTIONS/CAREER NOTES: Selected by Detroit Lions in sixth round (145th pick overall) of 1992 NFL draft. ... Signed by Lions (July 23, 1992). ... On injured reserve with back and knee injuries (September 4-October 14, 1992). ... On inactive list for 15 games with Lions (1994). ... Granted free agency (February 17, 1995). ... Signed by Arizona Cardinals (March 25, 1995); Lions received sixth-round pick (TE Kevin Hickman) in 1995 draft as compensation. ... Granted unconditional free agency (February 16, 1996). ... Signed by New England Patriots (April 29, 1996).
PLAYING EXPERIENCE: Detroit NFL, 1992 and 1993; Arizona NFL, 1995. ... Games: 1992 (11), 1993 (5), 1995 (16). Total: 32.

THIERRY, JOHN   DE   BEARS

PERSONAL: Born September 4, 1971, in Opelousas, La. ... 6-4/260. ... Full name: John Fitzgerald Thierry.
HIGH SCHOOL: Plaisance (Opelousas, La.).
COLLEGE: Alcorn State.
TRANSACTIONS/CAREER NOTES: Selected by Chicago Bears in first round (11th pick overall) of 1994 NFL draft. ... Signed by Bears (June 21, 1994).
PLAYING EXPERIENCE: Chicago NFL, 1994 and 1995. ... Games: 1994 (16), 1995 (16). Total: 32.
PRO STATISTICS: 1994—Returned one kickoff for no yards. 1995—Recovered four fumbles.

Year Team	G	SACKS
1994—Chicago NFL	16	0.0
1995—Chicago NFL	16	4.0
Pro totals (2 years)	32	4.0

THIGPEN, YANCEY   WR   STEELERS

PERSONAL: Born August 15, 1969, in Tarboro, N.C. ... 6-1/202. ... Full name: Yancey Dirk Thigpen.
HIGH SCHOOL: Southwest Edgecombe (Tarboro, N.C.).
COLLEGE: Winston-Salem (N.C.) State.
TRANSACTIONS/CAREER NOTES: Selected by San Diego Chargers in fourth round (90th pick overall) of 1991 NFL draft. ... Signed by Chargers (July 15, 1991). ... Released by Chargers (August 26, 1991). ... Re-signed by Chargers to practice squad (August 28, 1991). ... Activated (September 20, 1991). ... Released by Chargers (September 26, 1991). ... Re-signed by Chargers to practice squad (September 28, 1991). ... Activated (December 7, 1991). ... Released by Chargers (August 31, 1992). ... Signed by Pittsburgh Steelers (October 5, 1992).
CHAMPIONSHIP GAME EXPERIENCE: Played in AFC championship game (1994 and 1995 seasons). ... Played in Super Bowl XXX (1995 season).
HONORS: Played in Pro Bowl (1995 season).
PRO STATISTICS: 1995—Rushed once for one yard.
STATISTICAL PLATEAUS: 100-yard receiving games: 1995 (4).

Year Team	G	RECEIVING				KICKOFF RETURNS				TOTALS			
		No.	Yds.	Avg.	TD	No.	Yds.	Avg.	TD	TD	2pt.	Pts.	Fum.
1991—San Diego NFL	4	0	0	...	0	0	0	...	0	0	...	0	0
1992—Pittsburgh NFL	12	1	2	2.0	0	2	44	22.0	0	0	...	0	0
1993—Pittsburgh NFL	12	9	154	17.1	3	1	23	23.0	0	3	...	18	0
1994—Pittsburgh NFL	15	36	546	15.2	4	5	121	24.2	0	4	0	24	0
1995—Pittsburgh NFL	16	85	1307	15.4	5	0	0	...	0	5	0	30	1
Pro totals (5 years)	59	131	2009	15.3	12	8	188	23.5	0	12	0	72	1

THOMAS, BLAIR   RB

PERSONAL: Born October 7, 1967, in Philadelphia. ... 5-10/202.
HIGH SCHOOL: Frankford (Pa.).
COLLEGE: Penn State (degree in recreation and parks, 1990).
TRANSACTIONS/CAREER NOTES: Selected by New York Jets in first round (second pick overall) of 1990 NFL draft. ... Signed by Jets (August 26, 1990). ... On injured reserve with knee injury (November 29, 1992-remainder of season). ... Granted unconditional free agency (February 17, 1994). ... Signed by New England Patriots (March 30, 1994). ... Released by Patriots (November 23, 1994). ... Signed by Dallas Cowboys (November 30, 1994). ... Granted unconditional free agency (February 17, 1995). ... Signed by Atlanta Falcons (June 28, 1995). ... Released by Falcons (August 21, 1995). ... Signed by Carolina Panthers (November 7, 1995). ... Granted unconditional free agency (February 16, 1996).
CHAMPIONSHIP GAME EXPERIENCE: Played in NFC championship game (1994 season).
HONORS: Named running back on THE SPORTING NEWS college All-America second team (1989).
PRO STATISTICS: 1991—Attempted one pass with one completion for 16 yards and a touchdown. 1993—Recovered one fumble.
STATISTICAL PLATEAUS: 100-yard rushing games: 1990 (1), 1991 (1). Total: 2.

Year Team	G	RUSHING				RECEIVING				KICKOFF RETURNS				TOTALS			
		Att.	Yds.	Avg.	TD	No.	Yds.	Avg.	TD	No.	Yds.	Avg.	TD	TD	2pt.	Pts.	Fum.
1990—New York Jets NFL	15	123	620	5.0	1	20	204	10.2	1	0	0	...	0	2	...	12	3
1991—New York Jets NFL	16	189	728	3.9	3	30	195	6.5	1	0	0	...	0	4	...	24	3
1992—New York Jets NFL	9	97	440	4.5	0	7	49	7.0	0	0	0	...	0	0	...	0	2
1993—New York Jets NFL	11	59	221	3.8	1	7	25	3.6	0	2	39	19.5	0	1	...	6	0
1994—New England NFL	4	19	67	3.5	1	2	15	7.5	0	3	40	13.3	0	1	0	6	0
—Dallas NFL	2	24	70	2.9	1	2	1	.5	0	0	0	...	0	1	0	6	0
1995—Carolina NFL	7	22	90	4.1	0	3	24	8.0	0	0	0	...	0	0	0	0	0
Pro totals (6 years)	64	533	2236	4.2	7	71	513	7.2	2	5	79	15.8	0	9	0	54	8

T

THOMAS, BRODERICK   LB   COWBOYS

PERSONAL: Born February 20, 1967, in Houston. ... 6-4/242. ... Nephew of Mike Singletary, linebacker, Chicago Bears (1981-1992).
HIGH SCHOOL: James Madison (Houston).
COLLEGE: Nebraska.
TRANSACTIONS/CAREER NOTES: Selected by Tampa Bay Buccaneers in first round (sixth pick overall) of 1989 NFL draft. ... Signed by Buccaneers (August 29, 1989). ... Released by Buccaneers (June 30, 1994). ... Signed by Detroit Lions (July 15, 1994). ... Granted unconditional free agency (February 17, 1995). ... Signed by Minnesota Vikings (March 9, 1995). ... Released by Vikings (February 9, 1996). ... Signed by Dallas Cowboys (March 22, 1996).
HONORS: Named defensive lineman on THE SPORTING NEWS college All-America second team (1987). ... Named linebacker on THE SPORTING NEWS college All-America first team (1988).
PRO STATISTICS: 1990—Recovered two fumbles. 1991—Recovered two fumbles for 12 yards. 1992—Intercepted two passes for 81 yards and one touchdown and recovered three fumbles for minus one yard. 1993—Recovered one fumble. 1994—Recovered two fumbles for 11 yards. 1995—Recovered one fumble.

Year Team	G	SACKS
1989—Tampa Bay NFL	16	2.0
1990—Tampa Bay NFL	16	7.5
1991—Tampa Bay NFL	16	11.0
1992—Tampa Bay NFL	16	5.0
1993—Tampa Bay NFL	16	1.0
1994—Detroit NFL	16	7.0
1995—Minnesota NFL	16	6.0
Pro totals (7 years)	112	39.5

THOMAS, CHRIS   WR   49ERS

PERSONAL: Born July 16, 1971, in Ventura, Calif. ... 6-1/180. ... Full name: Chris Eric Thomas.
HIGH SCHOOL: Ventura (Calif.).
COLLEGE: Cal Poly-SLO.
TRANSACTIONS/CAREER NOTES: Signed as non-drafted free agent by San Diego Chargers (May 6, 1993). ... Released by Chargers (August 30, 1993). ... Re-signed by Chargers to practice squad (September 1, 1993). ... Granted free agency after 1993 season. ... Signed by San Francisco 49ers (May 16, 1995).
PLAYING EXPERIENCE: San Francisco NFL, 1995. ... Games: 1995 (15).
PRO STATISTICS: 1995—Caught six passes for 73 yards, returned one punt for 25 yards and returned three kickoffs for 49 yards.

THOMAS, DAMON   WR   BILLS

PERSONAL: Born December 15, 1970, in Clovis, Calif. ... 6-2/208. ... Full name: Damon Andrew Thomas.
HIGH SCHOOL: Clovis (Calif.).
JUNIOR COLLEGE: Fresno (Calif.) College.
COLLEGE: Wayne (Neb.) State.
TRANSACTIONS/CAREER NOTES: Signed as non-drafted free agent by Buffalo Bills (May 6, 1994). ... Released by Bills (August 23, 1994). ... Re-signed by Bills to practice squad (August 29, 1994). ... Activated (November 17, 1994).
PLAYING EXPERIENCE: Buffalo NFL, 1994 and 1995. ... Games: 1994 (3), 1995 (14). Total: 17.
PRO STATISTICS: 1994—Caught two passes for 31 yards. 1995—Caught one pass for 18 yards, returned one punt for no yards and fumbled once.

THOMAS, DAVE   CB   JAGUARS

PERSONAL: Born August 25, 1968, in Miami. ... 6-3/213.
HIGH SCHOOL: Miami Beach (Fla.).
COLLEGE: Tennessee.
TRANSACTIONS/CAREER NOTES: Selected by Dallas Cowboys in eighth round (203rd pick overall) of 1993 NFL draft. ... Signed by Cowboys (July 15, 1993). ... Selected by Jacksonville Jaguars from Cowboys in NFL expansion draft (February 15, 1995). ... Granted free agency (February 16, 1996). ... Re-signed by Jaguars (June 3, 1996).
PLAYING EXPERIENCE: Dallas NFL, 1993 and 1994; Jacksonville NFL, 1995. ... Games: 1993 (12), 1994 (16), 1995 (16). Total: 44.
CHAMPIONSHIP GAME EXPERIENCE: Played in NFC championship game (1993 and 1994 seasons). ... Member of Super Bowl championship team (1993 season).
PRO STATISTICS: 1995—Recovered one fumble.

THOMAS, DERRICK   LB   CHIEFS

PERSONAL: Born January 1, 1967, in Miami. ... 6-3/247. ... Full name: Derrick Vincent Thomas.
HIGH SCHOOL: South (Miami).
COLLEGE: Alabama.
TRANSACTIONS/CAREER NOTES: Selected by Kansas City Chiefs in first round (fourth pick overall) of 1989 NFL draft. ... Signed by Chiefs (August 24, 1989). ... Granted free agency (March 1, 1993). ... Re-signed by Chiefs (May 21, 1993).
CHAMPIONSHIP GAME EXPERIENCE: Played in AFC championship game (1993 season).
HONORS: Named linebacker on THE SPORTING NEWS college All-America second team (1987). ... Butkus Award winner (1988). ... Named linebacker on THE SPORTING NEWS college All-America first team (1988). ... Played in Pro Bowl (1989-1995 seasons). ... Named outside linebacker on THE SPORTING NEWS NFL All-Pro team (1990-1992).
RECORDS: Holds NFL single-game record for most sacks—7 (November 11, 1990, vs. Seattle).
PRO STATISTICS: 1989—Recovered one fumble. 1990—Recovered two fumbles for 14 yards. 1991—Recovered four fumbles for 23 yards

and one touchdown. 1992—Recovered three fumbles (including one in end zone for a touchdown). 1993—Recovered one fumble for 86 yards and a touchdown. 1994—Credited with one safety and recovered three fumbles for 11 yards. 1995—Recovered one fumble.

MISCELLANEOUS: Holds Kansas City Chiefs all-time record for most sacks (85).

Year Team	G	SACKS
1989—Kansas City NFL	16	10.0
1990—Kansas City NFL	15	*20.0
1991—Kansas City NFL	16	13.5
1992—Kansas City NFL	16	14.5
1993—Kansas City NFL	16	8.0
1994—Kansas City NFL	16	11.0
1995—Kansas City NFL	15	8.0
Pro totals (7 years)	110	85.0

THOMAS, ERIC — CB

PERSONAL: Born September 11, 1964, in Tucson, Ariz. ... 5-11/184. ... Full name: Eric Jason Thomas.
HIGH SCHOOL: Norte Del Rio (Sacramento).
JUNIOR COLLEGE: Pasadena (Calif.) City College.
COLLEGE: Tulane.
TRANSACTIONS/CAREER NOTES: Selected by Cincinnati Bengals in second round (49th pick overall) of 1987 NFL draft. ... Signed by Bengals (July 27, 1987). ... On reserve/non-football injury list (September 3-November 6, 1990). ... Granted free agency (February 1, 1991). ... Re-signed by Bengals (July 16, 1991). ... Granted unconditional free agency (March 1, 1993). ... Signed by New York Jets (April 3, 1993). ... Released by Jets (April 28, 1994). ... Re-signed by Jets (November 8, 1994). ... Granted unconditional free agency (February 17, 1995). ... Signed by Denver Broncos (March 23, 1995). ... Released by Broncos (February 5, 1996).
CHAMPIONSHIP GAME EXPERIENCE: Played in AFC championship game (1988 season). ... Played in Super Bowl XXIII (1988 season).
HONORS: Played in Pro Bowl (1988 season).
PRO STATISTICS: 1989—Credited with two sacks and recovered one fumble. 1991—Returned one kickoff for minus one yard and recovered one fumble. 1993—Recovered one fumble.

Year Team	G	INTERCEPTIONS No.	Yds.	Avg.	TD
1987—Cincinnati NFL	12	1	3	3.0	0
1988—Cincinnati NFL	16	7	61	8.7	0
1989—Cincinnati NFL	16	4	18	4.5	1
1990—Cincinnati NFL	4	0	0	...	0
1991—Cincinnati NFL	16	3	0	0.0	0
1992—Cincinnati NFL	16	0	0	...	0
1993—New York Jets NFL	16	2	20	10.0	0
1994—New York Jets NFL	1	0	0	...	0
1995—Denver NFL	14	0	0	...	0
Pro totals (9 years)	111	17	102	6.0	1

THOMAS, HENRY — DL — LIONS

PERSONAL: Born January 12, 1965, in Houston. ... 6-2/277. ... Full name: Henry Lee Thomas Jr.
HIGH SCHOOL: Dwight D. Eisenhower (Houston).
COLLEGE: Louisiana State.
TRANSACTIONS/CAREER NOTES: Selected by Minnesota Vikings in third round (72nd pick overall) of 1987 NFL draft. ... Signed by Vikings (July 14, 1987). ... Designated by Vikings as transition player (February 25, 1993). ... Designated by Vikings as franchise player (February 15, 1994). ... Free agency status changed by Vikings from franchise to unconditional (February 15, 1995). ... Signed by Detroit Lions (February 27, 1995).
CHAMPIONSHIP GAME EXPERIENCE: Played in NFC championship game (1987 season).
HONORS: Named defensive lineman on THE SPORTING NEWS college All-America second team (1986). ... Played in Pro Bowl (1991 and 1992 seasons).
PRO STATISTICS: 1987—Intercepted one pass for no yards and recovered one fumble. 1988—Intercepted one pass for seven yards and recovered one fumble for two yards and a touchdown. 1989—Recovered three fumbles for 37 yards and one touchdown. 1990—Recovered one fumble. 1991—Recovered one fumble. 1993—Credited with one safety. 1994—Recovered one fumble. 1995—Recovered two fumbles.

Year Team	G	SACKS
1987—Minnesota NFL	12	2.5
1988—Minnesota NFL	15	6.0
1989—Minnesota NFL	14	9.0
1990—Minnesota NFL	16	8.5
1991—Minnesota NFL	16	8.0
1992—Minnesota NFL	16	6.0
1993—Minnesota NFL	13	9.0
1994—Minnesota NFL	16	7.0
1995—Detroit NFL	16	10.5
Pro totals (9 years)	134	66.5

THOMAS, JOHNNY — CB — RAVENS

PERSONAL: Born August 3, 1964, in Houston. ... 5-9/191.
HIGH SCHOOL: Sterling (Houston).
COLLEGE: Baylor.
TRANSACTIONS/CAREER NOTES: Selected by Washington Redskins in seventh round (192nd pick overall) of 1987 NFL draft. ... Signed by Redskins (July 24, 1987). ... On injured reserve with ankle injury (August 31, 1987-entire season). ... On injured reserve with knee injury (September 30, 1988-remainder of season). ... Granted unconditional free agency (February 1, 1989). ... Signed by San Diego Chargers

(March 30, 1989). ... Released by Chargers (September 5, 1989). ... Re-signed by Chargers (September 13, 1989). ... Released by Chargers (December 16, 1989). ... Signed by Kansas City Chiefs (March 12, 1990). ... Released by Chiefs (August 28, 1990). ... Signed by Redskins (September 26, 1990). ... On injured reserve (October 17-November 16, 1990). ... Released by Redskins (November 27, 1990). ... Signed by Frankfurt Galaxy of World League (March 3, 1992). ... Signed by Redskins for 1992. ... Released by Redskins (August 31, 1992). ... Re-signed by Redskins (September 2, 1992). ... Released by Redskins (August 30, 1993). ... Re-signed by Redskins (August 31, 1993). ... Granted unconditional free agency (February 17, 1995). ... Signed by Cleveland Browns (April 17, 1995). ... Browns franchise moved to Baltimore and renamed Ravens for 1996 season (March 11, 1996).
PLAYING EXPERIENCE: Washington NFL, 1988, 1990 and 1992-1994; San Diego NFL, 1989; Frankfurt W.L., 1992; Cleveland NFL, 1995. ... Games: 1988 (4), 1989 (13), 1990 (4), 1992 W.L. (9), 1992 NFL (16), 1993 (16), 1994 (16), 1995 (16). Total NFL: 85. Total Pro: 94.
PRO STATISTICS: NFL: 1990—Returned one punt for no yards and fumbled once. 1992—Returned one punt for no yards, fumbled once and recovered one fumble. 1993—Recovered two fumbles. 1995—Recovered one fumble.

THOMAS, J.T.   WR   RAMS

PERSONAL: Born December 15, 1971, in San Bernardino, Calif. ... 5-10/173. ... Full name: Johnny Le'Mon Thomas.
HIGH SCHOOL: San Bernardino (Calif.).
JUNIOR COLLEGE: San Bernadino (Calif.) Valley.
COLLEGE: Arizona State.
TRANSACTIONS/CAREER NOTES: Selected after junior season by St. Louis Rams in seventh round (240th pick overall) of 1995 NFL draft. ... Signed by Rams (June 16, 1995).
PRO STATISTICS: 1995—Ran 61 yards with lateral from punt return and recovered one fumble for five yards.

		RECEIVING				KICKOFF RETURNS				TOTALS		
Year Team	G	No.	Yds.	Avg.	TD	No.	Yds.	Avg.	TD	TD	2pt.	Pts.	Fum.
1995—St. Louis NFL	15	5	42	8.4	0	32	752	23.5	0	0	0	0	1

THOMAS, LAMAR   WR   BUCCANEERS

PERSONAL: Born February 12, 1970, in Ocala, Fla. ... 6-2/173. ... Full name: Lamar Nathaniel Thomas.
HIGH SCHOOL: Buchholz (Gainesville, Fla.).
COLLEGE: Miami, Fla. (degree in sociology).
TRANSACTIONS/CAREER NOTES: Selected by Tampa Bay Buccaneers in third round (60th pick overall) of 1993 NFL draft. ... Signed by Buccaneers (July 14, 1993). ... Granted free agency (February 16, 1996).
HONORS: Named wide receiver on THE SPORTING NEWS college All-America second team (1992).
PRO STATISTICS: 1995—Rushed once for five yards.

		RECEIVING				TOTALS			
Year Team	G	No.	Yds.	Avg.	TD	TD	2pt.	Pts.	Fum.
1993—Tampa Bay NFL	14	8	186	23.3	2	2	...	12	0
1994—Tampa Bay NFL	11	7	94	13.4	0	0	0	0	0
1995—Tampa Bay NFL	11	10	107	10.7	0	0	0	0	0
Pro totals (3 years)	36	25	387	15.5	2	2	0	12	0

THOMAS, MARK   DE

PERSONAL: Born May 6, 1969, in Lilburn, Ga. ... 6-5/273. ... Full name: Mark Andrew Thomas.
HIGH SCHOOL: Parkview (Lilburn, Ga.).
COLLEGE: North Carolina State.
TRANSACTIONS/CAREER NOTES: Selected by San Francisco 49ers in fourth round (89th pick overall) of 1992 NFL draft. ... Signed by 49ers (July 16, 1992). ... On injured reserve with ankle injury (September 1-October 7, 1992). ... On practice squad (October 7-November 11, 1992). ... On injured reserve (November 11, 1992-remainder of season). ... Selected by Carolina Panthers from 49ers in NFL expansion draft (February 15, 1995). ... Granted free agency (February 17, 1995). ... On injured reserve with thumb injury (November 27, 1995-remainder of season). ... Granted unconditional free agency (February 16, 1996).
CHAMPIONSHIP GAME EXPERIENCE: Member of 49ers for NFC championship game (1993 and 1994 seasons); inactive. ... Member of Super Bowl championship team (1994 season).
PRO STATISTICS: 1993—Recovered one fumble.

Year Team	G	SACKS
1992—San Francisco NFL	Did not play.	
1993—San Francisco NFL	11	0.5
1994—San Francisco NFL	9	1.0
1995—Carolina NFL	10	2.0
Pro totals (3 years)	30	3.5

THOMAS, ORLANDO   S   VIKINGS

PERSONAL: Born October 21, 1972, in Crowley, La. ... 6-1/210.
HIGH SCHOOL: Crowley (La.).
COLLEGE: Southwestern Louisiana.
TRANSACTIONS/CAREER NOTES: Selected by Minnesota Vikings in second round (42nd pick overall) of 1995 NFL draft. ... Signed by Vikings (July 25, 1995).
PRO STATISTICS: 1995—Fumbled once and recovered four fumbles for 19 yards and one touchdown.

		INTERCEPTIONS			
Year Team	G	No.	Yds.	Avg.	TD
1995—Minnesota NFL	16	*9	108	12.0	1

THOMAS, ROBB — WR

PERSONAL: Born March 29, 1966, in Portland, Ore. ... 5-11/175. ... Full name: Robb Douglas Thomas. ... Son of Aaron Thomas, wide receiver, San Francisco 49ers and New York Giants (1961-1970).
HIGH SCHOOL: Corvallis (Ore.).
COLLEGE: Oregon State.
TRANSACTIONS/CAREER NOTES: Selected by Kansas City Chiefs in sixth round (143rd pick overall) of 1989 NFL draft. ... Signed by Chiefs (May 30, 1989). ... On injured reserve with dislocated shoulder (October 24-December 4, 1989). ... On developmental squad (December 5-23, 1989). ... Granted free agency (February 1, 1992). ... Re-signed by Chiefs (July 29, 1992). ... Released by Chiefs (August 31, 1992). ... Signed by Seattle Seahawks (September 8, 1992). ... Granted free agency (March 1, 1993). ... Re-signed by Seahawks (July 2, 1993). ... Released by Seahawks (August 30, 1993). ... Re-signed by Seahawks (August 31, 1993). ... Granted unconditional free agency (February 17, 1994). ... Re-signed by Seahawks (July 13, 1994). ... Granted unconditional free agency (February 17, 1996).
PRO STATISTICS: 1992—Rushed once for minus one yard.

		RECEIVING				TOTALS			
Year Team	G	No.	Yds.	Avg.	TD	TD	2pt.	Pts.	Fum.
1989—Kansas City NFL	8	8	58	7.3	2	2	...	12	1
1990—Kansas City NFL	16	41	545	13.3	4	4	...	24	0
1991—Kansas City NFL	15	43	495	11.5	1	1	...	6	0
1992—Seattle NFL	15	11	136	12.4	0	0	...	0	1
1993—Seattle NFL	16	7	67	9.6	0	0	...	0	0
1994—Seattle NFL	16	4	70	17.5	0	0	0	0	0
1995—Seattle NFL	15	12	239	19.9	1	1	0	6	0
Pro totals (7 years)	101	126	1610	12.8	8	8	0	48	2

THOMAS, RODNEY — RB — OILERS

PERSONAL: Born March 30, 1973, in Groveton, Texas. ... 5-10/213. ... Full name: Rodney Dejuane Thomas.
HIGH SCHOOL: Groveton (Texas).
COLLEGE: Texas A&M.
TRANSACTIONS/CAREER NOTES: Selected by Houston Oilers in third round (89th pick overall) of 1995 NFL draft. ... Signed by Oilers (August 1, 1995).
STATISTICAL PLATEAUS: 100-yard rushing games: 1995 (2).

		RUSHING				RECEIVING				KICKOFF RETURNS				TOTALS			
Year Team	G	Att.	Yds.	Avg.	TD	No.	Yds.	Avg.	TD	No.	Yds.	Avg.	TD	TD	2pt.	Pts.	Fum.
1995—Houston NFL	16	251	947	3.8	5	39	204	5.2	2	3	48	16.0	0	7	1	44	8

THOMAS, THURMAN — RB — BILLS

PERSONAL: Born May 16, 1966, in Houston. ... 5-10/198. ... Full name: Thurman Lee Thomas.
HIGH SCHOOL: Willow Ridge (Missouri City, Texas).
COLLEGE: Oklahoma State.
TRANSACTIONS/CAREER NOTES: Selected by Buffalo Bills in second round (40th pick overall) of 1988 NFL draft. ... Signed by Bills (July 14, 1988).
CHAMPIONSHIP GAME EXPERIENCE: Played in AFC championship game (1988 and 1990-1993 seasons). ... Played in Super Bowl XXV (1990 season), Super Bowl XXVI (1991 season), Super Bowl XXVII (1992 season) and Super Bowl XXVIII (1993 season).
HONORS: Named running back on The Sporting News college All-America second team (1985). ... Played in Pro Bowl (1989-1991 and 1993 seasons). ... Named to play in Pro Bowl (1992 season); replaced by Ronnie Harmon due to injury. ... Named running back on The Sporting News NFL All-Pro team (1990 and 1991). ... Named NFL Player of the Year by The Sporting News (1991).
RECORDS: Shares NFL record for most consecutive seasons with 1,000 or more yards rushing—7 (1989-1995).
POSTSEASON RECORDS: Shares NFL postseason career record for most games with 100 or more rushing yards—7. ... Shares NFL postseason single-game record for most receptions—13 (January 6, 1990, at Cleveland).
PRO STATISTICS: 1988—Recovered one fumble. 1989—Recovered two fumbles. 1990—Recovered two fumbles. 1992—Recovered one fumble. 1993—Attempted one pass without a completion and recovered one fumble. 1994—Recovered two fumbles.
STATISTICAL PLATEAUS: 100-yard rushing games: 1988 (2), 1989 (5), 1990 (5), 1991 (8), 1992 (9), 1993 (7), 1994 (4), 1995 (3). Total: 43. ... 100-yard receiving games: 1991 (2).
MISCELLANEOUS: Holds Buffalo Bills all-time record for most touchdowns (74).

		RUSHING				RECEIVING				TOTALS			
Year Team	G	Att.	Yds.	Avg.	TD	No.	Yds.	Avg.	TD	TD	2pt.	Pts.	Fum.
1988—Buffalo NFL	15	207	881	4.3	2	18	208	11.6	0	2	...	12	9
1989—Buffalo NFL	16	298	1244	4.2	6	60	669	11.2	6	12	...	72	7
1990—Buffalo NFL	16	271	1297	4.8	11	49	532	10.9	2	13	...	78	6
1991—Buffalo NFL	15	288	1407	*4.9	7	62	631	10.2	5	12	...	72	5
1992—Buffalo NFL	16	312	1487	4.8	9	58	626	10.8	3	12	...	72	6
1993—Buffalo NFL	16	*355	1315	3.7	6	48	387	8.1	0	6	...	36	6
1994—Buffalo NFL	15	287	1093	3.8	7	50	349	7.0	2	9	0	54	1
1995—Buffalo NFL	14	267	1005	3.8	6	26	220	8.5	2	8	0	48	6
Pro totals (8 years)	123	2285	9729	4.3	54	371	3622	9.8	20	74	0	444	46

THOMAS, WILLIAM — LB — EAGLES

PERSONAL: Born August 13, 1968, in Amarillo, Texas. ... 6-2/223. ... Full name: William Harrison Thomas Jr.
HIGH SCHOOL: Palo Duro (Amarillo, Texas).
COLLEGE: Texas A&M.
TRANSACTIONS/CAREER NOTES: Selected by Philadelphia Eagles in fourth round (105th pick overall) of 1991 NFL draft. ... Signed by Eagles (July 17, 1991). ... Granted free agency (February 17, 1994). ... Re-signed by Eagles (July 1994).

HONORS: Played in Pro Bowl (1995 season).
POSTSEASON RECORDS: Shares NFL postseason record for most touchdowns by interception return—1 (December 30, 1995, vs. Detroit).
PRO STATISTICS: 1991—Recovered one fumble. 1992—Recovered two fumbles for two yards. 1993—Recovered three fumbles. 1995—Recovered one fumble.

		INTERCEPTIONS				SACKS
Year Team	G	No.	Yds.	Avg.	TD	No.
1991—Philadelphia NFL	16	0	0	...	0	2.0
1992—Philadelphia NFL	16	2	4	2.0	0	1.5
1993—Philadelphia NFL	16	2	39	19.5	0	6.5
1994—Philadelphia NFL	16	1	7	7.0	0	6.0
1995—Philadelphia NFL	16	7	104	14.9	1	2.0
Pro totals (5 years)	80	12	154	12.8	1	18.0

THOMASON, JEFF   TE   PACKERS

PERSONAL: Born December 30, 1969, in San Diego. ... 6-4/233. ... Full name: Jeffrey David Thomason.
HIGH SCHOOL: Corona Del Mar (Newport Beach, Calif.).
COLLEGE: Oregon.
TRANSACTIONS/CAREER NOTES: Signed as non-drafted free agent by Cincinnati Bengals (1992). ... Placed on injured reserve with sprained knee (September 1, 1992). ... Activated off injured reserve for final four games (1992). ... Released by Bengals (August 30, 1993). ... Re-signed by Bengals (1993). ... Claimed on waivers by Green Bay Packers (August 2, 1994). ... Released by Packers (August 21, 1994). ... Re-signed by Packers (January 20, 1995).
CHAMPIONSHIP GAME EXPERIENCE: Played in NFC championship game (1995 season).
PRO STATISTICS: 1995—Returned one kickoff for 16 yards and recovered one fumble.

		RECEIVING				TOTALS			
Year Team	G	No.	Yds.	Avg.	TD	TD	2pt.	Pts.	Fum.
1992—Cincinnati NFL	4	2	14	7.0	0	0	...	0	0
1993—Cincinnati NFL	3	2	8	4.0	0	0	...	0	0
1994—			Did not play.						
1995—Green Bay NFL	16	3	32	10.7	0	0	0	0	0
Pro totals (3 years)	23	7	54	7.7	0	0	0	0	0

THOMPSON, BENNIE   S   RAVENS

PERSONAL: Born February 10, 1963, in New Orleans. ... 6-0/214.
HIGH SCHOOL: John McDonogh (New Orleans).
COLLEGE: Grambling State.
TRANSACTIONS/CAREER NOTES: Signed as non-drafted free agent by Kansas City Chiefs (May 9, 1985). ... Released by Chiefs (August 5, 1985). ... Signed by Winnipeg Blue Bombers of CFL (April 21, 1986). ... Granted free agency (March 1, 1989). ... Signed by New Orleans Saints (April 12, 1989). ... Released by Saints (September 5, 1989). ... Re-signed by Saints to practice squad (September 6, 1989). ... Activated (December 15, 1989). ... Granted unconditional free agency (February 1-April 1, 1991). ... Re-signed by Saints for 1991 season. ... Granted unconditional free agency (February 1, 1992). ... Signed by Chiefs (March 28, 1992). ... Granted unconditional free agency (February 17, 1994). ... Rights relinquished by Chiefs (April 29, 1994). ... Signed by Cleveland Browns (July 19, 1994). ... Browns franchise moved to Baltimore and renamed Ravens for 1996 season (March 11, 1996).
CHAMPIONSHIP GAME EXPERIENCE: Played in AFC championship game (1993 season).
HONORS: Played in Pro Bowl (1991 season).
PRO STATISTICS: CFL: 1987—Recovered one fumble. 1988—Fumbled once and recovered two fumbles for two yards. NFL: 1991—Recovered two fumbles. 1994—Recovered one fumble.

		INTERCEPTIONS				SACKS
Year Team	G	No.	Yds.	Avg.	TD	No.
1986—Winnipeg CFL	9	2	49	24.5	0	0.0
1987—Winnipeg CFL	8	1	0	0.0	0	0.0
1988—Winnipeg CFL	18	4	58	14.5	0	0.0
1989—New Orleans NFL	2	0	0	...	0	0.0
1990—New Orleans NFL	16	2	0	0.0	0	0.0
1991—New Orleans NFL	16	1	14	14.0	0	0.0
1992—Kansas City NFL	16	4	26	6.5	0	1.5
1993—Kansas City NFL	16	0	0	...	0	0.5
1994—Cleveland NFL	16	0	0	...	0	1.0
1995—Cleveland NFL	13	0	0	...	0	0.0
CFL totals (3 years)	35	7	107	15.3	0	0.0
NFL totals (7 years)	95	7	40	5.7	0	3.0
Pro totals (10 years)	130	14	147	10.5	0	3.0

THOMPSON, BRODERICK   OT   BRONCOS

PERSONAL: Born August 14, 1960, in Birmingham, Ala. ... 6-5/295. ... Full name: Broderick Lorenzo Thompson.
HIGH SCHOOL: Richard Gahr (Cerritos, Calif.).
JUNIOR COLLEGE: Cerritos College (Calif.).
COLLEGE: Kansas.
TRANSACTIONS/CAREER NOTES: Signed as non-drafted free agent by Dallas Cowboys (April 28, 1983). ... Released by Cowboys (August 2, 1983). ... Signed by San Antonio Gunslingers of USFL (November 12, 1983). ... Traded by Gunslingers with first-round pick in 1984 draft to Chicago Blitz for rights to QB Bob Gagliano (January 3, 1984). ... Released by Blitz (January 31, 1984). ... Signed by Los Angeles Express (February 10, 1984). ... Released by Express (February 13, 1984). ... Signed by Los Angeles Rams (May 4, 1984). ... Released by Rams (August 21, 1984). ... Signed by Portland Breakers of USFL (January 23, 1985). ... Claimed on waivers by Memphis Showboats (August 1, 1985). ... Released by Showboats (August 2, 1985). ... Signed by Cowboys (August 3, 1985). ... Released by Cowboys (August 26, 1986). ...

Signed by San Diego Chargers (April 13, 1987). ... Released by Chargers (September 7, 1987). ... Re-signed by Chargers (September 8, 1987). ... Granted free agency (February 1, 1991). ... Re-signed by Chargers (August 6, 1991). ... Granted free agency (February 1, 1992). ... Re-signed by Chargers (July 24, 1992). ... On injured reserve with bruised sternum (September 14-October 17, 1992). ... Traded by Chargers to Philadelphia Eagles for fourth-round pick (traded to Tampa Bay) in 1993 draft (April 25, 1993). ... Granted unconditional free agency (February 16, 1995). ... Signed by Denver Broncos (March 9, 1995).

PLAYING EXPERIENCE: Portland USFL, 1985; Dallas NFL, 1985; San Diego NFL, 1987-1992; Philadelphia NFL, 1993 and 1994; Denver NFL, 1995. ... Games: 1985 USFL (18), 1985 NFL (11), 1987 (8), 1988 (16), 1989 (16), 1990 (16), 1991 (16), 1992 (12), 1993 (10), 1994 (14), 1995 (16). Total NFL: 135. Total Pro: 153.

PRO STATISTICS: 1991—Recovered one fumble. 1994—Recovered one fumble.

THOMPSON, LEROY   RB

PERSONAL: Born February 3, 1968, in Knoxville, Tenn. ... 5-11/216. ... Full name: Ulys Leroy Thompson.
HIGH SCHOOL: Austin-East (Knoxville, Tenn.).
COLLEGE: Penn State (degree in speech communications).
TRANSACTIONS/CAREER NOTES: Selected by Pittsburgh Steelers in sixth round (158th pick overall) of 1991 NFL draft. ... Signed by Steelers (July 12, 1991). ... Granted free agency (February 17, 1994). ... Re-signed by Steelers (June 1, 1994). ... Traded by Steelers to New England Patriots for fourth-round pick (DL Oliver Gibson) in 1995 draft (August 10, 1994). ... Granted unconditional free agency (February 17, 1995). ... Signed by Kansas City Chiefs (July 13, 1995). ... Granted free agency after 1995 season.
PRO STATISTICS: 1991—Recovered one fumble. 1993—Recovered one fumble. 1994—Recovered one fumble.
STATISTICAL PLATEAUS: 100-yard rushing games: 1993 (2).

			RUSHING				RECEIVING				KICKOFF RETURNS				TOTALS			
Year Team	G	Att.	Yds.	Avg.	TD	No.	Yds.	Avg.	TD	No.	Yds.	Avg.	TD	TD	2pt.	Pts.	Fum.
1991—Pittsburgh NFL	13	20	60	3.0	0	14	118	8.4	0	1	8	8.0	0	0	...	0	1
1992—Pittsburgh NFL	15	35	157	4.5	1	22	278	12.6	0	2	51	25.5	0	1	...	6	2
1993—Pittsburgh NFL	15	205	763	3.7	3	38	259	6.8	0	4	77	19.3	0	3	...	18	7
1994—New England NFL	16	102	312	3.1	2	65	465	7.2	5	18	376	20.9	0	7	0	42	2
1995—Kansas City NFL	16	28	73	2.6	0	9	37	4.1	0	6	152	25.3	0	0	0	0	0
Pro totals (5 years)	75	390	1365	3.5	6	148	1157	7.8	5	31	664	21.4	0	11	0	66	12

THOMPSON, MIKE   DT   JAGUARS

PERSONAL: Born December 22, 1972, in Portage, Wis. ... 6-3/279. ... Full name: Michael John Thompson.
HIGH SCHOOL: Portage (Wis.).
COLLEGE: Wisconsin.
TRANSACTIONS/CAREER NOTES: Selected by Jacksonville Jaguars in fourth round (123rd pick overall) of 1995 NFL draft. ... Signed by Jaguars (June 1, 1995).
PLAYING EXPERIENCE: Jacksonville NFL, 1995. ... Games (2).

THOMPSON, TOMMY   P   49ERS

PERSONAL: Born April 27, 1972, in Ventura, Calif. ... 5-10/192.
HIGH SCHOOL: Lompoc (Calif.).
COLLEGE: Oregon.
TRANSACTIONS/CAREER NOTES: Signed as non-drafted free agent by San Francisco 49ers (May 4, 1994). ... Released by 49ers (August 20, 1994). ... Re-signed by 49ers (March 10, 1995).

		PUNTING					
Year Team	G	No.	Yds.	Avg.	Net avg.	In. 20	Blk.
1994—				Did not play.			
1995—San Francisco NFL	16	57	2312	40.6	33.7	14	0

THORNTON, JAMES   TE

PERSONAL: Born February 8, 1965, in Santa Rosa, Calif. ... 6-2/242. ... Full name: James Michael Thornton.
HIGH SCHOOL: Analy (Sebastopol, Calif.).
COLLEGE: Cal State Fullerton.
TRANSACTIONS/CAREER NOTES: Selected by Chicago Bears in fourth round (105th pick overall) of 1988 NFL draft. ... Signed by Bears (July 21, 1988). ... Granted free agency (February 1, 1991). ... Re-signed by Bears (August 9, 1991). ... On injured reserve with foot injury (September 2, 1992-entire season). ... Granted unconditional free agency (March 1, 1993). ... Signed by New York Jets (April 5, 1993). ... Released by Jets (April 27, 1995). ... Signed by Houston Oilers (July 10, 1995). ... Released by Oilers (November 21, 1995).
CHAMPIONSHIP GAME EXPERIENCE: Played in NFC championship game (1988 season).
PRO STATISTICS: 1989—Rushed once for four yards. 1994—Recovered two fumbles.

		RECEIVING				TOTALS			
Year Team	G	No.	Yds.	Avg.	TD	TD	2pt.	Pts.	Fum.
1988—Chicago NFL	16	15	135	9.0	0	0	...	0	1
1989—Chicago NFL	16	24	392	16.3	3	3	...	18	2
1990—Chicago NFL	16	19	254	13.4	1	1	...	6	1
1991—Chicago NFL	16	17	278	16.4	1	1	...	6	1
1992—Chicago NFL				Did not play—injured.					
1993—New York Jets NFL	13	12	108	9.0	2	2	...	12	0
1994—New York Jets NFL	15	20	171	8.6	0	0	0	0	0
1995—Houston NFL	4	0	0	...	0	0	0	0	0
Pro totals (7 years)	96	107	1338	12.5	7	7	0	42	5

THURE, BRIAN   OT   REDSKINS

PERSONAL: Born September 3, 1973, in Downey, Calif. ... 6-5/300.
HIGH SCHOOL: Salinas (Calif.).
COLLEGE: California.
TRANSACTIONS/CAREER NOTES: Selected by Washington Redskins in sixth round (176th pick overall) of 1995 NFL draft. ... Signed by Redskins (July 18, 1995).
PLAYING EXPERIENCE: Washington NFL, 1995. ... Games: 1995 (4).

TICE, MIKE   TE

PERSONAL: Born February 2, 1959, in Bayshore, N.Y. ... 6-7/253. ... Full name: Michael Peter Tice. ... Brother of John Tice, tight end, New Orleans Saints (1983-1992).
HIGH SCHOOL: Central Islip (N.Y.).
COLLEGE: Maryland.
TRANSACTIONS/CAREER NOTES: Signed as non-drafted free agent by Seattle Seahawks (April 30, 1981). ... On injured reserve with fractured ankle (October 15-December 7, 1985). ... Granted unconditional free agency (February 1, 1989). ... Signed by Washington Redskins (February 20, 1989). ... Released by Redskins (September 4, 1990). ... Signed by Seahawks (November 28, 1990). ... Granted unconditional free agency (February 1-April 1, 1991). ... Re-signed by Seahawks (July 19, 1991). ... Granted unconditional free agency (February 1, 1992). ... Signed by Minnesota Vikings (March 18, 1992). ... On injured reserve with back injury (September 25-October 21, 1992). ... Granted unconditional free agency (March 1, 1993). ... Re-signed by Vikings (May 4, 1993). ... Released by Vikings (August 30, 1993). ... Re-signed by Vikings (August 31, 1993). ... Granted unconditional free agency (February 17, 1994). ... Re-signed by Vikings (December 7, 1995). ... Granted unconditional free agency (February 16, 1996).
CHAMPIONSHIP GAME EXPERIENCE: Played in AFC championship game (1983 season).
PRO STATISTICS: 1982—Recovered one fumble. 1983—Recovered one fumble. 1986—Recovered one fumble. 1991—Recovered one fumble. 1992—Recovered one fumble for four yards.

| | | RECEIVING | | | | KICKOFF RETURNS | | | | TOTALS | | | |
Year Team	G	No.	Yds.	Avg.	TD	No.	Yds.	Avg.	TD	TD	2pt.	Pts.	Fum.
1981—Seattle NFL	16	5	47	9.4	0	0	0	...	0	0	...	0	0
1982—Seattle NFL	9	9	46	5.1	0	0	0	...	0	0	...	0	0
1983—Seattle NFL	15	0	0	...	0	2	28	14.0	0	0	...	0	0
1984—Seattle NFL	16	8	90	11.3	3	0	0	...	0	3	...	18	0
1985—Seattle NFL	9	2	13	6.5	0	1	17	17.0	0	0	...	0	0
1986—Seattle NFL	16	15	150	10.0	0	1	17	17.0	0	0	...	0	0
1987—Seattle NFL	12	14	106	7.6	2	0	0	...	0	2	...	12	0
1988—Seattle NFL	16	29	244	8.4	0	1	17	17.0	0	0	...	0	1
1989—Washington NFL	16	1	2	2.0	0	0	0	...	0	0	...	0	0
1990—Seattle NFL	5	0	0	...	0	0	0	...	0	0	...	0	0
1991—Seattle NFL	16	10	70	7.0	4	3	46	15.3	0	4	...	24	0
1992—Minnesota NFL	12	5	65	13.0	1	0	0	...	0	1	...	6	0
1993—Minnesota NFL	16	6	39	6.5	1	0	0	...	0	1	...	6	1
1994—						Did not play.							
1995—Minnesota NFL	3	3	22	7.3	0	0	0	...	0	0	0	0	0
Pro totals (14 years)	177	107	894	8.4	11	8	125	15.6	0	11	0	66	2

TILLMAN, CEDRIC   WR   JAGUARS

PERSONAL: Born July 22, 1970, in Natchez, Miss. ... 6-2/204. ... Full name: Cedric Cornel Tillman.
HIGH SCHOOL: Gulfport (Miss.).
COLLEGE: Alcorn State.
TRANSACTIONS/CAREER NOTES: Selected by Denver Broncos in 11th round (305th pick overall) of 1992 NFL draft. ... Signed by Broncos (1992). ... Released by Broncos (August 31, 1992). ... Re-signed by Broncos to practice squad (September 1, 1992). ... Activated (September 5, 1992). ... Released by Broncos (November 7, 1992). ... Re-signed by Broncos to practice squad (November 11, 1992). ... Activated (December 2, 1992). ... Selected by Jacksonville Jaguars from Broncos in NFL expansion draft (February 15, 1995). ... Granted free agency (February 17, 1995). ... Re-signed with Jaguars (May 19, 1995). ... Released by Jaguars (April 20, 1996).
PRO STATISTICS: 1993—Recovered one fumble. 1995—Returned two punts for six yards.
STATISTICAL PLATEAUS: 100-yard receiving games: 1994 (1).

| | | RECEIVING | | | | TOTALS | | | |
Year Team	G	No.	Yds.	Avg.	TD	TD	2pt.	Pts.	Fum.
1992—Denver NFL	9	12	211	17.6	1	1	...	6	0
1993—Denver NFL	14	17	193	11.4	2	2	...	12	1
1994—Denver NFL	16	28	455	16.3	1	1	0	6	1
1995—Jacksonville NFL	13	30	368	12.3	3	3	0	18	1
Pro totals (4 years)	52	87	1227	14.1	7	7	0	42	3

TILLMAN, LAWYER   TE

PERSONAL: Born May 20, 1966, in Mobile, Ala. ... 6-5/230. ... Full name: Lawyer James Tillman Jr.
HIGH SCHOOL: John LeFlore (Mobile, Ala.).
COLLEGE: Auburn.
TRANSACTIONS/CAREER NOTES: Selected by Cleveland Browns in second round (31st pick overall) of 1989 NFL draft. ... Signed by Browns (September 8, 1989). ... Granted roster exemption (September 8-18, 1989). ... On injured reserve with leg injury (September 4, 1990-entire season). ... On physically unable to perform list with ankle injury (August 26, 1991-entire season). ... Granted free agency (February 1, 1992). ... Re-signed by Browns (August 1, 1992). ... On physically unable to perform list with ankle injury (August 25-October 17, 1992). ... On injured reserve with ankle injury (November 19, 1993-remainder of season). ... Granted unconditional free agency (February 17, 1994). ...

Signed by Carolina Panthers (December 15, 1994). ... On injured reserve with knee injury (October 17, 1995-remainder of season). ... Released by Panthers (January 1996).
CHAMPIONSHIP GAME EXPERIENCE: Played in AFC championship game (1989 season).
HONORS: Named wide receiver on THE SPORTING NEWS college All-America second team (1987).
PRO STATISTICS: 1989—Recovered blocked punt in end zone for a touchdown. 1992—Rushed twice for 15 yards.

		RECEIVING				TOTALS			
Year Team	G	No.	Yds.	Avg.	TD	TD	2pt.	Pts.	Fum.
1989—Cleveland NFL	14	6	70	11.7	2	3	...	18	0
1990—Cleveland NFL				Did not play—injured.					
1991—Cleveland NFL				Did not play.					
1992—Cleveland NFL	11	25	498	19.9	0	0	...	0	1
1993—Cleveland NFL	7	5	68	13.6	1	1	...	6	0
1994—				Did not play.					
1995—Carolina NFL	5	2	22	11.0	0	0	0	0	0
Pro totals (4 years)	37	38	658	17.3	3	4	0	24	1

TILLMAN, LEWIS   RB

PERSONAL: Born April 16, 1966, in Oklahoma City. ... 6-0/204.
HIGH SCHOOL: Hazlehurst (Miss.).
COLLEGE: Jackson State (degree in business management, 1989).
TRANSACTIONS/CAREER NOTES: Selected by New York Giants in fourth round (93rd pick overall) of 1989 NFL draft. ... Signed by Giants (July 24, 1989). ... Granted free agency (February 1, 1992). ... Re-signed by Giants (July 31, 1992). ... Granted unconditional free agency (February 17, 1994). ... Signed by Chicago Bears (April 5, 1994). ... Released by Bears (February 23, 1996).
CHAMPIONSHIP GAME EXPERIENCE: Played in NFC championship game (1990 season). ... Member of Super Bowl championship team (1990 season).
PRO STATISTICS: 1991—Returned two kickoffs for 29 yards. 1995—Returned one kickoff for 20 yards and recovered one fumble.
STATISTICAL PLATEAUS: 100-yard rushing games: 1993 (2), 1994 (2). Total: 4.

		RUSHING				RECEIVING				TOTALS			
Year Team	G	Att.	Yds.	Avg.	TD	No.	Yds.	Avg.	TD	TD	2pt.	Pts.	Fum.
1989—New York Giants NFL	16	79	290	3.7	0	1	9	9.0	0	0	...	0	1
1990—New York Giants NFL	16	84	231	2.8	1	8	18	2.3	0	1	...	6	0
1991—New York Giants NFL	16	65	287	4.4	1	5	30	6.0	0	1	...	6	2
1992—New York Giants NFL	16	6	13	2.2	0	1	15	15.0	0	0	...	0	0
1993—New York Giants NFL	16	121	585	4.8	3	1	21	21.0	0	3	...	18	1
1994—Chicago NFL	16	275	899	3.3	7	27	222	8.2	0	7	0	42	1
1995—Chicago NFL	13	29	78	2.7	0	0	0	...	0	0	0	0	0
Pro totals (7 years)	109	659	2383	3.6	12	43	315	7.3	0	12	0	72	5

TIMMERMAN, ADAM   G   PACKERS

PERSONAL: Born August 14, 1971, in Cherokee, Iowa. ... 6-4/288. ... Full name: Adam Larry Timmerman.
HIGH SCHOOL: Washington (Cherokee, Iowa).
COLLEGE: South Dakota State (degree in agriculture business).
TRANSACTIONS/CAREER NOTES: Selected by Green Bay Packers in seventh round (230th pick overall) of 1995 NFL draft. ... Signed by Packers (June 2, 1995).
PLAYING EXPERIENCE: Green Bay NFL, 1995. ... Games: 1995 (13).
CHAMPIONSHIP GAME EXPERIENCE: Played in NFC championship game (1995 season).

TIMPSON, MICHAEL   WR   BEARS

PERSONAL: Born June 6, 1967, in Baxley, Ga. ... 5-10/180. ... Full name: Michael Dwain Timpson.
HIGH SCHOOL: Hialeah (Fla.) Miami Lakes.
COLLEGE: Penn State.
TRANSACTIONS/CAREER NOTES: Selected after junior season by New England Patriots in fourth round (100th pick overall) of 1989 NFL draft. ... Signed by Patriots (July 18, 1989). ... On injured reserve with hamstring injury (September 9-October 26, 1989). ... On developmental squad (October 27-November 3, 1989). ... On injured reserve with knee injury (November 16, 1989-remainder of season). ... On injured reserve with finger injury (September 4-December 1, 1990). ... Granted free agency (February 1, 1992). ... Re-signed by Patriots (July 27, 1992). ... Granted unconditional free agency (February 17, 1994). ... Re-signed by Patriots (May 24, 1994). ... Granted free agency (February 17, 1995). ... Tendered offer sheet by Chicago Bears (March 8, 1995). ... Patriots declined to match offer (March 15, 1995).
PRO STATISTICS: 1991—Rushed once for minus four yards. 1992—Returned eight punts for 47 yards. 1994—Rushed twice for 14 yards. 1995—Rushed three times for 28 yards and a touchdown and recovered one fumble.
STATISTICAL PLATEAUS: 100-yard receiving games: 1991 (1), 1994 (3). Total: 4.

		RECEIVING				KICKOFF RETURNS				TOTALS			
Year Team	G	No.	Yds.	Avg.	TD	No.	Yds.	Avg.	TD	TD	2pt.	Pts.	Fum.
1989—New England NFL	2	0	0	...	0	2	13	6.5	0	0	...	0	1
1990—New England NFL	5	5	91	18.2	0	3	62	20.7	0	0	...	0	0
1991—New England NFL	16	25	471	18.8	2	2	37	18.5	0	2	...	12	2
1992—New England NFL	16	26	315	12.1	1	2	28	14.0	0	1	...	6	0
1993—New England NFL	16	42	654	15.6	2	0	0	...	0	2	...	12	1
1994—New England NFL	15	74	941	12.7	3	1	28	28.0	0	3	0	18	0
1995—Chicago NFL	16	24	289	12.0	2	18	420	23.3	0	3	0	18	1
Pro totals (7 years)	86	196	2761	14.1	10	28	588	21.0	0	11	0	66	5

TINDALE, TIM   FB   BILLS

PERSONAL: Born April 15, 1971, in London, Ont. ... 5-11/220.
HIGH SCHOOL: Saunders (London, Ont.).
COLLEGE: Western Ontario.
TRANSACTIONS/CAREER NOTES: Signed as non-drafted free agent by Buffalo Bills (May 6, 1994). ... Active for one game (1994); did not play.
PLAYING EXPERIENCE: Buffalo NFL, 1995. ... Games: 1995 (16).
PRO STATISTICS: 1995—Rushed five times for 16 yards, returned six kickoffs for 62 yards and recovered one fumble for two yards.

TIPPINS, KEN   LB   FALCONS

PERSONAL: Born July 22, 1966, in Adel, Ga. ... 6-1/235.
HIGH SCHOOL: Cook (Adel, Ga.).
COLLEGE: Middle Tennessee State.
TRANSACTIONS/CAREER NOTES: Signed as non-drafted free agent by Dallas Cowboys (April 27, 1989). ... Released by Cowboys (September 5, 1989). ... Re-signed by Cowboys to developmental squad (September 11, 1989). ... Activated (September 15, 1989). ... Released by Cowboys (October 24, 1989). ... Re-signed by Cowboys to developmental squad (November 21, 1989). ... Released by Cowboys (January 5, 1990). ... Signed by Atlanta Falcons (May 9, 1990). ... Granted unconditional free agency (February 17, 1994). ... Re-signed by Falcons (June 16, 1994). ... Granted unconditional free agency (February 17, 1995). ... Re-signed by Falcons (April 3, 1995).
PRO STATISTICS: 1991—Intercepted one pass for 35 yards and recovered one fumble for 23 yards and a touchdown. 1992—Recovered one fumble. 1993—Recovered one fumble. 1994—Recovered one fumble. 1995—Returned one kickoff for 15 yards.

Year Team	G	SACKS
1989—Dallas NFL	6	0.0
1990—Atlanta NFL	16	0.0
1991—Atlanta NFL	16	1.0
1992—Atlanta NFL	16	3.0
1993—Atlanta NFL	14	0.0
1994—Atlanta NFL	16	0.0
1995—Atlanta NFL	16	0.0
Pro totals (7 years)	100	4.0

TOBECK, ROBBIE   C   FALCONS

PERSONAL: Born March 6, 1970, in Tarpon Springs, Fla. ... 6-4/287.
HIGH SCHOOL: New Port Richey (Fla.), did not play football.
COLLEGE: Washington State.
TRANSACTIONS/CAREER NOTES: Signed as non-drafted free agent by Atlanta Falcons (May 7, 1993). ... Released by Falcons (August 30, 1993). ... Re-signed by Falcons to practice squad (August 31, 1993). ... Activated (January 1, 1994).
PLAYING EXPERIENCE: Atlanta NFL, 1994 and 1995. ... Games: 1994 (5), 1995 (16). Total: 21.

TOLBERT, TONY   DE   COWBOYS

PERSONAL: Born December 29, 1967, in Tuskegee, Ala. ... 6-6/263. ... Full name: Tony Lewis Tolbert.
HIGH SCHOOL: Dwight Morrow (Englewood, N.J.).
COLLEGE: Texas-El Paso (degree in criminal justice, 1991).
TRANSACTIONS/CAREER NOTES: Selected by Dallas Cowboys in fourth round (85th pick overall) of 1989 NFL draft. ... Signed by Cowboys (July 23, 1989). ... Granted free agency (February 1, 1992). ... Re-signed by Cowboys (August 23, 1992). ... Granted roster exemption (August 23-September 2, 1992). ... Granted unconditional free agency (February 17, 1995). ... Re-signed by Cowboys (February 22, 1995).
CHAMPIONSHIP GAME EXPERIENCE: Played in NFC championship game (1992-1995 seasons). ... Member of Super Bowl championship team (1992, 1993 and 1995 seasons).
PRO STATISTICS: 1991—Recovered one fumble. 1994—Intercepted one pass for 54 yards and a touchdown and recovered one fumble.

Year Team	G	SACKS
1989—Dallas NFL	16	2.0
1990—Dallas NFL	16	6.0
1991—Dallas NFL	16	7.0
1992—Dallas NFL	16	8.5
1993—Dallas NFL	16	7.5
1994—Dallas NFL	16	5.5
1995—Dallas NFL	16	5.5
Pro totals (7 years)	112	42.0

TOMCZAK, MIKE   QB   STEELERS

PERSONAL: Born October 23, 1962, in Calumet City, Ill. ... 6-1/201. ... Full name: Michael John Tomczak. ... Name pronounced TOM-zak.
HIGH SCHOOL: Thornton Fractional North (Calumet City, Ill.).
COLLEGE: Ohio State.
TRANSACTIONS/CAREER NOTES: Selected by New Jersey Generals in 1985 USFL territorial draft. ... Signed as non-drafted free agent by Chicago Bears (May 9, 1985). ... Granted free agency (February 1, 1990). ... Re-signed by Bears (July 25, 1990). ... Granted unconditional free agency (February 1, 1991). ... Signed by Green Bay Packers (March 30, 1991). ... Granted free agency (February 1, 1992). ... Re-signed by Packers (August 19, 1992). ... Released by Packers (August 31, 1992). ... Signed by Cleveland Browns (September 16, 1992). ... Granted unconditional free agency (March 1, 1993). ... Signed by Pittsburgh Steelers (April 6, 1993).
CHAMPIONSHIP GAME EXPERIENCE: Member of Bears for NFC championship game (1985 season); did not play. ... Member of Super Bowl championship team (1985 season). ... Played in NFC championship game (1988 season). ... Member of Steelers for AFC championship game

(1994 and 1995 seasons); did not play. ... Member of Steelers for Super Bowl XXX (1995 season); did not play.

PRO STATISTICS: 1985—Fumbled once and recovered one fumble for minus 13 yards. 1986—Fumbled twice. 1987—Fumbled six times and recovered one fumble. 1988—Fumbled once. 1989—Fumbled twice. 1990—Caught one pass for five yards and fumbled twice. 1991—Fumbled five times and recovered two fumbles for minus one yard. 1992—Fumbled five times. 1993—Fumbled twice and recovered one fumble. 1994—Fumbled twice. 1995—Fumbled twice and recovered one fumble.

STATISTICAL PLATEAUS: 300-yard passing games: 1989 (1), 1991 (1), 1992 (1), 1994 (1). Total: 4.

MISCELLANEOUS: Regular-season record as starting NFL quarterback: 31-22 (.585).

Year Team	G	PASSING								RUSHING				TOTALS		
		Att.	Cmp.	Pct.	Yds.	TD	Int.	Avg.	Rat.	Att.	Yds.	Avg.	TD	TD	2pt.	Pts.
1985—Chicago NFL	6	6	2	33.3	33	0	0	5.50	52.8	2	3	1.5	0	0	...	0
1986—Chicago NFL	13	151	74	49.0	1105	2	10	7.32	50.2	23	117	5.1	3	3	...	18
1987—Chicago NFL	12	178	97	54.5	1220	5	10	6.85	62.0	18	54	3.0	1	1	...	6
1988—Chicago NFL	14	170	86	50.6	1310	7	6	7.71	75.4	13	40	3.1	1	1	...	6
1989—Chicago NFL	16	306	156	51.0	2058	16	16	6.73	68.2	24	71	3.0	1	1	...	6
1990—Chicago NFL	16	104	39	37.5	521	3	5	5.01	43.8	12	41	3.4	2	2	...	12
1991—Green Bay NFL	12	238	128	53.8	1490	11	9	6.26	72.6	17	93	5.5	1	1	...	6
1992—Cleveland NFL	12	211	120	56.9	1693	7	7	8.02	80.1	24	39	1.6	0	0	...	0
1993—Pittsburgh NFL	7	54	29	53.7	398	2	5	7.37	51.3	5	-4	-0.8	0	0	...	0
1994—Pittsburgh NFL	6	93	54	58.1	804	4	0	8.65	100.8	4	22	5.5	0	0	0	0
1995—Pittsburgh NFL	7	113	65	57.5	666	1	9	5.89	44.3	11	25	2.3	0	0	0	0
Pro totals (11 years)	121	1624	850	52.3	11298	58	77	6.96	66.8	153	501	3.3	9	9	0	54

TOVAR, STEVE　　　　　　　　LB　　　　　　　　BENGALS

PERSONAL: Born April 25, 1970, in Elyria, Ohio. ... 6-3/244. ... Full name: Steven Eric Tovar.

HIGH SCHOOL: West (Elyria, Ohio).

COLLEGE: Ohio State.

TRANSACTIONS/CAREER NOTES: Selected by the Cincinnati Bengals in third round (59th pick overall) of 1993 NFL draft. ... Signed by Bengals (July 19, 1993). ... Granted free agency (February 16, 1996). ... Re-signed by Bengals (April 15, 1996).

PRO STATISTICS: 1993—Recovered one fumble. 1994—Returned one kickoff for eight yards and recovered two fumbles.

Year Team	G	INTERCEPTIONS				SACKS
		No.	Yds.	Avg.	TD	No.
1993—Cincinnati NFL	16	1	0	0.0	0	0.0
1994—Cincinnati NFL	16	1	14	14.0	0	3.0
1995—Cincinnati NFL	14	1	13	13.0	0	1.0
Pro totals (3 years)	46	3	27	9.0	0	4.0

TRAPP, JAMES　　　　　　　　CB　　　　　　　　RAIDERS

PERSONAL: Born December 28, 1969, in Greenville, S.C. ... 6-0/180. ... Full name: James Harold Trapp.

HIGH SCHOOL: Lawton (Okla.).

COLLEGE: Clemson.

TRANSACTIONS/CAREER NOTES: Selected by Los Angeles Raiders in third round (72nd pick overall) of 1993 NFL draft. ... Signed by Raiders (July 13, 1993). ... Raiders franchise moved to Oakland (July 21, 1995). ... Granted free agency (February 16, 1996). ... Re-signed by Raiders (March 30, 1996).

PLAYING EXPERIENCE: Los Angeles Raiders NFL, 1993 and 1994; Oakland NFL, 1995. ... Games: 1993 (14), 1994 (16), 1995 (14). Total: 44.

PRO STATISTICS: 1993—Intercepted one pass for seven yards. 1994—Credited with one sack. 1995—Recovered one fumble.

TRAYLOR, KEITH　　　　　　　　DT　　　　　　　　CHIEFS

PERSONAL: Born September 3, 1969, in Malvern, Ark. ... 6-2/295. ... Full name: Byron Keith Traylor. ... Cousin of Isaac Davis, guard, San Diego Chargers.

HIGH SCHOOL: Malvern (Ark.).

JUNIOR COLLEGE: Coffeyville (Kan.) Community College.

COLLEGE: Oklahoma, then Central Oklahoma.

TRANSACTIONS/CAREER NOTES: Selected by Denver Broncos in third round (61st pick overall) of 1991 NFL draft. ... Released by Broncos (June 7, 1993). ... Signed by Los Angeles Raiders (June 1993). ... Released by Raiders (August 30, 1993). ... Signed by Green Bay Packers (September 14, 1993). ... Released by Packers (November 9, 1993). ... Signed by Kansas City Chiefs (January 7, 1994). ... Released by Chiefs (January 14, 1994). ... Re-signed by Chiefs (May 18, 1994). ... Released by Chiefs (August 28, 1994). ... Re-signed by Chiefs (February 28, 1995).

PLAYING EXPERIENCE: Denver NFL, 1991 and 1992; Green Bay NFL, 1993; Kansas City NFL, 1995. ... Games: 1991 (16), 1992 (16), 1993 (5), 1995 (16). Total: 53.

CHAMPIONSHIP GAME EXPERIENCE: Played in AFC championship game (1991 season).

PRO STATISTICS: 1992—Credited with one sack and returned one kickoff for 13 yards. 1995—Credited with 1½ sacks and recovered one fumble.

TREMBLE, GREG　　　　　　　　S

PERSONAL: Born April 16, 1972, in Warner Robbins, Ga. ... 5-11/188. ... Full name: Gregory Deshawn Tremble.

HIGH SCHOOL: Warner Robbins (Ga.).

JUNIOR COLLEGE: Northeast Oklahoma A&M.

COLLEGE: Georgia.

TRANSACTIONS/CAREER NOTES: Signed as non-drafted free agent by Cleveland Browns (May 2, 1994). ... Released by Browns (August 22, 1994). ... Signed by Dallas Cowboys (March 9, 1995). ... Released by Cowboys (October 16, 1995). ... Signed by Philadelphia Eagles (October 21, 1995). ... Released by Eagles (November 21, 1995).

PLAYING EXPERIENCE: Dallas (7)-Philadelphia (4) NFL, 1995. ... Games: 1995 (11).

TRUDEAU, JACK   QB

PERSONAL: Born September 9, 1962, in Forest Lake, Minn. ... 6-3/227. ... Full name: Jack Francis Trudeau.
HIGH SCHOOL: Granada (Livermore, Calif.).
COLLEGE: Illinois (degree in political science, 1986).
TRANSACTIONS/CAREER NOTES: Selected by Orlando Renegades in 1986 USFL territorial draft. ... Selected by Indianapolis Colts in second round (47th pick overall) of 1986 NFL draft. ... Signed by Colts (July 31, 1986). ... On injured reserve with knee injury (October 11, 1988-remainder of season). ... On injured reserve with knee injury (October 31, 1990-remainder of season). ... On injured reserve with thumb injury (October 16, 1991-remainder of season). ... Granted free agency (February 1, 1992). ... Re-signed by Colts (August 27, 1992). ... Granted roster exemption (August 27-September 7, 1992). ... Released by Colts (April 7, 1994). ... Signed by New York Jets (May 5, 1994). ... Selected by Carolina Panthers from Jets in NFL expansion draft (February 15, 1995). ... Granted unconditional free agency (February 16, 1996).
PRO STATISTICS: 1986—Led league with 13 fumbles and recovered six fumbles for minus 15 yards. 1987—Fumbled 10 times and recovered two fumbles for minus 28 yards. 1989—Fumbled 10 times and recovered seven fumbles for minus five yards. 1990—Fumbled 11 times and recovered four fumbles. 1992—Fumbled three times and recovered two fumbles for minus 12 yards. 1993—Fumbled twice and recovered one fumble for minus three yards. 1994—Fumbled twice and recovered one fumble for minus one yard. 1995—Fumbled once.
STATISTICAL PLATEAUS: 300-yard passing games: 1986 (2), 1990 (2), 1992 (1). Total: 5.
MISCELLANEOUS: Regular-season record as starting NFL quarterback: 19-30 (.388).

					PASSING						RUSHING				TOTALS		
Year Team	G	Att.	Cmp.	Pct.	Yds.	TD	Int.	Avg.	Rat.	Att.	Yds.	Avg.	TD	TD	2pt.	Pts.
1986—Indianapolis NFL	12	417	204	48.9	2225	8	18	5.34	53.5	13	21	1.6	1	1	...	6
1987—Indianapolis NFL	10	229	128	55.9	1587	6	6	6.93	75.4	15	7	0.5	0	0	...	0
1988—Indianapolis NFL	2	34	14	41.2	158	0	3	4.65	19.0	0	0	...	0	0	...	0
1989—Indianapolis NFL	13	362	190	52.5	2317	15	13	6.40	71.3	35	91	2.6	2	2	...	12
1990—Indianapolis NFL	6	144	84	58.3	1078	6	6	7.49	78.4	10	28	2.8	0	0	...	0
1991—Indianapolis NFL	2	7	2	28.6	19	0	1	2.72	0.0	0	0	...	0	0	...	0
1992—Indianapolis NFL	11	181	105	58.0	1271	4	8	7.02	68.6	13	6	0.5	0	0	...	0
1993—Indianapolis NFL	5	162	85	52.5	992	2	7	6.12	57.4	5	3	0.6	0	0	...	0
1994—New York Jets NFL	5	91	50	55.0	496	1	4	5.45	55.9	6	30	5.0	0	0	0	0
1995—Carolina NFL	1	17	11	64.7	100	0	3	5.88	40.9	0	0	...	0	0	0	0
Pro totals (10 years)	67	1644	873	53.1	10243	42	69	6.23	63.3	97	186	1.9	3	3	0	18

TRUITT, GREG   C   BENGALS

PERSONAL: Born December 8, 1965, in Sarasota, Fla. ... 6-0/235.
HIGH SCHOOL: Riverview (Sarasota, Fla.).
COLLEGE: Penn State.
TRANSACTIONS/CAREER NOTES: Signed as non-drafted free agent by Cincinnati Bengals (April 6, 1994).
PLAYING EXPERIENCE: Cincinnati NFL, 1994 and 1995. ... Games: 1994 (16), 1995 (16). Total: 32.

TRUITT, OLANDA   WR

PERSONAL: Born January 4, 1971, in Birmingham, Ala. ... 6-0/186.
HIGH SCHOOL: A.H. Parker (Birmingham, Ala.).
COLLEGE: Pittsburgh, then Mississippi State.
TRANSACTIONS/CAREER NOTES: Selected after junior season by Los Angeles Raiders in fifth round (125th pick overall) of 1993 NFL draft. ... Signed by Raiders (July 19, 1993). ... Claimed on waivers by Minnesota Vikings (August 31, 1993). ... Released by Vikings (August 27, 1994). ... Signed by Washington Redskins (August 29, 1994). ... Released by Redskins (August 27, 1995). ... Re-signed by Redskins (October 17, 1995). ... Granted unconditional free agency (February 16, 1996).

		RECEIVING				TOTALS			
Year Team	G	No.	Yds.	Avg.	TD	TD	2pt.	Pts.	Fum.
1993—Minnesota NFL	8	4	40	10.0	0	0	...	0	0
1994—Washington NFL	9	2	89	44.5	1	1	0	6	0
1995—Washington NFL	5	9	154	17.1	1	1	0	6	1
Pro totals (3 years)	22	15	283	18.9	2	2	0	12	1

TUAOLO, ESERA   DT   VIKINGS

PERSONAL: Born July 11, 1968, in Honolulu. ... 6-3/276. ... Full name: Esera Tavai Tuaolo. ... Name pronounced ess-ER-uh TOO-ah-OH-lo.
HIGH SCHOOL: Don Antonio Lugo (Chino, Calif.).
COLLEGE: Oregon State.
TRANSACTIONS/CAREER NOTES: Selected by Green Bay Packers in second round (35th pick overall) of 1991 NFL draft. ... Signed by Packers (July 19, 1991). ... Released by Packers (October 1, 1992). ... Signed by Minnesota Vikings (November 24, 1992). ... Granted free agency (February 17, 1994). ... Re-signed by Vikings (July 18, 1994). ... Granted unconditional free agency (February 17, 1995). ... Re-signed by Vikings (March 7, 1995).
PRO STATISTICS: 1991—Intercepted one pass for 23 yards. 1995—Recovered two fumbles.

Year Team	G	SACKS
1991—Green Bay NFL	16	3.5
1992—Green Bay NFL	4	1.0
—Minnesota NFL	3	0.0
1993—Minnesota NFL	11	0.0
1994—Minnesota NFL	16	0.0
1995—Minnesota NFL	16	3.0
Pro totals (5 years)	66	7.5

TUATAGALOA, NATU   DE

PERSONAL: Born May 25, 1966, in San Francisco. ... 6-4/275. ... Full name: Gerardus Mauritius Natuitasina Tuatagaloa. ... Name pronounced NA-too TOO-un-TAG-uh-LOW-uh.
HIGH SCHOOL: San Rafael (Calif.).
COLLEGE: California (degree in history, 1989).
TRANSACTIONS/CAREER NOTES: Selected by Cincinnati Bengals in fifth round (138th pick overall) of 1989 NFL draft. ... Signed by Bengals (July 22, 1989). ... Granted unconditional free agency (February 1-April 1, 1991). ... Re-signed by Bengals for 1991 season. ... Granted free agency (February 1, 1992). ... Rights relinquished by Bengals (September 11, 1992). ... Signed by Seattle Seahawks (September 16, 1992). ... Granted free agency (March 1, 1993). ... Re-signed by Seahawks (July 20, 1993). ... Granted unconditional free agency (February 17, 1994). ... Signed by New Orleans Saints (February 22, 1995). ... Released by Saints (August 27, 1995). ... Signed by Houston Oilers (November 21, 1995). ... Granted unconditional free agency (February 16, 1996).
PRO STATISTICS: 1990—Recovered two fumbles. 1992—Intercepted one pass for no yards. 1993—Returned one kickoff for 10 yards and recovered one fumble for no yards.

Year—Team	G	SACKS
1989—Cincinnati NFL	14	2.5
1990—Cincinnati NFL	16	4.5
1991—Cincinnati NFL	16	2.0
1992—Seattle NFL	13	3.0
1993—Seattle NFL	16	3.5
1994—	Did not play.	
1995—Houston NFL	1	0.0
Pro totals (6 years)	76	15.5

TUBBS, WINFRED   LB   SAINTS

PERSONAL: Born September 24, 1970, in Hollywood, Fla. ... 6-4/250. ... Full name: Winfred O'Neal Tubbs.
HIGH SCHOOL: Fairfield (Texas).
COLLEGE: Texas.
TRANSACTIONS/CAREER NOTES: Selected by New Orleans Saints in third round (79th pick overall) of 1994 NFL draft. ... Signed by Saints (July 20, 1994). ... On injured reserve with knee injury (December 22, 1995-remainder of season).
PRO STATISTICS: 1995—Recovered one fumble.

Year—Team	G	INTERCEPTIONS No.	Yds.	Avg.	TD	SACKS No.
1994—New Orleans NFL	13	1	0	0.0	0	1.0
1995—New Orleans NFL	7	1	6	6.0	0	1.0
Pro totals (2 years)	20	2	6	3.0	0	2.0

TUGGLE, JESSIE   LB   FALCONS

PERSONAL: Born February 14, 1965, in Spalding County, Ga. ... 5-11/230. ... Full name: Jessie Lloyd Tuggle.
HIGH SCHOOL: Griffin (Ga.).
COLLEGE: Valdosta (Ga.) State.
TRANSACTIONS/CAREER NOTES: Signed as non-drafted free agent by Atlanta Falcons (May 2, 1987). ... Granted free agency (February 1, 1991). ... Re-signed by Falcons (August 7, 1991). ... On reserve/did not report list (July 23-August 30, 1993). ... Granted roster exemption (August 30-September 3, 1993).
HONORS: Played in Pro Bowl (1992, 1994 and 1995 seasons).
RECORDS: Holds NFL career record for most touchdowns by recovery of opponents' fumbles—4. ... Shares NFL career record for most touchdowns by fumble recovery—4.
PRO STATISTICS: 1988—Recovered one fumble for two yards and a touchdown. 1989—Recovered one fumble. 1990—Recovered two fumbles for 65 yards and one touchdown. 1991—Recovered two fumbles for 18 yards and one touchdown. 1992—Recovered one fumble for 69 yards and a touchdown. 1993—Recovered one fumble. 1994—Recovered one fumble.

Year—Team	G	INTERCEPTIONS No.	Yds.	Avg.	TD	SACKS No.
1987—Atlanta NFL	12	0	0	...	0	1.0
1988—Atlanta NFL	16	0	0	...	0	0.0
1989—Atlanta NFL	16	0	0	...	0	1.0
1990—Atlanta NFL	16	0	0	...	0	5.0
1991—Atlanta NFL	16	1	21	21.0	0	1.0
1992—Atlanta NFL	15	1	1	1.0	0	1.0
1993—Atlanta NFL	16	0	0	...	0	2.0
1994—Atlanta NFL	16	1	0	0.0	0	0.0
1995—Atlanta NFL	16	3	84	28.0	1	1.0
Pro totals (9 years)	139	6	106	17.7	1	12.0

TUINEI, MARK   OT   COWBOYS

PERSONAL: Born March 31, 1960, in Nanakuli, Oahu, Hawaii. ... 6-5/305. ... Full name: Mark Pulemau Tuinei. ... Brother of Tom Tuinei, defensive end, Edmonton Eskimos of CFL (1982-1987). ... Name pronounced TOO-ee-nay.
HIGH SCHOOL: Punahou (Honolulu).
COLLEGE: UCLA, then Hawaii.
TRANSACTIONS/CAREER NOTES: Selected by Boston Breakers in 19th round (227th pick overall) of 1983 USFL draft. ... Signed as non-drafted free agent by Dallas Cowboys (April 28, 1983). ... On injured reserve with knee injury (December 2, 1987-remainder of season). ... On injured reserve with knee injury (October 19, 1988-remainder of season). ... Granted free agency (February 1, 1990). ... Re-signed by Cowboys (May 21, 1990).

PLAYING EXPERIENCE: Dallas NFL, 1983-1995. ... Games: 1983 (10), 1984 (16), 1985 (16), 1986 (16), 1987 (8), 1988 (5), 1989 (16), 1990 (13), 1991 (12), 1992 (15), 1993 (16), 1994 (15), 1995 (16). Total: 174.
CHAMPIONSHIP GAME EXPERIENCE: Played in NFC championship game (1992-1995 seasons). ... Member of Super Bowl championship team (1992, 1993 and 1995 seasons).
HONORS: Played in Pro Bowl (1994 and 1995 seasons).
PRO STATISTICS: 1984—Credited with one sack. 1986—Returned one kickoff for no yards, fumbled once and recovered three fumbles. 1987—Recovered one fumble. 1993—Recovered one fumble.
MISCELLANEOUS: Switched from defensive lineman to offensive lineman (1985).

TUPA, TOM　　　　　　　　　　P/QB　　　　　　　　　　PATRIOTS

PERSONAL: Born February 6, 1966, in Cleveland. ... 6-4/230. ... Full name: Thomas Joseph Tupa.
HIGH SCHOOL: Brecksville (Broadview Heights, Ohio).
COLLEGE: Ohio State.
TRANSACTIONS/CAREER NOTES: Selected by Phoenix Cardinals in third round (68th pick overall) of 1988 NFL draft. ... Signed by Cardinals (July 12, 1988). ... Granted free agency (February 1, 1991). ... Re-signed by Cardinals (July 17, 1991). ... Granted unconditional free agency (February 1, 1992). ... Signed by Indianapolis Colts (March 31, 1992). ... Released by Colts (August 30, 1993). ... Signed by Cleveland Browns (November 9, 1993). ... Released by Browns (November 24, 1993). ... Re-signed by Browns (March 30, 1994). ... Granted unconditional free agency (February 16, 1996). ... Signed by New England Patriots (March 14, 1996).
PRO STATISTICS: 1988—Attempted six passes with four completions for 49 yards. 1989—Rushed 15 times for 75 yards, attempted 134 passes with 65 completions for 973 yards (three touchdowns and nine interceptions), fumbled twice and recovered one fumble for minus six yards. 1990—Rushed once for no yards and fumbled once for minus seven yards. 1991—Rushed 28 times for 97 yards and a touchdown, attempted 315 passes with 165 completions for 2,053 yards (six touchdowns and 13 interceptions), fumbled eight times and recovered two fumbles. 1992—Rushed three times for nine yards, attempted 33 passes with 17 completions for 156 yards (one touchdown and two interceptions), fumbled once and recovered one fumble for minus one yard. 1995—Rushed once for nine yards, attempted one pass with one completion for 25 yards.
MISCELLANEOUS: Regular-season record as starting NFL quarterback: 4-9 (.308).

Year Team	G	No.	Yds.	Avg.	Net avg.	In. 20	Blk.
1988—Phoenix NFL	2	0	0	...	...	0	0
1989—Phoenix NFL	14	6	280	46.7	39.8	2	0
1990—Phoenix NFL	15	0	0	...	...	0	0
1991—Phoenix NFL	11	0	0	...	...	0	0
1992—Indianapolis NFL	3	0	0	...	...	0	0
1993—Cleveland NFL				Did not play.			
1994—Cleveland NFL	16	80	3211	40.1	35.4	27	0
1995—Cleveland NFL	16	65	2831	43.6	36.2	18	0
Pro totals (7 years)	77	151	6322	41.9	35.9	47	0

TURK, DAN　　　　　　　　　　C　　　　　　　　　　RAIDERS

PERSONAL: Born June 25, 1962, in Milwaukee. ... 6-4/290. ... Full name: Daniel Anthony Turk. ... Brother of Matt Turk, punter, Washington Redskins.
HIGH SCHOOL: James Madison (Milwaukee).
COLLEGE: Drake, then Wisconsin.
TRANSACTIONS/CAREER NOTES: Selected by Jacksonville Bulls in USFL territorial draft. ... USFL rights traded by Bulls with rights to RB Marck Harrison and TE Ken Whisenhunt to Tampa Bay Bandits for rights to RB Cedric Jones, K Bobby Raymond and DB Eric Riley (January 3, 1985). ... Selected by Pittsburgh Steelers in fourth round (101st pick overall) of 1985 NFL draft. ... Signed by Steelers (July 19, 1985). ... On injured reserve with broken wrist (September 16, 1985-remainder of season). ... Traded by Steelers to Tampa Bay Buccaneers for sixth-round pick (DE Tim Johnson) in 1987 draft (April 13, 1987). ... Crossed picket line during players strike (October 14, 1987). ... On injured reserve with knee injury (October 18-November 18, 1988). ... Granted free agency (February 1, 1989). ... Rights relinquished by Buccaneers (June 6, 1989). ... Signed by Los Angeles Raiders (June 21, 1989). ... Granted free agency (February 1, 1991). ... Re-signed by Raiders (July 12, 1991). ... Granted unconditional free agency (February 17, 1994). ... Re-signed by Raiders (February 23, 1994). ... Raiders franchise moved to Oakland (July 21, 1995).
PLAYING EXPERIENCE: Pittsburgh NFL, 1985 and 1986; Tampa Bay NFL, 1987 and 1988; Los Angeles Raiders NFL, 1989-1994; Oakland NFL, 1995. ... Games: 1985 (1), 1986 (16), 1987 (13), 1988 (12), 1989 (16), 1990 (16), 1991 (16), 1992 (16), 1993 (16), 1994 (16), 1995 (16). Total: 154.
CHAMPIONSHIP GAME EXPERIENCE: Played in AFC championship game (1990 season).
PRO STATISTICS: 1988—Fumbled once and recovered one fumble for minus 19 yards. 1989—Returned one kickoff for two yards and fumbled once for minus eight yards. 1990—Returned one kickoff for seven yards. 1991—Returned one kickoff for no yards. 1992—Returned one kickoff for three yards. 1993—Returned one kickoff for no yards and recovered one fumble.

TURK, MATT　　　　　　　　　　P　　　　　　　　　　REDSKINS

PERSONAL: Born June 16, 1968, in Greenfield, Wis. ... 6-5/230. ... Brother of Dan Turk, center, Oakland Raiders.
HIGH SCHOOL: Greenfield (Wis.).
COLLEGE: Wisconsin-Whitewater.
TRANSACTIONS/CAREER NOTES: Signed as non-drafted free agent by Green Bay Packers (July 13, 1993). ... Released by Packers (August 4, 1993). ... Signed by Los Angeles Rams (April 1994). ... Released by Rams (August 22, 1994). ... Signed by Washington Redskins (April 5, 1995).

Year Team	G	No.	Yds.	Avg.	Net avg.	In. 20	Blk.
1993—				Did not play.			
1994—				Did not play			
1995—Washington NFL	16	74	3140	42.4	37.7	29	0

TURNBULL, RENALDO DE SAINTS

PERSONAL: Born January 5, 1966, in St. Thomas, Virgin Islands. ... 6-4/250. ... Full name: Renaldo Antonio Turnbull.
HIGH SCHOOL: Charlotte Amalie (St. Thomas, Virgin Islands).
COLLEGE: West Virginia (degree in communications).
TRANSACTIONS/CAREER NOTES: Selected by New Orleans Saints in first round (14th pick overall) of 1990 NFL draft. ... Signed by Saints (July 15, 1990).
HONORS: Played in Pro Bowl (1993 season).
PRO STATISTICS: 1990—Recovered one fumble. 1991—Recovered one fumble. 1993—Intercepted one pass for two yards and recovered two fumbles. 1995—Recovered two fumbles.

Year Team	G	SACKS
1990—New Orleans NFL	16	9.0
1991—New Orleans NFL	16	1.0
1992—New Orleans NFL	14	1.5
1993—New Orleans NFL	15	13.0
1994—New Orleans NFL	16	6.5
1995—New Orleans NFL	15	7.0
Pro totals (6 years)	92	38.0

TURNER, ERIC S RAVENS

PERSONAL: Born September 20, 1968, in Ventura, Calif. ... 6-1/207. ... Full name: Eric Ray Turner.
HIGH SCHOOL: Ventura (Calif.).
COLLEGE: UCLA (degree in history, 1992).
TRANSACTIONS/CAREER NOTES: Selected by Cleveland Browns in first round (second pick overall) of 1991 NFL draft. ... Signed by Browns (July 14, 1991). ... On injured reserve with stress fracture in leg (August 28-November 2, 1991). ... Designated by Browns as transition player (February 25, 1993). ... Free agency status changed by Browns from transitional to franchise player (February 15, 1995). ... On injured reserve with back injury (December 15, 1995). ... Browns franchise moved to Baltimore and renamed Ravens for 1996 season (March 11, 1996).
HONORS: Played in Pro Bowl (1994 season).
PRO STATISTICS: 1991—Recovered one fumble. 1992—Credited with one sack and recovered two fumbles. 1994—Credited with one sack, returned one punt for no yards and recovered one fumble.

		INTERCEPTIONS			
Year Team	G	No.	Yds.	Avg.	TD
1991—Cleveland NFL	8	2	42	21.0	1
1992—Cleveland NFL	15	1	6	6.0	0
1993—Cleveland NFL	16	5	25	5.0	0
1994—Cleveland NFL	16	†9	199	22.1	1
1995—Cleveland NFL	8	0	0	...	0
Pro totals (5 years)	63	17	272	16.0	2

TURNER, FLOYD WR

PERSONAL: Born May 29, 1966, in Shreveport, La. ... 5-11/198.
HIGH SCHOOL: Mansfield (La.).
COLLEGE: Northwestern (La.) State (degree in education).
TRANSACTIONS/CAREER NOTES: Selected by New Orleans Saints in sixth round (159th pick overall) of 1989 NFL draft. ... Signed by Saints (July 22, 1989). ... On injured reserve with broken arm (December 6, 1989-remainder of season). ... Granted free agency (February 1, 1991). ... Re-signed by Saints (July 17, 1991). ... On injured reserve with leg injury (September 14, 1992-remainder of season). ... Granted free agency (March 1, 1993). ... Re-signed by Saints (July 23, 1993). ... Granted unconditional free agency (February 17, 1994). ... Signed by Indianapolis Colts (May 5, 1994). ... Granted unconditional free agency (February 16, 1996).
CHAMPIONSHIP GAME EXPERIENCE: Played in AFC championship game (1995 season).
PRO STATISTICS: 1989—Rushed twice for eight yards, returned one punt for seven yards and recovered three fumbles. 1992—Returned three punts for 10 yards. 1994—Rushed three times for minus three yards and recovered one fumble.
STATISTICAL PLATEAUS: 100-yard receiving games: 1991 (3).

		RECEIVING				TOTALS			
Year Team	G	No.	Yds.	Avg.	TD	TD	2pt.	Pts.	Fum.
1989—New Orleans NFL	13	22	279	12.7	1	1	...	6	7
1990—New Orleans NFL	16	21	396	18.9	4	4	...	24	0
1991—New Orleans NFL	16	64	927	14.5	8	8	...	48	1
1992—New Orleans NFL	2	5	43	8.6	0	0	...	0	2
1993—New Orleans NFL	10	12	163	13.6	1	1	...	6	0
1994—Indianapolis NFL	16	52	593	11.4	6	6	0	36	1
1995—Indianapolis NFL	14	35	431	12.3	4	4	2	28	0
Pro totals (7 years)	87	211	2832	13.4	24	24	2	148	5

TURNER, KEVIN FB EAGLES

PERSONAL: Born June 12, 1969, in Prattville, Ala. ... 6-1/231. ... Full name: Paul Kevin Turner.
HIGH SCHOOL: Prattville (Ala.).
COLLEGE: Alabama.
TRANSACTIONS/CAREER NOTES: Selected by New England Patriots in third round (71st pick overall) of 1992 NFL draft. ... Signed by Patriots (July 21, 1992). ... Granted free agency (February 17, 1995). ... Tendered offer sheet by Philadelphia Eagles (February 26, 1995). ... Patriots declined to match offer (March 2, 1995). ... On injured reserve with knee injury (September 15, 1995-remainder of season).
PRO STATISTICS: 1992—Returned one kickoff for 11 yards and recovered two fumbles. 1993—Attempted one pass without a completion

and recovered two fumbles for six yards. 1994—Recovered two fumbles for minus three yards.

Year Team	G	RUSHING				RECEIVING				TOTALS			
		Att.	Yds.	Avg.	TD	No.	Yds.	Avg.	TD	TD	2pt.	Pts.	Fum.
1992—New England NFL	16	10	40	4.0	0	7	52	7.4	2	2	...	12	2
1993—New England NFL	16	50	231	4.6	0	39	333	8.5	2	2	...	12	1
1994—New England NFL	16	36	111	3.1	1	52	471	9.1	2	3	0	18	4
1995—Philadelphia NFL	2	2	9	4.5	0	4	29	7.3	0	0	0	0	0
Pro totals (4 years)	50	98	391	4.0	1	102	885	8.7	6	7	0	42	7

TURNER, MARCUS — CB/S

PERSONAL: Born January 13, 1966, in Harbor City, Calif. ... 6-0/190. ... Full name: Marcus Jared Turner.
HIGH SCHOOL: David Starr Jordan (Long Beach, Calif.).
COLLEGE: UCLA.
TRANSACTIONS/CAREER NOTES: Selected by Kansas City Chiefs in 11th round (283rd pick overall) of 1989 NFL draft. ... Signed by Chiefs (July 21, 1989). ... Released by Chiefs (September 5, 1989). ... Signed by Phoenix Cardinals to developmental squad (September 6, 1989). ... Activated (September 29, 1989). ... Granted free agency (February 1, 1991). ... Re-signed by Cardinals (July 21, 1991). ... On injured reserve with ear injury (September 18, 1991-remainder of season). ... Granted unconditional free agency (February 1, 1992). ... Signed by New York Jets (March 31, 1992). ... Released by Jets (August 30, 1993). ... Re-signed by Jets (August 31, 1993). ... Granted unconditional free agency (February 17, 1995). ... Re-signed by Jets (February 21, 1995). ... On injured reserve with concussion (October 31, 1995-remainder of season). ... Traded by Jets to Green Bay Packers for conditional pick in 1997 draft (March 13, 1996). ... Released by Packers (April 2, 1996).
PRO STATISTICS: 1989—Recovered one fumble. 1990—Ran with lateral from interception 23 yards for a touchdown and recovered one fumble. 1991—Recovered one fumble. 1992—Recovered one fumble. 1993—Credited with one sack and recovered one fumble for seven yards. 1994—Recovered one fumble.

Year Team	G	INTERCEPTIONS			
		No.	Yds.	Avg.	TD
1989—Phoenix NFL	13	0	0	...	0
1990—Phoenix NFL	16	1	47	47.0	1
1991—Phoenix NFL	3	0	0	...	0
1992—New York Jets NFL	16	2	15	7.5	0
1993—New York Jets NFL	16	0	0	...	0
1994—New York Jets NFL	16	5	155	31.0	1
1995—New York Jets NFL	6	0	0	...	0
Pro totals (7 years)	86	6	202	33.7	2

TURNER, NATE — RB

PERSONAL: Born May 28, 1969, in Chicago. ... 6-1/255.
HIGH SCHOOL: Mount Carmel (Chicago).
COLLEGE: Nebraska.
TRANSACTIONS/CAREER NOTES: Selected by Buffalo Bills in sixth round (167th pick overall) of 1992 NFL draft. ... Signed by Bills (July 22, 1992). ... On injured reserve with back injury (September 5, 1992-entire season). ... Released by Bills (August 22, 1995). ... Signed by Carolina Panthers (October 3, 1995). ... On injured reserve with broken kneecap (November 8, 1995-remainder of season). ... Granted unconditional free agency (February 16, 1996).
CHAMPIONSHIP GAME EXPERIENCE: Member of Buffalo Bills for AFC championship game (1993 season); did not play. ... Member of Buffalo Bills for Super Bowl XXVIII (1993 season); did not play.

Year Team	G	RUSHING				RECEIVING				KICKOFF RETURNS				TOTALS			
		Att.	Yds.	Avg.	TD	No.	Yds.	Avg.	TD	No.	Yds.	Avg.	TD	TD	2pt.	Pts.	Fum.
1992—Buffalo NFL								Did not play—injured.									
1993—Buffalo NFL	13	11	36	3.3	0	0	0	...	0	1	10	10.0	0	0	...	0	0
1994—Buffalo NFL	13	2	4	2.0	0	1	26	26.0	1	6	102	17.0	0	1	0	6	0
1995—Carolina NFL	2	0	0	...	0	0	0	...	0	0	0	...	0	0	0	0	0
Pro totals (3 years)	28	13	40	3.1	0	1	26	26.0	1	7	112	16.0	0	1	0	6	0

TURNER, SCOTT — CB — REDSKINS

PERSONAL: Born February 26, 1972, in Richardson, Texas. ... 5-10/178.
HIGH SCHOOL: J.J. Pearce (Richardson, Texas).
COLLEGE: Illinois.
TRANSACTIONS/CAREER NOTES: Selected by Washington Redskins in seventh round (226th pick overall) of 1995 NFL draft. ... Signed by Redskins (July 18, 1995).
PLAYING EXPERIENCE: Washington NFL, 1995. ... Games: 1995 (16).
PRO STATISTICS: 1995—Intercepted one pass for no yards, returned one punt for no yards, credited with one sack, fumbled once and recovered one fumble.

TURNER, VERNON — RB/KR — BUCCANEERS

PERSONAL: Born January 6, 1967, in Brooklyn, N.Y. ... 5-8/185. ... Full name: Vernon Maurice Turner.
HIGH SCHOOL: Curtis (Staten Island, N.Y.).
COLLEGE: Carson-Newman (Tenn.).
TRANSACTIONS/CAREER NOTES: Signed as non-drafted free agent by Denver Broncos (May 1990). ... Released by Broncos (September 3, 1990). ... Signed by Buffalo Bills to practice squad (October 5, 1990). ... Activated (December 29, 1990). ... Deactivated for playoffs (January 11, 1991). ... Granted unconditional free agency (February 1-April 1, 1991). ... Re-signed by Bills for 1991 season. ... Claimed on waivers by

Los Angeles Rams (August 27, 1991). ... Released by Rams (December 2, 1992). ... Signed by Detroit Lions (March 17, 1993). ... Released by Lions (September 1, 1993). ... Re-signed by Lions (September 6, 1993). ... Claimed on waivers by Tampa Bay Buccaneers (December 30, 1993). ... Granted unconditional free agency (February 17, 1995). ... Signed by Carolina Panthers (March 20, 1995). ... Released by Panthers (August 27, 1995). ... Signed by Lions (October 10, 1995). ... Released by Lions (November 20, 1995). ... Signed by Tampa Bay Buccaneers (April 25, 1996).

PRO STATISTICS: 1991—Fumbled four times and recovered two fumbles for minus one yard. 1992—Fumbled three times. 1993—Fumbled once. 1994—Fumbled once and recovered one fumble. 1995—Fumbled once.

Year Team	G	RUSHING				RECEIVING				PUNT RETURNS				KICKOFF RETURNS				TOTALS		
		Att.	Yds.	Avg.	TD	No.	Yds.	Avg.	TD	No.	Yds.	Avg.	TD	No.	Yds.	Avg.	TD	TD	2pt.	Pts.
1990—Buffalo NFL	1	0	0	...	0	0	0	...	0	0	0	...	0	0	0	...	0	0	...	0
1991—L.A. Rams NFL	15	7	44	6.3	0	3	41	13.7	1	23	201	8.7	0	24	457	19.0	0	1	...	6
1992—L.A. Rams NFL	12	2	14	7.0	0	5	42	8.4	0	28	207	7.4	0	29	569	19.6	0	0	...	0
1993—Buffalo NFL	8	0	0	...	0	1	7	7.0	0	17	152	8.9	0	21	391	18.6	0	0	...	0
1994—Tampa Bay NFL	12	4	13	3.3	0	0	0	...	0	21	218	10.4	1	43	886	20.6	0	1	0	6
1995—Detroit NFL	6	0	0	...	0	0	0	...	0	6	39	6.5	0	17	323	19.0	0	0		0
Pro totals (6 years)	54	13	71	5.5	0	9	90	10.0	1	95	817	8.6	1	134	2626	19.6	0	2	0	12

TUTEN, MELVIN — OT — BENGALS

PERSONAL: Born November 11, 1971, in Washington, D.C. ... 6-6/305. ... Full name: Melvin Eugene Tuten.
HIGH SCHOOL: Woodrow Wilson (Washington, D.C.).
COLLEGE: Syracuse.
TRANSACTIONS/CAREER NOTES: Selected by Cincinnati Bengals in third round (69th pick overall) of 1995 NFL draft. ... Signed by Bengals (July 18, 1995).
PLAYING EXPERIENCE: Cincinnati NFL, 1995. ... Games: 1995 (16).
PRO STATISTICS: 1995—Caught two passes for 12 yards and one touchdown.

TUTEN, RICK — P

PERSONAL: Born January 5, 1965, in Perry, Fla. ... 6-2/221. ... Full name: Richard Lamar Tuten. ... Name pronounced TOOT-en.
HIGH SCHOOL: Forest (Ocala, Fla.).
COLLEGE: Miami (Fla.), then Florida State (degree in economics, 1986).
TRANSACTIONS/CAREER NOTES: Signed as non-drafted free agent by San Diego Chargers (May 10, 1988). ... Released by Chargers (August 23, 1988). ... Signed by Washington Redskins (June 2, 1989). ... Released by Redskins (August 27, 1989). ... Signed by Philadelphia Eagles (December 13, 1989). ... Granted unconditional free agency (February 1, 1990). ... Signed by Buffalo Bills (March 28, 1990). ... Released by Bills (August 15, 1990). ... Re-signed by Bills (September 19, 1990). ... Granted unconditional free agency (February 1-April 1, 1991). ... Re-signed by Bills for 1991 season. ... Released by Bills (August 20, 1991). ... Signed by Green Bay Packers (August 27, 1991). ... Released by Packers (August 30, 1991). ... Signed by Seattle Seahawks (October 9, 1991). ... Granted unconditional free agency (February 1-April 1, 1992). ... Re-signed by Seahawks for 1992 season. ... Granted unconditional free agency (February 16, 1996).
CHAMPIONSHIP GAME EXPERIENCE: Played in AFC championship game (1990 season). ... Played in Super Bowl XXV (1990 season).
HONORS: Played in Pro Bowl (1994 season).
PRO STATISTICS: 1992—Attempted one pass without a completion, rushed once for no yards, fumbled twice and recovered two fumbles for minus nine yards. 1993—Attempted one pass without a completion. 1994—Credited with one two-point conversion and attempted one pass without a completion.

Year Team	G	PUNTING					
		No.	Yds.	Avg.	Net avg.	In. 20	Blk.
1988—				Did not play.			
1989—Philadelphia NFL	2	7	256	36.6	33.6	1	0
1990—Buffalo NFL	14	53	2107	39.8	34.2	12	0
1991—Seattle NFL	10	49	2106	43.0	36.9	8	0
1992—Seattle NFL	16	*108	*4760	44.1	38.7	29	0
1993—Seattle NFL	16	90	*4007	44.5	37.3	21	1
1994—Seattle NFL	16	91	3905	42.9	36.7	33	0
1995—Seattle NFL	16	83	3735	*45.0	36.5	21	0
Pro totals (7 years)	90	481	20876	43.4	36.9	125	1

UHLENHAKE, JEFF — C

PERSONAL: Born January 28, 1966, in Indianapolis. ... 6-3/284. ... Full name: Jeffrey Alan Uhlenhake. ... Name pronounced you-lun-HAKE.
HIGH SCHOOL: Newark (Ohio) Catholic.
COLLEGE: Ohio State.
TRANSACTIONS/CAREER NOTES: Selected by Miami Dolphins in fifth round (121st pick overall) of 1989 NFL draft. ... Signed by Dolphins (July 21, 1989). ... Granted free agency (February 1, 1991). ... Re-signed by Dolphins (September 3, 1991). ... Activated (September 7, 1991). ... Granted free agency (March 1, 1993). ... Re-signed by Dolphins (August 3, 1993). ... On physically unable to perform list (August 3-August 30, 1993). ... On injured reserve with knee injury (November 10, 1993-remainder of season). ... Granted unconditional free agency (February 17, 1994). ... Signed by New Orleans Saints (April 22, 1994). ... Granted unconditional free agency (February 16, 1996).
PLAYING EXPERIENCE: Miami NFL, 1989-1993; New Orleans NFL, 1994 and 1995. ... Games: 1989 (16), 1990 (16), 1991 (13), 1992 (13), 1993 (5), 1994 (16), 1995 (14). Total: 93.
CHAMPIONSHIP GAME EXPERIENCE: Played in AFC championship game (1992 season).
HONORS: Named center on THE SPORTING NEWS college All-America first team (1988).
PRO STATISTICS: 1989—Fumbled once for minus 19 yards. 1992—Fumbled once and recovered two fumbles for minus four yards.

VALERIO, JOE — OT/C — CHIEFS

PERSONAL: Born February 11, 1969, in Swarthmore, Pa. ... 6-5/295. ... Full name: Joseph William Valerio. ... Son of Mike Valerio, former

professional middleweight boxer.
HIGH SCHOOL: Ridley Senior (Folsom, Pa.).
COLLEGE: Pennsylvania (degree in economics).
TRANSACTIONS/CAREER NOTES: Selected by Kansas City Chiefs in second round (50th pick overall) of 1991 NFL draft. ... Signed by Chiefs (July 17, 1991). ... Active for six games (1991); did not play. ... Assigned by Chiefs to Birmingham Fire in 1992 World League enhancement allocation program (February 20, 1992). ... Granted unconditional free agency (February 17, 1995). ... Re-signed by Chiefs (April 21, 1995). ... Released by Chiefs (February 15, 1996). ... Re-signed by Chiefs (April 12, 1996).
PLAYING EXPERIENCE: Birmingham W.L., 1992; Kansas City NFL, 1992-1995. ... Games: 1992 W.L. (10), 1992 NFL (16), 1993 (13), 1994 (16), 1995 (16). Total NFL: 61. Total Pro: 71.
CHAMPIONSHIP GAME EXPERIENCE: Played in AFC championship game (1993 season).
PRO STATISTICS: W.L.: 1992—Fumbled once and recovered one fumble for minus 26 yards. NFL: 1993—Caught one pass for one yard and a touchdown. 1994—Caught two passes for five yards and two touchdowns. 1995—Caught one pass for one yard and a touchdown and returned two kickoffs for 15 yards.

VANDERBEEK, MATT   LB   REDSKINS

PERSONAL: Born August 16, 1967, in Saugatuck, Mich. ... 6-3/243. ... Full name: Matthew James Vanderbeek.
HIGH SCHOOL: West Ottawa (Holland, Mich.).
COLLEGE: Michigan State.
TRANSACTIONS/CAREER NOTES: Signed as non-drafted free agent by Indianapolis Colts (April 30, 1990). ... Granted unconditional free agency (February 1, 1991). ... Signed by Minnesota Vikings (March 18, 1991). ... On injured reserve with hand injury (August 27-October 8, 1991). ... Released by Vikings (October 8, 1991). ... Signed by Colts (October 23, 1991). ... On injured reserve with knee injury (December 6, 1991-remainder of season). ... Granted unconditional free agency (February 1-April 1, 1992). ... Re-signed by Colts (June 5, 1992). ... Released by Colts (August 31, 1992). ... Re-signed by Colts (September 9, 1992). ... Granted free agency (March 1, 1993). ... Re-signed by Colts (July 23, 1993). ... Released by Colts (August 30, 1993). ... Signed by Dallas Cowboys (August 31, 1993). ... Granted unconditional free agency (February 17, 1994). ... Re-signed by Cowboys (July 13, 1994). ... Granted unconditional free agency (February 17, 1995). ... Signed by Washington Redskins (March 28, 1995).
PLAYING EXPERIENCE: Indianapolis NFL, 1990 and 1992; Minnesota (0)-Indianapolis (5) NFL, 1991; Dallas NFL, 1993 and 1994; Washington NFL, 1995. ... Games: 1990 (16), 1991 (5), 1992 (15), 1993 (16), 1994 (12), 1995 (16). Total: 80.
CHAMPIONSHIP GAME EXPERIENCE: Played in NFC championship game (1993 and 1994 seasons). ... Member of Super Bowl championship team (1993 season).
PRO STATISTICS: 1992—Returned one kickoff for six yards. 1995—Returned one kickoff for seven yards and recovered one fumble.

VANHORSE, SEAN   CB

PERSONAL: Born July 22, 1968, in Baltimore. ... 5-10/180. ... Full name: Sean Joseph Vanhorse.
HIGH SCHOOL: Northwestern (Baltimore).
COLLEGE: Howard.
TRANSACTIONS/CAREER NOTES: Selected by Miami Dolphins in sixth round (151st pick overall) of 1990 NFL draft. ... Signed by Dolphins (July 19, 1990). ... On physically unable to perform list (July 19-August 28, 1990). ... On physically unable to perform list with stress fracture in foot (August 28, 1990-entire season). ... Granted unconditional free agency (February 1, 1991). ... Signed by Detroit Lions (March 20, 1991). ... On injured reserve with ankle injury (August 27, 1991-entire season). ... Granted unconditional free agency (February 1, 1992). ... Signed by San Diego Chargers (March 31, 1992). ... Granted unconditional free agency (February 17, 1994). ... Re-signed by Chargers (May 19, 1994). ... Released by Chargers (February 6, 1995). ... Signed by Lions (April 23, 1995). ... Granted unconditional free agency (February 16, 1996).
CHAMPIONSHIP GAME EXPERIENCE: Played in AFC championship game (1994 season). ... Played in Super Bowl XXIX (1994 season).

| | | | INTERCEPTIONS | | |
Year Team	G	No.	Yds.	Avg.	TD
1990—Miami NFL		Did not play.			
1991—Detroit NFL		Did not play—injured.			
1992—San Diego NFL	16	1	11	11.0	0
1993—San Diego NFL	15	2	0	0.0	0
1994—San Diego NFL	16	2	56	28.0	1
1995—Detroit NFL	14	1	0	0.0	0
Pro totals (4 years)	61	6	67	11.2	1

VANOVER, TAMARICK   WR/KR   CHIEFS

PERSONAL: Born February 25, 1974, in Tallahassee, Fla. ... 5-11/213.
HIGH SCHOOL: Leon (Tallahassee, Fla.).
COLLEGE: Florida State.
TRANSACTIONS/CAREER NOTES: Signed after sophomore season with Las Vegas Posse of CFL (February 13, 1994). ... Selected by Kansas City Chiefs in third round (81st pick overall) of 1995 NFL draft.
HONORS: Named kick returner on THE SPORTING NEWS college All-America first team (1992). ... Named kick returner on THE SPORTING NEWS college All-America second team (1993).
PRO STATISTICS: CFL: 1994—Returned four unsuccessful field-goals for 31 yards, fumbled three times and recovered one fumble.

| | | RUSHING | | | | RECEIVING | | | | PUNT RETURNS | | | | KICKOFF RETURNS | | | | TOTALS | | |
Year Team	G	Att.	Yds.	Avg.	TD	No.	Yds.	Avg.	TD	No.	Yds.	Avg.	TD	No.	Yds.	Avg.	TD	TD	2pt.	Pts.
1994—Las Vegas CFL	15	1	6	6.0	0	23	385	16.7	3	36	341	9.5	1	31	718	23.2	1	5	1	32
1995—Kansas City NFL	15	6	31	5.2	0	11	231	21.0	2	51	*540	10.6	†1	43	1095	25.5	†2	5	0	30
Pro totals (2 years)	30	7	37	5.3	0	34	616	18.1	5	87	881	10.1	2	74	2336	31.6	3	10	1	62

VAN PELT, ALEX   QB   BILLS

PERSONAL: Born May 1, 1970, in Graffton, W.Va. ... 6-0/220. ... Full name: Gregory Alexander Van Pelt.

HIGH SCHOOL: Grafton (W.Va.), then Winston Churchill (San Antonio).
COLLEGE: Pittsburgh.
TRANSACTIONS/CAREER NOTES: Selected by Pittsburgh Steelers in eighth round (216th pick overall) of 1993 NFL draft. ... Released by Steelers (August 30, 1993). ... Signed by Kansas City Chiefs to practice squad (November 3, 1993). ... Activated (November 8, 1993); did not play. ... Released by Chiefs (November 17, 1993). ... Re-signed by Chiefs (May 18, 1994). ... Released by Chiefs (August 23, 1994). ... Signed by Buffalo Bills to practice squad (December 14, 1994). ... Activated (December 17, 1994).

					PASSING							RUSHING				TOTALS	
Year	Team	G	Att.	Cmp.	Pct.	Yds.	TD	Int.	Avg.	Rat.	Att.	Yds.	Avg.	TD	TD	2pt.	Pts.
1995—Buffalo NFL		1	18	10	55.6	106	2	0	5.89	110.0	0	0	...	0	0	0	0

VARDELL, TOMMY — FB — 49ERS

PERSONAL: Born February 20, 1969, in El Cajon, Calif. ... 6-2/230. ... Full name: Thomas Arthur Vardell.
HIGH SCHOOL: Granite Hills (El Cajon, Calif.).
COLLEGE: Stanford (degree in industrial engineering, 1992).
TRANSACTIONS/CAREER NOTES: Selected by Cleveland Browns in first round (ninth pick overall) of 1992 NFL draft. ... Signed by Browns (July 26, 1992). ... On injured reserve with calf injury (December 26, 1992-remainder of season). ... On injured reserve with knee injury (October 5, 1994-remainder of season). ... On physically unable to perform list with knee injury (July 17-23, 1995). ... Granted unconditional free agency (February 16, 1996). ... Signed by San Francisco 49ers (March 20, 1996).
STATISTICAL PLATEAUS: 100-yard rushing games: 1993 (1).

			RUSHING				RECEIVING				KICKOFF RETURNS				TOTALS			
Year	Team	G	Att.	Yds.	Avg.	TD	No.	Yds.	Avg.	TD	No.	Yds.	Avg.	TD	TD	2pt.	Pts.	Fum.
1992—Cleveland NFL		14	99	369	3.7	0	13	128	9.9	0	2	14	7.0	0	0	...	0	0
1993—Cleveland NFL		16	171	644	3.8	3	19	151	8.0	1	4	58	14.5	0	4	...	24	3
1994—Cleveland NFL		5	15	48	3.2	0	16	137	8.6	1	0	0	...	0	1	0	6	0
1995—Cleveland NFL		5	4	9	2.3	0	6	18	3.0	0	0	0	...	0	0	0	0	0
Pro totals (4 years)		40	289	1070	3.7	3	54	434	8.0	2	6	72	12.0	0	5	0	30	3

VAUGHN, JON — RB/KR — STEELERS

PERSONAL: Born March 12, 1970, in Florissant, Mo. ... 5-9/203. ... Full name: Jonathan Stewart Vaughn.
HIGH SCHOOL: McCluer North (Florissant, Mo.).
COLLEGE: Michigan (degree in criminal justice).
TRANSACTIONS/CAREER NOTES: Selected after sophomore season by New England Patriots in fifth round (112th pick overall) of 1991 NFL draft. ... Signed by Patriots (July 16, 1991). ... Traded by Patriots to Seattle Seahawks for sixth-round pick (OT Max Lane) in 1994 draft (August 25, 1993). ... Granted free agency (February 17, 1994). ... Re-signed by Seahawks (June 23, 1994). ... Released by Seahawks (November 23, 1994). ... Signed by Kansas City Chiefs (November 30, 1994). ... Released by Chiefs (August 22, 1995). ... Signed by Pittsburgh Steelers (April 9, 1996).
PRO STATISTICS: 1991—Attempted two passes with one completion for 13 yards and a touchdown and recovered one fumble for minus two yards.
STATISTICAL PLATEAUS: 100-yard rushing games: 1992 (1), 1993 (1). Total: 2.

			RUSHING				RECEIVING				KICKOFF RETURNS				TOTALS			
Year	Team	G	Att.	Yds.	Avg.	TD	No.	Yds.	Avg.	TD	No.	Yds.	Avg.	TD	TD	2pt.	Pts.	Fum.
1991—New England NFL		16	31	146	4.7	2	9	89	9.9	0	34	717	21.1	†1	3	...	18	1
1992—New England NFL		16	113	451	4.0	1	13	84	6.5	0	20	564	*28.2	1	2	...	12	6
1993—Seattle NFL		16	36	153	4.3	0	0	0	...	0	16	280	17.5	0	0	...	0	1
1994—Seattle NFL		9	27	96	3.6	1	1	5	5.0	1	18	443	24.6	1	3	1	20	3
—Kansas City NFL		3	0	0	...	0	0	0	...	0	15	386	25.7	1	1	0	6	0
1995—											Did not play.							
Pro totals (4 years)		60	207	846	4.1	4	23	178	7.7	1	103	2390	23.2	4	9	1	56	11

VEASEY, CRAIG — DT

PERSONAL: Born December 25, 1966, in Clear Lake City, Texas. ... 6-2/300. ... Full name: Anthony Craig Veasey. ... Name pronounced VEE-see.
HIGH SCHOOL: Clear Lake (Houston).
COLLEGE: Houston.
TRANSACTIONS/CAREER NOTES: Selected by Pittsburgh Steelers in third round (81st pick overall) of 1990 NFL draft. ... Signed by Steelers (August 13, 1990). ... On injured reserve with eye injury (September 5-October 13, 1990). ... Released by Steelers (August 25, 1992). ... Signed by Houston Oilers (September 2, 1992). ... Claimed on waivers by New England Patriots (October 26, 1992). ... Released by Patriots (October 30, 1992). ... Signed by Miami Dolphins (March 17, 1993). ... Claimed on waivers by Oilers (August 31, 1993). ... Released by Oilers (September 13, 1993). ... Signed by Dolphins (September 15, 1993). ... Granted unconditional free agency (February 17, 1995). ... Signed by Oilers (June 2, 1995). ... Released by Oilers (February 15, 1996).
HONORS: Named defensive end on THE SPORTING NEWS college All-America first team (1989).
PRO STATISTICS: 1990—Recovered one fumble. 1994—Intercepted one pass for seven yards.

Year	Team	G	SACKS
1990—Pittsburgh NFL		10	0.0
1991—Pittsburgh NFL		13	2.0
1992—Houston NFL		4	0.0
1993—Houston NFL		1	0.0
—Miami NFL		14	2.0
1994—Miami NFL		12	2.5
1995—Houston NFL		15	0.0
Pro totals (6 years)		69	6.5

VICKERS, KIPP   OL   COLTS

PERSONAL: Born August 27, 1969, in Holiday, Fla. ... 6-2/296.
HIGH SCHOOL: Tarpon Springs (Fla.).
COLLEGE: Miami (Fla.).
TRANSACTIONS/CAREER NOTES: Signed as non-drafted free agent by Indianapolis Colts (April 30, 1993). ... Released by Colts (August 30, 1993). ... Re-signed by Colts to practice squad (September 1, 1993). ... Activated (December 21, 1993).
PLAYING EXPERIENCE: Indianapolis NFL, 1994 and 1995. ... Games: 1994 (4), 1995 (9). Total: 13.
CHAMPIONSHIP GAME EXPERIENCE: Played in AFC championship game (1995 season).

VILLA, DANNY   G   CHIEFS

PERSONAL: Born September 21, 1964, in Nogales, Ariz. ... 6-5/308. ... Name pronounced VEE-uh.
HIGH SCHOOL: Nogales (Ariz.).
COLLEGE: Arizona State.
TRANSACTIONS/CAREER NOTES: Selected by New England Patriots in fifth round (113th pick overall) of 1987 NFL draft. ... Signed by Patriots (July 25, 1987). ... On injured reserve (October 4-November 8, 1991). ... On injured reserve with ankle injury (December 11, 1991-remainder of season). ... Traded by Patriots to Phoenix Cardinals for sixth-round pick (traded to Detroit) in 1992 draft (January 30, 1992). ... Granted unconditional free agency (March 1, 1993). ... Signed by Kansas City Chiefs (April 19, 1993).
PLAYING EXPERIENCE: New England NFL, 1987-1991; Phoenix NFL, 1992; Kansas City NFL, 1993-1995 . ... Games: 1987 (11), 1988 (16), 1989 (15), 1990 (16), 1991 (10), 1992 (16), 1993 (13), 1994 (14), 1995 (16). Total: 127.
CHAMPIONSHIP GAME EXPERIENCE: Played in AFC championship game (1993 season).
PRO STATISTICS: 1987—Fumbled once for minus 13 yards. 1988—Fumbled once for minus 39 yards. 1990—Recovered one fumble. 1991—Recovered two fumbles.

VINCENT, TROY   CB   EAGLES

PERSONAL: Born June 8, 1970, in Trenton, N.J. ... 6-0/184. ... Nephew of Steve Luke, safety, Green Bay Packers (1975-1980).
HIGH SCHOOL: Pennsbury (Fairless Hills, Pa.).
COLLEGE: Wisconsin.
TRANSACTIONS/CAREER NOTES: Selected by Miami Dolphins in first round (seventh pick overall) of 1992 NFL draft. ... Signed by Dolphins (August 8, 1992). ... Designated by Dolphins as transition player (February 25, 1993). ... On injured reserve with knee injury (December 15, 1993-remainder of season). ... Tendered offer sheet by Philadelphia Eagles (February 24, 1996). ... Dolphins declined to match offer (March 2, 1996).
CHAMPIONSHIP GAME EXPERIENCE: Played in AFC championship game (1992 season).
HONORS: Named defensive back on THE SPORTING NEWS college All-America first team (1991).
PRO STATISTICS: 1992—Recovered two fumbles. 1993—Recovered one fumble. 1994—Ran 58 yards with lateral from interception for a touchdown.

| | | INTERCEPTIONS | | | | PUNT RETURNS | | | | TOTALS | | | |
Year Team	G	No.	Yds.	Avg.	TD	No.	Yds.	Avg.	TD	TD	2pt.	Pts.	Fum.
1992—Miami NFL	15	2	47	23.5	0	5	16	3.2	0	0	...	0	2
1993—Miami NFL	13	2	29	14.5	0	0	0	...	0	0	...	0	0
1994—Miami NFL	13	5	113	22.6	1	0	0	...	0	1	0	6	0
1995—Miami NFL	16	5	95	19.0	1	0	0	...	0	1	0	6	0
Pro totals (4 years)	57	14	284	20.3	2	5	16	3.2	0	2	0	12	2

von OELHOFFEN, KIMO   DT   BENGALS

PERSONAL: Born January 30, 1971, in Kaunakaki, Hawaii. ... 6-4/300.
HIGH SCHOOL: Malokai (Hoolehua, Hawaii.).
JUNIOR COLLEGE: Walla Walla (Wash.) Junior College.
COLLEGE: Hawaii, then Boise State.
TRANSACTIONS/CAREER NOTES: Selected by Cincinnati Bengals in sixth round (162nd pick overall) of 1994 NFL draft. ... Signed by Bengals (May 9, 1994).
PLAYING EXPERIENCE: Cincinnati NFL, 1994 and 1995. ... Games: 1994 (7), 1995 (16). Total: 23.
PRO STATISTICS: 1995—Returned one kickoff for 10 yards.

WAGNER, BRYAN   P

PERSONAL: Born March 28, 1962, in Escondido, Calif. ... 6-2/200. ... Full name: Bryan Jeffrey Wagner.
HIGH SCHOOL: Hilltop (Chula Vista, Calif.).
COLLEGE: California Lutheran, then Cal State Northridge.
TRANSACTIONS/CAREER NOTES: Selected by Baltimore Stars in 15th round (216th pick overall) of 1985 USFL draft. ... Signed as non-drafted free agent by Dallas Cowboys (May 2, 1985). ... Released by Cowboys (August 27, 1985). ... Signed by New York Giants (May 10, 1986). ... Released by Giants (August 11, 1986). ... Signed by St. Louis Cardinals (August 19, 1986). ... Released by Cardinals (August 26, 1986). ... Signed by Denver Broncos (May 1, 1987). ... Traded by Broncos with undisclosed draft pick to Chicago Bears for G Stefan Humphries (August 25, 1987). ... On injured reserve with back injury (December 16, 1987-remainder of season). ... Granted unconditional free agency (February 1, 1989). ... Signed by Cleveland Browns (March 30, 1989). ... Granted unconditional free agency (February 1-April 1, 1991). ... Rights relinquished by Browns (April 1, 1991). ... Signed by New England Patriots (May 23, 1991). ... Released by Patriots (September 16, 1991). ... Signed by Green Bay Packers (May 4, 1992). ... Released by Packers (August 24, 1992). ... Re-signed by Packers (November 9, 1992). ... Granted unconditional free agency (February 17, 1994). ... Released by Packers (May 6, 1994). ... Released by Packers (August 1, 1994). ... Signed by San Diego Chargers (September 13, 1994). ... Granted unconditional free agency (February 17, 1995). ... Signed by New York Jets (July 27, 1995). ... Released by Jets (August 21, 1995). ... Signed by New England Patriots (October 31, 1995). ... Granted

unconditional free agency (February 16, 1996).

CHAMPIONSHIP GAME EXPERIENCE: Played in NFC championship game (1988 season). ... Played in AFC championship game (1989 and 1994 seasons). ... Played in Super Bowl XXIX (1994 season).

POSTSEASON RECORDS: Holds Super Bowl single-game record for highest average punt (minimum 4 punts)—48.8 (January 29, 1995, vs. San Francisco).

PRO STATISTICS: 1988—Attempted one pass with one completion for three yards, rushed twice for no yards, fumbled once and recovered one fumble for minus nine yards.

				PUNTING			
Year Team	G	No.	Yds.	Avg.	Net avg.	In. 20	Blk.
1987—Chicago NFL	10	36	1461	40.6	32.1	9	1
1988—Chicago NFL	16	79	3282	41.5	33.4	18	0
1989—Cleveland NFL	16	*97	3817	39.4	33.8	32	0
1990—Cleveland NFL	16	74	2879	38.9	30.9	13	*4
1991—New England NFL	3	14	548	39.1	29.1	0	0
1992—Green Bay NFL	7	30	1222	40.7	35.0	10	0
1993—Green Bay NFL	16	74	3174	42.9	36.3	19	0
1994—San Diego NFL	14	65	2705	41.6	35.3	20	0
1995—New England NFL	8	37	1557	42.1	35.4	13	0
Pro totals (9 years)	106	506	20645	40.8	33.8	134	5

WAINRIGHT, FRANK   TE

PERSONAL: Born October 10, 1967, in Peoria, Ill. ... 6-3/245. ... Full name: Frank Wesley Wainright.

HIGH SCHOOL: Pomona (Arvada, Colo.).

COLLEGE: Northern Colorado.

TRANSACTIONS/CAREER NOTES: Selected by New Orleans Saints in eighth round (210th pick overall) of 1991 NFL draft. ... Signed by Saints (July 14, 1991). ... Released by Saints (August 26, 1991). ... Re-signed by Saints to practice squad (August 28, 1991). ... Activated (September 14, 1991). ... Granted unconditional free agency (February 1-April 1, 1992). ... Re-signed by Saints for 1992 season. ... Granted unconditional free agency (February 17, 1995). ... Signed by Denver Broncos (April 17, 1995). ... Released by Broncos (August 22, 1995). ... Signed by Philadelphia Eagles (August 29, 1995). ... Released by Eagles (October 25, 1995). ... Signed by Miami Dolphins (November 15, 1995). ... Granted unconditional free agency (February 16, 1996).

PRO STATISTICS: 1995—Recovered one fumble.

		RECEIVING				TOTALS			
Year Team	G	No.	Yds.	Avg.	TD	TD	2pt.	Pts.	Fum.
1991—New Orleans NFL	14	1	3	3.0	0	0	...	0	0
1992—New Orleans NFL	13	9	143	15.9	0	0	...	0	0
1993—New Orleans NFL	16	0	0	...	0	0	...	0	0
1994—New Orleans NFL					Did not play.				
1995—Philadelphia NFL	7	0	0	...	0	0	0	0	0
—Miami NFL	6	0	0	...	0	0	0	0	0
Pro totals (4 years)	56	10	146	14.6	0	0	0	0	0

WALKER, ADAM   FB   EAGLES

PERSONAL: Born June 7, 1968, in Pittsburgh. ... 6-1/210.

HIGH SCHOOL: Steel Valley (Munhall, Pa.).

COLLEGE: Pittsburgh.

TRANSACTIONS/CAREER NOTES: Signed as non-drafted free agent by Philadelphia Eagles (1990). ... Released by Eagles (September 3, 1990). ... Signed by San Francisco 49ers (February 14, 1991). ... Released by 49ers (August 26, 1991). ... Re-signed by 49ers to practice squad (August 28, 1991). ... Released by 49ers (September 25, 1991). ... Re-signed by 49ers to practice squad (October 2, 1991). ... Released by 49ers (October 16, 1991). ... Re-signed by 49ers (February 3, 1992). ... Assigned by 49ers to Sacramento Surge in 1992 World League enhancement allocation program (February 20, 1992). ... Traded by Surge with S Greg Coauette to Ohio Glory for QB Chris Cochrane and future considerations (March 10, 1992). ... Released by 49ers (August 25, 1992). ... Re-signed by 49ers to practice squad (September 9, 1992). ... Activated (November 18, 1992). ... On injured reserve with knee injury (November 20-December 15, 1992). ... On practice squad (December 15, 1992). ... Released by 49ers (December 25, 1992). ... Re-signed by 49ers (December 26, 1992). ... Released by 49ers (August 30, 1993). ... Re-signed by 49ers (September 7, 1993). ... Released by 49ers (December 2, 1993). ... Re-signed by 49ers (December 7, 1993). ... Released by 49ers (February 17, 1994). ... Signed by Green Bay Packers (July 18, 1994). ... Released by Packers (August 17, 1994). ... Signed by 49ers (August 22, 1994). ... Granted unconditional free agency (February 16, 1996). ... Signed by Eagles (April 9, 1996).

CHAMPIONSHIP GAME EXPERIENCE: Member of 49ers for NFC championship game (1993 season); inactive. ... Played in NFC championship game (1994 season). ... Member of Super Bowl championship team (1994 season).

PRO STATISTICS: W.L.: 1992—Blocked punt out of end zone for safety and recovered one fumble. NFL: 1994—Recovered one fumble.

		RUSHING				RECEIVING				KICKOFF RETURNS				TOTALS			
Year Team	G	Att.	Yds.	Avg.	TD	No.	Yds.	Avg.	TD	No.	Yds.	Avg.	TD	TD	2pt.	Pts.	Fum.
1992—Ohio W.L.	10	38	144	3.8	0	31	236	7.6	0	32	733	22.9	0	0	1	2	4
—San Francisco NFL	1	0	0	...	0	0	0	...	0	0	0	...	0	0	...	0	0
1993—San Francisco NFL	10	5	17	3.4	0	1	4	4.0	0	3	51	17.0	0	0	...	0	0
1994—San Francisco NFL	8	13	54	4.2	1	0	0	...	0	6	82	13.7	0	1	0	6	0
1995—San Francisco NFL	13	14	44	3.1	1	11	78	7.1	0	1	17	17.0	0	1	0	6	2
W.L. totals (1 year)	10	38	144	3.8	0	31	236	7.6	0	32	733	22.9	0	0	1	2	4
NFL totals (4 years)	32	32	115	3.6	2	12	82	6.8	0	10	150	15.0	0	2	0	12	2
Pro totals (4 years)	42	70	259	3.7	2	43	318	7.4	0	42	883	21.0	0	2	1	14	6

WALKER, BRACEY   S   BENGALS

PERSONAL: Born October 28, 1970, in Spring Lake, N.C. ... 5-11/200. ... Full name: Bracey Wordell Walker.

HIGH SCHOOL: Pine Forest (Fayetteville, N.C.).

COLLEGE: North Carolina.

TRANSACTIONS/CAREER NOTES: Selected by Kansas City Chiefs in fourth round (127th pick overall) of 1994 NFL draft. ... Signed by Chiefs (July 20, 1994). ... Claimed on waivers by Cincinnati Bengals (October 12, 1994).
HONORS: Named defensive back on THE SPORTING NEWS college All-America second team (1993).
PRO STATISTICS: 1995—Recovered two fumbles for nine yards.

		INTERCEPTIONS			
Year Team	G	No.	Yds.	Avg.	TD
1994—Kansas City NFL	2	0	0	...	0
—Cincinnati NFL	7	0	0	...	0
1995—Cincinnati NFL	14	4	56	14.0	0
Pro totals (2 years)	23	4	56	14.0	0

WALKER, BRUCE DE PATRIOTS

PERSONAL: Born July 18, 1972, in Compton, Calif. ... 6-4/310.
HIGH SCHOOL: Dominguez (Compton, Calif.).
COLLEGE: UCLA.
TRANSACTIONS/CAREER NOTES: Selected after junior season by Philadelphia Eagles in second round (37th pick overall) of 1994 NFL draft. ... Signed by Eagles (June 28, 1994). ... Released by Eagles (August 27, 1994). ... Signed by New England Patriots (November 23, 1994).
PLAYING EXPERIENCE: New England NFL, 1995. ... Games: 1995 (11).

WALKER, DARNELL CB FALCONS

PERSONAL: Born January 17, 1970, in St. Louis. ... 5-8/168. ... Full name: Darnell Robert Walker.
HIGH SCHOOL: Sumner (St. Louis).
JUNIOR COLLEGE: Coffeyville (Kan.) Community College.
COLLEGE: Oklahoma.
TRANSACTIONS/CAREER NOTES: Selected by Atlanta Falcons in seventh round (178th pick overall) of 1993 NFL draft. ... Signed by Falcons (July 14, 1993). ... Granted free agency (February 16, 1996).
PRO STATISTICS: 1994—Credited with one sack.

		INTERCEPTIONS			
Year Team	G	No.	Yds.	Avg.	TD
1993—Atlanta NFL	15	3	7	2.3	0
1994—Atlanta NFL	16	3	105	35.0	1
1995—Atlanta NFL	16	0	0	...	0
Pro totals (3 years)	47	6	112	18.7	1

WALKER, DERRICK TE CHIEFS

PERSONAL: Born June 23, 1967, in Glenwood, Ill. ... 6-0/249. ... Full name: Derrick Norval Walker.
HIGH SCHOOL: Bloom (Chicago Heights, Ill.).
COLLEGE: Michigan (degree in communications).
TRANSACTIONS/CAREER NOTES: Selected by San Diego Chargers in sixth round (163rd pick overall) of 1990 NFL draft. ... Signed by Chargers (July 21, 1990). ... Granted free agency (March 1, 1993). ... Re-signed by Chargers for 1993 season. ... On injured reserve with knee injury (December 15, 1993-remainder of season). ... Released by Chargers (March 9, 1994). ... Signed by Kansas City Chiefs (August 29, 1994). ... Granted free agency (February 17, 1995). ... Tendered offer sheet by Washington Redskins (March 11, 1995). ... Offer matched by Chiefs (March 18, 1995).
PRO STATISTICS: 1991—Recovered one fumble.
STATISTICAL PLATEAUS: 100-yard receiving games: 1992 (1).

		RECEIVING				TOTALS			
Year Team	G	No.	Yds.	Avg.	TD	TD	2pt.	Pts.	Fum.
1990—San Diego NFL	16	23	240	10.4	1	1	...	6	1
1991—San Diego NFL	16	20	134	6.7	0	0	...	0	0
1992—San Diego NFL	16	34	393	11.6	2	2	...	12	0
1993—San Diego NFL	12	21	212	10.1	1	1	...	6	0
1994—Kansas City NFL	15	36	382	10.6	2	2	0	12	1
1995—Kansas City NFL	16	25	205	8.2	1	1	0	6	0
Pro totals (6 years)	91	159	1566	9.9	7	7	0	42	2

WALKER, GARY DE OILERS

PERSONAL: Born February 28, 1973, in Lavonia, Ga. ... 6-2/285.
HIGH SCHOOL: Franklin County (Lavonia, Ga.).
COLLEGE: Auburn.
TRANSACTIONS/CAREER NOTES: Selected by Houston Oilers in fifth round (159th pick overall) of 1995 NFL draft. ... Signed by Oilers (July 10, 1995).

Year Team	G	SACKS
1995—Houston NFL	15	2.5

WALKER, HERSCHEL RB GIANTS

PERSONAL: Born March 3, 1962, in Wrightsville, Ga. ... 6-1/225.
HIGH SCHOOL: Johnson County (Wrightsville, Ga.).
COLLEGE: Georgia (degree in criminal justice, 1984).

W

TRANSACTIONS/CAREER NOTES: Signed after junior season by New Jersey Generals of USFL (February 22, 1983); Generals forfeited first-round pick in 1984 draft. ... On developmental squad (April 8-14, 1984). ... Selected by Dallas Cowboys in fifth round (114th pick overall) of 1985 NFL draft. ... Granted free agency when USFL suspended operations (August 7, 1986). ... Signed by Cowboys (August 13, 1986). ... Granted roster exemption (August 13-23, 1986). ... Traded as part of a six-player, 12 draft-pick deal in which Cowboys sent Walker to Minnesota Vikings in exchange for DB Issiac Holt, LB David Howard, LB Jesse Solomon, RB Darrin Nelson, DE Alex Stewart, first-round pick in 1992 draft and conditional first-round picks in 1990 and 1991 drafts, conditional second-round picks in 1990, 1991 and 1992 drafts and conditional third-round pick in 1992 draft (October 12, 1989); Nelson refused to report to Cowboys and was traded to San Diego Chargers, with Vikings giving Cowboys a sixth-round pick in 1990 as well as the original conditional second-round pick in 1991 and Chargers sending a fifth-round pick in 1990 to Vikings through Cowboys (October 17, 1989); deal completed with Cowboys retaining Howard, Solomon and Holt and all conditional picks and Cowboys sending third-round picks in 1990 and 1991 and 10th-round pick in 1990 to Vikings (February 2, 1990). ... Granted free agency (February 1, 1991). ... Re-signed by Vikings (June 24, 1991). ... Granted free agency (February 1, 1992). ... Released by Vikings (May 29, 1992). ... Signed by Philadelphia Eagles (June 22, 1992). ... Released by Eagles (March 28, 1995). ... Signed by New York Giants (April 3, 1995).

HONORS: Named running back on THE SPORTING NEWS college All-America first team (1980-1982). ... Heisman Trophy winner (1982). ... Named College Football Player of the Year by THE SPORTING NEWS (1982). ... Maxwell Award winner (1982). ... Named running back on THE SPORTING NEWS USFL All-Star team (1983 and 1985). ... Named USFL Player of the Year by THE SPORTING NEWS (1985). ... Played in Pro Bowl (1987 and 1988 seasons).

PRO STATISTICS: USFL: 1983—Recovered four fumbles. 1984—Recovered two fumbles. 1985—Recovered three fumbles. NFL: 1986—Recovered two fumbles. 1987—Recovered one fumble. 1988—Recovered three fumbles. 1990—Attempted two passes with one completion for 12 yards. 1991—Recovered one fumble. 1992—Attempted one pass without a completion and recovered two fumbles. 1993—Recovered two fumbles. 1994—Recovered one fumble.

STATISTICAL PLATEAUS: USFL: 100-yard rushing games: 1983 (7), 1984 (5), 1985 (14). Total: 26. ... 100-yard receiving games: 1983 (1), 1985 (1). Total: 2. ... NFL: 100-yard rushing games: 1986 (2), 1987 (3), 1988 (4), 1991 (3), 1992 (5). Total: 17. ... 100-yard receiving games: 1986 (3), 1993 (2). Total: 5.

MISCELLANEOUS: Only player in NFL history to have a run from scrimmage, pass reception and kickoff return of 90 yards or more in one season (1994).

		RUSHING				RECEIVING				KICKOFF RETURNS				TOTALS			
YearTeam	G	Att.	Yds.	Avg.	TD	No.	Yds.	Avg.	TD	No.	Yds.	Avg.	TD	TD	2pt.	Pts.	Fum.
1983—New Jersey USFL	18	*412	*1812	4.4	*17	53	489	9.2	1	3	69	23.0	0	*18	1	*110	12
1984—New Jersey USFL	17	293	1339	4.6	16	40	528	13.2	5	0	0	...	0	*21	1	128	6
1985—New Jersey USFL	18	*438	*2411	5.5	*21	37	467	12.6	1	0	0	...	0	*22	0	*132	9
1986—Dallas NFL	16	151	737	4.9	12	76	837	11.0	2	0	0	...	0	14	...	84	5
1987—Dallas NFL	12	209	891	4.3	7	60	715	11.9	1	0	0	...	0	8	...	48	4
1988—Dallas NFL	16	361	1514	4.2	5	53	505	9.5	2	0	0	...	0	7	...	42	6
1989—Dallas NFL	5	81	246	3.0	2	22	261	11.9	1	0	0	...	0	3	...	18	2
—Minnesota NFL	11	169	669	4.0	5	18	162	9.0	1	13	374	28.8	†1	7	...	42	5
1990—Minnesota NFL	16	184	770	4.2	5	35	315	9.0	4	44	966	22.0	0	9	...	54	4
1991—Minnesota NFL	15	198	825	4.2	10	33	204	6.2	0	5	83	16.6	0	10	...	60	2
1992—Philadelphia NFL	16	267	1070	4.0	8	38	278	7.3	2	3	69	23.0	0	10	...	60	6
1993—Philadelphia NFL	16	174	746	4.3	1	75	610	8.1	3	11	184	16.7	0	4	...	24	3
1994—Philadelphia NFL	16	113	528	4.7	5	50	500	10.0	2	21	581	27.7	1	8	0	48	4
1995—New York Giants NFL	16	31	126	4.1	0	31	234	7.6	1	41	881	21.5	0	1	0	6	0
USFL totals (3 years)	53	1143	5562	4.9	54	130	1484	11.4	7	3	69	23.0	0	61	2	370	27
NFL totals (10 years)	155	1938	8122	4.2	60	491	4621	9.4	19	138	3138	22.7	2	81	0	486	41
Pro totals (13 years)	208	3081	13684	4.5	114	621	6105	9.8	26	141	3207	22.8	2	142	2	856	68

WALLACE, AARON　　　　　LB

PERSONAL: Born April 17, 1967, in Paris, Texas. ... 6-3/245.
HIGH SCHOOL: Franklin D. Roosevelt (Dallas).
COLLEGE: Texas A&M.
TRANSACTIONS/CAREER NOTES: Selected by Los Angeles Raiders in second round (37th pick overall) of 1990 NFL draft. ... Signed by Raiders (July 16, 1990). ... Granted free agency (March 1, 1993). ... Re-signed by Raiders (July 21, 1993). ... Raiders franchise moved to Oakland (July 21, 1995). ... Granted unconditional free agency (February 16, 1996).
CHAMPIONSHIP GAME EXPERIENCE: Played in AFC championship game (1990 season).
HONORS: Named linebacker on THE SPORTING NEWS college All-America second team (1988).
PRO STATISTICS: 1992—Recovered two fumbles. 1993—Recovered two fumbles. 1995—Recovered one fumble.

Year　Team	G	SACKS
1990—Los Angeles Raiders NFL	16	9.0
1991—Los Angeles Raiders NFL	16	2.0
1992—Los Angeles Raiders NFL	16	4.0
1993—Los Angeles Raiders NFL	16	2.0
1994—Los Angeles Raiders NFL	16	2.0
1995—Oakland NFL	13	2.0
Pro totals (6 years)	93	21.0

WALLACE, STEVE　　　　　OT　　　　　EAGLES

PERSONAL: Born December 27, 1964, in Atlanta. ... 6-5/280. ... Full name: Barron Steven Wallace. ... Related to Leonard Humphries, defensive back, Indianapolis Colts (1994).
HIGH SCHOOL: Chamblee (Ga.).
COLLEGE: Auburn.
TRANSACTIONS/CAREER NOTES: Selected by Birmingham Stallions in 1986 USFL territorial draft. ... Selected by San Francisco 49ers in fourth round (101st pick overall) of 1986 NFL draft. ... Signed by 49ers (July 18, 1986). ... Granted free agency (February 1, 1992). ... Re-signed by 49ers (August 1, 1992). ... Designated by 49ers as transition player (February 25, 1993). ... Released by 49ers (March 4, 1996). ... Signed by Philadelphia Eagles (April 18, 1996).
PLAYING EXPERIENCE: San Francisco NFL, 1986-1995. ... Games: 1986 (16), 1987 (11), 1988 (16), 1989 (16), 1990 (16), 1991 (16), 1992 (16), 1993 (15), 1994 (15), 1995 (13). Total: 150.
CHAMPIONSHIP GAME EXPERIENCE: Played in NFC championship game (1988-1990 and 1992-1994 seasons). ... Member of Super Bowl

W

championship team (1988, 1989 and 1994 seasons).
HONORS: Played in Pro Bowl (1992 season).
PRO STATISTICS: 1992—Recovered one fumble. 1993—Recovered one fumble. 1994—Recovered two fumbles.

WALLERSTEDT, BRETT — LB — BENGALS

PERSONAL: Born November 24, 1970, in Tacoma, Wash. ... 6-1/240. ... Full name: Brett Robert Wallerstedt.
HIGH SCHOOL: Manhattan (Kan.).
COLLEGE: Arizona State (degree in general business).
TRANSACTIONS/CAREER NOTES: Selected by Phoenix Cardinals in sixth round (143rd pick overall) of 1993 NFL draft. ... Signed by Cardinals (July 16, 1993). ... On injured reserve with knee injury (November 17, 1993-remainder of season). ... Cardinals franchise renamed Arizona Cardinals for 1994 season. ... Released by Cardinals (August 23, 1994). ... Signed by Denver Broncos (September 6, 1994). ... Claimed on waivers by Cincinnati Bengals (September 22, 1994). ... Granted free agency (February 16, 1996). ... Re-signed by Bengals (May 6, 1996).
PLAYING EXPERIENCE: Phoenix NFL, 1993; Cincinnati NFL, 1994 and 1995. ... Games: 1993 (7), 1994 (10), 1995 (11). Total: 28.

WALLS, WESLEY — TE — PANTHERS

PERSONAL: Born February 26, 1966, in Batesville, Miss. ... 6-5/250. ... Full name: Charles Wesley Walls.
HIGH SCHOOL: Pontotoc (Miss.).
COLLEGE: Mississippi.
TRANSACTIONS/CAREER NOTES: Selected by San Francisco 49ers in second round (56th pick overall) of 1989 NFL draft. ... Signed by 49ers (July 26, 1989). ... Granted free agency (February 1, 1992). ... Re-signed by 49ers (July 18, 1992). ... On injured reserve with shoulder injury (September 1, 1992-January 16, 1993). ... On injured reserve with shoulder injury (October 27, 1993-remainder of season). ... Granted unconditional free agency (February 17, 1994). ... Signed by New Orleans Saints (April 27, 1994). ... Granted unconditional free agency (February 16, 1996). ... Signed by Carolina Panthers (February 20, 1996).
CHAMPIONSHIP GAME EXPERIENCE: Played in NFC championship game (1989 and 1990 seasons). ... Member of Super Bowl championship team (1989 season).
HONORS: Named tight end on THE SPORTING NEWS college All-America second team (1988).
PRO STATISTICS: 1989—Recovered one fumble. 1990—Returned one kickoff for 16 yards. 1993—Recovered one fumble. 1995—Returned one kickoff for six yards and recovered one fumble.

| | | RECEIVING | | | | TOTALS | | | |
Year Team	G	No.	Yds.	Avg.	TD	TD	2pt.	Pts.	Fum.
1989—San Francisco NFL	16	4	16	4.0	1	1	...	6	1
1990—San Francisco NFL	16	5	27	5.4	0	0	...	0	0
1991—San Francisco NFL	15	2	24	12.0	0	0	...	0	0
1992—San Francisco NFL				Did not play—injured.					
1993—San Francisco NFL	6	0	0	...	0	0	...	0	0
1994—New Orleans NFL	15	38	406	10.7	4	4	1	26	0
1995—New Orleans NFL	16	57	694	12.2	4	4	1	26	1
Pro totals (6 years)	84	106	1167	11.0	9	9	2	58	2

WALSH, CHRIS — WR

PERSONAL: Born December 12, 1968, in Cleveland. ... 6-1/194. ... Full name: Christopher Lee Walsh.
HIGH SCHOOL: Ygnacio Valley (Concord, Calif.).
COLLEGE: Stanford (degree in quantitative economics).
TRANSACTIONS/CAREER NOTES: Selected by Buffalo Bills in ninth round (251st pick overall) of 1992 NFL draft. ... Signed by Bills (July 22, 1992). ... Released by Bills (August 31, 1992). ... Re-signed by Bills to practice squad (September 1, 1992). ... Activated (September 19, 1992). ... Released by Bills (October 2, 1992). ... Re-signed by Bills to practice squad (October 2, 1992). ... Granted free agency after 1992 season. ... Re-signed by Bills for 1993 season. ... Released by Bills (March 10, 1994). ... Signed by Minnesota Vikings (May 6, 1994). ... Granted unconditional free agency (February 16, 1996).
PLAYING EXPERIENCE: Buffalo NFL, 1992 and 1993; Minnesota NFL, 1994 and 1995. ... Games: 1992 (2), 1993 (3), 1994 (10), 1995 (16). Total: 31.
CHAMPIONSHIP GAME EXPERIENCE: Member of Bills for AFC championship game (1993 season); inactive. ... Member of Bills for Super Bowl XXVIII (1993 season); inactive.
PRO STATISTICS: 1994—Returned one kickoff for six yards. 1995—Caught seven passes for 66 yards and returned three kickoffs for 42 yards.

WALSH, STEVE — QB — RAMS

PERSONAL: Born December 1, 1966, in St. Paul, Minn. ... 6-3/205. ... Full name: Stephen John Walsh.
HIGH SCHOOL: Cretin-Derham (St. Paul, Minn.).
COLLEGE: Miami (Fla.).
TRANSACTIONS/CAREER NOTES: Selected by Dallas Cowboys in first round of 1989 NFL supplemental draft (July 7, 1989). ... Signed by Cowboys (July 29, 1989). ... Traded by Cowboys to New Orleans Saints for first-round and third-round (OT Erik Williams) picks in 1991 draft and second-round pick (traded to Cleveland) in 1992 draft (September 25, 1990). ... Active for two games (1992); did not play. ... Granted free agency (March 1, 1993). ... Re-signed by Saints (July 15, 1993). ... Released by Saints (April 23, 1994). ... Signed by Chicago Bears (April 26, 1994). ... Granted unconditional free agency (February 17, 1995). ... Re-signed by Bears (April 17, 1995). ... Granted unconditional free agency (February 16, 1996). ... Signed by St. Louis Rams (April 10, 1996).
PRO STATISTICS: 1989—Fumbled three times and recovered two fumbles for minus 14 yards. 1990—Fumbled six times and recovered two fumbles. 1991—Fumbled three times and recovered one fumble for minus 20 yards. 1994—Fumbled seven times and recovered three fumbles for minus eight yards.
STATISTICAL PLATEAUS: 300-yard passing games: 1991 (1).
MISCELLANEOUS: Regular-season record as starting NFL quarterback: 19-16 (.543).

W

Year Team	G	Att.	Cmp.	Pct.	Yds.	TD	Int.	Avg.	Rat.	Att.	Yds.	Avg.	TD	TD	2pt.	Pts.
					PASSING						RUSHING				TOTALS	
1989—Dallas NFL	8	219	110	50.2	1371	5	9	6.26	60.5	6	16	2.7	0	0	...	0
1990—Dallas NFL	1	9	4	44.4	40	0	0	4.45	57.6	1	0	0.0	0	0	...	0
—New Orleans NFL	12	327	175	53.5	1970	12	13	6.03	67.5	19	25	1.3		0	...	0
1991—New Orleans NFL	8	255	141	55.3	1638	11	6	6.42	79.5	8	0	0.0	0	0	...	0
1992—New Orleans NFL								Did not play.								
1993—New Orleans NFL	2	38	20	52.6	271	2	3	7.13	60.3	4	-4	-1.0	0	0	...	0
1994—Chicago NFL	12	343	208	60.6	2078	10	8	6.06	77.9	30	4	0.1	1	1	0	6
1995—Chicago NFL	1	0	0	...	0	0	0			0	0	...	0	0	0	0
Pro totals (6 years)	44	1191	658	55.3	7368	40	39	6.19	71.5	68	41	0.6	1	1	0	6

WALTER, JOE — OT — BENGALS

PERSONAL: Born June 18, 1963, in Dallas. ... 6-7/292. ... Full name: Joseph Follmann Walter Jr.
HIGH SCHOOL: North (Garland, Texas).
COLLEGE: Texas Tech.
TRANSACTIONS/CAREER NOTES: Selected by Denver Gold in 1985 USFL territorial draft. ... Selected by Cincinnati Bengals in seventh round (181st pick overall) of 1985 NFL draft. ... Signed by Bengals (July 15, 1985). ... On injured reserve with knee injury (December 30, 1988-remainder of season playoffs). ... On reserve/physically unable to perform list with knee injury (September 4-October 21, 1989). ... Granted free agency (February 1, 1992). ... Re-signed by Bengals (September 2, 1992). ... On injured reserve with knee injury (August 23, 1994-entire season).
PLAYING EXPERIENCE: Cincinnati NFL, 1985-1993 and 1995. ... Games: 1985 (14), 1986 (15), 1987 (12), 1988 (16), 1989 (10), 1990 (16), 1991 (15), 1992 (16), 1993 (16), 1995 (16). Total: 146.
PRO STATISTICS: 1987—Recovered two fumbles. 1991—Recovered one fumble. 1992—Recovered one fumble.

WARE, DEREK — TE

PERSONAL: Born September 17, 1967, in Sacramento. ... 6-2/255. ... Full name: Derek Gene Ware.
HIGH SCHOOL: Christian Brothers (Sacramento).
JUNIOR COLLEGE: Sacramento (Calif.) City College.
COLLEGE: Texas A&M, then Central Oklahoma.
TRANSACTIONS/CAREER NOTES: Selected by Phoenix Cardinals in seventh round (175th pick overall) of 1992 NFL draft. ... Signed by Cardinals (July 14, 1992). ... Cardinals franchise renamed Arizona Cardinals for 1994 season. ... Claimed on waivers by Cincinnati Bengals (December 21, 1994). ... Granted unconditional free agency (February 16, 1996).
PRO STATISTICS: 1994—Recovered one fumble.

Year Team	G	No.	Yds.	Avg.	TD	TD	2pt.	Pts.	Fum.
		RECEIVING				TOTALS			
1992—Phoenix NFL	15	1	13	13.0	0	0	...	0	0
1993—Phoenix NFL	16	3	45	15.0	0	0	...	0	0
1994—Arizona NFL	15	17	171	10.1	1	1	0	6	1
1995—Cincinnati NFL	7	2	36	18.0	0	0	0	0	0
Pro totals (4 years)	53	23	265	11.5	1	1	0	6	1

WARREN, CHRIS — RB — SEAHAWKS

PERSONAL: Born January 24, 1967, in Silver Spring, Md. ... 6-2/225. ... Full name: Christopher Collins Warren Jr.
HIGH SCHOOL: Robinson Secondary (Fairfax, Va.).
COLLEGE: Virginia, then Ferrum, Va. (degree in psychology).
TRANSACTIONS/CAREER NOTES: Selected by Seattle Seahawks in fourth round (89th pick overall) of 1990 NFL draft. ... Signed by Seahawks (July 24, 1990). ... Granted free agency (March 1, 1993). ... Tendered offer sheet by New York Jets (April 23, 1993). ... Offer matched by Seahawks (April 23, 1993).
HONORS: Played in Pro Bowl (1993-1995 seasons).
PRO STATISTICS: 1990—Fumbled three times and recovered one fumble. 1991—Fumbled three times and recovered one fumble. 1992—Fumbled twice and recovered two fumbles. 1993—Fumbled three times. 1994—Fumbled five times and recovered two fumbles. 1995—Fumbled five times and recovered two fumbles.
STATISTICAL PLATEAUS: 100-yard rushing games: 1992 (3), 1993 (3), 1994 (7), 1995 (8). Total: 21.

Year Team	G	Att.	Yds.	Avg.	TD	No.	Yds.	Avg.	TD	No.	Yds.	Avg.	TD	No.	Yds.	Avg.	TD	TD	2pt.	Pts.
		RUSHING				RECEIVING				PUNT RETURNS				KICKOFF RETURNS				TOTALS		
1990—Seattle NFL	16	6	11	1.8	1	0	0	...	0	28	269	9.6	0	23	478	20.8	0	1	...	6
1991—Seattle NFL	16	11	13	1.2	0	2	9	4.5	0	32	298	9.3	1	35	792	22.6	0	1	...	6
1992—Seattle NFL	16	223	1017	4.6	3	16	134	8.4	0	34	252	7.4	0	28	524	18.7	0	3	...	18
1993—Seattle NFL	14	273	1072	3.9	7	15	99	6.6	0	0	0	...	0	0	0	...	0	7	...	42
1994—Seattle NFL	16	333	1545	4.6	9	41	323	7.9	2	0	0	...	0	0	0	...	0	11	1	68
1995—Seattle NFL	16	310	1346	4.3	15	35	247	7.1	1	0	0	...	0	0	0	...	0	16	0	96
Pro totals (6 years)	94	1156	5004	4.3	35	109	812	7.5	3	94	819	8.7	1	86	1794	20.9	0	39	1	236

WARREN, LAMONT — RB — COLTS

PERSONAL: Born January 4, 1973, in Indianapolis. ... 5-11/211.
HIGH SCHOOL: Dorsey (Los Angeles).
COLLEGE: Colorado.
TRANSACTIONS/CAREER NOTES: Selected after junior season by Indianapolis Colts in sixth round (164th pick overall) of 1994 NFL draft. ... Signed by Colts (July 13, 1994).
CHAMPIONSHIP GAME EXPERIENCE: Played in AFC championship game (1995 season).

W

PRO STATISTICS: 1994—Attempted one pass without a completion.

			RUSHING				RECEIVING				KICKOFF RETURNS				TOTALS			
Year Team	G	Att.	Yds.	Avg.	TD	No.	Yds.	Avg.	TD	No.	Yds.	Avg.	TD	TD	2pt.	Pts.	Fum.
1994—Indianapolis NFL	11	18	80	4.4	0	3	47	15.7	0	2	56	28.0	0	0	0	0	0
1995—Indianapolis NFL	12	47	152	3.2	1	17	159	9.4	0	15	315	21.0	0	1	0	6	1
Pro totals (2 years)	23	65	232	3.6	1	20	206	10.3	0	17	371	21.8	0	1	0	6	1

WARREN, TERRENCE   WR/KR   JAGUARS

PERSONAL: Born August 2, 1969, in Suffolk, Va. ... 6-1/205. ... Full name: Terrence Lee Warren.
HIGH SCHOOL: John F. Kennedy (Suffolk, Va.).
COLLEGE: Hampton (Va.).
TRANSACTIONS/CAREER NOTES: Selected by Seattle Seahawks in fifth round (114th pick overall) of 1993 NFL draft. ... Signed by Seahawks (July 13, 1993). ... Assigned by Seahawks to London Monarchs in 1995 World League enhancement allocation program (February 20, 1995). ... Released by Seahawks (August 27, 1995). ... Signed by San Francisco 49ers (August 30, 1995). ... Released by 49ers (September 5, 1995). ... Signed by Jacksonville Jaguars (December 20, 1995).
PRO STATISTICS: 1994—Recovered one fumble.

			RUSHING				KICKOFF RETURNS				TOTALS			
Year Team	G	Att.	Yds.	Avg.	TD	No.	Yds.	Avg.	TD	TD	2pt.	Pts.	Fum.
1993—Seattle NFL	2	0	0	...	0	0	0	...	0	0	...	0	0
1994—Seattle NFL	14	3	15	5.0	0	14	350	25.0	0	0	0	0	0
1995—San Francisco NFL.....................	1	0	0	...	0	4	67	16.8	0	0	0	0	0
Pro totals (3 years)	17	3	15	5.0	0	18	417	23.2	0	0	0	0	0

WASHINGTON, BRIAN   S   CHIEFS

PERSONAL: Born September 10, 1965, in Richmond, Va. ... 6-1/210. ... Full name: Brian Wayne Washington.
HIGH SCHOOL: Highland Springs (Va.).
COLLEGE: Nebraska.
TRANSACTIONS/CAREER NOTES: Selected by Cleveland Browns in 10th round (272nd pick overall) of 1988 NFL draft. ... Signed by Browns (July 13, 1988). ... On injured reserve with broken nose and elbow (September 4-6, 1989). ... Released by Browns (September 7, 1989). ... Signed by New York Jets (September 12, 1989). ... On retired list (September 14-19, 1989). ... On retired/left camp list (September 20, 1989-February 12, 1990). ... Granted free agency (February 1, 1991). ... Re-signed by Jets (May 5, 1991). ... Granted free agency (March 1, 1993). ... Re-signed by Jets (April 30, 1993). ... Granted free agency (March 20, 1995). ... Signed by Kansas City Chiefs (March 29, 1995).
PRO STATISTICS: 1990—Recovered one fumble. 1991—Fumbled once and recovered one fumble. 1992—Recovered two fumbles. 1993—Recovered one fumble. 1994—Recovered three fumbles. 1995—Recovered one fumble for two yards.

		INTERCEPTIONS				SACKS
Year Team	G	No.	Yds.	Avg.	TD	No.
1988—Cleveland NFL............................	16	3	104	34.7	1	0.5
1989—			Did not play.			
1990—New York Jets NFL.....................	14	3	22	7.3	0	1.0
1991—New York Jets NFL.....................	16	1	0	0.0	0	2.0
1992—New York Jets NFL.....................	16	6	59	9.8	1	1.0
1993—New York Jets NFL.....................	16	6	128	21.3	1	0.0
1994—New York Jets NFL.....................	15	2	-3	-1.5	0	0.0
1995—Kansas City NFL	15	3	100	33.3	1	0.0
Pro totals (7 years)	108	24	410	17.1	4	4.5

WASHINGTON, DEWAYNE   CB   VIKINGS

PERSONAL: Born December 27, 1972, in Durham, N.C. ... 5-11/191. ... Full name: Dewayne Neron Washington.
HIGH SCHOOL: Northern (Durham, N.C.).
COLLEGE: North Carolina State.
TRANSACTIONS/CAREER NOTES: Selected by Minnesota Vikings in first round (18th pick overall) of 1994 NFL draft. ... Signed by Vikings (July 14, 1994).
PRO STATISTICS: 1994—Recovered two fumbles for 17 yards and one touchdown.

		INTERCEPTIONS			
Year Team	G	No.	Yds.	Avg.	TD
1994—Minnesota NFL	16	3	135	45.0	2
1995—Minnesota NFL	15	1	25	25.0	0
Pro totals (2 years)	31	4	160	40.0	2

WASHINGTON, JAMES   S   REDSKINS

PERSONAL: Born January 10, 1965, in Los Angeles. ... 6-1/209. ... Full name: James McArthur Washington.
HIGH SCHOOL: Jordan (Los Angeles).
COLLEGE: UCLA (degree in history).
TRANSACTIONS/CAREER NOTES: Selected by Los Angeles Rams in fifth round (137th pick overall) of 1988 NFL draft. ... Signed by Rams (July 12, 1988). ... On injured reserve with thigh injury (November 10-December 27, 1989). ... On developmental squad (December 28, 1989). ... Granted unconditional free agency (February 1, 1990). ... Signed by Dallas Cowboys (March 3, 1990). ... Granted free agency (February 1, 1992). ... Re-signed by Cowboys (August 11, 1992). ... Granted unconditional free agency (February 17, 1995). ... Signed by Washington Redskins (March 2, 1995).
CHAMPIONSHIP GAME EXPERIENCE: Played in NFC championship game (1989 and 1992-1994 seasons). ... Member of Super Bowl championship team (1992 and 1993 seasons).

W

HONORS: Named defensive back on THE SPORTING NEWS college All-America second team (1985).
POSTSEASON RECORDS: Shares Super Bowl career record for most touchdowns by fumble recovery—1 (January 30, 1994, vs. Buffalo).
PRO STATISTICS: 1989—Recovered one fumble. 1990—Recovered three fumbles. 1992—Recovered one fumble. 1993—Returned one punt for no yards, fumbled once and recovered one fumble. 1994—Recovered one fumble.

		INTERCEPTIONS			
Year Team	G	No.	Yds.	Avg.	TD
1988—Los Angeles Rams NFL	16	1	7	7.0	0
1989—Los Angeles Rams NFL	9	0	0	...	0
1990—Dallas NFL	15	3	24	8.0	0
1991—Dallas NFL	16	2	9	4.5	0
1992—Dallas NFL	16	3	31	10.3	0
1993—Dallas NFL	14	1	38	38.0	0
1994—Dallas NFL	16	5	43	8.6	0
1995—Washington NFL	12	2	35	17.5	0
Pro totals (8 years)	114	17	187	11.0	0

WASHINGTON, LIONEL   CB   BRONCOS

PERSONAL: Born October 21, 1960, in New Orleans. ... 6-0/185.
HIGH SCHOOL: Lutcher (La.).
COLLEGE: Tulane (degree in sports administration).
TRANSACTIONS/CAREER NOTES: Selected by Tampa Bay Bandits in 20th round (229th pick overall) of 1983 USFL draft. ... Selected by St. Louis Cardinals in fourth round (103rd pick overall) of 1983 NFL draft. ... Signed by Cardinals (May 6, 1983). ... On injured reserve with broken fibula (September 16-November 22, 1985). ... Granted free agency (February 1, 1987). ... Re-signed by Cardinals and traded to Los Angeles Raiders for fifth-round pick (P John Bruno) in 1987 draft (March 18, 1987). ... Granted free agency (February 1, 1992). ... Re-signed by Raiders (August 6, 1992). ... Granted unconditional free agency (February 17, 1995). ... Signed by Denver Broncos (March 6, 1995).
CHAMPIONSHIP GAME EXPERIENCE: Played in AFC championship game (1990 season).
PRO STATISTICS: 1983—Recovered one fumble. 1984—Recovered one fumble. 1986—Recovered one fumble. 1989—Recovered three fumbles for 44 yards and one touchdown. 1993—Credited with one sack. 1995—Fumbled once and recovered one fumble for 38 yards.

		INTERCEPTIONS			
Year Team	G	No.	Yds.	Avg.	TD
1983—St. Louis NFL	16	8	92	11.5	0
1984—St. Louis NFL	15	5	42	8.4	0
1985—St. Louis NFL	5	1	48	48.0	†1
1986—St. Louis NFL	16	2	19	9.5	0
1987—Los Angeles Raiders NFL	11	0	0	...	0
1988—Los Angeles Raiders NFL	12	1	0	0.0	0
1989—Los Angeles Raiders NFL	16	3	46	15.3	1
1990—Los Angeles Raiders NFL	16	1	2	2.0	0
1991—Los Angeles Raiders NFL	16	5	22	4.4	0
1992—Los Angeles Raiders NFL	16	2	21	10.5	0
1993—Los Angeles Raiders NFL	16	2	0	0.0	0
1994—Los Angeles Raiders NFL	11	3	65	21.7	1
1995—Denver NFL	16	0	0	...	0
Pro totals (13 years)	182	33	357	10.8	3

WASHINGTON, MARVIN   DE   JETS

PERSONAL: Born October 22, 1965, in Denver. ... 6-6/280. ... Full name: Marvin Andrew Washington. ... Cousin of Andrew Lang, center, Atlanta Hawks.
HIGH SCHOOL: Justin F. Kimball (Dallas).
JUNIOR COLLEGE: Hinds Community College (Miss.).
COLLEGE: Texas-El Paso, then Idaho.
TRANSACTIONS/CAREER NOTES: Selected by New York Jets in sixth round (151st pick overall) of 1989 NFL draft. ... Signed by Jets (July 21, 1989). ... Granted free agency (February 1, 1991). ... Re-signed by Jets (May 5, 1991). ... Granted free agency (March 1, 1993). ... Tendered offer sheet by Seattle Seahawks (March 25, 1993). ... Offer matched by Jets (March 31, 1993).
PRO STATISTICS: 1989—Returned one kickoff for 11 yards and recovered one fumble. 1992—Credited with one safety. 1994—Intercepted one pass for seven yards, fumbled once and recovered one fumble.

Year Team	G	SACKS
1989—New York Jets NFL	16	1.5
1990—New York Jets NFL	16	4.5
1991—New York Jets NFL	15	6.0
1992—New York Jets NFL	16	8.5
1993—New York Jets NFL	16	5.5
1994—New York Jets NFL	15	3.0
1995—New York Jets NFL	16	6.0
Pro totals (7 years)	110	35.0

W

WASHINGTON, MICKEY   CB   JAGUARS

PERSONAL: Born July 8, 1968, in Galveston, Texas. ... 5-10/191. ... Full name: Mickey Lynn Washington. ... Cousin of Joe Washington, running back with four NFL teams (1977-1985).
HIGH SCHOOL: West Brook Senior (Beaumont, Texas).
COLLEGE: Texas A&M (degree in sociology).
TRANSACTIONS/CAREER NOTES: Selected by Phoenix Cardinals in eighth round (199th pick overall) of 1990 NFL draft. ... Signed by Cardinals (July 23, 1990). ... Released by Cardinals (September 3, 1990). ... Signed by Indianapolis Colts to practice squad (September 3, 1990). ... Signed by New England Patriots off Colts practice squad (October 30, 1990). ... Granted unconditional free agency (February 1-April 1,

1991). ... Re-signed by Patriots for 1991 season. ... Granted free agency (February 1, 1992). ... Re-signed by Patriots (July 26, 1992). ... Claimed on waivers by Pittsburgh Steelers (August 25, 1992). ... Released by Steelers (August 31, 1992). ... Signed by Washington Redskins (November 18, 1992). ... Released by Redskins (December 16, 1992). ... Signed by Buffalo Bills (March 23, 1993). ... Granted unconditional free agency (February 17, 1995). ... Signed by Jacksonville Jaguars (March 14, 1995).

CHAMPIONSHIP GAME EXPERIENCE: Played in AFC championship game (1993 season). ... Played in Super Bowl XXVIII (1993 season).

PRO STATISTICS: 1993—Credited with ½ sack and recovered two fumbles for six yards. 1994—Credited with ½ sack and recovered one fumble. 1995—Recovered two fumbles.

			INTERCEPTIONS		
Year Team	G	No.	Yds.	Avg.	TD
1990—New England NFL	9	0	0	...	0
1991—New England NFL	16	2	0	0.0	0
1992—Washington NFL	3	0	0	...	0
1993—Buffalo NFL	16	1	27	27.0	1
1994—Buffalo NFL	16	3	63	21.0	0
1995—Jacksonville NFL	16	1	48	48.0	1
Pro totals (6 years)	76	7	138	19.7	2

WASHINGTON, TED   NT   BILLS

PERSONAL: Born April 13, 1968, in Tampa. ... 6-4/325. ... Son of Ted Washington, linebacker, Houston Oilers (1973-1982).

HIGH SCHOOL: Tampa Bay Vocational Tech Senior.

COLLEGE: Louisville.

TRANSACTIONS/CAREER NOTES: Selected by San Francisco 49ers in first round (25th pick overall) of 1991 NFL draft. ... Signed by 49ers (July 10, 1991). ... Traded by 49ers to Denver Broncos for fifth-round pick (traded to Green Bay) in 1994 draft (April 19, 1994). ... Granted unconditional free agency (February 17, 1995). ... Signed by Buffalo Bills (February 25, 1995).

CHAMPIONSHIP GAME EXPERIENCE: Played in NFC championship game (1992 and 1993 seasons).

PRO STATISTICS: 1993—Recovered one fumble. 1994—Intercepted one pass for five yards.

Year Team	G	SACKS
1991—San Francisco NFL	16	1.0
1992—San Francisco NFL	16	2.0
1993—San Francisco NFL	12	3.0
1994—Denver NFL	15	2.5
1995—Buffalo NFL	16	2.5
Pro totals (5 years)	75	11.0

WATERS, ANDRE   S

PERSONAL: Born March 10, 1962, in Belle Glade, Fla. ... 5-11/200.

HIGH SCHOOL: Pahokee (Fla.).

COLLEGE: Cheyney, Pa. (degree in business administration).

TRANSACTIONS/CAREER NOTES: Signed as non-drafted free agent by Philadelphia Eagles (June 20, 1984). ... Granted free agency (February 1, 1992). ... Re-signed by Eagles (August 20, 1992). ... On injured reserve with fractured fibula (October 19, 1992-January 8, 1993); on practice squad (January 6-8, 1992). ... Released by Eagles (June 3, 1994). ... Signed by Arizona Cardinals (July 30, 1994). ... Granted unconditional free agency (February 17, 1995). ... Re-signed by Cardinals (October 5, 1995). ... Granted unconditional free agency (February 16, 1996).

PRO STATISTICS: 1984—Recovered one fumble. 1985—Returned one punt for 23 yards and recovered one fumble. 1986—Recovered two fumbles for 81 yards. 1987—Recovered two fumbles for 11 yards. 1989—Recovered three fumbles for 21 yards and one touchdown. 1991—Recovered one fumble.

		INTERCEPTIONS				SACKS	KICKOFF RETURNS				TOTALS			
Year Team	G	No.	Yds.	Avg.	TD	No.	No.	Yds.	Avg.	TD	TD	2pt.	Pts.	Fum.
1984—Philadelphia NFL	16	0	0	...	0	0.0	13	319	24.5	†1	1	...	6	1
1985—Philadelphia NFL	16	0	0	...	0	0.0	4	74	18.5	0	0	...	0	1
1986—Philadelphia NFL	16	6	39	6.5	0	2.0	0	0	...	0	0	...	0	0
1987—Philadelphia NFL	12	3	63	21.0	0	0.0	0	0	...	0	0	...	0	0
1988—Philadelphia NFL	16	3	19	6.3	0	0.5	0	0	...	0	0	...	0	0
1989—Philadelphia NFL	16	1	20	20.0	0	1.0	0	0	...	0	1	...	6	0
1990—Philadelphia NFL	14	0	0	...	0	0.0	0	0	...	0	0	...	0	0
1991—Philadelphia NFL	16	1	0	0.0	0	0.0	0	0	...	0	0	...	0	0
1992—Philadelphia NFL	6	1	23	23.0	0	0.0	0	0	...	0	0	...	0	0
1993—Philadelphia NFL	9	0	0	...	0	0.0	0	0	...	0	0	...	0	0
1994—Arizona NFL	12	0	0	...	0	0.0	0	0	...	0	0	0	0	0
1995—Arizona NFL	7	0	0	...	0	0.0	0	0	...	0	0	0	0	0
Pro totals (12 years)	156	15	164	10.9	0	3.5	17	393	23.1	1	2	0	12	2

W

WATKINS, KENDELL   TE   COWBOYS

PERSONAL: Born March 8, 1973, in Jackson, Miss. ... 6-1/305. ... Full name: Kendell Mairo Watkins.

HIGH SCHOOL: Provine (Jackson, Miss.).

COLLEGE: Mississippi State.

TRANSACTIONS/CAREER NOTES: Selected by Dallas Cowboys in second round (59th pick overall) of 1995 NFL draft. ... Signed by Cowboys (July 17, 1995).

PLAYING EXPERIENCE: Dallas NFL, 1995. ... Games: 1995 (16).

CHAMPIONSHIP GAME EXPERIENCE: Played in NFC championship game (1995 season). ... Member of Super Bowl championship team (1995 season).

PRO STATISTICS: 1995—Caught one pass for eight yards, returned one kickoff for minus six yards and fumbled once.

WATSON, TIM   S   RAIDERS

PERSONAL: Born August 13, 1970, in Fort Valley, Ga. ... 6-1/215. ... Full name: James Timothy Watson Jr.
HIGH SCHOOL: Peach County (Fort Valley, Ga.).
COLLEGE: Howard (degree in business marketing and fashion merchandising).
TRANSACTIONS/CAREER NOTES: Selected by Green Bay Packers in sixth round (156th overall) in 1993 NFL draft. ... Signed by Packers (July 9, 1993). ... Released by Packers (August 23, 1993). ... Signed by Cleveland Browns (August 25, 1993). ... On non-injury football list (August 30-September 2, 1993). ... Released by Browns (September 2, 1993). ... Signed by Packers (September 6, 1993). ... Released by Packers (September 20, 1993). ... Signed by Kansas City Chiefs to practice squad (September 27, 1993). ... Activated (November 15, 1993). ... On injured reserve with knee injury (September 14, 1994-remainder of season). ... Released by Chiefs (September 27, 1995). ... Signed by New York Giants (November 8, 1995). ... Released by Giants (December 21, 1995). ... Signed by Oakland Raiders for 1996 season. ... Assigned by Raiders to Barcelona Dragons in 1996 World League enhancement allocation program (February 19, 1996).
PLAYING EXPERIENCE: Kansas City NFL, 1993 and 1994; Kansas City (4)-New York Giants (1) NFL, 1995. ... Games: 1993 (4), 1994 (1), 1995 (5). Total: 10.
CHAMPIONSHIP GAME EXPERIENCE: Played in AFC championship game (1993 season).

WATTERS, RICKY   RB   EAGLES

PERSONAL: Born April 7, 1969, in Harrisburg, Pa. ... 6-1/217. ... Full name: Richard James Watters.
HIGH SCHOOL: Bishop McDevitt (Harrisburg, Pa.).
COLLEGE: Notre Dame (degree in design).
TRANSACTIONS/CAREER NOTES: Selected by San Francisco 49ers in second round (45th pick overall) of 1991 NFL draft. ... Signed by 49ers (July 11, 1991). ... On injured reserve with foot injury (August 27, 1991-entire season). ... Designated by 49ers as transition player (February 15, 1994). ... Tendered offer sheet by Philadelphia Eagles (March 18, 1995). ... 49ers declined to match offer (March 25, 1995).
CHAMPIONSHIP GAME EXPERIENCE: Played in NFC championship game (1992-1994 seasons). ... Member of Super Bowl championship team (1994 season).
HONORS: Played in Pro Bowl (1992-1995 seasons).
POSTSEASON RECORDS: Shares Super Bowl single-game records for most points—18; and most touchdowns—3 (January 29, 1995, vs. San Diego). ... Holds NFL postseason single-game records for most points—30; most touchdowns—5; and most rushing touchdowns—5 (January 15, 1994, vs. New York Giants).
PRO STATISTICS: 1992—Attempted one pass without a completion and recovered one fumble. 1993—Recovered one fumble. 1994— Recovered two fumbles.
STATISTICAL PLATEAUS: 100-yard rushing games: 1992 (4), 1993 (3), 1994 (2), 1995 (4). Total: 13. ... 100-yard receiving games: 1994 (1).

Year Team	G	RUSHING				RECEIVING				TOTALS			
		Att.	Yds.	Avg.	TD	No.	Yds.	Avg.	TD	TD	2pt.	Pts.	Fum.
1991—San Francisco NFL				Did not play.									
1992—San Francisco NFL	14	206	1013	4.9	9	43	405	9.4	2	11	...	66	2
1993—San Francisco NFL	13	208	950	4.6	10	31	326	10.5	1	11	...	66	5
1994—San Francisco NFL	16	239	877	3.7	6	66	719	10.9	5	11	0	66	8
1995—Philadelphia NFL	16	337	1273	3.8	11	62	434	7.0	1	12	0	72	6
Pro totals (4 years)	59	990	4113	4.2	36	202	1884	9.3	9	45	0	270	21

WATTS, DAMON   DB   COLTS

PERSONAL: Born April 8, 1972, in Indianapolis. ... 5-10/173.
HIGH SCHOOL: Lawrence North (Indianapolis).
COLLEGE: Indiana.
TRANSACTIONS/CAREER NOTES: Signed as non-drafted free agent by Indianapolis Colts (July 12, 1994).
CHAMPIONSHIP GAME EXPERIENCE: Played in AFC championship game (1995 season).

Year Team	G	INTERCEPTIONS			
		No.	Yds.	Avg.	TD
1994—Indianapolis NFL	16	1	0	0.0	0
1995—Indianapolis NFL	13	1	9	9.0	0
Pro totals (2 years)	29	2	9	4.5	0

WAY, CHARLES   FB   GIANTS

PERSONAL: Born December 27, 1972, in Philadelphia. ... 6-0/245. ... Full name: Charles Christopher Way.
HIGH SCHOOL: Northeast (Philadelphia).
COLLEGE: Virginia.
TRANSACTIONS/CAREER NOTES: Selected by New York Giants in sixth round (206th pick overall) of 1995 NFL draft. ... Signed by Giants (July 23, 1995).
PRO STATISTICS: 1995—Returned one kickoff for eight yards.

Year Team	G	RUSHING				RECEIVING				TOTALS			
		Att.	Yds.	Avg.	TD	No.	Yds.	Avg.	TD	TD	2pt.	Pts.	Fum.
1995—New York Giants NFL	16	2	6	3.0	0	7	76	10.9	1	1	0	6	0

WEBB, RICHMOND   OT   DOLPHINS

PERSONAL: Born January 11, 1967, in Dallas. ... 6-6/303. ... Full name: Richmond Jewel Webb.
HIGH SCHOOL: Franklin D. Roosevelt (Dallas).
COLLEGE: Texas A&M (degree in industrial distribution).

TRANSACTIONS/CAREER NOTES: Selected by Miami Dolphins in first round (ninth pick overall) of 1990 NFL draft. ... Signed by Dolphins (July 27, 1990).
PLAYING EXPERIENCE: Miami NFL, 1990-1995. ... Games: 1990 (16), 1991 (14), 1992 (16), 1993 (16), 1994 (16), 1995 (16). Total: 94.
CHAMPIONSHIP GAME EXPERIENCE: Played in AFC championship game (1992 season).
HONORS: Named NFL Rookie of the Year by THE SPORTING NEWS (1990). ... Played in Pro Bowl (1990-1995 seasons). ... Named offensive tackle on THE SPORTING NEWS NFL All-Pro team (1992 and 1994).
PRO STATISTICS: 1995—Recovered one fumble.

WEBSTER, LARRY — DT — RAVENS

PERSONAL: Born January 18, 1969, in Elkton, Md. ... 6-5/288. ... Full name: Larry Melvin Webster Jr.
HIGH SCHOOL: Elkton (Md.).
COLLEGE: Maryland.
TRANSACTIONS/CAREER NOTES: Selected by Miami Dolphins in third round (70th pick overall) of 1992 NFL draft. ... Signed by Dolphins (July 10, 1992). ... Granted free agency (February 17, 1995). ... Signed by Cleveland Browns (May 4, 1995). ... On suspended list for violating league substance abuse policy (September 4-26, 1995). ... Browns franchise moved to Baltimore and renamed Ravens for 1996 season (March 11, 1996).
PLAYING EXPERIENCE: Miami NFL, 1992-1994; Cleveland NFL, 1995. ... Games: 1992 (16), 1993 (13), 1994 (16), 1995 (10). Total: 55.
CHAMPIONSHIP GAME EXPERIENCE: Played in AFC championship game (1992 season).
PRO STATISTICS: 1992—Credited with 1½ sacks. 1993—Recovered one fumble.

WEIDNER, BERT — G

PERSONAL: Born January 20, 1966, in Eden, N.Y. ... 6-2/295. ... Name pronounced WIDE-ner.
HIGH SCHOOL: Eden (N.Y.) Junior Senior.
COLLEGE: Kent.
TRANSACTIONS/CAREER NOTES: Selected by Miami Dolphins in 11th round (288th pick overall) of 1989 NFL draft. ... Signed by Dolphins (July 18, 1989). ... Released by Dolphins (September 4, 1989). ... Re-signed by Dolphins to developmental squad (September 5, 1989). ... Released by Dolphins (January 29, 1990). ... Re-signed by Dolphins (February 22, 1990). ... Granted free agency (February 1, 1992). ... Re-signed by Dolphins (July 14, 1992). ... Granted unconditional free agency (February 17, 1994). ... Re-signed by Dolphins (May 31, 1994). ... Granted unconditional free agency (February 17, 1995). ... Re-signed by Dolphins (July 14, 1995). ... On physically unable to perform list with ankle injury (July 20-August 22, 1995). ... Released by Dolphins (February 5, 1996).
PLAYING EXPERIENCE: Miami NFL, 1990-1995. ... Games: 1990 (8), 1991 (15), 1992 (16), 1993 (16), 1994 (14), 1995 (12). Total: 81.
CHAMPIONSHIP GAME EXPERIENCE: Played in AFC championship game (1992 season).
PRO STATISTICS: 1993—Recovered one fumble.

WELDON, CASEY — QB — BUCCANEERS

PERSONAL: Born February 3, 1969, in Americus, Ga. ... 6-1/206. ... Full name: William Casey Weldon.
HIGH SCHOOL: North Florida Christian (Tallahassee, Fla.).
COLLEGE: Florida State.
TRANSACTIONS/CAREER NOTES: Selected by Philadelphia Eagles in fourth round (102nd pick overall) of 1992 NFL draft. ... Signed by Eagles (July 26, 1992). ... On inactive list for all 16 games (1992). ... Claimed on waivers by Tampa Bay Buccaneers (September 1, 1993). ... Assigned by Buccaneers to Barcelona Dragons in 1995 World League enhancement allocation program (February 20, 1995).
HONORS: Named quarterback on THE SPORTING NEWS college All-America second team (1991).
PRO STATISTICS: 1995—Fumbled four times for minus three yards.

				PASSING						RUSHING				TOTALS		
Year Team	G	Att.	Cmp.	Pct.	Yds.	TD	Int.	Avg.	Rat.	Att.	Yds.	Avg.	TD	TD	2pt.	Pts.
1992—Philadelphia NFL						Did not play.										
1993—Tampa Bay NFL	3	11	6	54.6	55	0	1	5.00	30.5	0	0	...	0	0	...	0
1994—Tampa Bay NFL	2	9	7	77.8	63	0	0	7.00	95.8	0	0	...	0	0	0	0
1995—Barcelona W.L.	...	91	41	45.1	543	3	9	5.97	35.9	8	44	5.5	0	0	0	0
—Tampa Bay NFL	16	91	42	46.2	519	1	2	5.70	58.8	5	5	1.0	1	1	0	6
W.L. totals (1 year)	...	91	41	451	543	3	9	5.97	35.9	8	44	5.5	0	0	0	0
NFL totals (3 years)	21	111	55	496	637	1	3	5.74	59.0	5	5	1.0	1	1	0	6
Pro totals (3 years)	...	202	96	47.5	1180	4	12	5.84	47.9	13	49	3.8	1	1	0	6

WELLS, DEAN — LB — SEAHAWKS

W

PERSONAL: Born July 20, 1970, in Louisville, Ky. ... 6-3/244. ... Full name: Donald Dean Wells.
HIGH SCHOOL: Holy Cross (Louisville, Ky.).
COLLEGE: Kentucky (degree in marketing, 1992).
TRANSACTIONS/CAREER NOTES: Selected by Seattle Seahawks in fourth round (85th pick overall) of 1993 NFL draft. ... Signed by Seahawks (July 13, 1993).
PLAYING EXPERIENCE: Seattle NFL, 1993-1995. ... Games: 1993 (14), 1994 (15), 1995 (14). Total: 43.
PRO STATISTICS: 1995—Recovered one fumble for three yards.

WELLS, MIKE — DE — LIONS

PERSONAL: Born January 6, 1971, in Arnold, Mo. ... 6-3/287. ... Full name: Mike Allan Wells.
HIGH SCHOOL: Fox (Arnold, Mo.).
COLLEGE: Iowa.

TRANSACTIONS/CAREER NOTES: Selected by Minnesota Vikings in fourth round (125th pick overall) of 1994 NFL draft. ... Signed by Vikings (June 24, 1994). ... Released by Vikings (August 28, 1994). ... Signed by Detroit Lions (August 29, 1994).
PLAYING EXPERIENCE: Detroit NFL, 1994 and 1995. ... Games: 1994 (4), 1995 (15). Total: 19.
PRO STATISTICS: 1995—Credited with ½ sack.

WEST, DEREK   OT   COLTS

PERSONAL: Born March 28, 1972, in Denver. ... 6-8/303.
HIGH SCHOOL: Pomona (Arvada, Colo.).
COLLEGE: Colorado.
TRANSACTIONS/CAREER NOTES: Selected by Indianapolis Colts in fifth round (149th pick overall) of 1995 NFL draft. ... Signed by Colts (July 12, 1995).
PLAYING EXPERIENCE: Indianapolis NFL, 1995. ... Games: 1995 (3).
CHAMPIONSHIP GAME EXPERIENCE: Played in AFC championship game (1995 season).

WEST, ED   TE   EAGLES

PERSONAL: Born August 2, 1961, in Colbert County, Ala. ... 6-1/259. ... Full name: Edward Lee West III.
HIGH SCHOOL: Colbert County (Leighton, Ala.).
COLLEGE: Auburn.
TRANSACTIONS/CAREER NOTES: Selected by Birmingham Stallions in 1984 USFL territorial draft. ... Signed as non-drafted free agent by Green Bay Packers (May 3, 1984). ... Released by Packers (August 27, 1984). ... Re-signed by Packers (August 30, 1984). ... Granted free agency (February 1, 1992). ... Re-signed by Packers (July 27, 1992). ... Released by Packers (August 30, 1993). ... Re-signed by Packers (August 31, 1993). ... Granted unconditional free agency (February 17, 1994). ... Re-signed by Packers (June 22, 1994). ... Granted unconditional free agency (February 17, 1995). ... Signed by Indianapolis Colts (March 28, 1995). ... Released by Colts (August 27, 1995). ... Signed by Philadelphia Eagles (August 28, 1995). ... Granted unconditional free agency (February 16, 1996). ... Re-signed by Eagles (April 18, 1996).
PRO STATISTICS: 1984—Rushed once for two yards and a touchdown and recovered one fumble. 1985—Rushed once for no yards. 1986—Recovered one fumble. 1990—Returned one kickoff for no yards. 1992—Returned one kickoff for no yards. 1995—Recovered one fumble.
STATISTICAL PLATEAUS: 100-yard receiving games: 1986 (1), 1990 (1). Total: 2.

Year Team	G	RECEIVING					TOTALS			
		No.	Yds.	Avg.	TD	TD	2pt.	Pts.	Fum.
1984—Green Bay NFL	16	6	54	9.0	4	5	...	30	0
1985—Green Bay NFL	16	8	95	11.9	1	1	...	6	1
1986—Green Bay NFL	16	15	199	13.3	1	1	...	6	0
1987—Green Bay NFL	12	19	261	13.7	1	1	...	6	0
1988—Green Bay NFL	16	30	276	9.2	3	3	...	18	1
1989—Green Bay NFL	13	22	269	12.2	5	5	...	30	0
1990—Green Bay NFL	16	27	356	13.2	5	5	...	30	3
1991—Green Bay NFL	16	15	151	10.1	3	3	...	18	0
1992—Green Bay NFL	16	4	30	7.5	0	0	...	0	0
1993—Green Bay NFL	16	25	253	10.1	0	0	...	0	0
1994—Green Bay NFL	14	31	377	12.2	2	2	1	14	1
1995—Philadelphia NFL	16	20	190	9.5	1	1	0	6	0
Pro totals (12 years)	183	222	2511	11.3	26	27	1	164	6

WESTBROOK, MICHAEL   WR   REDSKINS

PERSONAL: Born July 7, 1972, in Detroit. ... 6-3/215.
HIGH SCHOOL: Chadsey (Detroit).
COLLEGE: Colorado.
TRANSACTIONS/CAREER NOTES: Selected by Washington Redskins in first round (fourth pick overall) of 1995 NFL draft. ... Signed by Redskins (August 14, 1995).
HONORS: Named wide receiver on THE SPORTING NEWS college All-America first team (1994).

Year Team	G	RUSHING				RECEIVING				TOTALS			
		Att.	Yds.	Avg.	TD	No.	Yds.	Avg.	TD	TD	2pt.	Pts.	Fum.
1995—Washington NFL	11	6	114	19.0	1	34	522	15.4	1	2	0	12	0

W

WETNIGHT, RYAN   TE   BEARS

PERSONAL: Born November 5, 1970, in Fresno, Calif. ... 6-2/240. ... Full name: Ryan Scott Wetnight.
HIGH SCHOOL: Hoover (Fresno, Calif.).
JUNIOR COLLEGE: Fresno (Calif.) City College.
COLLEGE: Stanford.
TRANSACTIONS/CAREER NOTES: Signed as non-drafted free agent by Chicago Bears (April 29, 1993). ... Released by Bears (October 10, 1993). ... Re-signed by Bears to practice squad (October 11, 1993). ... Activated (October 29, 1993). ... Released by Bears (October 7, 1994). ... Re-signed by Bears (October 10, 1994). ... On injured reserve with knee injury (December 7, 1995-remainder of season).

Year Team	G	RECEIVING					TOTALS			
		No.	Yds.	Avg.	TD	TD	2pt.	Pts.	Fum.
1993—Chicago NFL	10	9	93	10.3	1	1	...	6	0
1994—Chicago NFL	11	11	104	9.5	1	1	0	6	0
1995—Chicago NFL	12	24	193	8.0	2	2	0	12	0
Pro totals (3 years)	33	44	390	8.9	4	4	0	24	0

WHEATLEY, TYRONE — RB — GIANTS

PERSONAL: Born January 19, 1972, in Inkster, Mich. ... 6-0/228.
HIGH SCHOOL: Robichaud (Dearborn Heights, Mich.).
COLLEGE: Michigan.
TRANSACTIONS/CAREER NOTES: Selected by New York Giants in first round (17th pick overall) of 1995 NFL draft. ... Signed by Giants (August 9, 1995).

		RUSHING				RECEIVING				KICKOFF RETURNS				TOTALS			
Year Team	G	Att.	Yds.	Avg.	TD	No.	Yds.	Avg.	TD	No.	Yds.	Avg.	TD	TD	2pt.	Pts.	Fum.
1995—New York Giants NFL	13	78	245	3.1	3	5	27	5.4	0	10	186	18.6	0	3	0	18	2

WHEELER, LEONARD — CB — BENGALS

PERSONAL: Born January 15, 1969, in Taccoa, Ga. ... 5-11/189. ... Full name: Leonard Tyrone Wheeler.
HIGH SCHOOL: Stephens County (Taccoa, Ga.).
JUNIOR COLLEGE: Northwest Mississippi Community College.
COLLEGE: Lees-McRae College (N.C.), then Mississippi (did not play football), then Troy (Ala.) State.
TRANSACTIONS/CAREER NOTES: Selected by Cincinnati Bengals in third round (84th pick overall) of 1992 NFL draft. ... Signed by Bengals (July 25, 1992). ... On injured reserve with wrist injury (August 28, 1994-entire season). ... Granted free agency (February 17, 1995). ... Re-signed by Bengals (April 13, 1995). ... Granted unconditional free agency (February 16, 1996). ... Re-signed by Bengals (April 26, 1996).
PLAYING EXPERIENCE: Cincinnati NFL, 1992, 1993 and 1995. ... Games: 1992 (16), 1993 (16), 1995 (16). Total: 48.
PRO STATISTICS: 1992—Intercepted one pass for 12 yards. 1993—Recovered one fumble.

WHEELER, MARK — DT — PATRIOTS

PERSONAL: Born April 1, 1970, in San Marcos, Texas. ... 6-2/285.
HIGH SCHOOL: San Marcos (Texas).
JUNIOR COLLEGE: Navarro College (Texas).
COLLEGE: Texas A&M.
TRANSACTIONS/CAREER NOTES: Selected by Tampa Bay Buccaneers in third round (59th pick overall) of 1992 NFL draft. ... Signed by Buccaneers (July 9, 1992). ... Granted unconditional free agency (February 16, 1996). ... Signed by New England Patriots (March 21, 1996).

Year Team	G	SACKS
1992—Tampa Bay NFL	16	5.0
1993—Tampa Bay NFL	10	2.0
1994—Tampa Bay NFL	15	3.0
1995—Tampa Bay NFL	14	1.0
Pro totals (4 years)	55	11.0

WHIGHAM, LARRY — S — PATRIOTS

PERSONAL: Born June 23, 1972, in Hattiesburg, Miss. ... 6-2/202. ... Full name: Larry Jerome Whigham.
HIGH SCHOOL: Hattiesburg (Miss.).
COLLEGE: Northeast Louisiana.
TRANSACTIONS/CAREER NOTES: Selected by Seattle Seahawks in fourth round (110th pick overall) of 1994 NFL draft. ... Signed by Seahawks (June 9, 1994). ... Released by Seahawks (August 28, 1994). ... Re-signed by Seahawks to practice squad (August 29, 1994). ... Signed by New England Patriots off Seahawks practice squad (September 13, 1994).
PRO STATISTICS: 1994—Fumbled once. 1995—Recovered one fumble.

		INTERCEPTIONS			
Year Team	G	No.	Yds.	Avg.	TD
1994—New England NFL	12	1	21	21.0	0
1995—New England NFL	16	0	0	...	0
Pro totals (2 years)	28	1	21	21.0	0

WHITE, ALBERTO — DE — RAMS

PERSONAL: Born April 8, 1971, in Miami. ... 6-3/245.
HIGH SCHOOL: Southridge (Miami).
COLLEGE: Texas Southern.
TRANSACTIONS/CAREER NOTES: Selected after junior season by Los Angeles Raiders in 10th round (268th pick overall) of 1992 NFL draft. ... Released by Raiders (August 25, 1992). ... Re-signed by Raiders (July 1993). ... Released by Raiders (August 24, 1993). ... Re-signed by Raiders (May 4, 1994). ... Released by Raiders (August 28, 1994). ... Re-signed by Raiders to practice squad (August 29, 1994). ... Activated (November 4, 1994). ... Claimed on waivers by St. Louis Rams (August 23, 1995). ... Released by Rams (September 14, 1995). ... Signed by Green Bay Packers (October 11, 1995). ... Released by Packers (October 13, 1995). ... Signed by Rams (February 13, 1996).

Year Team	G	SACKS
1994—Los Angeles Raiders NFL	8	2.0
1995—St. Louis NFL	2	1.0
Pro totals (2 years)	10	3.0

W

WHITE, DAVID — LB — BILLS

PERSONAL: Born February 27, 1970, in New Orleans. ... 6-2/235.
HIGH SCHOOL: St. Augustine (New Orleans).

COLLEGE: Nebraska.
TRANSACTIONS/CAREER NOTES: Signed as non-drafted free agent by Buffalo Bills (May 7, 1993). ... Claimed on waivers by New England Patriots (August 31, 1993). ... Released by Patriots (September 29, 1993). ... Re-signed by Patriots to practice squad (October 1, 1993). ... Activated (November 27, 1993). ... Released by Patriots (August 20, 1994). ... Signed by Buffalo Bills (April 30, 1995).
PLAYING EXPERIENCE: New England NFL, 1993; Buffalo NFL, 1995. ... Games: 1993 (6), 1995 (15). Total: 21.
PRO STATISTICS: 1995—Credited with one sack and intercepted one pass for nine yards and recovered one fumble.

WHITE, DWAYNE   G   RAMS

PERSONAL: Born February 10, 1967, in Philadelphia. ... 6-2/315. ... Full name: Dwayne Allen White.
HIGH SCHOOL: South Philadelphia.
COLLEGE: Alcorn State (degree in political science, 1990).
TRANSACTIONS/CAREER NOTES: Selected by New York Jets in seventh round (167th pick overall) of 1990 NFL draft. ... Signed by Jets (July 12, 1990). ... On injured reserve with back injury (September 4-October 13, 1990). ... Granted unconditional free agency (February 17, 1995). ... Signed by Los Angeles Rams (March 24, 1995). ... Rams franchise moved to St. Louis (April 12, 1995).
PLAYING EXPERIENCE: New York Jets NFL, 1990-1994; St. Louis NFL, 1995. ... Games: 1990 (11), 1991 (16), 1992 (16), 1993 (15), 1994 (16), 1995 (15). Total: 89.
PRO STATISTICS: 1991—Recovered one fumble. 1992—Recovered one fumble for minus one yard. 1994—Recovered one fumble.

WHITE, LORENZO   RB   SAINTS

PERSONAL: Born April 12, 1966, in Hollywood, Fla. ... 5-11/222. ... Full name: Lorenzo Maurice White.
HIGH SCHOOL: Dillard (Fort Lauderdale).
COLLEGE: Michigan State.
TRANSACTIONS/CAREER NOTES: Selected by Houston Oilers in first round (22nd pick overall) of 1988 NFL draft. ... Signed by Oilers (July 23, 1988). ... Granted free agency (February 1, 1991). ... Re-signed by Oilers (September 5, 1991). ... Activated (September 16, 1991). ... Designated by Oilers as transition player (February 25, 1993). ... Re-signed by Oilers (August 23, 1993). ... Granted roster exemption (August 23-27, 1993). ... Free agency status changed by Oilers from transitional to unconditional (February 17, 1994). ... Re-signed by Oilers (August 26, 1994). ... Granted unconditional free agency (February 17, 1995). ... Signed by Cleveland Browns (April 25, 1995). ... Released by Browns after 1995 season. ... Signed by New Orleans Saints (May 15, 1996).
HONORS: Named running back on The Sporting News college All-America first team (1985). ... Named running back on The Sporting News college All-America second team (1987). ... Played in Pro Bowl (1992 season).
PRO STATISTICS: 1989—Recovered one fumble. 1990—Recovered three fumbles. 1992—Recovered two fumbles. 1994—Recovered one fumble for minus one yard. 1995—Recovered two fumbles.
STATISTICAL PLATEAUS: 100-yard rushing games: 1989 (1), 1990 (2), 1992 (3), 1994 (1). Total: 7. ... 100-yard receiving games: 1992 (1).

		RUSHING				RECEIVING				KICKOFF RETURNS				TOTALS			
Year Team	G	Att.	Yds.	Avg.	TD	No.	Yds.	Avg.	TD	No.	Yds.	Avg.	TD	TD	2pt.	Pts.	Fum.
1988—Houston NFL	11	31	115	3.7	0	0	0	0	0	8	196	24.5	†1	1	...	6	0
1989—Houston NFL	16	104	349	3.4	5	6	37	6.2	0	17	303	17.8	0	5	...	30	2
1990—Houston NFL	16	168	702	4.2	8	39	368	9.4	4	0	0	...	0	12	...	72	7
1991—Houston NFL	13	110	465	4.2	4	27	211	7.8	0	0	0	...	0	4	...	24	3
1992—Houston NFL	16	265	1226	4.6	7	57	641	11.3	1	0	0	...	0	8	...	48	2
1993—Houston NFL	8	131	465	3.6	2	34	229	6.7	0	0	0	...	0	2	...	12	1
1994—Houston NFL	15	191	757	4.0	3	21	188	9.0	1	8	167	20.9	0	4	0	24	2
1995—Cleveland NFL	12	62	163	2.6	1	8	64	8.0	0	0	0	...	0	1	0	6	0
Pro totals (8 years)	107	1062	4242	4.0	30	192	1738	9.1	6	33	666	20.2	1	37	0	222	17

WHITE, REGGIE   DT   PATRIOTS

PERSONAL: Born March 22, 1970, in Baltimore. ... 6-4/315. ... Full name: Reginald Eugene White.
HIGH SCHOOL: Milford Mill (Baltimore).
COLLEGE: North Carolina A&T.
TRANSACTIONS/CAREER NOTES: Selected by San Diego Chargers in sixth round (147th pick overall) of 1992 NFL draft. ... Signed by Chargers (July 16, 1992). ... On injured reserve with shoulder injury (November 7, 1992-remainder of season). ... Granted unconditional free agency (February 17, 1995). ... Signed by New England Patriots (April 3, 1995).
CHAMPIONSHIP GAME EXPERIENCE: Played in AFC championship game (1994 season). ... Member of Chargers for Super Bowl XXIX (1994 season); inactive.

Year Team	G	SACKS
1992—San Diego NFL	3	1.0
1993—San Diego NFL	8	0.0
1994—San Diego NFL	11	2.0
1995—New England NFL	16	1.5
Pro totals (4 years)	38	4.5

WHITE, REGGIE   DE   PACKERS

PERSONAL: Born December 19, 1961, in Chattanooga, Tenn. ... 6-5/300. ... Full name: Reginald Howard White.
HIGH SCHOOL: Howard (Chattanooga, Tenn.).
COLLEGE: Tennessee.
TRANSACTIONS/CAREER NOTES: Selected by Memphis Showboats in 1984 USFL territorial draft. ... Signed by Showboats (January 15, 1984). ... On developmental squad (March 9-24, 1984). ... Selected by Philadelphia Eagles in first round (fourth pick overall) of 1984 NFL supplemental draft. ... Released by Showboats (September 19, 1985). ... Signed by Eagles (September 21, 1985). ... Granted roster exemption (September 21-27, 1985). ... On reserve/did not report list (July 28-August 23, 1989). ... Designated by Eagles as franchise player (February 25, 1993). ... Signed by Green Bay Packers (April 6, 1993); Eagles received first-round pick (G Lester Holmes) in 1993 draft and

W

first-round pick (traded to Cleveland) in 1994 draft as compensation.

CHAMPIONSHIP GAME EXPERIENCE: Played in NFC championship game (1995 season).

HONORS: Named defensive end on THE SPORTING NEWS college All-America first team (1983). ... Named defensive end on THE SPORTING NEWS USFL All-Star team (1985). ... Played in Pro Bowl (1986-1993 and 1995 seasons). ... Named Outstanding Player of Pro Bowl (1986 season). ... Named defensive end on THE SPORTING NEWS NFL All-Pro team (1987, 1988, 1991, 1993 and 1995). ... Named to play in Pro Bowl (1994 season); replaced by Wayne Martin due to injury.

RECORDS: Holds NFL career record for most sacks—157.

POSTSEASON RECORDS: Shares NFL postseason single-game record for most safeties—1 (January 3, 1993, at New Orleans).

PRO STATISTICS: USFL: 1984—Recovered one fumble. 1985—Credited with one safety and recovered one fumble for 20 yards and a touchdown. NFL: 1985—Recovered two fumbles. 1987—Recovered one fumble for 70 yards and a touchdown. 1988—Recovered two fumbles. 1989—Recovered one fumble for 10 yards. 1990—Intercepted one pass for 33 yards and recovered one fumble. 1991—Intercepted one pass for no yards and recovered three fumbles for eight yards. 1992—Recovered one fumble for 37 yards and a touchdown. 1993—Recovered two fumbles for 10 yards. 1994—Recovered one fumble.

MISCELLANEOUS: Active NFC leader for career sacks (157). ... Holds Philadelphia Eagles all-time record for most sacks (124).

Year Team	G	SACKS
1984—Memphis USFL	16	12.0
1985—Memphis USFL	18	11.5
—Philadelphia NFL	13	13.0
1986—Philadelphia NFL	16	18.0
1987—Philadelphia NFL	12	*21.0
1988—Philadelphia NFL	16	*18.0
1989—Philadelphia NFL	16	11.0
1990—Philadelphia NFL	16	14.0
1991—Philadelphia NFL	16	15.0
1992—Philadelphia NFL	16	14.0
1993—Green Bay NFL	16	13.0
1994—Green Bay NFL	16	8.0
1995—Green Bay NFL	15	12.0
USFL totals (2 years)	34	23.5
NFL totals (11 years)	168	157.0
Pro totals (13 years)	202	180.5

WHITE, WILLIAM — S — CHIEFS

PERSONAL: Born February 19, 1966, in Lima, Ohio. ... 5-10/205. ... Full name: William Eugene White.

HIGH SCHOOL: Lima (Ohio).

COLLEGE: Ohio State.

TRANSACTIONS/CAREER NOTES: Selected by Detroit Lions in fourth round (85th pick overall) of 1988 NFL draft. ... Signed by Lions (July 11, 1988). ... Granted unconditional free agency (March 1, 1993). ... Re-signed by Lions (April 6, 1993). ... Traded by Lions to Kansas City Chiefs for conditional pick in 1995 draft (July 13, 1994).

CHAMPIONSHIP GAME EXPERIENCE: Played in NFC championship game (1991 season).

PRO STATISTICS: 1988—Recovered one fumble. 1989—Recovered one fumble for 20 yards and a touchdown. 1991—Returned blocked field-goal attempt 55 yards for a touchdown. 1992—Fumbled once.

			INTERCEPTIONS			SACKS
Year Team	G	No.	Yds.	Avg.	TD	No.
1988—Detroit NFL	16	0	0	...	0	0.0
1989—Detroit NFL	15	1	0	0.0	0	1.0
1990—Detroit NFL	16	5	120	24.0	1	0.0
1991—Detroit NFL	16	2	35	17.5	0	0.0
1992—Detroit NFL	16	4	54	13.5	0	0.0
1993—Detroit NFL	16	1	5	5.0	0	1.5
1994—Kansas City NFL	15	2	0	0.0	0	0.0
1995—Kansas City NFL	16	2	48	24.0	0	1.0
Pro totals (8 years)	126	17	262	15.4	1	3.5

WHITFIELD, BOB — OT — FALCONS

PERSONAL: Born October 18, 1971, in Carson, Calif. ... 6-5/300.

HIGH SCHOOL: Banning (Los Angeles).

COLLEGE: Stanford.

TRANSACTIONS/CAREER NOTES: Selected after junior season by Atlanta Falcons in first round (eighth pick overall) of 1992 NFL draft. ... Signed by Falcons (September 4, 1992). ... Granted roster exemption for one game (September 1992).

PLAYING EXPERIENCE: Atlanta NFL, 1992-1995. ... Games: 1992 (11), 1993 (16), 1994 (16), 1995 (16). Total: 59.

HONORS: Named offensive tackle on THE SPORTING NEWS college All-America first team (1991).

PRO STATISTICS: 1993—Recovered two fumbles.

W

WHITLEY, CURTIS — C — PANTHERS

PERSONAL: Born May 10, 1969, in Lowgrounds, N.C. ... 6-1/296. ... Full name: Curtis Wayne Whitley.

HIGH SCHOOL: Smithfield (N.C.)-Selma Senior.

COLLEGE: Chowan College (N.C.), then Clemson.

TRANSACTIONS/CAREER NOTES: Selected by San Diego Chargers in fifth round (117th pick overall) of 1992 NFL draft. ... Signed by Chargers (July 16, 1992). ... Released by Chargers (July 18, 1994). ... Re-signed by Chargers (August 20, 1994). ... Selected by Carolina Panthers from Chargers in NFL expansion draft (February 15, 1995). ... Granted free agency (February 17, 1995). ... Signed by Panthers (May 5, 1995). ... Granted unconditional free agency (February 16, 1996). ... Re-signed by Panthers (February 26, 1996).

PLAYING EXPERIENCE: San Diego NFL, 1992-1994; Carolina NFL, 1995. ... Games: 1992 (3), 1993 (15), 1994 (12), 1995 (16). Total: 46.

CHAMPIONSHIP GAME EXPERIENCE: Played in AFC championship game (1994 season). ... Member of Chargers for Super Bowl XXIX (1994 season); did not play.
PRO STATISTICS: 1994—Recovered one fumble. 1995—Recovered one fumble.

WHITMORE, DAVID   S

PERSONAL: Born July 6, 1967, in Daingerfield, Texas. ... 6-0/232. ... Full name: David Lawrence Whitmore.
HIGH SCHOOL: Daingerfield (Texas).
COLLEGE: Stephen F. Austin State (degree in criminal justice).
TRANSACTIONS/CAREER NOTES: Selected by New York Giants in fourth round (107th pick overall) of 1990 NFL draft. ... Signed by Giants (July 23, 1990). ... Granted unconditional free agency (February 1, 1991). ... Signed by San Francisco 49ers (March 13, 1991). ... On injured reserve with knee injury (October 19-November 25, 1991). ... Traded by 49ers with QB Joe Montana and third-round pick (WR Lake Dawson) in 1994 draft to Kansas City Chiefs for first-round pick (traded to Phoenix) in 1993 draft (April 20, 1993). ... On injured reserve with knee injury (November 5, 1993-remainder of season). ... Released by Chiefs (April 12, 1995). ... Signed by Philadelphia Eagles (July 21, 1995). ... Granted unconditional free agency (February 16, 1996).
CHAMPIONSHIP GAME EXPERIENCE: Played in NFC championship game (1990 and 1992 seasons). ... Member of Super Bowl championship team (1990 season).
PRO STATISTICS: 1990—Returned one kickoff for no yards and fumbled once. 1991—Credited with one sack and returned one kickoff for seven yards. 1994—Recovered one fumble.

		INTERCEPTIONS			
Year Team	G	No.	Yds.	Avg.	TD
1990—New York Giants NFL	16	0	0	...	0
1991—San Francisco NFL	11	1	5	5.0	0
1992—San Francisco NFL	16	1	0	0.0	0
1993—Kansas City NFL	6	0	0	...	0
1994—Kansas City NFL	12	0	0	...	0
1995—Philadelphia NFL	3	0	0	...	0
Pro totals (6 years)	**64**	**2**	**5**	**2.5**	**0**

WHITTINGTON, BERNARD   DE   COLTS

PERSONAL: Born July 20, 1971, in St. Louis. ... 6-6/278.
HIGH SCHOOL: Hazelwood East (St. Louis).
COLLEGE: Indiana.
TRANSACTIONS/CAREER NOTES: Signed as non-drafted free agent by Indianapolis Colts (May 5, 1994).
CHAMPIONSHIP GAME EXPERIENCE: Played in AFC championship game (1995 season).
PRO STATISTICS: 1995—Recovered one fumble.

Year Team	G	SACKS
1994—Indianapolis NFL	13	0.0
1995—Indianapolis NFL	16	2.0
Pro totals (2 years)	**29**	**2.0**

WIDELL, DAVE   C   JAGUARS

PERSONAL: Born May 14, 1965, in Hartford, Conn. ... 6-7/308. ... Full name: David Harold Widell. ... Brother of Doug Widell, guard, Indianapolis Colts. ... Name pronounced WY-dell.
HIGH SCHOOL: South Catholic (Hartford, Conn.).
COLLEGE: Boston College (degree in finance, 1988).
TRANSACTIONS/CAREER NOTES: Selected by Dallas Cowboys in fourth round (94th pick overall) of 1988 NFL draft. ... Signed by Cowboys (July 12, 1988). ... Traded by Cowboys to Denver Broncos for seventh-round pick (DT Leon Lett) in 1991 draft and eighth-round pick (traded to Cleveland) in 1992 draft (August 24, 1990). ... Granted unconditional free agency (February 17, 1994). ... Re-signed by Broncos (1994). ... Granted unconditional free agency (February 17, 1995). ... Signed by Jacksonville Jaguars (March 15, 1995).
PLAYING EXPERIENCE: Dallas NFL, 1988 and 1989; Denver NFL, 1990-1994; Jacksonville NFL, 1995. ... Games: 1988 (14), 1989 (15), 1990 (16), 1991 (16), 1992 (16), 1993 (15), 1994 (16), 1995 (16). Total: 124.
CHAMPIONSHIP GAME EXPERIENCE: Played in AFC championship game (1991 season).
PRO STATISTICS: 1988—Recovered one fumble. 1991—Fumbled once for minus 15 yards. 1994—Fumbled once.

WIDELL, DOUG   G   COLTS

W

PERSONAL: Born September 23, 1966, in Hartford, Conn. ... 6-4/290. ... Full name: Douglas Joseph Widell. ... Brother of Dave Widell, center, Jacksonville Jaguars. ... Name pronounced WY-dell.
HIGH SCHOOL: South Catholic (Hartford, Conn.).
COLLEGE: Boston College (degree in marketing, 1989).
TRANSACTIONS/CAREER NOTES: Selected by Denver Broncos in second round (41st pick overall) of 1989 NFL draft. ... Signed by Broncos (July 23, 1989). ... Granted free agency (February 1, 1992). ... Re-signed by Broncos (July 22, 1992). ... Traded by Broncos to Green Bay Packers for seventh-round pick (RB Butler By'not'e) in 1994 draft (August 24, 1993). ... Granted unconditional free agency (February 17, 1994). ... Signed by Detroit Lions (June 2, 1994). ... Granted unconditional free agency (February 16, 1996). ... Signed by Indianapolis Colts (March 15, 1996).
PLAYING EXPERIENCE: Denver NFL, 1989-1992; Green Bay NFL, 1993; Detroit NFL, 1994 and 1995. ... Games: 1989 (16), 1990 (16), 1991 (16), 1992 (16), 1993 (16), 1994 (16), 1995 (11). Total: 107.
CHAMPIONSHIP GAME EXPERIENCE: Played in AFC championship game (1989 and 1991 seasons). ... Played in Super Bowl XXIV (1989 season).
PRO STATISTICS: 1990—Recovered one fumble. 1991—Recovered one fumble. 1992—Caught one pass for minus seven yards and recovered two fumbles.

WIDMER, COREY   LB   GIANTS

PERSONAL: Born December 25, 1968, in Alexandria, Va. ... 6-3/250. ... Full name: Corey Edward Widmer.
HIGH SCHOOL: Bozeman (Mont.) Senior.
COLLEGE: Montana State.
TRANSACTIONS/CAREER NOTES: Selected by New York Giants in seventh round (180th pick overall) of 1992 NFL draft. ... Signed by Giants (July 21, 1992). ... On injured reserve with back injury (September 5-30, 1992). ... On practice squad (September 30-November 15, 1992). ... Granted free agency (February 17, 1995). ... Re-signed by Giants (April 18, 1995).
PLAYING EXPERIENCE: New York Giants NFL, 1992-1995. ... Games: 1992 (8), 1993 (11), 1994 (16), 1995 (16). Total: 51.
PRO STATISTICS: 1994—Credited with one sack. 1995—Returned one kickoff for no yards.

WIEGERT, ZACH   OT   RAMS

PERSONAL: Born August 16, 1972, in Fremont, Neb. ... 6-4/305. ... Name pronounced WEE-gert.
HIGH SCHOOL: Bergan (Fremont, Neb.).
COLLEGE: Nebraska.
TRANSACTIONS/CAREER NOTES: Selected by St. Louis Rams in second round (38th pick overall) of 1995 NFL draft. ... Signed by Rams (July 18, 1995).
PLAYING EXPERIENCE: St. Louis NFL, 1995. ... Games: 1995 (5).
HONORS: Outland Trophy Award winner (1994). ... Named offensive lineman on THE SPORTING NEWS college All-America first team (1994).

WILBURN, BARRY   CB   EAGLES

PERSONAL: Born December 9, 1963, in Memphis. ... 6-2/190.
HIGH SCHOOL: Melrose (Memphis).
COLLEGE: Mississippi.
TRANSACTIONS/CAREER NOTES: Selected by Washington Redskins in eighth round (219th pick overall) of 1985 NFL draft. ... Signed by Redskins (July 18, 1985). ... On injured reserve with knee injury (September 14-October 29, 1988). ... On non-football injury list with drug problem (November 4-28, 1989). ... Reinstated and granted roster exemption (November 29-December 3, 1989). ... On injured reserve with Achilles' heel injury (December 4, 1989-remainder of season). ... Released by Redskins (May 9, 1990). ... Signed by Cleveland Browns (April 3, 1992). ... Released by Browns (October 23, 1992). ... Signed by Saskatchewan Roughriders of CFL (June 2, 1993). ... Granted free agency after 1993 season. ... Signed by Kansas City Chiefs (May 18, 1994). ... Released by Chiefs (August 28, 1994). ... Signed by Philadelphia Eagles (March 22, 1995). ... Granted unconditional free agency (February 16, 1996). ... Re-signed by Eagles (June 5, 1996).
CHAMPIONSHIP GAME EXPERIENCE: Played in NFC championship game (1986 and 1987 seasons). ... Member of Super Bowl championship team (1987 season).
POSTSEASON RECORDS: Shares NFL postseason record for most touchdowns by interception return—1 (December 30, 1995, vs. Detroit).
PRO STATISTICS: 1985—Recovered one fumble. 1986—Recovered two fumbles. 1988—Recovered one fumble. 1992—Recovered one fumble for five yards. 1995—Recovered one fumble.

| | | | INTERCEPTIONS | | |
Year Team	G	No.	Yds.	Avg.	TD
1985—Washington NFL	16	1	10	10.0	0
1986—Washington NFL	16	2	14	7.0	0
1987—Washington NFL	12	*9	135	15.0	1
1988—Washington NFL	10	4	24	6.0	0
1989—Washington NFL	8	3	13	4.3	0
1990—			Did not play.		
1991—			Did not play.		
1992—Cleveland NFL	6	0	0	...	0
1993—Saskatchewan CFL	16	2	21	10.5	0
1994—			Did not play.		
1995—Philadelphia NFL	16	1	0	0.0	0
CFL totals (1 year)	16	2	21	10.5	0
NFL totals (7 years)	84	20	196	9.8	1
Pro totals (8 years)	100	22	217	9.9	1

WILHELM, ERIK   QB   BENGALS

W

PERSONAL: Born November 16, 1965, in Dayton, Ohio. ... 6-3/217. ... Full name: Erik Bradley Wilhelm.
HIGH SCHOOL: Gladstone (Ore.) and Lakeridge (Lake Oswego, Ore.).
COLLEGE: Oregon State.
TRANSACTIONS/CAREER NOTES: Selected by Cincinnati Bengals in third round (83rd pick overall) of 1989 NFL draft. ... Signed by Bengals (July 22, 1989). ... Granted free agency (February 1, 1992). ... Re-signed by Bengals (July 27, 1992). ... Released by Bengals (August 31, 1992). ... Signed by Phoenix Cardinals (September 16, 1992). ... On inactive list for three games (1992). ... Released by Cardinals (October 12, 1992). ... Signed by Bengals (April 19, 1993). ... Released by Bengals (June 16, 1994). ... Re-signed by Bengals (October 25, 1994). ... Released by Bengals (October 24, 1995). ... Signed by New York Jets (November 8, 1995). ... Inactive for six games (1995). ... Granted unconditional free agency (February 16, 1996). ... Signed by Bengals (February 21, 1996).
PRO STATISTICS: 1989—Fumbled twice and recovered one fumble. 1990—Fumbled once and recovered one fumble. 1991—Fumbled once.
MISCELLANEOUS: Regular-season record as starting NFL quarterback: 0-1 (.000).

| | | PASSING | | | | | | | RUSHING | | | | TOTALS | | |
Year Team	G	Att.	Cmp.	Pct.	Yds.	TD	Int.	Avg.	Rat.	Att.	Yds.	Avg.	TD	TD	2pt.	Pts.
1989—Cincinnati NFL	6	56	30	53.6	425	4	2	7.59	87.3	6	30	5.0	0	0	...	0
1990—Cincinnati NFL	7	19	12	63.2	117	0	0	6.16	80.4	6	6	1.0	0	0	...	0
1991—Cincinnati NFL	4	42	24	57.1	217	0	2	5.17	51.4	1	9	9.0	0	0	...	0
1992—Phoenix NFL						Did not play.										

Year	Team	G	PASSING								RUSHING				TOTALS		
			Att.	Cmp.	Pct.	Yds.	TD	Int.	Avg.	Rat.	Att.	Yds.	Avg.	TD	TD	2pt.	Pts.
1993—Cincinnati NFL		1	6	4	66.7	63	0	0	10.50	101.4	0	0	...	0	0	...	0
1994—Cincinnati NFL		1	0	0	...	0	0	0	...	...	0	0	...	0	0	0	0
1995—Cincinnati NFL							Did not play.										
Pro totals (5 years)		20	123	70	56.9	822	4	4	6.68	74.6	13	45	3.5	0	0	0	0

WILKERSON, BRUCE   OT/G   PACKERS

PERSONAL: Born July 28, 1964, in Loudon, Tenn. ... 6-5/305. ... Full name: Bruce Alan Wilkerson.
HIGH SCHOOL: Loudon (Tenn.).
COLLEGE: Tennessee.
TRANSACTIONS/CAREER NOTES: Selected by Los Angeles Raiders in second round (52nd pick overall) of 1987 NFL draft. ... Signed by Raiders (July 10, 1987). ... Crossed picket line during players strike (October 2, 1987). ... On injured reserve with knee injury (September 4-November 4, 1990). ... Granted free agency (February 1, 1991). ... Re-signed by Raiders (July 23, 1991). ... On injured reserve (December 22, 1992-remainder of season). ... Granted free agency (February 17, 1995). ... Signed by Jacksonville Jaguars (June 15, 1995). ... Released by Jaguars (April 16, 1996). ... Signed by Green Bay Packers (April 19, 1996).
PLAYING EXPERIENCE: Los Angeles Raiders NFL, 1987-1994; Jacksonville NFL, 1995. ... Games: 1987 (11), 1988 (16), 1989 (16), 1990 (8), 1991 (16), 1992 (15), 1993 (14), 1994 (11), 1995 (10). Total: 117.
CHAMPIONSHIP GAME EXPERIENCE: Played in AFC championship game (1990 season).
HONORS: Named offensive guard on THE SPORTING NEWS college All-America second team (1985).
PRO STATISTICS: 1989—Recovered two fumbles. 1992—Recovered one fumble. 1993—Recovered one fumble. 1994—Recovered one fumble.

WILKINS, GABE   DE   PACKERS

PERSONAL: Born September 1, 1971, in Cowpens, S.C. ... 6-4/310. ... Full name: Gabriel Nicholas Wilkins.
HIGH SCHOOL: Gettys D. Broome (Spartanburg, S.C.).
COLLEGE: Gardner-Webb (N.C.).
TRANSACTIONS/CAREER NOTES: Selected by Green Bay Packers in fourth round (126th pick overall) of 1994 NFL draft. ... Signed by Packers (June 17, 1994).
CHAMPIONSHIP GAME EXPERIENCE: Played in NFC championship game (1995 season).

Year Team	G	SACKS
1994—Green Bay NFL	15	1.0
1995—Green Bay NFL	13	3.0
Pro totals (2 years)	28	4.0

WILKINS, JEFF   K   49ERS

PERSONAL: Born April 19, 1972, in Youngstown, Ohio. ... 6-2/192.
HIGH SCHOOL: Austintown Fitch (Youngstown, Ohio).
COLLEGE: Youngstown State.
TRANSACTIONS/CAREER NOTES: Signed as non-drafted free agent by Dallas Cowboys (April 28, 1994). ... Released by Cowboys (July 18, 1994). ... Signed by Philadelphia Eagles (November 14, 1994). ... Released by Eagles (August 14, 1995). ... Signed by San Francisco 49ers (November 8, 1995).

Year Team	G	KICKING						
		XPM	XPA	FGM	FGA	Lg.	50+	Pts.
1994—Philadelphia NFL	6	0	0	0	0	...	0-0	0
1995—San Francisco NFL	7	27	29	12	13	40	0-0	63
Pro totals (2 years)	13	27	29	12	13	40	0-0	63

WILKINSON, DAN   DT   BENGALS

PERSONAL: Born March 13, 1973, in Dayton, Ohio. ... 6-5/313. ... Nickname: Big Daddy.
HIGH SCHOOL: Paul L. Dunbar (Dayton, Ohio).
COLLEGE: Ohio State.
TRANSACTIONS/CAREER NOTES: Selected after sophomore season by Cincinnati Bengals in first round (first pick overall) of 1994 NFL draft. ... Signed by Bengals (May 5, 1994).
HONORS: Named defensive lineman on THE SPORTING NEWS college All-America first team (1993).

Year Team	G	SACKS
1994—Cincinnati NFL	16	5.5
1995—Cincinnati NFL	14	8.0
Pro totals (2 years)	30	13.5

W

WILLIAMS, AENEAS   CB   CARDINALS

PERSONAL: Born January 29, 1968, in New Orleans. ... 5-10/190. ... Full name: Aeneas Demetrius Williams.
HIGH SCHOOL: Fortier (New Orleans).
COLLEGE: Southern, La. (degree in accounting, 1990).
TRANSACTIONS/CAREER NOTES: Selected by Phoenix Cardinals in third round (59th pick overall) of 1991 NFL draft. ... Signed by Cardinals (July 26, 1991). ... Granted free agency (February 17, 1994). ... Cardinals franchise renamed Arizona Cardinals for 1994 season. ... Re-signed by Cardinals (June 1, 1994). ... Granted unconditional free agency (February 16, 1996). ... Re-signed by Cardinals (February 27, 1996).
HONORS: Played in Pro Bowl (1994 and 1995 seasons). ... Named cornerback on THE SPORTING NEWS NFL All-Pro team (1995).

PRO STATISTICS: 1991—Fumbled once and recovered two fumbles for 10 yards. 1992—Recovered one fumble for 39 yards. 1993—Recovered two fumbles for 20 yards and a touchdown. 1994—Recovered one fumble. 1995—Fumbled once and recovered three fumbles.

			INTERCEPTIONS			
Year Team	G	No.	Yds.	Avg.	TD
1991—Phoenix NFL	16	6	60	10.0	0
1992—Phoenix NFL	16	3	25	8.3	0
1993—Phoenix NFL	16	2	87	43.5	1
1994—Arizona NFL	16	†9	89	9.9	0
1995—Arizona NFL	16	6	86	14.3	†2
Pro totals (5 years)	80	26	347	13.4	3

WILLIAMS, ALFRED   DE   BRONCOS

PERSONAL: Born November 6, 1968, in Houston. ... 6-6/265. ... Full name: Alfred Hamilton Williams.
HIGH SCHOOL: Jesse H. Jones Sr. (Houston).
COLLEGE: Colorado.
TRANSACTIONS/CAREER NOTES: Selected by Cincinnati Bengals in first round (18th pick overall) of 1991 NFL draft. ... Signed by Bengals (July 18, 1991). ... Granted free agency (February 17, 1994). ... Re-signed by Bengals (June 15, 1994). ... Granted unconditional free agency (February 17, 1995). ... Signed by San Francisco 49ers (July 15, 1995). ... Granted unconditional free agency (February 16, 1996). ... Signed by Denver Broncos (February 26, 1996).
HONORS: Named defensive end on THE SPORTING NEWS college All-America second team (1989). ... Butkus Award winner (1990). ... Named linebacker on THE SPORTING NEWS college All-America first team (1990).
PRO STATISTICS: 1991—Recovered two fumbles for 24 yards. 1993—Credited with one safety. 1994—Credited with one safety and recovered one fumble. 1995—Recovered one fumble.

Year Team	G	SACKS
1991—Cincinnati NFL	16	3.0
1992—Cincinnati NFL	15	10.0
1993—Cincinnati NFL	16	4.0
1994—Cincinnati NFL	16	9.5
1995—San Francisco NFL	16	4.5
Pro totals (5 years)	79	31.0

WILLIAMS, ALLEN   RB/KR   LIONS

PERSONAL: Born September 17, 1972, in Thomasville, Ga. ... 5-10/205.
HIGH SCHOOL: Thomasville (Ga.).
JUNIOR COLLEGE: Georgia Military College.
COLLEGE: Georgia.
TRANSACTIONS/CAREER NOTES: Signed as non-drafted free agent by Carolina Panthers (April 25, 1995). ... Released by Panthers (July 15, 1995). ... Claimed on waivers by Detroit Lions (July 19, 1995). ... Released by Lions (August 28, 1995). ... Re-signed by Lions to practice squad (August 29, 1995). ... Activated (November 20, 1995).
PRO STATISTICS: 1995—Fumbled once.
PLAYING EXPERIENCE: Detroit NFL, 1995. ... Games: 1995 (5).

WILLIAMS, BERNARD   OT   EAGLES

PERSONAL: Born July 18, 1972, in Memphis. ... 6-8/286. ... Full name: Bennie Bernard Williams.
HIGH SCHOOL: Hamilton (Memphis).
COLLEGE: Georgia.
TRANSACTIONS/CAREER NOTES: Selected by Philadelphia Eagles in first round (14th pick overall) of 1994 NFL draft. ... Signed by Eagles (July 18, 1994). ... On suspended list for violating league substance abuse policy (September 4-October 3, 1995). ... On suspended list for violating league substance abuse policy (October 23, 1996). ... Tentatively plans to apply to NFL for reinstatement, prior to 1996 season.
PLAYING EXPERIENCE: Philadelphia NFL, 1994. ... Games: 1994 (16).
HONORS: Named offensive lineman on THE SPORTING NEWS college All-America second team (1993).

WILLIAMS, BRENT   DE

PERSONAL: Born October 23, 1964, in Flint, Mich. ... 6-4/283. ... Full name: Brent Dione Williams.
HIGH SCHOOL: Northern (Flint, Mich.).
COLLEGE: Toledo (degree in marketing, 1986).
TRANSACTIONS/CAREER NOTES: Selected by New England Patriots in seventh round (192nd pick overall) of 1986 NFL draft. ... Signed by Patriots (July 16, 1986). ... Granted unconditional free agency (February 17, 1994). ... Signed by Seattle Seahawks (May 5, 1994). ... On injured reserve with knee injury (November 19, 1994-remainder of season). ... Granted free agency (February 17, 1995). ... Re-signed by Seahawks (April 26, 1995). ... Granted unconditional free agency (February 16, 1996).
PRO STATISTICS: 1986—Recovered four fumbles for 54 yards and one touchdown. 1988—Recovered one fumble. 1989—Recovered two fumbles for two yards. 1990—Recovered two fumbles for 45 yards and one touchdown. 1991—Recovered two fumbles. 1995—Fumbled once and recovered one fumble for minus one yard.

Year Team	G	SACKS
1986—New England NFL	16	7.0
1987—New England NFL	12	5.0
1988—New England NFL	16	8.0
1989—New England NFL	16	8.0
1990—New England NFL	16	6.0
1991—New England NFL	16	3.5
1992—New England NFL	16	4.0

W

Year Team	G	SACKS
1993—New England NFL	13	2.0
1994—Seattle NFL	10	1.0
1995—Seattle NFL	11	1.0
Pro totals (10 years)	142	45.5

WILLIAMS, BRIAN   LB   PACKERS

PERSONAL: Born December 17, 1972, in Dallas. ... 6-1/240.
HIGH SCHOOL: Bishop Dunne (Dallas).
COLLEGE: Southern California.
TRANSACTIONS/CAREER NOTES: Selected by Green Bay Packers in third round (73rd pick overall) of 1995 NFL draft. ... Signed by Packers (May 9, 1995).
PLAYING EXPERIENCE: Green Bay NFL, 1995; Games: 1995 (13).
CHAMPIONSHIP GAME EXPERIENCE: Played in NFC championship game (1995 season).

WILLIAMS, BRIAN   C   GIANTS

PERSONAL: Born June 8, 1966, in Mount Lebanon, Pa. ... 6-5/300. ... Full name: Brian Scott Williams.
HIGH SCHOOL: Mount Lebanon (Pittsburgh).
COLLEGE: Minnesota.
TRANSACTIONS/CAREER NOTES: Selected by New York Giants in first round (18th pick overall) of 1989 NFL draft. ... Signed by Giants (August 14, 1989). ... On injured reserve with knee injury (January 6, 1990-remainder of 1989 season playoffs). ... On injured reserve with knee injury (December 6, 1992-remainder of season). ... Granted free agency (March 1, 1993). ... Re-signed by Giants (July 12, 1993). ... Granted unconditional free agency (February 17, 1994). ... Re-signed by Giants (March 1, 1994).
PLAYING EXPERIENCE: New York Giants NFL, 1989-1995. ... Games: 1989 (14), 1990 (16), 1991 (14), 1992 (13), 1993 (16), 1994 (14), 1995 (16). Total: 103.
CHAMPIONSHIP GAME EXPERIENCE: Played in NFC championship game (1990 season). ... Member of Super Bowl championship team (1990 season).
PRO STATISTICS: 1994—Fumbled twice for minus 34 yards and recovered one fumble.

WILLIAMS, CALVIN   WR   EAGLES

PERSONAL: Born March 3, 1967, in Baltimore. ... 5-11/187. ... Full name: Calvin John Williams Jr.
HIGH SCHOOL: Dunbar (Baltimore).
COLLEGE: Purdue (degree in hotel and restaurant management).
TRANSACTIONS/CAREER NOTES: Selected by Philadelphia Eagles in fifth round (133rd pick overall) of 1990 NFL draft. ... Signed by Eagles (August 8, 1990). ... On injured reserve with dislocated shoulder (September 20-October 23, 1991). ... Granted free agency (February 1, 1992). ... Re-signed by Eagles (August 20, 1992).
PRO STATISTICS: 1990—Recovered two fumbles and returned two punts for minus one yard. 1994—Recovered one fumble.
STATISTICAL PLATEAUS: 100-yard receiving games: 1992 (1), 1993 (2), 1994 (2), 1995 (1). Total: 6.

		RUSHING				RECEIVING				TOTALS			
Year Team	G	Att.	Yds.	Avg.	TD	No.	Yds.	Avg.	TD	TD	2pt.	Pts.	Fum.
1990—Philadelphia NFL	16	2	20	10.0	0	37	602	16.3	9	9	...	54	2
1991—Philadelphia NFL	12	0	0	...	0	33	326	9.9	3	3	...	18	1
1992—Philadelphia NFL	16	0	0	...	0	42	598	14.2	7	7	...	42	0
1993—Philadelphia NFL	16	0	0	...	0	60	725	12.1	10	10	...	60	0
1994—Philadelphia NFL	16	2	11	5.5	0	58	813	14.0	3	3	0	18	0
1995—Philadelphia NFL	16	1	-2	-2.0	0	63	768	12.2	2	2	1	14	2
Pro totals (6 years)	92	5	29	5.8	0	293	3832	13.1	34	34	1	206	5

WILLIAMS, CHARLIE   S   COWBOYS

PERSONAL: Born February 2, 1972, in Detroit. ... 6-0/190.
HIGH SCHOOL: Henry Ford (Detroit).
COLLEGE: Bowling Green State.
TRANSACTIONS/CAREER NOTES: Selected by Dallas Cowboys in third round (92nd pick overall) of 1995 NFL draft. ... Signed by Cowboys (July 18, 1995).
PLAYING EXPERIENCE: Dallas NFL, 1995. ... Games: 1995 (16).
CHAMPIONSHIP GAME EXPERIENCE: Played in NFC championship game (1995 season). ... Member of Super Bowl championship team (1995 season).

W

WILLIAMS, DAN   DE   BRONCOS

PERSONAL: Born December 15, 1969, in Ypsilanti, Mich. ... 6-4/290.
HIGH SCHOOL: Ypsilanti (Mich.).
COLLEGE: Tennessee State, then Toledo.
TRANSACTIONS/CAREER NOTES: Selected by Denver Broncos in first round (11th pick overall) of 1993 NFL draft. ... Signed by Broncos (July 19, 1993). ... On injured reserve with knee injury (December 19, 1995-remainder of season).
PLAYING EXPERIENCE: Denver NFL, 1993-1995. ... Games: 1993 (13), 1994 (12), 1995 (6). Total: 31.
PRO STATISTICS: 1993—Credited with one sack and recovered one fumble. 1994—Intercepted one pass for minus three yards. 1995—Credited with two sacks.

WILLIAMS, DARRYL   S   SEAHAWKS

PERSONAL: Born January 7, 1970, in Miami. ... 6-0/191. ... Full name: Darryl Edwin Williams.
HIGH SCHOOL: American (Hialeah, Fla.).
COLLEGE: Miami (Fla.).
TRANSACTIONS/CAREER NOTES: Selected after junior season by Cincinnati Bengals in first round (28th pick overall) of 1992 NFL draft. ... Signed by Bengals (July 25, 1992). ... Designated by Bengals as transition player (February 15, 1994). ... Free agency status changed by Bengals from transitional to unconditional (February 16, 1996). ... Signed by Seattle Seahawks (February 21, 1996).
HONORS: Named defensive back on THE SPORTING NEWS college All-America second team (1991).
PRO STATISTICS: 1992—Recovered one fumble. 1993—Recovered two fumbles. 1994—Returned one punt for four yards and recovered two fumbles. 1995—Recovered three fumbles.

		INTERCEPTIONS				SACKS
Year Team	G	No.	Yds.	Avg.	TD	No.
1992—Cincinnati NFL	16	4	65	16.3	0	2.0
1993—Cincinnati NFL	16	2	126	63.0	1	2.0
1994—Cincinnati NFL	16	2	45	22.5	0	1.0
1995—Cincinnati NFL	16	1	1	1.0	0	1.0
Pro totals (4 years)	64	9	237	26.3	1	6.0

WILLIAMS, DAVID   OT   JETS

PERSONAL: Born June 21, 1966, in Mulberry, Fla. ... 6-5/292. ... Full name: David Wayne Williams.
HIGH SCHOOL: Lakeland (Fla.).
COLLEGE: Florida.
TRANSACTIONS/CAREER NOTES: Selected by Houston Oilers in first round (23rd pick overall) of 1989 NFL draft. ... Signed by Oilers (July 29, 1989). ... Granted free agency (March 1, 1993). ... Re-signed by Oilers (August 16, 1993). ... Designated by Oilers as franchise player (February 16, 1995). ... Released by Oilers (November 21, 1995). ... Signed by New York Jets (February 14, 1996).
PLAYING EXPERIENCE: Houston NFL 1989-1995. ... Games: 1989 (14), 1990 (15), 1991 (16), 1992 (16), 1993 (15), 1994 (16), 1995 (10). Total: 102.
PRO STATISTICS: 1989—Returned two kickoffs for eight yards. 1990—Recovered one fumble. 1991—Recovered one fumble. 1992—Recovered one fumble. 1993—Recovered one fumble for seven yards. 1994—Recovered one fumble.

WILLIAMS, ERIK   OT   COWBOYS

PERSONAL: Born September 7, 1968, in Philadelphia. ... 6-6/322. ... Full name: Erik George Williams.
HIGH SCHOOL: John Bartram (Philadelphia).
COLLEGE: Central State (Ohio).
TRANSACTIONS/CAREER NOTES: Selected by Dallas Cowboys in third round (70th pick overall) of 1991 NFL draft. ... Signed by Cowboys (July 14, 1991). ... Designated by Cowboys as transition player (February 15, 1994). ... On reserve/non-football injury list (November 21, 1994-remainder of season).
PLAYING EXPERIENCE: Dallas NFL, 1991-1995. ... Games: 1991 (11), 1992 (16), 1993 (16), 1994 (7), 1995 (15). Total: 65.
CHAMPIONSHIP GAME EXPERIENCE: Played in NFC championship game (1992, 1993 and 1995 seasons). ... Member of Super Bowl championship team (1992, 1993 and 1995 seasons).
HONORS: Named offensive tackle on THE SPORTING NEWS NFL All-Pro team (1993 and 1995). ... Played in Pro Bowl (1993 season).
PRO STATISTICS: 1991—Recovered one fumble.

WILLIAMS, GENE   OT/G   FALCONS

PERSONAL: Born October 14, 1968, in Blair, Neb. ... 6-2/305.
HIGH SCHOOL: Creighton Preparatory (Omaha, Neb.).
COLLEGE: Iowa State (degree in speech communications, 1991).
TRANSACTIONS/CAREER NOTES: Selected by Miami Dolphins in fifth round (121st pick overall) of 1991 NFL draft. ... Signed by Dolphins (July 11, 1991). ... Traded by Dolphins to Cleveland Browns for fourth-round pick (LB Ronnie Woolfork) in 1994 draft (July 12, 1993). ... Granted free agency (February 17, 1994). ... Re-signed by Browns (1994). ... Traded by Browns to Atlanta Falcons for fifth-round pick (WR Jermaine Lewis) in 1996 draft (August 28, 1995).
PLAYING EXPERIENCE: Miami NFL, 1991 and 1992; Cleveland NFL, 1993 and 1994; Atlanta NFL, 1995. ... Games: 1991 (10), 1992 (5), 1993 (16), 1994 (15), 1995 (12). Total: 58.

WILLIAMS, GERALD   DE   PANTHERS

PERSONAL: Born September 8, 1963, in Waycross, Ga. ... 6-3/293.
HIGH SCHOOL: Valley (Ala.).
COLLEGE: Auburn.
TRANSACTIONS/CAREER NOTES: Selected by Birmingham Stallions in 1986 USFL territorial draft. ... Selected by Pittsburgh Steelers in second round (36th pick overall) of 1986 NFL draft. ... Signed by Steelers (July 25, 1986). ... Crossed picket line during players strike (October 13, 1987). ... Granted free agency (February 1, 1990). ... Re-signed by Steelers (July 18, 1990). ... Granted free agency (February 1, 1992). ... Re-signed by Steelers (July 13, 1992). ... On injured reserve with knee injury (October 13-November 10, 1992). ... On practice squad (November 10-28, 1992). ... On injured reserve with tricep injury (November 22, 1994-remainder of season). ... Granted unconditional free agency (February 17, 1995). ... Signed by Carolina Panthers (March 28, 1995).
PRO STATISTICS: 1987—Recovered one fumble. 1988—Recovered one fumble for one yard. 1989—Recovered one fumble. 1994—Recovered one fumble in end zone for a touchdown.

Year Team	G	SACKS
1986—Pittsburgh NFL	16	3.5
1987—Pittsburgh NFL	9	1.0

W

Year Team	G	SACKS
1988—Pittsburgh NFL	16	3.5
1989—Pittsburgh NFL	16	3.0
1990—Pittsburgh NFL	16	6.0
1991—Pittsburgh NFL	16	2.0
1992—Pittsburgh NFL	10	3.0
1993—Pittsburgh NFL	10	1.0
1994—Pittsburgh NFL	11	1.5
1995—Carolina NFL	16	0.0
Pro totals (10 years)	136	24.5

WILLIAMS, HARVEY — RB — RAIDERS

PERSONAL: Born April 22, 1967, in Hempstead, Texas ... 6-2/215. ... Full name: Harvey Lavance Williams.
HIGH SCHOOL: Hempstead (Texas).
COLLEGE: Louisiana State.
TRANSACTIONS/CAREER NOTES: Selected by Kansas City Chiefs in first round (21st pick overall) of 1991 NFL draft. ... Signed by Chiefs (August 7, 1991). ... Released by Chiefs (April 6, 1994). ... Signed by Los Angeles Raiders (April 28, 1994). ... Granted unconditional free agency (February 17, 1995). ... Re-signed by Raiders (March 3, 1995). ... Raiders franchise moved to Oakland (July 21, 1995).
CHAMPIONSHIP GAME EXPERIENCE: Member of Chiefs for AFC championship game (1993 season); inactive.
PRO STATISTICS: 1991—Attempted one pass without a completion. 1994—Recovered two fumbles. 1995—Attempted one pass with one completion for 13 yards and a touchdown and recovered one fumble.
STATISTICAL PLATEAUS: 100-yard rushing games: 1991 (1), 1994 (2), 1995 (3). Total: 6.

		RUSHING				RECEIVING				KICKOFF RETURNS				TOTALS			
Year Team	G	Att.	Yds.	Avg.	TD	No.	Yds.	Avg.	TD	No.	Yds.	Avg.	TD	TD	2pt.	Pts.	Fum.
1991—Kansas City NFL	14	97	447	4.6	1	16	147	9.2	2	24	524	21.8	0	3	...	18	1
1992—Kansas City NFL	14	78	262	3.4	1	5	24	4.8	0	21	405	19.3	0	1	...	6	1
1993—Kansas City NFL	7	42	149	3.6	0	7	42	6.0	0	3	53	17.7	0	0	...	0	3
1994—Los Angeles Raiders NFL	16	282	983	3.5	4	47	391	8.3	3	8	153	19.1	0	7	1	44	4
1995—Oakland NFL	16	255	1114	4.4	9	54	375	6.9	0	0	0	...	0	9	0	54	5
Pro totals (5 years)	67	754	2955	3.9	15	129	979	7.6	5	56	1135	20.3	0	20	1	122	14

WILLIAMS, JAMES — CB — 49ERS

PERSONAL: Born March 30, 1967, in Osceola, Ark. ... 5-10/190. ... Full name: James Earl Williams.
HIGH SCHOOL: Coalinga (Calif.).
COLLEGE: Fresno State (degree in physical education, 1990).
TRANSACTIONS/CAREER NOTES: Selected by Buffalo Bills in first round (16th pick overall) of 1990 NFL draft. ... Signed by Bills (July 27, 1990). ... On injured reserve with knee injury (September 24-November 23, 1991). ... Granted free agency (March 1, 1993). ... Re-signed by Bills for 1993 season. ... Traded by Bills to Phoenix Cardinals for fourth-round pick (WR Justin Armour) in 1995 draft (March 8, 1994). ... Cardinals franchise renamed Arizona Cardinals for 1994 season. ... Granted unconditional free agency (February 17, 1995). ... Signed by Carolina Panthers (March 3, 1995). ... Released by Panthers (August 27, 1995). ... Signed by New York Giants (July 6, 1995). ... Released by Giants (August 22, 1995). ... Signed by San Francisco 49ers (May 30, 1996).
CHAMPIONSHIP GAME EXPERIENCE: Played in AFC championship game (1990-1993 seasons). ... Played in Super Bowl XXV (1990 season), Super Bowl XXVI (1991 season) and Super Bowl XXVII (1992 season). ... Member of Bills for Super Bowl XXVIII (1993 season); inactive.
HONORS: Named defensive back on THE SPORTING NEWS college All-America second team (1989).
PRO STATISTICS: 1990—Returned blocked punt 38 yards for a touchdown. 1993—Recovered two fumbles for 12 yards. 1994—Recovered two fumbles.

		INTERCEPTIONS			
Year Team	G	No.	Yds.	Avg.	TD
1990—Buffalo NFL	16	2	0	0.0	0
1991—Buffalo NFL	8	1	0	0.0	0
1992—Buffalo NFL	15	2	15	7.5	0
1993—Buffalo NFL	15	2	11	5.5	0
1994—Arizona NFL	15	4	48	12.0	0
1995—			Did not play.		
Pro totals (5 years)	69	11	74	6.7	0

WILLIAMS, JAMES — LB — FALCONS

W

PERSONAL: Born October 10, 1968, in Natchez, Miss. ... 6-0/230. ... Full name: James Edward Williams.
HIGH SCHOOL: Natchez (Miss.).
COLLEGE: Mississippi State.
TRANSACTIONS/CAREER NOTES: Selected by New Orleans Saints in sixth round (158th pick overall) of 1990 NFL draft. ... Signed by Saints (May 9, 1990). ... Granted unconditional free agency (February 1-April 1, 1991). ... Re-signed by Saints for 1991 season. ... Granted unconditional free agency (February 17, 1994). ... Re-signed by Saints (March 18, 1994). ... Selected by Jacksonville Jaguars from Saints in NFL expansion draft (February 15, 1995). ... Released by Jaguars (December 5, 1995). ... Signed by Atlanta Falcons (May 10, 1996).
PRO STATISTICS: 1991—Recovered one fumble. 1994—Intercepted two passes for 42 yards and one touchdown. 1995—Intercepted two passes for 19 yards.

Year Team	G	SACKS
1990—New Orleans NFL	14	0.0
1991—New Orleans NFL	16	1.0
1992—New Orleans NFL	16	0.0
1993—New Orleans NFL	16	2.0
1994—New Orleans NFL	16	0.0
1995—Jacksonville NFL	12	0.0
Pro totals (6 years)	90	3.0

WILLIAMS, JAMES   OT   BEARS

PERSONAL: Born March 29, 1968, in Pittsburgh. ... 6-7/335. ... Full name: James Otis Williams.
HIGH SCHOOL: Allderdice (Pittsburgh).
COLLEGE: Cheyney (Pa.).
TRANSACTIONS/CAREER NOTES: Signed as non-drafted free agent by Chicago Bears (April 25, 1991). ... Granted free agency (February 16, 1996). ... Re-signed by Bears (March 14, 1996).
PLAYING EXPERIENCE: Chicago NFL, 1991-1995. ... Games: 1991 (14), 1992 (5), 1993 (3), 1994 (16), 1995 (16). Total: 54.
PRO STATISTICS: 1991—Credited with one sack.
MISCELLANEOUS: Switched from defensive line to offensive line during the 1992 season.

WILLIAMS, JAY   DT   RAMS

PERSONAL: Born October 13, 1971, in Washington, D.C. ... 6-3/270. ... Full name: Jay Omar Williams.
HIGH SCHOOL: St. John's (Washington, D.C.).
COLLEGE: Wake Forest.
TRANSACTIONS/CAREER NOTES: Signed as non-drafted free agent by Miami Dolphins (April 28, 1994). ... Released by Dolphins (August 28, 1994). ... Signed by Los Angeles Rams to practice squad (September 27, 1994). ... Activated (December 7, 1994); did not play. ... Rams franchise moved from Los Angeles to St. Louis (April 12, 1995).
PLAYING EXPERIENCE: St. Louis NFL, 1995. ... Games: 1995 (7).

WILLIAMS, JOHN L.   FB

PERSONAL: Born November 23, 1964, in Palatka, Fla. ... 5-11/231.
HIGH SCHOOL: Palatka (Fla.).
COLLEGE: Florida.
TRANSACTIONS/CAREER NOTES: Selected by Tampa Bay Bandits in 1986 USFL territorial draft. ... Selected by Seattle Seahawks in first round (15th pick overall) of 1986 NFL draft. ... Signed by Seahawks (July 23, 1986). ... Granted roster exemption (July 25-August 5, 1991). ... Granted unconditional free agency (February 17, 1994). ... Signed by Pittsburgh Steelers (April 23, 1994). ... Released by Steelers (March 6, 1996).
CHAMPIONSHIP GAME EXPERIENCE: Played in AFC championship game (1994 and 1995 seasons). ... Played in Super Bowl XXX (1995 season).
HONORS: Played in Pro Bowl (1990 and 1991 seasons).
PRO STATISTICS: 1987—Recovered one fumble. 1988—Recovered two fumbles for minus two yards. 1989—Recovered one fumble. 1990—Recovered two fumbles. 1991—Recovered one fumble. 1992—Recovered one fumble. 1993—Attempted one pass without a completion and recovered one fumble. 1995—Recovered one fumble.
STATISTICAL PLATEAUS: 100-yard rushing games: 1987 (1), 1988 (3), 1991 (1), 1993 (1). Total: 6. ... 100-yard receiving games: 1987 (1), 1988 (1), 1989 (1), 1990 (1). Total: 4.

		RUSHING				RECEIVING				TOTALS			
Year Team	G	Att.	Yds.	Avg.	TD	No.	Yds.	Avg.	TD	TD	2pt.	Pts.	Fum.
1986—Seattle NFL	16	129	538	4.2	0	33	219	6.6	0	0	...	0	1
1987—Seattle NFL	12	113	500	4.4	1	38	420	11.1	3	4	...	24	2
1988—Seattle NFL	16	189	877	4.6	4	58	651	11.2	3	7	...	42	0
1989—Seattle NFL	15	146	499	3.4	1	76	657	8.6	6	7	...	42	2
1990—Seattle NFL	16	187	714	3.8	3	73	699	9.6	0	3	...	18	5
1991—Seattle NFL	16	188	741	3.9	4	61	499	8.2	1	5	...	30	2
1992—Seattle NFL	16	114	339	3.0	1	74	556	7.5	2	3	...	18	4
1993—Seattle NFL	16	82	371	4.5	3	58	450	7.8	1	4	...	24	2
1994—Pittsburgh NFL	15	68	317	4.7	1	51	378	7.4	2	3	0	18	0
1995—Pittsburgh NFL	11	29	110	3.8	0	24	127	5.3	1	1	0	6	2
Pro totals (10 years)	149	1245	5006	4.0	18	546	4656	8.5	19	37	0	222	20

WILLIAMS, KEVIN   WR/KR   COWBOYS

PERSONAL: Born January 25, 1971, in Dallas. ... 5-9/195. ... Full name: Kevin Ray Williams.
HIGH SCHOOL: Franklin D. Roosevelt (Dallas).
COLLEGE: Miami (Fla.).
TRANSACTIONS/CAREER NOTES: Selected after junior season by Dallas Cowboys in second round (46th overall) of 1993 NFL draft. ... Signed by Cowboys (April 29, 1993).
CHAMPIONSHIP GAME EXPERIENCE: Played in NFC championship game (1993-1995 seasons). ... Member of Super Bowl championship team (1993 and 1995 seasons).
PRO STATISTICS: 1993—Fumbled eight times and recovered four fumbles. 1994—Fumbled four times and recovered three fumbles. 1995—Fumbled three times.
STATISTICAL PLATEAUS: 100-yard receiving games: 1995 (1).

		RUSHING				RECEIVING				PUNT RETURNS				KICKOFF RETURNS				TOTALS		
Year Team	G	Att.	Yds.	Avg.	TD	No.	Yds.	Avg.	TD	No.	Yds.	Avg.	TD	No.	Yds.	Avg.	TD	TD	2pt.	Pts.
1993—Dallas NFL	16	7	26	3.7	2	20	151	7.6	2	36	381	10.6	†2	31	689	22.2	0	6	...	36
1994—Dallas NFL	15	6	20	3.3	0	13	181	13.9	0	39	349	9.0	1	43	1148	26.7	1	2	0	12
1995—Dallas NFL	16	10	53	5.3	0	38	613	16.1	2	18	166	9.2	0	49	1108	22.6	0	2	0	12
Pro totals (3 years)	47	23	99	4.3	2	71	945	13.3	4	93	896	9.6	3	123	2945	24.0	1	10	0	60

WILLIAMS, MARK   LB   JAGUARS

PERSONAL: Born May 17, 1971, in Camp Springs, Md. ... 6-3/243. ... Full name: Mark Anthony Williams. ... Cousin of Julius Erving, forward with Virginia Squires and New York Nets of ABA, Philadelphia 76ers (1971-72 through 1986-87) and member of Naismith Memorial

W

Basketball Hall of Fame.
HIGH SCHOOL: Bishop McNamara (Forestville, Md.).
COLLEGE: Ohio State.
TRANSACTIONS/CAREER NOTES: Signed as non-drafted free agent by Green Bay Packers (May 2, 1994). ... Selected by Jacksonville Jaguars from Packers in NFL expansion draft (February 15, 1995). ... On injured reserve with shoulder injury (November 21, 1995-remainder of season).
PLAYING EXPERIENCE: Green Bay NFL, 1994; Jacksonville NFL, 1995. ... Games: 1994 (16), 1995 (11). Total: 27.
PRO STATISTICS: 1994—Recovered one fumble.

WILLIAMS, MICHAEL — CB — 49ERS

PERSONAL: Born May 28, 1970, in Los Angeles. ... 5-10/185. ... Full name: Michael Dean Williams.
HIGH SCHOOL: Crenshaw (Los Angeles).
COLLEGE: UCLA (degree in history).
TRANSACTIONS/CAREER NOTES: Signed as non-drafted free agent by San Diego Chargers (April 27, 1993). ... Released by Chargers (August 30, 1993). ... Re-signed by Chargers to practice squad (September 1, 1993). ... Granted free agency after 1993 season. ... Re-signed by Chargers (March 11, 1994). ... Released by Chargers (August 22, 1994). ... Signed by San Francisco 49ers (April 25, 1995). ... Released by 49ers (August 19, 1995). ... Re-signed by 49ers to practice squad (August 30, 1995). ... Activated (September 5, 1995). ... Released by 49ers (October 3, 1995). ... Re-signed by 49ers to practice squad (October 5, 1995).
PLAYING EXPERIENCE: San Francisco NFL, 1995. ... Games: 1995 (4).

WILLIAMS, MIKE — WR

PERSONAL: Born October 9, 1966, in Mount Kisco, N.Y. ... 5-11/190.
HIGH SCHOOL: John Jay (Katonah, N.Y.).
COLLEGE: Northeastern.
TRANSACTIONS/CAREER NOTES: Selected by Los Angeles Rams in 10th round (269th pick overall) of 1989 NFL draft. ... Signed by Rams (July 15, 1989). ... On injured reserve with knee injury (September 2-25, 1989). ... Released by Rams (September 26, 1989). ... Signed by Detroit Lions to developmental squad (October 11, 1989). ... Activated (December 21, 1989). ... Granted unconditional free agency (February 1, 1990). ... Signed by Dallas Cowboys (March 3, 1990). ... Released by Cowboys (September 3, 1990). ... Signed by Atlanta Falcons (April 1, 1991). ... Released by Falcons (August 26, 1991). ... Signed by Miami Dolphins to practice squad (September 18, 1991). ... Activated (December 9, 1991). ... Granted unconditional free agency (February 1-April 1, 1992). ... Re-signed by Dolphins for 1992 season. ... On physically unable to perform list (July 20-August 2, 1993). ... On injured reserve with knee injury (December 22, 1993-remainder of season). ... Granted unconditional free agency (February 17, 1995). ... Signed by Jacksonville Jaguars (May 4, 1995). ... Traded by Jaguars to Dolphins for TE Pete Mitchell (August 27, 1995). ... Granted unconditional free agency (February 16, 1996).
CHAMPIONSHIP GAME EXPERIENCE: Played in AFC championship game (1992 season).
PRO STATISTICS: 1992—Recovered one fumble.

		RECEIVING				KICKOFF RETURNS				TOTALS			
Year Team	G	No.	Yds.	Avg.	TD	No.	Yds.	Avg.	TD	TD	2pt.	Pts.	Fum.
1989—Detroit NFL	1	0	0	...	0	0	0	...	0	0	...	0	0
1990—							Did not play.						
1991—Miami NFL	3	0	0	...	0	0	0	...	0	0	...	0	0
1992—Miami NFL	15	3	43	14.3	0	19	328	17.3	0	0	...	0	1
1993—Miami NFL	13	1	11	11.0	0	8	180	22.5	0	0	...	0	0
1994—Miami NFL	15	15	221	14.7	0	2	9	4.5	0	0	0	0	0
1995—Miami NFL	12	2	17	8.5	0	0	0	...	0	0	0	0	0
Pro totals (6 years)	59	21	292	13.9	0	29	517	17.8	0	0	0	0	2

WILLIAMS, RONNIE — TE — DOLPHINS

PERSONAL: Born January 19, 1966, in Wichita Falls, Texas. ... 6-3/258.
HIGH SCHOOL: Rider (Wichita Falls, Texas).
COLLEGE: Oklahoma State.
TRANSACTIONS/CAREER NOTES: Signed as non-drafted free agent by San Diego Chargers (1988). ... On injured reserve with groin injury (1988 season). ... Released by Chargers (1989). ... Signed by Indianapolis Colts to developmental squad (September 7, 1989). ... Released by Colts (September 13, 1989). ... Did not play in 1990. ... Selected by San Antonio Riders in first round (sixth pick overall) of 1991 WLAF draft. ... Signed by Philadelphia Eagles (June 11, 1992). ... Released by Eagles (August 25, 1992). ... Signed by New Orleans Saints (March 8, 1993). ... Released by Saints (August 30, 1993). ... Signed by Miami Dolphins (September 15, 1993). ... Granted free agency (February 17, 1995). ... Re-signed by Dolphins (March 13, 1995).
PRO STATISTICS: W.L.: 1991—Returned two punts for minus two yards. NFL: 1993—Recovered one fumble. 1994—Returned two kickoffs for 25 yards. 1995—Returned two kickoffs for 20 yards.

		RECEIVING				TOTALS			
Year Team	G	No.	Yds.	Avg.	TD	TD	2pt.	Pts.	Fum.
1991—San Antonio W.L.	10	30	321	10.7	0	0	...	0	0
1992—San Antonio W.L.	10	20	216	10.8	4	4	...	24	0
1993—Miami NFL	11	0	0	...	0	0	0	0	0
1994—Miami NFL	14	2	26	13.0	0	0	0	0	0
1995—Miami NFL	16	3	28	9.3	0	0	0	0	0
W.L. totals (2 years)	20	50	537	10.8	4	4	0	24	0
NFL totals (3 years)	41	5	54	10.8	0	0	0	0	0
Pro totals (5 years)	61	55	591	10.8	4	4	0	24	0

WILLIAMS, SHERMAN — RB — COWBOYS

PERSONAL: Born August 13, 1973, in Mobile, Ala. ... 5-8/190.
HIGH SCHOOL: M.T. Blount (Prichard, Ala.).

W

COLLEGE: Alabama.
TRANSACTIONS/CAREER NOTES: Selected by Dallas Cowboys in second round (46th pick overall) of 1995 NFL draft. ... Signed by Cowboys (July 21, 1995).
CHAMPIONSHIP GAME EXPERIENCE: Played in NFC championship game (1995 season). ... Member of Super Bowl championship team (1995 season).
HONORS: Named running back on THE SPORTING NEWS college All-America second team (1994).

		RUSHING				RECEIVING				TOTALS			
Year Team	G	Att.	Yds.	Avg.	TD	No.	Yds.	Avg.	TD	TD	2pt.	Pts.	Fum.
1995—Dallas NFL	11	48	205	4.3	1	3	28	9.3	0	1	0	6	2

WILLIAMS, WALLY — C — RAVENS

PERSONAL: Born February 19, 1971, in Tallahassee, Fla. ... 6-2/300. ... Full name: Wally James Williams Jr.
HIGH SCHOOL: James S. Rickards (Tallahassee, Fla.).
COLLEGE: Florida A&M.
TRANSACTIONS/CAREER NOTES: Signed as non-drafted free agent by Cleveland Browns (April 27, 1993). ... Browns franchise moved to Baltimore and renamed Ravens for 1996 season (March 11, 1996).
PLAYING EXPERIENCE: Cleveland NFL, 1993-1995. ... Games: 1993 (2), 1994 (11), 1995 (16). Total: 29.
PRO STATISTICS: 1994—Recovered one fumble.

WILLIAMS, WILLIE — CB — STEELERS

PERSONAL: Born December 26, 1970, in Columbia, S.C. ... 5-9/180. ... Full name: Willie James Williams Jr.
HIGH SCHOOL: Spring Valley (Columbia, S.C.).
COLLEGE: Western Carolina.
TRANSACTIONS/CAREER NOTES: Selected by Pittsburgh Steelers in sixth round (162nd pick overall) of 1993 NFL draft. ... Signed by Steelers (July 9, 1993). ... Granted free agency (February 16, 1996).
CHAMPIONSHIP GAME EXPERIENCE: Played in AFC championship game (1994 and 1995 seasons). ... Played in Super Bowl XXX (1995 season).
PRO STATISTICS: 1993—Returned one kickoff for 19 yards. 1995—Recovered one fumble.

		INTERCEPTIONS			
Year Team	G	No.	Yds.	Avg.	TD
1993—Pittsburgh NFL	16	0	0	...	0
1994—Pittsburgh NFL	16	0	0	...	0
1995—Pittsburgh NFL	16	7	122	17.4	1
Pro totals (3 years)	48	7	122	17.4	1

WILLIG, MATT — OT — FALCONS

PERSONAL: Born January 21, 1969, in Whittier, Calif. ... 6-8/317.
HIGH SCHOOL: St. Paul (Santa Fe Springs, Calif.).
COLLEGE: Southern California.
TRANSACTIONS/CAREER NOTES: Signed as non-drafted free agent by New York Jets (May 5, 1992). ... Released by Jets (August 24, 1992). ... Re-signed by Jets to practice squad (September 2, 1992). ... Activated (December 24, 1992). ... Active for one game (1992); did not play. ... Signed by Jets (February 14, 1995). ... Released by Jets (April 23, 1996). ... Recalled from waivers by Jets and traded to Atlanta Falcons for conditional seventh-round pick in 1998 NFL draft (May 2, 1996).
PLAYING EXPERIENCE: New York Jets NFL, 1993-1995. ... Games: 1993 (3), 1994 (16), 1995 (15). Total: 34.

WILLIS, JAMAL — RB — 49ERS

PERSONAL: Born December 12, 1972, in Lawton, Okla. ... 6-2/218.
HIGH SCHOOL: Bonanza (Las Vegas).
COLLEGE: Brigham Young.
TRANSACTIONS/CAREER NOTES: Signed as non-drafted free agent by San Francisco 49ers (May 5, 1995). ... Released by 49ers (July 12, 1995). ... Re-signed by 49ers (July 21, 1995). ... On injured reserve with knee injury (December 12, 1995-remainder of season).

		RUSHING				RECEIVING				KICKOFF RETURNS				TOTALS			
Year Team	G	Att.	Yds.	Avg.	TD	No.	Yds.	Avg.	TD	No.	Yds.	Avg.	TD	TD	2pt.	Pts.	Fum.
1995—San Francisco NFL	11	12	35	2.9	0	3	8	2.7	0	17	427	25.1	0	0	0	0	0

WILLIS, JAMES — LB — EAGLES

PERSONAL: Born September 2, 1972, in Huntsville, Ala. ... 6-2/237. ... Full name: James Edward Willis III.
HIGH SCHOOL: J.O. Johnson (Huntsville, Ala.).
COLLEGE: Auburn.
TRANSACTIONS/CAREER NOTES: Selected after junior season by Green Bay Packers in fifth round (119th pick overall) of 1993 NFL draft. ... Signed by Packers (May 21, 1993). ... On injured reserve with knee injury (December 23, 1993-remainder of season). ... Released by Packers (October 25, 1995). ... Signed by Philadelphia Eagles (October 31, 1995). ... Granted free agency (February 16, 1996). ... Re-signed by Eagles (March 1, 1996).
PRO STATISTICS: 1993—Recovered one fumble. 1994—Fumbled once and recovered one fumble.

		INTERCEPTIONS			
Year Team	G	No.	Yds.	Avg.	TD
1993—Green Bay NFL..................................	13	0	0	...	0

W

Year Team	G	No.	Yds.	Avg.	TD
		INTERCEPTIONS			
1994—Green Bay NFL	12	2	20	10.0	0
1995—Philadelphia NFL	5	0	0	...	0
Pro totals (3 years)	30	2	20	10.0	0

WILMOT, TREVOR　　　　　LB　　　　　COLTS

PERSONAL: Born October 30, 1972, in Evanston, Ill. ... 6-2/215.
HIGH SCHOOL: Evanston (Ill.) Township.
COLLEGE: Indiana.
TRANSACTIONS/CAREER NOTES: Signed as non-drafted free agent by Indianapolis Colts (April 27, 1995). ... Released by Colts (August 22, 1995). ... Re-signed by Colts to practice squad (August 28, 1995). ... Activated (November 10, 1995).
PLAYING EXPERIENCE: Indianapolis NFL, 1995. ... Games: 1995 (7).
CHAMPIONSHIP GAME EXPERIENCE: Played in AFC championship game (1995 season).

WILMSMEYER, KLAUS　　　　　P　　　　　SAINTS

PERSONAL: Born December 4, 1967, in Mississauga, Ont. ... 6-1/210.
HIGH SCHOOL: Lorne Park Secondary (Mississauga, Ont.).
COLLEGE: Louisville.
TRANSACTIONS/CAREER NOTES: Selected by Tampa Bay Buccaneers in 12th round (311th pick overall) of 1992 NFL draft. ... Signed by Buccaneers (June 9, 1992). ... Released by Buccaneers (August 24, 1992). ... Signed by San Francisco 49ers to practice squad (September 2, 1992). ... Activated (September 4, 1992). ... Granted unconditional free agency (February 17, 1995). ... Signed by New Orleans Saints (March 7, 1995).
CHAMPIONSHIP GAME EXPERIENCE: Played in NFC championship game (1992-1994 seasons). ... Member of Super Bowl championship team (1994 season).
PRO STATISTICS: 1992—Rushed twice for no yards, fumbled once and recovered one fumble. 1993—Rushed twice for no yards, fumbled twice and recovered one fumble for minus 10 yards. 1995—Attempted one pass with one completion for 18 yards.

Year Team	G	No.	Yds.	Avg.	Net avg.	In. 20	Blk.
				PUNTING			
1992—San Francisco NFL	15	49	1918	39.1	34.7	19	0
1993—San Francisco NFL	15	42	1718	40.9	34.5	11	0
1994—San Francisco NFL	16	54	2235	41.4	35.8	18	0
1995—New Orleans NFL	16	73	2965	40.6	35.6	21	1
Pro totals (4 years)	62	218	8836	40.5	35.2	69	1

WILNER, JEFF　　　　　TE　　　　　BRONCOS

PERSONAL: Born December 31, 1971, in East Meadowbrook, N.Y. ... 6-4/245. ... Full name: Jeffrey Scott Wilner.
HIGH SCHOOL: Phillips Exeter (N.H.) Academy.
COLLEGE: Wesleyan, Conn. (degree in economics and government).
TRANSACTIONS/CAREER NOTES: Signed as non-drafted free agent by Green Bay Packers (April 27, 1994). ... Traded by Packers with WR Bill Schroeder to New England Patriots for C Mike Arthur (August 11, 1995). ... Released by Patriots (August 27, 1995). ... Signed by Packers (September 26, 1995). ... Released by Packers (October 28, 1995). ... Signed by Denver Broncos (December 20, 1995).
PLAYING EXPERIENCE: Green Bay NFL, 1994 and 1995. ... Games: 1994 (11), 1995 (2). Total: 13.
PRO STATISTICS: 1994—Caught five passes for 31 yards.

WILSON, BERNARD　　　　　DT　　　　　CARDINALS

PERSONAL: Born August 17, 1970, in Nashville. ... 6-2/295.
HIGH SCHOOL: Maplewood (Nashville).
COLLEGE: Tennessee State.
TRANSACTIONS/CAREER NOTES: Signed as non-drafted free agent by Detroit Lions (May 1, 1992). ... Released by Lions (August 31, 1992). ... Re-signed by Lions to practice squad (September 1, 1992). ... Granted free agency after 1992 season. ... Re-signed by Lions for 1993 season. ... Released by Lions (September 6, 1993). ... Re-signed by Lions to practice squad (September 8, 1993). ... Signed by Tampa Bay Buccaneers off Lions practice squad (September 16, 1993). ... Claimed on waivers by Arizona Cardinals (September 7, 1994).
PLAYING EXPERIENCE: Tampa Bay NFL, 1993; Tampa Bay (1)-Arizona (13) NFL, 1994; Arizona NFL, 1995. ... Games: 1993 (13), 1994 (14), 1995 (16). Total: 43.
PRO STATISTICS: 1994—Credited with one sack. 1995—Credited with one sack.

W

WILSON, CHARLES　　　　　WR　　　　　BUCCANEERS

PERSONAL: Born July 1, 1968, in Tallahassee, Fla. ... 5-10/185. ... Full name: Charles Joseph Wilson.
HIGH SCHOOL: Godby (Tallahassee, Fla.).
COLLEGE: Memphis State (degree in general studies).
TRANSACTIONS/CAREER NOTES: Selected after junior season by Green Bay Packers in fifth round (132nd pick overall) of 1990 NFL draft. ... Signed by Packers (June 25, 1990). ... Granted free agency (February 1, 1992). ... Re-signed by Packers (August 5, 1992). ... On injured reserve (August-September 14, 1992). ... Released by Packers (September 14, 1992). ... Signed by San Diego Chargers (September 22, 1992). ... Released by Chargers (September 25, 1992). ... Signed by Tampa Bay Buccaneers (December 17, 1992). ... Granted unconditional free agency (February 17, 1995). ... Re-signed by Buccaneers (April 10, 1995). ... Traded by Buccaneers with DT Marc Spindler to New York Jets for fourth-round pick (OT Jason Odom) in 1996 draft (August 27, 1995). ... Released by Jets (April 23, 1996). ... Signed by Buccaneers (May 13, 1996).

PRO STATISTICS: 1991—Recovered one fumble. 1993—Recovered two fumbles.
STATISTICAL PLATEAUS: 100-yard receiving games: 1994 (1).

		RUSHING				RECEIVING				KICKOFF RETURNS				TOTALS			
Year Team	G	Att.	Yds.	Avg.	TD	No.	Yds.	Avg.	TD	No.	Yds.	Avg.	TD	TD	2pt.	Pts.	Fum.
1990—Green Bay NFL..............	15	0	0	...	0	7	84	12.0	0	35	798	22.8	0	0	...	0	0
1991—Green Bay NFL..............	15	3	3	1.0	0	19	305	16.1	1	23	522	22.7	†1	2	...	12	4
1992—Tampa Bay NFL.............	2	0	0	...	0	0	0	...	0	1	23	23.0	0	0	...	0	0
1993—Tampa Bay NFL.............	15	2	7	3.5	0	15	225	15.0	0	23	454	19.7	0	0	...	0	1
1994—Tampa Bay NFL.............	14	2	15	7.5	0	31	652	21.0	6	10	251	25.1	0	6	0	36	0
1995—New York Jets NFL..........	15	0	0	...	0	41	484	11.8	4	0	0	...	0	4	0	24	1
Pro totals (6 years)...................	76	7	25	3.6	0	113	1750	15.5	11	92	2048	22.3	1	12	0	72	6

WILSON, KARL   DT/DE

PERSONAL: Born September 10, 1964, in Amite, La. ... 6-5/274. ... Full name: Karl Wendell Wilson.
HIGH SCHOOL: Baker (La.).
COLLEGE: Louisiana State (degree in general studies, 1987).
TRANSACTIONS/CAREER NOTES: Selected by San Diego Chargers in third round (59th pick overall) of 1987 NFL draft. ... Signed by Chargers (July 29, 1987). ... On injured reserve with hamstring injury (November 3-December 5, 1987). ... Released by Chargers (September 5, 1989). ... Signed by Phoenix Cardinals (September 15, 1989). ... Granted unconditional free agency (February 1, 1990). ... Signed by Miami Dolphins (March 26, 1990). ... Granted unconditional free agency (February 1, 1991). ... Signed by Los Angeles Rams (March 5, 1991). ... Released by Rams (August 31, 1992). ... Signed by New York Jets (September 29, 1992). ... Released by Jets (October 23, 1992). ... Re-signed by Jets (March 1, 1993). ... Released by Jets (August 30, 1993). ... Re-signed by Jets (August 31, 1993). ... Released by Jets (October 22, 1993). ... Signed by Dolphins (October 27, 1993). ... Released by Dolphins (November 29, 1993). ... Signed by San Francisco 49ers (December 1, 1993). ... Released by 49ers (July 25, 1994). ... Re-signed by 49ers (July 26, 1994). ... Released by 49ers (August 22, 1994). ... Signed by Tampa Bay Buccaneers (August 26, 1994). ... Granted unconditional free agency (February 17, 1995). ... Signed by Buffalo Bills (June 8, 1995). ... Released by Bills (February 16, 1996).
CHAMPIONSHIP GAME EXPERIENCE: Played in NFC championship game (1993 season).
PRO STATISTICS: 1989—Credited with one safety. 1994—Recovered one fumble.

Year Team	G	SACKS
1987—San Diego NFL..	7	1.0
1988—San Diego NFL..	13	0.5
1989—Phoenix NFL..	15	1.0
1990—Miami NFL..	16	4.0
1991—Los Angeles Rams NFL..	13	2.0
1992—New York Jets NFL..	2	0.0
1993—New York Jets NFL..	5	0.0
—Miami NFL...	2	0.0
—San Francisco NFL..	5	3.0
1994—Tampa Bay NFL..	14	2.5
1995—Buffalo NFL..	11	1.0
Pro totals (9 years)...	103	15.0

WILSON, MARCUS   RB

PERSONAL: Born April 16, 1968, in Rochester, N.Y. ... 6-1/215. ... Full name: Edmond Marcus Wilson.
HIGH SCHOOL: Greece Olympia (Rochester, N.Y.).
COLLEGE: Virginia (degree in sports management).
TRANSACTIONS/CAREER NOTES: Selected after junior season by Los Angeles Raiders in sixth round (149th pick overall) of 1990 NFL draft. ... Claimed on waivers by Indianapolis Colts (August 29, 1990). ... Released by Colts (September 3, 1990). ... Signed by Raiders for 1991. ... Assigned by Raiders to Frankfurt Galaxy in 1991 WLAF enhancement allocation program (March 4, 1991). ... Released by Raiders (August 20, 1991). ... Re-signed by Raiders to practice squad (September 4, 1991). ... Activated (September 21, 1991). ... Released by Raiders (September 28, 1991). ... Re-signed by Raiders to practice squad (October 2, 1991). ... Granted free agency after 1991 season. ... Signed by Green Bay Packers (January 30, 1992). ... On injured reserve with foot injury (September 1-November 20, 1992). ... On injured reserve with hamstring injury (December 27, 1994-remainder of season). ... Selected by Jacksonville Jaguars from Packers in NFL expansion draft (February 15, 1995). ... Released by Jaguars (May 30, 1995). ... Signed by Packers (June 21, 1995). ... Released by Packers (February 16, 1996).
CHAMPIONSHIP GAME EXPERIENCE: Played in NFC championship game (1995 season).
PRO STATISTICS: 1993—Recovered one fumble.

		RUSHING				RECEIVING				KICKOFF RETURNS				TOTALS			
Year Team	G	Att.	Yds.	Avg.	TD	No.	Yds.	Avg.	TD	No.	Yds.	Avg.	TD	TD	2pt.	Pts.	Fum.
1990—							Did not play.										
1991—Los Angeles Raiders NFL....	1	6	21	3.5	0	0	0	...	0	0	0	...	0	0	...	0	0
1992—Green Bay NFL.................	6	0	0	...	0	0	0	...	0	0	0	...	0	0	...	0	0
1993—Green Bay NFL.................	16	6	3	.5	0	2	18	9.0	0	9	197	21.9	0	0	...	0	1
1994—Green Bay NFL.................	12	0	0	...	0	0	0	...	0	2	14	7.0	0	0	0	0	1
1995—Green Bay NFL.................	14	0	0	...	0	0	0	...	0	0	0	...	0	0	0	0	0
Pro totals (5 years)...................	49	12	24	2.0	0	2	18	9.0	0	11	211	19.2	0	0	0	0	2

WILSON, ROBERT   FB

PERSONAL: Born January 13, 1969, in Houston. ... 6-0/255. ... Full name: Robert Eugene Wilson.
HIGH SCHOOL: E.E. Worthing (Houston).
COLLEGE: Texas A&M.
TRANSACTIONS/CAREER NOTES: Selected after junior season by Tampa Bay Buccaneers in third round (80th pick overall) of 1991 NFL draft. ... Signed by Buccaneers (July 15, 1991). ... Released by Buccaneers (September 1, 1992). ... Signed by Green Bay Packers (February 8, 1993). ... Released by Packers (August 23, 1993). ... Signed by Dallas Cowboys (April 29, 1994). ... Released by Cowboys (October 25, 1994).

... Signed by Miami Dolphins (November 9, 1994). ... Granted unconditional free agency (February 16, 1996).
PRO STATISTICS: 1991—Returned two kickoffs for 19 yards and recovered one fumble. 1995—Recovered one fumble.

		RUSHING				RECEIVING				TOTALS			
Year Team	G	Att.	Yds.	Avg.	TD	No.	Yds.	Avg.	TD	TD	2pt.	Pts.	Fum.
1991—Tampa Bay NFL	16	42	179	4.3	0	20	121	6.1	2	2	...	12	3
1992—						Did not play.							
1993—Dallas NFL						Did not play.							
1994—Dallas NFL	2	1	-1	-1.0	0	0	0	...	0	0	0	0	0
—Miami NFL	2	0	0	...	0	0	0	...	0	0	0	0	0
1995—Miami NFL	16	1	5	5.0	0	1	3	3.0	0	0	0	0	0
Pro totals (3 years)	36	44	183	4.2	0	21	124	5.9	2	2	0	12	3

WILSON, TROY   LB/DE   CHIEFS

PERSONAL: Born November 22, 1970, in Topeka, Kan. ... 6-4/250.
HIGH SCHOOL: Shawnee Heights (Tecumseh, Kan.).
COLLEGE: Pittsburg (Kan.) State.
TRANSACTIONS/CAREER NOTES: Selected by San Francisco 49ers in seventh round (194th pick overall) of 1993 NFL draft. ... Signed by 49ers (May 12, 1993). ... On non-football injury list with back injury (August 24, 1993-October 16, 1993). ... Released by 49ers (August 27, 1995). ... Signed by Denver Broncos (September 28, 1995). ... Released by Broncos (October 30, 1995). ... Signed by Kansas City Chiefs (April 1996).
CHAMPIONSHIP GAME EXPERIENCE: Played in NFC championship game (1993 and 1994 seasons). ... Member of Super Bowl championship team (1994 season).

Year Team	G	SACKS
1993—San Francisco NFL	10	5.5
1994—San Francisco NFL	11	2.0
1995—Denver NFL	3	0.5
Pro totals (3 years)	24	8.0

WILSON, WADE   QB   COWBOYS

PERSONAL: Born February 1, 1959, in Greenville, Texas. ... 6-3/206. ... Full name: Charles Wade Wilson.
HIGH SCHOOL: Commerce (Texas).
COLLEGE: East Texas State.
TRANSACTIONS/CAREER NOTES: Selected by Minnesota Vikings in eighth round (210th pick overall) of 1981 NFL draft. ... On inactive list (September 12, 1982). ... On commissioner's exempt list (November 20-December 8, 1982). ... Active for four games with Vikings (1982); did not play. ... On injured reserve with broken thumb (September 26-November 24, 1990). ... On injured reserve with separated shoulder (December 26, 1990-remainder of season). ... Released by Vikings (July 9, 1992). ... Signed by Atlanta Falcons (July 15, 1992). ... Granted unconditional free agency (March 1, 1993). ... Signed by New Orleans Saints (April 12, 1993). ... Released by Saints (March 18, 1994). ... Re-signed by Saints (April 13, 1994). ... Released by Saints (March 20, 1995). ... Signed by Dallas Cowboys (May 22, 1995).
CHAMPIONSHIP GAME EXPERIENCE: Played in NFC championship game (1987 season). ... Member of Cowboys for NFC championship game (1995 season); did not play. ... Member of Super Bowl championship team (1995 season).
HONORS: Played in Pro Bowl (1988 season).
PRO STATISTICS: 1981—Fumbled twice and recovered one fumble. 1983—Fumbled once. 1984—Fumbled twice. 1986—Punted twice for 76 yards with one punt blocked, fumbled three times and recovered one fumble for minus two yards. 1987—Fumbled three times. 1988—Fumbled four times and recovered four fumbles for minus nine yards. 1989—Fumbled five times and recovered two fumbles for minus seven yards. 1990—Fumbled three times and recovered one fumble for minus two yards. 1991—Fumbled three times and recovered one fumble for minus three yards. 1993—Fumbled nine times and recovered four fumbles for minus three yards. 1994—Fumbled once. 1995—Fumbled once and recovered one fumble.
STATISTICAL PLATEAUS: 300-yard passing games: 1986 (2), 1988 (2), 1989 (2), 1990 (1), 1992 (3), 1993 (1). Total: 11.
MISCELLANEOUS: Regular-season record as starting NFL quarterback: 35-30 (.538).

		PASSING								RUSHING				TOTALS		
Year Team	G	Att.	Cmp.	Pct.	Yds.	TD	Int.	Avg.	Rat.	Att.	Yds.	Avg.	TD	TD	2pt.	Pts.
1981—Minnesota NFL	3	13	6	46.2	48	0	2	3.69	16.3	0	0	...	0	0	...	0
1982—Minnesota NFL								Did not play.								
1983—Minnesota NFL	1	28	16	57.1	124	1	2	4.43	50.3	3	-3	-1.0	0	0	...	0
1984—Minnesota NFL	8	195	102	52.3	1019	5	11	5.23	52.5	9	30	3.3	0	0	...	0
1985—Minnesota NFL	4	60	33	55.0	404	3	3	6.73	71.8	0	0	...	0	0	...	0
1986—Minnesota NFL	9	143	80	55.9	1165	7	5	8.15	84.4	13	9	.7	1	1	...	6
1987—Minnesota NFL	12	264	140	53.0	2106	14	13	*7.98	76.7	41	263	6.4	5	5	...	30
1988—Minnesota NFL	14	332	204	*61.5	2746	15	9	8.27	91.5	36	136	3.8	2	2	...	12
1989—Minnesota NFL	14	362	194	53.6	2543	9	12	7.03	70.5	32	132	4.1	1	1	...	6
1990—Minnesota NFL	6	146	82	56.2	1155	9	8	7.91	79.6	12	79	6.6	0	0	...	0
1991—Minnesota NFL	5	122	72	59.0	825	3	10	6.76	53.5	13	33	2.5	0	0	...	0
1992—Atlanta NFL	9	163	111	68.1	1366	13	4	8.38	110.1	15	62	4.1	0	0	...	0
1993—New Orleans NFL	14	388	221	57.0	2457	12	15	6.33	70.1	31	230	7.4	0	0	...	0
1994—New Orleans NFL	4	28	20	71.4	172	0	0	6.14	87.2	7	15	2.1	0	0	0	0
1995—Dallas NFL	7	57	38	66.7	391	1	3	6.86	70.1	10	12	1.2	0	0	0	0
Pro totals (14 years)	110	2301	1319	57.3	16521	92	97	7.18	75.5	222	998	4.5	9	9	0	54

WINANS, TYDUS   WR   REDSKINS

PERSONAL: Born July 26, 1972, in Los Angeles. ... 5-11/180. ... Full name: Tydus Oran Winans. ... Name pronounced TIE-dus WHY-nuns.
HIGH SCHOOL: Carson (Calif.).
COLLEGE: Fresno State.
TRANSACTIONS/CAREER NOTES: Selected by Washington Redskins in third round (68th pick overall) of 1994 NFL draft. ... Signed by

W

Redskins (July 18, 1994).
PRO STATISTICS: 1994—Rushed once for five yards.

			RECEIVING				TOTALS			
Year Team	G	No.	Yds.	Avg.	TD	TD	2pt.	Pts.	Fum.
1994—Washington NFL	15	19	344	18.1	2	2	1	14	0
1995—Washington NFL	8	4	77	19.3	0	0	0	0	1
Pro totals (2 years)	23	23	421	18.3	2	2	1	14	1

WINTERS, FRANK　　　　　C　　　　　PACKERS

PERSONAL: Born January 23, 1964, in Hoboken, N.J. ... 6-3/295. ... Full name: Frank Mitchell Winters.
HIGH SCHOOL: Emerson (Union City, N.J.).
JUNIOR COLLEGE: College of Eastern Utah.
COLLEGE: Western Illinois (degree in political science administration, 1987).
TRANSACTIONS/CAREER NOTES: Selected by Cleveland Browns in 10th round (276th pick overall) of 1987 NFL draft. ... Signed by Browns (July 25, 1987). ... Granted unconditional free agency (February 1, 1989). ... Signed by New York Giants (March 17, 1989). ... Granted unconditional free agency (February 1, 1990). ... Signed by Kansas City Chiefs (March 26, 1990). ... Granted unconditional free agency (February 1, 1992). ... Signed by Green Bay Packers (March 17, 1992). ... Granted unconditional free agency (February 17, 1994). ... Re-signed by Packers (April 1, 1994).
PLAYING EXPERIENCE: Cleveland NFL, 1987 and 1988; New York Giants NFL, 1989; Kansas City NFL, 1990 and 1991; Green Bay NFL, 1992-1995. ... Games: 1987 (12), 1988 (16), 1989 (15), 1990 (16), 1991 (16), 1992 (16), 1993 (16), 1994 (16), 1995 (16). Total: 139.
CHAMPIONSHIP GAME EXPERIENCE: Played in AFC championship game (1987 season). ... Played in NFC championship game (1995 season).
PRO STATISTICS: 1987—Fumbled once. 1990—Recovered two fumbles. 1992—Fumbled once. 1994—Fumbled once and recovered one fumble for minus two yards.

WISDOM, TERRENCE　　　　　G　　　　　JETS

PERSONAL: Born December 4, 1971, in Brooklyn, N.Y. ... 6-4/300.
HIGH SCHOOL: Roosevelt (N.Y.).
COLLEGE: Syracuse.
TRANSACTIONS/CAREER NOTES: Signed as non-drafted free agent by Seattle Seahawks (April 30, 1993). ... Released by Seahawks (July 22, 1993). ... Signed by New York Jets (April 30, 1994). ... Released by Jets (August 22, 1994). ... Re-signed by Jets to practice squad (August 30, 1994). ... Assigned by Jets to London Monarchs in 1995 World League enhancement allocation program (February 20, 1995). ... Released by Jets (August 27, 1995). ... Re-signed by Jets to practice squad (August 29, 1995). ... Activated (November 17, 1995).
PLAYING EXPERIENCE: New York Jets NFL, 1995. ... Games: 1995 (5).

WISNIEWSKI, STEVE　　　　　G　　　　　RAIDERS

PERSONAL: Born April 7, 1967, in Rutland, Vt. ... 6-4/285. ... Full name: Stephen Adam Wisniewski. ... Brother of Leo Wisniewski, nose tackle, Baltimore/Indianapolis Colts (1982-1984).
HIGH SCHOOL: Westfield (Houston).
COLLEGE: Penn State.
TRANSACTIONS/CAREER NOTES: Selected by Dallas Cowboys in second round (29th pick overall) of 1989 NFL draft. ... Draft rights traded by Cowboys with sixth-round pick (LB Jeff Francis) in 1989 draft to Los Angeles Raiders for second-round (RB Darryl Johnston), third-round (DE Rhondy Weston) and fifth-round (LB Willis Crockett) picks in 1989 draft (April 23, 1989). ... Signed by Raiders (July 22, 1989). ... Granted free agency (March 1, 1993). ... Re-signed by Raiders for 1993 season. ... Raiders franchise moved to Oakland (July 21, 1995).
PLAYING EXPERIENCE: Los Angeles Raiders NFL, 1989-1994; Oakland NFL, 1995. ... Games: 1989 (15), 1990 (16), 1991 (15), 1992 (16), 1993 (16), 1994 (16), 1995 (16). Total: 110.
CHAMPIONSHIP GAME EXPERIENCE: Played in AFC championship game (1990 season).
HONORS: Named guard on THE SPORTING NEWS college All-America first team (1987 and 1988). ... Named guard on THE SPORTING NEWS NFL All-Pro team (1990-1994). ... Played in Pro Bowl (1990, 1991, 1993 and 1995 seasons). ... Named to play in Pro Bowl (1992 season); replaced by Jim Ritcher due to injury.
PRO STATISTICS: 1989—Recovered three fumbles. 1995—Recovered one fumble.

WITHERSPOON, DERRICK　　　　　RB　　　　　EAGLES

PERSONAL: Born February 14, 1971, in Sumter, S.C. ... 5-10/196. ... Full name: Derrick Leon Witherspoon.
HIGH SCHOOL: Sumter (S.C.).
COLLEGE: Clemson.
TRANSACTIONS/CAREER NOTES: Signed as non-drafted free agent by New Enlgand Patriots (April 28, 1994). ... Released by Patriots (August 20, 1994). ... Signed by Philadelphia Eagles (April 20, 1995).

		RUSHING				KICKOFF RETURNS				TOTALS		
Year Team	G	Att.	Yds.	Avg.	TD	No.	Yds.	Avg.	TD	TD	2pt.	Pts.Fum.
1995—Philadelphia NFL	15	2	7	3.5	0	18	459	25.5	1	1	0	6 0

WOHLABAUGH, DAVE　　　　　C/G　　　　　PATRIOTS

PERSONAL: Born April 13, 1972, in Lackawanna, N.Y. ... 6-3/304. ... Full name: David Vincent Wohlabaugh. ... Name pronounced WOOL-uh-buh.
HIGH SCHOOL: Frontier (Hamburg, N.Y.).
COLLEGE: Syracuse.
TRANSACTIONS/CAREER NOTES: Selected by New England Patriots in fourth round (112th pick overall) of 1995 NFL draft. ... Signed by

W

Patriots (June 26, 1995).
PLAYING EXPERIENCE: New England NFL, 1995. ... Games: 1995 (11).
PRO STATISTICS: 1995—Recovered one fumble.

WOLF, JOE   G

PERSONAL: Born December 28, 1966, in Allentown, Pa. ... 6-6/296. ... Full name: Joseph Francis Wolf Jr.
HIGH SCHOOL: William Allen (Allentown, Pa.).
COLLEGE: Boston College (degree in communications, 1988).
TRANSACTIONS/CAREER NOTES: Selected by Phoenix Cardinals in first round (17th pick overall) of 1989 NFL draft. ... Signed by Cardinals (August 15, 1989). ... On injured reserve with shoulder injury (October 19-December 7, 1991). ... On injured reserve with torn pectoral muscle (September 3-December 4, 1992). ... Granted free agency (March 1, 1993). ... Re-signed by Cardinals (July 13, 1993). ... Granted unconditional free agency (February 17, 1994). ... Cardinals franchise renamed Arizona Cardinals for 1994 season. ... Re-signed by Cardinals (May 17, 1994). ... Granted unconditional free agency (February 17, 1995). ... Re-signed by Cardinals (June 16, 1995). ... Granted unconditional free agency (February 16, 1996).
PLAYING EXPERIENCE: Phoenix NFL, 1989-1993; Arizona NFL, 1994 and 1995. ... Games: 1989 (16), 1990 (15), 1991 (8), 1992 (3), 1993 (8), 1994 (7), 1995 (6). Total: 63.

WOLFLEY, RON   RB

PERSONAL: Born October 14, 1962, in Blasdell, N.Y. ... 6-0/225. ... Full name: Ronald Paul Wolfley. ... Brother of Craig Wolfley, guard, Pittsburgh Steelers and Minnesota Vikings (1980-1991).
HIGH SCHOOL: Frontier Central (Hamburg, N.Y.).
COLLEGE: West Virginia.
TRANSACTIONS/CAREER NOTES: Selected by Birmingham Stallions in 1985 USFL territorial draft.... Selected by St. Louis Cardinals in fourth round (104th pick overall) of 1985 NFL draft. ... Signed by Cardinals (July 21, 1985). ... Cardinals franchise moved to Phoenix (March 15, 1988). ... Granted free agency (February 1, 1990). ... Re-signed by Cardinals (August 1, 1990). ... On injured reserve with shoulder injury (September 27-October 24, 1990). ... Granted unconditional free agency (February 1, 1992). ... Signed by Cleveland Browns (April 1, 1992).... Released by Browns (1994).... Signed by St. Louis Rams (July 17, 1995).... Released by Rams (November 1, 1995).... Re-signed by Rams (November 15, 1995).... Released by Rams (December 5, 1995).
HONORS: Played in Pro Bowl (1986-1989 seasons).
PRO STATISTICS: 1985—Returned 13 kickoffs for 234 yards. 1986—Lost six yards on lateral from kickoff return. 1988—Recovered one fumble.

| | | RUSHING | | | | RECEIVING | | | | TOTALS | | | |
Year Team	G	Att.	Yds.	Avg.	TD	No.	Yds.	Avg.	TD	TD	2pt.	Pts.	Fum.
1985—St. Louis NFL	16	24	64	2.7	0	2	18	9.0	0	0	...	0	1
1986—St. Louis NFL	16	8	19	2.4	0	2	32	16.0	0	0	...	0	0
1987—St. Louis NFL	12	26	87	3.4	1	8	68	8.5	0	1	...	6	0
1988—Phoenix NFL	16	9	43	4.8	0	2	11	5.5	0	0	...	0	0
1989—Phoenix NFL	16	13	36	2.8	1	5	38	7.6	0	1	...	6	0
1990—Phoenix NFL	13	2	3	1.5	0	0	0	...	0	0	...	0	0
1991—Phoenix NFL	16	0	0	...	0	0	0	...	0	0	...	0	0
1992—Cleveland NFL	15	1	2	2.0	0	2	8	4.0	1	1	...	6	0
1993—Cleveland NFL	16	0	0	...	0	5	25	5.0	1	1	...	6	0
1994—							Did not play.						
1995—St. Louis NFL	9	3	9	3.0	0	0	0	...	0	0	0	0	0
Pro totals (10 years)	145	86	263	3.1	2	26	200	7.7	2	4	0	24	1

WOLFORD, WILL   OT   STEELERS

PERSONAL: Born May 18, 1964, in Louisville, Ky. ... 6-5/300. ... Full name: William Charles Wolford. ... Name pronounced WOOL-ford.
HIGH SCHOOL: St. Xavier (Louisville, Ky.).
COLLEGE: Vanderbilt.
TRANSACTIONS/CAREER NOTES: Selected by Memphis Showboats in 1986 USFL territorial draft. ... Selected by Buffalo Bills in first round (20th pick overall) of 1986 NFL draft. ... Signed by Bills (August 12, 1986). ... Granted roster exemption (August 12-22, 1986). ... Granted free agency (February 1, 1990). ... Re-signed by Bills (August 28, 1990). ... Granted roster exemption (September 9, 1990). ... Designated by Bills as transition player (February 25, 1993). ... Tendered offer sheet by Indianapolis Colts (March 28, 1993). ... Bills declined to match offer (April 23, 1993). ... On injured reserve with shoulder injury (December 10, 1993-remainder of season). ... Designated by Colts as transition player (February 15, 1994). ... Free agency status changed by Colts from transitional to unconditional (February 29, 1996). ... Signed by Pittsburgh Steelers (March 1, 1996).
PLAYING EXPERIENCE: Buffalo NFL, 1986-1992; Indianapolis NFL, 1993-1995 ... Games: 1986 (16), 1987 (9), 1988 (16), 1989 (16), 1990 (14), 1991 (15), 1992 (16), 1993 (12), 1994 (16), 1995 (16). Total: 146.
CHAMPIONSHIP GAME EXPERIENCE: Played in AFC championship game (1988, 1990-1992 and 1995 seasons). ... Played in Super Bowl XXV (1990 season), Super Bowl XXVI (1991 season) and Super Bowl XXVII (1992 season).
HONORS: Played in Pro Bowl (1990 and 1995 seasons). ... Named to play in Pro Bowl (1992 season); replaced by John Alt due to injury.
PRO STATISTICS: 1988—Recovered one fumble. 1994—Recovered one fumble.

WOODALL, LEE   LB   49ERS

PERSONAL: Born October 31, 1969, in Carlisle, Pa. ... 6-0/220.
HIGH SCHOOL: Carlisle (Pa.).
COLLEGE: West Chester (Pa.).
TRANSACTIONS/CAREER NOTES: Selected by San Francisco 49ers in sixth round (182nd pick overall) of 1994 NFL draft. ... Signed by 49ers (July 20, 1994).

W

CHAMPIONSHIP GAME EXPERIENCE: Played in NFC championship game (1994 season). ... Member of Super Bowl championship team (1994 season).
HONORS: Played in Pro Bowl (1995 season).
PRO STATISTICS: 1994—Recovered one fumble. 1995—Intercepted two passes for no yards and recovered two fumbles for 98 yards and one touchdown.

Year Team	G	SACKS
1994—San Francisco NFL	15	1.0
1995—San Francisco NFL	16	3.0
Pro totals (2 years)	31	4.0

WOODARD, MARC   LB   EAGLES

PERSONAL: Born February 21, 1970, in Kosciusko, Miss. ... 6-0/238.
HIGH SCHOOL: Kosciusko (Miss.).
COLLEGE: Mississippi State.
TRANSACTIONS/CAREER NOTES: Selected by Pittsburgh Steelers in fifth round (140th pick overall) of 1993 NFL draft. ... Signed by Steelers (July 26, 1993). ... Released by Steelers (August 30, 1993). ... Signed by Philadelphia Eagles to practice squad (October 12, 1993). ... Granted free agency after 1993 season. ... Re-signed by Eagles (April 6, 1994).
PLAYING EXPERIENCE: Philadelphia NFL, 1994 and 1995. ... Games: 1994 (16), 1995 (16). Total: 32.
PLAY EXPERIENCE: Credited with 1 ½ sack.

WOODEN, TERRY   LB   SEAHAWKS

PERSONAL: Born January 14, 1967, in Hartford, Conn. ... 6-3/239. ... Full name: Terrence Tylon Wooden.
HIGH SCHOOL: Farmington (Conn.).
COLLEGE: Syracuse (degree in sociology).
TRANSACTIONS/CAREER NOTES: Selected by Seattle Seahawks in second round (29th pick overall) of 1990 NFL draft. ... Signed by Seahawks (July 27, 1990). ... On injured reserve with knee injury (November 10, 1990-remainder of season). ... On injured reserve with knee injury (October 28, 1992-remainder of season). ... Granted free agency (March 1, 1993). ... Re-signed by Seahawks (August 25, 1993). ... Activated (September 4, 1993).
PRO STATISTICS: 1991—Recovered four fumbles for five yards. 1993—Recovered one fumble. 1994—Recovered two fumbles. 1995—Recovered one fumble for 20 yards.

		INTERCEPTIONS				SACKS
Year Team	G	No.	Yds.	Avg.	TD	No.
1990—Seattle NFL	8	0	0	...	0	0.0
1991—Seattle NFL	16	0	0	...	0	2.0
1992—Seattle NFL	8	1	3	3.0	0	0.0
1993—Seattle NFL	16	0	0	...	0	2.5
1994—Seattle NFL	16	3	78	26.0	1	1.5
1995—Seattle NFL	16	1	9	9.0	0	0.0
Pro totals (6 years)	80	5	90	18.0	1	6.0

WOODS, TONY   DE

PERSONAL: Born September 11, 1965, in Newark, N.J. ... 6-4/282. ... Full name: Stanley Anthony Woods.
HIGH SCHOOL: Seton Hall Prep (West Orange, N.J.).
COLLEGE: Pittsburgh.
TRANSACTIONS/CAREER NOTES: Selected by Seattle Seahawks in first round (18th pick overall) of 1987 NFL draft. ... Signed by Seahawks (July 20, 1987). ... Granted free agency (February 1, 1992). ... Re-signed by Seahawks (August 8, 1992). ... Granted unconditional free agency (March 1, 1993). ... Re-signed by Seahawks (July 22, 1993). ... Released by Seahawks (August 30, 1993). ... Signed by Los Angeles Rams (September 1, 1993). ... Granted unconditional free agency (February 17, 1994). ... Signed by Washington Redskins (April 4, 1994). ... Granted unconditional free agency (February 16, 1996).
HONORS: Named defensive lineman on THE SPORTING NEWS college All-America first team (1986).
PRO STATISTICS: 1987—Recovered one fumble. 1988—Recovered one fumble. 1989—Returned one kickoff for 13 yards and fumbled once. 1991—Recovered four fumbles for two yards. 1995—Recovered two fumbles for three yards and one touchdown.

Year Team	G	SACKS
1987—Seattle NFL	12	0.0
1988—Seattle NFL	16	5.0
1989—Seattle NFL	16	3.0
1990—Seattle NFL	16	3.0
1991—Seattle NFL	14	2.0
1992—Seattle NFL	15	3.0
1993—Los Angeles Rams NFL	14	1.0
1994—Washington NFL	15	4.5
1995—Washington NFL	16	2.0
Pro totals (9 years)	134	23.5

W

WOODSON, DARREN   S   COWBOYS

PERSONAL: Born April 25, 1969, in Phoenix. ... 6-1/215. ... Full name: Darren Ray Woodson.
HIGH SCHOOL: Maryvale (Phoenix).
COLLEGE: Arizona State.
TRANSACTIONS/CAREER NOTES: Selected by Dallas Cowboys in second round (37th pick overall) of 1992 NFL draft. ... Signed by Cowboys (April 26, 1992).
CHAMPIONSHIP GAME EXPERIENCE: Played in NFC championship game (1992-1995 seasons). ... Member of Super Bowl championship

team (1992, 1993 and 1995 seasons).
HONORS: Named strong safety on THE SPORTING NEWS NFL All-Pro team (1994 and 1995). ... Played in Pro Bowl (1994 and 1995 seasons).
PRO STATISTICS: 1992—Credited with a sack. 1993—Recovered three fumbles for three yards. 1994—Recovered one fumble.

Year Team	G	INTERCEPTIONS			
		No.	Yds.	Avg.	TD
1992—Dallas NFL	16	0	0	...	0
1993—Dallas NFL	16	0	0	...	0
1994—Dallas NFL	16	5	140	28.0	1
1995—Dallas NFL	16	2	46	23.0	1
Pro totals (4 years)	64	7	186	26.6	2

WOODSON, ROD   CB/KR   STEELERS

PERSONAL: Born March 10, 1965, in Fort Wayne, Ind. ... 6-0/200. ... Full name: Roderick Kevin Woodson.
HIGH SCHOOL: R. Nelson Snider (Fort Wayne, Ind.).
COLLEGE: Purdue.
TRANSACTIONS/CAREER NOTES: Selected by Pittsburgh Steelers in first round (10th pick overall) of 1987 NFL draft. ... On reserve/unsigned list (August 31-October 27, 1987). ... Signed by Steelers (October 28, 1987). ... Granted roster exemption (October 28-November 7, 1987). ... Granted free agency (February 1, 1991). ... Re-signed by Steelers (August 22, 1991). ... Activated (August 30, 1991).
CHAMPIONSHIP GAME EXPERIENCE: Played in AFC championship game (1994 season). ... Member of Steelers for AFC championship game (1995 season); inactive. ... Played in Super Bowl XXX (1995 season).
HONORS: Named defensive back on THE SPORTING NEWS college All-America second team (1985). ... Named kick returner on THE SPORTING NEWS college All-America first team (1986). ... Named kick returner on THE SPORTING NEWS NFL All-Pro team (1989). ... Played in Pro Bowl (1989-1994 seasons). ... Named cornerback on THE SPORTING NEWS NFL All-Pro team (1990 and 1992-1994).
PRO STATISTICS: 1987—Recovered two fumbles. 1988—Recovered three fumbles for two yards. 1989—Recovered four fumbles for one yard. 1990—Recovered three fumbles. 1991—Recovered three fumbles for 15 yards. 1992—Recovered one fumble for nine yards. 1993—Rushed once for no yards and recovered one fumble. 1994—Recovered one fumble.

Year Team	G	INTERCEPTIONS				SACKS	PUNT RETURNS				KICKOFF RETURNS				TOTALS			
		No.	Yds.	Avg.	TD	No.	No.	Yds.	Avg.	TD	No.	Yds.	Avg.	TD	TD	2pt.	Pts.	Fum.
1987—Pittsburgh NFL	8	1	45	45.0	1	0.0	16	135	8.4	0	13	290	22.3	0	1	...	6	3
1988—Pittsburgh NFL	16	4	98	24.5	0	0.5	33	281	8.5	0	37	850	23.0	*1	1	...	6	3
1989—Pittsburgh NFL	15	3	39	13.0	0	0.0	29	207	7.1	0	36	982	*27.3	†1	1	...	6	3
1990—Pittsburgh NFL	16	5	67	13.4	0	0.0	38	398	10.5	†1	35	764	21.8	0	1	...	6	3
1991—Pittsburgh NFL	15	3	72	24.0	0	1.0	28	320	11.4	0	*44	880	20.0	0	0	...	0	3
1992—Pittsburgh NFL	16	4	90	22.5	0	6.0	32	364	11.4	1	25	469	18.8	0	1	...	6	2
1993—Pittsburgh NFL	16	8	138	17.3	1	2.0	42	338	8.1	0	15	294	19.6	0	1	...	6	2
1994—Pittsburgh NFL	15	4	109	27.3	2	3.0	39	319	8.2	0	15	365	24.3	0	2	0	12	2
1995—Pittsburgh NFL	1	0	0	...	0	0.0	0	0	...	0	0	0	...	0	0	0	0	0
Pro totals (9 years)	118	32	658	20.6	4	12.5	257	2362	9.2	2	220	4894	22.3	2	8	0	48	21

WOOLFORD, DONNELL   CB   BEARS

PERSONAL: Born January 6, 1966, in Baltimore. ... 5-9/188.
HIGH SCHOOL: Douglas Byrd (Fayetteville, N.C.).
COLLEGE: Clemson.
TRANSACTIONS/CAREER NOTES: Selected by Chicago Bears in first round (11th pick overall) of 1989 NFL draft. ... Signed by Bears (August 16, 1989). ... Designated by Bears as transition player (February 25, 1993).
HONORS: Named kick returner on THE SPORTING NEWS college All-America second team (1987). ... Named defensive back on THE SPORTING NEWS college All-America first team (1988).
PRO STATISTICS: 1991—Recovered one fumble for 28 yards. 1992—Recovered one fumble. 1994—Returned one kickoff for 28 yards.

Year Team	G	INTERCEPTIONS				SACKS	PUNT RETURNS				TOTALS			
		No.	Yds.	Avg.	TD	No.	No.	Yds.	Avg.	TD	TD	2pt.	Pts.	Fum.
1989—Chicago NFL	11	3	0	0.0	0	0.0	1	12	12.0	0	0	...	0	0
1990—Chicago NFL	13	3	18	6.0	0	2.0	0	0	...	0	0	...	0	0
1991—Chicago NFL	15	2	21	10.5	0	1.0	0	0	...	0	0	...	0	0
1992—Chicago NFL	16	7	67	9.6	0	0.0	12	127	10.6	0	0	...	0	2
1993—Chicago NFL	16	2	18	9.0	0	0.0	0	0	...	0	0	...	0	0
1994—Chicago NFL	16	5	30	6.0	0	0.0	0	0	...	0	0	0	0	1
1995—Chicago NFL	9	4	21	5.3	0		0	0	...	0	0	...	0	0
Pro totals (7 years)	96	26	175	6.7	0	3.0	13	139	10.7	0	0	0	0	3

WOOTEN, TITO   S   GIANTS

PERSONAL: Born December 12, 1971, in Goldsboro, N.C. ... 6-0/195.
HIGH SCHOOL: Goldsboro (N.C.).
COLLEGE: North Carolina, then Northeast Louisiana.
TRANSACTIONS/CAREER NOTES: Selected by New York Giants in fourth round of 1994 NFL supplemental draft. ... Signed by Giants (July 22, 1994).
PLAYING EXPERIENCE: New York Giants NFL, 1994 and 1995. ... Games: 1994 (16), 1995 (16). Total: 32.
PRO STATISTICS: 1995—Intercepted one pass for 38 yards and recovered one fumble in end zone for a touchdown.

WORKMAN, VINCE   RB   COLTS

PERSONAL: Born May 9, 1968, in Buffalo. ... 5-10/205.

HIGH SCHOOL: Dublin (Ohio).

COLLEGE: Ohio State.

TRANSACTIONS/CAREER NOTES: Selected by Green Bay Packers in fifth round (127th pick overall) of 1989 NFL draft. ... Signed by Packers (July 23, 1989). ... Granted free agency (February 1, 1991). ... Re-signed by Packers (July 12, 1991). ... On injured reserve with shoulder injury (November 20, 1992-remainder of season). ... Granted free agency (March 1, 1993). ... Tendered offer sheet by Tampa Bay Buccaneers (April 23, 1993). ... Packers declined to match offer and received fifth-round pick (LB James Willis) in 1993 draft as compensation (April 24, 1993). ... Released by Buccaneers (August 27, 1995). ... Signed by Carolina Panthers (August 30, 1995). ... Released by Panthers (November 7, 1995). ... Signed by Indianapolis Colts (November 14, 1995). ... On injured reserve with neck injury (December 5, 1995-remainder of season).

PRO STATISTICS: 1989—Recovered one fumble. 1991—Recovered four fumbles for nine yards and returned one punt for no yards. 1992—Recovered two fumbles. 1993—Recovered one fumble. 1994—Recovered one fumble. 1995—Attempted one pass without a completion and recovered one fumble.

STATISTICAL PLATEAUS: 100-yard rushing games: 1992 (1).

		RUSHING				RECEIVING				KICKOFF RETURNS				TOTALS			
YearTeam	G	Att.	Yds.	Avg.	TD	No.	Yds.	Avg.	TD	No.	Yds.	Avg.	TD	TD	2pt.	Pts.	Fum.
1989—Green Bay NFL	15	4	8	2.0	1	0	0	...	0	33	547	16.6	0	1	...	6	1
1990—Green Bay NFL	15	8	51	6.4	0	4	30	7.5	1	14	210	15.0	0	1	...	6	0
1991—Green Bay NFL	16	71	237	3.3	7	46	371	8.1	4	8	139	17.4	0	11	...	66	3
1992—Green Bay NFL	10	159	631	4.0	2	47	290	6.2	0	1	17	17.0	0	2	...	12	4
1993—Tampa Bay NFL	16	78	284	3.6	2	54	411	7.6	2	5	67	13.4	0	4	...	24	2
1994—Tampa Bay NFL	15	79	291	3.7	0	11	82	7.5	0	0	0	...	0	0	0	0	2
1995—Carolina NFL	9	35	139	4.0	1	13	74	5.7	0	0	0	...	0	1	0	6	0
—Indianapolis NFL	1	9	26	2.9	0	0	0	...	0	0	0	...	0	0	0	0	0
Pro totals (7 years)	97	443	1667	3.8	13	175	1258	7.2	7	61	980	16.1	0	20	0	120	12

WORTHAM, BARRON   LB   OILERS

PERSONAL: Born November 1, 1969, in Everman, Texas. ... 5-11/244. ... Full name: Barron Winfield Wortham.

HIGH SCHOOL: Everman (Texas).

COLLEGE: Texas-El Paso.

TRANSACTIONS/CAREER NOTES: Selected by Houston Oilers in sixth round (194th pick overall) of 1994 NFL draft. ... Signed by Oilers (July 12, 1994).

PLAYING EXPERIENCE: Houston NFL, 1994 and 1995 . ... Games: 1994 (16), 1995 (16). Total: 32.

HONORS: Named linebacker on THE SPORTING NEWS college All-America second team (1993).

PRO STATISTICS: 1994—Recovered one fumble. 1995—Credited with one sack and returned one kickoff for minus three yards.

WRIGHT, ALEXANDER   WR   RAMS

PERSONAL: Born July 19, 1967, in Albany, Ga. ... 6-0/195.

HIGH SCHOOL: Albany (Ga.).

COLLEGE: Auburn (degree in adult education).

TRANSACTIONS/CAREER NOTES: Selected by Dallas Cowboys in second round (26th pick overall) of 1990 NFL draft. ... Signed by Cowboys (August 25, 1990). ... Traded by Cowboys to Los Angeles Raiders for fourth-round pick (OT Ron Stone) in 1993 draft (October 12, 1992). ... Granted free agency (March 1, 1993). ... Re-signed by Raiders (1993). ... Granted unconditional free agency (February 17, 1995). ... Signed by Los Angeles Rams (March 22, 1995). ... Rams franchise moved to St. Louis (April 12, 1995).

PRO STATISTICS: 1990—Recovered one fumble.

STATISTICAL PLATEAUS: 100-yard receiving games: 1993 (1), 1995 (1). Total: 2.

		RUSHING				RECEIVING				KICKOFF RETURNS				TOTALS			
YearTeam	G	Att.	Yds.	Avg.	TD	No.	Yds.	Avg.	TD	No.	Yds.	Avg.	TD	TD	2pt.	Pts.	Fum.
1990—Dallas NFL	15	3	26	8.7	0	11	104	9.5	0	12	276	23.0	1	1	...	6	1
1991—Dallas NFL	16	2	-1	-0.5	0	10	170	17.0	0	21	514	24.5	†1	1	...	6	0
1992—Dallas NFL	3	0	0	...	0	0	0	...	0	8	117	14.6	0	2	...	12	1
—Los Angeles Raiders NFL	10	0	0	...	0	12	175	14.6	0	18	325	18.1	0	2	...	12	1
1993—Los Angeles Raiders NFL	15	0	0	...	0	27	462	17.1	4	10	167	16.7	0	4	...	24	0
1994—Los Angeles Raiders NFL	16	0	0	...	0	16	294	18.4	2	10	282	28.2	0	2	0	12	0
1995—St. Louis NFL	8	1	17	17.0	0	23	368	16.0	2	0	0	...	0	2	0	12	0
Pro totals (6 years)	83	6	42	7.0	0	99	1573	15.9	10	79	1681	21.3	2	14	0	84	3

WRIGHT, SYLVESTER   LB   EAGLES

PERSONAL: Born December 30, 1971, in Detroit. ... 6-2/258.

HIGH SCHOOL: MacKenzie (Detroit).

COLLEGE: Kansas.

TRANSACTIONS/CAREER NOTES: Signed as non-drafted free agent by Philadelphia Eagles (April 26, 1995). ... Released by Eagles (August 27, 1995). ... Re-signed by Eagles to practice squad (September 6, 1995). ... Activated (October 13, 1995). ... Released by Eagles (December 1, 1995). ... Re-signed by Eagles to practice squad (December 4, 1995). ... Activated (December 22, 1995).

PLAYING EXPERIENCE: Philadelphia NFL, 1995 . ... Games: 1995 (6).

W

WRIGHT, TOBY   S   RAMS

PERSONAL: Born November 19, 1970, in Phoenix ... 5-11/203. ... Full name: Toby Lin Wright. ... Brother of Terry Wright, defensive back, Toronto Argonauts, Shreveport Pirates, Memphis Mad Dogs and Hamilton Tiger-Cats of CFL (1992-1995).

HIGH SCHOOL: Dobson (Mesa, Ariz.).

COLLEGE: Nebraska.

TRANSACTIONS/CAREER NOTES: Selected by Los Angeles Rams in second round (49th pick overall) of 1994 NFL draft. ... Signed by Rams (May 18, 1994). ... Rams franchise moved to St. Louis (April 12, 1995).

WYCHECK, FRANK — TE — OILERS

PERSONAL: Born October 14, 1971, in Philadelphia. ... 6-3/247.
HIGH SCHOOL: Archbishop Ryan (Philadelphia).
COLLEGE: Maryland.
TRANSACTIONS/CAREER NOTES: Selected after junior season by Washington Redskins in sixth round (160th pick overall) of 1993 NFL draft. ... Signed by Redskins (July 15, 1993). ... On suspended list for anabolic steroid use (November 29, 1994-remainder of season). ... Released by Redskins (August 17, 1995). ... Signed by Houston Oilers (August 18, 1995). ... Granted free agency (February 16, 1996).
PRO STATISTICS: 1993—Recovered one fumble. 1995—Rushed once for one yard and a touchdown and recovered one fumble for minus six yards.

Year Team		RECEIVING				KICKOFF RETURNS				TOTALS			
	G	No.	Yds.	Avg.	TD	No.	Yds.	Avg.	TD	TD	2pt.	Pts.	Fum.
1993—Washington NFL	9	16	113	7.1	0	0	0	...	0	0	...	0	1
1994—Washington NFL	9	7	55	7.9	1	4	84	21.0	0	1	0	6	0
1995—Houston NFL	16	40	471	11.8	1	0	0	...	0	2	0	12	0
Pro totals (3 years)	34	63	639	10.2	2	4	84	21.0	0	3	0	18	1

WYMAN, DAVID — LB

PERSONAL: Born March 31, 1964, in San Diego. ... 6-2/248. ... Full name: David Matthew Wyman.
HIGH SCHOOL: Earl Wooster (Reno, Nev.).
COLLEGE: Stanford.
TRANSACTIONS/CAREER NOTES: Selected by Seattle Seahawks in second round (45th pick overall) of 1987 NFL draft. ... Signed by Seahawks (July 21, 1987). ... Traded by Seahawks with draft pick to San Francisco 49ers for draft pick (November 3, 1987); trade voided after failing physical (November 4, 1987). ... On injured reserve with ankle injury (December 30, 1987-remainder of season). ... Granted free agency (February 1, 1990). ... Re-signed by Seahawks (July 18, 1990). ... On injured reserve with knee injury (September 4-November 10, 1990). ... On injured reserve with knee injury (September 25-December 14, 1991). ... Granted free agency (February 1, 1992). ... Re-signed by Seahawks (July 22, 1992). ... On injured reserve with foot injury (November 25, 1992-remainder of season). ... Granted unconditional free agency (March 1, 1993). ... Signed by Denver Broncos (June 17, 1993). ... Released by Broncos (May 1, 1995). ... Re-signed by Broncos (May 3, 1995). ... Granted unconditional free agency (February 16, 1996).
HONORS: Named linebacker on THE SPORTING NEWS college All-America first team (1986).
PRO STATISTICS: 1988—Recovered two fumbles. 1990—Recovered one fumble. 1992—Recovered one fumble for six yards. 1993—Caught one pass for one yard and a touchdown and recovered two fumbles for two yards.

Year Team		INTERCEPTIONS				SACKS
	G	No.	Yds.	Avg.	TD	No.
1987—Seattle NFL	4	0	0	...	0	0.0
1988—Seattle NFL	16	0	0	...	0	2.5
1989—Seattle NFL	16	0	0	...	0	0.0
1990—Seattle NFL	8	2	24	12.0	0	1.0
1991—Seattle NFL	6	0	0	...	0	0.0
1992—Seattle NFL	11	0	0	...	0	0.0
1993—Denver NFL	16	1	9	9.0	0	2.0
1994—Denver NFL	4	0	0	...	0	0.0
1995—Denver NFL	11	0	0	...	0	0.0
Pro totals (9 years)	92	3	33	11.0	0	5.5

YANCY, CARLOS — CB — PATRIOTS

PERSONAL: Born June 24, 1970, in Sarasota, Fla. ... 6-0/185. ... Full name: Carlos Delanio Yancy.
HIGH SCHOOL: Laurinburg (N.C.) Institute, then Sarasota (Fla.).
COLLEGE: Georgia.
TRANSACTIONS/CAREER NOTES: Selected by New England Patriots in seventh round (234th pick overall) of 1995 NFL draft. ... Signed by Patriots (June 26, 1995). ... Released by Patriots (August 27, 1995). ... Re-signed by Patriots to practice squad (August 28, 1995). ... Activated (November 20, 1995).
PLAYING EXPERIENCE: New England NFL, 1995. ... Games: 1995 (4).

YARBOROUGH, RYAN — WR — JETS

W
Y

PERSONAL: Born April 26, 1971, in Baltimore. ... 6-2/195.
HIGH SCHOOL: Rich East (Park Forest, Ill.).
COLLEGE: Wyoming.
TRANSACTIONS/CAREER NOTES: Selected by New York Jets in second round (41st pick overall) of 1994 NFL draft. ... Signed by Jets (June 21, 1994).
HONORS: Named wide receiver on THE SPORTING NEWS college All-America second team (1993).
STATISTICAL PLATEAUS: 100-yard receiving games: 1995 (1).

Year Team	G	No.	Yds.	Avg.	TD	TD	2pt.	Pts.	Fum.
		RECEIVING				**TOTALS**			
1994—New York Jets NFL	13	6	42	7.0	1	1	0	6	0
1995—New York Jets NFL	16	18	230	12.8	2	2	0	12	0
Pro totals (2 years)	29	24	272	11.3	3	3	0	18	0

YOUNG, BRYANT — DT — 49ERS

PERSONAL: Born January 27, 1972, in Chicago Heights, Ill. ... 6-2/276. ... Full name: Bryant Colby Young.
HIGH SCHOOL: Bloom (Chicago Heights, Ill.).
COLLEGE: Notre Dame.
TRANSACTIONS/CAREER NOTES: Selected by San Francisco 49ers in first round (seventh pick overall) of 1994 NFL draft. ... Signed by 49ers (July 26, 1994).
CHAMPIONSHIP GAME EXPERIENCE: Played in NFC championship game (1994 season). ... Member of Super Bowl championship team (1994 season).
PRO STATISTICS: 1994—Recovered one fumble. 1995—Recovered two fumbles.

Year Team	G	SACKS
1994—San Francisco NFL	16	6.0
1995—San Francisco NFL	12	6.0
Pro totals (2 years)	28	12.0

YOUNG, DUANE — TE

PERSONAL: Born May 29, 1968, in Kalamazoo, Mich. ... 6-1/270. ... Full name: Curtis Duane Young.
HIGH SCHOOL: Kalamazoo (Mich.) Central.
COLLEGE: Michigan State (degree in elementary education).
TRANSACTIONS/CAREER NOTES: Selected by San Diego Chargers in fifth round (123rd pick overall) of 1991 NFL draft. ... Signed by Chargers (July 15, 1991). ... On injured reserve with ankle injury (August 27-November 9, 1991). ... Granted free agency (February 17, 1994). ... Re-signed by Chargers (April 7, 1994). ... Released by Chargers (February 29, 1996).
CHAMPIONSHIP GAME EXPERIENCE: Played in AFC championship game (1994 season). ... Played in Super Bowl XXIX (1994 season).

Year Team	G	No.	Yds.	Avg.	TD	TD	2pt.	Pts.	Fum.
		RECEIVING				**TOTALS**			
1991—San Diego NFL	7	2	12	6.0	0	0	...	0	0
1992—San Diego NFL	16	4	45	11.3	0	0	...	0	0
1993—San Diego NFL	16	6	41	6.8	2	2	...	12	0
1994—San Diego NFL	14	17	217	12.8	1	1	0	6	0
1995—San Diego NFL	16	9	90	10.0	0	0	0	0	0
Pro totals (5 years)	69	38	405	10.7	3	3	0	18	0

YOUNG, GLEN — LB — CHARGERS

PERSONAL: Born May 2, 1969, in Scarborough, Ontario. ... 6-3/235.
HIGH SCHOOL: Neil McNeil (Toronto), then St. Mike's (Toronto).
COLLEGE: Syracuse.
TRANSACTIONS/CAREER NOTES: Signed as non-drafted free agent by Los Angeles Raiders (May 1993). ... Released by Raiders (August 22, 1993). ... Re-signed by Raiders to practice squad (August 30, 1993). ... Granted free agency after 1993 season. ... Signed by Buffalo Bills (April 14, 1994). ... Released by Bills (August 28, 1994). ... Signed by San Diego Chargers to practice squad (October 4, 1994). ... Granted free agency after 1994 season. ... Re-signed by Chargers (February 18, 1995).
PLAYING EXPERIENCE: San Diego NFL, 1995. ... Games: 1995 (16).
PRO STATISTICS: 1995—Credited with one sack.

YOUNG, LONNIE — S — JETS

PERSONAL: Born July 18, 1963, in Flint, Mich. ... 6-1/196.
HIGH SCHOOL: Beecher (Flint, Mich.).
COLLEGE: Michigan State (degree in communications, 1985).
TRANSACTIONS/CAREER NOTES: Selected by New Jersey Generals in eighth round (112th pick overall) of 1985 USFL draft. ... Selected by St. Louis Cardinals in 12th round (325th pick overall) of 1985 NFL draft. ... Signed by Cardinals (July 15, 1985). ... Cardinals franchise moved to Phoenix (March 15, 1988). ... On injured reserve with torn ligaments in elbow (November 22, 1988-remainder of season). ... On injured reserve with fractured shoulder (September 15-October 28, 1989). ... Traded by Cardinals to New York Jets for ninth-round pick (WR Tyrone Williams) in 1992 draft (June 12, 1991). ... On injured reserve with shoulder injury (November 8-December 7, 1991). ... Granted free agency (February 1, 1992). ... Re-signed by Jets (July 13, 1992). ... On injured reserve with knee injury (December 7, 1992-remainder of season). ... Released by Jets (July 13, 1993). ... Re-signed by Jets (October 14, 1993). ... Granted unconditional free agency (February 17, 1994). ... Signed by San Diego Chargers (September 7, 1994). ... Released by Chargers (February 16, 1995). ... Signed by Jets (October 10, 1995).
CHAMPIONSHIP GAME EXPERIENCE: Member of Chargers for AFC championship game and Super Bowl XXIX (1994 season); inactive.
PRO STATISTICS: 1985—Recovered one fumble. 1987—Recovered three fumbles. 1988—Recovered two fumbles. 1990—Recovered two fumbles. 1991—Recovered one fumble. 1992—Recovered two fumbles for nine yards. 1993—Recovered one fumble. 1995—Recovered two fumbles for four yards.

Year Team	G	No.	Yds.	Avg.	TD	No.
		INTERCEPTIONS				**SACKS**
1985—St. Louis NFL	16	3	0	0.0	0	0.0
1986—St. Louis NFL	13	0	0	...	0	1.5
1987—St. Louis NFL	12	1	0	0.0	0	0.0
1988—Phoenix NFL	12	1	2	2.0	0	0.0

Y

Year—Team	G	INTERCEPTIONS				SACKS
		No.	Yds.	Avg.	TD	No.
1989—Phoenix NFL	10	1	32	32.0	0	0.0
1990—Phoenix NFL	16	2	8	4.0	0	0.0
1991—New York Jets NFL	12	1	15	15.0	0	0.0
1992—New York Jets NFL	13	0	0	...	0	0.0
1993—New York Jets NFL	9	1	6	6.0	0	1.0
1994—San Diego NFL	12	0	0	...	0	1.0
1995—New York Jets NFL	7	0	0	...	0	0.0
Pro totals (11 years)	132	10	63	6.3	0	3.5

YOUNG, ROBERT   DE   RAMS

PERSONAL: Born January 29, 1969, in Jackson, Miss. ... 6-6/273.
HIGH SCHOOL: Carthage (Miss.).
COLLEGE: Mississippi State.
TRANSACTIONS/CAREER NOTES: Selected by Los Angeles Rams in fifth round (116th pick overall) of 1991 NFL draft. ... Signed by Rams (July 9, 1991). ... On injured reserve with shoulder injury (September 4-October 2, 1992); on practice squad (September 30-October 2, 1992). ... On injured reserve with knee injury (November 23, 1993-remainder of season). ... Granted free agency (February 17, 1994). ... Re-signed by Rams (May 13, 1994). ... Rams franchise moved to St. Louis (April 12, 1995). ... On reserve/non-football injury list with chest injury (July 21-August 22, 1995).

Year—Team	G	SACKS
1991—Los Angeles Rams NFL	16	1.0
1992—Los Angeles Rams NFL	11	2.0
1993—Los Angeles Rams NFL	6	7.0
1994—Los Angeles Rams NFL	16	6.5
1995—St. Louis NFL	14	0.0
Pro totals (5 years)	63	16.5

YOUNG, RODNEY   S   GIANTS

PERSONAL: Born January 25, 1973, in Grambling, La. ... 6-1/212. ... Full name: Rodney Menard Young.
HIGH SCHOOL: Ruston (La.).
COLLEGE: Louisiana State.
TRANSACTIONS/CAREER NOTES: Selected by New York Giants in third round (85th pick overall) of 1995 NFL draft. ... Signed by Giants (July 25, 1995).
PLAYING EXPERIENCE: New York Giants NFL, 1995. ... Games: 1995 (10).
PRO STATISTICS: 1995—Returned one punt for no yards and fumbled once.

YOUNG, STEVE   QB   49ERS

PERSONAL: Born October 11, 1961, in Salt Lake City. ... 6-2/205. ... Full name: Jon Steven Young.
HIGH SCHOOL: Greenwich (Conn.).
COLLEGE: Brigham Young (law degree, 1994).
TRANSACTIONS/CAREER NOTES: Selected by Los Angeles Express in first round (10th pick overall) of 1984 USFL draft. ... Signed by Express (March 5, 1984). ... Granted roster exemption (March 5-30, 1984). ... Selected by Tampa Bay Buccaneers in first round (first pick overall) of 1984 NFL supplemental draft. ... On developmental squad (March 31-April 16, 1985). ... Released by Express (September 9, 1985). ... Signed by Buccaneers (September 10, 1985). ... Granted roster exemption (September 10-23, 1985). ... Traded by Buccaneers to San Francisco 49ers for second-round (LB Winston Moss) and fourth-round (WR Bruce Hill) picks in 1987 draft and cash (April 24, 1987). ... Granted free agency (February 1, 1991). ... Re-signed by 49ers (May 3, 1991). ... Designated by 49ers as franchise player (February 25, 1993).
CHAMPIONSHIP GAME EXPERIENCE: Played in NFC championship game (1988-1990 and 1992-1994 seasons). ... Member of 49ers for Super Bowl XXIII (1988 season); did not play. ... Member of Super Bowl championship team (1989 and 1994 seasons).
HONORS: Davey O'Brien Award winner (1983). ... Named quarterback on THE SPORTING NEWS college All-America first team (1983). ... Named NFL Player of the Year by THE SPORTING NEWS (1992 and 1994). ... Named quarterback on THE SPORTING NEWS NFL All-Pro team (1992 and 1994). ... Played in Pro Bowl (1992-1995 seasons). ... Named Most Valuable Player of Super Bowl XXIX (1994 season).
RECORDS: Holds NFL career records for highest completion percentage—64.2; highest passer rating—96.1; and most consecutive seasons leading league in passer rating—4 (1991-1994). ... Holds NFL single-season record for highest passer rating—112.8 (1994).
POSTSEASON RECORDS: Holds Super Bowl single-game record for most touchdown passes—6 (January 29, 1995, vs. San Diego). ... Shares Super Bowl single-game record for most passes attempted without an interception—36 (January 29, 1995, vs. San Diego). ... Shares NFL postseason single-game record for most touchdown passes—6 (January 29, 1995, vs. San Diego).
PRO STATISTICS: USFL: 1984—Fumbled seven times and recovered four fumbles. 1985—Fumbled seven times and recovered one fumble for minus 11 yards. NFL: 1985—Fumbled four times and recovered one fumble for minus one yard. 1986—Fumbled 11 times and recovered four fumbles for minus 24 yards. 1988—Fumbled five times and recovered two fumbles for minus 10 yards. 1989—Fumbled twice and recovered one fumble. 1990—Fumbled once. 1991—Fumbled three times and recovered one fumble for minus six yards. 1992—Fumbled nine times and recovered three fumbles for minus 13 yards. 1993—Caught two passes for two yards, fumbled eight times and recovered two fumbles for minus four yards. 1994—Fumbled four times and recovered one fumble for minus four yards. 1995—Fumbled three times.
STATISTICAL PLATEAUS: USFL: 300-yard passing games: 1984 (2). ... 100-yard rushing games: 1984 (1), 1985 (1). Total: 2. ... NFL: 300-yard passing games: 1991 (3), 1992 (3), 1993 (3), 1994 (5), 1995 (5). Total: 19. ... 100-yard rushing games: 1990 (1).
MISCELLANEOUS: Regular-season record as starting NFL quarterback: 60-38 (.612).

Year—Team	G	PASSING								RUSHING				TOTALS		
		Att.	Cmp.	Pct.	Yds.	TD	Int.	Avg.	Rat.	Att.	Yds.	Avg.	TD	TD	2pt.	Pts.
1984—Los Angeles USFL	12	310	179	57.7	2361	10	9	7.62	80.6	79	515	6.5	7	7	3	48
1985—Los Angeles USFL	13	250	137	54.8	1741	6	13	6.97	63.1	56	368	6.6	2	2	0	12
—Tampa Bay NFL	5	138	72	52.2	935	3	8	6.78	56.9	40	233	5.8	1	1	...	6
1986—Tampa Bay NFL	14	363	195	53.7	2282	8	13	6.29	65.5	74	425	5.7	5	5	...	30
1987—San Francisco NFL	8	69	37	53.6	570	10	0	8.26	120.8	26	190	7.3	1	1	...	6

Year Team	G	Att.	Cmp.	Pct.	Yds.	TD	Int.	Avg.	Rat.	Att.	Yds.	Avg.	TD	TD	2pt.	Pts.
1988—San Francisco NFL	11	101	54	53.5	680	3	3	6.73	72.2	27	184	6.8	1	1	...	6
1989—San Francisco NFL	10	92	64	69.6	1001	8	3	10.88	120.8	38	126	3.3	2	2	...	12
1990—San Francisco NFL	6	62	38	61.3	427	2	0	6.89	92.6	15	159	10.6	0	0	...	0
1991—San Francisco NFL	11	279	180	64.5	2517	17	8	*9.02	*101.8	66	415	6.3	4	4	...	24
1992—San Francisco NFL	16	402	*268	*66.7	3465	*25	7	*8.62	*107.0	76	537	7.1	4	4	...	24
1993—San Francisco NFL	16	462	314	68.0	4023	*29	16	*8.71	*101.5	69	407	5.9	2	2	...	12
1994—San Francisco NFL	16	461	324	*70.3	3969	*35	10	*8.61	*112.8	58	293	5.1	7	7	0	42
1995—San Francisco NFL	11	447	299	*66.9	3200	20	11	7.16	92.3	50	250	5.0	3	0	0	0
USFL totals (2 years)	25	560	316	56.4	4102	16	22	7.33	72.8	135	883	6.6	9	9	3	60
NFL totals (11 years)	124	2876	1845	64.2	23069	160	79	8.02	96.1	539	3219	6.0	30	27	0	162
Pro totals (12 years)	149	3436	2161	62.9	27171	176	101	7.91	92.3	674	4102	6.1	39	36	3	222

ZANDOFSKY, MIKE — C/G — FALCONS

PERSONAL: Born November 30, 1965, in Corvallis, Ore. ... 6-2/305. ... Full name: Michael Leslie Zandofsky. ... Name pronounced zan-DOFF-skee.
HIGH SCHOOL: Corvallis (Ore.).
COLLEGE: Washington.
TRANSACTIONS/CAREER NOTES: Selected by Phoenix Cardinals in third round (67th pick overall) of 1989 NFL draft. ... Signed by Cardinals (July 22, 1989). ... Traded by Cardinals to San Diego Chargers for eighth-round pick (TE Jerry Evans) in 1991 draft (August 29, 1990). ... On injured reserve with knee injury (August 27-October 12, 1991). ... Granted free agency (February 1, 1992). ... Re-signed by Chargers (July 23, 1992). ... Granted free agency (March 1, 1993). ... Re-signed by Chargers (July 25, 1993). ... Granted unconditional free agency (February 17, 1994). ... Signed by Atlanta Falcons (March 6, 1994).
PLAYING EXPERIENCE: Phoenix NFL, 1989; San Diego NFL, 1990-1993; Atlanta NFL, 1994 and 1995. ... Games: 1989 (15), 1990 (13), 1991 (10), 1992 (15), 1993 (16), 1994 (16), 1995 (12). Total: 97.
HONORS: Named offensive tackle on THE SPORTING NEWS college All-America second team (1987).
PRO STATISTICS: 1995—Recovered one fumble.

ZATECHKA, ROB — OL — GIANTS

PERSONAL: Born December 1, 1971, in Lansing, Mich. ... 6-4/315. ... Name pronounced ZAT-es-ka.
HIGH SCHOOL: Lincoln (Neb.) East.
COLLEGE: Nebraska (degree in biological sciences).
TRANSACTIONS/CAREER NOTES: Selected by New York Giants in fourth round (128th pick overall) of 1995 NFL draft. ... Signed by Giants (July 6, 1995).
PLAYING EXPERIENCE: New York Giants NFL, 1995. ... Games: 1995 (16).
PRO STATISTICS: 1995—Returned one kickoff for five yards.

ZEIER, ERIC — QB — RAVENS

PERSONAL: Born September 6, 1972, in Marietta, Ga. ... 6-0/205. ... Full name: Eric Royce Zeier. ... Name pronounced ZY-er.
HIGH SCHOOL: Heidelberg (Germany), then Marietta (Ga.).
COLLEGE: Georgia.
TRANSACTIONS/CAREER NOTES: Selected by Cleveland Browns in third round (84th pick overall) of 1995 NFL draft. ... Signed by Browns (July 14, 1995). ... Browns franchise moved to Baltimore and renamed Ravens for 1996 season (March 11, 1996).
HONORS: Named quarterback on THE SPORTING NEWS college All-America second team (1994).
PRO STATISTICS: 1995—Fumbled three times for minus five yards.
STATISTICAL PLATEAUS: 300-yard passing games: 1995 (1).
MISCELLANEOUS: Regular-season record as starting NFL quarterback: 1-3 (.250).

Year Team	G	Att.	Cmp.	Pct.	Yds.	TD	Int.	Avg.	Rat.	Att.	Yds.	Avg.	TD	TD	2pt.	Pts.
1995—Cleveland NFL	7	161	82	50.9	864	4	9	5.37	51.9	15	80	5.3	0	0	1	2

ZELLARS, RAY — FB — SAINTS

PERSONAL: Born March 25, 1973, in Pittsburgh. ... 5-11/233. ... Full name: Raymond Mark Zellars.
HIGH SCHOOL: David B. Oliver (Pittsburgh).
COLLEGE: Notre Dame.
TRANSACTIONS/CAREER NOTES: Selected by New Orleans Saints in second round (44th pick overall) of 1995 NFL draft. ... Signed by Saints (July 19, 1995).

Year Team	G	Att.	Yds.	Avg.	TD	No.	Yds.	Avg.	TD	TD	2pt.	Pts.	Fum.
1995—New Orleans NFL	12	50	162	3.2	2	7	33	4.7	0	2	0	12	1

ZENDEJAS, TONY — K

PERSONAL: Born May 15, 1960, in Curimeo Michucan, Mexico. ... 5-8/165. ... Full name: Anthony Guerrero Zendejas. ... Cousin of Joaquin Zendejas, kicker, New England Patriots (1983); cousin of Max Zendejas, kicker, Washington Redskins and Green Bay Packers (1986-1988); and cousin of Luis Zendejas, kicker, Arizona Outlaws of USFL, Dallas Cowboys and Philadelphia Eagles (1985 and 1987-1989). ... Name pronounced zen-DAY-haas.
HIGH SCHOOL: Chino (Calif.).

COLLEGE: Nevada.
TRANSACTIONS/CAREER NOTES: Selected by Los Angeles Express in fifth round (90th pick overall) of 1984 USFL draft. ... Signed by Express (February 21, 1984). ... Selected by Washington Redskins in first round (27th pick overall) of 1984 NFL supplemental draft. ... Granted free agency (July 1, 1985). ... Signed by Redskins (July 3, 1985). ... Traded by Redskins to Houston Oilers for fifth-round pick in 1987 draft (August 27, 1985). ... Crossed picket line during players strike (October 14, 1987). ... On injured reserve with leg injury (October 24, 1990-remainder of season). ... Granted unconditional free agency (February 1, 1991). ... Signed by Los Angeles Rams (March 12, 1991). ... Granted unconditional free agency (March 1, 1993). ... Re-signed by Rams for 1993 season. ... Released by Rams (July 7, 1995). ... Signed by Atlanta Falcons (October 10, 1995). ... Claimed on waivers by San Francisco 49ers (October 18, 1995). ... Released by 49ers (November 8, 1995).
HONORS: Named kicker on The Sporting News USFL All-Star team (1984 and 1985).
RECORDS: Holds NFL single-season record for highest field-goal percentage—100.00 (1991).
PRO STATISTICS: NFL: 1985—Attempted one pass with one completion for minus seven yards and recovered one fumble. 1986—Punted once for 36 yards. 1989—Had only pass attempt intercepted and recovered one fumble.

| | | | | | KICKING | | | | |
Year Team	G	XPM	XPA	FGM	FGA	Lg.	50+	Pts.
1984—Los Angeles USFL	18	33	33	21	30	46	0-4	96
1985—Los Angeles USFL	18	22	23	*26	*34	52	2-7	100
—Houston NFL	14	29	31	21	27	52	3-3	92
1986—Houston NFL	15	28	29	22	27	51	1-3	94
1987—Houston NFL	13	32	33	20	26	52	1-1	92
1988—Houston NFL	16	48	50	22	34	52	2-4	114
1989—Houston NFL	16	40	40	25	37	52	2-2	115
1990—Houston NFL	7	20	21	7	12	45	0-0	41
1991—Los Angeles Rams NFL	16	25	26	17	17	50	2-2	76
1992—Los Angeles Rams NFL	16	38	38	15	20	49	0-0	83
1993—Los Angeles Rams NFL	16	23	25	16	23	54	6-8	71
1994—Los Angeles Rams NFL	16	28	28	18	23	47	0-0	82
1995—Atlanta NFL	1	0	0	2	3	45	0-0	6
—San Francisco NFL	3	5	6	1	3	38	0-0	8
USFL totals (2 years)	36	55	56	47	64	52	2-11	196
NFL totals (11 years)	149	316	327	186	252	54	17-23	874
Pro totals (12 years)	185	371	383	233	316	54	19-34	1070

ZGONINA, JEFF — DT — PANTHERS

PERSONAL: Born May 24, 1970, in Long Grove, Ill. ... 6-1/287. ... Full name: Jeffrey Marc Zgonina. ... Name pronounced skah-NEE-nah.
HIGH SCHOOL: Carmel (Long Grove, Ill.).
COLLEGE: Purdue (degree in community health promotion, 1992).
TRANSACTIONS/CAREER NOTES: Selected by Pittsburgh Steelers in seventh round (185th pick overall) of 1993 NFL draft. ... Signed by Steelers (July 16, 1993). ... Claimed on waivers by Carolina Panthers (August 28, 1995). ... Granted free agency (February 16, 1996).
PLAYING EXPERIENCE: Pittsburgh NFL, 1993 and 1994; Carolina NFL, 1995. ... Games: 1993 (5), 1994 (16), 1995 (2). Total: 23.
CHAMPIONSHIP GAME EXPERIENCE: Played in AFC championship game (1994 season).
PRO STATISTICS: 1993—Recovered one fumble. 1994—Returned two kickoffs for eight yards, fumbled once and recovered one fumble.

ZIMMERMAN, GARY — OT — BRONCOS

PERSONAL: Born December 13, 1961, in Fullerton, Calif. ... 6-6/294. ... Full name: Gary Wayne Zimmerman.
HIGH SCHOOL: Walnut (Calif.).
COLLEGE: Oregon.
TRANSACTIONS/CAREER NOTES: Selected by Los Angeles Express in second round (36th pick overall) of 1984 USFL draft. ... Signed by Express (February 13, 1984). ... Granted roster exemption (February 13-24, 1984). ... Selected by New York Giants in first round (third pick overall) of 1984 NFL supplemental draft. ... NFL rights traded by Giants to Minnesota Vikings for two second-round picks (CB Mark Collins and S Greg Lasker) in 1986 draft (April 29, 1986). ... Released by Express (May 19, 1986). ... Signed by Vikings (May 21, 1986). ... Granted free agency (February 1, 1988). ... Re-signed by Vikings (August 29, 1988). ... Placed on reserve/did not report list (July 20, 1993). ... Traded by Vikings to Denver Broncos for first-round (CB Dewayne Washington) and sixth-round (TE Andrew Jordan) picks in 1994 draft and second-round pick (DB Orlando Thomas) in 1995 draft (August 23, 1993).
PLAYING EXPERIENCE: Los Angeles USFL, 1984 and 1985; Minnesota NFL, 1986-1992; Denver NFL, 1993-1995. ... Games: 1984 (17), 1985 (17), 1986 (16), 1987 (12), 1988 (16), 1989 (16), 1990 (16), 1991 (16), 1992 (16), 1993 (16), 1994 (16), 1995 (16). Total Total NFL: 156. Total Pro: 190.
CHAMPIONSHIP GAME EXPERIENCE: Played in NFC championship game (1987 season).
HONORS: Named offensive tackle on The Sporting News college All-America second team (1983). ... Named offensive tackle on The Sporting News USFL All-Star team (1984 and 1985). ... Named offensive tackle on The Sporting News NFL All-Pro team (1987). ... Played in Pro Bowl (1987-1989, 1992 and 1994 seasons). ... Named to play in Pro Bowl (1995 season); replaced by Will Wolford due to injury.
PRO STATISTICS: USFL: 1984—Returned one kickoff for no yards, fumbled once and recovered two fumbles. NFL: 1986—Recovered two fumbles. 1987—Recovered one fumble for four yards. 1993—Recovered one fumble for no yards.

ZOLAK, SCOTT — QB — PATRIOTS

PERSONAL: Born December 13, 1967, in Pittsburgh. ... 6-5/222. ... Full name: Scott David Zolak.
HIGH SCHOOL: Ringgold (Monongahela, Pa.).
COLLEGE: Maryland (degree in business administration).
TRANSACTIONS/CAREER NOTES: Selected by New England Patriots in fourth round (84th pick overall) of 1991 NFL draft. ... On inactive list for all 16 games (1991). ... On injured reserve with ankle injury (December 18, 1992-remainder of season). ... Granted free agency (February 17, 1994). ... Re-signed by Patriots (April 2, 1994).
PRO STATISTICS: 1992—Fumbled five times and recovered three fumbles for minus 21 yards. 1995—Fumbled four times and recovered one fumble for minus two yards.
MISCELLANEOUS: Regular-season record as starting NFL quarterback: 2-3 (.400).

Year Team	G	Att.	Cmp.	Pct.	Yds.	TD	Int.	Avg.	Rat.	Att.	Yds.	Avg.	TD	TD	2pt.	Pts.
								PASSING				**RUSHING**			**TOTALS**	
1991—New England NFL...............								Did not play.								
1992—New England NFL...............	6	100	52	52.0	561	2	4	5.61	58.8	18	71	3.9	0	0	...	0
1993—New England NFL...............	3	2	0	0.0	0	0	0	.00	39.6	1	0	0.0	0	0	...	0
1994—New England NFL...............	16	8	5	62.5	28	0	0	3.50	68.8	1	-1	-1.0	0	0	0	0
1995—New England NFL...............	16	49	28	57.1	282	1	0	5.76	80.5	4	19	4.8	0	0	0	0
Pro totals (4 years)...................	41	159	85	53.5	871	3	4	5.48	65.3	24	89	3.7	0	0	0	0

ZOMALT, ERIC   S   EAGLES

PERSONAL: Born August 9, 1972, in Los Angeles. ... 5-11/201. ... Full name: Eric Lee Zomalt.
HIGH SCHOOL: Canyon Springs (Moreno Valley, Calif.).
COLLEGE: California.
TRANSACTIONS/CAREER NOTES: Selected by Philadelphia Eagles in third round (103rd pick overall) of 1994 NFL draft. ... Signed by Eagles (July 15, 1994).
PLAYING EXPERIENCE: Philadelphia NFL, 1994 and 1995. ... Games: 1994 (12), 1995 (15). Total: 27.

ZORDICH, MICHAEL   S   EAGLES

PERSONAL: Born October 12, 1963, in Youngstown, Ohio ... 6-1/212. ... Full name: Michael Edward Zordich.
HIGH SCHOOL: Chaney (Youngstown, Ohio).
COLLEGE: Penn State (degree in hotel, restaurant and institutional management, 1986).
TRANSACTIONS/CAREER NOTES: Selected by Baltimore Stars in 1986 USFL territorial draft. ... Selected by San Diego Chargers in ninth round (235th pick overall) of 1986 NFL draft. ... Signed by Chargers (June 24, 1986). ... Released by Chargers (August 22, 1986). ... Signed by New York Jets (April 9, 1987). ... Released by Jets (September 6, 1987). ... Re-signed by Jets (September 14, 1987). ... Granted unconditional free agency (February 1, 1989). ... Signed by Phoenix Cardinals (March 2, 1989). ... Granted free agency (February 1, 1991). ... Re-signed by Cardinals (July 22, 1991). ... Granted unconditional free agency (March 1, 1993). ... Re-signed by Cardinals (July 23, 1993). ... Granted unconditional free agency (February 17, 1994). ... Signed by Philadelphia Eagles (June 28, 1994).
PRO STATISTICS: 1990—Recovered one fumble. 1991—Recovered three fumbles for 19 yards. 1994—Returned one kickoff for no yards and recovered three fumbles for five yards. 1995—Recovered two fumbles for 58 yards and one touchdown.

Year Team	G	No.	Yds.	Avg.	TD	No.
			INTERCEPTIONS			**SACKS**
1987—New York Jets NFL	10	0	0	...	0	1.0
1988—New York Jets NFL	16	1	35	35.0	1	0.0
1989—Phoenix NFL	16	1	16	16.0	1	1.0
1990—Phoenix NFL	16	1	25	25.0	0	0.0
1991—Phoenix NFL	16	1	27	27.0	0	0.0
1992—Phoenix NFL	16	3	37	12.3	0	0.0
1993—Phoenix NFL	16	1	0	0.0	0	0.0
1994—Philadelphia NFL	16	4	39	9.8	1	1.0
1995—Philadelphia NFL	15	1	10	10.0	0	1.0
Pro totals (9 years)	137	13	189	14.5	3	4.0

ZORICH, CHRIS   DT   BEARS

PERSONAL: Born March 13, 1969, in Chicago. ... 6-1/280. ... Full name: Christopher Robert Zorich.
HIGH SCHOOL: Chicago Vocational.
COLLEGE: Notre Dame (degree in American studies).
TRANSACTIONS/CAREER NOTES: Selected by Chicago Bears in second round (49th pick overall) of 1991 NFL draft. ... Signed by Bears (June 24, 1991). ... Granted unconditional free agency (February 17, 1995). ... Re-signed by Bears (March 1, 1995).
HONORS: Named nose tackle on THE SPORTING NEWS college All-America first team (1989). ... Lombardi Award winner (1990). ... Named defensive lineman on THE SPORTING NEWS college All-America first team (1990).
PRO STATISTICS: 1992—Recovered one fumble for 42 yards and a touchdown. 1993—Recovered two fumbles. 1994—Recovered one fumble. 1995—Recovered two fumbles.

Year Team	G	SACKS
1991—Chicago NFL	12	0.0
1992—Chicago NFL	16	2.0
1993—Chicago NFL	16	7.0
1994—Chicago NFL	16	5.5
1995—Chicago NFL	16	1.0
Pro totals (5 years)	76	15.5

1996 DRAFT PICKS

ABDUL-JABBAR, KARIM   RB   DOLPHINS

PERSONAL: Born June 28, 1974, in Los Angeles. ... 5-10/194. ... Formerly known as Sharmon Shah.
HIGH SCHOOL: Dorsey (Los Angeles).
COLLEGE: UCLA.
TRANSACTIONS/CAREER NOTES: Selected after junior season by Miami Dolphins in third round (80th pick overall) of 1996 NFL draft.
HONORS: Named running back on THE SPORTING NEWS college All-America second team (1995).
MISCELLANEOUS: Granted medical redshirt due to knee injury (1993).

Year Team	G	RUSHING				RECEIVING				TOTALS	
		Att.	Yds.	Avg.	TD	No.	Yds.	Avg.	TD	TD	Pts.
1992—UCLA	7	48	124	2.6	1	0	0	...	0	1	6
1993—UCLA	3	54	260	4.8	0	2	34	17.0	0	0	0
1994—UCLA	11	210	1227	5.8	4	18	118	6.6	0	4	24
1995—UCLA	10	270	1419	5.3	11	16	154	9.6	1	12	72
College totals (4 years)	31	582	3030	5.2	16	36	306	8.5	1	17	102

ABRAHAM, DONNIE   CB   BUCCANEERS

PERSONAL: Born October 8, 1973, in Orangeburg, S.C. ... 5-10/181.
HIGH SCHOOL: Wilkinson (Orangeburg, S.C.).
COLLEGE: East Tennessee State.
TRANSACTIONS/CAREER NOTES: Selected by Tampa Bay Buccaneers in third round (71st pick overall) of 1996 NFL draft.

Year Team	G	INTERCEPTIONS			
		No.	Yds.	Avg.	TD
1991—East Tennessee State		Redshirted.			
1992—East Tennessee State	9	2	89	44.5	1
1993—East Tennessee State	11	7	20	2.9	0
1994—East Tennessee State	11	1	0	0.0	0
1995—East Tennessee State	11	5	189	37.8	2
College totals (4 years)	42	15	298	19.9	3

ACKERMAN, TOM   C   SAINTS

PERSONAL: Born September 6, 1972, in Bellingham, Wash. ... 6-3/290.
HIGH SCHOOL: Nooksack (Wash.).
COLLEGE: Eastern Washington.
TRANSACTIONS/CAREER NOTES: Selected by New Orleans Saints in fifth round (145th pick overall) of 1996 NFL draft.
COLLEGE PLAYING EXPERIENCE: Eastern Washington, 1992-1995. ... Games: 1992 (10), 1993 (7), 1994 (11), 1995 (11). Total: 39.

ALSTOTT, MIKE   FB   BUCCANEERS

PERSONAL: Born December 21, 1973, in Joliet, Ill. ... 6-0/240. ... Full name: Mike Joseph Alstott.
HIGH SCHOOL: Catholic (Joliet, Ill.).
COLLEGE: Purdue.
TRANSACTIONS/CAREER NOTES: Selected by Tampa Bay Buccaneers in second round (35th pick overall) of 1996 NFL draft.

Year Team	G	RUSHING				RECEIVING				TOTALS	
		Att.	Yds.	Avg.	TD	No.	Yds.	Avg.	TD	TD	Pts.
1992—Purdue	10	46	195	4.2	2	15	208	13.9	1	3	18
1993—Purdue	11	153	816	5.3	12	30	407	13.6	2	14	84
1994—Purdue	11	202	1188	5.9	14	23	298	13.0	0	14	84
1995—Purdue	11	243	1436	5.9	14	25	162	6.5	0	14	84
College totals (4 years)	43	644	3635	5.7	42	93	1075	11.6	3	45	270

ANDERSON, WILLIE   OT   BENGALS

PERSONAL: Born July 11, 1975, in Mobile, Ala. ... 6-5/325. ... Full name: Willie Aaron Anderson.
HIGH SCHOOL: Vigor (Mobile, Ala.).
COLLEGE: Auburn.
TRANSACTIONS/CAREER NOTES: Selected after junior season by Cincinnati Bengals in first round (10th pick overall) of 1996 NFL draft.
COLLEGE PLAYING EXPERIENCE: Auburn, 1993-1995. ... Games: 1993 (9), 1994 (11), 1995 (11). Total: 31.

ARCHIE, MIKE   RB   OILERS

PERSONAL: Born October 14, 1972, in Sharon, Pa. ... 5-8/205. ... Full name: Michael Lamont Archie.
HIGH SCHOOL: Sharon (Pa.).
COLLEGE: Penn State.
TRANSACTIONS/CAREER NOTES: Selected by Houston Oilers in seventh round (218th pick overall) of 1996 NFL draft.
MISCELLANEOUS: Attempted two passes with two completions for 106 yards and two touchdowns (1994).

Year Team	G	RUSHING				RECEIVING				PUNT RETURNS				KICKOFF RETURNS				TOTALS	
		Att.	Yds.	Avg.	TD	No.	Yds.	Avg.	TD	No.	Yds.	Avg.	TD	No.	Yds.	Avg.	TD	TD	Pts.
1991—Penn State						Redshirted.													
1992—Penn State	11	24	113	4.7	2	9	67	7.4	1	2	89	44.5	1	0	0	...	0	4	24
1993—Penn State	11	132	766	5.8	6	18	111	6.2	2	3	78	26.0	0	0	0	...	0	8	48
1994—Penn State	11	52	303	5.8	5	22	215	9.8	2	11	126	11.5	0	11	240	21.8	0	7	42
1995—Penn State	11	97	512	5.3	1	21	141	6.7	2	8	44	5.5	0	0	0	...	0	3	18
College totals (4 years)	44	305	1694	5.6	14	70	534	7.6	7	24	337	14.1	1	11	240	21.8	0	22	132

ARNOLD, JAHINE   WR   STEELERS

PERSONAL: Born June 19, 1973, in Rockville, Conn. ... 6-0/187.
HIGH SCHOOL: Homestead (Cupertino, Calif.)
COLLEGE: DeAnza (Cupertino, Calif.), then Fresno State.
TRANSACTIONS/CAREER NOTES: Selected by Pittsburgh Steelers in fourth round (132nd pick overall) of 1996 NFL draft.

Year Team	G	RECEIVING				PUNT RETURNS				KICKOFF RETURNS				TOTALS	
		No.	Yds.	Avg.	TD	No.	Yds.	Avg.	TD	No.	Yds.	Avg.	TD	TD	Pts.
1992—DeAnza College	...	0	0	...	0	0	0	...	0	0	0	...	0	0	0
1993—DeAnza College	...	47	1027	21.9	17	8	122	15.3	0	0	0	...	0	17	102
1994—Fresno State	...	3	27	9.0	0	0	0	...	0	0	0	...	0	0	0
1995—Fresno State	...	54	987	18.3	4	0	0	...	0	31	657	21.2	0	4	24
College totals (4 years)	...	104	2041	19.6	21	8	122	15.3	0	31	657	21.2	0	21	126

ASHER, JEREMY   LB   REDSKINS

PERSONAL: Born October 5, 1972, in Medford, Ore. ... 6-0/235. ... Full name: Jeremy Earl Asher.
HIGH SCHOOL: Tigard (Ore.).
COLLEGE: Oregon.
TRANSACTIONS/CAREER NOTES: Selected by Washington Redskins in seventh round (215th pick overall) of 1996 NFL draft.
HONORS: Named linebacker on THE SPORTING NEWS college All-America second team (1995).

Year Team	G	INTERCEPTIONS				SACKS
		No.	Yds.	Avg.	TD	No.
1991—Oregon				Redshirted.		
1992—Oregon	10	0	0	...	0	0.0
1993—Oregon	11	0	0	...	0	3.0
1994—Oregon	12	1	5	5.0	0	1.0
1995—Oregon	11	0	0	...	0	3.0
College totals (4 years)	44	1	5	5.0	0	7.0

AUSTIN, ERIC   S   BUCCANEERS

PERSONAL: Born June 7, 1973, in Moss Point, Miss. ... 5-10/217.
HIGH SCHOOL: Moss Point (Miss.).
COLLEGE: Jackson State.
TRANSACTIONS/CAREER NOTES: Selected by Tampa Bay Buccaneers in fourth round (104th pick overall) of 1996 NFL draft.

Year Team	G	INTERCEPTIONS				SACKS
		No.	Yds.	Avg.	TD	No.
1991—Jackson State				Did not play.		
1992—Jackson State	10	3	41	13.7	1	0.0
1993—Jackson State	10	0	0	...	0	0.0
1994—Jackson State				Redshirted.		
1995—Jackson State	11	2	112	56.0	1	8.0
College totals (3 years)	31	5	153	30.6	2	8.0

BAKER, DONNELL   WR   PANTHERS

PERSONAL: Born December 21, 1973, in Baton Rouge, La. ... 6-0/180.
HIGH SCHOOL: Baker (Baton Rouge, La.).
COLLEGE: Southern.
TRANSACTIONS/CAREER NOTES: Selected by Carolina Panthers in seventh round (217th pick overall) of 1996 NFL draft.

Year Team	G	RECEIVING			
		No.	Yds.	Avg.	TD
1992—Southern			Did not play.		
1993—Southern			Did not play.		
1994—Southern	8	12	209	17.4	1
1995—Southern	11	40	632	15.8	5
College totals (2 years)	19	52	841	16.2	6

BANDY, GARY   DE   FALCONS

PERSONAL: Born December 6, 1972, in Kansas City, Mo. ... 6-4/237.
HIGH SCHOOL: Kansas City (Mo.) Central.
JUNIOR COLLEGE: Coffeyville (Kan.) Junior College.

COLLEGE: Baylor.
TRANSACTIONS/CAREER NOTES: Selected by Atlanta Falcons in fifth round (164th pick overall) of 1996 NFL draft.

Year Team	G	SACKS
1991—Coffeyville Junior College	Redshirted.	
1992—Coffeyville Junior College	Statistics unavailable.	
1993—Coffeyville Junior College	Statistics unavailable.	
1994—Baylor	11	2.0
1995—Baylor	11	2.0
Junior College totals (2 years)	...	...
College totals (2 years)	22	4.0

BANKS, CHRIS — G — BRONCOS

PERSONAL: Born April 4, 1973, in Lexington, Mo. ... 6-1/286. ... Full name: Warren Christopher Banks.
HIGH SCHOOL: Lexington (Mo.).
COLLEGE: Kansas.
TRANSACTIONS/CAREER NOTES: Selected by Denver Broncos in seventh round (226th pick overall) of 1996 NFL draft.
COLLEGE PLAYING EXPERIENCE: Kansas, 1992-1995. ... Games: 1992 (4), 1993 (9), 1994 (8), 1995 (11). Total: 32.

BANKS, TONY — QB — RAMS

PERSONAL: Born April 5, 1973, in San Diego. ... 6-4/220. ... Cousin of Chip Banks, linebacker, Cleveland Browns, San Diego Chargers and Indianapolis Colts (1982-1992).
HIGH SCHOOL: Hoover (San Diego).
JUNIOR COLLEGE: Mesa (Ariz.) Community College.
COLLEGE: Michigan State.
TRANSACTIONS/CAREER NOTES: Selected by St. Louis Rams in second round (42nd pick overall) of 1996 NFL draft.

Year Team	G	PASSING								RUSHING				TOTALS	
		Att.	Cmp.	Pct.	Yds.	TD	Int.	Avg.	Rat.	Att.	Yds.	Avg.	TD	TD	Pts.
1992—Mesa Community College					Statistics unavailable.										
1993—Mesa Community College	10	312	145	46.5	2194	19	6	7.03	120.9	...	...	...	...	...	...
1994—Michigan State	11	238	145	60.9	2040	11	6	8.57	143.5	87	60	0.7	2	2	12
1995—Michigan State	8	214	134	62.6	1741	8	12	8.14	132.6	42	-56	-1.3	1	1	6
Junior College totals (1 year)	10	312	145	46.5	2194	19	6	7.03	120.9	...	...	...	...	...	...
College totals (2 years)	19	452	279	61.7	3781	19	18	7.82	138.1	129	4	0.0	3	3	18

RECORD AS BASEBALL PLAYER

TRANSACTIONS/CAREER NOTES: Threw right, batted left. ... Selected by Minnesota Twins organization in 10th round of free-agent draft (June 3, 1991).

Year Team (League)	Pos.	G	BATTING											FIELDING			
			AB	R	H	2B	3B	HR	RBI	Avg.	BB	SO	SB	PO	A	E	Avg.
1991—GC Twins (GCL)	DH	17	57	7	13	3	0	0	1	.228	4	16	2	0	0	0	...

BARBER, KANTROY — FB — PATRIOTS

PERSONAL: Born October 4, 1973, in Miami. ... 6-0/243. ... Son of Rudy Barber, linebacker, Miami Dolphins (1968).
HIGH SCHOOL: Carol City (Miami).
COLLEGE: Colorado, then West Virginia.
TRANSACTIONS/CAREER NOTES: Selected by New England Patriots in fourth round (124th pick overall) of 1996 NFL draft.

Year Team	G	RUSHING				RECEIVING				TOTALS	
		Att.	Yds.	Avg.	TD	No.	Yds.	Avg.	TD	TD	Pts.
1991—Colorado						Redshirted.					
1992—Colorado						Did not play.					
1993—West Virginia						Did not play.					
1994—West Virginia	12	72	337	4.7	5	6	38	6.3	0	5	30
1995—West Virginia	11	93	362	3.9	4	11	67	6.1	1	5	30
College totals (2 years)	23	165	699	4.2	9	17	105	6.2	1	10	60

BARLOW, REGGIE — WR — JAGUARS

PERSONAL: Born January 22, 1973, in Montgomery, Ala. ... 5-11/187. ... Full name: Reggie Devon Barlow.
HIGH SCHOOL: Lanier (Montgomery, Ala.).
COLLEGE: Alabama State.
TRANSACTIONS/CAREER NOTES: Selected by Jacksonville Jaguars in fourth round (110th pick overall) of 1996 NFL draft.

Year Team	G	RECEIVING				PUNT RETURNS				KICKOFF RETURNS				TOTALS	
		No.	Yds.	Avg.	TD	No.	Yds.	Avg.	TD	No.	Yds.	Avg.	TD	TD	Pts.
1991—Alabama State									Redshirted.						
1992—Alabama State	11	16	364	22.8	1	7	88	12.6	0	2	60	30.0	0	1	6
1993—Alabama State	9	19	384	20.2	2	21	208	9.9	0	2	71	35.5	0	2	12
1994—Alabama State	11	58	1267	21.8	12	13	104	8.0	0	1	37	37.0	0	12	72
1995—Alabama State	9	40	657	16.4	2	12	249	20.8	1	0	0	...	0	3	18
College totals (4 years)	40	133	2672	20.1	17	53	649	12.3	1	5	168	33.6	0	18	108

BARR, ROBERT   OT   SEAHAWKS

PERSONAL: Born June 7, 1973, in Freehold, N.J. ... 6-4/307.
HIGH SCHOOL: Hanover Area (Pa.).
JUNIOR COLLEGE: Nassau Community College (N.Y.).
COLLEGE: Rutgers.
TRANSACTIONS/CAREER NOTES: Selected by Seattle Seahawks in third round (77th pick overall) of 1996 NFL draft.
COLLEGE PLAYING EXPERIENCE: Nassau Community College, 1991 and 1992; Rutgers, 1994 and 1995. ... Games: 1991 (11), 1992 (11), 1994 (11), 1995 (11). Total: 44.

BATTAGLIA, MARCO   TE   BENGALS

PERSONAL: Born January 25, 1973, in Howard Beach, N.Y. ... 6-3/250.
HIGH SCHOOL: St. Francis (Queens, N.Y.).
COLLEGE: Rutgers.
TRANSACTIONS/CAREER NOTES: Selected by Cincinnati Bengals in second round (39th pick overall) of 1996 NFL draft.
HONORS: Named tight end on THE SPORTING NEWS college All-America first team (1995).

		RECEIVING			
Year Team	G	No.	Yds.	Avg.	TD
1991—Rutgers		Redshirted.			
1992—Rutgers	11	17	219	12.9	1
1993—Rutgers	11	27	329	12.2	1
1994—Rutgers	11	58	779	13.4	4
1995—Rutgers	11	69	894	13.0	10
College totals (4 years)	44	171	2221	13.0	16

BEASLEY, AARON   DB   JAGUARS

PERSONAL: Born July 7, 1973, in Pottstown, Pa. ... 6-0/194.
HIGH SCHOOL: Pottstown (Pa.), then Valley Forge Military Academy (Wayne, Pa.)
COLLEGE: West Virginia.
TRANSACTIONS/CAREER NOTES: Selected by Jacksonville Jaguars in third round (63rd pick overall) of 1996 NFL draft. ... Signed by Jaguars (May 25, 1996).

		INTERCEPTIONS				SACKS
Year Team	G	No.	Yds.	Avg.	TD	No.
1992—West Virginia	11	2	37	18.5	0	0.0
1993—West Virginia	11	1	0	0.0	0	0.0
1994—West Virginia	12	10	159	15.9	2	2.0
1995—West Virginia	11	5	171	34.2	1	0.0
College totals (4 years)	45	18	367	20.4	3	2.0

BIAKABUTUKA, TIM   RB   PANTHERS

PERSONAL: Born January 24, 1974, in Zaire. ... 6-0/210. ... Name pronounced bee-ah-kah-ba-TWO-kah.
HIGH SCHOOL: Vanier (Longueuil, Que.) College.
COLLEGE: Michigan.
TRANSACTIONS/CAREER NOTES: Selected after junior season by Carolina Panthers in first round (eighth pick overall) of 1996 NFL draft.

		RUSHING				RECEIVING				KICKOFF RETURNS				TOTALS	
Year Team	G	Att.	Yds.	Avg.	TD	No.	Yds.	Avg.	TD	No.	Yds.	Avg.	TD	TD	Pts.
1993—Michigan	6	43	209	4.9	5	0	0	...	0	0	0	...	0	5	30
1994—Michigan	11	126	783	6.2	7	8	73	9.1	0	2	31	15.5	0	7	42
1995—Michigan	12	279	1724	6.2	12	4	48	12.0	0	1	13	13.0	0	12	72
College totals (3 years)	29	448	2716	6.1	24	12	121	10.1	0	3	44	14.7	0	24	144

BLACKMAN, KEN   G/OT   BENGALS

PERSONAL: Born November 8, 1972, in Abilene, Texas. ... 6-6/315.
HIGH SCHOOL: Wylie (Abilene, Texas).
COLLEGE: Illinois.
TRANSACTIONS/CAREER NOTES: Selected by Cincinnati Bengals in third round (69th pick overall) of 1996 NFL draft.
COLLEGE PLAYING EXPERIENCE: Illinois, 1992-1995. ... Games: 1992 (8), 1993 (8), 1994 (10), 1995 (11). Total: 37.

BOLDEN, JURAN   CB   FALCONS

PERSONAL: Born June 27, 1974, in Tampa. ... 6-2/201.
HIGH SCHOOL: Hillsborough (Tampa).
JUNIOR COLLEGE: Mississippi Delta Community College.
TRANSACTIONS/CAREER NOTES: Signed by Winnipeg Blue Bombers of CFL for 1995 season. ... Selected by Atlanta Falcons in fourth round (127th pick overall) of 1996 NFL draft.
PRO STATISTICS: CFL: 1995—Returned one kick for two yards.
MISCELLANEOUS: Returned one fumble 42 yards for a touchdown (1993).

Year	Team		COLLEGIATE RECORD					SACKS
			INTERCEPTIONS					
		G	No.	Yds.	Avg.	TD		No.
1993—Mississippi Delta Community College		11	6	129	21.5	1		1.0
1994—Mississippi Delta Community College		9	6	137	22.8	2		0.0
Junior College totals (2 years)		20	12	266	22.2	3		1.0

Year	Team		PROFESSIONAL RECORD			
			INTERCEPTIONS			
		G	No.	Yds.	Avg.	TD
1995—Winnipeg CFL		9	6	28	4.7	0

BOYD, SEAN — S — VIKINGS

PERSONAL: Born December 19, 1972, in Gastonia, N.C. ... 6-3/206. ... Full name: Sean Lefell Boyd.
HIGH SCHOOL: Ashbrook (Gastonia, N.C.).
COLLEGE: North Carolina.
TRANSACTIONS/CAREER NOTES: Selected by Minnesota Vikings in fifth round (148th pick overall) of 1996 NFL draft.

Year	Team		INTERCEPTIONS			
		G	No.	Yds.	Avg.	TD
1991—North Carolina			Redshirted.			
1992—North Carolina		12	0	0	...	0
1993—North Carolina		12	4	24	6.0	0
1994—North Carolina		11	2	51	25.5	0
1995—North Carolina		11	1	0	0.0	0
College totals (4 years)		46	7	75	10.7	0

BRACKENS, TONY — DE — JAGUARS

PERSONAL: Born December 26, 1974, in Fairfield, Texas. ... 6-4/260.
HIGH SCHOOL: Fairfield (Texas).
COLLEGE: Texas.
TRANSACTIONS/CAREER NOTES: Selected after junior season by Jacksonville Jaguars in second round (33rd pick overall) of 1996 NFL draft.
HONORS: Named defensive lineman on THE SPORTING NEWS college All-America first team (1995).

Year	Team	G	SACKS
1993—Texas		11	10.0
1994—Texas		11	7.0
1995—Texas		9	7.0
College totals (3 years)		31	24.0

BRADLEY, FREDDIE — RB — CHARGERS

PERSONAL: Born June 12, 1970, in Helena, Ark. ... 5-10/208.
HIGH SCHOOL: Hueneme (Oxnard, Calif.)
JUNIOR COLLEGE: Moorpark (Calif.) College.
COLLEGE: Arkansas, then Sonoma State (Calif.).
TRANSACTIONS/CAREER NOTES: Selected by San Diego Chargers in seventh round (231st pick overall) of 1996 NFL draft.
MISCELLANEOUS: Granted medical redshirt due to knee injury (1993).

Year	Team		RUSHING				RECEIVING				KICKOFF RETURNS				TOTALS	
		G	Att.	Yds.	Avg.	TD	No.	Yds.	Avg.	TD	No.	Yds.	Avg.	TD	TD	Pts.
1989—Moorpark College	...	164	1266	7.7	15	...	...	...	...	...	...	...	...	15	90
1990—Moorpark College	...	235	1946	8.3	27	...	...	...	...	...	...	...	...	27	162
1991—Arkansas	...	49	197	4.0	1	0	0	...	0	16	388	24.3	0	1	6
1992—					Did not play.											
1993—Sonoma State	1	0	0	...	0	0	0	...	0	0	0	...	0	0	0
1994—Sonoma State					Did not play.											
1995—Sonoma State	9	155	726	4.7	2	9	43	4.8	0	3	53	17.7	0	2	12
Junior College totals (2 years)	...	399	3212	8.1	42	...	...	...	...	...	...	...	...	42	252
College totals (3 years)	10	204	923	4.6	3	9	43	4.8	0	19	441	23.2	0	3	18

BRANDENBURG, DAN — LB — BILLS

PERSONAL: Born February 2, 1973, in Rensselaer, Ind. ... 6-2/255.
HIGH SCHOOL: Rensselaer (Ind.) Central.
COLLEGE: Indiana State.
TRANSACTIONS/CAREER NOTES: Selected by Buffalo Bills in seventh round (237th pick overall) fo 1996 NFL draft.

Year	Team	G	SACKS
1991—Indiana State		Redshirted.	
1992—Indiana State		11	1.0
1993—Indiana State		11	13.0
1994—Indiana State		11	7.0
1995—Indiana State		11	11.0
College totals (4 years)		44	32.0

BREW, DORIAN   CB/PR   DOLPHINS

PERSONAL: Born July 19, 1974, in St. Louis. ... 5-10/182.
HIGH SCHOOL: McCluer North (Florissant, Mo.).
COLLEGE: Kansas.
TRANSACTIONS/CAREER NOTES: Selected by Miami Dolphins in third round (79th pick overall) of 1996 NFL draft.

Year Team	G	INTERCEPTIONS No.	Yds.	Avg.	TD	PUNT RETURNS No.	Yds.	Avg.	TD	KICKOFF RETURNS No.	Yds.	Avg.	TD	TOTALS TD	Pts.
1992—Kansas	9	0	0	...	0	0	0	...	0	0	0	...	0	0	0
1993—Kansas	7	2	0	0.0	0	7	97	13.9	0	11	251	22.8	0	0	0
1994—Kansas	11	1	0	0.0	0	12	152	12.7	1	0	0	...	0	1	6
1995—Kansas	11	4	79	19.8	1	4	15	3.8	0	0	0	...	0	1	6
College totals (4 years)	38	7	79	11.3	1	23	264	11.5	1	11	251	22.8	0	2	12

BROOKS, ETHAN   OT   FALCONS

PERSONAL: Born April 27, 1972, in Simsbury, Conn. ... 6-6/270.
HIGH SCHOOL: Westminster (Simsbury, Conn.).
COLLEGE: Williams (Williamstown, Conn.).
TRANSACTIONS/CAREER NOTES: Selected by Atlanta Falcons in seventh round (229th pick overall) of 1996 NFL draft.
COLLEGE PLAYING EXPERIENCE: Williams, 1992, 1994 and 1995. ... 1992 (8), 1994 (8), 1995 (8). Total: 24.
MISCELLANEOUS: Played defensive tackle during the 1992, 1993 and 1995 seasons. ... Credited with 10 sacks and intercepted one pass during college career.

BROWN, REGGIE   FB   SEAHAWKS

PERSONAL: Born June 26, 1973, in Detroit. ... 6-0/233.
HIGH SCHOOL: Henry Ford (Detroit).
JUNIOR COLLEGE: College of the Desert (Calif.).
COLLEGE: Fresno State.
TRANSACTIONS/CAREER NOTES: Selected by Seattle Seahawks in third round (91st pick overall) of 1996 NFL draft.

Year Team	G	RUSHING Att.	Yds.	Avg.	TD	RECEIVING No.	Yds.	Avg.	TD	TOTALS TD	Pts.
1992—College of the Desert					Statistics unavailable.						
1993—College of the Desert	10	110	777	7.1	13	...	...	...	...	13	78
1994—Fresno State	13	107	412	3.9	15	14	111	7.9	1	16	96
1995—Fresno State	10	131	719	5.5	9	18	183	10.2	3	12	72
Junior College totals (1 year)	10	110	777	7.1	13					13	78
College totals (2 years)	23	238	1131	4.8	24	32	294	9.2	4	28	168

BROWN, REGGIE   LB   LIONS

PERSONAL: Born September 28, 1974, in Austin, Texas. ... 6-2/241. ... Full name: Reginald Dwayne Brown.
HIGH SCHOOL: Reagan (Austin, Texas).
COLLEGE: Texas A&M.
TRANSACTIONS/CAREER NOTES: Selected by Detroit Lions in first round (17th pick overall) of 1996 NFL draft.

Year Team	G	INTERCEPTIONS No.	Yds.	Avg.	TD	SACKS No.
1992—Texas A&M	10	0	0	...	0	0.0
1993—Texas A&M	11	0	0	...	0	0.0
1994—Texas A&M	11	0	0	...	0	0.0
1995—Texas A&M	11	2	22	11.0	1	7.0
College totals (4 years)	43	2	22	11.0	1	7.0

BROWN, SHANNON   DT   FALCONS

PERSONAL: Born May 23, 1972, in Millbrook, Ala. ... 6-4/290.
HIGH SCHOOL: Stanhope-Elmore (Ala.).
COLLEGE: Alabama.
TRANSACTIONS/CAREER NOTES: Selected by Atlanta Falcons in third round (84th pick overall) of 1996 NFL draft.

Year Team	G	SACKS
1991—Alabama	Redshirted.	
1992—Alabama	9	2.0
1993—Alabama	10	2.0
1994—Alabama	11	5.0
1995—Alabama	10	0.0
College totals (4 years)	40	9.0

BROWNING, JOHN   DT   CHIEFS

PERSONAL: Born September 30, 1973, in Miami. ... 6-4/264.
HIGH SCHOOL: North Miami.

COLLEGE: West Virginia.
TRANSACTIONS/CAREER NOTES: Selected by Kansas City Chiefs in third round (68th pick overall) of 1996 NFL draft.

Year—Team	G	SACKS
1992—West Virginia	Did not play.	
1993—West Virginia	7	0.0
1994—West Virginia	10	4.0
1995—West Virginia	7	4.0
College totals (3 years)	24	8.0

BRUSCHI, TEDY — LB — PATRIOTS

PERSONAL: Born June 9, 1973, in San Francisco. ... 6-0/245. ... Full name: Tedy Lacap Bruschi. ... Stepson of Ronald Sandys, former professional tennis player. ... Name pronounced BREW-ski.
HIGH SCHOOL: Roseville (Calif.).
COLLEGE: Arizona.
TRANSACTIONS/CAREER NOTES: Selected by New England Patriots in third round (86th pick overall) of 1996 NFL draft.
HONORS: Named defensive lineman on THE SPORTING NEWS college All-America first team (1994 and 1995).
MISCELLANEOUS: Granted medical redshirt due to thumb injury (1991).

Year—Team	G	SACKS
1991—Arizona	2	0.0
1992—Arizona	11	4.5
1993—Arizona	11	19.0
1994—Arizona	11	10.0
1995—Arizona	11	14.5
College totals (5 years)	46	48.0

BUCKEY, JEFF — G — DOLPHINS

PERSONAL: Born August 7, 1974, in Bakersfield, Calif. ... 6-5/300.
HIGH SCHOOL: Bakersfield (Calif.).
COLLEGE: Stanford.
TRANSACTIONS/CAREER NOTES: Selected by Miami Dolphins in seventh round (230th pick overall) of 1996 NFL draft.
COLLEGE PLAYING EXPERIENCE: Stanford, 1992-1995. ... Games: 1992 (12), 1993 (11), 1994 (11), 1995 (11). Total: 45.

BURTON, KENDRICK — DE — OILERS

PERSONAL: Born September 7, 1973, in Decatur, Ala. ... 6-5/288.
HIGH SCHOOL: Hartselle (Ala.)
COLLEGE: Alabama.
TRANSACTIONS/CAREER NOTES: Selected by Houston Oilers in fourth round (107th pick overall) of 1996 NFL draft.

Year—Team	G	SACKS
1992—Alabama	Did not play.	
1993—Alabama	8	0.0
1994—Alabama	12	3.0
1995—Alabama	11	2.0
College totals (3 years)	31	5.0

BURTON, SHANE — DT — DOLPHINS

PERSONAL: Born January 18, 1974, in Catawba, N.C. ... 6-6/300. ... Full name: Franklin Shane Burton.
HIGH SCHOOL: Bandys (Catawba, N.C.).
COLLEGE: Tennessee.
TRANSACTIONS/CAREER NOTES: Selected by Miami Dolphins in fifth round (150th pick overall) of 1996 NFL draft.

Year—Team	G	SACKS
1992—Tennessee	11	0.0
1993—Tennessee	11	1.0
1994—Tennessee	11	4.0
1995—Tennessee	11	6.5
College totals (4 years)	44	11.5

CAMPBELL, MARK — DE — BRONCOS

PERSONAL: Born September 12, 1972, in Jamaica. ... 6-1/290. ... Full name: Mark Anthony Campbell.
HIGH SCHOOL: Sunset (Miami).
COLLEGE: Florida.
TRANSACTIONS/CAREER NOTES: Selected by Denver Broncos in third round (78th pick overall) of 1996 NFL draft.

Year—Team	G	SACKS
1991—Florida	Redshirted.	
1992—Florida	10	1.5
1993—Florida	12	5.0
1994—Florida	12	6.0
1995—Florida	12	4.5
College totals (4 years)	46	17.0

CAMPOS, ALAN   LB   COWBOYS

PERSONAL: Born March 3, 1973, in Miami. ... 6-3/236.
HIGH SCHOOL: Palmetto (Miami).
COLLEGE: Louisville.
TRANSACTIONS/CAREER NOTES: Selected by Dallas Cowboys in fifth round (167th pick overall) of 1996 NFL draft.

		INTERCEPTIONS				SACKS
Year Team	G	No.	Yds.	Avg.	TD	No.
1991—Louisville			Redshirted.			
1992—Louisville	11	0	0	...	0	0.0
1993—Louisville	11	0	0	...	0	0.0
1994—Louisville	11	1	2	2.0	0	2.0
1995—Louisville	11	3	58	19.3	1	2.0
College totals (4 years)	44	4	60	15.0	1	4.0

CAWLEY, MIKE   QB   COLTS

PERSONAL: Born August 28, 1972, in Mount Lebanon, Pa. ... 6-1/200. ... Full name: Michael Rodney Cawley.
HIGH SCHOOL: Mount Lebanon (Pa.).
COLLEGE: Syracuse, then James Madison.
TRANSACTIONS/CAREER NOTES: Selected by Indianapolis Colts in sixth round (205th pick overall) of 1996 NFL draft.

		PASSING								RUSHING				TOTALS	
Year Team	G	Att.	Cmp.	Pct.	Yds.	TD	Int.	Avg.	Rat.	Att.	Yds.	Avg.	TD	TD	Pts.
1991—Syracuse					Redshirted.										
1992—Syracuse	1	0	0	...	0	0	0	...	...	1	-2	-2.0	0	0	0
1993—James Madison	10	239	131	54.8	1988	14	11	8.32	135.9	97	108	1.1	6	6	36
1994—James Madison	11	263	152	57.8	2035	11	8	7.74	130.7	140	589	4.2	12	12	72
1995—James Madison	11	361	196	54.3	2459	17	11	6.81	120.7	99	70	0.7	4	4	24
College totals (4 years)	33	863	479	55.5	6482	42	30	7.51	128.0	337	765	2.3	22	22	132

CHEEVER, MICHAEL   C   JAGUARS

PERSONAL: Born June 24, 1973, in Newnan Ga. ... 6-3/296. ... Full name: Michael John Cheever.
HIGH SCHOOL: Newnan, Ga.
COLLEGE: Georgia Tech.
TRANSACTIONS/CAREER NOTES: Selected by Jacksonville Jaguars in second round (60th pick overall) of 1996 NFL draft. ... Signed by Jaguars (May 25, 1996).
COLLEGE PLAYING EXPERIENCE: Georgia Tech, 1992-1995. ... Games: 1992 (9), 1993 (11), 1994 (8), 1995 (11). Total: 39.

CHERRY, Je'ROD   S   SAINTS

PERSONAL: Born May 30, 1973, in Charlotte. ... 6-0/196. ... Name pronounced juh-ROD.
HIGH SCHOOL: Berkeley (Calif.).
COLLEGE: California (degree in political science, 1995).
TRANSACTIONS/CAREER NOTES: Selected by New Orleans Saints in second round (40th pick overall) of 1996 NFL draft.

		INTERCEPTIONS				KICKOFF RETURNS				TOTALS	
Year Team	G	No.	Yds.	Avg.	TD	No.	Yds.	Avg.	TD	TD	Pts.
1991—California				Redshirted.							
1992—California	11	0	0	...	0	0	0	...	0	0	0
1993—California	12	0	0	...	0	1	10	10.0	0	0	0
1994—California	11	0	0	...	0	4	62	15.5	0	0	0
1995—California	11	1	5	5.0	0	18	386	21.4	0	0	0
College totals (4 years)	45	1	5	5.0	0	23	458	19.9	0	0	0

CHURCH, JOHNIE   DE   SEAHAWKS

PERSONAL: Born January 1, 1974, in Fort Myers, Fla. ... 6-3/259.
HIGH SCHOOL: Cypress Lake (Fort Myers, Fla.)
COLLEGE: Florida.
TRANSACTIONS/CAREER NOTES: Selected by Seattle Seahawks in seventh round (225th pick overall) of 1996 NFL draft.

Year Team	G	SACKS
1992—Florida	11	4.0
1993—Florida	11	1.0
1994—Florida	12	3.0
1995—Florida	10	5.0
College totals (4 years)	44	13.0

CLARK, JON   OT   BEARS

PERSONAL: Born April 11, 1973, in Philadelphia ... 6-6/339.
HIGH SCHOOL: John Bartram (Philadelphia)
COLLEGE: Temple.

TRANSACTIONS/CAREER NOTES: Selected by Chicago Bears in sixth round (187th pick overall) of 1996 NFL draft.
COLLEGE PLAYING EXPERIENCE: Temple, 1992-1995. ... Games: 1992 (11), 1993 (11), 1994 (11), 1995 (11). Total: 44.

CLARK, SEDRIC — DE — RAIDERS

PERSONAL: Born January 28, 1973, in Missouri City, Texas. ... 6-1/248.
HIGH SCHOOL: Willowridge (Sugar Land, Texas).
COLLEGE: Tulsa.
TRANSACTIONS/CAREER NOTES: Selected by Oakland Raiders in seventh round (220th pick overall) of 1996 NFL draft.

Year Team	G	SACKS
1991—Tulsa	Redshirted.	
1992—Tulsa	11	2.0
1993—Tulsa	3	0.0
1994—Tulsa	11	8.0
1995—Tulsa	11	10.0
College totals (4 years)	36	20.0

CLAY, HAYWARD — TE — RAMS

PERSONAL: Born July 25, 1973, in Snyder, Texas. ... 6-4/256. ... Full name: Hayward John Clay.
HIGH SCHOOL: Snyder (Texas).
COLLEGE: Texas.
TRANSACTIONS/CAREER NOTES: Selected by St. Louis Rams in sixth round (201st pick overall) of 1996 NFL draft.

Year Team	G	RECEIVING No.	Yds.	Avg.	TD
1992—Texas A&M	...	1	11	11.0	0
1993—Texas A&M	...	5	85	17.0	0
1994—Texas A&M	9	4	37	9.3	0
1995—Texas A&M	11	19	235	12.4	3
College totals (4 years)	...	29	368	12.7	3

CLEMONS, DUANE — DE — VIKINGS

PERSONAL: Born May 23, 1974, in Riverside, Calif. ... 6-5/261.
HIGH SCHOOL: John W. North (Riverside, Calif.).
COLLEGE: California.
TRANSACTIONS/CAREER NOTES: Selected after junior season by Minnesota Vikings in first round (16th pick overall) of 1996 NFL draft.

Year Team	G	SACKS
1992—California	3	0.5
1993—California	11	2.5
1994—California	Redshirted.	
1995—California	11	10.5
College totals (3 years)	25	13.5

COLEMAN, MARCUS — S — JETS

PERSONAL: Born May 24, 1974, in Dallas. ... 6-2/208.
HIGH SCHOOL: Lake Highlands (Dallas).
COLLEGE: Texas Tech.
TRANSACTIONS/CAREER NOTES: Selected by New York Jets in fifth round (133rd pick overall) of 1996 NFL draft.
MISCELLANEOUS: Returned two blocked punts for 94 yards and one touchdown (1995).

Year Team	G	INTERCEPTIONS No.	Yds.	Avg.	TD	SACKS No.
1992—Texas Tech	11	2	72	36.0	1	0.0
1993—Texas Tech	11	3	87	29.0	1	4.0
1994—Texas Tech	11	2	44	22.0	2	2.0
1995—Texas Tech	11	2	43	21.5	0	2.0
College totals (4 years)	44	9	246	27.3	4	8.0

COLMAN, DOUG — LB — GIANTS

PERSONAL: Born June 4, 1973, in Somers Point, N.J. ... 6-2/252.
HIGH SCHOOL: Ocean City (N.J.)
COLLEGE: Nebraska.
TRANSACTIONS/CAREER NOTES: Selected by New York Giants in sixth round (171st pick overall) of 1996 NFL draft.

Year Team	G	SACKS
1991—Nebraska	5	0.0
1992—Nebraska	Redshirted.	
1993—Nebraska	11	0.0
1994—Nebraska	12	2.0
1995—Nebraska	11	2.0
College totals (4 years)	39	4.0

CONLEY, STEVEN   LB   STEELERS

PERSONAL: Born January 18, 1972, in Chicago. ... 6-1/231.
HIGH SCHOOL: Luther South (Chicago).
COLLEGE: Arkansas.
TRANSACTIONS/CAREER NOTES: Selected by Pittsburgh Steelers in third round (72nd pick overall) of 1996 NFL draft.

Year—Team	G	SACKS
1991—Arkansas	Redshirted.	
1992—Arkansas	7	0.0
1993—Arkansas	10	0.0
1994—Arkansas	11	7.0
1995—Arkansas	11	14.0
College totals (4 years)	39	21.0

CONLIN, KEITH   OT   COLTS

PERSONAL: Born November 9, 1972, in Glenside, Pa. ... 6-7/305. ... Full name: Keith Arthur Conlin.
HIGH SCHOOL: LaSalle (Glenside, Pa.).
COLLEGE: Penn State.
TRANSACTIONS/CAREER NOTES: Selected by Indianapolis Colts in sixth round (191st pick overall) of 1996 NFL draft.
COLLEGE PLAYING EXPERIENCE: Penn State, 1992-1995. ... Games: 1992 (7), 1993 (8), 1994 (11), 1995 (9). Total: 35.

CONRAD, J.R.   OT   PATRIOTS

PERSONAL: Born February 2, 1974, in Fairland, Okla. ... 6-3/300. ... Full name: James Robert Conrad.
HIGH SCHOOL: Fairland (Okla.).
COLLEGE: Oklahoma.
TRANSACTIONS/CAREER NOTES: Selected by New England Patriots in seventh round (247th pick overall) of 1996 NFL draft.
COLLEGE PLAYING EXPERIENCE: Oklahoma, 1992-1995. ... Games: 1992 (11), 1993 (11), 1994 (11), 1995 (9). Totals: 42.

CONWELL, ERNIE   TE   RAMS

PERSONAL: Born August 17, 1972, in Renton, Wash. ... 6-1/253.
HIGH SCHOOL: Kentwood (Kent, Wash.).
COLLEGE: Washington.
TRANSACTIONS/CAREER NOTES: Selected by St. Louis Rams in second round (59th pick overall) of 1996 NFL draft.

		RECEIVING			
Year—Team	G	No.	Yds.	Avg.	TD
1991—Washington		Redshirted.			
1992—Washington	11	3	40	13.3	0
1993—Washington	10	9	194	21.6	1
1994—Washington	11	11	154	14.0	2
1995—Washington	11	24	343	14.3	2
College totals (4 years)	43	47	731	15.6	5

CUNNINGHAM, T.J.   DB   SEAHAWKS

PERSONAL: Born October 24, 1972, in Aurora, Colo. ... 6-0/191.
HIGH SCHOOL: Overland (Aurora, Colo.).
COLLEGE: Colorado.
TRANSACTIONS/CAREER NOTES: Selected by Seattle Seahawks in sixth round (209th pick overall) of 1996 NFL draft.
MISCELLANEOUS: Played wide receiver during the 1992 and 1993 seasons. ... Caught 16 passes for 171 yards (1992); and caught five passes for 63 yards (1993).

		INTERCEPTIONS			
Year—Team	G	No.	Yds.	Avg.	TD
1991—Colorado		Redshirted.			
1992—Colorado	11	0	0	...	0
1993—Colorado	11	0	0	...	0
1994—Colorado	8	0	0	...	0
1995—Colorado	11	2	26	13.0	0
College totals (4 years)	41	2	26	13.0	0

DANIELS, DEXTER   LB   RAVENS

PERSONAL: Born December 8, 1973, in Valdosta, Ga. ... 6-1/241.
HIGH SCHOOL: Valdosta (Ga.).
COLLEGE: Florida.
TRANSACTIONS/CAREER NOTES: Selected by Baltimore Ravens in sixth round (172nd pick overall) of 1996 NFL draft.

		INTERCEPTIONS				SACKS
Year—Team	G	No.	Yds.	Avg.	TD	No.
1992—Florida	12	0	0	...	0	0.0
1993—Florida	12	1	0	0.0	0	0.5

Year Team	G	No.	INTERCEPTIONS Yds.	Avg.	TD	SACKS No.
1994—Florida	10	2	17	8.5	0	0.0
1995—Florida	12	0	0	...	0	4.0
College totals (4 years)	46	3	17	5.7	0	4.5

DANIELS, PHILLIP — DE — SEAHAWKS

PERSONAL: Born March 4, 1973, in Donalsonville, Ga. ... 6-5/263. ... Full name: Phillip Bernard Daniels.
HIGH SCHOOL: Seminole County (Ga.).
COLLEGE: Georgia.
TRANSACTIONS/CAREER NOTES: Selected by Seattle Seahawks in fourth round (99th pick overall) of 1996 NFL draft.

Year Team	G	No.	INTERCEPTIONS Yds.	Avg.	TD	SACKS No.
1992—Georgia	11	0	0	...	0	1.0
1993—Georgia	10	0	0	...	0	3.0
1994—Georgia	11	0	0	...	0	5.0
1995—Georgia	11	1	21	21.0	1	4.0
College totals (4 years)	43	1	21	21.0	1	13.0

DARKINS, CHRIS — RB — PACKERS

PERSONAL: Born April 30, 1974, in Houston. ... 6-0/211.
HIGH SCHOOL: Strake Jesuit College Prep (Houston).
COLLEGE: Minnesota.
TRANSACTIONS/CAREER NOTES: Selected by Green Bay Packers in fourth round (123rd pick overall) of 1996 NFL draft.

Year Team	G	RUSHING Att.	Yds.	Avg.	TD	RECEIVING No.	Yds.	Avg.	TD	KICKOFF RETURNS No.	Yds.	Avg.	TD	TOTALS TD	Pts.
1992—Minnesota	11	78	357	4.6	0	14	161	11.5	1	7	124	17.7	0	1	6
1993—Minnesota	10	124	610	4.9	4	18	180	10.0	2	11	251	22.8	0	6	36
1994—Minnesota	11	277	1443	5.2	11	22	299	13.6	2	0	0	...	0	13	78
1995—Minnesota	8	164	825	5.0	6	12	97	8.1	0	0	0	...	0	6	36
College totals (4 years)	40	643	3235	5.0	21	66	737	11.2	5	18	375	20.8	0	26	156

DAVIS, STEPHEN — RB — REDSKINS

PERSONAL: Born March 1, 1974, in Spartanburg, S.C. ... 6-0/227.
HIGH SCHOOL: Spartanburg (S.C.).
COLLEGE: Auburn.
TRANSACTIONS/CAREER NOTES: Selected by Washington Redskins in fourth round (102nd pick overall) of 1996 NFL draft.

Year Team	G	RUSHING Att.	Yds.	Avg.	TD	RECEIVING No.	Yds.	Avg.	TD	TOTALS TD	Pts.
1992—Auburn				Did not play.								
1993—Auburn	9	87	480	5.5	3	11	122	11.1	1	4	24
1994—Auburn	11	221	1263	5.7	13	12	92	7.7	0	13	78
1995—Auburn	11	180	1068	5.9	14	10	128	12.8	3	17	102
College totals (3 years)	31	488	2811	5.8	30	33	342	10.4	4	34	204

DAVIS, WENDELL — DB — COWBOYS

PERSONAL: Born June 27, 1973, in Wichita, Kan. ... 5-10/184.
HIGH SCHOOL: North (Wichita, Kan.).
JUNIOR COLLEGE: Coffeyville (Kan.) Junior College.
COLLEGE: Oklahoma.
TRANSACTIONS/CAREER NOTES: Selected by Dallas Cowboys in sixth round (207th pick overall) of 1996 NFL draft.

Year Team	G	No.	INTERCEPTIONS Yds.	Avg.	TD
1991—Coffeyville Junior College			Statistics unavailable.		
1992—Coffeyville Junior College			Statistics unavailable.		
1993—Oklahoma			Redshirted.		
1994—Oklahoma	11	1	20	20.0	0
1995—Oklahoma	11	0	0	...	0
Junior College totals (2 years)	...	...	...	...	...
College totals (2 years)	22	1	20	20.0	0

DAWKINS, BRIAN — S — EAGLES

PERSONAL: Born October 13, 1973, in Jacksonville. ... 5-11/188.
HIGH SCHOOL: Raines (Jacksonville).
COLLEGE: Clemson.
TRANSACTIONS/CAREER NOTES: Selected by Philadelphia Eagles in second round (61st pick overall) of 1996 NFL draft.
HONORS: Named defensive back on THE SPORTING NEWS college All-America second team (1995).

Year Team	G	No.	INTERCEPTIONS Yds.	Avg.	TD	SACKS No.
1992—Clemson	11	0	0	...	0	0.0

Year Team	G	INTERCEPTIONS No.	Yds.	Avg.	TD	SACKS No.
1993—Clemson	11	3	13	4.3	0	0.0
1994—Clemson	11	2	33	16.5	0	0.0
1995—Clemson	11	6	55	9.2	1	2.0
College totals (4 years)	44	11	101	9.2	1	2.0

DEXTER, JAMES — OT — CARDINALS

PERSONAL: Born March 3, 1973, in Springfield, Va. ... 6-5/300.
HIGH SCHOOL: West Springfield (Va.).
COLLEGE: South Carolina.
TRANSACTIONS/CAREER NOTES: Selected by Arizona Cardinals in fifth round (137th pick overall) of 1996 NFL draft.
COLLEGE PLAYING EXPERIENCE: South Carolina, 1992-1995. ... Games: 1992 (8), 1993 (8), 1994 (11), 1995 (11). Total: 38.

DOERING, CHRIS — WR — JAGUARS

PERSONAL: Born May 19, 1973, in Gainesville, Fla. ... 6-3/191. ... Name pronounced DOOR-ing.
HIGH SCHOOL: P.K. Yonge (Gainesville, Fla.).
COLLEGE: Florida.
TRANSACTIONS/CAREER NOTES: Selected by Jacksonville Jaguars in sixth round (185th pick overall) of 1996 NFL draft. ... Signed by Jaguars (June 5, 1996).

Year Team	G	RECEIVING No.	Yds.	Avg.	TD
1991—Florida		Redshirted			
1992—Florida	5	1	13	13.0	0
1993—Florida	12	43	553	12.9	7
1994—Florida	12	35	496	14.2	7
1995—Florida	12	70	1045	14.9	17
College totals (4 years)	41	149	2107	14.1	31

DORSETT, ANTHONY — CB — OILERS

PERSONAL: Born September 14, 1973, in Aliquippa, Pa. ... 5-11/190. ... Full name: Anthony Drew Dorsett Jr. ... Son of Tony Dorsett, Hall of Fame running back, Dallas Cowboys and Denver Broncos (1977-1988).
HIGH SCHOOL: Richland (Dallas), then J.J. Pearce (Dallas).
COLLEGE: Pittsburgh.
TRANSACTIONS/CAREER NOTES: Selected by Houston Oilers in sixth round (177th pick overall) of 1996 NFL draft.

Year Team	G	INTERCEPTIONS No.	Yds.	Avg.	TD	SACKS No.
1991—Pittsburgh		Redshirted.				
1992—Pittsburgh	11	0	0	...	0	1.0
1993—Pittsburgh	11	0	0	...	0	0.0
1994—Pittsburgh	9	0	0	...	0	0.0
1995—Pittsburgh	11	3	1	0.3	0	0.0
College totals (4 years)	42	3	1	0.3	0	1.0

DUDLEY, RICKEY — TE — RAIDERS

PERSONAL: Born July 15, 1972, in Henderson, Texas. ... 6-6/248.
HIGH SCHOOL: Henderson (Texas).
COLLEGE: Ohio State.
TRANSACTIONS/CAREER NOTES: Selected by Oakland Raiders in first round (ninth pick overall) of 1996 NFL draft.
MISCELLANEOUS: Member of Ohio State basketball team (1991-92 through 1993-94).

Year Team	G	RECEIVING No.	Yds.	Avg.	TD
1991—Ohio State		Did not play.			
1992—Ohio State		Did not play.			
1993—Ohio State		Did not play.			
1994—Ohio State	12	7	80	11.4	2
1995—Ohio State	12	32	469	14.7	6
College totals (2 years)	24	39	549	14.1	8

DUNN, JASON — TE — EAGLES

PERSONAL: Born November 15, 1973, in Harrodsburg, Ky. ... 6-4/257.
HIGH SCHOOL: Harrodsburg (Ky.).
COLLEGE: Eastern Kentucky.
TRANSACTIONS/CAREER NOTES: Selected by Philadelphia Eagles in second round (54th pick overall) of 1996 NFL draft.
MISCELLANEOUS: Played linebacker and defensive end during the 1991, 1992 and 1995 seasons. ... Granted medical redshirt due to knee injury (1992).

Year Team	G	RUSHING Att.	Yds.	Avg.	TD	RECEIVING No.	Yds.	Avg.	TD	TOTALS TD	Pts.
1991—Eastern Kentucky	11	0	0	...	0	0	0	...	0	0	0

Year Team	G	RUSHING				RECEIVING				TOTALS	
		Att.	Yds.	Avg.	TD	No.	Yds.	Avg.	TD	TD	Pts.
1992—Eastern Kentucky	2	0	0	...	0	0	0	...	0	0	0
1993—Eastern Kentucky	11	8	106	13.3	1	10	144	14.4	0	1	6
1994—Eastern Kentucky	11	8	51	6.4	0	13	266	20.5	1	1	6
1995—Eastern Kentucky	7	3	42	14.0	0	18	205	11.4	2	2	12
College totals (5 years)	42	19	199	10.5	1	41	615	15.0	3	4	24

EDWARDS, DONNIE — LB — CHIEFS

PERSONAL: Born April 6, 1973, in San Diego ... 6-2/225. ... Full name: Donald Lewis Edwards.
HIGH SCHOOL: Chula Vista (San Diego).
COLLEGE: UCLA.
TRANSACTIONS/CAREER NOTES: Selected by Kansas City Chiefs in fourth round (98th pick overall) of 1996 NFL draft.

Year Team	G	INTERCEPTIONS				SACKS
		No.	Yds.	Avg.	TD	No.
1991—UCLA				Redshirted.		
1992—UCLA	11	1	16	16.0	0	5.0
1993—UCLA	11	2	13	6.5	0	2.0
1994—UCLA	11	3	19	6.3	0	12.5
1995—UCLA	6	0	0	...	0	2.0
College totals (4 years)	39	6	48	8.0	0	21.5

ELMORE, JOHN — G — PATRIOTS

PERSONAL: Born March 2, 1973, in Sherman, Texas. ... 6-3/302.
HIGH SCHOOL: Sherman (Texas).
COLLEGE: Texas (degree in sports management, 1995).
TRANSACTIONS/CAREER NOTES: Selected by New England Patriots in fifth round (139th pick overall) of 1996 NFL draft.
COLLEGE PLAYING EXPERIENCE: Texas, 1992-1995. ... Games: 1992 (6), 1993 (8), 1994 (11), 1995 (11). Total: 36.

EMMONS, CARLOS — LB — STEELERS

PERSONAL: Born September 3, 1973, in Greenwood, Miss. ... 6-4/240.
HIGH SCHOOL: Greenwood (Miss.)
COLLEGE: Arkansas State.
TRANSACTIONS/CAREER NOTES: Selected by Pittsburgh Steelers in seventh round (242nd pick overall) of 1996 NFL draft.

Year Team	G	INTERCEPTIONS				SACKS
		No.	Yds.	Avg.	TD	No.
1992—Arkansas State	11	1	9	9.0	0	0.0
1993—Arkansas State	11	0	0	...	0	6.0
1994—Arkansas State	10	0	0	...	0	2.0
1995—Arkansas State	9	1	20	20.0	0	4.0
College totals (4 years)	41	2	29	14.5	0	12.0

ENGRAM, BOBBY — WR — BEARS

PERSONAL: Born January 7, 1973, in Camden, S.C. ... 5-10/187.
HIGH SCHOOL: Camden (S.C.).
COLLEGE: Penn State.
TRANSACTIONS/CAREER NOTES: Selected by Chicago Bears in second round (52nd pick overall) of 1996 NFL draft.
HONORS: Named wide receiver on The Sporting News college All-America second team (1994 and 1995).

Year Team	G	RUSHING				RECEIVING				PUNT RETURNS				KICKOFF RETURNS				TOTALS	
		Att.	Yds.	Avg.	TD	No.	Yds.	Avg.	TD	No.	Yds.	Avg.	TD	No.	Yds.	Avg.	TD	TD	Pts.
1991—Penn State	12	0	0	...	0	4	40	10.0	0	5	50	10.0	0	0	0	...	0	0	0
1992—Penn State								Did not play.											
1993—Penn State	11	3	15	5.0	0	48	873	18.2	13	33	402	12.2	0	1	34	34.0	0	13	78
1994—Penn State	11	3	46	15.3	0	52	1029	19.8	7	14	147	10.5	0	0	0	...	0	7	42
1995—Penn State	11	5	94	18.8	1	63	1084	17.2	11	19	187	9.8	0	2	42	21.0	0	12	72
College totals (4 years)	45	11	155	14.1	1	167	3026	18.1	31	71	786	11.1	0	3	76	25.3	0	32	192

EVANS, LEOMONT — DB — REDSKINS

PERSONAL: Born July 12, 1974, in Abbeville, S.C. ... 6-1/200.
HIGH SCHOOL: Abbeville (S.C.).
COLLEGE: Clemson.
TRANSACTIONS/CAREER NOTES: Selected by Washington Redskins in fifth round (138th pick overall) of 1996 NFL draft.

Year Team	G	INTERCEPTIONS			
		No.	Yds.	Avg.	TD
1992—Clemson	9	0	0	...	0
1993—Clemson	11	1	0	0.0	0
1994—Clemson	5	0	0	...	0
1995—Clemson	11	4	55	13.8	0
College totals (4 years)	36	5	55	11.0	0

FARMER, RAY   LB   EAGLES

PERSONAL: Born July 1, 1972, in White Plains, N.Y. ... 6-3/225.
HIGH SCHOOL: Glenn (Kernersville, N.C.).
COLLEGE: Duke.
TRANSACTIONS/CAREER NOTES: Selected by Philadelphia Eagles in fourth round (121st pick overall) of 1996 NFL draft.
MISCELLANEOUS: Selected by Seattle Mariners in 26th round of free-agent draft (June 1, 1992); did not sign. ... Played tight end during the 1992 season; caught 16 passes for 197 yards.

		INTERCEPTIONS			
Year Team	G	No.	Yds.	Avg.	TD
1992—Duke	11	0	0	...	0
1993—Duke	11	3	33	11.0	0
1994—Duke	11	2	0	0.0	0
1995—Duke	11	2	-2	-1.0	0
College totals (4 years)	44	7	31	4.4	0

FISCHER, SPENCE   QB   STEELERS

PERSONAL: Born November 30, 1972, in Atlanta ... 6-4/220.
HIGH SCHOOL: The Lovett School (Atlanta)
COLLEGE: Duke.
TRANSACTIONS/CAREER NOTES: Selected by Pittsburgh Steelers in sixth round (203rd pick overall) of 1996 NFL draft.

		PASSING								RUSHING				TOTALS	
Year Team	G	Att.	Cmp.	Pct.	Yds.	TD	Int.	Avg.	Rat.	Att.	Yds.	Avg.	TD	TD	Pts.
1991—Duke					Did not play.										
1992—Duke	9	197	113	57.4	1505	8	10	7.64	124.9	69	160	2.3	1	1	6
1993—Duke	11	388	213	54.9	2563	12	14	6.61	112.9	48	167	3.5	0	0	0
1994—Duke	11	346	204	59.0	2285	16	8	6.61	125.2	62	153	2.5	3	3	18
1995—Duke	11	438	256	58.5	2668	12	14	6.09	111.7	64	104	1.6	3	3	18
College totals (4 years)	42	1369	786	57.4	9021	48	46	6.59	117.6	243	584	2.4	7	7	42

FISHER, JOHN   S   JAGUARS

PERSONAL: Born July 28, 1973, in Oakland. ... 5-10/197.
HIGH SCHOOL: Skyline (Oakland).
COLLEGE: Missouri Western.
TRANSACTIONS/CAREER NOTES: Selected by Jacksonville Jaguars in sixth round (170th pick overall) of 1996 NFL draft. ... Signed by Jaguars (May 25, 1996).
MISCELLANEOUS: Played running back during the 1993, 1994 and 1995 seasons. ... Rushed three times for 45 yards and two touchdowns and returned one fumble for 85 yards and a touchown (1993); rushed 11 times for 17 yards and five touchdowns and returned one fumble for 73 yards and a touchdown (1994); rushed 240 times for 1,274 yards and 11 touchdowns and caught 14 passes for 163 yards and three touchdowns (1995).

		INTERCEPTIONS			
Year Team	G	No.	Yds.	Avg.	TD
1993—Missouri Western	11	2	114	57.0	1
1994—Missouri Western	11	6	126	21.0	1
1995—Missouri Western	10	1	25	25.0	0
College totals (3 years)	32	9	265	29.5	2

FLANAGAN, MIKE   C   PACKERS

PERSONAL: Born November 10, 1973, in Washington, D.C. ... 6-5/290. ... Full name: Michael Christopher Flanagan.
HIGH SCHOOL: Rio Americano (Sacramento).
COLLEGE: UCLA.
TRANSACTIONS/CAREER NOTES: Selected by Green Bay Packers in third round (90th pick overall) of 1996 NFL draft.
COLLEGE PLAYING EXPERIENCE: UCLA, 1992-1995. ... Games: 1992 (1), 1993 (11), 1994 (11), 1995 (11). Total: 34.

FOLEY, MIKE   DT   CARDINALS

PERSONAL: Born November 12, 1971, in Worcester, Mass. ... 6-3/290.
HIGH SCHOOL: St. John's (Worcester, Mass.), then Worcester (Mass.) Academy
COLLEGE: New Hampshire.
TRANSACTIONS/CAREER NOTES: Selected by Arizona Cardinals in sixth round (169th pick overall) of 1996 NFL draft.

Year Team	G	SACKS
1992—New Hampshire	9	3.0
1993—New Hampshire	9	11.0
1994—New Hampshire	10	12.0
1995—New Hampshire	10	4.0
College totals (4 years)	38	30.0

FORD, BRAD   CB   LIONS

PERSONAL: Born January 11, 1974, in Alexander City, Ala. ... 5-10/170.

HIGH SCHOOL: Dadeville (Ala.)
JUNIOR COLLEGE: Fresno (Calif.) City Community College.
COLLEGE: Alabama.
TRANSACTIONS/CAREER NOTES: Selected by Detroit Lions in fourth round (129th pick overall) of 1996 NFL draft.

Year Team	G	INTERCEPTIONS				PUNT RETURNS				KICKOFF RETURNS				TOTALS	
		No.	Yds.	Avg.	TD	No.	Yds.	Avg.	TD	No.	Yds.	Avg.	TD	TD	Pts.
1992—Fresno City Community College	10	4	136	34.0	1	12	67	5.6	0	29	838	28.9	0	1	6
1993—Fresno City Community College	10	2	30	15.0	0	14	115	8.2	0	0	0	...	0	0	0
1994—Alabama	12	0	0	...	0	1	2	2.0	0	0	0	...	0	0	0
1995—Alabama	11	2	46	23.0	1	0	0	...	0	0	0	...	0	1	6
Junior totals (2 years)	20	6	166	27.7	1	26	182	7.0	0	29	838	28.9	0	1	6
College totals (2 years)	23	2	46	23.0	1	1	2	2.0	0	0	0	...	0	1	6

GALYON, SCOTT LB GIANTS

PERSONAL: Born March 23, 1974, in Seymour, Tenn. ... 6-2/237.
HIGH SCHOOL: Seymour (Tenn.).
COLLEGE: Tennessee (degree in education business marketing, 1996).
TRANSACTIONS/CAREER NOTES: Selected by New York Giants in sixth round (182nd pick overall) of 1996 NFL draft.

Year Team	G	INTERCEPTIONS				SACKS
		No.	Yds.	Avg.	TD	No.
1992—Tennessee	12	0	0	...	0	0.5
1993—Tennessee	12	1	37	37.0	0	1.0
1994—Tennessee	12	1	0	0.0	0	1.0
1995—Tennessee	11	2	10	5.0	0	1.0
College totals (4 years)	47	4	47	11.8	0	3.5

GARDENER, DARYL DE DOLPHINS

PERSONAL: Born February 25, 1973, in Lawton, Okla. ... 6-6/320.
HIGH SCHOOL: Lawton (Okla.).
COLLEGE: Baylor.
TRANSACTIONS/CAREER NOTES: Selected by Miami Dolphins in first round (20th pick overall) of 1996 NFL draft. ... Signed by Dolphins (June 6, 1996).

Year Team	G	SACKS
1992—Baylor	10	3.0
1993—Baylor	11	4.0
1994—Baylor	11	4.5
1995—Baylor	11	3.5
College totals (4 years)	43	15.0

GARRIDO, NORBERTO OT PANTHERS

PERSONAL: Born October 4, 1972, in La Puente, Calif. ... 6-7/313.
HIGH SCHOOL: Workman (La Puente, Calif.).
COLLEGE: Southern California.
TRANSACTIONS/CAREER NOTES: Selected by Carolina Panthers in fourth round (106th pick overall) of 1996 NFL draft.
COLLEGE PLAYING EXPERIENCE: Southern California, 1993-1995. ... Games: 1993 (12), 1994 (11), 1995 (11). Total: 34.

GASKINS, PERCELL LB RAMS

PERSONAL: Born April 25, 1972, in Daytona Beach, Fla. ... 6-0/225.
HIGH SCHOOL: Seabreeze (Ormand Beach, Fla.).
COLLEGE: Northwestern Oklahoma State, then Kansas State.
TRANSACTIONS/CAREER NOTES: Selected by St. Louis Rams in fourth round (105th pick overall) of 1996 NFL draft.
MISCELLANEOUS: Won NCAA indoor high jump championship (1993).

Year Team	G	INTERCEPTIONS				SACKS
		No.	Yds.	Avg.	TD	No.
1991—Northwestern Oklahoma State	8	0	0	...	0	0.0
1992—Kansas State				Redshirted.		
1993—Kansas State	9	0	0	...	0	1.0
1994—Kansas State	10	0	0	...	0	5.0
1995—Kansas State	11	1	0	0.0	0	2.0
College totals (4 years)	38	1	0	0.0	0	8.0

GEORGE, EDDIE RB OILERS

PERSONAL: Born September 24, 1973, in Philadelphia. ... 6-3/232.
HIGH SCHOOL: Abington (Philadelphia), then Fork Union (Va.) Military Academy.
COLLEGE: Ohio State.
TRANSACTIONS/CAREER NOTES: Selected by Houston Oilers in first round (14th pick overall) of 1996 NFL draft.
HONORS: Heisman Trophy winner (1995). ... Maxwell Award winner (1995). ... Doak Walker Award winner (1995). ... Named running back on THE SPORTING NEWS college All-America first team (1995).

Year Team	G	RUSHING				RECEIVING				TOTALS	
		Att.	Yds.	Avg.	TD	No.	Yds.	Avg.	TD	TD	Pts.
1992—Ohio State	11	37	176	4.8	5	0	0	...	0	5	30
1993—Ohio State	10	42	223	5.3	3	0	0	...	0	3	18
1994—Ohio State	12	261	1353	5.2	12	16	117	7.3	0	12	72
1995—Ohio State	12	303	1826	6.0	23	44	399	9.1	1	24	144
College totals (4 years)	45	643	3578	5.6	43	60	516	8.6	1	44	264

GLENN, TERRY — WR — PATRIOTS

PERSONAL: Born July 23, 1974, in Columbus, Ohio. ... 5-10/184.
HIGH SCHOOL: Brookhaven (Columbus, Ohio).
COLLEGE: Ohio State.
TRANSACTIONS/CAREER NOTES: Selected after junior season by New England Patriots in the first round (seventh pick overall) of 1996 NFL draft.
HONORS: Fred Biletnikoff Award winner (1995). ... Named wide receiver on THE SPORTING NEWS college All-America first team (1995).

Year Team	G	RUSHING				RECEIVING				KICKOFF RETURNS				TOTALS	
		Att.	Yds.	Avg.	TD	No.	Yds.	Avg.	TD	No.	Yds.	Avg.	TD	TD	Pts.
1992—Ohio State						Redshirted.									
1993—Ohio State	9	1	-7	-7.0	0	8	156	19.5	0	10	241	24.1	0	0	0
1994—Ohio State	9	1	5	5.0	0	7	110	15.7	0	0	0	...	0	0	0
1995—Ohio State	11	3	37	12.3	0	57	1316	23.1	17	8	158	19.8	0	17	102
College totals (3 years)	29	5	35	7.0	0	72	1582	22.0	17	18	399	22.2	0	17	102

GLOVER, La'ROI — DT — RAIDERS

PERSONAL: Born July 4, 1974, in San Diego. ... 6-0/281. ... Full name: La'Roi Damon Glover. ... Name pronounced la-ROY.
HIGH SCHOOL: Point Loma (San Diego).
COLLEGE: San Diego State.
TRANSACTIONS/CAREER NOTES: Selected by Oakland Raiders in fifth round (166th pick overall) of 1996 NFL draft.

Year Team	G	SACKS
1992—San Diego State	10	3.0
1993—San Diego State	11	6.0
1994—San Diego State	11	5.0
1995—San Diego State	10	4.5
College totals (4 years)	42	18.5

GODFREY, RANDALL — LB — COWBOYS

PERSONAL: Born April 6, 1973, in Valdosta, Ga. ... 6-2/237. ... Full name: Randall Euralentris Godfrey.
HIGH SCHOOL: Lowndes County (Valdosta, Ga.).
COLLEGE: Georgia.
TRANSACTIONS/CAREER NOTES: Selected by Dallas Cowboys in second round (49th pick overall) of 1996 NFL draft.

Year Team	G	INTERCEPTIONS				SACKS
		No.	Yds.	Avg.	TD	No.
1992—Georgia	11	1	7	7.0	0	1.0
1993—Georgia	11	1	46	46.0	1	1.0
1994—Georgia	11	0	0	...	0	2.0
1995—Georgia	7	0	0	...	0	0.0
College totals (4 years)	40	2	53	26.5	1	4.0

GOODWIN, HUNTER — TE — VIKINGS

PERSONAL: Born October 10, 1972, in Bellville, Texas. ... 6-5/277. ... Full name: Robert Hunter Goodwin.
HIGH SCHOOL: Bellville (Texas).
COLLEGE: Texas A&I, then Texas A&M.
TRANSACTIONS/CAREER NOTES: Selected by Minnesota Vikings in fourth round (97th pick overall) of 1996 NFL draft.
MISCELLANEOUS: Credited with two two-point conversions (1992). ... Played offensive tackle during the 1994 and 1995 seasons.

Year Team	G	RECEIVING			
		No.	Yds.	Avg.	TD
1991—Texas A&I	...	0	0	...	0
1992—Texas A&I	...	12	192	16.0	1
1993—Texas A&M			Did not play.		
1994—Texas A&M	11	0	0	...	0
1995—Texas A&M	11	0	0	...	0
College totals (4 years)	...	12	192	16.0	1

GRAGERT, BRIAN — P — BRONCOS

PERSONAL: Born August 14, 1972, in Lincoln, Neb. ... 6-0/228.
HIGH SCHOOL: Elkhorn (Neb.).
COLLEGE: Wyoming.
TRANSACTIONS/CAREER NOTES: Selected by Denver Broncos in seventh round (236th pick overall) of 1996 NFL draft.

Year Team		G	No.	Yds.	Avg.	PUNTING Net avg.	In. 20	Blk.
1991—Wyoming						Redshirted.		
1992—Wyoming		12	67	2461	36.7	34.4	21	2
1993—Wyoming		11	53	2134	40.3	39.3	18	1
1994—Wyoming		12	72	3014	41.9	39.5	22	4
1995—Wyoming		11	40	1808	45.2	40.6	16	0
College totals (4 years)		46	232	9417	40.6	38.2	77	7

GRAHAM, AARON   C   CARDINALS

PERSONAL: Born May 22, 1973, in Las Vegas, N.M. ... 6-3/295.
HIGH SCHOOL: Denton (Texas)
COLLEGE: Nebraska.
TRANSACTIONS/CAREER NOTES: Selected by Arizona Cardinals in fourth round (112th pick overall) of 1996 NFL draft.
COLLEGE PLAYING EXPERIENCE: Nebraska, 1992-1995. ... Games: 1992 (11), 1993 (11), 1994 (12), 1995 (11). Total: 45.

GRASMANIS, PAUL   DT   BEARS

PERSONAL: Born August 2, 1974, in Grand Rapids, Mich. ... 6-2/295. ... Full name: Paul Ryan Grasmanis.
HIGH SCHOOL: Jenison (Mich.).
COLLEGE: Notre Dame.
TRANSACTIONS/CAREER NOTES: Selected by Chicago Bears in fourth round (116th pick overall) of 1996 NFL draft.

Year Team	G	SACKS
1992—Notre Dame	8	0.0
1993—Notre Dame	8	0.0
1994—Notre Dame	11	2.5
1995—Notre Dame	11	4.5
College totals (4 years)	38	7.0

GREEN, REGGIE   G   SEAHAWKS

PERSONAL: Born November 23, 1973, in Bradenton, Fla. ... 6-5/310.
HIGH SCHOOL: Southeast (Bradenton, Fla.)
COLLEGE: Florida.
TRANSACTIONS/CAREER NOTES: Selected by Seattle Seahawks in sixth round (184th pick overall) of 1996 NFL draft.
COLLEGE PLAYING EXPERIENCE: Florida, 1992-1995. ... Games: 1992 (12), 1993 (11), 1994 (11), 1995 (12). Total: 46.

GREENE, SCOTT   FB   PANTHERS

PERSONAL: Born June 1, 1972, in Honeoye, N.Y. ... 5-11/230.
HIGH SCHOOL: Canandaigua (N.Y.) Academy
COLLEGE: Michigan State.
TRANSACTIONS/CAREER NOTES: Selected by Carolina Panthers in sixth round (193rd pick overall) of 1996 NFL draft.

Year Team	G	RUSHING Att.	Yds.	Avg.	TD	RECEIVING No.	Yds.	Avg.	TD	KICKOFF RETURNS No.	Yds.	Avg.	TD	TOTALS TD	Pts.
1992—Michigan State	10	3	6	2.0	0	4	36	9.0	0	12	238	19.8	0	0	0
1993—Michigan State	11	1	10	10.0	0	31	306	9.9	4	2	32	16.0	0	4	24
1994—Michigan State	11	68	375	5.5	2	42	452	10.8	3	0	0	...	0	5	30
1995—Michigan State	11	125	590	4.7	17	33	291	8.8	0	2	17	8.5	0	17	102
College totals (4 years)	43	197	981	5.0	19	110	1085	9.9	7	16	287	17.9	0	26	156

GRIER, MARRIO   RB   PATRIOTS

PERSONAL: Born December 5, 1971, in Charlotte, N.C. ... 6-0/238.
HIGH SCHOOL: Independence (Charlotte).
COLLEGE: Clemson, then Tennessee-Chattanooga.
TRANSACTIONS/CAREER NOTES: Selected by New England Patriots in sixth round (195th pick overall) of 1996 NFL draft.

Year Team	G	RUSHING Att.	Yds.	Avg.	TD	RECEIVING No.	Yds.	Avg.	TD	TOTALS TD	Pts.
1991—Clemson					Redshirted.						
1992—Clemson	10	25	83	3.4	2	3	31	10.3	0	2	12
1993—Tennessee-Chattanooga	4	7	38	5.4	0	0	0	...	0	0	0
1994—Tennessee-Chattanooga	11	111	544	4.9	2	28	204	7.3	1	3	18
1995—Tennessee-Chattanooga	11	161	743	4.6	7	26	192	7.4	2	9	54
College totals (4 years)	36	304	1408	4.6	11	57	427	7.5	3	14	84

GRIFFIN, CHRIS   TE   PATRIOTS

PERSONAL: Born July 26, 1974, in Lafayette, La. ... 6-4/257. ... Full name: Chris David Griffin.
HIGH SCHOOL: Putnam North (Oklahoma City).
COLLEGE: New Mexico.

TRANSACTIONS/CAREER NOTES: Selected by New England Patriots in sixth round (173rd pick overall) of 1996 NFL draft.

		RECEIVING			
Year Team	G	No.	Yds.	Avg.	TD
1992—New Mexico	11	3	28	9.3	3
1993—New Mexico	11	8	87	10.9	1
1994—New Mexico	12	12	179	14.9	3
1995—New Mexico	7	7	107	15.3	2
College totals (4 years)	41	30	401	13.4	9

GUESS, TERRY — WR/KR — SAINTS

PERSONAL: Born September 22, 1974, in Orangeburg, S.C. ... 6-0/200.
HIGH SCHOOL: Edisto (Orangeburg, S.C.).
JUNIOR COLLEGE: Georgia Military College.
COLLEGE: Gardner-Webb (N.C.).
TRANSACTIONS/CAREER NOTES: Selected after junior season by New Orleans Saints in fifth round (165th pick overall) of 1996 NFL draft.

		RUSHING				RECEIVING				PUNT RETURNS				KICKOFF RETURNS				TOTALS	
Year Team	G	Att.	Yds.	Avg.	TD	No.	Yds.	Avg.	TD	No.	Yds.	Avg.	TD	No.	Yds.	Avg.	TD	TD	Pts.
1992—Georgia Military College							Statistics unavailable.												
1993—Georgia Military College							Redshirted.												
1994—Gardner-Webb	11	41	341	8.3	4	29	379	13.1	1	16	312	19.5	3	23	575	25.0	3	11	66
1995—Gardner-Webb	5	23	129	5.6	1	18	244	13.6	1	4	15	3.8	0	2	35	17.5	0	3	18
Junior College totals (1 year)	...	...	...	...	...	...	...	...	...	...	...	...	...	...	...	...	...	...	...
College totals (2 years)	16	64	470	7.4	5	47	623	13.3	2	20	327	16.4	3	25	610	24.4	3	14	84

HALL, TIM — RB — RAIDERS

PERSONAL: Born February 15, 1974, in Kansas City, Mo. ... 6-0/217.
HIGH SCHOOL: Northeast (Kansas City, Mo.).
JUNIOR COLLEGE: Kemper Military School and College (Mo.).
COLLEGE: Robert Morris.
TRANSACTIONS/CAREER NOTES: Selected by Oakland Raiders in sixth round (183rd pick overall) of 1996 NFL draft.

		RUSHING				RECEIVING				TOTALS	
Year Team	G	Att.	Yds.	Avg.	TD	No.	Yds.	Avg.	TD	TD	Pts.
1992—Kemper Military School and College						Statistics unavailable.					
1993—Kemper Military School and College						Statistics unavailable.					
1994—Robert Morris	9	154	1336	8.7	11	26	460	17.7	3	14	84
1995—Robert Morris	10	239	1572	6.6	16	31	333	10.7	4	20	120
Junior College totals (2 years)	...	...	...	...	...	...	...	...	...	...	...
College totals (2 years)	19	393	2908	7.4	27	57	793	13.9	7	34	204

HAMILTON, CONRAD — S — GIANTS

PERSONAL: Born November 5, 1974, in Alamogordo, N.M. ... 5-10/184.
HIGH SCHOOL: Alamogordo (N.M.).
JUNIOR COLLEGE: New Mexico Military Institute.
COLLEGE: New Mexico Military Institute, then Eastern New Mexico.
TRANSACTIONS/CAREER NOTES: Selected by New York Giants in seventh round (214th pick overall) of 1996 NFL draft.

		INTERCEPTIONS				SACKS
Year Team	G	No.	Yds.	Avg.	TD	No.
1992—New Mexico Military Institute	10	2	0	0.0	0	0.0
1993—Eastern New Mexico	10	0	0	...	0	3.0
1994—Eastern New Mexico	11	4	63	15.8	0	4.0
1995—Eastern New Mexico	9	2	26	13.0	0	0.0
Junior college totals (1 year)	10	2	0	0.0	0	0.0
College totals (3 years)	30	6	89	11.1	0	7.0

HARDY, KEVIN — LB — JAGUARS

PERSONAL: Born July 24, 1973, in Evansville, Ind. ... 6-4/245.
HIGH SCHOOL: Harrison (Evansville, Ind.).
COLLEGE: Illinois (degree in marketing, 1995).
TRANSACTIONS/CAREER NOTES: Selected by Jacksonville Jaguars in first round (second pick overall) of 1996 NFL draft.
HONORS: Butkus Award winner (1995). ... Named linebacker on THE SPORTING NEWS college All-America first team (1995).

		INTERCEPTIONS				SACKS
Year Team	G	No.	Yds.	Avg.	TD	No.
1991—Illinois				Redshirted.		
1992—Illinois	10	0	0	...	0	4.0
1993—Illinois	11	0	0	...	0	2.0
1994—Illinois	11	1	19	19.0	0	1.0
1995—Illinois	11	3	26	8.7	0	11.0
College totals (4 years)	43	4	45	11.3	0	18.0

HARRIS, DERRICK — RB — RAMS

PERSONAL: Born September 18, 1972, in Willowridge, Texas ... 6-0/253.
HIGH SCHOOL: Willowridge (Texas).
COLLEGE: Miami (Fla.).
TRANSACTIONS/CAREER NOTES: Selected by St. Louis Rams in sixth round (175th pick overall) of 1996 NFL draft.
MISCELLANEOUS: Played linebacker during the 1992 season.

| | | RUSHING | | | | RECEIVING | | | | TOTALS | |
Year Team	G	Att.	Yds.	Avg.	TD	No.	Yds.	Avg.	TD	TD	Pts.
1991—Miami (Fla.)				Redshirted.							
1992—Miami (Fla.)	11	0	0	...	0	0	0	...	0	0	0
1993—Miami (Fla.)	11	26	101	3.9	2	1	-3	-3.0	0	2	12
1994—Miami (Fla.)	10	4	3	.8	1	1	1	1.0	1	2	12
1995—Miami (Fla.)	11	16	42	2.6	1	10	77	7.7	0	1	6
College totals (4 years)	43	46	146	3.2	4	12	75	6.3	1	5	30

HARRIS, WALT — CB — BEARS

PERSONAL: Born August 10, 1974, in LaGrange, Ga. ... 5-11/188. ... Full name: Walter Lee Harris.
HIGH SCHOOL: LaGrange (Ga.).
COLLEGE: Mississippi State.
TRANSACTIONS/CAREER NOTES: Selected by Chicago Bears in first round (13th pick overall) of 1996 NFL draft.
MISCELLANEOUS: Returned one fumble 46 yards for a touchdown (1994).

| | | INTERCEPTIONS | | | |
Year Team	G	No.	Yds.	Avg.	TD
1992—Mississippi State	10	0	0	...	0
1993—Mississippi State	11	6	59	9.8	0
1994—Mississippi State	11	6	41	6.8	1
1995—Mississippi State	11	4	62	15.5	1
College totals (4 years)	43	16	162	10.1	2

HARRISON, MARVIN — WR — COLTS

PERSONAL: Born August 25, 1972, in Philadelphia. ... 6-0/188. ... Full name: Marvin Daniel Harrison.
HIGH SCHOOL: Roman Catholic (Philadelphia).
COLLEGE: Syracuse.
TRANSACTIONS/CAREER NOTES: Selected by Indianapolis Colts in first round (19th pick overall) of 1996 NFL draft.
HONORS: Named kick returner on THE SPORTING NEWS All-America first team (1995).
MISCELLANEOUS: Rushed three times for minus ten yards (1993); rushed five times for 65 yards and a touchdown (1994); and rushed five times for 69 yards (1995).

| | | RECEIVING | | | | PUNT RETURNS | | | | KICKOFF RETURNS | | | | TOTALS | |
Year Team	G	No.	Yds.	Avg.	TD	No.	Yds.	Avg.	TD	No.	Yds.	Avg.	TD	TD	Pts.
1991—Syracuse								Redshirted.							
1992—Syracuse	10	2	13	6.5	0	1	5	5.0	0	0	0	...	0	0	0
1993—Syracuse	11	41	813	19.8	7	1	3	3.0	0	1	18	18.0	0	7	42
1994—Syracuse	10	36	761	21.1	5	18	165	9.2	0	0	0	...	0	6	36
1995—Syracuse	11	56	1131	20.2	8	22	369	16.8	2	0	0	...	0	10	60
College totals (4 years)	42	135	2718	20.1	20	42	542	12.9	2	1	18	18.0	0	23	138

HARTINGS, JEFF — G — LIONS

PERSONAL: Born September 7, 1972, in Henry, Ohio. ... 6-3/283. ... Full name: Jeffrey Allen Hartings.
HIGH SCHOOL: St. Henry (Ohio).
COLLEGE: Penn State.
TRANSACTIONS/CAREER NOTES: Selected by Detroit Lions in first round (23rd pick overall) of 1996 NFL draft.
COLLEGE PLAYING EXPERIENCE: Penn State, 1992-1995. ... Games: 1992 (12), 1993 (11), 1994 (11), 1995 (11). Total: 45.
HONORS: Named offensive lineman on THE SPORTING NEWS college All-America second team (1994). ... Named offensive lineman on THE SPORTING NEWS college All-America first team (1995).

HAYES, CHRIS — DB — JETS

PERSONAL: Born May 7, 1972, in San Bernardino, Calif. ... 5-11/191.
HIGH SCHOOL: San Gorgonio (San Bernardino, Calif.).
COLLEGE: Washington State.
TRANSACTIONS/CAREER NOTES: Selected by New York Jets in seventh round (210th pick overall) of 1996 NFL draft.

| | | INTERCEPTIONS | | | | SACKS |
Year Team	G	No.	Yds.	Avg.	TD	No.
1991—Washington State				Redshirted.		
1992—Washington State	10	0	0	...	0	0.0
1993—Washington State	10	1	44	44.0	1	1.0
1994—Washington State	11	2	68	34.0	0	1.0
1995—Washington State	11	1	0	0.0	0	1.5
College totals (4 years)	42	4	112	28.0	1	3.5

HAYES, JARIUS   TE   CARDINALS

PERSONAL: Born March 27, 1973, in Sheffield, Ala. ... 6-3/255.
HIGH SCHOOL: Muscle Shoals (Ala.)
COLLEGE: North Alabama.
TRANSACTIONS/CAREER NOTES: Selected by Arizona Cardinals in seventh round (212th pick overall) of 1996 NFL draft.

		RUSHING				RECEIVING				TOTALS	
Year Team	G	Att.	Yds.	Avg.	TD	No.	Yds.	Avg.	TD	TD	Pts.
1992—North Alabama	10	0	0	...	0	3	94	31.3	0	0	0
1993—North Alabama	10	0	0	...	0	4	115	28.8	2	2	12
1994—North Alabama	10	8	97	12.1	2	7	86	12.3	1	3	18
1995—North Alabama	10	4	79	19.8	1	7	155	22.1	1	2	12
College totals (4 years)	40	12	176	14.7	3	21	450	21.4	4	7	42

HAYES, MERCURY   WR   SAINTS

PERSONAL: Born January 1, 1973, in Houston. ... 5-11/195.
HIGH SCHOOL: Washington (Houston).
COLLEGE: Michigan.
TRANSACTIONS/CAREER NOTES: Selected by New Orleans Saints in fifth round (136th pick overall) of 1996 NFL draft.

		RUSHING				RECEIVING				PUNT RETURNS				KICKOFF RETURNS				TOTALS	
Year Team	G	Att.	Yds.	Avg.	TD	No.	Yds.	Avg.	TD	No.	Yds.	Avg.	TD	No.	Yds.	Avg.	TD	TD	Pts.
1991—Michigan	11	4	27	6.8	0	28	469	16.8	5	7	73	10.4	0	5	102	20.4	0	5	30
1992—Michigan	11	1	5	5.0	0	9	126	14.0	2	8	74	9.3	0	10	204	20.4	0	2	12
1994—Michigan	11	5	37	7.4	0	33	548	16.6	0	0	0	...	0	15	276	18.4	0	0	0
1995—Michigan	12	9	105	11.7	0	46	888	19.3	4	6	21	3.5	0	14	224	16.0	0	4	24
College totals (4 years)	45	19	174	9.2	0	116	2031	17.5	11	21	168	8.0	0	44	806	18.3	0	11	66

HERNDON, JIMMY   OT   JAGUARS

PERSONAL: Born August 30, 1973, in Baytown, Texas. ... 6-8/304.
HIGH SCHOOL: Lee (Baytown, Texas).
COLLEGE: Houston.
TRANSACTIONS/CAREER NOTES: Selected by Jacksonville Jaguars in fifth round (146th pick overall) of 1996 NFL draft. ... Signed by Jaguars (May 25, 1996).
COLLEGE PLAYING EXPERIENCE: Houston, 1992-1995. ... Games: 1992 (11), 1993 (10), 1994 (11), 1995 (11). Total: 43.

HICKS, KERRY   DL   PANTHERS

PERSONAL: Born December 29, 1972, in McKay, Utah. ... 6-5/261.
HIGH SCHOOL: Highland (Salt Lake City).
COLLEGE: Colorado.
TRANSACTIONS/CAREER NOTES: Selected by Carolina Panthers in seventh round (234th pick overall) of 1996 NFL draft.

Year Team	G	SACKS
1991—Colorado	Redshirted.	
1992—Colorado	9	1.0
1993—Colorado	11	1.0
1994—Colorado	9	2.0
1995—Colorado	11	0.0
College totals (4 years)	40	4.0

HICKS, MICHAEL   RB   BEARS

PERSONAL: Born February 1, 1973, in Barnesville, Ga. ... 6-0/190.
HIGH SCHOOL: Robert E. Lee Institute (Thomaston, Ga.)
COLLEGE: South Carolina State.
TRANSACTIONS/CAREER NOTES: Selected by Chicago Bears in seventh round (253rd pick overall) of 1996 NFL draft.

		RUSHING				RECEIVING				TOTALS	
Year Team	G	Att.	Yds.	Avg.	TD	No.	Yds.	Avg.	TD	TD	Pts.
1991—South Carolina State			Did not play.									
1992—			Did not play.									
1993—South Carolina State	11	221	1388	6.3	17	1	11	11.0	0	17	102
1994—South Carolina State	11	252	1368	5.4	22	3	41	13.7	0	22	132
1995—South Carolina State	10	228	1299	5.7	13	6	78	13.0	1	14	84
College totals (3 years)	32	701	4055	5.9	52	10	130	13.0	1	53	318

HILLS, KENO   OT   SAINTS

PERSONAL: Born June 13, 1973, in Tampa. ... 6-6/320. ... Name pronounced KEY-no.
HIGH SCHOOL: Tampa Tech.
COLLEGE: Kent State, then Southwestern Louisiana.

TRANSACTIONS/CAREER NOTES: Selected by New Orleans Saints in sixth round (179th pick overall) of 1996 NFL draft.
COLLEGE PLAYING EXPERIENCE: Kent State, 1992; Southwestern Louisiana, 1993-1995. ... Games: 1992 (9), 1993 (11), 1994 (11), 1995 (11). Total: 42.

HOLMES, EARL — LB — STEELERS

PERSONAL: Born April 28, 1973, in Tallahassee, Fla. ... 6-1/238.
HIGH SCHOOL: Florida A&M University (Tallahassee, Fla.).
COLLEGE: Florida A&M.
TRANSACTIONS/CAREER NOTES: Selected by Pittsburgh Steelers in fourth round (126th pick overall) of 1996 NFL draft.

| | | INTERCEPTIONS | | | | SACKS |
Year Team	G	No.	Yds.	Avg.	TD	No.
1992—Florida A&M	11	1	40	40.0	1	4.0
1993—Florida A&M	11	0	0	...	0	2.0
1994—Florida A&M	11	2	72	36.0	1	0.5
1995—Florida A&M	11	5	71	14.2	0	0.0
College totals (4 years)	44	8	183	22.9	2	6.5

HORN, JOE — WR — CHIEFS

PERSONAL: Born January 16, 1972, in Tupelo, Miss. ... 6-1/195.
HIGH SCHOOL: Douglas Bird (Fayetteville, N.C.).
JUNIOR COLLEGE: Itawamba (Miss.) Junior College.
TRANSACTIONS/CAREER NOTES: Signed by Baltimore Stallions to practice squad for 1994 season. ... Signed by Memphis Mad Dogs for 1995 season. ... Selected by Kansas City Chiefs in fifth round (135th pick overall) of 1996 NFL draft.

| | | | | | COLLEGIATE RECORD | | | | | | |
| | | RECEIVING | | | | KICKOFF RETURNS | | | | TOTALS | |
Year Team	G	No.	Yds.	Avg.	TD	No.	Yds.	Avg.	TD	TD	Pts.
1991—Itawamba Junior College						Statistics unavailable.					
1992—Itawamba Junior College						Statistics unavailable.					

| | | | | | PROFESSIONAL RECORD | | | | | | |
| | | RECEIVING | | | | KICKOFF RETURNS | | | | TOTALS | |
Year Team	G	No.	Yds.	Avg.	TD	No.	Yds.	Avg.	TD	TD	Pts.
1994—Baltimore CFL						Did not play.					
1995—Memphis CFL	17	71	1415	19.9	5	2	17	8.5	5	5	30

HOYING, BOBBY — QB — EAGLES

PERSONAL: Born September 20, 1972, in St. Henry, Ohio. ... 6-3/221.
HIGH SCHOOL: St. Henry (Ohio).
COLLEGE: Ohio State.
TRANSACTIONS/CAREER NOTES: Selected by Philadelphia Eagles in third round (85th pick overall) of 1996 NFL draft.

| | | | | | PASSING | | | | | | RUSHING | | | | TOTALS | |
Year Team	G	Att.	Cmp.	Pct.	Yds.	TD	Int.	Avg.	Rat.	Att.	Yds.	Avg.	TD	TD	Pts.
1991—Ohio State					Redshirted.										
1992—Ohio State	7	14	8	57.1	58	1	1	4.14	100.9	5	-10	-2.0	0	0	0
1993—Ohio State	11	191	104	54.5	1515	8	8	7.93	125.8	33	-125	-3.8	0	0	0
1994—Ohio State	12	274	159	58.0	2155	17	13	7.87	133.8	58	65	1.1	2	2	12
1995—Ohio State	12	303	192	63.4	3023	28	11	9.98	168.5	52	33	0.6	2	2	12
College totals (4 years)	42	782	463	59.2	6751	54	33	8.63	146.6	148	-37	-0.3	4	4	24

HUNTER, BRICE — WR — DOLPHINS

PERSONAL: Born April 4, 1974, in Valdosta, Ga. ... 6-0/214.
HIGH SCHOOL: Valdosta (Ga.).
COLLEGE: Georgia.
TRANSACTIONS/CAREER NOTES: Selected by Miami Dolphins in seventh round (251st pick overall) of 1996 NFL draft.

| | | RECEIVING | | | | KICKOFF RETURNS | | | | TOTALS | |
Year Team	G	No.	Yds.	Avg.	TD	No.	Yds.	Avg.	TD	TD	Pts.
1992—Georgia	9	3	30	10.0	0	0	0	...	0	0	0
1993—Georgia	11	76	970	12.8	9	0	0	...	0	9	54
1994—Georgia	11	59	799	13.5	7	8	145	18.1	0	7	42
1995—Georgia	11	44	574	13.1	3	4	84	21.0	0	3	18
College totals (4 years)	42	182	2373	13.0	19	12	229	19.1	0	19	114

HUNTER, HUGH — DE — JETS

PERSONAL: Born June 19, 1972, in Portsmouth, Va. ... 6-3/260.
HIGH SCHOOL: Wilson (Portsmouth, Va.).
COLLEGE: Hampton (Va.).
TRANSACTIONS/CAREER NOTES: Selected by New York Jets in sixth round (168th pick overall) of 1996 NFL draft.

Year—Team	G	SACKS
1991—Hampton	Redshirted.	
1992—Hampton	5	0.0
1993—Hampton	11	9.0
1994—Hampton	11	19.0
1995—Hampton	11	16.0
College totals (4 years)	38	44.0

HUNTLEY, RICHARD   RB   FALCONS

PERSONAL: Born September 18, 1972, in Monroe, N.C. ... 5-11/224.
HIGH SCHOOL: Monroe (N.C.).
COLLEGE: Winston-Salem (N.C.) State.
TRANSACTIONS/CAREER NOTES: Selected by Atlanta Falcons in fourth round (117th pick overall) of 1996 NFL draft.

		RUSHING				RECEIVING				TOTALS	
Year—Team	G	Att.	Yds.	Avg.	TD	No.	Yds.	Avg.	TD	TD	Pts.
1991—Winston-Salem						Redshirted.					
1992—Winston-Salem	11	165	1012	6.1	12	15	333	22.2	2	14	84
1993—Winston-Salem	11	220	1570	7.1	10	10	68	6.8	0	10	60
1994—Winston-Salem	11	251	1815	7.2	18	3	34	11.3	0	18	108
1995—Winston-Salem	10	273	1889	6.9	16	9	89	9.9	1	17	102
College totals (4 years)	43	909	6286	6.9	56	37	524	14.2	3	59	354

IFEANYI, ISRAEL   DE   49ERS

PERSONAL: Born November 21, 1970, in Lagos, Nigeria. ... 6-3/246. ... Name pronounced IZ-ray-el if-ee-AHN-ee.
HIGH SCHOOL: Government Secondary School (Lagos, Nigeria).
JUNIOR COLLEGE: Orange Coast Community College (Calif.).
COLLEGE: Southern California.
TRANSACTIONS/CAREER NOTES: Selected by San Francisco 49ers in second round (46th pick overall) of 1996 NFL draft.

		INTERCEPTIONS				SACKS
Year—Team	G	No.	Yds.	Avg.	TD	No.
1992—Orange Coast Community College	9	0	0	...	0	2.0
1993—Orange Coast Community College	10	0	0	...	0	5.0
1994—Southern California	11	1	-2	-2.0	0	2.0
1995—Southern California	7	0	0	...	0	5.0
Junior college totals (2 years)	19	0	0	...	0	7.0
College totals (2 years)	18	1	-2	-2.0	0	7.0

IRWIN, HEATH   G   PATRIOTS

PERSONAL: Born June 27, 1973, in Boulder, Colo. ... 6-4/300. ... Nephew of Hale Irwin, professional golfer.
HIGH SCHOOL: Boulder (Colo.).
COLLEGE: Colorado.
TRANSACTIONS/CAREER NOTES: Selected by New England Patriots in fourth round (101st pick overall) of 1996 NFL draft.
COLLEGE PLAYING EXPERIENCE: Colorado, 1992-1995. ... Games: 1992 (5), 1993 (11), 1994 (11), 1995 (11). Total: 38.

JACKSON, RAYMOND   DB   BILLS

PERSONAL: Born February 17, 1973, in Denver. ... 5-10/189. ... Full name: Raymond DeWayne Jackson.
HIGH SCHOOL: Montbello (Denver).
COLLEGE: Colorado State.
TRANSACTIONS/CAREER NOTES: Selected by Buffalo Bills in fifth round (156th pick overall) of 1996 NFL draft.
MISCELLANEOUS: Returned blocked punt 30 yards for a touchdown (1994).

		INTERCEPTIONS			
Year—Team	G	No.	Yds.	Avg.	TD
1991—Colorado State			Did not play.		
1992—Colorado State	8	2	51	25.5	1
1993—Colorado State	11	5	117	23.4	1
1994—Colorado State	11	6	71	11.8	0
1995—Colorado State	11	5	113	22.6	1
College totals (4 years)	41	18	352	19.6	3

JAMES, TORY   CB   BRONCOS

PERSONAL: Born May 18, 1973, in New Orleans. ... 6-1/188.
HIGH SCHOOL: Archbishop Shaw (Marrero, La.).
COLLEGE: Louisiana State.
TRANSACTIONS/CAREER NOTES: Selected by Denver Broncos in second round (44th pick overall) of 1996 NFL draft.
MISCELLANEOUS: Played wide receiver during the 1992 season; rushed once for minus five yards and caught six passes for 78 yards and a touchdown (1992).

Year Team		G	No.	Yds.	Avg.	TD	No.
			INTERCEPTIONS				**SACKS**
1992—Louisiana State		9	0	0	...	0	0.0
1993—Louisiana State		11	4	87	21.8	0	1.0
1994—Louisiana State		11	5	23	4.6	1	0.0
1995—Louisiana State		8	2	0	0.0	0	1.0
College totals (4 years)		39	11	110	10.0	1	2.0

JEFFERS, PATRICK   WR   BRONCOS

PERSONAL: Born February 2, 1973, in Fort Campbell, Ky. ... 6-3/217. ... Full name: Patrick Christopher Jeffers.
HIGH SCHOOL: Fort Worth (Texas) Country Day.
COLLEGE: Virginia.
TRANSACTIONS/CAREER NOTES: Selected by Denver Broncos in fifth round (159th pick overall) of 1996 NFL draft.

Year Team		G	No.	Yds.	Avg.	TD
			RECEIVING			
1991—Virginia				Redshirted.		
1992—Virginia		11	9	128	14.2	3
1993—Virginia		9	32	580	18.1	6
1994—Virginia		11	33	560	17.0	3
1995—Virginia		8	34	517	15.2	3
College totals (4 years)		39	108	1785	16.5	15

ELLS, DIETRICH   WR   CHIEFS

PERSONAL: Born April 11, 1972, in Erie, Pa. ... 5-10/186. ... Name pronounced DEE-trick.
HIGH SCHOOL: Tech Memorial (Erie, Pa.).
COLLEGE: Pittsburgh.
TRANSACTIONS/CAREER NOTES: Selected by Kansas City Chiefs in sixth round (176th pick overall) of 1996 NFL draft.
MISCELLANEOUS: Granted medical redshirt due to knee injury (1993).

Year Team	G	No.	Yds.	Avg.	TD	No.	Yds.	Avg.	TD	TD	Pts.
		RECEIVING				**KICKOFF RETURNS**				**TOTALS**	
1991—Pittsburgh	10	12	339	28.3	3	0	0	...	0	3	18
1992—Pittsburgh	12	55	1091	19.8	8	7	143	20.4	0	8	48
1993—Pittsburgh	3	10	171	17.1	2	18	399	22.2	0	2	12
1994—Pittsburgh	11	35	613	17.5	4	3	83	27.7	0	4	24
1995—Pittsburgh	10	48	789	16.4	8	10	206	20.6	0	8	48
College totals (5 years)	46	160	3003	18.8	25	38	831	21.9	0	25	150

JENKINS, DeRON   CB   RAVENS

PERSONAL: Born November 14, 1973, in St. Louis. ... 5-11/177. ... Full name: DeRon Charles Jenkins.
HIGH SCHOOL: Ritenour (St. Louis).
COLLEGE: Tennessee.
TRANSACTIONS/CAREER NOTES: Selected by Baltimore Ravens in second round (55th pick overall) of 1996 NFL draft.

Year Team		G	No.	Yds.	Avg.	TD
			INTERCEPTIONS			
1992—Tennessee		11	2	5	2.5	0
1993—Tennessee		11	5	13	2.6	0
1994—Tennessee		8	1	0	0.0	0
1995—Tennessee		11	4	33	8.3	0
College totals (4 years)		41	12	51	4.3	0

JOHNSON, ANDRE   OT   REDSKINS

PERSONAL: Born August 25, 1973, in Southampton, N.Y. ... 6-5/309.
HIGH SCHOOL: Southhampton (N.Y.).
COLLEGE: Penn State.
TRANSACTIONS/CAREER NOTES: Selected by Washington Redskins in first round (30th pick overall) of 1996 NFL draft.
COLLEGE PLAYING EXPERIENCE: Penn State, 1992-1995. ... Games: 1992 (4), 1993 (11), 1994 (11), 1995 (11). Total: 37.

JOHNSON, DARRIUS   CB   BRONCOS

PERSONAL: Born September 17, 1972, in Terrell, Texas. ... 5-9/175.
HIGH SCHOOL: Terrell (Texas).
COLLEGE: Oklahoma.
TRANSACTIONS/CAREER NOTES: Selected by Denver Broncos in fourth round (122nd pick overall) of 1996 NFL draft.

Year Team	G	No.	Yds.	Avg.	TD	No.	Yds.	Avg.	TD	No.	Yds.	Avg.	TD	TD	Pts.
		INTERCEPTIONS				**PUNT RETURNS**				**KICKOFF RETURNS**				**TOTALS**	
1991—Oklahoma				Redshirted.											
1992—Oklahoma	11	3	65	21.7	1	0	0	...	0	0	0	...	0	1	6
1993—Oklahoma	11	5	36	7.2	0	25	212	8.5	0	7	162	23.1	0	0	0
1994—Oklahoma	11	4	54	13.5	0	34	254	7.5	1	4	54	13.5	0	1	6

Year Team	G	INTERCEPTIONS				PUNT RETURNS				KICKOFF RETURNS				TOTALS	
		No.	Yds.	Avg.	TD	No.	Yds.	Avg.	TD	No.	Yds.	Avg.	TD	TD	Pts.
1995—Oklahoma	11	0	0	...	0	12	75	6.3	0	4	60	15.0	0	0	0
College totals (4 years)	44	12	155	12.9	1	71	541	7.6	1	15	276	18.4	0	2	12

JOHNSON, KEYSHAWN   WR   JETS

PERSONAL: Born July 22, 1972, in Los Angeles. ... 6-3/215.
HIGH SCHOOL: Dorsey (Los Angeles).
JUNIOR COLLEGE: West Los Angeles College.
COLLEGE: Southern California.
TRANSACTIONS/CAREER NOTES: Selected by New York Jets in first round (first pick overall) of 1996 NFL draft.
HONORS: Named wide receiver on THE SPORTING NEWS college All-America first team (1995).
MISCELLANEOUS: Played safety during the 1991 season.

Year Team	G	RECEIVING			
		No.	Yds.	Avg.	TD
1991—West Los Angeles	4	0	0	...	0
1992—West Los Angeles		Did not play.			
1993—West Los Angeles	9	55	1245	22.6	22
1994—Southern California	10	58	1140	19.7	6
1995—Southern California	11	90	1218	13.5	6
Junior college totals (2 years)	13	55	1245	22.6	22
College totals (2 years)	21	148	2358	15.9	12

JOHNSON, TONY   TE   EAGLES

PERSONAL: Born February 5, 1972, in Como, Miss. ... 6-5/256.
HIGH SCHOOL: North Panola (Sardis, Miss.)
COLLEGE: Alabama.
TRANSACTIONS/CAREER NOTES: Selected by Philadelphia Eagles in sixth round (197th pick overall) of 1996 NFL draft.

Year Team	G	RECEIVING			
		No.	Yds.	Avg.	TD
1991—Alabama		Redshirted.			
1992—Alabama	12	0	0	...	0
1993—Alabama	12	12	117	9.8	1
1994—Alabama	12	2	48	24.0	0
1995—Alabama	11	7	132	18.9	0
College totals (4 years)	47	21	297	14.2	1

JOHNSTONE, LANCE   LB   RAIDERS

PERSONAL: Born June 11, 1973, in Philadelphia. ... 6-3/233.
HIGH SCHOOL: Germantown (Pa.).
COLLEGE: Temple.
TRANSACTIONS/CAREER NOTES: Selected by Oakland Raiders in second round (57th pick overall) of 1996 NFL draft.
MISCELLANEOUS: Recovered one fumble for five yards and a touchdown.

Year Team	G	INTERCEPTIONS				SACKS
		No.	Yds.	Avg.	TD	No.
1991—Temple			Redshirted.			
1992—Temple	11	1	0	0.0	0	9.0
1993—Temple	11	1	14	14.0	0	2.0
1994—Temple	11	1	8	8.0	0	1.0
1995—Temple	11	0	0	...	0	3.0
College totals (4 years)	44	3	22	7.3	0	15.0

JONES, CEDRIC   DE   GIANTS

PERSONAL: Born April 30, 1974, in Houston ... 6-4/275.
HIGH SCHOOL: Lamar (Houston).
COLLEGE: Oklahoma.
TRANSACTIONS/CAREER NOTES: Selected by New York Giants in first round (fifth pick overall) of 1996 NFL draft.
HONORS: Named defensive lineman on THE SPORTING NEWS college All-America first team (1995).

Year Team	G	SACKS
1992—Oklahoma	11	3.5
1993—Oklahoma	10	3.0
1994—Oklahoma	11	14.0
1995—Oklahoma	9	11.0
College totals (4 years)	41	31.5

JONES, CHARLIE   WR   CHARGERS

PERSONAL: Born December 1, 1972, in Hanford, Calif. ... 5-8/175.
HIGH SCHOOL: Lemoore (Calif.).

COLLEGE: Fresno State.
TRANSACTIONS/CAREER NOTES: Selected by San Diego Chargers in fourth round (114th pick overall) of 1996 NFL draft.

Year Team	G	RUSHING				RECEIVING				PUNT RETURNS				KICKOFF RETURNS				TOTALS	
		Att.	Yds.	Avg.	TD	No.	Yds.	Avg.	TD	No.	Yds.	Avg.	TD	No.	Yds.	Avg.	TD	TD	Pts.
1991—Fresno State									Redshirted.										
1992—Fresno State	12	5	34	6.8	0	15	305	20.3	3	14	168	12.0	1	1	12	12.0	0	4	24
1993—Fresno State	11	5	139	27.8	2	41	813	19.8	7	11	30	2.7	0	3	46	15.3	0	9	54
1994—Fresno State	13	7	32	4.6	0	54	971	18.0	6	9	55	6.1	0	2	22	11.0	0	6	36
1995—Fresno State	12	5	28	5.6	0	71	1171	16.5	9	2	25	12.5	0	0	0	...	0	9	54
College totals (4 years)	48	22	233	10.6	2	181	3260	18.0	25	36	278	7.7	1	6	80	13.3	0	28	168

JONES, CLARENCE — WR — JAGUARS

PERSONAL: Born March 12, 1973, in Vero Beach, Fla. ... 6-0/184. ... Full name: Clarence Edward Jones.
HIGH SCHOOL: Vero Beach (Fla.).
COLLEGE: Tennessee State.
TRANSACTIONS/CAREER NOTES: Selected by Jacksonville Jaguars in seventh round (227th pick overall) of 1996 NFL draft. ... Signed by Jaguars (May 25, 1996).

Year Team	G	RECEIVING				KICKOFF RETURNS				TOTALS	
		No.	Yds.	Avg.	TD	No.	Yds.	Avg.	TD	TD	Pts.
1991—Tennessee State					Redshirted.						
1992—Tennessee State	7	5	87	17.4	1	0	0	...	0	1	6
1993—Tennessee State	11	44	756	17.2	6	20	349	17.5	0	6	36
1994—Tennessee State	11	54	752	13.9	7	1	18	18.0	0	7	42
1995—Tennessee State					Did not play.						
College totals (3 years)	29	103	1595	15.5	14	21	367	17.5	0	14	84

JONES, LaCURTIS — LB — DOLPHINS

PERSONAL: Born June 23, 1972, in Waco, Texas ... 6-0/200.
HIGH SCHOOL: Waco (Texas)
COLLEGE: Baylor.
TRANSACTIONS/CAREER NOTES: Selected by Miami Dolphins in fourth round (125th pick overall) of 1996 NFL draft.

Year Team	G	SACKS
1991—Baylor	Redshirted.	
1992—Baylor	4	0.0
1993—Baylor	8	0.0
1994—Baylor	11	1.0
1995—Baylor	11	5.0
College totals (4 years)	34	6.0

JONES, MARCUS — DT — BUCCANEERS

PERSONAL: Born August 15, 1973, in Jacksonville. ... 6-6/280.
HIGH SCHOOL: Southwest Onslow (Jacksonville).
COLLEGE: North Carolina.
TRANSACTIONS/CAREER NOTES: Selected by Tampa Bay Buccaneers in first round (22nd pick overall) of 1996 NFL draft.
HONORS: Named defensive lineman on THE SPORTING NEWS college All-America second team (1995).

Year Team	G	SACKS
1992—North Carolina	11	1.0
1993—North Carolina	12	8.5
1994—North Carolina	11	7.5
1995—North Carolina	11	7.0
College totals (4 years)	45	24.0

JONES, ROD — G/OT — BENGALS

PERSONAL: Born January 11, 1974, in Detroit. ... 6-4/315.
HIGH SCHOOL: Henry Ford (Detroit).
COLLEGE: Kansas.
TRANSACTIONS/CAREER NOTES: Selected by Cincinnati Bengals in seventh round (219th pick overall) of 1996 NFL draft.
COLLEGE PLAYING EXPERIENCE: Kansas, 1992-1995. ... Games : 1992 (11), 1993 (11), 1994 (5), 1995 (11). Total: 38.

KANELL, DANNY — QB — GIANTS

PERSONAL: Born November 21, 1973, in Ft. Lauderdale. ... 6-3/222. ... Son of Dan Kanell, team physician, Miami Dolphins and spring training physician, New York Yankees.
HIGH SCHOOL: Westminster (Ft. Lauderdale) Academy.
COLLEGE: Florida State.
TRANSACTIONS/CAREER NOTES: Selected by New York Giants in fourth round (130th pick overall) of 1996 NFL draft.
MISCELLANEOUS: Selected by Milwaukee Brewers in 19th round of free-agent baseball draft (June 1, 1992); did not sign. ... Selected by New York Yankees in 25th round of free-agent baseball draft (June 1, 1995); did not sign.

Year Team	G		PASSING								RUSHING				TOTALS	
		Att.	Cmp.	Pct.	Yds.	TD	Int.	Avg.	Rat.	Att.	Yds.	Avg.	TD	TD	Pts.
1992—Florida State	6	20	9	45.0	135	1	0	6.8	118.2	11	-19	-1.7	0	0	0
1993—Florida State	4	49	36	73.5	499	7	0	10.2	204.7	3	-9	-3.0	0	0	0
1994—Florida State	11	380	227	59.7	2781	17	13	7.3	128.7	27	-127	-4.7	1	1	6
1995—Florida State	11	402	257	63.9	2957	32	13	7.4	146.2	19	-41	-2.2	0	0	0
College totals (4 years)	32	851	529	62.2	6372	57	26	7.5	142.0	60	-196	-3.3	1	1	6

KENDALL, PETE   G   SEAHAWKS

PERSONAL: Born July 9, 1973, in Weymouth, Mass. ... 6-5/292. ... Full name: Peter Marcus Kendall.
HIGH SCHOOL: Archbishop Williams (Weymouth, Mass.).
COLLEGE: Boston College.
TRANSACTIONS/CAREER NOTES: Selected by Seattle Seahawks in first round (21st pick overall) of 1996 NFL draft.
COLLEGE PLAYING EXPERIENCE: Boston College, 1992-1995. ... Games: 1992 (11), 1993 (11), 1994 (11), 1995 (12). Total: 45.

KENNISON, EDDIE   WR   RAMS

PERSONAL: Born January 20, 1973, in Lake Charles, La. ... 6-0/191. ... Full name: Eddie Joseph Kennison III. ... Nickname: Boo.
HIGH SCHOOL: Washington-Marion (Lake Charles, La.).
COLLEGE: Louisiana State.
TRANSACTIONS/CAREER NOTES: Selected after junior season by St. Louis Rams in first round (18th pick overall) of 1996 NFL draft.

Year Team	G	RECEIVING				PUNT RETURNS				KICKOFF RETURNS				TOTALS	
		No.	Yds.	Avg.	TD	No.	Yds.	Avg.	TD	No.	Yds.	Avg.	TD	TD	Pts.
1993—Louisiana State	11	28	466	16.6	3	20	256	12.8	0	18	410	22.8	0	3	18
1994—Louisiana State	10	25	349	14.0	5	36	438	12.2	1	16	397	24.8	0	6	36
1995—Louisiana State	11	45	739	16.4	2	19	253	13.3	0	17	371	21.8	0	2	12
College totals (3 years)	32	98	1554	15.9	10	75	947	12.6	1	51	1178	23.1	0	11	66

KEYES, MARCUS   DT   BEARS

PERSONAL: Born October 20, 1973, in Taylorsville, Miss. ... 6-3/310. ... Full name: Willis Marcus Keyes.
HIGH SCHOOL: Taylorsville (Miss.).
JUNIOR COLLEGE: Jones County Junior College (Miss.).
COLLEGE: North Alabama.
TRANSACTIONS/CAREER NOTES: Selected by Chicago Bears in seventh round (233rd pick overall) of 1996 NFL draft.

Year Team	G	SACKS
1992—Jones County Junior College	Statistics unavailable.	
1993—Jones County Junior College	Statistics unavailable.	
1994—North Alabama	10	4.0
1995—North Alabama	10	2.0
Junior College (2 years)	...	...
College totals (2 years)	20	6.0

KILLENS, TERRY   LB   OILERS

PERSONAL: Born March 24, 1974, in Cincinnati. ... 6-1/232. ... Full name: Terry Deleon Killens.
HIGH SCHOOL: Purcell (Cincinnati).
COLLEGE: Penn State.
TRANSACTIONS/CAREER NOTES: Selected by Houston Oilers in third round (74th pick overall) of 1996 NFL draft.
MISCELLANEOUS: Returned one punt for 25 yards and a touchdown (1995).

Year Team	G	SACKS
1992—Penn State	11	0.0
1993—Penn State	9	1.0
1994—Penn State	11	3.0
1995—Penn State	11	11.0
College totals (4 years)	42	15.0

KINNEY, KELVIN   DE   REDSKINS

PERSONAL: Born December 31, 1972, in Montgomery, W.Va. ... 6-6/250.
HIGH SCHOOL: Dupont (W.Va.), then Louisa (Va.).
COLLEGE: Virginia State.
TRANSACTIONS/CAREER NOTES: Selected by Washington Redskins in sixth round (174th pick overall) of 1996 NFL draft.

Year Team	G	SACKS
1992—Virginia State	Statistics unavailable.	
1993—Virginia State	Statistics unavailable.	
1994—Virginia State	Statistics unavailable.	
1995—Virginia State	10	9.0
College totals (4 years)	22	17.0

LANGFORD, JEVON   DE   BENGALS

PERSONAL: Born February 16, 1974, in Washington, D.C. ... 6-3/275.

1996 DRAFT PICKS

HIGH SCHOOL: Bishop Carroll (Washington, D.C.).
COLLEGE: Oklahoma State.
TRANSACTIONS/CAREER NOTES: Selected after junior season by Cincinnati Bengals in fourth round (108th pick overall) of 1996 NFL draft.

Year Team	G	SACKS
1993—Oklahoma State	11	3.0
1994—Oklahoma State	11	8.5
1995—Oklahoma State	11	1.0
College totals (3 years)	33	12.5

LAYMAN, JASON — OT/G — OILERS

PERSONAL: Born July 29, 1973, in Sevierville, Tenn. ... 6-5/306. ... Full name: Jason Todd Layman.
HIGH SCHOOL: Sevier County (Sevierville, Tenn.).
COLLEGE: Tennessee.
TRANSACTIONS/CAREER NOTES: Selected by Houston Oilers in second round (48th pick overall) of 1996 NFL draft.
COLLEGE PLAYING EXPERIENCE: Tennessee, 1991-1995. ... Games: 1991 (2), 1992 (8), 1993 (11), 1994 (11), 1995 (11). Total: 43.

LEVINE, L.T. — RB — BRONCOS

PERSONAL: Born December 27, 1973, in Colonia, N.J. ... 5-10/210. ... Name pronounced la-VEEN.
HIGH SCHOOL: Colonia (N.J.).
COLLEGE: Kansas.
TRANSACTIONS/CAREER NOTES: Selected by Denver Broncos in seventh round (235th pick overall) of 1996 NFL draft.

Year Team	G	RUSHING Att.	Yds.	Avg.	TD	RECEIVING No.	Yds.	Avg.	TD	KICKOFF RETURNS No.	Yds.	Avg.	TD	TOTALS TD	Pts.
1992—Kansas	5	15	62	4.1	0	0	0	...	0	0	0	...	0	0	0
1993—Kansas	9	123	588	4.8	2	10	46	4.6	0	5	102	20.4	0	2	12
1994—Kansas	11	128	812	6.3	11	6	31	5.2	0	1	15	15.0	0	11	66
1995—Kansas	10	156	841	5.4	8	25	117	4.7	1	0	0	...	0	9	54
College totals (4 years)	35	422	2303	5.5	21	41	194	4.7	1	6	117	19.5	0	22	132

LEWIS, JEFF — QB — BRONCOS

PERSONAL: Born April 17, 1973, in Columbus, Ohio. ... 6-1/217. ... Full name: Jeff Scott Lewis.
HIGH SCHOOL: Horizon (Scottsdale, Ariz.).
COLLEGE: Northern Arizona.
TRANSACTIONS/CAREER NOTES: Selected by Denver Broncos in fourth round (100th pick overall) of 1996 NFL draft.

Year Team	G	PASSING Att.	Cmp.	Pct.	Yds.	TD	Int.	Avg.	Rat.	RUSHING Att.	Yds.	Avg.	TD	TOTALS TD	Pts.
1991—Northern Arizona						Redshirted.									
1992—Northern Arizona	8	218	115	52.8	1377	4	7	6.32	106.7	80	-78	-1.0	5	5	30
1993—Northern Arizona	11	335	189	56.4	2497	15	6	7.45	127.8	100	32	0.3	2	2	12
1994—Northern Arizona	11	450	272	60.4	3355	26	8	7.46	138.5	108	32	0.3	6	6	36
1995—Northern Arizona	10	313	209	66.8	2426	22	3	7.75	153.2	51	120	2.4	2	2	12
College totals (4 years)	40	1316	785	59.7	9655	67	24	7.34	134.2	339	106	0.3	15	15	90

LEWIS, JERMAINE — WR — RAVENS

PERSONAL: Born October 16, 1974, in Lanham, Md. ... 5-7/172.
HIGH SCHOOL: Eleanor Roosevelt (Lanham, Md.).
COLLEGE: Maryland.
TRANSACTIONS/CAREER NOTES: Selected by Baltimore Ravens in fifth round (153rd pick overall) of 1996 NFL draft.

Year Team	G	RUSHING Att.	Yds.	Avg.	TD	RECEIVING No.	Yds.	Avg.	TD	PUNT RETURNS No.	Yds.	Avg.	TD	KICKOFF RETURNS No.	Yds.	Avg.	TD	TOTALS TD	Pts.
1992—Maryland	11	2	5	2.5	0	30	346	11.5	2	1	42	42.0	1	10	268	26.8	0	3	18
1993—Maryland	8	0	0	...	0	52	957	18.4	7	2	20	10.0	0	1	18	18.0	0	7	42
1994—Maryland	10	0	0	...	0	45	692	15.4	9	9	74	8.2	0	10	216	21.6	0	9	54
1995—Maryland	10	15	58	3.9	2	66	937	14.2	3	12	152	12.7	1	1	27	27.0	0	6	36
College totals (4 years)	39	17	63	3.7	2	193	2932	15.2	21	24	288	12.0	2	22	529	24.1	0	25	150

LEWIS, RAY — LB — RAVENS

PERSONAL: Born May 15, 1975, in Lakeland, Fla. ... 6-1/235. ... Full name: Ray Anthony Lewis.
HIGH SCHOOL: Kathleen (Lakeland, Fla.).
COLLEGE: Miami (Fla.).
TRANSACTIONS/CAREER NOTES: Selected after junior season by Baltimore Ravens in first round (26th pick overall) of 1996 NFL draft.
HONORS: Named linebacker on THE SPORTING NEWS college All-America second team (1995).

Year Team	G	INTERCEPTIONS No.	Yds.	Avg.	TD	SACKS No.
1993—Miami (Fla.)	9	0	0	...	0	2.0
1994—Miami (Fla.)	11	2	35	17.5	0	2.0
1995—Miami (Fla.)	11	2	75	37.5	1	2.0

College totals (3 years)		31	4	110	27.5	1	6.0

LUSK, HENRY   TE   SAINTS

PERSONAL: Born May 8, 1972, in Seaside, Calif. ... 6-1/240.
HIGH SCHOOL: Monterey (Calif.).
COLLEGE: Utah (degree in sociology, 1995).
TRANSACTIONS/CAREER NOTES: Selected by New Orleans Saints in seventh round (246th pick overall) of 1996 NFL draft.
MISCELLANEOUS: Granted extra year of eligibility with medical redshirt due to shoulder injury (1994).

			RECEIVING		
Year Team	G	No.	Yds.	Avg.	TD
1990—Utah			Redshirted.		
1991—Utah	10	1	34	34.0	0
1992—Utah	9	44	547	12.4	3
1993—Utah	12	42	692	16.5	3
1994—Utah			Medical redshirt.		
1995—Utah	11	37	534	14.4	4
College totals (4 years)	42	124	1807	14.6	10

LYNCH, BEN   C   CHIEFS

PERSONAL: Born November 18, 1972, in Santa Rosa, Calif. ... 6-3/291.
HIGH SCHOOL: Analy (Sebastopol, Calif.)
COLLEGE: California.
TRANSACTIONS/CAREER NOTES: Selected by Kansas City Chiefs in seventh round (211th pick overall) of 1996 NFL draft.
COLLEGE PLAYING EXPERIENCE: California, 1992-1995. ... Games: 1992 (1), 1993 (12), 1994 (11), 1995 (11). Total: 35.

MALONE, TODERICK   WR   SAINTS

PERSONAL: Born November 11, 1974, in Attalla, Ala. ... 5-10/177.
HIGH SCHOOL: Etowah (Attalla, Ala.).
COLLEGE: Alabama.
TRANSACTIONS/CAREER NOTES: Selected by New Orleans Saints in sixth round (204th pick overall) of 1996 NFL draft.

		RUSHING				RECEIVING				TOTALS	
Year Team	G	Att.	Yds.	Avg.	TD	No.	Yds.	Avg.	TD	TD	Pts.
1992—Alabama					Did not play.						
1993—Alabama	12	0	0	...	0	9	272	30.2	2	2	12
1994—Alabama	12	3	26	8.7	0	26	459	17.7	4	4	24
1995—Alabama	11	5	78	15.6	1	38	637	16.8	5	6	36
College totals (3 years)	35	8	104	13.0	1	73	1368	18.7	11	12	72

MANIECKI, JASON   DT   BUCCANEERS

PERSONAL: Born August 15, 1972, in Wisconsin Dells, Wis. ... 6-4/295. ... Name pronounced muh-NECK-ee.
HIGH SCHOOL: Wisconsin Dells (Wis.).
COLLEGE: Wisconsin.
TRANSACTIONS/CAREER NOTES: Selected by Tampa Bay Buccaneers in fifth round (140th pick overall) of 1996 NFL draft.

Year Team	G	SACKS
1991—Wisconsin	7	0.0
1992—Wisconsin		Redshirted.
1993—Wisconsin	9	1.0
1994—Wisconsin	10	2.0
1995—Wisconsin	11	4.0
College totals (4 years)	37	7.0

MANLEY, JAMES   DT   VIKINGS

PERSONAL: Born July 11, 1974, in Birmingham, Ala. ... 6-2/302.
HIGH SCHOOL: Huffman (Birmingham, Ala.)
COLLEGE: Vanderbilt.
TRANSACTIONS/CAREER NOTES: Selected by Minnesota Vikings in second round (45th pick overall) of 1996 NFL draft.

Year Team	G	SACKS
1992—Vanderbilt	11	3.0
1993—Vanderbilt	11	2.5
1994—Vanderbilt	11	9.0
1995—Vanderbilt	11	5.0
College totals (4 years)	44	19.5

MANUEL, SAM   LB   49ERS

PERSONAL: Born December 1, 1973, in Los Gatos, N.M. ... 6-2/235. ... Brother of Sean Manuel.
HIGH SCHOOL: Pinole Valley (El Sobrante, Calif.).
JUNIOR COLLEGE: Laney College (Calif.).

COLLEGE: New Mexico State.
TRANSACTIONS/CAREER NOTES: Selected by San Francisco 49ers in seventh round (254th pick overall) of 1996 NFL draft.

		INTERCEPTIONS				SACKS
Year Team	G	No.	Yds.	Avg.	TD	No.
1991—Laney College			Statistics unavailable.			
1992—Laney College			Did not play.			
1993—New Mexico State	11	0	0	...	0	3.0
1994—New Mexico State	11	1	0	0.0	0	0.0
1995—New Mexico State	11	0	0	...	0	5.5
College totals (3 years)	33	1	0	0.0	0	8.5

MANUEL, SEAN   TE   49ERS

PERSONAL: Born December 1, 1973, in Los Gatos, Calif. ... 6-2/245. ... Brother of Sam Manuel.
HIGH SCHOOL: Pinole Valley (El Sobrante, Calif.).
JUNIOR COLLEGE: Laney College (Calif.).
COLLEGE: New Mexico State.
TRANSACTIONS/CAREER NOTES: Selected by San Francisco 49ers in seventh round (239th pick overall) of 1996 NFL draft.

		RECEIVING			
Year Team	G	No.	Yds.	Avg.	TD
1991—Laney College	10	19	205	10.8	1
1992—Laney College	10	10	110	11.0	0
1993—New Mexico State			Redshirted.		
1994—New Mexico State	11	39	431	11.1	0
1995—New Mexico State	11	46	435	9.5	4
Junior college totals (2 years)	20	29	315	10.9	1
College totals (2 years)	22	85	866	10.2	4

MARSHALL, WHIT   LB   EAGLES

PERSONAL: Born January 6, 1973, in Atlanta. ... 6-2/247. ... Full name: Thomas Whitfield Marshall.
HIGH SCHOOL: The Lovett School (Atlanta).
COLLEGE: Georgia.
TRANSACTIONS/CAREER NOTES: Selected by Philadelphia Eagles in fifth round (147th pick overall) of 1996 NFL draft.

Year Team	G	SACKS
1991—Georgia		Redshirted.
1992—Georgia	11	1.0
1993—Georgia	11	0.0
1994—Georgia	11	2.0
1995—Georgia	11	1.0
College totals (4 years)	44	4.0

MARTIN, STEVE   DT   COLTS

PERSONAL: Born May 31, 1974, in St. Paul, Minn. ... 6-4/292. ... Full name: Steve Albert Martin.
HIGH SCHOOL: Jefferson City (Mo.).
COLLEGE: Missouri.
TRANSACTIONS/CAREER NOTES: Selected by Indianapolis Colts in fifth round (151st pick overall) of 1996 NFL draft.

Year Team	G	SACKS
1992—Missouri	11	2.0
1993—Missouri	11	1.0
1994—Missouri	11	8.0
1995—Missouri	10	6.0
College totals (4 years)	43	17.0

MATHIS, DEDRIC   CB   COLTS

PERSONAL: Born September 26, 1973, in Cuero, Texas. ... 5-10/196.
HIGH SCHOOL: Cuero (Texas).
COLLEGE: Houston.
TRANSACTIONS/CAREER NOTES: Selected by Indianapolis Colts in second round (51st pick overall) of 1996 NFL draft.

		INTERCEPTIONS			
Year Team	G	No.	Yds.	Avg.	TD
1992—Houston	4	0	0	...	0
1993—Houston	11	0	0	...	0
1994—Houston	11	0	0	...	0
1995—Houston	11	5	42	8.4	0
College totals (4 years)	37	5	42	8.4	0

MAXWELL, DeANDRE   WR   REDSKINS

PERSONAL: Born April 6, 1973, in Fresno, Calif. ... 6-1/200. ... Nephew of Henry Ellard, wide receiver, Washington Redskins.
HIGH SCHOOL: Bullard (Fresno, Calif.)

COLLEGE: San Diego State.
TRANSACTIONS/CAREER NOTES: Selected by Washington Redskins in seventh round (250th pick overall) of 1996 NFL draft.

			RECEIVING		
Year Team	G	No.	Yds.	Avg.	TD
1991—San Diego State			Redshirted.		
1992—San Diego State	4	11	226	20.6	4
1993—San Diego State	10	10	202	20.2	2
1994—San Diego State	11	47	591	12.6	3
1995—San Diego State	12	36	494	13.7	4
College totals (4 years)	37	104	1513	14.6	13

MAYBERRY, JERMANE — G/OT — EAGLES

PERSONAL: Born August 29, 1973, in Floresville, Texas. ... 6-4/325.
HIGH SCHOOL: Floresville (Texas).
COLLEGE: Texas A&M-Kingsville.
TRANSACTIONS/CAREER NOTES: Selected by Philadelphia Eagles in first round (25th pick overall) of 1996 NFL draft.
COLLEGE PLAYING EXPERIENCE: Texas A&M-Kingsville, 1992, 1994 and 1995. ... Games: 1992 (4), 1994 (10), 1995 (10). Total: 24.

MAYES, DERRICK — WR — PACKERS

PERSONAL: Born January 28, 1974, in Indianapolis. ... 6-0/201.
HIGH SCHOOL: North Central (Indianapolis).
COLLEGE: Notre Dame.
TRANSACTIONS/CAREER NOTES: Selected by Green Bay Packers in second round (56th pick overall) of 1996 NFL draft.

			RECEIVING		
Year Team	G	No.	Yds.	Avg.	TD
1992—Notre Dame	10	10	272	27.2	3
1993—Notre Dame	12	24	512	21.3	2
1994—Notre Dame	11	47	847	18.0	11
1995—Notre Dame	11	48	881	18.4	6
College totals (4 years)	44	129	2512	19.5	22

McDANIEL, EMMANUEL — DB — PANTHERS

PERSONAL: Born July 27, 1996, in Griffin, Ga. ... 5-9/178.
HIGH SCHOOL: Jonesboro (Ga.).
COLLEGE: East Carolina.
TRANSACTIONS/CAREER NOTES: Selected by Carolina Panthers in fourth round (111th pick overall) of 1996 NFL draft.

			INTERCEPTIONS		
Year Team	G	No.	Yds.	Avg.	TD
1991—East Carolina			Redshirted.		
1992—East Carolina	10	0	0	...	0
1993—East Carolina	11	2	0	0.0	0
1994—East Carolina	11	5	59	11.8	1
1995—East Carolina	11	6	111	18.5	1
College totals (4 years)	43	13	170	13.1	2

McDANIEL, KENNETH — G — COWBOYS

PERSONAL: Born December 20, 1973, in Mechanicsville, Va. ... 6-5/310.
HIGH SCHOOL: Lee-Davis (Mechanicsville, Va.).
COLLEGE: Norfolk State.
TRANSACTIONS/CAREER NOTES: Selected by Dallas Cowboys in fifth round (157th pick overall) of 1996 NFL draft.
COLLEGE PLAYING EXPERIENCE: Norfolk State, 1992-1995. ... Games: 1992 (10), 1993 (11), 1994 (8), 1995 (10). Total: 39.

McELROY, LEELAND — RB — CARDINALS

PERSONAL: Born June 25, 1974, in Beaumont, Texas. ... 5-9/198.
HIGH SCHOOL: Central (Beaumont, Texas).
COLLEGE: Texas A&M.
TRANSACTIONS/CAREER NOTES: Selected after junior season by Arizona Cardinals in second round (32nd pick overall) of 1996 NFL draft.
HONORS: Named kick returner on THE SPORTING NEWS college All-America first team (1994). ... Named kick returner on THE SPORTING NEWS college All-America second team (1995).

		RUSHING				RECEIVING				KICKOFF RETURNS				TOTALS	
Year Team	G	Att.	Yds.	Avg.	TD	No.	Yds.	Avg.	TD	No.	Yds.	Avg.	TD	TD	Pts.
1992—Texas A&M								Redshirted.							
1993—Texas A&M	11	72	613	8.5	7	19	224	11.8	4	15	590	39.3	3	14	84
1994—Texas A&M	10	130	707	5.4	9	9	42	4.7	0	6	301	50.2	1	10	60
1995—Texas A&M	10	246	1122	4.6	13	25	379	15.2	3	9	208	23.1	0	16	96
College totals (3 years)	31	448	2442	5.5	29	53	645	12.2	7	30	1099	36.6	4	40	240

McGEE, DELL — CB — CARDINALS

PERSONAL: Born September 7, 1973, in Columbus, Ga. ... 5-8/181.
HIGH SCHOOL: Kendrick (Columbus, Ga.)
COLLEGE: Auburn.
TRANSACTIONS/CAREER NOTES: Selected by Arizona Cardinals in fifth round (162nd pick overall) of 1996 NFL draft.
MISCELLANEOUS: Played wide receiver during the 1992 season.

			INTERCEPTIONS		
Year Team	G	No.	Yds.	Avg.	TD
1991—Auburn			Redshirted.		
1992—Auburn	2	0	0	...	0
1993—Auburn	11	1	0	0.0	0
1994—Auburn	11	0	0	...	0
1995—Auburn	11	1	66	66.0	0
College totals (4 years)	35	2	66	33.0	0

McKENZIE, KEITH — LB — PACKERS

PERSONAL: Born October 17, 1973, in Detroit. ... 6-2/242.
HIGH SCHOOL: Highland Park (Mich.).
COLLEGE: Ball State.
TRANSACTIONS/CAREER NOTES: Selected by Green Bay Packers in seventh round (252nd pick overall) of 1996 NFL draft.

			INTERCEPTIONS			SACKS
Year Team	G	No.	Yds.	Avg.	TD	No.
1991—Ball State			Redshirted.			
1992—Ball State	6	0	0	...	0	0.0
1993—Ball State	11	0	0	...	0	5.0
1994—Ball State	11	1	15	15.0	0	9.0
1995—Ball State	11	0	0	...	0	11.0
College totals (4 years)	39	1	15	15.0	0	25.0

McPHAIL, JERRIS — RB — DOLPHINS

PERSONAL: Born June 26, 1972, in Clinton, N.C. ... 5-11/201.
HIGH SCHOOL: Clinton (N.C.).
COLLEGE: Mount Olive (N.C.) College, then East Carolina.
TRANSACTIONS/CAREER NOTES: Selected by Miami Dolphins in fifth round (134th pick overall) of 1996 NFL draft.

		RUSHING				RECEIVING				TOTALS	
Year Team	G	Att.	Yds.	Avg.	TD	No.	Yds.	Avg.	TD	TD	Pts.
1991—Mount Olive				Did not play.							
1992—East Carolina				Redshirted.							
1993—East Carolina	10	30	173	5.8	0	34	410	12.1	4	4	24
1994—East Carolina	11	73	326	4.5	2	11	201	18.3	1	3	18
1995—East Carolina	10	185	910	4.9	5	38	342	9.0	2	7	42
College totals (3 years)	31	288	1409	4.9	7	83	953	11.5	7	14	84

McWILLIAMS, JOHNNY — TE — CARDINALS

PERSONAL: Born December 14, 1972, in Ontario, Calif. ... 6-4/261.
HIGH SCHOOL: Pomona (Calif.).
COLLEGE: Southern California.
TRANSACTIONS/CAREER NOTES: Selected by Arizona Cardinals in third round (64th pick overall) of 1996 NFL draft.

			RECEIVING		
Year Team	G	No.	Yds.	Avg.	TD
1991—Southern California			Redshirted.		
1992—Southern California	0	0	0	...	0
1993—Southern California	12	15	130	8.7	3
1994—Southern California	11	22	242	11.0	4
1995—Southern California	11	22	321	14.6	5
College totals (4 years)	34	59	693	11.8	12

MERRILL, JON — G — VIKINGS

PERSONAL: Born June 22, 1973, in Brevard, N.C. ... 6-3/292.
HIGH SCHOOL: Brevard (N.C.)
COLLEGE: Duke.
TRANSACTIONS/CAREER NOTES: Selected by Minnesota Vikings in seventh round (223rd pick overall) of 1996 NFL draft.
COLLEGE PLAYING EXPERIENCE: Duke, 1992, 1994 and 1995. ... Games: 1992 (7), 1994 (11), 1995 (11). Total: 29.

MICHELS, JOHN — OT — PACKERS

PERSONAL: Born March 19, 1973, in La Jolla, Calif. ... 6-7/290.

HIGH SCHOOL: La Jolla (Calif.).
COLLEGE: Southern California.
TRANSACTIONS/CAREER NOTES: Selected by Green Bay Packers in first round (27th pick overall) of 1996 NFL draft.
COLLEGE PLAYING EXPERIENCE: Southern California, 1993-1995. ... Games: 1993 (4), 1994 (10), 1995 (11). Total: 25.

MICKENS, RAY   CB   JETS

PERSONAL: Born January 4, 1973, in Frankfurt, West Germany. ... 5-8/178.
HIGH SCHOOL: Andress (El Paso, Texas).
COLLEGE: Texas A&M.
TRANSACTIONS/CAREER NOTES: Selected by New York Jets in third round (62nd pick overall) of 1996 NFL draft.
HONORS: Named defensive back on THE SPORTING NEWS college All-America second team (1995).

		INTERCEPTIONS			
Year Team	G	No.	Yds.	Avg.	TD
1991—Texas A&M			Redshirted.		
1992—Texas A&M	11	1	0	0.0	0
1993—Texas A&M	11	2	3	1.5	0
1994—Texas A&M	11	2	38	19.0	1
1995—Texas A&M	11	4	67	16.8	0
College totals (4 years)	44	9	108	12.0	1

MILLER, FRED   OT   RAMS

PERSONAL: Born February 6, 1973, in Aldine, Texas. ... 6-7/305.
HIGH SCHOOL: Aldine Eisenhower (Houston).
COLLEGE: Baylor.
TRANSACTIONS/CAREER NOTES: Selected by St. Louis Rams in fifth round (141st pick overall) of 1996 NFL draft.
COLLEGE PLAYING EXPERIENCE: Baylor, 1992-1995. ... Games: 1992 (11), 1993 (11), 1994 (11), 1995 (8). Total: 41.

MILLOY, LAWYER   S   PATRIOTS

PERSONAL: Born November 11, 1973, in St. Louis. ... 6-0/208.
HIGH SCHOOL: Lincoln (Tacoma, Wash.).
COLLEGE: Washington.
TRANSACTIONS/CAREER NOTES: Selected after junior season by New England Patriots in second round (36th pick overall) of 1996 NFL draft. ... Signed by Patriots (June 5, 1996).
HONORS: Named defensive back on THE SPORTING NEWS college All-America first team (1995).

		INTERCEPTIONS				SACKS
Year Team	G	No.	Yds.	Avg.	TD	No.
1992—Washington			Redshirted.			
1993—Washington	10	2	0	0.0	0	1.0
1994—Washington	11	1	0	0.0	0	0.0
1995—Washington	11	1	15	15.0	0	0.0
College totals (3 years)	32	4	15	3.8	0	1.0

MILLS, JIM   OT   CHARGERS

PERSONAL: Born March 30, 1973, in Marysville, Wash. ... 6-4/290.
HIGH SCHOOL: Marysville (Wash.).
COLLEGE: Idaho.
TRANSACTIONS/CAREER NOTES: Selected by San Diego Chargers in sixth round (190th pick overall) of 1996 NFL draft.
PLAYING EXPERIENCE: Idaho, 1992-1995. ... Games: 1992 (6), 1993 (11), 1994 (11), 1995 (10). Total: 38.

MILNE, BRIAN   FB   COLTS

PERSONAL: Born January 7, 1973, in Waterford, Pa. ... 6-3/254. ... Full name: Brian Fitzsimons Milne.
HIGH SCHOOL: LeBoeuf (Pa.).
COLLEGE: Penn State.
TRANSACTIONS/CAREER NOTES: Selected by Indianapolis Colts in fourth round (115th pick overall) of 1996 NFL draft.
MISCELLANEOUS: Won NCAA discus championship (1993).

		RUSHING				RECEIVING				TOTALS	
Year Team	G	Att.	Yds.	Avg.	TD	No.	Yds.	Avg.	TD	TD	Pts.
1991—Penn State						Redshirted.					
1992—Penn State						Did not play.					
1993—Penn State	11	19	94	5.0	4	2	10	5.0	0	4	24
1994—Penn State	11	56	267	4.8	8	15	78	5.2	0	8	48
1995—Penn State	11	39	151	3.9	4	15	141	9.4	0	4	24
College totals (3 years)	33	114	512	4.5	16	32	229	7.2	0	16	96

MIX, BRYANT   DE   OILERS

PERSONAL: Born July 28, 1972, in Water Valley, Miss. ... 6-3/301.

HIGH SCHOOL: Water Valley (Miss.).
JUNIOR COLLEGE: Northwest Mississippi Community College.
COLLEGE: Alcorn State.
TRANSACTIONS/CAREER NOTES: Selected by Houston Oilers in second round (38th pick overall) of 1996 NFL draft.

Year Team	G	SACKS
1992—Northwest Mississippi Community College	Statistics unavailable.	
1993—Northwest Mississippi Community College	Statistics unavailable.	
1994—Alcorn State	10	13.0
1995—Alcorn State	10	8.5
Junior College totals (2 years)	...	...
College totals (2 years)	20	21.5

MOBLEY, JOHN   LB   BRONCOS

PERSONAL: Born October 10, 1973, in Chester, Pa. ... 6-1/230.
HIGH SCHOOL: Chichester (Chester, Pa.).
COLLEGE: Kutztown (Pa.) State.
TRANSACTIONS/CAREER NOTES: Selected by Denver Broncos in first round (15th pick overall) of 1996 NFL draft.
MISCELLANEOUS: Played running back during the 1995 season; rushed 12 times for 17 yards and five touchdowns, returned 15 punts for 202 yards and returned seven kickoffs for 226 yards.

		INTERCEPTIONS				SACKS
Year Team	G	No.	Yds.	Avg.	TD	No.
1991—Kutztown State	11	0	0	...	0	2.0
1992—Kutztown State	10	2	89	44.5	1	7.0
1993—Kutztown State				Redshirted.		
1994—Kutztown State	10	1	4	4.0	0	7.0
1995—Kutztown State	10	5	63	12.6	1	4.0
College totals (4 years)	41	8	156	19.5	2	20.0

MOLDEN, ALEX   CB   SAINTS

PERSONAL: Born August 4, 1973, in Detroit. ... 5-10/190.
HIGH SCHOOL: Sierra (Colorado Springs, Colo.).
COLLEGE: Oregon.
TRANSACTIONS/CAREER NOTES: Selected by New Orleans Saints in first round (11th pick overall) of 1996 NFL draft.
HONORS: Named defensive back on The Sporting News college All-America second team (1995).

		INTERCEPTIONS				SACKS
Year Team	G	No.	Yds.	Avg.	TD	No.
1991—Oregon				Redshirted.		
1992—Oregon	11	3	19	6.3	0	0.0
1993—Oregon	11	1	8	8.0	0	0.0
1994—Oregon	12	3	41	13.7	0	0.0
1995—Oregon	10	3	17	5.7	0	1.0
College totals (4 years)	44	10	85	8.5	0	1.0

MOORE, JERALD   FB   RAMS

PERSONAL: Born November 20, 1974, in Houston. ... 5-9/233.
HIGH SCHOOL: Yates (Houston).
COLLEGE: Oklahoma.
TRANSACTIONS/CAREER NOTES: Selected after junior season by St. Louis Rams in third round (83rd pick overall) of 1996 NFL draft.

		RUSHING				RECEIVING				KICKOFF RETURNS				TOTALS	
Year Team	G	Att.	Yds.	Avg.	TD	No.	Yds.	Avg.	TD	No.	Yds.	Avg.	TD	TD	Pts.
1993—Oklahoma	8	70	325	4.6	3	4	51	12.8	0	0	0	...	0	3	24
1994—Oklahoma	9	129	659	5.1	10	12	138	11.5	1	3	27	9.0	0	11	66
1995—Oklahoma	10	165	1001	6.1	9	19	216	11.4	1	1	26	26.0	0	10	60
College totals (3 years)	27	364	1985	5.5	22	35	405	11.6	2	4	53	13.3	0	24	150

MORAN, SEAN   DE   BILLS

PERSONAL: Born June 5, 1973, in Denver. ... 6-3/255. ... Full name: Sean Farrell Moran.
HIGH SCHOOL: Overland (Aurora, Colo.).
COLLEGE: Colorado State.
TRANSACTIONS/CAREER NOTES: Selected by Buffalo Bills in fourth round (120th pick overall) of 1996 NFL draft.

Year Team	G	SACKS
1991—Colorado State		Redshirted.
1992—Colorado State	12	0.0
1993—Colorado State	11	3.0
1994—Colorado State	11	7.0
1995—Colorado State	11	6.0
College totals (3 years)	45	16.0

MOULDS, ERIC — WR — BILLS

PERSONAL: Born July 17, 1973, in Lucedale, Miss. ... 6-0/204. ... Full name: Eric Shannon Moulds.
HIGH SCHOOL: George County (Miss.).
COLLEGE: Mississippi State.
TRANSACTIONS/CAREER NOTES: Selected by Buffalo Bills in first round (24th pick overall) of 1996 NFL draft.

		RECEIVING				KICKOFF RETURNS				TOTALS	
Year Team	G	No.	Yds.	Avg.	TD	No.	Yds.	Avg.	TD	TD	Pts.
1992—Mississippi State				Did not play.							
1993—Mississippi State	10	17	398	23.4	4	7	143	20.4	0	4	24
1994—Mississippi State	11	39	845	21.7	7	13	426	32.8	0	7	42
1995—Mississippi State	10	62	779	12.6	6	9	259	28.8	0	6	36
College totals (3 years)	31	118	2022	17.1	17	29	828	28.6	0	17	102

MUHAMMAD, MUHSIN — WR — PANTHERS

PERSONAL: Born May 5, 1973, in Lansing, Mich. ... 6-2/217. ... Name pronounced moo-SEEN moo-HAH-med.
HIGH SCHOOL: Waverly (Lansing, Mich.).
COLLEGE: Michigan State.
TRANSACTIONS/CAREER NOTES: Selected by Carolina Panthers in second round (43rd pick overall) of 1996 NFL draft.

		RECEIVING			
Year Team	G	No.	Yds.	Avg.	TD
1991—Michigan State			Redshirted.		
1992—Michigan State	11	6	80	13.3	0
1993—Michigan State	2	3	32	10.7	0
1994—Michigan State	11	10	161	16.1	2
1995—Michigan State	11	41	696	17.0	2
College totals (4 years)	35	60	969	16.2	4

MYERS, GREG — S/PR — BENGALS

PERSONAL: Born September 30, 1972, in Tampa. ... 6-1/197. ... Full name: Gregory Jay Myers.
HIGH SCHOOL: Windsor (Colo.).
COLLEGE: Colorado State.
TRANSACTIONS/CAREER NOTES: Selected by Cincinnati Bengals in fifth round (144th pick overall) of 1996 NFL draft.
HONORS: Named defensive back on The Sporting News college All-America first team (1994 and 1995). ... Jim Thorpe Award winner (1995).

		INTERCEPTIONS				PUNT RETURNS				KICKOFF RETURNS				TOTALS	
Year Team	G	No.	Yds.	Avg.	TD	No.	Yds.	Avg.	TD	No.	Yds.	Avg.	TD	TD	Pts.
1991—Colorado State					Redshirted.										
1992—Colorado State	11	6	51	8.5	0	14	159	11.4	0	5	56	11.2	0	0	0
1993—Colorado State	11	2	39	19.5	0	27	325	12.0	0	14	316	22.6	0	0	0
1994—Colorado State	10	3	51	17.0	1	25	294	11.8	0	0	0	...	0	1	6
1995—Colorado State	11	3	55	18.3	0	35	555	15.9	3	0	0	...	0	3	18
College totals (4 years)	43	14	196	14.0	1	101	1333	13.2	3	19	372	19.6	0	4	24

NEAL, LEON — RB — BILLS

PERSONAL: Born September 11, 1972, in St. Paul, Minn. ... 5-9/185.
HIGH SCHOOL: Paramount (Calif.).
COLLEGE: Washington.
TRANSACTIONS/CAREER NOTES: Selected by Buffalo Bills in sixth round (196th pick overall) of 1996 NFL draft.

		RUSHING				RECEIVING				PUNT RETURNS				KICKOFF RETURNS				TOTALS	
Year Team	G	Att.	Yds.	Avg.	TD	No.	Yds.	Avg.	TD	No.	Yds.	Avg.	TD	No.	Yds.	Avg.	TD	TD	Pts.
1991—Washington											Redshirted.								
1992—Washington	1	2	15	7.5	0	0	0	...	0	0	0	...	0	0	0	...	0	0	0
1993—Washington	7	27	146	5.4	1	1	3	3.0	0	1	15	15.0	0	0	0	...	0	1	6
1994—Washington	11	51	220	4.3	1	8	60	7.5	0	25	139	5.6	0	8	185	23.1	0	1	6
1995—Washington	5	100	558	5.6	3	17	108	6.4	1	0	0	...	0	4	85	21.3	0	4	24
College totals (4 years)	24	180	939	5.2	5	26	171	6.6	1	26	154	5.9	0	12	270	22.5	0	6	36

NORTHERN, GABE — LB/DE — BILLS

PERSONAL: Born June 8, 1974, in Baton Rouge, La. ... 6-2/240. ... Full name: Gabriel O'Kara Northern.
HIGH SCHOOL: Glen Oaks (Baton Rouge, La.).
COLLEGE: Louisiana State.
TRANSACTIONS/CAREER NOTES: Selected by Buffalo Bills in second round (53rd pick overall) of 1996 NFL draft.

Year Team	G	SACKS
1992—Louisiana State	10	0.0
1993—Louisiana State	11	1.0
1994—Louisiana State	11	11.0
1995—Louisiana State	11	9.0
College totals (4 years)	43	21.0

OBEN, ROMAN — OT — GIANTS

PERSONAL: Born October 9, 1972, in Cameroon, West Africa. ... 6-4/297.
HIGH SCHOOL: Gonzaga (Washington, D.C.), then Fork Union (Va.) Military Academy.
COLLEGE: Louisville.
TRANSACTIONS/CAREER NOTES: Selected by New York Giants in third round (66th pick overall) of 1996 NFL draft.
COLLEGE PLAYING EXPERIENCE: Louisville, 1992-1995. ... Games: 1992 (11), 1993 (7), 1994 (11), 1995 (10). Total: 39.

ODOM, JASON — OT — BUCCANEERS

PERSONAL: Born March 31, 1974, in Bartow, Fla. ... 6-4/290. ... Full name: Jason Brian Odom.
HIGH SCHOOL: Bartow (Fla.).
COLLEGE: Florida.
TRANSACTIONS/CAREER NOTES: Selected by Tampa Bay Buccaneers in fourth round (96th pick overall) of 1996 NFL draft.
COLLEGE PLAYING EXPERIENCE: Florida, 1992-1995. ... Games: 1992 (11) 1993 (12) 1994 (11) 1995 (12). Total: 46.
HONORS: Named offensive lineman on THE SPORTING NEWS college All-America first team (1995).

OGDEN, JONATHAN — OT — RAVENS

PERSONAL: Born July 31, 1974, in Washington, D.C. ... 6-8/318. ... Full name: Jonathan Phillip Ogden.
HIGH SCHOOL: St. Alban's (Washington, D.C.).
COLLEGE: UCLA.
TRANSACTIONS/CAREER NOTES: Selected by Baltimore Ravens in first round (fourth pick overall) of 1996 NFL draft.
COLLEGE PLAYING EXPERIENCE: UCLA, 1992-1995. ... Games: 1992 (11), 1993 (8), 1994 (11), 1995 (11). Total: 41.
HONORS: Outland Trophy winner (1995). ... Named offensive lineman on THE SPORTING NEWS college All-America first team (1995).

OLIVER, WINSLOW — RB — PANTHERS

PERSONAL: Born March 3, 1973, in Houston. ... 5-7/180. ... Full name: Winslow Paul Oliver.
HIGH SCHOOL: Clements (Sugar Land, Texas), then Kempner (Houston).
COLLEGE: New Mexico.
TRANSACTIONS/CAREER NOTES: Selected by Carolina Panthers in third round (73rd pick overall) of 1996 NFL draft.

		RUSHING				RECEIVING				PUNT RETURNS				KICKOFF RETURNS				TOTALS	
Year Team	G	Att.	Yds.	Avg.	TD	No.	Yds.	Avg.	TD	No.	Yds.	Avg.	TD	No.	Yds.	Avg.	TD	TD	Pts.
1991—New Mexico					Redshirted.														
1992—New Mexico	10	245	1063	4.3	3	20	187	9.4	1	0	0	...	0	0	0	...	0	4	24
1993—New Mexico	9	146	648	4.4	2	11	130	11.8	0	0	0	...	0	6	180	30.0	0	2	12
1994—New Mexico	9	138	706	5.1	8	21	198	9.4	0	8	55	6.9	0	14	298	21.3	0	8	48
1995—New Mexico	11	162	915	5.7	4	22	228	10.4	2	16	101	6.3	0	21	666	31.7	1	7	42
College totals (4 years)	39	691	3332	4.8	17	74	743	10.1	3	24	156	6.5	0	41	1144	27.9	1	21	126

OSBORNE, CHUCK — DT — RAMS

PERSONAL: Born November 2, 1973, in Los Angeles. ... 6-2/281. ... Full name: Charles Wayne Osborne.
HIGH SCHOOL: Canyon (Calif.).
COLLEGE: Arizona.
TRANSACTIONS/CAREER NOTES: Selected by St. Louis Rams in seventh round (222nd pick overall) of 1996 NFL draft.

Year Team	G	SACKS
1992—Arizona	7	0.0
1993—Arizona	11	1.0
1994—Arizona	11	11.0
1995—Arizona	11	7.0
College totals (4 years)	40	19.0

OWENS, TERRELL — WR — 49ERS

PERSONAL: Born December 7, 1973, in Alexander City, Ala. ... 6-2/213.
HIGH SCHOOL: Benjamin Russell (Alexander City, Ala.).
COLLEGE: Tennessee-Chattanooga.
TRANSACTIONS/CAREER NOTES: Selected by San Francisco 49ers in third round (89th pick overall) of 1996 NFL draft.

		RUSHING				RECEIVING				KICKOFF RETURNS				TOTALS	
Year Team	G	Att.	Yds.	Avg.	TD	No.	Yds.	Avg.	TD	No.	Yds.	Avg.	TD	TD	Pts.
1992—Tennessee-Chattanooga	6	0	0	...	0	6	97	16.2	1	0	0	...	0	1	6
1993—Tennessee-Chattanooga	11	0	0	...	0	38	724	19.1	8	0	0	...	0	8	48
1994—Tennessee-Chattanooga	10	4	35	8.8	6	57	836	14.7	6	0	0	...	0	7	42
1995—Tennessee-Chattanooga	11	3	9	3.0	0	43	666	15.5	1	7	159	22.7	0	4	24
College totals (4 years)	38	7	44	6.3	6	144	2323	16.1	16	7	159	22.7	0	20	120

PETER, CHRISTIAN — DT

PERSONAL: Born October 5, 1972, in Locust, N.J. ... 6-3/304.

HIGH SCHOOL: South Middletown (N.J.), then Milford (Conn.) Academy.
COLLEGE: Nebraska.
TRANSACTIONS/CAREER NOTES: Selected by New England Patriots in fifth round (149th pick overall) of 1996 NFL draft. ... Patriots released rights (April 24, 1996).

Year Team	G	SACKS
1991—Nebraska	Did not play.	
1992—Nebraska	Redshirted.	
1993—Nebraska	11	0.0
1994—Nebraska	12	7.0
1995—Nebraska	11	2.0
College totals (3 years)	34	9.0

PHILLIPS, LAWRENCE — RB — RAMS

PERSONAL: Born May 12, 1975, in Little Rock, Ark. ... 6-0/229.
HIGH SCHOOL: Baldwin Park (Calif.).
COLLEGE: Nebraska.
TRANSACTIONS/CAREER NOTES: Selected after junior season by St. Louis Rams in first round (sixth pick overall) of 1996 NFL draft.

		RUSHING				RECEIVING				TOTALS	
Year Team	G	Att.	Yds.	Avg.	TD	No.	Yds.	Avg.	TD	TD	Pts.
1993—Nebraska	10	92	508	5.5	5	2	6	3.0	0	5	30
1994—Nebraska	12	286	1722	6.0	16	22	172	7.8	0	16	96
1995—Nebraska	5	71	547	7.7	9	4	14	3.5	0	9	54
College totals (3 years)	27	449	2777	6.2	30	28	192	6.9	0	30	180

PITTMAN, KAVIKA — DE — COWBOYS

PERSONAL: Born October 9, 1974, in Leesville, La. ... 6-5/263. ... Name pronounced kah-VEEK-ah.
HIGH SCHOOL: Leesville (La.).
COLLEGE: McNeese State.
TRANSACTIONS/CAREER NOTES: Selected by Dallas Cowboys in second round (37th pick overall) of 1996 NFL draft.

Year Team	G	SACKS
1993—McNeese State	5	0.0
1994—McNeese State	11	4.0
1995—McNeese State	11	13.0
College totals (3 years)	27	17.0

PITTS, STEPHEN — RB — 49ERS

PERSONAL: Born February 16, 1973, in Atlantic Highlands, N.J. ... 5-10/192. ... Full name: Stephen Michael Pitts.
HIGH SCHOOL: Middletown (N.J.) South.
COLLEGE: Penn State.
TRANSACTIONS/CAREER NOTES: Selected by San Francisco 49ers in sixth round (198th pick overall) of 1996 NFL draft.

		RUSHING				RECEIVING				KICKOFF RETURNS				TOTALS	
Year Team	G	Att.	Yds.	Avg.	TD	No.	Yds.	Avg.	TD	No.	Yds.	Avg.	TD	TD	Pts.
1991—Penn State								Redshirted.							
1992—Penn State	9	23	148	6.4	2	1	3	3.0	0	4	95	23.8	0	2	12
1993—Penn State	11	91	351	3.9	2	9	67	7.4	0	3	56	18.7	0	2	12
1994—Penn State	10	33	189	5.7	0	1	1	1.0	0	2	35	17.5	0	0	0
1995—Penn State	11	68	468	6.9	1	4	22	5.5	0	17	364	21.4	0	1	6
College totals (4 years)	41	215	1156	5.4	5	15	93	6.2	0	26	550	21.2	0	5	30

POINTER, KIRK — DB — DOLPHINS

PERSONAL: Born February 13, 1974, in Memphis. ... 5-11/178.
HIGH SCHOOL: Kingsbury (Memphis).
COLLEGE: Austin Peay.
TRANSACTIONS/CAREER NOTES: Selected by Miami Dolphins in fourth round (113th pick overall) of 1996 NFL draft.

		INTERCEPTIONS			
Year Team	G	No.	Yds.	Avg.	TD
1992—Austin Peay	11	6	0	0.0	0
1993—Austin Peay	10	2	37	18.5	0
1994—Austin Peay	10	4	32	8.0	0
1995—Austin Peay	11	4	1	.3	0
College totals (4 years)	42	16	70	4.4	0

PRICE, DARYL — DE — 49ERS

PERSONAL: Born October 23, 1972, in Galveston, Texas. ... 6-4/274.
HIGH SCHOOL: Central (Beaumont, Texas).
COLLEGE: Colorado.
TRANSACTIONS/CAREER NOTES: Selected by San Francisco 49ers in fourth round (128th pick overall) of 1996 NFL draft.

Year	Team	G	SACKS
1991—Colorado		Redshirted.	
1992—Colorado		10	0.0
1993—Colorado		9	0.0
1994—Colorado		8	1.0
1995—Colorado		11	4.0
College totals (4 years)		**38**	**5.0**

PRICE, J.C.   DT   PANTHERS

PERSONAL: Born January 13, 1973 in Prince George's County, Md. ... 6-2/280.
COLLEGE: Virginia Tech.
TRANSACTIONS/CAREER NOTES: Selected by Carolina Panthers in third round (88th pick overall) of 1996 NFL draft.

Year	Team	G	SACKS
1992—Virginia Tech		8	2.0
1993—Virginia Tech		11	4.0
1994—Virginia Tech		11	3.0
1995—Virginia Tech		11	8.0
College totals (4 years)		**41**	**17.0**

PRITCHETT, STANLEY   FB   DOLPHINS

PERSONAL: Born December 12, 1973, in Atlanta. ... 6-1/232.
HIGH SCHOOL: Frederick Douglass (College Park, Ga.).
COLLEGE: South Carolina.
TRANSACTIONS/CAREER NOTES: Selected by Miami Dolphins in fourth round (118th pick overall) of 1996 NFL draft.

Year	Team	G	RUSHING Att.	Yds.	Avg.	TD	RECEIVING No.	Yds.	Avg.	TD	TOTALS TD	Pts.
1992—South Carolina		11	0	0	...	0	0	0	...	0	0	0
1993—South Carolina		11	36	162	4.5	0	15	165	11.0	0	0	0
1994—South Carolina		11	130	601	4.6	8	34	212	6.2	2	10	60
1995—South Carolina		11	86	333	3.9	8	62	664	10.7	4	12	72
College totals (4 years)		**44**	**252**	**1096**	**4.4**	**16**	**111**	**1041**	**9.4**	**6**	**22**	**132**

PURNELL, LOVETT   TE   PATRIOTS

PERSONAL: Born April 7, 1972, in Seaford, Del. ... 6-2/250.
HIGH SCHOOL: Seaford (Del.).
COLLEGE: West Virginia.
TRANSACTIONS/CAREER NOTES: Selected by New England Patriots in seventh round (216th pick overall) of 1996 NFL draft.

Year	Team	G	RECEIVING No.	Yds.	Avg.	TD
1992—West Virginia				Redshirted.		
1993—West Virginia		11	1	12	12.0	0
1994—West Virginia		12	36	481	13.4	2
1995—West Virginia		11	37	614	16.6	6
College totals (3 years)		**34**	**74**	**1107**	**15.0**	**8**

RATLIFFE, LESLIE   OT   BRONCOS

PERSONAL: Born May 22, 1973, in Newport, Ark. ... 6-7/296. ... Full name: Leslie Tyrone Ratliffe.
HIGH SCHOOL: Newport (Ark.).
COLLEGE: Tennessee.
TRANSACTIONS/CAREER NOTES: Selected by Denver Broncos in seventh round (213rd pick overall) of 1996 NFL draft.
COLLEGE PLAYING EXPERIENCE: Tennessee, 1992-1994. ... Games: 1992 (6), 1993 (12), 1994 (12). Total: 30.

RAYBON, ISRAEL   DE   STEELERS

PERSONAL: Born February 5, 1973, in Lee, Ala. ... 6-6/293.
HIGH SCHOOL: Lee (Huntsville, Ala.)
COLLEGE: North Alabama.
TRANSACTIONS/CAREER NOTES: Selected by Pittsburgh Steelers in fifth round (163rd pick overall) of 1996 NFL draft.

Year	Team	G	INTERCEPTIONS No.	Yds.	Avg.	TD	SACKS No.
1992—North Alabama		10	0	0	...	0	2.0
1993—North Alabama		10	0	0	...	0	2.0
1994—North Alabama		10	1	11	11.0	1	5.0
1995—North Alabama		10	1	4	4.0	0	3.5
College totals (4 years)		**40**	**2**	**15**	**7.5**	**1**	**12.5**

RICE, SIMEON   DE   CARDINALS

PERSONAL: Born February 24, 1974, in Chicago. ... 6-5/265.

HIGH SCHOOL: Mt. Carmel (Chicago).
COLLEGE: Illinois.
TRANSACTIONS/CAREER NOTES: Selected by Arizona Cardinals in first round (third pick overall) of 1996 NFL draft.
HONORS: Named linebacker on THE SPORTING NEWS college All-America second team (1995).

Year Team	G	SACKS
1992—Illinois	11	9.0
1993—Illinois	11	8.0
1994—Illinois	11	16.0
1995—Illinois	11	12.0
College totals (4 years)	**44**	**45.0**

RIEMERSMA, JAY   TE   BILLS

PERSONAL: Born May 17, 1973, in Zeeland, Mich. ... 6-5/254. ... Name pronounced REE-mers-muh.
HIGH SCHOOL: Zeeland (Mich.).
COLLEGE: Michigan.
TRANSACTIONS/CAREER NOTES: Selected by Buffalo Bills in seventh round (244th pick overall) of 1996 NFL draft.
MISCELLANEOUS: Played quarterback during the 1992 and 1993 seasons. ... Attempted three passes with three completions for 43 yards and a touchdown and rushed twice for nine yards (1992); attempted eight passes with three completions for 36 yards (1993); and attempted three passes without a completion (1995).

		RECEIVING			
Year Team	G	No.	Yds.	Avg.	TD
1991—Michigan			Redshirted.		
1992—Michigan	11	0	0	...	0
1993—Michigan	11	0	0	...	0
1994—Michigan	11	33	306	9.3	2
1995—Michigan	12	40	360	9.0	1
College totals (4 years)	**45**	**73**	**666**	**9.1**	**3**

RILEY, PHILLIP   WR   EAGLES

PERSONAL: Born September 24, 1972, in Orlando. ... 5-11/189.
HIGH SCHOOL: Jones (Orlando).
JUNIOR COLLEGE: Garden City (Kan.) Community College.
COLLEGE: Florida State.
TRANSACTIONS/CAREER NOTES: Selected by Philadelphia Eagles in sixth round (199th pick overall) of 1996 NFL draft.

		RECEIVING				KICKOFF RETURNS				TOTALS	
Year Team	G	No.	Yds.	Avg.	TD	No.	Yds.	Avg.	TD	TD	Pts.
1991—Garden City Community College	10	25	513	20.5	5	10	317	31.7	0	5	30
1992—Garden City Community College					Did not play.						
1993—Florida State	9	6	59	9.8	0	3	106	35.3	0	1	6
1994—Florida State	7	2	34	17.0	1	7	107	15.3	0	1	6
1995—Florida State	11	30	340	11.3	3	0	0	...	0	3	18
Junior totals (1 years)	**10**	**25**	**513**	**20.5**	**5**	**10**	**317**	**31.7**	**0**	**5**	**30**
College totals (3 years)	**27**	**38**	**433**	**11.4**	**4**	**10**	**213**	**21.3**	**0**	**5**	**30**

RIVERA, MARCO   G   PACKERS

PERSONAL: Born April 26, 1972, in Elmont, N.Y. ... 6-5/295. ... Full name: Marco Anthony Rivera.
HIGH SCHOOL: Elmont (N.Y.) Memorial.
COLLEGE: Penn State.
TRANSACTIONS/CAREER NOTES: Selected by Green Bay Packers in sixth round (208th pick overall) of 1996 NFL draft.
COLLEGE PLAYING EXPERIENCE: Penn State, 1992-1995. ... Games: 1992 (9), 1993 (9), 1994 (11), 1995 (10). Total: 39.

ROBINSON, ADRIAN   S   COLTS

PERSONAL: Born July 25, 1974, in Edna, Texas. ... 6-2/216.
HIGH SCHOOL: Edna (Texas).
COLLEGE: Baylor.
TRANSACTIONS/CAREER NOTES: Selected by Indianapolis Colts in seventh round (232nd pick overall) of 1996 NFL draft.
MISCELLANEOUS: Played quarterback during the 1992 season. ... Attempted one pass with one completion for 46 yards and a touchdown and rushed 14 times for 62 yards and two touchdowns (1992).

		INTERCEPTIONS				SACKS
Year Team	G	No.	Yds.	Avg.	TD	No.
1992—Baylor	3	0	0	...	0	0.0
1993—Baylor	11	4	22	5.5	0	0.0
1994—Baylor	9	3	129	43.0	2	1.0
1995—Baylor	11	4	26	6.5	0	0.0
College totals (4 years)	**34**	**11**	**177**	**16.1**	**2**	**1.0**

ROCHE, BRIAN   TE   CHARGERS

PERSONAL: Born May 5, 1973, in Downey, Calif. ... 6-4/255.

HIGH SCHOOL: Damien (LaVerne, Calif.).
COLLEGE: Cal Poly-SLO, then San Jose State.
TRANSACTIONS/CAREER NOTES: Selected by San Diego Chargers in third round (81st pick overall) of 1996 NFL draft.

			RECEIVING		
Year Team	G	No.	Yds.	Avg.	TD
1991—Cal Poly-SLO		Did not play.			
1992—San Jose State		Redshirted.			
1993—San Jose State	11	5	57	11.4	0
1994—San Jose State	11	30	390	13.0	2
1995—San Jose State	11	66	729	11.1	5
College totals (3 years)	33	101	1176	11.7	7

ROE, JAMES WR RAVENS

PERSONAL: Born August 23, 1973, in Richmond, Va. ... 6-1/187.
HIGH SCHOOL: Henrico (Richmond, Va.).
COLLEGE: Norfolk State.
TRANSACTIONS/CAREER NOTES: Selected by Baltimore Ravens in sixth round (186th pick overall) of 1996 NFL draft.

			RECEIVING		
Year Team	G	No.	Yds.	Avg.	TD
1992—Norfolk State	10	46	850	18.5	9
1993—Norfolk State	11	52	916	17.6	5
1994—Norfolk State	10	77	1454	18.9	17
1995—Norfolk State	10	64	1248	19.5	15
College totals (4 years)	41	239	4468	18.7	46

ROYE, ORPHEUS DE/DT STEELERS

PERSONAL: Born January 21, 1974, in Miami. ... 6-3/295. ... Name pronounced OR-fee-us ROY.
HIGH SCHOOL: Miami Springs.
JUNIOR COLLEGE: Jones County Junior College (Miss.).
COLLEGE: Florida State.
TRANSACTIONS/CAREER NOTES: Selected by Pittsburgh Steelers in sixth round (200th pick overall) of 1996 NFL draft.

Year Team	G	SACKS
1992—Jones County Junior College	8	8.0
1993—Jones County Junior College	10	12.0
1994—Florida State	11	0.5
1995—Florida State	11	2.0
Junior totals (2 years)	18	20.0
College totals (2 years)	22	2.5

RUNYAN, JON OT/G OILERS

PERSONAL: Born November 27, 1973, in Flint, Mich. ... 6-7/308.
HIGH SCHOOL: Carman-Ainsworth (Flint, Mich.).
COLLEGE: Michigan.
TRANSACTIONS/CAREER NOTES: Selected after junior season by Houston Oilers in fourth round (109th pick overall) of 1996 NFL draft.
COLLEGE PLAYING EXPERIENCE: Michigan, 1993-1995. ... Games: 1993 (11), 1994 (10), 1995 (12). Total: 33.
HONORS: Named offensive lineman on THE SPORTING NEWS college All-America second team (1995).

RUSK, REGGIE CB BUCCANEERS

PERSONAL: Born October 19, 1972, in Galveston, Texas ... 5-10/182.
HIGH SCHOOL: Texas City (Texas).
JUNIOR COLLEGE: City College of San Francisco.
COLLEGE: Kentucky.
TRANSACTIONS/CAREER NOTES: Selected by Tampa Bay Buccaneers in seventh round (221st pick overall) of 1996 NFL draft.

			INTERCEPTIONS			SACKS
Year Team	G	No.	Yds.	Avg.	TD	No.
1992—City College of San Francisco		Statistics unavailable.				
1993—City College of San Francisco		Statistics unavailable.				
1994—Kentucky	11	0	0	...	0	0.0
1995—Kentucky	11	1	1	1.0	0	1.0
Junior College totals (2 years)	...	...	...	...	...	...
College totals (2 years)	22	1	1	1.0	0	11.0

SAPP, PATRICK LB CHARGERS

PERSONAL: Born May 11, 1973, in Jacksonville. ... 6-4/258.
HIGH SCHOOL: Raines (Jacksonville).
COLLEGE: Clemson.
TRANSACTIONS/CAREER NOTES: Selected by San Diego Chargers in second round (50th pick overall) of 1996 NFL draft.
MISCELLANEOUS: Played quarterback during the 1992, 1993 and 1994 seasons. ... Attempted 144 passes with 60 completions for 750 yards (three toucdowns and three interceptions) and rushed 50 times for 149 yards and one touchdown (1992); attempted 124 passes with 61

completions (three touchdowns and three interceptions) and rushed 65 times for 57 yards and a touchdown (1993); and attempted 88 passes with 39 completions for 444 yards (two touchdowns and three interceptions) and rushed 25 times for seven yards (1994).

			INTERCEPTIONS				SACKS
Year	Team	G	No.	Yds.	Avg.	TD	No.
1992—Clemson		6	0	0	...	0	0.0
1993—Clemson		9	0	0	...	0	0.0
1994—Clemson		7	0	0	...	0	0.0
1995—Clemson		11	2	34	17.0	0	4.5
College totals (4 years)		33	2	34	17.0	0	4.5

SAUER, CRAIG — LB — FALCONS

PERSONAL: Born December 13, 1972, in Sartell, Minn. ... 6-1/226.
HIGH SCHOOL: Sartell (Minn.).
COLLEGE: Minnesota.
TRANSACTIONS/CAREER NOTES: Selected by Atlanta Falcons in sixth round (188th pick overall) of 1996 NFL draft. ... Signed by Falcons (June 6, 1996).
MISCELLANEOUS: Played quarterback during the 1992 season.

			INTERCEPTIONS				SACKS
Year	Team	G	No.	Yds.	Avg.	TD	No.
1991—Minnesota					Redshirted.		
1992—Minnesota		1	0	0	...	0	0.0
1993—Minnesota		11	2	1	.5	0	3.0
1994—Minnesota		11	0	0	...	0	3.0
1995—Minnesota		11	1	25	25.0	0	1.0
College totals (4 years)		34	3	26	8.7	0	7.0

SHIVER, CLAY — C — COWBOYS

PERSONAL: Born December 7, 1972, in Tifton, Ga. ... 6-2/294.
HIGH SCHOOL: Tift (Tifton, Ga.).
COLLEGE: Florida State.
TRANSACTIONS/CAREER NOTES: Selected by Dallas Cowboys in third round (67th pick overall) of 1996 NFL draft.
COLLEGE PLAYING EXPERIENCE: Florida State, 1992-1995. ... Games: 1992 (11), 1993 (11), 1994 (11), 1995 (11). Total: 44.
HONORS: Named offensive lineman on THE SPORTING NEWS college All-America first team (1995).

SILVAN, NILO — WR — BUCCANEERS

PERSONAL: Born October 2, 1973, in Covington, La. ... 5-9/176.
HIGH SCHOOL: St. Paul (Covington, La.).
COLLEGE: Tennessee.
TRANSACTIONS/CAREER NOTES: Selected by Tampa Bay Buccaneers in sixth round (180th pick overall) of 1996 NFL draft.

			RECEIVING				PUNT RETURNS				KICKOFF RETURNS				TOTALS	
Year	Team	G	No.	Yds.	Avg.	TD	No.	Yds.	Avg.	TD	No.	Yds.	Avg.	TD	TD	Pts.
1992—Tennessee		11	2	28	14.0	0	1	38	38.0	0	1	21	21.0	0	0	0
1993—Tennessee		12	9	169	18.8	1	1	69	69.0	1	4	87	21.8	0	2	12
1994—Tennessee		12	9	95	10.6	1	15	272	18.1	0	16	340	21.3	0	1	6
1995—Tennessee		3	6	89	14.8	1	4	30	7.5	0	7	243	34.7	0	1	6
College totals (4 years)		38	26	381	14.7	3	21	409	19.5	1	28	691	24.7	0	4	24

SLUTZKER, SCOTT — TE — COLTS

PERSONAL: Born December 20, 1972, in Hasbrouck Heights, N.J. ... 6-4/250.
HIGH SCHOOL: Hasbrouck Heights, N.J.
COLLEGE: Iowa.
TRANSACTIONS/CAREER NOTES: Selected by Indianapolis Colts in third round (82nd pick overall) of 1996 NFL draft.

			RECEIVING			
Year	Team	G	No.	Yds.	Avg.	TD
1991—Iowa					Redshirted.	
1992—Iowa		11	0	0	...	0
1993—Iowa		11	29	307	10.6	2
1994—Iowa		9	27	379	14.0	2
1995—Iowa		11	35	509	14.5	1
College totals (4 years)		42	91	1195	13.1	5

SMEDLEY, ERIC — S/CB — BILLS

PERSONAL: Born July 23, 1973, in Charleston, W.Va. ... 5-11/199.
HIGH SCHOOL: Capital (Chesterton, W.Va.).
COLLEGE: Indiana.
TRANSACTIONS/CAREER NOTES: Selected by Buffalo Bills in seventh round (249th pick overall) of 1996 NFL draft.

			INTERCEPTIONS			
Year	Team	G	No.	Yds.	Avg.	TD
1991—Indiana					Redshirted.	

Year Team	G	INTERCEPTIONS			
		No.	Yds.	Avg.	TD
1992—Indiana	2	0	0	...	0
1993—Indiana	11	0	0	...	0
1994—Indiana	11	4	48	12.0	1
1995—Indiana	11	1	14	14.0	0
College totals (4 years)	35	5	62	12.4	1

SMITH, BRADY — DE — SAINTS

PERSONAL: Born June 5, 1973, in Royal Oak, Mich. ... 6-5/260. ... Full name: Brady McKay Smith. ... Son of Steve Smith, offensive tackle, Pittsburgh Steelers, Minnesota Vikings and Philadelphia Eagles (1966 and 1968-1974).
HIGH SCHOOL: Barrington (Ill.).
COLLEGE: Colorado State.
TRANSACTIONS/CAREER NOTES: Selected by New Orleans Saints in third round (70th pick overall) of 1996 NFL draft.

Year Team	G	SACKS
1991—Colorado State	Redshirted.	
1992—Colorado State	2	0.0
1993—Colorado State	6	3.0
1994—Colorado State	11	9.0
1995—Colorado State	11	15.0
College totals (4 years)	30	27.0

SMITH, DARIUS — C — RAIDERS

PERSONAL: Born October 9, 1972, in Dallas. ... 6-2/276.
HIGH SCHOOL: Carter (Dallas).
COLLEGE: Texas A&M, then Sam Houston State.
TRANSACTIONS/CAREER NOTES: Selected by Oakland Raiders in seventh round (224th pick overall) of 1996 NFL draft.
COLLEGE PLAYING EXPERIENCE: Sam Houston State, 1993-1995. ... Games: 1993 (5), 1994 (11), 1995 (10). Total: 26.

SMITH, DETRON — FB — BRONCOS

PERSONAL: Born February 25, 1974, in Dallas. ... 5-9/231. ... Full name: Detron Negil Smith.
HIGH SCHOOL: Lake Highlands (Dallas).
COLLEGE: Texas A&M.
TRANSACTIONS/CAREER NOTES: Selected by Denver Broncos in third round (65th pick overall) of 1996 NFL draft.

Year Team	G	RUSHING				RECEIVING				KICKOFF RETURNS				TOTALS	
		Att.	Yds.	Avg.	TD	No.	Yds.	Avg.	TD	No.	Yds.	Avg.	TD	TD	Pts.
1992—Texas A&M	9	2	6	3.0	0	1	13	13.0	0	2	30	15.0	0	0	0
1993—Texas A&M	11	24	86	3.6	0	6	73	12.2	0	1	3	3.0	0	0	0
1994—Texas A&M	10	16	73	4.6	1	11	115	10.5	0	1	14	14.0	0	1	6
1995—Texas A&M	11	15	19	1.3	0	15	99	6.6	0	1	7	7.0	0	0	0
College totals (4 years)	41	57	184	3.2	1	33	300	9.1	0	5	54	10.8	0	1	6

SMITH, JEFF — C — CHIEFS

PERSONAL: Born May 25, 1973, in Decatur, Tenn. ... 6-3/334.
HIGH SCHOOL: Meigs County (Decatur, Tenn.).
COLLEGE: Tennessee.
TRANSACTIONS/CAREER NOTES: Selected by Kansas City Chiefs in seventh round (241st pick overall) of 1996 NFL draft.
COLLEGE PLAYING EXPERIENCE: Tennessee, 1992-1995. ... Games: 1992 (12), 1993 (12), 1994 (12), 1995 (11). Total: 47.

SMITH, MARQUETTE — RB — PANTHERS

PERSONAL: Born July 14, 1972, in Casselberry, Fla. ... 5-7/195.
HIGH SCHOOL: Lake Howell (Winter Park, Fla.)
COLLEGE: Florida State, then Central Florida.
TRANSACTIONS/CAREER NOTES: Selected by Carolina Panthers in fifth round (142nd pick overall) of 1996 NFL draft.

Year Team	G	RUSHING				RECEIVING				TOTALS	
		Att.	Yds.	Avg.	TD	No.	Yds.	Avg.	TD	TD	Pts.
1991—Florida State	8	22	106	4.8	1	1	34	34.0	1	2	12
1992—Florida State		Redshirted.									
1993—Florida State	8	62	297	4.8	2	10	103	10.3	2	4	24
1994—Central Florida	11	194	1058	5.5	5	9	64	7.1	1	6	36
1995—Central Florida	11	274	1511	5.5	11	13	94	7.2	0	11	66
College totals (4 years)	38	552	2972	5.4	19	33	295	8.9	4	23	138

SOLI, JUNIOR — DT — CHARGERS

PERSONAL: Born November 15, 1974, in Samoa ... 6-2/290.

HIGH SCHOOL: Spencer (Columbus, Ga.)
COLLEGE: Arkansas.
TRANSACTIONS/CAREER NOTES: Selected by San Diego Chargers in fifth round (155th pick overall) of 1996 NFL draft.

		INTERCEPTIONS				SACKS
Year Team	G	No.	Yds.	Avg.	TD	No.
1992—Arkansas	9	0	0	...	0	0.0
1993—Arkansas	10	0	0	...	0	1.0
1994—Arkansas	11	1	51	51.0	1	1.0
1995—Arkansas	12	0	0	...	0	5.0
College totals (4 years)	42	1	51	51.0	1	7.0

SPANN, GREGORY WR JAGUARS

PERSONAL: Born April 16, 1973, in Macon, Miss. ... 6-0/215.
HIGH SCHOOL: Noxubee (Macon, Miss.).
COLLEGE: Jackson State.
TRANSACTIONS/CAREER NOTES: Selected by Jacksonville Jaguars in seventh round (228th pick overall) of 1996 NFL draft. ... Signed by Jaguars (May 28, 1996).

		RECEIVING				KICKOFF RETURNS				TOTALS	
Year Team	G	No.	Yds.	Avg.	TD	No.	Yds.	Avg.	TD	TD	Pts.
1991—Jackson State				Redshirted.								
1992—Jackson State	10	2	40	20.0	2	8	75	9.4	0	2	12
1993—Jackson State				Did not play.								
1994—Jackson State	11	39	721	18.5	5	13	339	26.1	0	5	30
1995—Jackson State	8	34	500	14.7	9	16	295	18.4	0	9	54
College totals (3 years)	29	75	1261	16.8	16	37	709	19.2	0	16	96

STAMPS, HARRY OT CARDINALS

PERSONAL: Born June 6, 1974, in Houston. ... 6-4/305. ... Full name: Harry Stamps Jr.
HIGH SCHOOL: M.B. Smiley (Houston).
COLLEGE: Oklahoma.
TRANSACTIONS/CAREER NOTES: Selected by Arizona Cardinals in fifth round (161st pick overall) of 1996 NFL draft.
COLLEGE PLAYING EXPERIENCE: Oklahoma, 1992-1995. ... Games: 1992 (10), 1993 (11), 1994 (11), 1995 (11). Total: 43.

STARK, JON QB RAVENS

PERSONAL: Born February 22, 1973, in Nashville. ... 6-4/222.
HIGH SCHOOL: Donelson Christian Academy (Nashville).
COLLEGE: Liberty, then Florida State, then Trinity International (Ill.).
TRANSACTIONS/CAREER NOTES: Selected by Baltimore Ravens in seventh round (238th pick overall) of 1996 NFL draft.

		PASSING								RUSHING				TOTALS	
Year Team	G	Att.	Cmp.	Pct.	Yds.	TD	Int.	Avg.	Rat.	Att.	Yds.	Avg.	TD	TD	Pts.
1991—Liberty						Redshirted.									
1992—Florida State						Did not play.									
1993—Florida State	5	35	25	71.4	328	2	3	9.37	151.5	8	0	0.0	0	0	0
1994—Florida State	6	38	24	63.2	291	3	1	7.66	148.3	6	-17	-2.8	0	0	0
1995—Trinity International	10	458	228	49.8	3142	21	10	6.86	118.2	52	-163	-3.1	0	0	0
College totals (3 years)	21	531	277	52.2	3761	26	14	7.08	122.6	66	-180	-2.7	0	0	0

STEPHENS, JAMAIN OT STEELERS

PERSONAL: Born January 9, 1974, in Lumberton , N.C. ... 6-5/315.
HIGH SCHOOL: Lumberton (N.C.).
COLLEGE: North Carolina A&T.
TRANSACTIONS/CAREER NOTES: Selected by Pittsburgh Steelers in first round (29th pick overall) of 1996 NFL draft.
COLLEGE PLAYING EXPERIENCE: North Carolina A&T, 1993-1995. ... Games: 1993 (11), 1994 (11), 1995 (11). Total: 33.

STEVENS, MATT CB BILLS

PERSONAL: Born June 15, 1973, in Chapel Hill, N.C. ... 6-0/206.
HIGH SCHOOL: Chapel Hill (N.C.).
COLLEGE: Appalachian State.
TRANSACTIONS/CAREER NOTES: Selected by Buffalo Bills in third round (87th pick overall) of 1996 NFL draft.

		INTERCEPTIONS			
Year Team	G	No.	Yds.	Avg.	TD
1991—Appalachian State			Redshirted.			
1992—Appalachian State	9	2	14	7.0	0
1993—Appalachian State	11	6	124	20.7	0
1994—Appalachian State	11	7	64	9.2	0
1995—Appalachian State	8	3	43	14.3	0
College totals (4 years)	39	18	245	13.6	0

STEWART, RAYNA   CB   OILERS

PERSONAL: Born June 18, 1973, in Oklahoma City. ... 5-10/192. ... Name pronounced ruh-NAY.
HIGH SCHOOL: Chatsworth (Calif.).
COLLEGE: Northern Arizona (degree in advertising, 1995).
TRANSACTIONS/CAREER NOTES: Selected by Houston Oilers in fifth round (143rd pick overall) of 1996 NFL draft.

		INTERCEPTIONS				SACKS	KICKOFF RETURNS				TOTALS	
Year—Team	G	No.	Yds.	Avg.	TD	No.	No.	Yds.	Avg.	TD	TD	Pts.
1991—Northern Arizona	10	0	0	...	0	0.0	8	191	23.9	0	0	0
1992—Northern Arizona						Redshirted.						
1993—Northern Arizona	10	1	0	0.0	0	1.0	4	47	11.8	0	0	0
1994—Northern Arizona	11	2	5	2.5	0	0.0	0	0	...	0	0	0
1995—Northern Arizona	11	1	23	23.0	0	0.0	0	0	...	0	0	0
College totals (4 years)	42	4	28	7.0	0	1.0	12	238	19.8	0	0	0

STEWART, RYAN   S   LIONS

PERSONAL: Born September 30, 1973, in Moncks Corner, S.C. ... 6-1/207.
HIGH SCHOOL: Berkeley (Moncks Corner, S.C.).
COLLEGE: Georgia Tech.
TRANSACTIONS/CAREER NOTES: Selected by Detroit Lions in third round (76th pick overall) of 1996 NFL draft.

		INTERCEPTIONS			
Year—Team	G	No.	Yds.	Avg.	TD
1991—Georgia Tech			Redshirted.		
1992—Georgia Tech	11	0	0	...	0
1993—Georgia Tech	11	0	0	...	0
1994—Georgia Tech	8	0	0	...	0
1995—Georgia Tech	11	3	62	20.7	1
College totals (4 years)	41	3	62	20.7	1

STILL, BRYAN   WR   CHARGERS

PERSONAL: Born June 3, 1974, in Newport News, Va. ... 5-11/174. ... Full name: Bryan Andrei Still.
HIGH SCHOOL: Huguenot (Richmond, Va.).
COLLEGE: Virginia Tech.
TRANSACTIONS/CAREER NOTES: Selected by San Diego Chargers in second round (41st pick overall) of 1996 NFL draft.

		RECEIVING				PUNT RETURNS				KICKOFF RETURNS				TOTALS	
Year—Team	G	No.	Yds.	Avg.	TD	No.	Yds.	Avg.	TD	No.	Yds.	Avg.	TD	TD	Pts.
1992—Virginia Tech	8	4	70	17.5	1	0	0	...	0	0	0	...	0	1	6
1993—Virginia Tech	11	15	260	17.3	3	0	0	...	0	0	0	...	0	3	18
1994—Virginia Tech	11	23	500	21.7	4	3	76	25.3	0	19	493	26.0	0	4	24
1995—Virginia Tech	9	32	628	19.6	3	4	18	4.5	0	3	43	14.3	0	3	18
College totals (4 years)	39	74	1458	19.7	11	7	94	13.4	0	22	536	24.4	0	11	66

STOLTENBERG, BRYAN   C   CHARGERS

PERSONAL: Born August 25, 1972, in Kearney, Neb. ... 6-1/293.
HIGH SCHOOL: Clements (Sugar Land, Texas).
COLLEGE: Colorado.
TRANSACTIONS/CAREER NOTES: Selected by San Diego Chargers in sixth round (192nd pick overall) of 1996 NFL draft.
COLLEGE PLAYING EXPERIENCE: Colorado, 1992-1995. ... Games: 1992 (11), 1993 (11), 1994 (11), 1995 (11). Total: 44.
HONORS: Named offensive lineman on THE SPORTING NEWS college All-America second team (1995).

SULLIVAN, CHRIS   DE   PATRIOTS

PERSONAL: Born March 14, 1973, in North Attleboro, Mass. ... 6-4/279. ... Full name: Christopher Patrick Sullivan.
HIGH SCHOOL: North Attleboro (Mass.).
COLLEGE: Boston College (degree in sociology, 1995).
TRANSACTIONS/CAREER NOTES: Selected by New England Patriots in fourth round (119th pick overall) of 1996 NFL draft.

Year—Team	G	SACKS
1991—Boston College	Redshirted.	
1992—Boston College	11	1.0
1993—Boston College	11	4.0
1994—Boston College	11	6.0
1995—Boston College	12	2.0
College totals (4 years)	45	13.0

THOMAS, FRED   DB   SEAHAWKS

PERSONAL: Born September 11, 1973, in Grand Rapids, Mich. ... 5-9/172.
HIGH SCHOOL: Bruce (Miss.).
JUNIOR COLLEGE: Northwest Mississippi Community College.

COLLEGE: Mississippi Valley State (did not play football), then Mississippi, then Tennessee-Martin.
TRANSACTIONS/CAREER NOTES: Selected by Seattle Seahawks in second round (47th pick overall) of 1996 NFL draft.
MISCELLANEOUS: Caught 21 passes for 349 yards and two touchdowns (1993).

		INTERCEPTIONS				PUNT RETURNS				KICKOFF RETURNS				TOTALS	
Year Team	G	No.	Yds.	Avg.	TD	No.	Yds.	Avg.	TD	No.	Yds.	Avg.	TD	TD	Pts.
1991—Mississippi Valley State	...						Did not play.								
1992—Northwest Mississippi CC	...	4	53	13.3	0	28	693	24.8	3	11	246	22.4	1	4	24
1993—Northwest Mississippi CC	...	1	80	80.0	0	12	256	21.3	1	8	252	31.5	1	4	24
1994—Mississippi	7	1	83	83.0	1	5	38	7.6	0	0	0	...	0	2	12
1995—Tennessee-Martin	11	5	61	12.2	1	23	208	9.0	1	12	267	22.3	0	2	12
Junior totals (2 years)	...	5	133	26.6	0	40	949	23.7	4	19	498	26.2	2	8	48
College totals (2 years)	18	6	144	24.0	2	28	246	8.8	2	12	267	22.3	0	4	24

THOMAS, ZACH — LB — DOLPHINS

PERSONAL: Born September 1, 1973, in Lubbock, Texas. ... 5-11/231.
HIGH SCHOOL: White Deer (Texas), then Pampa (Texas).
COLLEGE: Texas Tech.
TRANSACTIONS/CAREER NOTES: Selected by Miami Dolphins in fifth round (154th pick overall) of 1996 NFL draft.
HONORS: Named linebacker on THE SPORTING NEWS college All-America second team (1994). ... Named linebacker on THE SPORTING NEWS college All-America first team (1995).

		INTERCEPTIONS				SACKS
Year Team	G	No.	Yds.	Avg.	TD	No.
1992—Texas Tech	11	0	0	...	0	0.0
1993—Texas Tech	11	1	5	5.0	0	1.0
1994—Texas Tech	11	6	91	15.2	1	3.5
1995—Texas Tech	11	2	57	28.5	1	3.0
College totals (4 years)	44	9	153	17.0	2	7.5

TONGUE, REGGIE — CB/S — CHIEFS

PERSONAL: Born April 11, 1973, in Baltimore. ... 6-0/201. ... Full name: Reginald Clinton Tongue. ... Name pronounced TONG.
HIGH SCHOOL: Lathrop (Fairbanks, Alaska).
COLLEGE: Oregon State.
TRANSACTIONS/CAREER NOTES: Selected by Kansas City Chiefs in second round (58th pick overall) of 1996 NFL draft.
MISCELLANEOUS: Returned one fumble 75 yards for a touchdown (1993).

		INTERCEPTIONS			
Year Team	G	No.	Yds.	Avg.	TD
1991—Oregon State			Redshirted.			
1992—Oregon State	11	1	28	28.0	0
1993—Oregon State	11	3	35	11.7	1
1994—Oregon State	11	5	150	30.0	3
1995—Oregon State	11	0	0	...	0
College totals (4 years)	44	9	213	23.7	4

TOOMER, AMANI — WR — GIANTS

PERSONAL: Born September 8, 1974, in Berkely, Calif. ... 6-3/202. ... Name pronounced ah-MAH-nee.
HIGH SCHOOL: De La Salle Catholic (Concord, Calif.).
COLLEGE: Michigan.
TRANSACTIONS/CAREER NOTES: Selected by New York Giants in second round (34th pick overall) of 1996 NFL draft.

		RECEIVING				PUNT RETURNS				KICKOFF RETURNS				TOTALS	
Year Team	G	No.	Yds.	Avg.	TD	No.	Yds.	Avg.	TD	No.	Yds.	Avg.	TD	TD	Pts.
1992—Michigan	11	16	238	14.9	1	2	22	11.0	0	0	0	...	0	1	6
1993—Michigan	11	27	521	19.3	3	1	-10	-10.0	0	3	102	34.0	0	3	18
1994—Michigan	11	49	1033	21.1	5	17	116	6.9	1	0	0	...	0	6	36
1995—Michigan	12	39	623	16.0	5	21	177	8.4	1	11	204	18.6	0	6	36
College totals (4 years)	45	131	2415	18.4	14	41	307	7.5	2	14	306	21.9	0	16	96

TUMULTY, TOM — LB — BENGALS

PERSONAL: Born February 11, 1973, in Penn Hills, Pa. ... 6-2/242. ... Full name: Thomas Patrick Tumulty.
HIGH SCHOOL: Penn Hills (Pa.).
COLLEGE: Pittsburgh.
TRANSACTIONS/CAREER NOTES: Selected by Cincinnati Bengals in sixth round (178th pick overall) of 1996 NFL draft.
MISCELLANEOUS: Granted medical redshirt due to chest injury (1992).

		INTERCEPTIONS				SACKS
Year Team	G	No.	Yds.	Avg.	TD	No.
1991—Pittsburgh	11	0	0	...	0	0.0
1992—Pittsburgh	1	0	0	...	0	0.0
1993—Pittsburgh	11	2	6	3.0	0	3.0
1994—Pittsburgh	9	1	15	15.0	0	1.0
1995—Pittsburgh	11	0	0	...	0	1.0
College totals (5 years)	43	3	21	7.0	0	5.0

ULUFALE, MIKE　　　　　DE　　　　　COWBOYS

PERSONAL: Born February 1, 1972, in Honolulu. ... 6-4/282. ... Name pronounced oo-loo-FAH-lay.
HIGH SCHOOL: James Campbell (Honokai Hale, Hawaii).
JUNIOR COLLEGE: San Bernadino (Calif.) Valley.
COLLEGE: Brigham Young.
TRANSACTIONS/CAREER NOTES: Selected by Dallas Cowboys in third round (95th pick overall) of 1996 NFL draft.

Year　Team	G	INTERCEPTIONS No.	Yds.	Avg.	TD	SACKS No.
1991—San Bernardino Valley			Statistics unavailable.			
1992—San Bernardino Valley			Statistics unavailable.			
1993—Brigham Young			Redshirted.			
1994—Brigham Young	12	0	0	...	0	6.0
1995—Brigham Young	6	1	4	4.0	0	0.0
Junior College totals (2 years)	...	...	...	...	...	...
College totals (2 years)	18	1	4	4.0	0	6.0

UNVERZAGT, ERIC　　　　　LB　　　　　SEAHAWKS

PERSONAL: Born December 18, 1972, in Central Islip, N.Y. ... 6-1/236. ... Name pronounced UN-ver-zott.
HIGH SCHOOL: Central Islip (N.Y.).
COLLEGE: Wisconsin.
TRANSACTIONS/CAREER NOTES: Selected by Seattle Seahawks in fourth round (131st pick overall) of 1996 NFL draft.

Year　Team	G	INTERCEPTIONS No.	Yds.	Avg.	TD	SACKS No.
1991—Wisconsin	11	0	0	...	0	0.0
1992—Wisconsin			Redshirted.			
1993—Wisconsin	10	1	11	11.0	0	1.0
1994—Wisconsin	11	2	39	19.5	0	1.0
1995—Wisconsin	11	2	0	0.0	0	2.0
College totals (4 years)	43	5	50	10.0	0	4.0

UPSHAW, REGAN　　　　　DE　　　　　BUCCANEERS

PERSONAL: Born August 12, 1975, in Detroit. ... 6-4/260.
HIGH SCHOOL: Pittsburg (Calif.).
COLLEGE: California.
TRANSACTIONS/CAREER NOTES: Selected after junior season by Tampa Bay Buccaneers in first round (12th pick overall) of 1996 NFL draft.

Year　Team	G	INTERCEPTIONS No.	Yds.	Avg.	TD	SACKS No.
1993—California	12	1	0	0.0	0	7.5
1994—California	11	0	0	...	0	11.0
1995—California	11	0	0	...	0	9.5
College totals (3 years)	34	1	0	0.0	0	28.0

UWAEZUOKE, IHEANYI　　　　　WR　　　　　49ERS

PERSONAL: Born July 24, 1973, in Lagos, Nigeria ... 6-2/195. ... Name pronounced ee-HAHN-ee ooh-WAY-zoh-kay.
HIGH SCHOOL: Harvard (North Hollywood, Calif.)
COLLEGE: California.
TRANSACTIONS/CAREER NOTES: Selected by San Francisco 49ers in fifth round (160th pick overall) of 1996 NFL draft.

Year　Team	G	RECEIVING No.	Yds.	Avg.	TD
1991—California			Redshirted.		
1992—California	11	1	7	7.0	0
1993—California	12	25	422	16.9	2
1994—California	10	56	716	12.8	5
1995—California	7	30	506	16.9	3
College totals (4 years)	40	112	1651	14.8	10

VAN DYKE, ALEX　　　　　WR　　　　　JETS

PERSONAL: Born July 24, 1974, in Sacramento. ... 6-0/200. ... Full name: Frank Alexander Van Dyke.
HIGH SCHOOL: Luther Burbank (Sacramento).
JUNIOR COLLEGE: Sacramento City College.
COLLEGE: Nevada.
TRANSACTIONS/CAREER NOTES: Selected by New York Jets in second round (31st pick overall) of 1996 NFL draft.
HONORS: Named wide receiver on THE SPORTING NEWS college All-America second team (1995).

Year　Team	G	RECEIVING No.	Yds.	Avg.	TD	PUNT RETURNS No.	Yds.	Avg.	TD	KICKOFF RETURNS No.	Yds.	Avg.	TD	TOTALS TD Pts.
1992—Sacramento City College	11	28	786	28.1	...	...	...	...	...	...	...	...	...	... ...

Year	Team	G	RECEIVING No.	Yds.	Avg.	TD	PUNT RETURNS No.	Yds.	Avg.	TD	KICKOFF RETURNS No.	Yds.	Avg.	TD	TOTALS TD	Pts.
1993—Sacramento City College	11	52	1182	22.7	18	...	...	...	...	...	...	...	...	18	108
1994—Nevada	11	98	1246	12.7	10	2	5	2.5	0	21	451	21.5	1	11	66
1995—Nevada	11	129	1854	14.4	16	0	0	...	0	26	583	22.4	0	16	96
Junior College totals (2 years)	22	80	1968	24.6	...	...	...	...	...	...	...	...	...	...	...
College totals (2 years)	22	227	3100	13.7	26	2	5	2.5	0	47	1034	22.0	1	27	162

VELAND, TONY   S   BRONCOS

PERSONAL: Born March 11, 1973, in Omaha, Neb. ... 6-0/205.
HIGH SCHOOL: Benson (Omaha, Neb.).
COLLEGE: Nebraska.
TRANSACTIONS/CAREER NOTES: Selected by Denver Broncos in sixth round (181st pick overall) of 1996 NFL draft.
MISCELLANEOUS: Played quarterback during the 1992 and 1993 seasons. ... Rushed seven times for one yard (1992); and attempted nine passes with six completions for 76 yards and a touchdown and rushed eight times for 14 yards and a touchdown. (1993).

Year	Team	G	INTERCEPTIONS No.	Yds.	Avg.	TD
1991—Nebraska			Redshirted.			
1992—Nebraska	4	0	0	...	0	
1993—Nebraska	2	0	0	...	0	
1994—Nebraska	12	3	35	11.7	0	
1995—Nebraska	11	1	43	43.0	0	
College totals (4 years)	29	4	78	19.5	0	

VILLARRIAL, CHRIS   C/G   BEARS

PERSONAL: Born June 9, 1973, in Hummelstown, Pa. ... 6-4/300. ... Name pronounced vill-uh-ree-AL.
HIGH SCHOOL: Hershey (Pa.).
COLLEGE: Indiana (Pa.).
TRANSACTIONS/CAREER NOTES: Selected by Chicago Bears in fifth round (152nd pick overall) of 1996 NFL draft.
COLLEGE PLAYING EXPERIENCE: Indiana (Pa.), 1992-1995. ... Games: 1992 (10), 1993 (10), 1994 (11), 1995 (11). Total: 42.

WACHHOLTZ, KYLE   QB   PACKERS

PERSONAL: Born May 17, 1972, in Norco, Calif. ... 6-4/238.
HIGH SCHOOL: Norco (Corona, Calif.).
COLLEGE: Southern California.
TRANSACTIONS/CAREER NOTES: Selected by Green Bay Packers in seventh round (240th pick overall) of 1996 NFL draft.

Year	Team	G	PASSING Att.	Cmp.	Pct.	Yds.	TD	Int.	Avg.	Rat.	RUSHING Att.	Yds.	Avg.	TD	TOTALS TD	Pts.
1991—Southern California			Redshirted.												
1992—Southern California	3	10	6	60.0	54	0	1	5.40	85.4	4	-2	-0.5	0	0	0
1993—Southern California	6	25	17	68.0	184	2	0	7.36	156.2	2	11	5.5	0	0	0
1994—Southern California			Did not play.												
1995—Southern California	11	171	105	61.4	1231	11	3	7.20	137.3	42	-28	-0.7	0	0	0
College totals (3 years)	20	206	128	62.1	1469	13	4	7.13	133.7	48	-19	-0.4	0	0	0

WALDROUP, KERWIN   DL   LIONS

PERSONAL: Born August 1, 1974, in Chicago. ... 6-3/260.
HIGH SCHOOL: Rich Central (Olympia Fields, Ill.).
COLLEGE: Michigan, then Central State (Ohio).
TRANSACTIONS/CAREER NOTES: Selected by Detroit Lions in fifth round (158th pick overall) of 1996 NFL draft.

Year	Team	G	SACKS
1992—Michigan	Did not play.		
1993—Michigan	3	0.0	
1994—Michigan	8	2.0	
1995—Central State	11	9.0	
College totals (3 years)	22	11.0	

WHITE, STEVE   LB   EAGLES

PERSONAL: Born October 25, 1973, in Memphis. ... 6-2/246.
HIGH SCHOOL: Westwood (Memphis).
COLLEGE: Tennessee (degree in psychology, 1996).
TRANSACTIONS/CAREER NOTES: Selected by Philadelphia Eagles in sixth round (194th pick overall) of 1996 NFL draft.

Year	Team	G	SACKS
1991—Tennessee	Redshirted.		
1992—Tennessee	7	1.0	
1993—Tennessee	12	3.0	
1994—Tennessee	12	7.0	
1995—Tennessee	11	9.0	
College totals (4 years)	42	20.0	

WHITTLE, RICKY — RB — SAINTS

PERSONAL: Born December 21, 1971, in Fresno, Calif. ... 5-9/200. ... Full name: Ricky Jerome Whittle.
HIGH SCHOOL: Edison (Fresno, Calif.).
COLLEGE: Oregon.
TRANSACTIONS/CAREER NOTES: Selected by New Orleans Saints in fourth round (103rd pick overall) of 1996 NFL draft.

		RUSHING				RECEIVING				KICKOFF RETURNS				TOTALS	
Year Team	G	Att.	Yds.	Avg.	TD	No.	Yds.	Avg.	TD	No.	Yds.	Avg.	TD	TD	Pts.
1991—Oregon						Redshirted.									
1992—Oregon	11	126	607	4.8	1	6	75	12.5	0	0	0	...	0	1	6
1993—Oregon	11	67	284	4.2	1	15	196	13.1	1	14	326	23.3	0	2	12
1994—Oregon	8	118	561	4.8	7	9	81	9.0	1	5	230	46.0	0	8	48
1995—Oregon	11	248	971	3.9	12	51	419	8.2	1	18	414	23.0	0	13	78
College totals (4 years)	41	559	2423	4.3	21	81	771	9.5	3	37	970	26.2	0	24	144

WILLIAMS, DARRELL — DB/KR — CHIEFS

PERSONAL: Born June 29, 1973, in Augusta, Ga. ... 5-11/196.
HIGH SCHOOL: Laney (Augusta, Ga.).
COLLEGE: Tennessee State.
TRANSACTIONS/CAREER NOTES: Selected by Kansas City Chiefs in seventh round (245th pick overall) of 1996 NFL draft.
MISCELLANEOUS: Played safety during the 1994 season. ... Intercepted two passes for 50 yards (1994).

		RUSHING				RECEIVING				PUNT RETURNS				KICKOFF RETURNS				TOTALS	
Year Team	G	Att.	Yds.	Avg.	TD	No.	Yds.	Avg.	TD	No.	Yds.	Avg.	TD	No.	Yds.	Avg.	TD	TD	Pts.
1992—Tennessee State	8	23	56	2.4	0	5	45	9.0	0	0	0	...	0	3	33	11.0	0	0	0
1993—Tennessee State	11	59	264	4.5	3	34	293	8.6	1	2	0	0.0	0	1	8	8.0	0	4	24
1994—Tennessee State	11	0	0	...	0	0	0	...	0	40	445	11.1	1	24	585	24.4	0	0	0
1995—Tennessee State							Did not play.													
College totals (3 years)	30	82	320	3.9	3	39	338	8.7	1	42	445	10.6	1	28	626	22.4	0	4	24

WILLIAMS, MOE — RB — VIKINGS

PERSONAL: Born July 26, 1974, in Columbus, Ga. ... 6-1/203.
HIGH SCHOOL: Spencer (Columbus, Ga.).
COLLEGE: Kentucky.
TRANSACTIONS/CAREER NOTES: Selected after junior season by Minnesota Vikings in third round (75th pick overall) of 1996 NFL draft.

		RUSHING				RECEIVING				KICKOFF RETURNS				TOTALS	
Year Team	G	Att.	Yds.	Avg.	TD	No.	Yds.	Avg.	TD	No.	Yds.	Avg.	TD	TD	Pts.
1993—Kentucky	11	164	928	5.7	5	7	41	5.9	0	0	0	...	0	5	30
1994—Kentucky	11	160	805	5.0	4	12	119	9.9	1	0	0	...	0	5	30
1995—Kentucky	11	294	1600	5.4	17	19	153	8.1	0	4	73	18.3	0	17	102
College totals (3 years)	33	618	3333	5.4	26	38	313	8.2	1	4	73	18.3	0	27	162

WILLIAMS, STEPFRET — WR — COWBOYS

PERSONAL: Born June 14, 1973, in Minden, La. ... 6-0/170.
HIGH SCHOOL: Minden (La.).
COLLEGE: Northeast Louisiana.
TRANSACTIONS/CAREER NOTES: Selected by Dallas Cowboys in third round (94th pick overall) of 1996 NFL draft.

		RECEIVING				KICKOFF RETURNS				TOTALS	
Year Team	G	No.	Yds.	Avg.	TD	No.	Yds.	Avg.	TD	TD	Pts.
1991—Northeast Louisiana				Redshirted.							
1992—Northeast Louisiana	5	5	86	17.2	1	0	0	...	0	1	6
1993—Northeast Louisiana	11	40	929	23.2	10	1	8	8.0	0	10	60
1994—Northeast Louisiana	11	57	1106	19.4	10	3	60	20.0	0	10	60
1995—Northeast Louisiana	11	66	1056	16.0	12	12	275	22.9	0	12	72
College totals (4 years)	38	168	3177	18.9	33	16	343	21.4	0	33	198

WILLIAMS, TYRONE — CB — PACKERS

PERSONAL: Born May 31, 1973, in Bradenton, Fla. ... 5-11/190.
HIGH SCHOOL: Manatee (Bradenton, Fla.).
COLLEGE: Nebraska.
TRANSACTIONS/CAREER NOTES: Selected by Green Bay Packers in third round (93rd pick overall) of 1996 NFL draft.... Signed by Packers (May 15, 1996).

		INTERCEPTIONS			
Year Team	G	No.	Yds.	Avg.	TD
1992—Nebraska			Did not play.		
1993—Nebraska	11	1	15	15.0	0
1994—Nebraska	11	3	34	11.3	0
1995—Nebraska	11	1	11	11.0	0
College totals (3 years)	33	5	60	12.0	0

WITMAN, JON   FB   STEELERS

PERSONAL: Born June 1, 1972, in Wrightsville, Pa. ... 6-1/242. ... Full name: Jon Doyle Witman.
HIGH SCHOOL: Eastern York (Pa.).
COLLEGE: Penn State.
TRANSACTIONS/CAREER NOTES: Selected by Pittsburgh Steelers in third round (92nd pick overall) of 1996 NFL draft.
MISCELLANEOUS: Played linebacker during the 1992 season.

		RUSHING				RECEIVING				TOTALS	
Year Team	G	Att.	Yds.	Avg.	TD	No.	Yds.	Avg.	TD	TD	Pts.
1992—Penn State	11	0	0	...	0	0	0	...	0	0	0
1993—Penn State	11	14	125	8.9	0	1	7	7.0	0	0	0
1994—Penn State	10	49	241	4.9	5	4	21	5.3	1	6	36
1995—Penn State	11	84	316	3.8	9	14	87	6.2	1	10	60
College totals (4 years)	43	147	682	4.6	14	19	115	6.1	2	16	96

WOOD, RYAN   RB   COWBOYS

PERSONAL: Born June 13, 1972, in Fort Collins, Colo. ... 5-11/236.
HIGH SCHOOL: Loveland (Colo.), then Fork Union (Va.) Military Academy.
COLLEGE: Youngstown State, then Arizona State.
TRANSACTIONS/CAREER NOTES: Selected by Dallas Cowboys in seventh round (243rd pick overall) of 1996 NFL draft.

		RUSHING				RECEIVING				TOTALS	
Year Team	G	Att.	Yds.	Avg.	TD	No.	Yds.	Avg.	TD	TD	Pts.
1991—Youngstown State	11	11	47	4.3	1	0	0	...	0	1	6
1992—Youngstown State	11	59	212	3.6	0	5	28	5.6	0	0	0
1993—Arizona State				Did not play.							
1994—Arizona State	7	8	21	2.6	2	4	37	9.3	0	2	12
1995—Arizona State	11	35	100	2.9	2	1	3	3.0	0	2	12
College totals (4 years)	40	113	380	3.4	5	10	68	6.8	0	5	30

WOODEN, SHAWN   DB   DOLPHINS

PERSONAL: Born October 23, 1973, in Willow Grove, Pa. ... 5-11/186.
HIGH SCHOOL: Abington (Pa.).
COLLEGE: Notre Dame.
TRANSACTIONS/CAREER NOTES: Selected by Miami Dolphins in sixth round (189th pick overall) of 1996 NFL draft.

		INTERCEPTIONS			
Year Team	G	No.	Yds.	Avg.	TD
1991—Notre Dame	5	0	0	...	0
1992—Notre Dame			Redshirted.		
1993—Notre Dame	8	1	0	0.0	0
1994—Notre Dame	11	1	7	7.0	0
1995—Notre Dame	11	3	10	3.3	0
College totals (4 years)	35	5	17	3.4	0

WOODS, JEROME   CB/S   CHIEFS

PERSONAL: Born March 17, 1973, in Memphis. ... 6-2/198.
HIGH SCHOOL: Melrose (Memphis).
JUNIOR COLLEGE: Northeast Mississippi Junior College.
COLLEGE: Memphis.
TRANSACTIONS/CAREER NOTES: Selected by Kansas City Chiefs in first round (28th pick overall) of 1996 NFL draft.

		INTERCEPTIONS				PUNT RETURNS				KICKOFF RETURNS				TOTALS	
Year Team	G	No.	Yds.	Avg.	TD	No.	Yds.	Avg.	TD	No.	Yds.	Avg.	TD	TD	Pts.
1992—Northeast Mississippi Junior College				Did not play.											
1993—Northeast Mississippi Junior College	11	2	0	0.0	0	16	152	9.5	0	16	285	17.8	0	0	0
1994—Memphis	11	1	11	11.0	0	0	0	...	0	0	0	...	0	0	0
1995—Memphis	11	6	110	18.3	1	0	0	...	0	0	0	...	0	1	6
Junior College totals (1 year)	33	9	121	13.5	1	16	152	9.5	0	16	285	17.8	0	1	6
College totals (2 years)	33	9	121	13.5	1	16	152	9.5	0	16	285	17.8	0	1	6

WYLIE, JOEY   G   RAIDERS

PERSONAL: Born April 25, 1974, in Santa Fe, Texas. ... 6-4/301.
HIGH SCHOOL: Sante Fe (Texas).
COLLEGE: Stephen F. Austin State.
TRANSACTIONS/CAREER NOTES: Selected by Oakland Raiders in seventh round (248th pick overall) of 1996 NFL draft.
COLLEGE PLAYING EXPERIENCE: Stephen F. Austin State, 1992-1995. ... Games: 1992 (11), 1993 (11), 1994 (11), 1995 (10). Total: 43.

WYMAN, DEVIN   DT   PATRIOTS

PERSONAL: Born August 29, 1973, in East Palo Alto, Calif. ... 6-7/307.

HIGH SCHOOL: Carlmont (Belmont, Calif.).
JUNIOR COLLEGE: San Mateo (Calif.) Junior College.
COLLEGE: Kentucky State.
TRANSACTIONS/CAREER NOTES: Selected by New England Patriots in sixth round (206th pick overall) of 1996 NFL draft.

| Year Team | G | INTERCEPTIONS | | | | SACKS |
		No.	Yds.	Avg.	TD	No.
1992—San Mateo Junior College		Statistics unavailable.				
1993—San Mateo Junior College		Statistics unavailable.				
1994—Kentucky State		Statistics unavailable.				
1995—Kentucky State	11	2	78	39.0	1	9.0

ZEIGLER, DUSTY   C/G   BILLS

PERSONAL: Born September 27, 1973, in Rincon, Ga. ... 6-5/298. ... Full name: Curtis Dustin Zeigler.
HIGH SCHOOL: Effingham County (Springfield, Ga.).
COLLEGE: Notre Dame.
TRANSACTIONS/CAREER NOTES: Selected by Buffalo Bills in sixth round (202nd pick overall) of 1996 NFL draft.
COLLEGE PLAYING EXPERIENCE: Notre Dame, 1993-1995. ... Games: 1993 (7), 1994 (11), 1995 (11). Total: 29.

BROOKS, RICH — RAMS

PERSONAL: Born August 20, 1941, in Forest, Calif. ... Full name: Richard L. Brooks.
HIGH SCHOOL: Nevada Union (Grass Valley, Calif.).
COLLEGE: Oregon State (bachelor's degree in physical education, 1963; master's degree in education, 1964).

HEAD COACHING RECORD
BACKGROUND: Assistant freshman coach, Oregon State (1963). ... Assistant coach, Norte Del Rio High School, Calif. (1964). ... Defensive line coach, Oregon State (1965-1969). ... Linebackers coach, UCLA (1970). ... Special teams and fundamentals coach, Los Angeles Rams NFL (1971 and 1972). ... Defensive coordinator, Oregon State (1973). ... Defensive backs/special teams coach, San Francisco 49ers NFL (1974 and 1975). ...Linebackers coach, UCLA (1976).
HONORS: Named College Football Coach of the Year by THE SPORTING NEWS (1994).

	W	L	T	Pct.	REGULAR SEASON Finish	POST-SEASON W	L
1977—Oregon	2	9	0	.182	7th/Pacific-10 Conference	—	—
1978—Oregon	2	9	0	.182	8th/Pacific-10 Conference	—	—
1979—Oregon	6	5	0	.545	T3rd/Pacific-10 Conference	—	—
1980—Oregon	6	3	2	.636	5th/Pacific-10 Conference	—	—
1981—Oregon	2	9	0	.182	9th/Pacific-10 Conference	—	—
1982—Oregon	2	8	1	.227	9th/Pacific-10 Conference	—	—
1983—Oregon	4	6	1	.409	T6th/Pacific-10 Conference	—	—
1984—Oregon	6	5	0	.545	T7th/Pacific-10 Conference	—	—
1985—Oregon	5	6	0	.455	6th/Pacific-10 Conference	—	—
1986—Oregon	5	6	0	.455	7th/Pacific-10 Conference	—	—
1987—Oregon	6	5	0	.545	T4th/Pacific-10 Conference	—	—
1988—Oregon	6	6	0	.500	T6th/Pacific-10 Conference	—	—
1989—Oregon	7	4	0	.636	T2nd/Pacific-10 Conference	1	0
1990—Oregon	8	3	0	.727	3rd/Pacific-10 Conference	0	1
1991—Oregon	3	8	0	.273	T9th/Pacific-10 Conference	—	—
1992—Oregon	6	5	0	.545	T6th/Pacific-10 Conference	0	1
1993—Oregon	5	6	0	.455	T8th/Pacific-10 Conference	—	—
1994—Oregon	9	3	0	.750	1st/Pacific-10 Conference	0	1
1995—St. Louis NFL	7	9	0	.438	T3rd/NFC Western Divsion	—	—
College totals (18 years)	90	106	4	.460	**College totals (4 years)**	1	3
Pro totals (1 year)	7	9	0	.438			

NOTES:
1989—Defeated Tulsa, 27-24, in Independence Bowl.
1990—Lost to Colorado State, 32-31, in Freedom Bowl.
1992—Lost to Wake Forest, 39-35, in Independence Bowl.
1994—Lost to Penn State, 38-20, in Rose Bowl.

CAPERS, DOM — PANTHERS

PERSONAL: Born August 7, 1950 in Cambridge, Ohio. ... Full name: Dominic Capers.
HIGH SCHOOL: Meadowbrook (Byesville, Ohio).
COLLEGE: Mount Union, Ohio. (bachelor's degree in psychology and physical education), then Kent State (master's degree in administration).

HEAD COACHING RECORD
BACKGROUND: Graduate assistant, Kent State (1972-1974). ... Graduate assistant, Washington (1975). ... Defensive backs coach, Hawaii (1975). ... Defensive coordinator, Hawaii (1976). ... Defensive assistant coach, San Jose State (1977). ... Defensive assistant coach, California (1978 and 1979). ... Defensive backs coach, Tennessee (1980 and 1981). ... Defensive backs coach, Ohio State (1982 and 1983). ... Defensive backs coach, Philadelphia Stars USFL (1984). ... Defensive backs coach, Baltimore Stars USFL (1985). ... Defensive backs coach, New Orleans Saints NFL (1986-1991). ... Defensive coordinator, Pittsburgh Steelers NFL (1992-1994).

	W	L	T	Pct.	REGULAR SEASON Finish	POST-SEASON W	L
1995—Carolina NFL	7	9	0	.438	T3rd/NFC Western Division	—	—

COUGHLIN, TOM — JAGUARS

PERSONAL: Born August 31, 1946, in Waterloo, N.Y.
HIGH SCHOOL: Waterloo (N.Y.).
COLLEGE: Syracuse (bachelor's degree in education, 1968; master's degree in education, 1969).

HEAD COACHING RECORD
BACKGROUND: Graduate assistant/freshman coach, Syracuse (1969). ... Assistant coach, Rochester Institute of Technology (1969). ... Offensive coordinator, Syracuse (1974-1979). ... Quarterbacks coach, Boston College (1980-1983). ... Receivers coach, Philadelphia Eagles NFL (1984 and 1985). ... Receivers coach, Green Bay Packers NFL (1986 and 1987). ... Receivers coach, New York Giants NFL (1988-1990).

				REGULAR SEASON		POST-SEASON	
	W	L	T	Pct.	Finish	W	L
1970—Rochester Tech	4	3	0	.571	Eastern College Athletic Conference	—	—
1971—Rochester Tech	5	2	1	.688	Eastern College Athletic Conference	—	—
1972—Rochester Tech	4	5	0	.444	Eastern College Athletic Conference	—	—
1973—Rochester Tech	3	5	1	.389	Eastern College Athletic Conference	—	—
1991—Boston College	4	7	0	.364	7th/Big East Conference	0	0
1992—Boston College	8	2	1	.773	3rd/Big East Conference	0	1
1993—Boston College	8	3	0	.727	3rd/Big East Conference	1	0
1995—Jacksonville NFL	4	12	0	.250	5th/AFC Central Division	—	—
College totals (7 years)	**36**	**27**	**3**	**.568**	**College totals (2 years)**	**1**	**1**
Pro totals (1 year)	**4**	**12**	**0**	**.250**			

NOTES:
1992—Lost to Tennessee, 38-23, in Hall of Fame Bowl.
1993—Defeated Virginia, 31-13, in CarQuest Bowl.

COWHER, BILL — STEELERS

PERSONAL: Born May 8, 1957, in Pittsburgh. ... Full name: William Laird Cowher. ... Played linebacker.
HIGH SCHOOL: Carlynton (Crafton, Pa.).
COLLEGE: North Carolina State (degree in education, 1979).
TRANSACTIONS/CAREER NOTES: Signed as non-drafted free agent by Philadelphia Eagles (May 8, 1979). ... Released by Eagles (August 14, 1979). ... Signed by Cleveland Browns (February 27, 1980). ... On injured reserve with knee injury (August 20, 1981-entire season). ... Traded by Browns to Eagles for ninth-round pick (WR Don Jones) in 1984 draft (August 21, 1983). ... On injured reserve with knee injury (September 25, 1984-remainder of season).
PLAYING EXPERIENCE: Cleveland NFL, 1980 and 1982; Philadelphia NFL, 1983 and 1984. ... Games: 1980 (16), 1982 (9), 1983 (16), 1984 (4). Total: 45.
PRO STATISTICS: 1983—Recovered one fumble.

HEAD COACHING RECORD

BACKGROUND: Special teams coach, Cleveland Browns NFL (1985 and 1986). ... Defensive backs coach, Browns (1987 and 1988). ... Defensive coordinator, Kansas City Chiefs NFL (1989-1991).
HONORS: Named NFL Coach of the Year by THE SPORTING NEWS (1992).

				REGULAR SEASON		POST-SEASON	
	W	L	T	Pct.	Finish	W	L
1992—Pittsburgh NFL	11	5	0	.688	1st/AFC Central Division	0	1
1993—Pittsburgh NFL	9	7	0	.563	2nd/AFC Central Division	0	1
1994—Pittsburgh NFL	12	4	0	.750	1st/AFC Central Division	1	1
1995—Pittsburgh NFL	11	5	0	.689	1st/AFC Central Division	2	1
Pro totals (4 years)	**43**	**21**	**0**	**.672**	**Pro totals (4 years)**	**3**	**4**

NOTES:
1992—Lost to Buffalo, 24-3, in conference playoff game.
1993—Lost to Kansas City, 27-24 (OT), in first-round playoff game.
1994—Defeated Cleveland, 29-9, in conference playoff game; lost to San Diego, 17-13, in AFC championship game.
1995—Defeated Buffalo, 40-21, in conference playoff game; defeated Indianapolis, 20-16, in AFC championship game; lost to Dallas, 27-17, in Super Bowl XXX.

DUNGY, TONY — BUCCANEERS

PERSONAL: Born October 6, 1955 in Jackson, Mich. ... Full name: Anthony Kevin Dungy. ... Named pronounced DUN-gee. ... Played defensive back.
HIGH SCHOOL: Parkside (Jackson, Mich.).
COLLEGE: Minnesota (degree in business administration, 1978).
TRANSACTIONS/CAREER NOTES: Signed as non-drafted free agent by Pittsburgh Steelers (May 1977). ... Traded by Steelers to San Francisco 49ers for 10th-round pick in 1980 draft (August 21, 1979). ... Traded by 49ers with RB Mike Hogan to New York Giants for WR Jimmy Robinson and CB Ray Rhodes (March 27, 1980).
CHAMPIONSHIP GAME EXPERIENCE: Played in AFC championship game (1978 season). ... Member of Super Bowl championship team (1978 season).
PRO STATISTICS: 1977—Attempted eight passes with three completions for 43 yards and two interceptions, rushed three times for eight yards and fumbled once. 1978—Recovered two fumbles for eight yards. 1979—Recovered two fumbles.

		INTERCEPTIONS			
Year Team	G	No.	Yds.	Avg.	TD
1977—Pittsburgh NFL	14	3	37	12.3	0
1978—Pittsburgh NFL	16	6	95	15.8	0
1979—San Francisco NFL...	15	0	0	...	0
Pro totals (3 years)	**45**	**9**	**132**	**14.7**	**0**

HEAD COACHING RECORD

BACKGROUND: Defensive backs coach, Minnesota (1980). ... Defensive assistant, Pittsburgh Steelers NFL (1981). ... Defensive backs coach, Steelers (1982-1983). ... Defensive coordinator, Steelers (1984-1988). ... Defensive backs coach, Kansas City Chiefs NFL (1989-1991). ... Defensive coordinator, Minnesota Vikings NFL (1992-1995).

ERICKSON, DENNIS   SEAHAWKS

PERSONAL: Born March 24, 1947, in Everett, Wash.
HIGH SCHOOL: Everett (Wash.).
COLLEGE: Montana State (degree in physical education, 1970).

HEAD COACHING RECORD
BACKGROUND: Graduate assistant, Montana State (1969). ... Graduate assistant, Washington State (spring 1970). ... Head coach, Billings (Mont.) Central High (1970; record: 7-2). ... Offensive backs coach, Montana State (1971-1973). ... Offensive coordinator, Idaho (1974 and 1975). ... Offensive coordinator, Fresno State (1976-1978). ... Offensive coordinator, San Jose State (1979-1981).
HONORS: Named College Football Coach of the Year by THE SPORTING NEWS (1992)

		REGULAR SEASON				POST-SEASON	
	W	L	T	Pct.	Finish	W	L
1982—Idaho	8	3	0	.727	T2nd/Big Sky Conference	1	1
1983—Idaho	8	3	0	.727	T3rd/Big Sky Conference	—	—
1984—Idaho	6	5	0	.545	T3rd/Big Sky Conference	—	—
1985—Idaho	9	2	0	.818	1st/Big Sky Conference	0	1
1986—Wyoming	6	6	0	.500	T4th/Western Atletic Conference	—	—
1987—Washington State	3	7	1	.318	9th/Pacific-10 Conference	—	—
1988—Washington State	8	3	0	.727	T3rd/Pacific-10 Conference	1	0
1989—Miami	10	1	0	.909	Independent	1	0
1990—Miami	9	2	0	.818	Independent	1	0
1991—Miami	11	0	0	1.000	Independent	1	0
1992—Miami	11	0	0	1.000	1st/Big East Conference	0	1
1993—Miami	9	2	0	.818	2nd/Big East Conference	0	1
1994—Miami	10	1	0	.909	1st/Big East Conference	0	1
1995—Seattle NFL	8	8	0	.500	T3rd/AFC Western Divsion	—	—
College totals (13 years)	**108**	**35**	**1**	**.753**	**College totals (9 years)**	**5**	**5**
Pro totals (1 year)	**8**	**8**	**0**	**.500**			

NOTES:
1982—Defeated Montana, 21-7, in first round of NCAA Division I-AA playoffs; lost to Eastern Kentucky, 38-30, in second round of NCAA Division I-AA play-offs.
1985—Lost to Eastern Washington, 42-38, in first round of NCAA Division I-AA playoffs.
1988—Defeated Houston, 24-22, in Aloha Bowl.
1989—Defeated Alabama, 33-25, in Sugar Bowl.
1990—Defeated Texas, 46-3, in Cotton Bowl.
1991—Defeated Nebraska, 22-0, in Orange Bowl.
1992—Lost to Alabama, 34-13, in Sugar Bowl.
1993—Lost to Arizona, 29-0, in Fiesta Bowl.
1994—Lost to Nebraska, 24-17, in Orange Bowl.

FISHER, JEFF   OILERS

PERSONAL: Born February 25, 1958 in Culver City, Calif. ... Full name: Jeffrey Michael Fisher. ... Played safety.
HIGH SCHOOL: Woodland Hills (Calif.)-Taft.
COLLEGE: Southern California (degree in public administration, 1981).
TRANSACTIONS/CAREER NOTES. Selected by Chicago Bears in seventh round (177th pick overall) of 1981 NFL draft. ... On injured reserve with broken leg (October 24, 1983-remainder of season). ... On injured reserve with ankle injury (entire 1985 season).
CHAMPIONSHIP GAME EXPERIENCE: Played in NFC championship game (1984 season).
PRO STATISTICS: 1981—Recovered one fumble. 1984—Recovered one fumble.

		INTERCEPTIONS				PUNT RETURNS				KICKOFF RETURNS				TOTALS		
1981—Chicago NFL	16	2	3	1.5	0	43	509	11.8	1	7	102	14.6	0	1	...	6	3
1982—Chicago NFL	9	3	19	6.3	0	7	53	7.6	0	7	102	14.6	0	0	...	0	2
1983—Chicago NFL	8	0	0	...	0	13	71	5.5	0	0	0	...	0	0	...	0	0
1984—Chicago NFL	16	0	0	...	0	*57	492	8.6	0	0	0	...	0	0	...	0	4
1985—Chicago NFL						Did not play—injured.											
Pro totals (4 years)	**49**	**5**	**22**	**4.4**	**0**	**120**	**1125**	**9.4**	**1**	**14**	**204**	**14.6**	**0**	**1**	**...**	**6**	**9**

HEAD COACHING RECORD
BACKGROUND: Defensive backs coach, Philadelphia Eagles NFL (1986-1988). ... Defensive coordinator, Eagles (1989 and 1990). ... Defensive coordinator, Los Angeles Rams NFL (1991). ... Defensive backs coach, San Francisco 49ers NFL (1992 and 1993). ... Defensive coordinator, Houston Oilers NFL (February 9-November 14, 1994).

		REGULAR SEASON				POST-SEASON	
	W	L	T	Pct.	Finish	W	L
1994—Houston NFL	1	5	0	.167	4th/AFC Central Division	—	—
1995—Houston NFL	7	9	0	.438	T2nd/AFC Central Division	—	—
Pro totals (2 years)	**8**	**14**	**0**	**.364**			

NOTES:
1994—Replaced Jack Pardee as coach of Houston (November 14), with 1-9 record and in fourth place.

FONTES, WAYNE   LIONS

PERSONAL: Born February 2, 1940, at New Bedford, Mass. ... Full name: Wayne Howard Joseph Fontes. ... Name pronounced FONTS. ... Played defensive back. ... Brother of Len Fontes, former assistant coach, Cleveland Browns, New York Giants and Detroit Lions; and brother

of John Fontes, defensive backs coach, Lions.
HIGH SCHOOL: Wareham (Mass.), then McKinley (Canton, Ohio).
COLLEGE: Michigan State (degree in biological science, 1962; master's degree in administration, 1964).
TRANSACTIONS/CAREER NOTES: Selected (as future choice) by New York Titans in 22nd round of 1961 AFL draft.

Year Team	G	INTERCEPTIONS			
		No.	Yds.	Avg.	TD
1962—New York AFL	9	4	145	36.3	1

HEAD COACHING RECORD
BACKGROUND: Freshman coach, Michigan State (1965). ... Head coach, Visitation High School, Bay City, Mich. (1966 and 1967). ... Defensive backs coach, Dayton (1968). ... Defensive backs coach, Iowa (1969-1971). ... Defensive backs coach, Southern California (1972-1975). ... Defensive backs coach, Tampa Bay Buccaneers NFL (1976-1981). ... Defensive coordinator, Buccaneers (1982-1984). ... Defensive coordinator, Detroit Lions NFL (1985-November 14, 1988).

	REGULAR SEASON					POST-SEASON	
	W	L	T	Pct.	Finish	W	L
1988—Detroit NFL	2	3	0	.400	T4th/NFC Central Division	—	—
1989—Detroit NFL	7	9	0	.438	3rd/NFC Central Division	—	—
1990—Detroit NFL	6	10	0	.375	T2nd/NFC Central Division	—	—
1991—Detroit NFL	12	4	0	.750	1st/NFC Central Division	1	1
1992—Detroit NFL	5	11	0	.313	T3rd/NFC Central Division	—	—
1993—Detroit NFL	10	6	0	.625	1st/NFC Central Division	0	1
1994 Detroit NFL	9	7	0	.563	T2nd/NFC Central Division	0	1
1995 Detroit NFL	10	6	0	.625	2nd/NFC Central Division	0	1
Pro totals (8 years)	**61**	**56**	**0**	**.521**	**Pro totals (4 years)**	**1**	**4**

NOTES:
1988—Replaced Darryl Rogers as coach of Detroit (November 14), with 2-9 record and tied for fourth place.
1991—Defeated Dallas, 38-6, in conference playoff game; lost to Washington, 41-10, in NFC championship game.
1993—Lost to Green Bay, 28-24, in first-round playoff game.
1994—Lost to Green Bay, 16-12, in first-round playoff game.
1995—Lost to Philadelphia, 58-37, in first-round playoff game.

GREEN, DENNIS   VIKINGS

PERSONAL: Born February 17, 1949, at Harrisburg, Pa.
HIGH SCHOOL: John Harris (Harrisburg, Pa.).
COLLEGE: Iowa (degree in recreation education, 1971).

HEAD COACHING RECORD
BACKGROUND: Graduate assistant, Iowa (1972). ... Running backs/receivers coach, Dayton (1973). ... Running backs/receivers coach, Iowa (1974-1976). ... Running backs coach, Stanford (1977 and 1978). ... Special teams coach, San Francisco 49ers NFL (1979). ... Offensive coordinator, Stanford (1980). ... Receivers coach, 49ers (1986-1988).

	REGULAR SEASON					POST-SEASON	
	W	L	T	Pct.	Finish	W	L
1981—Northwestern	0	11	0	.000	10th/Big Ten Conference	—	—
1982—Northwestern	3	8	0	.273	T8th/Big Ten Conference	—	—
1983—Northwestern	2	9	0	.182	T8th/Big Ten Conference	—	—
1984—Northwestern	2	9	0	.182	9th/Big Ten Conference	—	—
1985—Northwestern	3	8	0	.273	T9th/Big Ten Conference	—	—
1989—Stanford	3	8	0	.273	T7th/Pacific-10 Conference	—	—
1990—Stanford	5	6	0	.455	T6th/Pacific-10 Conference	—	—
1991—Stanford	8	3	0	.727	T2nd/Pacific-10 Conference	0	1
1992—Minnesota NFL	11	5	0	.688	1st/NFC Central Division	0	1
1993—Minnesota NFL	9	7	0	.563	2nd/NFC Central Division	0	1
1994—Minnesota NFL	10	6	0	.625	1st/NFC Central Division	0	1
1995—Minnesota NFL	8	8	0	.500	4th/NFC Central Division	—	—
College totals (8 years)	**26**	**62**	**0**	**.296**	**College totals (1 year)**	**0**	**1**
Pro Totals (4 years)	**38**	**26**	**0**	**.594**	**Pro totals (3 years)**	**0**	**3**

NOTES:
1991—Lost to Georgia Tech, 18-17, in Aloha Bowl.
1992—Lost to Washington, 24-7, in first-round playoff game.
1993—Lost to New York Giants, 17-10, in first-round playoff game.
1994—Lost to Chicago, 35-18, in first-round playoff game.

HOLMGREN, MIKE   PACKERS

PERSONAL: Born June 15, 1948, in San Francisco. ... Full name: Michael George Holmgren.
HIGH SCHOOL: Lincoln (San Francisco).
COLLEGE: Southern California (degree in business finance, 1970).
TRANSACTIONS/CAREER NOTES: Selected by St. Louis Cardinals in eighth round of 1970 NFL draft. ... Released by Cardinals (1970). ... Tried out with New York Jets (1970).

HEAD COACHING RECORD
BACKGROUND: Assistant coach, Sacred Heart Cathedral Prep School, San Francisco (1972 and 1973). ... Assistant coach, Oak Grove High School, San Jose, Calif. (1975-1980). ... Offensive coordinator/quarterbacks coach, San Francisco State (1981). ... Quarterbacks coach, Brigham Young (1982-1985). ... Quarterbacks coach, San Francisco 49ers NFL (1986-1988). ... Offensive coordinator, 49ers (1989-1991).

HEAD COACHES

	REGULAR SEASON					POST-SEASON	
	W	L	T	Pct.	Finish	W	L
1992—Green Bay NFL	9	7	0	.563	2nd/NFC Central Division	—	—
1993—Green Bay NFL	9	7	0	.563	T2nd/NFC Central Division	1	1
1994—Green Bay NFL	9	7	0	.563	T2nd/NFC Central Division	1	1
1995—Green Bay NFL	11	5	0	.689	1st/NFC Central Division	2	1
Pro totals (4 years)	**38**	**26**	**0**	**.594**	**Pro totals (3 years)**	**4**	**3**

NOTES:
1993—Defeated Detroit, 28-24, in first-round playoff game; lost to Dallas, 27-17, in conference playoff game.
1994—Defeated Detroit, 16-12, in first-round playoff game; lost to Dallas, 35-9, in conference playoff game.
1995—Defeated Atlanta, 37-20, in first-round playoff game; defeated San Francisco, 27-17, in conference playoff game; lost to Dallas, 38-27, in NFC championship game.

INFANTE, LINDY   COLTS

PERSONAL: Born May 27, 1940 in Miami. ... Full name: Gelindo Infante. ... Played running back.
HIGH SCHOOL: Miami.
COLLEGE: Florida (degree in education, 1964).
TRANSACTIONS/CAREER NOTES: Selected by Cleveland Browns in 12th round of 1963 NFL draft. ... Selected by Buffalo Bills in 11th round of 1963 AFL draft. ... Signed by Bills (1963). ... Released by Bills (1963). ... Signed by Hamilton Tiger-Cats of CFL (1963).
PLAYING EXPERIENCE: Hamilton CFL, 1963. ... Games: 1963 (1).
PRO STATISTICS: 1963—Rushed three times for 12 yards.

HEAD COACHING RECORD
BACKGROUND: Assistant coach, Miami (Fla.) High School (1964). ... Head coach, Miami (Fla.) High School (1965). ... Assistant coach, Florida (1966-1971). ... Assistant coach, Memphis State (1972-1974). ... Assistant coach, Charlotte Hornets of WFL (1975). ... Assistant coach, Tulane (1976 and 1979). ... Assistant coach, New York Giants NFL (1977 and 1978). ... Assistant coach, Cincinnati Bengals NFL (1980-1982). ... Assistant coach, Cleveland Browns NFL (1986 and 1987). ... Offensive coordinator, Indianapolis Colts NFL (1995).
HONORS: Named NFL Coach of the Year by THE SPORTING NEWS (1989).

	REGULAR SEASON					POST-SEASON	
	W	L	T	Pct.	Finish	W	L
1984—Jacksonville USFL	6	12	0	.333	5th/Eastern Conference Southern Division	—	—
1985—Jacksonville USFL	9	9	0	.500	6th/Eastern Conference	—	—
1988—Green Bay NFL	4	12	0	.250	T4th/NFC Central Division	—	—
1989—Green Bay NFL	10	6	0	.625	T1st/NFC Central Division	—	—
1990—Green Bay NFL	6	10	0	.375	T2nd/NFC Central Division	—	—
1991—Green Bay NFL	4	12	0	.250	4th/NFC Central Division	—	—
USFL totals (2 years)	**15**	**21**	**0**	**.417**			
NFL totals (4 years)	**24**	**40**	**0**	**.375**			
Pro totals (6 years)	**39**	**61**	**0**	**.390**			

JOHNSON, JIMMY   DOLPHINS

PERSONAL: Born July 16, 1943, in Port Arthur, Texas. ... Full name: James William Johnson.
HIGH SCHOOL: Thomas Jefferson (Port Arthur, Texas).
COLLEGE: Arkansas (bachelor of arts degree in psychology, 1965).

HEAD COACHING RECORD
BACKGROUND: Assistant coach, Louisiana Tech (1965). ... Assistant coach, Wichita State (1967). ... Assistant coach, Iowa State (1968 and 1969). ... Assistant coach, Oklahoma (1970-1972). ... Assistant coach, Arkansas (1973-1976). ... Assistant coach, Pittsburgh (1977 and 1978).

	REGULAR SEASON					POST-SEASON	
	W	L	T	Pct.	Finish	W	L
1979—Oklahoma State	7	4	0	.636	3rd/Big Eight Conference	—	—
1980—Oklahoma State	3	7	1	.318	5th/Big Eight Conference	—	—
1981—Oklahoma State	7	4	0	.636	T3rd/Big Eight Conference	0	1
1982—Oklahoma State	4	5	2	.455	3rd/Big Eight Conference	—	—
1983—Oklahoma State	7	4	0	.636	T4th/Big Eight Conference	1	0
1984—Miami (Fla.)	8	4	0	.667	Independent	0	1
1985—Miami (Fla.)	10	1	0	.909	Independent	0	1
1986—Miami (Fla.)	11	0	0	1.000	Independent	0	1
1987—Miami (Fla.)	11	0	0	1.000	Independent	1	0
1988—Miami (Fla.)	10	1	0	.909	Independent	1	0
1989—Dallas NFL	1	15	0	.063	5th/NFC Eastern Division	—	—
1990—Dallas NFL	7	9	0	.438	4th/NFC Eastern Division	—	—
1991—Dallas NFL	11	5	0	.688	2nd/NFC Eastern Division	1	1
1992—Dallas NFL	13	3	0	.813	1st/NFC Eastern Division	3	0
1993—Dallas NFL	12	4	0	.750	1st/NFC Eastern Division	3	0
College totals (10 years)	**78**	**30**	**3**	**.716**	**College totals (7 years)**	**3**	**4**
Pro totals (5 years)	**44**	**36**	**0**	**.550**	**Pro totals (3 years)**	**7**	**1**

NOTES:
1980—Oklahoma State played to a 14-14 forfeited tie against Kansas (October 25).
1981—Lost to Texas A&M, 33-16, in Independence Bowl.
1983—Defeated Baylor, 24-14, in Bluebonnet Bowl.

1984—Lost to UCLA, 39-37, in Fiesta Bowl.
1985—Lost to Tennessee, 35-7, in Sugar Bowl.
1986—Lost to Penn State, 14-10, in Fiesta Bowl.
1987—Defeated Oklahoma, 20-14, in Orange Bowl.
1988—Defeated Nebraska, 23-3, in Orange Bowl.
1991—Defeated Chicago, 17-13, in first-round playoff game; lost to Detroit, 38-6, in conference playoff game.
1992—Defeated Philadelphia, 34-10, in conference playoff game; defeated San Francisco, 30-20, in NFC championship game; defeated Buffalo, 52-17, in Super Bowl XXVII.
1993—Defeated Green Bay, 27-17, in conference playoff game; defeated San Francisco, 38-21, in NFC championship game; defeated Buffalo, 30-13, in Super Bowl XXVIII.

JONES, JUNE — FALCONS

PERSONAL: Born February 19, 1953, in Portland, Ore. ... Full name: June Sheldon Jones III. ... Played quarterback.
HIGH SCHOOL: Grant (Portland, Ore.).
COLLEGE: Oregon, then Hawaii, then Portland State (degree in business administration, 1976).
TRANSACTIONS/CAREER NOTES: Signed as non-drafted free agent by Atlanta Falcons (May 1977). ... Released by Falcons (August 31, 1977). ... Re-signed by Falcons (September 13, 1977). ... On injured reserve with fractured ankle (August 19, 1980-entire season). ... Signed as free agent by Toronto Argonauts for 1982 season.
CHAMPIONSHIP GAME EXPERIENCE: Member of Argonauts for Grey Cup, CFL championship game (1982 season).
PRO STATISTICS: 1978—Fumbled four times for minus 12 yards. 1979—Fumbled four times for minus one yard.
MISCELLANEOUS: Regular-season record as starting NFL quarterback: 1-4 (.200).

Year Team	G	Att.	Cmp.	Pct.	Yds.	TD	Int.	Avg.	Rat.	Att.	Yds.	Avg.	TD	TD	2pt.	Pts.
				PASSING							RUSHING				TOTALS	
1977—Atlanta NFL	1	1	1	100.0	-1	0	0	-1.00	79.2	0	0	...	0	0	...	0
1978—Atlanta NFL	7	79	34	43.0	394	1	4	4.99	41.8	10	-3	-0.3	0	0	...	0
1979—Atlanta NFL	5	83	38	45.8	505	2	3	6.08	58.6	6	19	3.2	0	0	...	0
1980—Atlanta NFL						Did not play—injured.										
1981—Atlanta NFL	1	3	2	66.7	25	0	0	8.33	92.4	1	-1	-1.0	0	0	...	0
1982—Toronto CFL	1	5	2	40.0	17	0	0	3.40	49.6	0	0	...	0	0	0	0
CFL totals (1 year)	1	5	2	40.0	17	0	0	3.40	49.6	0	0	...	0	0	0	0
NFL totals (4 years)	14	166	75	45.2	923	3	7	5.56	51.4	17	15	0.9	0	0	...	8
Pro totals (5 years)	15	171	77	45.0	940	3	7	5.50	51.9	17	15	0.9	0	0	0	8

HEAD COACHING RECORD

BACKGROUND: Player/coach, Toronto Argonauts CFL (1982). ... Assistant coach, Hawaii (1983). ... Wide receivers coach, Houston Gamblers USFL (1984). ... Offensive coordinator, Denver Gold USFL (1985). ... Named assistant coach, Jacksonville Bulls USFL (1986; league suspended operations prior to start of season). ... Offensive assistant coach, Ottawa Rough Riders CFL (1986). ... Quarterbacks coach, Houston Oilers NFL (1987 and 1988). ... Quarterbacks/wide receivers coach, Detroit Lions NFL (1989 and 1990). ... Assistant head coach, Atlanta Falcons (1991-1993).

				REGULAR SEASON		POST-SEASON	
	W	L	T	Pct.	Finish	W	L
1994—Atlanta NFL	7	9	0	.438	T2nd/NFC Western Division	—	—
1995—Atlanta NFL	9	7	0	.563	2nd/NFC Western Division	0	1
Pro totals (2 years)	16	16	0	.500	Pro totals (1 year)	0	1

NOTES:
1995—Lost to Green Bay, 37-20, in first-round playoff game.

KOTITE, RICH — JETS

PERSONAL: Born October 13, 1942, in Brooklyn, N.Y. ... Full name: Richard Edward Kotite. ... Played tight end.
HIGH SCHOOL: Poly Prep Country Day School (Brooklyn, N.Y.).
COLLEGE: Miami (Fla.), then Wagner, N.Y. (degree in economics, 1967).
TRANSACTIONS/CAREER NOTES: Signed as non-drafted free agent by New York Giants (1967). ... Released by Giants (September 3, 1968). ... Signed by Pittsburgh Steelers (September 27, 1968). ... Released by Steelers (September 8, 1969). ... Signed by Giants (September 23, 1969). ... Released by Giants (September 7, 1970). ... Re-signed by Giants (September 16, 1970). ... Released by Giants (September 5, 1972). ... Re-signed by Giants (September 13, 1972).

Year Team	G	No.	Yds.	Avg.	TD	TD	2pt.	Pts.	Fum.
			RECEIVING				TOTAL		
1967—New York Giants NFL	4	0	0	...	0	0	...	0	0
1968—Pittsburgh NFL	12	6	65	10.8	2	2	...	12	0
1969—New York Giants NFL	3	1	2	2.0	1	1	...	6	0
1970—					Did not play.				
1971—New York Giants NFL	14	10	146	14.6	2	2	...	12	0
1972—New York Giants NFL	2	0	0	...	0	0	...	0	0
Pro totals (5 years)	35	17	213	12.5	5	5	...	30	0

HEAD COACHING RECORD

BACKGROUND: Assistant coach, UT-Chattanooga (1973-1976). ... Quality control coach, New Orleans Saints NFL (1977). ... Receivers coach, Cleveland Browns NFL (1978-1982). ... Offensive assistant, New York Jets NFL (1983 and 1984). ... Offensive coordinator, Jets (1985-1989). ... Offensive coordinator, Philadelphia Eagles NFL (1990).

				REGULAR SEASON		POST-SEASON	
	W	L	T	Pct.	Finish	W	L
1991—Philadelphia NFL	10	6	0	.625	3rd/NFC Eastern Division	—	—
1992—Philadelphia NFL	11	5	0	.688	2nd/NFC Eastern Division	1	1

HEAD COACHES

	REGULAR SEASON					POST-SEASON	
	W	L	T	Pct.	Finish	W	L
1993—Philadelphia NFL	8	8	0	.500	3rd/NFC Eastern Division	—	—
1994—Philadelphia NFL	7	9	0	.438	4th/NFC Eastern Division	—	—
1995—New York Jets NFL	3	13	0	.188	5th/AFC Eastern Division	—	—
Pro totals (5 years)	**39**	**41**	**0**	**.488**	**Pro totals (1 year)**	**1**	**1**

NOTES:

1992—Defeated New Orleans, 36-20, in first-round playoff game; lost to Dallas, 34-10, in conference playoff game.

LEVY, MARV   BILLS

PERSONAL: Born August 3, 1928, in Chicago. ... Full name: Marvin Daniel Levy.

HIGH SCHOOL: South Shore (Chicago).

COLLEGE: Coe College, Iowa (received degree, 1950), then Harvard (master's degree in English history, 1951).

HEAD COACHING RECORD

BACKGROUND: Head coach, St. Louis Country Day School (1951 and 1952; record: 13-0-1). ... Assistant coach, Coe College (1953-1955). ... Assistant coach, New Mexico (1956 and 1957). ... Kicking teams coach, Philadelphia Eagles NFL (1969). ... Special teams coach, Los Angeles Rams NFL (1970). ... Special teams coach, Washington Redskins NFL (1971 and 1972). ... Director of football operations, Montreal Alouettes CFL (1985).

HONORS: Named NFL Coach of the Year by THE SPORTING NEWS (1988).

	REGULAR SEASON					POST-SEASON	
	W	L	T	Pct.	Finish	W	L
1958—New Mexico	7	3	0	.700	2nd/Skyline Conference	—	—
1959—New Mexico	7	3	0	.700	3rd/Skyline Conference	—	—
1960—California	2	7	1	.250	4th/Athletic Assoc. of Western Universities	—	—
1961—California	1	8	1	.150	T4th/Athletic Assoc. of Western Universities	—	—
1962—California	1	9	0	.100	5th/Athletic Assoc. of Western Universities	—	—
1963—California	4	5	1	.450	4th/Athletic Assoc. of Western Universities	—	—
1964—William & Mary	4	6	0	.400	T4th/Southern Conference	—	—
1965—William & Mary	6	4	0	.600	1st/Southern Conference	—	—
1966—William & Mary	5	4	1	.550	T1st/Southern Conference	—	—
1967—William & Mary	5	4	1	.550	4th/Southern Conference	—	—
1968—William & Mary	3	7	0	.300	T3rd/Southern Conference	—	—
1973—Montreal CFL	7	6	1	.536	3rd/Eastern Conference	1	1
1974—Montreal CFL	9	5	2	.625	1st/Eastern Conference	2	0
1975—Montreal CFL	9	7	0	.563	2nd/Eastern Conference	2	1
1976—Montreal CFL	7	8	1	.469	T3rd/Eastern Conference	0	1
1977—Montreal CFL	11	5	0	.688	1st/Eastern Conference	2	0
1978—Kansas City NFL	4	12	0	.250	5th/AFC Western Division	—	—
1979—Kansas City NFL	7	9	0	.438	5th/AFC Western Division	—	—
1980—Kansas City NFL	8	8	0	.500	T3rd/AFC Western Division	—	—
1981—Kansas City NFL	9	7	0	.563	3rd/AFC Western Division	—	—
1982—Kansas City NFL	3	6	0	.333	11th/AFC	—	—
1984—Chicago USFL	5	13	0	.278	5th/Western Conference Central Division	—	—
1986—Buffalo NFL	2	5	0	.286	4th/AFC Eastern Division	—	—
1987—Buffalo NFL	7	8	0	.467	4th/AFC Eastern Division	—	—
1988—Buffalo NFL	12	4	0	.750	1st/AFC Eastern Division	1	1
1989—Buffalo NFL	9	7	0	.563	1st/AFC Eastern Division	0	1
1990—Buffalo NFL	13	3	0	.813	1st/AFC Eastern Division	2	1
1991—Buffalo NFL	13	3	0	.813	1st/AFC Eastern Division	2	1
1992—Buffalo NFL	11	5	0	.688	T1st/AFC Eastern Division	3	1
1993—Buffalo NFL	12	4	0	.750	1st/AFC Eastern Division	2	1
1994—Buffalo NFL	7	9	0	.438	4th/AFC Eastern Division	—	—
1995—Buffalo NFL	10	6	0	.625	1st/AFC Eastern Division	1	1
College totals (11 years)	**45**	**60**	**5**	**.432**			
CFL totals (5 years)	**43**	**31**	**4**	**.577**	**CFL totals (5 years)**	**7**	**3**
NFL totals (15 years)	**127**	**96**	**0**	**.570**	**NFL totals (7 years)**	**11**	**7**
USFL totals (1 year)	**5**	**13**	**0**	**.278**			
Pro totals (21 years)	**175**	**140**	**4**	**.555**	**Pro totals (12 years)**	**18**	**10**

NOTES:

1973—Defeated Toronto, 32-10, in conference playoff game; lost to Ottawa, 23-14, in conference championship game.

1974—Defeated Ottawa, 14-4, in conference championship game; defeated Edmonton, 20-7, in Grey Cup (CFL championship game).

1975—Defeated Hamilton, 35-12, in conference playoff game; defeated Ottawa, 20-10, in conference championship game; lost to Edmonton, 9-8, in Grey Cup.

1976—Lost to Hamilton, 23-0, in conference playoff game.

1977—Defeated Ottawa, 21-18, in conference championship game; defeated Edmonton, 41-6, in Grey Cup.

1986—Replaced Hank Bullough as coach of Buffalo (November 3), with 2-7 record and in fourth place.

1988—Defeated Houston, 17-10, in conference playoff game; lost to Cincinnati, 21-10, in AFC championship game.

1989—Lost to Cleveland, 34-30, in conference playoff game.

1990—Defeated Miami, 44-34, in conference playoff game; defeated Los Angeles Raiders, 51-3, in AFC championship game; lost to New York Giants, 20-19, in Super Bowl XXV.

1991—Defeated Kansas City, 37-14, in conference playoff game; defeated Denver, 10-7, in AFC championship game; lost to Washington, 37-24, in Super Bowl XXVI.

1992—Defeated Houston, 41-38, in first-round playoff game; defeated Pittsburgh, 24-3, in conference playoff game; defeated Miami, 29-10, in AFC championship game; lost to Dallas, 52-17, in Super Bowl XXVII.

1993—Defeated Los Angeles Raiders, 29-23, in conference playoff game; defeated Kansas City, 30-13, in AFC championship game; lost to Dallas, 30-13, in

Super Bowl XXVIII.
1995—On medical leave (October 22-November 12); team went 1-2 under assistant head coach Elijah Pitts. Defeated Miami, 37-22, in first-round playoff game; lost to Pittsburgh, 40-21, in conference playoff game.

MARCHIBRODA, TED — RAVENS

PERSONAL: Born March 15, 1931, in Franklin, Pa. ... Full name: Theodore Joseph Marchibroda. ... Played quarterback.
HIGH SCHOOL: Franklin (Pa.).
COLLEGE: St. Bonaventure, then Detroit (degree in physical education, 1953).
TRANSACTIONS/CAREER NOTES: Selected by Pittsburgh Steelers in first round of 1953 NFL draft. ... On military list (1954). ... Released by Steelers (1957). ... Signed by Chicago Cardinals (1957).
PRO STATISTICS: 1953—Returned one kickoff for 25 yards. 1957—Recovered one fumble.

				PASSING								RUSHING				TOTALS	
Year Team	G	Att.	Cmp.	Pct.	Yds.	TD	Int.	Avg.	Rat.	Att.	Yds.	Avg	TD	TD	2pt.	Pts.
1953—Pittsburgh NFL	4	22	9	40.9	66	1	2	3.00	25.9	1	15	15.0	0	0	0	0
1954—Pittsburgh NFL							Did not play.									
1955—Pittsburgh NFL	10	43	24	55.8	280	2	3	6.51	62.2	6	-1	-0.2	1	1	6	3
1956—Pittsburgh NFL	12	275	124	45.1	1585	12	19	5.76	49.4	39	152	3.9	2	2	12	3
1957—Chicago NFL	7	45	15	33.3	238	1	5	5.29	19.7	4	10	2.5	0	0	0	0
Pro totals (4 years)	33	385	172	44.7	2169	16	29	5.63	45.3	50	176	3.5	3	3	18	6

HEAD COACHING RECORD

BACKGROUND: Offensive backfield coach, Washington Redskins NFL (1961-1965). ... Offensive assistant coach, Los Angeles Rams NFL (1966-1970). ... Offensive coordinator, Redskins (1971-1974). ... Consultant, Philadelphia Eagles NFL (1980). ... Quarterbacks coach, Chicago Bears NFL (1981). ... Offensive coordinator, Detroit Lions NFL (1982 and 1983). ... Offensive coordinator, Eagles (1984 and 1985). ... Quarterbacks coach, Buffalo Bills NFL (1987 and 1988). ... Offensive coordinator, Bills (1989-1991).
HONORS: Named NFL Coach of the Year by THE SPORTING NEWS (1975).

	REGULAR SEASON					POST-SEASON	
	W	L	T	Pct.	Finish	W	L
1975—Baltimore NFL	10	4	0	.714	T1st/AFC Eastern Division	0	1
1976—Baltimore NFL	11	3	0	.786	T1st/AFC Eastern Division	0	1
1977—Baltimore NFL	10	4	0	.714	T1st/AFC Eastern Division	0	1
1978—Baltimore NFL	5	11	0	.313	T4th/AFC Eastern Division	—	—
1979—Baltimore NFL	5	11	0	.313	5th/AFC Eastern Division	—	—
1992—Indianapolis NFL	9	7	0	.563	3rd/AFC Eastern Division	—	—
1993—Indianapolis NFL	4	12	0	.250	5th/AFC Eastern Division	—	—
1994—Indianapolis NFL	8	8	0	.500	3rd/AFC Eastern Division	—	—
1995—Indianaplois NFL	9	7	0	.563	T2nd/AFC Eastern Division	2	1
Pro totals (9 years)	71	67	0	.514	Pro totals (4 years)	2	4

NOTES:
1975—Lost to Pittsburgh, 28-10, in conference playoff game.
1976—Lost to Pittsburgh, 40-14, in conference playoff game.
1977—Lost to Oakland, 37-31 (OT), in conference playoff game.
1995—Defeated San Diego, 35-20, in first-round playoff game; defeated Kansas City, 10-7, in conference playoff game; lost to Pittsburgh, 20-16, in AFC championship game.

MORA, JIM — SAINTS

PERSONAL: Born May 24, 1935, in Los Angeles. ... Full name: James Ernest Mora. ... Father of Jim Mora Jr., defensive backs coach, New Orleans Saints.
HIGH SCHOOL: University (Los Angeles).
COLLEGE: Occidental College (degree in physical education, 1957), then Southern California (master's degree in education, 1967).
MISCELLANEOUS: Played for U.S. Marines at Quantico (1957) and at Camp Lejeune (1958 and 1959).

HEAD COACHING RECORD

BACKGROUND: Assistant coach, Occidental College (1960-1963). ... Linebackers coach, Stanford (1967). ... Defensive assistant coach, Colorado (1968-1973). ... Linebackers coach, UCLA (1974). ... Defensive coordinator, Washington (1975-1977). ... Defensive line coach, Seattle Seahawks NFL (1978-1981). ... Defensive coordinator, New England Patriots NFL (1982). ... Vice president, New Orleans Saints NFL (1994 to present).
HONORS: Named USFL Coach of the Year by THE SPORTING NEWS (1984). ... Named NFL Coach of the Year by THE SPORTING NEWS (1987).

	REGULAR SEASON					POST-SEASON	
	W	L	T	Pct.	Finish	W	L
1964—Occidental	5	4	0	.556	3rd/Southern Calif. Intercollegiate Conference	—	—
1965—Occidental	8	1	0	.889	1st/Southern Calif. Intercollegiate Conference	—	—
1966—Occidental	5	4	0	.556	4th/Southern Calif. Intercollegiate Conference	—	—
1983—Philadelphia USFL	15	3	0	.833	1st/Atlantic Division	1	1
1984—Philadelphia USFL	16	2	0	.889	1st/Eastern Conference Atlantic Division	3	1
1985—Baltimore USFL	10	7	1	.583	4th/Eastern Conference	3	0
1986—New Orleans NFL	7	9	0	.438	4th/NFC Western Division	—	—
1987—New Orleans NFL	12	3	0	.800	2nd/NFC Western Division	0	1
1988—New Orleans NFL	10	6	0	.625	T1st/NFC Western Division	—	—
1989—New Orleans NFL	9	7	0	.563	3rd/NFC Western Division	—	—
1990—New Orleans NFL	8	8	0	.500	2nd/NFC Western Division	0	1
1991—New Orleans NFL	11	5	0	.688	1st/NFC Western Division	0	1
1992—New Orleans NFL	12	4	0	.750	2nd/NFC Western Division	0	1
1993—New Orleans NFL	8	8	0	.500	2nd/NFC Western Division	—	—

						POST- SEASON	
		REGULAR SEASON					
	W	L	T	Pct.	Finish	W	L
1994—New Orleans NFL	7	9	0	.438	T2nd/NFC Western Division	—	—
1995—New Orleans NFL	7	9	0	.438	T3rd/NFC Western Division	—	—
College totals (3 years)	18	9	0	.667			
USFL totals (3 years)	41	12	1	.769	**USFL totals (3 years)**	7	1
NFL totals (10 years)	91	68	0	.572	**NFL totals (4 years)**	0	4
Pro totals (13 years)	132	80	1	.622	**Pro totals (7 years)**	7	5

NOTES:
1983—Defeated Chicago, 44-38 (OT), in divisional playoff game; lost to Michigan, 24-22, in USFL championship game.
1984—Defeated New Jersey, 28-7, in conference playoff game; defeated Birmingham, 20-10, in conference championship game; defeated Arizona, 23-3, in USFL championship game.
1985—Defeated New Jersey, 20-17, in conference playoff game; defeated Birmingham, 28-14, in conference championship game; defeated Oakland, 28-24, in USFL championship game.
1987—Lost to Minnesota, 44-10, in wild-card playoff game.
1990—Lost to Chicago, 16-6, in conference playoff game.
1991—Lost to Atlanta, 27-20, in first-round playoff game.
1992—Lost to Philadelphia, 36-20, in first-round playoff game.

PARCELLS, BILL   PATRIOTS

PERSONAL: Born August 22, 1941, in Englewood, N.J. ... Full name: Duane Charles Parcells.
HIGH SCHOOL: River Dell (Oradell, N.J.).
COLLEGE: Colgate, then Wichita State (degree in education, 1964).

HEAD COACHING RECORD
BACKGROUND: Defensive assistant coach, Hastings (Neb.) College (1964). ... Defensive line coach, Wichita State (1965). ... Linebackers coach, Army (1966-1969). ... Linebackers coach, Florida State (1970-1972). ... Defensive coordinator, Vanderbilt (1973 and 1974). ... Defensive coordinator, Texas Tech (1975-1977). ... Linebackers coach, New England Patriots NFL (1980). ... Defensive coordinator and linebackers coach, New York Giants NFL (1981 and 1982).
HONORS: Named NFL Coach of the Year by THE SPORTING NEWS (1986).

						POST- SEASON	
		REGULAR SEASON					
	W	L	T	Pct.	Finish	W	L
1978—Air Force	3	8	0	.273	Independent	—	—
1983—New York Giants NFL	3	12	1	.219	5th/NFC Eastern Division	—	—
1984—New York Giants NFL	9	7	0	.563	T2nd/NFC Eastern Division	1	1
1985—New York Giants NFL	10	6	0	.625	T1st/NFC Eastern Division	1	1
1986—New York Giants NFL	14	2	0	.875	1st/NFC Eastern Division	3	0
1987—New York Giants NFL	6	9	0	.400	5th/NFC Eastern Division	—	—
1988—New York Giants NFL	10	6	0	.625	T1st/NFC Eastern Division	—	—
1989—New York Giants NFL	12	4	0	.750	1st/NFC Eastern Division	0	1
1990—New York Giants NFL	13	3	0	.813	1st/NFC Eastern Division	3	0
1993—New England NFL	5	11	0	.313	4th/AFC Eastern Division	—	—
1994—New England NFL	10	6	0	.625	T1st/AFC Eastern Division	0	1
1995—New England NFL	6	10	0	.375	4th/AFC Eastern Division	—	—
College totals (1 year)	3	8	0	.273			
Pro totals (11 years)	98	76	1	.563	**Pro totals (7 years)**	8	4

NOTES:
1984—Defeated Los Angeles Rams, 16-10, in wild-card playoff game; lost to San Francisco, 21-10, in conference playoff game.
1985—Defeated San Francisco, 17-3, in wild-card playoff game; lost to Chicago, 21-0, in conference playoff game.
1986—Defeated San Francisco, 49-3, in conference playoff game; defeated Washington, 17-0, in NFC championship game; defeated Denver, 39-20, in Super Bowl XXI.
1989—Lost to Los Angeles Rams, 19-13 (OT), in conference playoff game.
1990—Defeated Chicago, 31-3, in conference playoff game; defeated San Francisco, 15-13, in NFC championship game; defeated Buffalo, 20-19, in Super Bowl XXV.
1994—Lost to Cleveland, 20-13, in first-round playoff game.

REEVES, DAN   GIANTS

PERSONAL: Born January 19, 1944, in Americus, Ga. ... Full name: Daniel Edward Reeves. ... Played running back.
HIGH SCHOOL: Americus (Ga.).
COLLEGE: South Carolina.
TRANSACTIONS/CAREER NOTES: Signed as non-drafted free agent by Dallas Cowboys (1965).
CHAMPIONSHIP GAME EXPERIENCE: Played in NFL championship game (1966 and 1967 seasons). ... Played in NFC championship game (1970 and 1971 seasons). ... Played in Super Bowl V (1970 season). ... Member of Super Bowl championship team (1971 season).
HONORS: Named halfback on THE SPORTING NEWS NFL Eastern Conference All-Star team (1966).
PRO STATISTICS: 1965—Returned two kickoffs for 45 yards. 1966—Returned two punts for minus one yard, returned three kickoffs for 56 yards and fumbled six times. 1967—Fumbled seven times. 1969—Fumbled twice. 1970—Fumbled four times. 1971—Fumbled once.

				PASSING					RUSHING				RECEIVING				TOTALS	
Year Team	G	Att.	Cmp.	Pct.	Yds.	TD	Int.	Avg.	Att.	Yds.	Avg.	TD	No.	Yds.	Avg.	TD	TD	Pts.
1965—Dallas NFL	13	2	1	50.0	11	0	0	5.50	33	102	3.1	2	9	210	23.3	1	3	18
1966—Dallas NFL	14	6	3	50.0	48	0	0	8.00	175	757	4.3	8	41	557	13.6	8	*16	96
1967—Dallas NFL	14	7	4	57.1	195	2	1	27.86	173	603	3.5	5	39	490	12.6	6	11	66
1968—Dallas NFL	4	4	2	50.0	43	0	0	10.75	40	178	4.5	4	7	84	12.0	1	5	30
1969—Dallas NFL	13	3	1	33.3	35	0	1	11.67	59	173	2.9	4	18	187	10.4	1	5	30

Year Team	G	PASSING							RUSHING				RECEIVING				TOTALS	
		Att.	Cmp.	Pct.	Yds.	TD	Int.	Avg.	Att.	Yds.	Avg.	TD	No.	Yds.	Avg.	TD	TD	Pts.
1970—Dallas NFL	14	3	1	33.3	14	0	1	4.67	35	84	2.4	2	12	140	11.7	0	2	12
1971—Dallas NFL	14	5	2	40.0	24	0	1	4.80	17	79	4.7	0	3	25	8.3	0	0	0
1972—Dallas NFL	14	2	0	0.0	0	0	0	0.00	3	14	4.7	0	0	0	...	0	0	0
Pro totals (8 years)	100	32	14	43.8	370	2	4	11.56	535	1990	3.7	25	129	1693	13.1	17	42	252

HEAD COACHING RECORD

BACKGROUND: Player/coach, Dallas Cowboys NFL (1970 and 1971). ... Offensive backs coach, Cowboys (1972 and 1974-1976). ... Offensive coordinator, Cowboys (1977-1980).

HONORS: Named NFL Coach of the Year by THE SPORTING NEWS (1993).

Year Team	REGULAR SEASON					POST-SEASON	
	W	L	T	Pct.	Finish	W	L
1981—Denver NFL	10	6	0	.625	T1st/AFC Western Division	—	—
1982—Denver NFL	2	7	0	.222	12th/AFC	—	—
1983—Denver NFL	9	7	0	.563	T2nd/AFC Western Division	0	1
1984—Denver NFL	13	3	0	.813	1st/AFC Western Division	0	1
1985—Denver NFL	11	5	0	.688	2nd/AFC Western Division	—	—
1986—Denver NFL	11	5	0	.688	1st/AFC Western Division	2	1
1987—Denver NFL	10	4	1	.700	1st/AFC Western Division	2	1
1988—Denver NFL	8	8	0	.500	2nd/AFC Western Division	—	—
1989—Denver NFL	11	5	0	.688	1st/AFC Western Division	2	1
1990—Denver NFL	5	11	0	.313	5th/AFC Western Division	—	—
1991—Denver NFL	12	4	0	.750	1st/AFC Western Division	1	1
1992—Denver NFL	8	8	0	.500	3rd/AFC Western Division	—	—
1993—New York Giants NFL	11	5	0	.688	2nd/NFC Eastern Division	1	1
1994—New York Giants NFL	9	7	0	.563	2nd/NFC Eastern Division	—	—
1995—New York Giants NFL	5	11	0	.313	4th/NFC Eastern Division	—	—
Pro totals (15 years)	135	96	1	.584	Pro totals (7 years)	8	7

NOTES:
1983—Lost to Seattle, 31-7, in wild-card playoff game.
1984—Lost to Pittsburgh, 24-17, in conference playoff game.
1986—Defeated New England, 22-17, in conference playoff game; defeated Cleveland, 23-20 (OT), in AFC championship game; lost to New York Giants, 39-20, in Super Bowl XXI.
1987—Defeated Houston, 34-10, in conference playoff game; defeated Cleveland, 38-33, in AFC championship game; lost to Washington, 42-10, in Super Bowl XXII.
1989—Defeated Pittsburgh, 24-23, in conference playoff game; defeated Cleveland, 37-21, in AFC championship game; lost to San Francisco, 55-10, in Super Bowl XXIV.
1991—Defeated Houston, 26-24, in conference playoff game; lost to Buffalo, 10-7, in AFC championship game.
1993—Defeated Minnesota, 17-10, in first-round playoff game; lost to San Francisco, 44-3, in conference playoff game.

RHODES, RAY   EAGLES

PERSONAL: Born October 20, 1950 in Mexia, Texas. ... Full name: Raymond Earl Rhodes. ... Played wide receiver and defensive back.
HIGH SCHOOL: Mexia (Texas).
COLLEGE: Texas Christian, then Tulsa.
TRANSACTIONS/CAREER NOTES: Selected by New York Giants in 10th round of 1974 NFL draft. ... Traded by Giants with WR Jimmy Robinson to San Francisco 49ers for RB Mike Hogan and S Tony Dungy (March 27, 1980).
PRO STATISTICS: 1974—Rushed once for minus six yards, returned 10 punts for 124 yards and returned one kickoff for 27 yards. 1975—Rushed three times for minus four yards and recovered two fumbles. 1976—Rushed twice for 10 yards. 1977—Recovered two fumbles for 77 yards. 1979—Recovered two fumbles for seven yards. 1980—Recovered one fumble.

Year Team	G	RECEIVING				INTERCEPTIONS				TOTALS			
		No.	Yds.	Avg.	TD	No.	Yds.	Avg.	TD	TD	2pt.	Pts.	Fum.
1974—New York Giants NFL	14	9	138	15.3	0	0	0	...	0	0	...	0	1
1975—New York Giants NFL	14	26	537	20.7	6	0	0	...	0	6	...	36	3
1976—New York Giants NFL	13	16	305	19.1	1	0	0	...	0	1	...	6	0
1977—New York Giants NFL	14	0	0	...	0	2	59	29.5	0	0	...	0	0
1978—New York Giants NFL	13	0	0	...	0	3	74	24.7	0	0	...	0	0
1979—New York Giants NFL	15	0	0	...	0	2	0	0.0	0	0	...	0	0
1980—San Francisco NFL	14	0	0	...	0	1	25	25.0	0	0	...	0	0
NFL totals (7 years)	97	51	980	19.2	8	8	158	19.8	0	7	...	42	4

HEAD COACHING RECORD

BACKGROUND: Assistant defensive backs coach, San Francisco 49ers NFL (1981). ... Defensive backs coach, 49ers (1982-1991). ... Defensive coordinator, Green Bay Packers NFL (1992 and 1993). ... Defensive coordinator, 49ers (1994).
HONORS: Named NFL Coach of the Year by THE SPORTING NEWS (1995).

Year Team	REGULAR SEASON					POST-SEASON	
	W	L	T	Pct.	Finish	W	L
1995—Philadelphia NFL	10	6	0	.615	2nd/NFC Eastern Division	1	1

NOTES:
1995—Defeated Detroit, 58-37, in first-round playoff game; lost to Dallas, 30-11, in conference playoff game.

ROSS, BOBBY   CHARGERS

PERSONAL: Born December 23, 1936, in Richmond, Va. ... Full name: Robert Joseph Ross.

HIGH SCHOOL: Benedictine (Richmond, Va.).
COLLEGE: Virginia Military Institute (degree in English and history, 1959).

HEAD COACHING RECORD

BACKGROUND: Head coach, Benedictine High School, Richmond, Va. (1959; record: 1-8-1). ... Served in military (1960-1962). ... Assistant coach, Colonial Heights (Va.) High School (1962). ... Head coach, Colonial Heights High School (1963 and 1964). ... Freshman coach, Virginia Military Institute (1965). ... Defensive backs coach, VMI (1966). ... Offensive backs coach, William & Mary (1967 and 1968). ... Defensive backs coach, William & Mary (1969). ... Defensive coordinator, William & Mary (1970). ... Linebackers coach, Rice (1971). ... Linebackers coach, Maryland (1972). ... Special teams coach, Kansas City Chiefs NFL (1978 and 1979). ... Offensive backs coach, Chiefs (1980 and 1981).
HONORS: Named College Football Coach of the Year by THE SPORTING NEWS (1990).

			REGULAR SEASON			POST-SEASON	
	W	L	T	Pct.	Finish	W	L
1973—The Citadel	3	8	0	.273	T7th/Southern Conference	—	—
1974—The Citadel	4	7	0	.364	5th/Southern Conference	—	—
1975—The Citadel	6	5	0	.545	4th/Southern Conference	—	—
1976—The Citadel	6	5	0	.545	6th/Southern Conference	—	—
1977—The Citadel	5	6	0	.455	T3rd/Southern Conference	—	—
1982—Maryland	8	3	0	.727	2nd/Atlantic Coast Conference	0	1
1983—Maryland	8	3	0	.727	1st/Atlantic Coast Conference	0	1
1984—Maryland	8	3	0	.727	1st/Atlantic Coast Conference	1	0
1985—Maryland	8	3	0	.727	1st/Atlantic Coast Conference	1	0
1986—Maryland	5	5	1	.500	5th/Atlantic Coast Conference	—	—
1987—Georgia Tech	2	9	0	.182	8th/Atlantic Coast Conference	—	—
1988—Georgia Tech	3	8	0	.273	8th/Atlantic Coast Conference	—	—
1989—Georgia Tech	7	4	0	.636	T4th/Atlantic Coast Conference	—	—
1990—Georgia Tech	10	0	1	.955	1st/Atlantic Coast Conference	1	0
1991—Georgia Tech	7	5	0	.583	T2nd/Atlantic Coast Conference	1	1
1992—San Diego NFL	11	5	0	.688	1st/AFC Western Division	1	1
1993—San Diego NFL	8	8	0	.500	4th/AFC Western Division	—	—
1994—San Diego NFL	11	5	0	.688	1st/AFC Western Division	2	1
1995—San Diego NFL	9	7	0	.563	2nd/ AFC Western Division	0	1
College totals (15 years)	**90**	**74**	**2**	**.548**	**College totals (6 years)**	**4**	**2**
Pro totals (4 years)	**39**	**25**	**0**	**.609**	**Pro totals (3 years)**	**3**	**3**

NOTES:
1982—Lost to Washington, 21-10, in Aloha Bowl.
1983—Lost to Tennessee, 30-23, in Florida Citrus Bowl.
1984—Defeated Tennessee, 28-27, in Sun Bowl.
1985—Defeated Syracuse, 35-18, in Cherry Bowl.
1990—Defeated Nebraska, 45-21, in Florida Citrus Bowl.
1991—Defeated Stanford, 18-17, in Aloha Bowl.
1992—Defeated Kansas City, 17-0, in first-round playoff game; lost to Miami, 31-0, in conference playoff game.
1994—Defeated Miami, 22-21, in conference playoff game; defeated Pittsburgh, 17-13, in AFC championship game; lost to San Francisco, 49-26, in Super Bowl XXIX.
1995—Lost to Indianapolis, 35-20, in first-round playoff game.

SCHOTTENHEIMER, MARTY — CHIEFS

PERSONAL: Born September 23, 1943, in Canonsburg, Pa. ... Full name: Martin Edward Schottenheimer. ... Played linebacker. ... Brother of Kurt Schottenheimer, special teams/tight ends coach, Kansas City Chiefs.
HIGH SCHOOL: McDonald (Pa.).
COLLEGE: Pittsburgh (degree in English, 1964).
TRANSACTIONS/CAREER NOTES: Selected by Buffalo Bills in seventh round of 1965 AFL draft. ... Released by Bills (1969). ... Signed by Boston Patriots (1969). ... Patriots franchise renamed New Engand Patriots for 1971 season. ... Traded by New England Patriots to Pittsburgh Steelers for OT Mike Haggerty and a draft choice (July 10, 1971). ... Released by Steelers (1971).
CHAMPIONSHIP GAME EXPERIENCE: Member of AFL championship team (1965 season). ... Played in AFL championship (1966 season).
HONORS: Played in AFL All-Star Game (1965 season).
PRO STATISTICS: 1969—Returned one kickoff for 13 yards. 1970—Returned one kickoff for eight yards.

			INTERCEPTIONS			
Year Team	G	No.	Yds.	Avg.	TD
1965—Buffalo AFL	14	0	0	...	0
1966—Buffalo AFL	14	1	20	20.0	0
1967—Buffalo AFL	14	3	88	29.3	1
1968—Buffalo AFL	14	1	22	22.0	0
1969—Boston AFL	11	1	3	3.0	0
1970—Boston NFL	12	0	0	...	0
AFL totals (5 years)	**67**	**6**	**133**	**22.2**	**1**
NFL totals (1 year)	**12**	**0**	**0**	**...**	**0**
Pro totals (6 years)	**79**	**6**	**133**	**22.2**	**1**

HEAD COACHING RECORD

BACKGROUND: Linebackers coach, Portland Storm WFL (1974). ... Linebackers coach, New York Giants NFL (1975 and 1976). ... Defensive coordinator, Giants (1977). ... Linebackers coach, Detroit Lions NFL (1978 and 1979). ... Defensive coordinator, Cleveland Browns NFL (1980-October 22, 1984).

			REGULAR SEASON			POST-SEASON	
	W	L	T	Pct.	Finish	W	L
1984—Cleveland NFL	4	4	0	.500	3rd/AFC Central Division	—	—
1985—Cleveland NFL	8	8	0	.500	1st/AFC Central Division	0	1

	REGULAR SEASON					POST-SEASON	
	W	L	T	Pct.	Finish	W	L
1986—Cleveland NFL	12	4	0	.750	1st/AFC Central Division	1	1
1987—Cleveland NFL	10	5	0	.667	1st/AFC Central Division	1	1
1988—Cleveland NFL	10	6	0	.625	T2nd/AFC Central Division	0	1
1989—Kansas City NFL	8	7	1	.531	2nd/AFC Western Division	—	—
1990—Kansas City NFL	11	5	0	.688	2nd/AFC Western Division	0	1
1991—Kansas City NFL	10	6	0	.625	2nd/AFC Western Division	1	1
1992—Kansas City NFL	10	6	0	.625	2nd/AFC Western Division	0	1
1993—Kansas City NFL	11	5	0	.688	1st/AFC Western Division	2	1
1994—Kansas City NFL	9	7	0	.563	T2nd/AFC Western Division	0	1
1995—Kansas City NFL	13	3	0	.813	1st/AFC Western Division	0	1
Pro totals (12 years)	**116**	**66**	**1**	**.637**	**Pro totals (10 years)**	**5**	**10**

NOTES:

1984—Replaced Sam Rutigliano as coach of Cleveland (October 22), with 1-7 record and in third place.

1985—Lost to Miami, 24-21, in conference playoff game.

1986—Defeated New York Jets, 23-20 (2 OT), in conference playoff game; lost to Denver, 23-20 (OT), in AFC championship game.

1987—Defeated Indianapolis, 38-21, in conference playoff game; lost to Denver, 38-33, in AFC championship game.

1988—Lost to Houston, 24-23, in wild-card playoff game.

1990—Lost to Miami, 17-16, in conference playoff game.

1991—Defeated Los Angeles Raiders, 10-6, in first-round playoff game; lost to Buffalo, 37-14, in conference playoff game.

1992—Lost to San Diego, 17-0, in first-round playoff game.

1993—Defeated Pittsburgh, 27-24 (OT), in first-round playoff game; defeated Houston, 28-20, in conference playoff game; lost to Buffalo, 30-13, in AFC championship game.

1994—Lost to Miami, 27-17, in first-round playoff game.

1995—Lost to Indianapolis, 10-7, in conference playoff game.

SEIFERT, GEORGE   49ERS

PERSONAL: Born January 22, 1940, in San Francisco. ... Full name: George Gerald Seifert.
HIGH SCHOOL: Polytechnic (San Francisco).
COLLEGE: Utah (degree in zoology, 1963; master's degree in physical education, 1966).
MISCELLANEOUS: Served six months in U.S. Army after college.

HEAD COACHING RECORD
BACKGROUND: Graduate assistant, Utah (1964). ... Assistant coach, Iowa (1966). ... Defensive backs coach, Oregon (1967-1971). ... Defensive backs coach, Stanford (1972-1974 and 1977-1979). ... Defensive backs coach, San Francisco 49ers NFL (1980-1982). ... Defensive coordinator, 49ers (1983-1988).
HONORS: Named NFL Coach of the Year by THE SPORTING NEWS (1990 and 1994).

	REGULAR SEASON					POST-SEASON	
	W	L	T	Pct.	Finish	W	L
1965—Westminster College (Utah)	3	3	0	.500	Independent	—	—
1975—Cornell...............................	1	8	0	.111	8th/Ivy League	—	—
1976—Cornell...............................	2	7	0	.222	T7th/Ivy League	—	—
1989—San Francisco NFL	14	2	0	.875	1st/NFC Western Division	3	0
1990—San Francisco NFL	14	2	0	.875	1st/NFC Western Division	1	1
1991—San Francisco NFL	10	6	0	.625	T2nd/NFC Western Division	—	—
1992—San Francisco NFL	14	2	0	.875	1st/NFC Western Division	1	1
1993—San Francisco NFL	10	6	0	.625	1st/NFC Western Division	1	1
1994—San Francisco NFL	13	3	0	.813	1st/NFC Western Division	3	0
1995—San Francisco NFL	11	5	0	.688	1st/NFC Western Division	0	1
College totals (3 years)	**6**	**18**	**0**	**.250**			
Pro totals (7 years)	**86**	**26**	**0**	**.768**	**Pro totals (6 years)**	**9**	**4**

NOTES:

1989—Defeated Minnesota, 41-13, in conference playoff game; defeated Los Angeles Rams, 30-3, in NFC championship game; defeated Denver, 55-10, in Super Bowl XXIV.

1990—Defeated Washington, 28-10, in conference playoff game; lost to New York Giants, 15-13, in NFC championship game.

1992—Defeated Washington, 20-13, in conference playoff game; lost to to Dallas, 30-20, in NFC championship game.

1993—Defeated New York Giants, 44-3, in conference playoff game; lost to Dallas, 38-21, in NFC championship game.

1994—Defeated Chicago, 44-15, in conference playoff game; defeated Dallas, 38-28, in NFC championship game; defeated San Diego, 49-26, in Super Bowl XXIX.

1995—Lost to Green Bay, 27-17, in conference playoff game.

SHANAHAN, MIKE   BRONCOS

PERSONAL: Born August 24, 1952, in Oak Park, Ill. ... Full name: Michael Edward Shanahan.
HIGH SCHOOL: East Leyden (Franklin Park, Ill.).
COLLEGE: Eastern Illinois (bachelor's degree in physical education, 1974; master's degree in education, 1975).

HEAD COACHING RECORD
BACKGROUND: Graduate assistant, Eastern Illinois (1973 and 1974). ... Running backs/wide receivers coach, Oklahoma (1975 and 1976). ... Assistant coach, Northern Arizona (1977). ... Offensive coordinator, Eastern Illinois (1978). ... Offensive coordinator, Minnesota (1979). ... Offensive coordinator, Florida (1980-1983). ... Quarterbacks coach, Denver Broncos NFL (1984, 1989 and 1990). ... Offensive coordinator, Broncos (1985-1987 and 1991). ... Offensive coordinator, San Francisco 49ers NFL (1992-1994).

	W	L	T	Pct.	Finish	W	L
					REGULAR SEASON	POST-SEASON	
1988—LA Raiders NFL	7	9	0	.438	3rd/AFC Western Division	—	—
1989—LA Raiders NFL	1	3	0	.250		—	—
1995—Denver NFL	8	8	0	.500	T3rd/AFC Western Division	—	—
Pro totals (3 years)	16	20	0	.444		—	—

NOTES:
1989—Replaced as L.A. Raiders coach by Art Shell (October 3) with club tied for fourth place.

SHULA, DAVE — BENGALS

PERSONAL: Born May 28, 1959, in Lexington, Ky. ... Full name: David Donald Shula. ... Played wide receiver. ... Son of Don Shula, head coach, Baltimore Colts (1963-1969) and Miami Dolphins (1970-1995); and brother of Mike Shula, offensive coordinator, Tampa Bay Buccaneers.
HIGH SCHOOL: Chaminade (Hollywood, Fla.).
COLLEGE: Dartmouth (degree in history and educational studies, 1981).
TRANSACTIONS/CAREER NOTES: Signed as non-drafted free agent by Baltimore Colts (April 30, 1981). ... Released by Colts (August 1982).
PRO STATISTICS: 1981—Recovered two fumbles.

		PUNT RETURNS				KICK RETURNS				TOTALS			
Year Team	G	No.	Yds.	Avg.	TD	No.	Yds.	Avg.	TD	TD	2pt.	Pts.	Fum.
1981—Baltimore NFL	16	10	50	5.0	0	5	65	13.0	0	0	...	0	2

HEAD COACHING RECORD
BACKGROUND: Offensive assistant coach, Miami Dolphins NFL (1982-1988). ... Offensive coordinator, Dallas Cowboys NFL (1989 and 1990). ... Receivers coach, Cincinnati Bengals NFL (1991).

					REGULAR SEASON	POST-SEASON	
	W	L	T	Pct.	Finish	W	L
1992—Cincinnati NFL	5	11	0	.313	4th/AFC Central Division	—	—
1993—Cincinnati NFL	3	13	0	.188	4th/AFC Central Division	—	—
1994—Cincinnati NFL	3	13	0	.188	3rd/AFC Central Division	—	—
1995—Cincinnati NFL	7	9	0	.438	T2nd/AFC Central Divsiion	—	—
Pro totals (4 years)	18	46	0	.281			

SWITZER, BARRY — COWBOYS

PERSONAL: Born October 5, 1937, in Crossett, Ark.
HIGH SCHOOL: Crossett (Ark.).
COLLEGE: Arkansas (degree in business administration, 1960).

HEAD COACHING RECORD
BACKGROUND: Served in military (1960-1962). ... Scout team coach, Arkansas (1962 and 1963). ... Offensive ends coach, Arkansas (1964 and 1965). ... Offensive line coach, Oklahoma (1966). ... Offensive coordinator, Oklahoma (1967-1972).
HONORS: Named College Football Coach of the Year by The Sporting News (1973).

					REGULAR SEASON	POST-SEASON	
	W	L	T	Pct.	Finish	W	L
1973—Oklahoma	10	0	1	1.000	1st/Big Eight		
1974—Oklahoma	11	0	0	1.000	1st/Big Eight	—	—
1975—Oklahoma	11	1	0	.917	T1st/Big Eight	1	0
1976—Oklahoma	9	2	1	.826	T1st/Big Eight	1	0
1977—Oklahoma	10	2	0	.833	1st/Big Eight	0	1
1978—Oklahoma	11	1	0	.917	T1st/Big Eight	1	0
1979—Oklahoma	11	1	0	.917	1st/Big Eight	1	0
1980—Oklahoma	10	2	0	.833	1st/Big Eight	1	0
1981—Oklahoma	7	4	1	.625	2nd/Big Eight	1	0
1982—Oklahoma	8	4	0	.666	2nd/Big Eight	0	1
1983—Oklahoma	8	4	0	.666	2nd/Big Eight	—	—
1984—Oklahoma	9	2	1	.826	T1st/Big Eight	0	1
1985—Oklahoma	11	1	0	.917	1st/Big Eight	1	0
1986—Oklahoma	11	1	0	.917	1st/Big Eight	1	0
1987—Oklahoma	11	1	0	.917	1st/Big Eight	0	1
1988—Oklahoma	9	3	0	.750	2nd/Big Eight	0	1
1994—Dallas NFL	12	4	0	.750	1st/NFC Eastern Division	1	1
1995—Dallas NFL	12	4	0	.750	1st/NFC Eastern Division	3	0
College totals (16 years)	157	29	4	.837	**College totals (13 years)**	8	5
Pro totals (2 years)	24	8	0	.750	**Pro totals (2 years)**	4	1

NOTES:
1975—Defeated Michigan, 14-6, in Orange Bowl.
1976—Defeated Wyoming, 41-7, in Fiesta Bowl.
1977—Lost to Arkansas, 31-6, in Orange Bowl.
1978—Defeated Nebraska, 31-24, in Orange Bowl.
1979—Defeated Florida State, 24-7, in Orange Bowl.
1980—Defeated Florida State, 18-17, in Orange Bowl.
1981—Defeated Houston, 40-14, in Sun Bowl.
1982—Lost to Arizona State, 32-21, in Fiesta Bowl.
1984—Lost to Washington, 28-17, in Orange Bowl.

HEAD COACHES

NOTES:
1985—Defeated Penn State, 25-10, in Orange Bowl.
1986—Defeated Arkansas, 42-8, in Orange Bowl.
1987—Lost to Miami, 20-14, in Orange Bowl.
1988—Lost to Clemson, 13-6, in Citrus Bowl.
1994—Defeated Green Bay, 35-9, in conference playoff game; lost to San Francisco, 38-28, in NFC championship game.
1995—Defeated Philadelphia, 30-11, in conference playoff game; defeated Green Bay, 38-27, in NFC championship game; defeated Pittsburgh, 27-17, in Super Bowl XXX.

TOBIN, VINCE | CARDINALS

PERSONAL: Born September 29, 1943 in Burlington Junction, Mo. ... Full name: Vincent Michael Tobin.
HIGH SCHOOL: Maryville (Mo.).
COLLEGE: Missouri (degree in physical education, 1965; master's degree in guidance and counseling, 1966).

HEAD COACHING RECORD
BACKGROUND: Defensive ends coach, Missouri (1967-1970). ... Defensive coordinator, Missouri (1971-1976). ... Defensive coordinator, British Columbia Lions CFL (1977-1982). ... Defensive coordinator, Philadelphia/Baltimore Stars USFL (1983-1985). ... Defensive coordinator, Chicago Bears NFL (1986-1992). ... Defensive coordinator, Indianapolis Colts NFL (1994 and 1995).

TURNER, NORV | REDSKINS

PERSONAL: Born May 17, 1952, in LeJeune, N.C. ... Full name: Norval Eugene Turner. ... Brother of Ron Turner, offensive coordinator, Chicago Bears.
HIGH SCHOOL: Alhambra (Calif.).
COLLEGE: Oregon (degree in history, 1975).
BACKGROUND: Graduate assistant, Oregon (1975). ... Receivers coach, Southern California (1976-1979). ... Defensive backs coach, USC (1980). ... Quarterbacks coach, USC (1981-1983). ... Offensive coordinator, USC (1984). ... Receivers coach, Los Angeles Rams NFL (1985-1990). ... Offensive coordinator, Dallas Cowboys (1991-1993).

	W	L	T	Pct.	Finish	W	L
					REGULAR SEASON	POST-SEASON	
1994—Washington NFL	3	13	0	.188	5th/NFC Eastern Division	—	—
1995—Washington NFL	6	10	0	.375	3rd/NFC Eastern Division	—	—
Pro totals (2 years)	9	23	0	.281			

WANNSTEDT, DAVE | BEARS

PERSONAL: Born May 21, 1952, in Pittsburgh. ... Full name: David Raymond Wannstedt.
HIGH SCHOOL: Baldwin (Pittsburgh).
COLLEGE: Pittsburgh (degree in physical education, 1974; master's degree in education, 1975).
TRANSACTIONS/CAREER NOTES: Selected by Green Bay Packers in 15th round (376th pick overall) of 1974 NFL draft. ... On injured reserve with neck injury (entire 1974 season).

HEAD COACHING RECORD
BACKGROUND: Graduate assistant, Pittsburgh (1975). ... Defensive line coach, Pittsburgh (1976-1978). ... Defensive line coach, Oklahoma State (1979 and 1980). ... Defensive coordinator, Oklahoma State (1981 and 1982). ... Defensive line coach, Southern California (1983-1985). ... Defensive coordinator, Miami, Fla. (1986-1988). ... Defensive coordinator, Dallas Cowboys NFL (1989-1992).

	W	L	T	Pct.	Finish	W	L
					REGULAR SEASON	POST-SEASON	
1993—Chicago NFL	7	9	0	.438	4th/NFC Central Division	—	—
1994—Chicago NFL	9	7	0	.563	T2nd/NFC Central Division	1	1
1995—Chicago NFL	9	7	0	.563	3rd/NFC Central Division	—	—
Pro totals (3 years)	25	23	0	.521	**Pro totals (1 year)**	1	1

NOTES:
1994—Defeated Minnesota, 35-18, in first-round playoff game; lost to San Francisco, 44-15, in conference playoff game.

WHITE, MIKE | RAIDERS

PERSONAL: Born January 4, 1936, in Berkeley, Calif.
HIGH SCHOOL: Acalanes (Lafayette, Calif.).
COLLEGE: California (degree in business administration, 1958).

HEAD COACHING RECORD
BACKGROUND: Graduate assistant, California (1958). ... Assistant coach, California (1959-1963). ... Offensive coordinator, Stanford (1964-1971). ... Offensive line coach, San Francisco 49ers NFL (1978). ... Administrative assistant coach, 49ers (1979). ... Consultant, World League of American Football (1989). ... Quarterbacks coach, Los Angeles Raiders NFL (1990-1992). ... Offensive line coach, Raiders (1993 and 1994).
HONORS: Named College Football Coach of the Year by The Sporting News (1975).

	W	L	T	Pct.	Finish	W	L
					REGULAR SEASON	POST-SEASON	
1972—California	3	8	0	.273	5th/Pacific-8 Conference	—	—
1973—California	4	7	0	.364	T5th/Pacific-8 Conference	—	—
1974—California	7	3	1	.682	T3rd/Pacific-8 Conference	—	—

	W	L	T	Pct.	REGULAR SEASON Finish	POST-SEASON W	L
1975—California	8	3	0	.727	T1st/Pacific-8 Conference	—	—
1976—California	5	6	0	.455	T4th/Pacific-8 Conference	—	—
1977—California	7	4	0	.636	T5th/Pacific-8 Conference	—	—
1980—Illinois	3	7	1	.318	T6th/Big Ten Conference	—	—
1981—Illinois	7	4	0	.636	T3rd/Big Ten Conference	—	—
1982—Illinois	7	4	0	.636	4th/Big Ten Conference	0	1
1983—Illinois	10	1	0	.909	1st/Big Ten Conference	0	1
1984—Illinois	7	4	0	.636	T2nd/Big Ten Conference	—	—
1985—Illinois	6	4	1	.591	3rd/Big Ten Conference	0	1
1986—Illinois	4	7	0	.364	T6th/Big Ten Conference	—	—
1987—Illinois	3	7	1	.318	8th/Big Ten Conference	—	—
1995—Oakland NFL	8	8	0	.500	T3rd/AFC Western Division	—	—
College totals (14 years)	81	69	4	.539	**College totals (3 years)**	0	3
Pro totals (1 year)	8	8	0	.500			

NOTES:

1982—Lost to Alabama, 21-15, in Liberty Bowl.
1983—Lost to UCLA, 45-9, in Rose Bowl.
1985—Lost to Army, 31-29, in Peach Bowl.

HEAD COACHES

'For a very long time, Shula's name was synonymous with the NFL and all that was good about the league and the game. Every sport needs those types of images and Shula gave one to professional football.

"When people saw him or his name was used, it meant winning and doing it with class, character and dignity, and that's how he should be remembered first and foremost.'

— *Pete Rozelle, former NFL commissioner*

DON SHULA

THE NFL'S ALL-TIME WINNINGEST COACH

ALBERT DICKSON / TSN

PERSONAL: Born January 4, 1930, in Painesville, Ohio. ... Full name: Donald Francis Shula. ... Played defensive back. ... Father of David Shula, head coach, Cincinnati Bengals; and father of Mike Shula, offensive coordinator, Tampa Bay Buccaneers.
HIGH SCHOOL: Harvey (Painesville, Ohio).
COLLEGE: John Carroll, Ohio (degree in sociology, 1951).
TRANSACTIONS/CAREER NOTES: Selected by Cleveland Browns in ninth round of 1951 NFL draft. ... Traded by Browns with QB Harry Agganis, DB Bert Rechichar, DB Carl Taseff, E Gern Nagler, G Elmer Willhoite, G Ed Sharkey, G Art Spinney, T Dick Batten and T Stu Sheetz to Baltimore Colts for LB Tom Catlin, G Herschel Forester, HB John Petitbon, T Don Colo and T Mike McCormack (March 25, 1953). ... Sold by Colts to Washington Redskins (1957).
CHAMPIONSHIP GAME EXPERIENCE: Played in NFL championship game (1951 and 1952 seasons).
PRO STATISTICS: 1951—Returned one kickoff for six yards. 1953—Caught one pass for six yards and recovered one fumble. 1954—Rushed twice for three yards. 1955—Recovered two fumbles for 26 yards. 1956—Returned one kickoff for no yards and recovered one fumble for six yards.

			INTERCEPTIONS		
Year Team	G	No.	Yds.	Avg.	TD
1951—Cleveland NFL	12	4	23	5.8	0
1952—Cleveland NFL	5	0	0	...	0
1953—Baltimore NFL	12	3	46	15.3	0
1954—Baltimore NFL	12	5	84	16.8	0
1955—Baltimore NFL	9	5	64	12.8	0
1956—Baltimore NFL	12	1	2	2.0	0
1957—Washington NFL	11	3	48	16.0	0
Pro totals (7 years)	73	21	267	12.7	0

HEAD COACHING RECORD

BACKGROUND: Defensive backs coach, Virginia (1958). ... Running backs coach, Kentucky (1959). ... Defensive coordinator, Detroit Lions NFL (1960-1962).
HONORS: Named NFL Coach of the Year by THE SPORTING NEWS (1964, 1968, 1970 and 1972).
RECORDS: Holds NFL career records for most regular season wins—328; and most combined wins (regular season and postseason)—347.
POSTSEASON RECORDS: Holds Super Bowl record for most games coached—6. ... Shares Super Bowl record for most losses—4. ... Holds NFL postseason record for most losses—17. ... Shares NFL postseason record for most games—36.

				REGULAR SEASON		POST-SEASON	
	W	L	T	Pct.	Finish	W	L
1963—Baltimore NFL	8	6	0	.571	3rd/Western Conference	—	—
1964—Baltimore NFL	12	2	0	.857	1st/Western Conference	0	1
1965—Baltimore NFL	10	3	1	.750	2nd/Western Conference	0	1
1966—Baltimore NFL	9	5	0	.643	2nd/Western Conference	—	—
1967—Baltimore NFL	11	1	2	.857	2nd/Western Conference	—	—
1968—Baltimore NFL	13	1	0	.929	1st/Western Conference Coastal Division	2	1
1969—Baltimore NFL	8	5	1	.607	2nd/Western Conference Coastal Division	—	—
1970—Miami NFL	10	4	0	.714	2nd/AFC Eastern Division	0	1
1971—Miami NFL	10	3	1	.750	1st/AFC Eastern Division	2	1

	\ REGULAR SEASON					POST-SEASON	
	W	L	T	Pct.	Finish	W	L
1972—Miami NFL	14	0	0	1.000	1st/AFC Eastern Division	3	0
1973—Miami NFL	12	2	0	.857	1st/AFC Eastern Division	3	0
1974—Miami NFL	11	3	0	.786	1st/AFC Eastern Division	0	1
1975—Miami NFL	10	4	0	.714	T1st/AFC Eastern Division	—	—
1976—Miami NFL	6	8	0	.429	3rd/AFC Eastern Division	—	—
1977—Miami NFL	10	4	0	.714	T1st/AFC Eastern Division	—	—
1978—Miami NFL	11	5	0	.688	T1st/AFC Eastern Division	0	1
1979—Miami NFL	10	6	0	.625	1st/AFC Eastern Division	0	1
1980—Miami NFL	8	8	0	.500	3rd/AFC Eastern Division	—	—
1981—Miami NFL	11	4	1	.719	1st/AFC Eastern Division	0	1
1982—Miami NFL	7	2	0	.778	T2nd/AFC	3	1
1983—Miami NFL	12	4	0	.750	1st/AFC Eastern Division	0	1
1984—Miami NFL	14	2	0	.875	1st/AFC Eastern Division	2	1
1985—Miami NFL	12	4	0	.750	1st/AFC Eastern Division	1	1
1986—Miami NFL	8	8	0	.500	3rd/AFC Eastern Division	—	—
1987—Miami NFL	8	7	0	.533	T2nd/AFC Eastern Division	—	—
1988—Miami NFL	6	10	0	.375	5th/AFC Eastern Division	—	—
1989—Miami NFL	8	8	0	.500	T2nd/AFC Eastern Division	—	—
1990—Miami NFL	12	4	0	.750	2nd/AFC Eastern Division	1	1
1991—Miami NFL	8	8	0	.500	T2nd/AFC Eastern Division	—	—
1992—Miami NFL	11	5	0	.688	T1st/AFC Eastern Division	1	1
1993—Miami NFL	9	7	0	.563	2nd/AFC Eastern Division	—	—
1994—Miami NFL	10	6	0	.625	T1st/AFC Eastern Division	1	1
1995—Miami NFL	9	7	0	.563	T2nd/AFC Eastern Division	0	1
Pro totals (33 years)	328	156	6	.676	**Pro totals (19 years)**	19	17

NOTES:

1964—Lost to Cleveland, 27-0, in NFL championship game.
1965—Lost to Green Bay, 13-10, in conference playoff game.
1968—Defeated Minnesota, 24-14, in conference playoff game; defeated Cleveland, 34-0, in NFL championship game; lost to New York Jets, 16-7, in Super Bowl III.
1970—Lost to Oakland, 21-14, in conference playoff game.
1971—Defeated Kansas City, 27-24, in conference playoff game; defeated Baltimore, 21-0, in AFC championship game; lost to Dallas, 24-3, in Super Bowl VI.
1972—Defeated Cleveland, 20-14, in conference playoff game; defeated Pittsburgh, 21-17, in AFC championship game; defeated Washington, 14-7, in Super Bowl VII.
1973—Defeated Cincinnati, 34-16, in conference playoff game; defeated Oakland, 27-10, in AFC championship game; defeated Minnesota, 24-7, in Super Bowl VIII.
1974—Lost to Oakland, 28-26, in conference playoff game.
1978—Lost to Houston, 17-9, in conference playoff game.
1979—Lost to Pittsburgh, 34-14, in conference playoff game.
1981—Lost to San Diego, 41-38, (OT), in conference playoff game.
1982—Defeated New England, 28-13, in conference playoff game; defeated San Diego, 34-13, in conference playoff game; defeated New York Jets, 14-0, in AFC championship game; lost to Washington, 27-17, in Super Bowl XVII.
1983—Lost to Seattle, 27-20, in conference playoff game.
1984—Defeated Seattle, 31-10, in conference playoff game; defeated Pittsburgh, 45-28, in AFC championship game; lost to San Francisco, 38-16, in Super Bowl XIX.
1985—Defeated Cleveland, 24-21, in conference playoff game; lost to New England, 31-14, in AFC championship game.
1990—Defeated Kansas City, 17-16, in conference playoff game; lost to Buffalo, 44-34, in conference playoff game.
1992—Defeated San Diego, 31-0, in conference playoff game; lost to Buffalo, 29-10, in AFC championship game.
1994—Defeated Kansas City, 27-17, in first-round playoff game; lost to San Diego, 22-21, in conference playoff game.
1995—Lost to Buffalo, 37-22, in first-round playoff game; announced retirement (January 5, 1996).

Johnny U. and The Don

Johnny Unitas was one of 12 Hall of Fame players Shula coached during his 33-year career.

1995 NATIONAL FOOTBALL LEAGUE LEADERS

PASSING

Attempts
636	Drew Bledsoe, N.E.
606	Warren Moon, Min.
583	Scott Mitchell, Det.
570	Brett Favre, G.B.
567	Jeff Blake, Cin.
567	Jim Everett, N.O.

Completions
377	Warren Moon, Min.
359	Brett Favre, G.B.
346	Scott Mitchell, Det.
345	Jim Everett, N.O.
336	Jeff George, Atl.
326	Jeff Blake, Cin.

Yards
4413	Brett Favre, G.B.
4338	Scott Mitchell, Det.
4228	Warren Moon, Min.
4143	Jeff George, Atl.
3970	John Elway, Den.
3970	Jim Everett, N.O.

Touchdowns
38	Brett Favre, G.B.
33	Warren Moon, Min.
32	Scott Mitchell, Det.
29	Erik Kramer, Chi.
28	Jeff Blake, Cin.
26	John Elway, Den.
26	Jim Everett, N.O.

Interceptions
21	Dave Krieg, Ariz.
20	Rick Mirer, Sea.
19	Kerry Collins, Car.
18	Trent Dilfer, T.B.
17	Jeff Blake, Cin.
16	Drew Bledsoe, N.E.

Rating
100.7	Jim Harbaugh, Ind.
99.5	Brett Favre, G.B.
93.6	Troy Aikman, Dal.
93.5	Erik Kramer, Chi.
92.3	Steve Young, S.F.
92.3	Scott Mitchell, Det.
91.5	Warren Moon, Min.
90.8	Dan Marino, Mia.

300-Yard Games
7	Brett Favre, G.B.
5	John Elway, Den.
5	Scott Mitchell, Det.
5	Steve Young, S.F.
4	Dave Krieg, Ariz.
4	Warren Moon, Min.
4	Neil O'Donnell, Pit.

RUSHING

Carries
377	Emmitt Smith, Dal.
368	Curtis Martin, N.E.
338	Terry Allen, Was.
337	Ricky Watters, Phi.
332	Errict Rhett, T.B.
316	Edgar Bennett, G.B.
314	Barry Sanders, Det.

Yards
1773	Emmitt Smith, Dal.
1500	Barry Sanders, Det.
1487	Curtis Martin, N.E.
1346	Chris Warren, Sea.
1309	Terry Allen, Was.
1273	Ricky Watters, Phi.
1207	Errict Rhett, T.B.

Touchdowns
25	Emmitt Smith, Dal.
15	Chris Warren, Sea.
14	Curtis Martin, N.E.
11	Barry Sanders, Det.
11	Errict Rhett, T.B.
11	Ricky Watters, Phi.
11	Harvey Williams, Oak.

100 Yard Games
11	Emmitt Smith, Dal.
9	Curtis Martin, N.E.
8	Chris Warren, Sea.
7	Barry Sanders, Det.
5	Rashaan Salaam, Chi.
4	Terry Allen, Was.
4	Errict Rhett, Was.
4	Ricky Watters, Phi.

RECEIVING

Receptions
123	Herman Moore, Det.
122	Chris Carter, Min.
122	Jerry Rice, S.F.
119	Issac Bruce, St.L.
111	Michael Irvin, Dal.
108	Brett Perriman, Det.
104	Eric Metcalf, Atl.
102	Robert Brooks, G.B.
101	Larry Centers, Ariz.

Yards
1848	Jerry Rice, S.F.
1781	Issac Bruce, St.L.
1686	Herman Moore, Det.
1603	Michael Irvin, Dal.
1497	Robert Brooks, G.B.
1488	Brett Perriman, Det.

Touchdowns
17	Chris Carter, Min.
17	Carl Pickins, Cin.
15	Jerry Rice, S.F.
14	Anthony Miller, Den.
14	Herman Moore, Det.
13	Issac Bruce, St.L.
13	Robert Brooks, G.B.

100 Yard Games
11	Michael Irvin, Dal.
10	Herman Moore, Det.
9	Robert Brooks, G.B.
9	Issac Bruce, St.L.
9	Jerry Rice, S.F.
8	Brett Perriman, Det.

PUNT RETURNS

Returns
53	Todd Kinchen, St.L.
51	Tamarick Vanover, K.C.
48	Andre Hastings, Pit.
45	David Meggett, N.E.
43	Eric Guliford, Car.
39	Eric Metcalf, Atl.

Average
13.2	David Palmer, Min.
12.6	Brian Mitchell, Was.
11.6	Andre Coleman, S.D.
11.5	Jeff Burris, Buf.
11.4	Glyn Milburn, Den.
11.0	Eric Guliford, Car.

Touchdowns
1	10 players tied.

KICK RETURNS

Returns
66	Tyrone Hughes, N.O.
62	Andre Coleman, S.D.
58	Bobby Joe Edmonds, T.B.
56	Dexter Carter, NYJ-S.F.
55	Brian Mitchell, Was.
54	Ernie Mills, Pitt.

Average
27.7	Ron Carpenter, NYJ
27.0	Glyn Milburn, Den
26.0	Napoleon Kaufman, Oak.
25.6	Brian Mitchell, Was.
25.5	Tamarick Vanover, K.C.
25.4	David Meggett, N.E.

Touchdowns
2	Andre Coleman, S.D.
2	Tamarick Vanover, K.C.

KICKING

Points
141	Norm Johnson, Pit.
132	Jason Elam, Den.
132	Jason Hanson, Det.
127	Chris Boniol, Dal.
126	Steve Christie, Buf.
122	Morten Andersen, Atl.
122	Fuad Reveiz, Min.

Field Goals
34	Norm Johnson, Pit.
31	Morten Andersen, Atl.
31	Jason Elam, Den.
31	Steve Christie, Buf.
30	Greg Davis, Ariz.
29	Doug Pelfrey, Cin.
29	Matt Stover, Cle.

Longest Field Goals
59	Morten Andersen, Atl.
56	Jason Elam, Den.
56	Jason Hanson, Det.
55	Greg Davis, Ariz.
55	Matt Bahr, N.E.
53	Al Del Greco, Hou.
53	Mike Hollis, Jax.
53	Michael Husted, T.B.

PUNTING

Punts
99	Brian Hansen, NYJ
95	Tommy Barnhardt, Car.
91	Louie Aguiar, K.C.
86	Chris Mohr, Buf.
85	Tom Hutton, Phi.

Average
45.0	Rick Tuten, Sea.
44.7	Darren Bennett, S.D.
44.3	Sean Landeta, St.L.
43.8	Louie Aguiar, K.C.
43.8	Bryan Barker, Jax.
43.8	Jeff Feagles, Ariz.

Net Average
38.6	Bryan Barker, Jax.
38.6	Lee Johnson, Cin.
38.2	Jeff Feagles, Ariz.
37.7	Matt Turk, Was.
37.6	Tom Rouen, Den.
36.7	Sean Landeta, St.L.

Inside 20
29	Louie Aguiar, K.C.
29	Matt Turk, Was.
28	Darren Bennett, S.D.
27	Tommy Barnhardt, Car.
26	Rich Camarillo, Hou.
26	Brian Hansen, NYJ
26	Craig Hentrich, G.B.
26	Lee Johnson, Cin.

DEFENSE

Interceptions
9	Orlando Thomas, Min.
8	Willie Clay, Det.
7	William Thomas, Phi.
7	Willie Williams, Pit.
6	Ten players tied.

Sacks
17.5	Bryce Paup, Buf.
13.0	William Fuller, Phi.
13.0	Wayne Martin, N.O.
13.0	Pat Swilling, Oak.
12.5	Leslie O'Neal, S.D.
12.0	Neil Smith, K.C.
12.0	Reggie White, G.B.

Touchdowns (Passing)
10	Herman Moore, Det.
9	Robert Brooks, G.B.
9	Issac Bruce, St.L.
9	Jerry Rice, S.F.
8	Brett Perriman, Det.